THE

SAGA HOARD

Volume II

**Collecting Together
EnglishTranslations
of the
Icelandic Sagas**

**This Volume
is Dedicated
to Our
Ancestors**

Various English translations of the Icelandic Sagas are widely available in a digital format from a number of sources on the internet. There are also various collections available in book form.

Our goal with this collection was to present as many Icelandic Sagas as possible, at an affordable price. This is the second volume in a planned three-volume set of Icelandic Sagas.

The Saga Hoard - Volume 2 is part of the Temple library Collection. Any profits made from this book, will go directly to our fund to build a Hof and Hall in the Heartland of the United States.

Published by Jotun's Bane Kindred
Temple of Our Heathen Gods
P.O. Box 463
Liberty, MO 64069
mark@heathengods.com

http://www.heathengods.com

TABLE OF CONTENTS

TABLE OF CONTENTS

INTRODUCTION

The Icelandic Sagas are histories written in prose, describing life and events that took place during the Icelandic Commonweath period, around the 10th and 11th centuries. They are stories of families, adventures, feuding, deal-making, political maneuvers, wars, treasure amassed, great journeys, geneology, tribute given, kings, freemen, history, and myth. They are stories of the Norse and Celtic settlers and their descendants in Iceland during what is sometimes called the Saga Age.

It is believed that the Sagas were written down in the thirteenth and fourteenth centuries, and that at least some of them originated in the oral storytelling tradition. Their authors remain unknown, but the Sagas are recognized and respected as some of the best of world literature.

What is amazing about the Icelandic Sagas, is the wealth of information included in them and the storytelling with which it is presented. Though written hundreds of years ago, they are still enormously compelling to the modern reader. Their style is crisp and quick, and there is action, emotion, and humor to keep one entertained.

The stories describe actions and conversations among the characters, but at no point are we told directly what a character is thinking. But while reading of their deeds and words, we develop a sense of their psychology and their thoughts.

The Icelandic Sagas are more than just great literature about an entertaining subject matter. For Asatruars and Heathens, there is indispensable knowledge to be gained here. These tales give us a window into the world of our heathen ancestors. What did they value? How did they resolve conflicts and disputes? How did they uphold their responsibilities to their families and their friends? How did they approach life itself and their places within the community? How did they view and honor their Gods and Ancestors? What sort of men and women were they? While these great stories were compiled and written down by Christians after the conversion, they preserve in their tales of our pagan ancestors much that we should know.

Some Sagas have been lost to history. We read of their existence or see reference to these lost Sagas in other works, and it is impossible to not feel the tragic loss. But a large body of work has been preserved, and it forms an amazing resource and foundation for our reconstruction of the Heathenry of our Ancestors, in our modern times.

Contained in this volume are nearly 800 pages of Icelandic Sagas. Read, learn, and enjoy these tales of our Ancestors.

Mark Ludwig Stinson
July 15, 2010

THE SAGA OF GUNNLAUG THE WORM-TONGUE AND RAFN THE SKALD

Even as Ari Thorgilson the Learned, the Priest,
Hath told it, who was the man of all Iceland
Most learned in tales of the land's inhabiting
And in lore of time agone.

CHAPTER 1
Of Thorstein Egilson and His Kin

There was a man called Thorstein, the son of Egil, the son of Skallagrim, the son of Kveldulf the Hersir of Norway. Asgerd was the mother of Thorstein; she was the daughter of Biorn Hold. Thorstein dwelt at Burg in Burgfirth; he was rich of fee, and a great chief, a wise man, meek and of measure in all wise. He was nought of such wondrous growth and strength as his father Egil had been; yet was he a right mighty man, and much beloved of all folk.

Thorstein was goodly to look on, flaxen-haired, and the best-eyed of men; and so say men of lore that many of the kin of the Mere-men, who are come of Egil, have been the goodliest folk; yet, for all that, this kindred have differed much herein, for it is said that some of them have been accounted the most ill-favoured of men: but in that ken have been also many men of great prowess in many wise, such as Kiartan, the son of Olaf Peacock, and Slaying-Bardi, and Skuli, the son of Thorstein. Some have been great bards, too, in that kin, as Biorn, the champion of Hitdale, priest Einar Skulison, Snorri Sturluson, and many others.

Now, Thorstein had to wife Jofrid, the daughter of Gunnar, the son of Hlifar. This Gunnar was the best skilled in weapons, and the lithest of limb of all bonder-folk who have been in Iceland; the second was Gunnar of Lithend; but Steinthor of Ere was the third. Jofrid was eighteen winters old when Thorstein wedded her; she was a widow, for Thorodd, son of Odd of Tongue, had had her to wife aforetime. Their daughter was Hungerd, who was brought up at Thorstein's at Burg. Jofrid was a very stirring woman; she and Thorstein had many children betwixt them, but few of them come into this tale. Skuli was the eldest of their sons, Kollsvein the second, Egil the third.

2

CHAPTER 2
Of Thorstein's Dream

One summer, it is said, a ship came from over the main into Gufaros. Bergfinn was he hight who was the master thereof, a Northman of kin, rich in goods, and somewhat stricken in years, and a wise man he was withal.

Now, goodman Thorstein rode to the ship, as it was his wont mostly to rule the market, and this he did now. The Eastmen got housed, but Thorstein took the master to himself, for thither he prayed to go. Bergfinn was of few words throughout the winter, but Thorstein treated him well. The Eastman had great joy of dreams.

One day in spring-tide Thorstein asked Bergfinn if he would ride with him up to Hawkfell, where at that time was the Thing-stead of the Burg-firthers; for Thorstein had been told that the walls of his booth had fallen in. The Eastman said he had good will to go, so that day they rode, some three together, from home, and the house-carles of Thorstein withal, till they came up under Hawkfell to a farmstead called Foxholes. There dwelt a man of small wealth called Atli, who was Thorstein's tenant. Thorstein bade him come and work with them, and bring with him hoe and spade. This he did, and when they came to the tofts of the booth, they set to work all of them, and did out the walls.

The weather was hot with sunshine that day, and Thorstein and the Eastman grew heavy; and when they had moved out the walls, those two sat down within the tofts, and Thorstein slept, and fared ill in his sleep. The Eastman sat beside him, and let him have his dream fully out, and when he awoke he was much wearied. Then the Eastman asked him what he had dreamt, as he had had such an ill time of it in his sleep.

Thorstein said, If I tell thee the dream, then shalt thou unriddle it to me, as it verily is.

The Eastman said he would risk it.

Then Thorstein said: This was my dream; for methought I was at home at Burg, standing outside the men's-door, and I looked up at the house-roof, and on the ridge I saw a swan, goodly and fair, and I thought it was mine own, and deemed it good beyond all things. Then I saw a great eagle sweep down from the mountains, and fly thitherward and alight beside the swan, and chuckle over her lovingly; and methought the swan seemed well content thereat; but I noted that the eagle was black-eyed, and that on him were iron claws: valiant he seemed to me.

After this I thought I saw another fowl come flying from the south quarter, and he, too, came hither to Burg, and sat down on the house beside the swan, and would fain be fond with her. This also was a mighty eagle.

But soon I thought that the eagle first-come ruffled up at the coming of the other. Then they fought fiercely and long, and, this I saw that they both bled, and such was the end of their play, that each tumbled either way down from the house-roof, and there they lay both dead.

3

But the swan sat left alone, drooping much, and sad of semblance.

Then I saw a fowl fly from the west; that was a falcon, and he sat beside the swan and made fondly towards her, and they flew away both together into one and the same quarter, and therewith I awoke.

But a dream of no mark this is, he says, and will in all likelihood betoken gales, that they shall meet in the air from those quarters whence I deemed the fowl flew.

The Eastman spake: I deem it nowise such, saith he.

Thorstein said, Make of the dream, then, what seemeth likest to thee, and let me hear.

Then said the Eastman: These birds are like to be fetches of men: but thy wife sickens now, and she will give birth to a woman-child fair and lovely; and dearly thou wilt love her; but high born men shall woo thy daughter, coming from such quarters as the eagles seemed to fly from, and shall lover her with overweening love, and shall fight about her, and both lose their lives thereby. And thereafter a third man, from the quarter whence came the falcon, shall woo her and to that man shall she be wedded. Now, I have unravelled thy dream, and I think things will befall as I have said.

Thorstein answered: In evil and unfriendly wise is the dream interpreted, nor do I deem thee fit for the work of unriddling dreams.

The Eastman said, Thou shalt find how it will come to pass.

But Thorstein estranged himself from the Eastman thenceforward, and he left that summer, and now he is out of the tale.

CHAPTER 3
Of the Birth and Fostering of Helga The Fair

This summer Thorstein got ready to ride to the Thing, and spake to Jofrid his wife before he went from home. So is it, he says, that thou art with child now, but thy child shall be cast forth if thou bear a woman; but nourished if it be a man.

Now, at this time when all the land was heathen, it was somewhat the wont of such men as had little wealth, and were like to have many young children on their hands, to have them cast forth, but an evil deed it was always deemed to be.

And now, when Thorstein had said this, Jofrid answers, This is a word all unlike thee, such a man as thou art, and surely to a wealthy man like thee it will not seem good that this should be done.

Thorstein answered: Thou knowest my mind, and that no good will hap if my will be thwarted.

4

So he rode to the Thing; but while he was gone Jofrid gave birth to a woman-child wondrous fair. The woman would fain show her to the mother; she said there was little need thereof, but had her shepherd Thorvard called to her, and spake to him:

Thou shalt take my horse and saddle it, and bring this child west to Herdholt, to Thorgerd, Egil's daughter, and pray her to nourish it secretly, so that Thorstein may not know thereof. For with such looks of love do I behold this child, that surely I cannot bear to have it cast forth. Here are three marks of silver, have them in reward of thy work; but west there Thorgerd will get thee fare and food over the sea.

Then Thorvard did her bidding; he rode with the child to Herdholt, and gave it into Thorgerd's hands, and she had it nourished at a tenant's of hers who dwelt at Freedmans-stead up in Hvamfirth; but she got fare for Thorvard north in Steingrims-firth, in Shell-creek, and gave him meet outfit for his sea-faring: he went thence abroad, and is now out of the story.

Now when Thorstein came home from the Thing, Jofrid told him that the child had been cast forth according to his word, but that the herdsman had fled away and stolen her horse. Thorstein said she had done well, and got himself another herdsman. So six winters passed and this matter was nowise wotted of.

Now in those days Thorstein rode to Herdholt, being bidden there as guest of his brother-in-law, Olaf Peacock, the son of Hoskuld, who was then deemed to be the chief highest of worth among all men west there. Good cheer was made Thorstein, as was like to be; and one day at the feast it is said that Thorgerd sat in the high seat talking with her brother Thorstein, while Olaf was talking to other men; but on the bench right over against them sat three little maidens. Then said Thorgerd,---

How dost thou, brother, like the look of these three little maidens sitting straight before us?

Right well,he answers, but one is by far the fairest; she has all the goodliness of Olaf, but the whiteness and the countenance of us, the Mere-men.

Thorgerd answered: Surely this is true, brother, wherein thou sayest that she has the fairness and countenance of us Mere-folk, but the goodliness of Olaf Peacock she has not got, for she is not his daughter.

How can that be, says Thorstein, being thy daughter none the less?

She answered: To say sooth, kinsman, quoth she, this fair maiden is not my daughter, but thine.

And therewith she told him all as it had befallen, and prayed him to forgive her and his own wife that trespass.

Thorstein said: I cannot blame you two for having done this; most things will fall as they are fated, and well have ye covered over my folly: so look I on this maiden that I deem it great good luck to have so fair a child. But now, what is her name?

Helga she is called, says Thorgerd.

Helga the Fair, says Thorstein. But now shalt thou make her ready to come home with me.

She did go, and Thorstein was led out with good gifts, and Helga rode with him to his home, and was brought up there with much honour and great love from father and mother and all her kin.

CHAPTER 4
Of Gunnlaug Worm-Tongue and His Kin

Now at this time there dwelt at Gilsbank, up in White-water-side, Illugi the Black, son of Hallkel, the son of Hrosskel. The mother of Illugi was Thurid Dandle, daughter of Gunnlaug Worm-tongue.

Illugi was the next greatest chief in Burg-firth after Thorstein Egilson. He was a man of broad lands and hardy of mood, and wont to do well to his friends; he had to wife Ingibiorg, the daughter of Asbiorn Hordson, from Ornolfsdale; the mother of Ingibiorg was Thorgerd, the daughter of Midfirth-Skeggi. The children of Illugi and Ingibiorg were many, but few of them have to do with this story. Hermund was one of their sons, and Gunnlaug another; both were hopeful men, and at this time of ripe growth.

It is told of Gunnlaug that he was quick of growth in his early youth, big, and strong; his hair was light red, and very goodly of fashion; he was dark-eyed, somewhat ugly-nosed, yet of lovesome countenance; thin of flank he was, and broad of shoulder, and the best-wrought of men; his whole mind was very masterful; eager was he from his youth up, and in all wise unsparing and hardy; he was a great skald, but somewhat bitter in his rhyming, and therefore was he called Gunnlaug Worm-tongue.

Hermund was the best beloved of the two brothers, and had the mien of a great man.

When Gunnlaug was fifteen winters old he prayed his father for goods to fare abroad withal, and said he had will to travel and see the manners of other folk. Master Illugi was slow to take the matter up, and said he was unlike to be deemed good in the out-lands when I can scarcely shape thee to my own liking at home.

On a morning but a very little afterwards it happened that Illugi came out early, and saw that his storehouse was opened, and that some sacks of wares, six of them, had been brought out into the road, and therewithal too some pack-gear. Now, as he wondered at this, there came up a man leading four horses, and who should it be but his son Gunnlaug. Then said he:

I it was who brought out the sacks.

Illugi asked him why he had done so. He said that they should make his faring goods.

Illugi said: In nowise shalt thou thwart my will, nor fare anywhere sooner than I like! and in again he swung the ware-sacks therewith.

6

Then Gunnlaug rode thence and came in the evening down to Burg, and goodman Thorstein asked him to bide there, and Gunnlaug was fain of that proffer. He told Thorstein how things had gone betwixt him and his father, and Thorstein offered to let him bide there as long as he liked, and for some seasons Gunnlaug abode there, and learned law-craft of Thorstein, and all men accounted well of him.

Now Gunnlaug and Helga would be always at the chess-playing together, and very soon each found favour with the other, as came to be proven well enough afterwards: they were very nigh of an age.

Helga was so fair, that men of lore say that she was the fairest woman of Iceland, then or since; her hair was so plenteous and long that it could cover her all over, and it was as fair as a band of gold; nor was there any so good to choose as Helga the Fair in all Burgfirth, and far and wide elsewhere.

Now one day, as men sat in the hall at Burg, Gunnlaug spake to Thorstein: One thing in law there is which thou hast not taught me, and that is how to woo me a wife.

Thorstein said, That is but a small matter, and therewith taught him how to go about it.

Then said Gunnlaug, Now shalt thou try if I have understand all: I shall take thee by the hand and make as if I were wooing thy daughter Helga.

I see no need of that, says Thorstein. Gunnlaug, however, groped then and there after his hand, and seizing it said, Nay, grant me this though.

Do as thou wilt, then, said Thorstein; but be it known to all who are hereby that this shall be as if it had been unspoken, nor shall any guile follow herein.

Then Gunnlaug named for himself witnesses, and betrothed Helga to him, and asked thereafter if it would stand good thus. Thorstein said that it was well; and those who were present were mightily pleased at all this.

CHAPTER 5
Of Raven and His Kin

There was a man called Onund, who dwelt in the south at Mossfell: he was the wealthiest of men, and had a priesthood south there about the nesses. He was married, and his wife was called Geirny. She was the daughter of Gnup, son of Mold-Gnup, who settled at Grindwick, in the south country. Their sons were Raven, and Thorarin, and Eindridi; they were all hopeful men, but Raven was in all wise the first of them. He was a big man and strong, the sightliest of men and a good skald; and when he was fully grown he fared between sundry lands, and was well accounted of wherever he came.

Thorod the Sage, the son of Eyvind, then dwelt at Hjalli, south in Olfus, with Skapti his son, who was then the spokesman-at-law in Iceland. The mother of Skapti was Ranveig, daughter of Gnup, the son of Mold-Gnup; and Skapti and the sons of Onund were sisters' sons. Between these kinsmen was much friendship as well as kinship.

At this time Thorfin, the son of Selthorir, dwelt at Red-Mel, and had seven sons, who were all the hopefullest of men; and of them were these---Thorgils, Eyjolf, and Thorir; and they were all the greatest men out there.

But these men who have now been named lived all at one and the same time.

Next to this befell those tidings, the best that ever have befallen here in Iceland, that the whole land became Christian, and that all folk cast off the old faith.

CHAPTER 6
How Helga was Vowed to Gunnlaug,
and of Gunnlaug's Faring Abroad

Gunnlaug Worm-Tongue was, as is aforesaid, whiles at Burg with Thorstein, whiles with his father Illugi at Gilsbank, three winters together, and was by now eighteen winters old; and father and son were now much more of a mind.

There was a man called Thorkel the Black; he was a house-carle of Illugi, and near akin to him, and had been brought up in his house. To him fell an heritage north as As, in Water-dale, and he prayed Gunnlaug to go with him thither. This he did, and so they rode, the two together, to As. There they got the fee; it was given up to them by those who had the keeping of it, mostly because of Gunnlaug's furtherance.

But as they rode from the north they guested at Grimstongue, at a rich bonder's who dwelt there; but in the morning a herdsman took Gunnlaug's horse, and it had sweated much by then he got it back. Then Gunnlaug smote the herdsman, and stunned him; but the bonder would in nowise bear this, and claimed boot therefore. Gunnlaug offered to pay him one mark. The bonder thought it too little.

Then Gunnlaug sang:

> Bade I the middling mighty
> To have a mark of waves' flame;
> Giver of grey seas' glitter,
> This gift shalt thou make shift with.
> If the elf-sun of the waters
> From out of purse thou lettest,
> O waster of the worm's bed,
> Awaits thee sorrow later.

So the peace was made as Gunnlaug bade, and in such wise the two rode south.

Now, a little while after, Gunnlaug asked his father a second time for goods for going abroad.

Illugi says, Now shalt thou have thy will, for thou hast wrought thyself into something better than thou wert. So Illugi rode hastily from home, and bought for Gunnlaug half a ship which lay in Gufaros, from Audun Festargram -- this Audun was he who would not flit abroad the sons of Oswif the Wise, after the slaying of Kiartan Olafson, as is told in the story of the Laxdalemen, which thing though betid later than this. And when Illugi came home Gunnlaug thanked him well.

Thorkel the Black betook himself to seafaring with Gunnlaug, and their wares were brought to the ship; but Gunnlaug was at Burg while they made her ready, and found more cheer in talk with Helga than in toiling with chapmen.

Now one day Thorstein asked Gunnlaug if he would ride to his horses with him up to Longwater-dale. Gunnlaug said he would. So they ride both together till they come to the mountain-dairies of Thorstein, called Thorgilsstead. There were stud-horses of Thorstein, four of them together, all red of hue. There was one horse very goodly, but little tried: this horse Thorstein offered to give to Gunnlaug. He said he was in no need of horses, as he was going away from the country; and so they ride to other stud-horses. There was a grey horse with four mares, and he was the best of horses in Burgfirth. This one, too, Thorstein offered to give Gunnlaug, but he said, I desire these in no wise more than the others; but why dost thou not bid me what I will take?

What is that? said Thorstein.

Helga the Fair, thy daughter, says Gunnlaug.

That rede is not to be settled so hastily, said Thorstein; and therewithal got on other talk. And now they ride homewards down along Longwater.

Then said Gunnlaug, I must needs know what thou wilt answer me about the wooing.

Thorstein answers: I need not thy vain talk, says he.

Gunnlaug says, This is my whole mind, and no vain words.

Thorstein says, Thou shouldst first know thine own will. Art thou not bound to fare abroad? and yet thou makest as if thou wouldst go marry. Neither art thou an even match for Helga while thou art so unsettled, and therefore this cannot so much as be looked at.

Gunnlaug says, Where lookest thou for a match for thy daughter, if thou wilt not give her to the son of Illugi the Black; or who are they throughout Burg-firth who are of more note than he?

Thorstein answered: I will not play at men-mating, says he, but if thou wert such a man as he is, thou wouldst not be turned away.

Gunnlaug said, To whom wilt thou give thy daughter rather than to me?

Said Thorstein, Hereabout are many good men to choose from. Thorfin of Red-Mel hath seven sons, and all of them men of good manners.

Gunnlaug answers, Neither Onund nor Thorfin are men as good as my father. Nay, thou thyself clearly fallest short of him---or what hast thou to set against his strife with Thorgrim the Priest, the son of Kiallak, and his sons, at Thorsness Thing, where he carried all that was in debate?

Thorstein answers, I drave away Steinar, the son of Onund Sioni, which was deemed somewhat of a deed.

Gunnlaug says, Therein thou wast holpen by thy father Egil; and, to end all, it is for few bonders to cast away my alliance.

Said Thorstein, Carry thy cowing away to the fellows up yonder at the mountains; for down here, on the Meres, it shall avail thee nought.

Now in the evening they come home; but next morning Gunnlaug rode up to Gilsbank, and prayed his father to ride with him a-wooing out to Burg.

Illugi answered, Thou art an unsettled man, being bound for faring abroad, but makest now as if thou wouldst busy thyself with wife-wooing; and so much do I know, that this is not to Thorstein's mind.

Gunnlaug answers, I shall go abroad all the same, nor shall I be well pleased but if thou further this.

So after this Illugi rode with eleven men from home down to Burg, and Thorstein greeted him well. Early in the morning Illugi said to Thorstein, I would speak to thee.

Let us go, then, to the top of the Burg, and talk together there, said Thorstein; and so they did, and Gunnlaug went with them.

Then said Illugi, My kinsman Gunnlaug tells me that he has begun a talk with thee on his own behalf, praying that he might woo thy daughter Helga; but now I would fain know what is like to come of this matter. His kin is known to thee, and our possessions; from my hand shall be spared neither land nor rule over men, if such things might perchance further matters.

Thorstein said, Herein alone Gunnlaug pleases me not, that I find him an unsettled man; but if he were of a mind like thine, little would I hang back.

Illugi said, It will cut our friendship across if thou gainsayest me and my son an equal match.

Thorstein answers, For thy words and our friendship then, Helga shall be vowed, but not betrothed, to Gunnlaug, and shall bide for him three winters: but Gunnlaug shall go abroad and shape himself to the ways of good men; but I shall be free from all these matters if he does not then come back, or if his ways are not to my liking.

Thereat they parted; Illugi rode home, but Gunnlaug rode to his ship. But when they had wind at will they sailed for the main, and made the northern part of Norway, and sailed landward along Thrandheim to Nidaros; there they rode in the harbour, and unshipped their goods.

CHAPTER 7
Of Gunnlaug in the East and the West

In those days Earl Eric, the son of Hakon, and his brother Svein, ruled in Norway. Earl Eric abode as then at Hladir, which was left to him by his father, and a mighty lord he was. Skuli, the son of Thorstein, was with the earl at that time, and was one of his court, and well esteemed.

Now they say that Gunnlaug and Audun Festargram, and seven of them together, went up to Hladir to the earl. Gunnlaug was so clad that he had on a grey kirtle and white long-hose; he had a boil on his foot by the instep, and from this oozed blood and matter as he strode on. In this guise he went before the earl with Audun and the rest of them, and greeted him well. The earl knew Audun, and asked him tidings from Iceland. Audun told him what there was toward. Then the earl asked Gunnlaug who he was, and Gunnlaug told him his name and kin. Then the earl said: Skuli Thorstein's son, what manner of man is this in Iceland?

Lord, says he, give him good welcome, for he is the son of the best man in Iceland, Illugi the Black of Gilsbank, and my foster-brother withal.

The earl asked, What ails thy foot, Icelander?

A boil, lord, said he.

And yet thou wentest not halt.

Gunnlaug answers, Why go halt while both legs are long alike?

Then said one of the earl's men, called Thorir: He swaggereth hugely, this Icelander!It would not be amiss to try him a little.

Gunnlaug looked at him and sang:

> A courtman there is
> Full evil I wis,
> A bad man and black,
> Belief let him lack.

Then would Thorir seize an axe. The earl spake: Let it be, says he; to such things men should pay no heed. But now, Icelander, how old a man art thou?

Gunnlaug answers: I am eighteen winters old as now, says he.

Then says Earl Eric, My spell is that thou shalt not live eighteen winters more.

Gunnlaug said, somewhat under his breath: Pray not against me, but for thyself rather.

The earl asked thereat, What didst thou say, Icelander?

Gunnlaug answers, What I thought well befitting, that thou shouldst bid no prayers against me, but pray well for thyself rather.

What prayers, then? says the earl.

That thou mightest not meet thy death after the manner of Earl Hakon, thy father.

The earl turned red as blood, and bade them take the rascal in haste; but Skuli stepped up to the earl, and said: Do this for my words, lord, and give this man peace, so that he depart at his swiftest.

The earl answered, At his swiftest let him be off then, if he will have peace, and never let him come again within my realm.

Then Skuli went out with Gunnlaug down to the bridges, where there was an England-bound ship ready to put out; therein Skuli got for Gunnlaug a berth, as well as for Thorkel, his kinsman; but Gunnlaug gave his ship into Audun's ward, and so much of his goods as he did not take with him.

Now sail Gunnlaug and his fellows into the English main, and come at autumntide south to London Bridge, where they hauled ashore their ship.

Now at that time King Ethelred, the son of Edgar, ruled over England, and was a good lord; this winter he sat in London. But in those days there was the same tongue in England as in Norway and Denmark; but the tongues changed when William the Bastard won England, for thenceforward French went current there, for he was of French kin.

Gunnlaug went presently to the king, and greeted him well and worthily. The king asked him from what land he came, and Gunnlaug told him all as it was. But, said he, I have come to meet thee, lord, for that I have made a song on thee, and I would that it might please thee to hearken to that song. The king said it should be so, and Gunnlaug gave forth the song well and proudly; and this is the burden thereof: ---

> As God are all folk fearing
> The free lord King of England,
> Kin of all kings and all folk,
> To Ethelred the head bow.

The king thanked him for the song, and gave him as song-reward a scarlet cloak lined with the costliest of furs, and golden-broidered down to the hem; and made him his man; and Gunnlaug was with him all the winter, and was well accounted for.

One day, in the morning early, Gunnlaug met three men in a certain street, and Thororm was the name of their leader; he was big and strong, and right evil to deal with. He said, Northman, lend me some money.

Gunnlaug answered, That we're ill counselled to lend one's money to unknown men.

He said, I will pay it thee back on a named day.

Then shall it be risked, says Gunnlaug; and he lent him the fee withal.

But some time afterwards Gunnlaug met the king, and told him of the money-lending. The king answered, Now hast thou thriven little, for this is the greatest robber and reiver; deal with him in no wise, but I will give thee money as much as thine was.

Gunnlaug said, Then do we, your men, do after a sorry sort, if, treading sackless folk under foot, we let such fellows as this deal us out our lot. Nay, that shall never be.

Soon after he met Thororm and claimed the fee of him. He said he was not going to pay it.

Then sang Gunnlaug:

> Evil counselled art thou,
> Gold from us withholding;
> The reddener of the edges,
> Pricking on with tricking.
> Wot ye what? they called me,
> Worm-tongue, yet a youngling;
> Nor for nought so hight I;
> Now is time to show it!

Now I will make an offer good in law, says Gunnlaug; that thou either pay me my money, or else that thou go on holm with me in three nights' space.

Then laughed the viking, and said, Before thee none have come to that, to call me to holm, despite of all the ruin that many a man has had to take at my hands. Well, I am ready to go.

Thereon they parted for that time.

Gunnlaug told the king what had befallen; and he said, Now, indeed, have things taken a right hopeless turn; for this man's eyes can dull any weapon. But thou shalt follow my rede; here is a sword I will give thee -- with that thou shalt fight, but before the battle show him another.

Gunnlaug thanked the king well therefor.

Now when they were ready for the holm, Thororm asked what sort of sword it was that he had. Gunnlaug unsheathed it and showed him, but had a loop round the handle of the king's sword, and slipped it over his hand; the bearserk looked on the sword, and said, I fear not that sword.

But now he dealt a blow on Gunnlaug with his sword, and cut off from him nigh all his shield; Gunnlaug smote in turn with the king's gift; the bearserk stood shieldless before him, thinking he had the same weapon he had shown him, but Gunnlaug smote him his deathblow then and there.

The king thanked him for his work, and he got much fame therefor, both in England and far and wide elsewhere.

In the spring, when ships sailed from land to land, Gunnlaug prayed King Ethelred for leave to sail somewhither; the king asks what he was about then. Gunnlaug said, I would fulfil what I have given my word to do, and sang this stave withal:

> My ways must I be wending
> Three kings' walls to see yet,
> And earls twain, as I promised

Erewhile to land-sharers.
Neither will I wend me
Back, the worms'-bed lacking,
By war-lord's son, the wealth-free,
For work done gift well given.

So be it, then, skald, said the king, and withal he gave him a ring that weighed six ounces; but, said he, thou shalt give me thy word to come back next autumn, for I will not let thee go altogether, because of thy great prowess.

CHAPTER 8
Of Gunnlaug in Ireland

Thereafter Gunnlaug sailed from England with chapmen north to Dublin. In those days King Sigtrygg Silky-beard, son of King Olaf Kvaran and Queen Kormlada, ruled over Ireland; and he had then borne sway but a little while. Gunnlaug went before the king, and greeted them well and worthily. The king received him as was meet. Then Gunnlaug said, I have made a song on thee, and I would fain have silence therefor.

The king answered, No men have before now come forward with songs for me, and surely will I hearken to thine. Then Gunnlaug brought the song, whereof this is the burden:

Swaru's steed
Doth Sigtrygg feed.

And this is therein also:

Praise-worth I can
Well measure in man,
And kings, one by one---
Lo here, Kvaran's son!
Grudgeth the king
Gift of gold ring?
I, singer, know
His wont to bestow.
Let the high king say,
Heard he or this day,
Song drapu-measure
Dearer a treasure.

The king thanked him for the song, and called his treasurer to him, and said, How shall the song be rewarded?

What hast thou will to give, lord? says he.

How will it be rewarded if I give him two ships for it? said the king.

14

Then said the treasurer, This is too much, lord; other kings give in reward of songs good keepsakes, fair swords, or golden rings.

So the king gave him his own raiment of new scarlet, a gold-embroidered kirtle, and a cloak lined with choice furs, and a gold ring which weighed a mark. Gunnlaug thanked him well.

He dwelt a short time here, and then went thence to the Orkneys.

Then was lord in Orkney, Earl Sigurd, the son of Hlodver: he was friendly to Icelanders. Now Gunnlaug greeted the earl well, and said he had a song to bring him. The earl said he would listen thereto, since he was of such great kin in Iceland.

Then Gunnlaug brought the song; it was a shorter lay, and well done. The earl gave him for lay-reward a broad axe, all inlaid with silver, and bade him abide with him.

Gunnlaug thanked him both for his gift and his offer, but said he was bound east for Sweden; and thereafter he went on board ship with chapmen who sailed to Norway.

In the autumn they came east to King's Cliff, Thorkel, his kinsman, being with him all the time. From King's Cliff they got a guide up to West Gothland, and came upon a cheaping-stead, called Skarir: there ruled an earl called Sigurd, a man stricken in years. Gunnlaug went before him, and told him he had made a song on him; the earl gave a willing ear hereto, and Gunnlaug brought the song, which was a shorter lay.

The earl thanked him, and rewarded the song well, and bade him abide there that winter.

Earl Sigurd had a great Yule-feast in the winter, and on Yule-eve came thither men sent from Earl Eric of Norway, twelve of them together, and brought gifts to Earl Sigurd. The earl made them good cheer, and bade them sit by Gunnlaug through the Yule-tide; and there was great mirth at drinks.

Now the Gothlanders said that no earl was greater or of more fame than Earl Sigurd; but the Norwegians thought that Earl Eric was by far the foremost of the two. Hereon would they bandy words, till they both took Gunnlaug to be umpire in the matter.

Then he sang this stave:

Tell ye, staves of spear-din,
How on sleek-side sea-horse
Oft this earl hath proven
Over-toppling billows;
But Eric, victory's ash-tree,
Oft hath seen in east-seas
More of high blue billows
Before the bows a-roaring.

Both sides were content with his finding, but the Norwegians the best. But after Yule-tide those messengers left with gifts of goodly things, which Earl Sigurd sent to Earl Eric.

Now they told Earl Eric of Gunnlaug's finding: the earl thought that he had shown upright dealing and friendship to him herein, and let out some words, saying Gunnlaug should have good peace throughout his land. What the earl had said came thereafter to the ears of Gunnlaug.

But now Earl Sigurd gave Gunnlaug a guide east to Tenthland, in Sweden, as he had asked.

CHAPTER 9
Of the Quarrel Between Gunnlaug and Raven
Before the Swedish King

In those days King Olaf the Swede, son of King Eric the Victorious, and Sigrid the High-counselled, daughter of Skogul Tosti, ruled over Sweden. He was a mighty king and renowned, and full fain of fame.

Gunnlaug came to Upsala towards the time of the Thing of the Swedes in spring-tide; and when he got to see the king, he greeted him. The king took his greetings well, and asked who he was. He said he was an Iceland-man.

Then the king called out: Raven, says he, what man is he in Iceland?

Then one stood up from the lower bench, a big man and a stalwart, and stepped up before the king, and spake: Lord, says he, he is of good kin, and himself the most stalwart of men.

Let him go, then, and sit beside thee, said the king.

Then Gunnlaug said, I have a song to set forth before thee, king, and I would fain have peace while thou hearkenest thereto.

Go ye first, and sit ye down, says the king, for there is no leisure now to sit listening to songs.

So they did as he bade them.

Now Gunnlaug and Raven fell a-talking together, and each told each of his travels. Raven said that he had gone the summer before from Iceland to Norway, and had come east to Sweden in the forepart of winter. They soon got friendly together.

But one day, when the Thing was over, they were both before the king, Gunnlaug and Raven.

Then spake Gunnlaug, Now, lord, I would that thou shouldst hear the song.

That I may do now, said the king.

My song too willset forth now, says Raven.

Thou mayst do so, said the king.

Then Gunnlaug said, I will set forth mine first if thou wilt have it so, king.

Nay, said Raven, it behoveth me to be first, lord, for I myself came first to thee.

Whereto came our fathers forth, so that my father was the little boat towed behind? Whereto, but nowhere? says Gunnlaug. And in likewise shall it be with us.

Raven answered, Let us be courteous enough not to make this a matter of bandying of words. Let the king rule here.

The king said, Let Gunnlaug set forth his song first, for he will not be at peace till he has his will.

Then Gunnlaug set forth the song which he had made to King Olaf, and when it was at an end the king spake. Raven, says he, how is the song done?

Right well, he answered; it is a song full of big words and little beauty; a somewhat rugged song, as is Gunnlaug's own mood.

Well, Raven, thy song, said the king.

Raven gave it forth, and when it was done the king said, How is this song made, Gunnlaug?

Well it is, lord, he said; this is a pretty song, as is Raven himself to behold, and delicate of countenance. But why didst thou make a short song on the king, Raven? Didst thou perchance deem him unworthy of a long one?

Raven answered, Let us not talk longer on this; matters will be taken up again, though it be later.

And thereat they parted.

Soon after Raven became a man of King Olaf's, and asked him leave to go away. This the king granted him. And when Raven was ready to go, he spake to Gunnlaug, and said, Now shall our friendship be ended, for that thou must needs shame me here before great men; but in time to come I shall cast on thee no less shame than thou hadst will to cast on me here.

Gunnlaug answers: Thy threats grieve me nought. Nowhere are we likely to come where I shall be thought less worthy than thou.

King Olaf gave to Raven good gifts at parting, and thereafter he went away.

CHAPTER 10
How Raven Came Home to Iceland, and Asked for Helga to Wife

Now this spring Raven came from the east to Thrandheim, and fitted out his ship, and sailed in the summer to Iceland. He brought his ship to Leiruvag, below the Heath, and his friends and kinsmen were right fain of him. That winter

17

he was at home with his father, but the summer after he met at the Althing his kinsman, Skapti the law-man.

Then said Raven to him, Thine aid would I have to go a-wooing to Thorstein Egilson, to bid Helga his daughter.

Skapti answered, But is she not already vowed to Gunnlaug Worm-tongue?

Said Raven, Is not the appointed time of waiting between them passed by? And far too wanton is he withal, that he should hold or heed it aught.

Let us then do as thou wouldst, said Skapti.

Thereafter they went with many men to the booth of Thorstein Egilson, and he greeted them well.

Then Skapti spoke: Raven, my kinsman, is minded to woo thy daughter Helga. Thou knowest well his blood, his wealth, and his good manners, his many mighty kinsmen and friends.

Thorstein said, She is already the vowed maiden of Gunnlaug, and with him shall I hold all words spoken.

Skapti said, Are not the three winters worn now that were named between you?

Yes, said Thorstein; but the summer is not yet worn, and he may still come out this summer.

Then Skapti said, But if he cometh not this summer, what hope may we have of the matter then?

Thorstein answered, We are like to come here next summer, and then may we see what may wisely be done, but it will not do to speak hereof longer as at this time.

Thereon they parted. And men rode home from the Althing. But this talk of Raven's wooing of Helga was nought hidden.

That summer Gunnlaug came not out.

The next summer, at the Althing, Skapti and his folk pushed the wooing eagerly, and said that Thorstein was free as to all matters with Gunnlaug.

Thorstein answered, I have few daughters to see to, and fain am I that they should not be the cause of strife to any man. Now I will first see Illugi the Black. And so he did.

And when they met, he said to Illugi, Dost thou not think that I am free from all troth with thy son Gunnlaug?

Illugi said, Surely, if thou willest it. Little can I say herein, as I do not know clearly what Gunnlaug is about.

Then Thorstein went to Skapti, and a bargain was struck that the wedding should be at Burg, about winter-nights, if Gunnlaug did not come out that summer; but that Thorstein should be free from all troth with Raven if Gunnlaug should come and fetch his bride.

After this men rode home from the Thing, and Gunnlaug's coming was long drawn out. But Helga thought evilly of all these redes.

CHAPTER 11
Of How Gunnlaug Must Needs Abide Away from Iceland

Now it is to be told of Gunnlaug that he went from Sweden the same summer that Raven went to Iceland, and good gifts he had from King Olaf at parting.

King Ethelred welcomed Gunnlaug worthily, and that winter he was with the king, and was held in great favour.

In those days Knut the Great, son of Svein, ruled in Denmark, and had new-taken his father's heritage, and he vowed ever to wage war on England, for that his father had won a great realm there before he died west in that same land.

And at that time there was a great army of Danish men west there, whose chief was Heming, the son of Earl Strut-Harald, and brother to Earl Sigvaldi, and he held for King Knut that land that Svein had won.

Now in the spring Gunnlaug asked the king for leave to go away, but he said, It ill beseems that thou, my man, shouldst go away now, when all bodes such mighty war in the land.

Gunnlaug said, Thou shalt rule, lord; but give me leave next summer to depart, if the Danes come not.

The king answered, Then we shall see.

Now this summer went by, and the next winter, but no Danes came; and after midsummer Gunnlaug got his leave to depart from the king, and went thence east to Norway, and found Earl Eric in Thrandheim, at Hladir, and the earl greeted him well, and bade him abide with him. Gunnlaug thanked him for his offer, but said he would first go out to Iceland, to look to his promised maiden.

The earl said, Now all ships bound for Iceland have sailed.

Then said one of the court: Here lay, yesterday, Hallfred Troublous-Skald, out under Agdaness.

The earl answered, That may be well; he sailed hence five nights ago.

Then Earl Eric and Gunnlaug rowed out to Hallfred, who greeted him with joy; and forthwith a fair wind bore them from land, and they were right merry.

This was late in the summer: but now Hallfred said to Gunnlaug: Hast thou heard of how Raven, the son of Onund, is wooing Helga the Fair?

Gunnlaug said he had heard thereof, but dimly. Hallfred tells him all he knew of it, and therewith, too, that it was the talk of many men that Raven was in nowise less brave a man than Gunnlaug.

Then Gunnlaug sang this stave:

19

> Light the weather wafteth;
> But if this east wind drifted
> Week-long, wild upon us
> Little were I recking;
> More this word I mind of
> Me with Raven mated,
> Than gain for me the gold-foe
> Of days to make me grey-haired.

Then Hallfred said, Well, fellow, may'st thou fare better in thy strife with Raven than I did in mine. I brought my ship some winters ago into Leiruvag, and had to pay a half-mark in silver to a house-carle of Raven's, but I held it back from him. So Raven rode at us with sixty men, and cut the moorings of the ship, and she was driven up on the shallows, and we were bound for a wreck. Then I had to give selfdoom to Raven, and a whole mark I had to pay; and that is the tale of my dealings with him.

Then they two talked together alone of Helga the Fair, and Gunnlaug praised her much for her goodliness; and Gunnlaug sang:

> He who brand of battle
> Beareth over-wary,
> Never love shall let him
> Hold the linen-folded;
> For we when we were younger
> In many a way were playing
> On the outward nesses
> From golden land outstanding.

Well sung! said Hallfred.

CHAPTER 12
Of Gunnlaug's Landing,
and How He Found Helga Wedded to Raven

They made land north by Fox-Plain in Hraunhaven, half a month before winter, and there unshipped their goods. Now there was a man called Thord, a bonder's son of the Plain, there. He fell to wrestling with the chapmen, and they mostly got worsted at his hands.

Then a wrestling was settled between him and Gunnlaug. The night before Thord made vows to Thor for the victory; but the next day, when they met, they fell-to wrestling. Then Gunnlaug tripped both feet from under Thord, and gave him a great fall; but the foot that Gunnlaug stood on was put out of joint, and Gunnlaug fell together with Thord.

Then said Thord: Maybe that other things go no better for thee.

What then? says Gunnlaug.

20

Thy dealings with Raven, if he wed Helga the Fair at winter-nights. I was anigh at the Thing when that was settled last summer.

Gunnlaug answered naught thereto.

Now the foot was swathed, and put into joint again, and it swelled mightily; but he and Hallfred ride twelve in company till they come to Gilsbank, in Burg-firth, the very Saturday night when folk sat at the wedding at Burg. Illugi was fain of his son Gunnlaug and his fellows; but Gunnlaug said he would ride then and there down to Burg. Illugi said it was not wise to do so, and to all but Gunnlaug that seemed good. But Gunnlaug was then unfit to walk, because of his foot, though he would not let that be seen. Therefore there was no faring to Burg.

On the morrow Hallfred rode to Hreda-water, in North-water dale, where Galti, his brother and a brisk man, managed their matters.

CHAPTER 13
Of the Winter-Wedding at Skaney,
and How Gunnlaug Gave the King's Cloak to Helga

Tells the tale of Raven, that he sat at his wedding-feast at Burg, and it was the talk of most men that the bridge was but drooping; for true is the saw that saith, Long we remember what youth gained us, and even so it was with her now.

But this new thing befell at the feast, that Hungerd, the daughter of Thorod and Jofrid, was wooed by a man named Sverting, the son of Hafr-Biorn, the son of Mold-Gnup, and the wedding was to come off that winter after Yule, at Skaney, where dwelt Thorkel, a kinsman of Hungerd, and son of Torfi Valbrandsson; and the mother of Torfi was Thorodda, the sister of Odd of the Tongue.

Now Raven went home to Mossfell with Helga his wife. When they had been there a little while, one morning early before they rose up, Helga was awake, but Raven slept, and fared ill in his sleep. And when he woke Helga asked him what he had dreamt. Then Raven sang:

> In thine arms, so dreamed I,
> Hewn was I, gold island!
> Bride, in blood I bled there,
> Bed of thine was reddened.
> Never more then mightst thou,
> Mead-bowls' pourer speedy,
> Bind my gashes bloody---
> Lind-leek-bough thou lik'st it.

Helga spake: Never shall I weep therefor, quoth she; ye have evilly beguiled me, and Gunnlaug has surely come out. And therewith she wept much.

But, a little after, Gunnlaug's coming was bruited about, and Helga became so hard with Raven, that he could not keep her at home at Mossfell; so that back they had to go to Burg, and Raven got small share of her company.

21

Now men get ready for the winter-wedding. Thorkel of Skaney bade Illugi the Black and his sons. But when master Illugi got ready, Gunnlaug sat in the hall, and stirred not to go. Illugi went up to him and said, Why dost thou not get ready, kinsman?

Gunnlaug answered, I have no mind to go.

Says Illugi, Nay, but certes thou shalt go, kinsman, says he; and cast thou not grief over thee by yearning for one woman. Make as if thou knewest nought of it, for women thou wilt never lack.

Now Gunnlaug did as his father bade him; so they came to the wedding, and Illugi and his sons were set down in the high seat; but Thorstein Egilson, and Raven his son-in-law, and the bride-groom's following, were set in the other high seat, over against Illugi.

The women sat on the dais, and Helga the Fair sat next to the bride. Oft she turned her eyes on Gunnlaug, thereby proving the saw, Eyes will betray if maid love man.

Gunnlaug was well arrayed, and had on him that goodly raiment that King Sigtrygg had given him; and now he was thought far above all other men, because of the many things, both strength, and goodliness, and growth.

There was little mirth among folk at this wedding. But on the day when all men were making ready to go away the women stood up and got ready to go home. Then went Gunnlaug to talk to Helga, and long they talked together: but Gunnlaug sang:

> Light-heart lived the Worm-tongue
> All day long no longer
> In mountain-home, since Helga
> Had name of wife of Raven;
> Nought foresaw thy father,
> Hardener white of fight-thaw,
> What my words should come to.
> ---The maid to gold was wedded.

And again he sang:

> Worst reward I owe them,
> Father thine, O wine-may,
> And mother, that they made thee
> So fair beneath thy maid-gear;
> For thou, sweet field of sea-flame,
> All joy hast slain within me.
> Lo, here, take it, loveliest
> E'er made of lord and lady!

And therewith Gunnlaug gave Helga the cloak, Ethelred's gift, which was the fairest of things, and she thanked him well for the gift.

Then Gunnlaug went out, and by that time riding-horses had been brought home and saddled, and among them were many very good ones; and they were all tied up in the road. Gunnlaug leaps on to a horse, and rides a hand-gallop along the homefield up to a place where Raven happened to stand just before him; and Raven had to draw out of his way. Then Gunnlaug said:

No need to slink aback, Raven, for I threaten thee nought as at
this time; but thou knowest forsooth, what thou hast earned.

Raven answered and sang:

God of wound-flames glitter,
Glorier of fight-goddess,
Must we fall a-fighting
For fairest kirtle-bearer?
Death-staff, many such-like
Fair as she is are there
In south-lands o'er the sea-floods.
Sooth saith he who knoweth.

Maybe there are many such, but they do not seem so to me, said Gunnlaug.

Therewith Illugi and Thorstein ran up to them and would not have them fight.

Then Gunnlaug sang:

The fair-hued golden goddess
For gold to Raven sold they,
(Raven my match as men say)
While the mighty isle-king,
Ethelred, in England
From eastward way delayed me,
Wherefore to gold-waster
Waneth tongue's speech-hunger.

Hereafter both rode home, and all was quiet and tidingless that winter through; but Raven had nought of Helga's fellowship after her meeting with Gunnlaug.

CHAPTER 14
Of the Holmgang at the Althing

Now in summer men ride a very many to the Althing: Illugi the Black, and his sons with him, Gunnlaug and Hermund; Thorstein Egilson and Kolsvein his son; Onund, of Mossfell, and his sons all, and Sverting, Hafr-Biorn's son. Skapti yet held the spokesmanship-at-law.

One day at the Thing, as men went thronging to the Hill of Laws, and when the matters of the law were done there, then Gunnlaug craved silence and said:

Is Raven, the son of Onund, here?

He said he was.

Then spake Gunnlaug, Thou well knowest that thou hast got to wife my avowed bride, and thus hast thou made thyself my foe. Now for this I bid thee to holm here at the Thing, in the holm of the Axe-water, when three nights are gone by.

Raven answers, This is well bidden, as was to be looked for of thee, and for this I am ready, whenever thou willest it.

Now the kin of each deemed this a very ill thing. But, at that time it was lawful for him who thought himself wronged by another to call him to fight on the holm.

So when three nights had gone by they got ready for the holmgang, and Illugi the Black followed his son thither with a great following. But Skapti, the lawman, followed Raven, and his father and other kinsmen of his.

Now before Gunnlaug went upon the holm he sang:

> Out to isle of eel-field
> Dight am I to hie me:
> Give, O God, thy singer With glaive to end the striving.
> Here shall I the head cleave
> Of Helga's love's devourer,
> At last my bright sword bringeth
> Sundering of head and body.

Then Raven answered and sang:

> Thou, singer, knowest not surely
> Which of us twain shall gain it;
> With edge for leg-swathe eager,
> Here are the wound-scythes bare now.
> In whatso-wise we wound us,
> The tidings from the Thing here,
> And fame of thanes' fair doings,
> The fair young maid shall hear it.

Hermund held shield for his brother, Gunnlaug; but Sverting, Hafr-Biorn's son, was Raven's shield-bearer. Whoso should be wounded was to ransom himself from the holm with three marks of silver.

Now, Raven's part it was to deal the first blow, as he was the challenged man. He hewed at the upper part of Gunnlaug's shield, and the sword brake asunder just beneath the hilt, with so great might he smote; but the point of the sword flew up from the shield and struck Gunnlaug's cheek, whereby he got just grazed; with that their fathers ran in between them, and many other men.

Now, said Gunnlaug, I call Raven overcome, as he is weaponless.

But I say that thou art vanquished, since thou art wounded, said Raven.

Now, Gunnlaug was nigh mad, and very wrathful, and said it was not tried out yet.

Illugi, his father, said they should try no more for that time.

Gunnlaug said, Beyond all things I desire that I might in such wise meet Raven again, that thou, father, wert not anight to part us.

And thereat they parted for that time, and all men went back to their booths.

But on the second day after this it was made law in the law-court that, henceforth, all holmgangs should be forbidden; and this was done by the counsel of all the wisest men that were at the Thing; and there, indeed, were all the men of most counsel in the land. And this was the last holmgang fought in Iceland, this, wherein Gunnlaug and Raven fought.

But this Thing was the third most thronged Thing that has been held in Iceland; the first was after Njal's burning, the second after the Heath-slaughters.

Now, one morning, as the brothers Hermund and Gunnlaug went to Axe-water to wash, on the other side went many women towards the river, and in that company was Helga the Fair. Then said Hermund:

Dost thou see thy friend Helga there on the other side of the river?

Surely, I see her, says Gunnlaug, and withal he sang:

> Born was she for men's bickering:
> Sore bale hath wrought the war-stem,
> And I yearned every madly
> To hold that oak-tree golden.
> To me then, me destroyer
> Of swan-mead's flame, uneedful
> This looking on the dark-eyed,
> This golden land's beholding.

Therewith the crossed the river, and Helga and Gunnlaug spake awhile together, and as the brothers crossed the river eastward back again, Helga stood and gazed long after Gunnlaug.

Then Gunnlaug looked back and sang:

> Moon of linen-lapped one,
> Leek-sea-bearing goddess,
> Hawk-keen out of heaven
> Shone all bright upon me;
> But that eyelid's moonbeam
> Of gold-necklaced goddess
> Her hath all undoing
> Wrought, and me made nought of.

CHAPTER 15
How Gunnlaug and Raven Agreed to Go East to Norway, to Try the Matter Again

Now after these things were gone by men rode home from the Thing, and Gunnlaug dwelt at home at Gilsbank.

On a morning when he awoke all men had risen up, but he alone still lay abed; he lay in a shut-bed behind the seats. Now into the hall came twelve men, all full armed, and who should be there but Raven, Onund's son; Gunnlaug sprang up forthwith, and got to his weapons.

But Raven spake, Thou art in risk of no hurt this time, quoth he, but my errand hither is what thou shalt now hear: Thou didst call me to a holmgang last summer at the Althing, and thou didst not deem matters to be fairly tried therein; now I will offer thee this, that we both fare away from Iceland, and go abroad next summer, and go on holm in Norway, for there our kinsmen are not like to stand in our way.

Gunnlaug answered, Hail to thy words, stoutest of men! this thine offer I take gladly; and here, Raven, mayest thou have cheer as good as thou mayest desire.

It is well offered, said Raven, but this time we shall first have to ride away. Thereon they parted.

Now the kinsmen of both sore misliked them of this, but could in no wise undo it, because of the wrath of Gunnlaug and Raven; and, after all, that must betide that drew towards.

Now it is to be said of Raven that he fitted out his ship in Leiruvag; two men are named that went with him, sisters' sons of his father Onund, one hight Grim, the other Olaf, doughty men both. All the kinsmen of Raven thought it great scathe when he went away, but he said he had challenged Gunnlaug to the holmgang because he could have no joy soever of Helga; and he said, withal, that one must fall before the other.

So Raven put to sea, when he had wind at will, and brought his ship to Thrandheim, and was there that winter and heard nought of Gunnlaug that winter through; there he abode him the summer following: and still another winter was he in Thrandheim, at a place called Lifangr.

Gunnlaug Worm-tongue took ship with Hallfred Troublous-Skald, in the north at The Plain; they were very late ready for sea.

They sailed into the main when they had a fair wind, and made Orkney a little before the winter. Earl Sigurd Lodverson was still lord over the isles, and Gunnlaug went to him and abode there that winter, and the earl held him of much account.

In the spring the earl would go on warfare, and Gunnlaug made ready to go with him; and that summer they harried wide about the South-isles and Scotland's firths, and had many fights, and Gunnlaug always showed himself the bravest and doughtiest of fellows, and the hardiest of men wherever they came.

Earl Sigurd went back home early in the summer, but Gunnlaug took ship with chapmen, sailing for Norway, and he and Earl Sigurd parted in great friendship.

Gunnlaug fared north to Thrandheim, to Hladir, to see Earl Eric, and dwelt there through the early winter; the earl welcomed him gladly, and made offer to Gunnlaug to stay with him, and Gunnlaug agreed thereto.

The earl had heard already how all had befallen between Gunnlaug and Raven, and he told Gunnlaug that he laid ban on their fighting within his realm; Gunnlaug said the earl should be free to have his will herein.

So Gunnlaug abode there the winter through, ever heavy of mood.

CHAPTER 16
How the Two Foes Met and Fought at Dingness

But on a day in spring Gunnlaug was walking abroad, and his kinsman Thorkel with him; they walked away from the town, till on the meads before them they saw a ring of men, and in that ring were two men with weapons fencing; but one was named Raven, the other Gunnlaug, while they who stood by said that Icelanders smote light, and were slow to remember their words.

Gunnlaug saw the great mocking hereunder, and much jeering was brought into the play; and withal he went away silent.

So a little while after he said to the earl that he had no mind to bear any longer the jeers and mocks of his courtiers about his dealings with Raven, and therewith he prayed the earl to give him a guide to Lifangr: now before this the earl had been told that Raven had left Lifangr and gone east to Sweden; therefore, he granted Gunnlaug leave to go, and gave him two guides for the journey.

Now Gunnlaug went from Hladir with six men to Lifangr; and, on the morning of the very day whereas Gunnlaug came in in the evening, Raven had left Lifangr with four men. Thence Gunnlaug went to Vera-dale, and came always in the evening to where Raven had been the night before.

So Gunnlaug went on till he came to the uppermost farm in the valley, called Sula, wherefrom had Raven fared in the morning; there he stayed not his journey, but kept on his way through the night.

Then in the morning at sunrise they saw one another. Raven had got to a place where were two waters, and between them flat meads, and they are called Gleipni's meads: but into one water stretched a little ness called Dingness. There on the ness Raven and his fellows, five together, took their stand. With Raven were his kinsmen, Grim and Olaf.

Now when they met, Gunnlaug said, It is well that we have found one another.

Raven said that he had nought to quarrel with therein; But now, says he, thou mayest choose as thou wilt, either that we fight alone together, or that we fight all of us man to man.

Gunnlaug said that either way seemed good to him.

Then spake Raven's kinsmen, Grim and Olaf, and said that they would little like to stand by and look on the fight, and in like wise spake Thorkel the Black, the kinsman of Gunnlaug.

Then said Gunnlaug to the earl's guides, Ye shall sit by and aid neither side, and be here to tell of our meeting; and so they did.

So they set on, and fought dauntlessly, all of them. Grim and Olaf went both against Gunnlaug alone, and so closed their dealings with him that Gunnlaug slew them both and got no wound. This proves Thord Kolbeinson in a song that he made on Gunnlaug the Worm-tongue: ----

> Grim and Olaf, great-hearts
> In Gondul's din, with thin sword
> First did Gunnlaug fell there
> Ere at Raven fared he;
> Bold, with blood be-drifted
> Bane of three the thane was;
> War-lord of the wave-horse
> Wrought for men folks' slaughter.

Meanwhile Raven and Thorkel the Black, Gunnlaug's kinsman, fought until Thorkel fell before Raven and lost his life; and so at last all their fellowship fell. Then they two alone fought together with fierce onsets and mighty strokes, which they dealt each the other, falling on furiously without stop or delay.

Gunnlaug had the sword Ethelred's-gift, and that was the best of weapons. At last Gunnlaug dealt a mighty blow at Raven, and cut his leg from under him; but none the more did Raven fall, but swung round up to a tree-stem, whereat he steadied the stump.

Then said Gunnlaug, Now thou art no more meet for battle, nor will I fight thee any longer, a maimed man.

Raven answered: So it is, said he, that my lot is now all the worser lot, but it were well with me yet, might I but drink somewhat.

Gunnlaug said, Betray me not if I bring thee water in my helm.

I will not betray thee, said Raven.

Then went Gunnlaug to a brook and fetched water in his helm, and brought it to Raven; but Raven stretched forth his left hand to take it, but with his right hand drave his sword into Gunnlaug's head, and that was a mighty great wound.

Then Gunnlaug said, Evilly hast thou beguiled me, and done traitorously wherein I trusted thee.

Raven answers, Thou sayest sooth, but this brought me to it, that I begrudged thee to lie in the bosom of Helga the Fair.

Thereat they fought on, recking of nought; but the end of it was that Gunnlaug overcame Raven, and there Raven lost his life.

Then the earl's guides came forward and bound the head-wound of Gunnlaug, and in meanwhile he sat and sang:

> O thou sword-storm stirrer,
> Raven, stem of battle
> Famous, fared against me

Fiercely in the spear din.
Many a flight of metal
Was borne on me this morning,
By the spear-walls' builder,
Ring-bearer, on hard Dingness.

After that they buried the dead, and got Gunnlaug on to his horse thereafter, and brought him right down to Lifangr. There he lay three nights, and got all his rights of a priest , and died thereafter, and was buried at the church there.

All men thought it great scathe of both of these men, Gunnlaug and Raven, amid such deeds as they died.

CHAPTER 17
The News of the Fight Brought to Iceland

Now this summer, before these tidings were brought out hither to Iceland, Illugi the Black, being at home at Gilsbank, dreamed a dream: he thought that Gunnlaug came to him in his sleep, all bloody, and he sang in the dream this stave before him; and Illugi remembered the song when he woke, and sang it before others:

Knew I of the hewing
Of Raven's hilt-finned steel-fish
Byrny-shearing----sword-edge
Sharp clave leg of Raven. ----
Of warm wounds drank the eagle,
When the war-rod slender,
Cleaver of the corpses,
Clave the head of Gunnlaug.

This portent befel south at Mossfell, the selfsame night, that Onund dreamed how Raven came to him, covered all over with blood, and sang:

Red is the sword, but I now
Am undone by Sword-Odin.
'Gainst shields beyond the sea-flood
The ruin of shields was wielded.
Methinks the blood-fowl blood-stained
In blood o'er men's heads stood there,
The wound-erne yet wound-eager
Trod over wounded bodies.

Now the second summer after this, Illugi the Black spoke at the Althing from the Hill of Laws, and said:

Wherewith wilt thou make atonement to me for my son, whom Raven, thy son, beguiled in his troth?

Onund answers, Be it far from me to atone for him, so sorely as their meeting hath wounded me. Yet will I not ask atonement of thee for my son.

Then shall my wrath come home to some of thy kin, says Illugi. And withal after the Thing was Illugi at most times very sad.

Tells the tale how this autumn Illugi rode from Gilsbank with thirty men, and came to Mossfell early in the morning. Then Onund got into the church with his sons, and took sanctuary; but Illugi caught two of his kin, one called Biorn and the other Thorgrim, and had Biorn slain, but the feet smitten from Thorgrim. And thereafter Illugi rode home, and there was no righting of this for Onund.

Hermund, Illugi's son, had little joy after the death of Gunnlaug his brother, and deemed he was none the more avenged even though this had been wrought.

Now there was a man called Raven, brother's son to Onund of Mossfell; he was a great seafarer, and had a ship that lay up in Ramfirth: and in the spring Hermund Illugison rode from home alone north over Holt-beacon Heath, even to Ramfirth, and out as far as Board-ere to the ship of the chapmen. The chapmen were then nearly ready for sea; Raven, the ship-master, was on shore, and many men with him; Hermund rode up to him, and thrust him through with his spear, and rode away forthwith: but all Raven's men were bewildered at seeing Hermund.

No atonement came for this slaying, and there with ended the dealings of Illugi the Black and Onund of Mossfell.

CHAPTER 18
The Death of Helga the Fair

As time went on, Thorstein Egilson married his daughter Helga to a man called Thorkel, son of Hallkel, who lived west in Hraundale. Helga went to his house with him, but loved him little, for she cannot cease to think of Gunnlaug, though he be dead. Yet was Thorkel a doughty man, and wealthy of goods, and a good skald.

They had children together not a few, one of them was called Thorarin, another Thorstein, and yet more they had.

But Helga's chief joy was to pluck at the threads of that cloak, Gunnlaug's-gift, and she would be ever gazing at it.

But on a time there came a great sickness to the house of Thorkel and Helga, and many were bed-ridden for a long time. Helga also fell sick, and yet she could not keep abed.

So one Saturday evening Helga sat in the firehall, and leaned her head upon her husband's knees, and had the cloak Gunnlaug's-gift sent for; and when the cloak came to her she sat up and plucked at it, and gazed thereon awhile, and then sank back upon her husband's bosom, and was dead. Then Thorkel sang this:

Dead in mine arms she droopeth,
My dear one, gold-rings bearer,
For God hath changed the life-days
Of this Lady of the linen.
Weary pain hath pined her,
But unto me, the seeker
Of hoard of fishes highway,
Abiding here is wearier.

Helga was buried in the church there, but Thorkel dwelt yet at Hraundale: but a great matter seemed the death of Helga to all, as was to be looked for.

And here endeth the story.

THE STORY OF HEN-THORIR

CHAPTER 1
Of Men of Burgfirth

There was a man hight Odd, the son of Onund Broadbeard, the son of Wolf of Fitiar, the son of Thorir the Stamper; he dwelt at Broadlairstead in Reekdale of Burgfirth. His wife was Jorun, a wise woman and well spoken of. Four children had they, two sons of good conditions, and. two daughters: one of their sons hight Thorod, and the other Thorwald; Thurid was one daughter of Odd, and Jofrid the other. Odd was by-named Odd-a-Tongue; he was not held for a man of fair dealings.

A man named Torn, the son of Valbrand, the son of Valthiof, the son of Orlyg of Esjuberg, had wedded Thurid, daughter of Odd-a-Tongue, and they dwelt at the other Broadlairstead.

There was a man hight Arngrim, the son of Helgi, the son of Hogni, who came out with Hromund; he dwelt at Northtongue; he was called Arngrim the priest, and his son was Helgi.

There was a man hight Blundketil, son of Geir the Wealthy, the son of Ketil Blund, after whom as Blundwater named: he dwelt at Ornolfsdale somewhat above where the house now standeth; there were many steads upward from it; and his son was Herstein. Blundketil was the wealthiest of all men, and the best conditioned of all men of the ancient faith; thirty tenants he had, and was the best-beloved man of the countryside.

There was a man called Thorkel Welt, the son of Red Biorn; he dwelt at Swigniskarth, west-away of Northwater. Helgi his brother dwelt at Hwamm in

Northwaterdale.; another brother was Gunnwald, who had to wife Helga, daughter of Thorgeir of Withymere. Thorkel Welt was a wise man and well-befriended, very wealthy of goods.

There was a certain man hight Thorir, needy of money, not well-loved of the folk: his wont it was to go a-huokstering in summer-tide from one countryside to the other, selling in one place what he had bought in another; by which peddling his wealth waxed fast; and on a time when he went from the south over Holtbeacon Heath, he had hens with him in his journey to the north country, and sold them with his other wares, wherefore was he called Hen Thorir.

Now throve Thorir so much that he bought him land at a place called the Water, up from North-tongue, and but a few winters had he set up house before he became so very wealthy that he had moneys out with well-nigh every man. Yet though his fortune were amended, yet still prevailed his ill favour amongst men, for hardly was there any so well-hated as was Hen Thorir.

CHAPTER 2
Hen-Thorir Fosters Helgi Arngrimson

On a day Thorir went his ways from home and rode to Northtongue to see Arngrim the priest, and craved to have the fostering of a child of his. "I would," said he, "take to me Helgi thy son, and heed him all I can, and have thy friendship in return, and furtherance herein, to wit, the getting of my rights from men."

Arngrim answered: "Little furtherance to me do I see in this fostering." Answered Thorir: "I will give the lad my money to the half-part rather than lose the fostering of him : but thou shalt right me and be bound thereto, with whomsoever I may have to do."

Arngrim answered: "Sooth to say, I will not put from me so good an offer."

So Helgi went home with Thorir, and the stead has been called thenceforward Heigiwater. And now Arngrim gave an eye to Thorir's business, and straightway men deemed him harder yet to deal with; he got his rights now of every man, and throve exceedingly in wealth, and became an exceeding rich man, but his ill favour stuck to him.

On a summer came a ship into Burgfirth, but lay not in the river-mouth, but in the roads without. Erne was the shipmaster's name, a man well-liked, and the best of chapman-lads. Now Odd heard of the ship's coming, and he was wont to come in good time to the opening of markets, and settle the prices of men's ladings, for he had the rule of

the countryside; neither durst any man fall to chaffer before they wotted what he would do. So now he went to the chapmen, and asked them what they had a mind to do about their voyage, and how soon they would have their market; and therewithal he told them of his wont of settling the prices of men's ladings. Erne answered : "We have a mind to be masters of our own for all thou mayst have to say; since not a penny's worth in the lading is thine; so this time thy words will be mightier than thy deeds."

Odd answered: "I misdoubt me that it will do worse for thee than for me: so be it then; for hereby I proclaim that I forbid all men to have any chaffer with you, or to land any goods; yea, I shall take money from all such as give you any help ; and I know that ye shall not away out of the haven before the spring-tide."

Erne answered: "Say what thou wilt; but none the more for that will we let ourselves be cowed."

Now Odd rides home, but the Eastmen lie in the haven wind-bound.

CHAPTER 3
Blundketil Takes the Eastmen to Him

The next day Herstein, Blundketil's son, rode west to Akraness, and he met the Eastmen as he came back, and found an old acquaintance in the master, and that was much to his mind.

Erne told Herstein what great wrong Odd had offered them. "And," quoth he, "we misdoubt us how we shall go about; our affair." So they talked together daylong and at eve rides Herstein home, and tells his father of the mariners to what pass their business has come. Blundketil answered: "I know the man now from thy story of him, for I was with his father when I was a child, nor ever fell I in with a fellow better at need than was he; so ill it is that his son is hard bestead, and his father would look to me to take some heed to his fortune if need were; so betimes tomorrow shalt thou ride down to the Haven, and bid him hither with as many men as he will; or he be liefer thereto, then will I flit him north or south, or where he will; and I will help him with all my heart as far as in me lies."

Herstein said it was good rede and manly: "Yet it is to be looked for that we shall have some folks' displeasure for it." Blundketil answered: "Whereas we have to carry about nought worse than Odd, we may lightly bear it." So weareth the night, and betimes on the morrow Blundketil let gather horses from the pastures, and when all was ready Herstein drave an hundred horses to meet the chapmen, nor need they crave any from any other stead. So he came thither to them, and told Erne what his father had taken on himself. Erne said he would take that with a good heart, but that he deemed the father and son would have the enmity of others for it; but Herstein said they heeded it nought. Then said Erne : "Well, my crew shall be flitted into other countrysides, for the risk is enough, though we be not all in one and the same house." So Herstein had Erne and his lading home with him, and left not before all the chapmen were gone, and the ship laid up, and all brought into due order.

Blundketil received Erne wondrous well, and there he abode in good entertainment.

But now were tidings brought to Odd of what Blundketil had done, and men talk over it, and say that he had set himself up against Odd thereby. Odd answereth:

"So may folk say; but Blundketil is such a man as is both sturdy and well-beloved, so I will even let the matter alone."

And so all is quiet.

CHAPTER 4
Hay-Need this Season

That summer was the grass light and bad, and hay-harvest poor because of the wet, and men had exceeding small hay-stores. Blundketil went round to his tenants that autumn, and told them that he would have his rents paid in hay on all his lands: "For I have much cattle to fodder, and little hay enow; but I will settle how much is to be slaughtered this autumn in every house of my tenants, and then will matters go well." Now weareth summer away and cometh winter, and there soon began to be exceeding scarcity north about the Lithe, and but little store there was to meet it, and men were hard pressed. So weareth the time over Yule, and when Thorri-tide was come folk were sore pinched, and for many the game was up.

But on an evening came to Blundketil one of his tenants, and told him that hay had failed him, and prayed deliverance of him. Master Blundketil answered: "How cometh that? I deemed that I had so looked to it in the autumn that things would be like to go well."

The man answered that less had been slaughtered than he had commanded. . Then said Blundketil: "Well, let us make a bargain together: I will deliver thee from thy trouble this time, but thou shalt tell no man thereof; because I would not that folk should fall to coming on me: all the less since ye have not kept my commandment"

So that man fared home, and told his friend that Blundketil was peerless among men in all dealings, and that he had helped him at his need ; and that man in turn told his friend, and so the matter became known all over the countryside.

Time wore and Goi came, and therewith came two more of the tenants to Blundketil, and told him that they were out of hay. Blundketil answered ; "Ye have done ill in departing from my counsel; for so it is, that though I have hay good store, yet have I more beasts therewithal: now if I help you, then shall I have nought for my own stock; lo you! that is the choice herein. But they pressed the case, and bewailed their misery, till he thought it pity of their moans, and so let drive home an hundred and forty horses, and let slay forty of the worst of them, and gave his tenants the fodder these should have had: so they fare home glad at. heart. But the winter worsened as it wore, and the hope of many a man was quenched.

CHAPTER 5
Blundketil Would Buy Hay of Hen Thorir

Now when One-month was come came two more of Blundketil's tenants to him; they were somewhat better to do, but their hay had failed them now, arid they prayed him to deliver them. He answered and said that he had not wherewithal, and that he would slaughter no more beasts. Then they asked if he knew of any man who had hay to sell, and he said he knew not for certain; but they drive on the matter, saying that their beasts must; die if they get no help of him ; he said : "It is your own doing; but I am told that Hen Thorir will have hay to sell."

They said : "We shall get nought of him unless thou go along with us, but he will straightway sell to us if thou become our surety in the bargain."

He answers: "I may do as much as to go?with you, for it is meet that they should sell who have."

So they fare betimes in the morning, and there was a drift of wind from the north, which Was somewhat cold ; master Thorir was standing without at the time, and when he saw folk coming toward the garth, in he walks again, shuts to the door, draws the bolt, and goes to his day-meal. Now was the door smitten on, and the lad Helgi took up the word and said : "Go thou out, foster-father, for here be men come to see thee." Thorir said he would eat his meat first; but the lad ran from the table, and came to the door and greeted the new-comers well. Blundketil asked ,if Thorir were within and the lad said that so it was. "Bid him come out to us then" said Blundketil. The lad did so, and said that Blundketil was without, and would seeThorir. He answered: "Wherefore must Blundketil be sniffing about here? It is wondrous if he come for any good. I have nought to do with him." Then goes the lad and says that Thorir will not come out. "Then shall we go in" said Blundketil.

So they go into the chamber and are greeted there; but Thorir held his peace. "Things are come to this, Thorir" said Blundketil "that we would buy hay of thee."

Thorir answered: "Thy money is no better to me than mine own."

"That is as it may be," said Blundketil. Thorir said: "How comest thou, rich man as thou art, to lack hay?". "Nay, I am not come to that,"said Blundketil; "I am dealing for my tenants here, who verily need help, and. I would fain get it for them if it were to be got." Said Thorir: "Thou art right welcome to give to others of thine own, but not of mine."

Blundketil answered: "We will not ask a gift: let Odd and Arngrim be thine umpires, and I will give thee gifts moreover."

Thorir said: "I have no hay to sell;, and, moreover, I will not sell it." Then went Blundketil out, and those fellows and the lad with them; and then Blunketil took up the word and said : "Which is it, that thy foster-father has no hay, or that he will not sell it?"

"Hay enough he has to sell if he would," answers the lad. Blundketil said: "Bring us to where the haystacks are."

35

He did so, and then Blundketil made a reckoning of the fodder for Thorir's stock, and made out that if they were all stall-fed up to the time of the Althing, there would still be of the hay five stacks over; so herewith they go in again, and Blundketil says: " I reckon about thy stock of hay, Thorir, that if all thy beasts were fed at stall till the Althing, there would yet be a good deal left over; and that would I buy of thee.' Thorir answered : "And ' what shall I do for hay next winter then, if it is like this or worse?" Says Blundketil: "I will give thee the choice to take just the same lot of hay and no worse in the summer, and I will bring it into thy garth for thee."

Thorir answered: "If thou hast no store of hay now, why shouldst thou have more in the summer? but I know there is such odds of might between us, that thou mayest take my hay in despite of me if thou wilt."

Blundketil answers: "That is not the way to take it: thou wottest that silver goeth in all the markets of the land here, and therein will I pay thee."

"I will not have thy silver," said Thorir.

"Then take thou such wares as Odd and Arn-grim shall award thee," said Blundketil.

"Here are but few workmen," said Thorir, "and I like going about but little, nor will I be dragged hither and thither in such dealings."

Blundketil answereth: " Then shall I let bear the goods home for thee." Thorir said: "I have no house-room for them, and they shall certainly be spoilt.

Answereth Blundketil: "I shall get thee hides, then, to do over them, so that they shall be safe."

Thorir answers: "I will not have other men scratching about in my storehouses."

Says Blundketil: "Then shall they be at my house through the winter, and I will take care of them for thee."

"I know all thy babble now," said Thorir, "and

I will in no wise deal with thee;"

Blundketil said: "Then must things go a worser road; for the hay will we have all the same, though thou forbid it, and lay the price thereof in its stead, making the most of it that we are many."

Then Thorir held his peace, but his mind was nothing good. Blundketil let take ropes and bind up the hay, and then they hove it up in loads on to the horses and bore it away; but made up the price in full.

CHAPTER 6
Thorir Would Make a Case Against Blundketil

Now shall we tell what Thorir fell to : he gat him gone from home with Helgi his Foster-son, and they ride to Northtongue, and are greeted there wondrous well, and Arngrim asks for tidings. Thorir answered: "I have heard of nought newer than the robbery." "Nay, now, what robbery?" said Arngrim.

Thorir answered: "Blundketil has robbed me of all my hay so that there is hardly a wisp left to throw to the neat in the cold weather."

"Is it so, Helgi?" asked Arngrim.

"Not one whit," said Helgi; "Blundketil did right well in the matter." And therewith he told how the thing had gone between them.

Then said Arngrim ; "Yea, that is more like; and the hay that he hath gotten is better bestowed than that which shall rot on thine hands."

Thorir answered: "In an evil hour I offered; fostering to thy child ; forsooth, whatsoever ill deed is done to me in mine own house none the more, shall I be righted here, or holpen at thine hands; a mighty shame is that to thee."

Arngrim answers: "Forsooth, that, was a rash deed from the first, for I wot that in thee I have to do with an evil man."

"Nay, words will not slay me," said Thorir; "but I am ill content that thou rewardest my good deeds in such wise ; but so it is that:what men rob from me is taken from thee no less." They parted with things in such a plight. Thorir rides away, and comes to Broadlairstead, where Odd greeted him well, and asked for tidings.

"Nought have I heard newer than the robbery," said Thorir. "Nay, now, what robbery?" said Odd.

Thorir. answered : "Blundketil took all my hay, so that my store is clean gone; and I would fain have thy furtherance; moreover, the matter toucheth thee, whereas thou art a ruler in the countryside, to right what is wrong; and thou mayest call to mind withal that he hath made himself thy foe."

Odd asked: "Is it so, Helgi?" He answered that Thorir had wrested the matter clean away from the truth, and he set forth how the whole thing had gone. Odd answered "I will have nought to do with it; I should have done likewise if need had been." Said Thorir: "'True is the saw that saith, 'Best but to hear of woeful thanes;' and this also: 'A man's foes are those of his own house.'"

Therewithal rides Thorir away, and Helgi with him, and home he fareth ill-content.

CHAPTER 7
Of Thorwald, Odd-a-Tongue's Son

Thorwald, the son of Odd-a-Tongue, had come ashore that summer in the north country, and had guested there through the winter; but as it drew toward summer, he fared from the north to go see his father and abode a night at Northtongue in good cheer. Now there was a man guesting there already, called Vidfari, a gangrel man who went from one corner of the land to the other; he was nigh akin to Thorir, and like to him in mind and mood. So that same evening he gathered up his clothes and took to his heels, and ran away and stayed not till he came to Thorir, who welcomed him with open arms, saying "Surely something good will come to me of thy homing." He answered: "That may well be, for now is Thorwald Oddson come to Northtongue, and is a-guesting there now."

Said Thorir: "I thought I saw somegood coming to me from thine hands, so well was all with me!"

So weareth the night, and the first thing on the morrow rideth Thorir with his foster-son to North-tongue : thereto was come much folk, but the lad had a seat given to him; while Thorir wandered about the floor.

Now Thorwald, a-sitting on the dais, sets eyes on him as he talks privily to Arngrim, of whom he asketh: "What man is he wandering about the floor yonder?"

Arngrim answereth: "That is my son's fosterer" "Yea," says Thorwald; " why shall he not have a seat then?"

Arngrim says: "That is no matter of thine."

"Well, it shall not be so," says Thorwald and he lets call Thorir to him therewith, and gives him a seat beside himself, and asks for the tidings most spoken about. Thorir answered : "Sore was I tried whereas Blundketil robbed me."

"Are ye at one on it?" said Thorwald.

"Far from it," said Thorir.

"How cometh it, Arngrim," said Thorwald, "that ye great men let such shameful doings go on?"

Arngrim answered: "It is mostly lies, and there is but little in the bottom of the matter."

"Yet it was true that he had the hay?" said Thorwald,

"Yea," said Arngrim, "he had it sure enough."

"Every man has a right to rule his own," says Thorwald; "and withal your friendship for him goes for little if thou let him be trodden under foot."

"Thou art dear to my heart, Thorwald," said Hen Thorir, "and my heart tells me'that thou wilt right my case somewhat."

Said Thorwald: "I am but feeble to lean on."

Thorir said: "I will give thee half my wealth for the righting of my case, that I may have either outlawry or self-doom, so that my foes may not sit over mine own."

Arngrim said: "Do it not, Thorwald, for in him ye have no trusty fellow to backup; and 'in Blundketil thou wilt have to do with a man both wise and mighty, and well befriended on all sides."

"I see," said Thorwald, "that envy hath got hold of thee for my taking of his money, and that thou grudgest it me."

38

Said Thorir: "Consider, Thorwald, that my wealth will be found to be in good kind and other men wot that far and wide money for mine own goods is withheld from me."

Arngrim said: "I would fain hinder thee still; Thorwald, from taking up this case, but thou must even do as it seemeth good to thee ; I misdoubt me though, that things great and evil will come of this."

Thorwald answers: "Well, I will not refuse wealth offered."

Now hansels Thorir half his wealth to him, and therewith the case against Blundketil.

Then spake Arngrim again: "How art thou minded to set about the case?" Thorwald answered: "I shall first go see my father, and take counsel with him."

"Nay," said Thorir, "that is not to my mind: I will not hang back now I have staked so much hereon; I will have you go summon Blundketil forthwith tomorrow." Thorwald answereth : "It will be seen of thee that thou art no lucky man, and ill will be born of thee; yet now thou must needs have thy way."

So he and Thorir bind themselves to meet on the morrow at a place appointed.

CHAPTER 8
The Summoning of Master Blundketil

Betimes on the morrow, therefore, rides Thorwald, and Arngrim with him, thirty men in company, and meet Thorir, who had but two with him, Helgi Arngrimson, to wit, and Vidfari, Thorir's kinsman. "Why are ye so few, Thorir" said Thorwald. Thorir answered: "I knew well that ye would not lack men." So they ride up along the Lithe, and their going was seen from the steads, and every man ran from out his house, and he thought himself happiest who got first to Blundketil's, so that a many men awaited them there.

Thorwald and his folk ride up to the garth, and leap off their horses, and walk up to the house. Blundketil sees it and goes to meet them and bids them take due entertainment. Said Thorwald: "Other errand have we here than the eating of meat; I willl wot how thou wilt answer for that matter of the taking of Thorir's hay in his despite." "Even as to him," said Blundketil, "award it at what price soever ye will; and to thee will I give gifts over and above; the better and the more to thee as thou art the more worthy than Thorir; and I shall make thine honour so great that all men shall be a-talking of it how thou art well honoured:" "Thorwald was silent, for he deemed this well offered, but Thorir answered, and said: "We will not 'take it; there is no need to think of it; this choice I had erewhile, and little do I deem me holpen if so it be; and it avails me little that I have given thee my wealth."

Then said Thorwald: "What wilt thou do, Blundketil, as to the law herein?" "Nothing but this; that thou award and shape it thyself alone, even as thou wilt." Then answered Thorwald : "Well, meseemeth, there is nothing for it but to take the case into court." And therewith he summoned Blundketil for robbery, naming witnesses thereto, and his words and the summoning were of the hardest that are.

Now turneth Blundketil back toward the house, and meeteth Erne the Eastman a-going about his wares. Erne asked : "Art thou wounded, master, that thou art red as blood?"

"Nay, I am not wounded," said he, "but I had as lief be, for I haye had words said to me that never have been uttered before ; I am called thief and robber."

Ernie takes his bow and sets an arrow on the string, and he comes out just as the others were a-leaping a-horseback; he shot, and a man met the arrow, and sank down from his horse -- who but Helgi, son of Arngrim the priest -- they ran to him, but Thorir pushed forward between them, and thrust the men from, him, bidding them give place: "For this concerneth me most." He bent down over Helgi, who was verily dead by now; but Thorir said; "Is there yet a little might in thee, foster-son?" Then he arose from the corpse and said: "The lad spake twice to me in the same wise, even thus: "Burn! Burn Blundketil In!"

Then answered Arngrim and said: "Now it fares as I misdoubted; for, Oft cometh ill from an ill man; and verily I feared that great ill would come from thee, Thorir, and now, in spite of thy babble, I wot not if the lad really spoke it, though it is not unlike that it will come to that; for evilly the thing began, and in likewise shall end mayhap." "Meseemeth" said Thorir, "that something lieth nearer to thine hand than scolding at me."

So Arngrim and his folk ride away to the edge of a wood and leap off their horses, and abide there till nightfall.

Blundketil thanked his men well for their helping, and so bade every man ride his ways home as he best might.

CHAPTER 9
The Burning of Blundketil

So it is said that at nightfall Thorwald and his company ride to the house at Ornolfe-dale, where all folk were now asleep; there they drag a stack of brushwood to the house, and sef fire thereto; and Blundketil and his folk awoke not before the house was ablaze over them.

Blundketil asked who had lighted that hot fire, and Thorir told who they were. Blundketil asked

if aught might get him peace; but Thorir said "There is nought for it but to burn." And they departed not before every man's child therein was burnt up.

Now Herstein, Blundketil's ;son, had gone that evening to his foster-father Thorbiorn, who was by-named the Strider, and of whom it was said that he was not always all utterly there where he was seen. So Herstein awoke the next morning; and asked his foster-father if he were awake. "Yea," said he, "what wilt thou?" "Medreamed that my father came in hither with his raiment all ablaze, and even as one flame, he seemed to me." Then they arise and go out, and see the fire presently: so they take their weapons, and go thither in haste; but .all men were gone away by then they came thither. Said Herstein:

"Woeful tidings have befallen here; what rede now?"

Thorbiorn answers; "Now will I make the most of the offer which Odd-a-Tongue hath often made me, to come to him if I were in any need." "Nought hopeful I deem that," saith Herstein. But they go nevertheless, and Come to Broadlair-stead, and call out Odd; who cometh out and greeteth them, and asketh for tidings ; so they told him what had come to pass, and he spake as deeming it ill. Then Thorbiorn taketh up the word: "So it is, master Odd," saith he, "that thou hast promised me thy furtherance; now therefore will I take; it of thee if thou wilt give us some good rede, and bring it to pass." Odd said that he would do even so; and so they ride to Ornolfsdale, and come there before day; by then were the houses fallen in, and the fire was growing pale.

So Odd rideth to a certain house that, was not utterly burned; there he laid hold of a birch rafter, and pulled it down from the house, and then rode with the burning brand withershins round about the house, and spake: "Here take I land to my self, for here I see no house inhabited; hearken; ye to this all witnesses hereby;" And therewithal he smote his horse, and rode away. Then said Herstein: "What rede now? This one has turned out ill." Said Thorbiorn: "Hold thou thy peace if thou mayest, whatsoever befall."

Herstein answered and said that all he had spoken hitherto was not overmuch forsooth. Now the outbower wherein was the lading of the East-men was unburned and much other goods was therein moreover. Herewith old Thorbiorn vanished away, and as Herstein looked on the house, he saw this outbower opened, and the goods borne out, but yet beheld no man: Then are the goods bound up into loads; and then he hears a great clatter in the home-mead, and lo ! his father's horses are being driven home, and the sheep, and the neat from the byre, and all the live-stock': then were the loads heaved up, and the whole drove went their ways, and every penny's-worth brought off. Then Herstein turned about, and saw that master Thorbiorn was driving the cattle.

So they wend their ways down along the country side to Staff holts-tongue, and so west over North water.

CHAPTER 10
Of Thorkel Welt and Gunnar Hlifarson

The shepherd of Thorkel Welt of Swigni-skarth went to his sheep that morning, and he saw them a-faring on and driving all kind of cattle; so he told Thorkel thereof, who answers: "I wot how it will be; these will be the men of Thwartlithe, my friends, who have been sore pinched by the winter, and will be driving their beasts hither: they shall be welcome, for I have hay enough, and here are enough winter pastures open for grazing beasts." So he went out when they came into the home-mead, and gave them good welcome, and bade them to all good things that they would have; yea, scarce might they get off their horses, he was so eager-kind with them. But Thorbiorn said: "Thy good welcome is a great matter, and much lies on thy holding to all thou hast promised us."

Said Thorkel: "I wot of thine errand, that ye would leave the beasts behind here, where forsooth there lacketh not open pastures and good." Thorbiorn said : "That will we take,"

Then he taketh Thorkel aside by the houses, and said: "Great tidings and evil are abroad."

Thorkel asked what they were.

"Master Blundketil was burned in his house last night," said Thorbiorn.

"Who wrought that deed of shame?" said Thorkel.

So Thorbiorn told the whole story of it, saying moreover: "Herstein here hath need of thine wholesome redes."

Thorkel says: "It is not so sure that I should have been so busy with my offers had I known hereof before; but my redes shall even go down the road they set out on ; and first come ye in to meat."

They said yea thereto. Thorkel Welt was of few words, and somewhat thoughtful; but when they had eaten, he bade them to horse; and they take their weapons, and get a-horseback, but Thorkel rode first that day, and gave command that the beasts in the pasture should be well heeded, and those at stall fed plenteously. So ride they now to Woodstrand, to Gunnarstead, which lieth on the inner side of the Strand. There dwelt a man named Gunnar, the son of Hlifar, a big man and a strong, and the greatest of champions; he was wedded to a sister of Thord Gellir called Helga, and had two daughters, Jofrid and Thurid.

Thither they come late in the day, and get off their horses up above the house; the wind was in the north, and it was somewhat cold. So Thorkel goes to the door and knocks, and a house-carle comes thereto, and greets the new-comer well, asking who he might be. Thorkel says he would be none the wiser though he tell him, and bids him bid Gunnar come out. He said that Gunnar was gotten to bed; but Thorkel bids him say that a man would see him. The house-carle does so, goes in, and tells Gunnar that here is a man will see him. Gunnar asks who it might be; the house-carle said he wotted not, but that he was great of growth.

Gunnar said : "Go and tell him to abide here to-night."

The house-carle went and did as Gunnar bade; but Thorkel said he would not take that bidding from a thrall, but from the master himself. The house-carle said that, be that as true as it might be, Gunnar was not wont to arise benights. "Do one of two things," said he; "either go away, or come in and abide here to-night."

"Do thou one of two things," said Thorkel, "either go bear my errand doughtily to Gunnar, or have my sword-hilt on the nose of thee." The house-carle ran in, and shut to the door, and Gunnar asked why he went on so wildly; but he said that he would talk no more with the newcomer, for that he was exceeding rough of speech. Then Gunnar arose, and went out into the home-mead ; and he was clad in shirt and linen breeches, with a cloak cast over him, black shoes on his feet, and his sword in his hand; he greeted Thorkel well, and bade him come in, but he said there were more of them in company. So Gunnar goeth out into the home-mead; but Thorkel catcheth hold of the door-ring, and shutteth to the door, and then they go round to the back of the house. There Gunnar welcomes them, but Thorkel said: "Sit we down, because we have many things to say to thee, Gunnar."

They did so, sitting on either hand of him, and so close that they sat on the very skirts of the cloak that Gunnar had over him. Then spake Thorkel: " So it falleth out, master Gunnar, that here is a man in my company called Herstein, son of Blundketil, nor need we hide our errand from thee, that he comes a-wooing Thurid thy daughter of thee; and for this cause have I come hither with him, that I would not thou turn the man away, for meseemeth it is a most meet match ; withal we shall deem it no little matter if he be deemed unworthy, he and my furtherance, yea, or if he be answered coldly."

Gunnar said: "I may not answer to this matter alone; I will take counsel with her mother, and with my daughter herself, and especially with Thord Gellir, her kinsman; yet have we heard nought but good of the man, or his father either, and it is a matter to be looked to."

Then answered Welt: "Thou must know that we will not be dangling about the woman, and we think the match no less for thine honour than for ours; wondrous I deem it that a wise man like thee should ponder matters in such a good match as is this ; moreover, we will not have come from home for nothing; wherefore, Herstein, I will give thee whatso help thou wilt to bring this about if he know not his own honour."

Gunnar answered: "I cannot make out why ye are so hasty in this, or why ye go nigh even to threaten me; for the match is an even one; but I may look for any mischief from you; so I must even take the rede of stretching forth my hand."

So did he, and Herstein named witnesses for himself, and betrothed himself to the woman. Then they stand up, and go in, and are well served.

Now Gunnar asks for tidings; and Thorkel says that there is none newer than the burning of Blundketil.

Gunnar asked who brought it to pass, and Thorkel says that Thorwald Oddson and Arngrim the priest were the leaders therein. Gunnar answered in few words; blamed but little, and praised nought at all.

CHAPTER 11
Thord Betrotheth Herstein and Thurid

Next morning forthwith is Gunnar afoot, and coming to Thorkel bids him clothe himself: so do they, and go to their meat, and then are the horses got ready, and they leap a-horseback; and Gunnar rides ahead in along the firth, and it is much under ice. So they stay not till they come to Thord Gellir's at Hwamm, who greeted them well, and asked for tidings; but they told him what seemed good to them. Then Gunnar calls Thord apart to talk with him, and says that here in his company are Herstein, Blund-ketil's son, and Thorkel Welt: "And their errand is that Herstein speaketh of tying himself to me by wedding Thurid my daughter; what thinkest thou of the match? the man is goodly and doughty, and lacketh not wealth, for his father hath said that he would give up the house, and that Herstein is to take the same?"

Thord answereth: "I like Blundketil well; for on a time I strove with Odd-a-Tongue at the Althing for weregild for a thrall which had been awarded me against him. I went to fetch it in exceeding foul weather with two men in my company ; and so we came benight to Blundketil, and had very fair welcome, and we abode there a week; and he shifted horses with us, giving me certain good stallions; such treatment I had from him; and yet meseemeth it were no ill rede not to strike the bargain."

"Well," said Gunnar, "thou must know that she will not be betrothed to any other wooer; for the man is both doughty and a good man in my eyes; and there is danger in what may befall if he be turned away."

Then Gunnar goes and finds his daughter, for she was a-fostering with Thord there, and asked her what her mind was about the wooing; she an-swereth that she was not so desirous of men but that she would deem it just as well to abide at home : "For I am well looked after with Thord my kinsman; yet will I do thy pleasure and his, in this, as in other things"

Now comes Gunnar to talk with Thord again, saying that the match looks very seemly to him.

Says Thord : "Why shouldst thou not give thy daughter to him if thou wilt?" Gunnar answers:

"I will give her only if thy will be as mine herein."

So Thord says it shall be done by the rede of them both.

"I will,Thord,"said Gunnar," that thou betroth the woman unto Herstein." Thord answers: "Nay, it is for thee thyself to betroth thine own daughter."

Says Gunnar: "I should deem myself the more honoured if thou betroth her, for it were seemlier so."

So Thord let it be so; and the betrothal went on: then spake Gunnar: "I pray thee, moreover, to let the wedding be holden here at Hwamm, for then it will be done with all honour."

Thord bade him have his way if he thought it better so.

Gunnar says : "We should be minded to have it in a week's space." Then they get a-horseback, and go their ways, but Thord brought them on their road, and asked at last if there were anything new to tell.

Gunnar answereth: "We have heard nought newer than the burning of master Blundketil."

Thord asked how that had come about, and Gunnar told him all the tale of how the burning had betid, and who was he that stirred it, and who were they who did it.

Said Thord: "I would not have counselled this match so hastily had I known this ; ye will deem that ye have got round me altogether in wit, and have overcome me with wiles. I see how it is, however ; ye are not so sure that ye are enough for this case by yourselves."

Gunnar said: "We deem ourselves safe in leaning on thy help, for thou art bound to help thy son-in-law even as we are bound to help thee ; for many heard thee betroth the woman, and all was done with thy goodwill. Well, good it were to try once for all which of you great men may hold out longest; for ye have long been eating each the other with the wolfs mouth."

CHAPTER 12
A Wedding at Hwamm

So parted they, and Thord is as wroth as wroth may be, deeming himself bemocked of them; but they ride to Gunnarstead first, thinking how they have played their game well to have brought Thord into the case, and right joyous are they. They rode not south as yet, but bade men to the feast, and made for Hwamm at the time appointed. There had Thord a many guests, and marshalled men to their seats in the evening: he himself sat on one bench with Gunnar his brother-in-law and his men, but Thorkel Welt sat beside the bridegroom on the other bench with their guests; the women filled the dais-bench.

So when the boards were set, Herstein the bridegroom leapt up and over the board to where was a certain stone; then he set one foot upon the stone, and spake: "This oath I swear hereby, that before the Althing is over this summer I shall have had Arngrim the priest made fully guilty, or gained self-doom else." Then back he strode to his seat.

Then sprang forth Gunnar and spake: "This oath swear I, that before the Althing is over this summer I shall have Thorwald Oddson to outlawry, or else self-doom to our side."

Then he stepped back and sat himself down at the board, and saith to Thord : "Why sittest thou there, Thord, and vowest nought of thine own about it? we wot thou hast e'en such things in thy heart as we have."

Thord answers: "It shall lie quiet, though, for this time."

Answers Gunnar: "If thou wilt that we speak for thee, then are we ready thereto, and we wot thou art minded to take Odd-a-Tongue."

Thord said: "Ye may rule your own speech, but I will be master over my words; bring that ye have . spoken to a good end."

Nought more to tell of befell at the feast, but it went on in noble fashion, and when it came to an end, each went about his own business, and winter wore away.

But in springtide they gathered men, and fared south to Burgfirth, and, coming to Northtongue, summoned Arngrim and Hen Thorir to the Thing of Thingness: but Herstein parted company from them with thirty men to go thither whereas he said he had heard tell of Thorwald Oddson's last night-harbour ; for Thorwald was gone from his winter guest-quarters. So the countryside is astir, and there is much talk, and mustering of men on either side.

CHAPTER 13
Battle on Whitewater

Now it fell out that Hen Thorir vanished away from the countryside, with twelve men, when he knew who had come into the case, and nought was to be heard of him.

Odd gathers force now from the Dales, either Reekdale and Skorradale, and all the country south of Whitewater, and had moreover many from other countries. Arngrim the priest gathered men from all Thwartwaterlithe, and some part of Northwater-dale. Thorkel Welt gathered men from the Nether Mires, and from Staffholtstongue; and some of the men of Northwaterdale also he had with him, because Helgi his brother dwelt at Hwamm, and he followed him.

Now gathers Thord Gellir men from the west, but had not many men : so all they who are in the case meet, and are two hundred men in all: they ride down to the west of Northwater, and over it at Eyiaford above Staff holt, with the mind to cross Whitewater by the ford of Thrall stream; then they see a many men going south of the river, and there is Odd-a-Tongue with hard on four hundred men : so they speed on their way, being wishful to come first to the ford ; they meet by the river, and Odd's folk leap off their horses, and guard the ford, so that Thord's company may not pass forth, how fain soever they were to come to the Thing. Then they fell to fight, and men were presently hurt, and four of Thord's men fell, amongst whom was Thorolf Fox, brother of Alf-a-dales, and a man of account; therewith they turn away, but one man fell of Odd's and three were sorely hurt.

So now Thord laid the case to the Althing; they ride home west, and men deem the honour of the west-country folk to be falling. But Odd rides to the Thing, and sends his thralls home with the horses ; of whom when they came home Jorun his wife asked for tidings; they said they had no other to tell save that he was come from Broadfirth out of the west country who alone was able to answer Odd-a-Tongue, and whose voice and speech were as the roaring of a bull.

She said it was no tidings though he were answered as other men, and that nought had befallen save what was likeliest to befall. "Ah, there was a battle though," said they," and five men fell in all, and many were hurt." For they had told no whit of this before.

The Thing wears with nought to tell of; but when those kinsmen-in-law came home they changed dwellings; Gunnar goes into Ornolfsdale, and Herstein takes Gunnarstead. Then let Gunnar flit to him from the west all that timber which Eastman Erne had owned, and so gat him home to Ornolfsdale; then he falls to and builds up again the houses at the stead there; for he was the handiest of men, and in all things well skilled, the best of men at arms, and the briskest in all wise.

CHAPTER 14
Of Matters at the Althing

So weareth the time on till men ride to the Thing, and there is much arraying of men in the countryside, and either company rides wondrous many.

But when Thord Gellir and his men come to Gunnarstead, then is Herstein sick, and may not fare to the Thing; so he hands his cases over to others: thirty men abode behind with him; but Thord rides to the Thing. He gathereth to him kinsfolk and friends, and cometh to the Thing betimes, which in those days was held under Armans-fell, and as the companies come in Thord has a great gathering.

Now is Odd-a-Tongue seen coming. Thord rideth to meet him, and would not that he should get him the peace of the hallowed Thing. Odd is riding with three hundred men. So Thord and his folk guard the Thingstead, and men fall to fight straightway, and very many are hurt.

There fell six of Odd's men, for Thord had many more than he. Now worthy men see that great troubles will come of it if the whole Thing gets to fighting, and late will it be amended; so they go betwixt them and part them, and turn the case to a peaceful awarding; for Odd was overborne by numbers and had to give way; yea, both because he was deemed to have the heavier case to back, and because he had the weaker force.

So it was proclaimed that Odd was to pitch his tents away from the peace of the Thing, and to go to the courts, and about his errands, and to fare with meek demeanour, showing no stiff-neckedness, neither he nor his men.

Then men sit over the cases, and seek how they may appease them, and it went heavily with Odd, mostly, indeed, because there was over-mastery against him.

CHAPTER 15
Of Hen Thorir's Ending

But now shall we tell somewhat of Herstein; for his sickness presently left him after men were gone to the Thing, and he fared to Ornolfsdale : there early one morning he was in the stithy, for he was the handiest of men with iron; so there came to him thither a goodman called Ornolf, and said: "My cow is sick, and I

47

pray thee, Herstein, to come and see her; we are rejoiced that thou art come back, for thus we have some of thy father's heart left us, who was of the greatest avail to us."

Herstein answered: "I take no keep of thy cow, nor may I know what aileth her."

Said the goodman : "Ah, well I great is the difference betwixt thee and thy father, for he gave me the cow, and thou wilt not so much as come and look at her."

Herstein said: "I will give thee another cow if this one dies."

The goodman said: "Yea, but first of all I would have thee come and see this." Then Herstein sprang up, and was, wroth, and went with the goodman, and they turned into a way that led into the wood; for a byway went there with the wood on either hand: but as Herstein went on the cliff-road he stood still, and he was the keenest-eyed of men. He said: "A shield peeped out in the wood yonder."

The goodman held his peace, and Herstein said: "Hast thou betrayed me, hound? now if thou art bound to silence by any oaths, lie down in the path here, and speak no word; but if thou do not so, I will slay thee."

So the goodman lay down, but Herstein turned back and called on his men, who take their weapons and go to the wood, and find Ornolf yet in the path, and bid him go take them to the place where the meeting was appointed. So they go till they come to a clearing, and then Herstein said to Ornolf: "I will not compel thee to speak, but do thou now even as thou hast been ordered to do."

So Ornolf ran up a certain knoll and whistled shrilly, and forth sprang twelve men, and who but Hen Thorir was the leader of that band.

So Herstein and his company take them and slay them, and Herstein himself smites the head from Thorir, and has it along with him. Then they ride south to the Thing and tell these tidings, and Herstein is much honoured for the deed, and his good renown furthered, as was like to be.

Now is peace made in these cases, and the end of it was that Arngrim the priest was fully outlawed, and all those that were at the burning except Thorwald Oddson, who was to be away for three winters, and then be free to come back; money was given for the faring over the sea of other men. Thorwald went abroad that summer, and was taken captive in Scotland and enthralled there.

After this the Thing was ended, and men deem that Thord has carried out the case well and mightily. Arngrim the priest also went abroad that summer, but as to what money was paid is nothing certain. Such was the end of this case.

So then folk ride home from the Thing, and those of the outlawed fare who were appointed to.

CHAPTER 16
Thorod Oddson Wooeth Gunnar's Daughter Jofrid

Gunnar Hlifarson sitteth now at Ornolfsdale, and has housed himself well there; he had much of mountain pastures, and ever had but few men at home; Jofrid, Gunnar's daughter, had a tent without doors, for she deemed it less dreary so.

It befell on a day that Thorod, son of Odd-a-Tongue, rode to Thwartwaterlithe; he came to Ornolfsdale by the beaten way, and went into Jo-frid's tent, and she greeted him well; he sat down beside her, and they fell to talk together; but therewith in comes a lad from the mountain-pasture, and bids Jofrid help take off the loads. Thorod goes and takes off the loads, and then the lad goes his way, and comes to the mountain-stead; there Gunnar asked him why he was so speedily back, but he answered nought. Gunnar said : "Sawest thou ought to tell of?"

"Nought at all," said the lad. "Nay," said Gunnar, "there is something in the look of thee as if a thing had passed before thine eyes which thou deemest worth talking of; so tell me what it is, or if any man has come to the house?" "I saw no one new-come," said the lad. "Nay, but thou shalt tell me," said Gunnar; and took up a stout switch to beat the boy withal, but got no more out of him than before; so then he mounts and rides swiftly down along the Lithe by the winter-fold. Jofrid caught sight of her father as he went, and told Thorod, and bade him ride away: "For I were loth for any ill to come to thee by me." Thorod said he would ride presently; but Gunnar came on apace, and leaping from his horse went into the tent.

Thorod greeted him well, and Gunnar took his greeting, and then asked him why he was come thither. Thorod told him why he was come: "But this I do, not out of enmity to thee, but rather I would wot how thou wouldst answer me, were I to woo Jofrid thy daughter of thee."

Gunnar answered : "I will not give her to thee amidst these goings-on; for matters have long stood on a ticklish point betwixt us."

So therewithal rides Thorod home.

CHAPTER 17
Thorod Weddeth Jofrid

On a day Odd says that it were not ill to have a little avail of the lands of Ornolfs-dale: "whereas other men have wrongfully sat upon my possessions."

The women said that it were good so to do, for that the beasts were very scant of milk, and that they would milk much the better for such change. "Well, thither shall they," said Odd, "for there is much good pasture there."

Then said Thorod: "I would go with the cattle, for then will they deem it a harder matter to set on us."

Odd said he was right fain thereof; so they go with the cattle, and when they are come a long way, Thorod bids them drive the beasts where the pasture is worst and stoniest. So wears the night away, and they drive the beasts home in the morning, and when the women have milked them, they say they have never been so dry before; wherefore the thing is not tried again.

Weareth a while away now, till on a morning early Odd falleth to talk with Thorod his son: "Go thou down along the countryside, and gather folk; for now will I drive those men from our possessions; but Torfi shall fare north aver the Neck, and make this muster known, and we will meet at Stoneford."

So do they, and gather folk. Thorod and his folk muster, ninety men in all, and so ride for the ford; thereto come first Thorod and his company, and he biddeth them ride on : "I will await my father."

Now as they come to the garth at Ornolfsdale, Gunnar was making up a wain-load; then saith a lad who was with Gunnar: "Men are faring to the stead, no little company." "Yea," said Gunnar, "so it is;" and he went home to his house, and took his bow, for he was the best shooter among men, and came nighest therein to matching Gunnar of Lithend. He had built a fair house at the stead, and there was a window in the outer door wherethrough a man might thrust out his head; by this door he stood, bow in hand. Now comes Thorod to the house, and, going up to the house with but few men, asks if Gunnar will offer any atonement.

He answers: "I wot not of aught to be atoned for, and I look for it that before ye have your will of me, my handmaidens here will have set the Sleepthorn into some of yon fellows, or ever I bow adown in the grass."

Said Thorod: "True it is that thou art wellnigh peerless among the men that now are, yet may such a company come against thee as thou mayest not withstand, for my father is riding to the garth now with a great company, and is minded to slay thee."

Gunnar answered: "It is well, but I would have wished to have had a man before me ere I fall to field. But I wonder at it nowise, though thy father keep but little to the peace."

Said Thorod: "Nay, 'tis all the other way; we wish indeed that thou and I should make a good and true peace, and that thou stretch forth thine hand, and give me Jofrid thy daughter."

Gunnar answers: "Thou cowest me not to give thee my daughter; yet would the match be not far from equal as to thee, for thou art a brave man and a truer

Thorod saith: "It will not be so accounted of amongst men of worth; and I must needs give thee many thanks for thy taking this choice on such condition as befitteth."

So what with the talking over of his friends, what with thinking that Thorod had ever fared well of his ways, Gunnar stretched forth his hand, and so the matter ended.

But even therewith came Odd into the home-mead, and Thorod straightway turned to meet his father, and asked him of his intent. Odd said he was minded to burn up the house and the men therein; but Thorod answered: "Another road have matters gone, for Gunnar and I have made peace together." And he told how the thing had betid. "Hearken to the fool!" saith Odd; "would it be any the worse for thee to have the woman if Gunnar our greatest foe were first slain? And an ill deed have I done in ever having furthered thee."

Thorod answered and said: " Thou shalt have Hen Thorir to do with me first, if it may no otherwise be done."

Then men go between them, and the father and son are appeased, and the end of the matter was that Thorod was wedded to Jofrid, and Odd was very ill content.

So folk go home with matters thus done, and later on men sit at the wedding, and Thorod deems his lot happy. But at the end of the winter Thorod fared abroad because he had heard that Thorwald his brother was in bondage, and he would ransom him with money; he came to Norway, but never back to Iceland again, neither he nor his brother.

Now waxed Odd very old, and when he knew that neither of his sons would come back to him, a great sickness took him, and when it grew heavy on him, he spake to his friends, bidding them bear him up to Skaney-fell when he was dead, and saying that thence would he look down on all the Tongue ; and even so was it done.

As for Jofrid, Gunnar's daughter, she was wedded afterwards to Thorstein Egilson of Burg, and was the greatest-hearted of women. Thus endeth the story of Hen Thorir.

THE STORY OF HOWARD THE HALT

CHAPTER 1
Of Thorbiorn and the Icefirthers

Here beginneth this story, and telleth of a man named Thorbiorn, the son of Thiodrek, who dwelt in Icefirth at a house called Bathstead, and had the priesthood over Icefirth ; he was a man of great kin and a mighty chief, but the most unjust of men, neither was there any throughout Icefirth who bore any might to gainsay him: he would take the daughters of men or their kinswomen, and handfast them awhile, and then send them home again. From some men he took their goods and chattels in their despite, and other some he drave away from their lands. He had taken a woman, Sigrid by name, young and high-born, to be over his household; great wealth she had, which Thorbiorn would hold for her behoof, but not put out to usury while she was with him.

A man named Howard dwelt at the stead of Bluemire: he was of great kin, but now sunk unto his latter days , in his earlier life he had been a great viking, and the best of champions; but in a certain fight he had gotten many sore hurts, and amongst them one under his kneepan, whereby he went halt ever after. Howard was a wedded man, and his wife was hight Biargey, a woman of good kin, and the most stirring of women. One son they had, hight Olaf, young of years, the. doughtiest of men, great of growth, and goodly of aspect: Howard and Biargey loved him much, and he was obedient and kind unto them.

Thormod was the name of a man who dwelt at Bank, whose wife was hight Thorgerd: he was little to people's minds, and was now somewhat stricken in years; it was said of him that he had more shapes than one, and all folk deemed him most ill to deal with.

Liot was the name of one who dwelt at Moonberg in Icefirth, a big man and a strong, brother to Thor-biorn, and in all wise as like him as might be.

A man named Thorkel dwelt on an isle called Eider-isle : he was a wise man, but of feeble heart, though of great kin : he was of all men the least outspoken : he was the Lawman of those of Icefirth. Two more men are named in the story ; one named Brand, and the other Vakr, homemen of Thorbiorn of Bathstead: Brand was great of growth and mighty of strength; it was his business to go hither and thither in the summer, and fetch home things of need for the stead; but in winter he had to watch the full-grown sheep; he was a man well-beloved, and no busybody.

Vakr was sister's son of Thorbiorn, a little man, and freckled of face, murderous of speech, and foul-mouthed; he would ever be egging Thorbiorn, his kinsman, of two minds to be of the worser: wherefore was he unbefriended, and folk grudged him no true word about himself: he did no work save going about with Thorbiorn at home and abroad, and doing his errands for him, and that more especially when he was about some evil deed.

A woman named Thordis dwelt at the Knoll in Icefirth; she was sister of Thorbiorn, and mother of Vakr, and had another son named Scart, a big and strong man, who abode with his mother, and was master over her household.

Thoralf was the name of a man who abode at Loonsere, a man well befriended, albeit of no great account; he was nigh akin to Sigrid, Thorbiorn's housekeeper, and had craved to have her home to him, and to put her money out to usury; but Thorbiorn would not have it so, but once more showed forth his injustice, forbidding him ever speak a word hereof again.

CHAPTER 2
Of the Great Manhood of Olaf Howardson

Here taketh up the tale the telling of how that Olaf waxed up at Bluemire, and became a hopeful man: men say that Olaf Howardson had bear's-warmth; for there was never that frost or cold wherein he would go in more raiment than breeches alone, with shirt girded thereinto ; never went he forth from the house clad in more raiment than that.

There was a man named Thorhall, a homeman of Howard, and akin to him, a young man of the briskest, who used to get things together for the household.

One autumn the men of Icefirth fared to their, sheep-walks, and gathered but little there, and Thorbiorn of Bathstead lacked sixty wethers. Winter-nights wore, and they were not found, but a little before winter Olaf Howardson went up into the sheep-walks, and all the fells, and searched for men's sheep, and found many, both those of Thorbiorn, and his own and his fathers, and other folk's besides: then he drave the sheep home, and brought his own to each man : whereby he became well-beloved, and he had all men's thanks therefor.

Early on a day Olaf drave Thorbiorn's wethers down to Bathstead, and he got there by then all folk were set down to table, and there was no man without; so he smote on the door and a woman came thereto, Sigrid to wit, Thorbiorn's housekeeper, and she greeted him well, and asked him what he would ; Olaf answered : "I have brought Thorbiorn's wethers here, even those that he lost in the autumn."

But when Thorbiorn heard that the door was smitten on, he bade Vakr go see who was come thither, so Vakr arose and went to the wicket, and there he saw how Olaf and Sigrid were a-talking together; so he got up on the ledge of the door and stood there while they talked. Now Olaf was saying; "No need to go further then; thou Sigrid shalt tell where the wethers are."

She said that so it should be, and bade him farewell: whereon Vakr ran back whooping into the hall: then Thorbiorn asked him why he went on so, or who was to hand: said he: "I believe verily that he, Olaf Howardson the Bluemire booby, has been here, driving home thy sheep that were missing last harvest." "A good deed" said Thorbiorn.

"Ah, methinks there was something else behind his coming, though," said Vakr, "for he and Sigrid have been talking away all the morning, and I could see that she liked well enough to lay her arms about his neck."

Quoth Thorbiorn: "Dauntless though Olaf be, yet is he overbold thus to go about to win my hatred."

So Olaf fared home. Time weareth, and, as saith the tale, ever would Olaf be coming to Bath-stead, and seeing Sigrid; and things went well betwixt them, and the rumour went abroad presently that Olaf was beguiling her.

Next harvest went men to their sheep-walks, and again brought home but little, and again Thorbiorn lacked most: so when the folding was over, Olaf gat him away alone, and went into the sheep-walks far and wide, over mount and moor, and again found many sheep and drave them into the peopled parts, and once more brought each man his own; whereby he became so beloved of the bonders that all men gave him good thanks, saving Thorbiorn, who waxed exceeding grim at him for all this; both that others praised him, and that he heard folk say the country over, of how he came to Sigrid: neither spared Vakr to slander Olaf to Thorbiorn. Now once more it has come to pass that Olaf is gotten to Bathstead with as many wethers as aforetime; and when he came thither no man was without; so went he into the hall, and master Thorbiorn was therein, and Vakr his kinsman, and many homemen: Olaf went well-nigh up to the dais, and smote his axe-shaft down on to the floor and leaned thereon: but none greeted him, and all kept silence; so Olaf, when he found that no man gave any heed to him, sang a stave :

This silence shall I break And to Thanes speechless speak. Stems of the spear-wood tall Why sit ye hushed in hall ? What honour then have those Who keep their mouths shut close ? Now long have I stood here And had no word of cheer.

Spake Olaf then: "It is my errand hither, goodman Thorbiorn, that I have brought home thy wethers."

"Yea," said Vakr, "men know, Olaf, that thou art become the Icefirth sheep-drover; and we wot of thine errand hither, that thou art come to claim a share in the sheep; after the fashion of beggars. ?And it were best to remember him, little as the alms may be."

Olaf answered: "Nay, that is not my errand, neither will I drive sheep here the third time." And he turned away, and Vakr sprang up and whooped after him, but Olaf gave no heed at all to it, but went his ways home.

So wear the seasons; and that harvest men get home their sheep well, save Thorbiorn, who again lacked sixty wethers, and found them not at all: so those kinsmen let out the word that Olaf had a mind to claim share in them, or to steal them else. Now on an evening as Olaf and his father sat at the board together there lay a leg of mutton on' the dish, and Olaf took it up, and said: "A wondrous big and fat leg is this."

"Yea," said Howard, "but methinks, kinsman, it came from our sheep and not from Master Thorbiorn's: a heavy thing to have to bear such injustice!"

Olaf laid the leg down on the board, and flushed red; and it seemed to them that sat by as though; he had smitten on the board; anyhow, the leg brake asunder so sharply that one part thereof flew up into the gable wainscot and stuck there: Howard looked up arid smiled, but said nought. Even therewith walked a woman into the hall, and there was come Thorgerd of Bank: Howard greeted her well, and asked for tidings, and she said that her husband Thormod was dead.

"Yea, but things go amiss with us," she said, "for he cometh home to his bed every night: wherefore I fain would have some help from thee, goodman: for whereas my men deemed it ill dealing with Thormod aforetime, now are things come to such a pass that they are all minded to be gone." Howard answered: "I am passed the briskest way of my life now, and am unmeet for such dealings: why goest thou not to Bathstead? it is to be looked for of chieftains that they should presently use their might in the country-side for the settling of such matters."

She answered : "No good do I look for thence; nay, I am well content if he do me no harm."

Said Howard; "Then do I counsel thee to ask Olaf, my son; meet it is for young men to try their manliness in such wise : time was when we should have deemed it good game."

Even so she did, and Olaf promised to go, and bade her abide there that night; but the next day Olaf went home with Thorgerd, at whose house were all folk down-hearted.

But at night folk went to bed and Olaf lay in a gable-end bed out by the door. In such wise burnt light in the hall, that it was bright aloft and dim below. Olaf lay down in his shirt and breeches (for he never wore other clothes) and cast a fell over him. Now at nightfall Thormod walked into the hall wagging his bald head, and saw that there was a man abed where none was wont to lie; and forsooth he was not over hospitable, so he turned thither, and caught hold of the fell; Olaf would not let it go, but held on till they tore it atwain betwixt them ; so when Thormod saw there was might in him that lay there, he leapt up into the settle by the bed. Olaf sprang up and laid hold on his axe to smite him, but things went quicker than he looked for, and Thormod ran in under his hand, and Olaf had to grapple with him. The struggle was of the fiercest; Thormod was so hard a gripper that the flesh gave way before him wheresoever he took hold: and . most things flew about that were before them. Even in that nick of time the light died out, and Olaf deemed matters nowise amended thereby. Thormod fell on furiously, and it came, to pass in the end that they drave out of doors. In the home-mead lay a great drift-log, and as hap would have it Thormod tripped both his heels against the log and fell aback: Olaf let his knee follow the belly of him and served Thormod in such wise that he did with him as he would. All folk were silent when Olaf came back into the hall; but when he let himself be heard, folk were afoot and the light kindled at one and the same time, and they fell to stroking of him up and down, for he was all bruised by Thormod's handling; every child of man that could speak gave thanks to him, and he said he deemed that they would have no more hurt of Thormod.

Olaf abode there certain days, and then went back to Bluemire; but the fame of that deed of his spread wide through Icefirth, and all the -quarters of the land. Nevertheless from all. this also the hatred of Thorbiorn to him did but wax the more.

CHAPTER 3
Howard Shifteth his Dwelling-Place

It is next to be told how a whale came ashofe in Icefirth : now Thorbiorn and Howard had rights of drift adjoining one to the other, and men said straightway that this whale was Howard's of right; and it was the best of whales. Either side went thither, and would have the judgment of the Lawman thereon : many men were come together there, and it seemed clear to all that Howard should have the whale.

But now Thorkel the Lawman being come, he was asked whose the whale was: he answered, speaking, very low, "Certainly the whale is theirs." Then went Thorbiorn to him with drawn sword, "Whose, thou wretch?" said he. "O thine, thine, surely," said Thorkel in all haste, letting his head fall. So then Thorbiorn set to work, and with wrongdoing took to him all the whale, and Howard went home ill content with his lot, and all men now deemed that Thorbiorn's utter wrongdoing was again made manifest.

On a day Olaf went to his sheep-folds because the weather was hard that winter, and men had great need to look to their sheep, and that night had been exceeding hard; so when he was about going he sees a man coming up to the house, Brand the Strong to wit. Olaf greeted him, and Brand took his greeting well; Olaf asked what made him there so late. Brand said: "It is an ugly tale. I went to my sheep early in the day, but they had all got driven down on to the foreshore ; there were two places whereby to drive them up, but so oft as I tried to do that, there was a man in the way, and withstood them, so that they all came back into my arms; and thus has it gone on all day until now, wherefore am I fain that we go there both together."

"That will I do for thy prayer," said Olaf.

So they went both together down to the foreshore, and when they would drive up the sheep thence, they saw Thormod, Olaf's wrestling-fellow, standing in the way, and staying the sheep, so that they cajne back into their arms. Then said Olaf, "Which wilt thou, Brand, drive the sheep, or play with Thormod?"

"The easiest will I choose," said Brand, "driving the sheep to wit."

Then Olaf went there whereas stood Thormod against him up above. There lay a great snowdrift over the face of the bank. Olaf ran forthwith up the bank at Thormod, who gave back before him ; but when he came up on to the bank Thormod ran under the arms of him, and Olaf caught hold and wrestled with all his might; they played a long while, and Olaf thought that Thormod had lost but little of his strength from that handling of his: so it came to pass that they both fell together on the face of the bank, and rolled over and over one another till they tumbled into the drift below, and now one, now the other, was atop, till they came on to the foreshore; by then as it happed Thormod was under, so Olaf made the most of it, and brake the back of him asunder, and served him as he would, and then swam out to sea with him and sank him in the depths of the sea; and ever after have men deemed it uncouth for men sailing anigh there.

Then Olaf swam ashore, and Brand had by then driven up all the sheep, and he gave Olaf fair welcome, and so each went his ways home.

But when Brand came home, the night was far spent, and Thorbiorn asked what had belated him. Brand told him how things had gone, and how Olaf had stood him in stead. Then said Vakr: "Thou must have been sore afraid, whereas thou praisest that booby: his fame will mostly come of his dealings with ghosts, forsooth."

Brand answered: "Thou wouldst havebeen more afraid ; for ever art thou greatest in talk, as the fox in his tail, and in nowise art thou a match for him."

So they talked till either grew hot; then Thor-biorn bade Brand not to champion Olaf: " It shall be ill for thee or any other to make more of Olaf than me or my kin."

So weareth winter, and when spring is come, Howard falleth to talk with Olaf his son, saying: "Things have come to this, kinsman, that I have no heart to live any longer so nigh to Thorbiorn, for we have no might to hold our own against him."

Olaf said : "It is little to my mind to have such boot for our wrongs as to flee before Thorbiorn ; yet will I that thou rule; whither wilt thou, then?"

Howard answered : "Out on the other side of the firth are many empty tofts' and wide lands owned of no man ; there will I that we set up our dwelling, and then we shall be nigher to our friends and kinsfolk."

That rede they take and flit all their stock and such goods as they had, and set up there a very goodly house, which was afterward called Howard-stead.

Now there were no bonders in Icefirth in those days, but were land-settlers.

CHAPTER 4
The Slaying of Olaf Howardson

Now Thorbiorn Thiodrekson rode every summer to the Thing with his men; he was a mighty chief, of great stock, and had many kinsmen.

In those days Guest Oddleifson dwelt at the Mead on Bardstrand; he was a great sage, and wise and, well-befriended, the most foreseeing of all men, and had rule over many.

Now the same summer that the father and son shifted their dwelling Thorbiorn rode to the Thing a-wooing, and craved the sister of Guest Oddleifson. Guest was cold over the match, saying that Thorbiorn was little to his mind because of his injustice and violence; but whereas many furthered Thorbiorn in his wooing, Guest gave him this choice, that the match should be if he promised by hand given to lay aside his injustice and. wrongdoing, and to render his own to each man, and hold by law and right; but if he would not bring himself to this, then was Guest to be quit of the bargain, and the match to be clean voided.

Thorbiorn assented hereto, and the bargain was struck on these terms. Then Thorbiorn rode from the Thing home with Guest to Bardstrand, and the wedding was holden in the summer, and that was the best of bridals.

But when these tidings were known in. Icefirth, Sigrid and Thoralf her kinsman take counsel together, and summon the bonders, and let appraise for Sigrid her goods out of Bathstead. and thereafter she fared to Thoralf at Loonsere.

So when Thorbiorn came home to Bathstead he was wondrous wroth that Sigrid was gone; and he threatened the bonders with measureless evil in that they had appraised those goods, and he grew as hard as hard might be, for he deemed his might waxen by this alliance of his.

Master Howard's live stock was very wild that summer, and on a morning early the herdsman came in, and Olaf asked how it went with him. "So it goes," quoth he, " that there is a deal of the beasts missing, and I may not do both at once, seek for those that are lost, and heed them that are found." "Keep a good heart, fellow," answered Olaf, "heed what thou hast, and I will go seek the missing."

Now by this time he was grown to be the most hopeful of men, and the goodliest to look on, and both big and strong: he was eighteen winters old. So

Olaf took his axe in his hand, and went down along by the firth till he came to Loonsere, and there he sees that those sheep are all gotten to the place where they first came aland; so he turned toward the house early in the morning-tide, and smote on the door, and thither came Sigrid, and greeted him well, and well he took her greeting.

But now when they had talked awhile, Sigrid said: "Lo a boat coming over the firth, and therein I see clearly Thorbiorn Thiodrekson and Vakr his kinsman; and I can see their weapons lying forward in the prow, and Warflame is there, Thorbiorn's sword; and now either he will have done an ill deed or be minded for one; wherefore I pray thee Olaf meet him not; this long while have ye been ill seen one of another, and belike matters will not be bettered since ye were at the appraising of the goods for me from Bathstead."

Olaf answered : "I fear not Thorbiorn whiles I have done him no wrong, and but a little way will I run before him alone."

"A brave word of thine" she said, "that thou, a lad of eighteen winters, must needs yield nought before one who is any man's match in fight, and beareth a sword whose stroke will not be stayed by aught; yea, and I deem that if their intent is to meet thee, as indeed my mind forebodes me, wicked Vakr will not sit idle by the fight."

Olaf answered : "I have no errand with Thorbiorn, and I will not go meet them, yet if we do meet, thou shalt have to ask after brave deeds if need there be."

"Nay, I shall never ask thereof," said Sigrid.

Then Olaf sprang up quickly, and bade her live long and happy, and she bade him farewell; and therewith he went down to the foreshore whereas lay the sheep; and Thorbiorn and Vakr were come to land now, over against that very place; so he went his ways down to the boat and met it, and drew it up under them on to the beach. Thorbiorn greeted Olaf well, and he took the greeting, and asked whither away, and Thorbiorn said he would go see his sister Thordis. "So go we all together," said Olaf; "it falleth amiss, because I must needs drive my sheep home; and verily it might well be said that sheep-drovers shall be getting great men in Icefirth if thou shouldst lower thyself so far as to take to that craft."

"Nay, I heed that nought" said Thorbiorn.

Now there was a big heap of wood on the beach, whereon lay a great forked cudgel with the ends broken off: this Olaf caught up and bore in his hand, and so drave the sheep before him, and they went their ways all together.

Thorbiorn talked with Olaf, and was as merry as might be: but Olaf found that they would ever be hanging back; so he looked to that, and then on they went all abreast, till they came past the knoll, and there the ways sundered.

Then Thorbiorn turned about and said : "Kinsman Vakr, there is no longer any need to put off that which we would do."

Olaf saw the intent of them, and turned up on to the bent, and they set on him from below: Olaf warded himself with the cudgel, but Thorbiorn smote hard and oft with the sword Warflame, and sliced away the cudgel as if it had been a stalk of angelica: yet gat they heavy strokes from the cudgel whiles it held out; but when it was all smitten to pieces Olaf took to his axe, and defended himself so well that they deemed it doubtful how it would go between them; and they were all wounded.

Now Thordis, Thorbiorn's sister, went out that morning of the fight, and heard the noise thereof, but might not see aught; so she sent her foot-page to see what was toward ; who came back and told her that there were Thorbiorn her brother and Vakr her son fighting against Olaf Howardson : so she turned back into the house, and told her son Skart of these tidings, and bade him go help his kinsmen; but he said: "I am more like to go fight for Olaf against them, for I hold it shame for three to fall upon one man, they being as like to win the day as any four other; I will nowise go." Thordis answered: "I was deeming that I had two stout-hearted sons; but sooth is that which is said,' Many a thing lieth long hidden :' for now I know that thou art rather a daughter than a son of mine, since thou durst not help thy kin: wherefore now shall I show full surely that I am a braver daughter than thou art a son."

Therewith she went away, but he waxed wondrous wroth, and he leapt up and caught hold of his axe, and ran out, and down along the bent to where they were fighting. Thorbiorn saw him, and set on all the more fiercely, but Olaf saw him not: and as soon as Skart came within reach of Olaf he fetched a blow at him with both hands, and drave the axe deep in between the shoulders. Olaf was about smiting at Thorbiorn, but when he got that stroke he turned about with axe raised aloft on Skart, who was weaponless now, and smote him on the head so that the axe stood in the brain: but even therewith was Thorbiorn beside Olaf, and smote him into the breast, and that was enough for the death of him, and the twain, Skart and Olaf, tumbled down dead.

Then Thorbiorn went up to Olaf and smote him across the face so that the front teeth and jaw-teeth fell out. Vakr said, "Why dost thou so to a dead man?"

Thorbiorn answered that it might yet serve him somewhat, and he took a clout therewith, and knit up the teeth in it, and kept them. Then they went into the house, and told Thordis the tidings; and they were both grievously wounded.

Thordis was much overcome thereat, and bewailed bitterly that eager egging-on of her son: but she gave them help and service there.

Now are these tidings told far and wide about Icefirth; and all thought it the greatest scathe of Olaf, such a defence as he had made withal, as the rumour of men told: for herein did Thor-biorn well, in that he told everything even as it had happened, and gave Olaf his due in the story.

So they fared home when they deemed they had might thereto, and their weariness had run off, and Thorbiorn went to Loonsere and asked for Sigrid: but he was told that she had not been seen since she went out with Olaf that other morning. She was sought for far and wide, but, as the tale goes, she was never seen again.

So Thorbiorn went home and abode in peace at his own house.

CHAPTER 5
Howard Claimeth Atonement of Thorbiorn

Howard and Biargey, saith the tale, got these tidings of the death of their son Olaf, and old Howard sighed heavily and went to his bed; and so say folk that he lay there in his bed all the next twelve months, and never came out of it. But Biargey took such rede that she rowed out to sea every day with Thorhall, and worked benights at what there was need to work in the house.

So wear away those seasons, and all is quiet: there was no blood-suit after Olaf, and men deemed it likely that his kin would never right their case; for Howard was deemed fit for nought, and withal he had to do with men mighty, and little like to deal fairly. So wear the seasons.

On a morning it fell that Biargey went to master Howard, and asked if he were waking, and he said so it was, and asked what she would: she said, "I would have thee arise and go to Bathstead, and see Thorbiorn; for it is manly for one who is unmeet for hardy deeds not to spare his tongue from Speaking that which may avail: nor shalt thou claim overmuch if he bear himself well" He answered: "I see nought good herein; yet shalt thou have thy will."

So old master Howard goes his way to Bath-stead, and Thorbiorn gave him good greeting, and he took the same. Then spake old Howard: "This is the matter in hand, Thorbiorn, that I am come to claim weregild for my son Olaf, whom thou slewest sackless."

Thorbiorn answered: "It is well known, Howard, that I have slain many men, and though folk called them sackless, yet have I paid weregild for none: but whereas thou hast lost a brave son and the matter touches thee so closely, meseemeth it were better to remember thee somewhat, were' it never so little : now here above the garth goeth a horse that the lads call Dodderer: grey is he, Sorebacked, and hath lain cast a long while until now; for he is exceeding old: but now he hath, been fed on chaff these days past, and belike is somewhat amended; come, take him home, and keep him if thou wilt"

Howard reddened, and might not answer aught: he gat him gone straightway, wondrous wroth, and Vakr whooped after him as he walked all bent down to his boat, where Thorhall had awaited him meanwhile.

So they rowed home, and Howard went to his bed, and lay down, and never stood up for the next, twelvemonth.

This was heard of far and wide, and folk deemed that Thorbiorn had again showed his evil heart and unrighteousness in that answer. And so wear the seasons.

CHAPTER 6
Biargey will have Howard go to the Thing

But the next summer Thorbiorn rides to the Thing with his men from Icefirth. And on a day Biargey goes again to talk to Howard, and he asked her what she would; she answered: "I would have thee ride to the Thing, and see if aught may be done in thy case." He answered : "This is clean contrary to my mind : thinkest thou that I have not been mocked enough of Thorbiorn my son's bane, but that he must needs mock me also whereas all the chieftains are gathered together ?"

Said she: "It will not fare so. This I guess, that thou wilt have someone to help thee in thy case, Guest Oddleifson to wit: and if it hap, as I think, that he bring about peace between thee and Thorbiorn, so that he shall have to pay thee much money, then meseemeth he will let many men be thereby, and there will be a ring of men round about, and thou wilt be within the ring when Thorbiorn payeth thee the money: and now if it come to pass that Thorbiorn, before he pay thee that money, doeth somewhat to grieve the soul in thee, trying thee sorely, then shalt thou get thee gone at thy most speed; and then if it be that thou art lighter of heart than thou mightest look for, thou shalt not make peace in thy suit; because then thou mayest hope, as unlike as it looketh, that Olaf our son shall be avenged: but if thou wax not light-hearted, then go not away from the Thing unappeased, because then no avenging shall be."

Said Howard: "I know not what all this meaneth; but if I knew that Olaf my son should be avenged, nought should I heed any toil herein."

CHAPTER 7
Old Howard Rideth to the Thing

So she gat him ready, and he rode his ways: somewhat bent was the old man as he came to the Thing; by which time were the booths tilted, and all men come.

He rode to a great booth, even that which was owned of Steinthor of Ere, a mighty man and a great chief, of the stoutest and best heart: he leapt from his horse, and went into the booth, and there sat Steinthor and his men beside him: so Howard went up to him, and greeted him well, and well he took his greeting, and asked him who he was, Howard told of himself. Said Steinthor: "Art thou he who had that well-renowned son whom Thorbiorn slew, and whose stout defence is in all men's mouths ? "

Howard said that even so it was: " And I will, master, that thou give me leave to abide in thy booth throughout the Thing."

He answered: "Surely I will give thee leave; but be quiet, and abstain from meddling ; for the lads here are ever gamesome, and thou hast a great sorrow in thine heart, and art little fit to hold thine own, an old man, and a helpless."

The tale tells that old Howard took to himself a berth somewhere within the booth, and lay down there, and never stirred thence, nor ever fell into talk with any until the Thing was far spent: but on a morning Steinthor came to him, and said : "Why earnest thou hither to lie there like a bedes? man and a losel?"

Said Howard; "I had it in my mind to seek atonement for Olaf my son, but my heart faileth me, for Thorbiorn is unsparing of foul words and dastardliness."

Said Steinthor: "Take my counsel; go thou to Thorbiorn and complain of thy case; and I deem that if Guest goes with thee thou shalt get righting of Thorbiorn." So Howard arose, and went forth all bent, and fared to the booth of Guest and Thorbiorn, and went in. Thorbiorn was therein, but not Guest: so Howard was greeted of Thorbiorn, who asked him why he was come thither. Howard answered: "So mindful am I of the slaying of Olaf my son that it seemeth to me but newly done; and my errand here is to claim weregild of thee for the slaying."

Thorbiorn answered: "Now give I good rede to thee; come to me at home in my own country and then may I comfort thee somewhat: but here am I busy over many things, and will not have thee whining against me."

Howard answered: "If thou wilt do nought?now, I have well proven that thou wilt do none?the more in thine own country: but I was deeming that someone might perchance back my case?here."

Then spake Thorbiorn: "Hear a wonder!" said he, "he is minded now to draw men upon me! get thee gone, and never henceforward speak to me hereof if thou wilt be unbeaten."

Then Howard waxed very wroth, and turned away from the booth, saying: "Too old am I now, but those days of mine have been, wherein I little looked to bear such wrong."

Now as he went, came men meeting him, Guest Oddleifson to wit, and his folk. Howard was so wroth that he scarce heeded where he went nor would he meet those men, so home he went to his booth; but Guest cast a glance at the man going past him.

Howard went to his berth, and lay down and drew a heavy sigh : so Steinthor asked him how he had fared, and he told him. Steinthor answered: "Such deeds are injustice unheard of ! great shame to him may be looked for some time or other."

Now when Guest came back to his booth he was well greeted of Thorbiorn, but he said: "What man went from the booth even now?"

Thorbiom answered : "A wondrous question from so wise a man! More come and go hereabout than I may make account of."

Guest answered : " Yea, but this man was unlike to other men: a man big-grown, albeit somewhat old and haltfoot, yet most manly of mien withal; and meseemed he was full of sorrow and little-ease and heart-burning: and so wroth he was that he heeded not whither he went: yea, and the man looked lucky too, and not one to be lightly dealt with."

Answered Thorbiorn : "This will have been old Howard, my Thingman."

Guest asked: "Was it his son that thou slewest sackless?"

"Yea, sure," said Thorbiorn.

Said Guest: "How deemest thou that thou hast held to the promise that thou madest me when I gave thee my sister?" Now there was a man named Thorgils, called Hallason after his mother, a man most renowned and great-hearted, who abode as then with Guest his kinsman, and this was in the days of his fast-waxing fame. Him Guest bade go after Howard and bid him thither; so he went to Howard's booth, and told him that Guest would see him : but Howard said: "Loth am I to go and endure the injustice of Thorbiorn and his shameful words."

Thorgils bade him fare. "Guest will back thy case," said he. So Howard went, how loth soever he were, and came to Guest, who stood up to meet him, and welcomed him, and set him down beside him, and spake: "Now shalt thou, Howard, begin, and tell forth all thy dealings with Thorbiorn"

He did so, and when he had spoken, Guest asked of Thorbiorn if that were in any wise true: and Thorbiorn said it was no vain babble. Then said Guest: "Heard any of suchlike injustice! Now hast thou two choices; either I break our bargain utterly, or thou shalt suffer me alone to doom and deal in this your case."

To this said Thorbiorn yea, and so they all went from out the booth. Then Guest called to him a many men, and they stood in a ring round about, but some stood together within the ring, and talked the matter over. Then spoke Guest: "I may not, Thorbiorn, award as much money as ought to be paid, because thou hast not wherewithal to pay it: but I award a threefold mangild for the slaying of Olaf. But as to the other wrong thou hast done to Howard, I offer thee, Howard, that thou come to me every spring and autumn tide, and I will honour thee with gifts, and will promise never to fail thee whiles we both live."

Thorbiorn said: "This will I yeasay, and will pay him at my ease at home in the country-side."

"Nay," said Guest, " thou shalt pay all the money here at the Thing, and pay it well and duly : but I myself will lay down one mangild."

And this same he delivered out of hand well paid down. But Howard sat down, and poured the money into his cloak-skirt. Thereon Thorbiorn went thereto, and paid up little by little, and when he had got through one mangild he said he had come to the end of what he had. Guest bade hint not to shirk the matter, and thereon Thorbiorn took a folded cloth, and undid it, and spake: "Surely now he will not deem himself paid short if he have this withal."

And thereon he draveit on to Howards face so that the blood fell adown him. " Lo there," said he, " the teeth and jaw-teeth of Olaf thy son I"

Then Howard beheld how these were tumbling into his cloak-skirt, and he leapt up mad-wroth, and the pennies rolled this way and that, and staff in hand he rushed at the ring of men, and thrust his staff so hard against the breast of one, that he fell aback, and lay long in a swoon: then leapt Howard over the ring of men, and touched none, and came down afar from any, and so ran home to his booth like a young man; but when he came to the booth, he would give no word to any, but cast himself down and lay as one sick.

After these things spake Guest unto Thorbiorn.: "No man is like to thee for evil heart and wrongdoing : nor can I see aught into a man if thou dost not repent it one day, thou or thy kin ? "

And so wroth and wood was Guest, that he rode straight from the Thing to Icefirth, and took away Thorgerd from Thorbiorn: whereby Thorbiorn and all his kin deemed their honour sorely minished, . but nought might they do. Guest said withal that Thorbiorn would have to abide a greater shame yet, and one more meet for him; and he rideth therewith away to Bardstrand with his kinswoman and a deal of money. The tale tells that Howard got him away home after these things and was by now exceeding stiff; but Steinthor said to him or ever they parted: "If ever thou need a little help, Howard, come thou to me."

Howard thanked him, and so rode home, and lay down in his bed and abode there the third twelvemonth and was by then waxen much stiffen

Biargey still held to her wont of rowing out to sea every day along with Thorhall.

CHAPTER 8
Of Biargey and her Brethren

On a day in summer as they rowed out to sea they saw a craft coming east up the firth, and they knew that it was Thorbiorn and his homemen. Then spake Biargey: "Now shall we take up our lines, and row to meet Thorbiorn, for I would see him: thou shalt row towards the cutter's beam, and I will talk with him a little, whiles thou rowest about the craft." They did so and rowed toward the cutter: Biargey cast a word at Thorbiorn, hailing him, and asking him whither he would: he said he was going west to Vadil: "Thither is come out Sturla my brother, and Thio-drek his son, and I shall flit them down hither to me."

"How long wilt thou be gone, master?" said she.

" Nigh upon a week," said Thorbiorn.

Thorhall had by now rowed all about the cutter, and so when she had what she wanted they bent to their oars, and rowed off all they might. Then cried Thorbiorn: "To the devil with the wretched hag I let us straightway row after them, and slay him and maim her."

Then spake Brand : "Lo here again the truth of what men say of thee, that thou wilt never spare to do all the ill thou mayest: but I shall help them with all my might; so thou wilt have a dear bargain of it." So, what with Brand's words, what with their having by now gotten far away, Thorbiorn kept quiet and went his ways.

Now spake Biargey: "As little as it seemeth likely, I deem that there will be an avenging for Olaf my son; now will we not go straight home."

"Whither away ? " said Thorhall.

" We will go. see Valbrand my brother," said she. Now he dwelt at Valbrandstead, a very old man in these days, but once of great renown: two sons he had, exceeding hopeful, but young in years, Torfi and Eyjulf to wit.

So they make no stay till they came there : Valbrand was abroad in the home-mead and manymen with him; he went to meet his sister, and greeted her, and prayed her to abide; but she said; "It may not be, I must be home to-night."

"What wilt thou, sister ? " said he.

She said: "I will that thou lend me thy seal-nets."

"Here be three," he said : "one old and grown untrustworthy now, though once it was strong enow, and two new and unproven : which wilt thou, two or three?"

She said : " The new ones will I have, but I will not risk taking the old : get them ready against I send for them."

He said that so it should be, and therewith they, went away.

Then said Thorhall: "Whither now?" She answered : "We will go see Thorbrand my brother." He dwelt at Thorbrandstead and was now very old: he had two sons, young and hopeful, hight Odd and Thorir.

So when they came thither Thorbrand gave them good greeting and bade them abide : she said it might not be.

" What wilt thou then, sister?" said he.

Quoth she: "I would have the loan of thy trout-nets."

He answered: "Here have I three, one very old, and two new that have not been used : which wilt thou, two or three?"

She said she would have but those new ones, and they parted therewith. Then they go their ways, and Thorhall asked: "Whither now?"

"Let us go see master Asbrand, my brother," said she. He dwelt at Asbrandstead, and was the eldest of those brethren, and had wedded a sister of master Howard: he had a son named Hallgrim,. young of years, but both big and strong; ill-favoured, but most manlike to behold. So when Biargey came there, Asbrand greeted her, and bade her abide, but she said she must home that evening. "What wilt thou," said he, "so seldom as thou comest to see thy kin ? "

" A little errand " said she; "we be unfurnished of turf-tools, so I would that thou lend me thy turf-axe."

He answered, smiling:" Here be two, one exceeding rusty, old and notched, and now deemed fit for nought; but the other new and big, though unused as yet."

She said she would have the new one when she came to fetch it: he answered that she should have her way : and so they fare home to Howardstead in the evening.

CHAPTER 9
Howard Goeth to Bathstead

Now weareth certain days, until Biargey thought she might look for Thorbiorn's return from the west; then on a day she went to Howard's bed, and asked him if he slept: he sat up thereon, and sang:

Never sleep besetteth Mine eyelids since that morning? Grief driveth the ship-dweller To din of steel a-meeting? Never since the sword-stems Wrought that brunt of bucklers; E'en those that slew my Olaf Utterly unguilty.

"Full surely," said she, "that is a huge lie, that thou hast not slept for three years long; but now is it time to arise, and make thee as valiant as may be, if thou wouldst avenge Olaf thy son; for never will he be avenged in thy lifetime but if that be tonight."

So when he heard her words he leapt up from his bed and forth on to the floor, and sang:

Once more amid my old age I ask for quiet hearing, Although the speech of song-craft Scarce in my heart abideth

Since then when first I wotted Of weapon-god downfallen. O son, how surely wert thou The strength of all my welfare I

And now was Howard as brisk as might be, and halt no longer: he went to a big chest that was full of weapons, and unlocked it, and set a helm on his head,and did on him a strong byrny: then he-looked up, and saw a mew flying across the windowy and therewith he sang a stave:

High Screaming, hail-besmitten,

Lo here the bird of slaughter,

Who coming to the corpse-sea

Craveth his meal of morning! '

E'en so in old days bygone

From the old tree croaked the raven

When the sworn hawks of the slaughter

The warrior's mead went seeking.

He armed himself speedily and deftly, and arrayed Thorhall also with goodly weapons: and so when they were ready he turned to Biargey and kissed her, saying it was not all so sure when they should meet again.

So she bade him farewell: "No need to egg thee on to the avenging of Olaf our son, for I wot that in thee might and a hardy heart are fellows."

So they parted: but those twain went down to the sea, and ran out a six-oared boat, and took the oars, and made no stay till they came off the stead of Valbrand : there a long tongue of the ere runneth out into the sea, and there they laid their boat: then Howard bade Thorhall watch the boat while he went up to the stead; and he had a spear in his hand, a noble weapon : but when he came up on to the home-mead there were the father and sons: the brethren were stripped and raking up the hay, and had taken off their shoes, and had laid them down in the meadow beside them; and they were high shoes.

So Valbrand went to meet Howard, and greeted him well, bidding him abide: he said it might not be.

"For I am come to fetch the seal-nets that thou didst lend to my wife, thy sister."

Then went Valbrand to his sons, and said to them: "Hither is come Howard your kinsman, and he is so arrayed as if he had some mighty deed on hand."

But when they heard that, they cast by their rakes and ran to their clothes, and when they came to take their shoes, lo! they were shrunken with the sun: nevertheless they thrust their feet into them at their speediest, so that they tore the skin off their heels, and when they came home their shoes were full of blood.

Valbrand gave his sons good weapons, and said; "Follow Howard well, and think more on your vengeance than on what may come after."

Then they went their ways to Thorbrandstead, and there also were Odd and Thorir speedily arrayed. Thence fared they till they came to Asbrandstead, and there Howard claimed his turf-cutter, whereon Hallgrim his kinsman arrayed himself to go with him, in whose company also went one An, a homeman of Asbrand, who did housecarle's service, and was fosterer of Hall-grim.

So when they were ready they went to where the boat lay, and Thorhall greeted them well. They were now eight in company, and each more warriorlike than the other. Now spake Hallgrim to Howard his kinsman, saying: "Why wentest thou from home, kinsman, lacking both sword and axe?"

He answered: "Maybe we shall fall in with Thorbiorn Thiodrekson, and then after our parting thou shalt speak another word, for most like I shall have the sword Warflame, the best of weapons."

Then they rejoiced, blessing the word of his mouth: "For much lies upon it that we fall to work in manly wise."

The day was now far spent, and so they ran out the boat, and leapt into her, and fell a-rowing: and even therewith they saw a great flock of ravens flying on before them over the tongue of the ere that lay ahead : then sang Howard this stave:

> A sign I deem yon blood-fowl
> Over the ere a-sweeping;
> Since even now fat-feeding
> To Odin's fowl I promised.
> All we shall have to hearken,
> O Hallgrim, to Hild's uproar,
> And well are we, O fellows,
> Whom happy hour awaiteth.

They fared over the sound, and out in the firth it blew hard, whereby they snipped many a sea forward : but they fell to work in manly wise, and made no stay till they came off Bathstead: thereat was a place good to lay a craft in, for Thorbiorn had let make a goodly haven there, and had had all cleaned and cleared out right up to land: the shore went down steep into the sea, and a cutter might lie there, or a craft bigger yet, if need were : great whale-ribs also were laid down there for slips, and the ends of them made fast with big stones: nor needed any man be wet going off board or on, were the ship bigger or lesser.

But above this haven ran a ridge of shingle, above which stood a great boat-house well found in all wise; and on the other hand above the ridge on one side was a big pool; from the boat-house one might not see the foreshore, but from the shingle-ridge both boat-house and foreshore were in sight

So when they came to land they leapt from the boat, and Howard spake, saying : "We will bear the boat up over the ridge unto the pool, and we ourselves also will be up the other side of the ridge, so that they may not see us at once; neither will we be over hasty in our hunting: let none leap up before I give the word." And now was it quite dusk.

CHAPTER 10
Of the Metting of Those Men at Bathstead

Now must we tell how Thorbiorn and his fellows fare from the west, ten in company in a cutter: Sturla was there, and Thiodrek his son, Thorbiorn and Vakr, Brand the Strong and two house-carles; and their cutter was deeply laden.

That same evening they came to Bathstead just before dark, and Thorbiorn said: "We will fare nought hastily; we will let the cutter lie here tonight, and bear up nought save our weapons and clothes, for the weather is fine and like to be dry : and thou, Vakr, shalt bear ashore our weapons." So he took their swords first and their spears, and bore them up to the boat-house.

Then said Torfi : "Let us take their swords and him that goes with them."

"Nay, let it be yet," said Howard. But he bade Hallgrim go and take the sword Warflame, and bring it him: so when Vakr went down again, Hallgrim ran and took the sword and brought it to Howard, and he drew it forth and brandished it aloft.

Now Vakr came up again, and had laden his back with shields and his arms with steel-hoods, and he had a helm on his head. So when he was gotten to the pool-side they sprang up to take him : but he, hearing the clatter of them deemed full surely that war was abroad, and was minded to run back to his friends with their weapons, but as he turned round sharply, his feet stumbled by the pool, so that he fell down therein head foremost; the mud was deep there, and the water shallow, and the man heavy-laden with all those weapons; so he might not get up again, neither would any there help him, and that was Vakr's latter end, that there he died. So when they had seen that, they ran down to the shingle-ridge, and when Thorbiorn beheld them he cast himself into the sea, and struck out from shore. Master Howard was the first to see this hap, and he ran and cast himself also into the sea, and swam after Thorbiorn.

But of Brand the Strong they say, that rushing forward, he caught hold of a ship-runner, a great whale-rib, and drove it into the head of An, Hallgrim's fosterer; Hallgrim was just come down from the ridge when he saw An fall; so he ran up with axe raised aloft, and smote Brand on the head, cleaving him down to the shoulders, and it was even therewith that Thorbiorn and Howard leapt into the sea; and Hallgrim when he saw it leapt in after them.

Torfi Valbrandson ran to meet Sturla, a big and strong man, unmatched in arms, and he had all his war-gear on him: so they fought long, and in manly wise withal.

CHAPTER 11
Of the Slaying of Thorbiorn Thiodrekson

Turn we now to Howard and Thorbiorn : they made from land, and a long swim it was till they came to a skerry that lay off there; and when Thorbiorn came up on to the skerry, Howard was but just off it: that seeth Thorbiorn, who being weaponless before him, catcheth up a big stone to drive at his head withal.

But when Howard saw that, it came into his mind of how he had heard tell of the Outlands that another faith was put forth there than the faith of the Northlands; and therewith he vowed that If any could show him that that faith was better and fairer, then would he trow in it if he might but overcome Thorbiorn.

And therewithal he struck out his hardest for the skerry. And so as Thorbiorn was a-casting the stone, his feet slipped up, for it was slippery on the stones, and he fell aback, and the stone fell on his breast, so that he was stunned thereby; and even therewith came Howard on to the skerry, and thrust him through with the Sword Warflame. Then was Hallgrim also come on to the skerry; but Howard smote Thorbiorn across the face, and clave out the teeth and jaw-teeth of him, and down right through. Hallgrim asked wherefore he did so to a dead man; but Howard said: "I had this stroke in my mind when Thorbiorn smote me in the face with that cloth knit up; for then the teeth that he had smitten from Olaf, my son with this same sword, tumbled about me."

Then they made for the land again. Men deemed afterward when that was told them, that Howard did valiantly to swim out into the firth, not knowing that there was any skerry before him: and a very long swim was that even as things went.

As they came up toward the shingle-ridge, a man came running to meet them with axe raised aloft, a man in a blue frock girt into his breeches; they turned toward him, and when they met they knew Torfi Valbrandson, and greeted him well, and he asked them if Thorbiorn were dead. Then sang Howard:

    I drave adown the sword-edge
    To jaw of sword-clash dealer;
    I set the venomed sword-dew
    Seeking the chieftain's eyen;

Nought saw I any shrinking
In that dweller in the scabbard

Warflame, when his old wielder
Who once was mighty fell there.

He asked what their deeds were, and Torfi said that Sturla was fallen, and the house-carles, but that An was slain withal. Then sang Howard :

So have we slain full swiftly
Four of the men who slew him,
The blood-stained son of Biargey;
Brave is the gain we bring you.
But one of our own fellows
An, unto earth is fallen
By bone of sea-wolf smitten
As Hallgrim sayeth soothly.

Then they went up to the boat-house, and found their fellows, who greeted them well. Then asked Eyjulf Valbrandson if they should slay the thralls; but Howard said that the slaying of thralls was no revenge for Olaf his son. "Let them abide here to-night, and watch that none steal aught of. the spoil."

Then Hallgrim asked what to do now, and Howard answered: "We will take the cutter and all we deem of avail, and make for under Moon-berg to see Liot the champion: somewhat of a revenge were there in such a man as that, if we might get it done."

So they take the cutter and manifold good things of those kinsmen, and row out along the firth, and up to Moonberg. Then spake Howard : "Now must we fare wisely. Liot is well ware of himself, for he hath ever feuds on hand; he hath watch held over him every night, and lieth in a shut-bed bolted every night: an earth-house is there under the sleeping-chamber, and the mouth of the same cometh up at the back of the houses, and many men he hath with him."

Then said Torfi Valbrandson: "My rede it is to bear fire to the stead, and burn every man's son within."

Howard said it should not be so: "But thou and Hallgrim my kinsman shall be upon the housetop to watch thence the mouth of the earth-house, lest any go out thereby, thee I trust best for this: here also be two doors in the front of the stead and two doors to the hall: now shall Eyjulf and I go in by one, and the brethren Odd and Thorir by the other, and so into the hall: but thou Thorhall shalt watch the cutter here, and defend it manly if there be need thereof."

So when he had ordered them as he would, they go up to the house. There stood a great out-bower in the home-mead, and a man armed sat under the wall thereof: so when they were drawn nigh the same, the man sees them, and springs up with the mind to give warning of their coming: now Hallgrim went foremost of that company, and he shot a spear after that man, and pinned him to the house-wall, and there he died on the spear. So then they went whither they were minded; Torfi and Hallgrim going to the outgate of the house.

70

CHAPTER 12
Of the Slaying of Liot Thiodrekson

So tells the tale that Howard went into the hall; light burned above, but below it was dim: so he went into the bedchamber: and as it happed the mistress was not yet gone to bed, but was yet in the women's bower, and women with her, and the bed-chamber was not locked. So Howard smote with the flat of his sword on the door, and Liot waked therewith, and asked who made that clatter, and so master Howard named himself.

"Why art thou there, carle Howard ? " said Liot, "we were told the day before yesterday that thou wert hard at death's door."

Howard answered: "Of another man's death mayest thou first hear : for hearken, I tell thee of the death of thy brethren, Thorbiorn and Sturla."

When he heard that, he sprang up in his bed, and caught down a sword that hung over him, and cried on the men in the hall to arise and take their weapons: but Howard leapt up into the bedchamber, and smote Liot on the left shoulder; but Liot turned sharply therewith, and the sword glanced from the shoulder, and tore down the arm, and took it off at the elbow joint: Liot leapt forth from the chamber with brandished sword, with the mind to hew down Howard; but then was Eyjulf come up, and he smote him on the right shoulder, and struck off his hand, and there they slew Liot.

Then arose great uproar in the hall, and Liot's house-carles would stand up and take to their weapons; but now were Thorbrand's sons come in, and here and there men got a scratch or a knock. Then spake Howard : "Let all be as quiet as may be, and do ye no manner of mischief, or else will we slay every man's son of you, one on the heels of the other."

So they deemed it better to be all quiet; nor had they much sorrow of Liot's death, though they were of his house.

So those fellows turned away, nor would Howard do more therein. Torfi and Hallgrim came to meet them, for they were about going in; and they asked what had been done; so Howard sang a stave:

> Wrought good work Geirdi's offspring
> >On grove of water's sunshine,
> Beheld I Knott there brandish
> The blood-ice sharp and bitter;
> Eyjolf was fain of edge-play
> With eager kin of warriors;
> The wary one, the well-known
> Would deal out flame of war-sheen.

Then they went down to the cutter, and Thor-hall greeted them well there.

Torfi Valbrandson asked what to do now. Said Howard: "Now shall we seek after some safeguard; for though the revenge be not as great as would, yet shall we not be able to keep ourselves after this work; for there are many of Thorbiorn's kin of great account: and the likeliest thing I deem it to go to Steinthor of Ere; for he of all men has promised to help me in my need."

So they all bade him look to it, and they would do his will, and not depart from him till he deemed it meet. So then they put forth into the firth and lay hard on their oars, but Howard sat by the tiller. Then spake Hallgrim, bidding Howard sing somewhat; and he sang :

How have all we, O Hallgrim, Well wreaked a mighty vengeance On Thiodrek's son I full surely We never shall repent it. For Thorbiorn's sake the ship-lords In storm of steel were smitten; And I wot that the people's wasters Yet left would fain repay us.

CHAPTER 13
Of Those Fellows and Steinthor of Ere

Of their voyage is nought to tell till they come to Ere; and it was then the time of day whenas Steinthor was sitting at table with his men : so they went into the hall with their weapons, four in company; and Howard went before Steinthor, and greeted him; Steinthor took his. greeting well, and asked who he was, and he said he was called Howard.

"Wert thou in our booth last summer?" He said that so it was. Then said Steinthor: "Lads, have ye seen any man less like to what he is now than the man he was then ? Meseems he might scarce go staffless from booth to booth, and we deemed him like to be a man bedridden, such grief of heart lay upon him : but now a wight man under weapons he seemeth to be. What tell ye any tidings?"

Howard answered: "Tidings we tell of: the slaying of Thorbiorn Thiodrekson, and his brethren Liot and Sturla, sons of Thiodrek, of Brand the Strong and the seven of them."

Steinthor answered: "Great tidings ye tell: who is it hath done this, and smitten down these the greatest of champions, these so mighty men ?"

Howard spake and said that he and his kinsmen had done it. Then spake Steinthor, and asked where Howard would seek for safeguard after such great deeds. Said Howard : "I was minded for that which has now come to pass, to wit, to come unto thee, for methought thou saidst last summer at the Thing, that if ever I needed some little help I should come to thee no later than to other chiefs."

Steinthor answered: "I know not when thou mayest deem thyself in want of great help if now thou deemest thy need but a little one; but thou mightest well think that I were no good friend in need, if I were slow to answer thee herein: neither shall it be so. I will bid thee, Howard, to abide here with thy fellows till this matter is brought to an end; and 1 promise to right your case for you all: for meseemeth ye are such men, that he will have the better part who taketh you to him; nor is it sure that such doughty men as ye be are lightly to be gotten:

forsooth matters have gone herein more according to right than according to likelihood."

Then sang Howard a stave:

Due is it for the dealers Of Firth's-sun to be stirring If they be fain to further

The folk of Valkyrs'fire; For the pride of Icefirth people Men tell hath had a down-fall By a blow that bodeth unpeace, By sackless sword-stems smitten.

They thanked Steinthor for his noble bidding; and he bade take their clothes and weapons, and let them dry clothes; and when Howard did off is helm, and put his byrny from him, he sang :

> Laughed the lords of bloodwolf
> Loud about my sorrow
> When with steel-shower smitten
> Fell my son the well-loved.
> Well, since Odin's woodmen
> Went along the death-road
> Otherwise wolf-wailing
> Echoeth o'er the mountains.

Steinthor bade Howard go to the bench and sit over against him, and to marshal those fellows beside him, and Howard did so, marshalling his kinsman Hallgrim inward from him, and then inward yet sit Thorbrand's sons Thorir and Odd; but outward from Howard sit Torfi and Eyjulf, the sons of Valbrand, then Thorhall, and then the homemen who sat there afore.

And when they sat down Howard sang a stave:

In this house, 0 Hallgrim, We shall have abiding; War-gale we deny not Warriors' wrath that bringeth; Yet that slaying surely Unto straw shall tumble Scarce for those spear-heeders Shall I spend my substance.

Then said Steinthor : "Easy to hear of thee that things are going after thy will; and so forsooth would it be, if there were no blood-feud after such bold and mighty men as were those kinsmen all; who have left behind them such great men to follow up the feud."

Howard said that he heeded not the feud, and that there was an end from henceforth of sorrow or grief in his heart, neither should he think any end to the case aught but well. He was as glad and merry with every child of man there as if he were young again. Now are these tidings heard of far and wide, and were deemed to have fallen out clean contrary to what was like to have been. So there they sat at eve with master Steinthor lacking neither plenteous company nor goodly cheer; and there were no fewer there than sixty men defensible. Leave we them now a-sitting at Ere with master Steinthor in good welcome, and costly entertainment.

CHAPTER 14
Of the Slaying of Holmgang-Liot

Liot was the name of a man who dwelt at Redsand; he was called Holmgang-Liot: he was both big and strong, and the greatest of Holmgang-fighters. Thorbiorn Thiodrekson had had his sister to wife : it is said of him that he was a most unjust man, who had had his axe in the head of every man who would not yield all to his will; nor was there any who might hold his head up in freedom against him all around Redsand, and far and wide otherwhere.

Now there was one called Thorbiorn, who dwelt at a stead called Ere, a man well stricken in years, a wealthy man, but of no great heart: two sons he had, one called Grim, and the other Thorstein.

Now as tells the tale, Liot and Thorbiorn had a water-meadow in common, a right good possession, which was so divided betwixt them that they should have it summer and summer about: but the brook which flooded the meadow in spring ran below Liot's house, and there were water-hatches therein, and all was well arrayed. But so it fell out that whensoever it was Thorbiorn's turn for the meadow he gat no water, and at last it came to this, that Liot gave out that the meadow was none of Thorbiorn's, and he were best not dare to claim it; and when Thorbiorn heard that, he deemed well that Liot would keep his word. It was but a little way between their houses, so on a day they met, and Thorbiorn asked Liot if he would verily take his meadow from him. Liot answered and bade him speak not another word of it: "It is not for thee any more than for others to go whining against what I will have; do one of two things : either be well content with my will herein, or I drive thee away from thine own, and thou wilt have neither the meadow nor aught else."

So when Thorbiorn saw Liot's injustice, and whereas he had wealth and to spare, he bought the meadow at Liot's own price, paying him sixty hundreds then and there; wherewith they parted.

But when those lads his sons heard hereof, they were full evil content, saying that it was the greatest robbery of their heritage to have to buy what was their own.

And this thing was heard of far and wide.

Now those brethren kept their father's sheep. Thorstein being of twelve winters, and Grim of ten : and on a day in the early winter they went to the sheep-houses; for there had been a great snow-storm, and they would wot whether all the sheep were come home. Now herewith it befell that Liot had gone that morning to see to his drifts ; for he was a man busy in his matters; so just as the lads came to the sheep-house they saw how Liot came up from the sea shore ; then spake Grim to Thorstein his brother : "Seest thou Holmgang-Liot yonder, coming up from the sea ? "

"How may I fail to see him?" said Grim.

Then said Thorstein: "Great wrong hath he . done to us and to others, and I have it in my mind to avenge it if I might."

Said Grim : "An unwise word that thou wouldst do a mischief to such a champion as is Liot, a man mightier than four or five men might deal with, even were they full-grown : this is no game for children." Thorstein answered : "It availeth not to stay me, I will follow him all the same; but thou art likest to thy father, and wilt be a robbing-stock for Liot like many others."

Grim answered : "Whereas this hath got into thy head, kinsman, for as little avail as I may be to thee, I will help thee all I may." "Then is it well done of thee," said Thorstein, "and maybe that things will follow our right." Now, they bore hand-axes little out sharp. There they stand, and bide till Liot makes for the sheep-house: he passed by them quickly, having a poleaxe in his hand, and so went on his way, making as if he saw not the lads; but when he was even passing by them Thorstein smote on his shoulder; the axe bit not, but so great was the stroke that the arm was put out of joint at the shoulder. But when Liot saw (as he deemed) that the lads would bait him, he turned on them, and hove up his axe to smite Thorstein ; but even as he hove it aloft, ran Grim in on him, and smote the hand from him above the wrist, and down fell hand and axe together. Short space then they left betwixt their strokes; nor is aught more likely to be told hereof, than that there fell Holmgang-Liot, and neither of them hurt.

So they buried him in the snowdrift and left him there; and when they came home their father was out in the doorway; and he asked them what made them so late, and why their clothes were bloody.

They told of the slaying of Liot. He asked if they had slain him; and they said that so it was. Then said he : "Get ye gone, luckless wretches! ye have wrought a most unhappy deed, and have slain the greatest of lords and our very chieftain; and this withal have ye brought to pass, that I shall be driven from my lands and all that I have, and ye will be slain, and that is right well."

And therewith he rushed out away from the house.

Said Grim: "Let us have nothing to do with the old devil, so loathly as he goeth on! to hear how he goeth on, the sneaking wretch !"

Thorstein answered: "Nay, let us go find him, for I doubt me he is nought so wroth as he would make believe." So they go' to him, and Thorbiorn spake gladly to them, and bade them bide him there; then he went home, and was away but a little while till he came back with two horses well arrayed; so he bade them leap a-horseback. "I will send you," said he, "to Steinthor of Ere, my friend, whom ye shall bid to take you in; and here is a gold ring, a right dear thing, which ye shall give him: he hath oft asked me for it, and never got it, but now it shall be free to him because of your necessity." Then the old man kissed his sons, and bade them to fare well, and that they might all meet again safe and sound. Nought is told of their journey till they came unto Ere betimes of a morning; so they went into the hall, and it was all hung about and both benches were full, and neither game nor glee was lacking* They went before Steinthor and greeted him. well,* and well he took their greeting, and asked, them who they were; so they told of their names and of their father, and withal Thorstein said: "Here is a ring which my father sendeth thee, and therewithal his greeting, and biddeth thee give us quarters this winter, or longer, if we need it.

Steinthor took the ring, and said: "Tell ye any tidings?"

They said : " The slaying of Liot, and we have slain him."

Steinthor answered: " Lo here another wonder, that two little lads should make an end of such a champion as was Liot! and what was his guilt?" They said what they deemed thereof. Steinthor said : "My rede it is that ye go across the floor up to Howard, the hoary carle who sits right over against me, and ask of him whether he will or will not take you into his company."

So do they, and go before Howard; he greeted them well, and asked for tidings, making as if he had not heard, and they told him the very innermost thereof; and when their tale was done, Howard sprang up to meet them, and sang a stave:

Ye, O fir-stems of the fight-sun, Thank we now for manly service; Men by valiant deeds left luckless Do I love, and ye are loved. Of all men on mould abiding Do I deem his slaughter meetest Let this fearful word go flying To my foemen of the westward.

Howard gave those brethren place outward from himself, and they sat there glad and merry.

These tidings are heard all about Redsand, and far and wide otherwhere. Liot was found dead there under the wall; and folk went to Thorbiorn and asked him thereof, and Thorbiorn denied not that his sons had slain him. But whereas Liot was unbeloved in Redsand, and that Thorbiorn said he had taken their deed amiss and driven them away, wherein the home-men bore him out, there was no taking up of the feud as at that time; and Thorbiorn sat at home in peace.

CHAPTER 15
Steinthor Goes to Seek Stores in Otterdale

FALL we now to telling how they sit all together at Ere well holden; very costly it was unto Steinthor, so many men as he had, and so much as he must expend in his bounteous housekeeping.

Now there was a man named Atli, who dwelt at Otterdale, and was wedded to a sister of Steinthor of Ere, Thordis to wit; he was the smallest of men, a very mannikin, and it was said of him that- his mind was even as his body, and that he was the greatest of misers; yet was he come of great men, and was so.rich that he might scarce tell his wealth; and Thordis, Steinthor's sister, had been wedded to him for his wealth's sake.

As goes the tale the house at Otterdale was far. from the highway, and stood on the other side of the firth over against Ere.

Atli was not free enough of his money to keep workmen.; he himself worked night and day all he migh, and he was so self-willed, that he would have nought to do with other men either for good or ill. He was the greatest, husbandman, and had a.big store-house, wherein were all kinds of goods: there were huge piles of dried fish and all kinds of flesh-meat, and cheese and all things needful, and in that house had he made his bed, and he and his wife slept there every night.

Now. tells the tale that on a morning was Steinthor early, afoot, and he went to Howard's bed, and took him by the foot and bade him stand up; and Howard sprang up speedilyand forth on to the floor, and when he was arisen his fellows stood up one after another, even as their wont was, that all went whithersoever one had need to go; and when they were allarrayed they went forth into thehome-mead, where was Steinthor with certain of his men. Then said Howard: "We are ready, master, to fare whitherso thou wilt have us; and we will follow thee heartily, recking or reckless; but that is left me of my pride, that I go not on any journey but if I wot whither I be going."

Steinthor said : "I would fare to Atli my brother-in-law, and I would have you bear me fellowship on the road."

So they went down to the sea, where was the cutter they had taken from Thorbiorn ; so they ran it out and took to their oars, and rowed out into the firth. But Steinthor deemed that that company took all things with hardy heart

That morning master Atli arose up early and went from his bed ; he was so clad, that he had on a white doublet, short and strait. The man was not speedy of foot; he was both a starveling and foul of favour, bald and sunken-eyed. He went out and looked at the weather ; it was cold and very frosty. Now he saw a boat faring thitherward over the firth and nigh come to shore, and he knew master Steinthor his brother-in-law, and was ill-content thereat. There was a garth in the home-mead, standing somewhat out into the fields; therein stood a haystack drawn together from all about: so what must Atli do but run into the garth, and tumble the hay stack down on himself and lie thereunder.

But of Steinthor and that company it is to?told that they come aland and go up to the house,?and when they came to the store-house Thordis?sprang up and greeted well her brother and all of?them, and said he was seldom seen there. Steinthor asked where was Atli his brother-in-law; and?she said he was gone out but a little while; so?Steinthor bade seek him, and they sought him about?the stead and found him not, and so came back and?told Steinthor. Then said Thordis : "What wilt?thou of us, kinsman?" He answered: "I was?deeming that Atli would have given or sold me some?stores."

Said she: "Meseemcth I have no less to do herewith than Atli; and I will that thou have hence what thou wilt." He said that he would take that willingly; so they clear out the store-house, and bear what was in it down aboard the cutter till it was laden with all kinds of good things. Then said Steinthor : " Now shall ye go back home with the cutter, but I will abide behind with my sister; for I am fain to see how my brother-in-law Atli bears himself when he cometh back."

" Meseems, kinsman," said Thordis, "there is no food in this; it will be nothing merry to hear him. \\xt do as thou wilt; only thou shalt promise me to be no worse friend to Atli than before, whatsoever he may say or do."

Steinthor said yea to this; and so she set him behind certain hangings where none might see him, but the others went their ways back home with the cutter; they had rough weather on the firth and shipped many seas before they came to land.

CHAPTER 16
Of Atli the Little and His Words

Turn we now to Atli lying under the haystack, who, when he saw them depart from the shore, crept out from under the stack; and was so stiff that he might scarce stand up; he drags himself home to the store-house, and every tooth in his head chattered again ; he stared wide and wild round about, and seeth that the storehouse hath been cleared; then saith he: "What robbers have been here ?"

Thordis answered: "None have robbed here; but here have been Steinthor my brother, and his men, and I have given them what thou callest robbed"

Atli answered: "Of all things I shall rue most that ever I wedded thee; wretched man that I am for that wedding I I wot of none worse than is Steinthor thy brother, nor greater robbers than they of his house. Now is all taken and stolen and harried from me, so that we shall soon have td take to the road."

Then said Thordis: "We shall never lack for wealth : come thou to bed and let me warm thee somewhat, for meseems thou art wondrous cold."

So he crawled under the bedclothes to her. Steinthor deemed his brother-in-law a very starveling: he had nought on his feet; his cowl was pulled over his head, and came nowhere down him.

So Atli nestles under the clothes beside her, and is mad of speech, ever scolding at Steinthor, and calling him a robber. Then he was silent for awhile.

But when he waxed warm, then said.he; "Sooth to say, I have a great treasure in thee,; and truly no such a noble-minded man may be found as is Steinthor my brother-in-law, and that is well bestowed which he hath gotten; it is even as if I had it myself."

And so he went on a long while praising Steinthor. Then Steinthor came forth to the bed, and Atli seeth him and standeth up and greeteth him.

Then said Steinthor: "What thinkest thou, brother-in-law Atli, have we cleared out thy storehouse?"

Atli answered: " It is most sooth that all is best bestowed! which thou hast, and I bid thee take all thou wilt of my goods, for nought is lacking here: thou hast done as most befitteth a chieftain in taking to. thee those men who have wreaked their griefs, and thou wilt be minded to see them through it as a great man should."

Said Steinthor: "Atli, I will bid thee be nought so miserly as thou hast been hitherto; live thy life well, and get thee workmen, and mingle with men; I know thee for no paltry man, though thou makest thyself such for perverseness sake.' r Atli promised this; and Steinthor went home that day, and the brothers-in-law parted in all kindness. Steinthor cometh home to Ere, and deemeth he hath sped well. There they sit at home now, and the. winter wears: there were holden sturdy skin-plays and hall-plays.

CHAPTER 17
Men Get Ready for the Thing

There was one Swart, a thrall at Ere, a big man, and so'strong that he had four men's might; he was handy about the stead, and did much work. Now on a day Stein-thor let call this thrall to him, and said: "They will have thee in the game with us to-day, for we lack a man." Swart answered: "It is idle to bid me this, for I have much work to do, and I deem not that thy champions will do it for me; yet I will grant thee this if thou wilt."

So saith it that Hallgrim was matched against Swart, and the best one may tell of it is, that every time they fell to, Swart went down, and after every fall his shoes came off, and he would be a long while binding them on again. This went on for long in the day, and men made great jeering and laughter thereat; but Howard sang a stave:

> The lords of sea-king's stallion,
> Valbrand's sons the doughty,
> Nought so long they louted
> Low o'er shoe-thongs, mind we,
> When we went, O Valkyr,
> Toward my son's avenging,
> And Gylfi's garth swelled round me
> On that day of summer.

The play was of the best. Hallgrim was then eighteen winters old, and was deemed like to be a most doughty man by then he came to his full growth. .

So sayeth it that the winter wore, and nought befell to tell of, yea and until they were ready to go to the Thing.

Steinthor said he knew not what he would do for those fellows; he would not have them with him to the Thing, and he thought it not good to let them abide at his house the while. But a few days before the Thing he and Atli his brother-in-law met, and Atli asked what He was minded to do with his guests while the Thing lasted. Steinthor said he knew not where he could bestow them, so as to be unafraid for them: "Unless thou take them." Atli said : "I will bind myself to take these men." "Thou dost well therein," said Steinthor. Said Atli: "I will help thee in all thou wilt so far as my might goeth.'"

"Right well I trust thee so to do," said Steinthor.

CHAPTER 18
Men Ride to the Thing

After this Howard and his fellows went their ways with Atli, and came to Otter-dale, and there Atli welcomed Howard with both hands. Nought lacked there that they needed, and Atli made them the most goodly feast: there were ten stout men there now. Atli cleared out the store-house, and made their beds there, and hung up their weapons, and all was arrayed in the best wise. But Steinthor summoned men to him, and lacked neither for friends nor kin, and with great men also was he allied : so he rode to the Thing with three hundred men, all which were his Thingmen, kin, friends, or men allied to him.

CHAPTER 19
Of the Men of Dyrafirth

There was a man hight Thorarin, the priest of Dyrafirth in the west country, a great chief, and somewhat stricken in years; He was the brother of those sons of Thiodrek, but by far the thoughtfullest and wisest of them. He had heard of these tidings and of the slaying of his brethren and kinsmen, and deemed himself nigh touched by it, and that he might not sit idle in the matter whereas the blood-feud fell to him most of all. So before folk rode to the Thing, he summoned to him the men of Dyrafirth, his friends and kinsfolk. There was one Dyri, next of account after Thorarin the priest, and a great friend of his; Thorgrim was the name of his son, a man full grown at this time: it is told of him that he was both big and strong, and a wizard of the cunningest, who dealt much in spells. Now when Thorarin laid this matter before his friends, they were of one accord in this, that Thorarin and Dyri should ride to the Thing with two hundred men; but Thorgrim, Dyri's son, offered himself to compass the slaying of Howard, and all those kinsmen and fellows : he said how the word went that Steinthor of Ere had held them through the winter, and that he had promised to uphold their case at law to the uttermost against such as had the blood-feud after those kinsmen.

Thorgrim said that he knew how Steinthor was ridden from home, a great company, to the Thing, and that those fellows were gotten to Otterdale to Atli the Miser, brother-in-law of Steinthor: "And there is nought to hinder our slaying them one on the heels of the other."

So this rede was taken, that Thorgrim should ride from home with eighteen men: of whose journey is nought to tell till they come to Atli's stead in Otterdale early of a morning, and ride into a hollow whence they might not be seen from the house; then bade Thorgrim to light down, and they did so, and baited their horses; but Thorgrim said that he was so sleepy that he might not sit up, so. he slept with a skin drawn over his head, and was ill at ease in his sleep.

CHAPTER 20
Of Atli's Dreaming

Now must we take up the tale of what they were about in the house at Otterdale : they slept in the store-house that night according to wont, arid in the morning they were waked, because Atli in his sleep laboured so, that none of them might sleep because of it; for he tossed about and breathed heavily, and beat about with hand and foot in the bed; till Torfi Valbrandson leapt up and woke him, laying, that they might not sleep for him and his goings on. Then sat up Atli, stroking his bald head.

Howard asked if aught had been shown to him, and he said verily it was so: "Methought I went forth from the store-house, and I saw how wolves ran over the wold from the south eighteen in company, and before the wolves went a vixen fox, and so sly a creature as was that, saw I never erst; exceeding ogre-like was it and evil; it peered all about, and would have its eyes on everything", and right grimly methought all the beasts did look. But even as they were come to the stead Torfi woke me; and well I wot that these are fetches of men ; so stand we up straightway."

Nor did Atli depart from his wont, but sprang up and cast his cape on him, and so out as swift as a bolt is shot, while they take their weapons and clothes and array themselves at their briskest; and when they were well-nigh dight, cometh Atli back clad in a strong byrny, and with a drawn sword in his hand; then spake Atli: "Most like it is that it falleth out now as many guessed it would, to wit, that it would avail not Steinthor my brother-in-law to find you a harbour here; but I pray you to let me rule in what now lies before us ; and first it is my rede that we go out under the house-wall, and let them not gore us indoors ; as for fleeing away, I deem that hath not come into your heads.' And they say that so it shall be.

CHAPTER 21
Of the Otterdalers

Tell we now how Thorgrim woke, and was waxen hot; then spake he: "I have been up to the house and about it awhile ; but all was so dim to me that I wot not what shall befall me; yet let us go home to the house: meseems we should burn them in, so may we the speediest bring the end about."

So they take their weapons, and fare into the home-mead. And when Atli and his fellows saw the men, Atli said: "Here be come the Dyrafirthers, I think, with;Thorgrim, Dyri's son, at the head of them, the worst man and the greatest wizard in Dyraflrth; he is the most friend of Thorarin, who has the blood-feud for Thorbiorn his brother: now I am minded, as unlike as it may seem, to go against Thorgrim ; but thee, Howard, I will have to do deal with two, for thou art proven and a great champion. To Hallgrim thy kinsman I allot those twain who are stoutest; to Torfi and Eyjulf, Valbrand's sons, I allot four; and to Thor-brand's sons, Odd and Thorir, other four; to Thor-biorn's sons, Grim and Thorstein, I allot three, and to Thorhall and my house-carle each one his man."

So when Atli had ordered them as he would, Thorgrim and his men come on from the south toward the house ; and they see that things have gone otherwise than they looked for, arid that men are standing there with weapons, ready to deal with them; then said Thorgrim: "Who may know but that Atli the craven hath more shifts than we wotted of; yet all the same shall we go against them.!'

Then men fell on as they had been ordered; and the first onset was of Atli the. Little against Thorgrim, smiting at him two-handed with his sword; but never it bit on him. So a while they smote, and never bit the sword on Thorgrim. Then said Atli: "As a troll art thou, Thorgrim; and not as a man, that the iron biteth not on thee." Thorgrim answered: "How durst thou say such things, whereas I hewed on thee e'en now at my best, and the sword bit not on thine evil pilled pate."

Then seeth Atli that things will not go well on this wise; so he casteth by his sword, and runneth under Thorgrim's hands, and casteth him down on the field. Now is there no weapon beside him, and he knew that the odds were great between them, so he grovelleth down on him, and biteth the throat of him asunder, and then draggeth him to where his sword lay, and smiteth the head from off him. Then he looked round about wide-eyed, and saw that Howard had slain one of those whom he had to deal with. Thither ran Atli first, and for no long while they gave and took before the man fell dead. Hallgrim had slain both those he had to deal with, and Torfi in likewise: Eyjulf had slain one of his: Thorir and Odd had slain three, and one was left: Thorstein and Grim had slain two and left one: Thorhall had slain his man; but the house-carle had not slain his. Then bade Howard to hold their hands; but Thorstein Thorbiornson said: "Our father shall not have to hear west there in Redsand that we brethren could not do our allotted day's work as other men." And therewith he ran at one of those with axe aloft and smote it into his head that he gat his bane. Atli asked why not slay them all; but Howard said that was of no use. Then Atli sat down and bade lead the men before him; then he shaved the hair from them and polled them, and tarred them thereafter; he drew his knife from the sheath, and sheared the ears from each of them, bidding them so ear-marked go find Dyri and Thorarin; and said that now perchance they would mind them how they had come across Atli the Little. So they went thence, three of them, who had come there eighteen in company, stout men and well arrayed.

Now sang Howard a stave:

> West and east is wafted
> Word to Icefirth's dwellings,
> Word of weapons reddened
> In the spear-storm's waxing;
> Now for spear-play's speeding
> Sped the war-lords hither,
> Soothly small the matter
> Unto sons of Valbrand.

Then they went their ways and buried the slain, and thereafter gat them rest and peace even as they would.

CHAPTER 22
Of the Peace Made at the Thing

Tell we now how men come to the Thing a very many: many chieftains there were and of great account; there were Guest Oddleifson, and Steinthor of Ere, and Dyri and Thorarin.

82

So they fell all together to talking of the case, and Steinthor was for Howard and his fellows, and he craved peace for them, and; Guest Oddleifson to be judge, whereas the matter was fully known to him; and because they were well ware afore of their privy dealings, they fell in to it gladly.

Then spake Guest: "Forasmuch as ye both will have an award of me, I shall not be slow to give it: and first we must turn back to what was said last summer about the slaying of Olaf Howard-son, for the which I award three man-fines; against this shall the slaying be set of Sturla and Thiodrek and Liot, who were slain quite sackless; but Thorbiorn Thiodrekson shall have fallen unatoned be*cause of his injustice, and those his unheard-of dealings with Howard, and many other ill-deeds : unatoned also shall be Vakr and Scart, his sister's sons; but the slaying of Brand the Strong shall be set against An's slaying, the fosterer of Hall-grim : one man-fine shall be paid for the serving-man of Liot of Moonberg, whom Howard and his folk slew.

"So is it concerning the slaying of Holmgang-Liot that I can award no atonement for him, for plain to see is the wrongfulness of his dealings with Thorbiorn, and all them over whom he might prevail; and according to right was it that two little lads should slay such a champion as was Liot. Thorbiorn also shall have freely all the meadow that they had in common. On the other hand, to ease the mind of Thorarin, these men shall fare abroad; to wit: Hallgrim Asbrand's son, Torfi and Eyjulf, sons of Valbrand, Thorir and Odd, sons of Thorbrand, Thorstein and Grim, sons of Thorbiorn : and whereas thou, Thorarin, art old exceedingly, they shall not come back before they hear that thou art passed away ; but Howard shall change his dwelling, and not abide in this quarter of the land, and Thorhall his kinsman in likewise.

"Now will I that ye hold the peace well and truly without guile on either side."

Then came Steinthor forth, and took peace for Howard and all those fellows on the terms aforesaid by Guest; and he paid also the hundred of silver due. And Thorarin and Dyri stood forth ill seeming manly wise, and were well content with the award.

But when the case was ended, thither to the Thing came those earless ones, and in the hearing of all told what was betid in their journey. To all seemed the tidings great, and yet that things had gone as meet was: men deemed that Thorgrim had thrust himself into enmity against them, and had gotten but his due.

But now spake Guest: "Most sooth it is to say that ye kinsmen are unlike to other men for evil heart and unmanliness: how came it into thine head, Thorarin, to make as if thou wouldst have peace, and yet fare so guilefully ? But whereas I have spoken somewhat afore, so that this thy case might have a peaceful end, even so will I let it abide according to my word and my judgment; though forsooth, ye Thorarm and Dyri, were well worthy to come off the worser for your fraud's sake; for which cause indeed I will nevermore be at your back in whatever case ye may have on hand. But thou, Steinthor, be well content, for henceforward I will help thee in thy cases, with whomsoever thou hast to do; for herein hast thou fared well and manly."

Steinthor said that Guest should have his will herein: "Meseemeth they have come to the worse, losing many of their men and their honour withal." Therewith came the Thing to an end, and Guest and Steinthor parted in all friendship, but Thorarin and Dyri are very ill-pleased. So when Steinthor came home he sent after the folk in Otterdale, and when they met either told each other how they had sped, and they deemed that things had gone well considering the plight of matters.

They thanked Steinthor well for his furtherance, and said withal that Atli his brother-in-law had done well by them, and had been doughty of deeds moreover, and they called him the valiantest of fellows. So the greatest friendship grew up between the brethren-in-law, and Atli was holden thenceforward for the doughtiest of men wheresoever he came.

CHAPTER 23
Of the Feast at Howard's House

After these things fared Howard and all of them home to Icefirth, and Biargey was exceeding fain of them, and the fathers of those brethren withal, who deemed themselves grown young a second time. Then took Howard such rede, that he arrayed a great feast, and his house was great and noble, and nought was lacking there: he bade thereto Steinthor of Ere, and Atli his brother-in-law, Guest Oddleifson and all his kindred and alliance. Great was the throng there, and the feast of the fairest; there sat they altogether a week's space joyful and merry.

Howard was a man very rich of all manner of stock, and at the feast's ending he gave to Steinthor thirty wethers and five oxen, a shield, a sword, and a gold ring, the best of treasures. To Guest Oddleifson he gave two gold rings and nine oxen : to master Atli he gave good gifts : to the sons of Valbrand, and the sons of Thorbrand, and the sons of Thorbiorn he gave the best of gifts: good weapons to some, and other things to others. To Hallgrim his kinsman gave he the sword Warflame, and full array of war therewith exceeding goodly. And he thanked them all for their good service and doughty deeds. Good gifts withal he gave to all that he had bidden thither, for he lacked neither gold nor silver.

So after this feast rideth Steinthor home to Ere, Guest to Bardstrand, and Atli to Otterdale; and now all part with the greatest love. But they who had to fare abroad went west to Vadil, and thence to sea in the summertide: they had a fair wind and made Norway.

In those days Earl Hakon ruled over Norway. So they were there the winter, and in spring got them a ship and went a-warring, and became most famous men. This was their business for certain seasons, and then they fared out hither whenas Thorarin was dead ; great men they became, and much are they told of in tale here in the land, and far and wide otherwhere.

So leave we to tell of them.

CHAPTER 24
How Howard Died Full of Years and Honour

But of Howard it is told that he sold his lands, and they went their ways north to Swarfadardale, and up into a dale called Oxdale. There he built a house, and abode there certain winters, calling that stead Howardstead.

But within certain winters heard Howard these tidings, that Earl Hakon was dead, and King Olaf Trygvison come to the land and gotten to be sole king over Norway, and that he set forth new beliefs and true. So when Howard heard hereof he broke up his household, and fared out with Biargey and Thorhall his kinsman. They came to King Olaf and he gave them good welcome. There was Howard christened with all his house, and abode there that winter well accounted of by King Olaf. That same winter died Biargey; but the next summer Howard and Thorhall his kinsman fared out to Iceland. Howard had out with him church-wood exceeding big: he set up house in the nether part of Thorhallsdale, and abode there no long time before he fell sick; then he called to him Thorhall his kinsman, and spake: "Things have come to this that I am sick with the sickness that will bring me to my death; so I will that thou take the goods after me, whereof I wish thee joy; for thou hast served me well and given me good fellowship. Thou shalt flit thine house to the upper part of Thorhallsdale and there shalt thou build a church, wherein I would be buried."

So when he had ordered things as he would, he died a little after.

Thorhall fell to speedily, and brought his house up the dale, and made a goodly stead there, and called it Thorhallstead : he wedded well, and many men are come from him; and there he dwelt till eld.

Moreover it is said that when Christ's faith came to Iceland Thorhall let make a church of that wood which Howard had brought out hither.

The stateliest house was that, and therein was set Howard's grave, and he was held for a very great man.

Wherewith make we an end of this tale as for this time.

THE SAGA OF
THE HEATH SLAYINGS

(The first fifteen chapters of this saga were lost during the Great Fire of Copenhagen).

CHAPTER 16
Thorarin Bids Bardi Concerning The Choosing Of Men

Now Bardi and his brethren had on hand much wright's work that summer, and the work went well the summer through, whereas it was better ordered than heretofore. Now summer had worn so far that but six weeks thereof were left. Then fares Bardi to Lechmote to meet Thorarin his fosterer; often they talked together privily a long while, and men knew not clearly what they said.

"Now will there be a man-mote," says Thorarin, "betwixt the Hope and Huna-water, at the place called Thing-ere. But I have so wrought it that heretofore none have been holden.

"Now shalt thou fare thither and prove thy friends; because now I look for it that many men will be together there, since man-motes have so long been put off. In crowds they will be there, and I ween that Haldor thy foster-brother will come thither. Crave thou fellowship of him and avail, if thine heart is anywise set on faring away from the country-side and the avenging of thy brother.

"A stead there is called Bank, lying west of Huna-water;" there dwelt a woman hight Thordis, by-named Gefn, a widow; there was a man with her over her housekeeping, hight Odd, a mighty man of his hands, not exceeding wealthy nor of great kin, but a man well renowned. "Of him shalt thou crave following; for he shall rule his answer himself."

"In that country is a place called Blizzard-mere, where are many steads, one of which is Middleham;" there dwelt a man hight Thorgisl; he was by kin mother's sister's son of Gefn's-Odd; a valiant man and a good skald, a man of good wealth, and a mighty man of his hands. "Call thou on him to fare with thee.'

"A stead there is hight Bowerfell, twixt Swinewater and Blanda; it is on the Necks to the westward." There dwelt a man hight Eric, by-named Wide-sight; he was a skald and no little man of might. "Him shalt thou call to thy fellowship."

"In Longdale is a house called Audolfstead," where dwelt the man hight Audolf; "he is a good fellow and mighty of his hands; his brother is Thorwald." He is not told of as having aught to do with the journey; he dwelt at the place called Evendale, which lieth up from Swinewater. "There are two steads so called." He was the strongest man of might of all the North-country. "Him shalt thou not call on for this journey, and the mood of his mind is the reason for why."

"There is a stead called Swinewater;" and there dwelt the man hight Summerlid, who was by-named the Yeller, wealthy of fee and of good account. There dwelt in the house with him his daughter's son who hight Thorliot, Yeller's fosterling, a valiant man. "Pray him to be of thy fellowship."

A man hight Eyolf dwelt at Asmund's-nip, "which is betwixt the Water and Willowdale." "Him shalt thou meet and bid him fare with thee; he is our friend."

"Now meseemeth," saith he, "that little will come of it though thou puttest this forward at the man-mote; but sound them there about the matter, and say thou. that they shall not be bound to fare with thee, if thou comest not to each one of them on the Saturday whenas it lacketh yet five weeks of winter. And none such shalt thou have with thee who is not ready to go, for such an one is not right trusty. Therefore shalt thou the rather choose these men to fare with thee than others of the country- side, whereas they are near akin to each other; they are men of good wealth, and so also their kinsmen no less; so that they are all as one man. Withal they are the doughtiest men of all who are here in Willowdale, and in all our parishes; and they will be best willed towards thy furtherance who are most our friends. Now is it quite another thing to have with one good men and brave, rather than runagates untried, men of nought, to fall back upon, if any trouble happen. Now withal thy home-men are ready to fare with thee, and thy neighbours, who are both of thy kindred and thine alliance: such as Eyolf of Burg thy brother- in-law, a doughty man, and a good fellow."

"There is a stead called Ternmere in Westhope, where dwell two brothers." One was hight Thorod, the other Thorgisl; they were the sons of Hermund, and nephews of Bardi as to kinship; men of good wealth, great champions, and good of daring. "These men will be ready to fare with thee."

Two brothers yet are named who lived at Bardi's home, one hight Olaf, the other Day, sons of a sister of Bardi s mother, and they had grown up there in Gudmund's house; "they be ready to fare with thee."

Two men more are named, one hight Gris and by-named Kollgris, a man reared there at Asbiorn's-ness. He was a deft man and the foreman of them there, and had for long been of good-will toward them.

The other hight Thord, by-named Fox; he was the fosterling of Thurid and Gufimund. They had taken him a little bairn from off the road, and had reared him. He was a full ripe man, and well of his hands; and men say that there was nought either of word or deed that might not be looked for of him; Gudmund and his wife loved him much, and made more of him than he was of worth. "This man will be ready to fare from home with thee."

Now are the men named who were to fare with Bardi.

And when they had held such talk, they sundered.

CHAPTER 17
Of Bardi's Way-Fellows

The Lord's day cometh Bardi to Lechmote, and rideth on thence to the man-mote; and by then he came was much folk there come, and good game is toward. Now were men eager for game, whereas the man-motes had been dropped so long. Little was done in the case, though men were busy in talk at that meeting.

Now the foster-brethren Haldor and Bardi fell to talk together, and Bardi asks whether he would fare with him somewhat from out the country-side that autumn. Says Haldor: "Belike it will be found that on my part I utter not a very manly word, when I say that my mind is not made up for this journey. Now all things are ready for my faring abroad, on which faring I have been twice bent already. But I have settled this in my mind, if ever perchance I may have my will, to be to thee of avail that may be still greater, shouldst thou be in need of it, and ever hereafter if thou be hard bestead; and this also is a cause hereof, that there are many meeter than I for the journey that, as my mind tells me, thou art bent on."

Bardi understood that so it was as he said, and he said that he would be no worse friend to him than heretofore.

"But I will bid thee somewhat," says Haldor; "it befell here last summer, that I fell out with a man hight Thorarin, and he was wounded by my onslaught. He is of little account for his own sake, but those men claim boot for him of whose Thing he is, and of much account are they. Now it is not meet for me to put Eilif and Hoskuld from the boot, so I will thou make peace for me in the matter, as I cannot bring myself to it, whereas I have nay- said hitherto to offer them atonement."

Then goeth Bardi forthwith to meet Eilif and Hoskuld, and straightway takes up the word on behalf of Haldor, and they bespeak a meeting between themselves for the appeasing of the case, when it lacked four weeks of winter, at the Cliffs, Thorarin's dwelling.

Now cometh Bardi to speech with Gefn's-Odd that he should fare with him south to Burgfirth.

Odd answereth his word speedily: "Yea, though thou hadst called on me last winter, or two winters ago, I had been all ready for this journey."

Then met Bardi Thorgisl, the sister's son of Odd's mother, and put the same words before him. He answereth: "That will men say, that thou hast not spoken hereof before it was to be looked for, and fare shall I if thou willest."

Then meeteth he Arngrim, the fosterling of Audolf, and asked him if he would be in the journey with him; and he answereth: "Ready am I, when thou art ready."

The same talk held he with all them afore-named, and all they took his word well.

Now spake Bardi: "In manly wise have ye dealt with me herein; now therefore will I come unto you on the Saturday, when it lacketh five weeks of winter; and if I come not thus, then are ye nowise bound to fare with me."

Now ride men home from the man-mote, and they meet, the foster-father and son, Thorarin and Bardi, and Bardi tells him of the talk betwixt him and Haldor. Thorarin showed that it liked him well, and said that the journey would happen none the less though Haldor fared not. "Yea, he may yet stand thee in good stead. And know that I have made men ware of this journey for so short a while, because I would that as late as might be aforehand should it be heard of in the country of those Burgfirthers."

CHAPTER 18
Of Bardi And His Workman Thord The Fox

Now wears the time, till Friday of the sixth week, and at nones of that day home came the home-men of Bardi, and had by then pretty much finished with their hay-work.

Bardi and his brethren were without, when the workmen came, and they greeted them well. They had their work-tools with them, and Thord the Fox was dragging his scythe behind him.

Quoth Bardi: "Now draggeth the Fox his brush behind him."

"So is it," saith Thord, "that I drag my brush behind me, and cock it up but little or nought; but this my mind bodes me, that thou wilt trail thy brush very long or ever thou avenge Hall thy brother."

Bardi gave him back no word in revenge, and men go to table.

Those brethren were speedy with their meat, and stood up from table straightway, and Bardi goeth up to Thord the Fox and spake with him, laying before him the work he shall do that evening and the day after, Saturday to wit.

Forty haycocks lay yet ungathered together in Asbiorn's-ness; and he was to gather them together, and have done with it that evening. "Moreover, to-morrow shalt thou fare to fetch our bell-wether hight the Flinger, whereas our wethers be gone from the sheepwalks, and come into the home-pastures."

Now he bade Thord to this, because the wether was worse to catch than other sheep, and swifter withal. "Now further to-morrow shalt thou go to Ambardale, and fetch home the five-year-old ox which we have there, and slaughter him, and bring all the carcass south to Burg on Saturday. Great is the work, but if thou win it not, then shalt thou try which of us bears the brush most cocked thenceforward."

Thord answered and said that often he had heard his big threats; and thereof he is nowise blate.

Now rideth Bardi in the evening to Lechmote, and the brethren together, and Bardi and Thorarin talk together the evening through.

CHAPTER 19
Concerning Thord The Fox

Now it is to be told of Thord's business, how he got through with it. He gathered together the hay which had stood less safely; and when he came home, then was the shepherd about driving the sheep out to the Cliffs, and Thord rides the horse whereon he had been carting the evening long. Now he finds the flock of wethers to which he had been told off, but could not overhaul them till he got out to Hope-oyce; so he slaughters that wether and rideth home with the carcass. By this time he has foundered the horse; so he takes another, and gallops over the dale, as forthright the way lay, nor did he heed whether he was faring by night or by day. He cometh to Ambardale in early morn, and getteth the ox, and slaughtereth him and dighteth him, bindeth the carcass on his horse, and going his ways cometh home again, and layeth down the carcass. Then he taketh out the carcass of the wether, and when he cometh back one limb of the ox is gone. No good words spake Thord thereover; but a man owneth that he had taken it away, and bids him be nought so bold as to speak aught thereof unless he would have a clout. So Thord taketh the rest of the carcass, and fareth south to Burg as he had been bidden.

There Alof, the sister of Bardi, and her foster-mother taketh in the flesh-meat. The foster-mother also hight Alof, a wise woman, and foster-mother also of Bardi and the other sons of Gudmund. She was called Kiannok, and thus by that name were the two Alofs known apart. Alof, Bardi's fosterer, was wise exceedingly; she could see clearly a many things, and was well-wishing to the sons of Gudmund. She was full of lore, and ancient things were stored in her mind.

CHAPTER 20
Of The Horses Of Thord Of Broadford

Now must it be told what wise they talked together, Thorarin his fosterer and Bardi, before Bardi got to the road; they talked of a many things.

It was early of the Saturday morning, whereon he should go meet his fellows who were to fare with him. But when he was ready to ride, there were led forth two horses, white with black ears either of them. Those horses did Thord of Broadford own, and they had vanished away that summer from the Thing.

Now spake Thorarin: "Here are Thord's horses; thou shalt go and bring them to him, and take no reward therefor: neither is it worth rewarding; for I it was who caused them to vanish away, and they have been in my keeping, and hard enough matter for me has it been to see to their not being taken and used. But for this cause let I take these horses, that meseemed it would be more of an errand to ask after these horses than mere jades. So I have often sent men south to Burgfirth this summer to ask after them. Meseemed that was a noteworthy errand, and that they would not see through my device; and I have but newly sent a man south, and from the south will he come to-morrow, and tell us tidings of the South-country."

Now just then was there a market toward at Whitewater-meads, and ships were come from the main but a little while before these things befell.

CHAPTER 21
Bardi Gathers In His Following

Now rideth Bardi thence and cometh to Bank, whereas dwelt Thordis, and there stood a saddled horse and a shield there beside him, and they rode home to the house with much din in the home-mead over the hard field.

Without there was a man, and a woman with him, who was washing his head; and these were Thordis and Odd, and she had not quite done the washing of his head, and had not yet washed the lather therefrom.

So straightway when he saw Bardi he sprang up, and welcomed him laughing.

Bardi took his greeting well, and bade the woman finish her work and wash him better.

Even so he let her do, and arrayed himself and went with Bardi.

Now came they north over Blanda to Broadford, and brought Thord his horses.

It is to be told that, at that time in the week just worn, was Thorgisl Arason ridden north to Eyiafirth, whereas he was to be wedded at Thwartwater, and he was to be looked for from the north the next week after. Thord takes his horses well, and offers some good geldings as a reward. But Bardi said that he would take no reward therefor; and such, he said, was the bidding of him who had found the horses. "Thou, friend," saith he, "shalt be my friend at need."

Then Bardi rides into Longdale, and over the meadows close anigh to the stead of Audolf; and they saw how a man rode down from the home-mead, and they deemed it would be Arngrim their fellow; and he rideth with them.

Now ride they west over Blanda to Eric Widesight, and they came there by then the sheep were being tended at morning-meal time, betwixt noon and day-meal, and they come on the shepherd and ask him whether Eric were at home.

He said that Eric was a-horseback at sunrise, "and now we know not whither he has ridden."

"What thinkest thou mostlike as to where he has ridden?" says Bardi. For it cometh into his mind that he will have slunk away, and will not fare with them. But nought was it found to be so that he had slunk off away. Now they saw two men riding down along Swinewater; for thence from the stead one could see wide about, and they knew them for Eric Wide-sight and Thorliot, Yeller's fosterling. They met there whereas the water hight Laxwater falleth out of Swinewater, and either greeted the other well.

Now they ride till they come to Thorgisl of Middleham; they greeted each other well and ride away thence and come hard on Gorge-water. Then said Bardi that men should ride to the stead at Asmund's-nip and meet Eyolf Oddson. "There rideth a man," said he, "nor laggardly either, from the stead, and down along the river; and meseemeth," saith he, "that there will be Eyolf; I deem that he will be at the ford by then we come there; so ride we forth."

So did they, and saw a man by the ford, and knew him for Eyolf; and they met and greeted each other well. Then they go their ways and come to the place called Ash in Willowdale. Then there came riding up to meet Bardi and his fellowship three men in coloured raiment, and they met presently, whereas each were riding towards the other; and two sister's sons of Bardi were in that company, and one hight Lambkar and the other Hun; but the third man in their fellowship was a Waterdaler. They had all come out and landed west in Willowdale, but Gudbrand their father and Gudrun their mother dwelt west in Willowdale, at the stead called thereafter Gudbrandstead.

Now was there a joyful meeting betwixt those kinsmen, whereas Bardi met his sister's sons, and either told the other what tidings there were.

Bardi tells of his journey, whither he was bound.

These men were eighteen winters old, and had been abroad one winter. They were the noblest of men both for goodlihead and might, and goodly crafts and deftness, and moreover they would have been accounted of as doughty of deed even had they come already to their full age.

Now they took counsel together, and said that they were minded to betake them to the journey with them, but their fellow fared away into Willowdale.

Now Bardi rides till he comes to Lechmote, and tells his fosterer how matters stood. Thorarin says: "Now shalt thou ride home to Asbiorn's-ness; but to-morrow will I ride to meet thee, and Thorberg my son with me; and then will I ride on the way with you."

CHAPTER 22
Of The Egging-On of Thurid

Now fares Bardi home with his fellowship, and abides at home that night. On the morrow Kollgris arrays them breakfast; but the custom it was that the meat was laid on the board before men, and no dishes there were in those days. Then befell this unlooked-for thing, that three portions were gone from three men. Kollgris went and told Bardi thereof.

"Go on dighting the board," said he, "and speak not thereof before other men."

But Thurid said that to those sons of hers he should deal no portion of breakfast, but she would deal it.

Kollgris did even so, and set forth the board, a trencher for each man, and set meat thereon.

Then went in Thurid and laid a portion before each of those brethren, and there was now that ox-shoulder cut up in three.

Taketh up Steingrim the word and said: "Hugely is this carved, mother, nor hast thou been wont to give men meat in such measureless fashion. Unmeasured mood there is herein, and nigh witless of wits art thou become."

She answereth: "No marvel is this, and nought hast thou to wonder threat; for bigger was Hall thy brother caryen, and I heard ye tell nought thereof that any wonder was that."

She let a stone go with the flesh-meat for each one of them; and they asked what that might betoken. She answereth: "Of that ye brethren have most which is no more likely for avail than are these stones (for food), insomuch as ye have not dared to avenge Hall your brother, such a man as he was; and far off have ye fallen away from your kinsmen, the men of great worth, who would not have sat down under such shame and disgrace as yea long while have done, and gotten the blame of many therefor."

Then she walked up along the floor shrieking, and sang a stave:

> "I say that the cravers of songs of the battle
> Now soon shall be casting their shame-word on Bardi.
> The tale shall be told of thee, God of the wound-worm,
> That thy yore-agone kindred with shame thou undoest;
> Unless thou, the ruler of light once a-lying
> All under the fish-road shall let it be done,
> That the lathe-fire's bidders at last be red-hooded.
> Let all folk be hearkening this song of my singing."

CHAPTER 23
How Foster-Father And Foster-Mother Array Bardi

Now Bardi and his flock ride their ways till they are but a little short of Burg. Then ride up certain men to meet them, who but Thorarin the Priest, Bardi's fosterer, and Thorberg his son.

They straightway fall to talk, and the fosterer and fosterling come to speech. "Nay, foster-father," saith Bardi, "great is the sword which thou layest there across thy knee."

"Hast thou not seen me have this weapon before, thou heedful and watchful?" saith Thorarin. "So it is, I have not had it before. And now shall we two shift weapons; I shall have that which thou now hast."

So did they; and Bardi asks whence it came to him. He told him, with all the haps of how it fared betwixt him who owned it and Lyng-Torfi, and how he had drawn him in to seek the weapons. "But Thorberg my son hath the other weapon, and Thorbiorn owns that, but Thorgaut owns that which thou hast. Most meet it seemed to me, that their own weapons should lay low their pride and masterful mood; therefore devised I this device, and therewithal this, that thou mightest avenge thee of the shame that they have done to thee and thy kindred. Now will I that thou be true to my counsel with me, such labour as I have put forth for thine honour."

Now ride they into the home-mead of Burg unto Eyolf, the brother-in-law of those brethren. There were two harnessed horses before the door when Bardi came into the garth; and on one of them was the victual of the brethren, and were meant for provision for their journey; and that was the meaning of the new-slain flesh-meat which Bardi let bring thither erst; but Alof their sister and Kiannok, Bardi's foster-mother, had dight the same.

Now Eyolf leaps a-horseback and is all ready to ride into the home-mead from the doors. Then came out a woman and called on Bardi, and said that he should ride back to the doors, and that she had will to speak with him; and she was Alof, his sister. He bade the others ride on before, and said that he would not tarry them.

So he cometh to the door and asketh her what she would. She biddeth him light down and come see his foster-mother. So did he, and went in. The carline was muttering up at the further end of the chamber, as she lay in her bed there. "Who goeth there now?" says she.

He answereth: "Now is Bardi here; what wilt thou with me, foster-mother?"

"Come thou hither," saith she; "welcome art thou now. Now have I slept," saith she, "but I waked through the night arraying thy victual along with thy sister. Come thou hither, and I will stroke thee over."

Bardi did according to her word, for he loved her much.

She fell to work, beginning with the crown of his head and stroked him all over right down to the toes.

Bardi said: "What feelest thou herein, and what art thou minded will be, that thou strokest me so carefully?"

She answereth: "I think well of it; nowhere meseemeth is aught in the way of a big bump, to come upon."

Bardi was a big man and stark of pith, and thick was the neck of him; she spans his neck with her hands, and taketh from her sark a big pair of beads which was hers, and winds it about his neck, and draggeth his shirt up over it.

He had a whittle at his neck in a chain, and that she let abide. Then she bade him farewell; and he rideth away now after his fellows; but she called after him, "Let it now abide so arrayed, as I have arrayed it; and meseemeth that then things will go well."

CHAPTER 24
Of Thorarin's Arraying

Now when he cometh up with his fellowship, they ride their ways. Thorarin fared long on the road with them, and layeth down, how they shall go about their journey, deeming that much lay on it that they should fare well.

94

"A place for guesting have I gotten you," saith he, "in Nipsdale, which ye shall take. The bonder whereas ye shall harbour to-night is one Nial. So it is told," said he, "that, as to other men, he is no great thane with his wealth, though he hath enough; but this I wot that he will take you in at the bidding of my word. But now is the man come hither who last night rode from Burgfirth and the south, he whom I sent south this week to wot tidings of the country-side. And this he knoweth clearly as a true tale, that Hermund Illugison will be at the market the beginning of this week with many other men of the country-side. This also ye will have heard, that those brethren, the sons of Thorgaut, have a business on their hands this summer, to wit, to mow the meadow which is called Goldmead; and now is the work well forward, so that it will be done on Wednesday of this week; so that they must needs be at home. Now I have heard that which they are wont to fall to speech of, those Gislungs, when there is any clatter or noise; then say they, 'What! Will Bardi be come?' and thereof make they much jeering and mocking for the shaming of you. Now it is also told north here, and avouched to be thoroughly true, that this have the men of the country-side agreed to, that if any tidings befall in the country such as be of men's fashioning, then shall all men be bound to ride after them, the reason thereof being that Snorri the Priest and his folk slept but a short way from the steads after that slaying and big deed of his. And everyone who is not ready hereto shall be fined in three marks of silver, if he belong to those who have 'thingfare-pay' to yield, from Havenfells to North-water, whereas there dwelleth the greatest number of the Thingmen of the Sidefolk and those of Flokis-dale. So ride ye on the Monday from Nial's, and fare leisurely and have night-harbour on the Heath" (thence gat it the name of Two-day's Heath), "and ye shall come to those two fighting-steads which be on the Heath, as ye go south, and look to it if they be as I tell you. There is a place called the Mires on the Heath, whence the fall of water is great; and in the northern Mire is a water whereinto reacheth a ness, no bigger at its upper part than nine men may stand abreast thereon; and from that mere waters run northward to our country-sides; and thither would I bid you to. But another fighting-stead is there in the southern Mire, which I would not so much have you hold as the other, and it will be worse for you if you shall have to make a shift there for safeguard. There also goeth a ness into the water. Thereon may eighteen men stand abreast, and the waters fall thence from that mere south into the country.

"But ye shall come south on Wednesday to the fell-bothies whenas all men are gone from the bothies all up and down Copsedale; for all the Sidemen have mountain business there, and there hitherto have tarried. Now meseemeth that ye will come thither nigh to nones of the day. Then shall two of your company ride down into the country-side there, and along the fell, and so to the Bridge, and not come into the peopled parts till ye are south of the river. Then shall ye come to the stead called Hallward-stead, and ask the goodman for tidings, and ask after those horses which have vanished away from the North-country. Ye shall ask also of tidings from the market. Then will ye see on Goldmead, whereas ye fare down along the river, whether men be a mowing thereon, even as the rumour goes.

"Then shall ye ride up along to the ford, and let the goodman show you the way to the ford; and so ride thence up towards the Heath and on to the Heath, whence ye may look down on Goldmead whereas ye fare along the river. Now on Wednesday morning shalt thou fare down on to the bridge, whence ye may see what may be toward in the country-side; and thou shalt sunder thy company for three places, to wit, the eighteen all told; but the nineteenth shall abide behind to heed your horses, and that shall be Kollgris, and let them be ready when ye need to take to them.

"Now six men shall be up on the bridge; and I shall make it clear who they shall be, and why it shall be arrayed that way. There shall be those kinsmen Thorgisl of Middleham and Arngrim, and Eric Wide-sight, and Thorliot, Yeller's fosterling, and Eyolf of Asmund's-nip; and for this reason shall they sit there, because they would be the stiffest to thee and the hardest to sway whenas ye come into the country-side, and it behoveth you not that ye lack measure and quieting now and again.

"But midway shall sit other six: the brethren Thorod and Thorgisl of Ternmere" (the sons of the brother of Bardi's father), "then the third man who came instead of Haldor; therewithal shall be the sons of thy mother's sister, Hun and Lambkar; and Eyolf, thy brother-in-law, for the sixth; they shall be somewhat more obedient to thy counsel, and not fare with suchlike fury. And for this reason shall they sit there, that they may look on the goings of men about the country-side.

"But ye six shall fare down (into the country), to wit, thou and Stein and Steingrim, thy brethren, and Olaf and Day and Thord. They will be the most obedient to thy word; yet shall ye have strength enough for those on the Mead.

"Now shall ye fare away forthright after ye have done them a scathe whereas the chase will not fail you, and less labour will they lay thereon, if there be but seen six men of you, and there will not be a great throng at your heels if so ye go on.

"Now shall ye ride away at your swiftest until ye are come to the northern fighting-stead upon the Heath; because that thence all verdicts go to the north, and therein is the greatest avail to you that so things should turn out.

"And yet I misdoubt me that thou wilt not bring this about, because of the frowardness of them that follow thee.

"Now must we sunder for this while, and meet we hail hereafter."

CHAPTER 25
Of Bardi's Two Spies

Now comes Bardi with his flock to Nial's in the evening. Nial is standing without, and bids them all guesting as one merry with ale; that they take, let loose their horses, and sit them down on either bench. Nial is without that evening, and his wife with him, dighting victual for their guests; but his young lad was within, and made game with them.

Bardi asked the lad if he had ever a whetstone. "I wot," saith he, "of a hard-stone which my father owns, but I durst not take it."

"I will buy it of thee," saith Bardi, "and give thee a whittle therefor."

"Yea," said the lad, "why then should I not strike a bargain with thee;" and goeth and findeth the hard-stone, and giveth it to Bardi. Bardi handles it, and taketh the whittle from his neck, and therewith was somewhat shifted the pair of beads which the carline had done about his neck, whereof is told sithence.

Now they whet their weapons, and the lad thinketh he hath done them a good turn, whereas they have what they needed. So there they abide the night through, and have good cheer.

They ride their ways on the Monday in good weather, and go not hard. Bardi asks of Eric Wide-sight what wise he deemed things would go. He answereth:

> "O Lime-tree, upbearer of board of the corpses,
> We nineteen together have gone from the Northland;
> All over the Heath have we wended together,
> And our will is to nourish the bloodfowl with victual.
> But, O lad of the steed that is stalled on the rollers,
> The steed of the sea-rover Heite, well wot we
> That fewer shall wend we our ways from the Southland.
> Now the mind of the singer is bent on the battle."

CHAPTER 26
Portents At Walls

Now must somewhat be told about the men of that country who now come into our matter. Thorbiorn Brunison rose up early at Walls, and bade his house-carle rise with him. "To-day shall we fare to Thorgaut to the stithy, and there shall we smithy."

Now that was early, just at the sun's uprising. Thorbiorn called for their breakfast, and nought is told of what of things was brought forward, but that the goodwife set a bowl on the board. Thorbiorn cried out that he was nought well served, and he drave the bowl betwixt the shoulders of her. She turned about thereat, and cried out aloud, and was shrewish of tongue, and either was hard on the other.

"Thou hast brought that before me," said he, "wherein there is nought save blood, and a wonder it is that thou seest nothing amiss therein."

Then she answereth calmly: "I brought nought before thee which thou mightest not well eat; and none the worse do I think of the wonder thou seest, whereas it betokens that thou shalt be speedily in hell. For assuredly this will be thy fetch."

He sang a stave:

> "The wealth-bearing stem that for wife we are owning,
> The black coif of widowhood never shall bear
> For my death; though I know that the field of the necklace
> All the days of my life neath the mould would be laying:
> She who filleth the ale round would give for my eating

The apples of hell-orchard. Evil unheard of!
But that wealth-bearing board now will scarcely meseemeth
Have might for the bringing this evil about."

CHAPTER 27
The Slaying Of Gisli

Now has Bardi arrayed his folk in their lurking-places, as his fosterer had taught him, even as is aforesaid, and he tells them all what he had forecast in his mind.

Then they were somewhat better content therewith, and deemed that what was minded would be brought about; and they gave out that they liked this array, so to say, but they said nevertheless that to their minds the doings would be but little.

There was then a big wood on Whitewater-side, such as in those days were wide about the land here, and six of them sat down above the wood, and saw clearly what befell on Goldmead. Bardi was in the wood, and well-nigh he and the six of them within touch of them that were a-mowing. Now Bardi scans heedfully how many men were at the mowing; and he deemed that he did not clearly know whether the third man, who was white about the head, would be a woman, or whether it would be Gisli.

Now they went down from under the wood one after other; and it seemed first to those sons of Thorgaut as if but one man went there; and Thormod, who mowed the last in the meadow, took up the word. "There go men," said he.

"But it seemeth to me," said Gisli, "that but one man goeth there;" but they went hard, yet did not run.

"That is not so," said Ketil Brusi; "men are there, and not so few."

So they stood still, and looked thereon, and Ketil said: "Will not Bardi be there? That is not unlike him; and no man have I skill to know if yon be not he. And that wise was he arrayed last summer at the Thing."

Those brethren, Ketil and Thormod, looked on; but Gisli went on mowing and took up the word. "So speak .ye," said he, "as if Bardi would be coming from out of every bush all the summer. And he has not come yet."

Bardi and his folk had portioned out the men to them beforehand, that two should fall on each one of them. Bardi and Stein were to take Ketil Brusi, who was mighty of strength; Day and Olaf were to go against Gisli; Steingrim and Thord were to go against Thormod. So now they turn on them.

Now spake Ketil: "No lie it was that Bardi is come!"

They would fain catch up their weapons, but none of them gat hold of the weapons.

Now when they see into what plight they were come, Gisli and Ketil would run for the homemead garth, and Bardi and four of his fellows followed after them;

but Thormod turns down to the river, and after him went Thord and Steingrim, and chased him into the river and stoned him from the shore; he got him over the river, and came off well.

Now came those brethren to the garth, and Ketil was the swifter, and leapt over it into the mead; but whenas Gisli leapt at the garth, a turf fell therefrom, and he slipped; therewith came up Bardi, who was the swiftest of those men, and hewed at him with the sword Thorgaut's-loom, and hewed off well-nigh all the face of him.

Straightway then he turns to meet his fellows, and tells them that something of a wound had been wrought. They said that the onset was but little and unwarrior-like. But he said that things would have to be as they were. "And now shall we turn back."

Needs must he rule, though it was much against their will.

But Ketil dragged Gisli in over the garth, and cast him on his back, and they saw that he was no heavy burden to him; and he ran home to the stead.

Thorbiorn and Thorgaut were in the stithy abiding till the house- carle should come back with the smithying stuff.

Now Thorgaut spake: "Yea, there is great noise and clatter; is not Bardi come?"

Even in that nick of time came Ketil into the stithy, and said: "That found Gisli thy son, that come he is;" and he cast him dead before his feet.

Now Bardi turns to meet his fellows, and said that he was minded that now man was come to be set against man. Quoth they, that the men were nowise equal, and that little had been done though one man had been slain, and so long a way as they had fared thereto.

So when all the fellowship met, then said they who had been higher up in the lurking-places, that full surely they would not have fared if they had known they should thus have to leave off in this way, that no more vengeance should follow after such a grief as had been done them, and they said that Gisli and Hall were men nowise equal. And they laid blame on Bardi, and said that they were minded to think that more would have been done if they had stood anear. Then they went to their horses, and said that they would have breakfast. Bardi bade them have no heed of breakfast, but they said that they had no will to fast. "And we know not how to think whatwise thou wouldst have come away if thou hadst done that wherein was some boldness."

Bardi said that he heeded not what they said. So they had their meat.

CHAPTER 28
The Call For The Chase

Now Thorgaut and Thorbiorn and Ketil, they talk together at home there. Thorgaut says that great is the hap befallen; "and the blow has lighted nigh to me; yet meseemeth that no less may be looked for yet, and I will that there be no tiding after them."

They say both that that shall never be. The women heard what had been said, and Ketil sends them out to Frodistead and Side-mull to tell the tidings; and then might each tell the other thence-forth, till the word should come into Thwartwater-lithe, and over Northwater-dale, for men to ride after them who have wrought this deed, and so put off from them forfeits and fines.

They fare then, and take their horses and ride to Highfell to see Arni Thorgautson; he there might welcome men allied to him, for thither was come Thorarin of Thwartwater-lithe, the father of Astrid his wife: thence ride they five together.

Now it is to be told of Thormod that he fared up along south of the river till he came to the Ridge. In that time south of the river was scantily housed. There were but few folk at home there, for the men were gone to Whitewater-meads, and the house- carles were at work. Eid was sitting at the chess, and his sons with him, the one hight Illugi, the other Eystein. Thormod tells him of the tidings that have befallen. There was, in those days and long after, a bridge over the river beside Biarnisforce. Eid nowise urged the journey, but his two sons grip their weapons and take to the way. The brethren go to Thorgisl of Hewerstead, and by then was come home Eyolf his son, who had come out to Iceland that same summer.

Thormod fares up to Hallkeldstead, and comes thither and tells the tidings. Tind was the one carle at home there; but men were come thither to the stithy.

A woman dwelt next thereto who hight Thorfinna, and was called the Skald-woman; she dwelt at Thorwardstead. She had a son hight Eyolf, and a brother who hight Tanni, and was called the Handstrong, for his might was unlike the sons of men; and of like kind was Eyolf, his sister's son; full-hearted in daring they were moreover. These had come to Tind for the smithying. But for that cause folk came not to Gilsbank, that Hermund was ridden to the ship and his house-carles with him.

Tind and the others were four, and Thormod the fifth, and it was now late in the day.

The sons of Eld came to Thorgisl the Hewer, and the folk there bestir them speedily, and fare thence six in company. Eyolf, the son of Thorgisl, fared with him and four others.

CHAPTER 29
The Chasing Of Bardi

Now must it be told what tidings Bardi and his folk see. He rideth the first of them, and somewhat the hardest, so that a gate's space was betwixt him and them; but they rode after him somewhat leisurely, and said that he was wondrous fearful.

Now see they the faring of men who chase them, and that flock was not much less than they themselves had. Then were Bardi's fellows glad, and thought it good that there would be a chance of some tale to tell of their journey.

Then spake Bardi: "Fare we away yet a while, for it is not to be looked for that they will spur on the chase any the less."

Then sang Eric Wide-sight a stave:

"Now gather together the warriors renowned,
Each one of them eager-fain after the fray.
Now draweth together a folk that is fight-famed,
Apace on the heathways from out of the Southland;
But Bardi in nowise hard-counselled is bidding
The warriors fare fast and be eager in fleeing
The blast of the spear-storm that hitherward setteth,
The storm of the feeders of fight from the South."

CHAPTER 30
The First Brunt Of Battle On The Heath

Now they come face to face, Bardi and the Southern men, who now got off their horses. Bardi's folk had arrayed them athwart the ness. "Go none of you forth beyond these steps," says Bardi, "because I misdoubt me that more men are to be looked for."

The breadth of the ness went with the rank of the eighteen of them, and there was but one way of falling on them. Says Bardi: "It is most like that ye will get the trying of weapons; but better had it been to hold the northernmost fight-stead, nor had any blame been laid upon us if we had so done; and better had it been for the blood-feuds. Yet shall we not be afraid, even though we are here."

There stood they with brandished weapons. On the one hand of Bardi stood Thorberg, and on the other side Gefn's-Odd, and on the other hand of them the brethren of Bardi.

Now those Southern men, they fall not on so speedily as the others looked for, for more folk had they to face than they had wotted of. The leaders of them were Thorgaut, Thorbiorn, and Ketil. Spake Thorgaut: "Wiser it were to bide more folk of ours; much deeper in counsel have they proved, inasmuch as they came but few of them within the country-side."

Now they fall not on; and when the Northern men see that, they take to their own devices. Saith Thorberg: "Is Brusi amidst the folk perchance?" He said that he was there.

Says Thorberg: "Knowest thou perchance this sword, which here I hold?" He said that he knew not how that should be looked for. "Or who art thou?"

"Thorberg I hight," says he; "and this sword Lyng-Torfi, thy kinsman, gave to me; thereof shalt thou abide many a stroke to-day, if it be as I will. But why fall ye not on, so boldly as ye have followed on to-day, as it seemeth to me, now running, and now riding."

He answereth: "Maybe that is a sword I own; but before we part to-day thou shalt have little need to taunt us."

Then said Thorberg: "If thou art a man full-fashioned for fight, why wilt thou tarry for more odds against us?"

Then Bardi took up the word: "What are the tidings of the country-side?"

Said Ketil: "Tidings are such as shall seem good to thee, to wit, the slaying of Gisli, my brother."

Saith Bardi: "We blame it nowise; and I deemed not that my work had been done anywise doubtfully. Come! Deemest thou, Ketil, that thou and thy father have nought at all wherefor to avenge you on us. I mind me that it was but a little since thou camest home, Ketil, bearing a back burden, a gift in hand for thy father. Now if thou bearest it not in mind, here is there a token thereof, this same sword, to wit, not yet dry of the brains of him."

And he shaketh the sword at him therewith.

This they might not abide, so now they run on them. Thorbiorn leaps at Bardi, and smites him on the neck, and wondrous great was the clatter of the stroke, and it fell on that stone of the beads which had been shifted whenas he took the knife and gave it to Nial's son; and the stone brake asunder, and blood was drawn on either side of the band, but the sword did not bite.

Then said Thorbiorn: "Troll! No iron will bite on thee."

Now were they joined in battle together, and after that great stroke he (Thorbiorn) turns him forthwith to meet Thorod, and they fall to fight together; Ketil goeth against Bardi, and Thorgaut against Thorberg. There lacked not great strokes and eggings-on.

The Southlanders had the lesser folk, and the less trusty.

Now first is to be told of the dealings betwixt Bardi and Ketil. Ketil was the strongest of men and of great heart. Long they had to do together, till it came to this, that Bardi slashed into the side of him, and Ketil fell. Then leapt Bardi unto Thorgaut and gave him his death-wound, and there they both lay low before the very weapon which they owned themselves.

Now is it to be told of Thorbiorn and Thorod. They fall to in another place; and there lacked not for great strokes, which neither spared to the other, most of them being huge in sooth. But one stroke Thorod fetched at Thorbiorn, and smote off his foot at the ankle-joint; but none the less he fought on, and thrust forth his sword into Thorod's belly, so that he fell, and his gut burst out.

But Thorbiorn, seeing how it had fared with his kinsmen (namely, Ketil and Thorgaut), he heeded nought of his life amidst these maimings.

Now turn the sons of Gudbrand on Thorbiorn. He said: "Seek ye another occasion; erst it was not for young men to strive with us." Therewith he leaps at Bardi and fights with him. Then said Bardi: "What! A very troll I deem thee, whereas thou tightest with one foot off. Truer of thee is that which thou spakest to me."

"Nay," quoth Thorbiorn, "nought of trollship is it for a man to bear his wounds, and not to be so soft as to forbear warding him whiles he may. That may be accounted for manliness rather; and so shouldst thou account it, and betroll men not, whereas thou art called a true man. But this shall ye have to say hereof before I bow me in the grass, that I had the heart to make the most of weapons."

There fell he before Bardi and won a good word.

Now lacks there never onset, but it came to this at last, that the Southern men gave way.

But it is told that there was a man hight Thorliot, a great champion, who had his abode at Walls; but some say that he was of Sleybrook: he fought with Eric Wide-sight; and before they fought, Eric sang this stave:

> "O warrior that reddenest the war-brand thin-whetted,
> 'Tis the mind of us twain to make shields meet together
> In the wrath of the war-fray. O bider of Wall-stead,
> Now bear we no ruth into onset of battle.
> O hider of hoards of the fire that abideth
> In the fetter of earth, I have heard of thine heart,
> High-holden, bepraised amongst men for its stoutness;
> And now is the time that we try it together."

CHAPTER 31
The Second Brunt Of Battle And The Third

Now is there somewhat of a lull; but therewith were seen six men a-riding: there were Thorgisl the Hewer, and Eyolf his son, and the sons of Eid. They see the evil plight of their folk, and that their lot was sinking much, and they were ill content therewith.

Now the sons of Gudbrand were ware that there was Eyolf, and they crave leave of Bardi to take his life and avenge them. For it had befallen, that whenas they were east-away he had thrust them from a certain gallery down into a muck-pit, and therein they had fared shamefully; so they would now avenge them; and they had made this journey with Bardi from the beginning that they might get the man.

Said Bardi: "Ye are doughty men, and of much worth, and much teen it were if ye were cast away. Still, I will see to it that your will have its way; but I will bid you go not from out the ranks." But they might not withhold themselves, and they run off to meet him eagerly, and they fall to fight. Eyolf was the greatest of champions, and a man of showy ways, like his father before him; full-fashioned of might, well proven in onslaught; and the battle betwixt them was long and hard; and suchwise it ended, that either was so wilful and eager, and so mighty of heart and hand, that they all lay dead at their parting.

Fast fought the sons of Eid withal, and go forward well and warrior-like; against them fought Stein and Steingrim, and now they all fight and do a good stroke of work; and there fall the sons of Eid, and Bardi was standing hard by, when they lost their lives.

Thorgisl the Hewer spared nought; he deemed great scathe wrought him by the death of his son. He was the mightiest man of his hands, and defter of weapons than other men. He heweth on either hand and deemeth life no better than death.

These are most named amongst the foremost herein, to wit, Thorgisl and Eric and Thorod.

Thorgisl spared him nought, and there was no man of the country who seemed to all a wayfellow of more avail than he. Thorgisl (son of Hermund, brother of Thorod) betook him to meet him; and they dealt long together, nor was either of them lacking in hardihood. Now Thorgisl (Hermundson) smites a stroke on him down his nose from the brow, and said:

"Now hast thou gotten a good mark befitting thee; and even such should more of you have."

Then spake Thorgisl (the Hewer): "Nought good is the mark; yet most like it is, that I shall have the heart to bear it manfully; little have ye yet to brag over." And he smote at him so that he fell and is now unfightworthy.

Now was there a lull for a while, and men bind their wounds.

Now is seen the riding of four men, and there was Tind and Tanni, Eyolf and Thormod; and when they came up they egg on much; and they themselves were of championship exceeding great; and battle was joined the third time.

Tanni fell on against Bardi, and there befell fight of wondrous daring.

Tanni hewed at him, and it fell out as before, that Bardi is hard to deal with, and the business betwixt them ended herewith, that Tanni fell before Bardi.

Eyolf went against Odd, and they fight, each of them the best of stout men. Now Eyolf smiteth at Odd, and it came on to his cheek and on to his mouth, and a great wound was that.

Then spake Eyolf: "Maybe the widow will think the kissing of thee worsened."

Odd answereth: "Long hath it been not over good, and now must it be much spoilt forsooth; yet it may be that thou wilt not tell thereof to thy sweetheart."

And he smote at him, so that he gat a great wound.

Here it befell as of the rest, that Bardi was standing hard by, and did him scathe.

Withal Thormod Thorgautson was a bold man, and went well forward. Eyolf of Burg fared against him, and got a sore hurt.

Now though these above said be the most named amongst the Northlanders, yet all of them fared forth well and in manly wise, whereas they had a chosen company.

So when these were fallen there was a lull in the battle. And now Thorberg spake that they should seek to get away; but eight men from the South were fallen, and three from the North. Now Bardi asks Thorod if he thought he would have the might to fare with them, and he gave out there was no hope thereof, and bids them ride off.

Now Bardi beheld his hurt, and therewithal they saw the band that now fared up from the South like a wood to look upon. So Bardi asks if they be minded to bide, but they said they would ride off; and so they did, and were now sixteen in company, and the more part of them wounded.

CHAPTER 32
Bardi Puts Away His Wife

Now it is to be told of Illugi that he cometh upon the field of deed, and seeth there things unlooked for, and great withal. Then sang Tind a song when Illugi asked how many they had been:

> "The stem of the battle-craft here was upbearing
> His spear-shaft with eight and with ten of the ash-trees
> That bear about ever the moon of the ocean;
> With us five less than thirty men were they a-fighting.
> But nine of the flingers of hail of the bow,
> Yea, nine of our folk unto field there have fallen,
> And surely meseemeth that dead they are lying,
> Those staves of the flame by the lathe that is fashioned.
> "Of the North the two cravers of heirship from Eid
> In the field are they fallen as seen is full clearly,
> And Gudbrand's two sons they fell there moreover,
> Where the din of the spear-play was mighty mid men.
> But never henceforward for boot are we biding;
> Unless as time weareth the vengeance befall.
> Now shall true folk be holding a mind of these matters,
> As of sword-motes the greatest ere fought amongst men."

CHAPTER 33
The Speaking Out Of Truce

Now they hear a great din, in that many men ride to the river. Here was come Thorgisl Arason, having journeyed from the North- country from his bridal; in his company was Snorri the Priest, and eighty men together they rode.

Then said Bardi: "Let us drop our visors, and ride we into their band, but never more than one at a time, and then they will find out nothing, seeing that it is dark."

So Bardi rideth up to Snorri the Priest, having a mask over his face, and hath talk with him while they cross the ford, and tells him the tidings. And as they ride out of the river Snorri the Priest took up the word, and said:

"Here let us bait, Thorgisl, and tarry and talk together, before we betake ourselves to quarters for the night." Bardi and his were riding beside the company, and folk heeded it not. Thorgisl was minded in the evening for Broadlairstead.

Now when they had sat down, spake Snorri: "I am told, Thorgisl," says he, "that no man can set forth as well as thou the speech of truce and other in law matters."

"That is a tale that goeth not for much," says Thorgisl.

"Nay," says Snorri, "there must be much therein, since all men speak in one way thereof."

Thorgisl answers: "Truly there is nothing in it that I deliver the speech of truce better than other men, though it may be good in law notwithstanding."

Says Snorri: "I would that thou wouldst let me hear it."

He answers: "What need is there thereof? Are any men here at enmity together?"

He said he knew nought thereof, "but this can never be a misdoing; so do as I will."

So Thorgisl said it should be so, and therewithal he fell to speaking:

"This is the beginning of our speech of truce, that God may be at peace with us all; so also shall we be men at peace between ourselves and of good accord, at ale and at eating, at meets and at man-motes, at church-goings and in king's house; and wherever the meetings of men befall, we shall be so at one as if enmity had never been between us. Knife we shall share and shorn meat, yea, and all other things between us, even as friends and not foes. Should henceforth any trespass happen amongst us, let boot be done, but no blade be reddened. But he of us who tramples on truce settled, or fights after full troth given, he shall be so far wolf-driven and chased, as men furthest follow up wolves, Christian men churches seek, heathen men their temples tend, fires flare up, earth grows green, son names a mother's name, ships sail, shields glitter, sun shines, snow wanes, Fin skates, fir groweth, a falcon flieth the springlong day with wind abaft under both his wings standing, as heaven dwindles, the world is peopled, wind waxeth, water sheds to sea, and carles sow corn.

"He shall shun churches and Christian men, God's houses and men's, and every home but hell.

"Each one of us taketh troth from the other for himself and his heirs born and unborn, begotten and not begotten, named and not named, and each one giveth in turn troth, life troth, dear troth, yea, main troth, such as ever shall hold good while mold and men be alive.

"Now are we at one, and at peace wheresoever we meet on land or on water, on ship or on snowshoe, on high seas or horseback:

"Oars to share,
Or bailing-butt,
Thoft or thole plank
If that be needful."

CHAPTER 34
Snorri Tells The Whole Tale

And when Thorgisl had done giving out the words of truce, Snorri spoke: "Have thanks, friend; right well hast thou spoken, and it is clear enough that he who trespasseth there against is truly a truce-breaker, most especially if he be here present." And now Snorri tells the tidings which had befallen, and also this, that Bardi and his men had come into the band of Thorgisl and those with him.

In that band there were many friends and close kindred of the men of the South; moreover, Thorgisl had aforetime had for wife Grima, the daughter of Halkel, and sister of Illugi the Black.

Then said Thorgisl: "For this once we might well have done without thee, Snorri."

He answers: "Say not so, good friend; troubles between men have now grown full great, though here they be stayed."

So now Thorgisl would not go against the truce which he himself had bespoken, and so folk parted asunder.

Snorri rode away with a company of twenty men to Lechmote, and Bardi and his folk were with him, and Thorarin received them well, and cheery of mood they were and bespoke their counsels.

[Here a lacuna of one leaf in the old MS. interrupts the story, which begins again when, apparently at the Althing, the affairs of Bardi were settled at law.]

CHAPTER 35
Bardi's Affairs Settled

Then stands up an old man, Eid Skeggison to wit, and said: "We like it ill that men should bandy words about here, whether it be done by our men or others; to nought good will that come, while often evil proceedeth therefrom. It behoveth men here to speak what may tend to peace. I am minded to think that not another man among us has more to miss, nor that on any, much greater grief hath been brought than on me; yet a wise counsel do I deem it to come to peace, and therefore I shall have no ruth on anyone bandying words about here. Moreover, it is most likely now, as ever, that it will only come to evil if folk will be casting words of shame at each other."

He got good cheer for his speech. And now men search about for such as be likeliest for the peacemaking. Snorri is most chiefly spoken of as seeking to bring about the peace. He was then far sunk in age. Another such was Thorgisl, the friend of Snorri, for their wives were sisters. Now both sides did it to wit that matters should be put to award, and the pairing of man to man; though erst folk had been sore of their kinsmen.

Now we know no more to tell thereof than that the fallen were paired man to man, and for the award Snorri was chosen on behalf of Bardi, together with Gudmund, the son of Eyolf, while Thorgisl, the son of Ari, and I11ugi, were appointed on behalf of the Southerners. So they fell to talking over the matter between them, as to what would most likely lead to peace. And it seemed good to them to pair men together in this wise:

The sons of Eid and the sons of Gudbrand were evened, as was also Thorod, the son of Hermund, and Thorbiorn. But now as to Hall Gudmundson, the Burgfirthers thought the mangild for him was pushed too far, so they drew off, and broke the peace; yet they knew that Bardi had set his heart on that matter. But of the close thereof this is to be told, that the sons of Thorgaut, Ketil and Gisli, were paired against Hall Gudmundson. In all there were nine lives lost of the Southerners, and now four from the North have been set off against five Gislungs; for nought else would like the kinsmen of Bardi because of the disparity of kin there was.

Then matters were talked over with both sides as to what next was most like to do. There were now four Southernmen unatoned, Thorgisl to wit, and Eyolf his son, Tanni the Handstrong, and Eyolf, his sister's son.

Now Bardi declared that he was no man of wealth any more than his brothers or their kindred, "nor do we mean to claim money in atonement on our side."

Answered Snorri: "Yet it behoveth not, that neither fine nor outlawry come about." Bardi said he would not gainsay that people should go abroad, so that they were free to come back again, nor that then all the more of them should fare. "Yet one there is who cannot fare; for him let fee be yolden, though it may hap that ye deem ye have some guilt to square with him. My fellow Gris will not be found to be bitten by guilt." Hesthofdi, who now dwells at the place called Stead in Skagafirth, who was a kinsman of his, took him in.

So matters came about, that on this they made peace, as they were most willing to agree to men faring abroad. Now this was deemed to be about the only boot to be got, since Bardi might not bite at-fines; they hoped, too, that thereby unpeace would somewhat abate, and on the other hand they deemed no less honour done to themselves by their having to be abroad. By wise men it was deemed most like to allay their rage, so great as it was, if for a while they should not be living within one and the same land.

Fourteen of the men who had had share in the Heath-slaughters were to fare abroad, and be abroad for three winters, and be free to come back in the third summer, but no money should be found for their faring.

Thus were men appeased on these matters without taking them into court. And so it was accounted that Bardi and those who came forth for his avail had had the fuller share, for as hopeless as it had seemed for a while.

CHAPTER 36
Bardi Fares And Is Shipwrecked

Now Bardi sends men into the country-side. He and his had got rid of their land and stock in case this should be the end of the matter; the which they could not surely tell beforehand. The messenger was hight Thorod, and was by-named Kegward, not beloved of folk; he was to have three winters; he was akin to the sons of Gudround, wealthy in chattels withal. And now the purchase of their lands as aforesaid was all but settled.

Now there cometh withal a ship from the high seas into the mouth of Blanda, which was the keel of Haldor, Bardi's foster-brother.

Therewithal folk came back from the Thing, and when Haldor hears that Bardi must needs go abroad, he has the freight of the craft unshipped, and brings himself, ship and all, up into the Hope over against Bardi's house, and a joyful meeting was theirs.

"Kinsman," says Haldor, "ever hast thou handled matters well as concerning me; thou hast often been bounteous to me, nor didst thou wax wrath on me when I did not go with thee on that journey of thine, so therefore I will now promise thee some avail in return, as now thou shalt hear: this ship will I give thee with yard and gear."

Bardi thanked him, saying he deemed he had done the deed of a great man. So now he dights this craft, and has with him five- and-twenty men. Somewhat late they were bound for sea; then put off to the main, and are eleven days out at sea; but in such wise their faring befell that they wreck their ship against Sigluness in the north, and goods were lost, but the men saved.

Gudmund the Elder had ridden out to Galmastrand, and heareth the tidings and hasteneth homeward. And in the evening spake Eyolf, his son: "Maybe it is Bardi yonder on the other side, that we see from here." Many said it was not unlike.

"Now how wouldst thou go about it?" says Eyolf, even he, "if it should hap that he had been driven back here?"

He answers: "What seemeth good to thee?"

He answers: "To bid them all home here to guesting. Meet were that."

Gudmund answers: "Large of mind thou, nor wot I if that be altogether so ill counselled."

Answers Eyolf, even he: "Speak thou, hailest of men! Now I can tell thee that Bardi, he and his, have been driven back, and broken to splinters against Sigluness, and have lost the best part of their goods. From this thou wilt have honour."

So he closed his mouth; but Gudmund thought he liked the matter none the better for that, yet lets him have his will.

CHAPTER 37
Bardi's Abiding With Gudmund

So Eyolf dights him for the journey, and goes with five-and- twenty horses to meet them, and happens on them on Galmastrand. He greets them well, and bids them go home with him, by the will of his father.

They did so, and there they had to themselves the second bench throughout the winter; and Gudmund was cheery to them, and did to them after the fashion of a great man and well. And that was widely rumoured.

Einar, the son of Jarnskeggi, often bids them go to his house and stay with him. And thus now they are right happy.

Now we have to bring to mind, that it was Thorarin's rede that with Bardi there were men who were of great worth and had much to fall back upon. And they now sent to the west for their moneys, being still bent on faring abroad in the summer.

CHAPTER 38
Eric's Song On The Heathslayings

Some time that winter it befell that there was one who asked Eric the Skald as to what had befallen, and how many lives had been lost. He sang:

> "Famed groves of the race-course whereon the sword runneth,
> All up on the Heath 'twas eleven lay dead
> In the place where the lime-board, the red board of battle,
> Went shivering to pieces midst din of the shields.
> And thereof was the cause of the battle, that erewhile
> It was Gisli fell in with his fate and his ending
> In the midst of the fray of the fire of the fight:
> 'Gainst the wielder of wound-shaft we thrust forth the onslaught."

CHAPTER 39
Bardi Goeth To Norway
And Afterwards To Iceland Again

Now Bardi's fellows took their money and made them ready for faring abroad with a goodly deal of wealth.

Bardi and his brethren sent a word to say that they will have their lands to sell them, for they deem that they are in need of chattels. But he (Thorolf Kegward) would not give up the land, and claims that the bargain should stand even as it was erst purposed. So that now they must either forego their money or slay him.

Now Eyolf (Gudmundson) says he will hand over to them as much money as the land is worth, and that he will himself see to further dealings with Eyolf of Burg, and declareth that that summer he shall have him either killed or driven out of the lands, and made himself the owner thereof.

Now Bardi buys a ship which stood up in Housewick; and then he went abroad, and Eyolf saw them off with all honour, and now, this time, they fared well, and Bardi cometh up from the main north in Thrandheim-bay into the Cheaping, and has his ship drawn up and well done to withal.

At that time King Olaf the Holy ruled over Norway, and was now at the cheaping-stead. Bardi and his fellows went before the king, and they greeted the king well, even as beseemed, "and this is the way with us, lord," says Bardi, "that we would fain be of thy winter-guests."

The king answers in this way: "We have had news of thee, Bardi," says he, "that thou art a man of great kin, a mighty man of thine hands; moreover, that ye are doughty men, that ye have fallen in with certain great deeds, and have wreaked your wrongs, yet waited long before so doing. Howbeit ye have still some ancient ways about you, and such manner of faith as goeth utterly against my mind. Now for the reason that I have clean parted from such things, our will is not to take you in; yet shall I be thy friend, Bardi," says he, "for methinks that some great things may be in store for thee. But it may often befall to those who fall in with suchlike matters, should they grow to be over-weighty to deal with, then if there be certain ancient lore blended therewith, therein are men given to trow overmuch."

Then spake Bardi: "No man there is," says he, "whom I would rather have for a friend than thee, and thanks we owe thee for thy words."

Now that winter long Bardi had his abode in the town, and all men held him of good account. But the next spring he dights his ship for Denmark, and there he was for another winter, and was well beholden withal, though tidings be not told thereof.

Thereafter he dights his ship for Iceland, and .they came out upon the north of the land, and were in great straits for money.

By this time Gudmund was dead, and Eyolf came to see them and bid them come to his house, and anon each went to his own, all being now guiltless.

Eyolf gave up to Bardi and his brethren their lands inherited from their father, showing forth again his large-heartedness as before, nor was any other man such avail to them as he was.

Now Bardi betook himself to Gudbrand his brother-in-law, a wealthy man and of high kin withal, but said to be somewhat close-fisted.

But the brethren of Bardi went to Burg, the southernmost, to Eyolf their brother-in-law, and by that time their foster-mother was dead.

Now Eyolf redeemed all the land for the hand of those brothers, and buys Bardi out of his share, with chattels. And so the brothers now set up house on their father's lands, and they died there in old age -- men of avail, though not abreast with the greatness of their family; they were married both, and men are come from them.

CHAPTER 40
The Second Wedding Of Bardi

Bardi rideth to the Thing after he had been one winter here in the land. Then he wooed for himself a wife, hight Aud, daughter of Snorri the Priest, and betrothed to him she was, and the bridals were settled to be at Saelings-dale in the harvest tide, at the home of Snorri her father. It is not set forth what jointure there should go with her from home, though like enough it be that it would be a seemly portion. She was a right stirring woman and much beloved by Snorri. Her mother was Thurid, the daughter of Illugi the Red.

Bardi rides after the Thing to Waterdale to his alliances, being now well content with his journey and having good honour of men. And things turned out even as wise men had foreseen, that the peace amongst men was well holden, even as it had been framed erst, nor telleth the tale that aught of dealings they had further together.

Now Snorri dights the bridals in the harvest tide as had been settled, and a great multitude of folk gathered there; bravely the banquet turned out as might be looked for, and there Bardi and his wife tarry the winter long. But in the spring they get them away with all their belongings, and as good friends they parted, Snorri and Bardi.

Now Bardi goeth north to Waterdale, where he tarrieth with Gudbrand his brother-in-law. And in the following spring he dighteth a journey of his, and buyeth a ship and goeth abroad, and his wife with him. The tale telleth that the journey sped well with him, and he hove in from the main up against Halogaland, where the next winter long he dwelt in Thiotta with Svein, son of Harek, being well accounted of, for men deemed they saw in him the tokens of a great man; so Svein held him dear, both him and his wife withal.

CHAPTER 41
The End Of Bardi

So it befell one morning, as they were both together in their sleeping loft, away from other folk, that Bardi would sleep on, but she would be rousing him, and so she took a small pillow and cast it into his face as if for sport. He threw it back again from him; and so this went on sundry times. And at last he cast it at her and let his hand go with it. She was wroth thereat, and having gotten a stone she throweth it at him in turn.

So that day, when drinking was at an end, Bardi riseth to his feet, and nameth witnesses for himself, and declareth that he is parted from Aud, saying that he will take masterful ways no more from her than from anyone else. And so fast was he set in this mind herein, that to bring words to bear was of no avail.

So their goods were divided between them, and Bardi went his ways next spring, and made no stay in his journey till he cometh into Garthrealm, where he taketh warrior's wages, and becometh one of the Vaerings, and all the Northmen held him of great account, and had him for a bosom-friend amongst themselves.

Always, when that king's realm was to be warded, he is on the ways of war, gaining good renown from his valiance, so that he has about him always a great company of men. There Bardi spent three winters, being much honoured by the king and all the Vaerings. But once it befell, as they were out on their war-galleys with an host and warded the king's realm, that there fell an host upon them; there make they a great battle, and many of the king's men fell, as they had to struggle against an overwhelming force, though ere they fell they wrought many a big deed; and therewithal fell Bardi amidst good renown, having used his weapons after the fashion of a valiant man unto death.

Aud was married again to a mighty man, the son of Thorir Hound, who was hight Sigurd. And thence are sprung the men of Birchisle, the most renowned among men.

And there endeth this story.

THE STORY OF HRAFNKELL, FREY'S PRIEST

CHAPTER 1

It was in the days of King Harold Fairhair that a man brought his ship to Iceland into Breiðdal, his name being Hallfreðr. Breiðdal is a countryside down below that of Fljótsdalr. On board his ship was his wife and son, who was hight Hrafnkell, who was then fifteen winters old, a hopeful man and a goodly. Hallfreðr set up household. In the course of the winter there died a servant-maid of foreign kin, whose name was Arnthrúðr; hence the name of the place Arnthruðr-staðir. In the spring Hallfreðr moved his house northward over the heath, and set up a home at a place called Geitdalr. One night he dreamt that there came a man to him, and said : "There liest thou, Hallfreðr, and rather unwarily; flit thy house away west across the Lagarfljót, for there all thy good luck awaits thee." Thereupon he awoke and flitted his belongings down valley across Rangá, into the Tongue, to a spot, which has since been called Hallfreðr-staðir, and there he dwelt into a good old age. In breaking up from Geitdalr he had left a goat and a buck behind, and the same day that Hallfreðr left, an earthslip struck the house, and there these two creatures were lost. Hence the name Geitdalr, which this place has borne ever since.

CHAPTER 2

Hrafnkell made it his wont to ride upon the heaths in the summer-seasons. At this time Jökuldalr was all settled as high as the bridge. Once Hrafnkell rode up along Fljótsdalhérað and saw that a certain void valley stretched up beyond Jökuldalr, which seemed to him to be a better settlement than other valleys which he had seen already. And when he came home, he asked his father to share him out his part in the property, saying, that he was minded to set up house in the valley. This his father granted him, and in the valley he had found, he made an abode for himself, which he called Aðalból. Hrafnkell got him for wife Oddbjörg, daughter of Skjaldúlfr, from Laxárdalr, with whom he begat two sons, the older hight Thórir, the younger Ásbjörn. But when Hrafnkell had hallowed for himself the land of Aðalból, he held a great sacrificial feast, and a great temple, too, he reared up there. Hrafnkell loved no other god before Frey, and to him he made offerings of all the best things he had, going half-shares. Hrafnkell settled the whole of the valley, bestowing lands on other people, on condition of being their chief; and thus he assumed priesthood over them. From this it came to pass that his name was lengthened, and he was called Freysgoði. He was a man of right unruly ways, but a well-mannered man notwithstanding. He asserted the authority of a priest over all the men of Jokuldalr. Hrafnkell was meek and blithe towards his own people, but stern and crossgrained towards those of Jokuldalr, who never got fair dealings with him. He busied himself much with single combats, and for no man did he pay a weregild, and one ever brought him to do boot for whatsoever he might have done.

The country side of Fljótsdalr is a right difficult one to traverse, stony and sloughy. Yet father and son would be constantly riding to see each other, for between them there was much fondness of love. Hallfreðr thought the common way was too difficult of passing, so he sought for a new road above the fells, which stand in the country-sides of Fljótsdalr, where he found a drier one, although a longer, which ever since has been called the "gate" of Hallfreðr. This road is traversed only by those who are well acquainted with the country-sides.

CHAPTER 3

There was a man named Bjarni, who dwelt at a stead called Langarhús, in Hrafnkelsdalr. He was married, and had begotten sons with his wife, one of whom was called Sámr, the other Eyvindr, goodly men and promising; Eyvindr stayed at home with his father, but Sámr was married, and had his abode on the northern side of the valley at a place called Leikskálar, and was right well off for live-stock. Sámr was a turbulent fellow, and skilled in law withal; but Eyvindr became a traveller, and went to Norway, where he dwelt for the first winter; from there he went abroad into foreign lands, coming at last to a stay in Constantinople, where he was right honourably received by the Greek king, and where, for a while, he spent his time.

Of all his possessions there was one for which Hrafnkell had greater fondness than any other. This was a horse of a roan colour, which he called "Freymane." He gave unto his friend Frey the half of this horse, and so great a love had he for it, that he made a solemn vow that he would kill any one who should ride the horse without his leave.

CHAPTER 4

A man was hight Thorbjörn, brother of Bjarni, who dwelt at a stead in Hrafnkelsdalr, called Hóll, situated across the valley right against Aðalból, on the eastern side. Thorbjörn was a man of scanty means, but of many useless mouths. The eldest of his sons was called Einarr; he was a tall man and well-mannered withal. It so happened one spring that Thorbjörn said to Einarr that he had better try to secure some place for himself; "for," said he, "I am in want of no more work than can be done by the hands that are here already, but thou wilt find it easy to secure a situation, able and skilful as thou art. It is not for any want of love that I thus call upon thee to go away, for thou art to me the most useful of all my children; but it is because of my small means and poverty; but my other children must grow up labourers, but as for thee, thou wilt find it easier to get a place than they." Einarr answered : "Too late hast thou let me know of this, as now all places and situations, the best of them at least, are already arranged for, and I deem it an undesirable thing to have to accept only the worst." Now Einarr took his horse and rode to Aðalból, where Hrafnkell sat in his chamber, and received him well and joyfully. Einarr applied for a situation with Hrafnkell, and he answered : "Why askest so late for this? otherwise I should have taken thee the first of all men. Now I have secured all my servants, except for that one business which, I fear, thou art not minded to undertake." Einarr asked what it was. Hrafnkell answered, he had got no one to take charge of his sheep, but said he was in great need of one. Einarr said he did not mind what work he did, whether this or any other; but said he would like to settle with him for cloth and board wages. "I'll make a short bargain with thee," said Hrafnkell. "Thy business shall be to watch fifteen ewes at the mountain dairy, and gather and carry home faggots for summer fuel. On these terms thou shalt take service with me for two 'half-years.' But a one thing I must give thee, as all my shepherds, to understand: 'Freymane' goes grazing in the valley with his band of mares; thou shalt take care of him winter and summer; but I warn thee of one thing, namely, that thou never be on his back on any condition whatever, for I am bound by a mighty vow to slay the man that ever should have a ride on him. There are twelve mares with him; whichever one of these thou mayest want, night or day, is at your service. Do now as I tell thee, and mind the old saw: 'No blame is borne by those who warn.' Now thou knowest what I have said." Einarr said he trusted he was under no such luckless spell as to ride on a horse which was forbidden, least of all when there were other horses at his disposal.

CHAPTER 5

Now Einarr goes home for his clothes, and betakes himself to Aðalból. Thereupon they brought the milking-stock to the mountain-dairy up in Hrafnkelsdalr, which was set up at a place called Grjótteigssel. During the summer all went in a fair way with Einarr, so that never a ewe was missing up to mid-summer; but then, one night, it came to pass that nearly thirty of them had strayed away. Einarr went all over the sheep-walks, searching without finding any, and for nearly a week the sheep were missing. One morning Einarr rose early, and, coming out, found that all the fog from the south and the drizzle had lifted. And so he takes into his hand a staff and a bridle, and a riding-rug. Then he went on, passing Grjótteigsá, which ran above the dairy. On the shingly flats by the river were lying about all the sheep that had been home in the evening before. These he drove home towards the dairy, and then went in search of those that were wanting. He now saw the stud-horses further afield on the flats, and was minded to secure one of them to ride on, knowing that he would cover ground more quickly by riding than by walking: and when he came to the horses, he had to run about after them, they being now shy, though never before they used to run away from any one -- except "Freymane" alone. He was as quiet as if stuck buried in the ground. Einarr, seeing that the morning was passing off, thought that Hrafnkell surely would never know if he rode upon the horse, and so he took it, put on it the bridle, and the riding-rug on his back under himself, and rode up past the gorge of Grjóta, and farther up towards the glaciers, then along the "jökul," beneath whick Jökulsá runs, and then down along the river unto the dairy of Reykir. He asked all shepherds at the sundry dairies if any of them had set their eye upon the sheep, but no one professed to have seen them. Einarr rode "Freymane" from the first streak of dawn until middle eve, and the horse took him quickly over the ground and far, for it was the best of horses. Then it came into Einarr's mind that it was time already to drive home to the dairy the sheep which were still in safe keeping, letting alone those that he could not find. So he rode to the eastward over the mountain-necks into Hrafnkelsdalr. But as he came down by Grjótteigr, he heard the bleating of sheep along the river-gorge, even where he had ridden close by before; and turning thither, sees how thirty ewes come running along towards him, even the very ones which had been missing for a whole week already, and these, with the rest of the ewes, he drove along home to the dairy. The horse was all foaming with sweat, so that every hair on him was dripping; bespattered he was all over with mire, and mightily blown. Twelve times he rolled himself, and then he set up a mighty neighing, and then set off at a swift pace down along the beaten tracks. Einarr ran forthwith after him, endeavouring to overtake him, and to lay hand on him and bring him back to the horses. But now "Freymane" was so shy, that Einarr could get nowhere near him. Thus the horse ran down all along the valley, never stopping until it came home to Aðalból. At the time Hrafnkell sat at table, and when the horse came before the door it neighed aloud. Hrafnkell told one of the handmaidens who were serving at table, to go to the door, "for I heard the neighing of a horse, and meseemed the neighing was like to that of 'Frey-mayne.'" She went out to the door, and there beheld "Freymane" in a most ungainly plight. She told Hrafnkell that "Freymane" stood outside the door most ill-favoured of look. "What is the matter with the

116

champion that he should come home as at this time," says Hrafnkell; "sure that bodes no good." Then he went out and saw "Freymane," and spoke to him: "I am sorry to see thee in this kind of plight, my pet; however, thou hadst all thy wits about thee in thus coming to let me know what is the matter; due revenge shall be taken for this, and now thou mayest go back to thy company." And forthwith "Freymane" walked up the valley again to join the stud.

CHAPTER 6

In the evening Hrafnkell went to his bed as usual, and slept through the night. In the morning he had a horse brought home to him, and ordered it to be saddled, and rode up to the dairy. He rode in blue raiment: he had an axe in his hand, but no other weapons about him. At that time Einarr had just driven the ewes into the pen, and lay on the wall of the pen, casting up the number of the sheep; but the women were busy a-milking. They all greeted Hrafnkell, and he asked how they got on. Einarr answered: "I have had no good speed myself, for no less than thirty ewes were missing for a week, though now I have found them again." Hrafnkell said, he had no fault to find with tilings of that kind; "It has not happened so often as might have been expected, that thou hast lost the ewes. But has not something worse befallen than that? Didst thou not have a ride on 'Freymane' yesterday?" Einarr said he could not gainsay that utterly. "Why didst thou ride on this horse which was forbidden thee, while there were plenty of others on which thou art free to ride? Now this one trespass I should have forgiven thee, if I had not used words of such earnest already. And yet thou hast manfully confessed thy guilt." But by reason of the belief that those who fulfil their vows never come to grief, he leaped off his horse, sprang upon Einarr, and dealt him his death-blow. After that, having done the deed, he rode home to Aðalból and there told these tidings. He got him another shepherd to take charge of the dairy. But he had Einarr's dead body brought westward upon the terrace by the dairy, and there set up a beacon beside his cairn; and it is called Einarr's beacon, where, when the sun is right above it, they count mid-eve hour (six o'clock) at the dairy.

CHAPTER 7

The news of Einarr, his son's, death, was brought over to Thorbjörn at Hóll, and he was mightily grieved at the tidings. He now took his horse, and rode over to Aðalból to ask Hrafnkell to do boot for his son. Hrafnkell said that he had slain many a man beside this one; "for thou must know that I never pay weregild to any man, and yet people have to rest content with things so done. Yet I allow it, that I think that this my deed is rather of the worse kind among the manslaughters which I have wrought hitherto; thou, too, hast been a neighbour of mine for a long while, and I have had a good liking for thee, and we have enjoyed one another's favour; and no small tiling would have brought matters to an evil pass between me and Einarr, if only he had not ridden this horse; but now I have to regret that I spoke too much; and seldomer, indeed, should we have to regret that which we say too little than that which we say too much, and now I shall show that I consider this deed of mine a worse one than other deeds that I have done, inasmuch as I will supply thy house with dairy-produce during the summer, and with slaughtered meat when autumn comes; and in the same way I will do to thee as long as thou art minded to keep a house. Thy sons and daughters we shall fit out at my cost, and so endow them, as to make their conditions desirable. And all that thou knowest my house to contain, and of which thou mayest stand in need in future, thou shalt let me know of, nor henceforth shalt thou be in want of those things which may be requisite unto thee. Thou shalt keep house as long as thou takest pleasure therein, but when thou art tired thereof, thou shalt come to me, and I will take care of thee unto thy dying day. Let this be our atonement; and likely, it seems to me, that most people will say, that this man was dearly paid for." "This offer I will not accept," says Thorbjörn. "What then?" says Hrafnkell. Then spake Thorbjörn: "I will, that we name an umpire between us." Answered Hrafnkell: "Then thou holdest thyself as good a man as I; the peace between us is at an end." Then Thorbjörn rode away, and down along Hrafnkelsdalr. He came to Langarhus, and met his brother Bjarni, and told him the tidings, asking him at the same time to lend him a hand in these matters. Bjarni answered, saying that Hrafnkell was his equal to deal with; "for though we have plenty of money to dispose of, we are not the men to plunge into a strife with such a man; and sooth, indeed, is the old saw; 'Know one thing, know thyself!' He has made lawsuits difficult for many a one who have been mightier men of their hands than we are; and it seems to me that thou hast been somewhat short of wits in refusing such a good offer, and I will have nothing to do with this." Thorbjörn overwhelmed his brother with abuse, saying that there was in him the less of manhood, the more he was to be depended upon. So he rode away, and the two brothers parted in little love. He did not stop until he came down to Leikskálar, where he knocked at the door, and people answered the knock and came out. Thorbjörn asked Sámr to come out and see him. Sámr greeted his kinsman well, and asked him to put up there. Thorbjörn answered it slowly somewhat. Seeing that Thorbjörn was downcast, Sámr asked him for tidings, and Thorbjörn told him the slaughter of his son Einarr. "That is no great tidings," said Sámr, "if Hrafnkell slays a man." Thorbjörn asks if Sámr was minded to lend him any help: "for such is the nature of the case, that though the man is nearest and dearest to me, yet the blow has been dealt no way from malice." "Hast thou tried to have any redress of Hrafnkell?" said Sámr. Thorbjörn told all truthfully as to what had passed between him and Hrafnkell. "Never before did I know Hrafnkell to make such offer to any man, as those he has made to thee," says Sámr. "Now I will ride with thee up to Aðalból, and let us come before Hrafnkell in a humble mind, and see if he will still hold to the same offers; and I doubt not that he will behave honourably in the matter." Says Thorbjörn: "This is to be said, both that Hrafnkell will now refuse, and that such is no more in my mind now than it was when I rode away from there." Sámr says: "Heavy enough, I guess, will it be to strive with Hrafnkell in matters at law." Thorbjörn answers: "That is why ye young men never come to aught, that you flinch at all things, and I am minded to think that no man has got such milksops for kinsmen as I have. It seems to me that a man like you is putting himself in a right false position, being skilled in law and eager for petty cases, but refusing to take up this case, a great and urgent one. Thou shalt be widely reviled for this, as, indeed, thou deservest, being known as the most boisterous man in our kin. And I now see how the matter turns." Sámr answered: "By how much art thou the better off than before, even if I should take up the case, and we should both be worsted together?" Thorbjörn answered: "It would be a great relief to my mind, if thou shouldst undertake it, no matter how after that it should turn out." Sámr said: "I am right unwilling to engage in this, and it is only for the sake of kinship that I do it; but thou must know, that in thee I deem that I have no avail of any kind." Then Sámr gave his hand, and took the case off Thorbjörn's hand.

CHAPTER 8

Now Sámr took a horse, and rode up the valley unto a certain stead, where he declared the manslaughter, and after that he gathered men against Hrafnkell. Hrafnkell heard of this, and thought it a laughable affair that Sámr should have undertaken a blood-suit against him. And thus the winter and the next summer pass away. When the days of the summonses pass by, Sámr rode away from home up to Aðalból, and summoned Hrafnkell for the manslaughter of Einarr. After that he rode down the valley, and called upon the goodmen to come to the "Þing." Hrafnkell, too, sent messengers down along Jokuldalr and charged his men to come; and thus from his own jurisdiction he brought together seventy men. With this band he rode eastward over Fljótsdalshérað, across it past the upper end of the water, then straight across the neck unto Skriðudalr, and up along the same valley and south unto Öxarheiði on the way to Berufjörðr and the straight "Þing" road to Siða. From Fljotsdalr there are seventeen days' journey unto Þingvellir. Now when Hallfreðr had ridden away from the country-side, Sámr gathered men together, and most of those that he brought together, and who formed his following, were only country tramps; unto these men Sámr gave both weapons and clothes and victuals. Sámr struck another route out of the valley. He first went north to the bridge and then over the bridge, and thence unto Moðrudalsheiði, putting up at Moðrudalr for the night. Thence they rode unto Herðirbreiðstunga, and so on above Bláfjöll, and thence into Króksdalr, and so southward unto the Sand, until they came down unto Sauðafell, whence unto Þingvöll, where Hrafnkell had not arrived as yet, the reason of his slower travelling being the longer road he had to do. Sámr tilts a booth for his men, but nowhere near where the Eastfirth-men were wont to tilt. Now shortly after this Hallfreðr arrived and tilted his booth as had been his wont here before. He heard that Sámr was at the "Þing," and that he found right laughable. The "Þing" was a very crowded one, and at it there were most of the lords of the land. Sámr went to all the chieftains, asking them for help and avail, but they all answered one way, saying each that they had nothing good to requite Sámr so as to join him in strife at law against priest Hrafnkell and thus to hazard their honour. They also say that most of those who ever had contentions at law with Hrafnkell had fared one way; that in all such cases as had men set up against him, he had worsted them all. Sámr went home to his booth, and in a downcast frame of mind; the two kinsmen were misdoubting that their affairs would come to such an utter downfall, as that they would only reap from it shame and disgrace, and in so deep an anxiety were both of them fallen, that they might have no enjoyment either of food or sleep, because all the chieftains refused all assistance to them, even those upon whose help they had counted most.

CHAPTER 9

It so fell early one morning, that the old carl Thorbjörn was awake; he roused Sámr from his sleep and bade him stand up, "for now it behoves not to slumber." Sámr stood up and put on his raiment. They went abroad, walking down to Oxará below the bridge, where they washed themselves. Thorbjörn spake to Sámr, "It is my counsel now, that thou cause our horses to be driven up, and that we get ready to return home, for it is easy to see that here nothing is awaiting us but utter shame." Sámr answered: "That is well enough, since thou wouldst hear of nothing but striving with Hrafnkell, and didst not choose to accept offers that many a man, who had lost a near kinsman, would have been fain to take. With hard reproaches thou didst egg on my mind, doing the same to others, who were not willing to enter the case with thee. But as for me I shall never give in, until I deem that all hope is past of my ever being able to bring things further about." This came so close home to Thorb-jörn, that he wept. Then they saw how, on the western side of the river, only a bit further down than where they were sitting, five men walk together out of a certain booth. He who was at the head of them, and walked abreast of them, was a tall man, not of a stout build to look at, arrayed in a leaf-green kirtle, in his hand a sword ornamented; a straight-faced man he was, and ruddy of hue, and of a goodly presence, light-auburn of hair, which was fast growing hoary. This was a man easy to know, as he had a light lock in his hair on the left side. Then Sámr spake: "Stand we up, and go we west across the river to meet these men." Now they went down along the river, and the leader of those men is the first to greet them, asking them who they were, to which they answered as asked. Sámr asked this man for his name; he said he was named Thorkell, and was the son of Thjostar. Sámr asked where his family was, and where he had got a home. The other said he was a West-firther by kin and origin, and that his abode was in Thorskafjörðr. Questioned Sámr: "Art thou a man of a priesthood?" "Far from it," said the other. "Art thou a bonder then?" said Sámr. He said that was not so. Sámr asked: "What of a man art thou then?" He answered: "I am only a country tramp. I came out here last summer, having been for seven winters abroad, having fared all the way to Constantinople, being now a henchman of the King of the Greeks, and at this time staying with my brother, whose name is Thorgeirr." "Is he a man of a priesthood?" said Sámr. Thorkell answered: "A man of a priesthood he is indeed, both in Thorskafjörðr and wide about elsewhere in the West-firths." "Is he here at the Þing?" said Sámr. "To be sure," said Thorkell. "How many men has he got with him?" said Sámr. "About seventy men," said Thorkell. "Are there more of ye brothers?" said Sámr. "A third one still," says Thorkell. "Who is he?" says Sámr. "He is hight Thormoðr," says Thorkell, "and dwells at Garðar on Álptanes, and is married to Thórdís, the daughter of Thórólfr Skalla-grimsson of Borg." "Art thou minded at all to bear us a hand?" says Sámr. "What is it you want?" says Thorkell. "To be backed up by the might of chieftains," says Sámr, "for we have affairs at law on hand against Hrafnkell the priest, for the manslaughter of Einarr Thorbjarnar-son; and if thou shouldst back us up, we, as plaintiffs, are confident of the case." Thorkell answered: "As I told you, I am not a man of a priesthood." "Why art thou so stinted of thy share," said Sámr, "being the son of a chieftain like the rest of thy

120

brothers?" Thorkell answered: "I did not say that I was not possessed of a priesthood, but I handselled to my brother Thorgeirr my rule of men before I went abroad; and since my return I have not resumed it, because I deem it well cared for, while he takes charge of it. Go ye to meet him, and ask him to look to you; he is a lordly-minded man, and a noble-hearted, and in every way of good conditions; a young man too, and ambitious withal. Such are the likeliest men to yield the assistance ye want." Sámr says: "We shall get nothing out of him unless thou backest up our suit as well." Thorkell answers: "I will promise to be rather with than against you, as it seems to me the necessity is urgent, that a suit should be brought on for a close relative. Go ye now to the booth, and go ye into the booth, now that all men are asleep; ye will see, where there stands, athwart the upper part of the floor, a couple of sleeping-bags, out of one of which I have just arisen, and in the other of which there is resting still Thorgeirr, my brother. Since he came to the 'Þing' he has suffered much from a suppurated foot, and has therefore slept little a-night, but last night, the boil burst, and the core is out: since that he has been asleep, and has stretched the foot from under the clothes out over the foot-board for relief from over-heat. Let the old man go first, and let him go up the booth. It seems to me that he is a right decrepit old fellow, both as to sight and as to age. Now, my man," says Thorkell, "when thou comest up to the sleeping-bag, take care to trip hard and come flopping down upon the footboard, and catch in the fall at the toe which is bandaged, and pull at it, and just see how he likes it." Sámr said: "No doubt that thou art a man of wholesome counsel to us, but this seems to me hardly a wise thing to do." Thorkell answered: "One of two things you must do -- to take what I advise, or not to come to me for a counsel at all." Sámr spake, and said: "As he has counselled, so the thing shall be done." Thorkell said that he would come on later, "for I am waiting for my men."

CHAPTER 10

Now Sámr and Thorbjörn went away and came into the booth, where all men were asleep; they soon saw where Thorgeirr was lying. The old carl Thorbjörn went first, and in a stumbling manner he walked. But when he came up to the sleeping-bag, then he stumbled on to the footboard and clutched at the sore toe and pulled hard at it, while Thorgeirr woke and jumped up in the sleeping-bag, and asked who he was who was going on so headlong as to rush upon people's sore feet. But Sámr and his men had nothing to say for themselves; but in the same moment Thorkell sprang into the booth and said to Thorgeirr his brother: "Be not so hasty and furious, kinsman, about this; it will do thee no harm, and people often do by chance things worse than they would; and to many a man it has happened to be unable to have his eye on all things, when his mind is overloaded with great things. No wonder, kinsman, that thou shouldst be so hurt in thy foot which has so long been painful, and, indeed, that pain pinches thyself sharpest. But even so it may be, that no less painful to an old man is the death of his son, for whom he can get no redress, being moreover a man pinched by every kind of want. No doubt he knows best his own pain, and it is not to be wondered at that he should not be very heedful of all things, in whose mind mighty things are abiding." Thorgeirr answered: "I did not know that he was to

121

hold me responsible for this, for I did not kill his son, and he cannot therefore revenge this on me." "He nowise minded to be avenged on thee," says Thorkell, "but he came to thee at a faster pace than he could help, and paid for his dimness of sight in his eager hope of finding some support in thee. And a noble deed it would be to lend one's help to an old and needy man. This is to him a matter of necessity, not of choice, seeing that it is his son, after whom he has to take up the suit. But now all the chieftains back out of all help to these men, and show therein a great want of great-mindedness." Thorgeirr answered: "Against whom have these men the plaint to bring?" Thorkell answered: "Hrafnkell the priest has slain the son of Thorbjörn, sackless. One deed after another he works, never allowing redress to any one therefor." Thorgeirr answered: "I shall, belike, fare the way of others, in not finding that I have any such good deed to requite to these men, as that I should go willingly into law struggles with Hrafnkell. For it seems that every summer he deals with those who have got cases to contest with him, so that most of them get little or no honour thereof in the end. In this way I have seen them fare every one. This, I guess, must be the cause why most men are so unwilling, whom necessity does not urge along." Thorkell answered: "It may be, if I were a chieftain, that I should fare in the same way, and that I should deem it ill to have to strive with Hrafnkell, but as I am, I look on that matter otherwise, for I should above all things choose to deal with such a man before whom all men had come to grief already; and greatly should I deem that my honour had advanced, or the honour of any chieftain, by Hrafnkell being brought into some straits; whereas, I should deem it undiminished if I fared no worse than others, as the proverbs say, 'Tis not my curse what's common fate,' and 'nothing venture, nothing gain.'" "Now I see," says Thorgeirr, "how thy mind stands in the matter; thou wilt lend these men thy assistance. Now I shall hand over to thee my priesthood and my rule of men, and have thou that which I have had before, but after that we go even shares, and now thou back up whomsoever thou choosest" Answered Thorkell: "It seems to me that our priesthood will be best looked after by being longest in thy hands; and I should like no one better to have it than thee, for thou hast many things to make thee a man above all of us brothers, whereas I have not made up my mind as to what I shall do with myself as at this time. Thou knowest, kinsman, that I have meddled in few things since I came to Iceland. I shall see what my counsels are held worth, for now I have pleaded this cause all I can at present. May be that Thorkell Leppr may come forward hereafter in such a manner as that his words may be held of greater account." Thorgeirr answered: "I see now, kinsman, how the matter stands, that thou art not pleased, which I cannot bear to think of, so we will lend these men our assistance if it be thy will, whatsoever end the affair may have." Thorkell answered: "Therefore I asked that it is my pleasure that the request be granted." "What do these men consider themselves able to do?" says Thorgeirr, "so that thereby the success of their case may be better insured?" "As I said before today," said Sámr, "we want the assistance of chieftains, but the pleading of the case is in my hand." Thorgeirr said that it was then for him to show what he was good for: "And now the thing to be done is to start the suit in the most correct manner. But methinks it is Thorkell's will that you come to meet him before judgment fall; and then ye will have something for your pertinacity -- either some comfort, or otherwise a humiliation still greater than before, and grief and heartburn. Now go ye home and be merry, for if ye are to strive with Hrafnkell it behoves you to bear yourselves well and straightly for a while. But let no man be told that we have promised you any support." Now they went home to their booth and bore themselves right merrily. People wondered much at this, how they had so suddenly come to change their mind, seeing how downcast they were when they went away.

CHAPTER 11

And now they sit quietly until the time when judgments were to be passed. Then Sámr called together his men and went to the Mount of Laws, where the court was set. Then Sámr came boldly forth to the court; calling witnesses forthwith, he pleaded his cause in a manner good in law against Hrafnkell the priest, without making mistakes and with a frank and fearless manner of pleading. Then came up the sons of Thjóstar with a large following of men, all men from the west country joining them, whereby it was seen how well befriended the sons of Thjóstar were. Sámr pleaded the cause unto judgment, until Hrafnkell was called upon to defend, or then he who should be there present who should come forward to keep up law defence for him, according as might be good and right in law. Sámr's pleading was received with good cheer, and the question was put whether no one would bring forward a lawful defence on behalf of Hrafnkell. People rushed to the booth of Hrafnkell and told him what was doing. He started quickly, calling together his men, and went to the court, thinking that there would be but a poor "defence of the coast," and thinking in his mind how he should make small men loth to set up cases against him ; and was minded to break up the court for Sámr and to hustle him out of the case. This, however, was not to be done now; there being already there such a crowd of people that he could get nowhere near; and so was himself hustled away with great violence, even so that he could not hear the speaking of those who pleaded against him, and therefore was deprived of means to bring forward a lawful defence on his own behalf. But Sámr pushed the suit to the full extent of law, until Hrafnkell, at this very "Þing," was made full outlaw. Hrafnkell went forthwith to his booth and had his horses brought up and rode away from the "Þing" mightily ill-contented at the end of these affairs, for such he had never before experienced. So he rode east, over Lyngdalsheiði and further on to Siða, and did not halt travelling until he came to Hrafnkelsdalr, and settled in his home at Aðalból. He behaved as if nothing had happened. But Sámr remained behind at the "Þing," going about and bearing himself right struttingly. Many people thought it well that the case should have come about in this way, and that Hrafnkell should have to come down once in a way, calling now to mind how many people he had dealt with unfairly before.

CHAPTER 12

Sámr waited until the "Þing" broke up, and men got ready to return home. He thanked the brothers well for their assistance, and Thorgeirr asked Sámr, laughingly, how he was pleased at the turn matters had taken? He signified his pleasure thereat; but Thorgeirr asked: "Deemest thou thyself now in any better case than before?" Sámr said: "Methinks that Hrafnkell has had a right great shame of this, such as shall be long remembered, and I deem it to be worth as much as a great lot of money." Thorgeirr said: "A full outlaw the man is not yet, as long as the act of distress has not been executed, which must be done at his own home, not later than a fortnight after 'Wapentake' " (but it is called Wapentake when all men ride away from the "Þing"). "But I guess," said Thorgeirr, "that Hrafnkell is come home, and means to sit at Aðalból, and I also hold likely that he will have taken to himself thy rule over men. But thou, I guess, art minded to ride home and to settle at thy house as best thou mayest, if such be possible. I guess, too, that thou deemest thou hast so brought about thy affairs as to declare him an outlaw, but I am minded to think that he will overawe people in the same manner as before, excepting that, as for thyself, thou wilt have to stoop even lower than ever." "That I never mind," said Sámr. "Thou art a brave man," said Thorgeirr, "and I think that my kinsman, Thorkell, is minded not to let it come to a poor end with thee, having made up his mind to accompany thee until a settlement of thy case with Hrafnkell be brought about, so that thou mayest sit at thy home in quiet. And thou, too, wilt think that it is most due to us now to give thee our support, since already we had the most to do in thy affairs. Now for this once we shall accompany thee to the Eastfirths; but art thou acquainted with any road thither which is not a highroad?" Sámr said he would go back the same way he had come from the east, and was now right glad at this offer.

CHAPTER 13

Thorgeirr selected the best men from his band, and charged forty of them to accompany him. Sámr, likewise, had forty men in his following, and the whole band was well fitted out, both as to weapons and horses. So they rode all along die same way until they came into Jokuldalr one night, as the fire of dawn was first lighting. They passed over the bridge on the river in the very morning when the act of distress was to be executed. Then asked Thorgeirr how they could best come there unawares; for this Sámr said he had a good advice. And out of the road he turned and up to the mountain side, and so along the neck, between Hrafnkelsdalr and Jokuldalr, until they came to the outer spur of the mountain, beneath which stood the homestead of Aðalból. There some grassy deans stretched up into the heath and a steep slope stretched down into the valley, underneath which was the farmstead. Then Sámr got off his horse and said: "Let our horses be loose and be guarded by twenty men, while we, sixty together, rush upon the stead, where, I guess, few people will be upon their feet as yet." Now they did so, and there the deans are called horse-deans unto this day. They were swiftly upon the farm. The time for rising was past, and yet the people had not got up. They broke the door open by a beam and rushed in. Hrafnkell lay in his bed, and him, together with all his housecarls, those who were able to bear weapons, they made prisoners; but women and children they drove all into one chamber. On the lawn there stood a storehouse, between which and the hall there was laid a beam for drying clothes on; unto this storehouse they brought Hrafnkell and his men. He made many offers for himself and his people; but when that was not heeded, he asked the life of his men to be spared, "for they have done nothing to offend you; but it is no shame to me to be killed; and from that I beg not to be excused; only ill-treatment I pray to be spared, for that is no honour to you." Thorkell said: "We have heard, that hitherto thou hast not let thyself be easily led by thy enemies, and it is now well that thou shouldst take a lesson for it to-day." Then they took Hrafnkell and his men, and tied their hands behind their back; whereupon they broke up the storehouse, and took down from pegs some ropes hanging therein ; and next they took out their knives, making slits through their hough sinews, drawing therethrough the ropes which then they slung over the aforenamed beam, and there tied them up, eight together. Then said Thorgeirr: "Now thou hast been brought to such a plight, Hrafnkell, as thou deservest, unlikely as thou wouldst have deemed it, that thou shouldst ever have received such a shame at any man's hands as now has come to pass. Now which wilt thou do, Thorkell, sit here beside Hrafnkell and watch them, or go outside the farmstead with Sámr within the distance of an arrow shot, and there execute the act of distress on some stony knoll where there be neither field nor meadow." (This was to be done at the time when the sun was in due south.) Thorkell answered: "I will sit there beside Hrafnkell, and thus have less to do." Then Thorgeirr and Sámr executed the act of distress. Now after this they walked home and took down Hrafnkell and his men, and set them down in a field; and then blood had already filled their eyes. Then said Thorgeirr to Sámr that he should now deal with Hrafnkell as he liked, "for meseems it is now a matter of small difficulty to deal with him." Then answered Sámr: "Two choices are set before thee, Hrafnkell; one to be taken outside the stead, together with those of thy men that I choose, and to be slaughtered; but whereas thou hast a great number of useless mouths to provide for, I will allow thee to look thereto. So the second choice is, if thou wilt have thy life, that thou betake thyself from Aðalból with all thy folk and with so much money only as I share to thee, which shall be mighty little; but I shall settle on thy property and have the rule of all thy men; and to neither shalt thou ever raise a claim, nor thy heirs, nor shalt thou ever live nearer this place than somewhere to the east of Fljotsdalsherað; and this thou mayest handsel me if thou art ready to accept it." Hrafnkell answered: "Many a man would think a swift death better than such hard dealings, but, belike, I shall fare after the manner of many, 'that life be chosen while choice there is;' which I do, mostly because of my sons, for theirs will be a scanty prospect if I die from them." Then Hrafnkell was let loose and he handselled self-doom unto Sámr. Sámr allowed Hrafnkell so much of the wealth as he chose, which was a slight portion indeed. His spear Hrafnkell retained, but no weapon besides; and this very day he betook himself from Aðalból together with all his folk. Then said Thorkell to Sámr: "I wonder at thy doing this, for no man will regret more than thyself having given Hrafnkell his life." Sámr said that could not be helped now.

CHAPTER 14

Hrafnkell brought his household east over Fljótsdals-heraö and right across Fljótsdalr unto the eastern side of Lagarfljót. At the bottom of that water stood a small stead, which was called Lokhylla. This land Hrafnkell bought on credit, for his means went no further than to cover the cost of household implements.

People had much talk about this, how Hrafnkell's masterfulness had suddenly come down to nought; and many a man now recalls the ancient saw: "Short is the age of over-boldness." This was a good woodland and large in extent, but the house was a poor one, and therefore he bought the land at a low price. But Hrafnkell spared no cost; he felled the wood, which was large, and raised there a lofty abode, which since has been called Hrafnkelsstaðir, and has always been accounted of as a good stead. During the first seasons Hrafnkell lived there in battle with hard distress. He had much ado in storing his home with fish. He went much about common labour while the stead was being built. The first half-year he embarked on the winter with one calf and one kid. But it turned well out for him, so that nearly everything lived in the way of live stock, which was added to it; and it might be said that nearly every creature was with two heads. That same summer there happened to be a large catch in Lagarfljót, which brought the householders of the country-side many a comfort, and this held on well every summer.

CHAPTER 15

Sámr set up his house at Aðalból after Hrafnkell, and set up a great banquet there, and invited to him all those who formerly had been Hrafnkell's retainers. Sámr offered to be the lord over them instead of Hrafnkell, and they accepted the offer, although they had various misgivings about the matter. The sons of Thjóstar counselled him to be bounteous of his money, and helpful to his men, and a support to whomsoever might be in want; "And then they are not men if they do not faithfully follow thee in whatsoever thou mayest stand in need of. But this we counsel thee, therefore, that we should like to see thee successful in all things, for thou seemest to us to be a stalwart man. Now take care of thyself and be wary of thy ways: 'for evil foes 'tis hard to heed.'" The sons of Thjóstar sent for "Freymane" and the stud; said they would like to see the beasts of which there were so many stories abroad. Then the horses were brought home and they were viewed by the brothers. Thorgeirr said: "These horses seem to me to be serviceable to the household, and it is my counsel that they be made to work all they can in the service of man until they can live no longer by reason of old age; but this horse 'Freymane' seems to me no better than other horses, nay, the worse, indeed, that he has brought many an evil thing about; and I will not that he be the cause of any more manslaughters than he has been already, so it is fittest that he be received by him who owns him." Now they led the horse down the field. Beside the river there stood a precipitous rock, and below it there was a deep eddy in the river, and so they led the horse forth unto the rock. The sons of Thjóstar wound a certain cloth over the head of the horse, tied a stone round his neck, and thereupon seized long poles wherewith they thrust the horse over the precipice and destroyed him so. Sithence this rock is called Freymane's Rock. Above it stands the temple which Hrafnkell had had. Thorkell wished to come there, and he let strip all the gods, and after that he set the temple on fire and burnt there up everything together. After that the guests prepared to leave, and Sámr presented the brothers with things most precious, and they bespoke a firm friendship between them, and thereupon parted the best of friends. After this they rode west to the firths and arrived in Thorskafjörðr in great honour. Sámr settled Thorbjörn in the house at Leikskálar, where he was to keep house; but the wife of Sámr went to his house at Aðalból where he farmed for a while.

CHAPTER 16

The news was brought east into Fljótsdalr, to Hrafnkell, that the sons of Thjóstar had destroyed "Freymane" and burnt the temple. Then said Hrafnkell: "I deem it a vain thing to believe in the gods," and he vowed that henceforth he would set his trust in them no more. And to this he kept ever afterwards, and never made a sacrifice again. Now Hrafnkell sat at Hrafnkelsstaðir, raking money together fast. He became a much honoured man in the country-side, and every one chose to sit and stand as it pleased him. At that time there was a great going of ships from Norway to Iceland, and people were taking up claims in the country as fast as might be during Hrafnkell's days. No one might settle freely in Hrafnkell's country-side without his leave; and all those who settled had to promise him their aid, against which he promised his protection. Thus he brought under himself all the land on the eastern side of Lagarfljót. This jurisdiction soon became much more thickly peopled than that which he had ruled over before, stretching all the way up Skriðudal as well as up all along Lagarfljót. Now his mind, too, had undergone a change; he was much better liked than heretofore; he was still of the same temper as to helpful husbandry and lordly household ways; but now the man was much milder and meeker in all things than ever before. He and Sámr often met at public gatherings, but never a word fell betwixt them as to their former dealings. In this manner six winters passed away. Sámr also was well liked among his retainers, for he was gentle and quiet and ready to help, and bore in mind always the counsel which those brothers had given him; he, too, was a man of much splendour in outfit and raiment.

CHAPTER 17

It is stated that there came a certain ship into Reiðarfjörðr, the master of which was Eyvindr Bjarnason, who had been abroad for seven winters together. Eyvindr had bettered himself greatly as to manners, and had now become the briskest of men. Now he soon was told of the tidings which had come to pass, and he made as if he took little heed thereof, being a man of unmeddlesome ways. When Sámr heard this he rode to the ship, and a great joyful meeting there was between the brothers. Sámr asked him to come up west to his place, and Eyvindr accepted it, and bade Sámr ride home first, and afterwards send him horses for his chattels. He hauled his ship aland, and made her snug. Now Sámr did as Eyvindr bade, and went home, and had horses sent down to meet Eyvindr, and when he had made his chattels ready for the journey, he set off unto Hrafnkelsdalr, riding up along Reiðarfjörðr. They were five in company together, and a sixth there was, an attendant of Eyvindr, an Icelander by kin, and a relative of his. This youth Eyvindr had redeemed from poverty, and brought him now home in his own company, and had done to him as to himself, which good deed of Eyvindr was loudly praised, and the common talk was that few people could be found to match him. Now they rode up along Thorsdalsheiði, driving before them sixteen horses loaded. They were there together, two of Sámr's house-carls, and three of the sailors; all arrayed in vari-coloured clothes, and carrying glittering shields. They rode across Skriðudalr, and across the neck, over the country-side, and unto Fljótsdalr, to a spot called Bulunyarvellir, and thence unto the shingly flats of Gilsá -- a river that flows into the Fljot from the east, between Hallormsstaðr and Hrafnkelstaðir: then they rode up along Lagarfljót, down below the home-field of Hrafnkelsstaðir, and thus round the upper end of the water, crossing Jökulsá at the ford of Skali. This was midway between the hour of rising and the hour of day-meal (i.e. nine o'clock A.M.). A certain woman was there by the waterside washing her linen, and, seeing the men travelling, the handmaiden gathers up her linen and rushes homeward. The linen she threw down beside a certain pile of wood, running into the house herself. At this time Hrafnkell was not up as yet; his chosen men lay about in the hall, but the workmen had already gone each about his business, the time being the hay-making season. Now when the maiden came in she took up the wood, saying: "Sooth, indeed, are most of the old saws; 'so one grows craven as one grows old;' that honour mostly cometh to but little which, beginning early, is allowed to drop into dishonour, the bearer having no courage to wreak his right at any time, and such must be held a great wonder in a man who, once upon a time, has had bravery to boast of. Now the thing is changed; those who grow up with their fathers, and are deemed as of no worth against you, yet, when they grow up in another country, they are deemed of the greatest worth in whatsoever place they show themselves, and come back again from abroad and hold themselves better even than any chieftains. Now Eyvindr Bjarnarson has just crossed the river at the ford of Skuli, riding with a shield so fair that it beamed again; surely he is so much of a man as to be worth taking in revenge." These things the handmaiden said in great eagerness of temper. Hrafnkell rose and answered her: "May be the words thou speakest are only too true; not because that thou meanest anything good thereby; but it is well that thou have something for thy ado, and go forthwith, as hard as thou canst run, south to Viðivellir, to the sons of Hallsteinn, Sighvatr, and Snorri, and bid them at once come to me with as many men as they have about them able to bear weapons." Another handmaiden he sent down to Hrólfstadir to fetch the sons of Hrólfr, Thordr, and Halli, together with such men as might happen to be there able-bodied. All these were the stoutest of men, and were skilled in all manly parts. Hrafnkell also sent for his house-carls. And thus they were at last eighteen together. They armed themselves trustily, and rode across the river where the others had crossed it before.

CHAPTER 18

By this time Eyvindr and his men had got upon the heath, and on he rode until he had crossed the heath half-way, and had come to a spot called Bessagötur, where there is a boggy mire like a slough to ride through, where the horses waded all the way knee-deep, haunch-deep, or even belly-deep; but

128

underneath the bottom was as hard as a frozen earth. On the western side of this bog is a large lava, and, when they got upon the lava, the youth looked back and said to Eyvindr: "Some men there be riding after us, no less than eighteen in number, among whom there is one, a big man on his horse, riding in blue raiment, and to me he seems to bear the likeness of Hrafnkell, the priest, although I have now not seen him for a long while." Eyvindr answered: "What is that to us? I know nothing whereby I need fear the anger of Hrafnkell, having never done aught to offend him. No doubt he has some errand into the next valley, desiring, may be, to go see his friends." The youth answered: "My mind bodes me that he be minded to meet thee." "I am not aware," says Eyvindr, "that aught has happened between him and my brother Sámr since their atonement." The youth answered: "I wish thou wouldst ride away west to the dale, where thou shalt be in safety; but I know so much of Hrafnkell's temper, that he will do nothing to us, if he should miss thee; for, if thou alone be safe, then all things are well seen to; then there 'be no bear to tug along,' and that is well, whatsoever may become of us." Eyvindr said he felt no desire to ride so hurriedly away, "for I know not who the men may be, and many a man would find a matter good to laugh at if I should run away before it came to any trial at all." Now they rode west over the lava, when they came upon another mire called Oxemire, a grassy spot, with bogs which are all but impassable. Hence old Hallfreðr struck the higher tracks, though they were longer. Now Eyvindr rode westward into the bog-land, where the horses came by, plentifully weltering in the mire; and they were much delayed because thereof. The others, riding loose, quickly covered the ground, and Hrafnkell and his men rode their way towards the bog-land. And just as Eyvindr had got over the bogs, he saw that there was come Hrafnkell and both his sons. Now Eyvindr's men bade him ride away, now all trammels are past, "And thou wilt have time to reach Aðalból while the bog-land lies between thee and Hrafnkell." Eyvindr answered: "I mean not to fly away from any man to whom I never did any harm." So now they rode upon the neck of the land where some small hills rise above the ground. On this neck, spurring off from the mountain, there was a certain hummock and a windswept place surrounded by high banks. Up to this spot Eyvindr rode, and got there off his horse and waited for them. Then Eyvindr said: "Now we shall soon know their errand." After this they betook themselves up on to the hummock, where they broke up some stones. Now Hrafnkell turned off the road, making for the hummock. Without accosting Eyvindr with a word, he set on them forthwith. Eyvindr defended himself well and manfully; but his attendant, not deeming himself the stoutest of men for fighting, took his horse and rode west over the neck to Aðalból, and told Sámr what was going on. Sámr bestirred himself quickly, gathering men together, so that there was twenty of them in a band, and right well-armed following he had. Now Sámr rode eastward unto the heath, and to the spot where the fight had stood, and saw how matters had come about between them, and how Hrafnkell rode eastward again from his work; Eyvindr lying there fallen, and all his men. The first thing Sámr did, was to try if there still lingered life in the body of his brother, and carefully he was searched; but they had all lost their lives, five of them together. Of Hrafnkell's men, twelve had fallen, but six had been able to ride away. Now Sámr made a short stay here, and rode, together with his men, in pursuit of Hrafnkell, who rode away as fast as they could on their weary horses. Then said Sámr: "We shall be able to overtake them, they having their horses jaded, ours being all fresh; yet it will be a hard thing to reach them, though, probably, if they cross the heath before, it will be at a close shave." At this time Hrafnkell had passed Oxemire again to the eastward.

Now both parties ride until Sámr reaches the brow of the heath, and saw that Hrafnkell had already got far down the slopes, and perceives that he will be able to fly away into the country-side, and said: "Now here we must return, for Hrafnkell will have no lack of men to help him." And so Sámr returns, at things thus done, and came back to the spot where Eyvindr was lying, and set about throwing up a how over Eyvindr and his followers. In these parts, even to this day, the hummock is called Evindr-hummock, the mountains Eyvindr-hills, the valley Eyvindr-dale.

CHAPTER 19

Now Sámr brought all the chattels home to Aðalból; and when he came home Sámr sent for his retainers to be there with him the next morning by the hour of day-meal (9 o'clock A.M.), being minded to set off eastward over the heath, "And let our journey now take its own turn." In the evening Sámr went to bed, and a goodly gathering of people there was there. Hrafnkell rode home and told the tidings that had befallen. Having partaken of a repast, he gathers to him men, even to the number of seventy, with which gathering he rides west over the heath, and coming unawares upon Aðalból, he took Sámr in his bed, and had him brought out. Then Hrafnkell spoke : "Now thy conditions have come to such a pass, Sámr, as surely a short while ago thou wouldst not have believed, I having now in my hand the power of thy life. Yet I shall not deal with thee in more unmanly manner than thou didst to me. Now two conditions I put before thee -- one, to be slain; the other, that I settle and arrange all things between me and thee." Sámr said that he would rather choose to live, though he well knew that that condition would be hard enough. To that Hrafnkell bade him be sure to make up his mind, "For that is a requital I owe thee; and I should deal with thee better by half, if thou art worthy of it. Thou shalt be off from Aðalból, and betake thee to Leikskálar, and there set up thy house; thou shalt take with thee all the wealth that belonged to Eyvindr, but from hence thou shalt take with thee of money's worth, so much as thou didst bring hither; that only shalt thou bring away. I shall overtake again my priesthood, and my house, and my property; and great as I see the increase of my wealth has grown, thou shalt enjoy nought thereof notwithstanding; for Eyvindr, thy brother, no weregild shall be forthcoming, even for this reason, that thou didst plead so provokingly after thy kinsman: for thou hast, indeed, had plentiful weregild for Einarr, thy relation, in having enjoyed my rule and my wealth for six years together; but the slaying of Eyvindr and his men, I value no more than the mutilation wrought on me and my men. Thou didst drive me out of my country-side; but I am content that thou abide at Leikskálar; and that will do for thee, if thou rush not into over-boldness, that may bring about thy shame. My underling thou shalt remain while we are both alive. Be thou sure of this, too, that things shall fare the worse with thee, the more ill-dealings we have together." Now Sámr went away with his folk down to Leikskálar, and there set up his household. Now Hrafnkell committed his household of Aðalból to his chosen men and on Thórir, his son, he settled his house at Hrafnkelsstaðir; but he himself had the priesthood over all these country-sides, and his son Ásbjörn, being younger, remained with him.

CHAPTER 20

Now Sámr sat at Leikskálar this winter: he was few-spoken and unmeddlesome, and many people found that he was right ill-content with his lot. But in the winter, when the days began to lengthen, Sámr rode in company with another man, having a train of three horses, across the bridge, and thence onward across the heath of Möðrudalr; thence again across Jökulsá-of-the-Ferry, to Mývatn; thence across the Fljótsheiði, and past Ljósavatn's Pass, never halting on his way until he made Thorskafjörðr, where a good cheer was made for him. At that time Thorkell had just arrived from a journey abroad, having spent four winters together in foreign lands. Sámr stayed there for a week, giving himself some rest. He now told them of all the dealings between himself and Hrafnkell, and charged the brothers to lend him now, as afore, their aid and avail. This time Thorgeirr was chief spokesman on his own and his brother's behalf; said he was settled afar; "The way between us is a long way indeed, and before we left thee we thought we had made matters snug enough for thee, so much so, that it would have been an easy matter for thee to maintain thyself. But now things have come to what I foretold thee, when thou gavest life to Hrafnkell, that that would be the matter of thy sorest regret. I urged thee to take Hrafnkell's life, but thou wantedst to have thy way. Now it is easy to see the disparity of wisdom there is between ye two: he allowing thee to sit in peace all along, and only seized the chance of attack when he saw his way to destroying him in whom he deemed there was a greater man than in thyself. Now we may nowise allow thy lucklessness to be the bringer-about of our ruin. Nor have we any such eager desire to plunge into a strife with Hrafnkell again, as that we should want to risk our honour in that matter again. But we are willing to offer thee to come here with all thy relatives, and are ready to afford thee our protection, shouldst thou find thy mind more at ease here, than in the neighbourhood of Hrafnkell." Sámr said he was not of a mind to close such a bargain; said he wanted to be home again, and bade them afford him relay-horses which was granted him forthwith. The brothers wanted to give Sámr good gifts, but he would take none such; rejoined only that they were men of little hearts. Now Sámr rode home unto his house of Leikskálar, where he lived unto old age, nor ever, as long as he lived, did he get a redress against Hrafnkell. But Hrafnkell sat at home and maintained his lordly title, until he died in his bed. His "how" is in Hrafnkelsdalr, down below Aðalból. In his "how" there was laid down great wealth, all his armour, and his good spear. His sons stepped into his rule; Thórir dwelling at Hrafnkelstaðir, and Ásbjörn at Aðalból; both owning the priesthood conjointly, and were deemed to be right mighty men of their hands. And here the tale of Hrafnkell cometh to a close.

THE SAGE OF
CORMAC THE SKALD

CHAPTER 1
Cormac's Fore-Elders

Harald Fairhair was king of Norway when this tale begins. There was a chief in the kingdom in those days and his name was Cormac; one of the Vik-folk by kindred, a great man of high birth. He was the mightiest of champions, and had been with King Harald in many battles.

He had a son called Ogmund, a very hopeful lad; big and sturdy even as a child; who when he was grown of age and come to his full strength, took to sea-roving in summer and served in the king's household in winter. So he earned for himself a good name and great riches.

One summer he went roving about the British Isles and there he fell in with a man named Asmund Ashenside, who also was a great champion and had worsted many vikings and men of war. These two heard tell of one another and challenges passed between them. They came together and fought. Asmund had the greater following, but he withheld some of his men from the battle: and so for the length of four days they fought, until many of Asmund's people were fallen, and at last he himself fled. Ogmund won the victory and came home again with wealth and worship.

His father said that he could get no greater glory in war, - "And now," said he, "I will find thee a wife. What sayest thou to Helga, daughter of Earl Frodi?"

"So be it," said Ogmund.

Upon this they set off to Earl Frodi's house, and were welcomed with all honour. They made known their errand, and he took it kindly, although he feared that the fight with Asmund was likely to bring trouble. Nevertheless this match was made, and then they went their ways home. A feast was got ready for the wedding and to that feast a very great company came together.

Helga the daughter of Earl Frodi had a nurse that was a wise woman, and she went with her. Now Asmund the viking heard of this marriage, and set out to meet Ogmund. He bade him fight, and Ogmund agreed.

Helga's nurse used to touch men when they went to fight: so she did with Ogmund before he set out from home, and told him that he would not be hurt much.

Then they both went to the fighting holm and fought. The viking laid bare his side, but the sword would not bite upon it. Then Ogmund whirled about his sword swiftly and shifted it from hand to hand, and hewed Asmund's leg from under him: and three marks of gold he took to let him go with his life.

132

CHAPTER 2
How Cormac Was Born and Bred

About this time King Harald Fairhair died, and Eric Bloodaxe reigned in his stead. Ogmund would have no friendship with Eric, nor with Gunnhild, and made ready his ship for Iceland.

Nor Ogmund and Helga had a son called Frodi: but when the ship was nearly ready, Helga took a sickness and died; and so did their son Frodi.

After that, they sailed to sea. When they were near the land, Ogmund cast overboard his high-seat-pillars; and where the high- seat-pillars had already been washed ashore, there they cast anchor, and landed in Midfiord.

At this time Skeggi of Midfiord ruled the countryside. He came riding toward them and bade them welcome into the firth, and gave them the pick of the land: which Ogmund took, and began to mark out ground for a house. Now it was a belief of theirs that as the measuring went, so would the luck go: if the measuring-wand seemed to grow less when they tried it again and again, so would that house's luck grow less: and if it grew greater, so would the luck be. This time the measure always grew less, though they tried it three times over.

So Ogmund built him a house on the sandhills, and lived there ever after. He married Dalla, the daughter of Onund the Seer, and their sons were Thorgils and Cormac. Cormac was dark-haired, with a curly lock upon his forehead: he was bright of blee and somewhat like his mother, big and strong, and his mood was rash and hasty. Thorgils was quiet and easy to deal with.

When the brothers were grown up, Ogmund died; and Dalla kept house with her sons. Thorgils worked the farm, under the eye of Midfiord-Skeggi.

CHAPTER 3
How Cormac Fell In Love

There was a man named Thorkel lived at Tunga (Tongue). He was a wedded man, and had a daughter called Steingerd who was fostered in Gnupsdal (Knipedale).

Now it was one autumn that a whale came ashore at Vatnsnes (Watsness), and it belonged to the brothers, Dalla's sons. Thorgils asked Cormac would he rather go shepherding on the fell, or work at the whale. He chose to fare on the fell with the house-carles.

Tosti, the foreman, it was should be master of the sheep- gathering: so he and Cormac went together until they came to Gnupsdal. It was night: there was a great hall, and fires for men to sit at.

That evening Steingerd came out of her bower, and a maid with her. Said the maid, "Steingerd mine, let us look at the guests."

"Nay," she said, "no need": and yet went to the door, and stepped on the threshold, and spied across the gate. Now there was a space between the wicker and the threshold, and her feet showed through. Cormac saw that, and made this song:

> "At the door of my soul she is standing,
> So sweet in the gleam of her garment:
> Her footfall awakens a fury,
> A fierceness of love that I knew not,
> Those feet of a wench in her wimple,
> Their weird is my sorrow and troubling,
> - Or naught may my knowledge avail me -
> Both now and for aye to endure."

Then Steingerd knew she was seen. She turned aside into a corner where the likeness of Hagbard was carved on the wall, and peeped under Hagbard's beard. Then the firelight shone upon her face.

"Cormac," said Tosti, "seest eyes out yonder by that head of Hagbard?"

Cormac answered in song:

> "There breaks on me, burning upon me,
> A blaze from the cheeks of a maiden,
> - I laugh not to look on the vision -
> In the light of the hall by the doorway.
> So sweet and so slender I deem her,
> Though I spy bug a glimpse of an ankle
> By the threshold: and through me there flashes
> A thrill that shall age never more."

And then he made another song:

> "The moon of her brow, it is beaming
> 'Neath the bright-litten heaven of her forehead:
> So she gleams in her white robe, and gazes
> With a glance that is keen as the falcon's.
> But the star that is shining upon me
> What spell shall it work by its witchcraft?
> Ah, that moon of her brow shall be mighty
> With mischief to her - and to me?"

Said Tosti, "She is fairly staring at thee!" - And he answered:

> "She's a ring-bedight oak of the ale-cup,
> And her eyes never left me unhaunted.
> The strife in my heart I could hide not,
> For I hold myself bound in her bondage.
> O gay in her necklet, and gainer
> In the game that wins hearts on her chessboard, -
> When she looked at me long from the doorway
> Where the likeness of Hagbard is carved."

134

Then the girls went into the hall, and sat down. He heard what they said about his looks, - the maid, that he was black and ugly, and Steingerd, that he was handsome and everyway as best could be, - "There is only one blemish," said she, "his hair is tufted on his forehead:" - and he said:

"One flaw in my features she noted
- With the flame of the wave she was gleaming
All white in the wane of the twilight -
And that one was no hideous blemish.
So highborn, so haughty a lady
- I should have such a dame to befriend me:
But she trows me uncouth for a trifle,
For a tuft in the hair on my brow!"

Said the maid, "Black are his eyes, sister, and that becomes him not." Cormac heard her, and said in verse:

"Yes, black are the eyes that I bring ye,
O brave in your jewels, and dainty.
But a draggle-tail, dirty-foot slattern
Would dub me ill-favoured and sallow.
Nay, many a maiden has loved me,
Thou may of the glittering armlet:
For I've tricks of the tongue to beguile them
And turn them from handsomer lads."

At this house they spent the night. In the morning when Cormac rose up, he went to a trough and washed himself; then he went into the ladies' bower and saw nobody there, but heard folk talking in the inner room, and he turned and entered. There was Steingerd, and women with her.

Said the maid to Steingerd, "There comes thy bonny man, Steingerd."

"Well, and a fine-looking lad he is," said she.

Now she was combing her hair, and Cormac asked her, "Wilt thou give me leave?"

She reached out her comb for him to handle it. She had the finest hair of any woman. Said the maid, "Ye would give a deal for a wife with hair like Steingerd's, or such eyes!"

He answered:

"One eye of the far of the ale-horn
Looking out of a form so bewitching,
Would a bridegroom count money to buy it
He must bring for it ransom three hundred.
The curls that she combs of a morning,
White-clothed in fair linen and spotless,
They enhance the bright hoard of her value, -
Five hundred might barely redeem them!"

135

Said the maid, "It's give and take with the two of ye! But thou'lt put a big price upon the whole of her!" He answered:

> "The tree of my treasure and longing,
> It would take this whole Iceland to win her:
> She is dearer than far-away Denmark,
> And the doughty domain of the Hun-folk.
> With the gold she is combing, I count her
> More costly than England could ransom:
> So witty, so wealthy, my lady
> Is worth them, - and Ireland beside!"

Then Tosti came in, and called Cormac out to some work or other; but he said:

> "Take m swift-footed steel for thy tiding,
> Ay, and stint not the lash to him, Tosti:
> On the desolate downs ye may wander
> And drive him along till he weary.
> I care not o'er mountain and moorland
> The murrey-brown weathers to follow, -
> Far liefer, I'd linger the morning
> In long, cosy chatter with Steingerd."

Tosti said he would find it a merrier game, and went off; so Cormac sat down to chess, and right gay he was. Steingerd said he talked better than folk told of; and he sat there all the day; and then he made this song:

> " 'Tis the dart that adorneth her tresses,
> The deep, dewy grass of her forehead.
> So kind to my keeping she gave it,
> That good comb I shall ever remember!
> A stranger was I when I sought her
> - Sweet stem with the dragon's hoard shining -"
> With gold like the sea-dazzle gleaming -
> The girl I shall never forget."

Tosti came off the fell and they fared home. After that Cormac used to go to Gnupsdal often to see Steingerd: and he asked his mother to make him good clothes, so that Steingerd might like him the most that could be. Dalla said there was a mighty great difference betwixt them, and it was far from certain to end happily if Thorkel at Tunga got to know.

CHAPTER 4
How Cormac Liked Black-Puddings

Well Thorkel soon heard what was going forward, and thought it would turn out to his own shame and his daughter's if Cormac would not pledge himself to take her or leave her. So he sent for Steingerd, and she went home.

Thorkel had a man called Narfi, a noisy, foolish fellow, boastful, and yet of little account. Said he to Thorkel, "If Cormac's coming likes thee not, I can soon settle it."

"Very well," says Thorkel.

Now, in the autumn, Narfi's work it was to slaughter the sheep. Once, when Cormac came to Tunga, he saw Steingerd in the kitchen. Narfi stood by the kettle, and when they had finished the boiling, he took up a black-pudding and thrust it under Cormac's nose, crying:

> "Cormac, how would ye relish one?
> Kettle-worms I call them."

To which he answered:

> "Black-puddings boiled, quoth Ogmund's son,
> Are a dainty, - fair befall them!"

And in the evening when Cormac made ready to go home he saw Narfi, and bethought him of those churlish words. "I think, Narfi," said he, "I am more like to knock thee down, than thou to rule my coming and going." And with that struck him an axe- hammer-blow, saying:

> "Why foul with thy clowning and folly,
> The food that is dressed for thy betters?
> Thou blundering archer, what ails thee
> To be aiming thy insults at me?"

And he made another song about:

> "He asked me, the clavering cowherd
> If I cared for - what was it he called them? -
> The worms of the kettle. I warrant
> He'll be wiping his eyes by the hearth-stone.
> I deem that yon knave of the dunghill
> Who dabbles the muck on the meadow
> - Yon rook in his mud-spattered raiment -
> Got a rap for his noise - like a dog."

CHAPTER 5
They Waylay Cormac: And The Witch Curses Him

There was a woman named Thorveig, and she knew a deal too much. She lived at Steins-stadir (Stonestead) in Midfiord, and had two sons; the elder was Odd, and the younger Gudmund. They were great braggarts both of them.

This Odd often came to see Thorkel at Tunga, and used to sit and talk with Steingerd. Thorkel made a great show of friendship with the brothers, and egged them on to waylay Cormac. Odd said it was no more than he could do.

So one day when Cormac came to Tunga, Steingerd was in the parlour and sat on the dais. Thorveig's sons sat in the room, ready to fall upon him when he came in; and Thorkel had put a drawn sword on one side of the door, and on the other side Narfi had put a scythe in its shaft. When Cormac came to the hall-door the scythe fell down and met the sword, and broke a great notch in it. Out came Thorkel and began to upbraid Cormac for a rascal, and got fairly wild with his talk: then flung into the parlour and bade Steingerd out of it. Forth they went by another door, and he locked her into an outhouse, saying that Cormac and she would never meet again.

Cormac went in: and he came quicker than folk thought for, and they were taken aback. He looked about, and no Steingerd: but he saw the brothers whetting their weapons: so he turned on his heel and went, saying:

> "The weapon that mows in the meadow
> It met with the gay painted buckler,
> When I came to encounter a goddess
> Who carries the beaker of wine.
> Beware! for I warn you of evil
> When warriors threaten me mischief.
> It shall not be for nought that I pour ye
> The newly mixed mead of the gods."

And when he could find Steingerd nowhere, he made this song:

> "She has gone, with the glitter of ocean
> Agleam on her wrist and her bosom,
> And my heart follows hard on her footsteps,
> For the hall is in darkness without her.
> I have gazed, but my glances can pierce not
> The gloom of the desolate dwelling;
> And fierce is my longing to find her,
> The fair one who only can heal me."

After a while he came to the outhouse where Steingerd was, and burst it open and had talk with her.

"This is madness," cried she, "to come talking with me; for Thorveig's sons are meant to have thy head."

But he answered:

> "There wait they within that would snare me;
> There whet they their swords for my slaying.
> My bane they shall be not, the cowards,
> The brood of the churl and the carline.
> Let the twain of them find me and fight me
> In the field, without shelter to shield them,
> And ewes of the sheep should be surer
> To shorten the days of the wolf."

So he sat there all day. By that time Thorkel saw that the plan he had made was come to nothing; and he bade the sons of Thorveig waylay Cormac in a dale near his garth. "Narfi shall go with ye two," said he; "but I will stay at home, and bring you help if need be."

In the evening Cormac set out, and when he came to the dale, he saw three men, and said in verse:

> "There sit they in hiding to stay me
> From the sight of my queen of the jewels:
> But rude will their task be to reave me
> From the roof of my bounteous lady.
> The fainer the hatred they harbour
> For him that is free of her doorway,
> The fainer my love and my longing
> For the lass that is sweeter than samphire."

Then leaped up Thorveig's sons, and fought Cormac for a time: Narfi the while skulked and dodged behind them. Thorkel saw from his house that they were getting but slowly forward, and he took his weapons. In that nick of time Steingerd came out and saw what her father meant. She laid hold on his hands, and he got no nearer to help the brothers. In the end Odd fell, and Gudmund was so wounded that he died afterwards. Thorkel saw to them, and Cormac went home.

A little after this Cormac went to Thorveig and said he would have her no longer live there at the firth. "Thou shalt flit and go thy way at such a time," said he, "and I will give no blood- money for thy sons."

Thorveig answered, "It is like enough ye can hunt me out of the countryside, and leave my sons unatoned. But this way I'll reward thee. Never shalt thou have Steingerd."

Said Cormac, "That's not for thee to make or to mar, thou wicked old hag!"

CHAPTER 6
Cormac Wins His Bride and Loses Her

After this, Cormac went to see Steingerd the same as ever: and once when they talked over these doings she said no ill of them: whereupon he made this song:

> "There sat they in hiding to slay me
> From the sight of my bride and my darling:
> But weak were the feet of my foemen
> When we fought on the island of weapons.
> And the rush of the mightiest rivers
> Shall race from the shore to the mountains
> Or ever I leave thee, my lady,
> And the love that I feast on to-day!"

"Say no such big words about it," answered she; "Many a thing may stand in the road."

Upon which he said:

> "O sweet in the sheen of thy raiment,
> The sight of thy beauty is gladdening!
> What man that goes marching to battle,
> What mate wouldst thou choose to be thine?"

And she answered:

> "O giver of gold, O ring-breaker,
> If the gods and the high fates befriend me,
> I'd pledge me to Frodi's blithe brother
> And bind him that he should be mine."

Then she told him to make friends with her father and get her in marriage. So for her sake Cormac gave Thorkel good gifts. Afterwards many people had their say in the matter; but in the end it came to this, - that he asked for her, and she was pledged to him, and the wedding was fixed: and so all was quiet for a while.

Then they had words. There was some falling-out about settlements. It came to such a pass that after everything was ready, Cormac began to cool off. But the real reason was, that Thorveig had bewitched him so that they should never have one another.

Thorkel at Tunga had a grown-up son, called Thorkel and by-named Tooth-gnasher. He had been abroad some time, but this summer he came home and stayed with his father.

Cormac never came to the wedding at the time it was fixed, and the hour passed by. This the kinsfolk of Steingerd thought a slight, deeming that he had broken off the match; and they had much talk about it.

CHAPTER 7
How Steingerd Was Married To Somebody Else

Bersi lived in the land of Saurbae, a rich man and a good fellow: he was well to the fore, a fighter, and a champion at the holmgang. He had been married to Finna the Fair: but she was dead: Asmund was their son, young in years and early ripe. Helga was the sister of Bersi: she was unmarried, but a fine woman and a pushing one, and she kept house for Bersi after Finna died.

At the farm called Muli (the Mull) lived Thord Arndisarson: he was wedded to Thordis, sister of Bork the Stout. They had two sons who were both younger than Asmund the son of Bersi.

There was also a man with Vali. His farm was named Vali's stead, and it stood on the way to Hrutafiord.

Now Thorveig the spaewife went to see Holmgang Bersi and told him her trouble. She said that Cormac forbade her staying in Midfiord: so Bersi bought land for her west of the firth, and she lived there for a long time afterwards.

Once when Thorkel at Tunga and his son were talking about Cormac's breach of faith and deemed that it should be avenged, Narfi said, "I see a plan that will do. Let us go to the west- country with plenty of goods and gear, and come to Bersi in Saurbae. He is wifeless. Let us entangle him in the matter. He would be a great help to us."

That counsel they took. They journeyed to Saurbae, and Bersi welcomed them. In the evening they talked of nothing but weddings. Narfi up and said there was no match so good as Steingerd, - "And a deal of folk say, Bersi, that she would suit thee."

"I have heard tell," he answered, "that there will be a rift in the road, though the match is a good one."

"If it's Cormac men fear," cried Narfi, "there is no need; for he is clean out of the way."

When Bersi heard that, he opened the matter to Thorkel Toothgnasher, and asked for Steingerd. Thorkel made a good answer, and pledged his sister to him.

So they rode north, eighteen in all, for the wedding. There was a man named Vigi lived at Holm, a big man and strong of his hands, a warlock, and Bersi's kinsman. He went with them, and they thought he would be a good helper. Thord Arndisarson too went north with Bersi, and many others, all picked men.

When they came to Thorkel's, they set about the wedding at once, so that no news of it might get out through the countryside: but all this was sore against Steingerd's will.

Now Vigi the warlock knew every man's affairs who came to the steading or left it. He sat outmost in the chamber, and slept by the hall door.

Steingerd sent for Narfi, and when they met she said, - "I wish thee, kinsman, to tell Cormac the business they are about: I wish thee to take this message to him."

So he set out secretly; but when he was a gone a little way Vigi came after, and bade him creep home and hatch no plots. They went back together, and so the night passed.

Next morning Narfi started forth again; but before he had gone so far as on the evening, Vigi beset him, and drove him back without mercy.

When the wedding was ended they made ready for their journey. Steingerd took her gold and jewels, and they rode towards Hrutafiord, going rather slowly. When they were off, Narfi set out and came to Mel. Cormac was building a wall, and hammering it with a mallet. Narfi rode up, with his shield and sword, and carried on strangely, rolling his eyes about like a hunted beast. Some men were up on the wall with Cormac when he came, and his horse shied at them. Said Cormac, - "What news, Narfi? What folk were with you last night?"

"Small tidings, but we had guests enough," answered he.

"Who were the guests?"

"There was Holmgang Bersi, with seventeen more to sit at his wedding."

"Who was the bride?"

"Bersi wed Steingerd Thorkel's daughter," said Narfi. "When they were gone she sent me here to tell thee the news."

"Thou hast never a word but ill," said Cormac, and leapt upon him and struck at the shield: and as it slipped aside he was smitten on the breast and fell from his horse; and the horse ran away with the shield (hanging to it).

Cormac's brother Thorgils said this was too much. "It serves him right," cried Cormac. And when Narfi woke out of his swoon they got speech of him.

Thorgils asked, "What manner of men were at the wedding?"

Narfi told him.

"Did Steingerd know this before?"

"Not till the very evening they came," answered he; and then told of his dealings with Vigi, saying that Cormac would find it easier to whistle on Steingerd's tracks and go on a fool's errand than to fight Bersi. Then said Cormac:

> "Now see to thy safety henceforward,
> And stick to thy horse and thy buckler;
> Or this mallet of mine, I can tell thee,
> Will meet with thine ear of a surety.
> Now say no more stories of feasting,
> Though seven in a day thou couldst tell of,
> Or bumps thou shalt comb on thy brainpan,
> Thou that breakest the howes of the dead.

Thorgils asked about the settlements between Bersi and Steingerd. Her kinsmen, said Narfi, were now quit of all farther trouble about that business, however it might turn out; but her father and brother would be answerable for the wedding.

CHAPTER 8
How Cormac Chased Bersi And His Bride

Cormac took his horse and weapons and saddle-gear.

"What now, brother?" asked Thorgils.

He answered:

> "My bride, my betrothed has been stolen,
> And Bersi the raider has robbed me.
> I who offer the song-cup of Odin -

Who else? - should be riding beside her.
She loved me - no lord of them better:
I have lost her - for me she is weeping:
The dear, dainty darling that kissed me,
For day upon day of delight."

Said Thorgils, "A risky errand is this, for Bersi will get home before you catch him. And yet I will go with thee."

Cormac said he would away and bide for no man. He leapt on his horse forthwith, and galloped as hard as he could. Thorgils made haste to gather men, - they were eighteen in all, - and came up with Cormac on the hause that leads to Hrutafiord, for he had foundered his horse. So they turned to Thorveig the spaewife's farmsteading, and found that Bersi was gone aboard her boat.

She had said to Bersi, "I wish thee to take a little gift from me, and good luck follow it."

This was a target bound with iron; and she said she reckoned Bersi would hardly be hurt if he carried it to shield him, - "but it is little worth beside this steading thou hast given me." He thanked her for the gift, and so they parted. Then she got men to scuttle all the boats on the shore, because she knew beforehand that Cormac and his folk were coming.

When they came and asked her for a boat, she said she would do them no kindness without payment; - "Here is a rotten boat in the boathouse which I would lend for half a mark."

Thorgils said it would be in reason if she asked two ounces of silver. Such matters, said Cormac, should not stand in the way; but Thorgils said he would sooner ride all round the water-head. Nevertheless Cormac had his will, and they started in the boat; but they had scarcely put off from shore when it filled, and they had hard work to get back to the same spot.

"Thou shouldst pay dearly for this, thou wicked old hag," said Cormac, "and never be paid at all."

That was no mighty trick to play them, she said; and so Thorgils paid her the silver; about which Cormac made this song:

"I'm a tree that is tricked out in war-gear,
She, the trim rosy elf of the shuttle:
And I break into singing about her
Like the bat at the well, never ceasing.
With the dew-drops of Draupnir the golden
Full dearly folk buy them their blessings;
Then lay down three ounces and leave them
For the leaky old boat that we borrowed."

Bersi got hastily to horse, and rode homewards; and when Cormac saw that he must be left behind, he made this song:

"I tell you, the goddess who glitters
With gold on the perch of the falcon,

143

The bride that I trusted, by beauty,
From the bield of my hand has been taken.
On the boat she makes glad in its gliding
She is gone from me, reft from me, ravished!
O shame, that we linger to save her,
Too sweet for the prey of the raven!

They took their horses and rode round the head of the firth. They met Vali and asked about Bersi; he said that Bersi had come to Muli and gathered men to him, - "A many men."

"Then we are too late," said Cormac, "if they have got men together."

Thorgils begged Cormac to let them turn back, saying there was little honour to be got; but Cormac said he must see Steingerd.

So Vali went with them and they came to Muli where Bersi was and many men with him. They spoke together. Cormac said that Bersi had betrayed him in carrying off Steingerd, "But now we would take the lady with us, and make him amends for his honour."

To this said Thord Arndisarson, "We will offer terms to Cormac, but the lady is in Bersi's hands."

"There is no hope that Steingerd will go with you," said Bersi; "but I offer my sister to Cormac in marriage, and I reckon he will be well wedded if take Helga."

"This is a good offer," said Thorgils; "let us think of it, brother."

But Cormac started back like a restive horse.

CHAPTER 9
Of Another Witch, And Two Magic Swords

There was a woman called Thordis - and a shrew she was - who lived at Spakonufell (Spaequean's-fell), in Skagastrand. She, having foresight of Cormac's goings, came that very day to Muli, and answered this matter on his behalf, saying, "Never give him yon false woman. She is a fool, and not fit for any pretty man. Woe will his mother be at such a fate for her lad!"

"Aroint thee, foul witch!" cried Thord. They should see, said he, that Helga would turn out fine. But Cormac answered, "Said it may be, for sooth it may be: I will never think of her."

"Woe to us, then," said Thorgils, "for listening to the words of yon fiend, and slighting this offer!"

Then spoke Cormac, "I bid thee, Bersi, to the holmgang within half a month, at Leidholm, in Middal."

Bersi said he would come, but Cormac should be the worse for his choice.

After this Cormac went about the steading to look for Steingerd. When he found her he said she had betrayed him in marrying another man.

"It was thou that made the first breach, Cormac," said she, "for this was none of my doing."

Then said he in verse:

> "Thou sayest my faith has been forfeit,
> O fair in thy glittering raiment;
> But I wearied my steed and outwore it,
> And for what but the love that bare thee?
> O fainer by far was I, lady,
> To founder my horse in the hunting -
> Nay, I spared not the jade when I spurred it -
> Than to see thee the bride of my foe."

After this Cormac and his men went home. When he told his mother how things had gone, "Little good," she said, "will thy luck do us. Ye have slighted a fine offer, and you have no chance against Bersi, for he is a great fighter and he has good weapons."

Now, Bersi owned the sword they call Whitting; a sharp sword it was, with a life-stone to it; and that sword he had carried in many a fray.

"Whether wilt thou have weapons to meet Whitting?" she asked. Cormac said he would have an axe both great and keen.

Dalla said he should see Skeggi of Midfiord and ask for the loan of his sword, Skofnung. So Cormac went to Reykir and told Skeggi how matters stood, asking him to lend Skofnung. Skeggi said he had no mind to lend it. Skofnung and Cormac, said he, would never agree: "It is cold and slow, and thou art hot and hasty."

Cormac rode away and liked it ill. He came home to Mel and told his mother that Skeggi would not lend the sword. Now Skeggi had the oversight of Dalla's affairs, and they were great friends; so she said, "He will lend the sword, though not all at once."

That was not what he wanted, answered Cormac, - "If he withhold it not from thee, while he does withhold it from me." Upon which she answered that he was a thwart lad.

A few days afterwards Dalla told him to go to Reykir. "He will lend thee the sword now," said she. So he sought Skeggi and asked for Skofnung.

"Hard wilt thou find it to handle," said Skeggi. "There is a pouch to it, and that thou shalt let be. Sun must not shine on the pommel of the hilt. Thou shalt not wear it until fighting is forward, and when ye come to the field, sit all alone and then draw it. Hold the edge toward thee, and blow on it. Then will a little worm creep from under the hilt. Then slope thou the sword over, and make it easy for that worm to creep back beneath the hilt."

"Here's a tale of tricks, thou warlock!" cried Cormac

"Nevertheless," answered Skeggi, "it will stand thee in good stead to know them."

So Cormac rode home and told his mother, saying that her will was of great avail with Skeggi. He showed the sword, and tried to draw it, but it would not leave the sheath.

"Thou are over wilful, my son," said she.

Then he set his feet against the hilts, and pulled until he tore the pouch off, at which Skofnung creaked and groaned, but never came out of the scabbard.

Well, the time wore on, and the day came. He rode away with fifteen men; Bersi also rode to the holm with as many. Cormac came there first, and told Thorgils that he would sit apart by himself. So he sat down and ungirt the sword.

Now, he never heeded whether the sun shone upon the hilt, for he had girt the sword on him outside his clothes. And when he tried to draw it he could not, until he set his feet upon the hilts. Then the little worm came, and was not rightly done by; and so the sword came groaning and creaking out of the scabbard, and the good luck of it was gone.

CHAPTER 10
The Fight On Leidarholm

After that Cormac went to his men. Bersi and his party had come by that time, and many more to see the fight.

Cormac took up Bersi's target and cut at it, and sparks flew out.

Then a hide was taken and spread for them to stand on. Bersi spoke and said, "Thou, Cormac, hast challenged me to the holmgang; instead of that, I offer thee to fight in simple sword- play. Thou art a young man and little tried; the holmgang needs craft and cunning, but sword-play, man to man, is an easy game."

Cormac answered, "I should fight no better even so. I will run the risk, and stand on equal footing with thee, every way."

"As thou wilt," said Bersi.

It was the law of the holmgang that the hide should be five ells long, with loops at its corners. Into these should be driven certain pins with heads to them, called tjosnur. He who made it ready should go to the pins in such a manner that he could see sky between his legs, holding the lobes of his ears and speaking the forewords used in the rite called "The Sacrifice of the tjosnur." Three squares should be marked round the hide, each one foot broad. At the outermost corners of the squares should be four poles, called hazels; when this is done, it is a hazelled field. Each man should have three shields, and when they were cut up he must get upon the hide if he had given way from it before, and guard himself with his weapons alone thereafter. He who had been challenged should strike the first stroke. If one was wounded so that blood fell upon the hide, he should fight no longer. If either set one foot outside the hazel poles "he went on his heel," they said; but he "ran" if both feet were outside. His own man was to hold the shield before each of the fighters. The one who was wounded should pay three marks of silver to be set free.

So the hide was taken and spread under their feet. Thorgils held his brother's shield, and Thord Arndisarson that of Bersi. Bersi struck the first blow, and cleft Cormac's shield; Cormac struck at Bersi to the like peril. Each of them cut up and spoilt three shields of the other's. Then it was Cormac's turn. He struck at Bersi, who parried with Whitting. Skofnung cut the point off Whitting in front of the ridge. The sword-point flew upon Cormac's hand, and he was wounded in the thumb. The joint was cleft, and blood dropped upon the hide. Thereupon folk went between them and stayed the fight.

Then said Cormac, "This is a mean victory that Bersi has gained; it is only from my bad luck; and yet we must part."

He flung down his sword, and it met Bersi's target. A shard was broken out of Skofnung, and fire flew out of Thorveig's gift.

Bersi asked the money for release, Cormac said it would be paid; and so they parted.

CHAPTER 11
The Songs That Were Made About The Fight

Steinar was the name of a man who was the son of Onund the Seer, and brother of Dalla, Cormac's mother. He was an unpeaceful man, and lived at Ellidi.

Thither rode Cormac from the holme, to see his kinsman, and told him of the fight, at which he was but ill pleased. Cormac said he meant to leave the country, - "And I want thee to take the money to Bersi."

"Thou art no bold man," said Steinar, "but the money shall be paid if need be."

Cormac was there some nights; his hand swelled much, for it was not dressed.

After that meeting, Holmgang Bersi went to see his brother. Folk asked how the holmgang had gone, and when he told them they said that two bold men had struck small blows, and he had gained the victory only through Cormac's mishap. When Bersi met Steingerd, and she asked how it went, he made this verse:

> "They call him, and truly they tell it,
> A tree of the helmet right noble:
> But the master of manhood must bring me
> Three marks for his ransom and rescue.
> Though stout in the storm of the bucklers
> In the stress of the Valkyrie's tempest
> He will bid me no more to the battle,
> For the best of the struggle was ours."

Steinar and Cormac rode from Ellidi and passed through Saurbae. They saw men riding towards them, and yonder came Bersi. He greeted Cormac and asked how the wound was getting on. Cormac said it needed little to be healed.

"Wilt thou let me heal thee?" said Bersi; "though from me thou didst get it: and then it will be soon over."

Cormac said nay, for he meant to be his lifelong foe. Then answered Bersi:

> "Thou wilt mind thee for many a season
> How we met in the high voice of Hilda.
> Right fain I go forth to the spear-mote
> Being fitted for every encounter.
> There Cormac's gay shield from his clutches
> I clave with the bane of the bucklers,
> For he scorned in the battle to seek me
> If we set not the lists of the holmgang."

Thus they parted; and then Cormac went home to Mel and saw his mother. She healed his hand; it had become ugly and healed badly. The notch in Skofnung they whetted, but the more they whetted the bigger it was. So he went to Reykir, and flung Skofnung at Skeggi's feet, with this verse:

> "I bring thee, thus broken and edgeless,
> The blade that thou gavest me, Skeggi!
> I warrant thy weapon could bite not:
> I won not the fight by its witchcraft.
> No gain of its virtue nor glory
> I got in the strife of the weapons,
> When we met for to mingle the sword-storm
> For the maiden my singing adorns."

Said Skeggi, "It went as I warned thee." Cormac flung forth and went home to Mel: and when he met with Dalla he made this song:-

> "To the field went I forth, O my mother
> The flame of the armlet who guardest, -
> To dare the cave-dweller, my foeman
> And I deemed I should smite him in battle.
> But the brand that is bruited in story
> It brake in my hand as I held it;
> And this that should thrust men to slaughter
> Is thwarted and let of its might.
>
> For I borrowed to bear in the fighting
> No blunt-edged weapon of Skeggi:
> There is strength in the serpent that quivers
> By the side of the land of the girdle.
> But vain was the virtue of Skofnung
> When he vanquished the sharpness of Whitting;
> And a shard have I shorn, to my sorrow,
> From the shearer of ringleted mail.

Yon tusker, my foe, wrought me trouble
When targe upon targe I had carven:
For the thin wand of slaughter was shattered
And it sundered the ground of my handgrip.
Loud bellowed the bear of the sea-king
When he brake from his lair in the scabbard,
At the hest of the singer, who seeketh
The sweet hidden draught of the gods.

Afar must I fare, O my mother,
And a fate points the pathway before me,
For that white-wreathen tree may woo not
- Two wearisome morrows her outcast.
And it slays me, at home to be sitting,
So set is my heart on its goddess,
As a lawn with fair linen made lovely
- I can linger no third morrow's morn."

After that, Cormac went one day to Reykir and talked with Skeggi, who said the holmgang had been brought to scorn. Then answered Cormac:

"Forget it, O Frey of the helmet,
- Lo, I frame thee a song in atonement -
That the bringer of blood, even Skofnung,
I bare thee so strangely belated.
For by stirrers of storm was I wounded;
They smote me where perches the falcon:
But the blade that I borrowed, O Skeggi,
Was borne in the clashing of edges.

I had deemed, O thou Grey of fighting,
Of the fierce song of Odin, - my neighbour,
I had deemed that a brand meet for bloodshed
I bare to the crossways of slaughter.
Nay, - thy glaive, it would gape not nor ravin
Against him, the rover who robbed me:
And on her, as the surge on the shingle,
My soul beats and breaks evermore."

CHAPTER 12
Bersi's Bad Luck At The Thor's-Ness Thing

In the winter, sports were held at Saurbae. Bersi's lad, Asmund, was there, and likewise the sons of Thord; but they were younger than he, and nothing like so sturdy. When they wrestled Asmund took no heed to stint his strength, and the sons of Thord often came home blue and bleeding. Their mother Thordis was ill pleased, and asked her husband would he give Bersi a hint to make it up on behalf of his son. Nay, Thord answered, he was loath to do that.

"Then I'll find my brother Bork," said she, "and it will be just as bad in the end."

Thord bade her do no such thing. "I would rather talk it over with him," said he; and so, at her wish, he met Bersi, and hinted that some amends were owing.

Said Bersi, "Thou art far too greedy of getting, nowadays. This kind of thing will end in losing thee thy good name. Thou wilt never want while anything is to be got here."

Thord went home, and there was a coolness between them while that winter lasted.

Spring slipped by, until it was time for the meeting at Thor's-ness. By then, Bersi thought he saw through this claim of Thord's, and found Thordis at the bottom of it. For all that, he made ready to go to the Thing. By old use and wont these two neighbours should have gone riding together; so Bersi set out and came to Muli, but when he got there Thord was gone.

"Well," said he, "Thord has broken old use and wont in awaiting me no longer."

"If breach there be," answered Thordis, "it is thy doing. This is nothing to what we owe thee, and I doubt there will be more to follow."

They had words. Bersi said that harm would come of her evil counsel; and so they parted.

When he left the house he said to his men, "Let us turn aside to the shore and take a boat; it is a long way to ride round the waterhead." So they took a boat - it was one of Thord's - and went their way.

They came to the meeting when most other folks were already there, and went to the tent of Olaf Peacock of Hjardarholt (Herdholt), for he was Bersi's chief. It was crowded inside, and Bersi found no seat. He used to sit next Thord, but that place was filled. In it there sat a big and strong-looking man, with a bear-skin coat, and a hood that shaded his face. Bersi stood a while before him, but the seat was not given up. He asked the man for his name, and was told he might call him Bruin, or he might call him Hoodie - which-ever he liked; whereupon he said in verse:

> "Who sits in the seat of the warriors,
> With the skin of the bear wrapped around him,
> So wild in his look? - Ye have welcomed
> A wolf to your table, good kinsfolk!
> Ah, now may I know him, I reckon!
> Doth he name himself Bruin, or Hoodie? -
> We shall meet once again in the morning,
> And maybe he'll prove to be - Steinar."

"And it's no use for thee to hide thy name, thou in the bearskin," said he.

"No more it is," he answered. "Steinar I am, and I have brought money to pay thee for Cormac, if so be it is needed. But first I bid thee to fight. It will have to be seen whether thou get the two marks of silver, or whether thou lose them both."

Upon which quoth Bersi:

> "They that waken the storm of the spear-points -
> For slaughter and strife they are famous -
> To the island they bid me for battle,
> Nor bitter I think it nor woeful;
> For long in that craft am I learned
> To loosen the Valkyrie's tempest
> In the lists, and I fear not to fight them -
> Unflinching in battle am I.

"Well I wot, though," said he, "that ye and your gang mean to make away with me. But I would let you know that I too have something to say about it - something that will set down your swagger, maybe."

"It is not thy death we are seeking," answered Steinar; "all we want is to teach thee thy true place."

Bersi agreed to fight him, and then went out to a tent apart and took up his abode there.

Now one day the word went round for bathing in the sea. Said Steinar to Bersi, "Wilt try a race with me, Bersi?"

"I have given over swimming," said he, "and yet I'll try."

Bersi's manner of swimming was to breast the waves and strike out with all his might. In so doing he showed a charm he wore round his neck. Steinar swam at him and tore off the lucky-stone with the bag it was in, and threw them both into the water, saying in verse:

> "Long I've lived,
> And I've let the gods guide me;
> Brown hose I never wore
> To bring the luck beside me.
> I've never knit
> All to keep me thriving
> Round my neck a bag of worts,
> - And lo! I'm living!"

Upon that they struck out to land.

But this turn that Steinar played was Thord's trick to make Bersi lose his luck in the fight. And Thord went along the shore at low water and found the luck-stone, and hid it away.

Now Steinar had a sword that was called after Skrymir the giant: it was never fouled, and no mishap followed it. On the day fixed, Thord and Steinar went out of the tent, and Cormac also came to the meeting to hold the shield of Steinar. Olaf Peacock got men to help Bersi at the fight, for Thord had been used to hold his shield, but this time failed him. So Bersi went to the trysting-place with

151

a shield-bearer who is not named in the story, and with the round target that once had belonged to Thorveig.

Each man was allowed three shields. Bersi cut up two, and then Cormac took the third. Bersi hacked away, but Whitting his sword stuck fast in the iron border of Steinar's shield. Cormac whirled it up just when Steinar was striking out. He struck the shield-edge, and the sword glanced off, slit Bersi's buttock, sliced his thigh down to the knee-joint, and stuck in the bone. And so Bersi fell.

"There!" cried Steinar, "Cormac's fine is paid."

But Bersi leapt up, slashed at him, and clove his shield. The sword-point was at Steinar's breast when Thord rushed forth and dragged him away, out of reach.

"There!" cried Thord to Bersi, "I have paid thee for the mauling of my sons."

So Bersi was carried to the tent, and his wound was dressed. After a while, Thord came in; and when Bersi saw him he said:

> "When the wolf of the war-god was howling
> Erstwhile in the north, thou didst aid me:
> When it gaped in my hand, and it girded
> At the Valkyries' gate for to enter.
> But now wilt thou never, O warrior,
> At need in the storm-cloud of Odin
> Give me help in the tempest of targes
> - Untrusty, unfaithful art thou.

> "For when I was a stripling I showed me
> To the stems of the lightning of battle
> Right meet for the mist of the war-maids;
> - Ah me! that was said long ago.
> But now, and I may not deny it
> My neighbours in earth must entomb me,
> At the spot I have sought for grave-mound
> Where Saurbae lies level and green."

Said Thord, "I have no wish for thy death; but I own it is no sorrow to see thee down for once."

To which Bersi answered in song:

> "The friend that I trusted has failed me
> In the fight, and my hope is departed:
> I speak what I know of; and note it,
> Ye nobles, - I tell ye no leasing.
> Lo, the raven is ready for carnage,
> But rare are the friends who should succour.
> Yet still let them scorn me and threaten,
> I shrink not, I am not dismayed."

After this, Bersi was taken home to Saurbae, and lay long in his wounds.

But when he was carried into the tent, at that very moment Steinar spoke thus to Cormac:

> "Of the reapers in harvest of Hilda
> - Thou hast heard of it - four men and eight men
> With the edges of Skrymir to aid me
> I have urged to their flight from the battle.
> Now the singer, the steward of Odin,
> Hath smitten at last even Bersi
> With the flame of the weapon that feedeth
> The flocks of the carrion crows."

"I would have thee keep Skrymir now for thy own, Cormac," said he, "because I mean this fight to be my last."

After that, they parted in friendly wise: Steinar went home, and Cormac fared to Mel.

CHAPTER 13
Steingerd Leaves Bersi

Next it is told of Bersi. His wound healed but slowly. Once on a time a many folk were met to talk about that meeting and what came of it, and Bersi made this song:

> "Thou didst leave me forlorn to the sword-stroke,
> Strong lord of the field of the serpent!
> And needy and fallen ye find me,
> Since my foeman ye shielded from danger.
> Thus cunning and counsel are victors,
> When the craft of the spear-shaft avails not;
> But this, as I think, is the ending,
> O Thord, of our friendship for ever!"

A while later Thord came to his bedside and brought back the luck-stone; and with it he healed Bersi, and they took to their friendship again and held it unbroken ever after.

Because of these happenings, Steingerd fell into loathing of Bersi and made up her mind to part with him; and when she had got everything ready for going away she went to him and said: "First ye were called Eygla's-Bersi, and then Holmgang-Bersi, but now your right name will be Breech-Bersi!" and spoke her divorce from him.

She went north to her kinsfolk, and meeting with her brother Thorkel she bade him seek her goods again from Bersi - her pin- money and her dowry, saying that she would not own him now that he was maimed. Thorkel Toothgnasher never blamed her for that, and agreed to undertake her errand; but the winter slipped by and his going was put off.

CHAPTER 14
The Bane Of Thorkel Toothgnasher

Afterwards, in the spring, Thorkel Toothgnasher set out to find Bersi and to seek Steingerd's goods again. Bersi said that his burden was heavy enough to bear, even though both together underwent the weight of it. "And I shall not pay the money!" said he.

Said Thorkel, "I bid thee to the holmgang at Orrestholm beside Tjaldanes (Tentness)."

"That ye will think hardly worth while," said Bersi, "such a champion as you are; and yet I undertake for to come."

So they came to the holme and fell to the holmgang. Thord carried the shield before Bersi, and Vali was Thorkel's shield-bearer. When two shields had been hacked to splinters, Bersi bade Thorkel take the third; but he would not. Bersi still had a shield, and a sword that was long and sharp.

Said Thorkel, "The sword ye have, Bersi, is longer than lawful."

"That shall not be," cried Bersi; and took up his other sword, Whitting, two-handed, and smote Thorkel his deathblow. Then sang he:-

> "I have smitten Toothgnasher and slain him,
> And I smile at the pride of his boasting.
> One more to my thirty I muster,
> And, men! say ye this of the battle:
> In the world not a lustier liveth
> Among lords of the steed of the oar-bench;
> Though by eld of my strength am I stinted
> To stain the black wound-bird with blood."

After these things Vali bade Bersi to the holmgang, but he answered in this song:

> "They that waken the war of the mail-coats,
> For warfare and manslaying famous,
> To the lists they have bid me to battle,
> Nor bitter I think it not woeful.
> It is sport for yon swordsmen who goad me
> To strive in the Valkyries' tempest
> On the holme; but I fear not to fight them -
> Unflinching in battle am I!"

The were even about to begin fighting, when Thord came and spoke to them saying: "Woeful waste of life I call it, if brave men shall be smitten down for the sake of any such matters. I am ready to make it up between ye two."

To this they agreed, and he said: "Vali, this methinks is the most likely way of bringing you together. Let Bersi take thy sister Thordis to wife. It is a match that may well be to thy worship."

Bersi agreed to this, and it was settled that the land of Brekka should go along with her as a dowry; and so this troth was plighted between them. Bersi afterwards had a strong stone wall built around his homestead, and sat there for many winters in peace.

CHAPTER 15
The Rescue Of Steinvor Slim-ankles

There was a man named Thorarin Alfsson, who lived in the north at Thambardal; that is a dale which goes up from the fiord called Bitra. He was a big man and mighty, and he was by-named Thorarin the Strong. He had spent much of his time in seafaring (as a chapman) and so lucky was he that he always made the harbour he aimed at.

He had three sons; one was named Alf, the next Loft, and the third Skofti. Thorarin was a most overbearing man, and his sons took after him. They were rough, noisy fellows.

Not far away, at Tunga (Tongue) in Bitra, lived a man called Odd. His daughter was named Steinvor, a pretty girl and well set up; her by-name was Slim-ankles. Living with Odd were many fisherman; among them, staying there for the fishing-season, was one Glum, an ill-tempered carle and bad to deal with.

Now once upon a time these two, Odd and Glum, were in talk together which were the greatest men in the countryside. Glum reckoned Thorarin to be foremost, but Odd said Holmgang Bersi was better than he in every way.

"How can ye make that out?" asked Glum.

"Is there any likeness whatever," said Odd, "between the bravery of Bersi and the knavery of Thorarin?"

So they talked about this until they fell out, and laid a wager upon it.

Then Glum wend and told Thorarin. He grew very angry and made many a threat against Odd. And in a while he went and carried off Steinvor from Tunga, all to spite her father; and he gave out that if Odd said anything against it, the worse for him: and so took her home to Thambardal.

Things went on so for a while, and then Odd went to see Holmgang Bersi, and told him what had happened. He asked him for help to get Steinvor back and to wreak vengeance for that shame. Bersi answered that such words had been better unsaid, and bade him go home and take no share in the business. "But yet," added he, "I promise that I will see to it."

No sooner was Odd gone than Bersi made ready to go from home. He rode fully armed, with Whitting at his belt, and three spears; he came to Thambardal

155

when the day was far spent and the women were coming out of the bower. Steinvor saw him and turning to meet him told of her unhappiness.

"Make ready to go with me," said he; and that she did.

He would not go to Thambardal for nothing, he said; and so he turned to the door where men were sitting by long fires. He knocked at the door, and out there came a man - his name was Thorleif. But Thorarin knew Bersi's voice, and rushed forth with a great carving-knife and laid on to him. Bersi was aware of it, and drew Whitting, and struck him his death-blow.

Then he leapt on horseback and set Steinvor on his knee and took his spears which she had kept for him. He rode some way into the wood, where in a hidden spot he left his horse and Steinvor, bidding her await him. Then he went to a narrow gap through which the high-road ran, and there made ready to stand against his foes.

In Thambardal there was anything but peace. Thorleif ran to tell the sons of Thorarin that he lay dead in the doorway. They asked who had done the deed. He told them. Then they went after Bersi and steered the shortest way to the gap, meaning to get there first; but by that time he was already first at the gap.

When they came near him, Bersi hurled a spear at Alf, and it went right through him. Then Loft cast at Bersi, but he caught the spear on his target and it dropped off. Then Bersi threw at Loft and killed him, and so he did by Skofti.

When all was over, the house-carles of the brothers came up. Thorleif turned back to meet them, and they all went home together.

After that Bersi went to find Steinvor, and mounted his horse. He came home before men were out of bed. They asked him about his journey and he told them. When Odd met him he asked about the fight and how it had passed, and Bersi answered in this verse:

"There was one fed the wolves has encountered
His weird in the dale of the Bowstring -
Thorarin the Strong, 'neath the slayer
Lay slain by the might of my weapon.
And loss of their lives men abided
When Loft fell, and Alf fell, and Skofti.
They were four, yonder kinsmen, and fated -
They were fey - and I met them, alone!"

After that Odd went home, but Steinvor was with Bersi, though it misliked Thordis, his wife. By this time his stone wall was some-what broken down, but he had it built up again; and it is said that no blood-money was ever paid for Thorarin and his sons. So the time went on.

CHAPTER 16
How Vali Fell Before An Old Man And A Boy

Once on a day when Thordis and Bersi were talking together, said he, "I have been thinking I might ask Olaf Peacock for a child of his to foster."

"Nay," said she, "I think little of that. It seems to me a great trouble, and I doubt if folk will reckon more of us for it."

"It means that I should have a sure friend," answered he. "I have many foes, and I am growing heavy with age."

So he went to see Olaf, and asked for a child to foster. Olaf took it with thanks, and Bersi carried Halldor home with him and got Steinvor to be nurse. This too misliked Thordis, and she laid hands on every penny she could get (for fear it should go to Steinvor and the foster-child).

At last Bersi took to ageing much. There was one time when men riding to the Thing stayed at his house. He sat all by himself, and his food was brought him before the rest were served. He had porridge while other folk had cheese and curds. Then he made this verse:

> "To batten the black-feathered wound-bird
> With the blade of my axe have I stricken
> Full thirty and five of my foemen;
> I am famed for the slaughter of warriors.
> May the fiends have my soul if I stain not
> My sharp-edged falchion once over!
> And then let the breaker of broadswords
> Be borne - and with speed - to the grave!"

"What?" said Halldor; "hast thou a mind to kill another man, then?"

Answered Bersi, "I see the man it would rightly serve!"

Now Thordis let her brother Vali feed his herds on the land of Brekka. Bersi bade his house-carles work at home, and have no dealings with Vali; but still Halldor thought it a hardship that Bersi had not his own will with his own wealth. One day Bersi made this verse:

> "Here we lie,
> Both on one settle -
> Halldor and I,
> Men of no mettle.
> Youth ails thee,
> But thou'lt win through it;
> Age ails me,
> And I must rue it!"

"I do hate Vali," said Halldor; and Bersi answered thus in verse:

"Yon Vali, so wight as he would be,
Well wot I our pasture he grazes;
Right fain yonder fierce helmet-wearer
Under foot my dead body would trample!
But often my wrongs have I wreaked
In wrath on the mail-coated warrior -
On the stems of the sun of the ocean
I have stained the wound-serpent for less!"

And again he said:

"With eld I am listless and lamed -
I, the lord of the gold of the armlet:
I sit, and am still under many
A slight from the warders of spear-meads.
Though shield-bearers shape for the singer
To shiver alone in the grave-mound,
Yet once in the war would I redden
The wand that hews helms ere I fail."

"Thy heart is not growing old, foster-father mine!" cried Halldor.

Upon that Bersi fell into talk with Steinvor, and said to her "I am laying a plot, and I need thee to help me."

She said she would if she could.

"Pick a quarrel," said he, "with Thordis about the milk-kettle, and do thou hold on to it until you whelm it over between you. Then I will come in and take her part and give thee nought but bad words. Then go to Vali and tell him how ill we treat thee."

Everything turned out as he had planned. She went to Vali and told him that things were no way smooth for her; would he take her over the gap (to Bitra to her father's): and so he did.

But when he was on the way back again, out came Bersi and Halldor to meet him. Bersi had a halberd in one hand and a staff in the other, and Halldor had Whitting. As soon as Vali saw them he turned and hewed at Bersi. Halldor came at his back and fleshed Whitting in his hough-sinews. Thereupon he turned sharply and fell upon Halldor. Then Bersi set the halberd-point betwixt his shoulders. That was his death-wound.

Then they set his shield at his feet and his sword at his head, and spread his cloak over him; and after that got on horseback and rode to five homesteads to make known the deed they had done and then rode home. Men went and buried Vali, and the place where he fell has ever since been called Vali's fall.

Halldor was twelve winters old when these doings came to pass.

CHAPTER 17
How Steingerd Was Married Again

Now there was a man named Thorvald, the son of Eystein, bynamed the Tinker: he was a wealthy man, a smith, and a skald; but he was mean-spirited for all that. His brother Thorvard lived in the north country at Fliot (Fleet); and they had many kinsmen, - the Skidings they were called, - but little luck or liking.

Now Thorvald the Tinker asked Steingerd to wife. Her folk were for it, and she said nothing against it; and so she was wed to him in the very same summer in which she left Bersi.

When Cormac heard the news he made as though he knew nothing whatever about the matter; for a little earlier he had taken his goods aboard ship, meaning to go away with his brother. But one morning early he rode from the ship and went to see Steingerd; and when he got talk with her, he asked would she make him a shirt. To which she answered that he had no business to pay her visits; neither Thorvald nor his kinsmen would abide it, she said, but have their revenge.

Thereupon he made his voice:

> "Nay, think it or thole it I cannot,
> That thou, a young fir of the forest
> Enwreathed in the gold that thou guardest,
> Shouldst be given to a tinkering tinsmith.
> Nay, scarce can I smile, O thou glittering
> In silk like the goddess of Baldur,
> Since thy father handfasted and pledged thee,
> So famed as thou art, to a coward."

"In such words," answered Steingerd, "an ill will is plain to hear. I shall tell Thorvald of this ribaldry: no man would sit still under such insults."

Then sang Cormac:

> "What gain is to get if he threatens,
> White goddess in raiment of beauty,
> The scorn that the Skidings may bear me?
> I'll set them a weft for their weaving!
> I'll rhyme you the roystering caitiffs
> Till rocks go afloat on the water;
> And lucky for them if they loosen
> The line of their fate that I ravel!"

Thereupon they parted with no blitheness, and Cormac went to his ship.

CHAPTER 18
Cormac's Voyage To Norway

The two brothers had but left the roadstead, when close beside their ship, uprose a walrus. Cormac hurled at it a pole-staff, which struck the beast, so that it sank again: but the men aboard thought that they knew its eyes for the eyes of Thorveig the witch. That walrus came up no more, but of Thorveig it was heard that she lay sick to death; and indeed folk say that this was the end of her.

Then they sailed out to sea, and at last came to Norway, where at that time Hakon, the foster-son of Athelstan, was king. He made them welcome, and so they stayed there the winter long with all honour.

Next summer they set out to the wars, and did many great deeds. Along with them went a man called Siegfried, a German of good birth; and they made raids both far and wide. One day as they were gone up the country eleven men together came against the two brothers, and set upon them; but this business ended in their overcoming the whole eleven, and so after a while back to their ship. The vikings had given them up for lost, and fain were their folk when they came back with victory and wealth.

In this voyage the brothers got great renown: and late in the summer, when winter was coming on, they made up their minds to steer for Norway. They met with cold winds; the sail was behung with icicles, but the brothers were always to the fore. It was on his voyage that Cormac made the song:

> "O shake me yon rime from the awning;
> Your singer's a-cold in his berth;
> For the hills are all hooded, dear Skardi,
> In the hoary white veil of the firth.
> There's one they call Wielder of Thunder
> I would were as chill and as cold;
> But he leaves not the side of his lady
> As the lindworm forsakes not its gold."

"Always talking of her now!" said Thorgils; "and yet thou wouldst not have her when thou couldst."

"That was more the fault of witchcraft," answered Cormac, "that any want of faith in me."

Not long after they were sailing hard among crags, and shortened sail in great danger.

"It is a pity Thorvald Tinker is not with us here!" said Cormac.

Said Thorgils with a smile, "Most likely he is better off than we, to-day!"

But before long they came to land in Norway.

CHAPTER 19
How Cormac Fought In Ireland,
And Went Home To Iceland;
And How He Met Steingerd Again

While they were abroad there had been a change of kings; Hakon was dead, and Harald Greyfell reigned in his stead. They offered friendship to the king, and he took their suit kindly; so they went with him to Ireland, and fought battles there.

Once upon a time when they had gone ashore with the king, a great host came against him, and as the armies met, Cormac made this song:

"I dread not a death from the foemen,
Though we dash at them, buckler to buckler,
While our prince in the power of his warriors
Is proud of me foremost in battle.
But the glimpse of a glory comes o'er me
Like the gleam of the moon on the skerry,
And I faint and I fail for my longing,
For the fair one at home in the North."

"Ye never get into danger," said Thorgils, "but ye think of Steingerd!"

"Nay," answered Cormac, "but it's not often I forget her."

Well: this was a great battle, and king Harald won a glorious victory. While his men drove the rout before him, the brothers were shoulder to shoulder; and they fell upon nine men at once and fought them. And while they were at it, Cormac sang:

"Fight on, arrow-driver, undaunted,
And down with the foemen of Harald!
What are nine? they are nought! Thou and I, lad,
Are enough; - they are ours! - we have won them!
But - at home, - in the arms of an outlaw
That all the gods loathe for a monster,
So white and so winsome she nestles
- Yet once she was loving to me!"

"It always comes down to that!" said Thorgils. When the fight was over, the brothers had got the victory, and the nine men had fallen before them; for which they won great praise from the king, and many honours beside.

But while they were ever with the king in his warfarings, Thorgils was aware that Cormac was used to sleep but little; and he asked why this might be. This was the song Cormac made in answer:

"Surf on a rock-bound shore of the sea-king's blue domain-
Look how it lashes the crags, hark how it thunders again!

But all the din of the isles that the Delver heaves in foam
In the draught of the undertow glides out to the sea-gods' home.

Now, which of us two should test? Is it thou, with thy heart at
ease,
Or I that am surf on the shore in the tumult of angry seas?
- Drawn, if I sleep, to her that shines with the ocean-
- Dashed, when I wake, to woe, for the want of my glittering
dream."

"And now let me tell you this, brother," he went on. "Hereby I give out that I am
going back to Iceland."

Said Thorgils, "There is many a snare set for thy feet, brother, to drag thee
down, I know not whither."

But when the king heard of his longing to begone, he sent for Cormac, and said
that he did unwisely, and would hinder him from his journey. But all this availed
nothing, and aboard ship he went.

At the outset they met with foul winds, so that they shipped great seas, and the
yard broke. Then Cormac sang:

"I take it not ill, like the Tinker
If a trickster had foundered his muck-sled;
For he loves not rough travelling, the losel,
And loath would he be of this uproar.
I flinch not, - nay, hear it, ye fearless
Who flee not when arrows are raining, -
Though the steeds of the ocean be storm-bound
And stayed in the harbour of Solund."

So they pushed out to sea, and hard weather they tholed. Once on a time when
the waves broke over the deck and drenched them all, Cormac made this song:

"O the Tinker's a lout and a lubber,
And the life of a sailor he dares not,
When the snow-crested surges caress us
And sweep us away with their kisses,
He bides in a berth that is warmer,
Embraced in the arms of his lady;
And lightly she lulls him to slumber,
- But long she has reft me of rest!"

They had a very rough voyage, but landed at last in Midfiord, and anchored off
shore. Looking landward they beheld where a lady was riding by; and Cormac
knew at once that it was Steingerd. He bade his men launch a boat, and rowed
ashore. He went quickly from the boat, and got a horse, and rode to meet her.
When they met, he leapt from horseback and helped her to alight, making a
seat for her beside him on the ground.

Their horses wandered away: the day passed on, and it began to grow dark. At last Steingerd said, "It is time to look for our horses."

Little search would be needed, said Cormac; but when he looked about, they were nowhere in sight. As it happened, they were hidden in a gill not far from where the two were sitting.

So, as night was hard at hand, they set out to walk, and came to a little farm, where they were taken in and treated well, even as they needed. That night they slept each on either side of the carven wainscot that parted bed from bed: and Cormac made this song:

"We rest, O my beauty, my brightest,
But a barrier lies ever between us.
So fierce are the fates and so mighty
- I feel it - that rule to their rede.
Ah, nearer I would be, and nigher,
Till nought should be left to dispart us,
- The wielder of Skofnung the wonder,
And the wearer of sheen from the deep."

"It was better thus," said Steingerd: but he sang:

"We have slept 'neath one roof-tree - slept softly,
O sweet one, O queen of the mead-horn,
O glory of sea-dazzle gleaming,
These grim hours, - these five nights, I count them.
And here in the kettle-prow cabined
While the crow's day drags on in the darkness,
How loathly me seems to be lying,
How lonely, - so near and so far!"

"That," said she, "is all over and done with; name it no more." But he sang:

"The hot stone shall float, - ay, the hearth-stone
Like a husk of the corn on the water,
- Ah, woe for the wight that she loves not! -
And the world, - ah, she loathes me! - shall perish,
And the fells that are famed for their hugeness
Shall fail and be drowned in the ocean,
Or ever so gracious a goddess
Shall grow into beauty like Steingerd."

Then Steingerd cried out that she would not have him make songs upon her: but he went on:

"I have known it and noted it clearly,
O neckleted fair one, in visions,
- Is it doom for my hopes, - is it daring
To dream? - O so oft have I seen it! -
Even this, - that the boughs of thy beauty,
O braceleted fair one, shall twine them

163

Round the hill where the hawk loves to settle,
The hand of thy lover, at last."

"That," said she, "never shall be, if I can help it. Thou didst let me go, once for all; and there is no more hope for thee."

So then they slept the night long; and in the morning, when Cormac was making ready to be gone, he found Steingerd, and took the ring off his finger to give her.

"Fiend take thee and thy gold together!" she cried. And this is what he answered:

> "To a dame in her broideries dainty
> This drift of the furnace I tendered;
> O day of ill luck, for a lover
> So lured, and so heartlessly cheated!
> Too blithe in the pride of her beauty -
> The bliss that I crave she denies me;
> So rich that no boon can I render,
> - And my ring she would hurl to the fiends!"

So Cormac rode forth, being somewhat angry with Steingerd, but still more so with the Tinker. He rode home to Mel, and stayed there all the winter, taking lodgings for his chapmen near the ship.

CHAPTER 20
Of A Spiteful Song That Cormac Never Made;
And How Angry Steingerd Was

Now Thorvald the Tinker lived in the north-country at Svinadal (Swindale), but his brother Thorvard at Fliot. In the winter Cormac took his way northward to see Steingerd; and coming to Svinadal he dismounted and went into the chamber. She was sitting on the dais, and he took his seat beside her; Thorvald sat on the bench, and Narfi by him.

Then said Narfi to Thorvald, "How canst thou sit down, with Cormac here? It is no time, this, for sitting still!"

But Thorvald answered, "I am content; there is no harm done it seems to me, though they do talk together."

"That is ill," said Narfi.

Not long afterwards Thorvald met his brother Thorvard and told him about Cormac's coming to his house.

"Is it right, think you," said Thorvard, "to sit still while such things happen?"

He answered that there was no harm done as yet, but that Cormac's coming pleased him not.

164

"I'll mend that," cried Thorvard, "if you dare not. The shame of it touches us all."

So this was the next thing, - that Thorvard came to Svinadal, and the Skiding brothers and Narfi paid a gangrel beggar-man to sing a song in the hearing of Steingerd, and to say that Cormac had made it, - which was a lie. They said that Cormac had taught this song to one called Eylaug, a kinswoman of his; and these were the words:

> "I wish an old witch that I know of,
> So wealthy and proud of her havings,
> Were turned to a steed in the stable
> - Called Steingerd - and I were the rider!
> I'd bit her, and bridle, and saddle,
> I'd back her and drive her and tame her;
> So many she owns for her masters,
> But mine she will never become!"

Then Steingerd grew exceedingly angry, so that she would not so much as hear Cormac named. When he heard that, he went to see her. Long time he tried in vain to get speech with her; but at last she gave this answer, - that she misliked his holding her up to shame, - "And now it is all over the country-side!"

Cormac said it was not true; but she answered, "Thou mightest flatly deny it, if I had not heard it."

"Who sang it in thy hearing?" asked he.

She told him who sang it, - "And thou needest not hope for speech with me if this prove true."

He rode away to look for the rascal, and when he found him the truth was forced out at last. Cormac was very angry, and set on Narfi and slew him. That same onset was meant for Thorvald, but he hid himself in the shadow and skulked, until men came between then and parted them. Said Cormac:

> "There, hide in the house like a coward,
> And hope not hereafter to scare mc
> With the scorn of thy brethren the Skidings, -
> I'll set them a weft for their weaving!
> I'll rhyme on the swaggering rascals
> Till rocks go afloat on the water;
> And lucky for you if ye loosen
> The line of your fate that I ravel!"

This went all over the country-side and the feud grew fiercer between them. The brothers Thorvald and Thorvard used big words, and Cormac was wroth when he heard them.

CHAPTER 21
How Thorvard Would Not Fight,
But Tried To Get The Law Of Cormac

After this Thorvard sent word from Fliot that he was fain to fight Cormac, and he fixed time and place, saying that he would now take revenge for that song of shame and all other slights.

To this Cormac agreed; and when the day came he went to the spot that was named, but Thorvard was not there, nor any of his men. Cormac met a woman from the farm hard by, who greeted him, and they asked each other for news.

"What is your errand?" said she; "and why are you waiting here?"

Then he answered with this song:

> "Too slow for the struggle I find him,
> That spender of fire from the ocean,
> Who flung me a challenge to fight him
> From Fleet in the land of the North.
> That half-witted hero should get him
> A heart made of clay for his carcase,
> Though the mate of the may with the necklace
> Is more of a fool than his fere!"

"Now," said Cormac, "I bid Thorvard anew to the holmgang, if he can be called in his right mind. Let him be every man's nithing if he come not!" and then he made this song:

> "The nithing shall silence me never,
> Though now for their shame they attack me,
> But the wit of the Skald is my weapon,
> And the wine of the gods will uphold me.
> And this they shall feel in its fulness;
> Here my fame has its birth and beginning;
> And the stout spears of battle shall see it,
> If I 'scape from their hands with my life."

Then the brothers set on foot a law-suit against him for libel. Cormac's kinsmen backed him up to answer it, and he would let no terms be made, saying that they deserved the shame put upon them, and no honour; he was not unready to meet them, unless they played him false. Thorvard had not come to the holmgang when he had been challenged, and therefore the shame had fallen of itself upon him and his, and they must put up with it.

So time passed until the Huna-water Thing. Thorvard and Cormac both went to the meeting, and once they came together.

"Much enmity we owe thee," said Thorvard, "and in many ways. Now therefore I challenge thee to the holmgang, here at the Thing."

Said Cormac, "Wilt thou be fitter than before? Thou hast drawn back time after time."

"Nevertheless," said Thorvard, "I will risk it. We can abide thy spite no longer."

"Well," said Cormac, "I'll not stand in the way;" and went home to Mel.

CHAPTER 22
What The Witch Did For Them In Their Fights

At Spakonufell (Spae-wife's-fell) lived Thordis the spae-wife, of whom we have told before, with her husband Thorolf. They were both at the Thing, and many a man thought her good-will was of much avail. So Thorvard sought her out, to ask her help against Cormac, and gave her a fee; and she made him ready for the holmgang according to her craft.

Now Cormac told his mother what was forward, and she asked if he thought good would come of it.

"Why not?" said he.

"That will not be enough for thee," said Dalla. "Thorvard will never make bold to fight without witchcraft to help him. I think it wise for thee to see Thordis the spae-wife, for there is going to be foul play in this affair."

"It is little to my mind," said he; and yet went to see Thordis, and asked her help.

"Too late ye have come," said she. "No weapon will bite on him now. And yet I would not refuse thee. Bide here to-night, and seek thy good luck. Anyway, I can manage so that iron bite thee no more than him."

So Cormac stayed there for the night; and, awaking, found that some one was groping round the coverlet at his head. "Who is there?" he asked, but whoever it was made off, and out at the house-door, and Cormac after. And then he saw it was Thordis, and she was going to the place where the fight was to be, carrying a goose under her arm.

He asked what it all meant, and she set down the goose, saying, "Why couldn't ye keep quiet?"

So he lay down again, but held himself awake, for he wanted to know what she would be doing. Three times she came, and every time he tried to find out what she was after. The third time, just as he came out, she had killed two geese and let the blood run into a bowl, and she had taken up the third goose to kill it.

"What means this business, foster-mother?" said he.

"True it will prove, Cormac, that you are a hard one to help," said she. "I was going to break the spell Thorveig laid on thee and Steingerd. Ye could have loved one another been happy if I had killed the third goose and no one seen it."

"I believe nought of such things," cried he; and this song he made about it:

"I gave her an ore at the ayre,
That the arts of my foe should not prosper;
And twice she has taken the knife,
And twice she has offered the offering;
But the blood is the blood of a goose -
What boots it if two should be slaughtered? -
Never sacrifice geese for a Skald
Who sings for the glory of Odin!"

So they went to the holmgang: but Thorvald gave the spae-wife a still greater fee, and offered the sacrifice of geese; and Cormac said:

"Trust never another man's mistress!
For I know, on this woman who weareth
The fire of the field of the sea-king
The fiends have been riding to revel.
The witch with her hoarse cry is working
For woe when we go to the holmgang,
And if bale be the end of the battle
The blame, be assured, will be hers."

"Well," she said, "I can manage so that none shall know thee." Then Cormac began to upbraid her, saying she did nought but ill, and wanting to drag her out to the door to look at her eyes in the sunshine. His brother Thorgils made him leave that: "What good will it do thee?" said he.

Now Steingerd gave out that she had a mind to see the fight; and so she did. When Cormac saw her he made this song:

"I have fared to the field of the battle,
O fair one that wearest the wimple!
And twice for thy sake have I striven;
What stays me as now from thy favour?
This twice have I gotten thee glory,
O goddess of ocean! and surely
To my dainty delight, to my darling
I am dearer by far than her mate."

So then they set to. Cormac's sword bit not at all, and for a long while they smote strokes one upon the other, but neither sword bit. At last Cormac smote upon Thorvard's side so great a blow that his ribs gave way and were broken; he could fight no more, and thereupon they parted. Cormac looked and saw where a bull was standing, which he slew for a sacrifice; and being heated, he doffed his helmet from his head, saying this song:

"I have fared to the field of the battle,
O fair one that wearest the bracelet!
Even three times for thee have I striven,
And this thou canst never deny me.
But the reed of the fight would not redden,
Though it rang on the shield-bearer's harness;

For the spells of a spae-wife had blunted
My sword that was eager for blood."

He wiped the sweat from him on the corner of Steingerd's mantle; and said:

"So oft, being wounded and weary,
I must wipe my sad brow on thy mantle.
What pangs for thy sake are my portion,
O pine-tree with red gold enwreathed!
Yet beside thee he snugs on the settle
As thou seamest thy broidery, - that rhymester!
And the shame of it whelms me in sorrow,
O Steingerd! - that rascal unslain!"

And then Cormac prayed Steingerd that she would go with him: but Nay, she said; she would have her own way about men. So they parted, and both were ill pleased.

Thorvard was taken home, and she bound his wounds. Cormac was now always meeting with Steingerd. Thorvard healed but slowly; and when he could get on his feet he went to see Thordis, and asked her what was best to help his healing.

"A hill there is," answered she, "not far away from here, where elves have their haunt. Now get you the bull that Cormac killed, and redden the outer side of the hill with its blood, and make a feast for the elves with its flesh. Then thou wilt be healed."

So they sent word to Cormac that they would buy the bull. He answered that he would sell it, but then he must have the ring that was Steingerd's. So they brought the ring, took the bull, and did with it as Thordis bade them do. On which Cormac made a song:

"When the workers of wounds are returning,
And with them the sacrifice reddened,
Then a lady in raiment of linen,
Who loved me, time was, - she will ask:
My ring, - have ye robbed me? - where is it?
- I have wrought them no little displeasure:
For the swain that is swarthy has won it,
The son of old Ogmund, the skald."

It fell out as he guessed. Steingerd was very angry because they had sold her ring.

CHAPTER 23
How Cormac Beat Thorvard Again

After that, Thorvard was soon healed, and when he thought he was strong again, he rode to Mel and challenged Cormac to the holmgang.

"It takes thee long to tire of it," said Cormac: "but I'll not say thee nay."

So they went to the fight, and Thordis met Thorvard now as before, but Cormac sought no help from her. She blunted Cormac's sword, so that it would not bite, but yet he struck so great a stroke on Thorvard's shoulder that the collarbone was broken and his hand was good for nothing. Being so maimed he could fight no longer, and had to pay another ring for his ransom.

Then Thorolf of Spakonufell set upon Cormac and struck at him. He warded off the blow and sang this song:

> "This reddener of shields, feebly wrathful,
> His rusty old sword waved against me,
> Who am singer and sacred to Odin!
> Go, snuffle, most wretched of men, thou!
> A thrust of thy sword is as thewless
> As thou, silly stirrer of battle.
> What danger to me from thy daring,
> Thou doited old witch-woman's carle?"

Then he killed a bull in sacrifice according to use and wont, saying, "Ill we brook your overbearing and the witchcraft of Thordis:" and he made this song:

> "The witch in the wave of the offering
> Has wasted the flame of the buckler,
> Lest its bite on his back should be deadly
> At the bringing together of weapons.
> My sword was not sharp for the onset
> When I sought the helm-wearer in battle;
> But the cur got enough to cry craven,
> With a clout that will mind him of me!"

After that each party went home, and neither was well pleased with these doings.

CHAPTER 24
How They All Went Out To Norway

Now all the winter long Cormac and Thorgils laid up their ship in Hrutafiord; but in spring the chapmen were off to sea, and so the brothers made up their minds for the voyage. When they were ready to start, Cormac went to see Steingerd: and before they two parted he kissed her twice, and his kisses were not at all

170

hasty. The Tinker would not have it; and so friends on both sides came in, and it was settled that Cormac should pay for this that he had done.

"How much?" asked he.

"The two rings that I parted with," said Thorvard. Then Cormac made a song:

> "Here is gold of the other's well gleaming
> In guerdon for this one and that one, -
> Here is treasure of Fafnir the fire-drake
> In fee for the kiss of my lady.
> Never wearer of ring, never wielder
> Of weapon has made such atonement;
> Never dearer were deeply-drawn kisses, -
> For the dream of my bliss is betrayed."

And then, when he started to go aboard his ship he made another song:

> "One song from my heart would I send her
> Ere we shall, ere I leave her and lose her,
> That dainty one, decked in her jewels
> Who dwells in the valley of Swindale.
> And each word that I utter shall enter
> The ears of that lady of bounty,
> Saying - Bright one, my beauty, I love thee,
> Ah, better by far than my life!"

So Cormac went abroad and his brother Thorgils went with him; and when they came to the king's court they were made welcome.

Now it is told that Steingerd spoke to Thorvald the Tinker that they also should abroad together. He answered that it was mere folly, but nevertheless he could not deny her. So they set off on their voyage: and as they made their way across the sea, they were attacked by vikings who fell on them to rob them and to carry away Steingerd. But it so happened that Cormac heard of it; and he made after them and gave good help, so that they saved everything that belonged to them, and came safely at last to the court of the king of Norway.

One day Cormac was walking in the street, and spied Steingerd sitting within doors. So he went into the house and sat down beside her, and they had a talk together which ended in his kissing her four kisses. But Thorvald was on the watch. He drew his sword, but the women-folk rushed in to part them, and word was sent to King Harald. He said they were very troublesome people to keep in order. - "But let me settle this matter between you," said he; and they agreed.

Then spake the king: "One kiss shall be atoned for by this, that Cormac helped you to get safely to land. The next kiss is Cormac's, because he saved Steingerd. For the other two he shall pay two ounces of gold."

Upon which Cormac sang the same song that he had made before:

> "Here is gold of the otter's well gleaming
> In guerdon for this one and that one, -
> Here is treasure of Fafnir the fire-drake

In fee for the kiss of my lady.
Never wearer of ring, never wielder
Of weapon has made such atonement;
Never dearer were deeply-drawn kisses -
And the dream of my bliss is betrayed."

Another day he was walking in the street and met Steingerd again. He turned to
her and prayed her to walk with him. She would not; whereupon he laid hand on
her, to lead her along. She cried out for help; and as it happened, the king was
standing not far off, and went up to them. He thought this behaviour most
unseemly, and took her away, speaking sharply to Cormac. King Harald made
himself very angry over this affair; but Cormac was one of his courtiers, and it
was not long before he got into favour again, and then things went fair and
softly for the rest of the winter.

CHAPTER 25
How They Cruised With The King's Fleet,
And Quarrelled, And Made It Up

In the following spring King Harald set forth to the land of Permia with a great
host. Cormac was one of the captains in that warfaring, and in another ship was
Thorvald: the other captains of ships are not named in our story.

Now as they were all sailing in close order through a narrow sound, Cormac
swung his steering-oar and hit Thorvald a clout on the ear, so that he fell from
his place at the helm in a swoon; and Cormac's ship hove to, when she lost her
rudder. Steingerd had been sitting beside Thorvald; she laid hold of the tiller,
and ran Cormac down. When he saw what she was doing, he sang:

> "There is one that is nearer and nigher
> To the noblest of dames than her lover:
> With the haft of the helm is he smitten
> On the hat-block - and fairly amidships!
> The false heir of Eystein - he falters -
> He falls in the poop of his galley!
> Nay! steer not upon me, O Steingerd,
> Though stoutly ye carry the day!"

So Cormac's ship capsized under him; but his crew were saved without loss of
time, for there were plenty of people round about. Thorvald soon came round
again, and they all went on their way. The king offered to settle the matter
between them; and when they both agreed, he gave judgment that Thorvald's
hurt was atoned for by Cormac's upset.

In the evening they went ashore; and the king and his men sat down to supper.
Cormac was sitting outside the door of a tent, drinking out of the same cup with
Steingerd. While they were busy at it, a young fellow for mere sport and
mockery stole the brooch out of Cormac's fur cloak, which he had doffed and

laid aside; and when he came to take his cloak again, the brooch was gone. He sprang up and rushed after the young fellow, with the spear that he called Vigr (the spear) and shot at him, but missed. This was the song he made about it:

> "The youngster has pilfered my pin,
> As I pledged the gay dame in the beaker;
> And now must we brawl for a brooch
> Like boys when they wrangle and tussle.
> Right well have I shafted my spear,
> Though I shot nothing more than the gravel:
> But sure, if I missed at my man,
> The moss has been prettily slaughtered!"

After this they went on their way to the land of Permia, and after that they went home again to Norway.

CHAPTER 26
How Cormac Saved Steingerd Once More From Pirates; And How They Parted For Good And All

Thorvald the Tinker fitted out his ship for a cruise to Denmark, and Steingerd sailed with him. A little afterwards the brothers set out on the same voyage, and late one evening they made the Brenneyjar.

There they saw Thorvald's ship riding, and found him aboard with part of his crew; but they had been robbed of all their goods, and Steingerd had been carried off by Vikings. Now the leader of those Vikings was Thorstein, the son of that Asmund Ashenside, the old enemy of Ogmund, the father of Cormac and Thorgils.

So Thorvald and Cormac met, and Cormac asked how came it that his voyage had been so unlucky.

"Things have not turned out for the best, indeed," said he.

"What is the matter?" asked Cormac. "Is Steingerd missing?"

"She is gone," said Thorvald, "and all our goods."

"Why don't you go after her?" asked Cormac.

"We are not strong enough," said Thorvald.

"Do you mean to say you can't?" said Cormac.

"We have not the means to fight Thorstein," said Thorvald. "But if thou hast, go in and fight for thy own hand."

"I will," said Cormac.

So at nightfall the brothers went in a boat and rowed to the Viking fleet, and boarded Thorstein's ship. Steingerd was in the cabin on the poop; she had been allotted to one of the Vikings; but most of the crew were ashore round the cooking-fires. Cormac got the story out of the men who were cooking, and they told all the brothers wanted to know. They clambered on board by the ladder; Thorgils dragged the bridegroom out to the gunwale, and Cormac cut him down then and there. Then he dived into the sea with Steingerd and swam ashore; but when he was nearing the land a swarm of eels twisted round his hands and feet, so that he was dragged under. On which he made this song:

"They came at me yonder in crowds,
O kemp of the shield-serpents' wrangle!
When I fared on my way through the flood,
That flock of the wights of the water.
And ne'er to the gate of the gods
Had I got me, if there had I perished;
Yet once and again have I won,
Little woman, thy safety in peril!"

So he swam ashore and brought Steingerd back to her husband.

Thorvald bade Steingerd to go, at last, along with Cormac, for he had fairly won her, and manfully. That was what he, too, desired, said Cormac; but "Nay," said Steingerd, "she would not change knives."

"Well," said Cormac, "it was plain that this was not to be. Evil beings," he said, "ill luck, had parted them long ago." And he made this song:

"Nay, count not the comfort had brought me,
Fair queen of the ring, thy embrace!
Go, mate with the man of thy choosing,
Scant mirth will he get of thy grace!
Be dearer henceforth to thy dastard,
False dame of the coif, than to me; -
I have spoken the word; I have sung it; -
I have said my last farewell to thee."

And so he bade her begone with her husband.

CHAPTER 27
The Swan-Songs of Cormac

After these things the brothers turned back to Norway, and Thorvald the Tinker made his way to Iceland. But the brothers went warfaring round about Ireland, Wales, England and Scotland, and they were reckoned to be the most famous of men. It was they who first built the castle of Scarborough; they made raids into Scotland, and achieved many great feats, and led a mighty host; and in all that host none was like Cormac in strength and courage.

Once upon a time, after a battle, Cormac was driving the flying foe before him while the rest of his host had gone back aboard ship. Out of the woods there rushed against him one as monstrous big as an idol - a Scot; and a fierce struggle began. Cormac felt for his sword, but it had slipped out of the sheath;

he was over-matched, for the giant was possessed; but yet he reached out, caught his sword, and struck the giant his death-blow. Then the giant cast his hands about Cormac, and gripped his sides so hard that the ribs cracked, and he fell over, and the dead giant on top of him, so that he could not stir. Far and wide his folk were looking for him, but at last they found him and carried him aboard ship. Then he made this song:

> "When my manhood was matched in embraces
> With the might of yon horror, the strangler,
> Far other I found it than folding
> That fair one ye know in my arms!
> On the high-seat of heroes with Odin
> From the horn of the gods I were drinking
> O'er soon - let me speak it to warriors -
> If Skrymir had failed of his aid."

Then his wounds were looked to; they found that his ribs were broken on both sides. He said it was no use trying to heal him, and lay there in his wounds for a time, while his men grieved that he should have been so unwary of his life.

He answered them in song:

> "Of yore never once did I ween it,
> When I wielded the cleaver of targets,
> That sickness was fated to foil me -
> A fighter so hardy as I.
> But I shrink not, for others must share it,
> Stout shafts of the spear though they deem them,
> - O hard at my heart is the death-pang, -
> Thus hopeless the bravest may die."

And this song also:

> "He came not with me in the morning,
> Thy mate, O thou fairest of women,
> When we reddened for booty the broadsword,
> So brave to the hand-grip, in Ireland:
> When the sword from its scabbard was loosened
> And sang round my cheeks in the battle
> For the feast of the Fury, and blood-drops
> Fell hot on the neb of the raven."

And then he began to fail.

This was his last song:

> "There was dew from the wound smitten deeply
> That drained from the stroke of the sword-edge;
> There was red on the weapon I wielded
> In the war with the glorious and gallant:
> Yet not where the broadsword, - the blood wand, -
> Was borne by the lords of the falchion,

But low in the straw like a laggard,
O my lady, dishonoured I die!"

He said that his will was to give Thorgils his brother all he had - the goods he owned and the host he led; for he would like best, he said, that his brother should have the use of them.

So then Cormac died. Thorgils became captain over the host, and was long time in viking.

And so ends the story.

THE LAXDALE SAGA

CHAPTER 1
Of Ketill Flatnose and his Descendants, 9th Century A.D.

Ketill Flatnose was the name of a man. He was the son of Bjorn the Ungartered. Ketill was a mighty and high-born chieftain (hersir) in Norway. He abode in Raumsdale, within the folkland of the Raumsdale people, which lies between Southmere and Northmere. Ketill Flatnose had for wife Yngvild, daughter of Ketill Wether, who was a man of exceeding great worth. They had five children; one was named Bjorn the Eastman, and another Helgi Bjolan. Thorunn the Horned was the name of one of Ketill's daughters, who was the wife of Helgi the Lean, son of Eyvind Eastman, and Rafarta, daughter of Kjarval, the Irish king. Unn "the Deep-minded" was another of Ketill's daughters, and was the wife of Olaf the White, son of Ingjald, who was son of Frodi the Valiant, who was slain by the Svertlings. Jorunn, "Men's Wit-breaker," was the name of yet another of Ketill's daughters. She was the mother of Ketill the Finn, who settled on land at Kirkby. His son was Asbjorn, father of Thorstein, father of Surt, the father of Sighat the Speaker-at-Law.

CHAPTER 2
Ketill and his Sons prepare to leave Norway

In the latter days of Ketill arose the power of King Harald the Fairhaired, in such a way that no folkland king or other great men could thrive in the land unless he alone ruled what title should be theirs. When Ketill heard that King Harald was minded to put to him the same choice as to other men of might - namely, not only to put up with his kinsmen being left unatoned, but to be made himself a hireling to boot - he calls together a meeting of his kinsmen, and began his speech in this wise: "You all know what dealings there have been between me and King Harald, the which there is no need of setting forth; for a greater need besets us, to wit, to take counsel as to the troubles that now are in store for us. I have true news of King Harald's enmity towards us, and to me it seems that we may abide no trust from that quarter. It seems to me that there are two choices left us, either to fly the land or to be slaughtered each in his own seat. Now, as for me, my will is rather to abide the same death that my kinsmen suffer, but I would not lead you by my wilfulness into so great a trouble, for I know the temper of my kinsmen and friends, that ye would not desert me, even though it would be some trial of manhood to follow me." Bjorn, the son of Ketill, answered: "I will make known my wishes at once. I will follow the example of noble men, and fly this land. For I deem myself no greater a man by abiding at home the thralls of King Harald, that they may chase me away from my own possessions, or that else I may have to come by utter death at their hands." At this there was made a good cheer, and they all thought it was spoken bravely. This counsel then was settled, that they should leave the country, for the sons of Ketill urged it much, and no one spoke against it. Bjorn and Helgi wished to go to Iceland, for they said they had heard many pleasing news thereof. They had been told that there was good land to be had there, and no need to pay money for it; they said there was plenty of whale and salmon and other fishing all the year round there. But Ketill said, "Into that fishing place I shall never come in my old age." So Ketill then told his mind, saying his desire was rather to go west over the sea, for there was a chance of getting a good livelihood. He knew lands there wide about, for there he had harried far and wide.

CHAPTER 3
Ketill's Sons go to Iceland

After that Ketill made a great feast, and at it he married his daughter Thorunn the Horned to Helgi the Lean, as has been said before. After that Ketill arrayed his journey west over the sea. Unn, his daughter, and many others of his relations went with him. That same summer Ketill's sons went to Iceland with Helgi, their brother-in-law. Bjorn, Ketill's son, brought his ship to the west coast of Iceland, to Broadfirth, and sailed up the firth along the southern shore, till he came to where a bay cuts into the land, and a high mountain stood on the ness on the inner side of the bay, but an island lay a little way off the land. Bjorn said that they should stay there for a while. Bjorn then went on land with a few men, and wandered along the coast, and but a narrow strip of land was there between fell and foreshore. This spot he thought suitable for habitation. Bjorn found the pillars of his temple washed up in a certain creek, and he thought that showed where he ought to build his house. Afterwards Bjorn took for himself all the land between Staff-river and Lavafirth, and abode in the place that ever after was called Bjornhaven. He was called Bjorn the Eastman. His wife, Gjaflaug, was the daughter of Kjallak the Old. Their sons were Ottar and Kjallak, whose son was Thorgrim, the father of Fight-Styr and Vemund, but the daughter of Kjallak was named Helga, who was the wife of Vestar of Eyr, son of Thorolf "Bladder-skull," who settled Eyr. Their son was Thorlak, father of Steinthor of

Eyr. Helgi Bjolan brought his ship to the south of the land, and took all Keelness, between Kollafirth and Whalefirth, and lived at Esjuberg to old age. Helgi the Lean brought his ship to the north of the land, and took Islefirth, all along between Mastness and Rowanness, and lived at Kristness. From Helgi and Thornunn all the Islefirthers are sprung.

CHAPTER 4
Ketill goes to Scotland, A.D. 890

Ketill Flatnose brought his ship to Scotland, and was well received by the great men there; for he was a renowned man, and of high birth. They offered him there such station as he would like to take, and Ketill and his company of kinsfolk settled down there - all except Thorstein, his daughter's son, who forthwith betook himself to warring, and harried Scotland far and wide, and was always victorious. Later on he made peace with the Scotch, and got for his own one-half of Scotland. He had for wife Thurid, daughter of Eyvind, and sister of Helgi the Lean. The Scotch did not keep the peace long, but treacherously murdered him.

Ari, Thorgil's son, the Wise, writing of his death, says that he fell in Caithness. Unn the Deep-minded was in Caithness when her son Thorstein fell. When she heard that Thorstein was dead, and her father had breathed his last, she deemed she would have no prospering in store there. So she had a ship built secretly in a wood, and when it was ready built she arrayed it, and had great wealth withal; and she took with her all her kinsfolk who were left alive; and men deem that scarce may an example be found that any one, a woman only, has ever got out of such a state of war with so much wealth and so great a following. From this it may be seen how peerless among women she was. Unn had with her many men of great worth and high birth. A man named Koll was one of the worthiest amongst her followers, chiefly owing to his descent, he being by title a "Hersir." There was also in the journey with Unn a man named Hord, and he too was also a man of high birth and of great worth. When she was ready, Unn took her ship to the Orkneys; there she stayed a little while, and there she married off Gro, the daughter of Thorstein the Red. She was the mother of Greilad, who married Earl Thorfinn, the son of Earl Turf-Einar, son of Rognvald Mere-Earl. Their son was Hlodvir, the father of Earl Sigurd, the father of Earl Thorfinn, and from them come all the kin of the Orkney Earls. After that Unn steered her ship to the Faroe Isles, and stayed there for some time. There she married off another daughter of Thorstein,named Olof, and from her sprung the noblest race of that land, who are called the Gate-Beards.

CHAPTER 5
Unn goes to Iceland, A.D. 895

Unn now got ready to go away from the Faroe Isles, and made it known to her shipmates that she was going to Iceland. She had with her Olaf "Feilan," the

178

son of Thorstein, and those of his sisters who were unmarried. After that she put to sea, and, the weather being favourable, she came with her ship to the south of Iceland to Pumice-Course (Vikrarskeid). There they had their ship broken into splinters, but all the men and goods were saved. After that she went to find Helgi, her brother, followed by twenty men; and when she came there he went out to meet her, and bade her come stay with him with ten of her folk. She answered in anger, and said she had not known that he was such a churl; and she went away, being minded to find Bjorn, her brother in Broadfirth, and when he heard she was coming, he went to meet her with many followers, and greeted her warmly, and invited her and all her followers to stay with him, for he knew his sister's high-mindedness. She liked that right well, and thanked him for his lordly behaviour. She stayed there all the winter, and was entertained in the grandest manner, for there was no lack of means, and money was not spared. In the spring she went across Broadfirth, and came to a certain ness, where they ate their mid-day meal, and since that it has been called Daymealness, from whence Middlefell-strand stretches (eastward). Then she steered her ship up Hvammsfirth and came to a certain ness, and stayed there a little while. There Unn lost her comb, so it was afterwards called Combness. Then she went about all the Broadfirth-Dales, and took to her lands as wide as she wanted. After that Unn steered her ship to the head of the bay, and there her high-seat pillars were washed ashore, and then she deemed it was easy to know where she was to take up her abode. She had a house built there: it was afterwards called Hvamm, and she lived there. The same spring as Unn set up household at Hvamm, Koll married Thorgerd, daughter of Thorstein the Red. Unn gave, at her own cost, the bridal-feast, and let Thorgerd have for her dowry all Salmonriver-Dale; and Koll set up a household there on the south side of the Salmon-river. Koll was a man of the greatest mettle: their son was named Hoskuld.

CHAPTER 6
Unn Divides her Land

After that Unn gave to more men parts of her land-take. To Hord she gave all Hord-Dale as far as Skramuhlaups River. He lived at Hordabolstad (Hord-Lair-Stead), and was a man of the greatest mark, and blessed with noble offspring. His son was Asbjorn the Wealthy, who lived in Ornolfsdale, at Asbjornstead, and had to wife Thorbjorg, daughter of Midfirth-Skeggi. Their daughter was Ingibjorg, who married Illugi the Black, and their sons were Hermund and Gunnlaug Worm-tongue. They are called the Gilsbecking-race. Unn spoke to her men and said: "Now you shall be rewarded for all your work, for now I do not lack means with which to pay each one of you for your toil and good-will. You all know that I have given the man named Erp, son of Earl Meldun, his freedom, for far away was it from my wish that so high-born a man should bear the name of thrall." Afterwards Unn gave him the lands of Sheepfell, between Tongue River and Mid River. His children were Orm and Asgeir, Gunbjorn, and Halldis, whom Alf o' Dales had for wife. To Sokkolf Unn gave Sokkolfsdale, where he abode to old age. Hundi was the name of one of her freedmen. He was of Scottish kin. To him she gave Hundidale. Osk was the name of the fourth daughter of Thorstein the Red. She was the mother of Thorstein Swart, the Wise, who found the "Summer eeke." Thorhild was the name of a fifth daughter of Thorstein. She was the mother of Alf o' Dales, and many great men trace back their line of descent to him. His daughter was Thorgerd, wife of Ari Marson of Reekness, the son of Atli, the son ofUlf the Squinter and Bjorg, Eyvond's daughter, the sister of Helgi the Lean. From them come all the Reeknessings. Vigdis was the name of the sixth daughter of Thorstein the Red. From her come the men of Headland of Islefirth.

CHAPTER 7
Of the Wedding of Olaf "Feilan," A.D. 920

Olaf "Feilan" was the youngest of Thorstein's children. He was a tall man and strong, goodly to look at, and a man of the greatest mettle. Unn loved him above all men, and made it known to people that she was minded to settle on Olaf all her belongings at Hvamm after her day. Unn now became very weary with old age, and she called Olaf "Feilan" to her and said: "It is on my mind, kinsman, that you should settle down and marry." Olaf took this well, and said he would lean on her foresight in that matter. Unn said: "It is chiefly in my mind that your wedding-feast should be held at the end of the summer, for that is the easiest time to get in all the means needed, for to me it seems a near guess that our friends will come hither in great numbers, and I have made up my mind that this shall be the last bridal feast arrayed by me." Olaf answered: "That is well spoken; but such a woman alone I mean to take to wife who shall rob thee neither of wealth nor rule (over thine own)." That same summer Olaf "Feilan" marriedAlfdis. Their wedding was at Hvamm. Unn spent much money on this feast, for she let be bidden thereto men of high degree wide about from other parts. She invited Bjorn and Helgi "Bjolan," her brothers, and they came with many followers. There came Koll o' Dales, her kinsman-in-law, and Hord of Hord-Dale, and many other great men. The wedding feast was very crowded; yet there did not come nearly so many as Unn had asked, because the Islefirth people had such a long way to come. Old age fell now fast upon Unn, so that she did not get up till mid-day, and went early to bed. No one did she allow to come to her for advice between the time she went to sleep at night and the time she was aroused, and she was very angry if any one asked how it fared with her strength. On this day Unn slept somewhat late; yet she was on foot when the guests came, and went to meet them and greeted her kinsfolk and friends with great courtesy, and said they had shown their affection to her in "coming hither from so far, and I specially name for this Bjorn and Helgi, but I wish to thank you all who are here assembled." After that Unn went into the hall and a great company with her, and when all seats were taken in the hall, every one was much struck by the lordliness of the feast. Then Unn said: "Bjorn and Helgi, my brothers, and all my other kindred and friends, I call witnesses to this, that this dwelling with all its belongings that you now see before you, I give into the hands of mykinsman, Olaf, to own and to manage." After that Unn stood up and said she would go to the bower where she was wont to sleep, but bade every one have for pastime whatever was most to his mind, and that ale should be the cheer of the common folk. So the tale goes, that Unn was a woman both tall and portly. She walked at a quick step out along the hall, and people could not help saying to each other how stately the lady was yet. They feasted that evening till they thought it time to go to bed. But the day after Olaf went to the sleeping bower of Unn, his grandmother, and when he came into the chamber there was Unn sitting up against her pillow, and she was dead. Olaf went into the hall after that and told these tidings. Every one thought it a wonderful thing, how Unn had upheld her dignity to the day of her death. So they now drank together Olaf's wedding and Unn's funeral honours, and the last day of the feast Unn was carried to the howe (burial mound) that was made for her. She was laid in a ship in the cairn, and much treasure with her, and after that the cairn was closed up. Then Olaf "Feilan" took over the household of Hvamm and all charge of the wealth there, by the advice of his kinsmen who were there. When the feast came to an end Olaf gave lordly gifts to the men most held in honour before they went away. Olaf became a mighty man and a great chieftain. He lived at Hvamm to old age. The children of Olaf and Alfdis were Thord Yeller, whomarried Hrodny, daughter of Midfirth Skeggi; and their sons were, Eyjolf the Grey, Thorarin Fylsenni, and Thorkell Kuggi. One daughter of Olaf Feilan was Thora, whom Thorstein Cod-biter, son of Thorolf Most-Beard, had for wife; their sons were Bork the Stout, and Thorgrim, father of Snori the Priest. Helga was another daughter of Olaf; she was the wife of Gunnar Hlifarson; their daughter was Jofrid, whom Thorodd, son of Tongue-Odd, had for wife, and afterwards Thorstein, Egil's son. Thorunn was the name of yet one of his daughters. She was the wife of Herstein, son of Thorkell Blund-Ketill's son. Thordis was the name of a third daughter of Olaf: she was the wife of Thorarin, the Speaker-at-Law, brother of Ragi. At that time, when Olaf was living at Hvamm, Koll o' Dales, his brother-in-law, fell ill and died. Hoskuld, the son of Koll, was young at the time of his father's death: he was fulfilled of wits before the tale of his years. Hoskuld was a hopeful man, and well made of body. He took over his father's goods and household. The homestead where Koll lived was named after him, being afterwards called Hoskuldstead. Hoskuld was soon in his householding blessed with friends, for that many supports stood thereunder, both kinsmen and friends whom Koll had gathered round him. Thorgerd, Thorstein's daughter, the mother of Hoskuld, was still a young woman and most goodly; she did not care for Iceland after the death of Koll. She told Hoskuld her son that she wished to goabroad, and take with her that share of goods which fell to her lot. Hoskuld said he took it much to heart that they should part, but he would not go against her in this any more than in anything else. After that Hoskuld bought the half-part in a ship that was standing beached off Daymealness, on behalf of his mother. Thorgerd betook herself on board there, taking with her a great deal of goods. After that Thorgerd put to sea and had a very good voyage, and arrived in Norway. Thorgerd had much kindred and many noble kinsmen there. They greeted her warmly, and gave her the choice of whatever she liked to take at their hands. Thorgerd was pleased at this, and said it was her wish to settle down in that land. She had not been a widow long before a man came forward to woo her. His name was Herjolf; he was a "landed man" as to title, rich, and of much account. Herjolf was a tall and strong man, but he was not fair of feature; yet the most high-mettled of men, and was of all men the best skilled at arms. Now as they sat taking counsel on this matter, it was Thorgerd's place to reply to it herself, as she was a widow; and, with the advice of her relations, she said she would not refuse the offer. So Thorgerd married Herjolf, and went with him to his home, and they loved each other dearly. Thorgerd soon showed by her ways that she was a woman of the greatest mettle, and Herjolf's manner of life was deemed much better and more highly to be honoured now that he had got such an one as she was for his wife.

CHAPTER 8
The Birth of Hrut and
Thorgerd's Second Widowhood, A.D. 923

Herjolf and Thorgerd had not long been together before they had a son. The boy was sprinkled with water, and was given the name of Hrut. He was at an early age both big and strong as he grew up; and as to growth of body, he was goodlier than any man, tall and broad-shouldered, slender of waist, with fine limbs and well-made hands and feet. Hrut was of all men the fairest of feature, and like what Thorstein, his mother's father, had been, or like Ketill Flatnose. And all things taken together, he was a man of the greatest mettle. Herjolf now fell ill and died, and men deemed that a great loss. After that Thorgerd wished to go to Iceland to visit Hoskuld her son, for she still loved him best of all men, and Hrut was left behind well placed with his relations. Thorgerd arrayed her journey to Iceland, and went to find Hoskuld in his home in Salmonriver-Dale. He received his mother with honour. She was possessed of great wealth, and remained with Hoskuld to the day of her death. A few winters after Thorgerd came to Iceland she fell sick and died. Hoskuld took to himself all her money, but Hrut his brother owned one-half thereof.

CHAPTER 9
Hoskuld's Marriage, A.D. 935

At this time Norway was ruled by Hakon, Athelstan's fosterling. Hoskuld was one of his bodyguard, and stayed each year, turn and turn about, at Hakon's court, or at his own home, and was a very renowned man both in Norway and in Iceland. Bjorn was the name of a man who lived at Bjornfirth, where he had taken land, the firth being named after him. This firth cuts into the land north from Steingrim's firth, and a neck of land runs out between them. Bjorn was a man of high birth, with a great deal of money: Ljufa was the name of his wife. Their daughter was Jorunn: she was a most beautiful woman, and very proud and extremely clever, and so was thought the best match in all the firths of the West. Of this woman Hoskuld had heard, and he had heard besides that Bjorn was the wealthiest yeoman throughout all the Strands. Hoskuld rode from home with ten men, and went to Bjorn's house at Bjornfirth. He was well received, for to Bjorn his ways were well known. Then Hoskuld made his proposal, and Bjorn said he was pleased, for his daughter could not be better married, yet turned the matter over to her decision. And when the proposal was set before Jorunn, she answered in this way: "From all the reports I have heard of you, Hoskuld, I cannot but answer yourproposal well, for I think that the woman would be well cared for who should marry you; yet my father must have most to say in this matter, and I will agree in this with his wishes." And the long and short of it was, that Jorunn was promised to Hoskuld with much money, and the wedding was to be at Hoskuldstead. Hoskuld now went away with matters thus settled, and home to his abode, and stays now at home until this wedding feast was to be held. Bjorn came from the north for the wedding with a brave company of followers. Hoskuld had also asked many guests, both friends and relations, and the feast was of the grandest. Now, when the feast was over each one returned to his home in good friendship and with seemly gifts. Jorunn Bjorn's daughter sits behind at Hoskuldstead, and takes over the care of the household with Hoskuld. It was very soon seen that she was wise and well up in things, and of manifold knowledge, though rather high-tempered at most times. Hoskuld and she loved each other well, though in their daily ways they made no show thereof. Hoskuld became a great chieftain; he was mighty and pushing, and had no lack of money, and was thought to be nowise less of his ways than his father, Koll. Hoskuld and Jorunn had not been married long before they came to have children. A son of theirs was named Thorliek. He was the eldest of their children. Bard was another son of theirs. One of their daughters was called Hallgerd, afterwards surnamed "Long-Breeks."Another daughter was called Thurid. All their children were most hopeful. Thorliek was a very tall man, strong and handsome, though silent and rough; and men thought that such was the turn of his temper, as that he would be no man of fair dealings, and Hoskuld often would say, that he would take very much after the race of the men of the Strands. Bard, Hoskuld's son, was most manly to look at, and of goodly strength, and from his appearance it was easy to see that he would take more after his father's people. Bard was of quiet ways while he was growing up, and a man lucky in friends, and Hoskuld loved him best of all his children. The house of Hoskuld now stood in great honour and renown. About this time Hoskuld gave his sister Groa in marriage to Velief the Old, and their son was "Holmgang"-Bersi.

CHAPTER 10
Of Viga Hrapp

Hrapp was the name of a man who lived in Salmon-river-Dale, on the north bank of the river on the opposite side to Hoskuldstead, at the place that was called later on Hrappstead, where there is now waste land. Hrapp was the son of Sumarlid, and was called Fight-Hrapp. He was Scotch on his father's side, and his mother's kin came from Sodor, where he was brought up. He was a very big,strong man, and one not willing to give in even in face of some odds; and for the reason that was most overbearing, and would never make good what he had misdone, he had had to fly from West-over-the-sea, and had bought the land on which he afterwards lived. His wife was named Vigdis, and was Hallstein's daughter; and their son was named Sumarlid. Her brother was named Thorstein Surt; he lived at Thorsness, as has been written before. Sumarlid was brought up there, and was a most promising young man. Thorstein had been married, but by this time his wife was dead. He had two daughters, one named Gudrid, and the other Osk. Thorkell trefill married Gudrid, and they lived in Svignaskard. He was a great chieftain, and a sage of wits; he was the son of Raudabjorn. Osk, Thorstein's daughter, was given in marriage to a man of Broadfirth named Thorarin. He was a valiant man, and very popular, and lived with Thorstein, his father-in-law, who was sunk in age and much in need of their care. Hrapp was disliked by most people, being overbearing to his neighbours; and at times he would hint to them that theirs would be a heavy lot as neighbours, if they held any other man for better than himself. All the goodmen took one counsel, and went to Hoskuld and told him their trouble. Hoskuld bade them tell him if Hrapp did any one any harm, "For he shall not plunder me of men or money."

CHAPTER 11
About Thord Goddi and Thorbjorn Skrjup

Thord Goddi was the name of a man who lived in Salmon-river-Dale on the northern side of the river, and his house was Vigdis called Goddistead. He was a very wealthy man; he had no children, and had bought the land he lived on. He was a neighbour of Hrapp's, and was very often badly treated by him. Hoskuld looked after him, so that he kept his dwelling in peace. Vigdis was the name of his wife. She was daughter of Ingjald, son of Olaf Feilan, and brother's daughter of Thord Yeller, and sister's daughter of Thorolf Rednose of Sheepfell. This Thorolf was a great hero, and in a very good position, and his kinsmen often went to him for protection. Vigdis had married more for money than high station. Thord had a thrall who had come to Iceland with him, named Asgaut. He was a big man, and shapely of body; and though he was called a thrall, yet few could be found his equal amongst those called freemen, and he knew well how to serve his master. Thord had many other thralls, though this one is the only one mentioned here. Thorbjorn was the name of a man. He lived in Salmon-river-Dale, next to Thord, up valley away from his homestead, and was called Skrjup. He was very rich in chattels, mostly in gold and silver.

He was an huge man and of great strength. No squanderer of money on common folk was he. Hoskuld, Dalakoll's son, deemed it a drawback to his state that his house was worse built than he wished it should be; so he bought a ship from a Shetland man. The ship lay up in the mouth of the river Blanda. That ship he gets ready, and makes it known that he is going abroad, leaving Jorunn to take care of house and children. They now put out to sea, and all went well with them; and they hove somewhat southwardly into Norway, making Hordaland, where the market-town called Biorgvin was afterwards built. Hoskuld put up his ship, and had there great strength of kinsmen, though here they be not named. Hakon, the king, had then his seat in the Wick. Hoskuld did not go to the king, as his kinsfolk welcomed him with open arms. That winter all was quiet (in Norway).

CHAPTER 12
Hoskuld Buys a Slave Woman

There were tidings at the beginning of the summer that the king went with his fleet eastward to a tryst in Brenn-isles, to settle peace for his land, even as the law laid down should be done every third summer. This meeting was held between rulers with a view to settling such matters as kings had toadjudge - matters of international policy between Norway, Sweden, and Denmark. It was deemed a pleasure trip to go to this meeting, for thither came men from well-nigh all such lands as we know of. Hoskuld ran out his ship, being desirous also to go to the meeting; moreover, he had not been to see the king all the winter through. There was also a fair to be made for. At the meeting there were great crowds of people, and much amusement to be got - drinking, and games, and all sorts of entertainment. Nought, however, of great interest happened there. Hoskuld met many of his kinsfolk there who were come from Denmark. Now, one day as Hoskuld went out to disport himself with some other men, he saw a stately tent far away from the other booths. Hoskuld went thither, and into the tent, and there sat a man before him in costly raiment, and a Russian hat on his head. Hoskuld asked him his name. He said he was called Gilli: "But many call to mind the man if they hear my nickname - I am called Gilli the Russian." Hoskuld said he had often heard talk of him, and that he held him to be the richest of men that had ever belonged to the guild of merchants. Still Hoskuld spoke: "You must have things to sell such as we should wish to buy." Gilli asked what he and his companions wished to buy. Hoskuld said he should like to buy some bonds-woman, "if you have one to sell." Gilli answers: "There, you mean to give me trouble by this, in asking for things you don'texpect me to have in stock; but it is not sure that follows." Hoskuld then saw that right across the booth there was drawn a curtain; and Gilli then lifted the curtain, and Hoskuld saw that there were twelve women seated behind the curtain. So Gilli said that Hoskuld should come on and have a look, if he would care to buy any of these women. Hoskuld did so. They sat all together across the booth. Hoskuld looks carefully at these women. He saw a woman sitting out by the skirt of the tent, and she was very ill-clad. Hoskuld thought, as far as he could see, this woman was fair to look upon. Then said Hoskuld, "What is the price of that woman if I should wish to buy her?" Gilli replied, "Three silver pieces is what you must weigh me out for her." "It seems to me," said Hoskuld, "that you charge very highly for this bonds-woman, for that is the price of three (such)." Then Gilli said, "You speak truly, that I value her worth more than the others. Choose any of the other eleven, and pay one mark of silver for her, this one being left in my possession." Hoskuld said, "I must first see how much silver there is in the purse I have on my belt," and he asked Gilli to take the scales while he searched the purse. Gilli then said, "On my side there shall be no guile in this matter; for, as to the ways of this woman, there is a great drawback which I wish, Hoskuld, that you know before we strike this bargain." Hoskuld asked what it was. Gilli replied, "The woman is dumb. I have triedin many ways to get her to talk, but have never got a word out of her, and I feel quite sure that this woman knows not how to speak." Then, said Hoskuld, "Bring out the scales, and let us see how much the purse I have got here may weigh." Gilli did so, and now they weigh the silver, and there were just three marks weighed. Then said

185

Hoskuld, "Now the matter stands so that we can close our bargain. You take the money for yourself, and I will take the woman. I take it that you have behaved honestly in this affair, for, to be sure, you had no mind to deceive me herein." Hoskuld then went home to his booth. That same night Hoskuld went into bed with her. The next morning when men got dressed, spake Hoskuld, "The clothes Gilli the Rich gave you do not appear to be very grand, though it is true that to him it is more of a task to dress twelve women than it is to me to dress only one." After that Hoskuld opened a chest, and took out some fine women's clothes and gave them to her; and it was the saying of every one that she looked very well when she was dressed. But when the rulers had there talked matters over according as the law provided, this meeting was broken up. Then Hoskuld went to see King Hakon, and greeted him worthily, according to custom. The king cast a side glance at him, and said, "We should have taken well your greeting, Hoskuld, even if you had saluted us sooner; but so shall it be even now."

CHAPTER 13
Hoskuld Returns to Iceland, A.D. 948

After that the king received Hoskuld most graciously, and bade him come on board his own ship, and "be with us so long as you care to remain in Norway." Hoskuld answered: "Thank you for your offer; but now, this summer, I have much to be busy about, and that is mostly the reason I was so long before I came to see you, for I wanted to get for myself house-timber." The king bade him bring his ship in to the Wick, and Hoskuld tarried with the king for a while. The king got house-timber for him, and had his ship laden for him. Then the king said to Hoskuld, "You shall not be delayed here longer than you like, though we shall find it difficult to find a man to take your place." After that the king saw Hoskuld off to his ship, and said: "I have found you an honourable man, and now my mind misgives me that you are sailing for the last time from Norway, whilst I am lord over that land." The king drew a gold ring off his arm that weighed a mark, and gave it to Hoskuld; and he gave him for another gift a sword on which there was half a mark of gold. Hoskuld thanked the king for his gifts, and for all the honour he had donehim. After that Hoskuld went on board his ship, and put to sea. They had a fair wind, and hove in to the south of Iceland; and after that sailed west by Reekness, and so by Snowfellness in to Broadfirth. Hoskuld landed at Salmon-river-Mouth. He had the cargo taken out of his ship, which he took into the river and beached, having a shed built for it. A ruin is to be seen now where he built the shed. There he set up his booths, and that place is called Booths'-Dale. After that Hoskuld had the timber taken home, which was very easy, as it was not far off. Hoskuld rode home after that with a few men, and was warmly greeted, as was to be looked for. He found that all his belongings had been kept well since he left. Jorunn asked, "What woman that was who journeyed with him?" Hoskuld answered, "You will think I am giving you a mocking answer when I tell you that I do not know her name." Jorunn said, "One of two things there must be: either the talk is a lie that has come to my ears, or you must have spoken to her so much as to have asked her her name." Hoskuld said he could not gainsay that, and so told her the truth, and bade that the woman should be kindly treated, and said it was his wish she should stay in service with them. Jorunn said, "I am not going to wrangle with the mistress you have brought out of Norway, should she find living near me no pleasure; least of all should I think of it if she is both deaf and dumb." Hoskuld slept with his wife every night after he camehome, and had very little to say to the mistress. Every one clearly saw that there was something betokening high birth in the way she bore herself, and that she was no fool. Towards the end of the winter Hoskuld's mistress gave birth to a male child. Hoskuld was called, and was shown the child, and he thought, as others did, that he had never seen a goodlier or a more noble-looking child. Hoskuld was asked what the boy should be called. He said it should be named Olaf, for Olaf Feilan had died a little time before, who was his mother's brother. Olaf was far before other children, and Hoskuld bestowed great love on the boy. The next summer Jorunn said, "That the woman must do some work or other, or else go away." Hoskuld said she should wait on him and his wife, and take care of her boy besides. When the boy was two years old he had got full speech, and ran about like children of four years old. Early one morning, as Hoskuld had gone out to look about his manor, the weather being fine, and the sun, as yet little risen in the sky, shining brightly, it happened that he heard some voices of people talking; so he went down to where a little brook ran past the home-field slope, and he saw two people there whom he recognised as his son Olaf and his mother, and he discovered she was not speechless, for she was talking a great deal to the boy. Then Hoskuld went to her and asked her her name, and said it was useless for her to hide it any longer. She said so it should be, and they satdown on the brink of the field. Then she said, "If you want to know my name, I am called Melkorka." Hoskuld bade her tell him more of her kindred. She answered, "Myr Kjartan is the name of my father, and he is a king in Ireland; and I was taken a prisoner of war from there when I was fifteen winters old." Hoskuld said she had kept silence far too long about so noble a descent. After that Hoskuld went on, and told Jorunn what he had just found out during his walk. Jorunn said that she "could not tell if this were true," and said she had no fondness for any manner of wizards; and so the matter dropped. Jorunn was no kinder to her than before, but Hoskuld had somewhat more to say to her. A little while after this, when Jorunn was going to bed, Melkorka was undressing her, and put her shoes on the floor, when Jorunn took the stockings and smote her with them about the head. Melkorka got angry, and struck Jorunn on the nose with her fist, so that the blood flowed. Hoskuld came in and parted them. After that he let Melkorka go away, and got a dwelling ready for her up in Salmon-river-Dale, at the place that was afterwards called Melkorkastad, which is now waste land on the south of the Salmon river. Melkorka now set up household there, and Hoskuld had everything brought there that she needed; and Olaf, their son, went with her. It was soon seen that Olaf, as he grew up, was far superior to other men, both on account of his beauty and courtesy.

CHAPTER 14
The Murder of Hall, Ingjald's Brother

Ingjald was the name of a man. He lived in Sheepisles, that lie out in Broadfirth. He was called Sheepisles' Priest. He was rich, and a mighty man of his hand. Hall was the name of his brother. He was big, and had the makings of a man in him; he was, however, a man of small means, and looked upon by most people as an unprofitable sort of man. The brothers did not usually agree very well together. Ingjald thought Hall did not shape himself after the fashion of doughty men, and Hall thought Ingjald was but little minded to lend furtherance to his affairs. There is a fishing place in Broadfirth called Bjorn isles. These islands lie many together, and were profitable in many ways. At that time men went there a great deal for the fishing, and at all seasons there were a great many men there. Wise men set great store by people in outlying fishing-stations living peacefully together, and said that it would be unlucky for the fishing if there was any quarrelling; and most men gave good heed to this. It is told how one summer Hall, the brother of Ingjald, the Sheepisles' Priest, came to Bjorn isles for fishing. He took ship as one of the crew with a man called Thorolf. He was a Broadfirth man, and was well-nigh a penniless vagrant, and yet a brisk sort of a man. Hall was there for some time, and palmed himself off as being much above other men. It happened one evening when they were come to land, Hall and Thorolf, and began to divide the catch, that Hall wished both to choose and to divide, for he thought himself the greater man of the two. Thorolf would not give in, and there were some high words, and sharp things were said on both sides, as each stuck to his own way of thinking. So Hall seized up a chopper that lay by him, and was about to heave it at Thorolf's head, but men leapt between them and stopped Hall; but he was of the maddest, and yet unable to have his way as at this time. The catch of fish remained undivided. Thorolf betook himself away that evening, and Hall took possession of the catch that belonged to them both, for then the odds of might carried the day. Hall now got another man in Thorolf's place in the boat, and went on fishing as before. Thorolf was ill-contented with his lot, for he felt he had come to shame in their dealings together; yet he remained in the islands with the determination to set straight the humble plight to which he had been made to bow against his will. Hall, in the meantime, did not fear any danger, and thought that no one would dare to try to get even with him in his own country. So one fair-weather day it happened that Hall rowed out, and there were three of them together in the boat. The fish bit well through the day, and as they rowed home in the evening they were very merry. Thorolf kept spying about Hall's doings during the day, and is standing in the landing-place when Hall came to land. Hall rowed in the forehold of the boat, and leapt overboard, intending to steady the boat; and as he jumped to land Thorolf happens to be standing near, and forthwith hews at him, and the blow caught him on his neck against the shoulder, and off flew his head. Thorolf fled away after that, and Hall's followers were all in a flurried bustle about him. The story of Hall's murder was told all over the islands, and every one thought it was indeed great news; for the man was of high birth, although he had had little good luck. Thorolf now fled from the islands, for he knew no man there who would shelter him after such a deed, and he had no kinsmen he could expect help from; while in the neighbourhood were men from whom it might be surely looked for that they would beset his life, being moreover men of much power, such as was Ingjald, the Sheepisles' Priest, the brother of Hall. Thorolf got himself ferried across to the mainland. He went with great secrecy. Nothing is told of his journey, until one evening he came to Goddistead. Vigdis, the wife of Thord Goddi, was some sort of relation to

Thorolf, and on that account he turned towards that house. Thorolf had also heard before how matters stood there, and how Vigdis was endowed with a good deal more courage than Thord, her husband. And forthwith the same evening that Thorolf came to Goddistead he went to Vigdis to tell her his trouble, and to beg her help. Vigdis answered his pleading in this way: "I do not deny our relationship, and in this way alone I can look upon the deed you have done, that I deem you in no way the worser man for it. Yet this I see, that those who shelter you will thereby have at stake their lives and means, seeing what great men they are who will be taking up the blood-suit. And Thord," she said, "my husband, is not much of a warrior; but the counsels of us women are mostly guided by little foresight if anything is wanted. Yet I am loath to keep aloof from you altogether, seeing that, though I am but a woman, you have set your heart on finding some shelter here." After that Vigdis led him to an outhouse, and told him to wait for her there, and put a lock on the door. Then she went to Thord, and said, "A man has come here as a guest, named Thorolf. He is some sort of relation of mine, and I think he will need to dwell here some long time if you will allow it." Thord said he could not away with men coming to put up at his house, but bade him rest there over the next day if he had no trouble on hand, but otherwise he should be off at his swiftest. Vigdis answered, "I have offered him already to stay on, and I cannot take back my word, though he be not in even friendship with all men." Afterthat she told Thord of the slaying of Hall, and that Thorolf who was come there was the man who had killed him. Thord was very cross-grained at this, and said he well knew how that Ingjald would take a great deal of money from him for the sheltering that had been given him already, seeing that doors here have been locked after this man. Vigdis answered, "Ingjald shall take none of your money for giving one night's shelter to Thorolf, and he shall remain here all this winter through." Thord said, "In this manner you can checkmate me most thoroughly, but it is against my wish that a man of such evil luck should stay here." Still Thorolf stayed there all the winter. Ingjald, who had to take up the blood-suit for his brother, heard this, and so arrayed him for a journey into the Dales at the end of the winter, and ran out a ferry of his whereon they went twelve together. They sailed from the west with a sharp north-west wind, and landed in Salmon-river-Mouth in the evening. They put up their ferry-boat, and came to Goddistead in the evening, arriving there not unawares, and were cheerfully welcomed. Ingjald took Thord aside for a talk with him, and told him his errand, and said he had heard of Thorolf, the slayer of his brother, being there. Thord said there was no truth in that. Ingjald bade him not to deny it. "Let us rather come to a bargain together: you give up the man, and put me to no toil in the matter of getting at him. I have three marks of silver that you shall have, and I will overlook the offences you have broughton your hands for the shelter given to Thorolf." Thord thought the money fair, and had now a promise of acquittal of the offences for which he had hitherto most dreaded and for which he would have to abide sore loss of money. So he said, "I shall no doubt hear people speak ill of me for this, none the less this will have to be our bargain." They slept until it wore towards the latter end of the night, when it lacked an hour of day.

CHAPTER 15
Thorolf's Escape with Asgaut the Thrall

Ingjald and his men got up and dressed. Vigdis asked Thord what his talk with Ingjald had been about the evening before. Thord said they had talked about many things, amongst others how the place was to be ransacked, and how they should be clear of the case if Thorolf was not found there. "So I let Asgaut, my thrall, take the man away." Vigdis said she had no fondness for lies, and said she should be very loath to have Ingjald sniffing about her house, but bade him, however, do as he liked. After that Ingjald ransacked the place, and did not hit upon the man there. At that moment Asgaut came back, and Vigdis asked him where he had parted with Thorolf. Asgaut replied, "I took him to our sheephouses asThord told me to." Vigdis replied, "Can anything be more exactly in Ingjald's way as he returns to his ship? nor shall any risk be run, lest they should have made this plan up between them last night. I wish you to go at once, and take him away as soon as possible. You shall take him to Sheepfell to Thorolf; and if you do as I tell you, you shall get something for it. I will give you your freedom and money, that you may go where you will." Asgaut agreed to this, and went to the sheephouse to find Thorolf, and bade him get ready to go at once. At this time Ingjald rode out of Goddistead, for he was now anxious to get his money's worth. As he was come down from the farmstead (into the plain) he saw two men coming to meet him; they were Thorolf and Asgaut. This was early in the morning, and there was yet but little daylight. Asgaut and Thorolf now found themselves in a hole, for Ingjald was on one side of them and the Salmon River on the other. The river was terribly swollen, and there were great masses of ice on either bank, while in the middle it had burst open, and it was an ill-looking river to try to ford. Thorolf said to Asgaut, "It seems to me we have two choices before us. One is to remain here and fight as well as valour and manhood will serve us, and yet the thing most likely is that Ingjald and his men will take our lives without delay; and the other is to tackle the river, and yet that, I think, is still a somewhat dangerous one." Asgaut said that Thorolf should have his way, and hewould not desert him, "whatever plan you are minded to follow in this matter." Thorolf said, "We will make for the river, then," and so they did, and arrayed themselves as light as possible. After this they got over the main ice, and plunged into the water. And because the men were brave, and Fate had ordained them longer lives, they got across the river and upon the ice on the other side. Directly after they had got across, Ingjald with his followers came to the spot opposite to them on the other side of the river. Ingjald spoke out, and said to his companions, "What plan shall we follow now? Shall we tackle the river or not?" They said he should choose, and they would rely on his foresight, though they thought the river looked impassable. Ingjald said that so it was, and "we will turn away from the river;" and when Thorolf and Asgaut saw that Ingjald had made up his mind not to cross the river, they first wring their clothes and then make ready to go on. They went on all that day, and came in the evening to Sheepfell. They were well received there, for it was an open house for all guests; and forthwith that same evening Asgaut went to see Thorolf Rednose, and told him all the matters concerning their errand, "how Vigdis, his kinswoman, had sent him this man to keep in safety." Asgaut also told him all that had happened between Ingjald and Thord Goddi;

190

therewithal he took forth the tokens Vigdis had sent. Thorolf replied thus, "I cannot doubt these tokens. I shall indeed take this man in ather request. I think, too, that Vigdis has dealt most bravely with this matter and it is a great pity that such a woman should have so feeble a husband. And you, Asgaut, shall dwell here as long as you like." Asgaut said he would tarry there for no length of time. Thorolf now takes unto him his namesake, and made him one of his followers; and Asgaut and they parted good friends, and he went on his homeward journey. And now to tell of Ingjald. He turned back to Goddistead when he and Thorolf parted. By that time men had come there from the nearest farmsteads at the summons of Vigdis, and no fewer than twenty men had gathered there already. But when Ingjald and his men came to the place, he called Thord to him, "You have dealt in a most cowardly way with me, Thord," says he, "for I take it to be the truth that you have got the man off." Thord said this had not happened with his knowledge; and now all the plotting that had been between Ingjald and Thord came out. Ingjald now claimed to have back his money that he had given to Thord. Vigdis was standing near during this talk, and said it had fared with them as was meet, and prayed Thord by no means to hold back this money, "For you, Thord," she said, "have got this money in a most cowardly way." Thord said she must needs have her will herein. After that Vigdis went inside, and to a chest that belonged to Thord, and found at the bottom a large purse. She took out the purse, and went outside withit up to where Ingjald was, and bade him take the money. Ingjald's brow cleared at that, and he stretched out his hand to take the purse. Vigdis raised the purse, and struck him on the nose with it, so that forthwith blood fell on the earth. Therewith she overwhelmed him with mocking words, ending by telling him that henceforth he should never have the money, and bidding him go his way. Ingjald saw that his best choice was to be off, and the sooner the better, which indeed he did, nor stopped in his journey until he got home, and was mightily ill at ease over his travel.

CHAPTER 16
Thord becomes Olaf's Foster Father, A.D. 950

About this time Asgaut came home. Vigdis greeted him, and asked him what sort of reception they had had at Sheepfell. He gave a good account of it, and told her the words wherewith Thorolf had spoken out his mind. She was very pleased at that. "And you, Asgaut," she said, "have done your part well and faithfully, and you shall now know speedily what wages you have worked for. I give you your freedom, so that from this day forth you shall bear the title of a freeman. Therewith you shall take the money that Thord took as the price for the head of Thorolf, mykinsman, and now that money will be better bestowed." Asgaut thanked her for her gift with fair words. The next summer Asgaut took a berth in Day-Meal-Ness, and the ship put to sea, and they came in for heavy gales, but not a long sea-voyage, and made Norway. After that Asgaut went to Denmark and settled there, and was thought a valiant and true man. And herewith comes to an end the tale of him. But after the plot Thord Goddi had made up with Ingjald, the Sheepisles priest, when they made up their minds to compass the death of Thorolf, Vigdis' kinsman, she returned that deed with hatred, and divorced herself from Thord Goddi, and went to her kinsfolk and told them the tale. Thord Yeller was not pleased at this; yet matters went off quietly. Vigdis did not take away with her from Goddistead any more goods than her own heirlooms. The men of Hvamm let it out that they meant to have for themselves one-half of the wealth that Thord was possessed of. And on hearing this he becomes exceeding faint-hearted, and rides forthwith to see Hoskuld to tell him of his troubles. Hoskuld said, "Times have been that you have been terror-struck, through not having with such overwhelming odds to deal." Then Thord offered Hoskuld money for his help, and said he would not look at the matter with a niggard's eye. Hoskuld said, "This is clear, that you will not by peaceful consent allow any man to have the enjoyment of your wealth." Answers Thord, "No, not quite that though; for I fain would that you shouldtake over all my goods. That being settled, I will ask to foster your son Olaf, and leave him all my wealth after my days are done; for I have no heir here in this land, and I think my means would be better bestowed then, than that the kinsmen of Vigdis should grab it." To this Hoskuld agreed, and had it bound by witnesses. This Melkorka took heavily, deeming the fostering too low. Hoskuld said she ought not to think that, "for Thord is an old man, and childless, and I wish Olaf to have all his money after his day, but you can always go to see him at any time you like." Thereupon Thord took Olaf to him, seven years old, and loved him very dearly. Hearing this, the men who had on hand the case against Thord Goddi thought that now it would be even more difficult than before to lay claim to the money. Hoskuld sent some handsome presents to Thord Yeller, and bade him not be angry over this, seeing that in law they had no claim on Thord's money, inasmuch as Vigdis had brought no true charges against Thord, or any such as justified desertion by her. "Moreover, Thord was no worse a man for casting about for counsel to rid himself of a man that had been thrust upon his means, and was as beset with guilt as a juniper bush is with prickles." But when these words came to Thord from Hoskuld, and with them large gifts of money, then Thord allowed himself to be pacified, and said he thought the money was well placed that Hoskuld looked after, and tookthe gifts; and all was quiet after that, but their friendship was rather less warm than formerly. Olaf grew up with Thord, and became a great man and strong. He was so handsome that his equal was not to be found, and when he was twelve years old he rode to the Thing meeting, and men in other countrysides looked upon it as a great errand to go, and to wonder at the splendid way he was made. In keeping herewith was the manner of Olaf's war-gear and raiment, and therefore he was easily distinguished from all other men. Thord got on much better after Olaf came to live with him. Hoskuld gave Olaf a nickname, and called him Peacock, and the name stuck to him.

CHAPTER 17
About Viga Hrapp's Ghost, A.D. 950

The tale is told of Hrapp that he became most violent in his behaviour, and did his neighbours such harm that they could hardly hold their own against him. But from the time that Olaf grew up Hrapp got no hold of Thord. Hrapp had the same temper, but his powers waned, in that old age was fast coming upon him, so that he had to lie in bed. Hrapp called Vigdis, his wife, to him, and said, "I have never been of ailing health in life," said he, "and it is therefore most likely that this illness willput an end to our life together. Now, when I am dead, I wish my grave to be dug in the doorway of my fire hall, and that I be put: thereinto, standing there in the doorway; then I shall be able to keep a more searching eye on my dwelling." After that Hrapp died, and all was done as he said, for Vigdis did not dare do otherwise. And as evil as he had been to deal with in his life, just so he was by a great deal more when he was dead, for he walked again a great deal after he was dead. People said that he killed most of his servants in his ghostly appearances. He caused a great deal of trouble to those who lived near, and the house of Hrappstead became deserted. Vigdis, Hrapp's wife, betook herself west to Thorstein Swart, her brother. He took her and her goods in. And now things went as before, in that men went to find Hoskuld, and told him all the troubles that Hrapp was doing to them, and asked him to do something to put an end to this. Hoskuld said this should be done, and he went with some men to Hrappstead, and has Hrapp dug up, and taken away to a place near to which cattle were least likely to roam or men to go about. After that Hrapp's walkings-again abated somewhat. Sumarlid, Hrapp's son, inherited all Hrapp's wealth, which was both great and goodly. Sumarlid set up household at Hrappstead the next spring; but after he had kept house there for a little time he was seized of frenzy, and died shortly afterwards. Now it was the turn of his mother, Vigdis, totake there alone all this wealth; but as she would not go to the estate of Hrappstead, Thorstein Swart took all the wealth to himself to take care of. Thorstein was by then rather old, though still one of the most healthy and hearty of men.

CHAPTER 18
Of the Drowning of Thorstein Swart

At that time there rose to honour among men in Thorness, the kinsmen of Thorstein, named Bork the Stout and his brother, Thorgrim. It was soon found out how these brothers would fain be the greatest men there, and were most highly accounted of. And when Thorstein found that out, he would not elbow them aside, and so made it known to people that he wished to change his abode, and take his household to Hrappstead, in Salmon-river-Dale. Thorstein Swart got ready to start after the spring Thing, but his cattle were driven round along the shore. Thorstein got on board a ferry-boat, and took twelve men with him; and Thorarin, his brother-in-law, and Osk, Thorstein's daughter, and Hild, her daughter, who was three years old, went with them too. Thorstein fell in with a high south-westerly gale, and they sailed up towards the roosts, and into that roost which is called Coal-chest-Roost,which is the biggest of the currents in Broadfirth. They made little way sailing, chiefly because the tide was ebbing, and the wind was not favourable, the weather being squally, with high wind when the squalls broke over, but with little wind between whiles. Thorstein steered, and had the braces of the sail round his shoulders, because the boat was blocked up with goods, chiefly piled-up chests, and the cargo was heaped up very high; but land was near about, while on the boat there was but little way, because of the raging current against them. Then they sailed on to a hidden rock, but were not wrecked. Thorstein bade them let down the sail as quickly as possible, and take punt poles to push off the ship. This shift was tried to no avail, because on either board the sea was so deep that the poles struck no bottom; so they were obliged to wait for the incoming tide, and now the water ebbs away under the ship. Throughout the day they saw a seal in the current larger by much than any others, and through the day it would be swimming round about the ship, with flappers none of the shortest, and to all of them it seemed that in him there were human eyes. Thorstein bade them shoot the seal, and they tried, but it came to nought. Now the tide rose; and just as the ship was getting afloat there broke upon them a violent squall, and the boat heeled over, and every one on board the boat was drowned, save one man, named Gudmund, who drifted ashore with some timber. The place where he was washedup was afterwards called Gudmund's Isles. Gudrid, whom Thorkell Trefill had for wife, was entitled to the inheritance left by Thorstein, her father. These tidings spread far and near of the drowning of Thorstein Swart, and the men who were lost there. Thorkell sent straightway for the man Gudmund, who had been washed ashore, and when he came and met Thorkell, he (Thorkell) struck a bargain with him, to the end that he should tell the story of the loss of lives even as he (Thorkell) was going to dictate it to him. Gudmund agreed. Thorkell now asked him to tell the story of this mishap in the hearing of a good many people. Then Gudmund spake on this wise: "Thorstein was drowned first, and then his son-in-law, Thorarin" - so that then it was the turn of Hild to come in for the money, as she was the daughter of Thorarin. Then he said the maiden was drowned, because the next in inheritance to her was Osk, her mother, and she lost her life the last of them, so that all the money thus came to Thorkell Trefill, in that his wife Gudrid must take inheritance after her sister. Now this tale is spread abroad by Thorkell and his men; but Gudmund ere this had told the tale in somewhat another way. Now the kinsmen of Thorarin misdoubted this tale somewhat, and said they would not believe it unproved, and claimed one-half of the heritage against Thorkell; but Thorkell maintained it belonged to him alone, and bade that ordeal should be taken on the matter, according to their custom. This was the ordealat that time, that men had had to pass under "earth-chain," which was a slip of sward cut loose from the soil, but both ends thereof were left adhering to the earth, and the man who should go through with the ordeal should walk thereunder. Thorkell Trefill now had some misgivings himself as to whether the deaths of the people had indeed taken place as he and Gudmund had said the second time. Heathen men deemed that on them rested no less responsibility when ceremonies of this kind had to be gone through than Christian men do when ordeals are decreed. He who passed under "earth-chain" cleared himself if the sward-slip did not fall down upon him. Thorkell made an arrangement with two men that they should feign quarrelling over something or another, and be close to the spot when the ordeal was being gone through with, and touch the sward-slip so unmistakably that all men might see that it was they who knocked it down. After this comes forward he who was to go through with the ordeal, and at the nick of time when he had got under the "earth-chain," these men who had been put up to it fall on each other with weapons, meeting close to the arch of the sward-slip, and lie there fallen, and down tumbles the "earth-chain", as was likely enough. Then men rush up between them and part them, which was easy enough, for they fought with no mind to do any harm. Thorkell Trefill then asked people as to what they thought about the ordeal, and all his men now said that it would have turned out allright

194

if no one had spoilt it. Then Thorkell took all the chattels to himself, but the land at Hrapstead was left to lie fallow.

CHAPTER 19
Hrut Comes to Iceland

Now of Hoskuld it is to be told that his state is one of great honour, and that he is a great chieftain. He had in his keep a great deal of money that belonged to his (half) brother, Hrut, Herjolf's son. Many men would have it that Hoskuld's means would be heavily cut into if he should be made to pay to the full the heritage of his (Hrut's) mother. Hrut was of the bodyguard of King Harald, Gunnhild's son, and was much honoured by him, chiefly for the reason that he approved himself the best man in all deeds of manly trials, while, on the other hand, Gunnhild, the Queen, loved him so much that she held there was not his equal within the guard, either in talking or in anything else. Even when men were compared, and noblemen therein were pointed to, all men easily saw that Gunnhild thought that at the bottom there must be sheer thoughtlessness, or else envy, if any man was said to be Hrut's equal. Now, inasmuch as Hrut had in Iceland much money to look after, and many noble kinsfolk to go and see, he desired to go there, and now arrays his journey for Iceland. The king gave him a ship at parting, and said he had proved a brave man and true. Gunnhild saw Hrut off to his ship, and said, "Not in a hushed voice shall this be spoken, that I have proved you to be a most noble man, in that you have prowess equal to the best man here in this land, but are In wits a long way before them". Then she gave him a gold ring and bade him farewell. Whereupon she drew her mantle over her head and went swiftly home. Hrut went on board his ship, and put to sea. He had a good breeze, and came to Broadfirth. He sailed up the bay, up to the island, and, steering in through Broadsound, he landed at Combness, where he put his gangways to land. The news of the coming of this ship spread about, as also that Hrut, Herjolf's son, was the captain. Hoskuld gave no good cheer to these tidings, and did not go to meet Hrut. Hrut put up his ship, and made her snug. He built himself a dwelling, which since has been called Combness. Then he rode to see Hoskuld, to get his share of his mother's inheritance. Hoskuld said he had no money to pay him, and said his mother had not gone without means out of Iceland when she met with Herjolf. Hrut liked this very ill, but rode away, and there the matter rested. All Hrut's kinsfolk, excepting Hoskuld, did honour to Hrut. Hrut now lived three winters at Combness, and was always demanding the money from Hoskuld at the Thing meetings and other law gatherings, and he spoke well on the matter. And most men held that Hrut had right on his side. Hoskuld said that Thorgerd had not married Herjolf by his counsel, and that he was her lawful guardian, and there the matter dropped. That same autumn Hoskuld went to a feast at Thord Goddi's, and hearing that, Hrut rode with twelve men to Hoskuldstead and took away twenty oxen, leaving as many behind. Then he sent some men to Hoskuld, telling them where he might search for the cattle. Hoskuld's house-carles sprang forthwith up, and seized their weapons, and words were sent to the nearest neighbours for help, so that they were a party of fifteen together, and they rode each one as fast as they possibly could. Hrut and his followers did not see the pursuit till they were a little way from the enclosure at Combness. And forthwith he and his men jumped off their horses, and tied them up, and went forward unto a certain sandhill. Hrut said that there they would make a stand, and added that though the money claim against Hoskuld sped slowly, never should that be said that he had run away before his thralls. Hrut's followers said that they had odds to deal with. Hrut said he would never heed that; said they should fare all the worse the more they were in number. The men of Salmon-river-Dale now jumped off their horses, and got ready to fight. Hrut bade his men not trouble themselves about the odds, and goes for them at a rush. Hrut had a helmet on his head, a drawn sword in one hand and a shield in the other. He was of all men the most skilled at arms. Hrut was then so wild that few could keep up with him. Bothsides fought briskly for a while; but the men of Salmon-river-Dale very soon found that in Hrut they had to deal with one for whom they were no match, for now he slew two men at every onslaught. After that the men of Salmon-river-Dale begged for peace. Hrut replied that they should surely have peace. All the house-carles of Hoskuld who were yet alive were wounded, and four were killed. Hrut then went home, being somewhat wounded himself; but his followers only slightly or not at all, for he had been the foremost in the fight. The place has since been called Fight-Dale where they fought. After that Hrut had the cattle killed. Now it must be told how Hoskuld got men together in a hurry when he heard of the robbery and rode home. Much at the same time as he arrived his house-carles came home too, and told how their journey had gone anything but smoothly. Hoskuld was wild with wrath at this, and said he meant to take at Hrut's hand no robbery or loss of lives again, and gathered to him men all that day. Then Jorunn, his wife, went and talked to him, and asked him what he had made his mind up to. He said, "It is but little I have made up my mind to, but I fain would that men should oftener talk of something else than the slaying of my house-carles". Jorunn answered, "You are after a fearful deed if you mean to kill such a man as your brother, seeing that some men will have it that it would not have been without cause if Hrut had seized these goods even before this; and now he has shown that, taking after the race he comes from, he means no longer to be an outcast, kept from what is his own. Now, surely he cannot have made up his mind to try his strength with you till he knew that he might hope for some backing-up from the more powerful among men; for, indeed, I am told that messages have been passing in quiet between Hrut and Thord Yeller. And to me, at least, such matters seem worthy of heed being paid to them. No doubt Thord will be glad to back up matters of this kind, seeing how clear are the bearings of the case. Moreover you know, Hoskuld, that since the quarrel between Thord Goddi and Vigdis, there has not been the same fond friendship between you and Thord Yeller as before, although by means of gifts you staved off the enmity of him and his kinsmen in the beginning. I also think, Hoskuld," she said, "that in that matter, much to the trial of their temper, they feel they have come off worst at the hands of yourself and your son, Olaf. Now this seems to me the wiser counsel: to make your brother an honourable offer, for there a hard grip from greedy wolf may be looked for. I am sure that Hrut will take that matter in good part, for I am told he is a wise man, and he will see that that would be an honour to both of you." Hoskuld quieted down greatly at Jorunn's speech, and thought this was likely to be true. Then men went between them who were friends of both sides, bearing words of peace from Hoskuld to Hrut. Hrut received them well, and said he would indeed make friends with Hoskuld, and added that he had long been ready for their coming to terms as behoved kinsmen, if but Hoskuld had been willing to grant him his right. Hrut also said he was ready to do honour to Hoskuld for what he on his side had misdone. So now these matters were shaped and settled between the brothers, who now take to living together in good brotherhood from this time forth. Hrut now looks after his homestead, and became mighty man of his ways. He did not mix himself up in general things, but in whatever matter he took a part he would have his own way. Hrut now moved his dwelling, and abode to old age at a place which now is called Hrutstead. He made a temple in his home-field, of which the remains are still to be seen. It is called Trolls' walk now, and there is the high road. Hrut married a woman named Unn, daughter of Mord Fiddle. Unn left him, and thence sprang the quarrels between the men of Salmon-river-Dale and the men of Fleetlithe. Hrut's second wife was named Thorbjorg. She was Armod's daughter. Hrut married a third wife, but her we do not name. Hrut had sixteen sons and ten daughters by these two wives. And men say that one summer Hrut rode to the Thing meeting, and fourteen of his sons were with him. Of this mention is made, because it was thought a sign of greatness and might. All his sons were right goodly men.

CHAPTER 20
Melkorka's Marriage
and Olaf the Peacock's Journey, A.D. 955

Hoskuld now remained quietly at home, and began now to sink into old age, and his sons were now all grown up. Thorliek sets up household of his own at a place called Combness, and Hoskuld handed over to him his portion. After that he married a woman named Gjaflaug, daughter of Arnbjorn, son of Sleitu Bjorn, and Thordaug, the daughter of Thord of Headland. It was a noble match, Gjaflaug being a very beautiful and high-minded woman. Thorliek was not an easy man to get on with, but was most warlike. There was not much friendship between the kinsmen Hrut and Thorliek. Bard Hoskuld's son stayed at home with his father, looked after the household affairs no less than Hoskuld himself. The daughters of Hoskuld do not have much to do with this story, yet men are known who are descended from them. Olaf, Hoskuld's son, was now grown up, and was the handsomest of all men that people ever set eyes on. He arrayed himself always well, both as to clothes and weapons. Melkorka, Olaf's mother, lived at Melkorkastead, as has been told before. Hoskuld looked less after Melkorka's household ways than he used to do, saying that that matter concerned Olaf, her son. Olaf said he would give her such help as he had to offer her. Melkorka thought Hoskuld had done shamefully by her, and makes up her mind to do something to him at which he should not be over pleased. Thorbjorn Skrjup had chiefly had on hand the care of Melkorka's household affairs. He had made her an offer of marriage, after she had been an householder for but a little while, but Melkorka refused him flatly. There was a ship up by Board-Ere in Ramfirth, and Orn was the name of the captain. He was one of the bodyguard of King Harald, Gunnhild's son. Melkorka spoke to Olaf, her son, and said that she wished he should journey abroad to find his noble relations, "For I have told the truth that Myrkjartan is really my father, and he is king of the Irish and it would be easy for you betake you on board the ship that is now at Board-Ere." Olaf said, "I have spoken about it to my father, but he seemed to want to have but little to do with it; and as to the manner of my foster-father's money affairs, it so happens that his wealth is more in land or cattle than in stores of islandic market goods." Melkorka said, "I cannot bear your being called the son of a slave-woman any longer; and if it stands in the way of the journey, that you think you have not enough money, then I would rather go to the length even of marrying Thorbjorn, if then you should be more willing than before to betake yourself to the journey. For I think he will be willing to hand out to you as much wares as you think you may need, if I give my consent to his marrying me. Above all I look to this, that then Hoskuld will like two things mightily ill when hecomes to hear of them, namely, that you have gone out of the land, and that I am married." Olaf bade his mother follow her own counsel. After that Olaf talked to Thorbjorn as to how he wished to borrow wares of him, and a great deal thereof. Thorbjorn answered, "I will do it on one condition, and that is that I shall marry Melkorka for them; it seems to me, you will be as welcome to my money as to that which you have in your keep." Olaf said that this should then be settled; whereupon they talked between them of such matters as seemed needful, but all these things they agreed should be kept quiet. Hoskuld wished Olaf to ride with him to the Thing. Olaf said he could not do that on account of household affairs, as he also wanted to fence off a grazing paddock for lambs by Salmon River. Hoskuld was very pleased that he should busy himself with the homestead. Then Hoskuld rode to the Thing; but at Lambstead a wedding feast was arrayed, and Olaf settled the agreement alone. Olaf took out of the undivided estate thirty hundred ells' worth of wares, and should pay no money for them. Bard, Hoskuld's son, was at the wedding, and was a party with them to all these doings. When the feast was ended Olaf rode off to the ship, and found Orn the captain, and took berth with him. Before Olaf and Melkorka parted she gave him a great gold finger-ring, and said, "This gift my father gave me for a teething gift, and I know he will recognise it when he sees it." She also put into his hands a knife and a belt, and bade him give them to her nurse: "I am sure she will not doubt these tokens." And still further Melkorka spake, "I have fitted you out from home as best I know how, and taught you to speak Irish, so that it will make no difference to you where you are brought to shore in Ireland." After that they parted. There arose forthwith a fair wind, when Olaf got on board, and they sailed straightway out to sea.

CHAPTER 21
Olaf the Peacock goes to Ireland, A.D. 955

Now Hoskuld came back from the Thing and heard these tidings, and was very much displeased. But seeing that his near akin were concerned in the matter, he quieted down and let things alone. Olaf and his companions had a good voyage, and came to Norway. Orn urges Olaf to go to the court of King Harald, who, he said, bestowed goodly honour on men of no better breeding than Olaf was. Olaf said he thought he would take that counsel. Olaf and Orn now went to the court, and were well received. The king at once recognised Olaf for the sake of his kindred, and forthwith bade him stay with him. Gunnhild paid great heed to Olaf when sheknew he was Hrut's brother's son; but some men would have it, that she took pleasure in talking to Olaf without his needing other people's aid to introduce him. As the winter wore on, Olaf grew sadder of mood. Orn asked him what was the matter of his sorrow? Olaf answered, "I have on hand a journey to go west over the sea; and I set much store by it and that you should lend me your help, so that it may be undertaken in the course of next summer." Orn bade Olaf not set his heart on going, and said he did not know of any ships going west over the sea. Gunnhild joined in their talk, and said, "Now I hear you talk together in a manner that has not happened before, in that each of you wants to have his own way!" Olaf greeted Gunnhild well, without letting drop their talk. After that Orn went away, but Gunnhild and Olaf kept conversing together. Olaf told her of his wish, and how much store he set by carrying it out, saying he knew for certain that Myrkjartan, the king, was his mother's father. Then Gunnhild said, "I will lend you help for this voyage, so that you may go on it as richly furnished as you please." Olaf thanked her for her promise. Then Gunnhild had a ship prepared and a crew got together, and bade Olaf say how many men he would have to go west over the sea with him. Olaf fixed the number at sixty; but said that it was a matter of much concern to him, that such a company should be more like warriors than merchants. She said that so it should be; and Orn is the only man mentioned by name in company with Olaf on this journey. The company were well fitted out. King Harald and Gunnhild led Olaf to his ship, and they said they wished to bestow on him their good-luck over and above other friendship they had bestowed on him already. King Harald said that was an easy matter; for they must say that no goodlier a man had in their days come out of Iceland. Then Harald the king asked how old a man he was. Olaf answered, "I am now eighteen winters." The king replied, "Of exceeding worth, indeed, are such men as you are, for as yet you have left the age of child but a short way behind; and be sure to come and see us when you come back again." Then the king and Gunnhild bade Olaf farewell. Then Olaf and his men got on board, and sailed out to sea. They came in for unfavourable weather through the summer, had fogs plentiful, and little wind, and what there was was unfavourable; and wide about the main they drifted, and on most on board fell "sea-bewilderment." But at last the fog lifted over-head; and the wind rose, and they put up sail. Then they began to discuss in which direction Ireland was to be sought; and they did not agree on that. Orn said one thing, and most of the men went against him, and said that Orn was all bewildered: they should rule who were the greater in number. Then Olaf was asked to decide. He said, "I think we should follow the counsel of the wisest; for the counsels of foolish men I think will be of all the worseservice for us in the greater number they gather together." And now they deemed the matter settled, since Olaf spake in this manner; and Orn took the steering from that time. They sailed for days and nights, but always with very little wind. One night the watchmen leapt up, and bade every one wake at once, and said they saw land so near that they had almost struck on it. The sail was up, but there was but little wind. Every one got up, and Orn bade them clear away from the land, if they could. Olaf said, "That is not the way out of our plight, for I see reefs all about astern; so let down the sail at once, and we will take our counsel when there is daylight, and we know what land this is." Then they cast anchors, and they caught bottom at once. There was much talk during the night as to where they could be come to; and when daylight was up they recognised that it was Ireland. Orn said, "I don't think we have come to a good place, for this is far away from the harbours or market-towns, whose strangers enjoy peace; and we are now left high and dry, like sticklebacks, and near enough, I think, I come to the laws of the Irish in saying that they will lay claim to the goods we have on board as their lawful prize, for as flotsam they put down ships even when sea has ebbed out shorter from the stern (than here)." Olaf said no harm would happen, "But I have seen that to-day there is a gathering of men up inland; so the Irish think, no doubt, the arrival of this ship a great thing.During the ebb-tide to-day I noticed that there was a dip, and that out of the dip the sea fell without emptying it out; and if our ship has not been damaged, we can put out our boat and tow the ship into it." There was a bottom of loam where they had been riding at anchor, so that not a plank of the ship was damaged. So Olaf and his men tow their boat to the dip, cast anchor there. Now, as day drew on, crowds drifted down to the shore. At last two men rowed a boat out to the ship. They asked what men they were who had charge of that ship, and Olaf answered, speaking in Irish, to their inquiries. When the Irish knew they were Norwegians they pleaded their law, and bade them give up their goods; and if they did so, they would do them no harm till the king had sat in judgment on their case. Olaf said the law only held good when merchants had no interpreter with them. "But I can say with truth these are peaceful men, and we will not give ourselves up untried." The Irish then raised a great war-cry, and waded out into the sea, and wished to drag the ship, with them on board, to the shore, the water being no deeper than reaching up to their armpits, or to the belts of the tallest. But the pool was so deep where the ship was floating that they could not touch the bottom. Olaf bade the crew fetch out their weapons, and range in line of battle from stem to stern on the ship; and so thick they stood, that shield overlapped shield all round the ship, and a spear-point stood out at the lower end of every shield.Olaf walked fore to the prow, and was thus arrayed: he had a coat of mail, and a gold-reddened helmet on his head; girt with a sword with gold-inlaid hilt, and in his hand a barbed spear chased and well engraved. A red shield he had before him, on which was drawn a lion in gold. When the Irish saw this array fear shot through their hearts, and they thought it would not be so easy a matter as they had thought to master the booty. So now the Irish break their journey, and run all together to a village near. Then there arose great murmur in the crowd, as they deemed that, sure enough, this must be a warship, and that they must expect many others; so they sent speedily word to the king, which was easy, as he was at that time a short way off, feasting. Straightway he rides with a company of men to where the ship was. Between the land and the place where the ship lay afloat the space was no greater than that one might well hear men talking together. Now Olaf stood forth in the same arrayal whereof is written before, and men marvelled much how noble was the appearance of the man who was the captain of the ship. But when the shipmates of Olaf see how a large company of knights rides towards them, looking a company of the bravest, they grow hushed, for they deemed here were great odds to deal with. But when Olaf heard the murmur which went round among his followers, he bade them take heart, "For now our affairs are in a fair way; the Irish are now greeting Myrkjartan, their king." Then they rodeso near to the ship, that each could hear what the other said. The king asked who was the master of the ship. Olaf told his name, and asked who was the valiant-looking knight with whom he then was talking. He answered, "I am called Myrkjartan." Olaf asked, "Are you then a king of the Irish?" He said he was. Then the king asked Olaf for news commonly talked of, and Olaf gave good answers as to all news he was asked about. Then the king asked whence they had put to sea, and whose men they were.

And still the king asked, more searchingly than before, about Olaf's kindred, for the king found that this man was of haughty bearing, and would not answer any further than the king asked. Olaf said, "Let it be known to you that we ran our ship afloat from the coast of Norway, and these are of the bodyguard of King Harald, the son of Gunnhild, who are here on board. And as for my race, I have, sire, to tell you this, that my father lives in Iceland, and is named Hoskuld, a man of high birth; but of my mother's kindred, I think you must have seen many more than I have. For my mother is called Melkorka, and it has been told me as a truth that she is your daughter, king. Now, this has driven me upon this long journey, and to me it is a matter most weighty what answer you give in my case." The king then grew silent, and had a converse with his men. The wise men asked the king what might be the real truth of the story that this man was telling. The king answered,"This is clearly seen in this Olaf, that he is high-born man, whether he be a kinsman of mine or not, as well as this, that of all men he speaks the best of Irish." After that the king stood up, and said, "Now I will give answer to your speech, in so far as we grant to you and all your shipmates peace; but on the kinship you claim with us, we must talk more before I give answer to that." After that they put out their gangways to the shore, and Olaf and his followers went on land from the ship; and the Irish now marvel much how warrior-like these men are. Olaf greeted the king well, taking off his helmet and bowing to the king, who welcomes Olaf with all fondness. Thereupon they fall to talking together, Olaf pleading his case again in a speech long and frank; and at the end of his speech he said he had a ring on his hand that Melkorka had given him at parting in Iceland, saying "that you, king, gave it her as a tooth gift." The king took and looked at the ring, and his face grew wondrous red to look at; and then the king said, "True enough are the tokens, and become by no means less notable thereby that you have so many of your mother's family features, and that even by them you might be easily recognised; and because of these things I will in sooth acknowledge your kinship, Olaf, by the witnessing of these men that here are near and hear my speech. And this shall also follow that I will ask you to my court, with all your suite, but the honour of you all will depend thereon of what worth as a man I find you to be when I try you more." After that the king orders riding-horses to be given to them, and appoints men to look after their ship, and to guard the goods belonging to them. The King now rode to Dublin, and men thought this great tidings, that with the king should be journeying the son of his daughter, who had been carried off in war long ago when she was only fifteen winters old. But most startled of all at these tidings was the foster-mother of Melkorka, who was then bed-ridden, both from heavy sickness and old age; yet she walked with no staff even to support her, to meet Olaf. The king said to Olaf, "Here is come Melkorka's foster-mother, and she will wish to hear all the tidings you can tell about Melkorka's life." Olaf took her with open arms, and set the old woman on his knee, and said her foster-daughter was well settled and in a good position in Iceland. Then Olaf put in her hands the knife and the belt, and the old woman recognised the gifts, and wept for joy, and said it was easy to see that Melkorka's son was one of high mettle, and no wonder, seeing what stock he comes of. The old woman was strong and well, and in good spirits all that winter. The king was seldom at rest, for at that time the lands in the west were at all times raided by war-bands. The king drove from his land that winter both Vikings and raiders. Olaf was with his suite in the king's ship, and those who came against them thought his was indeed a grim company to deal with. The king talked over with Olaf and his followers all matters needing counsel,for Olaf proved himself to the king both wise and eager-minded in all deeds of prowess. But towards the latter end of the winter the king summoned a Thing, and great numbers came. The king stood up and spoke. He began his speech thus: "You all know that last autumn there came hither a man who is the son of my daughter, and high-born also on his father's side; and it seems to me that Olaf is a man of such prowess and courage that here such men are not to be found. Now I offer him my kingdom after my day is done, for Olaf is much more suitable for a ruler than my own sons." Olaf thanked him for this offer with many graceful and fair words, and said he would not run the risk as to how his sons might behave when Myrkjartan was no more; said it was better to gain swift honour than lasting shame; and added that he wished to go to Norway when ships could safely journey from land to land, and that his mother would have little delight in life if he did not return to her. The king bade Olaf do as he thought best. Then the Thing was broken up. When Olaf's ship was ready, the king saw him off on board; and gave him a spear chased with gold, and a gold-bedecked sword, and much money besides. Olaf begged that he might take Melkorka's foster-mother with him; but the king said there was no necessity for that, so she did not go. Then Olaf got on board his ship, and he and the king parted with the greatest friendship. Then Olaf sailed out to sea. They had a good voyage, and made landin Norway; and Olaf's journey became very famous. They set up their ship; and Olaf got horses for himself, and went, together with his followers, to find King Harald.

CHAPTER 22
Olaf the Peacock comes Home to Iceland, A.D. 957

Olaf Hoskuldson then went to the court of King Harald. The king gave him a good welcome, but Gunnhild a much better. With many fair words they begged him to stay with them, and Olaf agreed to it, and both he and Orn entered the king's court. King Harald and Gunnhild set so great a store by Olaf that no foreigner had ever been held in such honour by them. Olaf gave to the king and Gunnhild many rare gifts, which he had got west in Ireland. King Harald gave Olaf at Yule a set of clothes made out of scarlet stuff. So now Olaf stayed there quietly all the winter. In the spring, as it was wearing on, Olaf and the king had a conversation together, and Olaf begged the king's leave to go to Iceland in the summer, "For I have noble kinsfolk there I want to go and see." The king answered, "It would be more to my mind that you should settle down with us, and take whatever position in our service you like best yourself." Olafthanked the king for all the honour he was offering him, but said he wished very much to go to Iceland, if that was not against the king's will. The king answered, "Nothing shall be done in this in an unfriendly manner to you, Olaf. You shall go out to Iceland in the summer, for I see you have set your heart on it; but neither trouble nor toil shall you have over your preparations, for I will see after all that," and thereupon they part talking. King Harald had a ship launched in the spring; it was a merchant ship, both great and good. This ship the king ordered to be laden with wood, and fitted out with full rigging. When the ship was ready the king had Olaf called to him, and said, "This ship shall be your own, Olaf, for I should not like you to start from Norway this summer as a passenger in any one else's ship." Olaf thanked the king in fair words for his generosity. After that Olaf got ready for his journey; and when he was ready and a fair wind arose, Olaf sailed out to sea, and King Harald and he parted with the greatest affection. That summer Olaf had a good voyage. He brought his ship into Ramfirth, to Board-Ere. The arrival of the ship was soon heard of, and also who the captain was. Hoskuld heard of the arrival of Olaf, his son, and was very much pleased, and rode forthwith north to Hrutafjord with some men, and there was a joyful meeting between the father and son. Hoskuld invited Olaf to come to him, and Olaf said he would agree to that; so he set up his ship, but his goods were brought (on horseback)from the north. And when this business was over Olaf himself rode with twelve men home to Hoskuldstead, and Hoskuld greeted his son joyfully, and his brothers also received him fondly, as well as all his kinsfolk; but between Olaf and Bard was love the fondest. Olaf became very renowned for this journey; and now was proclaimed the descent of Olaf, that he was the daughter's son of Myrkjartan, king of Ireland. The news of this spread over the land, as well as of the honour that mighty men, whom he had gone to see, had bestowed on him. Melkorka came soon to see Olaf, her son, and Olaf greeted her with great joy. She asked about many things in Ireland, first of her father and then of her other relations. Olaf replied to everything she asked. Then she asked if her foster-mother still lived. Olaf said she was still alive. Melkorka asked why he had not tried to give her the pleasure of bringing her over to Iceland. Olaf replied, "They would not allow me to bring your foster-mother out of Ireland, mother." "That may be so," she replied, and it could be seen that this she took much to heart. Melkorka and Thorbjorn had one son, who was named Lambi. He was a tall man and strong, like his father in looks as well as in temper. When Olaf had been in Iceland a month, and spring came on, father and son took counsel together. "I will, Olaf," said Hoskuld, "that a match should be sought for you, and that then you should take over the house of your foster-father at Goddistead, where still there aregreat means stored up, and that then you should look after the affairs of that household under my guidance." Olaf answered, "Little have I set my mind on that sort of thing hitherto; besides, I do not know where that woman lives whom to marry would mean any great good luck to me. You must know I shall look high for a wife. But I see clearly that you would not have broached this matter till you had made up your mind as to where it was to end." Hoskuld said, "You guess that right. There is a man named Egil. He is Skallagrim's son. He lives at Borg, in Borgarfjord. This Egil has a daughter who is called Thorgerd, and she is the woman I have made up my mind to woo on your behalf, for she is the very best match in all Borgarfjord, and even if one went further afield. Moreover, it is to be looked for, that an alliance with the Mere-men would mean more power to you." Olaf answered, "Herein I shall trust to your foresight, for if this match were to come off it would be altogether to my liking. But this you must bear in mind, father, that should this matter be set forth, and not come off, I should take it very ill." Hoskuld answered, "I think I shall venture to bring the matter about." Olaf bade him do as he liked. Now time wears on towards the Thing. Hoskuld prepares his journey from home with a crowded company, and Olaf, his son, also accompanies him on the journey. They set up their booth. A great many people were there. Egil Skallagrim's son was at the Thing. Every one who saw Olaf remarkedwhat a handsome man he was, and how noble his bearing, well arrayed as he was as to weapons and clothes.

CHAPTER 23
The Marriage of Olaf Peacock and Thorgerd, the Daughter of Egil, A.D. 959

It is told how one day the father and son, Hoskuld and Olaf, went forth from their booth to find Egil. Egil greeted them well, for he and Hoskuld knew each other very well by word of mouth. Hoskuld now broaches the wooing on behalf of Olaf, and asks for the hand of Thorgerd. She was also at the Thing. Egil took the matter well, and said he had always heard both father and son well spoken of, "and I also know, Hoskuld," said Egil, "that you are a high-born man and of great worth, and Olaf is much renowned on account of his journey, and it is no wonder that such men should look high for a match, for he lacks neither family nor good looks; but yet this must be talked over with Thorgerd, for it is no man's task to get Thorgerd for wife against her will." Hoskuld said, "I wish, Egil, that you would talk this over with your daughter." Egil said that that should be done. Egil now went away to find his daughter, and they talked together. Egil said, "There is here a mannamed Olaf, who is Hoskuld's son, and he is now one of the most renowned of men. Hoskuld, his father, has broached a wooing on behalf of Olaf, and has sued for your hand; and I have left that matter mostly for you to deal with. Now I want to know your answer. But it seems to me that it behoves you to give a good answer to such a matter, for this match is a noble one." Thorgerd answered, "I have often heard you say that you love me best of all your children, but now it seems to me you make that a falsehood if you wish me to marry the son of a bonds-woman, however goodly and great a dandy he may be." Egil said, "In this matter you are not so well up, as in others. Have you not heard that he is the son of the daughter of Myrkjartan, king of Ireland? so that he is much higher born on his mother's side than on his father's, which, however, would be quite good enough for us." Thorgerd would not see this; and so they dropped the talk, each being somewhat of a different mind. The next day Egil went to Hoskuld's booth. Hoskuld gave him a good welcome, and so they fell a-talking together. Hoskuld asked how this wooing matter had sped. Egil held out but little hope, and told him all that had come to pass. Hoskuld said it looked like a closed matter, "Yet I think you have behaved well." Olaf did not hear this talk of theirs. After that Egil went away. Olaf now asks, "How speeds the wooing?" Hoskuld said, "It pointed to slow speed on her side." Olaf said, "It is now as I told you,father, that I should take it very ill if in answer (to the wooing) I should have to take shaming words, seeing that the broaching of the wooing gives undue right to the wooed. And now I shall have my way so far, that this shall not drop here. For true is the saw, that 'others' errands eat the wolves'; and now I shall go straightway to Egil's booth." Hoskuld bade him have his own way. Olaf now dressed himself in this way, that he had on the scarlet clothes King Harald had given him, and a golden helmet on his head, and the gold-adorned sword in his hand that King Myrkjartan had given him. Then Hoskuld and Olaf went to Egil's booth. Hoskuld went first, and Olaf followed close on his heels. Egil greeted him well, and Hoskuld sat down by him, but Olaf stood up and looked about him. He saw a woman sitting on the dais in the booth, she was goodly and had the looks of one of high degree, and very well dressed. He thought to himself this must be Thorgerd, Egil's daughter. Olaf went up to the dais and sat down by her. Thorgerd greeted the man, and asked who he was. Olaf told his own and his father's name, and "You must think it very bold that the son of a slave should dare to sit down by you and presume to talk to you!" She said, "You cannot but mean that you must be thinking you have done deeds of greater daring than that of talking to women." Then they began to talk together, and they talked all day. But nobody heard their conversation. And before they parted Egil and Hoskuld were called to them; and the matter of Olaf's wooing was now talked over again, and Thorgerd came round to her father's wish. Now the affair was all easily settled and the betrothal took place. The honour was conceded to the Salmon-river-Dale men that the bride should be brought home to them, for by law the bride-groom should have gone to the bride's home to be married. The wedding was to take place at Hoskuldstead when seven weeks summer had passed. After that Egil and Hoskuld separated. The father and son rode home to Hoskuldstead, and all was quiet the rest of the summer. After that things were got ready for the wedding at Hoskuldstead, and nothing was spared, for means were plentiful. The guests came at the time settled, and the Burgfirthmen mustered in a great company. Egil was there, and Thorstein, his son. The bride was in the journey too, and with her a chosen company out of all the countryside. Hoskuld had also a great company awaiting them. The feast was a brave one, and the guests were seen off with good gifts on leaving. Olaf gave to Egil the sword, Myrkjartan's gift, and Egil's brow brightened greatly at the gift. Nothing in the way of tidings befell, and every one went home.

CHAPTER 24
The Building of Herdholt, A. D. 960

Olaf and Thorgerd lived at Hoskuldstead and loved each other very dearly; it was easily seen by every one that she was a woman of very high mettle, though she meddled little with every-day things, but whatever Thorgerd put her hand to must be carried through as she wished. Olaf and Thorgerd spent that winter turn and turn about at Hoskuldstead, or with Olaf's foster-father. In the spring Olaf took over the household business at Goddistead. The following summer Thord fell ill, and the illness ended in his death. Olaf had a cairn raised over him on the ness that runs out into the Salmon-river and is called Drafn-ness, with a wall round which is called Howes-garth. After that liegemen crowded to Olaf and he became a great chieftain. Hoskuld was not envious of this, for he always wished that Olaf should be consulted in all great matters. The place Olaf owned was the stateliest in Salmon-river-Dale. There were two brothers with Olaf, both named An. One was called An the White and the other An the Black. They had a third brother who was named Beiner the Strong. These were Olaf's smiths, and very valiant men. Thorgerd and Olaf had a daughter who was named Thurid. The land that Hrapp had owned all lay waste, as has been told before. Olaf thought that it laywell and set before his father his wishes on the matter; how they should send down to Trefill with this errand, that Olaf wished to buy the land and other things thereto belonging at Hrappstead. It was soon arranged and the bargain settled, for Trefill saw that better was one crow in the hand than two in the wood. The bargain arranged was that Olaf should give three marks of silver for the land; yet that was not fair price, for the lands were wide and fair and very rich in useful produce, such as good salmon fishing and seal catching. There were wide woods too, a little further up than Hoskuldstead, north of the Salmon-river, in which was a space cleared, and it was well-nigh a matter of certainty that the flocks of Olaf would gather together there whether the weather was hard or mild. One autumn it befell that on that same hill Olaf had built a dwelling of the timber that was cut out of the forest, though some he got together from drift-wood strands. This was a very lofty dwelling. The buildings stood empty through the winter. The next spring Olaf went thither and first gathered together all his flocks which had grown to be a great multitude; for, indeed, no man was richer in live stock in all Broadfirth. Olaf now sent word to his father that he should be standing out of doors and have a look at his train as he was moving to his new home, and should give him his good wishes. Hoskuld said so it should be. Olaf now arranged how it should be done. He ordered that all the shiest of his cattle should be driven first and then the milking live stock, then came the dry cattle, and the pack horses came in the last place; and men were ranged with the animals to keep them from straying out of straight line. When the van of the train had got to the new homestead, Olaf was just riding out of Goddistead and there was nowhere a gap breaking the line. Hoskuld stood outside his door together with those of his household. Then Hoskuld spake, bidding Olaf his son welcome and abide all honour to this new dwelling of his, "And somehow my mind forebodes me that this will follow, that for a long time his name will be remembered." Jorunn his wife said, "Wealth enough the slave's son has got for his name to be long remembered." At the moment that the house-carles had unloaded the pack horses Olaf rode into the place. Then he said, "Now you shall have your curiosity satisfied with regard to what you have been talking about all the winter, as to what this place shall be called; it shall be called Herdholt." Every one thought this a very happy name, in view of what used to happen there. Olaf now sets up his household at Herdholt, and a stately one it soon became, and nothing was lacking there. And now the honour of Olaf greatly increased, there being many causes to bring it about: Olaf was the most beloved of men, for whatever he had to do with affairs of men, he did so that all were well contented with their lot. His father backed him up very much towards being a widely honoured man, and Olaf gained much in power from his alliance with the Mere-men. Olaf was considered the noblest of all Hoskuld's sons. The first winter that Olaf kept house at Herdholt, he had many servants and workmen, and work was divided amongst the house-carles; one looked after the dry cattle and another after the cows. The fold was out in the wood, some way from the homestead. One evening the man who looked after the dry cattle came to Olaf and asked him to make some other man look after the neat and "set apart for me some other work." Olaf answered, "I wish you to go on with this same work of yours." The man said he would sooner go away. "Then you think there is something wrong," said Olaf. "I will go this evening with you when you do up the cattle, and if I think there is any excuse for you in this I will say nothing about it, but otherwise you will find that your lot will take some turn for the worse." Olaf took his gold-set spear, the king's gift, in his hand, and left home, and with him the house-carle. There was some snow on the ground. They came to the fold, which was open, and Olaf bade the house-carle go in. "I will drive up the cattle and you tie them up as they come in." The house-carle went to the fold-door. And all unawares Olaf finds him leaping into his open arms. Olaf asked why he went on so terrified? He replied, "Hrapp stands in the doorway of the fold, and felt after me, but I have had my fill of wrestling with him." Olaf went to the folddoor and struck at him with his spear. Hrapp took the socket of the spear in both hands and wrenched it aside, so that forthwith the spear shaft broke. Olaf was about to run at Hrapp but he disappeared there where he stood, and there they parted, Olaf having the shaft and Hrapp the spear-head. After that Olaf and the house-carle tied up the cattle and went home. Olaf saw the house-carle was not to blame for his grumbling. The next morning Olaf went to where Hrapp was buried and had him dug up. Hrapp was found undecayed, and there Olaf also found his spear-head. After that he had a pyre made and had Hrapp burnt on it, and his ashes were flung out to sea. After that no one had any more trouble with Hrapp's ghost.

CHAPTER 25
About Hoskuld's Sons

Now Hoskuld's sons shall be told about. Thorliek, Hoskuld's son, had been a great seafarer, and taken service with men in lordly station when he was on his merchant voyages before he settled down as a householder, and a man of mark he was thought to be. He had also been on Viking raids, and given good account of himself by reason of his courage. Bard, Hoskuld's son, had also been a seafarer, and waswell accounted of wherever he went, for he was the best of brave men and true, and a man of moderation in all things. Bard married a Broadfirth woman, named Astrid, who came of a good stock. Bard's son was named Thorarin, and his daughter Gudney, who married Hall, the son of Fight Styr, and from them are descended many great families. Hrut, Herjolf's son, gave a thrall of his, named Hrolf, his freedom, and with it a certain amount of money, and a dwelling-place where his land joined with Hoskuld's. And it lay so near the landmark that Hrut's people had made a mistake in the matter, and settled the freedman down on the land belonging to Hoskuld. He soon gained there much wealth. Hoskuld took it very much to heart that Hrut should have placed his freedman right up against his ear, and bade the freedman pay him money for the lands he lived on "for it is mine own." The freedman went to Hrut and told him all they had spoken together. Hrut bade him give no heed, and pay no money to Hoskuld. "For I do not know," he said, "to which of us the land belonged." So the freedman went home, and goes on with his household just as before. A little later, Thorliek, Hoskuld's son, went at the advice of his father to the dwelling of the freedman and took him and killed him, and Thorliek claimed as his and his father's own all the money the freedman had made. Hrut heard this, and he and his sons liked it very ill. They were most of them grown up, and the band of kinsmen was deemeda most forbidding one to grapple with. Hrut fell back on the law as to how this ought to turn out, and when the matter was searched into by lawyers, Hrut and his son stood at but little advantage, for it was held a matter of great weight that Hrut had set the freedman down without leave on Hoskuld's land, where he had made money, Thorliek having slain the man within his and his father's own lands. Hrut took his lot very much to heart; but things remained quiet. After that Thorliek had a homestead built on the boundary of Hrut and Hoskuld's lands, and it was called Combness. There

Thorliek lived for a while, as has been told before. Thorliek begat a son of his wife. The boy was sprinkled with water and called Bolli. He was at an early age a very promising man.

CHAPTER 26
The Death of Hoskuld, A.D. 985

Hoskuld, Koll o' Dales' son, fell ill in his old age, and he sent for his sons and other kinsfolk, and when they were come Hoskuld spoke to the brothers Bard and Thorliek, and said, "I have taken some sickness, and as I have not been much in the way of falling ill before, I think this may bring me to death; and now, as you know, you are both begotten inwedlock, and are entitled to all inheritance left by me. But there is a third son of mine, one who is not born in wedlock, and I will ask you brothers to allow him, Olaf to wit, to be adopted, so that he take of my means one-third with you." Bard answered first, and said that he would do as his father wished, "for I look for honour from Olaf in every way, the more so the wealthier he becomes." Then Thorliek said, "It is far from my wish that Olaf be adopted; he has plenty of money already; and you, father, have for a long time given him a great deal, and for a very long time dealt unevenly with us. I will not freely give up the honour to which I am born." Hoskuld said, "Surely you will not rob me of the law that allows me to give twelve ounces to my son, seeing how high-born Olaf is on his mother's side." To this Thorliek now agreed. Then Hoskuld took the gold ring, Hakon's gift, that weighed a mark, and the sword, King's gift whereon was half a mark of gold, and gave them to Olaf, his son, and therewith his good luck and that of the family, saying he did not speak in this way because he did not know well enough that the luck had already come to him. Olaf took his gifts, and said he would risk how Thorliek would like it. Thorliek liked it very ill, and thought that Hoskuld had behaved in a very underhand way to him. Olaf said, "I shall not give up the gifts, Thorliek, for you agreed to the gift in the face of witnesses; and I shall run the risk to keep it." Bard said he would obey his father's wishes. After that Hoskuld died, and his death was very much grieved for, in the first place by his sons, and next by all his relations and friends. His sons had a worthy cairn made for him; but little money was put into it with him. And when this was over, the brothers began to talk over the matter of preparing an "arvale" (burial feast) after their father, for at that time such was the custom. Olaf said, "It seems to me that we should not be in a hurry about preparing this feast, if it is to be as noble as we should think right; now the autumn is very far worn, and the ingathering of means for it is no longer easy; most people who have to come a long way would find that a hard matter in the autumn days; so that it is certain that many would not come of the men we most should like to see. So I will now make the offer, next summer at the Thing, to bid men to the feast, and I will bear one-third of the cost of the wassail." The brothers agreed to that, and Olaf now went home. Thorliek and Bard now share the goods between them. Bard had the estate and lands, which was what most men held to, as he was the most popular; but Thorliek got for his share more of the chattels. Olaf and Bard got on well together, but Olaf and Thorliek rather snappishly. Now the next winter passed, and summer comes, and time wears on towards the Thing. The sons of Hoskuld got ready to go to the Thing. It was soon seen clearly enough how Olaf took the lead of the brothers. When they got to the Thing theyset up three booths, and make themselves comfortable in a handsome manner.

CHAPTER 27
The Funeral Feast for Hoskuld

It is told how one day when people went to the law rock Olaf stood up and asked for a hearing, and told them first of the death of his father, "and there are now here many men, kinsmen and friends of his. It is the will of my brothers that I ask you to a funeral feast in memory of Hoskuld our father. All you chieftains, for most of the mightier men are such, as were bound by alliances to him, I let it be known that no one of the greater men shall go away giftless. And herewith I bid all the farmers and any who will accept - rich or poor - to a half month's feast at Hoskuldstead ten weeks before the winter." And when Olaf finished his speech good cheer was made thereto, and his bidding was looked upon as a right lordly one. And when Olaf came home to the booth he told his brothers what he had settled to do. The brothers were not much pleased, and thought that this was going in for far too much state. After the Thing the brothers rode home and the summer now wears on. Then the brothers got ready for the feast, and Olaf put forward unstintedly his third part, and the feast wasfurnished with the best of provisions. Great stores were laid in for this feast, for it was expected many folk would come. And when the time came it is said that most of the chief men came that were asked. There were so many that most men say that there could not be far short of nine hundred (1080). This is the most crowded burial feast that has been in Iceland, second to that which the sons of Hialti gave at the funeral of their father, at which time there were 1440 guests. But this feast was of the bravest in every way, and the brothers got great honour therefrom, Olaf being at the head of the affair throughout. Olaf took even share with his brothers in the gifts; and gifts were bestowed on all the chiefs. When most of the men had gone away Olaf went to have a talk with Thorliek his brother, and said, "So it is, kinsman, as you know, that no love has been lost between us; now I would beg for a better understanding in our brotherhood. I know you did not like when I took the heirlooms my father gave me on his dying day. Now if you think yourself wronged in this, I will do as much for gaining back your whole good-will as to give fostering to your son. For it is said that ever he is the lesser man who fosters another's child." Thorliek took this in good part, and said, as was true, that this was honourably offered. And now Olaf took home Bolli, the son of Thorliek, who at this time was three winters old. They parted now with the utmost affection, and Bolli went home to Herdholt withOlaf. Thorgerd received him well, and Bolli grew up there and was loved no less than their own children.

CHAPTER 28
The Birth of Kjartan, Olaf's Son, A.D. 978

Olaf and Thorgerd had a son, and the boy was sprinkled with water and a name was given him, Olaf letting him be called Kjartan after Myrkjartan his mother's father. Bolli and Kjartan were much of an age. Olaf and Thorgerd had still more children; three sons were called Steinthor and Halldor and Helgi, and Hoskuld was the name of the youngest of Olaf's sons. The daughters of Olaf and his wife were named Bergthora, Thorgerd, and Thorbjorg. All their children were of goodly promise as they grew up. At that time Holmgang Bersi lived in Saurby at an abode called Tongue. He comes to see Olaf and asked for Halldor his son to foster. Olaf agreed to this and Halldor went home with him, being then one winter old. That summer Bersi fell ill, and lay in bed for a great part of the summer. It is told how one day, when all the men were out haymaking at Tongue and only they two, Bersi and Halldor, were left in the house, Halldor lay in his cradle and the cradle fell over under the boyand he fell out of it on to the floor, and Bersi could not get to him. Then Bersi said this ditty:

Here we both lie
In helpless plight,
Halldor and I,
Have no power left us;
Old age afflicts me,
Youth afflicts you,
You will get better
But I shall get worse.

Later on people came in and picked Halldor up off the floor, and Bersi got better. Halldor was brought up there, and was a tall man and doughty looking. Kjartan, Olaf's son, grew up at home at Herdholt. He was of all men the goodliest of those who have been born in Iceland. He was striking of countenance and fair of feature, he had the finest eyes of any man, and was light of hue. He had a great deal of hair as fair as silk, falling in curls; he was a big man, and strong, taking after his mother's father Egil, or his uncle Thorolf. Kjartan was better proportioned than any man, so that all wondered who saw him. He was better skilled at arms than most men; he was a deft craftsman, and the best swimmer of all men. In all deeds of strength he was far before others, more gentle than any other man, and so engaging that every child loved him; he was light of heart, and free with his money. Olaf loved Kjartan best of all his children. Bolli, his foster-brother, was a great man, he came next to Kjartan in all deeds of strength and prowess; he was strong, and fair of face and courteous, and most warrior-like, and a great dandy. The foster-brothers were very fond of each other. Olaf now remained quietly in his home, and for a good many years.

CHAPTER 29
Olaf's Second Journey to Norway, A.D. 975

It is told how one spring Olaf broke the news to Thorgerd that he wished to go out voyaging "And I wish you to look after our household and children." Thorgerd said she did not much care about doing that; but Olaf said he would have his way. He bought a ship that stood up in the West, at Vadill. Olaf started during the summer, and brought his ship to Hordaland. There, a short way inland, lived a man whose name was Giermund Roar, a mighty man and wealthy, and a great Viking; he was an evil man to deal with, but had now settled down in quiet at home, and was of the bodyguard of Earl Hakon. The mighty Giermund went down to his ship and soon recognised Olaf, for he had heard him spoken of before. Giermund bade Olaf come and stay with him, with as many of his men as he liked to bring. Olaf accepted his invitation, and went there with seven men. The crew of Olaf went into lodgings about Hordaland. Giermund entertained Olaf well. His house was a lofty one, and there were many men there, and plenty of amusement all the winter. And towards the end of the winter Olaf told Giermund the reason of his voyage, which was that he wished to get for himself some house-timber, and said he set great store by obtaining timber of a choice kind. Giermund said, "Earl Hakon has the best of woods, and I know quite well if you went to see him you would be made welcome to them, for the Earl receives well, men who are not half so well-bred as you, Olaf, when they go to see him." In the spring Olaf got ready to go and find Hakon Earl; and the Earl gave him exceeding good welcome, and bade Olaf stay with him as long as he liked. Olaf told the Earl the reason of his journey, "And I beg this of you, sir, that you give us permission to cut wood for house-building from your forests." The Earl answered, "You are welcome to load your ship with timber, and I will give it you. For I think it no every-day occurrence when such men as you come from Iceland to visit me." At parting the Earl gave him a gold-inlaid axe, and the best of keepsakes it was; and therewith they parted in the greatest friendship. Giermund in the meantime set stewards over his estates secretly, and made up his mind to go to Iceland in the summer in Olaf's ship. He kept this secret from every one. Olaf knew nothing about it till Giermund brought his money to Olaf's ship, and very great wealth it was. Olaf said, "You should not have gone in my ship if I had known of this before-hand, for I think there are those in Iceland for whom it would be better never to have seen you. But since you have come with so much goods, I cannot drive you out like a straying cur." Giermund said, "I shall not return for all your high words, for I mean to be your passenger." Olaf and his got on board, and put out to sea. They had a good voyage and made Broadfirth, and they put out their gangways and landed at Salmon-river-Mouth. Olaf had the wood taken out of his ship, and the ship put up in the shed his father had made. Olaf then asked Giermund to come and stay with him. That summer Olaf had a fire-hall built at Herdholt, a greater and better than had ever been seen before. Noble legends were painted on its wainscoting and in the roof, and this was so well done that the hall was thought even more beautiful when the hangings were not up. Giermund did not meddle with every-day matters, but was uncouth to most people. He was usually dressed in this way - he wore a scarlet kirtle below and a grey cloak outside, and a bearskin cap on his head, and a sword in his hand.

This was a great weapon and good, with a hilt of walrus tooth, with no silver on it; the brand was sharp, and no rust would stay thereon. This sword he called Footbiter, and he never let it out of hishands. Giermund had not been there long before he fell in love with Thured, Olaf's daughter, and proposed to Olaf for her hand; but he gave him a straight refusal. Then Giermund gave some money to Thorgerd with a view to gaining the match. She took the money, for it was offered unstintedly. Then Thorgerd broached the matter to Olaf, and said she thought their daughter could not be better married, "for he is a very brave man, wealthy and high-mettled." Then Olaf answered, "I will not go against you in this any more than in other things, though I would sooner marry Thured to some one else." Thorgerd went away and thought her business had sped well, and now told Giermund the upshot of it. He thanked her for her help and her determination, and Giermund broached the wooing a second time to Olaf, and now won the day easily. After that Giermund and Thured were betrothed, and the wedding was to be held at the end of the winter at Herdholt. The wedding feast was a very crowded one, for the new hall was finished. Ulf Uggason was of the bidden guests, and he had made a poem on Olaf Hoskuldson and of the legends that were painted round the hall, and he gave it forth at the feast. This poem is called the "House Song," and is well made. Olaf rewarded him well for the poem. Olaf gave great gifts to all the chief men who came. Olaf was considered to have gained in renown by this feast.

CHAPTER 30
About Giermund and Thured, A.D. 978

Giermund and Thured did not get on very well together, and little love was lost between them on either side. When Giermund had stayed with Olaf three winters he wished to go away, and gave out that Thured and his daughter Groa should remain behind. This little maid was by then a year old, and Giermund would not leave behind any money for them. This the mother and daughter liked very ill, and told Olaf so. Olaf said, "What is the matter now, Thorgerd? is the Eastman now not so bounteous as he was that autumn when he asked for the alliance?" They could get Olaf to do nothing, for he was an easygoing man, and said the girl should remain until she wished to go, or knew how in some way to shift for herself. At parting Olaf gave Giermund the merchant ship all fitted out. Giermund thanked him well therefor, and said it was a noble gift. Then he got on board his ship, and sailed out of the Salmon-river-Mouth by a north-east breeze, which dropped as they came out to the islands. He now lies by Oxe-isle half a month without a fair wind rising for a start. At that time Olaf had to leave home to look after his foreshore drifts. Then Thured, his daughter, called to his house-carles, and bade them come with her. She had the maid Groa with her, and they were a party of ten together. She lets run out into the water a ferry-boat that belonged to Olaf, and Thured bade them sail and row down along Hvamfirth, and when they came out to the islands she bade them put out the cock-boat that was in the ferry. Thured got into the boat with two men, and bade the others take care of the ship she left behind until she returned. She took the little maid in her arms, and bade the men row across the current until they should reach the ship (of Giermund). She took a gimlet out of the boat's locker, and gave it to one of her companions, and bade him go to the cockle-boat belonging to the merchant ship and bore a hole in it so as to disable it if they needed it in a hurry. Then she had herself put ashore with the little maid still in her arms. This was at the hour of sunrise. She went across the gangway into the ship, where all men were asleep. She went to the hammock where Giermund slept. His sword Footbiter hung on a peg pole. Thured now sets the little maid in the hammock, and snatched off Footbiter and took it with her. Then she left the ship and rejoined her companions. Now the little maid began to cry, and with that Giermund woke up and recognised the child, and thought he knew who must be at the bottom of this. He springs up wanting to seize his sword, and misses it, as was to be expected, and then went to the gunwale, and saw that they were rowing away from the ship. Giermund called to his men, and bade them leap into the cockle-boatand row after them. They did so, but when they got a little way they found how the coal-blue sea poured into them, so they went back to the ship. Then Giermund called Thured and bade her come back and give him his sword Footbiter, "and take your little maid, and with her as much money as you like." Thured answered, "Would you rather than not have the sword back?" Giermund answered, "I would give a great deal of money before I should care to let my sword go." Thured answered, "Then you shall never have it again, for you have in many ways behaved cowardly towards me, and here we shall part for good." Then Giermund said, "Little luck will you get with the sword." Thured said she would take the risk of that. "Then I lay thereon this spell," said Giermund, "That this sword shall do to death the man in your family in who would be the greatest loss, and in a manner most ill-fated." After that Thured went home to Herdholt. Olaf had then come home, and showed his displeasure at her deed, yet all was quiet. Thured gave Bolli, her cousin, the sword Footbiter, for she loved him in no way less than her brothers. Bolli bore that sword for a long time after. After this Giermund got a favourable wind, and sailed out to sea, and came to Norway in the autumn. They sailed one night on to some hidden rocks before Stade, and then Giermund and all his crew perished. And that is the end of all there is to tell about Giermund.

CHAPTER 31
Thured's Second Marriage, A.D. 980

Olaf Hoskuldson now stayed at home in much honour, as has been told before. There was a man named Gudmund, who was the son of Solmund, and lived at Asbjornness north in Willowdale. He wooed Thured, and got her and a great deal of wealth with her. Thured was a wise woman, high-tempered and most stirring. Their sons were called Hall and Bard and Stein and Steingrim. Gudrun and Olof were their daughters. Thorbjorg, Olaf's daughter, was of women the most beautiful and stout of build. She was called Thorbjorg the Stout, and was married west in Waterfirth to Asgier, the son of Knott. He was a noble man. Their son was Kjartan, father of Thorvald, the father of Thord, the father of Snorri, the father of Thorvald, from whom is sprung the Waterfirth race. Afterwards, Vermund, the son of Thorgrim, had Thorbjorg for wife. Their daughter was Thorfinna, whom Thorstein Kuggason had for wife. Bergthora, Olaf's daughter, was married west in Deepfirth to Thorhall the Priest. Their son was Kjartan, father of Smith-Sturla, the foster son of Thord Gilson. Olaf Peacock had many costly cattle. He had one very good ox named Harri; it was dapple-grey of coat, and bigger than any other of his cattle. It had four horns,two great and fair ones, the third stood straight up, and a fourth stood out of its forehead, stretching down below its eyes. It was with this that he opened the ice in winter to get water. He scraped snow away to get at pasture like a horse. One very hard winter he went from Herdholt into the Broadfirth-Dales to a place that is now called Harristead. There he roamed through the winter with sixteen other cattle, and got grazing for them all. In the spring he returned to the home pastures, to the place now called Harris'-Lair in Herdholt land. When Harri was eighteen winters old his ice-breaking horn fell off, and that same autumn Olaf had him killed. The next night Olaf dreamed that a woman came to him, and she was great and wrathful to look at. She spoke and said, "Are you asleep?" He said he was awake. The woman said, "You are asleep, though it comes to the same thing as if you were awake. You have had my son slain, and let him come to my hand in a shapeless plight, and for this deed you shall see your son, blood-stained all over through my doing, and him I shall choose thereto whom I know you would like to lose least of all." After that she disappeared, and Olaf woke up and still thought he saw the features of the woman. Olaf took the dream very much to heart, and told it to his friends, but no one could read it to his liking. He thought those spoke best about this matter who said that what had appeared to him was only a dream or fancy.

CHAPTER 32
Of Osvif Helgeson

Osvif was the name of a man. He was the son of Helgi, who was the son of Ottar, the son of Bjorn the Eastman, who was the son of Ketill Flatnose, the son of Bjorn Buna. The mother of Osvif was named Nidbiorg. Her mother was Kadlin, the daughter of Ganging-Hrolf, the son of Ox-Thorir, who was a most renowned "Hersir" (war-lord) east in Wick. Why he was so called, was that he owned three islands with eighty oxen on each. He gave one island and its oxen to Hakon the King, and his gift was much talked about. Osvif was a great sage. He lived at Laugar in Salingsdale. The homestead of Laugar stands on the northern side of Salingsdale-river, over against Tongue. The name of his wife was Thordis, daughter of Thjodolf the Low. Ospak was the name of one of their sons. Another was named Helgi, and a third Vandrad, and a fourth Jorrad, and a fifth Thorolf. They were all doughty men for fighting. Gudrun was the name of their daughter. She was the goodliest of women who grew up in Iceland, both as to looks and wits. Gudrun was such a woman of state that at that time whatever other women wore in the way of finery of dress was looked upon as children's gewgaws beside hers. She was the most cunning and the fairest spoken of all women, and an open-handedwoman withal. There was a woman living with Osvif who was named Thorhalla, and was called the Chatterer. She was some sort of relation to Osvif. She had two sons, one named Odd and the other Stein. They were muscular men, and in a great measure the hardest toilers for Osvif's household. They were talkative like their mother, but ill liked by people; yet were upheld greatly by the sons of Osvif. At Tongue there lived a man named Thorarin, son of Thorir Sæling (the Voluptuous). He was a well-off yeoman, a big man and strong. He had very good land, but less of live stock. Osvif wished to buy some of his land from him, for he had lack of land but a multitude of live stock. So this then came about that Osvif bought of the land of Thorarin all the tract from Gnupaskard along both sides of the valley to Stackgill, and very good and fattening land it was. He had on it an out-dairy. Osvif had at all times a great many servants, and his way of living was most noble. West in Saurby is a place called Hol, there lived three kinsmen-in-law - Thorkell the Whelp and Knut, who were brothers, they were very well-born men, and their brother-in-law, who shared their household with them, who was named Thord. He was, after his mother, called Ingun's-son. The father of Thord was Glum Gierison. Thord was a handsome and valiant man, well knit, and a great man of law-suits. Thord had for wife the sister of Thorkell and Knut, who was called Aud, neither a goodly nor a bucksome woman. Thord loved her little, ashe had chiefly married her for her money, for there a great wealth was stored together, and the household flourished from the time that Thord came to have hand in it with them.

CHAPTER 33
Of Gest Oddleifson and Gudrun's Dreams

Gest Oddleifson lived west at Bardastrand, at Hagi. He was a great chieftain and a sage; was fore-seeing in many things and in good friendship with all the great men, and many came to him for counsel. He rode every summer to the Thing, and always would put up at Hol. One time it so happened once more that Gest rode to the Thing and was a guest at Hol. He got ready to leave early in the morning, for the journey was a long one and he meant to get to Thickshaw in the evening to Armod, his brother-in-law's, who had for wife Thorunn, a sister of Gest's. Their sons were Ornolf and Haldor. Gest rode all that day from Saurby and came to the Sælingsdale spring, and tarried there for a while. Gudrun came to the spring and greeted her relative, Gest, warmly. Gest gave her a good welcome, and they began to talk together, both being wise and of ready speech. And as the day was wearing on, Gudrun said, "I wish, cousin, you would ride home with us with all your followers, for itis the wish of my father, though he gave me the honour of bearing the message, and told me to say that he would wish you to come and stay with us every time you rode to or from the west." Gest received the message well, and thought it a very manly offer, but said he must ride on now as he had purposed. Gudrun said, "I have dreamt many dreams this winter; but four of the dreams do trouble my mind much, and no man has been able to explain them as I like, and yet I ask not for any favourable interpretation of them." Gest said, "Tell me your dreams, it may be that I can make something of them." Gudrun said, "I thought I stood out of doors by a certain brook, and I had a crooked coif on my head, and I thought it misfitted me, and I wished to alter the coif, and many people told me I should not do so, but I did not listen to them, and I tore the hood from my head, and cast it into the brook, and that was the end of that dream." Then Gudrun said again, "This is the next dream. I thought I stood near some water, and I thought there was a silver ring on my arm. I thought it was my own, and that it fitted me exceeding well. I thought it was a most precious thing, and long I wished to keep it. But when I was least aware of it, the ring slipped off my arm and into the water, and nothing more did I see of it afterwards. I felt this loss much more than it was likely I should ever feel the loss of a mere keepsake. Then I awoke." Gest answered this alone: "No lesser a dream is that one."Gudrun still spoke: "This is the third dream, I thought I had a gold ring on my hand, which I thought belonged to me, and I thought my loss was now made good again. And the thought entered my mind that I would keep this ring longer than the first; but it did not seem to me that this keepsake suited me better than the former at anything like the rate that gold is more precious than silver. Then I thought I fell, and tried to steady myself with my hand, but then the gold ring struck on a certain stone and broke in two, and the two pieces bled. What I had to bear after this felt more like grief than regret for a loss. And it struck me now that there must have been some flaw in the ring, and when I looked at the pieces I thought I saw sundry more flaws in them; yet I had a feeling that if I had taken better care of it, it might still have been whole; and this dream was no longer." Gest said, "The dreams are not waning." Then said Gudrun, "This is my fourth dream. I thought I had a helm of gold upon my head, set with many precious stones. And I thought this precious thing belonged to me, but what I chiefly found fault with was that it was rather too heavy, and I could scarcely bear it, so that I carried my head on one side; yet I did not blame the helm for this, nor had I any mind to part with it. Yet the helm tumbled from my head out into Hvammfirth, and after that I awoke. Now I have told you all my dreams." Gest answered, "I clearly see what these dreams betoken; but you will find my unravelling savouring much of sameness, for I must read them all nearly in the same way. You will have four husbands, and it misdoubts me when you are married to the first it will be no love match. Inasmuch as you thought you had a great coif on your head and thought it ill-fitting, that shows you will love him but little. And whereas you took it off your head and cast it into the water, that shows that you will leave him. For that, men say, is 'cast on to the sea,' when a man loses what is his own, and gets nothing in return for it." And still Gest spake: "Your second dream was that you thought you had a silver ring on your arm, and that shows you will marry a nobleman whom you will love much, but enjoy him for but a short time, and I should not wonder if you lose him by drowning. That is all I have to tell of that dream. And in the third dream you thought you had a gold ring on your hand; that shows you will have a third husband; he will not excel the former at the rate that you deemed this metal more rare and precious than silver; but my mind forebodes me that by that time a change of faith will have come about, and your husband will have taken the faith which we are minded to think is the more exalted. And whereas you thought the ring broke in two through some misheed of yours, and blood came from the two pieces, that shows that this husband of yours will be slain, and then you will think you see for the first time clearly all the flaws of that match." Still Gest went on to say: "This is your fourth dream, that you thought you had a helm on your head, of gold set with precious stones, and that it was a heavy one for you to bear. This shows you will have a fourth husband who will be the greatest nobleman (of the four), and will bear somewhat a helm of awe over you. And whereas you thought it tumbled out into Hvammfirth, it shows that that same firth will be in his way on the last day of his life. And now I go no further with this dream." Gudrun sat with her cheeks blood red whilst the dreams were unravelled, but said not a word till Gest came to the end of his speech. Then said Gudrun, "You would have fairer prophecies in this matter if my delivery of it into your hands had warranted; have my thanks all the same for unravelling the dreams. But it is a fearful thing to think of, if all this is to come to pass as you say." Gudrun then begged Gest would stay there the day out, and said that he and Osvif would have many wise things to say between them. He answered, "I must ride on now as I have made up my mind. But bring your father my greeting and tell him also these my words, that the day will come when there will be a shorter distance between Osvif's and my dwellings, and then we may talk at ease, if then we are allowed to converse together." Then Gudrun went home and Gest rode away. Gest met a servant of Olaf's by the home-field fence, who invited Gest to Herdholt, at the bidding of Olaf. Gest said he would go and see Olaf during the day, but would stay (the night) at Thickshaw. The servant returned home and told Olaf so. Olaf had his horse brought and rode with several men out to meet Gest. He and Gest met up at Lea-river. Olaf greeted him well and asked him in with all his followers. Gest thanked him for the invitation, and said he would ride up to the homestead and have a look and see how he was housed, but he must stay with Armod. Gest tarried but a little while, yet he saw over the homestead and admired it and said, "No money has been spared for this place." Olaf rode away with Gest to the Salmon-river. The foster-brothers had been swimming there during the day, and at this sport the sons of Olaf mostly took the lead. There were many other young men from the other houses swimming too. Kjartan and Bolli leapt out of the water as the company rode down and were nearly dressed when Olaf and Gest came up to them. Gest looked at these young men for a while, and told Olaf where Kjartan was sitting as well as Bolli, and then Gest pointed his spear shaft to each one of Olaf's sons and named by name all of them that were there. But there were many other handsome young men there who had just left off swimming and sat on the river-bank with Kjartan and Bolli. Gest said he did not discover the family features of Olaf in any of these young men. Then said Olaf: "Never is there too much said about your wits, Gest, knowing, as you do, men you have never seen before. Now I wish you to tell me which of those young men will be the mightiest man." Gest replied, "That will fall out much in keeping with your own love, for Kjartan will be the most highly accounted of so long as he lives." Then Gest smote his horse and rode away. A little while after Thord the Low rode up to his side, and said, "What has now come to pass, father, that you are shedding tears?" Gest answered, "It is needless to tell it, yet I am loath to keep silence on matters that will happen in your own days. To me it will not come unawares if Bolli one day should *have* at his feet the head of Kjartan slain, and should by the deed bring about his own death, and this is an ill thing to know of such sterling men." Then they rode on to the Thing, and it was an uneventful meeting.

CHAPTER 34
Gudrun's First Marriage, A.D. 989

Thorvald was the name of a man, son of Haldor Garpdale's Priest. He lived at Garpsdale in Gilsfirth, a wealthy man, but not much of a hero. At the Thing he wooed Gudrun, Osvif's daughter, when she was fifteen years old. The matter

217

was not taken up in a very adverse manner, yet Osvif said that againstthe match it would tell, that he and Gudrun were not of equal standing. Thorvald spoke gently, and said he was wooing a wife, not money. After that Gudrun was betrothed to Thorvald, and Osvif settled alone the marriage contract, whereby it was provided that Gudrun should alone manage their money affairs straightway when they came into one bed, and be entitled to one-half thereof as her own, whether their married life were long or short. He should also buy her jewels, so that no woman of equal wealth should have better to show. Yet he should retain his farm-stock unimpaired by such purchases. And now men ride home from the Thing. Gudrun was not asked about it, and took it much to heart; yet things went on quietly. The wedding was at Garpsdale, in Twinmonth (latter part of August to the latter part of September). Gudrun loved Thorvald but little, and was extravagant in buying finery. There was no jewel so costly in all the West-firths that Gudrun did not deem it fitting that it should be hers, and rewarded Thorvald with anger if he did not buy it for her, however dear it might be. Thord, Ingun's son, made himself very friendly with Thorvald and Gudrun, and stayed with them for long times together, and there was much talk of the love of Thord and Gudrun for each other. Once upon a time Gudrun bade Thorvald buy a gift for her, and Thorvald said she showed no moderation in her demands, and gave her a box on the ear. Then said Gudrun, "Now you have given me that which we women set great store by having to perfection - a fine colour in the cheeks - and thereby have also taught me how to leave off importuning you." That same evening Thord came there. Gudrun told him about the shameful mishandling, and asked him how she should repay it. Thord smiled, and said: "I know a very good counsel for this: make him a shirt with such a large neck-hole that you may have a good excuse for separating from him, because he has a low neck like a woman." Gudrun said nothing against this, and they dropped their talk. That same spring Gudrun separated herself from Thorvald, and she went home to Laugar. After that the money was divided between Gudrun and Thorvald, and she had half of all the wealth, which now was even greater than before (her marriage). They had lived two winters together. That same spring Ingun sold her land in Crookfirth, the estate which was afterwards called Ingunstead, and went west to Skalmness. Glum Gierison had formerly had her for wife, as has been before written. At that time Hallstein the Priest lived at Hallsteinness, on the west side of Codfirth. He was a mighty man, but middling well off as regards friends.

CHAPTER 35
Gudrun's Second Marriage, A.D. 991

Kotkell was the name of a man who had only come to Iceland a short time before, Grima was the name of his wife. Their sons were Hallbjorn Whetstone-eye, and Stigandi. These people were natives of Sodor. They were all wizards and the greatest of enchanters. Hallstein Godi took them in and settled them down at Urdir in Skalm-firth, and their dwelling there was none of the best liked. That summer Gest went to the Thing and went in a ship to Saurby as he was wont. He stayed as guest at Hol in Saurby. The brothers-in-law found him in horses as was their former wont. Thord Ingunson was amongst the followers of

Gest on this journey and came to Laugar in Salingsdale. Gudrun Osvif's daughter rode to the Thing, and Thord Ingunson rode with her. It happened one day as they were riding over Blueshaw-heath, the weather being fine, that Gudrun said, "Is it true, Thord, that your wife Aud always goes about in breeches with gores in the seat, winding swathings round her legs almost to her feet?" Thord said, "He had not noticed that." "Well, then, there must be but little in the tale," said Gudrun, "if you have not found it out, but for what then is she called Breeches And?" Thord said, "I think she has been called so for but a short time." Gudrun answered, "What is of more moment to her is that she bear the name for a long time hereafter." After that people arrived at the Thing and no tidings befell there. Thord spent much time in Gest's booth and always talked to Gudrun. One day Thord Ingunson asked Gudrun what the penalty was for a woman who went about always in breeches like men. Gudrun replied, "She deserves the same penalty as a man who is dressed in a shirt with so low a neck that his naked breast be seen - separation in either case." Then Thord said, "Would you advise me to proclaim my separation from And here at the Thing or in the country by the counsel of many men? For I have to deal with high-tempered men who will count themselves as ill-treated in this affair." Gudrun answered after a while, "For evening waits the idler's suit." Then Thord sprang up and went to the law rock and named to him witnesses, declared his separation from Aud, and gave as his reason that she made for herself gored breeches like a man. Aud's brothers disliked this very much, but things kept quiet. Then Thord rode away from the Thing with the sons of Osvif. When Aud heard these tidings, she said, "Good! Well, that I know that I am left thus single." Then Thord rode, to divide the money, west into Saurby and twelve men with him, and it all went off easily, for Thord made no difficulties as to how the money was divided. Thord drove from the west unto Laugar a great deal of live stock. After that he wooed Gudrun and that matter was easily settled; Osvif and Gudrun said nothing against it. The wedding was to take place in the tenth week of the summer, and that was a right noble feast. Thord and Gudrun lived happily together. What alone withheld Thorkell Whelp and Knut from setting afoot a lawsuit against Thord Ingunson was, that they got no backing up to that end. The next summer the men of Hol had an out-dairy business in Hvammdale, and Aud stayed at the dairy. The men of Laugar had their out-dairy in Lambdale, which cuts westward into the mountains off Salingsdale. Aud asked the man who looked after the sheep how often he met the shepherd from Laugar. He said nearly always as was likely since there was only a neck of land between the two dairies. Then said Aud, "You shall meet the shepherd from Laugar to-day, and you can tell me who there are staying at the winter-dwelling or who at the dairy, and speak in a friendly way of Thord as it behoves you to do." The boy promised to do as she told him. And in the evening when the shepherd came home And asked what tidings he brought. The shepherd answered, "I have heard tidings which you will think good, that now there is a broad bedroom-floor between the beds of Thord and Gudrun, for she is at the dairy and he is swinging at the rear of the hall, he and Osvif being two together alone at the winter-dwelling." "You have espied well," said she, "and see to have saddled two horses at the time when people are going to bed." The shepherd did as she bade him. A little before sunset Aud mounted, and was now indeed in breeches. The shepherd rode the other horse and could hardly keep up with her, so hard did she push on riding. She rode south over Salingsdale-heath and never stopped before she got to the home-field fence at Laugar. Then she dismounted, and bade the shepherd look after the horses whilst she went to the house. And went to the door and found it open, and she went into the fire-hall to the locked-bed in the wall. Thord lay asleep, the door had fallen to, but the bolt was not on, so she walked into the bedroom. Thord lay asleep on his back. Then And woke Thord, and he turned on his side when he saw a man had come in. Then she drew a sword and thrust it at Thord and gave him great wounds, the sword striking his right arm and wounding him on both nipples. So hard did she follow up the stroke that the sword stuck in the bolster. Then Aud went away and to her horse and leapt on to its back, and thereupon rode home. Thord tried to spring up when he got the blow, but could not, because of his loss of blood. Then Osvif awoke and asked what had happened, and Thord told that he had been wounded somewhat. Osvif asked if he knew who had done the deed on him, and got up and bound up his wounds. Thord said he was minded to think that Audhad done it. Osvif offered to ride after her, and said she must have gone on this errand with few men, and her penalty was ready-made for her. Thord said that should not be done at all, for she had only done what she ought to have done. Aud got home at sunrise, and her brothers asked her where she had been to. Aud said she had been to Laugar, and told them what tidings had befallen in her journey. They were pleased at this, and said that too little was likely to have been done by her. Thord lay wounded a long time. His chest wound healed well, but his arm grew no better for work than before (*i.e.* when it first was wounded). All was now quiet that winter. But in the following spring Ingun, Thord's mother, came west from Skalmness. Thord greeted her warmly: she said she wished to place herself under his protection, and said that Kotkell and his wife and sons were giving her much trouble by stealing her goods, and through witchcraft, but had a strong support in Hallstein the Priest. Thord took this matter up swiftly, and said he should have the right of these thieves no matter how it might displease Hallstein. He got speedily ready for the journey with ten men, and Ingun went west with him. He got a ferry-boat out of Tjaldness. Then they went to Skalmness. Thord had put on board ship all the chattels his mother owned there, and the cattle were to be driven round the heads of the firths. There were twelve of them altogether in the boat, withIngun and another woman. Thord and ten men went to Kotkell's place. The sons of Kotkell were not at home. He then summoned Kotkell and Grima and their sons for theft and witchcraft, and claimed outlawry as award. He laid the case to the Althing, and then returned to his ship. Hallbjorn and Stigandi came home when Thord had got out but a little way from land, and Kotkell told his sons what had happened there. The brothers were furious at that, and said that hitherto people had taken care not to show them in so barefaced a manner such open enmity. Then Kotkell had a great spell-working scaffold made, and they all went up on to it, and they sang hard twisted songs that were enchantments. And presently a great tempest arose. Thord, Ingun's son, and his companions, continued out at sea as he was, soon knew that the storm was raised against him. Now the ship is driven west beyond Skalmness, and Thord showed great courage with seamanship. The men who were on land saw how he threw overboard all that made up the boat's lading, saving the men; and the people who were on land expected Thord would come to shore, for they had passed the place that was the rockiest; but next there arose a breaker on a rock a little way from the shore that no man had ever known to break sea before, and smote the ship so that forthwith up turned keel uppermost. There Thord and all his followers were drowned, and the ship was broken to pieces, and the keel was washed up at a

220

place now called Keelisle. Thord's shield was washed up on an island that has since been called Shieldisle. Thord's body and the bodies of his followers were all washed ashore, and a great howe was raised over their corpses at the place now called Howesness.

CHAPTER 36
About Kotkell and Grima

These tidings spread far and wide, and were very ill-spoken of; they were accounted of as men of doomed lives, who wrought such witchcraft as that which Kotkell and his had now shown. Gudrun took the death of Thord sorely to heart, for she was now a woman not hale, and coming close to her time. After that Gudrun gave birth to a boy, who was sprinkled with water and called Thord. At that time Snorri the Priest lived at Holyfell; he was a kinsman and a friend of Osvif's, and Gudrun and her people trusted him very much. Snorri went thither (to Laugar), being asked to a feast there. Then Gudrun told her trouble to Snorri, and he said he would back up their case when it seemed good to him, but offered to Gudrun to foster her child to comfort her. This Gudrun agreed to, and said she would rely on his foresight. This Thord was surnamed the Cat, and was father of the poet Stúf. After that Gest Oddleifson went to see Hallstein, and gave him choice of two things, either that he should send away these wizards or he said that he would kill them, "and yet it comes too late." Hallstein made his choice at once, and bade them rather be off, and put up nowhere west of Daleheath, adding that it was more justly they ought to be slain. After that Kotkell and his went away with no other goods than four stud-horses. The stallion was black; he was both great and fair and very strong, and tried in horse-fighting. Nothing is told of their journey till they came to Combeness, to Thorliek, Hoskuld's son. He asked to buy the horses from them, for he said that they were exceeding fine beasts. Kotkell replied, "I'll give you the choice. Take you the horses and give me some place to dwell in here in your neighbourhood." Thorliek said, "Will the horses not be rather dear, then, for I have heard tell you are thought rather guilty in this countryside?" Kotkell answers, "In this you are hinting at the men of Laugar." Thorliek said that was true. Then Kotkell said, "Matters point quite another way, as concerning our guilt towards Gudrun and her brothers, than you have been told; people have overwhelmed us with slander for no cause at all. Take the horses, nor let these matters stand in the way. Such tales alone are told of you, moreover, as would show that we shall not be easily tripped up by the folk of this countryside, if we have your help to fall back upon." Thorliek now changed his mind in this matter, for the horses seemed fair to him, and Kotkell pleaded his case cunningly; so Thorliek took the horses, and gave them a dwelling at Ludolfstead in Salmon-river-Dale, and stocked them with farming beasts. This the men of Laugar heard, and the sons of Osvif wished to fall forthwith on Kotkell and his sons; but Osvif said, "Let us take now the counsel of Priest Snorri, and leave this business to others, for short time will pass before the neighbours of Kotkell will have brand new cases against him and his, and Thorliek, as is most fitting, will abide the greatest hurt from them. In a short while many will become his enemies from whom heretofore he has only had good will. But I shall not stop you from doing whatever hurt you please to Kotkell and his, if other men do not come forward to drive them out of the countryside or to take their lives, by the time that three winters have worn away." Gudrun and her brothers said it should be as he said. Kotkell and his did not do much in working for their livelihood, but that winter they were in no need to buy hay or food; but an unbefriended neighbourhood was theirs, though men did not see their way to disturbing their dwelling because of Thorliek.

CHAPTER 37
About Hrut and Eldgrim, A.D. 995

One summer at the Thing, as Thorliek was sitting in his booth, a very big man walked into the booth. He greeted Thorliek, who took well the greeting of this man and asked his name and whence he was. He said he was called Eldgrim, and lived in Burgfirth at a place called Eldgrimstead - but that abode lies in the valley which cuts westward into the mountains between Mull and Pigtongue, and is now called Grimsdale. Thorliek said, "I have heard you spoken of as being no small man." Eldgrim said, "My errand here is that I want to buy from you the stud-horses, those valuable ones that Kotkell gave you last summer." Thorliek answered, "The horses are not for sale." Eldgrim said, "I will offer you equally many stud-horses for them and some other things thrown in, and many would say that I offer you twice as much as the horses are worth." Thorliek said, "I am no haggler, but these horses you will never have, not even though you offer three times their worth." Eldgrim said, "I take it to be no lie that you are proud and self-willed, and I should, indeed, like to see you getting a somewhat less handsome price for them than I have now offered you, and that you should have to let the horses go none the less." Thorliek got angered at these words, and said, "You need, Eldgrim, to come to closer quarters if you mean to frighten out me the horses." Eldgrim said, "You think it unlikely that you will be beaten by me, but this summer I shall go and see the horses, and we will see which of us will own them after that." Thorliek said, "Do as you like, but bring up no odds against me." Then they dropped their talk. The man who heard this said that for this sort of dealing together here were two just fitting matches for each other. After that people went home from the Thing, and nothing happened to tell tidings of. It happened one morning early that a man looked out at Hrutstead at goodman Hrut's, Herjolf's son's, and when he came in Hrut asked what news he brought. He said he had no other tidings to tell save that he saw a man riding from beyond Vadlar towards where Thorliek's horses were, and that the man got off his horse and took the horses. Hrut asked where the horses were then, and the house-carle replied, "Oh, they have stuck well to their pasture, for they stood as usual in your meadows down below the fence-wall." Hrut replied, "Verily, Thorliek, my kinsman, is not particular as to where he grazes his beasts; and I still think it more likely that it is not by his order that the horses are driven away." Then Hrut sprang up in his shirt and linen breeches, and cast over him a grey cloak and took in his hand his gold inlaid halberd that King Harald had given him. He went out quickly and saw where a man was riding after horses down below the wall. Hrut went to meet him, and saw that it was Eldgrim driving the horses. Hrut greeted him, and Eldgrim returned his greeting, but rather slowly. Hrut asked him why he was driving the horses. Eldgrim replied, "I will not hide it from you, though I know what kinship there is between you and Thorliek; but I tell you I have come after these horses, meaning that he shall never have them again. I have also kept what I promised him at the Thing, that I have not gone after the horses with any great company." Hrut said, "That is no deed of fame to you to take away the horses while Thorliek lies in his bed and sleeps; you would keep best what you agreed upon if you go and meet himself before you drive the horses out of the countryside." Eldgrim said, "Go and warn Thorliek if you wish, for you may see I have prepared myself in such a manner as that I should like it well if we were to meet together, I and Thorliek," and therewith he brandished the barbed spear he had in his hand. He had also a helmet on his head, and a sword girded on his side, and a shield on his flank, and had on a chain coat. Hrut said, "I think I must seek for something else than to go to Combeness for I am heavy of foot; but I mean not to allow Thorliek to be robbed if I have means thereto, no matter how little love there may go with our kinship." Eldgrim said, "And do you mean to take the horses away from me?" Hrut said, "I will give you other stud-horses if you will let these alone, though they may not be quite so good as these are." Eldgrim said, "You speak most kindly, Hrut, but since I have got hold of Thorliek's horses you will not pluck them out of my hands either by bribes or threats." Hrut replied, "Then I think you are making for both of us the choice that answers the worst." Eldgrim now wanted to part, and gave the whip to his horse, and when Hrut saw that, he raised up his halberd and struck Eldgrim through the back between the shoulders so that the coat of mail was torn open and the halberd flew out through the chest, and Eldgrim fell dead off his horse, as was only natural. After that Hrut covered up his body at the place called Eldgrim's-holt south of Combeness. Then Hrut rode over to Combeness and told Thorliek the tidings. Thorliek burst into a rage, and thought a great shame had been done him by this deed, while Hrut thought he had shown him great friendship thereby. Thorliek said that not only had he done this for an evil purpose, but that, moreover, no good would come in return for it. Hrut said that Thorliek must do what pleased him, and so they parted in no loving kindness. Hrut was eighty years old when he killed Eldgrim, and he was considered by that deed to have added much to his fame. Thorliek thought that Hrut was none the worthier of any good from him for being more renowned for this deed, for he held it was perfectly clear he would have himself have got the better of Eldgrim if they had had a trial of arms between them, seeing how little was needed to trip Eldgrim up. Thorliek now went to see his tenants Kotkell and Grima, and bade them do something to the shame of Hrut. They took this up gladly, and said they were quite ready to do so. Thorliek now went home. A little later they, Kotkell and Grima and their sons, started on a journey from home, and that was by night. They wentto Hrut's dwelling, and made great incantations there, and when the spell-working began, those within were at a loss to make out what could be the reason of it; but sweet indeed was that singing they heard. Hrut alone knew what these goings-on meant, and bade no man look out that night, "and let every one who may keep awake, and no harm will come to us if that counsel is followed." But all the people fell asleep. Hrut watched longest, and at last he too slept. Kari was the name of a son of Hrut, and he was then twelve winters old. He was the most promising of all Hrut's sons, and Hrut loved him much. Kari hardly slept at all, for to him the play was made; he did not sleep very soundly, and at last he got up and looked out, and walked in the direction of the enchantment, and fell down dead at once. Hrut awoke in the morning, as also did his household, and missed his son, who was found dead a short way from the door. This Hrut felt as the greatest bereavement, and had a cairn raised over Kari. Then he rode to Olaf Hoskuldson and told him the tidings of what had happened there. Olaf was madly wroth at this, and said it showed great lack of forethought that they had allowed such scoundrels as Kotkell and his family to live so near to him, and said that Thorliek had shaped for himself an evil lot by dealing as he had done with Hrut, but added that more must have been done than Thorliek had ever could have wished. Olaf said too that forthwith Kotkell and his wife and sons mustbe slain, "late though it is now." Olaf and Hrut set out with fifteen men. But when Kotkell and his family saw the company of men riding up to their dwelling, they took to their heels up to the mountain. There Hallbjorn Whetstone-eye was caught and a bag was drawn over his head, and while some men were left to guard him others went in pursuit of Kotkell, Grima, and Stigandi up on the mountain. Kotkell and Grima were laid hands on on the neck of land between Hawkdale and Salmon-river-Dale, and were stoned to death and a heap of stones thrown up over them, and the remains are still to be seen, being called Scratch-beacon. Stigandi took to his heels south over the neck towards Hawkdale, and there got out of their sight. Hrut and his sons went down to the sea with Hallbjorn, and put out a boat and rowed out from land with him, and they took the bag off his head and tied a stone round his neck. Hallbjorn set gloating glances on the land, and the manner of his look was nowise of the goodliest. Then Hallbjorn said, "It was no day of bliss when we, kinsfolk, came to this Combeness and met with Thorliek. And this spell I utter," says he, "that Thorliek shall from henceforth have but few happy days, and that all who fill his place have a troublous life there." And this spell, men deem, has taken great effect. After that they drowned him, and rowed back to land.

A little while afterwards Hrut went to find Olaf his kinsman, and told him that he wouldnot leave matters with Thorliek as they stood, and bade him furnish him with men to go and make a house-raid on Thorliek. Olaf replied, "It is not right that you two kinsmen should be laying hands on each other; on Thorliek's behalf this has turned out a matter of most evil luck. I would sooner try and bring about peace between you, and you have often waited well and long for your good turn." Hrut said, "It is no good casting about for this; the sores between us two will never heal up; and I should like that from henceforth we should not both live in Salmon-river-Dale." Olaf replied, "It will not be easy for you to go further against Thorliek than I am willing to allow; but if you do it, it is not unlikely that dale and hill will meet." Hrut thought he now saw things stuck hard and fast before him; so he went home mightily ill pleased; but all was quiet or was called so. And for that year men kept quiet at home.

CHAPTER 38
The Death of Stigandi. Thorliek Leaves Iceland

Now, to tell of Stigandi, he became an outlaw and an evil to deal with. Thord was the name of a man who lived at Hundidale; he was a rich man, but had no manly greatness. A startling thing happened that summer in Hundidale, in that the milking stock did not yield much milk, but a woman looked after the beast there. At last people found out that she grew wealthy in precious things, and that she would disappear long and often, and no one knew where she was. Thord brought pressure to bear on her for confession, and when she got frightened she said a man was wont to come and meet her, "a big one," she said, "and in my eyes very handsome." Thord then asked how soon the man would come again to meet her, and she said she thought it would be soon. After that Thord went to see Olaf, and told him that Stigandi must be about, not far away from there, and bade him bestir himself with his men and catch him. Olaf got ready at once and came to Hundidale, and the bonds-woman was fetched for Olaf to have talk of her. Olaf asked her where the lair of Stigandi was. She said she did not know. Olaf offered to pay her money if she would bring Stigandi within reach of him and his men; and on this they came to a bargain together. The next day she went out to herd her cattle, and Stigandi comes that day to meet her. She greeted him well, and offers to look through (the hair of) his head. He laid his head down on her knee, and soon went to sleep. Then she slunk away from under his head, and went to meet Olaf and his men, and told them what had happened. Then they went towards Stigandi, and took counsel between them as to how it should not fare with him as his brother, that he should cast his glance on many things from which evil would befall them. They take now a bag, and draw it over his head. Stigandi woke at that, and made no struggle, for now there were many men to one. The sack had a slit in it, and Stigandi could see out through it the slope on the other side; there the lay of the land was fair, and it was covered with thick grass. But suddenly something like a whirlwind came on, and turned the sward topsy-turvy, so that the grass never grew there again. It is now called Brenna. Then they stoned Stigandi to death, and there he was buried under a heap of stones. Olaf kept his word to the bonds-woman, and gave her her freedom, and she went home to Herdholt. Hallbjorn Whetstone-eye was washed up by the surf a short time after he was drowned. It was called Knorstone where he was put in the earth, and his ghost walked about there a great deal. There was a man named Thorkell Skull who lived at Thickshaw on his father's inheritance. He was a man of very dauntless heart and mighty of muscle. One evening a cow was missing at Thickshaw, and Thorkell and his house-carle went to look for it. It was after sunset, but was bright moonlight. Thorkell said they must separate in their search, and when Thorkell was alone he thought he saw the cow on a hill-rise in front of him, but when he came up to it he saw it was Whetstone-eye and no cow. They fell upon each in mighty strength. Hallbjorn kept on the defensive, and when Thorkell least expected it he crept down into the earth out of his hands. After that Thorkell went home. The house-carle had come home already, and had found the cow. No more harm befell ever again from Hallbjorn. Thorbjorn Skrjup was dead by then, and so was Melkorka, and they both lie in a cairn in Salmon-river-Dale. Lambi, their son, kept house there after them. He was very warrior-like, and had a great deal of money. Lambi was more thought of by people than his father had been, chiefly because of his mother's relations; and between him and Olaf there was fond brotherhood. Now the winter next after the killing of Kotkell passed away. In the spring the brothers Olaf and Thorliek met, and Olaf asked if Thorliek was minded to keep on his house. Thorliek said he was. Olaf said, "Yet I would beg you, kinsman, to change your way of life, and go abroad; you will be thought an honourable man whereever you come; but as to Hrut, our kinsman, I know he feels how your dealings with him come home to him. And it is little to my mind that the risk of your sitting so near to each other should be run any longer. For Hrut has a strong run of luck to fall back upon, and his sons are but reckless bravos. On account of my kinship I feel I should be placed in a difficulty if you, my kinsman, should come to quarrel in full enmity." Thorliek replied, "I am not afraid of not being able to hold myself straight in the face of Hrut and his sons, and that is no reason why I should depart the country. But if you, brother, set much store by it, and feel yourself in a difficult position in this matter, then, for your words I will do this; for then I was best contented with my lot in life when I lived abroad. And I know you will not treat my son Bolli any the worse for my being nowhere near; for of all men I love him the best." Olaf said, "You have, indeed, taken an honourable course in this matter, if you do after my prayer; but as touching Bolli, I am minded to do to him henceforth as I have done hitherto, and to be to him and hold him no worse than my own sons." After that the brothers parted in great affection. Thorliek now sold his land, and spent his money on his journey abroad. He bought a ship that stood up in Daymealness; and when he was full ready he stepped on board ship with his wife and household. That ship made a good voyage, and they made Norway in the autumn. Thence he went south to Denmark, as he did not feel at home in Norway, his kinsmen and friends there being either dead or driven out of the land. After that Thorliek went to Gautland. It is said by most men that Thorliek had little to do with old age; yet he was held a man of great worth throughout life. And there we close the story of Thorliek.

CHAPTER 39
Of Kjartan's Friendship for Bolli

At that time, as concerning the strife between Hrut and Thorliek, it was ever the greatest gossip throughout the Broadfirth-Dales how that Hrut had had to abide a heavy lot at the hands of Kotkell and his sons. Then Osvif spoke to Gudrun and her brothers, and bade them call to mind whether they thought now it would have been the best counsel aforetime then and there to have plunged into the danger of dealing with such "hell-men" (terrible people) as Kotkell and his were. Then said Gudrun, "He is not counsel-bereft, father, who has the help of thy counsel." Olaf now abode at his manor in much honour, and all his sons are at home there, as was Bolli, their kinsman and foster-brother. Kjartan was foremost of all the sons of Olaf. Kjartan and Bolli loved each other the most, and Kjartan went nowhere that Bolli did not follow. Often Kjartan would go to the Sælingdale-spring, and mostly it happened that Gudrun was at the spring too. Kjartan liked talking to Gudrun, for she was both a woman of wits and clever of speech. It was the talk of all folk that of all men who were growing up at the time Kjartan was the most even match for Gudrun. Between Olaf and Osvif there was also great friendship, and often they would invite one another, and not the less frequently so when fondness was growing up between the young folk. One day when Olaf was talking to Kjartan, he said: "I do not know why it is that I always take it to heart when you go to Laugar and talk to Gudrun. It is not because I do not consider Gudrun the foremost of all other women, for she is the one among womenkind whom I look upon as a thoroughly suitable match for you. But it is my foreboding, though I will not prophesy it, that we, my kinsmen and I, and the men of Laugar will not bring altogether good luck to bear on our dealings together." Kjartan said he would do nothing against his father's will where he could help himself, but he hoped things would turn out better than he made a guess to. Kjartan holds to his usual ways as to his visits (to Laugar), and Bolli always went with him, and so the next seasons passed.

CHAPTER 40
Kjartan and Bolli Voyage to Norway, A.D. 996

Asgeir was the name of a man, he was called Eider-drake. He lived at Asgeir's-river, in Willowdale; he was the son of Audun Skokul; he was the first of his kinsmen who came to Iceland; he took to himself Willowdale. Another son of Audun was named Thorgrim Hoaryhead; he was the father of Asmund, the father of Gretter. Asgeir Eider-drake had five children; one of his sons was called Audun, father of Asgeir, father of Audun, father of Egil, who had for wife Ulfeid, the daughter of Eyjolf the Lame; their son was Eyjolf, who was slain at the All Thing. Another of Asgeir's sons was named Thorvald; his daughter was Wala, whom Bishop Isleef had for wife; their son was Gizor, the bishop. A third son of Asgeir was named Kalf. All Asgeir's sons were hopeful men. Kalf Asgeirson was at that time out travelling, and was accounted of as the worthiest of men. One of Asgeir's daughters was named Thured; she married Thorkell Kuggi, the son of Thord Yeller; their son was Thorstein. Another of Asgeir's daughters was named Hrefna; she was the fairest woman in those northern countrysides and very winsome. Asgeir was a very mighty man. It is told how one time Kjartan Olafson went on a journey south to Burgfirth. Nothing is told of his journey before he got to Burg. There at that time lived Thorstein, Egil's son, his mother's brother. Bolli was with him, for the foster-brothers loved each other so dearly that neither thought he could enjoy himself if they were not together. Thorstein received Kjartan with loving kindness, and said he should be glad for his staying there a long rather than a short time. So Kjartan stayed awhile at Burg. That summer there was a ship standing up in Steam-river-Mouth,and this ship belonged to Kalf Asgeirson, who had been staying through the winter with Thorstein, Egil's son. Kjartan told Thorstein in secret that his chief errand to the south then was, that he wished to buy the half of Kalf's ship, "for I have set my mind on going abroad," and he asked Thorstein what sort of a man he thought Kalf was. Thorstein said he thought he was a good man and true. "I can easily understand," said Thorstein, "that you wish to see other men's ways of life, and your journey will be remark-able in one way or another, and your kinsfolk will be very anxious as to how the journey may speed for you." Kjartan said it would speed well enough. After that Kjartan, bought a half share in Kalf's ship, and they made up half-shares partnership between them; Kjartan was to come on board when ten weeks of summer had passed. Kjartan was seen off with gifts on leaving Burg, and he and Bolli then rode home. When Olaf heard of this arrangement he said he thought Kjartan had made up his mind rather suddenly, but added that he would not foreclose the matter. A little later Kjartan rode to Laugar to tell Gudrun of his proposed journey abroad. Gudrun said, "You have decided this very suddenly, Kjartan," and she let fall sundry words about this, from which Kjartan got to understand that Gudrun was displeased with it. Kjartan said, "Do not let this displease you. I will do something else that shall please you." Gudrun said, "Be then a man of your word, for I shall speedily let you know what I want." Kjartan bade her do so. Gudrun said, "Then, I wish to go out with you this summer; if that comes off, you would have made amends to me for this hasty resolve, for I do not care for Iceland." Kjartan said, "That cannot be, your brothers are unsettled yet, and your father is old, and they would be bereft of all care if you went out of the land; so you wait for me three winters." Gudrun said she would promise nothing as to that matter, and each was at variance with the other, and therewith they parted. Kjartan rode home. Olaf rode to the Thing that summer, and Kjartan rode with his father from the west out of Herdholt, and they parted at North-river-Dale. From thence Kjartan rode to his ship, and his kinsman Bolli went along with him. There were ten Icelanders altogether who went with Kjartan on this journey, and none would part with him for the sake of the love they bore him. So with this following Kjartan went to the ship, and Kalf Asgeirson greeted them warmly. Kjartan and Bolli took a great many goods with them abroad. They now got ready to start, and when the wind blew they sailed out along Burgfirth with a light and good breeze, and then out to sea. They had a good journey, and got to Norway to the northwards and came into Thrandhome, and fell in with men there and asked for tidings. They were told that change of lords over the land had befallen, in that Earl Hakon had fallen and King Olaf Tryggvason had come in, and all Norway had fallen under his power. King Olaf was ordering a change of faith in Norway, and the people took to it most unequally. Kjartan and his companions took their craft up to Nidaross. At that time many Icelanders had come to Norway who were men of high degree. There lay beside the landing-stage three ships, all owned by Icelanders. One of the ships belonged to Brand the Bounteous, son of Vermund Thorgrimson. And another ship belonged to Hallfred the Trouble-Bard. The third ship belonged to two brothers, one named Bjarni, and the other Thorhall; they were sons of Broad-river-Skeggi, out of Fleetlithe in the east. All these men had wanted to go west to Iceland that summer, but the king had forbidden all these ships to sail because the Icelanders would not take the new faith that he was preaching. All the Icelanders greeted Kjartan warmly, but especially Brand, as they had known each other already before. The Icelanders now took counsel together and came to an agreement among themselves that they would refuse this faith that the king preached, and all the men previously named bound themselves together to do this. Kjartan and his companions brought their ship up to the landing-stage and unloaded it and disposed of their goods. King Olaf was then in the town. He heard of the coming of the ship and that men of great account were on board. It happened one fair-weather day in the autumn that the men went out of the town to swim in the river Nid. Kjartan and his friends saw this. Then Kjartan said to his companions that they should also go and disport themselves that day. They did so. There was one man who was by much the best at this sport. Kjartan asked Bolli if he felt willing to try swimming against the townsman. Bolli answered, "I don't think I am a match for him." "I cannot think where your courage can now have got to," said Kjartan, "so I shall go and try." Bolli replied, "That you may do if you like." Kjartan then plunges into the river and up to this man who was the best swimmer and drags him forthwith under and keeps him down for awhile, and then lets him go up again. And when they had been up for a long while, this man suddenly clutches Kjartan and drags him under; and they keep down for such a time as Kjartan thought quite long enough, when up they come a second time. Not a word had either to say to the other. The third time

228

they went down together, and now they keep under for much the longest time, and Kjartan now misdoubted him how this play would end, and thought he had never before found himself in such a tight place; but at last they come up and strike out for the bank. Then said the townsman, "Who is this man?" Kjartan told him his name. The townsman said, "You are very deft at swimming. Are you as good at other deeds of prowess as at this?" Kjartan answered rather coldly, "It was said when I was in Iceland that the others kept pace with this one. But now this one is not worth much." The townsman replied, "It makes some odds with whom you have had to do. But why do you not ask me anything?" Kjartan replied, "I do not want to know your name." The townsman answered, "You are not only a stalwart man, but you bear yourself very proudly as well, but none the less you shall know my name, and with whom you have been having a swimming match. Here is Olaf the king, the son of Tryggvi." Kjartan answered nothing, but turned away forthwith without his cloak. He had on a kirtle of red scarlet. The king was then well-nigh dressed; he called to Kjartan and bade him not go away so soon. Kjartan turned back, but rather slowly. The king then took a very good cloak off his shoulders and gave it to Kjartan, saying he should not go back cloakless to his companions. Kjartan thanked the king for the gift, and went to his own men and showed them the cloak. His men were nowise pleased as this, for they thought Kjartan had got too much into the king's power; but matters went on quietly. The weather set in very hard that autumn, and there was a great deal of frost, the season being cold. The heathen men said it was not to be wondered at that the weather should be so bad; "it is all because of the newfangled ways of the king and this new faith that the gods are angry." The Icelanders kept all together in the town during the winter, and Kjartan took mostly the lead among them. On the weather taking a turn for the better, many people came to the town at the summons of King Olaf. Many people had become Christians in Thrandhome, yet there were a great many more who withstood the king. One day the king had a meeting out at Eyrar, and preached the new faith to men - a long harangue and telling. The people of Thrandhome had a whole host of men, and in turn offered battle to the king. The king said they must know that he had had greater things to cope with than fighting there with churls out of Thrandhome. Then the good men lost heart and gave the whole case into the king's power, and many people were baptized then and there. After that, the meeting came to an end. That same evening the king sent men to the lodgings of the Icelanders, and bade them get sure knowledge of what they were saying. They did so. They heard much noise within. Then Kjartan began to speak, and said to Bolli, "How far are you willing, kinsman, to take this new faith the king preaches?" "I certainly am not willing thereto," said Bolli, "for their faith seems to me to be most feeble." Kjartan said, "Did ye not think the king was holding out threats against those who should be unwilling to submit to his will?" Bolli answered, "It certainly seemed to me that he spoke out very clearly that they would have to take exceeding hard treatment at his hands." "I will be forced under no one's thumb," said Kjartan, "while I have power to stand up and wield my weapons. I think it most unmanly, too, to be taken like a lamb in a fold or a fox in a trap. I think that is a better thing to choose, if a man must die in any case, to do first some such deed as shall be held aloft for a long time afterwards." Bolli said, "What will you do?" "I will not hide it from you," Kjartan replied; "I will burn the king in his hall." "There is nothing cowardly in that," said Bolli; "but this is not likely to come to pass, as far as I can see. The king, I take it, is one of great good luck and his guardian spirit mighty, and, besides, he has a faithful guard watching both day and night." Kjartan said that what most men failed in was daring, however valiant they might otherwise be. Bolli said it was not so certain who would have to be taunted for want of courage in the end. But here many men joined in, saying this was but an idle talk. Now when the king's spies had overheard this, they went away and told the king all that had been said. The next morning the king wished to hold a meeting, and summoned all the Icelanders to it; and when the meeting was opened the king stood up and thanked men for coming, all those who were his friends and had taken the new faith. Then he called to him for a parley the Icelanders. The king asked them if they would be baptized, but they gave little reply to that. The king said they were making for themselves the choice that would answer the worst. "But, by the way, who of you thought it the best thing to do to burn me in my hall?" Then Kjartan answered, "You no doubt think that he who did say it would not have the pluck to confess it; but here you can see him." "I can indeed see you," said the king, "man of no small counsels, but it is not fated for you to stand over my head, done to death by you; and you have done quite enough that you should be prevented making a vow to burn more kings in their houses yet, for the reason of being taught better things than you know and because I do not know whether your heart was in your speech, and that you have bravely acknowledged it, I will not take your life. It may also be that you follow the faith the better the more outspoken you are against it; and I can also see this, that on the day you let yourself be baptized of your own free will, several ships' crews will on that day also take the faith. And I think it likely to happen that your relations and friends will give much heed to what you speak to them when you return to Iceland. And it is in my mind that you, Kjartan, will have a better faith when you return from Norway than you had when you came hither. Go now in peace and safety wheresoever you like from the meeting. For the time being you shall not be tormented into Christianity, for God says that He wills that no one shall come to Him unwillingly." Good cheer was made at the king's speech, though mostly from the Christian men; but the heathen left it to Kjartan to answer as he liked. Kjartan said, "We thank you, king, that you grant safe peace unto us, and the way whereby you may most surely draw us to take the faith is, on the one hand, to forgive us great offences, and on the other to speak in this kindly manner on all matters, in spite of your this day having us and all our concerns in your power even as it pleases you. Now, as for myself, I shall receive the faith in Norway on that understanding alone that I shall give some little worship to Thor the next winter when I get back to Iceland." Then the king said and smiled, "It may be seen from the mien of Kjartan that he puts more trust in his own weapons and strength than in Thor and Odin." Then the meeting was broken up. After a while many men egged the king on to force Kjartan and his followers to receive the faith, and thought it unwise to have so many heathen men near about him. The king answered wrathfully, and said he thought there were many Christians who were not nearly so well-behaved as was Kjartan or his company either, "and for such one would have long to wait." The king caused many profitable things to be done that winter; he had a church built and the market-town greatly enlarged. This church was finished at Christmas. Then Kjartan said they should go so near the church that they might see the ceremonies of this faith the Christians followed; and many fell in, saying that would be right good pastime. Kjartan with his following and Bolli went to the church; in that train was also Hallfred and many other Icelanders. The king preached the faith before the people, and spoke both long and tellingly, and the

Christians made good cheer at his speech. And when Kjartan and his company went back to their chambers, a great deal of talk arose as to how they had liked the looks of the king at this time, which Christians accounted of as the next greatest festival. "For the king said, so that we might hear, that this night was born the Lord, in whom we are now to believe, if we do as the king bids us." Kjartan says: "So greatly was I taken with the looks of the king when I saw him for the first time, that I knew at once that he was a man of the highest excellence, and that feeling has kept steadfast ever since, when I have seen him at folk-meetings, and that but by much the best, however, I liked the looks of him to-day; and I cannot help thinking that the turn of our concerns hangs altogether on our believing Him to be the true God in whom the king bids us to believe, and the king cannot by any means be more eager in wishing that I take this faith than I am to let myself be baptized. The only thing that puts off my going straightway to see the king now is that the day is far spent, and the king, I take it, is now at table; but that day will be delayed, on which we, companions, will let ourselves all be baptized." Bolli took to this kindly, and bade Kjartan alone look to their affairs. The king had heard of the talk between Kjartan and his people before the tables were cleared away, for he had his spies in every chamber of the heathens. The king was very glad at this, and said, "In Kjartan has come true the saw: 'High tides best for happy signs.'" And the first thing the next morning early, when the king went to church, Kjartan met him in the street with a great company of men. Kjartan greeted the king with great cheerfulness, and said he had a pressing errand with him. The king took his greeting well, and said he had had a thoroughly clear news as to what his errand must be, "and that matter will be easily settled by you." Kjartan begged they should not delay fetching the water, and said that a great deal would be needed. The king answered and smiled. "Yes, Kjartan," says he, "on this matter I do not think your eager-mindedness would part us, not even if you put the price higher still." After that Kjartan and Bolli were baptized and all their crew, and a multitude of other men as well. This was on the second day of Yule before Holy Service. After that the king invited Kjartan to his Yule feast with Bolli his kinsman. It is the tale of most men that Kjartan on the day he laid aside his white baptismal-robes became a liegeman of the king's, he and Bolli both. Hallfred was not baptized that day, for he made it a point that the king himself should be his godfather, so the king put it off till the next day. Kjartan and Bolli stayed with Olaf the king the rest of the winter. The king held Kjartan before all other men for the sake of his race and manly prowess, and it is by all people said that Kjartan was sowinsome that he had not a single enemy within the court. Every one said that there had never before come from Iceland such a man as Kjartan. Bolli was also one of the most stalwart of men, and was held in high esteem by all good men. The winter now passes away, and, as spring came on, men got ready for their journeys, each as he had a mind to.

CHAPTER 41
Bolli Returns to Iceland, A.D. 999

Kalf Asgeirson went to see Kjartan and asks what he was minded to do that summer. Kjartan said, "I have been thinking chiefly that we had better take our ship to England, where there is a good market for Christian men. But first I will go and see the king before I settle this, for he did not seem pleased at my going on this journey when we talked about it in the spring." Then Kalf went away and Kjartan went to speak to the king, greeting him courteously. The king received him most kindly, and asked what he and his companion (Kalf) had been talking about. Kjartan told what they had mostly in mind to do, but said that his errand to the king was to beg leave to go on this journey. "As to that matter, I will give you your choice, Kjartan. Either you will go to Iceland this summer, and bring men to Christianity by force or by expedients; but if you think this too difficult a journey, I will not let you go away on any account, for you are much better suited to serve noble men than to turn here into a chapman." Kjartan chose rather to stay with the king than to go to Iceland and preach the faith to them there, and said he could not be contending by force against his own kindred. "Moreover, it would be more likely that my father and other chiefs, who are near kinsmen of mine, would go against thy will with all the less stubbornness the better beholden I am under your power." The king said, "This is chosen both wisely and as beseems a great man." The king gave Kjartan a whole set of new clothes, all cut out of scarlet cloth, and they suited him well; for people said that King Olaf and Kjartan were of an even height when they went under measure. King Olaf sent the court priest, named Thangbrand, to Iceland. He brought his ship to Swanfirth, and stayed with Side-Hall all the winter at Wash-river, and set forth the faith to people both with fair words and harsh punishments. Thangbrand slew two men who went most against him. Hall received the faith in the spring, and was baptized on the Saturday before Easter, with all his household; then Gizor the White let himself be baptized, so did Hjalti Skeggjason and many other chiefs, though there were many more who spoke against it; and then dealings between heathen men and Christians became scarcely free of danger. Sundry chiefs even took counsel together to slay Thangbrand, as well as such men who should stand up for him. Because of this turmoil Thangbrand ran away to Norway, and came to meet King Olaf, and told him the tidings of what had befallen in his journey, and said he thought Christianity would never thrive in Iceland. The king was very wroth at this, and said that many Icelanders would rue the day unless they came round to him. That summer Hjalti Skeggjason was made an outlaw at the Thing for blaspheming the gods. Runolf Ulfson, who lived in Dale, under Isles'-fells, the greatest of chieftains, upheld the lawsuit against him. That summer Gizor left Iceland and Hjalti with him, and they came to Norway, and went forthwith to find King Olaf. The king gave them a good welcome, and said they had taken a wise counsel; he bade them stay with him, and that offer they took with thanks. Sverling, son of Runolf of Dale, had been in Norway that winter, and was bound for Iceland in the summer. His ship was floating beside the landing stage all ready, only waiting for a wind. The king forbade him to go away, and said that no ships should go to Iceland that summer. Sverling went to the king and pleaded his case, and begged leave to go, and said it mattered a great deal to him, that they should not have to unship their cargo again. The king spake, and then he was wroth: "It is well for the son of a sacrificer to be where he likes it worst." So Sverling went no whither. That winter nothing to tell of befell. The next summer the king sent Gizor and Hjalti Skeggjason to Iceland to preach the faith anew, and kept four men back as hostages Kjartan Olafson, Halldor, the son of Gudmund the Mighty, Kolbein, son of Thord the priest of Frey, and Sverling, son of Runolf of Dale. Bolli made up his mind to journey with Gizor and Hjalti, and went to Kjartan, his kinsman, and said, "I am now ready to depart; I should wait for you through the next winter, if next summer you were more free to go away than you are now. But I cannot help thinking that the king will on no account let you go free. I also take it to be the truth that you yourself call to mind but few of the things that afford pastime in Iceland when you sit talking to Ingibjorg, the king's sister." She was at the court of King Olaf, and the most beautiful of all the women who were at that time in the land. Kjartan said, "Do not say such things, but bear my greeting to both my kinsfolk and friends."

CHAPTER 42
Bolli Makes Love to Gudrun, A.D. 1000

After that Kjartan and Bolli parted, and Gizor and Hjalti sailed from Norway and had a good journey, and came to the Westmen's Isles at the time the Althing was sitting, and went from thence to the mainland, and had there meetings and parleys with their kinsmen. Thereupon they went to the Althing and preached the faith to the people in an harangue both long and telling, and then all men in Iceland received the faith. Bolli rode from the Thing to Herdholt in fellowship with his uncle Olaf, who received him with much loving-kindness. Bolli rode to Laugar to disport himself after he had been at home for a short time, and a good welcome he had there. Gudrun asked very carefully about his journey and then about Kjartan. Bolli answered right readily all Gudrun asked, and said there were no tidings to tell of his journey. "But as to what concerns Kjartan there are, in truth, the most excellent news to be told of his ways of life, for he is in the king's bodyguard, and is there taken before every other man; but I should not wonder if he did not care to have much to do with this country for the next few winters to come." Gudrun then asked if there was any other reason for it than the friendship between Kjartan and the king. Bolli then tells what sort of way people were talking about the friendship of Kjartan with Ingibjorg the king's sister, and said he could not help thinking the king would sooner marry Ingibjorg to Kjartan than let him go away if the choice lay between the two things. Gudrun said these were good tidings, "but Kjartan would be fairly matched only if he got a good wife." Then she let the talk drop all of a sudden and went away and was very red in the face; but other people doubted if she really thought these tidings as good as she gave out she thought they were. Bolli remained at home in Herdholt all that summer, and had gained much honour from his journey; all his kinsfolk and acquaintances set great store by his valiant bearing; he had, moreover, brought home with him a great deal of wealth. He would often go over to Laugar and while away time talking to Gudrun. One day Bolli asked Gudrun what she would answer if he were to ask her in marriage. Gudrun replied at once, "No need for you to bespeak such a thing, Bolli, for I cannot marry any man whilst I know Kjartan to be still alive." Bolli answered, "I think then you will have to abide husbandless for sundry winters if you are to wait for Kjartan; he might have chosen to give me some message concerning the matter if he set his heart at all greatly on it." Sundry words they gave and took, each at variance with the other. Then Bolli rode home.

CHAPTER 43
Kjartan Comes Back to Iceland, A.D. 1001

A little after this Bolli talked to his uncle Olaf, and said, "It has come to this, uncle, that I have it in mind to settle down and marry, for I am now grown up to man's estate. In this matter I should like to have the assistance of your words and your backing-up, for most of the men hereabouts are such as will set much store by your words." Olaf replied, "Such is the case with most women, I am minded to think, that they would be fully well matched in you for a husband. And I take it you have not broached this matter without first having made up your mind as to where you mean to come down." Bolli said, "I shall not go beyond this countryside to woo myself a wife whilst there is such an goodly match so near at hand. My will is to woo Gudrun, Osvif's daughter, for she is now the most renowned of women." Olaf answered, "Ah, that is just a matter with which I will have nothing to do. To you it is in no way less well known, Bolli, than to me, what talk there was of the love between Kjartan and Gudrun; but if you have set your heart very much on this, I will put no hindrance in the way if you and Osvif settle the matter between you. But have you said anything to Gudrun about it?" Bolli said that he had once hinted at it, but that she had not given much heed to it, "but I think, however, that Osvif will have most to say in the matter." Olaf said Bolli could go about the business as it pleased himself. Not very long after Bolli rode from home with Olaf's sons, Halldor and Steinthor; there were twelve of them together. They rode to Laugar, and Osvif and his sons gave them a good welcome. Bolli said he wished to speak to Osvif, and he set forth his wooing, and asked for the hand ofGudrun, his daughter. Osvif answered in this wise, "As you know, Bolli, Gudrun is a widow, and has herself to answer for her, but, as for myself, I shall urge this on." Osvif now went to see Gudrun, and told her that Bolli Thorliekson had come there, "and has asked you in marriage; it is for you now to give the answer to this matter. And herein I may speedily make known my own will, which is, that Bolli will not be turned away if my counsel shall avail." Gudrun answered, "You make a swift work of looking into this matter; Bolli himself once bespoke it before me, and I rather warded it off, and the same is still uppermost in my mind." Osvif said, "Many a man will tell you that this is spoken more in overweening pride than in wise forethought if you refuse such a man as is Bolli. But as long as I am alive, I shall look out for you, my children, in all affairs which I know better how to see through things than you do." And as Osvif took such a strong view of the matter, Gudrun, as far as she was concerned, would not give an utter refusal, yet was most unwilling on all points. The sons of Osvif's urged the matter on eagerly, seeing what great avail an alliance with Bolli would be to them; so the long and short of the matter was that the betrothal took place then and there, and the wedding was to be held at the time of the winter nights. Thereupon Bolli rode home and told this settlement to Olaf, who did not hide his displeasure thereat. Bolli stayed on at home till he was to go to the wedding. He asked his uncle to it, but Olaf accepted it nowise quickly, though, at last, he yielded to the prayers of Bolli. It was a noble feast this at Laugar. Bolli stayed there the winter after. There was not much love between Gudrun and Bolli so far as she was concerned. When the summer came, and ships began to go and come between Iceland and Norway, the tidings spread to Norway that Iceland was all Christian. King Olaf was very glad at that, and gave leave to go to Iceland unto all those men whom he had kept as hostages, and to fare whenever they liked. Kjartan answered, for he took the lead of all those who had been hostages, "Have great thanks, Lord King, and this will be the choice we take, to go and see Iceland this summer." Then King Olaf said, "I must not take back my word, Kjartan, yet my order pointed rather to other men than to yourself, for in my view you, Kjartan, have been more of a friend than a hostage through your stay here. My wish would be, that you should not set your heart on going to Iceland though you have noble relations there; for, I take it, you could choose for yourself such a station in life in Norway, the like of which would not be found in Iceland." Then Kjartan answered, "May our Lord reward you, sire, for all the honours you have bestowed on me since I came into your power, but I am still in hopes that you will give leave to me, no less than to the others you have kept back for a while." The king said so it should be, but avowed that it would be hard for him to get in his place any untitled man such as Kjartan was. That winter Kalf Asgeirson had been in Norway and had brought, the autumn before, west-away from England, the ship and merchandise he and Kjartan had owned. And when Kjartan had got leave for his journey to Iceland Kalf and he set themselves to get the ship ready. And when the ship was all ready Kjartan went to see Ingibjorg, the king's sister. She gave him a cheery welcome, and made room for him to sit beside her, and they fell a-talking together, and Kjartan tells Ingibjorg that he has arranged his journey to Iceland. Then Ingibjorg said, "I am minded to think, Kjartan, that you have done this of your own wilfulness rather than because you have been urged by men to go away from Norway and to Iceland." But thenceforth words between them were drowned in silence. Amidst this Ingibjorg turns to a "mead-cask" that stood near her, and takes out of it a white coif inwoven with gold and gives it to Kjartan, saying, that it was far too good for Gudrun Osvif's daughter to fold it round her head, yet "you will give her the coif as a bridal gift, for I wish the wives of the Icelanders to see as much as that she with whom you have had your talks in Norway comes of no thrall's blood." It was in a pocket of costly stuff, and was altogether a most precious thing. "Now I shall not go to see you off," said Ingibjorg. "Fare you well, and hail!" After that Kjartan stood up and embraced Ingibjorg, and people told it as a true story that they took it sorely to heart being parted. And now Kjartan went away and unto the king, and told the king he now was ready for his journey. Then the king led Kjartan to his ship and many men with him, and when they came to where the ship was floating with one of its gangways to land, the king said, "Here is a sword, Kjartan, that you shall take from me at our parting; let this weapon be always with you, for my mind tells me you will never be a 'weapon-bitten' man if you bear this sword." It was a most noble keepsake, and much ornamented. Kjartan thanked the king with fair words for all the honour and advancement he had bestowed on him while he had been in Norway. Then the king spoke, "This I will bid you, Kjartan, that you keep your faith well." After that they parted, the king and Kjartan in dear friendship, and Kjartan stepped on board his ship. The king looked after him and said, "Great is the worth of Kjartan and his kindred, but to cope with their fate is not an easy matter."

CHAPTER 44
Kjartan Comes Home, A.D. 1001

Now Kjartan and Kalf set sail for the main. They had a good wind, and were only a short time out at sea. They hove into White-river, in Burgfirth. The tidings spread far and wide of the coming of Kjartan. When Olaf, his father, and his other kinsfolk heard of it they were greatly rejoiced. Olaf rode at once from the west out of the Dales and south to Burgfirth, and there was a very joyful meeting between father and son. Olaf asked Kjartan to go and stay with him, with as many of his men as he liked to bring. Kjartan took that well, and said that there only of all places in Iceland he meant to abide. Olaf now rides home to Herdholt, and Kjartan remained with his ship during the summer. He now heard of the marriage of Gudrun, but did not trouble himself at all over it; but that had heretofore been a matter of anxiety to many. Gudmund, Solmund's son, Kjartan's brother-in-law, and Thurid, his sister, came to his ship, and Kjartan gave them a cheery welcome. Asgeir Eider-drake came to the ship too to meet his son Kalf, and journeying with him was Hrefna his daughter, the fairest of women. Kjartan bade his sister Thurid have such of his wares as she liked, and the same Kalf said to Hrefna. Kalf now unlocked a great chest and bade them go and have a look at it. That day a gale sprang up, and Kjartan and Kalf had to go out to moor their ship, and when that was done they went home to the booths. Kalf was the first to enter the booth, where Thurid and Hrefna had turned out most of the things in the chest. Just then Hrefna snatched up the coif and unfolded it, and they had much to say as to how precious a thing it was. Then Hrefna said she would coif herself with it, and Thurid said she had better, and Hrefna did so. When Kalf saw that he gave her to understand that she had done amiss, and bade her take it off at her swiftest. "For that is the one thing that we, Kjartan and I, do not own in common." And as he said this Kjartan came into the booth. He had heard their talk, and fell in at once and told them there was nothing amiss. So Hrefna sat still with the head-dress on. Kjartan looked at her heedfully and said, "I think the coif becomes you very well, Hrefna," says he, "and I think it fits the best that both together, coif and maiden, be mine." Then Hrefna answered, "Most people take it that you are in no hurry to marry, and also that the woman you woo, you will be sure to get for wife." Kjartan said it would not matter much whom he married, but he would not stand being kept long a waiting wooer by any woman. "Now I see that this gear suits you well, and it suits well that you become my wife." Hrefna now took off the head-dress and gave it to Kjartan, who put it away in a safe place. Gudmund and Thurid asked Kjartan to come north to them for a friendly stay some time that winter, and Kjartan promised the journey. Kalf Asgeirson betook himself north with his father. Kjartan and he now divided their partnership, and that went off altogether in good-nature and friendship. Kjartan also rode from his ship westward to the Dales, and they were twelve of them together. Kjartan now came home to Herdholt, and was joyfully received by everybody. Kjartan had his goods taken to the west from the ship during the autumn. The twelve men who rode with Kjartan stayed at Herdholt all the winter. Olaf and Osvif kept to the same wont of asking each other to their house, which was that each should go to the other every other autumn. That autumn the wassail was to be at Laugar, and Olaf and all the Herdholtings were to go thither. Gudrun now spoke to Bolli, and said she did not think he had told her the truth in all things about the coming back of Kjartan. Bolli said he had told the truth about it as best he knew it. Gudrun spoke little on this matter, but it could be easily seen that she was very displeased, and most people would have it that she still was pining for Kjartan, although she tried to hide it. Now time glides on till the autumn feast was to be held at Laugar. Olaf got ready and bade Kjartan come with him. Kjartan said he would stay at home and look after the household. Olaf bade him not to show that hewas angry with his kinsmen. "Call this to mind, Kjartan, that you have loved no man so much as your foster-brother Bolli, and it is my wish that you should come, for things will soon settle themselves between you, kinsmen, if you meet each other." Kjartan did as his father bade him. He took the scarlet clothes that King Olaf had given him at parting, and dressed himself gaily; he girded his sword, the king's gift, on; and he had a gilt helm on his head, and on his side a red shield with the Holy Cross painted on it in gold; he had in his hand a spear, with the socket inlaid with gold. All his men were gaily dressed. There were in all between twenty and thirty men of them. They now rode out of Herdholt and went on till they came to Laugar. There were a great many men gathered together already.

CHAPTER 45
Kjartan marries Hrefna, A.D. 1002

Bolli, together with the sons of Osvif, went out to meet Olaf and his company, and gave them a cheery welcome. Bolli went to Kjartan and kissed him, and Kjartan took his greeting. After that they were seen into the house, Bolli was of the merriest towards them, and Olaf responded to that most heartily, but Kjartan was rather silent. The feast went off well. Now Bolli had some stud-horses which were looked upon as the best of their kind. The stallion was great and goodly, and had never failed at fight; it was light of coat, with red ears and forelock. Three mares went with it, of the same hue as the stallion. These horses Bolli wished to give to Kjartan, but Kjartan said he was not a horsey man, and could not take the gift. Olaf bade him take the horses, "for these are most noble gifts." Kjartan gave a flat refusal. They parted after this nowise blithely, and the Herdholtings went home, and all was quiet. Kjartan was rather gloomy all the winter, and people could have but little talk of him. Olaf thought this a great misfortune. That winter after Yule Kjartan got ready to leave home, and there were twelve of them together, bound for the countrysides of the north. They now rode on their way till they came to Asbjornness, north in Willowdale, and there Kjartan was greeted with the greatest blitheness and cheerfulness. The housing there was of the noblest. Hall, the son of Gudmund, was about twenty winters old, and took much after the kindred of the men of Salmon-river-Dale; and it is all men's say, there was no more valiant-looking a man in all the north land. Hall greeted Kjartan, his uncle, with the greatest blitheness. Sports are now at once started at Asbjornness, and men were gathered together from far and near throughout the countrysides, and people came from the west from Midfirth and from Waterness and Waterdale all the way and from out of Longdale, and there was a great gathering together. It was the talk of all folk how strikingly Kjartan showed above other men. Now the sports were set going,

237

and Hall took the lead. He asked Kjartan to join in the play, "and I wish, kinsman, you would show your courtesy in this." Kjartan said, "I have been training for sports but little of late, for there were other things to do with King Olaf, but I will not refuse you this for once." So Kjartan now got ready to play, and the strongest men there were chosen out to go against him. The game went on all day long, but no man had either strength or litheness of limb to cope with Kjartan. And in the evening when the games were ended, Hall stood up and said, "It is the wish and offer of my father concerning those men who have come from the farthest hither, that they all stay here over night and take up the pastime again to-morrow." At this message there was made a good cheer, and the offer deemed worthy of a great man. Kalf Asgeirson was there, and he and Kjartan were dearly fond of each other. His sister Hrefna was there also, and was dressed most showily. There were over a hundred (*i.e.* over 120) men in the house that night. And the next day sides were divided for the games again. Kjartan sat by and looked on at the sports. Thurid, his sister, went to talk to him, and said, "It is told me, brother, that you have been rather silent all the winter, and men say it must be because you are pining after Gudrun, and set forth as a proof thereof that no fondness now is shown between you and Bolli, such as through all time there had been between you. Do now the good and befitting thing, and don't allow yourself to take this to heart, and grudge not your kinsman a good wife. To me it seems your best counsel to marry, as you bespoke it last summer, although the match be not altogether even for you, where Hrefna is, for such a match you cannot find within this land. Asgeir, her father, is a noble and a high-born man, and he does not lack wealth wherewith to make this match fairer still; moreover, another daughter of his is married to a mighty man. You have also told me yourself that Kalf Asgeirson is the doughtiest of men, and their way of life is of the stateliest. It is my wish that you go and talk to Hrefna, and I ween you will find that there great wits and goodliness go together." Kjartan took this matter up well, and said she had ably pleaded the case. After this Kjartan and Hrefna are brought together that they may have their talk by themselves, and they talked together all day. In the evening Thurid asked Kjartan how he liked the manner in which Hrefna turned her speech. He was well pleased about it, and said he thought the woman was in all ways one of the noblest as far as he could see. The next morning men were sent to Asgeir to ask him to Asbjornness. And now they had a parley between them on this affair, and Kjartan wooed Hrefna, Asgeir's daughter. Asgeir took up the matter with a good will, for he was a wise man, and saw what an honourableoffer was made to them. Kalf, too, urged the matter on very much, saying, "I will not let anything be spared (towards the dowry)." Hrefna, in her turn, did not make unwilling answers, but bade her father follow his own counsel. So now the match was covenanted and settled before witnesses. Kjartan would hear of nothing but that the wedding should be held at Herdholt, and Asgeir and Kalf had nothing to say against it. The wedding was then settled to take place at Herdholt when five weeks of summer had passed. After that Kjartan rode home with great gifts. Olaf was delighted at these tidings, for Kjartan was much merrier than before he left home. Kjartan kept fast through Lent, following therein the example of no man in this land; and it is said he was the first man who ever kept fast in this land. Men thought it so wonderful a thing that Kjartan could live so long without meat, that people came over long ways to see him. In a like manner Kjartan's other ways went beyond those of other men. Now Easter passed, and after that Kjartan and Olaf made ready a great feast.

At the appointed time Asgeir and Kalf came from the north as well as Gudmund and Hall, and altogether there were sixty men. Olaf and Kjartan had already many men gathered together there. It was a most brave feast, and for a whole week the feasting went on. Kjartan made Hrefna a bridal gift of the rich head-dress, and a most famous gift was that; for no one was there so knowing or so rich as ever to have seen or possessed such a treasure, for it is the saying of thoughtful men that eight ounces of gold were woven into the coif. Kjartan was so merry at the feast that he entertained every one with his talk, telling of his journey. Men did marvel much how great were the matters that entered into that tale; for he had served the noblest of lords - King Olaf Tryggvason. And when the feast was ended Kjartan gave Gudmund and Hall good gifts, as he did to all the other great men. The father and son gained great renown from this feast. Kjartan and Hrefna loved each other very dearly.

CHAPTER 46
Feast at Herdholt
and the Loss of Kjartan's Sword, A.D. 1002

Olaf and Osvif were still friends, though there was some deal of ill-will between the younger people. That summer Olaf had his feast half a month before winter. And Osvif was also making ready a feast, to be held at "Winter-nights," and they each asked the other to their homes, with as many men as each deemed most honourable to himself. It was Osvif's turn to go first to the feast at Olaf's, and he came to Herdholt at the time appointed. In his company were Bolli and Gudrun and the sons of Osvif. In the morning one of the women on going down the hall was talking howthe ladies would be shown to their seats. And just as Gudrun had come right against the bedroom wherein Kjartan was wont to rest, and where even then he was dressing and slipping on a red kirtle of scarlet, he called out to the woman who had been speaking about the seating of the women, for no one else was quicker in giving the answer, "Hrefna shall sit in the high seat and be most honoured in all things so long as I am alive." But before this Gudrun had always had the high seat at Herdholt and everywhere else. Gudrun heard this, and looked at Kjartan and flushed up, but said nothing. The next day Gudrun was talking to Hrefna, and said she ought to coif herself with the head-dress, and show people the most costly treasure that had ever come to Iceland. Kjartan was near, but not quite close, and heard what Gudrun said, and he was quicker to answer than Hrefna. "She shall not coif herself with the headgear at this feast, for I set more store by Hrefna owning the greatest of treasures than by the guests having it to feast thereon their eyes at this time." The feast at Olaf's was to last a week. The next day Gudrun spoke on the sly to Hrefna, and asked her to show her the head-dress, and Hrefna said she would. The next day they went to the out-bower where the precious things were kept, and Hrefna opened a chest and took out the pocket of costly stuff, and took from thence the coif and showed it to Gudrun. She unfolded the coif and looked at it a while, but said no word of praise or blame. After that Hrefna put it back, and they went to their places, and after that all was joy and amusement. And the day the guests should ride away Kjartan busied himself much about matters in hand, getting change of horses for those who had come from afar, and speeding each one on his journey as he needed. Kjartan had not his sword "King's-gift" with him while he was taken up with these matters, yet was he seldom wont to let it go out of his hand. After this he went to his room where the sword had been, and found it now gone. He then went and told his father of the loss. Olaf said, "We must go about this most gently. I will get men to spy into each batch of them as they ride away," and he did so. An the White had to ride with Osvif's company, and to keep an eye upon men turning aside, or baiting. They rode up past Lea-shaws, and past the homesteads which are called Shaws, and stopped at one of the homesteads at Shaws, and got off their horses. Thorolf, son of Osvif, went out from the homestead with a few other men. They went out of sight amongst the brushwood, whilst the others tarried at the Shaws' homestead. An followed him all the way unto Salmon-river, where it flows out of Sælingsdale, and said he would turn back there. Thorolf said it would have done no harm though he had gone nowhere at all. The night before a little snow had fallen so that footprints could be traced. An rode back to the brushwood, and followed the footprints of Thorolf to a certain ditch or bog. He gropeddown with his hand, and grasped the hilt of a sword. An wished to have witnesses with him to this, and rode for Thorarin in Sælingsdale Tongue, and he went with An to take up the sword. After that An brought the sword back to Kjartan. Kjartan wrapt it in a cloth, and laid it in a chest. The place was afterwards called Sword-ditch, where An and Thorarin had found the "King's-gift." This was all kept quiet. The scabbard was never found again. Kjartan always treasured the sword less hereafter than heretofore. This affair Kjartan took much to heart, and would not let the matter rest there. Olaf said, "Do not let it pain you; true, they have done a nowise pretty trick, but you have got no harm from it. We shall not let people have this to laugh at, that we make a quarrel about such a thing, these being but friends and kinsmen on the other side." And through these reasonings of Olaf, Kjartan let matters rest in quiet. After that Olaf got ready to go to the feast at Laugar at "winter nights," and told Kjartan he must go too. Kjartan was very unwilling thereto, but promised to go at the bidding of his father. Hrefna was also to go, but she wished to leave her coif behind. "Goodwife," Thorgerd said, "whenever will you take out such a peerless keepsake if it is to lie down in chests when you go to feasts?" Hrefna said, "Many folk say that it is not unlikely that I may come to places where I have fewer people to envy me than at Laugar." Thorgerd said, "I have no great belief in people who let suchthings fly here from house to house." And because Thorgerd urged it eagerly Hrefna took the coif, and Kjartan did not forbid it when he saw how the will of his mother went. After that they betake themselves to the journey and came to Laugar in the evening, and had a goodly welcome there. Thorgerd and Hrefna handed out their clothes to be taken care of. But in the morning when the women should dress themselves Hrefna looked for the coif and it was gone from where she had put it away. It was looked for far and near, and could not be found. Gudrun said it was most likely the coif had been left behind at home, or that she had packed it so carelessly that it had fallen out on the way. Hrefna now told Kjartan that the coif was lost. He answered and said it was no easy matter to try to make them take care of things, and bade her now leave matters quiet; and told his father what game was up. Olaf said, "My will is still as before, that you leave alone and let pass by this trouble and I will probe this matter to the bottom in quiet; for I would do anything that you and Bolli should not fall out. Best to bind up a whole flesh, kinsman," says he. Kjartan said, "I know well, father, that you wish the best for everybody in this affair; yet I

240

know not whether I can put up with being thus overborne by these folk of Laugar." The day that men were to ride away from the feast Kjartan raised his voice and said, "I call on you, Cousin Bolli, to show yourself more willing henceforth than hitherto to do to us as behoves a good man and true. I shall not set this matter forth in a whisper, for within the knowledge of many people it is that a loss has befallen here of a thing which we think has slipped into your own keep. This harvest, when we gave a feast at Herdholt, my sword was taken; it came back to me, but not the scabbard. Now again there has been lost here a keepsake which men will esteem a thing of price. Come what may, I will have them both back." Bolli answered, "What you put down to me, Kjartan, is not my fault, and I should have looked for anything else from you sooner than that you would charge me with theft." Kjartan says, "I must think that the people who have been putting their heads together in this affair are so near to you that it ought to be in your power to make things good if you but would. You affront us far beyond necessity, and long we have kept peaceful in face on your enmity. But now it must be made known that matters will not rest as they are now." Then Gudrun answered his speech and said, "Now you rake up a fire which it would be better should not smoke. Now, let it be granted, as you say, that there be some people here who have put their heads together with a view to the coif disappearing. I can only think that they have gone and taken what was their own. Think what you like of what has become of the head-dress, but I cannot say I dislike it though it should be bestowed in such a way as that Hrefna should have little chance to improve her apparel with it henceforth." After that they parted heavy of heart, and the Herdholtings rode home. That was the end of the feasts, yet everything was to all appearances quiet. Nothing was ever heard of the head-dress. But many people held the truth to be that Thorolf had burnt it in fire by the order of Gudrun, his sister. Early that winter Asgeir Eider-drake died. His sons inherited his estate and chattels.

CHAPTER 47
Kjartan Goes to Laugar,
and of the Bargain for Tongue, A.D. 1003

After Yule that winter Kjartan got men together, and they mustered sixty men altogether. Kjartan did not tell his father the reason of his journey, and Olaf asked but little about it. Kjartan took with him tents and stores, and rode on his way until he came to Laugar. He bade his men get off their horses, and said that some should look after the horses and some put up the tents. At that time it was the custom that outhouses were outside, and not so very far away from the dwelling-house, and so it was at Laugar. Kjartan had all the doors of the house taken, and forbade all the inmates to go outside, and for three nights he made them do their errands within the house. After that Kjartan rode home to Herdholt, and each of his followers rode to his own home. Olaf was veryill-pleased with this raid, but Thorgerd said there was no reason for blame, for the men of Laugar had deserved this, yea, and a still greater shame. Then Hrefna said, "Did you have any talk with any one at Laugar, Kjartan?" He answered, "There was but little chance of that," and said he and Bolli had exchanged only a few words. Then Hrefna smiled and said, "It was told me as truth that you and

Gudrun had some talk together, and I have likewise heard how she was arrayed, that she had coifed herself with the head-dress, and it suited her exceeding well." Kjartan answered, and coloured up, and it was easy to see he was angry with her for making a mockery of this. "Nothing of what you say, Hrefna, passed before my eyes, and there was no need for Gudrun to coif herself with the head-dress to look statelier than all other women." Thereat Hrefna dropped the talk. The men of Laugar bore this exceedingly ill, and thought it by much a greater and worse disgrace than if Kjartan had even killed a man or two of them. The sons of Osvif were the wildest over this matter, but Bolli quieted them rather. Gudrun was the fewest-spoken on the matter, yet men gathered from her words that it was uncertain whether any one took it as sorely to heart as she did. Full enmity now grows up between the men of Laugar and the Herdholtings. As the winter wore on Hrefna gave birth to a child, a boy, and he was named Asgier. Thorarin, the goodman of Tongue, let it beknown that he wished to sell the land of Tongue. The reason was that he was drained of money, and that he thought ill-will was swelling too much between the people of the countryside, he himself being a friend of either side. Bolli thought he would like to buy the land and settle down on it, for the men of Laugar had little land and much cattle. Bolli and Gudrun rode to Tongue at the advice of Osvif; they thought it a very handy chance to be able to secure this land so near to themselves, and Osvif bade them not to let a small matter stand in the way of a covenant. Then they (Bolli and Gudrun) bespoke the purchase with Thorarin, and came to terms as to what the price should be, and also as to the kind wherein it should be paid, and the bargain was settled with Thorarin. But the buying was not done in the presence of witnesses, for there were not so many men there at the time as were lawfully necessary. Bolli and Gudrun rode home after that. But when Kjartan Olafson hears of these tidings he rides off with twelve men, and came to Tongue early one day. Thorarin greeted him well, and asked him to stay there. Kjartan said he must ride back again in the morning, but would tarry there for some time. Thorarin asked his errand, and Kjartan said, "My errand here is to speak about a certain sale of land that you and Bolli have agreed upon, for it is very much against my wishes if you sell this land to Bolli and Gudrun." Thorarin said that to do otherwise would be unbecoming to him, "For the price that Bolli has offered for the land is liberal, and is to be paid up speedily." Kjartan said, "You shall come in for no loss even if Bolli does not buy your land; for I will buy it at the same price, and it will not be of much avail to you to speak against what I have made up my mind to have done. Indeed it will soon be found out that I shall want to have the most to say within this countryside, being more ready, however, to do the will of others than that of the men of Laugar." Thorarin answered, "Mighty to me will be the master's word in this matter, but it would be most to my mind that this bargain should be left alone as I and Bolli have settled it." Kjartan said, "I do not call that a sale of land which is not bound by witnesses. Now you do one of two things, either sell me the lands on the same terms as you agreed upon with the others, or live on your land yourself." Thorarin chooses to sell him the land, and witnesses were forthwith taken to the sale, and after the purchase Kjartan rode home. That same evening this was told at Laugar. Then Gudrun said, "It seems to me, Bolli, that Kjartan has given you two choices somewhat harder than those he gave Thorarin - that you must either leave the countryside with little honour, or show yourself at some meeting with him a good deal less slow than you have been heretofore." Bolli did not answer, but went forthwith away from this talk. All was

242

quiet now throughout what was left of Lent. The third day after Easter Kjartan rode from home with one other man, on the beach, for a follower. They came to Tongue in the day. Kjartan wished Thorarin to ride with them to Saurby to gather in debts due to him, for Kjartan had much money-at-call in these parts. But Thorarin had ridden to another place. Kjartan stopped there awhile, and waited for him. That same day Thorhalla the Chatterbox was come there. She asked Kjartan where he was minded to go. He said he was going west to Saurby. She asked, "Which road will you take?" Kjartan replied, "I am going by Sælingsdale to the west, and by Swinedale from the west." She asked how long he would be. Kjartan answered, "Most likely I shall be riding from the west next Thursday (the fifth day of the week)." "Would you do an errand for me?" said Thorhalla. "I have a kinsman west at Whitedale and Saurby; he has promised me half a mark's worth of homespun, and I would like you to claim it for me, and bring it with you from the west." Kjartan promised to do this. After this Thorarin came home, and betook himself to the journey with them. They rode westward over Sælingsdale heath, and came to Hol in the evening to the brothers and sister there. There Kjartan got the best of welcomes, for between him and them there was the greatest friendship. Thorhalla the Chatterbox came home to Laugar that evening. The sons of Osvif asked her who she had met during the day. She said she had met Kjartan Olafson. They asked where he was going. She answered, tellingthem all she knew about it, "And never has he looked braver than now, and it is not wonderful at all that such men should look upon everything as low beside themselves;" and Thorhalla still went on, "and it was clear to me that Kjartan liked to talk of nothing so well as of his land bargain with Thorarin." Gudrun spoke, "Kjartan may well do things as boldly as it pleases him, for it is proven that for whatever insult he may pay others, there is none who dares even to shoot a shaft at him." Present at this talk of Gudrun and Thorhalla were both Bolli and the sons of Osvif. Ospak and his brothers said but little, but what there was, rather stinging for Kjartan, as was always their way. Bolli behaved as if he did not hear, as he always did when Kjartan was spoken ill of, for his wont was either to hold his peace, or to gainsay them.

CHAPTER 48
The Men of Laugar and Gudrun
Plan an Ambush for Kjartan, A.D. 1003

Kjartan spent the fourth day after Easter at Hol, and there was the greatest merriment and gaiety. The night after An was very ill at ease in his sleep, so they waked him. They asked him what he had dreamt. He answered, "A woman came to me most evil-looking and pulled me forth unto the bedside.She had in one hand a short sword, and in the other a trough; she drove the sword into my breast and cut open all the belly, and took out all my inwards and put brushwood in their place. After that she went outside." Kjartan and the others laughed very much at this dream, and said he should be called An "brushwood belly," and they caught hold of him and said they wished to feel if he had the brushwood in his stomach. Then Aud said, "There is no need to mock so much at this; and my counsel is that Kjartan do one of two things: either tarry here longer, or, if he will ride away, then let him ride with more followers hence than hither he did." Kjartan said, "You may hold An 'brushwood belly' a man very sage as he sits and talks to you all day, since you think that whatever he dreams must be a very vision, but go I must, as I have already made up my mind to, in spite of this dream." Kjartan got ready to go on the fifth day in Easter week; and at the advice of Aud, so did Thorkell Whelp and Knut his brother. They rode on the way with Kjartan a band of twelve together. Kjartan came to Whitedale and fetched the homespun for Thorhalla Chatterbox as he had said he would. After that he rode south through Swinedale. It is told how at Laugar in Sælingsdale Gudrun was early afoot directly after sunrise. She went to where her brothers were sleeping. She roused Ospak and he woke up at once, and then too the other brothers. And when Ospak saw that therewas his sister, he asked her what she wanted that she was up so early. Gudrun said she wanted to know what they would be doing that day. Ospak said he would keep at rest, "for there is little work to do." Gudrun said, "You would have the right sort of temper if you were the daughters of some peasant, letting neither good nor bad be done by you. Why, after all the disgrace and shame that Kjartan has done to you, you none the less lie quietly sleeping, though he rides past this place with but one other man. Such men indeed are richly endowed with the memory of swine. I think it is past hoping that you will ever have courage enough to go and seek out Kjartan in his home, if you dare not meet him now that he rides with but one other man or two; but here you sit at home and bear yourselves as if you were hopeful men; yea, in sooth there are too many of you." Ospak said she did not mince matters and it was hard to gainsay her, and he sprang up forthwith and dressed, as did also each of the brothers one after the other. Then they got ready to lay an ambush for Kjartan. Then Gudrun called on Bolli to bestir him with them. Bolli said it behoved him not for the sake of his kinship with Kjartan, set forth how lovingly Olaf had brought him up. Gudrun answered, "Therein you speak the truth, but you will not have the good luck always to do what pleases all men, and if you cut yourself out of this journey, our married life must be at an end." And through Gudrun's harping onthe matter Bolli's mind swelled at all the enmity and guilts that lay at the door of Kjartan, and speedily he donned his weapons, and they grew a band of nine together. There were the five sons of Osvif - Ospak, Helgi, Vandrad, Torrad, and Thorolf. Bolli was the sixth and Gudlaug, the son of Osvif's sister, the hopefullest of men, the seventh. There were also Odd and Stein, sons of Thorhalla Chatterbox. They rode to Swinedale and took up their stand beside the gill which is called Goat-gill. They bound up their horses and sat down. Bolli was silent all day, and lay up on the top of the gill bank. Now when Kjartan and his followers were come south past Narrowsound, where the dale begins to widen out, Kjartan said that Thorkell and the others had better turn back. Thorkell said they would ride to the end of the dale. Then when they came south past the out-dairies called Northdairies Kjartan spake to the brothers and bade them not to ride any farther. "Thorolf the thief," he said, "shall not have that matter to laugh at that I dare not ride on my way with few men." Thorkell Whelp said, "We will yield to you in not following you any farther; but we should rue it indeed not to be near if you should stand in need of men to-day." Then Kjartan said, "Never will Bolli, my kinsman, join hands with plotters against my life. But if the sons of Osvif lie in wait for me, there is no knowing which side will live to tell the tale, even though I may have some odds to deal with." Thereupon the brothers rode back to the west.

CHAPTER 49
The Death of Kjartan

Now Kjartan rode south through the dale, he and they three together, himself, An the Black, and Thorarin. Thorkell was the name of a man who lived at Goat-peaks in Swinedale, where now there is waste land. He had been seeing after his horses that day, and a shepherd of his with him. They saw the two parties, the men of Laugar in ambush and Kjartan and his where they were riding down the dale three together. Then the shepherd said they had better turn to meet Kjartan and his; it would be, quoth he, a great good hap to them if they could stave off so great a trouble as now both sides were steering into. Thorkell said, "Hold your tongue at once. Do you think, fool as you are, you will ever give life to a man to whom fate has ordained death? And, truth to tell, I would spare neither of them from having now as evil dealings together as they like. It seems to me a better plan for us to get to a place where we stand in danger of nothing, and from where we can have a good look at their meeting, so as to have some fun over theirplay. For all men make a marvel thereof, how Kjartan is of all men the best skilled at arms. I think he will want it now, for we two know how overwhelming the odds are." And so it had to be as Thorkell wished. Kjartan and his followers now rode on to Goat-gill. On the other hand the sons of Osvif misdoubt them why Bolli should have sought out a place for himself from where he might well be seen by men riding from the west. So they now put their heads together, and, being of one mind that Bolli was playing them false, they go for him up unto the brink and took to wrestling and horse-playing with him, and took him by the feet and dragged him down over the brink. But Kjartan and his followers came up apace as they were riding fast, and when they came to the south side of the gill they saw the ambush and knew the men. Kjartan at once sprung off his horse and turned upon the sons of Osvif. There stood near by a great stone, against which Kjartan ordered they should wait the onset (he and his). Before they met Kjartan flung his spear, and it struck through Thorolf's shield above the handle, so that therewith the shield was pressed against him, the spear piercing the shield and the arm above the elbow, where it sundered the main muscle, Thorolf dropping the shield, and his arm being of no avail to him through the day. Thereupon Kjartan drew his sword, but he held not the "King's-gift." The sons of Thorhalla went at Thorarin, for that was the task allotted to them. That outset was a hard one, for Thorarin was mightily strong, and it was hard to tell which would outlast the other. Osvif's sons and Gudlaug set on Kjartan, they being five together, and Kjartan and An but two. An warded himself valiantly, and would ever be going in front of Kjartan. Bolli stood aloof with Footbiter. Kjartan smote hard, but his sword was of little avail (and bent so), he often had to straighten it under his foot. In this attack both the sons of Osvif and An were wounded, but Kjartan had no wound as yet. Kjartan fought so swiftly and dauntlessly that Osvif's sons recoiled and turned to where An was. At that moment An fell, having fought for some time, with his inwards coming out. In this attack Kjartan cut off one leg of Gudlaug above the knee, and that hurt was enough to cause death. Then the four sons of Osvif made an onset on Kjartan, but he warded himself so bravely that in no way did he give them the chance of any advantage. Then spake Kjartan, "Kinsman Bolli, why did you leave home if you meant quietly to stand by? Now the choice lies before you, to help one side or the other, and try now how Footbiter will do." Bolli made as if he did not hear. And when Ospak saw that they would no how bear Kjartan over, he egged on Bolli in every way, and said he surely would not wish that shame to follow after him, to have promised them his aid in this fight and not to grant it now. "Why, heavy enough in dealings with us was Kjartan then, when by none so big a deed as this we had offended him; but ifKjartan is now to get away from us, then for you, Bolli, as even for us, the way to exceeding hardships will be equally short." Then Bolli drew Footbiter, and now turned upon Kjartan. Then Kjartan said to Bolli, "Surely thou art minded now, my kinsman, to do a dastard's deed; but oh, my kinsman, I am much more fain to take my death from you than to cause the same to you myself." Then Kjartan flung away his weapons and would defend himself no longer; yet he was but slightly wounded, though very tired with fighting. Bolli gave no answer to Kjartan's words, but all the same he dealt him his death-wound. And straightway Bolli sat down under the shoulders of him, and Kjartan breathed his last in the lap of Bolli. Bolli rued at once his deed, and declared the manslaughter due to his hand. Bolli sent the sons of Osvif into the countryside, but he stayed behind together with Thorarin by the dead bodies. And when the sons of Osvif came to Laugar they told the tidings. Gudrun gave out her pleasure thereat, and then the arm of Thorolf was bound up; it healed slowly, and was never after any use to him. The body of Kjartan was brought home to Tongue, but Bolli rode home to Laugar. Gudrun went to meet him, and asked what time of day it was. Bolli said it was near noontide. Then spake Gudrun, "Harm spurs on to hard deeds (work); I have spun yarn for twelve ells of homespun, and you have killed Kjartan." Bolli replied, "Thatunhappy deed might well go late from my mind even if you did not remind me of it." Gudrun said "Such things I do not count among mishaps. It seemed to me you stood in higher station during the year Kjartan was in Norway than now, when he trod you under foot when he came back to Iceland. But I count that last which to me is dearest, that Hrefna will not go laughing to her bed to-night." Then Bolli said and right wroth he was, "I think it is quite uncertain that she will turn paler at these tidings than you do; and I have my doubts as to whether you would not have been less startled if I had been lying behind on the field of battle, and Kjartan had told the tidings." Gudrun saw that Bolli was wroth, and spake, "Do not upbraid me with such things, for I am very grateful to you for your deed; for now I think I know that you will not do anything against my mind." After that Osvif's sons went and hid in an underground chamber, which had been made for them in secret, but Thorhalla's sons were sent west to Holy-Fell to tell Snorri Godi the Priest these tidings, and therewith the message that they bade him send them speedily all availing strength against Olaf and those men to whom it came to follow up the blood-suit after Kjartan. At Sælingsdale Tongue it happened, the night after the day on which the fight befell, that An sat up, he who they had all thought was dead. Those who waked the bodies were very much afraid, and thought this a wondrous marvel. Then An spake to them, "I beg you, in God'sname, not to be afraid of me, for I have had both my life and my wits all unto the hour when on me fell the heaviness of a swoon. Then I dreamed of the same woman as before, and methought she now took the brushwood out of my belly and put my own inwards in instead, and the change seemed good to me." Then the wounds that An had were bound up and he became a hale man, and was ever afterwards called An Brushwood-belly. But now when Olaf Hoskuld's son heard these tidings he took the slaying of Kjartan most sorely to heart, though he bore it like a brave man. His sons wanted to set on Bolli forthwith and kill him. Olaf said, "Far be it from me, for my son is none the more atoned to me though Bolli be slain; moreover, I loved Kjartan before all men, but as to Bolli, I could not bear any harm befalling him. But I see a more befitting business for you to do. Go ye and meet the sons of Thorhalla, who are now sent to Holy-Fell with the errand of summoning up a band against us. I shall be well pleased for you to put them to any penalty you like." Then Olaf's sons swiftly turn to journeying, and went on board a ferry-boat that Olaf owned, being seven of them together, and rowed out down Hvamsfirth, pushing on their journey at their lustiest. They had but little wind, but fair what there was, and they rowed with the sail until they came under Scoreisle, where they tarried for some while and asked about the journeyings of men thereabouts. A little while after they saw a ship coming from the west across the firth, and soon they saw who the men were, for there were the sons of Thorhalla, and Halldor and his followers boarded them straightway. They met with no resistance, for the sons of Olaf leapt forthwith on board their ships and set upon them. Stein and his brother were laid hands on and beheaded overboard. The sons of Olaf now turn back, and their journey was deemed to have sped most briskly.

CHAPTER 50
The End of Hrefna. The Peace Settled, A.D. 1003

Olaf went to meet Kjartan's body. He sent men south to Burg to tell Thorstein Egilson these tidings, and also that he would have his help for the blood-suit; and if any great men should band themselves together against him with the sons of Osvif, he said he wanted to have the whole matter in his own hands. The same message he sent north to Willowdale, to Gudmund, his son-in-law, and to the sons of Asgeir; with the further information that he had charged as guilty of the slaying of Kjartan all the men who had taken part in the ambush, except Ospak, son of Osvif, for he was already under outlawry because of a woman who was called Aldis, the daughter of Holmganga-Ljot of Ingjaldsand. Their son was Ulf,who later became a marshal to King Harold Sigurdsson, and had for wife Jorunn, the daughter of Thorberg. Their son was Jon, father of Erlend the Laggard, the father of Archbishop Egstein. Olaf had proclaimed that the blood-suit should be taken into court at Thorness Thing. He had Kjartan's body brought home, and a tent was rigged over it, for there was as yet no church built in the Dales. But when Olaf heard that Thorstein had bestirred him swiftly and raised up a band of great many men, and that the Willowdale men had done likewise, he had men gathered together throughout all the Dales, and a great multitude they were. The whole of this band Olaf sent to Laugar, with this order: "It is my will that you guard Bolli if he stand in need thereof, and do it no less faithfully than if you were following me; for my mind misgives me that the men from beyond this countryside, whom, coming soon, we shall be having on our hands, will deem that they have somewhat of a loss to make up with Bolli. And when he had put the matter in order in this manner, Thorstein, with his following, and also the Willowdale men, came on, all wild with rage. Hall Gudmund's son and Kalf Asgeirson egged them on most to go and force Bolli to let search be made for the sons of Osvif till they should be found, for they could be gone nowhere out of the countryside. But because Olaf set himself so much against their making a raid on Laugar, messages of peace were borne between the two parties, and Bolli was most willing, and bade Olaf settle all terms on his behalf, and Osvif said it was not in his power to speak against this, for no help had come to him from Snorri the Priest. A peace meeting, therefore, took place at Lea-Shaws, and the whole case was laid freely in Olaf's hand. For the slaughter of Kjartan there were to come such fines and penalties as Olaf liked. Then the peace meeting came to an end. Bolli, by the counsel of Olaf, did not go to this meeting. The award should be made known at Thorness Thing. Now the Mere-men and Willowdale men rode to Herdholt. Thorstein Kuggison begged for Asgeir, son of Kjartan, to foster, as a comfort to Hrefna. Hrefna went north with her brothers, and was much weighed down with grief, nevertheless she bore her sorrow with dignity, and was easy of speech with every man. Hrefna took no other husband after Kjartan. She lived but a little while after coming to the north; and the tale goes that she died of a broken heart.

CHAPTER 51
Osvif's Sons are Banished

Kjartan's body lay in state for a week in Herdholt. Thorstein Egilson had had a church built at Burg. He took the body of Kjartan home with him, and Kjartan was buried at Burg. The church was newly consecrated, and as yet hung in white. Now time wore on towards the Thorness Thing, and the award was given against Osvif's sons, who were all banished the country. Money was given to pay the cost of their going into exile, but they were forbidden to come back to Iceland so long as any of Olaf's sons, or Asgeir, Kjartan's son, should be alive. For Gudlaug, the son of Osvif's sister, no weregild (atonement) should be paid, because of his having set out against, and laid ambush for, Kjartan, neither should Thorolf have any compensation for the wounds he had got. Olaf would not let Bolli be prosecuted, and bade him ransom himself with a money fine. This Halldor and Stein, and all the sons of Olaf, liked mightily ill, and said it would go hard with Bolli if he was allowed to stay in the same countryside as themselves. Olaf saw that would work well enough as long as he was on his legs. There was a ship in Bjornhaven which belonged to Audun Cable-hound. He was at the Thing, and said, "As matters stand, the guilt of these men will be no less in Norway, so long as any of Kjartan's friends are alive." Then Osvif said, "You, Cable-hound, will be no soothsayer in this matter, for my sons will be highly accounted of among men of high degree, whilst you, Cable-hound, will pass, this summer, into the power of trolls." Audun Cable-hound went out a voyage that summer and the ship was wrecked amongst the Faroe Isles and every man's child on board perished, and Osvif's prophecy was thought to have come thoroughly home. The sons of Osvif went abroad that summer, and none ever came back again. In such a manner the blood-suit came to an end that Olaf was held to have shown himself all the greater a man, because where it was due, in the case of the sons of Osvif, to wit, he drove matters home to the very bone, but spared Bolli for the sake of their kinship. Olaf thanked men well for the help they had afforded him. By Olaf's counsel Bolli bought the land at Tongue. It is told that Olaf lived three winters after Kjartan was slain. After he was dead his sons shared the inheritance he left behind. Halldor took over the manor of Herdholt. Thorgerd, their mother, lived with Halldor; she was most hatefully-minded towards Bolli, and thought the reward he paid for his fostering a bitter one.

CHAPTER 52
The Killing of Thorkell of Goat's Peak

In the spring Bolli and Gudrun set up householding at Sælingsdale-Tongue, and it soon became a stately one. Bolli and Gudrun begat a son. To that boy a name was given, and he was called Thorleik; he was early a very fine lad, and a right nimble one. Halldor Olafson lived at Herdholt, as has before been written, and he was in most matters at the head of his brothers. The spring that Kjartan was slain Thorgerd Egil's daughter placed a lad, as kin to her, with Thorkell of Goat-Peaks, and the lad herded sheep there through the summer. Like other people he was much grieved over Kjartan's death. He could never speak of Kjartan if Thorkell was near, for he always spoke ill of him, and said he had been a "white" man and of no heart; he often mimicked how Kjartan had taken his death-wound. The lad took this very ill, and went to Herdholt and told Halldor and Thorgerd and begged them to take him in. Thorgerd bade him remain in his service till the winter. The lad said he had no strength to bear being there any longer. "And you would not ask this of me if you knew what heart-burn I suffer from all this." Then Thorgerd's heart turned at the tale of his grief, and she said that as far as she was concerned, she would make a place for him there. Halldor said, "Give no heed to this lad, he is not worth taking inearnest." Then Thorgerd answered, "The lad is of little account," says she, "but Thorkell has behaved evilly in every way in this matter, for he knew of the ambush the men of Laugar laid for Kjartan, and would not warn him, but made fun and sport of their dealings together, and has since said many unfriendly things about the matter; but it seems a matter far beyond you brothers ever to seek revenge where odds are against you, now that you cannot pay out for their doings such scoundrels as Thorkell is." Halldor answered little to that, but bade Thorgerd do what she liked about the lad's service. A few days after Halldor rode from home, he and sundry other men together. He went to Goat-Peaks, and surrounded Thorkell's house. Thorkell was led out and slain, and he met his death with the utmost cowardice. Halldor allowed no plunder, and they went home when this was done. Thorgerd was well pleased over this deed, and thought this reminder better than none. That summer all was quiet, so to speak, and yet there was the greatest ill-will between the sons of Olaf and Bolli. The brothers bore themselves in the most unyielding manner towards Bolli, while he gave in to his kinsmen in all matters as long as he did not lower himself in any way by so doing, for he was a very proud man. Bolli had many followers and lived richly, for there was no lack of money. Steinthor, Olaf's son, lived in Danastead in Salmon-river-Dale. He had for wife Thurid, Asgeir's daughter, who had before been married to Thorkell Kuggi. Their son was Steinthor, who was called "Stone-grig."

CHAPTER 53
Thorgerd's Egging, A.D. 1007

The next winter after the death of Olaf Hoskuldson, Thorgerd, Egil's daughter, sent word to her son Steinthor that he should come and meet her. When the mother and son met she told him she wished to go up west to Saurby, and see her friend Aud. She told Halldor to come too. They were five together, and Halldor followed his mother. They went on till they came to a place in front of the homestead of Sælingsdale Tongue. Then Thorgerd turned her horse towards the house and asked, "What is this place called?" Halldor answered, "You ask this, mother, not because you don't know it. This place is called Tongue." "Who lives here?" said she. He answered, "You know that, mother." Thorgerd said and snorted, "I know that well enough," she said. "Here lives Bolli, the slayer of your brother, and marvellously unlike your noble kindred you turn out in that you will not avenge such a brother as Kjartan was; never would Egil, your mother's father, have behaved in such a manner; and a piteous thing it is to have dolts for sons; indeed, I think it would have suited you better if you had been your father's daughter and had married. For here, Halldor, it comes to the old saw: 'No stock without a duffer,' and this is the ill-luck of Olaf I see most clearly, how he blundered in begetting his sons. This I would bring home to you, Halldor," says she, "because you look upon yourself as being the foremost among your brothers. Now we will turn back again, for all my errand here was to put you in mind of this, lest you should have forgotten it already." Then Halldor answered, "We shall not put it down as your fault, mother, if this should slip out of our minds." By way of answer Halldor had few words to say about this, but his heart swelled with wrath towards Bolli. The winter now passed and summer came, and time glided on towards the Thing. Halldor and his brothers made it known that they will ride to the Thing. They rode with a great company, and set up the booth Olaf had owned. The Thing was quiet, and no tidings to tell of it. There were at the Thing from the north the Willowdale men, the sons of Gudmund Solmundson. Bardi Gudmundson was then eighteen winters old; he was a great and strong man. The sons of Olaf asked Bardi, their nephew, to go home with them, and added many pressing words to the invitation. Hall, the son of Gudmund, was not in Iceland then. Bardi took up their bidding gladly, for there was much love between those kinsmen. Bardi rode west from the Thing with the sons of Olaf. They came home to Herdholt, and Bardi tarried the rest of the summer time.

CHAPTER 54
Halldor Prepares to Avenge Kjartan

They plan revenge. Now Halldor told Bardi in secret that the brothers had made up their minds to set on Bolli, for they could no longer withstand the taunts of their mother. "And we will not conceal from you, kinsman Bardi, that what mostly lay behind the invitation to you was this, that we wished to have your help and fellowship." Then Bardi answered, "That will be a matter ill spoken of, to break the peace on one's own kinsmen, and on the other hand it

250

seems to me nowise an easy thing to set on Bolli. He has many men about him and is himself the best of fighters, and is not at a loss for wise counsel with Gudrun and Osvif at his side. Taking all these matters together they seem to me nowise easy to overcome." Halldor said, "There are things we stand more in need of than to make the most of the difficulties of this affair. Nor have I broached it till I knew that it must come to pass, that we make earnest of wreaking revenge on Bolli. And I hope, kinsman, you will not withdraw from doing this journey with us." Bardi answered, "I know you do not think it likely that I will draw back, neither do I desire to do so if I see that I cannot get you to give it up yourselves." "There you do your share in the matter honourably," said Halldor, "as was to be looked forfrom you." Bardi said they must set about it with care. Halldor said he had heard that Bolli had sent his house-carles from home, some north to Ramfirth to meet a ship and some out to Middlefell strand. "It is also told me that Bolli is staying at the out-dairy in Sælingsdale with no more than the house-carles who are doing the haymaking. And it seems to me we shall never have a better chance of seeking a meeting with Bolli than now." So this then Halldor and Bardi settled between them. There was a man named Thorstein the Black, a wise man and wealthy; he lived at Hundidale in the Broadfirth-Dales; he had long been a friend of Olaf Peacock's. A sister of Thorstein was called Solveig; she was married to a man who was named Helgi, who was son of Hardbein. Helgi was a very tall and strong man, and a great sailor; he had lately come to Iceland, and was staying with his brother-in-law Thorstein. Halldor sent word to Thorstein the Black and Helgi his brother-in-law, and when they were come to Herdholt Halldor told them what he was about, and how he meant to carry it out, and asked them to join in the journey with him. Thorstein showed an utter dislike of this undertaking, saying, "It is the most heinous thing that you kinsmen should go on killing each other off like that; and now there are but few men left in your family equal to Bolli." But though Thorstein spoke in this wise it went for nought. Halldor sent word to Lambi, his father's brother, and when he came and met Halldor he told him what he was about, and Lambi urged hard that this should be carried out. Goodwife Thorgerd also egged them on eagerly to make an earnest of their journey, and said she should never look upon Kjartan as avenged until Bolli paid for him with his life. After this they got ready for the journey. In this raid there were the four sons of Olaf and the fifth was Bardi. There were the sons of Olaf, Halldor, Steinthor, Helgi, and Hoskuld, but Bardi was Gudmund's son. Lambi was the sixth, the seventh was Thorstein, and the eighth Helgi, his brother-in-law, the ninth An Brushwood-belly. Thorgerd betook herself also to the raid with them; but they set themselves against it, and said that such were no journeys for women. She said she would go indeed, "For so much I know of you, my sons, that whetting is what you want." They said she must have her own way.

CHAPTER 55
The Death of Bolli

After that they rode away from home out of Herdholt, the nine of them together, Thorgerd making the tenth. They rode up along the foreshore and so to Lea-shaws during the early part of the night. They did not stop before they got to

Sælingsdale in the early morning tide. There was a thick wood in the valley at that time. Bolli was there in the out-dairy, as Halldor had heard. The dairy stood near the river at the place now called Bolli's-tofts. Above the dairy there is a large hill-rise stretching all the way down to Stack-gill. Between the mountain slope above and the hill-rise there is a wide meadow called Barni; it was there Bolli's house-carles were working. Halldor and his companions rode across Ran-meads unto Oxgrove, and thence above Hammer-Meadow, which was right against the dairy. They knew there were many men at the dairy, so they got off their horses with a view to biding the time when the men should leave the dairy for their work. Bolli's shepherd went early that morning after the flocks up into the mountain side, and from there he saw the men in the wood as well as the horses tied up, and misdoubted that those who went on the sly in this manner would be no men of peace. So forthwith he makes for the dairy by the straightest cut in order to tell Bolli that men were come there. Halldor was a man of keen sight. He saw how that a man was running down the mountain side and making for the dairy. He said to his companions that "That must surely be Bolli's shepherd, and he must have seen our coming; so we must go and meet him, and let him take no news to the dairy." They did as he bade them. An Brushwood-belly went the fastest of them and overtook the man, picked him up, and flung him down. Such was that fall that the lad's back-bone was broken. After that they rode to the dairy. Now the dairy was divided into two parts, the sleeping-room and the byre. Bolli had been early afoot in the morning ordering the men to their work, and had lain down again to sleep when the house-carles went away. In the dairy therefore there were left the two, Gudrun and Bolli. They awoke with the din when they got off their horses, and they also heard them talking as to who should first go on to the dairy to set on Bolli. Bolli knew the voice of Halldor, as well as that of sundry more of his followers. Bolli spoke to Gudrun, and bade her leave the dairy and go away, and said that their meeting would not be such as would afford her much pastime. Gudrun said she thought such things alone would befall there worthy of tidings as she might be allowed to look upon, and held that she would be of no hurt to Bolli by taking her stand near to him. Bolli said that in this matter he would have his way, and so it was that Gudrun went out of the dairy; she went down over the brink to a brook that ran there, and began to wash some linen. Bolli was now alone in the dairy; he took his weapon, set his helm on his head, held a shield before him, and had his sword, Footbiter, in his hand: he had no mail coat. Halldor and his followers were talking to each other outside as to how they should set to work, for no one was very eager to go into the dairy. Then said An Brushwood-belly, "There are men here in this train nearer in kinship to Kjartan than I am, but notone there will be in whose mind abides more steadfastly than in mine the event when Kjartan lost his life. When I was being brought more dead than alive home to Tongue, and Kjartan lay slain, my one thought was that I would gladly do Bolli some harm whenever I should get the chance. So I shall be the first to go into the dairy." Then Thorstein the Black answered, "Most valiantly is that spoken; but it would be wiser not to plunge headlong beyond heed, so let us go warily now, for Bolli will not be standing quiet when he is beset; and however underhanded he may be where he is, you may make up your mind for a brisk defence on his part, strong and skilled at arms as he is. He also has a sword that for a weapon is a trusty one." Then An went into the dairy hard and swift, and held his shield over his head, turning forward the narrower part of it. Bolli dealt him a blow with Footbiter, and cut off the tail-end of the shield, and clove

An through the head down to the shoulder, and forthwith he gat his death. Then Lambi went in; he held his shield before him, and a drawn sword in his hand. In the nick of time Bolli pulled Footbiter out of the wound, whereat his shield veered aside so as to lay him open to attack. So Lambi made a thrust at him in the thigh, and a great wound that was. Bolli hewed in return, and struck Lambi's shoulder, and the sword flew down along the side of him, and he was rendered forthwith unfit to fight, and never after that time for the rest of his life was his arm anymore use to him. At this brunt Helgi, the son of Hardbien, rushed in with a spear, the head of which was an ell long, and the shaft bound with iron. When Bolli saw that he cast away his sword, and took his shield in both hands, and went towards the dairy door to meet Helgi. Helgi thrust at Bolli with the spear right through the shield and through him. Now Bolli leaned up against the dairy wall, and the men rushed into the dairy, Halldor and his brothers, to wit, and Thorgerd went into the dairy as well. Then spoke Bolli, "Now it is safe, brothers, to come nearer than hitherto you have done," and said he weened that defence now would be but short. Thorgerd answered his speech, and said there was no need to shrink from dealing unflinchingly with Bolli, and bade them "walk between head and trunk." Bolli stood still against the dairy wall, and held tight to him his kirtle lest his inside should come out. Then Steinthor Olafson leapt at Bolli, and hewed at his neck with a large axe just above his shoulders, and forthwith his head flew off. Thorgerd bade him "hale enjoy hands," and said that Gudrun would have now a while a red hair to trim for Bolli. After that they went out of the dairy. Gudrun now came up from the brook, and spoke to Halldor, and asked for tidings of what had befallen in their dealings with Bolli. They told her all that had happened. Gudrun was dressed in a kirtle of "rám"-stuff, and a tight-fitting woven bodice, a high bent coif on her head, and she had tied a scarf round her with dark-blue stripes, and fringed at the ends. Helgi Hardbienson went up to Gudrun, and caught hold of the scarf end, and wiped the blood off the spear with it, the same spear with which he had thrust Bolli through. Gudrun glanced at him and smiled slightly. Then Halldor said, "That was blackguardly and gruesomely done." Helgi bade him not be angry about it, "For I am minded to think that under this scarf end abides undoer of my life." Then they took their horses and rode away. Gudrun went along with them talking with them for a while, and then she turned back.

CHAPTER 56
Bolli Bollison is Born, A.D. 1008

The followers of Halldor now fell a-talking how that Gudrun must think but little of the slaying of Bolli, since she had seen them off chatting and talked to them altogether as if they had done nothing that she might take to heart. Then Halldor answered, "That is not my feeling, that Gudrun thinks little of Bolli's death; I think the reason of her seeing us off with a chat was far rather, that she wanted to gain a thorough knowledge as to who the men were who had partaken in this journey. Nor is it too much said of Gudrun that in all mettleof mind and heart she is far above other women. Indeed, it is only what might be looked for that Gudrun should take sorely to heart the death of Bolli, for, truth to tell, in such men as was Bolli there is the greatest loss, though we kinsmen, bore not about the good luck to live in peace together." After that they rode home to Herdholt. These tidings spread quickly far and wide and were thought startling, and at Bolli's death there was the greatest grief. Gudrun sent straightway men to Snorri the Priest, for Osvif and she thought that all their trust was where Snorri was. Snorri started quickly at the bidding of Gudrun and came to Tongue with sixty men, and a great ease to Gudrun's heart his coming was. He offered her to try to bring about a peaceful settlement, but Gudrun was but little minded on behalf of Thorleik to agree to taking money for the slaughter of Bolli. "It seems to me, Snorri, that the best help you can afford me," she said, "is to exchange dwellings with me, so that I be not next-door neighbour to the Herdholtings." At that time Snorri had great quarrels with the dwellers at Eyr, but said he would do this for the sake of his friendship with Gudrun. "Yet, Gudrun, you will have to stay on this year at Tongue." Snorri then made ready to go away, and Gudrun gave him honourable gifts. And now Snorri rides away, and things went pretty quietly on that year. The next winter after the killing of Bolli Gudrun gave birth to a child; it was a male, and he was named Bolli. He was at an early age both big and goodly, and Gudrun loved him very much. Now as the winter passed by and the spring came the bargain took place which had been bespoken in that Snorri and Gudrun changed lands. Snorri went to Tongue and lived there for the rest of his life, and Gudrun went to Holyfell, she and Osvif, and there they set up a stately house. There Thorleik and Bolli, the sons of Gudrun, grew up. Thorleik was four years old at the time when Bolli his father was slain.

CHAPTER 57
About Thorgils Hallason, A.D. 1018

There was a man named Thorgils Hallason; he was known by his mother's name, as she lived longer than his father, whose name was Snorri, son of Alf o' Dales. Halla, Thorgil's mother, was daughter of Gest Oddliefson. Thorgils lived in Horddale at a place called Tongue. Thorgils was a man great and goodly of body, the greatest swaggerer, and was spoken of as one of no fairness in dealings with men. Between him and Snorri the Priest there was often little love lost, for Snorri found Thorgils both meddlesome and flaunting of demeanour. Thorgils would get up many errands on which to go west into the countryside, and always came to Holyfell offering Gudrun to look after her affairs, but she only took the matter quietly and made but little of it all. Thorgils asked for her son Thorleik to go home with him, and he stayed for the most part at Tongue and learnt law from Thorgils, for he was a man most skilled in law-craft. At that time Thorkell Eyjolfson was busy in trading journeys; he was a most renowned man, and of high birth, and withal a great friend of Snorri the Priest. He would always be staying with Thorstein Kuggison, his kinsman, when he was out here (in Iceland). Now, one time when Thorkell had a ship standing up in Vadil, on Bardistrand, it befell, in Burgfirth, that the son of Eid of Ridge was killed by the sons of Helga from Kropp. Grim was the name of the man who had done the manslaughter, and that of his brother was Nial, who was drowned in White-river; a little later on Grim was outlawed to the woods because of the manslaughter, and he lay out in the mountains whilst he was under the award of outlawry. He was a great man and strong. Eid was then very old when this happened, so the case was not followed up. People blamed Thorkell very much that he did not see matters righted. The next spring when Thorkell had got his ship ready he went south across Broadfirth-country, and got a horse there and rode alone, not stopping in his journey till he got as far as Ridge, to Eid, his kinsman. Eid took him in joyfully. Thorkell told him his errand, how that he would go and find Grimhis outlaw, and asked Eid if he knew at all where his lair was. Eid answered, "I am nowise eager for this; it seems to me you have much to risk as to how the journey may speed, seeing that you will have to deal with a man of Hel's strength, such as Grim. But if you will go, then start with many men, so that you may have it all your own way." "That to me is no prowess," said Thorkell, "to draw together a great company against one man. But what I wish is, that you would lend me the sword Skofnung, for then I ween I shall be able to overcome a mere runagate, be he never so mighty a man of his hands." "You must have your way in this," said Eid, "but it will not come to me unawares, if, some day, you should come to rue this wilfulness. But inasmuch as you will have it that you are doing this for my sake, what you ask for shall not be withheld, for I think Skofnung well bestowed if you bear it. But the nature of the sword is such that the sun must not shine upon its hilt, nor must it be drawn if a woman should be near. If a man be wounded by the sword the hurt may not be healed, unless the healing-stone that goes with the sword be rubbed thereon." Thorkell said he would pay careful heed to this, and takes over the sword, asking Eid to point out to him the way to where Grim might have his lair. Eid said he was most minded to think that Grim had his lair north on Twodays-Heath by the Fishwaters. Then Thorkell rode northward upon the heath theway which Eid did point out to him, and when he had got a long way onward over the heath he saw near some great water a hut, and makes his way for it.

CHAPTER 58
Thorkell and Grim, and Their Voyage Abroad

Thorkell now comes to the hut, he sees where a man is sitting by the water at the mouth of a brook, where he was line-fishing, and had a cloak over his head. Thorkell leapt off his horse and tied it up under the wall of the hut. Then he walks down to the water to where the man was sitting. Grim saw the shadow of a man cast on the water, and springs up at once. By then Thorkell had got very nearly close up to him, and strikes at him. The blow caught him on his arm just above the wolf-joint (the wrist), but that was not a great wound. Grim sprang forthwith upon Thorkell, and they seized each other wrestling-wise, and speedily the odds of strength told, and Thorkell fell and Grim on the top of him. Then Grim asked who this man might be. Thorkell said that did not at all matter to him. Grim said, "Now things have befallen otherwise than you must have thought they would, for now your life will be in my power." Thorkell said he would not pray for peace for himself, "for lucklessly I have taken this in hand." Grim said he had had enough mishapsfor him to give this one the slip, "for to you some other fate is ordained than that of dying at this our meeting, and I shall give you your life, while you repay me in whatever kind you please." Now they both stand up and walk home to the hut. Thorkell sees that Grim was growing faint from loss of blood, so he took Skofnung's-stone and rubbed it on, and ties it to the arm of Grim, and it took forthwith all smarting pain and swelling out of the wound. They stayed there that night. In the morning Thorkell got ready to go away, and asked if Grim would go with him. He said that sure enough that was his will. Thorkell turns straightway westward without going to meet Eid, nor halted he till he came to Sælingsdale Tongue. Snorri the Priest welcomes him with great blitheness. Thorkell told him that his journey had sped lucklessly. Snorri said it had turned out well, "for Grim looks to me a man endowed with good luck, and my will is that you make matters up with him handsomely. But now, my friend, I would like to counsel you to leave off trade-journeyings, and to settle down and marry, and become a chief as befits your high birth." Thorkell answered, "Often your counsels have stood me in good stead," and he asked if Snorri had bethought him of the woman he should woo. Snorri answers, "You must woo the woman who is the best match for you, and that woman is Gudrun, Osvif's daughter." Thorkell said it was true that a marriage with her would be an honourable one. "But," says he, "I think her fierceheart and reckless-mindedness weigh heavily, for she will want to have her husband, Bolli, avenged. Besides, it is said that on this matter there is some understanding between her and Thorgils Hallason, and it may be that this will not be altogether to his liking. Otherwise, Gudrun pleases me well." Snorri said, "I will undertake to see that no harm shall come to you from Thorgils; but as to the revenge for Bolli, I am rather in hopes that concerning that matter some change will have befallen before these seasons (this year) are out." Thorkell answered, "It may be that these be no empty words you are speaking now. But as to the revenge of Bolli, that does not seem to me more likely to happen now than it did a while ago, unless into that strife some of the greater men may be drawn." Snorri said, "I should be well pleased to see you go abroad once more this summer, to let us see then what happens." Thorkell said so it should be, and they parted, leaving matters where they now stood. Thorkell went west over Broadfirth-country to his ship. He took Grim with him abroad. They had a good summer-voyage, and came to the south of Norway. Then Thorkell said to Grim, "You know how the case stands, and what things happened to bring about our acquaintance, so I need say nothing about that matter; but I would fain that it should turn out better than at one time it seemed likely it would. I have found you a valiant man, and for that reason I will so part from you, as if I had never borne you anygrudge. I will give you as much merchandise as you need in order to be able to join the guild of good merchants. But do not settle down here in the north of this land, for many of Eid's kinsmen are about on trading journeys who bear you heavy ill-will." Grim thanked him for these words, and said he could never have thought of asking for as much as he offered. At parting Thorkell gave to Grim a goodly deal of merchandise, and many men said that this deed bore the stamp of a great man. After that Grim went east in the Wick, settled there, and was looked upon as a mighty man of his ways; and therewith comes to an end what there is to be told about Grim. Thorkell was in Norway through the winter, and was thought a man of much account; he was exceeding wealthy in chattels. Now this matter must be left for a while, and the story must be taken up out in Iceland, so let us hear what matters befell there for tidings to be told of whilst Thorkell was abroad.

CHAPTER 59
Gudrun Demands Revenge for Bolli, A.D. 1019

In "Twinmonth" that summer Gudrun, Osvif's daughter, went from home up into the Dales. She rode to Thickshaw; and at this time Thorleik was sometimes at Thickshaw with the sonsof Armod Halldor and Ornolf, and sometimes Tongue with Thorgils. The same night Gudrun sent a man to Snorri Godi saying that she wished to meet him without fail the next day. Snorri got ready at once and rode with one other man until he came to Hawkdale-river; on the northern side of that river stands a crag by the river called Head, within the land of Lea-Shaw. At this spot Gudrun had bespoken that she and Snorri should meet. They both came there at one and the same time. With Gudrun there was only one man, and he was Bolli, son of Bolli; he was now twelve years old, but fulfilled of strength and wits was he, so much so, that many were they who were no whit more powerful at the time of ripe manhood; and now he carried Footbiter. Snorri and Gudrun now fell to talking together; but Bolli and Snorri's follower sat on the crag and watched people travelling up and down the countryside. When Snorri and Gudrun had asked each other for news, Snorri inquired on what errand he was called, and what had come to pass lately that she sent him word so hurriedly. Gudrun said, "Truth to tell, to me is ever fresh the event which I am about to bring up, and yet it befell twelve years ago; for it is about the revenge of Bolli I wish to speak, and it ought not to take you unawares. I have called it to your mind from time to time. I must also bring this home to you that to this end you have promised me some help if I but waited patiently, but now I think it past hopethat you will give any heed to our case. I have now waited as long as my temper would hold out, and I must have whole-hearted counsel from you as to where this revenge is to be brought home." Snorri asked what she chiefly had in her mind's eye. Gudrun said, "It is my wish that all Olaf's sons should not go scatheless." Snorri said he must forbid any onset on the men who were not only of the greatest account in the countryside, but also closely akin to those who stand nearest to back up the revenge; and it is high time already that these family feuds come to an end. Gudrun said, "Then Lambi shall be set upon and slain; for then he, who is the most eager of them for evil, would be put out of the way." Snorri said, "Lambi is guilty enough that he should be slain; but I do not think Bolli any the more revenged for that; for when at length peace should come to be settled, no such disparity between them would be acknowledged as ought to be due to Bolli when the manslaughters of both should come up for award." Gudrun spoke, "It may be that we shall not get our right out of the men of Salmon-river-Dale, but some one shall pay dear for it, whatever dale he may dwell in. So we shall turn upon Thorstein the Black, for no one has taken a worse share in these matters than he." Snorri spake, "Thorstein's guilt against you is the same as that of the other men who joined in the raid against Bolli, but did not wound him. But you leave such men to sit by in quiet onwhom it seems to me revenge wrought would be revenge indeed, and who, moreover, did take the life of Bolli, such as was Helgi Hardbienson." Gudrun said, "That is true, but I cannot be sure that, in that case, all these men against whom I have been stirring up enmity will sit quietly by doing nothing." Snorri said, "I see a good way to hinder that. Lambi and Thorstein shall join the train of your sons, and that is a fitting ransom for those fellows, Lambi and Thorstein; but if they will not do this, then I shall not plead for them to be let off, whatever penalty you may be pleased to put upon them." Gudrun spake: "How shall we set about getting these men that you have named to go on this journey?" Snorri spake: "That is the business of them who are to be at the head of the journey." Gudrun spake: "In this we must have your foresight as to who shall rule the journey and be the leader." Then Snorri smiled and said, "You have chosen your own men for it." Gudrun replied, "You are speaking of Thorgils." Snorri said so it was. Gudrun spake: "I have talked the matter over already with Thorgils, but now it is as good as all over, for he gave me the one choice, which I would not even look at. He did not back out of undertaking to avenge Bolli, if he could have me in marriage in return; but that is past all hope, so I cannot ask him to go this journey." Snorri spoke: "On this I will give you a counsel, for I do not begrudge Thorgils this journey. You shall promisemarriage to him, yet you shall do it in language of this double meaning, that of men in this land you will marry none other but Thorgils, and that shall be holden to, for Thorkell Eyjolfson is not, for the time being, in this land, but it is he whom I have in my mind's eye for this marriage." Gudrun spake: "He will see through this trick." Snorri answered, "Indeed he will not see through it, for Thorgils is better known for foolhardiness than wits. Make the covenant with but few men for witnesses, and let Halldor, his foster-brother, be there, but not Ornolf, for he has more wits, and lay the blame on me if this will not work out." After that they parted their talk and each bade the other farewell, Snorri riding home, and Gudrun unto Thickshaw. The next morning Gudrun rode from Thickshaw and her sons with her, and when they ride west along Shawstrand they see that men are riding after them. They ride on quickly and catch them up swiftly, and lo, there was Thorgils Hallason. They greeted each other well, and now ride on in the day all together, out to Holyfell.

CHAPTER 60
The Egging of Gudrun

A few nights after Gudrun had come home she called her sons to her to have a talk with them in her orchard; and when they were come there they saw how there were lying out some linen clothes, a shirt and linen breeches, and they were much stained with blood. Then spake Gudrun: "These same clothes you see here cry to you for your father's revenge. I will not say many words on this matter, for it is past hope that you will heed an egging-on by words alone if you bring not home to your minds such hints and reminders as these." The brothers were much startled as this, and at what Gudrun had to say; but yet this way they made answer that they had been too young to seek for revenge without a leader; they knew not, they felt, how to frame a counsel for themselves or others either. "But we might well bear in mind what we have lost." Gudrun said, "They would be likely to give more thought to horse-fights or sports." After that they went away. The next night the brothers could not sleep. Thorgils got aware of this, and asked them what was the matter. They told him all the talk they had had with their mother, and this withal that they could no longer bear their grief or their mother's taunts. "We will seek revenge," said Bolli, "now that we brothers have come to so ripe an age that men will be much after us if we do not take the matter in hand." The next day Gudrun and Thorgils had a talk together, and

Gudrun started speaking in this wise: "I am given to think, Thorgils, that my sons brook it ill to sit thus quietly on any longer without seeking revenge for their father's death. But what mostly has delayed the matter hitherto is that up to now I deemed Thorleik and Bolli too young to be busy in taking men's lives. But need enough there has been to call this to mind a good long time before this. Thorgils answered, "There is no use in your talking this matter over with me, because you have given a flat denial to 'walking with me' (marrying me). But I am in just the same frame of mind as I have been before, when we have had talks about this matter. If I can marry you, I shall not think twice about killing either or both of the two who had most to do with the murder of Bolli." Gudrun spoke: "I am given to think that to Thorleik no man seems as well fitted as you to be the leader if anything is to be done in the way of deeds of hardihood. Nor is it a matter to be hidden from you that the lads are minded to go for Helgi Hardbienson the 'Bareserk,' who sits at home in his house in Skorridale misdoubting himself of nothing." Thorgils spake: "I never care whether he is called Helgi or by any other name, for neither in Helgi nor in any one else do I deem I have an over-match in strength to deal with. As far as I am concerned, the last word on this matter is now spoken if you promise before witnesses to marry me when, together with your sons, I have wreaked the revenge." Gudrun said she would fulfil all she should agree to, even though such agreement were come to before few men to witness it. "And," said she, "this then we shall settle to have done." Gudrun bade becalled thither Halldor, Thorgils' foster-brother, and her own sons. Thorgils bade that Ornolf should also be with them. Gudrun said there was no need of that, "For I am more doubtful of Ornolf's faithfulness to you than I think you are yourself." Thorgils told her to do as she liked. Now the brothers come and meet Gudrun and Thorgils, Halldor being also at the parley with them. Gudrun now sets forth to them that "Thorgils has said he will be the leader in this raid against Helgi Hardbienson, together with my sons, for revenge of Bolli, and Thorgils has bargained in return for this undertaking to get me for wife. Now I avow, with you to witness, that I promise this to Thorgils, that of men in this land I shall marry none but him, and I do not purpose to go and marry in any other land." Thorgils thought that this was binding enough, and did not see through it. And now they broke up their talk. This counsel is now fully settled that Thorgils must betake himself to this journey. He gets ready to leave Holyfell, and with him the sons of Gudrun, and they rode up into the Dales and first to the homestead at Tongue.

CHAPTER 61
Of Thorstein the Black and Lambi

The next Lord's day a leet was held, and Thorgils rode thither with his company, Snorri Godi was not at the leet, but there was a great many people together. During the day Thorgils fetched up Thorstein the Black for a talk with him, and said, "As you know, you were one in the onset by the sons of Olaf when Bolli was slain, and you have made no atonement for your guilt to his sons. Now although a long time is gone since those things befell, I think their mind has not given the slip to the men who were in that raid. Now, these brothers look in this light upon the matter, that it beseem them least, by reason of kinship, to seek revenge on the sons of Olaf; and so the brothers purpose to turn for revenge upon Helgi Hardbienson, for he gave Bolli his death-wound. So we ask this of you, Thorstein, that you join in this journey with the brothers, and thus purchase for yourself peace and good-will." Thorstein replied, "It beseems me not at all to deal in treason with Helgi, my brother-in-law, and I would far rather purchase my peace with as much money as it would be to their honour to take." Thorgils said, "I think it is but little to the mind of the brothers to do aught herein for their own gain; so you need not hide it away from yourself, Thorstein, that at your hands there lie two choices: either to betake yourself to this journey, or to undergo the harshest of treatments from them as soon as they may bring it about; and my will is, that you take this choice in spite of the ties that bind you to Helgi; for when men find themselves in such straits, each must look after himself." Thorstein spake: "Will the same choice be given to more of the men who are charged with guilt by the sons of Bolli?" Thorgils answered, "The same choice will be put to Lambi." Thorstein said he would think better of it if he was not left the only one in this plight. After that Thorgils called Lambi to come and meet him, and bade Thorstein listen to their talk. He said, "I wish to talk over with you, Lambi, the same matter that I have set forth to Thorstein; to wit, what amends you are willing to make to the sons of Bolli for the charges of guilt which they have against you? For it has been told me as true that you wrought wounds on Bolli; but besides that, you are heavily guilt-beset, in that you urged it hard that Bolli should be slain; yet, next to the sons of Olaf, you were entitled to some excuse in the matter." Then Lambi asked what he would be asked to do. Thorgils said the same choice would be put to him as to Thorstein, "to join with the brothers in this journey." Lambi said, "This I think an evil price of peace and a dastardly one, and I have no mind for this journey." Then said Thorstein, "It is not the only thing open to view, Lambi, to cut so quickly away from this journey; for in thismatter great men are concerned, men of much worth, moreover, who deem that they have long had to put up with an unfair lot in life. It is also told me of Bolli's sons that they are likely to grow into men of high mettle, and that they are exceeding masterful; but the wrong they have to wreak is great. We cannot think of escaping from making some amends after such awful deeds. I shall be the most open to people's reproaches for this by reason of my alliance with Helgi. But I think most people are given to 'setting all aside for life,' and the trouble on hand that presses hardest must first be thrust out of the way." Lambi said, "It is easy to see what you urge to be done, Thorstein; and I think it well befitting that you have your own way in this matter, if you think that is the only way you see open, for ours has been a long partnership in great troubles. But I will have this understood if I do go into this business, that my kinsmen, the sons of Olaf, shall be left in peace if the revenge on Helgi shall be carried out." Thorgils agreed to this on behalf of the brothers. So now it was settled that Lambi and Thorstein should betake themselves to the journey with Thorgils; and they bespoke it between them that they should come early on the third day (Tuesday) to Tongue, in Hord-Dale. After that they parted. Thorgils rode home that evening to Tongue. Now passes on the time within which it was bespoken they should come to Tongue. In the morning of the third day (Tuesday), before sunrise, Thorstein and Lambi came to Tongue, and Thorgils gave them a cheerful welcome.

CHAPTER 62
Thorgils and his Followers Leave Home

Thorgils got himself ready to leave home, and they all rode up along Hord-Dale, ten of them together. There Thorgils Hallason was the leader of the band. In that train the sons of Bolli, Thorleik and Bolli, and Thord the Cat, their brother, was the fourth, the fifth was Thorstein the Black, the sixth Lambi, the seventh and eighth Haldor and Ornolf, the ninth Svein, and the tenth Hunbogi. Those last were the sons of Alf o' Dales. They rode on their way up to Sweeping-Pass, and across Long-waterdale, and then right across Burgfirth. They rode across North-river at Isleford, but across White-river at Bankford, a short way down from the homestead of By. Then they rode over Reekdale, and over the neck of land to Skorradale, and so up through the wood in the neighbourhood of the farmstead of Water-Nook, where they got off their horses, as it was very late in the evening. The homestead of Water-Nook stands a short way from the lake on the south side of the river. Thorgils said to his followers that they must tarry there over night, "and I will go to the house and spy and see if Helgi be at home. I am told Helgi has at most times very few men with him, but that he is of all men the wariest of himself, and sleeps on a strongly made lock-bed." Thorgils' followers bade him follow his own foresight. Thorgils now changed his clothes, and took off his blue cloak, and slipped on a grey foul-weather overall. He went home to the house. When he was come near to the home-field fence he saw a man coming to meet him, and when they met Thorgils said, "You will think my questions strange, comrade, but whose am I come to in this countryside, and what is the name of this dwelling, and who lives here?" The man answered, "You must be indeed a wondrous fool and wit-bereft if you have not heard Helgi Hardbienson spoken of, the bravest of warriors, and a great man withal." Thorgils next asked how far Helgi took kindly to unknown people coming to see him, such as were in great need of help. He replied, "In that matter, if truth is told, only good can be said of Helgi, for he is the most large-hearted of men, not only in giving harbour to comers, but also in all his high conduct otherwise." "Is Helgi at home now?" asked Thorgils; "I should like to ask him to take me in." The other then asks what matters he had on his hands. Thorgils answered, "I was outlawed this summer at the Thing, and I want to seek for myself the help of some such man as is a mighty one of his hands and ways, and I will in return offer my fellowship and service. So now you take me home to the house to see Helgi." "I can do that very well, to show you home," he said, "for you will be welcome to quarters for the night, but you will not see Helgi, for he is not at home." Then Thorgils asked where he was. The man answered, "He is at his out-dairy called Sarp." Thorgils asked where that was, and what men were with him. He said his son Hardbien was there, and two other men, both outlaws, whom he had taken in to shelter. Thorgils bade him show the nearest way to the dairy, "for I want to meet Helgi at once, when I can get to him and plead my errand to him." The house-carle did so and showed him the way, and after that they parted. Thorgils returned to the wood to his companions, and told them what he had found out about Helgi. "We must tarry here through the night, and not go to the dairy till to-morrow morning." They did as he ordained, and in the morning Thorgils and his band rode up through the wood till they were within a short way from the dairy. Then Thorgils bade them get off their horses and eat their morning meal, and so they did, and kept them for a while.

CHAPTER 63
The Description of his Enemies Brought to Helgi

Now we must tell what happened at the dairy where Helgi was, and with him the men that were named before. In the morning Helgi told his shepherd to go through the woods in the neighbourhood of the dairy and look out for people passing, and take heed of whatever else he saw, to tell news of, "for my dreams have gone heavily to-night." The lad went even as Helgi told him. He was away awhile, and when he came back Helgi asked what he had seen to tell tidings of. He answered, "I have seen what I think is stuff for tidings." Helgi asked what that was. He said he had seen men, "and none so few either, and I think they must have come from beyond this countryside." Helgi spoke: "Where were they when you saw them, and what were they doing, or did you take heed of the manner of raiment, or their looks?" He answered, "I was not so much taken aback at the sight as not to mind those matters, for I knew you would ask about them." He also said they were but short away from the dairy, and were eating their morning meal. Helgi asked if they sat in a ring or side by side in a line. He said they sat in a ring, on their saddles. Helgi said, "Tell me now of their looks, and I will see if I can guess from what they looked like who the men may be." The lad said, "There sat a man in a stained saddle, in a blue cloak. He was great of growth, and valiant-looking; he was bald in front and somewhat 'tooth-bare.'" Helgi said, "I know that man clearly from your tale. There you have seen Thorgils Hallason, from west out of Hord-Dale. I wonder what he wants with us, the hero." The lad spoke: "Next to him sat a man in a gilded saddle; he had on a scarlet kirtle, and a gold ring on his arm, and a gold-embroidered fillet was tied round his head. This man had yellow hair, waving down over his shoulders; he was fair of hue, with a knot on his nose, which was somewhat turned up at the tip, with very fine eyes - blue-eyed and swift-eyed, and with a glance somewhat restless, broad-browed and full-cheeked; he had his hair cut across his forehead. He was well grown as to breadth of shoulders and depth of chest. He had very beautiful hands, and strong-looking arms. All his bearing was courteous, and, in a word, I have never seen a man so altogether doughty-looking. He was a young-looking man too, for his lips had grown no beard, but it seemed to me he was aged by grief." Then Helgi answers: "You have paid a careful heed, indeed, to this man, and of much account he must needs be; yet this man, I think, I have never seen, so I must make a guess at it who he is. There, I think, must have been Bolli Bollison, for I am told he has in him the makings of a man." Then the lad went on: "Next there sat a man on an enamelled saddle in a yellow green kirtle; he had a great finger ring on his hand. This man was most goodly to behold, and must still be young of age; his hair was auburn and most comely, and in every way he was most courtly." Helgi answers, "I think I know who this man is, of whom you have now been telling. He must be Thorleik Bollison, and a sharp and mindful man you are." The lad said again, "Next sat a young man; he was in a blue kirtle and black breeches, and his tunic tucked into them. This man was straight-faced, light of hair, with a goodly-featured face, slender and graceful." Helgi answered, "I know that man, for I must have seen him, though at a time when he was quite young; for it must be Thord Thordson, fosterling of Snorri the Priest. And a very courtly band they have, the Westfirthers. What is there yet to tell?" Then the lad said, "There sat a man on a Scotch saddle, hoary of beard and very sallow of hue, with black curly hair, somewhat unsightly and yet warrior like; he had on a grey pleated cape." Helgi said, "I clearly see who that man is; there is Lambi, the son of Thorbjorn, from Salmon-river-Dale; but I cannot think why he should be in the train of these brothers." The lad spake: "There sat a man on a pommelled saddle, and had on a blue cloak for an overall, with a silver ring on his arm; he was a farmer-looking sort of man and past the prime of life, with dark auburn long curly hair, and scars about his face." "Now the tale grows worse by much," said Helgi, "for there you must have seen Thorstein the Black, my brother-in-law; and a wondrous thing indeed I deem it, that he should be in this journey, nor would I ever offer him such a home-raid. But what more is there still to tell?" He answered, "Next there sat two men like each other to look upon, and might have been of middle age; most brisk they looked, red of hair, freckled of face, yet goodly to behold." Helgi said, "I can clearly understand who those men are. There are the sons of Armod, foster-brothers of Thorgils, Halldor and Ornolf. And a very trustworthy fellow you are. But have you now told the tale of all the men you saw?" He answered, "I have but little to add now. Next there sat a man and looked out of the circle; he was in a plate-corselet and had a steel cap on his head, with a brim a hand's breadth wide; he bore a shining axe on his shoulder, the edge of which must have measured an ell in length. This man was dark of hue, black-eyed, and most viking like." Helgi answered, "I clearly know this man from your tale. There has been Hunbogi the Strong, son of Alf o' Dales. But what I find so hard to make out is, what they want journeying with such a very picked company." The lad spoke again: "And still there sat a man next to this strong-looking one, dark auburn of hair, thick-faced and red-faced, heavy of brow, of a tall middle size." Helgi said, "You need not tell the tale further, there must have been Svein, son of Alf o' Dales, brother of Hunbogi. Now it would be as well not to stand shiftless in the face of these men; for near to my mind's foreboding it is, that they are minded to have a meeting with me or ever they leave this countryside; moreover, in this train there are men who would hold that it would have been but due and meet, though this our meeting should have taken a good long time before this. Now all the women who are in the dairy slip on quickly men's dress and take the horses that are about the dairy and ride as quickly as possible to the winter dwelling; it may be that those who are besetting us about will not know whether men or women be riding there; they need give us only a short respite till we bring men together here, and then it is not so certain on which side the outlook will be most hopeful." The women now rode off, four together. Thorgils misdoubts him lest news of their coming may have reached Helgi, and so bade the others take their horses and ride after them at their swiftest, and so they did, but before they mounted a man came riding up to them openly in all men's sight. He was small of growth and all on the alert, wondrously swift of glance and had a lively horse. This man greeted Thorgils in a familiar manner, and Thorgils asked him his name and family and also whence he had come. He said his name was Hrapp, and he was from Broadfirth on his mother's side. "And then I grew up, and I bear the name of Fight-Hrapp, with the name follows that I am nowise an easy one to deal with, albeit I am small of growth; but I am a southlander on my father's

263

side, and have tarried in the south for some winters. Now this is a lucky chance, Thorgils, I have happened of you here, for I was minded to come and see you anyhow, even though I should find it a business somewhat hard to follow up. I have a trouble on hand; I have fallen out with my master, and have had from him a treatment none of the best; but it goes with the name, that I will stand no man such shameful mishandling, so I made an outset at him, but I guess I wounded him little or not at all, for I did not wait long enough to see for myself, but thought myself safe when I got on to the back of this nag, which I took from the goodman." Hrapp says much, but asks for few things; yet soon he got to know that they were minded to set on Helgi, and that pleased him very much, and he said they would not have to look for him behind.

CHAPTER 64
The Death of Helgi, A.D. 1019

Thorgils and his followers, as soon as they were on horseback, set off at a hard ride, and rode now out of the wood. They saw four men riding away from the dairy, and they rode very fast too. Seeing this, some of Thorgils' companions said they had better ride after them at their swiftest. Then said Thorleik Bollison, "We will just go to the dairy and see what men are there, for I think it less likely that these be Helgi and his followers. It seems to me that those are only women." A good many of them gainsaid this. Thorgils said that Thorleik should rule in the matter, for he knew that he was a very far-sighted man. They now turned to the dairy. Hrapp rode first, shaking the spear-stick he carried in his hand, and thrusting it forward in front of himself, and saying now was high time to try one's self. Helgi and his followers were not aware of anything till Thorgils and his company had surrounded the dairy. Helgi and his men shut the door, and seized their weapons. Hrapp leapt forthwith upon the roof of the dairy, and asked if old Reynard was in. Helgi answered, "You will come to take for granted that he who is here within is somewhat hurtful, and will know how to bite near the warren." And forthwith Helgi thrust his spear out through the window and through Hrapp, so that he fell dead to earth from the spear. Thorgils bade the others go heedfully and beware of mishaps, "for we have plenty of means wherewith to get the dairy into our power, and to overcome Helgi, placed as he is now, for I am given to think that here but few men are gathered together." The dairy was rigged over one roof-beam,resting on two gables so that the ends of the beam stuck out beyond each gable; there was a single turf thatch on the house, which had not yet grown together. Then Thorgils told some of his men to go to the beam ends, and pull them so hard that either the beam should break or else the rafters should slip in off it, but others were to guard the door lest those within should try and get out. Five they were, Helgi and his within the dairy - Hardbien, his son, to wit, he was twelve years old - his shepherd and two other men, who had come to him that summer, being outlaws - one called Thorgils, and the other Eyolf. Thorstein the Black and Svein, son of Alf o' Dales, stood before the door. The rest of the company were tearing the roof off the dairy. Hunbogi the Strong and the sons of Armod took one end of the beam, Thorgils, Lambi, and Gudrun's sons the other end. They now pull hard at the beam till it broke asunder in the middle; just at this Hardbien thrust a halberd out through where the door was broken, and the thrust struck the steel cap of Thorstein the Black and stuck in his forehead, and that was a very great wound. Then Thorstein said, as was true, that there were men before them. Next Helgi leapt so boldly out of the door so that those nearest shrunk aback. Thorgils was standing near, and struck after him with a sword, and caught him on the shoulder and made a great wound. Helgi turned to meet him, and had a wood-axe in his hand, and said, "Still the old one will dare to look at and face weapons," and therewith he flung the axe at Thorgils, and the axe struck his foot, and a great wound that was. And when Bolli saw this he leapt forward at Helgi with Footbiter in his hand, and thrust Helgi through with it, and that was his death-blow. Helgi's followers leapt out of the dairy forthwith, and Hardbien with them. Thorleik Bollison turned against Eyolf, who was a strong man. Thorleik struck him with his sword, and it caught him on the leg above the knee and cut off his leg, and he fell to earth dead. Hunbogi the Strong went to meet Thorgils, and dealt a blow at him with an axe, and it struck the back of him, and cut him asunder in the middle. Thord Cat was standing near where Hardbien leapt out, and was going to set upon him straightway, but Bolli rushed forward when he saw it, and bade no harm be done to Hardbien. "No man shall do a dastard's work here, and Hardbien shall have life and limbs spared." Helgi had another son named Skorri. He was brought up at Gugland in Reekdale the southernmost.

CHAPTER 65
Of Gudrun's Deceit

After these deeds Thorgils and his band rode away over the neck to Reekdale, where they declared these manslaughters on their hands. Then they rode the same way eastward as they had ridden from the west, and did not stop their journey till they came to Hord-Dale. They now told the tidings of what had happened in their journey, which became most famous, for it was thought a great deed to have felled such a hero as was Helgi. Thorgils thanked his men well for the journey, and the sons of Bolli did the same. And now the men part who had been in Thorgils' train; Lambi rode west to Salmon-river-Dale, and came first to Herdholt and told his kinsmen most carefully the tidings of what had happened in Skorradale. They were very ill-pleased with his journey and laid heavy reproaches upon him, saying he had shown himself much more of the stock of Thorbjorn "Skrjup" than of that of Myrkjartan, the Irish king. Lambi was very angry at their talk, and said they knew but little of good manners in overwhelming him with reproaches, "for I have dragged you out of death," says he. After that they exchanged but few words, for both sides were yet more fulfilled of ill-will than before. Lambi now rode home to his manor. Thorgils Hallason rode out to Holyfell, and with him the sons of Gudrun and his foster-brothers Halldor and Ornolf. They came late in the evening to Holyfell, when all men were in bed. Gudrun rose up and bade the household get up and wait upon them. She went into the guest-chamber and greeted Thorgils and all the others, and asked for tidings. Thorgils returned Gudrun's greeting; he had laid aside his cloak and his weapons as well, and sat then up against the pillars.

Thorgils had on a red-brown kirtle, and had round his waist a broad silver belt. Gudrun sat down on the bench by him. Then Thorgils said this stave -

"To Helgi's home a raid we led,
Gave ravens corpse-repast to swallow,
We dyed shield-wands with blood all red,
As Thorleik's lead our band did follow.
And at our hands there perished three
Keen helmet-stems, accounted truly
As worthies of the folk - and we
Claim Bolli now's avenged full duly."

Gudrun asked them most carefully for the tidings of what had happened on their journey. Thorgils told her all she wished. Gudrun said the journey had been most stirringly carried out, and bade them have her thanks for it. After that food was set before them, and after they had eaten they were shown to bed, and slept the rest of the night. The next day Thorgils went to talk to Gudrun, and said, "Now the matter stands thus, as you know, Gudrun, that I have brought to an end the journey you bade me undertake, and I must claim that, in a full manly wise, that matter has been turned out of hand; you will also call to mind what you promised me in return, and I think I am now entitled to that prize." Then Gudrun said, "It is not such a long time since we last talked together that I should have forgotten what we said, and my only aim is to hold to all I agreed to as concerning you. Or what does your mind tell you as to how matters were bespoken between us?" Thorgils said she must remember that, and Gudrun answered, "I think I said that of men within this land I would marry none but you; or have you aught to say against that?" Thorgils said she was right. "That is well then," said Gudrun, "that our memory should be one and the same on this matter. And I will not put it off from you any longer, that I am minded to think that it is not fated to me to be your wife. Yet I deem that I fulfil to you all uttered words, though I marry Thorkell Eyjolfson, who at present is not in this land." Then Thorgils said, and flushed up very much, "Clearly I do see from whence that chill wave comes running, and from thence cold counsels have always come to me. I know that this is the counsel of Snorri the Priest." Thorgils sprang up from this talk and was very angry, and went to his followers and said he would ride away. Thorleik disliked very much that things should have taken such a turn as to go against Thorgils' will; but Bolli was at one with his mother's will herein. Gudrun said she would give Thorgils some good gifts and soften him by that means, but Thorleik said that would be of no use, "for Thorgils is far too high-mettled a man to stoop to trifles in a matter of this sort. "Gudrun said in that case he must console himself as best he could at home. After this Thorgils rode from Holyfell with his foster-brothers. He got home to Tongue to his manor mightily ill at ease over his lot.

CHAPTER 66
Osvif and Gest Die

That winter Osvif fell ill and died, and a great loss that was deemed, for he had been the greatest of sages. Osvif was buried at Holyfell, for Gudrun had had a church built there. That same winter Gest Oddliefson fell ill, and as the sickness grew heavy on him, he called to him Thord the Low, his son, and said, "My mind forebodes me that this sickness will put an end to our living together. I wish my body to be carried to Holyfell, for that will be the greatest place about these countrysides, for I have often seen a light burning there." Thereupon Gest died. The winter had been very cold, and there was much ice about, and Broadfirth was laid under ice so far out that no ship could get over it from Bardistrand. Gest's body lay in state two nights at Hegi, and that very night there sprang up such a gale that all the ice was drawn away from the land, and the next day the weather was fair and still. Then Thord took a ship and put Gest's body on board, and went south across Broadfirth that day, and came in the evening to Holyfell. Thord had a good welcome there, and stayed there through the night. In the morning Gest's body was buried, and he and Osvif rested in one grave. So Gest's soothsaying was fulfilled, in that now it was shorter between them than at the time when one dwelt at Bardistrand and the other in Sælingsdale. Thord the Low then went home as soon as he was ready. That next night a wild storm arose, and drove the ice on to the land again, where it held on long through the winter, so that there was no going about in boats. Men thought this most marvellous, that the weather had allowed Gest's body to be taken across when there was no crossing before nor afterwards during the winter.

CHAPTER 67
The Death of Thorgils Hallason, A.D. 1020

Thorarin was the name of a man who lived at Longdale: he was a chieftain, but not a mighty one. His son was named Audgisl, and was a nimble sort of a man. Thorgils Hallason took the chieftainship from them both, father and son. Audgisl went to see Snorri Godi, and told him of this unfairness, and asked him to help. Snorri answered only by fair words, and belittled the whole affair; but answered, "Now that Halla's-grig is getting too forward and swaggering. Will Thorgils then happen on no man that will not give in to him in everything? No doubt he is a big man and doughty, but men as good as he is have also been sent to Hel." And when Audgisl went away Snorri gave him an inlaid axe. The next spring Thorgils Hallason and Thorstein the Black went south to Burgfirth, and offered atonement to the sons of Helgi and his other kinsmen, and they came to terms of peace on the matter, and fair honour was done (to Helgi's side). Thorstein paid two parts of the atonement for the manslaughter, and the third part Thorgils was to pay, payment being due at the Thing. In the summer Thorgils rode to the Thing, but when he and his men came to the lava field by Thingvellir, they saw a woman coming to meet them, and a mighty big one she was. Thorgils rode up to her, but she turned aside, and said this –

> "Take care
> If you go forward,
> And be wary
> Of Snorri's wiles,
> No one can escape,
> For so wise is Snorri."

And after that she went her way. Then Thorgils said, "It has seldom happened sobefore, when luck was with me, that you were leaving the Thing when I was riding to it." He now rode to the Thing and to his own booth. And through the early part the Thing was quiet. It happened one day during the Thing that folk's clothes were hung out to dry. Thorgils had a blue hooded cloak, which was spread out on the booth wall, and men heard the cloak say thus -

> "Hanging wet on the wall,
> A hooded cloak knows a braid (trick);
> I do not say he does not know two,
> He has been lately washed."

This was thought a most marvellous thing. The next day Thorgils went west over the river to pay the money to the sons of Helgi. He sat down on the lava above the booths, and with him was his foster-brother Halldor and sundry more of them were there together. The sons of Helgi came to the meeting. Thorgils now began to count out the money. Audgisl Thorarinson came near, and when Thorgils had counted ten Audgisl struck at him, and all thought they heard the head say eleven as it flew off the neck. Audgisl ran to the booth of the Waterfirthers and Halldor rushed after him and struck him his death-blow in the door of the booth. These tidings came to the booth of Snorri Godi how Thorgils was slain. Snorri said, "You must be mistaken; it must be that Thorgils Hallason has slain some one." The man replied, "Why, the head flew off his trunk." "Then perhaps it is time," said Snorri. This manslaughter was peacefully atoned, as is told in the Saga of Thorgils Hallason.

CHAPTER 68
Gudrun's Marriage with Thorkell Eyjolfson

The same summer that Thorgils Hallason was killed a ship came to Bjorn's-haven. It belonged to Thorkell Eyjolfson. He was by then such a rich man that he had two merchant ships on voyages. The other ship came to Ramfirth to Board-Eyr; they were both laden with timber. When Snorri heard of the coming of Thorkell he rode at once to where the ship was. Thorkell gave him a most blithe welcome; he had a great deal of drink with him in his ship, and right unstintedly it was served, and many things they found to talk about. Snorri asked tidings of Norway, and Thorkell told him everything well and truthfully. Snorri told in return the tidings of all that had happened here while Thorkell had been away. "Now it seems to me," said Snorri, "you had better follow the counsel I set forth to you before you went abroad, and should give up voyaging about and settle down in quiet, and get for yourself the same woman to wife of whomwe spoke then." Thorkell replied, "I understand what you are driving at; everything we bespoke then is still uppermost in my mind, for indeed I begrudge me not the noblest of matches could it but be brought about." Snorri spake, "I am most willing and ready to back that matter up on your behalf, seeing that now we are rid of both the things that seemed to you the most troublesome to overcome, if you were to get Gudrun for wife at all, in that Bolli is revenged and Thorgils is out of the way." Thorkell said, "Your counsels go very deep, Snorri, and into this affair I go heart and soul." Snorri stayed in the ship several nights, and then they took a ten-oared boat that floated alongside of the merchant ship and got ready with five-and-twenty men, and went to Holyfell. Gudrun gave an exceeding affectionate welcome to Snorri, and a most goodly cheer they had; and when they had been there one night Snorri called Gudrun to talk to him, and spake, "Matters have come to this, that I have undertaken this journey for my friend Thorkell, Eyjolf's son, and he has now come here, as you see, and his errand hither is to set forth the wooing of you. Thorkell is a man of noble degree. You know yourself all about his race and doings in life, nor is he short of wealth either. To my mind, he is now the one man west about here who is most likely to become a chieftain, if to that end he will put himself forward. Thorkell is held in great esteem when he is out there, but by much is he more honoured when he is in Norway in the train of titled men." Then answers Gudrun: "My sons Thorleik and Bolli must have most to say in this matter; but you, Snorri, are the third man on whom I shall most rely for counsels in matters by which I set a great store, for you have long been a wholesome guide to me." Snorri said he deemed it a clear case that Thorkell must not be turned off. Thereupon Snorri had the sons of Gudrun called in, and sets forth the matter to them, laying down how great an help Thorkell might afford them by reason of his wealth and wise foresight; and smoothly he framed his speech on this matter. Then Bolli answered: "My mother will know how most clearly to see through this matter, and herein I shall be of one mind with her own will. But, to be sure, we shall deem it wise to set much store by your pleading this matter, Snorri, for you have done to us mightily well in many things." Then Gudrun spake: "In this matter we will lean most on Snorri's foresight, for to us your counsels have been wholesome." Snorri urged the matter on by every word he spoke, and the counsel taken was, that Gudrun and Thorkell should be joined in marriage. Snorri offered to have the wedding at his house; and Thorkell, liking that well, said: "I am not short of means, and I am ready to furnish them in whatever measure you please." Then Gudrun spake: "It is my wish that the feast be held here at Holyfell. I do not blench at standing the cost of it, nor shall I call upon Thorkell or any one else to trouble themselves about this matter." "Often, indeed, you show, Gudrun," said Snorri, "that you are the most high-mettled of women." So this was now settled that the wedding should take place when it lacked six weeks of summer. At matters thus settled Snorri and Thorkell went away, Snorri going home and Thorkell to his ship, and he spent the summer, turn and turn about, at Tongue or at his ship. Time now wore on towards the wedding feast. Gudrun made great preparation with much ingatherings. Snorri came to the feast together with Thorkell, and they brought with them well-nigh sixty men, and a very picked company that was, for most of the men were in dyed raiments. Gudrun had well-nigh a hundred and twenty first-bidden guests. The brothers Bolli and Thorleik, with the first-bidden guests, went to meet Snorri and his train; and to him and his fellowship was given a right cheery welcome, and their horses are taken in hand, as well as their clothes. They were shown into the guest-chamber, and Thorkell and Snorri and their followers took seats on the bench that was the upper one, and Gudrun's guests sat on the lower.

CHAPTER 69
The Quarrel about Gunnar at the Feast

That autumn Gunnar, the slayer of Thridrandi, had been sent to Gudrun for "trust and keep," and she had taken him in, his name being kept secret. Gunnar was outlawed because of the slaying of Thridrandi, Geitir's son, as is told in the Niard-wickers' Saga. He went about much "with a hidden head," for that many great men had their eyes upon him. The first evening of the feast, when men went to wash, a big man was standing by the water; he was broad of shoulder and wide of chest, and this man had a hat on his head. Thorkell asked who he was. He named himself as it seemed best to him. Thorkell says: "I think you are not speaking the truth; going by what the tale tells you would seem more like to Gunnar, the slayer of Thridrandi. And if you are so great a hero as other men say, you will not keep hidden your name." Then said Gunnar: "You speak most eagerly on this matter; and, truth to tell, I think I have no need to hide myself from you. You have rightly named your man; but then, what have you chiefly bethought yourself of having done to me?" Thorkell said he would like that he should soon know it, and spake to his men, ordering them to lay hands on him. Gudrun sat on the dais at the upper end of the hall, together with other womenall becoifed with white linen, and when she got aware of this she rises up from the bridal bench and calls on her men to lend Gunnar help, and told them to give quarter to no man who should show any doubtful behaviour. Gudrun had the greatest number of followers, and what never was meant to happen seemed like to befall. Snorri Godi went between both sides and bade them allay this storm. "The one thing clearly to be done by you, Thorkell, is not to push things on so hotly; and now you can see what a stirring woman Gudrun is, as she overrules both of us together." Thorkell said he had promised his namesake, Thorleik Geitir's son, that he would kill Gunnar if he came into the countrysides of the west. "And he is my greatest friend," Snorri spake. "You are much more in duty bound to act as we wish; and for yourself, it is a matter of the greatest importance, for you will never find such another woman as Gudrun, however far you may seek." And because of Snorri's reasoning, and seeing that he spoke the truth, Thorkell quieted down, and Gunnar was sent away that evening. The feast now went forward well and bravely, and when it was over the guests got ready to go away. Thorkell gave to Snorri very rich gifts, and the same to all the chief men. Snorri asked Bolli Bollison to go home with him, and to live with him as long as he liked. Bolli accepted this with thanks, and rides home to Tongue. Thorkell now settled down at Holyfell, and took in hand the affairs of the household, and it was soon seen that he was no worse a hand at that than at trade-voyaging. He had the hall pulled down in the autumn and a new one built, which was finished when the winter set in, and was both large and lofty. Between Gudrun and Thorkell dear love now grew up, and so the winter passed on. In the spring Gudrun asked how Thorkell was minded to look out for Gunnar the slayer of Thridrandi. He said that Gudrun had better take the management of that matter, "for you have taken it so hard in hand, that you will put up with nothing but that he be sent away with honour." Gudrun said he guessed aright: "I wish you to give him a ship, and therewithal such things as he cannot do without." Thorkell said and smiled, "You think nothing small on most matters, Gudrun, and would be ill served if you had a mean-minded man for a husband; nor has that ever been your heart's aim. Well, this shall be done after your own will" - and carried out it was. Gunnar took the gifts most gratefully. "I shall never be so 'long-armed' as to be able to repay all this great honour you are doing to me," he said. Gunnar now went abroad and came to Norway, and then went to his own estates. Gunnar was exceeding wealthy, most great-hearted, and a good and true man withal.

CHAPTER 70
Thorleik Goes to Norway

Thorkell Eyjolfson became a great chieftain; he laid himself out much for friendships and honours. He was a masterful man within his own countryside, and busied himself much about law-suits; yet of his pleadings at court there is no tale to tell here. Thorkell was the richest man in Broadfirth during his lifetime next after Snorri. Thorkell kept his house in good order. He had all the houses at Holyfell rebuilt large and strong. He also had the ground of a church marked out, and gave it out that he had made up his mind to go abroad and fetch timber for the building of his church. Thorkell and Gudrun had a son who was called Gellir; he looked early most likely to turn out well. Bolli Bollison spent his time turn and turn about at Tongue or Holyfell, and Snorri was very fond of him. Thorleik his brother lived at Holyfell. These brothers were both tall and most doughty looking, Bolli being the foremost in all things. Thorkell was kind to his stepsons, and Gudrun loved Bolli most of all her children. He was now sixteen, and Thorleik twenty years old. So, once on a time, Thorleik came to talk to his stepfather and his mother, and said he wished to go abroad. "I am quite tired of sitting at home like a woman, and I wish thatmeans to travel should be furnished to me." Thorkell said, "I do not think I have done against you two brothers in anything since our alliance began. Now, I think it is the most natural thing that you should yearn to get to know the customs of other men, for I know you will be counted a brisk man wheresoever you may come among doughty men." Thorleik said he did not want much money, "for it is uncertain how I may look after matters, being young and in many ways of an unsettled mind." Thorkell bade him have as much as he wanted. After that Thorkell bought for Thorleik a share in a ship that stood up in Daymeal-Ness, and saw him off to his ship, and fitted him well out with all things from home. Thorleik journeyed abroad that summer. The ship arrived in Norway. The lord over the land then was King Olaf the Holy. Thorleik went forthwith to see King Olaf, who gave him a good welcome; he knew Thorleik from his kindred, and so asked him to stay with him. Thorleik accepted with thanks, and stayed with the king that winter and became one of his guard, and the king held him in honour. Thorleik was thought the briskest of men, and he stayed on with King Olaf for several months. Now we must tell of Bolli Bollison. The spring when he was eighteen years old he spoke to his stepfather and his mother, and said that he wished they would hand him out his father's portion. Gudrun asked him what he had set his mind on doing, since he asked them to give him this money. Bolli answered, "It is my wish that a woman be wooed on my behalf, and I wish," said Bolli, "that you, Thorkell, be my spokesman and carry this through." Thorkell asked what woman it was Bolli wished to woo. Bolli answered, "The woman's name is

Thordis, and she is the daughter of Snorri the Priest; she is the woman I have most at heart to marry; I shall be in no hurry to marry if I do not get this one for wife. And I set a very great store by this matter being carried out." Thorkell answered, "My help is quite welcome to you, my son, if you think that if I follow up this matter much weight lies thereon. I think the matter will be easily got over with Snorri, for he will know well enough how to see that a fair offer is made him by such as you." Gudrun said, "I will say at once, Thorkell, that I will let spare nothing so that Bolli may but have the match that pleases him, and that for two reasons, first, that I love him most, and then he has been the most whole-hearted of my children in doing my will." Thorkell gave it out that he was minded to furnish Bolli off handsomely. "It is what for many reasons is due to him, and I know, withal, that in Bolli a good husband will be purchased." A little while after Thorkell and Bolli went with a good many followers to Tongue. Snorri gave to them a kind and blithe welcome, and they were treated to the very best of cheers at Snorri's hands. Thordis, the daughter of Snorri, was at home with her father; she wasa woman both goodly and of great parts. When they had been a few nights at Tongue Thorkell broached the wooing, bespeaking on behalf of Bolli an alliance with Snorri by marriage with Thordis, his daughter. Snorri answers, "It is well you come here on this errand; it is what I might have looked for from you. I will answer the matter well, for I think Bolli one of the most hopeful of men, and that woman I deem well given in marriage who is given in marriage to him. It will, however, tell most in this matter, how far this is to Thordis' own mind; for she shall marry such a man only on whom she sets her heart." This matter coming before Thordis she answered suchwise as that therein she would lean on the foresight of her father, saying she would sooner marry Bolli, a man from within her own countryside, than a stranger from farther away. And when Snorri found that it was not against her wish to go with Bolli, the affair was settled and the betrothal took place. Snorri was to have the feast at his house about the middle of summer. With that Thorkell and Bolli rode home to Holyfell, and Bolli now stayed at home till the time of the wedding-feast. Then Thorkell and Bolli array themselves to leave home, and with them all the men who were set apart therefor, and a crowded company and the bravest band that was. They then rode on their way and came to Tongue, and had a right hearty welcome there. There were great numbers there, and the feast was of the noblest, and when the feast comes to an end the guests get ready to depart. Snorri gave honourable gifts to Thorkell, yea and to both of them, him and Gudrun, and the same to his other friends and relations. And now each one of those who had gone to the feast rode to his own home. Bolli abode at Tongue, and between him and Thordis dear love sprang speedily up. Snorri did all he could to entertain Bolli well, and to him he was even kinder than to his own children. Bolli received all this gratefully, and remained at Tongue that year in great favour. The next summer a ship came to White-river. One-half of the ship belonged to Thorleik Bollison and the other half of it belonged to some Norwegian man. When Bolli heard of the coming of his brother he rode south to Burgfirth and to the ship. The brothers greeted each other joyfully. Bolli stayed there for several nights, and then both brothers ride together west to Holyfell; Thorkell takes them in with the greatest blitheness, as did also Gudrun, and they invited Thorleik to stay with them for the winter, and that he took with thanks. Thorleik tarried at Holyfell awhile, and then he rode to White-river and lets his ship be beached and his goods be brought to the West. Thorleik had had good luck with him both as to wealth and honours, for that he had become the henchman of that noblest of lords, King Olaf. He now stayed at Holyfell through the winter, while Bolli tarried at Tongue.

CHAPTER 71
The Peace between the Sons of Bolli and the Sons of Olaf, A.D. 1026

That winter the brothers would always be meeting, having talks together, and took no pleasure in games or any other pastime; and one time, when Thorleik was at Tongue, the brothers talked day and night together. Snorri then thought he knew that they must be taking counsel together on some very great matter, so he went and joined the talk of the brothers. They greeted him well, but dropped their talk forthwith. He took their greeting well; and presently Snorri spoke: "What are you taking counsels about so that ye heed neither sleep nor meat?" Bolli answers: "This is no framing of counsels, for that talk is one of but little mark which we talk together." Now Snorri found that they wanted to hide from him all that was in their minds, yet misdoubted him, that they must be talking chiefly of things from which great troubles might arise, in case they should be carried out. He (Snorri) spoke to them: "This I misdoubt me now, that it be neither a vain thing nor a matter of jest you are talking about for such long hours together, and I hold you quite excused, even if such should be the case. Now, be so good as to tell it me and not to hide it away from me. We shall not, when gathered all together, be worse able to take counsel in this matter, for that I shall nowhere stand in the way of anything going forward whereby your honour grows the greater." Thorleik thought Snorri had taken up their case in a kindly manner, and told him in a few words their wishes, and how they had made up their minds to set on the sons of Olaf, and to put them to sore penalties; they said that now they lacked of nothing to bring the sons of Olaf to terms of equality, since Thorleik was a liegeman of King Olaf, and Bolli was the son-in-law of such a chief as Snorri was. Snorri answered in this way: "For the slaying of Bolli enough has come in return, in that the life of Helgi Hardbeinson was paid therefor; the troubles of men have been far too great already, and it is high time that now at last they be put a stop to." Bolli said, "What now, Snorri? are you less keen now to stand by us than you gave out but a little while ago? Thorleik would not have told you our mind as yet if he had first taken counsel with me thereon. And when you claim that Helgi's life has come in revenge for Bolli, it is a matter well known to men that a money fine was paid for the slaying of Helgi, while my father is still unatoned for." When Snorri saw he could not reason them into a change of mind, he offered them to try to bring about a peaceful atonement between them and the sons of Olaf, rather than that any more manslaughters should befall; and the brothers agreed to this. Then Snorri rode with some men to Herdholt. Halldor gave him a good welcome, and asked him to stay there, but Snorri said he must ride back that night. "But I have an urgent errand with you." So they fell to talking together, and Snorri made known his errand, saying it had come to his knowledge that Thorleik and Bolli would put up with it no longer that their father should be unatoned at the hands of the sons of Olaf. "And now I would endeavour to bring about peace, and see if an end cannot be put to the evil luck that besets you kinsmen." Halldor did not flatly refuse to deal further with the case. "I know only too well that Thorgils Hallason and Bolli's sons were minded to fall on me and my brothers, until you turned elsewhere their vengeance, so that thence-forward it seemed to them best to slay Helgi Hardbeinson. In these matters you have taken a good part, whatever your counsels may have been like in regard to earlier dealings between us kinsmen." Snorri said, "I set a great store by my errand turning out well and that it might be brought about which I have most at heart, that a sound peace should be settled between you kinsmen; for I know the minds of the men who have to deal with you in this case so well, that they will keep faithfully to whatever terms of peace they agree to." Halldor said, "I will undertake this, if it be the wish of my brothers, to pay money for the slaying of Bolli, such as shall be awarded by the umpires chosen, but I bargain that there be no outlawing of anybody concerned, nor forfeiture of my chieftainship or estate; thesame claim I make in respect of the estates my brothers are possessed of, and I make a point of their being left free owners thereof whatever be the close of this case, each side to choose their own umpire." Snorri answered, "This is offered well and frankly, and the brothers will take this choice if they are willing to set any store by my counsel." Thereupon Snorri rode home and told the brothers the outcome of his errand, and that he would keep altogether aloof from their case if they would not agree to this. Bolli bade him have his own way, "And I wish that you, Snorri, be umpire on our behalf." Then Snorri sent to Halldor to say that peaceful settlement was agreed to, and he bade them choose an umpire against himself. Halldor chose on his behalf Steinthor Thorlakson of Eyr. The peace meeting should be at Drangar on Shawstrand, when four weeks of summer were passed. Thorleik Bollison rode to Holyfell, and nothing to tell tidings of befell that winter, and when time wore unto the hour bespoken for the meeting, Snorri the Priest came there with the sons of Bolli, fifteen together in all; Steinthor and his came with the same number of men to the meeting. Snorri and Steinthor talked together and came to an agreement about these matters. After that they gave out the award, but it is not told how much money they awarded; this, however, is told, that the money was readily paid and the peace well holden to. At the Thorness Thing the fines were paid out; Halldor gave Bolli a good sword, and SteinthorOlafson gave Thorleik a shield, which was also a good gift. Then the Thing was broken up, and both sides were thought to have gained in esteem from these affairs.

CHAPTER 72
Bolli and Thorleik go Abroad, A. D. 1029

After the peace between Bolli and Thorleik and the sons of Olaf had been settled and Thorleik had been one winter in Iceland, Bolli made it known that he was minded to go abroad. Snorri, dissuading him, said, "To us it seems there is a great risk to be run as to how you may speed; but if you wish to have in hand more than you have now, I will get you a manor and stock it for you; therewithal I shall hand over to you chieftainship over men and uphold you for honours in all things; and that, I know, will be easy, seeing that most men bear you good-will." Bolli said, "I have long had it in my mind to go for once into southern lands; for a man is deemed to grow benighted if he learns to know nothing farther afield than what is to be seen here in Iceland." And when Snorri saw that Bolli had set his mind on this, and that it would come to nought to try to stop him, he bade him take as much money as he liked for his journey. Bolli was all for having plenty of money, "for I will not," he said, "be beholden to any man either here or in any foreign land." Then Bolli rode south to Burgfirth to White-river and bought half of a ship from the owners, so that he and his brother became joint owners of the same ship. Bolli then rides west again to his home. He and Thordis had one daughter whose name was Herdis, and that maiden Gudrun asked to bring up. She was one year old when she went to Holyfell. Thordis also spent a great deal of her time there, for Gudrun was very fond of her.

CHAPTER 73
Bolli's Voyage

Now the brothers went both to their ship. Bolli took a great deal of money abroad with him. They now arrayed the ship, and when everything was ready they put out to sea. The winds did not speed them fast, and they were a long time out at sea, but got to Norway in the autumn, and made Thrandheim in the north. Olaf, the king, was in the east part of the land, in the Wick, where he had made ingatherings for a stay through the winter. And when the brothers heard that the king would not come north to Thrandheim that autumn, Thorleik said he would go east along the land to meet King Olaf. Bolli said, "I have little wish to driftabout between market towns in autumn days; to me that is too much of worry and restraint. I will rather stay for the winter in this town. I am told the king will come north in the spring, and if he does not then I shall not set my face against our going to meet him." Bolli has his way in the matter, and they put up their ship and got their winter quarters. It was soon seen that Bolli was a very pushing man, and would be the first among other men; and in that he had his way, for a bounteous man was he, and so got speedily to be highly thought of in Norway. Bolli kept a suite about him during the winter at Thrandheim, and it was easily seen, when he went to the guild meeting-places, that his men were both better arrayed as to raiment and weapons than other townspeople. He alone also paid for all his suite when they sat drinking in guild halls, and on a par with this were his openhandedness and lordly ways in other matters. Now the brothers stay in the town through the winter. That winter the king sat east in Sarpsborg, and news spread from the east that the king was not likely to come north. Early in the spring the brothers got their ship ready and went east along the land. The journey sped well for them, and they got east to Sarpsborg, and went forthwith to meet King Olaf. The king gave a good welcome to Thorleik, his henchman, and his followers. Then the king asked who was that man of stately gait in the train of Thorleik; and Thorleik answered, "He is my brother, and is named Bolli." "He looks,indeed, a man of high mettle," said the king. Thereupon the king asks the brothers to come and stay with him, and that offer they took with thanks, and spend the spring with the king. The king was as kind to Thorleik as he had been before, yet he held Bolli by much in greater esteem, for he deemed him even peerless among men. And as the spring went on, the brothers took counsel together about their journeys. And Thorleik asked Bolli if he was minded to go back to Iceland during the summer, "or will you stay on longer here in Norway?" Bolli answered, "I do not mean to do either. And sooth to say, when I left Iceland, my thought was settled on this, that people should not be asking for news of me from the house next door; and now I wish, brother, that you take over our ship." Thorleik took it much to heart that they should have to part. "But you, Bolli, will have your way in this as in other things." Their matter thus bespoken they laid before the king, and he answered thus: "Will you not tarry with us any longer, Bolli?" said the king. "I should have liked it best for you to stay with me for a while, for I shall grant you the same title that I granted to Thorleik, your brother." Then Bolli answered: "I should be only too glad to bind myself to be your henchman, but I must go first whither I am already bent, and have long been eager to go, but this choice I will gladly take if it be fated to me to come back." "You will have your way as to your journeyings, Bolli," says the king, "for you Icelanders are self-willed in most matters. But with this word I must close, that I think you, Bolli, the man of greatest mark that has ever come from Iceland in my days." And when Bolli had got the king's leave he made ready for his journey, and went on board a round ship that was bound south for Denmark. He also took a great deal of money with him, and sundry of his followers bore him company. He and King Olaf parted in great friendship, and the king gave Bolli some handsome gifts at parting. Thorleik remained behind with King Olaf, but Bolli went on his way till he came south to Denmark. That winter he tarried in Denmark, and had great honour there of mighty men; nor did he bear himself there in any way less lordly than while he was in Norway. When Bolli had been a winter in Denmark he started on his journey out into foreign countries, and did not halt in his journey till he came to Micklegarth (Constantinople). He was there only a short time before he got himself into the Varangian Guard, and, from what we have heard, no Northman had ever gone to take war-pay from the Garth king before Bolli, Bolli's son. He tarried in Micklegarth very many winters, and was thought to be the most valiant in all deeds that try a man, and always went next to those in the forefront. The Varangians accounted Bolli most highly of whilst he was with them in Micklegarth.

CHAPTER 74
Thorkell Eyjolfson Goes to Norway

Now the tale is to be taken up again where Thorkell Eyjolfson sits at home in lordly way. His and Gudrun's son, Gellir, grew up there at home, and was early both a manly fellow and winning. It is said how once upon a time Thorkell told Gudrun a dream he had had. "I dreamed," he said, "that I had so great a beard that it spread out over the whole of Broadfirth." Thorkell bade her read his dream. Gudrun said, "What do you think this dream betokens?" He said, "To me it seems clear that in it is hinted that my power will stand wide about the whole of Broadfirth." Gudrun said, "Maybe that such is the meaning of it, but I rather should think that thereby is betokened that you will dip your beard down into Broadfirth." That same summer Thorkell runs out his ship and gets it ready for Norway. His son, Gellir, was then twelve winters old, and he went abroad with his father. Thorkell makes it known that he means to fetch timber to build his church with, and sails forthwith into the main sea when he was ready. He had an easy voyage of it, but not a very short one, and they hove into Norway northwardly. King Olaf then had his seat in Thrandheim, and Thorkell sought forthwith a meeting with King Olaf, and his son Gellir with him. They had there a good welcome. So highly was Thorkell accounted of that winter by the king, that all folk tell that the king gave him not less than one hundred marks of refined silver. The king gave to Gellir at Yule a cloak, the most precious and excellent of gifts. That winter King Olaf had a church built in the town of timber, and it was a very great minster, all materials thereto being chosen of the best. In the spring the timber which the king gave to Thorkell was brought on board ship, and large was that timber and good in kind, for Thorkell looked closely after it. Now it happened one morning early that the king went out with but few men, and saw a man up on the church which then was being built in the town. He wondered much at this, for it was a good deal earlier than the smiths were wont to be up. Then the king recognised the man, and, lo! there was Thorkell Eyjolfson taking the measure of all the largest timber, crossbeams, sills, and pillars. The king turned at once thither, and said: "What now, Thorkell, do you mean after these measurements to shape the church timber which you are taking to Iceland?" "Yes, in truth, sire," said Thorkell. Then said King Olaf, "Cut two ells off every main beam, and that church will yet be the largest built in Iceland." Thorkell answered, "Keep your timber yourself if you think you have given me too much, or your hand itches to take it back, but not an ell's length shall I cut off it. I shall both know how to go about and how to carry out getting other timber for me." Then says the king most calmly, "So it is, Thorkell, that you are not only a man of much account, but you are also now making yourself too big, for, to be sure, it is too overweening for the son of a mere peasant to try to vie with us. But it is not true that I begrudge you the timber, if only it be fated to you to build a church therewith; for it will never be large enough for all your pride to find room to lie inside it. But near it comes to the foreboding of my mind, that the timber will be of little use to men, and that it will be far from you ever to get any work by man done with this timber." After that they ceased talking, and the king turned away, and it was marked by people that it misliked him how Thorkell accounted as of nought what he said. Yet the king himself did not let people get the wind of it, and he and Thorkell parted in great good-will. Thorkell got on board his ship and put to sea. They had a good wind, and were not long out about the main. Thorkell brought his ship to Ramfirth, and rode soon from his ship home to Holyfell, where all folk were glad to see him. In this journey Thorkell had gained much honour. He had his ship hauled ashore and made snug, and the timber for the church he gave to a caretaker, where it was safely bestowed, for it could not be brought from the north this autumn, as he was at all time full of business. Thorkell now sits at home at his manor throughout the winter. He had Yule-drinking at Holyfell, and to it there came a crowd of people; and altogether he kept up a great state that winter. Nor did Gudrun stop him therein; for she said the use of money was that people should increase their state therewith; moreover, whatever Gudrun must needs be supplied with for all purposes of high-minded display, that (she said) would be readily forthcoming (from her husband). Thorkell shared that winter amongst his friends many precious things he had brought with him out to Iceland.

CHAPTER 75
Thorkell and Thorstein and Halldor Olafson, A.D. 1026

That winter after Yule Thorkell got ready to go from home north to Ramfirth to bring his timber from the north. He rode first up into the Dales and then to Lea-shaws to Thorstein, his kinsman, where he gathered together men and horses. He afterwards went north to Ramfirth and stayed there awhile, taken up with the business of his journey, and gathered to him horses from about the firth, for he did not want to make more than one journey of it, if that could be managed. But this did not speed swiftly, and Thorkell was busy at this work even into Lent. At last he got under way with the work, and had the wood dragged from the north by more than twenty horses, and had the timber stacked on Lea-Eyr, meaning later on to bring it in a boat out to Holyfell. Thorstein owned a large ferry-boat, and this boat Thorkell was minded to use for his homeward voyage. Thorkell stayed at Lea-shaws through Lent, for there was dear friendship between these kinsmen. Thorstein said one day to Thorkell, they had better go to Herdholt, "for I want to make a bid for some land from Halldor, he having but little money since he paid the brothers the weregild for their father, and the land being just what I want most." Thorkell bade him do as he liked; so they left home a party of twenty men together. They come to Herdholt, and Halldor gave them good welcome, and was most free of talk with them. There were few men at home, for Halldor had sent his men north to Steingrims-firth, as a whale had come ashore there in which he owned a share. Beiner the Strong was at home, the only man now left alive of those who had been there with Olaf, the father of Halldor. Halldor had said to Beiner at once when he saw Thorstein and Thorkell riding up, "I can easily see what the errand of these kinsmen is - they are going to make me a bid for my land, and if that is the case they will call me aside for a talk; I guess they will seat themselves each on either side of me; so, then, if they should give me any trouble you must not be slower to set on Thorstein than I on Thorkell. You have long been true to us kinsfolk. I have also sent to the nearest homesteads for men, and at just the same moment I should like these two things to happen: the coming in of the men summoned, and the breaking up of our talk." Now as the day wore on, Thorstein hinted to Halldor that they should all go aside and have some talk together, "for we have an errand with you." Halldor said it suited him well. Thorstein told his followers they need not come with them, but Beiner went with them none the less, for he thought things came to pass very much after what Halldor had guessed they would. They went very far out into the field. Halldor had on a pinned-up cloak with a long pin brooch, as was the fashion then. Halldor sat down on the field, but on either side of him each of these kinsmen, so near that they sat well-nigh on his cloak; but Beiner stood over them with a big axe in his hand. Then said Thorstein, "My errand here is that I wish to buy land from you, and I bring it before you now because my kinsman Thorkell is with me; I should think that this would suit us both well, for I hear that you are short of money, while your land is costly to husband. I will give you in return an estate that will beseem you, and into the bargain as much as we shall agree upon." In the beginning Halldor took the matter as if it were not so very far from his mind, and they exchanged words concerning the terms of the purchase; and when they felt that he was not so far from coming to terms, Thorkell joined eagerly in the talk, and tried to bring the bargain to a point. Then Halldor began to draw back rather, but they pressed him all the more; yet at last it came to this, that he was the further from the bargain the closer they pressed him. Then said Thorkell, "Do you not see, kinsman Thorstein, how this is going? Halldor has delayed the matter for us all day long, and we have sat here listening to his fooling and wiles. Now if you want to buy the land we must come to closer quarters." Thorstein then said he must know what he had to look forward to, and bade Halldor now come out of the shadow as to whether he was willing to come to the bargain. Halldor answered, "I do not think I need keep you in the dark as to this point, that you will have to go home to-night without any bargain struck." Then said Thorstein, "Nor do I think it needful to delay making known to you what we have in our mind to do; for we, deeming that we shall get the better of you by reason of the odds on our side, have bethought us of two choices for you: one choice is, that you do this matter willingly and take in return our friendship; but the other, clearly a worse one, is, that you now stretch out your hand against your own will and sell me the land of Herdholt." But when Thorstein spoke in this outrageous manner, Halldor leapt up so suddenly that the brooch was torn from his cloak, and said, "Something else will happen before I utter that which is not my will." "What is that?" said Thorstein. "A pole-axe will stand on your head from one of the worst of men, and thus cast down your insolence and unfairness." Thorkell answered, "That is an evil prophecy, and I hope it will not be fulfilled; and now I think there is ample cause why you, Halldor, should give up your land and have nothing for it." Then Halldor answered, "Sooner you will be embracing the sea-tangle in Broadfirth than I sell my land against my own will." Halldor went home after that, and the men he had sent for came crowding up to the place. Thorstein was of the wrothest, and wanted forthwith to make an onset on Halldor. Thorkell bade him not to do so, "for that is the greatest enormity at such a season as this; but when this season wears off, I shall not stand in the way of his and ours clashing together." Halldor said he was given to think he would not fail in being ready for them. After that they rode away and talked much together of this their journey; and Thorstein, speaking thereof, said that, truth to tell, their journey was most wretched. "But why, kinsman Thorkell, were you so afraid of falling on Halldor and putting him to some shame?" Thorkell answered, "Did you not see Beiner, who stood over you with the axe reared aloft? Why, it was an utter folly, for forthwith on seeing me likely to do anything, he would have driven that axe into your head." They rode now home to Lea-shaws; and Lent wears and Passion Week sets in.

CHAPTER 76
The Drowning of Thorkell, A.D. 1026

On Maundy Thursday, early in the morning, Thorkell got ready for his journey. Thorstein set himself much against it: "For the weather looks to me uncertain," said he. Thorkell said the weather would do all right. "And you must not hinder me now, kinsman, for I wish to be home before Easter." So now Thorkell ran out the ferry-boat, and loaded it. But Thorstein carried the lading ashore from out the boat as fast as Thorkell and his followers put it on board. Then Thorkell said, "Give over now, kinsman, and do not hinder our journey this time; you must not have your own way in this." Thorstein said, "He of us two will now follow the counsel that will answer the worst, for this journey will cause the happening of great matters." Thorkell now bade them farewell till their next meeting, and Thorstein went home, and was exceedingly downcast. He went to the guest-house, and bade them lay a pillow under his head, the which was done. The servant-maid saw how the tears ran down upon the pillow from his eyes. And shortly afterwards a roaring blast struck the house, and Thorstein said, "There, we now can hear roaring the slayer of kinsman Thorkell." Now to tell of the journey of Thorkell and his company: they sail this day out, down Broadfirth, and were ten on board. The wind began to blow very high, and rose to full gale before it blew over. They pushed on their way briskly, for the men were most plucky. Thorkell had with him the sword Skofnung, which was laid in the locker. Thorkell and his party sailed till they came to Bjorn's isle, and people could watch them journey from both shores. But when they had come thus far, suddenly a squall caught the sail and overwhelmed the boat. There Thorkell was drowned and all the men who were with him. The timber drifted ashore wide about the islands, the corner-staves (pillars) drove ashore in the island called Staff-isle. Skofnung stuck fast to the timbers of the boat, and was found in Skofnungs-isle. That same evening that Thorkell and his followers were drowned, it happened at Holyfell that Gudrun went to the church, when other people had gone to bed, and when she stepped into the lich-gate she saw a ghost standing before her. He bowed over her and said, "Great tidings, Gudrun." She said, "Hold then your peace about them, wretch." Gudrun went on to the church, as she had meant to do, and when she got up to the church she thought she saw that Thorkell and his companions were come home and stood before the door of the church, and she saw that water was running off their clothes. Gudrun did not speak to them, but went into the church, and stayed there as long as it seemed good to her. After that she went to the guest-room, for she thought Thorkell and his followers must have gone there; but when she came into the chamber, there was no one there. Then Gudrun was struck with wonder at the whole affair. On Good Friday Gudrun sent her men to find out matters concerning the journeying of Thorkell and his company, some up to Shawstrand and some out to the islands. By then the flotsam had already come to land wide about the islands and on both shores of the firth. The Saturday before Easter the tidings got known and great news they were thought to be, for Thorkell had been a great chieftain. Thorkell was eight-and-forty years old when he was drowned, and that was four winters before Olaf the Holy fell. Gudrun took much to heart the death of Thorkell, yet bore her bereavement bravely. Only very little of the church timber could ever be gathered in. Gellir was now fourteen years old, and with his mother he took over the business of the household and the chieftainship. It was soon seen that he was made to be a leader of men. Gudrun now became a very religious woman. She was the first woman in Iceland who knew the Psalter by heart. She would spend long time in the church at nights saying her prayers, and Herdis, Bolli's daughter, always went with her at night. Gudrun loved Herdis very much. It is told that one night the maiden Herdis dreamed that a woman came to her who was dressed in a woven cloak, and coifed in a head cloth, but she did not think the woman winning to look at. She spoke, "Tell your grandmother that I am displeased with her, for she creeps about over me every night, and lets fall down upon me drops so hot that I am burning all over from them. My reason for letting you know this is, that I like you somewhat better, though there is something uncanny hovering about you too. However, I could get on with you if I did not feel there was so much more amiss with Gudrun." Then Herdis awoke and told Gudrun her dream. Gudrun thought the apparition was of good omen. Next morning Gudrun had planks taken up from the church floor where she was wont to kneel on the hassock, and she had the earth dug up, and they found blue and evil-looking bones, a round brooch, and a wizard's wand, and men thought they knew then that a tomb of some sorceress must have been there; so the bones were taken to a place far away where people were least likely to be passing.

CHAPTER 77
The Return of Bolli, A.D. 1030

When four winters were passed from the drowning of Thorkell Eyjolfson a ship came into Islefirth belonging to Bolli Bollison, most of the crew of which were Norwegians. Bolli brought out with him much wealth, and many precious things that lords abroad had given him. Bolli was so great a man for show when he came back from this journey that he would wear no clothes but of scarlet and fur, and all his weapons were bedight with gold: he was called Bolli the Grand. He made it known to his shipmasters that he was going west to his own countrysides, and he left his ship and goods in the hands of his crew. Bolli rode from the ship with twelve men, and all his followers were dressed in scarlet, and rode on gilt saddles, and all were they a trusty band, though Bolli was peerless among them. He had on the clothes of fur which the Garth-king had given him, he had over all a scarlet cape; and he had Footbiter girt on him, the hilt of which was dight with gold, and the grip woven with gold; he had a gilded helmet on his head, and a red shield on his flank, with a knight painted on it in gold. He had a dagger in his hand, as is the custom in foreign lands; and whenever they took quarters the women paid heed to nothing but; gazing at Bolli and his grandeur, and that of his followers. In this state Bolli rode into the western parts all the way till he came to Holyfell with his following. Gudrun was very glad to see her son. Bolli did not stay there long till he rode up to Sælingsdale Tongue to see Snorri, his father-in-law, and his wife Thordis, and their meeting was exceeding joyful. Snorri asked Bolli to stay with him with as many of his men as he liked. Bolli accepted the invitation gratefully, and was with Snorri all the winter, with the men who had ridden from the north with him. Bolli got great renown from this journey. Snorri made it no less his business Snorri' now to treat Bolli with every kindness than death when he was with him before.

CHAPTER 78
The Death of Snorri, and the End, A.D. 1031

When Bolli had been one winter in Iceland Snorri the Priest fell ill. That illness did not gain quickly on him, and Snorri lay very long abed. But when the illness gained on him, he called to himself all his kinsfolk and affinity, and said to Bolli, "It is my wish that you shall take over the manor here and the chieftainship after my day, for I grudge honours to you no more than to my own sons, nor is there

281

within this land now the one of my sons who I think will be the greatest man among them, Halldor to wit." Thereupon Snorri breathed his last, being seventy-seven years old. That was one winter after the fall of St. Olaf, so said Ari the Priest "Deep-in-lore." Snorri was buried at Tongue. Bolli and Thordis took over the manor of Tongue as Snorri had willed it, and Snorri's sons put up with it with a good will. Bolli grew a man of great account, and was much beloved. Herdis, Bolli's daughter, grew up at Holyfell, and was the goodliest of all women. Orm, the son of Hermund, the son of Illugi, asked her in marriage, and she was given in wedlock to him; their son was Kodran, who had for wife Gudrun, the daughter of Sigmund. The son of Kodran was Hermund, who had for wife Ulfeid, the daughter of Runolf, who was the son of Bishop Kelill; their sons were Kelill, who was Abbot of Holyfell, and Reinn and Kodran and Styrmir; their daughter was Thorvor, whom Skeggi, Bard's son, had for wife, and from whom is come the stock of the Shaw-men. Ospak was the name of the son of Bolli and Thordis. The daughter of Ospak was Gudrun, whom Thorarin, Brand's son, had to wife. Their son was Brand, who founded the benefice of Housefell. Gellir, Thorleik's son, took to him a wife, and married Valgerd, daughter of Thorgils Arison of Reekness. Gellir went abroad, and took service with King Magnus the Good, and had given him by the king twelve ounces of gold and many goods besides. The sons of Gellir were Thorkell and Thorgils, and a son of Thorgils was Ari the "Deep-in-lore." The son of Ari was named Thorgils, and his son was Ari the Strong. Now Gudrun began to grow very old, and lived in such sorrow and grief as has lately been told. She was the first nun and recluse in Iceland, and by all folk it is said that Gudrun was the noblest of women of equal birth with her in this land. It is told how once upon a time Bolli came to Holyfell, for Gudrun was always very pleased when he came to see her, and how he sat by his mother for a long time, and they talked of many things. ThenBolli said, "Will you tell me, mother, what I want very much to know? Who is the man you have loved the most?" Gudrun answered, "Thorkell was the mightiest man and the greatest chief, but no man was more shapely or better endowed all round than Bolli. Thord, son of Ingun, was the wisest of them all, and the greatest lawyer; Thorvald I take no account of." Then said Bolli, "I clearly understand that what you tell me shows how each of your husbands was endowed, but you have not told me yet whom you loved the best. Now there is no need for you to keep that hidden any longer." Gudrun answered, "You press me hard, my son, for this, but if I must needs tell it to any one, you are the one I should first choose thereto." Bolli bade her do so. Then Gudrun said, "To him I was worst whom I loved best." "Now," answered Bolli, "I think the whole truth is told," and said she had done well to tell him what he so much had yearned to know. Gudrun grew to be a very old woman, and some say she lost her sight. Gudrun died at Holyfell, and there she rests. Gellir, Thorkell's son, lived at Holyfell to old age, and many things of much account are told of him; he also comes into many Sagas, though but little be told of him here. He built a church at Holyfell, a very stately one, as Arnor, the Earls' poet, says in the funeral song which he wrote about Gellir, wherein he uses clear words about that matter. When Gellir was somewhat sunk into his latter age, he prepared himself for a journey away from Iceland.

He went to Norway, but did not stay there long, and then left straightway that land and "walked" south to Rome to "see the holy apostle Peter." He was very long over this journey; and then journeying from the south he came into Denmark, and there he fell ill and lay in bed a very long time, and received all the last rites of the church, whereupon he died, and he rests at Roskild. Gellir had taken Skofnung with him, the sword that had been taken out of the barrow of Holy Kraki, and never after could it be got back. When the death of Gellir was known in Iceland, Thorkell, his son, took over his father's inheritance at Holyfell. Thorgils, another of Gellir's sons, was drowned in Broadfirth at an early age, with all hands on board. Thorkell Gellirson was a most learned man, and was said to be of all men the best stocked of lore. Here is the end of the Saga of the men of Salmon-river-Dale.

THE STORY OF
Thórðr Hreða

CHAPTER 1

Thórðr hight a man, who was the son of Hörða-Kári, a man of great reputation; he was chief over the counties which lay next to his. He was Lord by title, but superior to Earls in many things. He had a noble wife, by whom he had three sons and one daughter. The eldest son was called Steingrímrr, the second Klyppr, the third Eyjúlfr, and the daughter Sigríðr. All the bairns were promising, but Klyppr was the foremost of his brothers. They were all mighty men, wonderfully fine and strong fellows, as their forefathers had been. Their sister Sigríðr was the finest of women, dressy and high-minded. She was more skilful than any of her mates that grew up with her. When the brothers were nearly of age, their father took illness and died, and his burial was magnificent according to ancient custom. And when the funeral feast was over (drunk), the wife of Thórðr gave birth to a fine boy; to him a name was given, and, according to the wife's wishes, was called Thórðr after his father, as she thought he would become a great man, if he was like his kinsmen. And when Thórðr grew up, he was mighty and strong, promising, hard and furious against all whom he thought little of, but friendly towards the people; he was munificent with his money, gentle of conversation, and a steadfast friend; he was a great jovial man, the most nimble at sports, could swim better than any one, and was a good poet At the time when this happened, the sons of Gunnhildr reigned over Norway; and when Thórðr grew up, he wished to become one of the men of King Gamli, the son of Gunnhildr, who of all men was the most beloved King of Norway, with the exception of Hákon Aðalsteinsfóstri. Thórðr was twelve years of age when he went to the Court of King Gamli, and the King considered him a great man in everything he had to do; and he was with the King for three winters. He always went before the King in every danger and peril, when the King was engaged in warfare, wherefore he received great honour and fame, for which he was widely known. When Thórðr had stayed three winters with King Gamli, he said to the King that he wished to seek his possessions. The King replied: "You have given us good assistance, and you will become a great man." The King unfastened his sword (sabre), which he was wont to carry daily, and said to Thórðr, "Here is a sword, which I wish to give to you, and I think good luck will attend it, and with it shall my friendship follow." Thórðr thanked him for this honour and everything else which he had shown him. The King said: "This I beg of you, that you give it to no one, and never part with it, except you have to redeem your own head; and it is not unlikely that you will want to do that." Then Thórðr answers: "I intend, my Lord, not to stay for a long time away from you, while I have the chance to accompany you." The King replies: "That will not be so; for we shall never see one another, now that we part." Thórðr became silent at the King's words, and answered nought; then he took leave of the King, went home to his possessions, and his relatives were glad to see him. Klyppr, his brother, had taken possession of all their property, and had become a chief over all the counties over which his father had ruled; he was also a Lord by title. But short time after Thórðr went away from King Gamli, King Hákon the Good and King Gamli had a fight, and in that battle fell King Gamli. which is narrated in the Sagas of the Kings of Norway.

King Sigurðr "Slefa," the son of Gunnhildr, was a very licentious man; he had induced Alöf, the daughter of Skeggi of Yrjum, to leave her husband the Lord Klyppr, the son of Thórðr (the elder). Thórðr did often invite (egg) his brother Klyppr to seek a revenge, and one day Thórðr came to speak with his brother, and said: "How is this? Are you not going to drive off your hands the disgrace which lies on your shoulders with regard to King Sigurðr, and become such a wonder as to have every one's reproof, and will never be looked upon as such a man as your former kinsmen were, if you can bear such an insult on the part of King Sigurðr, without seeking revenge? Although we have to contend with great difference as regards strength, yet it is better to die with honour, if that should be our fate, than to suffer such a disgrace without doing anything at all. I offer myself to go with you, as well as all my brothers, rather than endure this any longer without any revenge, however it may fare." Then answers Klyppr: "True it is, brother, what thou sayest, that it was fully necessary to revenge this disgrace, if an opportunity should offer; and I am heartily willing to take revenge upon him for the insult." After this interview, all the brothers betake themselves from home with a large troop of men in the direction of the Uplands, where they heard that King Sigurðr was at a banquet. And when they arrive at the house in which the King was present and sat at table, the brothers arrange their men for entering, and Thórðr said that the man who was the last to enter should be the first to go out. Klyppr was to be the first to enter, next to him Thórðr, then Steingrímrr, then Eyjúlfr, and then the others according to arrangement. They were all fully armed with helms, shields, and drawn swords. And when Lord Klyppr came before King Sigurðr, he drew his sword and struck the King on the head, and split it open right down to the shoulders; the King then fell dead on to the table. After this the brothers retire farther out into the hall, and in the same moment Thórðr heard a crash behind him, and observed that his brother Klyppr had been struck a death-blow. The man who did this was called Hróaldr, the son of Ögmundr, the son of Hörda-Kári; he was a near relative of the sons of Thórðr; he was waiting at the King's table when they entered, wherefore they did not notice him; another man did he kill, who was hight Ögmundr, and he was the son of Valþjófr; and when Thórðr observes the fall of his brother, he struck at Hróaldr and split him asunder above the hips. Then the men sprang up all about the hall, drew their swords, and attacked the brothers furiously, but they defended themselves well and manly. Þórðr made good use of the sword which King Gamli had presented him with, and became slayer of many before he could get out. It came to pass here as it always does, that, when one suddenly loses his chief, most of the men become disorderly, when they should follow their enemies, and so it was here, and the brothers returned to their homes. King Haraldr quickly heard this news -- the fall of his brother, King Sigurðr -- and intends to send men against the brothers for the purpose of killing them. At that time the King was north in the land, wherefore it took longer time than otherwise would have been the case; he summoned "Þing," and had the brothers outlawed from the whole of Norway, but took possession of their property.

CHAPTER 2

Now there is to be said, that the brothers came home and related the fall of King Sigurðr and their brother Klyppr. It now seemed to the brothers that they would not be able to remain in the land on account of the power of King Haraldr and Gunnhildr. Their kinsmen and friends then wished to sell their estates for ready money, and added that Þórðr should go in search for Iceland, whither many noble men had gone, who had to flee from the country before the Kings of Norway. Then Þórðr answers: "Not had I intended to flee from my property (go in exile), but as there are many noble men, who have been content with settling in Iceland, then it may be that something similar may be my fate." After this Þórðr made himself ready for a journey to Iceland, and with him his brothers Steingrímr and Eyjulfr and his sister Sigríðr. They had with them great many chattels. He had nineteen men on board his ship. He then proceeded to sea, and this was in the early summer. They were a month at sea, and touched the Vestman Islands; thence they sailed to the west coast of the land, and to the north beyond the Strands ; they sailed into the bay, and kept themselves nearer to the north coast. They then put into one firth and took there land about the beginning of winter. Soon people came to them, and they asked them the name of the firth they had come to. They were informed that they had come to Miðfjörðr. They landed in the mouth of Miðfjörðr, and at that time Miðfjörðr was completely peopled. Skeggi, who was called Miðfjarðar-Skeggi, dwelt at Reykir. He was the son of Skinna-Bjöm. The reason for him being called Skinna-Björn was, that he was wont to sail on mercantile business to the East, and bring thence grey skins (grey fur), beaver-skins, and sable-fur. Skeggi was a great hero and fighter in single combats. He had been long journeying as viking, and once he came to Denmark, and went to Hleiðr, where the mound of King Hrólfr ("the Crow") was, broke into the mound and took away the sword of King Hrólfr, "Sköfnungr," which is the best sword ever came to Iceland. He also took the axe, which Hjalti ("the Stout-hearted") had owned, but he could not get Laufi from Böðvar "bjarki," for he could in no way bend his arms. From that time Skeggi carried the sword "Sköfnungr." Miðfjarðar-Skeggi was great chief and wealthy. He had mighty kinsmen. All the inhabitants of Miðfjörðr had chosen him as their chief. His father, Björn, had taken possession of the whole of Miðfjörðr before him. He was a "goðarð" man (temple priest) in Miðfjörðr, and in many other places. Eyjúlfr hight a good farmer; he dwelt at Ós, and was a rich man.

There was another farmer, named Thorkell; he dwelt at a farm named Sandar, on the west side of the firth, opposite Ós. He was a mean man, but rich in money, and a friend of Skeggi of Reykir. Thorkell had offered Skeggi to bring up one of his children, and when Thórðr came to Miðfjörðr, Eiðr, the son of Skeggi, was being brought up at Sandar. Eyjúlfr, the farmer from Ós, was the first man who came to the chapmen and had a talk with them. Thórðr asked how it was the farmers were so slow in coming to the ship. Eyjúlfr said it was a custom, that Skeggi, as a rule, came first to the ship, and took that of the goods which he liked. Also did he receive those of the chapmen he liked for wintering at his house. Thórðr said that his pride was great, "but, on the contrary, I am told, that it is the custom of the inhabitants of the land to visit the chapmen, who have newly arrived from sea to inquire after news." Eyjúlfr answered: "Let us go and see Skeggi, and he will receive well such a man as thou art." Thórðr said: "On board my ship I intend to stay, and await there what will happen." Then quoth Eyjúfr: "I shall go and see Skeggi, and inform him of the arrival of the ship." Thórðr answers: Can you not do as you like?" and then they parted. Eyjulfr went to Reykir to meet Skeggi, and told him of the ship's arrival, also who the master was. Skeggi said that he knew well Thórðr and his parents; said that he was a serviceable man, and never had a more noble or a better person come to this land, and praised him highly. Eyjulfr asked Skeggi to ride down to the ship and choose those of the chapmen whom he liked to invite home. Skeggi answered: "It always pains me that you show me honour in all things, but once will I show you that honour, to elect those of the chapmen you like, for none of this crew shall I receive in my home. But this I advise you, that you give Thórðr no promise, unless you mean keeping it, for he thinks little of making one or another bow to the earth, if he takes that into his head." Then they parted, and Eyjulfr rode to the ship, saw the master, and told Thórðr of the interview with Skeggi. Thórðr said: "You fare well (behave generously), but it seems to me from this, that Skeggi intends picking quarrel with me; and I fancy therefore, it is more likely that I should show him a little deference." Eyjulfr said: "That would be my wish, that we should visit Skeggi." Thórðr answered: "I shall not go at all; but as Skeggi will receive no chapman to sit by his side this winter, then let him keep his pride to himself as long as he likes." Eyjúlfr invited Thórðr to stay with him for the winter at Ós, but asked him to get an abode for the other chapmen round the firth. Thórðr thanked him for his invitation, but said that he would not take up his abode with him. Thórðr asked if Eyjulfr would let his farm during the winter, and that Eyjulfr did, but betook himself to Torfastaðir, for there he possessed another farm; but Thórðr took the farm at Ós. Thereafter he had the whole cargo brought home, and the ship drawn on shore. With Thórðr went home his brothers and sister and all the crew, and dwelt there quiet during the winter. Skeggi behaved as if nothing had happened, but he and Thórðr did not speak when they met. Skeggi did not make as if he knew about the agreement or action of Thórðr and Eyjulfr. Thórðr had many men, and was himself a very jovial one, and so were his brothers. Thórðr soon became beloved by the people of his district. Skeggi did not like that much, and thought likely that he would wish to become chief over Miðfjörðr, wherefore he envied Thórðr, for he was hard-tempered, and could not endure that others should be held in the same honour as himself. Thórðr had sports during the winter, and the brothers, as well as the men from Baer, took part in them, but none equalled Thórðr, neither in agility nor in strength. Thórðr was a great active man, as well as a fine handicraftsman.

During the winter Thórðr built a boat down by the mouth of Miðfjörðr, where he, as a rule, spent his days. His intention was, that this boat should go in the spring to the Strands for fishing. Thus time lasted to Yule, and towards Yule Skeggi sent a man to Thorkell of Sandar, and invited him and his wife to a Yule feast; he also asked, that the boy Eiðr might accompany them; he was then young, but still grown pretty strong. They prepared themselves to go away from Sandar on the day before Yule, and with them the boy Eiðr. Such was the weather that thaw had set in with rain, and the river of Miðfjörðr impassable. The ice on the river began to thaw higher up, but down by the firth it was passable in a boat, and when Thorkell put forward the boat, Thórðr addressed him, saying, "Man! the river is impassable." Thorkell answers, "Look after your work, I will see to my journey." Thorkell put the boat into the river, and the three were now on board; when they had got fairly out, the ice began to thaw very quickly, so they got on slowly. They drifted down the river before the ice and the current, which ended in the capsizing of the boat. They had a ducking, and were nearly drowned; but there was a longer life in store for them, and Thorkell got them on the keel of the boat. The boat now drifted towards the sea, and opposite where Thórðr was at work, and his brother Steingrímrr with him. Then Thorkell called to Thórðr and asked him for help, but answers Thórðr: "I will look after my work, you attend to your journey." Steingrímrr said, "Do well, my brother, and save the people, for now their lives are in danger, and show thy skill." Then Thórðr casts off the outer clothes, throws himself into the water, and swims out to the boat; he had to break the ice, and push it away from him in all directions. And when he reached the boat, he first took the boy Eiðr, put him between his shoulders, fastened him with a string, and swam with him on shore: and asked his brother, Steingrímrr, to help the boy, that he might get warm. Thereupon he swam to the boat again, took the wife of Thorkell, who had become much exhausted, and brought her to land. For the third time he swims out to the boat, and brings Thorkell to land, who was nearly dead from the cold. Steingrímrr asked, "Why did you bring the boy first?" Thórðr says: "Therefore did I bring Eiðr first, because my mind tells me, that to me this youth will be of much use, and he will save my life. But therefore did I bring Thorkell last, thinking he would best stand the cold, and again I thought, that in him was the least loss even if he had perished." Thereupon changes Thorkell his clothes, and recovered his strength as well as his wife. After this they went to Reykir, but Thórðr invited Eiðr home with him to Ós. Eiðr says that he will willingly accept the invitation, and stayed there for a long time. But now there is to be related, that Thorkell came to Reykir and spoke of his unfortunate journey. Skeggi says, that a most unfortunate journey had he had, and moreover left my son with that man, who is the most violent man; he added, that his mind told him, time would come when one would give a great deal that Eiðr had never come to Thórðr. But when Yule had passed, Thorkell went home, and on his way called at Ós, and asked Eiðr to go with him. Eiðr answers: "I shall not go with thee, and you shall not again try to destroy my life." "I would no more have caused your death than I would my own," answered Thorkell; went home, and is now out of the Saga.

CHAPTER 3

Eiðr was a constant faithful follower of Thórðr, and so was Thórðr very yielding to him. Thórðr was mostly engaged in building the boat, and the boy Eiðr with him. Thórðr had always with him the sword which Gamli gave him, and so it was this time. Eiðr took up the sword and played with it. Thórðr saw this, and said: "Do you like the sword, my foster-son?" He answered, "Very well." Thórðr said: "Then I will give you the sword." Eiðr answered: "Never shall I be able to reward you for such a valuable gift, but friendship will I give you, my foster-father, if it be thought of little worth." Thórðr replied: "Accept my thanks for this, my foster-son, and your reward will be both often and great." Thereupon went they home, and Eiðr showed the sword to all the inmates, and was greatly pleased with it. A short time after went Eiðr to Reykir, to see his father. Skeggi received him coolly, and asked: "Why did you think the fostering-place at Thórðr was better than the one I got you at Thorkell?" Eiðr replied: "Totally is the place different in all respects; for Thórðr is a great man, and one can gain some good from him, but Thorkell is both a mean man and a fool; he would have killed me through his foolishness and want of foresight, but Thórðr saved my life, and he has also given me the most valuable gift." "Through the care of Thorkell is it, that you hold the life; he did not wish any more for your death than he did for his own or his wife's; but I will look at this costly thing which you praise so highly, that I may see if I think it of much worth." Eiðr showed him the sword. Skeggi drew it out, liked it very much, and said: "That is evident, that this valuable thing has belonged to some nobleman, and it is a great jewel; and I do not believe that he has given you such a valuable and rare thing." Eiðr said: "It seems to me then unlikely, that you would assist me as to rewards, as you do not believe that he has given it me." Skeggi said: "Gladly wish I, that you had not accepted this costly gift." Eiðr answered: "As to this we have to differ." After this Eiðr went home, and the parting of father and son this time was anything but friendly. Thórðr received his foster-son well, and inquired as to the conversation which took place between father and son. Eiðr explained everything which had passed. Thórðr answered: "This I expected, and very much wishes your father to show me enmity; and this is my opinion that some further difficulties will spring up between me and your father and his kinsmen, and it is not easily foreseen to what end they will come; so that you will often, with great danger, be obliged to go between." Eiðr answered: "Pleased should I be, if I could do some good between you."

There was a man called Ásbjörn; he was the son of Thorstein "the White" and Sigríðr, the sister of Miðfjarðar-Skeggi. He came out to Iceland this summer, and landed at Blönduós in Langidalr. When Skeggi ascertained the arrival of his kinsman, he rode down to the ship, receives him well, and invites him to go home with him, and take as many men with him as he liked. Ásbjörn accepted this invitation, landed his ship, and went home to Reykir, and two men with him. Ásbjörn was a very tall man, handsome, and highly esteemed. He was so strong, that his equal could scarcely be found. He was a cheery man, and went mostly to a bath for pleasure's sake. One day went he and Skeggi to bathe, as their wont was, and lay by the side of the bath in conversation. Sigríðr of Ós went the same day to a hot spring with her linen, and was making herself ready to go home. She went by where they lay. Ásbjörn was a very pompous man with

288

regard to dress. They saw where the woman went. She had on a red kirtle (gown) and a blue cloak. The woman was both handsome and tall, and altogether very smart. Ásbjörn raised himself up on his elbow, and looked at her over his shoulder. Then Ásbjörn asked who this handsome woman was: "It seems to me possible that this woman will find my love." Skeggi answered: "Her name is Sigríðr, and she is the daughter of Thórðr, the son of Hörða-Kári; but this advice I give you, that you have nothing to do with her." Ásbjörn asked, "Why should that be so?" Skeggi answered: "Her brothers are full of fierceness, and very unruly." Ásbjörn replied, "I had thought to be my own adviser before every man here in this land." Skeggi said, "It will show itself, whether you need no help before you part, if you should take any more liberty with them than they like." After this they went home.

Now there is to be said, that Sigríðr came home to Ós. Her brother Thórðr went to meet her. He said: "Why are you so pale, my sister? It seems as if Ásbjörn 'Veisugalti,' has made you change colour, but many things will pass between us before he gets you for his wife." So the winter passed; all was quiet. Ásbjörn never mentioned Sigríðr. There was ball-playing on the ice in Miðfjörðr between Reykir and Ós, for the firth was early covered with ice. At this time there were many vigorous men in Miðfjörðr. Thórðr and Ásbjörn, the kinsman of Skeggi, were the most vigorous of those who took part in the sports. Skeggi did not take part in the sports, as he was getting old, but was quite strong to use his weapon. He therefore looked on, and enjoyed himself much. He and Thórðr never spoke together, and much coolness seemed to exist between them. It happened one day that Thórðr and Ásbjörn took part in the sports, and were to play together, and once Thórðr threw Ásbjörn on the ice with a huge thump. "There fell 'Veisugalti,'" said Thórðr, but he made no reply. Another time, when they had to go together, Ásbjörn seized Thórðr with such strength that he fell on his knees. "And there fell the man with the maiden-cheek," said Ásbjörn, "and you ought scarcely to take part in sports with vigorous men." Thórðr said: "That you will first see, 'Veisugalti,' when we try weapons, which of us has to look up when we leave off that sport." Ásbjörn said he was quite ready, and seized his weapons. People went then between them, and they were parted. Now the winter passes. Ásbjörn rode to his ship in the spring, and prepared it ready for sea. Skeggi accompanied Ásbjörn to the ship with many men, because he thought there was nothing bad that one could not expect from Thórðr. Thórðr stayed at home and pretended to know nothing. Ásbjörn said to Skeggi: "The case is this, kinsman, that I am thinking of marrying, and I should like to be my own counsellor." Skeggi said, "Where is the woman to whom your mind mostly looks to?" Ásbjörn answered; "I will not conceal it; it is Sigríðr, the sister of Thórðr of Ós; she is the woman to whom my mind looks most forward to to get for a wife." Skeggi answered: "I do not think it likely that we shall succeed in this, and also I am unwilling to bring this case before Thórðr, on account of the coolness which has reigned between you before." Ásbjörn said that the only enmity, which had been between them, had been of little worth, and added, that he would not lose the best match on account of that, if he could obtain it. At last Skeggi promised to woo the woman on his behalf. "My advice is, that you do not give up your journey abroad on account of this." Skeggi rode home, but Ásbjörn went abroad that summer. Short time after Skeggi arrived home, there was news about that a ship had arrived in the White River in Borgarfjörðr, and when the news came, great number of people from the northern districts, both from

Miðfjörðr and other places, went to trade with the chapmen. Skeggi also prepared himself to ride to the ship with many men. And when Eiðr heard that his father intended going to the ship, he said to Thorðr: "Have you any intention of going to the ship, foster-father?" Thórðr said: "Why should I want my goods any less than other farmers? and I shall certainly go." Eiðr said: "Then I will ride with you, and hear other people's conversation, and thus acquaint myself with the market." Thórðr answered: "It will do better for our journey, if you accompany me, my foster-son, for so my mind tells me, that I shall greatly need you on this journey, if my dreams forebode anything." Eiðr said: "What did you dream, my foster-father?" Thórðr said: "I dreamt I had come to the White River in Borgar-fjörðr, and was conversing with some foreign men, especially with regard to some bargain, and in the same moment a quantity of wolves entered the shop, and I had a great disgust for them; then they turned upon me, tore my clothes, and wished to kill me, but I drew my sword, hewed one of the wolves across the middle, and the head of another. Thereupon they ran at me from all sides, but I seemed to defend myself, and became very wroth; but it seemed as if I could not foresee how it would fare with me. In the same moment a young bear leapt before me, and would defend me, and I woke up. It seems to me this dream forebodes great tidings." Eiðr said: "It is evident that this forebodes some men's evil minds towards you. Now it is my advice, that you ride from home at the same time as my father, though you do not converse together." Thórðr said: "That will I do for the sake of your request." Thórðr made himself ready, and Eiðr with him. And when Thórðr prepared himself, his sister Sigríðr said: "Brother! I wish you would buy me a cloak, a very choice one." Thórðr answered: "That will I do, but it strikes me it will be dear enough before the end."

CHAPTER 4

Thórðr and Eiðr rode to the ship at the same time as Skeggi, for Eiðr requested Thórðr to do so. And when they arrived at the ship, they both threw their tent over one booth.

A man by the name of Jón is now introduced into the Saga. He lived at Hvassafelli in Norðrárdalr. He was a wealthy man, unforbearing and much disliked. Guðrún was his wife's name. She was very gaudy in dress, and ambitious. Her brother hight Auðúlfr: Glúmr hight their father. He lived at Skarðshamrar. They intended to ride to the ship at the same time Thórðr and Skeggi were there. And as they were riding from home Guðrún said to her husband, that he ought to buy her a fine mantle, for she was a dressy woman. This the husband promised. They now continue their journey until they come to Hvítárvellir. Then was the market at the fullest. They, Jón and Auðúlfr, went through the booths. They came into a booth of a man whose name was Thórir ("the Rich"), and asked for a cloak if it could be had. He said that he had a cloak, "but, farmer, you will think it dear." Jón answered: "Let us hear what there is to pay." The Eastman valued the cloak, but Jón thought it too dear. Auðúlfr would that he should buy the cloak, and offered him some of his money. Jón went away, and when they came out, Auðúlfr egged him on to buy the cloak, as he had promised his sister to do so. "Why should you not have your own will?"

said Jón, "and we will go home for the price." But this caused some delay. It is said that Thórðr and Eiðr went through the booths demanding goods for purchase. They came into the booth of Thórir ("the Rich") and wished to buy the cloak. Thórir says that he knows Thórðr and his parents, "so I will not put any price on it for you, but wish that you would accept it." Thórðr thanked him, and said: "This I will accept, and let the cloak lie here while I go and fetch its worth." "I do wish," says Thórir, "that you had it with you." "That is of no consequence," says Thórðr; and he and Eiðr went to fetch its worth. When Thórðr had gone, Jón and Auðúlfr entered the booth, and asked the Eastman to hand them over the cloak. He said the cloak was sold, "for you would not give as much for it as I valued it." Jón said that he would have it; and in the same moment Thórðr and Eiðr came into the booth with the price for it. Thórðr seized the cloak, but Auðúlfr drew his sword, and was going to smite Thórðr. Jón also ran against Thórðr and was going to deal him a blow, but Thórðr immediately drew his sword, turned against Auðúlfr, and smote him in the head, and he fell there and then dead on the floor. Eiðr ran before Thórðr, when he saw Jón's outrage, and warded off the blow with the shield, but took the cloak under his hand. This saw Thórðr, and smote at Jón with the sword; the blow hit him in the middle and cut him in two above the hips. Jón's and Auðúlfr's companions then attacked him, but Thórðr retreated out of the booth, jumped on a pile of rafters, wherefrom he defended himself well and bravely. The men of the district and those from Borgarfjörðr flocked to the place and wished to revenge the death of Jón and Auðúlfr, but Eiðr went to see his father, and asked him with his men to come and help Thórðr. Skeggi says: "What has Thórðr been doing that he is not capable to help himself?" Eiðr answered: "He has killed two men." "Who are they?" says Skeggi. "Auðúlfr and Jón," says Eiðr. "What was the reason?" says Skeggi. Eiðr says: "They would rob him of a cloak which he had bought; and one of the two would have killed him, had I not defended him. Do not let the coolness which has reigned between you go so far, that you take more notice of that than of the fact that he is from the same district as yourself; he is also my life's saviour and foster-father." Skeggi did not answer. Thereupon Eiðr went away, and to the place where they attacked Thórðr, and drew his sword. And when Thórðr saw Eiðr, his foster-son, he said: "Do not endanger thy life for my sake." But when Eiðr had gone out of the tent, Skeggi stood up and said: "The pig is sure to squeal, if the sow be killed." Thereupon he took the sword, Sköfnungr, and went to the place where they were still attacking Thórðr; but he had defended himself so bravely, that they had not been able to inflict a wound upon him, but he had wounded many. When Skeggi came, he went on so furiously, that those who had attacked Thórðr had to retreat. Thereupon Skeggi effected a settlement reconciliation between them; he was to be the sole judge in the whole affair, and he there and then gave his verdict. Thórðr was to pay two hundred of silvers for the murder of Jón, but Auðúlfr should fall unholy because of his outrage and plot against the life of Thórðr. Those who had been wounded should carry their wounds without reward, for the sake of their plot against him and attack on him, and thus they parted. When Skeggi was ready, he rode home. At the same time Thórðr rode to the north and Eiðr went with him, but he and Skeggi had no conversation during the whole of the journey. They ride on until they come to the river Miðfjarðará. Then Skeggi said: "Here we will alight, for I have something to say to you, Thórðr," and so they did. Then said Skeggi: "Ásbjörn, my kinsman, asked me to make a proposal on his behalf, and wished me to woo your sister, Sigríðr, for him; and I should now like to know what your answer might be in this case." Thórðr says: "Little friendship exists between me and Ásbjörn. Neither have you been much of a friend hitherto, and never came it into my mind that you would seek here an alliance for your kinsman; well do I know that Ásbjörn is a highborn man, rich and a strong fellow, but I do not know how my brothers or herself will like this bargain." Skeggi answers: "Therefore did I mention the case to you, rather than to your brothers, because I know that they will follow your advice, both as regards this and other matters." Thórðr answers: "Most likely will they act according to my will, but to no man shall I give her without her sanction; but I expect she will not go contrary to my advice." Then says Eiðr: "I wish you would give my father a satisfactory answer as regards this wooing, and value highly his recommendation." Thórðr says: "So it shall be; for Skeggi gave me a great assistance in this journey, and I will recognise it; for I will come to terms with you, Skeggi, as to the courting of Sigríðr. She shall sit in troth for three winters, and if Ásbjörn does not arrive within these three winters, then this agreement is of no worth, but should he come to the country before, then he has a right to the marriage of Sigríðr." Skeggi consented to this. Thereupon held Thórðr out his hand, and Skeggi took it, thus concluding the bargain. Witnesses were then taken as to this promise. Then said Skeggi: "Now have you fared well, Thórðr! but lucky was it that your sister got the cloak rather than the wife of Jón. It seems to me very likely that the men of Borgarfjörðr will remember what kind of meeting yours was. I will therefore lengthen your name, and call you Thórðr Hreða ('the Terror')." Thórðr said: "I am well pleased if they have some memory of my coming there, and then I have no dislike to the name, but methinks seldom will this district be without a Terror." After this they rode home. When Thórðr came home he was well received ; he was asked what news there was. He told everything in the clearest manner. Thereupon he asked his brothers and sister to have a talk with him, and told them of his promise. Sigríðr answered: "It seems to me, brother, that you have acted rather rashly as regards the promise of marriage on my behalf, as I was not consulted before." Thórðr answered: "This agreement shall have no further value than yourself will consent to." "This I could expect from you, and, with your foresight, I will be content in the matter." Thórðr thanked her for the answer, gave her the cloak, and told her of his quarrel with Jón and Auðúlfr. After this, Thórðr kept at home quiet, and Eiðr constantly with him.

CHAPTER 5

This same summer a ship arrived in Blönduós in Langidalr. By that ship came Ormr, nephew of Skeggi and brother of Ásbjörn. But when Skeggi hears of the arrival of his kinsman, he rides to the ship, and invites Ormr home to stay the winter over, and Ormr went home with him. Ormr was this kind of a man, that he was stronger than any other, and a most valiant man; he was full of fierceness, considered no one his equal, was a great fighter in single combats, and full of injustice. It happened one day when Ormr went to the Springs, that Sigríðr from Ós was there, and another woman with her. He thought much of her, and inquired who she was. He was told her name and her kin. He spoke to Skeggi and said: "The fact of the matter is this, that I wish you to woo Sigríðr of Ós on my behalf." Skeggi answered: "This woman I will not woo for you, but any other woman you may wish I will propose to for you." Ormr said: "Either must you woo Sigríðr or no one else." Skeggi answered: "Why should I woo on your behalf your brother's betrothed?" Ormr said: "I don't care, if she is my brother's betrothed, but if you do not woo her for me there will be some quarrel in the district, for then I shall beguile her, and the brothers will hinder that, but I shall not mind it, and so you will have to assist in the case." Then Skeggi said: "Sigríðr will not allow herself to be beguiled by you, and you are much conceited to think you can get her so dishonourably, and this will be to your shame, for a heavier load has Thórðr overturned, when he and his brothers killed King Sigurðr "Slefa," the son of Gunnhildr." Ormr said: "That will take its own course; I shall chance it, if you will not woo her on my behalf." Skeggi answered: "Rather will I undertake this task than some difficulties should be caused by it; and I feel sure you will be discontented whatever the answer may be." Eiðr got to know this, as he was on a visit at his father's at Reykir. Skeggi and Eiðr (father and son) send a word to Thórðr, asking him to come to Reykir. Thórðr went, and his brothers with him. Skeggi greets Thórðr gladly. He received his greeting well, and asked, what was the meaning of his sending for him. Skeggi says: "That his kinsman, Ormr, wished to marry his sister Sigríðr." Thórðr says: "This is a strange negotiation on your part, for it seems to me that your kinsman, Ormr, is more possessed of wrath and foolishness than of luck, and it is not unlikely that it will soon be found to be so; or does he not know that the woman is betrothed to his brother?" Skeggi said: "Ormr is not at home, he has gone to the ship in Langidalr." Eiðr said: "That would I, my foster-father, that you could come to some terms for the sake of my father's pleading." "So it shall be as you wish," said Thórðr; "I will come to terms on account of your asking and the pleading of Skeggi; but none should I have come to if Ormr himself had wooed the woman." "This answer will I give you, Skeggi, as regards this case, that I shall break nothing which I have promised Ásbjörn. I will that Ormr go abroad this summer and stay for two winters, but that he may expect to get the match if Ásbjörn did not return." Skeggi thought the answer very good, and they had witnesses as to this transaction. Thórðr and Eiðr rode home to Ós. Sigríðr gave little heed to this. Now, time passed until Ormr came home after having prepared his ship for sailing. Ormr asked what the result was with regard to the wooing of the woman. Skeggi told him all. Ormr thought that Skeggi had pushed this matter very lightly. Skeggi asked him to value the transaction as he pleased. Ormr requested him to have no thanks for the result, and became very angry; he said he should never care whether Thórðr liked it well or not, and that she should be his mistress. Skeggi said that he was a wonderfully unwise man to talk in such way. Ormr had not been at home for a few nights before he went to Ós, and began conversing with Sigríðr. She asked him not to do it, and said Thórðr would not care for it, adding: "You will soon find the mistake out if you do not stop it." Ormr said that in no way should he be unprepared against Thórðr, whatsoever they might try. She said: "You will find that out, if you frequent your visits hither; you must also expect, that I shall pay no attention to it as long as I hear nothing of your brother

Ásbjörn." They broke off the conversation. Thórðr was building a boat down by the mouth of the river, which he intended to send to the Strands for fish, and he was going with the boat himself. Ormr came for three successive days to Ós, and then Thórðr spoke to him, saying: "I request you, Ormr, not to frequent your

293

visits hither to my dislike or to my sister's disgrace." To this Ormr gave a crossgrained answer, saying, that hitherto he had taken his own counsel as to his journeyings despite of any man; and said he rather thought that so this time too the matter would have to stand. Thórðr said that they would not be likely both to stand upright, if he came there for the fourth time. Ormr left off his visits for several nights. Now Thórðr went on busying himself about his boat, and, when he had done, one morning, as the weather was fine, he proposed to have sail out of the river. At Ós, one of the handmaids, going into the house, said that now the weather was good for the washing of linen. Now Sigríðr was wont to wash her linen in the rivulet that passed the enclosure of Ós, and now took her linen there in company with the handmaid. This morning Ormr had an inkling of Thórðr's intention to sail away, and bade his horse be fetched without Skeggi's knowledge; whereupon he took his weapons and rode to Ós, and went to the very dean where Sigríðr was. He got off his horse and tied it up, laid aside his weapons, and went to Sigríðr, setting her down beside him, laying his head in her lap, and putting her hands round his head. She asked how he could take into his head to do such a thing as this?" For this is altogether against my will; or mindest thou not the last words of threats of my brother's, which he will be only too sure to keep, so you had better see to your affairs." He answers: "I am not going to be frightened at your wraiths." Now, when Ormr came into the dean, the handmaiden started off down to the ferry, and told Thórðr that Ormr had come to Sigríðr in the dean. Thórðr bestirred himself quickly, and took his sword and his shield, and ran up to the dean, where Ormr still lay in the lap of Sigríðr. Thórðr sprang at Ormr, and said: "Stand up, thou, and defend thyself; that is a manlier deed than to crouch up to women, and to sneak behind me." Ormr started up and stretched for his sword, and in the same moment Thórðr hewed at Ormr, and through his right arm. Then Ormr drew his sword, and, as he started about, his right leg broke, whereupon Thórðr hewed the head of Ormr, and went home to Ós, and there declared the manslaughter to have been done by his hand. Sigríðr bade her brother Thórðr save himself. He smiled at her word and said: "I shall go nowhere away, for I know no roads whereby to go; I shall send a messenger to Reykir, to tell Skeggi of the manslaughter of Ormr." She answers: "What a strange man thou art, brother, for surely Skeggi will speedily come here with many men to revenge his brother, and, stalwarth as thou art, thou hast no might to withstand him in such a strife." Thórðr said that he did not care for that. Thereupon he found his shepherd, and bade him go to Reykir and tell Skeggi of the manslaughter. He said he was unwilling to do so, but that he would go if he wished it. "Tell Skeggi also that he must have his fool removed." The youth went as he was ordered, and told Skeggi of the manslaughter of Ormr, his kinsman. Skeggi became very angry. The youth said: "Thórðr asked me to tell you that you must have your fool removed." Now Skeggi gathers men together, and rides to Ós. But Thórðr was at home with nine men, and when he sees Skeggi advancing, he prepares himself for defence. His two brothers were there, and all the men were well armed. Thórðr says that in no way will he give way to Skeggi, adding, that now it would be well they tried their strength. It is to be said that this morning Eiðr had gone to his stud-horses in Linak-radalr; these Thórðr had given him. And when he heard of the murder of Ormr, he hurried home to Ós in order to be there before his father; and so he was. But when he came home he saw their preparations, took his weapons, and joined the party of Thórðr, his foster-father. Thórðr said: "I did not wish that you were at this meeting, for I shall no more spare your father than any one else if he should make an attack." Eiðr said: "By you shall I stand, my foster-father, whatever may happen, for the same fate shall be shared by us; thus I thought, when you saved my life, that I should unite yours with mine." Thórðr said: "Then you will assist me best when I need it mostly." When they had conversed together, then Skeggi came with many men. Skeggi was most wroth; and when he saw his son Eiðr one of Thórðr's party, he stopped his men. Thórðr accosted Skeggi, and bade him attack, saying: "For now I am quite ready to hew the ox, though it be fat, as it is getting rather old." Then said Skeggi: "I shall not attack, for I will not fight against Eiðr, but you will be the cause of many crimes." Thórðr said: "I think it is more because of fright than mercy, if you do not attack." Skeggi answered nought, and rode away home. Ormr was buried in a how in Miðfjarðarnes.

CHAPTER 6

Now we have to name more men in the Saga. Thorvaldr hight a man; he was a good farmer, and lived in Langidalr at a farm called Engihlíð: he was a good leech, had two sons, one named Einarr, the other Bjarni. Indriði hight a man, a comrade of Ormr; he was a great man, a better fighter than any other person, but a most noble fellow. He had come to Iceland and landed in Kolbeinsárós. When this happened he was ready for sailing. Össurr hight a man, who dwelt in Skagafjörðr, at a farm called Grund; his father was Arngrimr and his mother Jorunn, who was sister to Miðfjarðar-Skeggi. Össurr was a great chief, for he had a "goðorð" at the upper part of Skagafjörðr, which reached towards the one of the sons of Hjalti. Össurr was overbearing, disliked, bigger and stronger than most men, faithless and guileful. Thormóðr hight a man, who lived at Miklibær in Óslandshlíð; his wife was Ólöf, a fine woman and a most noble character. Thórhallr was immensely rich; a champion he was never called, but rather a coward, and altogether a most mean man; he was boasting, and the greatest bragger, and thought he knew the best advice for everything. His wife Ólöf was the daughter of Hrolleifr, who was the one who took possession of Hrolleifsdalr, situate above Sléttahlíð. She was superior to them in every respect, and had been given to him in marriage for his wealth's sake. She was young, but Thórhallr getting old. Ólöf was also a good leech. Kálfr hight a man in Hjaltadalr, who dwelt at Kálfastaðir; he was a good man of great consideration.

CHAPTER 7

Now we take up the story again at Ós, after Skeggi had had his kinsman, Ormr, buried. He sends a man north to Indriði, the fellow of Ormr, to tell him about the manslaughter, and asks him to prepare himself for a journey from the north, if he intends trying to revenge his comrade, for he had sworn brotherhood with Ormr ere they went to Iceland. Indriði made himself ready at once, and took his weapons. He had a helm and a red shield, a great barbed spear, and girt with a sharp sword. With him went two Eastmen and two Icelanders. Indriði rode from the ship as soon as he was ready. Now we begin the story again when Thórðr and Skeggi parted at Ós. Eiðr said then to Thórðr: "I do wish, my foster-father, that you would ride out of the district at present, but I will look after your farm while you are away." Thórðr said: "You shall have your way, but I do not care much for leaving my dwelling-place." "So it must be at present," said Eiðr, "for ill do I know my father's contest, if he allow you to dwell so close to him for some time to come." Then Thórðr prepared himself from home; he took his weapons with him, shield, helm, sword, and spear. His brothers made themselves ready for the journey with him. "This I will not," said Thórðr, "for I wish not to lead you into any difficulties with me, as you have had no share in the murders with me; stay, therefore, here with my foster-son, until you hear some further news." Then he mounted his horse, and bade all his people a farewell. Thereupon he rode up the mountain-ridge towards Linakradalr with one man as guide. He did not halt until he came to the farm Engihlíð, in Langidalr, late in the evening; he had a mask over the helm, and thus disguised himself. The sons of Thorvaldr thought they knew him, and told their father. "And if it be he, it means some news, that he goes disguised through the district." The farmer asked the great man his name, who said it was Thórðr. "And art thou Thórðr Terror?" He says: "So you may call me, if you like; I am the man." The farmer said: "What is the meaning of your journey?" Thórðr told him of the manslaughter of Ormr, and all the circumstances connected therewith. Thorvaldr said: "Great tidings do you bring: the manslaughter of Ormr, the kinsman of Skeggi, and many will the kinsmen be, who will make a common cause with Skeggi for a redress; but whither art thou riding now?" Thórðr said: "First I intend going north to a ship, which is at the mouth of the river Kolbeinsá, whatever may then take place." Thorvaldr offered him his son Einarr as guide, as the way was unknown to Thórðr. Einarr was to guide him north over Vatnsskarð to a place,

where the roads divided. Thórðr thanked him, drew a gold ring off his hand and gave to Thorvaldr. The good man thanked him for the gift, and asked him to call on him, if he would. "My mind tells me that during this journey you will be tried as to your skill in arms and your valour; you may expect that Össurr, the kinsman of Ormr, will waylay you, when he gets to know, for he is a great chief and an overbearing man." Thórðr said: "What the fate had destined would have to come to pass; but unless the tokens of my family fetches are greatly at fault, I am minded to think that some of Ormr's kinsmen may have to lose their life at my hand, or ever my nose has done breathing; well do you act, my good man, and have my thanks, but I will accept your friendship, should I ever be in need." Then Thórðr rode away and Einarr with him; Thórðr and Thorvaldr parted in good friendship; and now they went up Langi-dalr and north towards Vatnsskarð; when they came out of the pass they disagreed as to the road. Thórðr would ride over Grindarhólar, and he had his own will; they ride to Arnarstapi, and baited there. Thórðr said he was sleepy, and that some fetches of enemies were pursuing him.

Now we come to the story when Indriði heard of the murder of his comrade, Ormr. He rode from the ship and four men with him, two were Norse-men; was the one hight Sigurðr, the other Thorgrimr, but both most brave fellows. The other two were Icelanders; the one hight Bárðr, the other Thorfinnr. They were both great and strong, and were all well armed. They took the usual road from Skagafjörðr up to the Vatnsskarð this same day that Thórðr rode through the pass. Thórðr and his guide now saw where five men rode with weapons. Thórðr asked his guide if he knew any of them. He said: "Much am I mistaken if that is not Indriði master, the foster-brother of Ormr, with the red shield and a great barbed spear in his hand." Thórðr answers: "May be that Indriði wants to meet me, but what help can I expect from you?" He said: "I am not a fighting man, and I cannot stand to see human blood, but it is very bad should you lose your life through them." Thórðr said, that it was uncertain who that night would be the commander over Indriði's ship. Thereupon Thórðr prepared himself for defence, but said it was a great drawback that his guide was so fainthearted. Now when they met, Indriði inquired what delayed Ormr. Thórðr spake, and said that Ormr had bought for himself property in Miðfjörðrnes. Then he told him the manslaughter --" And avenge him now, for thou wilt not have a better chance of me again than thou hast now." Said Indriði: "Let it be so then." Whereupon they all set on Thórðr. Sigurðr the Eastman aimed a thrust at him with a spear, which, striking the shield, glanced off it down into the ground. He stooped after the thrust, and Thórðr, seeing that, dealt him a blow, which striking Sigurðr amidmost cut him in twain above the hips. At this nick of time Thorfinnr dealt a blow at Thórðr and struck the shield and chopped a large slice thereof. Thórðr hewed at the leg of Thorfinnr above the knee, and forthwith cut it off. Then he challenged Indriði to make a brisker onset of it, "if thou hast a will to avenge thy comrade." Indriði made a leap at Thórðr and made an eager onslaught on him, and long they fought, and the end of it was, that Indriði fell before Thórðr, all slit up with yawning wounds. Then leapt Thórðr upon the companions of Indriði, and after an assault at arms, brief and swift, Thórðr finished by slaughtering both. After this he sat him down, and bound up his wounds, for many a one he had got and great. He then went up to Indriði, and asked if he stood to healing. He answered: "Belike, if leeches be fetched." Then Thórðr took hold of Indriði, pulled him out of his blood and put him on his nag. Whereupon he mounted his own horse and rode west into Bolstaðahlíð and there gave out what had befallen, and rode on with Indriði unto Engihlíð. Thorvaldr gave a good welcome to Thórðr, and offered him every cheer that he would accept, and asked him for tidings. He told him of the fight at Arnarstapi and the death of five men. "But therefore have I here come, that I wish that you would heal Indriði, for never was there a braver man." Thorvaldr said that was no more than his duty. He received Indriði, made him a tub-bath, and cleansed his wounds, none of which, however, were deadly. Thorvaldr offered to cure Thórðr, but he would not, and said: "I am going to the north, whatever may befall me." Indriði said: "Now have I, as you know, tried to avenge Ormr's manslaughter upon Thórðr, but thus it turned out that four of my companions fell before him, and I myself deadly wounded, and the result of my fight with Thórðr ended as might be expected, for he is not like any one as regards skill in arms. But now it is my counsel, Thórðr, that you ride north to my ship and wait me there. Olöf is the name of the mistress at Miklibær; she is a great lady and one of the best of leeches; ask her to receive you, until I come to the north, and she will heal your wounds. Össurr hight a good man, who lives at Þverá in Skagafjörðr; he is a kinsman of Ormr, whom you slew, and will be sure to waylay you." Thórðr bade him have his thanks for his good advice. "But I shall go my way in spite of Össurr, as I have determined." After this Thórðr rode northward through the pass to Skagafjörðr and straight to the ship. He came to Miklibær in the evening, found the good man, who asked him his name. Thórðr gave it him. Thor-hallr said: "Often have I heard you mentioned, but what is the reason for coming here?" Thórðr told him of the meeting with Indriði, and of the manslaughters.

297

Thórhallr said that he was a great hero: "But so it seems to me as if you are severely wounded." Thórðr said the wounds were of very little consequence, but that he only had some few scratches. At this moment the good wife came out and said: "Who is this great man just come?" Thórðr gave his name. She said she had often heard him talked of, bade him dismount, and dwell there for the night. Thórðr thanked the good woman. Thórhallr said: "Dangerous seems it to me to receive this man, who has been implicated in so many slaughters, is himself greatly wounded, and needs cure; there are also great men who will pursue him and avenge Ormr; and I think that he who renders him any help neither will take care of his goods nor life." Then says the mistress: "In this matter we do not think one way; I think that one who helps him will get the best of it; I therefore invite you, Thórðr, to stay here as long as you like; I will bind up your wounds and heal you, if it be possible." Thórðr thanked her, and said he would accept the offer, if her goodman would consent thereto. Thórhallr said, once more, "As you are wont, you will have your own way; I will promise Thórðr to be faithful to him in all things, but I must hold my tongue as to his dwelling here." Then Thórðr dismounted, and the good wife took him to an outhouse, while the good man unsaddled his horse. The good woman laid out a table before Thórðr, and he commenced his meal. After that she made him a tub-bath, and cleansed his wounds, which were both many and great. Thórðr dwelt at Miklibær in concealment until he was healed from all his wounds. Then Thórðr spoke to the good man Thórhallr and his mistress: "It has now come to this, that I am healed from all my wounds, and I will no longer keep disguised, or be here longer than you wish." The mistress said: "It is my will that you be here until this case in one way or another is settled." Thórhallr said: "This I will, that Thórðr be here this winter; still I have been told that Össurr at Þverá intends having his revenge upon you." Thórðr said: "I do not mind that, but uncertain it is which of us two would be the one to lay the stone over the other's head." One day rode Thórðr to the ship, which lay out by Elinarholmr, and at the same time Indriði came there. The sailors had made the ship ready whilst Indriði was at Engihlíð. Indriði invited Thórðr to go with him abroad, but said he could not take him to Norway because of Ormr's kinsmen, who were both mighty and rich; "but I have come to terms on your behalf as to all the manslaughters done at our meeting, for I have paid weregild out of my money." Thórðr thanked him for all this, and drew a gold ring off his hand and gave him; but he did not think he would go abroad for the present. After this they parted friendly. Indriði went abroad, and is now out of the Saga. Thórðr rode to Miklibær. Thórhallr received him very well, and said: "Glad am I you did not go abroad; you have dwelt here now for some time, and I like you well; I know also that my wife wishes that you dwell here as long as you like; I am without children, and it is well to make such men one's friends, and help them with money, even if there should be a flaw in their affairs. I am neither in want of courage, nor of intellect to give good counsel if Össurr should commence hostility against you." Thórðr was pleased with this; but then said the wife: "I do not wish, Thórðr, that you should put much faith in Thórhallr's wisdom or help, but I think it would be well that you would try for once his courage should you need it." Thórðr dwells with Thórhallr during the winter.

CHAPTER 8

Ketill hight a farmer, who lived within Ósland; he had given Thórðr a good horse called Sviðgrímr, after which Sviðgrímshólar have taken their name. The farmer Kálfr, at Kálfstaðir, invited Thórðr and Thórhallr to a Yule feast, and Thórðr accepted the invitation, but before they rode from home, the housewife said to Thórðr: "I wish you to be cautious, for Össurr at Þverá is waylaying you; he has made a vow to avenge his kinsman Ormr." Then said Thórhallr: "Rely you may upon this, my goodwife, that we are not lost, neither for good plans nor valour, even if we have to try, although there is some difference in strength, and not a very small one either." The housewife said: "May your self-praise never thrive; and I advise you, Thórðr, that you do not trust to the valour of Thórhallr." Thórðr says: "He will prove himself good." Thereupon they rode to Kálfstaðir and were received well; the Yule feast was a good one. Now it is to be said about Össurr of Þverá, that he keeps spies for the purpose of finding out about Thórðr's journey, when he be likely to leave after the Yule feast. He gathers together men, and on the night before the last day in Yule he rides to Hjaltadalr, and eighteen men with him; he halted near the farm of Viðvik in a small dale called Garðshvammr. Early in the morning after Yule, Thórðr bade his men prepare themselves for returning home, and said, that many things had passed before him during the night. Goodman Kálfr asked, what he had dreamt. "I dreamt," he says, "that we comrades were riding up Hjaltadalr; and when we came nigh Viðvik, there sprang up before us eighteen wolves; one of them was the biggest and ran at me with open mouth, and attacked me and my men; methought they bit my men to death, but I thought that I killed many of the wolves, and the biggest one I thought I wounded, and then I woke." Farmer Kálfr thought this signified hostilities, and said: "This means evil-minded men," and bade him stay the day over, and let spies go down to Viðvik. Thórðr would not. "Then I will," said Kálfr, "give you some more men to increase your company.'" Thórðr said: "Never shall it get abroad that Thórðr 'Terror' is frightened at mere dreams and increases his company because that he, for this reason, dare not go through the county." They now rode from Kálfstaðir, seven altogether, Thórðr and Thórhallr and five men-servants. The farmer Kálfr gave Thórðr one of his house-carls for accompanying him; his name was Hallr, and a strong man he was. Eyvindr hight a man, who lived at Ás in Hjaltadalr; he had been at Kálfstaðir during Yule; he had given Thórðr a spear inlaid with gold, and promised him his assistance whenever he was in want of men. Eyvindr went with Thórðr; they went down the dale, and not very far, before a man met them; this man had been sent by Kálfr to spy, and he informed them, that no fewer than eighteen men were waylaying them down in Garðshvammr. Thórhallr asked who they were. He said that Össurr of Þverá was the leader. Thórðr said, that here was an opportunity to try men's alacrity and skill in arms. Thórhallr said: "It is not wise to go and meet them with so many odds against us, but I will give you my counsel." "And what may that be?" says Thórðr. Thórhallr says: "Let us turn here over to the tongue, thence into Kolbeinsdalr and then home, that they may not become aware of us." Thórðr says: "Small odds against us it seems to me, if they are eighteen and we nine; I know, that often have men fared well against such odds; and not would my kinsman Hörða-Kári have fled, even had it been more odds, and so much methinks I take after him, and other noble kinsmen of mine, as not to run away before we have tried. Now will I go and meet Össurr, whatever may happen, but thou, Thórhallr, shalt not be at this meeting; I will not reward your wife or yourself for your well-doing by having you in any life's danger." Thórhallr bade him have his own way, but said: "My enemies will say that I leave you unmanfully." Thórðr also requested Eyvindr to ride home, but he said: "Badly should I keep comradeship with a brave fellow as you, if I were to run away from you at the moment you need me most; it shall never come to pass that such shame had befallen me." Thereupon they go to the place from where they could see Össurr sit in ambush. Thórðr said: "Let us turn up the slope yonder nigh by; there is a good stronghold." They did so, and broke up some stones there. When Össurr and his men saw this, they ran up the slope. Thórðr asked: "Who are these that behave so hostile?" Össurr gave his name and said: "Is it Thórðr Terror standing there on the hill?" He answered: "That is the man, and the best for you to do is to avenge your kinsman Ormr, if there be any valour in you, for you have got odds enough against us." Össurr bade his men attack. There was a hard fight. Thórðr soon did for one of them. Thórðr and his men let stones fly at Össurr's men thick and fast, but they defended themselves with shields. Some of Össurr's men fell while the stones lasted. Thereupon Thórðr and his men ran down the slope and then commenced the slaughter. A man named Örn hewed at Thórðr while he turned his face, and hit him on the leg, for a man attacked him in the front; his name was Hafthorr, a kinsman of Össurr. But when Thórðr received the blow, he turned round, and with one hand struck the other man with his sword in the middle, and split him in twain. The second blow he dealt Hafthórr, which hit him in the shoulder and cut the arm from his side, and he fell dead to the ground. Now Thórðr had killed three men, and when Össurr saw this, he bade his men advance. He, with five men, attacked Thórðr, and the others Thórðr's men. But the result of this fight was, that Thórðr killed six men, and wounded Össurr so severely, that he was unable to fight. Of Össurr's men fell nine, and five of Thórðr's. After the fight Thórðr went up to Össurr and dragged him out of the blood, and covered him with a shield, so that ravens should not tear him, for he could in no way help himself. All Össurr's men fled. Thórðr's men were not able to pursue them, for none escaped unwounded from this meeting. Thórðr offered Össurr to have him cured, but Össurr said: "You need not offer me cure, for as soon as I have an opportunity I shall kill you."

Thórðr said he did not care for that, and sent Thórhallr over to Ás to Thorgrimr, who lived there, with a message that he wished him to come and fetch Össurr and heal him. He did so, and brought him home; he was long laid up of his wounds, but at length became healed. Cairns were made over the bodies of the men who fell. After the meeting at Garðshvammr, Thórðr went home with Thórhallr; he had received many wounds, but none deadly. Ólöf asked Thórðr about the meeting, and he told her all what had passed. She said: "These are great tidings;" she healed Thórðr; but the winter passed over without any tidings of importance.

CHAPTER 9

In the spring Thórðr rode up into the district, for a farmer, by name of Thorgrimr, had sent him word to build up his hall, as Thórðr was the most handy of men.

Thorgrimr dwelt at Flatatunga; that farm is in the upper part of Skagafjörðr. Thórðr was busy building the hall during summer, and, when he had nearly finished, a ship from the ocean arrived at Gasir in Eyjafjörðr. Thórðr said to the good man that he would ride to the ship and buy the timber that he thought was most needed. The farmer bade him have his own way, and gave him three house-carls to bring home the timber. Thereupon they went northwards, and stayed at the market as long as they wanted, and brought from the north timber on many horses. Thórðr rode with them and was fully armed. He had a helm, a shield, was girt with a sword and the good spear. They went over Hörgárdalr-heiði down Norðrárdalr, then over the river above the farm Egilsá, and down the banks. Then they see twelve men start up before them with weapons. These were Össurr and his men of Þverá. Thórðr at once jumped off his horse and put his shield before him. His companions immediately show much bravery, dismount, and draw their swords. Thórðr bade them not place themselves in any life's danger. They said that he who stood by should never thrive while he wanted men. Then said Thórðr to Össurr: "You have not left off yet to lie in wait for me; I thought our last meeting was memorable enough, but you will not fare any better than last time before we part." Össurr answered: "I told you I should never be faithful to you, if my life were spared, and this vow I shall fulfil. Let us now attack him, and avail ourselves of our greater strength." Thórðr says: "Yet have I not given up all hope. It seems to me uncertain what you could do, even if I be by myself, but more uncertain now that these men follow me." Then Thórðr ran forth against Össurr and thrust his spear through the man who stood foremost. Thórðr said: "There is one gone, and not unlikely another will follow." Össurr with six men now attack Thórðr; but four of Össurr's followers assailed the companions of Thórðr, resulting in the falling of them all. But with regard to the fight between Thórðr and Össurr, there is to be said, that Thórðr killed four of Össurr's men, and inflicted upon Össurr himself many wounds. Now we come to where the herdsman of the good man Thorgrimr sees the fight from the hill, and thinks he knows who the men are; he is also aware that Thórðr wants men; he runs, therefore, home to Flatatunga and tells the good man of the strife, and asks him to hasten to help Thórðr. The good man started off quickly, and rode up the banks with nine men. When Össurr sees the men coming, he hastens to his horse, mounts it with great difficulty, and rides away as fast as he can, until he comes to Þverá, much dissatisfied with his journey. He had lost his men, and was himself much wounded The three men of Thórðr who fell were buried on the banks where the fight took place. Thorgrimr, the farmer, asked Thórðr what news there was; and Thórðr told him. Thórðr now dwelt at Flatatunga and finished the building of the hall, which was a wonderfully strong house. (This hall stood until the time that Bishop Egill was at Holar, 1331-41.) And when Thórðr was going away, Thorgrimr, the farmer, accompanied him with nine men, and they all rode down Skagafjörðr. When Össurr saw them, he thought he had not strength enough to follow them. They continue their journey until they come to Miklibær in Óslands-hlíð. Thórhallr received him well, but the good wife better. Thorgrimr rode home, and he and Thórðr parted good friends. Thórðr became very famous all over the country. This heard Miðfjarðar-Skeggi, and pretended not to know what was going on between his kinsman Össurr and Thórðr.

Now Thórðr sat at rest nearly to Yule. It so happened that, one morning before Yule, Thórðr wished to go and see his horse, Sviðgrímr, a-grazing in the walks with four mares. Thórhallr asked Thórðr to wait, and rather go three nights later, "when I want to bring hay from my stack-yards." Thórðr bade him have his own way; "but I shall not be taken by surprise even if it comes to an encounter." Thórhallr answered: "Nay, to some odds we should not give in." Thórðr smiled at his words, and said: "So it would be, if you stood by my side." The housewife said: "May your self-praise never thrive; I thought Thórðr received little assistance from you at the last encounter you had, and badly is that woman married who has got you for a husband, for you are as boastful as you are faint-hearted." Thórðr said: "That is not so; Thórhallr is not a man of dash; he is wary, but let it come to a trial, and he will show himself the smartest of warriors." Says Thórhallr: "You need not, my good wife, be so hard spoken, for I do not intend to draw back for one, if we are equally well armed." They now left off their conversation. During their talk a vagrant was present; he took to his heels, and came in the evening to Þverá. Össurr asked him for tidings. He says he has no news to tell. "But at Miklibær in Óslandshlíð slept I last night." Össurr said: "What was the hero, Thórðr the Terror, doing?" The boy said: "Certainly can you call him a hero, considering how disgracefully you have fared before him; but nothing did I see him do, except to rivet the clinch of his sword. But this I heard Thórhallr say, that they intended fetching hay from the stack-yards within three nights." Össurr says: "How many men are they likely to muster?" The boy answers: "No more than Thórðr, and Eyvindr, and Thórhallr." "Well do you say, my boy," says Össurr. Thereupon he got twelve men to follow him, and they

all rode to Óslandshlíð. This same morning Thórðr, Eyvindr, and Thórhallr rode from home. Thórðr asked Eyvindr to take his weapons with him, and said: "That would not be in vain." He did so. They rode out to Sviðgrímshólar. Then said Thórðr: "My wish is, Thórhallr, that you stay here behind; but Eyvindr and I will go to look for the horses upon the hill." Thórhallr bade him have his own way. They went up the hill, which in many places was covered with hard snow. Össurr with his twelve men came up to the stack-yard, and made a ring around Thórhallr, drawing their weapons, and bade the rascal tell where Thórðr was. Thórhallr was awfully frightened, and sank down by the wall, and said that Thórðr had gone up the slope with another man. Össurr said: "Bad to have a thrall for a bosom-friend," and struck him with the back of his axe, so that he lay in a swoon. Then said Thórðr to Eyvindr: "There are men coming from down below up the hill, and I know them well. It is Össurr who is there, and once more wants to fight me. Now we will try to get to Skeggjahamar, and thence to Sviðgrímshólar, where there is a good stand." Eyvindr answers: "Easy it is to get upon the crag;" and so up they got; but in the same moment Össurr and his men came up to the rock Thórðr goes right out to the edge of the crag. A mass of snow lay on it, and right down to the bottom, and it was awfully steep. It was the greatest danger possible to go down; but they put their spears between their legs, and thus slid right down all the way on to Sviðgrímshólar. Össurr and his men soon were there. Thórðr said: "Much eagerness do you display in trying to have my life, Össurr; it would not be a bad job if you did suffer for it, nor shall we both of us go away from this meeting alive." Össurr said that it was just what he had intended, that Thórðr should not escape any longer. Thereupon they attacked Thórðr and Eyvindr. Thórðr threw a spear at Össurr, but one of his men in the same moment ran before him, and the spear flew right through him. One man hewed at Thórðr, but he put up his shield, and the blow hit it, so he was not wounded. Thórðr smote at this man, and dealt him a death-blow. He struck another, the blow came on the neck, and the sword ran down into the breast, and he fell dead to the ground. The third he pierced through with his sword, and Eyvindr killed the fourth. Össurr now made an attack with great vehemence, and again fell two of his men, but Eyvindr also became wounded. He was much exhausted through the loss of blood, and sat himself down, and was very weary. Then six men attacked Thórðr, but in such way did he defend himself that no one was able to inflict a wound upon him. Then Thórðr said to Össurr: "Difficult seems the attack for six men, and certainly I should not wish to be called these men's foreman, and use them only as a shield to-day; now you ought rather to make an attack and avenge your kinsman Ormr, and all the disasters you have met with at my hands." Össurr now became exceedingly enraged at the whole affair, both because of Thórðr's provoking language as well as on account of the hatred he bore him. He now runs up to him, and hews with both hands at Thórðr. The sword hit the shield, and took a good slice off it. At the same moment Thórðr hewed at Össurr, and the blow struck him below the left armpit, slicing the flesh along the spine so as, at last, to sever it from the ribs, whereupon the sword flew into the hollow of the body, and Össurr fell dead down on the spot. Össurr's companions, who were alive, ran away, and related the manslaughter of Össurr. Thórðr had Eyvindr brought home; he was much wounded, and was laid up for a long time, but was healed at last. A cairn was cast up over Össurr. Thórðr narrated at Miklibær the manslaughter of Össurr.

Olöf was much displeased with Thórhallr for having told where Thórðr was, and so much so, that she for this reason was almost going to be separated from him. Thórðr laid himself out to smooth matters between them, and said it was not to be wondered at that he should try to save his life, since from Össurr there was nothing but evil to be looked for. So time wore away past Yule tide, that no tidings came to pass, and Thórðr kept quiet at home.

CHAPTER 10

Now it is to be told that Miðfjarðar-Skeggi heard from the north the news of the fall of his kinsman Össurr, and thought that Thórðr had dealt a blow close enough to him, and filled with a mighty wrath against him, though he let it out to no man, because he did not desire that his son Eiðr, or the brothers of Thórðr, should have any misgivings as to what he was about until he should come forward openly. Secretly he had twelve of his horses stabled, with a view to riding at Thórðr after Yule. And secretly he rode away from his home at Reykir with a band of twelve men; and riding north through Vatnsskarð and down through Hegranes, and out along the country-side, they arrived, shortly before dawn of day, at Miklibær. The moon shone bright. They rapped hard at the door, and out there came a man, who asked who the new-comers might be. Skeggi told him who he was, and asked if Thórðr the Terror were there. The man answered: "What wilt thou with him?" He answered: "Ask him whether he will abide the blows of Sköfnungr outside or in." And when the message came in as to on what errand Skeggi had come there, Thórðr stood up and seized his weapons. Then spake Olöf, the housewife: "Stand up, men, to arms, and defend ye a brave man, for here are many stalwarth fellows among you, and take care that Skeggi's journey hither come to a disgraceful close." Then answered Thórhallr: "I forbid every man of my household to join in an onset on Skeggi; let no one dare to cover my house with shame in thus dealing with a chieftain of another district." Answered the housewife: "Long enough did I know that at weapons you were as worthless, as in deed you have no heart in matters of manhood." Answered Thórðr: "The head shall rule in the house, good wife," and went out to the door. Skeggi charged him to step forth, so as to have room to strike out. "I shall step out," said Thórðr, "on condition that I may accompany you to the spot where I slew your kinsman

Össurr; for in that manner your memory may serve you as to what 'family blow' I have dealt you." Skeggi said: "Be sure that your biting words will stand thee in no stead, but I deem it well enough that on the spot the revenge be wrought." Thereupon went Thórðr with them to the place where Össurr had been buried, and they walked round the cairn. Skeggi then drew his sword, Sköfnungr, and said: "On this spot no one is justified to kill Thórðr but me." Thórðr drew his sword and said: "You cannot expect, Skeggi, that I shall stand quiet before your blows while I am unbound." At this moment eighteen men ran at them, all with drawn swords. Thither had come Eiðr, Eyjulfr, and Steingrímrr, the brothers of Thórðr. Eiðr asked if Thórðr were alive. Thórðr said that death was not near him. They all dismounted. Eiðr offered his father two conditions to choose between -- either to make peace with Thórðr, so that he might ride home to Ós, and stay there in quietness, or that he (Eiðr) should help his foster-father and fight for him. Skeggi says: "Long ago should I have killed Thórðr, had I seen an opportunity, if I had not found that you value more, Eiðr, having been brought up by Thórðr, than kinship with me." Eiðr said Thórðr was deserving of it all, and that Thórðr had not committed any murders but in self-defence, with the exception of the murder of Ormr, and that was excusable. Skeggi answered: "It seems most likely that you will have your own way, for I should not fight against you." After this, Skeggi rides to Miklibær in the night, walks in with drawn sword to Thórhallr's bedstead, and bade the housewife to get up, and said that she had too long submitted to this dastard. She did so, but asked that Thórhallr might be spared. He said that this rascal had lived long enough. Thereupon he took him by the hair, dragged him to the bedside, hewed his head off, and said: "Sooner by a great deal would I sheath Sköfnungr in thine than Thórðr's blood, for in him to lose his life there would be a great loss, but in thee there is none at all, and now I have atoned Sköf-nungr for being drawn." Skeggi rode now away home to Reykir, and was by no means pleased with his journey. Thórðr and Eiðr arrived at Mik-libær just at the time Skeggi was riding away. Ólöf told them of the murder of Thórhallr. Eiðr said that less than this he could not have expected, for his father had been extremely wroth when they parted. Olöf bade them stay there as long as they wished. Eiðr said that her offer was generous, and they stayed there for a week and rested their horses. Then they prepared themselves to go away. Thórðr went to Ólöf and said: "This I beg of you, that you do not marry again within two winters, if you hear I am alive, for you are the woman who would be likely to win my affection." She answered thus: "This I will promise you, for I do not expect a better offer of marriage than this." They now ride west to Miðfjörðr and home to Ós. Eyvindr went with Thórðr, but left a man to manage his farm; because he would not leave Thórðr while he was not reconciled as to his manslaughters. Now the winter passed over, and all was quiet.

CHAPTER 11

Now it is said, that a ship came across the ocean to Blönduós; with it came Ásbjörn skipper, kinsman of Skeggi. Skeggi rides to the ship and bids Ásbjörn home with him. They went to Reykir eighteen together. Ásbjörn was not in good spirits during the winter. Thórðr the Terror dwelt at home at Ós, and had many brave fellows with him, amongst them Eiðr with eight men. Ásbjörn had been but a short time at Reykir, when he told Skeggi what his intention was with regard to the affairs between him and Thórðr, and said it was sad to have no atonement for the slaughter of his brother, Ormr, while he had strength enough for revenge. Skeggi said this was a difficult case: "because Eiðr is always on Thórðr's side, and may not clearly see which side may prevail in end in the dealings I have on hand with the men of Ós," and so they dropped their talk. This very summer a ship arrived in White River in Borgarfjörðr. Men rode to the market from the northern districts, both from Miðfjörðr and other places. Thórðr the Terror rode to the ship with eleven men, all well armed. Both his brothers, Eyjulfr and Steingrímrr, were of the company. It was said that he intended to ride up along the Borgarfjörðr on his errands, but from the south over Arnarvatnsheiði. Skeggi heard of this, and prepares himself secretly to start from home with seventeen men ; so that Eiðr did not know, intending to waylay Thórðr on his return from the south. Ásbjörn was one amongst them. They ride north over the ridge to Viðidalr, south of all habitations, then south over the heath, where the roads divide, and slants down towards Viðidalr. A man went with Skeggi, hight Thorbjörn, and was called the Paltry; he lived on some land belonging to Skeggi, and had become his client; he was very wealthy, but he was so stingy, that he grudged using his wealth himself or giving it to others, and for this reason he was called "the Paltry." He had few people by him except his wife. Eiðr had gone out to Miðfjarðarnes, to look after the house of a man named Thorbjörn, and who was called the Puny. He was the client of Thórðr the Terror, and had gone with him; he possessed a quantity of live-stock of all kinds; he lived on the northern part of Miðfjarðarnes, and his sheep went self-feeding about the woods. Thórðr had as much of his money as he wished for. Eiðr dwelt there for a few nights, and then he rode home to Ós, and ascertained what was going on. He collected some men and rode with fourteen men south on to the heath after his father. Now there is to be said that Thórðr was at the market as long as he wanted, and when he was ready, he rode up the Borgarfjörðr, and north on to the heath so far, that he could see the ambush. Thórðr said: "What men do you know here?" Eyjulfr says: "I do not know for certain, but I think most likely Skeggi." Thórðr said: "Long do they persevere lying in wait for me, but although there is a vast difference in strength, yet they shall find resistance." They then rode against them with drawn swords. Skeggi then started up and said: "Ásbjörn, my kinsman, let us now attack them, and let them feel the superiority of our power, and avenge now your brother, Ormr." "So it shall be," says Ásbjörn. Thórðr answered: "There is many a slip 'tween cup and lip."

They then attacked Thórðr and his men. Thórðr cast a spear at Skeggi and aimed it at his middle, but a man ran before him, hight Halldórr, who was a near kinsman of Skeggi. The spear hit him in the middle and went through him, and into the breast of another man, who stood behind him, and they both fell down dead. The third he struck on the neck with the sword in such a manner that the head flew off. Now the attack became the strongest. Thórðr and Skeggi fought the best part of the day in such a way, that nothing was gained on either side. Eyjúlfr and Ásbjörn fought furiously, and it could not be foreseen which of them would gain the victory; they inflicted on each other great wounds. Steingrímrr fought very boldly and killed four men. The fighting now changed thus, that Steingrímrr was against Skeggi; but Thórðr with his men fought against Skeggi's, and killed five of them. The namesakes, Thorbjörn the Paltry and Thorbjörn the Puny fought one another with great vehemence, and the result was, that both fell dead. This very moment Eiðr burst forth with his fifteen men. Eiðr there and then dismounted, went between them, and parted them. Skeggi was very wroth, rode home to Reykir and Ásbjörn with him, but they were anything but pleased with their journey. Ásbjörn was laid up for a long time from his wounds, but at last was healed. Thórðr and Eiðr rode home to Ós after the meeting. Thirteen of Skeggi's men fell in the fight, but seven of Thórðr's. Now both parties kept quiet, and the winter wore on. It happened one day, that Eiðr rode to Reykir with nine men. His father received him well. Eiðr said that he wanted to make peace. Skeggi replied, that there was time enough for that, "and stay here for the rest of the winter." Eiðr said that so it should be. There was a great deal of coolness between Eiðr and Ásbjörn during the winter. Eiðr had a suspicion, from the talk of Skeggi and Ásbjörn, that they were seeking the life of Thórðr, his foster-father: he therefore sent Thórðr word, and told him to be on the look-out.

CHAPTER 12

It so happened once during the winter, that Eiðr became aware of his father riding from home secretly and going up the district; he felt sure that his father meant some great undertaking; he therefore rode after him with nine men. They met up by Krdksmelar. Skeggi asked Eiðr where he intended going. Eiðr says: "I was minded to fill your flock, my father." Says Skeggi: "Your intention is good, my kinsman, but I am going home, because I am unwell." "May be," said Eiðr, "but I will ride to Torfastaðir, for I have an errand there." Then they parted. Ásbjörn, and six men with him, had gone the same day to the baths. Now there is to be said about Thórðr the Terror, that he woke up this same morning, and said to his brothers: "Thus my dreams have told me, that Miðfjarðar-Skeggi and Ásbjörn are seeking my life; I shall therefore leave home to-day, and cast about for some catch or another, if an opportunity should offer, for I will no longer have the two, Ásbjörn and Skeggi, over my head. Let us go seven together, my brothers and Eyvindr and three other men." Thereupon they take their weapons and ride to Reykir. Ásbjörn was going from the bath just that moment, and saw the men riding. Ásbjörn spoke to his men and said: "There goes Thórðr the Terror, and seems unruly, and I suppose he wants me; let us therefore turn up on the hill and wait there." They did so. Now Thórðr approached and commenced fighting at once; both fought most vigorously, for there was no difference in strength. Thórðr became quickly a man-slayer. Three men fell there of Ásbjorn's men, but one of Thórðr's. Then Thórðr attacked Ásbjörn and

306

inflicted several wounds upon him, and he was nearly unfit for fighting. At this very moment Skeggi appeared with his sword, Sköfnungr, drawn; he said to Ásbjörn: "Why do you not flee, poor fellow?" Ásbjörn sat himself down, for he was much exhausted because of the loss of blood. Skeggi hewed at Thórðr and hit him in the shoulder, inflicting on him a yawning wound. At the nick of time Eiðr came there with nine men; he ran at once between them, and said that they should not fight any longer: he said also that he should kill Ásbjörn, except that he alone was given permission to settle affairs. Ásbjörn said: "My errand to the country was, to fetch my betrothed; but when I heard of my brother's slaughter, I made the resolution to avenge him; but our fighting has become such, that I prefer peace with Thórðr." Thórðr answered: "I will grant my foster-son the honour of settling this case, but otherwise I do not care for any peace. The play might go on in the same way as it has gone before." The result, however, was, that they came to terms, and Eiðr was to decide as to all their charges and manslaughters. Thórðr, Asbjörn, and Skeggi all of them joined hands. Thórðr's hand swelled. Eiðr cut from the wound the flesh where the edge of the sword had touched. Now Eiðr summoned a district meeting. They were all present, Skeggi, Ásbjörn, and Thórðr. Then Eiðr made the following agreement between them. "This is my verdict," said Eiðr, "that for the manslaughter of Össurr I make two hundred silvers; the third hundred will be dropped on account of the plot against Thórðr's life and all other hostilities; all Össurr's men shall be unholy because of their attack on Thórðr; but for the manslaughter of Ormr I make two hundred silvers, and for the wound my father inflicted upon Thórðr I give a hundred silvers; thereupon shall Ásbjörn have Sigríðr, as had been decided from the first, and Thórðr shall have the wedding at his house. Here is also one hundred in silver, Ásbjörn, that I and my foster-father will give you as weregild for your kinsman." All thanked Eiðr; Skeggi was not much satisfied, but said that he should keep peace and truce. Thórðr thanked his foster-son for his verdict; "but I will not have the hundred silvers, which you awarded me; Skeggi shall not pay this money, for neither would my father, Thórðr, nor Hörða-Kári, have taken a bribe for their body, therefore I shall not do so." This won great approbation, and

Thórðr had great honour of his speech. Now Thórðr prepared for the wedding, and invites many guests. And in the evening Ei'ðr showed the guests to their seats. Skeggi occupied the first high seat on the upper bench, and Thórðr sat next to him; but opposite Skeggi, in the second high seat, sat Ásbjörn, the bridegroom, and next to him Eiðr. The bridesmaids occupied the cross-benches in the upper part of the hall. All were well entertained during the evening, and all seemed merry except Skeggi; he was rather frowning. In the evening the guests went to sleep, but in the morning went to the banquet as was customary. Skeggi was in an angry mood, and fell asleep at the table; he had put his sword, Sköfnungr, at his back. Thórðr was much displeased that Skeggi was so gloomy at the banquet; he therefore took the sword, Sköfnungr, and drew it. Eiðr said: "This is useless, my foster-father." Thórðr answers: "What has that to do with the case?" Eiðr says: "It is the nature of the sword, that something must be hewed with it each time it is drawn." Thórðr says: "That shall be tried," and ran out, and said that it should gnaw horsebones, and hewed at a mare, which stood in the homefield. Eiðr said that it was sad that this had happened. Now Skeggi wakes, and misses both the sword and Thórðr; he became wroth and ran out, and asked if Thórðr had taken the sword. Eiðr says: "I am the cause of

Thórðr hewing the mare, because I told him the nature of the sword." Thórðr said that he himself was the cause of it. Then Skeggi, very wroth, said: "I will now, that we try our strength." Thórðr said, that he was quite ready. Eiðr and Ásbjörn went between, so they did not get near enough one another to have a fight. Then said Thórðr: "As they do not wish, that we should try each other's strength, I consider it most proper that Skeggi alone should make the conditions of peace, if he thinks that any disgrace has been done him." Eiðr said: "This is a good offer, father, to take self-judgment from the hands of such a man as Thórðr is." Skeggi accepted this offer, and awarded himself ten cows. Thórðr said: "This shall be paid." Both parties were well satisfied, and parted in friendship.

CHAPTER 13

Shortly after the wedding, Thórðr spoke to Eiðr, and said: "I do wish, my foster-son, that you would ride with me north to Miklibær, and woo Olöf Hrolleif's daughter, on my behalf." Eiðr says: "My duty it is, my foster-father, to ride whithersoever you wish me." Thereupon they all ride from home, Thórðr, and Eiðr, Ásbjörn, Eyjulfr, and Steingrímrr, until they come to Miklibær. They were well received there. In the morning Thórðr told his errand, and wooed Olöf. She willingly accepted the offer, and the bargain was soon concluded; there were witnesses as to the promise of marriage, and after that they rode home. The housewife, Olöf, held the wedding at her place. Thórðr bade Eiðr to the feast, as well as his brother-in-law Ásbjörn, and on their return presented them with fine gifts. In the spring Thórðr commenced farming at Miklibær, but his brothers, Eyjulfr and Steingrímrr, lived at Ós, in Miðfjörðr. Thórðr soon became a wealthy man through his skill in his craft.

A man is named Thorgils, who was a good farmer; he lived at Hrafhagili in Eyjafjörðr. He sent Thórðr word to come north to him, and build his hall. Thórðr promised to go, and when he was ready, he rode from home and had one man with him; they went up Skagafjörðr and north over Öxnadalsheiði. About this time a ship came across the ocean and put in at Gásir in Eyjafjörðr. On board this ship was a man hight Sörli, and called Sörli the Strong; he was the strongest of all men, and better fighter than any one; he was a fine man and well liked by everybody. He was an uncle of Ormr, whom Thórðr slew, and of Ásbjörn. Sörli gets himself horses, and intends riding west to Miðfjörðr, to his kinsmen. He had heard of the manslaughter of his kinsman Ormr; he rode from the ship with seventeen men up the Öxnadalr and over the heath to Lurkasteinn. This same day Thórðr the Terror rode across the heath on to the hills above Lurkasteinn. He observed then where eighteen men made their appearance; he thought he knew who they were, and dismounted. They soon came nearer. Thórðr greets them, and asks what the name of their chief is. He answered and said that his name was Sörli. "Are you called Sörli the Strong?" says Thórðr. "You may call me so if you like," says Sörli, "and who are you?" "I am hight Thórðr," says he. "Are you Thórðr the Terror, who slew my kinsman Ormr?" "That is the same man," says Thórðr, "and you may avenge him if you like; I have not, however, prepared myself to meet you, for I did not know you had arrived in this country, and weregild have I paid for the manslaughter of your kinsman." Sörli said: "Nothing have you paid me, but I shall not take advantage over you. All my men shall sit by, but we two will fight together; and should I fall, I forbid each one of my men to do you any harm." Thereupon they advanced towards one another, and fought very boldly. Thórðr soon found that Sörli was a great man because of his skill in arms, and he thought that a stronger man he had never met. They inflicted great wounds upon one another, but so it ended, that Sörli fell dead to the ground, and Thórðr was so exhausted that he could not help himself on to the horse, without being supported by his companions, and that was as much as they could do: they now rode down Öxnadalr to a farm called Þverá. There lived a good man by name of Einarr. He received Thórðr well, and Thórðr was laid up there for á long time, but at last healed. Sörli was buried in a cairn on the hill where the fight took place, and his death was thought a very great loss.

CHAPTER 14

Now there is to be said, that when Thórðr had recovered from his wounds he rode to Hrafnagil and built there a hall in the summer, which is standing to the present day. He has also built the hall at Höfði in Höfðahverfi. After this Thórðr rode west through the counties, and came to terms with his brother-in-law Ásbjörn and Skeggi as to the manslaughter of Sörli. Thereupon he rode north to his estate at Miklibær. Ásbjörn purchased Rakkaland in Miðfjörðr and dwelt there for three winters. He was very turbulent-minded, so much so that he could not stop there with his kinsmen; therefore he sold the land and went abroad, and took up his abode in Norway, and there increased his kin. Their married life turned out a happy one, and Sigríðr was accounted of as the most notable of women, wherein, indeed, she took after her kin. Eiðr spent his life mostly in trading voyages, or as a henchman of noble lords, and was always held of great worth. But when tired of that kind of life, he settled down as a householder. In his advanced age, Skeggi went south to Ás in Borgar-fjörðr to his son Eiðr, and remained there unto his death. He was laid in a how to the north of the "garth;" and still his bones may be seen in the "night-meal-beacon." Eiðr lived at Ás to a good old age, and he and his foster-father, Thórðr, were always in the habit of visiting each other, and to exchange fair gifts, nor was there ever a flaw in their friendship as long as they lived. After his departure from Norway, Thórðr never saw that country again, having been made an outlaw from it, together with his brothers, for the slaughter of King Sigurðr, "Slefa," the son of Eric.

From Thórðr a great family has descended, and many noble men both in Norway and Iceland. It is commonly said, that the prophecy of Thórðr that in Miðfjörðr there would always be disturbances, has come true; for there folk have been always more quarrelsome than in other districts. Thórðr himself died in his bed, and no more have we heard truthfully told of him, and so here cometh to an end the story of Thórðr Hreða (the Terror).

THE SAGA OF VIGA-GLUM

CHAPTER 1

There was a man called Ingiald, who lived at Thverá, on the Eyjafirth; he was one of the original priests and a great chief, and he was already in years when this story begins.

Ingiald was married, and had two sons, Steinolf and Eyiolf, both right good men and fair to see. Ingiald himself was self-willed, reserved, hard to deal with, and obstinate. He cared little for merchants, and did not choose to submit to their arrogance. If he wanted anything from them, he preferred sending other people for it to going himself.

One summer a ship came into Eyjafirth, the master of which was named Hreidar: he was a man of great family, who had his home at Vorz in Norway, and was very courageous and very popular. Ingialds son, Eyiolf, was often about the ship in the course of the summer, and he and Hreidar became great friends. Hreidar told him he should like to pass the winter here in some house, and from the report he had heard he should prefer that of Ingiald. Eyiolf said that such was not his fathers wont, but still that he would see about it. When he came home, he spoke to his father and asked him to take the master of the ship into his house--that he was a good, worthy fellow--and pleaded strongly in his behalf. Ingiald replied, If youhave invited him already, what is the use of talking about it? I must bear my part in meeting the expense, and you must bear yours in taking all the trouble; but he added that he had never had a foreigner staying with him before and that he was still not desirous of doing so. Then Eyiolf answered, It has not yet been settled without your consent; but I have not had much share in the management of the house as yet, and it seems your will that I should not have much, if a guest is not to be received whom I have invited hither. Well, said Ingiald, you shall have your own way in this matter, and the master and one other man may come here. I shall make no charge, for your sake; but you must take all the trouble for them, and I will defray the cost. I am well pleased, replied Eyiolf, that so it should be.

Eyiolf went the next day, found Hreidar, and told him how matters stood, whereupon Hreidar expressed his satisfaction and betook himself, with his cargo, to Ingialds house. A short time afterwards he learned that there was to be a great gathering there at Christmas. In the meantime Ingiald, though reserved, was on good terms with him.

One day Hreidar asked Ingiald to go into the outhouse where his cargo was; and when he went he invited him to choose whatever he liked out of his goods. Ingiald said that he did not wish to take any of his property, but acknowledged his liberality. Hreidar replied, I have, however, thought of something that you may want from us. I have been in several of the best dwellings here in Eyjafirth, and I have seen none so good as this; but the hangings for your hall are not such as to surpass those of other people. So saying, he took from his chests a set of hangings of such quality that no better had ever come to Iceland, and gave them to Ingiald, who thanked him; and a friendly feeling was now established between them. In the course of the winter Eyiolf said that he should like to sail with Hreidar on his outward voyage, but Hreidar did not answer him very readily. Why, says Eyiolf, will you not take me with you? Do you not like me? I like you right well, but your father will not approve of such a return for his hospitality, and I should not like to repay his kindness by taking away a son who is such a credit to him. If he approves, I shall willingly take you with me, and be truly thankful for your going.

Now the traders prepared for their voyage, and when they were ready, Eyiolf again asked Hreidar about taking him out: he told him what he wanted, and how he did not mean to act in this matter against his fathers wishes. Afterwards, he told his father how anxious he was to go, and what had passed between himself and Hreidar. Ingiald said there were few such mean as Hreidar to be found, and what with your own conduct and his tried worth, I shall allow you to go, for I am sure you had better make the voyage with him than with any one else.

CHAPTER 2

Then they sailed and arrived in Norway; and Heidar laid before Eyiolf many schemes for disposing of himself, but he would not agree to anything which was proposed. Well, said Hreidar, what are your plans, then? I really do not know. Will you not visit the king, or some of the other great men? You would, as a matter of course, be entitled to every assistance from us. (At this time Hacon, the ward of Athelstan, ruled in Norway.) Such chiefs are the persons whom you ought to serve. Eyiolf answered, I am not well fitted for a kings service; and though things might turn out as I should desire, yet I decline the proposal. Hreidar said, What will you do, then? Why, replied Eyiolf, do you shirk asking me to your own house? for that is what I want. I do not like to offer you that which it is not good you should accept, and good alone ought you to have at my hands. I am curious, said Eyiolf, to know how this matter stands. You shall know all about it, answered Hreidar, although it befits me ill to speak of it. I have a brother named Ivar; we live together, and hold our property jointly, and are very fond of one another; but we are not of the same mind in one thing, for he cannot bear any Icelander; so that they are not safe where he is. He is out sea-roving all the summer; but when he comes home, he takes up his quarters in my house, with ten or twelve men, and everybody there has to look to their wishes. All these fellows will be so ill-disposed towards you, that you would not in any way be comfortable there.

I am very curious, said Eyiolf, to learn what these men are like, and whatever happens, it will be no fault of yours, if you let the visit take place. Hreidar replied, I owe this to my brother, seeing that he brings me home the excellent gifts which he does--not to let a difference arise between us on your account-- and I shall be very much vexed if they mock and insult you. Ah! you want terribly to get out of having me at your house, remarked Eyiolf; but how will he bear himself towards me--will he beat me? It will be something worse than beating; he has many ill-conditioned men with him, and they will put the worst construction on all you do or say. Eyiolf said, Thats no great trial. If a man knows it before, it is folly not to bear that sort of thing: that shall be no hindrance. Hreidar replied, There is a difficulty both ways--you are my friend, and he is my brother, whom I love much.

The end of it was that Eyiolf went to stay at Hreidars, on the promontory; and when Ivar was expected home, he put on a great fur cloak, which he wore every day; he was a tall man, and sat always at Hreidars side.

CHAPTER 3

Now, when Ivar arrived, they went out to meet him as a mark of honour, and received him joyfully. Either brother then aksed the other for tidings and Ivar inquired of Hreidar where he had been through the winter. Hreidar told him he had been in Iceland, and then Ivar asked no more about the matter; but tell me, said he, is that great rough lump I see there a man, or is it some animal? Eyiolf answered, I am a man of Iceland, my name is Eyiolf, and I intend to be here all the winter. I guess one thing, said Ivar; we shall not be without mischief of some kind, if an Icelander is here. Hreidar replied, If you deal badly with him, so that he cannot stay here, the affection between us, as near kinsmen, will suffer. It was a bad voyage of yours to Iceland, said Ivar, if we on that account are to be dependent on Icelanders, or cast off our own friends and kindred: nor do I know why you chose to visit that most hateful people; and then too you have escaped telling me what has happened to you. It is very different from what you suppose, said Hreidar; there are many good fellows there. Well, replied Ivar, at any rate that rough and shaggy beast does not look particularly well on the high seat. But when he saw that his brother set great store by Eyiolf he did not speak so strongly as before against Icelanders. What can I call him, said he, except Lump? and Eyiolf did not seem to object to the name; but they made the worst of everything that he did.

There was a man named Vigfuss, lord of the district of Vorz, the son of Sigurd, who was the son of Kari-Viking; and Vigfuss had a daughter, called Astrida. Hreidar and Ivar were great friends of Vigfuss, and they used to entertain one another alternate winters, at Christmas. At this time it was the turn of the brothers to prepare for the feast. In fact Hreidar had got everything ready, and had then to invite his guest. He asked Eyiolf to go with him, for, said he, I have no curiosity to try how they will behave towards you here. I am not well, replied Eyiolf, and I cannot go. That evening, when Hreidar was gone and they took their places, Ivars companions exclaimed, Now we shall amuse ourselves as we please, for old Lump is left at home. Nay, said Ivar, we must think of something which befits us. Here we are, two brothers, holding our property jointly, and he has all the trouble of it, whilst I have none. This is a man to whom he wishes to be kind, and we act in such a way that he can scarcely stay here, but at the same time we have no fault to find with him. No man shall say anything injurious to him whilst Hreidar is absent. They replied it was just the time to have some sport. No, said Ivar, there is little true manhood in what you say. Every one waits on us here, and we have all the sport we choose, but others have the labour and care. If that man had killed my brother, I would not, for Hreidars sake, do him any harm, and no one shall dare to make sport of him. He shall not be called Lump any longer. In the morning Ivar spoke with Eyiolf: Will you go into the wood with us and amuse yourself He assented to this and went with them: they took to cutting down trees and carrying them home. Eyiolf had with him his sword and a hatchet. I advise you, Icelander, said Ivar, if our men go each his on way, that you get home before dark. So each man went his own way, and Eyiolf went off by himself, and taking off his rough cloak, laid upon it the sword which he hand in his hand. Then he turned into the wood to amuse himself with his hatchet, and cut down the trees which he fancied. As the day advanced it came on to snow, and he thought of going home; but when he came to the spot where he had left his cloak it was gone, and the sword remained behind. He saw a track in the snow as if the cloak had been dragged along. A bear had come and carried off the cloak, but had hardly had strength to hold it off the ground, for it was a young bear, just come out of its lair, that had never killed a man. They Eyiolf went and saw the bear sitting before him, so he drew his sword and cut off its snout close to the eyes and took it home with him in his hand. Ivar came home first, missed Eyiolf, and exclaimed, We have made a bad expedition of it, and we have done wrong in parting from our comrade in the wood, for he does not know his way in it. It is likely that there are wild beasts there, and considering the footing on which we have been with him, it would be much talked about, if he did not get safe back. I advise that we should go and look for him till we find him. When they got out before the door, there was Eyiolf coming to meet them, and Ivar greeted him well, and asked how he came to be covered with blood. Eyiolf showed them what he held in his hand, and Ivar said, I fear you are wounded? but he answered, Dont trouble yourself about me; I have no hurt. Ivar exclaimed, What folly it is to mock men whom we do not know! He has shown in this matter a courage which I doubt if any of us would come up to.

The following evening Hreidar came home, and Ivar asked him, Why are you so moody, brother? Are you anxious about Lump? How do you think I am likely to have dealt with him? No doubt, said Hreidar, it is of some consequence how you have acted in this matter. What will you give me, if I should be on the same terms with him as you are yourself? I will give you, answered Hreidar, that gold ring which belongs to both of us and which you have long liked. Ivar replied, I dont covet your property, but I shall for the future stand to him in the same relation as to yourself, and henceforth he shall sit by my side, and not by yours. Then both of them held Eyiolf in high honour, and felt that the place he sat in was worthily filled; and so it went on.

CHAPTER 4

Now people came to the Christmas feast, and those who were to sit together were told off in messes of twelve. Lots were cast to see who should sit next to Astrida, the daughter of the chief Vigfuss, and Eyiolf always drew the lot for sitting by her side. No one observed that they talked together more than other persons did, but still men said that it was fated to come about in that way that he should marry her. The feast came to an end, after being celebrated with great splendour, and the guest were dismissed with presents. Eyiolf went sea-roving for four summers, and was held to be a very valiant man. He gained great reputation and much booty. It happened one winter that a certain Thorstein came to Vorz, who was a great friend of the brothers, and lived in the upland country. He told them of the strait he was in; how the Berserker, who was called Asgaut, had challenged him to the holmgang, because he had refused to give him his sister, and he asked them to escort him to the field with a large number of men, so that the pirate might not seize on his property. He added that Asgaut had killed many of his people, and that he must give up his sister to him if they would not support him; for, said he, I have no confidence in the result of the holmgang, unless I have the benefit of the good luck which attends you.

They did not like to refuse to go with him, and so they went into the upland with thirty men in their company; when they got to the place of meeting the question was put to all the people there, Was there any man who desired to win a wife by fighting Asgaut? but though the lady was attractive enough, there was no one ready to win her a that price. Then the brothers asked Eyiolf to bear Thorsteins shield for him in the fight, but he replied that he never defended any other man, and not even himself in that way. I shall not like it, said he, if he is killed whilst he is under my care, and there could be no honour in that. But if this young fellow is slain on our hands now, what are we to do? Are we to go away again when that is done, or are we to get a second and third man to fight the Berserker? Our disgrace will only increase in proportion as more men are killed on our side, and we shall get little credit by our journey if we go back without avenging him who thus falls, as it were, on our behalf. Ask me, if you like, to fight the Berserker myself; that is a thing one may do for ones friends, but what you now ask I will not grant. They thanked him much, but the stake to be risked seemed very great in his case.

Well, observed Eyiolf, my opinion is, that none of our people ought to go back to their homes again, if the man who falls is not avenged, and I think it worse to fight the Berserker after your kinsman is killed than it would be before. So he stepped forward, and Ivar offered to hold the shield for him. Eyiolf answered-- It is well offered, but the matter concerns me most, and the old proverb is true, a mans own hand is most to be trusted. Then he went on to the holm, and the Berserker called out, Is that fellow going to fight with me? Is it not true, said Eyiolf, that you are afraid to fight with me? It may be that you are not of the right sort when you fear a big man, and crow over a little one. That has never been laid to my charge, replied the Berserker, but I will explain to you the laws of the combat. If I am wounded I am to get off by paying five marks. Oh, said Eyiolf, I do not feel bound to keep any rules with you, when you set your own price on yourself, and that price is one which in our country would be paid for a thrall. Eyiolf had to strike the first blow, and that first blow he struck in such a way that if fell on the point of the Berserkers shield, and cut it off, and his foot along with it. He got great honour by this feat, and returned home with the brothers. A good deal of money was offered for his acceptance, but he said he had not done the deed for the sake of money, nor for the sake of the lady, but out of friendship for Hreidar and Ivar. Asgaut paid the fine to be released from the duel, and lived a maimed man.

After all this Eyiolf wooed Astrida, the daughter of Vigfuss, and the brothers went to press his suit for him. They said he was a man of great family, who held a good position in Iceland, and had many kinsmen to back him, and they thought it probable his career would be a distinguished one. Eyiolf himself then said, It may be that Astridas friends think we are boasting in what we say, but many know the fact of my having in Iceland an honourable descent and a good property. Vigfuss answered, This will be her destiny, though we did not look lower for our kinswoman, and so she was betrothed to him and they sailed out to Iceland together.

CHAPTER 5

There was a man named Bödvar; he was the son of Vikingakari, and the brother of Sigurd the father of Vigfuss, whose daughter was Astrida, the mother of Erik father of another Astrida, the mother of Olaf, the son of Tryggvi. Vikingakari was the son of Eymund the pirate, the son of Thorir. Bödvar was the father of Oluf the mother of Gizor the white. When Eyiolf and his wife Astrida got out to Iceland, Ingiald was dead, and Eyiolf succeeded to his property and his office as priest. Ingiald had a daughter named Ulfeida, who was married to Narvi of Hrisey. Four children of Eyiolf and Astrida are mentioned, of whom Thorstein was the eldest, but his share of the inheritance was paid him when he married, and he dwelt on Eyjafirth as long as he lived, and has little to do with our story. The second was Vigfuss, who married Halfrida, the daughter of Thorkel the tall from Myvain. Glum was the youngest of their sons, and the daughter was named Helga. She was wedded to Steingrim of Sigluvik, and their son was Thorvald Tafalld, who comes up afterwards in this story. Vigfuss, however, died very soon after his marriage, leaving one child, who survived him a short time only, and thus it came to pass that all his property vested half in Halfrida and half in Glum and Astrida, for Eyiolf was dead before this happened. Then Thorkel the tall moved his establishment to Thverà, and Sigmund his son with him. The latter was a man of much importance, an looked forward to becoming chief of the district, if he made a good match, and got the support of good kinsmen.

Thorir was the name of a man who lived at Espihole, the son of Hamund of the dark-skin, and of Ingunna, the daughter of Helgi the thin. He had married Thordis, the daughter of Kadal, and their children were Thorarin and Thorvald the crooked, who lived at Grund on the Eyjafirth, Thorgrim, who lived at Mödrufell, Ingunna, the wife of Thord the priest of Frey, and Vigdis, who married Sigmund.

Now Thorkel and Sigmund took to disturbing the property of Astrida, and they divided the land in half, but Glum and his mother got that part which had no house on it. So they made their dwelling at Borgarhole, but Glum took very little trouble about household matters, and seemed to be somewhat slow in coming to his full faculties. He was for the most part silent and undemonstrative, tall, of a dark complexion, with straight white hair; a powerful man, who seemed rather awkward and shy, and never went to the places where men met together.

The temple of Frey was on the south of the river at Hripkelstad. Thorarin, of Espihole, was a prudent and popular man, but his brother Thorvald the crooked was a bully and hard to deal with. Sigmund thought he should be a great man if he could ally himself to the people at Espihole. In the meantime the property of

Glum and Astrida was getting less every day, and their condition became uncomfortable, for Sigmund and Thorkel thwarted them, so that in everything they got less than their share. Then Glum says to his mother that he will go abroad, for I see clearly I shall never get on here, but it may be I shall meet with more luck by means of the reputation of my kindred: I do not like to bear the encroachments of Sigmund, for whom as yet I am no match. However, do not you let go your hold on the land, through your position may be a difficult one. Glum at that time, when he desired to go abroad, was fifteen years of age.

CHAPTER 6

Now we have to tell of Glums voyage. As soon as he landed in Norway he went up to Vigfusss house; and when he came thither he saw a great crowd of people, and all sorts of amusements and games going on. He understood at once that everything there must be on a great scale, but he saw many men of mark, and did not know which was his kinsman Vigfuss. He made him out by observing a tall and distinguished-looking man, in a full blue cloak, on the high seat, playing with a gold-mounted spear. Then Glum went up to him and greeted him, and his greeting was received courteously. Vigfuss asked who he was; he replied that he was an Icelander from Eyjafirth. Vigfuss inquired after his son-in-law, and his daughter Astrida. Glum told him that the former was dead, but that the latter was still living. Then he asked what children of theirs were alive, and Glum gave an account of his brothers and his sister, and added that he who now stood before him was one of the sons, but when he had said that, the conversation went no further. Glum asked Vigfuss to assign him a seat, but he said he did not know how much of what had been told him was true, told him to take a seat on the outside of the lower bench, and took little notice of him. Glum spoke little, and was unsociable in his habits, and when men were drinking or amusing themselves in other ways, he used to lie with his cloak wrapt round his head, so that he seemed a sort of fool. At the commencement of winter there was a feast prepared, and a sacrifice to the gods, in which observance all were expected to take part, but Glum sat in his place and did not attend it. As evening passed on, and the guests had arrived, there was not so much merriment, on account of the meeting of friends and the welcoming one another, as might have been expected when so many had come together. On the day on which the people came, Glum had not stirred out to meet them, nor did he ask any one to sit by him ort to take his place.

After they were set down to table, it was said that the man called Biörn with the Iron Skull, and eleven others with him, were come into the homestead. He was a great Berserker, who used to go about to feasts where many people were assembled, and picked a quarrel with any one who chose to say anything which he could take hold of; the he challenged them to the holmgang: and Vigfuss therefore desired that every one should take care what he said. For, said he, it is less disgrace to do that than to get something worse at his hands. This all men promised to observe, and Biörn walked into the hall and looked for compliments, and asked the last man on the upper bench whether he thought himself as good a man as he (Biörn) was? to which the reply was Very far from it. Then he asked the same question of one man after the other, until he got up in front of the high seat. People used different words in answering him, but the end of it was that no one professed to be his match. When he came up to Vigfuss he asked him if he knew where to find such champions as he (Biörn) was? Vigfuss said he did not know any men equal to him. Well, said Biörn, that is a proper and discreet answer, as might have been expected from you, for you are an honourable man, and your life has been according to your wishes, without any check to your prosperity or any stain on your reputation. It is well therefore that I need address nothing but fair words to you, but I wish to ask you one question--Do you think yourself as good a man as I am? Vigfuss replied, When I was young, out sea-roving and getting some honour of my own--well, I do not know whether I might then have been your match, but now I am not half as good, for I am old and decrepid. Biörn turned away and proceeded further out along the second bench, and went on asking men whether they were his equals, but they all answered that they were not so. At last he came to the place where Glum lay stretched out on the bench. Why does this fellow lie there, said Biörn, and not sit up? Glums comrades answered for him and spoke on his behalf, and said that he was so dull that it mattered little what he said. Biörn gave him a kick, told him to sit up like other people, and asked him if he was as brave a man as he? Glum replied that Biörn had no need to meddle with him, and that he (Glum) knew nothing about his courage; but there is one reason, he added, why I should not like to be put on the same footing with you, and that is because out there, in Iceland, a man would be called a fool who conducted himself as you do, but here I see everybody regulates his speech in the most perfect manner. Then he jumps up, pulls Biörns helmet off, catches up a stick of firewood, and brings it down between his shoulders, so that the great champion bends beneath the stroke. Glum gives him one blow after another till he is down, and then, as he tries to get on his feet, he smites him on the head, and so he goes on till he gets him outside the door. When Glum wanted to return to his seat, Vigfuss had come down from the dais to the floor of the hall and greeted his kinsman, telling him that he had now shown what he was, and proved that he belonged to the race. Now I shall honour you as befits us, said Vigfuss; and he added that he acted as he had done at first, because Glum seemed slow and stupid. I chose to wait till you on your way into our family by some act of manhood. Then he led him up to a seat next himself, and Glum told him he would have accepted that place before, If it had been offered to him. The next day they heard of Biörns death, and Vigfuss offered Glum to succeed to himself in his position and dignity. The latter said he would accept the offer, but he must first go to Iceland in order to see that his inheritance there did not fall into the hands of those whom he did not choose should enjoy it, but that he would return as soon as possible. Vigfuss expressed his conviction that Glum would do credit to his race and increase his reputation in Iceland. So when summer came he got a ship ready for Glum, and put a cargo on board, with much store of gold and silver, and said to him, I feel sure we shall not see one another again; but certain special gifts I will give you, that is to say, a cloak, a spear, and a sword, which we in this family have put great trust in. Whilst you retain these articles, I expect that you will never lose your honour; but if you part with them, then I have my fears: and so they separated.

317

CHAPTER 7

Glum sailed out to Iceland, and went home to Thverá, where he straightway found his mother. She received him gladly, and told him the unfairness of Sigmund and his father towards her. She bade him however have patience, for that she was not able to cope with them. Then he rode to the homestead, and saw that the fence ran in such a way as to encroach on his property, and he sung these verses:--

Yes! closer than I thought, fair dame,
This hedge so green hath hemmd us in;
Our peace at home is spoilt, and shame
Must cling to us and all our kin.
I sing it now, but in the fray
I soon shall have to draw my sword.
Too surely, whilst Ive been away,
My land hath found a wrongful lord.

What had occurred whilst he was absent, was that Sigmund had worried Astrida, and evidently wanted to drive her off her land. In the autumn, before Glum returned, Sigmund and Thorkel had lost two heifers, and supposed they had been stolen. Their suspicions fell on the serfs of Astrida, who, they said, had no doubt killed and eaten them off hand, and they caused these serfs to be summoned in the spring for the theft. Now these were the best men Astrida had, and she thought she could hardly mange her farm if they went away. So she went to her son Thorstein, and told him what wrong Sigmund and his father were doing her, and asked him to answer for her serfs. I would rather atone for them in money, she said, than that they should be found guilty on a false charge, and I should think it your business now to stand before us, and to show yourself worthy of a good name. Thorstein seemed to think that the prosecutors would so follow up the matter as to bring the full force of their family interest to bear on it. And if, said he, these serfs are essential to your household, we had better take such a share of the fine as will make it possible to get the money to pay it. Yes, she answered, but I hear that the only atonement they will take is one which is intended to ruin us. However, as I see there is a little help to be got where you are, the matter must rest in their hands.

One of the best things about the estate at Thverá was a certain field known by the name of the Suregiver, which was never without a crop. It had been so arranged in the partition of the land that either party should have this field year and year about. Then Astrida said to Thorkel and Sigmund, It is clear thay you wish to push me hard, and you see that I have no one to manage for me, but rather than give up my serfs I will leave the affair to be settled on your own terms. They replied that was very prudent on her part, and after consulting together they decided that they must either declare the men guilty, or award what damages they thought proper. But Thorstein did not stir in the case, so as to take the award out of their hands, and they assigned to the field to themselves, as sole owners, with the intention of getting hold of all her land, by thus depriving her of the main prop of her housekeeping. And that very summer which was coming on, she ought, if she had her rights, to have had the field.

Now, in the summer, when men were gone to the Thing, and when this suit had been thus settled, the herdsmen going round the pastures found the two heifers in a landslip, where the snow had drifted over them early in the winter, and thus the calumny against Astridas serfs was exposed. When Thorkel and Sigmund heard that the heifers had bee found, they offered money to pay for the field, but they refused to renounce the conveyance which had been made of it to them. Astrida however answered that it would not be too great a compensation for the false charge which had been go up, if she were allowed to have what was her own. So, said she, I will either have what belongs to me, or I will submit to the loss; and though there is no one here to set the matter straight, I will wait, and I expect that Glum will come out and put it in the right way. Sigmund replied, It will be a long time before he ploughs for that harvest. Why, there is that son of yours, who is a much fitter man to help you, sitting by and doing nothing. Pride and wrong, said she, often end badly, and this may happen in your case.

It was somewhat late in the summer when Glum came out; he stayed a little while with the ship, and then went home with his goods. His temper and character were the same as thy had been. He gave little sign of what he thought, and seemed as if he did not hear what had happened whilst he was away. He slept every day till nine oclock, and took no thought about the management of the farm. If they had had their right, the field would, as had been said, have been that summer in the hands of Glum and his mother. Sigmunds cattle moreover did them much injury, and were to be found every morning in their home-field.

One morning Astrida waked Glum up, and told him that many of Sigmunds cattle had got Into their home-field, and wanted to break in among the hay which was laid in heaps, and I am not active enough to drive them out, and the men are all at work. He answered, Well, you have not often asked me to work, and there shall be no offence in your doing so now. So he jumped up, took his horse, and a large stick in his hand, drove the cattle briskly off the farm, thrashing them well till they came to the homestead of Thorkel and Sigmund, and then he let them do what mischief they please. Thorkel was looking after the hay and the fences that morning, and Sigmund was with the labourers. The former called out to Glum, You may be sure people will not stand this at your hands--that you should damage their beasts in this way, though you may have got some credit while you were abroad. Glum answered, The beasts are not injured yet, but if they come again and trespass upon us some of them will be lamed, and you will have to make the best of it; it is all you will get; we are not going to suffer damage by your cattle any longer. Sigmund cried, out, You talk big, Glum, but in our eyes you are now just as great a simpleton as when you went away, and we shall not regulate our affairs according to your nonsense. Glum went home, and then a fit of laughter came upon him, and affected him in such a manner that he turned quite pale, and tears burst from his eyes, just like large hailstones. He was often afterwards taken in this way when the appetite for killing some one came upon him.

319

CHAPTER 8

We are told that as the autumn went on Astrida came and spoke to Glum another morning, and, waking him up, asked him to give directions about the work, for the haymaking, she said, would be finished this day if all was ordered as it ought to be. Sigmund and Thorkel had already finished their hay, and they had gone early in the morning to the field Sure-giver; and they are no doubt very well pleased in having that field, which we should have, if all were as it should be. Then Glum got up, but he was not ready before nine oclock. He took his blue cloak, and his spear with gold about it in his hand, and got his horse saddled. But Astrida said to him, You take a good deal of pains about your dress, my son, for haymaking. His answer was, I do not often go out to labour, but I shall do a good stroke of work, and I will be well dressed for it. However, I am not able to give directions for the farm-work, and I shall ride up to Hole and accept the invitation of my brother Thorstein. So he crossed over to the south side of the river, and as he came to the field he took the brooch out of his cloak. Vigdis and her husband Sigmund were in the field, and when she saw Glum she came towards him and greeted him, saying, We are sorry that our intercourse as relations is so little, and we wish in everything to do our part to increase it. Glum told her, I have turned in here because the brooch is gone from my cloak, and I want you to put a stitch in it for me. She said she would do it with pleasure, and did it accordingly. Glum looked over the field and remarked, Sure-giver has not yet lost his character. Then he put on his cloak again, took his spear in his hand, and turned sharp on Sigmund, with it uplifted. Sigmund sprang up to meet him, but Glum struck him on the head so that he needed no second blow. Then he went up to Vigdis, and told her to go home, and tell Thorkel, on Glums part, nothing is yet done which will necessarily hinder our being on the footing of kinsmen, but that Sigmund is unable to leave the field. Glum rode on to Hole, and said nothing to his brother of what had happened; but when Thorstein saw how he was equipped, and how he had his cloak and spear, and perceived the blood in the ornaments of the weapon, he asked him if he had used it within a short time. Oh, cried Glum, it is quite true; I forgot to mention it, I killed Sigmund, Thorkels son, with it to-day. That will be some news, replied Thorstein, for Thorkel and his kinsmen at Espihole. Yes, said glum; however, as the old saying is, The nights of blood are the nights of most impatience. No doubt they will think less of it as time goes on. He staid three nights at his brothers house, and then got ready to return home. Thorstein was preparing to ride with him, but Glum told him, Look after your won household--I shall ride the straight path home to Thverá; they will not be so very keen in this business. So he went home to Thverá.

Thorkel went to see Thorarin, and asked him for counsel as to the course to be taken. His answer was, It may now be that Astrida will say, Glum has not got on his legs for nothing. Yes, said Thorkel, but I trow that he has got on that leg which will not bear him long. Thorarin replied, That is as it may be. You have long dealt unfairly with them, and tried to turn them out, without considering what was to be expected from the descendants of one such as Eyiolf, a man of great family and withal himself of great courage. We are closely connected with Glum by kindred, and with you by marriage, and the suit seems a difficult one, if Glum follows it up, as I think he will. Thorkel then returned home, and the whole matter was kept quiet through the winter; but Glum had somewhat more men about him than he usually had.

CHAPTER 9

It is said that Glum had a dream one night, in which he seemed to be standing out in front of his dwelling, looking towards the firth; and he thought he saw the form of a woman stalking up straight through the district from the sea towards Thverá. She was of such height and size that her shoulders touched the mountains on each side, and he seemed to go out of the homestead to meet her and asked her to come to his house; and then he woke up. This appeared very strange to every one, but he said, The dream is no doubt a very remarkable one, and I interpret it thus--My grandfather, Vigfuss, must be dead, and that woman who was taller than the mountains, must be his guardian spirit, for he too was far beyond other men in honour and in most things, and his spirit must have been looking for a place of rest where I am. But in the summer, when the ships arrived, the news of Vigfusss death became known, and then Glum sang as follows--

At dead of night, beneath the sky,
Upon the banks of Eyjafirth,
I saw the spirit stalking by,
In giant stature oer the earth.

The goddess of the sword and spear
Stood, in my dream, upon this ground;
And whilst the valley shook with fear,
She towerd above the mountains round.

In the spring Thorkel met Thorvald the crooked, and other sons of Thorir, and asked them to follow up this suit of his, referring to the tie which united them throurgh Thorirs daughter, and to all the friendship which he and his son Sigmund had shown to them. Thorvald spoke to Thorarin, and said that it would be discreditable to them not to help their brothcr-in-law, and he replied that he was ready to do all he could, and besides, he said, It is now clear that Glum means to turn the slaying of Sigmund to account, so as to make himself a great man, and we think ourselves worth as much as he is in the district. Yes, replied Thorarin, but it seems to me it will be hard to follow up the suit, so as to make sure that we shall get any advantage by it, and on the other hand it is not unexpected that Glum should take after his race and kindred. I am slower to move in it than you are, because I doubt if any honour is to be got in a quarrel with Glum; yet I should not like to see our credit lowered. Hoever, after a certain pressure, Thorarin, the son of Thorir, set on foot at the Althing the suit against Glum for the slaying of Sigmund; and Glum set on foot a suit against Thorkel the tall, for slander against Astridas serfs; and another against Sigmund, whom he charged with theft, and whom he alleged that he had killed while trespassing on his own property. So he summoned him as outlawed, inasmuch as he fell on his, Glums, land, and he dug his body up. In this condition matters were when they went to the Althing. Then Glum visited his kinsmen, and sought for help at the hands of Gizor the white, and Teit, the son of Ketilbiörn of Mosfell, and

Asgrim, the son of Ellidagrim; and he told them the whole course of the proceedings, and how Thorkel and Sigmund had encroached on his rights, and all the wrong and disgrace they had inflicted on him. But from them, he said, he expected help to put matters in a better condition. He himself would conduct the suit. They all professed themselves bound to take care that his cause was not left in unfriendly hands, and said they should be glad to see him distinguish himself among their kin.

The Thing went on till the court sat, and the men of Espihole preferred their suit for the slaying of Sigmund, rather as if they were egged on by those who had wrongs to revenge, than by those who felt sure that there were no flaws in their case. Glum too moved in the case against Thorkel, and the two suits came before the court. Glum had many kinsmen and friends to back him, and when, as defendant, he was called on to answer, he said, The matter is on this wise. Every one may see that you have gone into this suit more as a question of temper than because there were no defects in your case, for I slew Sigmund trespassing on my own property, and before I rode to the Thing I proclaimed him as an outlaw. Then he named his witnesses on this point, and defended his suit with the help of his kinsmen, in such sort that judgment was given to the effect that Sigmund had been killed out of the pale of the law. Glum next took up the charge against Thorkel for trespass on his property, and the case looked ill for Thorkel, for the witnesses were on Glums side, and there was no legal defence, so that it ended in seeking to compound the matter with the plaintiff. Glum said two courses were open--either he would follow the case out to its conclusion, or Thorkel must reconvey the land that Thverá at such a price as he should put on it, which was not more than half its worth. And Thorkel may be sure, he added, if he is convicted, that we shall not both of us be at the Thing next summer. The friends of Thorkel now interfered to get him to compound the suit, and he took the course which was expedient, settled the matter, and conveyed the land to Glum. He was to live on the land for the year, and thus, so to speak, they were on terms again. But the men of Espihole were ill pleased with the conclusion of these suits, and from that time they were never on a good footing with Glum. Indeed, before Thorkel left Thverá, he went to Freys temple, and taking an old steer up thither, made this speech:--Thou, Frey, said he, wert long my protector, and many offerings hast thou had at my hands, which have borne good fruit to me. Now do I present this steer to thee, in the hope that Glum hereafter may be driven by force off this land, as I am driven off it; and, I pray thee, give me some token whether thou acceptest this offering or not. Then the steer was stricken in such a way that he bellowed loud and fell down dead, and Thorkel took this a a favourable omen. Afterwards he was in better spirits, as if he thought his offering was accepted and his wish ratified by the god. Then he removed to Myvatn, and we have doe with him in this story.

CHAPTER 10

Glum now assumed a high position in the district. There was a man named Gunnstein, who lived at Lón in Högardal, a great and rich man, reckoned to be one of the most important persons in the land. He had a wife called Hlif, and their son was Thorgrim, generally known as Thorgrim the son of Hlif, being called after his mother because she outlived his father. She was a woman of a high spirit, and Thorgrim himself was all that a man ought to be, and became eminent. Another son of theirs was Grim, surnamed Eyrarleggr, and their daughter was Halldora, who was a beautiful woman of a gentle temper. She was esteemed to be about the best match in the country both on account of her kindred and of her own accomplishments and great qualities. Glum paid his addresses to her, stating that he did not want the help of kinsmen to explain what his family or his property and personal merits were. All that you know well enough, and I have set my mind on this marriage is so be that it is agreeable to her friends. He received a favourable answer to his suit, and Halldora was betrothed to him with a great portion; so the wedding went of prosperously, and Glums position became one of more dignity that it was before.

Thorvald was the son of Reim, who lived at Bard, in the Fleets: he had to wife Thurida, the daughter of Thord of Höfdi. Their children were Klaufi and Thorgerda, whom Thorarin of Espihole had married. Thorvald the crooked of Grund wedded Thorkatla of Thiorsádal. Hlenni the Old, the son of Ornolf Wallet-back, dwelt at Vidines, and he had to wife Otkatla, the daughter of Otkel of Thiorsádal. Gizor was the son of Kadal, and lived at The Tarns, in the valley of Eyjafirth; his wife was named Saldis, and she was a worthy matron. Gizor was one of the most considerable landowners, well to do in respect of property, with two daughters, named Thordis and Herpruda, both handsome women, who were distinguished in dress and appearance and were considered good matches. They grew up to womanhood at home. Gizors brother was called Runolf, and he was the father of Valgerda, mother of Eyiolf of Mödrufell. Thordis was Kadals daughter, and she was married to Thorir of Espihole, and they had the children who have been named before. Thorgrim, however, the son of Thorir, although born in wedlock, was not the child of Thordis. He was a brave and well conditioned man, and he set out to meet Gizor and ask Thordis his daughter to wife for himself. His brothers and kinsmen too were engaged in pressing this suit. The maidens relatives thought that they ought all to have a voice in the disposal of their kinswoman, and they all considered the proposal an excellent one; but notwithstanding this Thorgrim was refused. It seemed to pepole in general that Thorgrim had proposed a fair and equal match, and his brothers and kinsmen were offended at his rejection.

CHAPTER 11

We must now bring into the story the man named Arnor, who was called Red-cheek, the son of Steinolf, the son of Ingiald and first cousin of Glum. He had been long abroad, but was highly esteemed, and constantly with Glum when he was in Iceland. He suggested to Glum to get him a wife. Glum asked him what woman he wished to woo? He replied, Thordis, the daughter of Gizor, who was refused to Thorgrim, the son of Thorir. Well, said Glum, that seems to me a hopeless proposal, for there is nothing to choose betwixt you two personally; but Thorgrim has a good establishment, plenty of money, and many kinsmen to back him, whereas you, on the other hand, have no household and not much property. I do not want to offer an unequal match to Gizor, so as to prevent him doing the best for his daughter, as he wishes, for Gizor deserves well at my hands. Arnor answered him, I get the benefit of having good friends, if I make a better match in consequence of your urging my suit. Promise him your friendship, and then he will give me the girl. Indeed, it might have been called a fair match enough, if she had not been already refused to so good a man as Thorgrim. Glum allowed himself to be persuaded and went with Arnor to Gizor and pressed the matter on his behalf. Gizors answer was, It may be, Glum, that people will say I have made a mistake, if I give to Arnor, your kinsman, my daughter, whom I did not choose to give to Thorgrim. Well, said Glum, there is some reason in that; but it may also be said, if you will give proper weight to what I say, that my hearty friendship is to be thrown into the balance. Gizor replied, Yes; but, on the other side, I suspect there will be the emnity of other people. Well, said Glum, you see your way before you; but I tell you that what you do makes a great difference in my disposition towards you. Then said Gizor, You shall not go away this time without succeeding; so he gave him his and, and the girl was betrothed to Arnor. Glum insisted on one condition--that the bridal was to be at Thverá in the autumn; and they parted on this understanding.

Now Arnor had some malt out at Gásar, and he himself and one of his men were to fetch it. Thorgrim, son of Thorir, went to the warm spring on the very day on which they were expected in with the malt, and he was at the bath at Hrafnagil with six of his own men in his company. So when Arnor was coming up and wanted to cross the river, Thorgrim exclaimed, Is not this a lucky hit, now, to stumble on Arnor? Do not let us miss the malt, at any rate, if we have missed the lady. They went at them with their swords uplifted, and Arnor, when he saw what the difference in their number was, jumped right into the river and got across; but his pack-horses remained on the west side of the stream. Ah! exclaimed Thorgrim, we are not altogether out of luck; we shall drink the ale, if they get the wife. So he rode off to South Espihole. Thorir was then quite blind, and Thorgrims companions were very merry and laughed aloud. Then Thorir asked what seemed so laughable to them. They said they did not know which party would have thier feast first; and they told him what they had got, and how the owners of the malt had been driven off, and how the bridegroom had jumped into the water. When Thorir heard the story he said, Do you think you have made a good business of it now, that you laugh so heartily? How do you suppose you will get out of it? Do you imagine you will sleep quietly here to-night and want nothing else? Do you not know what Glums disposition will be, if he approves of his kinsmans journey? I say it is good counsel to get our men together; it is most probable that Glum has already assembled a good many of his.

There was at that time a ford in the river at the place where now there is none. In the course of the night they collected some eighty good men, and stationed them on the edge of the rising ground, because the ford was just at that very point. On the other hand, it is to be told how Arnor found Glum and gave him an account of his expedition. Yes, answered Glum, this is pretty much what I expected; I did not think they would be quiet; and the matter is somewhat difficult to handle. If we do nothing there is disgrace for us, and the honour is not so clear if we try to set it right. However, we must get our men together. So when day broke Glum came to the river with sixty men and wanted to ride across, but the men of Espihole pelted them with stones, so that they did not advance; and Glum turned back whilst they fought with stones and missiles across the water. A good many men were wounded, but their names are not recorded. When the men of the district became aware of what was going on they came up in the course of the day and interfered, and the two parties came to a parley about terms. The men of Espihole were asked what satisfaction they would make for the insult offered to Arnor, and they said that no satisfaction was due from them, though Arnor had run away from his malt-sacks. Then a proposal was made that Glum should take part in asking, on behalf of Thorgrim, for Herpruda, the other daughter of Gizor, and that the marriage of Arnor and Thordis should take place only on condition of Glums getting this second match agreed to. In fact, the one who was to be married to Thogrim was thought to have the best bargain. In consequence of the intervention of so many people, Glum promised his assistance in this matter, and he went to Gizor and spoke to him upon it. It may seem, he said, to be officiousness on my part, if I take on myself to woo a wife for my own kinsman and for the men of Espihole too; but in order to stop disturbances in our district, I think I am bound to pledge my faith and friendship to you, if you will do as I wish. Gizpr replied, It seems best to me that you should have you way, inasmuch as the offer to my daughter is a good one; and so both matches were agreed on. Arnor went to live at Upsal, and Thorgrim at Mödrufell. Shortly after this Gizor died, and Saldis moved her household to Upsal. Arnor had a son by Thordis, who was called Steinolf, and Thorgrim had one who was named Arngrim, and was, as he grew up, a promising lad.

CHAPTER 12

Saldis invited both her grandsons to stay with her. Arngrim was two winters older than Steinolf; there was not in the whole of the Eyjafirth any boys of a better disposition or greater promise, and they were very fond of each other. When one was four years old and the other six, they were one day playing together, and Steinolf asked Arngrim to lend him the little brass horse which he had. Arngrim answered, I will give it you, for looking to my age, it is more fit for your plaything than mine. Steinolf went and told hls foster-mother what a fair gift he had got, and she said it was quite right that they should be on such good terms with one another.

There was a woman who went about in that part of the country, named Oddbiörg, who amused people by story telling, and was a spaewife. A feeling existed that it was of some consequence for the mistress of the house to receive her well, for that what she said depended more or less on how she was entertained. She came to Upsal, and Saldis asked her to spae something, and that something good, of those boys. Her answer was, Hopeful are these lads; but what their future luck may be it is difficult for me to discern. Saldis exclaimed, If I am to judge by this unsatisfactory speech of yours, I suppose you are not pleased with your treatment here. You must not, said Oddbiörg, let this affect your hospitality, nor need you be so particular about a word of this kind. The less you say the better, replied Saldis, if you can tell us nothing good. I have not yet said too much, she answered; but I do not think this love of theirs will last long. Then Saldis said, I should have thought my good treatment of you deserved some other omen; and if you deal with evil bodings, you will have a chance of being turned out of doors. Well, said Oddbiörg, since you are so angry about nothing, I see no need for sparing you, and I shall never trouble you again. But, take it as you will, I can tell you that these boys will hereafter be the death each of the other, and one mischief worse than another for this district will spring from them. So Oddbiörg is out of our story.

CHAPTER 13

It happened one summer, at the Althing, that the Northern men and those of the West-firths met one another on the wrestling ground in a match according to their districts. The Northerners had rather the worst of it, and their leader was Márr, the son of Glum. Now a certain man of the name of Ingolf, the son of Thorvald, came up, whose father lived at Rangavellir. Márr addressed him thus--You are a strong-limbed fellow, and ought to be sturdy; do me the favour of going into the match and taking hold. his answer was--I will do so for your sake, and forthwith the man he grappled with went down, and thus it was with the second, and the third, so that the Northerners were well pleased. Then said Márr, If you want a good word on my part, I shall be ready to help you. What may be your plans? I have no plans, he answered, but I had an inclination to go northward and get work. Well, rejoined Márr, I should like you to go with me; I will get you a place. Ingolf had a good horse of his own, which he called b the name of Snækoll, and he went northward to Thverá, after the Thing was over, and staid there some time. Márr asked him one day what he intended to do. There is and over-looker wanted here, who ought to be somewhat handy; for instance, here is this sledge to be finished, and if you can do that you can do something worth having. I should be too glad of such a place, said Ingolf, but it has sometimes happened that my horses have caused trouble in the pastures of the cattle. No one will talk about that here, answered Márr; so Ingiolf set to work on the sledge. Glum came up, and looked at what he was doing. That is a good piece of work, he observed. What are your plans? Ingolf answered, I have no plans. Glum replied, I want an over-looker, are you used to that sort of business? Not much, in such a place as this, but I should be glad to stay with you. Why should it not be so? said Glum; for I see that you and Márr get on well together. When Márr came home Ingolf told him what had passed. I should like it much, he answered, if it turns out well, and I will take care, if anything displeases my father, to tell you of it three times; but if you do not set it right then I must stop. So Ingolf took to his business, and Glum was pleased with him.

One day Glum and Ingolf, his over-looker, went to a horse-fight; the latter rode a mare, but the horse ran along by their side. The sport was good; Kálf, of Stockahlad was there, and he had an old working horse who beat all the others. He called out, why dont they bring into the ring that fine-jawed beast of the Thverá people? They are no fair match, said Glum, your cart-horse and that stallion. Ah! exclaimed Kálf, the real reason why you will not fight him is because he has no spirit in him. It may be the old proverb is proved true, the cattle are like their master. You know nothing about that, answered Glum, and I will not refuse on Ingolfs part, but the fight must not go on longer than he chooses. He will probably know well enough, said Kálf, that little will be done against your wishes, The two horses were led out, and fought well, and all thought Ingolfs horse had the best of it; Glum then chose to separate them, and they rode home. Ingolf remained that year in his place, and Glum was well satisfied with him.

Not long after this there was a meeting at Diupadal, whither Glum, and Ingolf with his horse, came; Kálf also was there. This last man was a friend of the people of Espihole, and he demanded that they should now let the horses fight it out. Glum said it depended on Ingolf, but that he himself was against it; howerer, he did not like to back out of it, and the horses were led out accordingly. Kálf spurred his horse on, but Ingolfs horse had the best of it in every contest. Then Kálf struck Ingolfs horse over the ears with his staff in such a way as to make him giddy, but immediately afterwards he went at his adversary again. Glum came up, and fair fighting was restore, till in the end Kálfs horse bolted from the ring. Then there wars a great shout, and at last Kálf smote Ingolf with his stick. People interfered, and Glum said, Let us take no note of such a matter as this; this is the end of every horse-fight. Márr, on the other hand, said to Ingolf, Depend upon it, my father does not intend that any disgrace shall attach to you for this blow.

CHAPTER 14

There was a man named Thorkel, who lived at Hamar. Ingolf went thither, and met this mans daughter, who was a handsome woman. Her father was well enough off, but he was not a person of much consideration in the country. Ingolf, however, attended properly to his duties as over-looker, but he did not work as a craftsman so much as he had done, and Márr spoke to him once about it saying, I see that my father is not pleased at your being often away from home. Ingolf gave a fair answer, but it came to the same thing again, and Márr warned him again a second and third time, but it was no use.

One evening it happened that he came home late, and when the men had had their supper Glum said, Now let us amuse ourselves, and let each of us say what or whom he most relies on, and I will have first choice. Well, I choose three things on which I most rely; the first is my purse, the second is my axe, and the third is my larder. Then one man after another made his choice, and Glum called out, whom do you chose, Ingolf? His answer was, Thorkel, of Hamar. Glum jumped up, held up a the hilt of his sword, and going up to him said, A pretty sort of patron you have chosen. All men saw that Glum was wroth. He went out, and Ingolf went with him, and then Glum said to him, Go now to your patron and tell him you have killed Kálf. Why, replied he, how can I tell him this lie? You shall do as I please, answered Glum, so they both went together, and Glum turned into the barn, where he saw a calf before him. Cut its head off, he cried, and then go southward across the river and tell Thorkel that you look to him alone for protection, and show him your bloody sword as the token of the deed you have done. Ingolf did this; went to Thorkel, and told him as news how he had not forgooten the blow Kálf had given him, and how he had killed him. The answer was, You are a fool, and you have killed a good man; get you gone as quick as you can, I do not choose that you should be slain on my premises. Then Ingolf came back again to meet Glum, who asked him Well, how did your patron turn out? Not over well, said he. You will have trouble on your hands, remarked Glum, if Kálf, of Stockahlad should really be killed.

Now Glum himself had killed Kálf, at Stöckahlad, whilst Ingolf was away, and had thus taken vengeance for him, and the following day Kálfs death was publicly known. Thorkel said at once that a fellow had come thither who had taken the death on himself, so that everybody thought it was really so. The winter passed on, and Glum sent Ingolf northward, to the house of Einar, the son of Konál, and gave him nine hundred ells of cloth. You have had no wages, he said, from me, but with your saving habits you may turn this to good account, and as regards this matter which is laid to your charge I will take care of that. It shall not hurt you; I paid you off for your perverseness in this way, and when you come home you may come and pay me a visit. Ingolf answered, One thing I beg of you, do not let the woman be married to any one else. This, I promise you, said Glum. Ingolfs horses were left where they were. Einar, the son of Konál, got Ingolf conveyed abroad, but Thorvald began a suit at the Hegranes Thing for the slaughter of Kálf, and it looked as if Ingolf would be found guilty. Glum was at the Thing, and some of Ingolfs kinsmen came to him, and asked him to look after the case, professing their readiness to contribute to pay the fine for him. Glum told them, I will se to the suit without any fine being paid.

When the court went out to sit, and the defendant was called on for his defence, Glum stated that the suit was null and void, for you have proceeded against the wrong man; I did the deed. Then he named his witnesses, who were to certify that the suit was void; for though Ingolf did kill the calf in the barn, I did not make any charge against him for that. Now, I will offer an atonement more according to the worth of the man killed, ant according to the pride of you men of Espihole. So he did, and the people left the Thing.

Ingolf was abroad that winter, and could stand it no longer, but turned his cash into goods, and purchased valuable articles, and tapestry hangings of rare quality. Glum had given him a good cloak, and he exchanged that for a scarlet kirtle. The summer that he had sailed there came out to Iceland the man called Thiodolf, whose mother lived at Æsustad. He visited Hamar, and fell in with Helga. One day Glum was riding up to Hole, and a he went down the hill at Saurbæ, Thiodolf met him. Glum said to him, I do not like your visits to Hamar; I mean myself to provide for Helgas marriage, and if you do not give this up I shall challenge you to the Holmgang. He answered that he was not going to math himself with Glum, and so he left off going thither.

CHAPTER 15

Then Ingolf came out to Iceland and went to Thverá, and asked Glum to take him in, which was granted. One day he said, Now, Glum, I should like you to look over my merchandize. So he did, and it seemed to him that Ingolf had laid out his money well. Then Ingolf said, You gave me the capital for this voyage, and I consider all the goods as belonging to you. No, answered Glum, what you have got is not enough for me to take anything from you. Here, answered Ingolf, are some hangings which I purchased for you--these you shall accept; and here is a kirtle. I will accept your gifts, replied Glum.

Another time Glum asked him if he wished to remain at home with him, and Ingolf answered that his intention was not to part from him if he had the choice o staying. My stud-horses I will give you, he said, and Glum replied, The horses I will accept, and now to-day we will go and find Thorkel, at Hamar. Thorkel received Glum well, and the latter said, You have wronged Ingolf, and now you must make it up to him by giving him your daughter in marriage--he is a proper man for this match. I will lay down some money for him, and I have proved him to be a worthy fellow. If you do not act thus, you will see that you have made a bad business of it. So Thorkel consented, and Ingolf got his wife and settled down as a householder and a good useful man.

CHAPTER 16

Glum married his daughter Thorlauga to Vigu-Skuta, of Myvatn, in the north country, but on account of disagreement the husband caused her to return to Thverà, and divorced her, which annoyed Glum much. Afterwards Arnor Kerlingarnef wooed her and had her to wife, and good men are sprung from that marriage. From this time there was a great feud between Glum and Skuta. One summer it happened that a vagabond fellow came to Skuta and asked to be taken in. He inquired what he had been doing, and the answered was that he had slain a man and could not stay in the district to which he belonged. Skuta replied, Well, what are you ready to do to earn my protection? What do you ask for? said the other. Why, you shall go, as sent from me, to Glums house, and tell him that you want him to take charge of your affair. I think it will turn out with reference to your meeting that he is now on his way to the Thing. He is a good man to help any one in trouble, if people want his aid; and it may be that he will tell you to go to Thverà and wait for him there. You will then say that you are in too great a strait for this, and that you would rather have some talk with him alone, and it may be that he will tell you what to do. An any rate ask him to let you meet in the Midárdal, which runs up from the homestead at Thverà and in which his pasture-huts stand; say that you would be glad to find him there on some day named for the purpose. The man assented to all this, and it was arranged as Skuta had proposed. Now this fellow, who was to serve as a bait, came back to Skuta and told him the whole. You have done your work well, said he, and you had better stay with me. Time passed on until the day came when Glum had promised the meeting, and then Skuta gets ready to start from home with thirty men. He rides southward, and then west, over the heath of Vadla, and so on to the bank which is called Red-bank, and there they dismount. Then Skuta says to his men, You will have to stay here a little while, and I will ride further into the valley, along the side of the hill, to see if there is anything to be got. When he looks along the valley he sees a tall man, in a green cloak, riding up from Thverà, whom he knows to be Glum, and gets off his horse. He has a cape on him of two colours, one side black and the other white, and he leaves his horse in the clearing and goes up to the pasture-hut into which Glum has entered. Skuta holds in his hand the sword named Fluga, with a helmet on his head; he goes up to the door, knocks upon the wall, and then steps on one side close to the hut. Glum comes out, without any weapon in his hand, and sees no one by the hut, but Skuta rushes forward between Glum and the doorway. Then Glum knows his man, and starts away from him. The gorge in which the river runs is near the hut. Skuta calls to him to wait, but he says it would be all right if they were armed in the same way, and makes for the gorge with Skuta after him. Glum jumps right into the gorge, but Skuta looks about to see where he can get down. Then he sees in the gorge a cloak driven along in the water, and runs towards it, thrusting at it with his sword; but he hears a voice calling out above him, There is little honour to be won by spoiling peoples clothes. He looks up and recognizes Glum; who in fact knew that there was a grassy bank on the edge of the stream where he jumped down. Well, says Skuta, remember one thing, Glum, you have run for it, and would not wait for Skuta. Glums answer is, That is true enough, and I only wish that, before sunset this day, you may have to run for it as far as I have done. Glum sung a verse--

> South of the river here, I trow,
> Each bush is worth a crown;
> Elsewhere the forest often saves
> The outlaw hunted down.

So they parted at that time; but Glum went home, got his people together, told them what a trap had been set for him, and expressed his desire to take vengeance for it at once. In a short time he collected sixty men and rode up into the valley. Skuta, after parting with Glum, got back to his horse, and riding along the hill-side he saw the men on their way. He thought it would not be good for him to meet them, so he made his plan, broke his spear-head off its shaft, handled this as if it were a pole, unsaddled his horse and rode bareback, with his cape turnd inside out, shouting as if he were looking for sheep. Glums men overtook him and inquired if he had seen any man fully armed riding over the hill? He replied that he had seen one. What is your name? they asked. I am called, he says, Plenty in the Myvatn country, but at Fiskelæk people call me Scarce. They answered, You are making sport of us; but he said he could not tell them anything truer than what he had told them, and so he parted from them. As soon as this was done he took up his daddle again and rode sharply off to his own men. Glums people came up to him and told him they had met a man who had answered them with a jest, and they said what his name was. You have made a blunder, said Glum; it was Skuta himself that you fell in with. What could he say that was more true? In the Myvatn country caves (Skuta) are plenty, and in Fiskelæk they are scarce. He has come pretty close to us, and we must ride after him. So they came up to the bank where Skuta and his men were, but there was only one path up to it, and the position was easier to defend with thirty men that it was to attack with sixty. Skuta then called out, You have taken a good deal of trouble to follow me up, and I suppose you think you haves something to pay me for on account of your escape. No doubt you showed great presence of mind in jumping into the gorge, and you were pretty quick of foot about it. Yes, said Glum, and you had some reason to be afraid when you pretended to be a sheperd belonging to the Eyjafirth people, and hid your arms or broke some of them. I fancy you had to run quite as far as I did. Skuta replied, However things may have gone up this time, try now to attack us with double our number. Glums answer was, I think we will part this time, whatever people may say of either of us. So Skuta rode away north, and Glum went home to Thverà.

CHAPTER 17

When Thorir died his son Thorarin set up his household to the north of Espihole and lived there. Glum had two children by his wife, of whom one was Márr, as has been said above, and the other was Vigfuss; both promising, but utterly unlike each other. Márr was quiet and silent, but Vigfuss was a dashing fellow, ready to do an unfair thing, strong and full of courage. There was a man living with Glum, who was called Hallvard, and was a freedman of his; he had brought Vigfuss up, and having got a good deal of property together by cheating in money matters , he had made over the reversion if it to his foster-child. Hallvard had a bad name, and went to live at a place called The Tarns, in the valley of the Eyjafirth: nor did his reputation impove on account of the spot where he dwelt, for he was sharp in dealing with the cattle in the common pastures up there. Vigfuss was a great traveller

A man hight Halli lived at Jorunnarstad, who was called Halli the white, and he was the son of Thorbiörn, whilst his mother was Vigdis, the daughter of Andun the bald. Now Halli had fostered Einar, the son of Eyiolf, who then lived at Saurbæ. Halli was blind, and was mixed up in all the lawsuits in the country because he was both a wise man and sound in his judgment. His sons were Orm and Brusi the Skald, who lived at Törfufell, and Bárd, who lived at Skállstad. Bárd was a noisy, quarrelsome fellow, better able to fight than anybody, and reckless and abusive in his language; he had for a wife Una, the daughter of Oddkell, in Thiorsádal.

One autumn Halli missed some ten or twelve wethers out of the hill pastures, and they could not be found, so when Bárd and his father met, Halli asked his son what he thought had become of the wethers. Bárd replied, I dont wonder if sheep disappear, when a thief lives next door to you, ever since Hallvard came into the district. Yes, says Halli, I should like you to set on foot a suit against him, and summon him for theft. I dont think, if I make this charge against him, Glum will go the lengths of clearing him by the oath of twelve men. No, answered Bárd, it will be a difficult matter for him to get the oath of twelve men out of Glum and Vigfuss and their people.

CHAPTER 18

Then Bárd set his suit on foot, and when Vigfuss knew it, he told his father that he should not like proceedings for a theft to be commenced against his foster-father. Glums answer was, You know he is not to be trusted, and it will not be a popular thing to swear him guiltless. Vigfuss said, Then I would rather that we had to deal with a matter of greater consequence. Glum replied, It seems to me better to pay something on his account and let him change his residence and come hither, than to risk my credit for a man of his character.

When men came up to the Thing, the case was brought on in court, and Glum had to swear one way or the other with his twelve men. Vigfuss became aware of the fact that his father intended to find Hallvard guilty, so he went to the court and said that he would take care Glum should pay dearly for it, if his foster-father was declared guilty. It ended in Glum quashing the suit by swearing that Hallvard was innocent, and he got discredit by doing so. In the course of a winter or two it happened that Halli lost a pig of his, which was so fat that it could hardly get on its legs. Bárd came in one day and asked if he pig had been killed, and Halli said it had disappeared. Bárd replied, he is gone, no doubt, to look for the sheep which were stolen last autumn. I suppose, said Halli, they are both gone the same way. Will you summon Hallvard? Well, replied Bárd, so it shall be, for I do not think Glum will this time swear Hallvard free; Vigfuss was the cause of he previous acquittal, and he is not now in the country. Bárd took up the case and proceeded to serve the summons; but when he met Hallvard he made a short matter of the suit by cutting of his head, and went and told his father. Halli did not like it; he straightway found Glum, told him what had happened, and offered to leave the matter in his hands. Glum accepted the offer, assessed the damage at a small sum, and caused the pig and the sheep to be paid for, by doing which he was well spoken of. When Vigfuss returned he was displeased at Hallvards death; but his father said, I shall not allow this settlement to be disturbed now it is made; and when Vigfuss and Bárd met nothing passed between them.

The next summer there was a meeting appointed for a horse-fight, in which all the horses in that district were to be fought; those from the upper against those from the lower rape, and either party were to select their man as umpire to decide which had the best of it. The judgment of the men thus chosen was to be abided by. From the upper rape Bárd was taken, and from the lower Vigfuss, the son of Glum. There were many horses, and the sport was good, but the fight was pretty equal, and many matches came off, with the result however that the number of those which fought well, and those which bolted was the same. so they agreed that it was an equal match; but Vigfuss said he had a horse which had not fought, which was the best on the ground that day. Come, said he, do you match some one with him. Bárd answered, He looks a poor beast to us, we will not match any horse with him; let us say it is a tie. Oh, replied Vigfuss, the fact is you have none to meet him, but you do not choose to own that you have got the worst of it. Up to this time, said Bárd, You have acted impartially, but now the sky is clouding over. Now we see the truth, that you have stood by your mother at the dresser in the pantry, and talked about cooking oftener than you have been at horse-fights, and that is the reason why your beard has never got any colour in it. Vigfuss and other people laughed at this joke.

Hallis servant came home, and his mater asked him about the horse-fights. He said the match was held to be a tie. Then Halli asked, Did Bárd and Vigfuss agree? Yes, pretty well, but Bárd said one thing to Vigfuss. What was that? he inquired; then the servant repeated it, and Halli said, That will lead to mischief. The servant said, Vigfuss laughed at it. Yes, but it is the way of Glum and his son to laugh when the fit for killing somebody comes upon them.

When Halli and Bárd met, the former asked his son, How came you to talk in that reckless way? I fear it will lead to great evil. You have but one thing to do,

332

and that is to go abroad and get house timber; you must stay away three winters or your death is certain. Bárd answered, There is nothing in it if you were not a coward, but old age causes you to be afraid on account of your sons. You are no doubt a very brave fellow, said Halli, but you will find it difficult to stay in the district. So Bárd took his fathers advice and went abroad, and Halli bribed a vagrant fellow to go into Skagafirth, or to the westward of it, and tell the story how Bárd was gone away; and how for the sake of one word, on account of Glum and his son, the only safe course for him had been to become an exile; and ho no one in the district dared to do anything which they disliked. This fellow did what Halli wished, and they had recourse to this plan in order that Bárds kinsmen might not be molested for his sake. Bárd stopped out one winter, and then returned to his home.

CHAPTER 19

Whilst Bárd was away Halli took care of his property, and got some timber cut in a wood in Midárdal which belonged to him, and Bárd brought out a good deal of timber with him. Sometimes he stayed at his own home, and sometimes with his father. Bárd said he would go and fetch his timber home, when Halli remarked, I would not have you go yourself, for it is not good to trust that father and son. Oh, said Bárd, nobody will know that I am going. So he went, and a servant with him, to fetch the timber, and they took a good many horses with them, but his wife Una had gone to Vidines to see her sister Oddkatla, and Bárd went thither on his way. Hlenni begged him to send some one else into the wood, and to stay where he was himself; it seemed more prudent to do so, but Bárd answered there was no need of it.

The two sisters went with him out of the homestead, but when they were returning Una looked back at him over her shoulder, and fell down in a swoon. Her sister asked her what she had seen? I saw dead men coming to meet Bárd, said she; he must be fey. We shall never see one another again. Bárd and his men made their way into the wood, and when they were there, they got their loads of timber together, and tied up their horses, but a great mist had come on. Very early that morning the shepherd from Thverà had been a-foot, and Vigfuss met him and asked him for tidings, as he often did. It is wonderful to me, he said, that you never fail to find your sheep in such a fog as there is now. The shepherd answered, It is a small matter for me to find my flock, but those men whom I saw in the wood in the morning had more trouble to find their horses, which were really standing close to them. They were fine looking fellows; one was in a green kirtle, and they had shields by their sides. Vigfuss asked him if he knew the man? He said he thought it was Bárd, for he was the owner of the wood where they were. Get my three horses, said Vigfuss. There were two Easterlings staying there whom Vigfuss asked to ride with him, saying that he was going to the warm spring; but when he got out of the homestead he made as if he would ride southward over Laugardal. The Easterlings asked him, Whither are you riding now? On some business of my own first, said he, so he rode a good way in front of them, and they went southward above the enclosures, until they saw Bárd coming out of the wood with his loaded horses. Bárds servant saw some one riding after them, and remarked, These men are riding sharp after us. Who is that? said Bárd. It is Vigfuss, he replied, and I think we had better get away from him. There is no disgrace in doing so, whilst we know nothing of their intentions. Bárd said, He will not set on me with three men, if you are not with me. I would sooner go with the horses, answered the man, and do you ride to Vidines. You cannot be blamed for going where you have business, and you do not know for a certainty what they who are riding after us want, thought Hlenni told you not to trust them. Bárd told him then, You shall ride on forward and, if I am delayed, tell our men what is going on, for it is likely that I and Vigfuss shall be some time about it, if we look one another fairly in the face; and he is too good a man to set on me with three against one. If, on the other hand, we are two and they are three, they will take the benefit of the difference in strength.

The servant did what Bárd told him, and Bárd himself unstrapped his shield, and got ready in the best way he could. When they came up he asked what they wanted? Vigfuss said that both of them would not quit the meeting-place alive. Bárd replied that he was ready, if they two only were to play the game out; but there is no manhood in it if three are to set on one. The Easterlings then said they would have staid at home if they had known their errand, but that they could not take part unless, in consequence of Bárds companion having ridden off, men should come to his assistance. Vigfuss told them to see first how matters went. So he and Bárd fought for some time without either being wounded, but it looked worse for Vigfuss, inasmuch as he had to give ground every time without being able to make a single blow tell. Bárd had his sword, and defended himself admirable without being touched. In the mean time the Easterlings thought it would be a bad business if Vigfuss should be slain, while they stood by doing nothing, and if men should come up to help Bárd. They they rushed at him, so that he was dying when Hlenni and his men got there. Vigfuss and his friends rode home, but Glum was ill pleased with what they had done, and said that the difficulties in the district would be greatly increased. Halli went to his foster-son Einar, at Saurbæ, and asked him to take the case in hand, and he admitted that he was bound to avenge his kinsman and foster-brother.

Then they rode to Thorarin, and asked for his support; he replied that he knew no man he would rather have to deal with than Vigfuss, and they confirmed with oaths their alliance with reference to that and all other matters. The cause went to the Thing, and attempts were made to compound it, but there was so much in the way that it was difficult to effect a compromise, as both the men of Mödrufell and those of Espihole, who resisted it, were bold in spirit, and well versed in the law. The case was closed by a verdict against the Easterlings, and by money being given to allow Vigfuss a safe conduct. He was to have three summers to get a passage out, and to have three places of refuge in each year, but he was an outlaw on peril of his life elsewhere, and not allowed to be at home on account of the sacredness of the place. However, he stayed long at Upsal, though people thought he was in other quarters of the island, and he would not go abroad within the period fixed. Then he became completely outlawed, and Glum kept him concealed, but outlawed men were not allowed to live there because Frey, who owned the temple, did not permit it. So matters went on for six winters.

CHAPTER 20

We must now go back to the point where the foster-brothers Arngrim and Steinolf were growing up together. When Thorgrim of Mödrufell died, Arngrim went to his own house, and Steinolf remained with him, and there was as much affection between them as there had ever been. Arngrim took a wife, Thordis, the daughter of Biörn, and the sister of Arnor Kerlingarnef. Steinolf was at that time abroad, engaged in trading voyages, but when he was in Iceland he was at Arngrims house. It happened one summer, on his arrival in the Eyjafirth, that Arngrim did not invite him to his house, and though they met he did not speak to him, imputing to him that he had talked with his wife, Thordis, more than was proper; but the report of most men was that there was little or nothing in the matter. Then Glum asked Steinolf to visit him, and he was there for a year or two when he was in Iceland, and they regarded one another with much affection as kinsmen. Steinolf was an active merry fellow. One summer Glum did not ask him to his house, and said that he preferred that he should be with his father at Upsal, and my reason is, I do not approve of men living in other peoples house, but if you are with your father then you can come over hither to Thverà, and I shall be glad to see you. Vigfuss, for some winters, whilst he was an outlaw, was at Upsal with Arnor Red-cheek, and Steinolf was there also. One autumn a yeoman at Öxnafell married his daughter, and invited all those land-owners in Eyjafirth, who were of most consequence; Steinolf too was invited. He came over to Thverà, and wanted to go with Glum, bout Glum said he should not be at the wedding. Then Steinolf observed, What I do not like is that you do not abide by what you say. Well, said Glum, my want of consistency will not do so much harm as your want of prudence, and I will not go. It is a piece of presumption at any rate, if there is no deeper design in it, for a yeoman to ask so many men of consequence to his house. But I suspect that something more is meant that appears, and that the yeoman did not get up this scheme himself, so I think it better that I and my friends should stay away. Steinolf, however, and those who were asked, with the exception of Glum, went to the wedding. Einar, the son of Eyiolf, Thorvald, and Steingrim had a good deal of talk together. When people were going away, Einar made a long speech about the management of affairs in the district, and said it was fitting that when they met in any number they should talk over the matters of most urgency; that in this way things would get into a better state. For instance, he said, there has long been a bad feeling among men of the highest spirit, and I allude particularly to the fact that there is a quarrel between the two kinsmen Arngrim and Steinolf, whilst we think that some lie or calumny is at the bottom of it all. Now Arngrim wishes to invite Steinolf to his house, and will receive him honourably if he choose to accept the invitation. So get rid of all unfriendly feeling between you. Steinolf professed his readiness to accept the offer, and his unconsciousness of any cause of offence, and he added that he loved Arngrim above all men. The each man returned to his home, and Steinolf went back with Arngrim, and remained with him, for several nights with all honour.

CHAPTER 21

One day Arngrim asked Steinolf if he would go down with him to Grund to a club-feast, and stay two or three nights. He replied, I will stay at home now and go some other time when you are here. Arngrim expressed a hope that he would wait for his return, if he would not accompany him, and he went on to Grund, but Steinolf stayed over the night. In the morning Steinolf was sitting by the fire, with some work in hand; it was a certain casket which belonged to the lady of the house. At that moment Arngrim returned home with Thorvald the crooked, and as they came into the sitting-room Steinolf was bending down over his work. Then Arngrim struck him on the head in such a way as to cause his death; but the mistress of the house came up to him and exclaimed, Wretch that thou are to strike this blow! This is the work of wiser men than thou art; but from this day I will never be they wife. She went to the house of Arnor Kerlingarnef and never came together with Arngrim again; but before she rode off she said, It will be some consolation, Arngrim, that your days are to be few, for those which are to come will be worse for you. Afterwards she became the wife of Asgrim, Ellidagrims son.

Arngrim and Thorvald rode to Espihole and told Thorarin what had happened, asking for his protection, and adding that whilst they had neither the wisdom nor the popularity to hold their own against Glum, he (Thorarin) had abundance of both. He replied to them and said that the deed seemed to be bad, and one from which apprehended evil consequences. Thorvald thought it was no use to find fault with what had been done, and that if he did not support them, he would soon have greater difficulties on his hands. They hoped to get other people to help them, if he would speak on their behalf. My counsel, says Thorarin, is that you should both remove from Grund and Mödrufell, and that we should collect men as soon as we may, and join our households together, before Glum is informed of it. They did this before Glum heard what had occurred; but when he learnt it he assembled his people, who proceeded to attack them. However, there was no opportunity for doing so with effect, as the men of Espihole had the larger force, and so they remained quiet for the winter. Glum, on the other hand, was never to be got at; he was so cautious about himself that he never slept in the bed which had been prepared for him. Very often he rested little at night, but he and Márr walked up and down and talked about lawsuits. One night Márr asked him how he had slept, and Glum answered by a stanza--

> Mid all this strife and tumult now
> Sleep doth mine eyelids flee.
> These men will find it hard, I trow,
> To make their peace with me,
>
> Before upon their crests shall ring
> My sword in battle-fray.
> I've slain men for a small thing,
> And why not these, I pray?

Now I will tell you of my dream. Methought I went out of the homestead here by myself and without arms, and Thorarin seemed to come at me with a large whetstone in his hand, and I felt ill prepared for our meeting; but whilst I was thinking about it I saw another whetstone lying close by me, so I cuaght it up and attacked him, and when we met either tried to strike the other, but the two stones came against one another and there was a tremendous crash. Was it such, asked Márr, as might be considered a conflict between the two houses? More than that, replied Glum. Did it seem that it might represent a conflict between the two districts? Yes, said Glum, the omen may well be reckoned such, for I thought the crash could be heard all over the district, and when I woke I sung as follows

> I thought this night to see in sleep
> that chief, who o'er the sea
> guides the fierce raven of the deep,
> Smite with a stone at me.

> The lord of Limafirths broad strand
> Came on in all his pride,
> I met him fearless hand to hand
> And dashed the blow aside.

Márr observed it was very likely the old saying would come true, Each of you will smite the other with and evil stone before it is over. Yes, said Glum, it is not improbable; there are many bodings tending that way. There is another dream to tell you. Methought I was standing out of doors, and that I saw two women who had a trough between them, and they took their stations at Hrisateig and sprinkled the whole district with blood. I woke up, and I think this portends something which is to happen. Then I sung these verses--

> The gods--methought, they swept along
> Across the path of men.
> the clash of swords and the javelins song
> We shall hear full soon again.

> I saw the maids of carnage stand,
> In grim and vengeful mood,
> As the battle raged, and they drenched the land
> In slaughtered warriors blood.

That morning Márr rode to Mödrufell, with seventeen other men, to summon Arngrim for the death of Steinolf; but Glum remained at home with five men besides himself, and told them to be quick in getting back again. In the house with Glum were Jöd, and Eyiolf, the son of Thorleif the tall, Thorvald Tafalld, Glums nephew, and two thralls.

CHAPTER 22

Helga, Glum's sister, who had been married to Steingrim of Sigluvik, had at that time come to Laugaland; she was the mother of Thorvald Tafalld, who was then eighteen years of age. There was a man named Thorvard, the son of Ornolf and of Yngvillda, who went by the name of Everybodys sister. He lived at Krisnes, and had a son named Gudbrand, who was then twelve years old. Thorvard was

337

a prudent man, and tolerably well inclined to help any one, but he was then old. That morning he was early a-foot, and told his man to get his horses. Then they rode to Thverà, and when they got there Márr had just started. Glum welcomed Thorvard well, and the latter inquired if any attempt had been made to procure a settlement between the parties. Glum told him None. Thorvard asked, Is the suit set on foot? Glum said it was not. Then said the other, A day like this would be a good one for this business: there is much mist, and no one would know what was going on, if one went quietly about it. Glum went on to say how matters stood, and how six men only remained at home. Thorvard answered, You have rather a small number with you, but the steps you have taken will no doubt be sufficient. Then Thorvard rode to Espihole, and when he came thither the men were not up; but he found Thorarin, and inquired, What do you intend to do? Do you intend to offer Glum any composition for the death? Thorarin answered, We do not think it an easy matter to offer to compound with Glum. Is the suit set on foot? asked Thorvard. I have not heard, said Thorarin; but what do you know about the matter? Oh, replied he, Márr rode off this morning with seventeen others to proceed with the suit, and Glum remained at home with five men; no doubt it would now be a famous chance for setting matters straight, but you fellows here never get the best of it, because you are not so sharp in your movements as Glum is. Well, said Thorarin, the fact is I do not like to set up mere gossip and nonsense on our side to meet this charge. Thorvard answered, Whether there was any sufficient cause or not is a point which ought to have been considered before Steinolf was killed. Did he not try to seduce Arngrims wife? Of a surety I think such a matter as that is not to be reckoned as nothing. Thorarin persisted, I do not like having to do with such a business. What do you mean, said Thorvard, by talking thus? Glum got something by that outlawry of your relative, Sigmund, and your clear course is not to let yourself be thus insulted by him. I am not sure, said Thorarin, whether that is or is not a wise course.

After this conversation the people of the house got up, and Thorvald the crooked pressed that they should ride to Upsal and give notice of outlawry as against Steinolf for his conduct to Arngrims wife, so that he might be taken to have been rightly killed. Thorarin said, That does not seem very advisable, but we will do it. There were fifteen of them in all, of whom seven are named, that is to say, Thorarin, Thorvald the crooked, his son Ketill, Arngrim, Eystein the Berserker, Thord the son of Rafn, who lived as Stockahlad, and had married Vigdis, the daughter of Thorir and widow of Sigmund, and Eyvind, the Norwegian who was staying with Thord. They went to Upsal, but Thorvard rode to Öngulstad (where there lived a good yeoman, Halli the fat), and sent his son to Thverà, desiring him to tell Glum the purpose of the men of Espihole, and afterwards, he added, you will ride back quickly to meet me.

When Thorvard came to Öngulstad, Halli asked what news he had to tell. Nothing as yet, he replied; but then he told him what was the position of things, and Halli thought he saw pretty clearly that Thorvard had brought all this trouble on, and he told him that such men as he were born for mischief, inasmuch as he desired that every man should be at variance with his neighbour; and he added, It would serve you right if you were killed. Then Halli went in a great hurry with all the people, men and women, whom he had got, with the intention of interfering between the two parties, if it were necessary. Gudbrand,

Thorvards son, got to Thverà, and said that his father had sent him thither; he told Glum what had occurred, and how my father thought himself bound to tell you this which concerns you nearly, that the men of Espihole intend to give notice of outlawry as attaching to Steinolf. Glums answer was, Why did not your father come himself? The lad said, I consider it all the same which of us two came. Glum replied, Your father has done well in sending you hither, if we are in want of men: so he made him dismount, and fastened up his horse. Gudbrand exclaimed, My father told me I must get back quickly. Oh, rejoined Glum, it cannot be so; he was desirous, no doubt, that you should show your manhood to-day.

In the meantime Thorvard began to say, My son Gudbrand is late. Halli inquired whither he had sent him. I sent him to Thverà, answered Thorvard. It is well, said Halli, that you should meet with some cunning people, and it serves you right.

The men of Espihole rode across the river with the intention of passing at the Ship-ford. Glum saw them riding, and remarked that Márr was somewhat too late. Then he ran out of the homestead with six men, of whom Gudbrand was one, and followed the other party. He had his shield and a halberd, with his sword by his side, and hastened on the road, with his men after him, to come up with them. When Thorarin saw them coming he had his people ride their own way, no faster and no slower on that account, and no one can blame us for that. Thord, the son of Rafn, asked Thorarin whether they with twenty men were to let themselves be chased by Glum with his six? Thorarins answer was, Let us ride on, for Glums object is to delay us and to wait for his own people. Thord said, It is no wonder that when he stands on equal vantage-ground with us we often get the worst of it with Glum; seeing that now, when he has only a few men with him, you do not dare to wait for him; but he shall not make me run, and so he dismounted. Eystein the Berserker said too that he would not ride away from Glum, so that they should profess to have driven us off. Thorarin observed that this course seemed to him inexpedient; but when Glum saw that they did not go on, he slackened his pace, and addressed Thorarin, asking what their errand was at Upsal. Thorarin replied that they had determined to proclaim Steinolf as liable to outlawry. Then Glum said, Is not this rather too strong a measure? Should not some offer of satisfaction be tried first, and we might possibly hit upon some method for bringing this suit to a close. Thorarin said that he wanted to delay them and had them ride on, and so they did. Glum asked them, Will you stay a little bit longer? but they rode away from him, and as they rode slower, so Glum slackened his pace and waited for his men, and said, Your cause will not find much favour, if you rake up a parcel of lies, and it will end only in disgrace. We shall not look to that now, replied Thorarin; it is a hard matter to come to terms with you. Whilst they rode on, Glum kept going forward alongside of them, talking with them, and thus delayed them. But when he saw he could not keep them back any longer, and felt sure of his own men coming up, then he threw his spear at Arngrim so that it went through the mans thigh and the saddle-bow also, and Arngrim was disabled for the day. Eystein was the first who then rushed at Glum, but Thorvald Tafalld stood out to meet him, and they two fought with each other. Every other man thought he was well off in proportion as he kept away from them; for they were both full of courage and strength, and each of them dealt the other many and sore strokes. Thorvald the crooked attacked Glum sharply and many more with him, but Glum and his men got out of their way and protected themselves as well as they could. Thorarin did not get off his horse, for he thought that they were quite enough to set on one man.

CHAPTER 23

Whilst they were fighting a man came up at full speed, wearing a hood of skins, with a sword in his hand. He came where Thorvald Tafalld had fallen before Eystein, and rushing at the latter, gave him a death-blow. Then he joined himself to Glums side, and Glum called out to him, Good luck to you Thundarbenda! I made a good bargain when I bought you. You will pay me well to-day for the outlay. Now Glum had a thrall who was called by that name, and that is why he spoke thus; but in reality it was Vigfuss, Glums son, though few or none except Glum himself knew him, for he had been three winters outlawed and living in concealment, so that most people thought he had gone abroad. It happened that whilst Glum was getting away he fell, and lay on the ground, and his two thralls lay over him, and were killed with spear-thrusts; but at that moment Márr with his men came up. Then Thorarin got off his horse, and he and Márr fought, without any other men meddling with them. Glum sprung up, and joined heartily in the fight, and there was then no advantage of number on either side. A servant of Thorarins, named Eirik, who had been about his work in the morning, came too his maters aid with a club in his hand, but without other arms of offence of defence; and Glum suffered much by him because his men were injured both in person and in their arms by that club which he bore. It is told too that Halldor, Glums wife, called on the women to go with her, saying, We will bind up the wounds of those men who have any hope of life, whichever party they belong to. When she came up Thorarin was just struck down by Márr, his shoulder was cut away in such fashion that the lungs were exposed. But Halldor bound up his wound, and kept watch over him till the fight was over.

Halli the fat was the first who came up to interfere, and may men were with him. The end of the combat was that five men of those from Espihole were killed, that is to say, Thorvald the crooked, Arngrim, Eysein, Eirik, and Eyvind the Norwegian. On Glums side there fell Thorvald Tafalld, Eyiolf son of Thorleif, Jöd, and the two thralls. Thorarin got home with his people; Glum also returned with his men, and had the dead carried into an outbuilding, where the utmost honour was done to the body of Thorvald, for garments were placed under it, and it was sewn up in a skin. When the men had returned, Glum said to Halldora, Our expedition to-day would have been successful, if you had staid at home, and if Thorarin had not escaped with his life. She replied, There is little of life in Thorarin, and if he lives you will not be able to remain in the district long; but if he dies you will not be able to remain in the country at all. After this Glum said to Gudbrand, You got much honour by your prowess to-day in killing Thorvald the crooked, and you did us good service. Gudbrand replied that nothing of the sort had happened; he had only defended himself as well as he could. Oh, said Glum, that is all very well. I saw clearly what took place; a mere child in age to kill such a champion as Thorvald! You will always be talked of for this deed. I got credit abroad in the same way for killing the Berserker. I never slew Thorvald, answered Gudbrand. It is no use trying to conceal it, my good friend, you gave him the wound which killed him. Do not shirk the good luck which has fallen to you. Glum maintained his point with Gudbrand till the latter believed what he said, admitted that he had done it, and thought it an honour to himself, so that it could no longer be concealed, and the death was formally laid to his charge. This seemed to those who took up the suit for Thorvalds slaughter to be less promising than had been expected: Thorvald was chosen as the man whose death was to be avenged.

People report a speech of Glums--One thing I do not like, and that is that Márr should have his head tied up, though he has gat a bump on it. What he called a bump was in fact a cut crosswise over his head. Márrs answer was, I should not need this so much if I had lain down and use a couple of thralls as a shield. Well, my lad, said Glum, our field Hrisateig (Bush acre) was hard to mow to-day. Márr replied, It will turn out a bad mowing for you in one way, for you have mowed the land at Thverà out of your own hands. I do not think you know that for a certainty, rejoined Glum. I may not know it, but it will turn out for you as if I did now it, was Márrs answer. Now, when Helga, Glums sister, heard the tidings, she came over to Thverà and asked how her son had borne himself. There was no better man, said Glum. I should like to see him dead, said she, if that is all that is left for me. they allowed her to do so, and she caused him to be lifted into the waggon, and tenderly handled, and when she got home she cleansed his wounds and bound them up, and dealt with him in such a way that he recovered his speech.

The law was then that if an equal number of men were killed on either side they were set off against each other, though there might be a difference in the men themselves; but if one party had the worst of it they had to select the man for whom atonement was to be demanded. If anything however, happened to turn up afterwards, by which it would have seemed better to have made a different choice, they could not change their selection. When Thorarin heard that Thorvald Tafalld was alive, he chose his own brother Thorvald the crooked, as the man to be atoned for. When, however, he found a little afterwards that the latters death was laid to the charge of Gudbrand, he would gladly have selected another man, but he had to abide by his first choice. Then they found Einar the son of Eyiolf, and Thorarin told him he should now take advantage of that agreement which they had formerly made with each other. Einar replied, My mind is the same now that it was formerly when Bárd was killed. he then took up the suit to carry it on at the Thing, in the summer, and he made the charge against Glum. Thorarin was laid up with his wounds the whole summer, and so was Thorvald Tafalld, but they both recovered. Glum had a great number of men with him at the Thing, and so in fact had both parties. An attempt was now made by persons of consideration connected with both sides to bring about a settlement of the case. The suit was compounded on these conditions, that is to say, that the death of Steinolf was to be considered as atoned for, if Vigfuss, Glums son, were proclaimed free from his penalty. Gudbrand, however, was convicted of the death of Thorvald, and Glum got him taken abroad. They returned home with affairs in this condition; but Thorvard and Thorarin were very much dissatisfied, and the latter thought he had obtained no honourable satisfaction for the death of his brother Thorvald. Glum remained at home much looked up to, and in the course of the winter there got abroad a stanza which he had lately composed:

> She asks--he nymph that pours the wine--
> the deeds of death that I have done.
> Theyre past and gone, those deeds of mine;
> But no man yet has talked of one.

CHAPTER 24

One day, when men had got together at the warm bath of Hrafnagil, Thorvard came thither. He was a merry fellow, and amused himself in many ways. What men, he asked, have you got here who can entertain us with some fresh stories? There is plenty of amusement and fun where you are, they said. Well, he replied, nothing amuses me more than reciting Glums verses; but I keep thinking over what can be the faulty reckoning he speaks of in one of his stanzas, when he says he did not get credit for all the people he had killed. What are we to suppose to be the real state of the case? Which is more likely, that Gudbrand killed Thorvald, or that Glum did it? This view seemed to many men worth consideration, and Thorvard rode to meet Thorarin, and said to him, I have been thinking the matter out, and I am convinced that the truth has not been known about the death of Thorvald the crooked. You will find in Glums verses, that he says he has not got credit for all the men he has killed. Thorarin answered, I can hardly take the case up again, though you should be right, and so things shall remain as they are. Thorvard rejoined, That is not a proper course, although if the matter had not been revived, all might have gone on quietly; no I shall talk of it publicly, and there will fall on you disgrace greater than any which has yet ensued in this affair. Well, said Thorarin, it seems to me an awkward matter to carry this cause to the Althing, in the face of the power of Glum and his kinsmen. Thorvard replied, I can give you a piece of advice on that point. Summon him to the Hegranes Thing: you have plenty of kinsmen there, and he will find it hard to defend the case. That we will do, said Thorarin, an so they parted.

The spring was a bad one, and everything became difficult to procure. At that time Thorarin set on foot the suit as against Glum at Hegranes Thing, inasmuch as all the priests of the different division in the district who belonged to that Thing, were bound to Thorarin by the ties of kindred. It was scarcely possible to get across the moors with horses, on account of the snow. So Glum adopted the plan of putting a large vessel into the charge of his brother, Thorstein, who was to sail in her to the westward, and convey arms and provisions to the Thing. When, however, they came off Ulfsdal, the ship went to pieces, and all the men and property on board her were lost. Glum got to the Thing with a hundred and twenty men, but he could not encamp nearer to the place itself than in the outer circle, or verge of the court. Einar, the son of Eyiolf, with the men of Espihole, was already there. Word was sent to Glum that he was to present himself to the court, and produce his plea in answer to the indictment. Glum went accordingly, but the men were drawn up on both sides in such a way that there was not more space than would allow of one man passing, and Glum was desired to go into the enclosure if he wanted to get to the court. He did not think this an advisable course, so he said to his men, It is easy to see that they think they have got our affair in their own hands now. Well, it may be so, but I should like you to fall back and change your order. I will march first, then two men following me in a line, and then four in a line after them, and so on; and we will march right at them, keeping our spears before us, and this sort of wedge must make its way in if you follow close up. They did this, and pushed without interruption right into the ring which was cleared for the court, but it was night long before they could be got of the ground again, so as to allow the court to sit; so great was the crush and press. At last it was brought about that the court was reconstituted, and they were proceeding to sum up the case when Glum came forward on the bank were the court was held, and called his witnesses to the fact that the sun had risen again on the field of the Thing; then he protested solemnly against any judgment being given in the case before them. It followed from this protest that every suit before the court at once discontinued and fell to the ground. Men rode away, and the people of Espihole were very ill pleased with what had happened.

Thorarin declared that Glum had dealt vexatiously with them, but Einar replied, The matter does not appear to me to be so very ugly, for the suit may be taken up again at the point where it left off. Afterwards the men of Espihole rode to the Althing with Einar, and with many of their friends who had promised them their support against glum. Glums kinsmen gave him their help also in securing the benefit of the point of law, and the matter was settled by the advice of skilled men, on condition that Glum would take an oath in the case to the effect that he did not kill Thorvald the crooked. So when many men interceded, they compounded the matter on these terms--that Glum should swear he had not slain him; and the time was appointed when the oath should be taken, that is to say, in the autumn, five weeks before winter. They followed up the suit with such vigour that they were determined to bring it on again, if he did not take the necessary oath in three temples on the Eyjafirth, and if it were not done at the prescribed time the right to clear himself by the oath was to be forfeited. There was much talk about this business, and what Gums oaths would be, and how he would get on with them.

CHAPTER 25

Now men returned from the Thing, and Glum staid at home all the summer: everything was quiet in the district till it came to the time of the Leet, when they assembled at that court. Glum, however, was not there, and nothing was heard of him. Márr was at home in his dwelling; but in the autumn, five weeks before winter, he held a wedding-feast, and invited men to it, so that not less than a hundred and twenty people came together. This invitation appeared strange to everybody, for those who were concerned in the wedding were not persons of any consequence. That evening all the men of Eyjafirth were seen riding in from the dales two or five at a time, and the people who came down into the district were all collected in one body. Glum was there, and Asgrim, and Gizor, with three hundred and sixty men, and they came in the course of the night to the homestead, and sat at the wedding-feast.

343

The morning after Glum sent to find Thorarin, and told him to come to Diupadal, not later than six in the morning, to hear the oaths. Thorarin bestirred himself and got together a hundred and twenty men, and when they came to the temple, six people went into it, that is to say, Gizor and Asgrim with Glum, and Einar and Hlenni the old with Thorarin. Whoever had to take the temple oath laid hold with his hand of the silver ring, which was stained red with the blood of the cattle sacrificed, and which ought not to weigh less than three ounces. Then Glum said word for word thus: I name Asgrim to bear witness, and Gizor in the second place to bear witness, that I take the temple oath, on the ring, and I say it to the God. When Thorvald the crooked got his death-blow--

Vark at þar--ok vák ek þar--ok raudk at þ odd ok egg.

Now let those men who are skilled in such matters, and who stand by, look to my oath.

Thorarin and his friends were not prepared to find any fault, but they said they had never heard the form of words used before. In the same manner the oaths were taken by Glum at Gnupafell and at Thverà. Gizor and Asgrim stayed some nights at Thverà, and when they went away Glum gave Gizor the blue cloak, and he gave Asgrim the gold-mounted spear (which Vigfuss had given him).

In the course of the winter Thorvard met Thorarin, and asked him, Did Glum take the oath properly? We found nothing to take hold of, said Thorarin. It is a wonderful thing, replied Thorvard, that wise people should make such mistakes. I have known men who have declared themselves to have slain others, but I have never known a case of a man swearing explicitly that he was guilty, as Glum did. How could he say more than he did when he declared that he was there at the doing of the deed, that he took part in the death, and that he reddened point and edge, when Thorvald the crooked fell at Hrisateig?--though I admit that he did not pronounce the words as they are commonly pronounced. That scandal will never be done away with. Thorarin replied, I did not observe this, but I am tired of having to do with Glum. Well, said Thorvard, if you are tired because your health is not equal to it, let Einar take the matter up. He is a prudent man, with a great kindred, and many will follow him. His brother Gudmund will not be neutral, and he himself is most anxious for one thing-to get to Thverà. Then they met Einar and consulted with him, and Thorarin said, If you will take the lead in the suit many men will back you in it, and we will bring it about that you shall have Glums land, at a price not exceeding that which he paid to Thorkel the tall. Einar observed, Glum has now parted with those two things, his cloak and his spear, which his mothers father, Vigfuss, gave him, and bad him keep, if he wished to hold his position, telling him that he would fall away in dignity from the time that he let them out of his hands. Now will I take up the suit and follow it out.

CHAPTER 26

Einar now set the suit on foot afresh for the Althing, and both sides collected their people together, but before Glum left home he dreamt that many persons came to Thverà to visit the god Frey, and he thought he saw a great crowd on the sand-banks by the river, with Frey sitting on a chair. He dreamt that he asked who they were who had come thither, and they said, We are thy departed kindred, and we are now begging Frey that thou mayst not be driven out of Thverà, but it is no use, for he answers shortly and angrily, and calls to mind now the gift of the ox by Thorkel the tall. At that point Glum woke up, and ever afterwards he professed that he was on worse terms with Frey.

Men rode to the Thing, and the suit was brought to a close in such a way that Glum admitted the killing of Thorvald; but his kinsmen and friends exerted themselves to secure the acceptance of a settlement rather than the imposition of outlawry or banishment. So they compounded the matter at the Thing, on the condition that Glum was to forfeit the land at Thverà, half absolutely as an atonement to Ketell, the son of Thorvald the crooked, and to convey the other half at a valuation; but he was allowed to live there till the spring, and was then to be outlawed in the district, and not to live nearer than in Hörgardal. So they left the Thing. Einar afterwards bought the land, as had been promised to him. In the spring his men came thither to work on the farm, and Einar told them that they should give an account to him of every word which Glum spoke. One day he came and talked with them on this wise, It is easy to see that Einar has got good workmen about him; the work is well done on the land, and it is now of consequence that great and little matters should both be attended to. You would do well to put up posts here by the water side for drying clothes; it is convenient for the women washing the larger articles; the wells at home are indifferent.

When they got home Einar asked what Glum had said to them. They told him how careful he was with reference to all the work done. Did it appear to you, said he, that he was desirous of getting everything ready for my hands? Yes, they replied, so we think. Well, replied Einar, I think differently. I think he meant very likely to hang you on these posts, or stick on them some insult to me. You must not go there, however.

Einar transferred his household to Thverà in the spring, but Glum remained where he was till the last day for moving, and when people were all ready to start he sat down on the high seat and did not move, although he was summoned to do so. He had the hall decorated with hangings, and refused to turn out like mere cottage tenants. Hallbera, the daughter of Thorodd, the son of Hialm, was the mother of Gudmund and Einar, and lived at Hanakamb. She came to Thverà, and saluted Glum, saying, Good morning to you, Glum, but you cannot stay here any longer. I have marked out the land of Thverà with fire, and I eject you and all yours formally from it, as made over to my son Einar.

Then Glum rose up and told her she might chatter away like a miserable old woman as she was; but as he rode away he looked over his shoulder towards the homestead and sung a stanza--

> With sword and spear, as fame hath told,
> Like many a gallant earl of old,
> I won these lands by might and main.
> But now the wielder of the brand
> Has dashd at last from out his hand,
> Broad lands and lordships lost again.

Glum lived at Mödrufell, in Hörgardal, with Thorgrim Fiuk, but he was not content to remain there more than one winter. Then he dwelt two winters in Myrkárdal, but a landslip fell near the homestead and destroyed some of the buildings. After that he bought land at Thverbrek, in Öxnadal, and dwelt there as long as he lived, and became aged and blind.

CHAPTER 27

There was a man named Narvi who dwelt at Hrisey. He had as his wife Ulfeida, the daughter of Ingiald, son of Helgi the thin. Their sons were Eyiolf, Klængr, Thorbrand, and Thorvald, all distinguished men and kinsmen of Glums. Two of these, Klæengr and Eyiolf, lived at Hrisey, after their fathers death. A man named Thorvald, who had married Helga, the daughter of Thord, the son of Hraf, of Stöckahlad, and who was nicknamed Menni, dwelt at Hagi at that time. One spring Thorvald came from Hagi, and lay off Hrisey in his vessel, intending to fish, and when Klængr was aware of this he stared with him. They got out into the firth, and fell in with a whale which was just dead, which they made fast and towed into the firth in the course of the day. Klængr wanted to bring the carcass into Hrisey, because the distance was shorter, but Thorvald desired to tow it to Hagi, and said he had and equal right to do so. Klængr maintained that it was not the law to take it anywhere except to the nearest point where any of the men engaged in the capture owned land. Thorvald asserted his rights, and said that Glums kinsmen had no business to interfere with the fair partition of the fish. Whatever the laws were, the strongest should now have their way. At that moment Thorvald had the largest number of men with him, and so they took the drift fish from Klængr by force, though both of them were land-owners. Klængr went home very much dissatisfied, and Thorvald and his people laughed at him and his party, telling them they did not dare to hold on to their booty.

One morning Klængr got up early, and went with three other men in to Hagi, so as to be there in good time whilst people were still asleep. Then Klængr said-- Well try a scheme; here are cattle about in the homestead; we will drive them on to the buildings, under which Thorvald is asleep, and so we shall get him to come out. They did this, and Thorvald woke up and rushed out of doors. Klængr made at him, and gave him a mortal wound; but went away again without daring to declare himself the slayer, because there were so many people about on the spot. So he went out to one of the islands, and there declared that he had killed Thorvald. The right of claiming atonement belonged to Thorarin and Thord, and they treated the case as one of murder. When the suit was being brought before the Thing, Glum was quiet at home, but whilst the Thing was going on he went about in the districts of Fliot and Svarvadardal, begging for help to meet the execution of the anticipated sentence of forfeiture; however, he asked men to say nothing of this intention of his. Klaufi, of Bárd, exclaimed, To be sure we will help Glum; he married Halldora, the daughter of Arnor Red-cheek; and many men besides promised to support him. Then Glum returned home, but the suit ran its course at the Thing, and when that was over they got ready to carry out the sentence of forfeiture with four ships, and thirty men in each ship. Einar, Thorarn, and Thord commanded the ships, and when they came in-shore at the island, in the twilight of morning, they saw a smoke rising over the buildings. Einar asked his people whether it appeared to them, as it did to him, that the smoke was not a clear blue. They answered that so it seemed to them. Then, said Einar, it appears likely to me from that smoke that there are a good many people in the house, and that steam hanging in the air must be the steam from men. If this be so we shall find out about it by rowing away from the island openly and then we shall be sure if there by any number of men there. They did this, and when the men who were in the island saw them they rushed out to their vessels, and put out after them, for Glum had come thither with two hundred and forty men, and they chased them right up to Oddaeyr, so that the sentence of forfeiture was not carried out, and the men of Eyjafirth got dishonour by the failure.

Glum remained in his own dwelling through the summer. He had to open an Autumn court; but the place of holding it is on the east of the firth, not far from Kaupáng, and the men of Eyjafirth got a large force together, whilst Glum had only thirty men. Many people spoke to Glum and told him that he ought not to go with a small number of followers. His answer was, The finest portion of my life is gone by, and I am pleased that they have not driven me so hard that I cannot ride the straight path. He went up the firth in a ship, and then disembarked and went to he booths. Now between the firth and the booths there are certain steep ascents covered with loose gravel, and when Glum came opposite to the booth which belonged to Einar, men rushed out upon him and his people and dashed their shields against them so as to push them down the slope. Glum fell and rolled shield and all down the bank on to the spit of sand below. He was not wounded, but three spears had stuck in his shield. Thorvald Tafalld had then come to shore and saw that Glum was in a strait: he jumped on land with his oar in his hand and, running up the slope, hurled it at Gudmund the powerful: it came against his shield, which broke, and the handle of the oar struck him on the breast so that he fell down senseless and was carried off by four men to his booth. Then they challenged one another to come on, and cast weapons and stones on both sides, and the contest was a hard one; many were wounded; but all said the same thing--that it was impossible for a small number to fight better than Glum and his men had done. Einar and his men made a vigorous onslaught; but people interfered, and it ended in Glum losing two men, Klængr, the son of Narvi, and Grim Eyrarlegg, the brother of his wife Halldora. Then Brusi, the son of Halli, made these verses:

> Thou warrior-goddess of the shield!
> We held our own in battle fray--
> I know tis so--we did not yield
> The honour of the day.

> Those chiefs forsooth, the while we fought,
> (Bright nymph! it may not be denied)
> Strode somewhat faster than I though
> Adown the steep hill side.

Then Einar composed a stanza:

> he had to run away perforce
> From out the fight--that swordsman bold--

I trow twas hard to stop his course
As down the bank he rolled.

Well used the pirates spear to wield,
In vain that chieftain fought,
And the loose shingle failed to yield
The foothold which he sought.

Then Glum composed some verses in answer to him:

Though standing on the band so high
Their helmets made a gallant show,
They did not dare their luck to try
Upon the beach below.

They did not dare to risk the path,
Whilst on the sandy shore we stood,
And faced the dread Valkyries wrath
With shields that dripped with blood.

The matter was settled upon the ground that the death of Klængr and Thorvald of Hagi were set off one against the other, and the slaying of Grim Eyrarlegg was considered equal to the injury caused to Gudmund; but Glum was much dissatisfied with this close of the suit, as he expressed himself in the following stanza, which he made afterwards:

The world is worthless; and my life
With all the keen delights of strife
Hath well-nigh passed away.
Too weak, when gallant Grim lay low,
To strike mid men th'avenging blow,
And blood with blood repay!

CHAPTER 28

It happened one summer that the brothers Gudmund and Einar were riding back from the Thing, when Glum invited some guests to his house, and he sent men up to Öxnadal-heath and asked those brothers also, professing that he wished to be reconciled to them wholly and entirely. For, said he, on account of old age I am fit for nothing, and I will not invite them only to a meal. Glum was then blind, but he caused a look-out to be kept for their coming. Gudmund wished to accept the invitation, but Einar did not; and each of them rode on his own side of the river, till Glum was told that one of the two troops was coming that way. Then, said he, Einar will not accept the invitation; he is so distrustful that he will put confidence in no man. It is reported that Einar called out to Gudmund and said, If you go thither this evening, I will be sure to be there tomorrow; but Gudmund reflected on those words and said, Well, you must mean that you will have to take measures for avenging my death; and so he turned round and followed Einar. It was told to Glum that neither of the two was coming. Then it is a bad business, exclaimed he, for if I had gone to meet them, I had made up my mind not to miss both of them. He had a drawn sword under his cloak. So this was the last thing which passed between Glum and the men of Eyjafirth.

When Christianity was introduced in these parts Glum was baptized, and lived three winters afterwards. He was confirmed in his last illness by Bishop Kol, and died in white vestments. Márr, Glums son, lived at Forn-Hagi, and caused a church to be built there, in which Glum and Márr himself, when he died, were buried. Many other people also were buried there, because for a long time there was but that one church in Hörgárdal. People relate that for twenty years Glum was the greatest chief on Eyjafirth; and for another twenty years there were no greater men there, though some were on an equal footing with him. They say too that of all the valiant men that have been in this land he had the noblest spirit. And so ends the Story of Glum.

THE SAGA OF VIGLUND THE FAIR

CHAPTER 1
Of King Harald Fair-Hair

Harald Fair-hair, son of Halfdan the Black, was sole King of Norway in the days of this story; and young he was when he gat the kingdom. The wisest of all men was Harald, and well furnished of all prowess that befitted the kingly dignity. The king had a great court, and chose therefor men of fame, even such as were best proven for hardihood and many doughty deeds: and whereas the king was fain to have with him the best men that might be chosen, so also were they held in more account than other men in the land; because the king was niggard to them neither of wealth nor furtherance if they knew how to bear themselves. Nor, on the other hand, did this thing go for little, that none of those who were against the king's will throve ever; for some were driven from the land and some slain; but the king stretched his hand out over all the wealth they left behind. But many men of account fled from Norway, and would not bear the burden of the king, even men of great kin; for rather would they forego the free lands their fathers owned, their kin and their friends, than lie under the thraldom of the king and the hard days he laid upon them. These went from land to land; and in those days was Iceland peopled, for many fled thither who might not abide the lordship of King Harald.

CHAPTER 2
Of Olof Sunbeam

There was a lord named Thorir, a man of mighty power in Norway, a man of fame, and wedded to a noble wife: this earl begat on his wife a woman-child, Olof by name, who was wondrous fair-mannered from her youth up; and she was the fairest fashioned of all women of Norway, so that her name was lengthened and she was called Olof Sunbeam.The earl loved his daughter much, and was so jealous of her that no son of man might speak with her.He let build a bower of her, and let adorn that house with all kinds of craft.Wide about was it carven and fretted, with gold run through the carving; roofed with lead was this dwelling, and fair bepainted within; round about it was a wall of pales, and therein a wicket iron-bolted strongly: neither was the house adorned in meaner wise without than within.

So in this bower dwelt the earl's daughter, and her serving-women; and the earl sent after those women whom he knew to be the most courteous, and let them teach his daughter all the deeds of women which it befitted high-born maidens to know: for the earl had mind, as indeed it came to pass, that his daughter should excel all other women in skill and learning as she did in fairness.

But as soon as she was of age thereto, many noble men fell to wooing her.But the earl was hard to please concerning her, and so it came to pass that he gave her to none, but turned them away with courteous words; and for her, she mocked none either by word or deed.So slipped away a while and she had the praise of all men.

Now must the tale tell of other folk.There was a man named Ketil, who bare sway over Raum-realm; he was a mighty man and a wealthy, wise and well befriended.Ketil was wedded, and Ingibiorg was the name of his wife, and she was come of noble blood: two sons they had, Gunnlaug and Sigurd; bynames had those brethren, for Gunnlaug was called the Masterful, and Sigurd the Sage.Ketil let learn his sons all the craft that it was the wont of those days to learn, for he himself was better furnished with such things than most other men.So the brethren had playmates, and they gave them gold and other good things; and ever they rode out with their men to shoot the wild things and fowls of the air, for of the greatest prowess and craft were they.

Goodman Ketil was a great fighting man, four-and-twenty holmgangs had he fought, and had won the victory in all.

There was good friendship between King Harald and Ketil.

This Ketil was so great a lawyer, that he never had to do in any case, with whomsoever he dealt, that he did not prevail; for so soon as he began to talk, all folk deemed that so it must be as he said.

The king bade Ketil take a higher dignity, saying, that it well befitted him, both for his wealth's sake and for many other matters; but Ketil would not, and said he had liefer be just a very franklin, and hold himself none the less equal to folk of higher dignity.

Ketil loved his wife so well, that he would not have her know a sorrow.

Thus wore the time away.

CHAPTER 3
Of the Sons of Earl Eric

It befell on a time that King Harald called out his sea-folk, with the mind to go south along the land, and arrayed his journey well, both with ships and men.Ketil got his sons to go with a very fair company in the king's fellowship, but he himself sat at home, for he was now sunken into eld.

Now when the king was ready he sailed south along the land; but when he came south to Rogaland, there was an earl held sway there called Eric; a great chieftain, and well beloved of his men: who, when he heard of the king's coming, let array a fair feast and bade the king thereto with all his company; that the king took, and went ashore with his host, and the earl led him home to his hall, with all his court and all kinds of minstrelsy and songs and harp-playing, and every disport that might be.With such welcoming the earl brought the king to his hall, and set him in the high seat, and there befell the fairest feast, and the king was exceeding joyous, and all his men, because the earl spared in nought to serve the king with all loving-kindness; and the best of drink was borne forth, and men were speedily merry with drink.

The king ever set Ketil's sons beside him, and they had great honour of him: the earl stood before the king, and served himself at his board, and great grew the glee in the hall.Then the king caused those brethren to pour out, and set the earl in the high seat beside him; and the brethren did straightway as the king bade, and gat great praise of men for their courtesy.But when the boards were taken up, the earl let bear forth good things which he had chosen for the king, yea, and to all his men he gave some good gift or other; and at the end of this gift-giving the earl let bear forth a harp, whose strings were this one of gold and that one of silver, and the fashion of it most glorious; and the king stretched forth his hand to meet it, and began to smite it; and so great and fair a voice had this harp, that all wondered, and thought they had never heard the like before.

Then spake the earl: "I would, lord, that thou wentest with me for thy disport, and then will I show thee all I have, within and without, and both cornfield and orchard."

So the king did as the earl bade, and went and beheld all about, and made much of it; and they came to a certain apple-orchard wherein was a fair grove, and under the grove three lads a-playing: fair were they all, but one much the most fair.So they sat a-playing at tables, and that one played against the twain; then these deemed that their game was coming to nought before him, and so they cast the board together; thereat was the better one wroth, and he smote each of them with his fist: then they fell to and wrestled, the two against him alone, and he prevailed no less in the wrestling than in the table-play.

Then the earl bade them forbear and be at one, and they did so, and played at tables as before.And the king and his company went home to the hall, and sat

351

them down; and it was well seen of the king that he thought much of that youngling; and he asked the earl concerning what those lads were.

"They are my sons," said the earl.

"Are they of one mother? "said the king.

"Nay," said the earl.

Then the king asked what they hight, and the earl said, "Sigmund and Helgi, but Thorgrim is the third, and love-born is he."

So a little after came all those brethren into the hall, and Thorgrim went the hindermost; for in this, as in other matters, was he less honoured.

The earl called the boys to him, and bade them go before the king; and they did so, and greeted him: but when they came before him, Thorgrim put a hand on each of his brethren, and pushed them from him, and passed forth betwixt them, and stood up on the footpace and greeted the king, and kissed him: but the king laughed and took the lad, and set him down beside him, and asked him of his mother; but he said he was the sister's son of Hersir Thorir of Sogn.Then the king, pulled a gold ring off his arm, and gave it to Thorgrim.

Then Thorgrim went back to his brethren, and the feast endured with the greatest honour till the king declared his will to depart.

"Now," said he, "because of the great-heartedness thou hast shown to me, shalt thou thyself choose thy reward."

The earl was glad thereat, and said, that he would have the king take Thorgrim his son of him: "Better," saith he, "do I deem that than store of pennies, because that everything that thou wouldst do to me, I shall deem so much the better if thou doest it to him; and for that cause am I fain he should go with thee, because I love him the best of all my sons."

So the king said yea thereto, and departed, and Thorgrim with him, who right soon grew to be most gentle of manner in all service to the king; wherefore began many of the king's men to envy him.

CHAPTER 4
Thorgrim Wooeth Olof Sunbeam

The tale tells, that on a time the king went a-guesting to a man named Sigurd, and the feast was well arrayed with all things needful: and the king bade Thorgrim stand forth that day, and pour out for him and his chosen friends.Now many men misliked the great honour in which the king held Thorgrim: and Sigurd had a kinsman called Grim, a man wealthy of money; a man of such dignity, that he accounted all men nought beside him: this man was at the feast, and sat on the dais at the higher bench.So Thorgrim served that day; and as he bare a great beaker of drink before Grim, the liquor was spilt out of it because Thorgrim stumbled, and it fell on Grim's raiment.He grew wroth thereat, and sprang up with big words, saying, that it was well seen that the son of a whore was more wont to herding swine, and giving them their wash, than to serving any men of account.

Thorgrim waxed wroth at his words, and drew his sword and thrust him through, and men pulled him dead from under the board.Then Sigurd called on his men and bade them stand up and lay hands on Thorgrim: but the king said: "Nay, Sigurd, do it not!for Grim should fall unatoned because of his word; yet will I atone him with a full weregild, if thou wilt that I deal with the matter as I will: for thus will our friendship be better holden."

So it must be as the king would, and he paid so much money that Sigurd was well content; and the feast wore away, and there is nought more to tell of it.

Then the king went his way home: and now he bade the great men to him, and first of these Earl Thorir, and Master Ketil of Raum-realm; who now lacked a wife, because Ingibiorg had died in child-bed, when she had born a daughter, who was called Ingibiorg after her mother: but after these the king bade many men and a great company, for there was no lack of all things needful.

So men came as they were bidden to the feast; and Olof Sunbeam came thereto with her father.So men were marshalled to their seats and noble drink was borne forth.

Thorgrim went a-serving, and folk heeded much what a sprightly and goodly man he was: he was seemly clad, for the king honoured him exceedingly, and that misliked many of his men, and they hated Thorgrim therefor; and a byname was given him, and he was called Thorgrim the Proud.

But when Thorgrim saw Olof his heart yearned toward her, and even so it fared with her toward him, for she loved him; but folk noted it not, though as time served them they met together, and either was well-liking to other: so Thorgrim asked her how she would answer if he bade her in wedlock; and she said that for her part she would not gainsay it, if her father would have it so.So at the end of the feast Thorgrim set forth his wooing and craved Olof Sunbeam.Earl Thorir was not swift in assenting thereto, and they parted with so much done.

CHAPTER 5
The Wedding of Olof Sunbeam

A little after Thorgrim gat speech of the king, and craved leave to go see Earl Thorir, and the king granted the same; and when Thorgrim came to Earl Thorir's he had good welcome there.

Then again Thorgrim fell to his wooing, and would now know for sure what answer the earl would give; but the earl said he would not wed his daughter to him.

Thorgrim was there three nights, and he and Olof met lovingly; and some folk say that at that tide they plighted their troth.And so Thorgrim went back to the king for that time.

Now he went on warfare, and was fully come to man's estate; so he was a-warring through the summer, and was accounted the stoutest of men in all dangers, and he gat to him in this journey both riches and renown.

But after these things it befell that Ketil of Raumarik came a-riding to Earl Thorir's with thirty men, and King Harald also was a-guesting there. Then Ketil fell a-wooing Olof Sunbeam to wed her, and with the furtherance of the king Earl Thorir gave his daughter Olof to Ketil: but Olof neither said yea thereto nor thought it in her heart: and when the betrothals were to be fulfilled she sang a stave: ---

> "Sure glad ring-warder singeth
> Sweeter than any other;
> O Voice amid Earth's voices
> Henceforth but woe unto me!
> No ring-warder so white is
> That he may win look from me:
> One man have I made oath for,
> And well beloved is he."

Now most men held it for sooth that Olof had been fain to wed Thorgrim, but it behoved to go the other way.

So the day was appointed whereon the wedding was to be, and that was at winter-nights in the house of Earl Thorir: so wore away the summer.

But in the autumn came Thorgrim back from warfare, and heard that Olof was betrothed; so he went straightway to the king, and craved help of him to get the woman, whether Earl Thorir liked it better or worse, or Ketil either. But the king utterly gainsayed all help to Thorgrim, saying that Ketil was his best friend.

"And I will give thee this counsel," said the king, "that thou raise no strife with Ketil: I will woo Ingibiorg his daughter for thee, and in such wise shall ye make good peace between you!"

Thorgrim said he would not have it so: "I will hold," says he, "to my words, and the oaths that Olof and I swore betwixt us; and her will I have or no woman else. And since thou wilt help me not, I will serve thee no longer."

Said the king: "Thou must even rule the matter as thou wilt; but methinks it is most like that thy honour shall wax no greater in another place than with me."

So Thorgrim took leave of the king, and the king gave him a gold ring at parting which weighed a mark; and so he went to his own men.

Now it lacked three nights of the wedding-day; so Thorgrim went up a-land alone for any of his own men, and went till he came to the house of Earl Thorir.

Thither he came by then that the bride was set on the bench, and all the drinking-hall was full of men, and the king was set in the highseat, and the feast was at its full height.

So Thorgrim went into the drinking-hall, yea, unto the midst of the floor, and stood there; and so many lights were there in the hall, that no shadow fell from aught. All men knew Thorgrim, and to many, forsooth, he was no unwelcome guest.

So he spake: "Hast thou, Ketil, wooed and won Olof? "

Ketil said that so it was.

"Was it aught with her assent? " said he.

Says Ketil: "I am minded to think that Earl Thorir might give his daughter away himself, and that the match so made would be lawful forsooth."

"This is my word," says Thorgrim, "that Olof and I have sworn oath each to each that she should have no man but me.Let her say if it be so."

And Olof said it was true.

"Then meseemeth the woman is mine," said Thorgrim.

"Thou shalt never have her," said Ketil."I have striven with greater men than thou, and prevailed against them."

Said Thorgrim: "Well, meseems thou dost these things in trust of the king's furtherance; so here I bid thee to holm.Let us fight it out and he shall have the woman who winneth her on holm."

"Nay, I am minded to make the most of it that I have more men than thou," said Ketil.

But lo, while they were a-talking thus, all lights died out throughout the hall, and there was a mighty uproar and jostling; but when lights were brought again the bride was gone, and Thorgrim withal; and all men deemed it clear that he had brought it about: and true it was that Thorgrim had taken the bride and brought her to his ship.His men had made all ready even as he had aforetime appointed them, and now they were arrayed for sea; so they hoisted sail as soon as Thorgrim was ready, for the wind blew from off the land.

These things befell in the thick of the land-settling-time of Iceland; and Thorgrim thought sure enough that he might not hold himself in Norway after this business: so he made for Iceland.They put forth into the sea and had a fair wind, and made Snowfellness, and went a-land at Hraunhaven.

But the king and the earl heard of Thorgrim's journey, and Ketil was deemed to have won the greatest shame, in that he had lost his wife, and it was not well seen that he would have right of Thorgrim.The king made Thorgrim an outlaw for this deed at Ketil's urging: but turn we from these a while.

CHAPTER 6
Of Ketilrid and Her Kin

There was a man named Holmkel, who dwelt at Foss on Snowfellness, by Holmkel's River: he had to wife Thorbiorg, the daughter of Einar of Bath-brent, and they had two sons together, one named Jokul and the other Einar.Holmkel was the son of Alfarin, who was the son of Vali; his brothers were Ingiald ofIngialdsknoll, and Hauskuld of Hauskuldstead, and Goti of Gotisbrook.

355

So Thorgrim the Proud bought the lands of Ingialdsknoll, and Ingiald on the other hand went a-trading, and comes not into our tale.Thorgrim soon became a great chieftain, and a most bounteous man; and he got to be great friends with Holmkel of Foss.

Now tells the tale that he made a wedding for Olof, and the winter after they set up house at Ingialdsknoll Olof bore a child, a man-child that had to name Trusty; the next winter she bore another boy, who was called Viglund, and he soon grew both strong and fair.

The same year Thorbiorg bore a woman-child, and it was named Ketilrid; so she and Viglund were of an age: but Trusty was one winter older.

So they grew up in that country, and all would be saying thereabout that there was neither man nor maid of fairer promise or of better conditions in all things than were Viglund and Ketilrid.

Holmkel loved his daughter so much that he would do nought against her will, but Thorbiorg loved her little.

Now whenas Viglund was ten and Trusty eleven winters old, there were none of that age as strong as they in all the country side, and Viglund was the stronger; their other conditions were according to this, and moreover Thorgrim spared in nought to teach his sons.

But Thorbiorg of Foss would learn her daughter no skill, and Holmkel thought it great pity of that; so he took the rede at last to ride to Ingialdsknoll with his daughter; and Thorgrim greeted him well, for great was the friendship between them.Holmkel was seeking fostering there for his daughter with Olof, that she might teach her skill, for Olof was accounted the most skilled of all women of Iceland; she took her rejoicing and got to love her exceeding well.

By this had Olof a young daughter named Helga, a year younger than Ketilrid; and so these young folk drew together in all joyance and glee: but in all games betwixt them it ever so befell that Viglund and Ketilrid would fall into company together, and the brother and sister Trusty and Helga.And now great love grew up between Viglund and Ketilrid, and many would be saying that it would make an even match for many causes.But ever when they were together would either gaze at other and turn to nought else.And on a time Viglund spoke and said that he was fain they should bind their love with oath and troth; but Ketilrid was slow thereover.

Said she: "There are many things against it: first, that thou mayest not be in the same mind when thou art fully come to man's estate; for about such things are ye men's minds nought steadfast.And again, it is not meet, neither will I have it, that we go against my father's counsels herein.And a third thing I see that may fret it all away is, that I am of no might in my matters; for so it is that these things go mostly after my mother's will, and she has little love for me: yet, indeed, I know none that I would rather have than thee, if I might rule matters; but my heart tells me that troubles great and sore lie in the way of it, however it may be in the end."

Full oft got Viglund's talk on to the same road, and ever she answered in like wise; and yet men deem indeed that they must have sworn troth each to each.

CHAPTER 7
Those Brethren of Foss Come to Ingialdsknoll

Now must we tell of the brethren Jokul and Einar, how they became exceeding ill-ruled in the country-side, treading herein in the footsteps of their mother.Holmkel was ill-content therewith, but might not better it, and they got to be hated because of their goings on.

Now on a time Einar fell to speech with his mother, and said: "I am ill-content with the honour of Thorgrim the Proud has in the countryside; and I am minded to try if I may not do my will on Olof his wife; and then it would either be that he would strive to avenge it, or else would his honour lie alow: neither is it all so sure that he would get the better of it, if he strove to get the thing avenged."

She said it was well spoken and just her very mind.So on a certain day, when Holmkel was from home, rode Einar to Ingialdsknoll, and Jokul his brother with him.

Olof the good-wife had bidden a home-woman of hers to lock the men's door every morning whenas the men were gone to work; and in such wise did she the morning those twain came to the stead.So the home-woman was ware of their coming, and went to Olof's bedchamber and told her that the Foss-dwellers were come thither.So Olof arose and clad herself, and went to her sewing-bower, and set down on the dais there a handmaiden, casting her own mantle over her, and saying: "Take it nought strange though they think thee to be me, and I shall look to it that thou get no shame of them."

Therewith she sent another home-woman to the door, for there was no man in the house.So Einar asked where Olof was, and it was told him that she was in her sewing-bower.Thither turned both those brethren, and when they came into the chamber, they beheld how Olof sat on the dais; so Einar sat down by her and began his talk with her.

But therewith came one into the hall clad in blue and with a drawn sword in hand, not great of growth, but exceeding wroth of aspect.

They asked of his name, and he called himself Ottar; they knew him not, and yet they waxed somewhat adrad of the man.

Now he took up the word and spake: "All must out, and welcome home Thorgrim the goodman, who is a-riding to the garth."Then up sprang the brethren, and went out, and beheld where the goodman rode with a great company; so they leapt on their horses and rode away home.

But it turned out that that great company was but the beasts being driven home; yea, and the blue-clad man was even Olof herself: and when the Foss-folk knew that, they thought their journey but pitiful: so ever waxed great hatred betwixt the houses.

But when goodman Thorgrim came home Olof told him all that was befallen, and he spake: "Let us tell nought hereof abroad, because of Holmkel my friend: for Einar did it not with his consenting."

CHAPTER 8
Of a Horsefight

Now those brethren had a stallion, brown of colour and a savage beast; every horse he dealt with he drave away: and two tusks he had, so huge that they were like no teeth of horses.Viglund also had a stallion, light-dun of colour, the best and fairest of horses, and held of great account amongst them.Thorgrim the Proud withal had two oxen, blaze-faced, and with horns like polished bone, and these oxen he liked well.

Now on a day the brethren Einar and Jokul rode to Ingialdsknoll, and there found the father and sons all three standing without the door: so Jokul asked Viglund to give him his light-dun horse.Viglund said he had scarce made up his mind to that; then said Jokul that it was niggardly done: but Viglund said he took no keep thereof.

"Then let us fight the horses," said Jokul.

"That meseems maybe," quoth Viglund.

"And that," said Jokul, "I deem better than the gift of thine to me."

"Good," says Viglund; "let the thing go as it will."

Therewith they appoint a day for the horsefight.So when the day was came the brown of those brethren was led forth, and devilish was his demeanour; so both the brethren got ready to follow him.Then in came Viglund's light-dun, and when he came into the ring he went about circling, till he reared up and smote both his forefeet on the brown's muzzle so that the tusks were driven from out him; thereafter he made at the brown with his teeth, and smote him in the belly, and tore him through, and the brown fell down dead.But when the Foss-folk saw that, they ran to their weapons, and so did the others, and there they fought till Holmkel and Thorgrim gat them parted; and by then was fallen one man of Viglund's, but two of the brethren's men; and in such wise man departed.

But still held the friendship between Holmkel and Thorgrim; and Holmkel withal got to know of the love between Ketilrid and Viglund, and did nought to hinder it: but Thorbiorg and her sons were exceeding ill-content therewith.

So wore away the time, till it was the talk of all men, that none of that day in Iceland were as fair as Viglund and Ketilrid, or as good in all skill and courtesy.

CHAPTER 9
Evil Deeds of Those Brethren

The tale tells, that on a time those brethren, Einar and Jokul, went from home a nighttide when it was bright and clear and came to the fell-common whereas dwelt Viglund's light-dun: they went up to the horses and would drive them home, but might not in anywise, for the dun warded the horses from their driving, but they had been minded to drive all the horses about him to impound him.

So when they might not bring it about they waxed exceeding wroth, and set on the stallion with weapons to slay him; but he defended himself with hoofs and teeth so mightily, that the night was far spent and nothing done: but it came to pass in the end that they got within spear-thrust of him and slew him so.

But when they had done it they were loth to drive the horses home, for they deemed that then it would be clearly seen that they had slain the stallion, and they were fain to hide the same; so they dragged him over a shear rock, with the intent that it should be thought that he had tumbled over of himself: then they fared home, and made as if nought had happened.

Again a little after went the brethren Einar and Jokul to a hill-common of Thorgrim the Proud wherein went his gelded beasts: and there had he a herd of fifty oxen.

So the brethren knew the goodly blaze-faced oxen, and took them and cast halters over them and led them along to Foss, and there slew them both, and then went and hung them up in an outhouse. This was a-night time, and they had made an end of their work before the home-men arose.

Their mother knew all about it, and was, forsooth, exceeding busy in helping her sons over this work of theirs.

CHAPTER 10
Holmkel Rides to Ingialdsknoll

Now must it be told, how that the brethren, Viglund and Trusty, went one day to their horses; and when they came to the hill-common to them, they missed their stallion, and, seeking him far and wide, found him at last stark dead under a great cliff; many and great wounds they found on him, and he had been thrust clean through.

So Viglund and his brother thought it clear that the Foss-folk had done it; so they went home and told how their horse was dead, and how it must have been done by the Foss-folk.

Thorgrim bade them keep it quiet; says he, "They were the first to lose their horse; and ye will have your turn again, if things go as I deem, even though ye let this pass over."

So for that time they let it pass at first: but not long after Thorgrim was told that his goodly blaze-faced oxen were gone, even those that he held in most account, and withal that folk deemed it the work of men.

Thorgrim made few words thereover, but said that it was most like that thieves who dwelt abroad in the mountains would have done such a deed; neither did he let any search be made for the oxen.

So this was heard far and wide, and men deemed that those of Ingialdsknoll had great scathe hereby.

Thorbiorg of Foss made plentiful mocking about this, and let eat the slaughtered oxen: but when goodman Holmkel came to know where the oxen were gotten to, he takes his horse and rides off to Ingialdsknoll: but when he finds goodman Thorgrim he tells him that he thinks his goodly oxen have gotten to his house, and that his sons must have done it."And now," says he, "I will pay for the oxen out and out, even as much as thou thyself wilt, if thou bring not their guilt home to them by law."

Thorgrim says that so it shall be; and so he took as much money as made him well content, and he and Holmkel parted with great friendship.

CHAPTER 11
The Brewing of a Witch-Storm

A woman named Kiolvor dwelt at Hraunskard, a great witch-wife of very ill conditions and hateful to all folk; and there was great friendship between her and Thorbiorg of Foss.So the mother and sons, Thorbiorg to wit, Einar and Jokul, bargained with Kiolvor and gave her a hundred in silver, so that she should overcome those brethren, Viglund and Trusty, by some such manner of witchcraft as she might see her way to.For the greatest envy beat about the hearts of these; and they had heard withal of the true love of Viglund and Ketilrid, and grudged that they should have joy one of the other, as was well proven afterwards.

But they twain loved ever hotter and hotter, with secret love and desire enfolded in their breasts, even from the time they first grew up; so that the roots of love and the waxing of desire were never torn up from the hearts of them; even as the nature of love is, that the fire of longing and flame of desire burneth ever the hotter, and knitteth the more together the breast and heart of the lovers, as folk stand more in the way thereof, as kith and kin cast greater hindrances before those betwixt whom sweet love and yearning lieth.Even so it fared with these folk, Viglund and Ketilrid; for ever all the days while they both lived they loved so hotly, that neither might look away from the other, from the time they first looked each on each, if they might but do as their hearts' yearning was.

Now there was a man named Biorn, a homeman of Thorgrim the Proud, and he was called Biorn of the Billows, because he was such a sea-dog that he deemed no weather unmeet to put to sea in; and he would ever say that he heeded nought the idle tricks of the billows.He had come out with Thorgrim, and his business it was to look to his craft; and there was good fishing off the ness.He never rowed out with more than two men, though he had a stout ten-oared yawl; but now this autumn it befell by Kiolvor's witchcraft that both his fellows lay sick, and all men else were busy about the hay.So Biorn would row a-fishing, wherefore he bade Viglund and Trusty go with him that day.They did so, because the weather was fair, and they all good friends together.But Kiolvor knew all this, and went up on to her witch-house, and waved her veil out toward the east quarter, and thereby the weather grew thick speedily.

So when they were gotten on to the fishing-banks there was fish enough under them, till they beheld how a cloud-fleck came up from the east and north-east.Then said Viglund: "Meseems it were good to make for land, for I like not the look of the weather."

Says Biorn: "Nay, let us wait till the ship is laden."

"Thou shalt be master," said Viglund.

Therewith the cloud-fleck drew all over the sky, and brought with it both wind and frost, and such an ill sea, that the waters were nowhere still, but drave about like grains of salt.

And now Biorn said they would make for land."Better before," said Viglund; "but I will say nought against it now."So Biorn and Trusty rowed, and made no way forward; but they drove south-west out to sea; and the craft began to fill under them.

Then Viglund bade Biorn bale and Trusty steer, but he himself took the oars, and rowed so mightily that they made land at Daymealness.There dwelt Thorkel Skinhood, who came out with Bardi the Snowfell-sprite, and was now old.

Now when it was told Ketilrid that they had been driven out to sea and were dead, she fell into a faint; but when she came to herself she sang this stave as she looked out toward the sea.:

> "No more now may my eyes
> meet the sea ungreeting,
> Since the day my speech-friend
> Sank below the seabanks.
> I loathe the sea-flood's swartness
> And the swallowing billow,
> Full sore for me the sorrow
> Born in sea-wave's burden.

But Thorkel gave the brethren a good welcome, and the next day they went home; and sweet and joyful was the meeting betwixt Viglund and Ketilrid

CHAPTER 12
Of Hakon the East-Man

Now must we take up the story whereas we left it awhile agone; for Ketil Ram was ill-content with such an ending of his case with Thorgrim the Proud; but he was fast getting old now, and he deemed it not easy to get aught done.His sons Sigurd and Gunnlaug were become hardy men and goodly, and Ingibiorg his daughter was the fairest of all women.

Now there was a man named Hakon, a Wickman of kin, wealthy and warlike: this man went his ways to Ketil of Raum-realm, and craved his daughter in wedlock; and Ketil gave this answer to his asking: "I will give thee my daughter on these wise; thou wilt first fare out to Iceland and slay Thorgrim the Proud, and bring me the head of him."

Hakon said he thought that no great matter; and so they struck the bargain.Hakon fared to Iceland that summer, and brought his ship into Frodaroyce; and the Foss-folk Jokul and Einar came first to the ship: the ship-master gave them good welcome, and asked them many things; and they were free of tidings to him.

Then he asked concerning lodging, and they said there was none better than at their father's house at Foss.

"A sister we have," said they, "so fair and courteous, that her like is not to be found; and we will do for thee which thou wilt; either give her to thee as a wife, or let thee have her as a concubine: so come, we bid thee thither to guest with us."

The master thought this a thing to be desired, so he said he would go thither; and tells them withal what errand he had in Iceland; and they liked the thing well: and now all bind themselves as fellows in the plot.

A little after went the ship-master home to Foss; forsooth clean against the will of Holmkel the goodman: but so it had to be.In a little while withal the ship-master got to be great friends with Thorbiorg; for he gave her many goodly things.

So on a time this Hakon fell to talk with the mother and sons, and asked where the woman was whereof the brethren had told him; "for I would see her," says he.

They said she was being fostered with Olof at Ingialdsknoll; so he bade them see to it and have her home: "For," said he, "I trust full well to have thy furtherance in the getting of my will of her, because of our friendship."

So a little after this Thorbiorg fell a-talking with goodman Holmkel."I will," she said, "that my daughter Ketilrid come home to me."

"Well," said the goodman, "I deem it better that she be left in peace where she is gotten to."

"Nay, it shall not be," says she; "rather will I go fetch her msyelf, then that she should have such rumour from Viglund as now lieth on her: yea, I will rather wed her to Hakon; for that methinks were a seemly match."

Therewith they make an end of talking; and Holmkel thought he could see, that Thorbiorg would send after Ketilrid, and he deems it better to go fetch her himself.So he rode to Ingialdsknoll, and had good welcome there.

But when he was come thither Viglund went to Ketilrid and spake thus with her: "Thy father is come hither; and methinks he is come after thee to bring thee home with him, and he must needs have his will.But now, Ketilrid, I am full fain that thou keep in memory all the privy talk we have had together, for indeed I know that thou wilt never be out of my mind."

Then said Ketilrid, sore weeping: "Long have I seen that we might not long have this joy in peace; and now belike it were better that we had not said so much: but not all so sure it is that thou lovest me better than I love thee; though my words be less than thine.But now herein do I see the redes of my mother; because for a long while I have had but little love of her; and most like it is that the days of our bliss are over and done if she may have her will of me: nevertheless should I be well content if I wist that all went well with thee.But howsoever it be, we shall never come together in bliss, but if the will of my father prevail; and a heavy yoke he has to drive, whereas my mother and brothers are afield, for in all things will they be against me.But thou, let all these things slip from off thee!"

Then went Viglund to Ketilrid and kissed her; and it was easily seen of her, yea and of both of them, how hard it was for them to part as at that time.

Moreover, Viglund sang a stave: ----

"Young now I shall not ever
Love any silken goddess,
That son of man shall say it,
Save thee alone, O Sweetling!
Therefore fair maid remember
The oath we swore aforetime,
Howso that women wilful
Would waste the love between us."

Then Ketilrid went into the house to her father, who straightway told her that she must away home with him.Ketilrid says that he must have his will; "But good," says she, "would I deem it to abide here ever: yet must it be even as it must."

A great matter it was to all to part with Ketilrid, for she was a joy to the heart of every man.

But now they ride home to Foss: and the shipmaster was wondrous fain of her coming home: but Thorbiorg her mother appointed her to serve Hakon; which thing she would in nowise do,but told her father thereof weeping; and he said: "Thou shalt not serve Hakon but if thou wilt: yea that alone shalt thou do which thou willest, and thou shalt be by me both day and night."

She said she was right glad of that: and so the time wore away a space, in such wise that Hakon got never a word with her.

CHAPTER 13
Ball-Play on Esja-tarn

Now was ball-play set up on Esja-tarn, and the Foss-men were the setters forth of the sport: and the first day when men came home from these games, Ketilrid asked if none had come thither from Ingialdsknoll; and she was told that they had all been there, both the father and sons, and Olof and her daughter Helga: so Ketilrid craved of her father next day that she might go to the play; he said yea thereto; and so they went all together that day, and great was the glee: for Thorgrim's sons were come and none other from Ingialdsknoll.

So the brethren went up on to the bank whereas the women sat; and Ketilrid stood up to meet them, and greeted them lovingly, and they sat down on either hand of her, Viglund and Trusty.

Then spake Ketilrid: "Now will I be just as kind to one of you as the other, and hoodwink folk thereby."

Therewith she gazed ever on Viglund and said: "Thy name will I lengthen this day, and call thee Viglund the Fair: and this ring I will give thee, which my father gave me as a toothing-token, and it shall be to thee a naming-token."

So he took the ring and drew it on to his hand; and gave her again the ring Harald's-gift, for his father had given it to him.And so, long was their talk drawn out: but when the Foss-men saw that, they took it sore to heart.

So either fare home that evening; and Hakon fell to speech with Thorbiorg, and bade her forbid her daughter to go to any more such meetings of men-folk, in such a mood as she was.She assented thereto, and told Holmkel the goodman not to let his daughter go to any play; but let her abide at home in peace rather: and he did so and Ketilrid's gladness departed from her.Then her father said, she should be ever by him at home if she thought it better so; and she said it pleased her well.

But men go to the play as aforetime; and one had one side, one the other in the play, the Foss-folk and Thorgrim's sons.And on a time Viglund drave the ball out beyond Jokul.Jokul waxed wroth thereat, and when he got the ball, he took it and drave it into Viglund's face, so hard that the skin of his brow fell down over his eyes.Then Trusty ripped a rag from his shirt, and bound up his brother's brow, and when that was done the Foss-folk were departed.

So the brethren went home; and when they came into the hall, Thorgrim cried out as he sat on the dais, "Welcome, dear son and daughter!"

"Why dost thou make women of us, father? " said Trusty.

"Belike," said Thorgrim, "a coif-wearer should be a woman."

"No woman am I," said Viglund."Yet may happen I am not so far short of it."

"Why didst thou not pay Jokul back? "said Thorgrim.

"They were gone," said Trusty, "by then I had bound up his face."And so the talk came to an end.

The next day both the brethren went to the play; and so when it was least to be looked for, Viglund drave the ball right into Jokul's face, so that the skin burst.Then Jokul went to smite Viglund with his bat, but Viglund ran in under the blow and cast Jokul down on the ice, so that he lay long swooning; and therewith were they parted, and either side went home.Jokul had no might to get a-horseback, and was borne home betwixt the four corners of a cloth: but he mended speedily, and the play was set up at Foss.So Thorgrim's sons arrayed them for the play.Thorgrim would have stayed them, saying that he deemed sore troubles would come of it; but they went none the less.

So when they came into the hall at Foss the play was begun, but folk were all in their seats in the hall.So Viglund went in and up to the dais, whereon sat the goodman and his daughter; and Ketilrid greeted him well.

He took her up from her seat, and sat himself down therein, and set her on his knee.But when the goodman saw that, he edged away and gave place, and then Ketilrid sat her down between them, and they fell to talk together.

Then let the goodman get them a pair of tables, and there they played daylong.

Hakon was ill at ease at that; and ever that winter had he been talking to goodman Holmkel and craving his daughter; but Holmkel answered ever in one wise, and said it might not be.

So wore the day till the brethren got them ready to go; but when they were on the causeway, lo, Ketilrid was in the path before them, and bade them not fare home that night."Because," quoth she, "I know that my brethren will waylay you."

But Viglund said he would go as he had been minded afore, and they did so; and each of them had his axe in his hand.But when they came to a certain stackgarth, lo the Foss-folk, twelve in company.

Then said Jokul: "Good that we have met, Viglund; now shall I pay thee back for the stroke of ball and felling on the ice."

"I have nought to blame my luck herein," said Viglund.

So they fell on the two brethren, who defended themselves well and manly.Viglund fought no great while before he had slain a man, and then another, and Trusty slew a third.

Then said Jokul: "Now let us hold our hands, and lay all these feuds on those brethren."

So did they, and either side went their ways home; and Jokul tells his father that Viglund and Trusty had slain three of his home-men."But we," quoth he, "would do nought against them till we had seen thee."

Now Holmkel was exceeding wroth at this tale.

CHAPTER 14
Ketilrid Betrothed to Hakon

Jokul kept on egging his father to wed Ketilrid his daughter to Hakon; so, what with the urging of those brethren, Holmkel did betroth her to him, but utterly against her will.Hakon was well minded to abide in Iceland, whereas he saw he could not bring to pass the slaying of Thorgrim the Proud.

So this was heard of at Ingialdsknoll, and Viglund took it much to heart.

But when Holmkel knew the very sooth about the waylaying of the brethren, he deemed he had done overmuch in giving Ketilrid to Hakon.

Now still came the sons of Thorgrim to the games at Foss as heretofore; and Viglund had speech of Ketilrid, and blamed her much with hard words in that she was betrothed.But when they arrayed them to go that night, lo, Hakon had vanished, and the sons of Holmkel, and many others with them.Then spake the goodman with Viglund: "I would," said he, "that ye went not home tonight: for meseemeth the departure of those brethren looks untrustworthy."

But Viglund said he would go, as he had afore been minded: but when they came out a-doors, there was Ketilrid in the way before them, who prayed Viglund to go another road."No great things will I do for thy word,"said he; and he sang withal: ----

> "Stem where the gathered gold meets,
> All trust I gave unto thee:
> Last thought of all thoughts was it
> That thou couldst wed another.
> But now no oaths avail us,
> Nought are our many kisses;
> Late learn we of women: ----
> Her word to me is broken."

"I think not that I have done any such thing," said Ketilrid; "but indeed I would that thou wentest not!"

"It shall not be," said Viglund; "for I have more mind to try the matter out with Hakon, than to let him cast his arms about thee, while I am alive to see it."And he sang: ---

> "I would abide the bale-fire,
> Or bear the steel-tree's smiting,
> As other men may bear it;
> But heavy maidens' redes are:
> Sorely to me it seemeth,
> Gold spoilers' shoulder-branches,
> The sweet that was my maiden
> Other than mine entwining."

CHAPTER 15
The Battle of the Foss-folk and Thorgrim's Sons

So they went on their way till they came to the stackgarth, whereas they had had to do before: and there were the Foss-folk, twelve in company.

Then the sons of Thorgrim gat them up on to the hay, which was in the garth, so that the others were not ware of them, till they had torn up great store of the frozen turf.

But when they had so done, they saw Thorgrim's sons, and fell on them, and there befell the fiercest of fights: till the Foss-folk saw that they made way slowly against Thorgrim's sons whiles they were up on the hay: then cried Jokul----

"Thou wert well counselled, Viglund, not to slink away; and we shall hold for certain that thou art no good man and true, but if thou come down from the hay there, and try the matter to its end."

So, because of Jokul's egging on, Viglund leapt down from the hay with Trusty his brother, and they met fiercely; and all the men of Hakon and those brethren fell, so that of the Foss-dwellers these alone stood on their feet, Jokul, Einar, and Hakon, with two men more who were hurt and unmeet for fight.

Thus said Jokul: "Now let us set to work in manly and generous wise; let Trusty and Einar fight together, and Viglund and Hakon, and I will sit beside the while."

Now Trusty was both sore and weary; and they fought, Trusty and Einar, till either fell.

Then fell to fight Viglund and Hakon; and Viglund was exceeding weary, but unwounded.

The fight was both hard and long, because Hakon was strong and stout-hearted, but Viglund strong of hand, and skilled in arms and eager of heart: but the end of their dealings was, that Hakon fell dead to earth, while Viglund was sore hurt.

Then up sprung Jokul, fresh, and without a hurt, and turned against Viglund, and they fell to fight: and a long space they fought, and hard enow, till none could see which would win the day; when Viglund sees that it is a hard matter to prevail against Jokul to the end because of his wounds and weariness; and so being as good with one hand as the other, he cast aloft axe and shield, and caught his shield with his right hand and his axe with his left, in such wise that Jokul noted it not, and then smote the right arm off him at the crook of the elbow. Then Jokul took to flight, nor might Viglund follow after him; but he caught up a spear from the ground, wheras many lay beside him, and cast it after Jokul; and that spear smote him, and went in at the shoulders and out at the breast of him; and Jokul fell down dead.

But Viglund was grown faint with the flow of blood, and he fell swooning and lay there as one dead.

Then the two Foss-men who were left, crawled away to their horses and rode home to Foss, and got into the hall; and there sat the goodman, with his wife on one side and his daughter on the other: then they tell out the tidings: that Hakon is fallen and the brethren, and seven other men besides, and the sons of Thorgrim withal.

When Ketilrid heard that, she fell fainting, and when she came to herself, her mother laid heavy words on her. "Now," quoth she, "is thy light-o'-love well seen, and the desire thou hadst toward Viglund: ---good it is that ye must needs be parted now."

Then said the goodman: "Why must thou needs turn this blame on her? She loved her brethren so well, that she may well be astonied at hearing of their fall."

"Maybe that it is so," said Thorbiorg; "yet surely I think not. But now the business in hand is to gather a company of men and go slay Thorgrim the Proud, as swiftly as may be."

"Yea, is that our due business? "said Holmkel."Meseems he at least is sackless of the slaying of those brethren; and as for his sons, they can lose no more than their lives; and soothly, it was but their due to defend themselves."

CHAPTER 16
Ketil's Sons Come Out to Iceland

Now Viglund and Trusty lay among the slain, till Viglund came to himself, and sought after his brother, and found there was yet life in him; wherefore he was minded to do what he might for him there, for he looked not to be of might to bear him to a dwelling: but now he heard the sound of ice breaking on the way, and lo, their father coming with a sledge.So Thorgrim brought Trusty into the sledge and drave him home to Ingialdsknoll; but Viglund rode unholpen.So he set them into an earthdug house under his bed, and there Olof awaited them, and bound their wounds: there they abode privily, and were fully healed in the end, though they lay full a twelvemonth wounded.

Holmkel let set his sons in mound, and those men who had fallen with them, and that place is now called Mound-knowes.

These things were now told of far and wide, and all thought it great tidings, deeming it wellnigh sooth that Thorgrim's sons were slain.

Thorgrim and Holmkel met, nor did this matter depart their friendship, and they made peace on such terms that the case should not be brought to law or judgment.But when Thorbiorg wist thereof, she sent privily to her father Einar, and bade him take up the feud after her sons; and follow up the sons of Thorgrim for full penalty, if yet they lived: and albeit Einar were old, yet he threw himself into this case, and beguilted the sons of Thorgrim to the full at the Thorsness-thing.

And all this came home to the ears of the countryside.

Now Hakon's shipmates sailed away in the summer when they were ready, and made Norway, and coming to Ketil told him throughout how all things had gone: wherefore it seemed to him that the revenge on Thorgrim and his sons was like to be tardy.Gunnlaug and Sigurd, the sons of Ketil, were come from a viking cruise in those days, and were grown most famous men: Gunnlaug the Masterful had sworn this oath, never to deny to any man a berth in his ship, if so be his life lay theron; and Sigurd the Sage had sworn never to reward good with evil.

So Ketil told his sons of the fall of Hakon, and bade them fare to Iceland and revenge his shame, and slay Thorgrim the Proud.

They came into this tardily, yet for the prayer's sake of their father they went; but as soon as they came into the main sea there drave a storm down on them, and a mighty wind, and they weltered about right up to winter-nights.They came on Snowfellness amidst a great fog, and struck on Onverdaness, and were wrecked; so all men got a-land alive, but of the goods was little saved.

Now Thorgrim heard hereof, and who the men were, and rode to meet them, and they took that joyfully, and abode the winter through.

And now Sigurd began to think much of Helga, though he said but little to her.

And they knew nought of Thorgrim's sons.

But on a time got Gunnlaug a-talking with Sigurd his brother, and said, "Were it not meet that we should seek revenge on Thorgrim, for certes we may have a right good chance against him? "

Sigurd answered: "It had been better unspoken; for thus meseems should I reward good with evil, if I were to slay the man who has taken me from shipwreck; and in every wise doth better and better to me: nay, rather would I defend him than do him a mischief if it should come to such a pass."

So they made an end of talking, and Gunnlaug never got on this talk again with Sigurd.So the winter wears, and those brethren let array their ship, being desirous to be ready to depart against summer-tide.

And some men would be saying that things went sweetly between Helga and Sigurd; howbeit, it was scarce known openly to all folk.

CHAPTER 17
The Parting of Viglund and Ketilrid

Now turns the tale to Earl Eric, who became an old man, and died of eld; but Sigmund his son took his possessions after him, but gat no dignity from King Harald, because the King bore all the kin of Thorgrim something of a grudge for his friendship's sake with Ketil.

Helgi had wedded in Norway, but his wife was dead before the tale gets so far as this: he had a daughter called Ragnhild, the fairest of women.So Helgi was weary of Norway, and went to Iceland, and came thither late in the land-settling time, and bought land in Gautwick of that Gaut who had settled the land there; and there he dwelt till old age.

Now tells the tale of more folk: Steinolf, to wit, who dwelt in Hraundale, who had a son hight Thorleif, a big man and a proper.This Thorleif wooed Ketilrid, but she would nought of him.Then Thorleif made many words about it, to the end that he should get her, howsoever she might gainsay it; and Thorbiorg was utterly of his way of thinking.

But now, when Thorgrim's sons were clean healed of their hurts, they asked their father what he would counsel them to do.He said, "I deem it good rede for you to take berth in the ship of the brethren Gunnlaug and Sigurd, and pray a passage of them over the Iceland sea, saying that your lives lie thereon, as the sooth is, keeping your names hidden meanwhile.Then shall Sigurd keep to his oath, and grant you passage: for this Sigurd is a good man and true, and ye will get but good at his hands: and soothly ye will need it, for over there ye will have to answer for me."

So it was settled that this was to be done.Men say that Ketilrid was weighed down with sorrow that winter; that oft she slept little, and sat awake in her sewing-bower nightlong.But that same night before the day whenas Viglund should fare to the ship, for now Ketil's sons were all ready for sea, Viglund and Trusty went to Foss, and into the chamber whereas sat Ketilrid awake, while her handmaids slept.

Sweetly she welcomed the brethren."It is long since we met," said she; "but right good it is that ye are whole and about on your feet again."

So the two brethren sat down beside her, and talked a long while; and Viglund told her all he was minded to do, and she was glad thereat.

"All is right well," she said, "so long as thou art well, howsoever it fare with me."

"Let thyself not be wedded whiles I am away," said Viglund.

"My father must rule that," she said, "for I have no might herein; moreover, I will not be against him: but belike it will be no happier for me than for thee, if things go otherwise: yet all must needs go its own ways."

Then Viglund bade her cut his hair and wash his head, and she did so; and when it was done, Viglund said: "This I swear, that none shall cut my hair or wash my head but thou only while thou art alive."

Then they all went out together, and parted without in the home-mead: and Viglund kissed Ketilrid weeping sore; and it was well seen of them, that their hearts were sore to part thus: but so must it be: and she went into her bower, but they went on their way.

And Viglund, or ever he parted from Ketilrid, sang this stave: ----

> "Maiden, my songs remember,
> Fair mouth, if thou mayst learn them;
> For, clasp-mead, they may gain thee
> At whiles some times beguiling.
> Most precious, when thou wendest
> Abroad, where folk are gathered,
> Me, O thou slender isle-may,
> Each time shalt thou remember."

But when they were come a little way from the garth Viglund sang another stave: ----

> "Amid the town we twain stood,
> And there she wound around me
> Her hands, the hawk-eyed woman,
> The fair-haired, greeting sorely.
> Fast fell tears from the maiden,
> And sorrow told of longing;
> Her cloth the drift-white dear one
> Over bright brows was drawing."

A little after, when Ketilrid came into her bower, thither came the goodman Holmkel, and saw his daughter weeping sorely: then he asked her why she was so sleepless: but for all answer she sang: ---

"A little way I led him,
The lord of sheen, from green garth;
But farther than all faring,
My heart it followeth after.
Yea, longer had I led him,
If land lay off the haven,
And all the waste of Ægir
Were into green meads waxen."

Then spake Ketilrid and answered her father: "My brothers' death was in my mind."

"Wilt thou have them avenged? " said he.

"That should be soon seen," she said, "if I were as much a man and of might in matters, as I am now but a woman."

The goodman said: "Daughter, know in good sooth, that it is for thy sake that I have done nought against those brethren; for I wot well that they are alive: so come now, hide not from me how thou wouldst have the matter go; for I will get them slain if that is thy will."

"So far from having them slain," said she, "if I might rule, I would never have made themoutlaws if I might have ruled; and, moreover, I would have given them money for their journey if I had had it; and never would I have any other but Viglund, if I might choose."

Then Holmkel arose and went forth, and took his horse and rode after the brethren.But when they saw him, then said Trusty, "There rideth Holmkel alone; and if thou wilt get Ketilrid, there is one thing to be done----nought good though it be----to slay Holmkel and carry off Ketilrid."

Said Viglund: "Though it were on the board that I should never see Ketilrid from this time henceforward, yet rather would I have it so than that I do Holmkel any hurt, and forget the trustiness he hath dealt me withal, when he hath had such sorrow to pay me back for: yea, moreover, Ketilrid hath grief enow to bear though she see not her father slain, who hath ever wished all things good for her."

"Yea, so it is best," said Trusty.

"Now shall we," said Viglund, "ride into our home-mead to meet him, for the increasing of his honour."

They did so; but Holmkel rode on past them and then turned back: so the brethren went back to the road, and found money there, and a gold ring, and a rune-staff: and on the rune-staff were cut all those words of Ketilrid and Holmkel, and this withal, that she gave that money to Viglund.

CHAPTER 18
The Sons of Thorgrim Fare Out from Iceland

Thereafter they went to the ship, and Gunnlaug and his brother were ready for sea, and the wind blowing off shore: so Viglund hailed the ship, and asked whether Gunnlaug were aboard, and whether he would give them passage over the Iceland seas.He asked who they were: They said one was named Troubleman, and the other Hardfellow.Then Gunnlaug asked what dragged them toward the outlands; and they said, very fear for their lives.So he bade them come out to the ship, and they did so.Then they hoisted sail, and sailed out to sea; and when they had made some way Gunnlaug said, "Big fellow, why art thou named Troubleman? "

"Well," said he, "I am called Troubleman, because I have troubles enough and to spare of my own; but I am also called Viglund, and my brother here is Trusty, and we are the sons of Thorgrim the Proud."

Then Gunnlaug was silent, but spake at last: "What do we, brother Sigurd? "said he; "for now have we a hard matter to get out of, seeing that I wot well that Ketil our father will let slay them as soon as they come to Norway."

Said Sigurd: "Thou didst not ask me this when thou tookest them in; but I knew Viglund when I saw him, by Helga his sister.But meseems thou hast might to bring it about that our father Ketil have no more power over them than thou wilt; and a most meet reward will that be for that wherein Thorgrim has done well to us."

"It is well spoken," said Gunnlaug: "let us do so."

Now they had a fair wind and made Norway, and fared home to Raumsdale, and Ketil was from home; and when he came home, there were his sons in the hall, with Thorgrim's sons sitting in their midst; and they were a company of four-and-twenty.

Now they greeted not their father when he set him down in the high seat; but he knew his sons, but not the sons of Thorgrim: so he asked why they greeted him not, or who the stranger men were.

And Sigurd said, "One is called Viglund, and the other Trusty, the sons of Thorgrim the Proud."

Said Ketil: "Stand up, all ye my men, and take them!And I would that Thorgrim the Proud also were come hither; and then should they all fare by one road."

Sigurd the Sage answered and said: "Great is the difference between us here and Thorgrim the Proud; for he took us brethren from shipwreck, and did to us ever better and better, when he had us utterly at his will: but thou wilt slay his sons sackless: and belike, good fellows, we may do you a mischief before Thorgrim" sons be slain: and one fate shall be over us all."

Then Ketil says that it is unmeet for him to fight against his own sons, and the wrath runs off him.

Then spake Sigurd: "This is my counsel, that my brother Gunnlaug take the whole matter in hand, for he is well proven in rightfulness."

"Well, it must be so," said Ketil, "rather than that we, father and sons, begin an ill strife together."

So this was settled to be; and Gunnlaug spake: "This is my doom: Thorgrim shall keep the woman himself; but withal she shall forego the heritage of Earl Thorir her father, and my father shall duly take the said heritage; and my father shall give his daughter Ingibiorg to Trusty, Thorgrim's son; and Sigurd the Sage shall wed Helga, Thorgrim's daughter.And this my doom I hold to firmly."

All thought it done well and wisely, and Ketil was well pleased with matters having come hereto.

So there they abode in good entertainment, the winter through, and Trusty wedded Ingibiorg: but in the summer they went a-warring, all the foster-brethren together, and became the most renowned of men, but Viglund bare away the prize from them all: and they were close upon three winters in this warfare.

But Viglund was never in more joyous mood than at the first; for Ketilrid was never out of his mind.

CHAPTER 19
The Wedding of Ketilrid

Now must the story be taken up, whereas goodman Holmkel sat at home at Foss.And on a day he rode to Ingialdsknoll, and no man knew what he spake to Thorgrim: and thereafter he went home.Still Thorleif Steinolfson was importunate in the wooing of Ketilrid; but she was slow enough over it.

A little after Thorgrim sent three of his men from home, and they were away three weeks, and when they came home none knew what their errand had been.

Now this befell one day at Foss, that thither came thirty men.Holmkel asked their leader to name himself; and he said he was called Thord, and had his abode in the Eastfirths, and that his errand thither was the wooing of Ketilrid.The goodman put the matter before his daughter, and she was asked thereof, and she said it was as far as might be from her mind, for she deemed the man old, and she said she had no heart to be wedded at all.

Thorbiorg was exceeding eager that the bargain should be struck, and the end of it was, that Holmkel betrothed her to Thord, whether she were lieve or loth; and she went away with Thord at once, and the wedding was to be in the Eastfirths.So they made no stay till they got home, and Ketilrid took the rule of all things there; yet men never saw her glad.

But Thord wedded her not; they both lay in one bed, but in such wise that there was a curtain between them.

So wore away a long space.

Thorlief was ill content that Ketilrid was wedded; but thought it not easy to do aught, whereas she was a long way off.

Thord did well to Ketilrid in all wise, but no gain that seemed to Ketilrid, because of the love she had for Viglund: for ever she bare about the flame of desire in her breast for his sake.

CHAPTER 20
Viglund Comes Out to Iceland Again

Viglund and all the foster-brethren came home that summer from warfare, and Ketil gave them good welcome.

On a day were folk called to head-washing, but Viglund answered thereto: "Nay, I will have nought of this head-washing, nor havesince we parted, Ketilrid and I."Then he sang a stave: ----

> "The linen-oak bath-lovely
> Laid last on me the lather:
> So nought have I to hurry
> Unto another head-bath.
> And me no more shall any
> Gold glittering of the maidens
> Henceforth, in all my life-days,
> In ashen bath bewash me."
> Nor would Viglund let himself be bathed.

So there they abode in peace that winter; but in summer they made ready for Iceland, each company in their own ship; so they sailed into the sea, and parted company at sea; and Ketil's sons made White-water, and went to quarters at Ingialdsknoll, and told Thorgrim of the peace made twixt him and Ketil, and also that his sons were soon to be looked for: and Thorgrim was glad at all these things.But Viglund and his brother sailed on till they saw Snowfell-Jokul; then sang Viglund a stave: ----

> "Behold the hill whereunder
> My bond of love high-hearted,
> My well-beloved one sitteth:
> Lo Love's eyes turn I to her.
> Sweet, sing I of the gold-brent,
> The proud by proud that sitteth.
> O hill-side among hill-sides,
> Beloved, if any have been!"

And again he sang: ---

> "Leek-bearer, bright the looking
> Over the heaths sun-litten,
> The sun sinks slow thereunder:
> How sore I long to be there!
> Lovesome she makes the mountains;

> Sweet, therefore must I hush me:
> The goodliest goddess have I
> To greet, who sits thereunder."

And therewith there came a wind down from the ness so great, that they drave out into the sea; and a west wind fell on them, and the weather became exceeding stormy, and men must ever stand a-baling.And on a day, as Viglund sat on the bulk amid weather of the roughest, he sang: ---

> "Ketilrid her carle bade
> Quail not mid swift sailing,
> Though the beat of billows
> Overboar the foredeck.
> Still her word is with me,
> Be we wight now, Trusty!
> Stormy heart of sorrow
> I have for Ketilrid."

"A mighty matter, forsooth," said Trusty, "whenas thou must needs name her first and last in thy singing."

"Yea, kinsman, thinkest thou so? "said Viglund.

So they were out at sea many days, and at last amid great danger and pain made Gautwick in the Eastfirths.

Then said Viglund, "Whereas we have a feud on us, methinks it were well, brother, that thou shouldst call thyself Raven, and I should call myself Erne."

So the goodman from the stead of Gautwick came to the ship; and the shipmen gave him good welcome, and bade him take what he would of the lading.The goodman said he had a young wife."She," quoth he, "shall come to the ship and take of your lading what she will."So the goodman rode home now, and the mistress came thither the next morning; and she knew Viglund as soon as she saw him, but made little of it; but Viglund was much astonished when he knew her.

So she took what she would of the lading, for all things were at her will.

The bonder had bidden the ship-masters home, and when they came thither, the master and mistress went to meet them: then stumbled the goodman, for he was stiff with eld: then the mistress said, somewhat under her breath, "An evil mate is an old man."

"It was so slippery, though," said the master.

So they were brought in with all honour; but Viglund deemed that Ketilrid knew him not.But she sang: ----

> "The fight-grove of Van's fire,
> The fair, I knew at even---
> Marvel that he would meet me!
> I knew gold-master Trusty.
> The ship of gold all slender
> To such an one is wedded,

That ne'er another older
In all the world one findeth."

So they abode there that winter, and Viglund was exceeding heavy-hearted, but Trusty as blithe as might be, and the goodman exceeding blithe, who served them with all kindness.

But it is told that Ketilrid had a veil ever before her face, for she would not that Viglund should know her, and that Viglund also for his part was not all so sure that it was she.

CHAPTER 21
Guesting at Gautwick

On a day Ketilrid was standing without, and she was exceeding warm, and had rent the veil from her face: and in that nick of time Viglund came out and saw her visage clearly; and thereat was he much astonished, and flushed red as blood.He went into the hall, wherein was Trusty sitting, who asked him what was toward and what he had seen that he was so changed.Then Viglund sang a stave: ----

> "Nought shall I say thee lie now:
> Ne'er saw I eyen sweeter
> Since when we twain were sundered,
> O sweet one of the worm-lair.
> This craven carle her clippeth;
> Shall I not carve from off him
> His head? all grief go with him!---
> Grief from the gold one gat I."

Now Ketilrid never had a veil before her face from that time forward that she wotted that Viglund knew her.

So Trusty said, "The last thing to be done I deem is to do the goodman any harm, as well as he has done to us; a luckless deed it will be to slay her husband sackless: let it be far from thee!"And he sang: ---

> "Never, burnt-rings breaker,
> Shall ye be brought together.
> If felon's deed thou doest
> On Fafnir's-land's good dealer.
> Not ever, nor in all things,
> Availeth shielded onset;
> Aright must we arede us,
> O brother wise in trials."

So the day wears away to evening, and folk go to rest.But in the night Viglund arose and went to the bed wherein slept Ketilrid and the goodman; the light was drawn up into the hall roof, so that aloft it was light, but all below was dim.So he lifted up the curtains and saw Ketilrid lying turned towards the wall, and the

376

goodman turned away thence towards the bedstock, with his head laid thereon, handy to be smitten off.

Then was Viglund at the point to draw his sword, but therewith came Trusty to him, and said, "Nay, beware of thyself, and do no such fearful and shameful deed as to slay a sleeping man.Let none see in thee that thy heart is in this woman!bear thyself like a man!"And he sang: ---

> "My friend, mind here the maiden
> Who murdereth all thy gladness;
> See there thy fair fame's furtherer,
> Who seemeth fain of saying:
> Though one, the lovely woman,
> Hath wasted all thy life-joy,
> Yet keep it close within thee,
> Nor cry aloud thereover."

Therewith was Viglund appeased, and he wondered withal that there was so wide a space in the bed betwixt them.

So the brethren went to their beds; but Viglund slept but little that night, and the next morning was he exceeding downcast; but the goodman was very joyous, and he asked Viglund what made him so sorrowful.

Then Viglund, whom all deemed was called Erne, sang a stave: ----

> "The white hands' ice-hill's wearer
> Hath wasted all my joyance:
> O strong against me straineth
> The stream of heaped-up waters!
> This sapling oak thy wife here
> From out my heart ne'er goeth;
> Well of tormenting wotteth
> The woman mid her playing."

"Like enough it is so," said the master; "but come, it were good that we disported us and played at the chess."

And they did so; but little heed had Erne of the board because of the thought he had of the goodwife, so that he was like to be mated: but therewith came the mistress thither, and looked on the board, and sang this half-stave: ----

> "O battles' thunder-bearer
> Be glad and shift thy board-piece
> On to this square thou seest;
> So saith the staff of hangings."
> Then the master looked on her and sang: ---
> "Again to-day gold-goddess
> Against her husband turneth,
> Though I the wealth-god owe thee
> For nought but eld meseemeth."

So Erne played as he was bidden, and the game was a drawn game.

The goodwife talked little with Erne; but on a day when they met without alone, they two, Viglund and Ketilrid, they did talk together somewhat; yet not for long; and when they had made an end of talking, Viglund sang: ----

> "O slender sweet, O fair-browed,
> Meseemeth this thy husband
> As ferry-boat all foredone
> Amid the Skerries floating.
> But thee, when I behold thee
> Go forth so mighty waxen,
> 'Tis as a ship all stately
> O'er sea-mews' pasture sweeping."

Then they left off talking, and Ketilrid went in; but Erne fell to talk with the goodman, who was joyous with the shipmaster; but Erne sang: ---

> "Friend, watch and ward now hold thou
> Of this thy wife, the fair one;
> And heed lest that spear-Goddess
> Should go about to waste me.
> If oft we meet without doors,
> I and the twined-thread's Goddess,
> Who knows whose most she should be,
> Or mine or thine, that gold-wife? "

And another stave he sang: ----

> "Fight-grove full fain would not
> Be found amidst of man-folk,
> So tame to maids' enticing
> To take a man's wife wedded.
> But if amid the mirk-tide
> She came here made as woman,
> I cannot soothly swear it
> But soft I should enfold her."

Said the master; "O, all will go well enough if she sees to it herself."And so they left this talk.

Ever did the goodman do better and better to the shipmaster, but it availed him nought; a sorrowful man he was ever, and never spake one joyous word.But Trusty, his brother, thought such harm of this, that he talked to him full oft, bidding him put it from his mind and take another woman.But Erne said, "It may not be; I should not love her; yea, moreover, I could not set the thing afoot."And he sang: ----

> "Another man's wife love I,
> Unmanly am I holden,
> Though old, and on her beam-ends,
> Fallen is the fallow oak-keel.
> I wot not if another,
> At any time hereafter,
> Shall be as sweet unto me----
> The ship drave out of peril."

"It may be so," said Raven.So they went together into the hall: and there sat the master with the goodwife on his knees, and he with his arms about her middle: but Erne saw that she was not right glad thereat.

Now she slipped from his knees, and went and sat down on the bench, and wept.Erne went thither, and sat down by her, and they talked together softly.And he sang: ----

> "Sweet linen-bride, full seldom
> In such wise would I find thee,
> An hoary dotard's hand-claws
> Hanging about thee, bright one.
> Rather, O wristfires' lady,
> Would I around thy midmost
> Cast as my longing led me,
> These lands of gold light-shinging."

"Mayhappen," said the goodwife, "it will never be."Therewith she arose and went away: but the master was exceeding joyous and said: "Now, Erne, I will that thou have care of my household, and all else that concerns me, whiles I am away, because I am going from home and shall be away for a month at the least; and thee I trust best of all in all matters that concern me."

Erne said little to this.

CHAPTER 22
A Wedding at Gautwick

Then the master went from home with fourteen men; and when he was gone Erne spake to his brother and said: "Methinks it were well if we went from home, and abode not here whiles the master is away; for otherwise folk will deem that I am about beguiling his wife; and then would a mighty difference be seen betwixt me and the master."

So they rode from home, and abode by their shipmates till the goodman came home on the day named.

And now were there many more with him than before: for in his company were Thorgrim the Proud, and Olof his wife, and Helga his daughter, and Sigurd the Sage, and Gunnlaug his brother, and Holmkel the master of Foss: and they were fifty all told.Therewith also came home the two mariners.

And now Ketilrid had arrayed all things as the goodman had commanded her, with the intent to hold his wedding.

But when they were all set down in the hall the master stood up and said: "So stands the case, Shipmaster Erne, that thou hast abided here through the winter, and thy brother with thee, and I know that thou art called Viglund and thy brother Trusty, and that ye are the sons of Thorgrim the Proud: no less I know all thy mind toward Ketilrid; and with many trials and troubles have I tried thee, and all hast thou borne well: nevertheless thy brother hath holden thee that thou hast not fallen into any dreadful case or done any dreadful thing: and I myself indeed had ever something else to fall back upon.For now will I no longer hide from thee that I am called Helgi, and am the son of Earl Eric, and thine own father's brother: therefore wooed I Ketilrid, that I might keep her safe for thee, and she is a clean maiden as for me.Ketilrid hath borne all well and womanly: for I and the others hid these things from her: forsooth we have lain never under one sheet, for the bedstock cometh up between the berths we lay in, though we had one coverlet over all: and I deem indeed that it would be no trial nor penance to her though she knew no man whiles thou wert alive.But all these things were done by the rede of Master Holmkel, and methinks it were well that thou pray him for peace, and crave his daughter of him thereafter: and surely he will give thee peace, for things better and nobler than this he hath done to thee in your dealings together."

Then went Viglund to Master Holmkel, and laid his head on his knee, and bade him do therewith whatso he would; and he answered in this wise---

"That shall be done with thine head which shall please my daughter Ketilrid best, and assuredly we will be at peace together."

So Holmkel gave his daughter Ketilrid to Viglund, and Thorgrim gave Helga his daughter to Sigurd the Sage, and Helgi gave Ragnhild his daughter to Gunnlaug the Masterful; and folk sat down to all these weddings at one and the same time.

Then each went to his own house: Viglund and Ketilrid loved their life exceeding well now, and dwelt at Foss after Holmkel, Ketilrid's father: but Gunnlaug the Masterful and Sigurd his brother fared abroad and set up house in Norway: but Trusty abode at Ingialdsknoll after Thorgrim his father.

So here endeth the tale.

THE STORY OF THE VOLSUNGS AND NIBLUNGS

Translated by William Morris and Eirikr Magnusson.

INTRODUCTION

It would seem fitting for a Northern folk, deriving the greater and better part of their speech, laws, and customs from a Northern root, that the North should be to them, if not a holy land, yet at least a place more to be regarded than any part of the world beside; that howsoever their knowledge widened of other men, the faith and deeds of their forefathers would never lack interest for them, but would always be kept in remembrance. One cause after another has, however, aided in turning attention to classic men and lands at the cost of our own history. Among battles, "every schoolboy" knows the story of Marathon or Salamis, while it would be hard indeed to find one who did more than recognise the name, if even that, of the great fights of Hafrsfirth or Sticklestead. The language and history of Greece and Rome, their laws and religions, have been always held part of the learning needful to an educated man, but no trouble has been taken to make him familiar with his own people or their tongue. Even that Englishman who knew Alfred, Bede, Caedmon, as well as he knew Plato, Caesar, Cicero, or Pericles, would be hard bestead were he asked about the great peoples from whom we sprang; the warring of Harold Fairhair or Saint Olaf; the Viking (1) kingdoms in these (the British) Western Isles; the settlement of Iceland, or even of Normandy. The knowledge of all these things would now be even smaller than it is among us were it not that there was one land left where the olden learning found refuge and was kept in being. In England, Germany, and the rest of Europe, what is left of the traditions of pagan times has been altered in a thousand ways by foreign influence, even as the peoples and their speech have been by the influx of foreign blood; but Iceland held to the old tongue that was once the universal speech of northern folk, and held also the great stores of tale and poem that are slowly becoming once more the common heritage of their descendants. The truth, care, and literary beauty of its records; the varied and strong life shown alike in tale and history; and the preservation of the old speech, character, and tradition—a people placed apart as the Icelanders have been—combine to make valuable what Iceland holds for us. Not before 1770, when Bishop Percy translated Mallet's "Northern Antiquities", was anything known here of Icelandic, or its literature. Only within the latter part of this century has it been studied, and in the brief book-list at the end of this volume may be seen the little that has been done as yet. It is, however, becoming ever clearer, and to an increasing number, how supremely important is Icelandic as a word-hoard to the English-speaking peoples, and that in its legend, song, and story there is a very mine of noble and pleasant beauty and high manhood. That which has been done, one may hope, is but the beginning of a great new birth, that shall give back to our language and literature all that heedlessness and ignorance bid fair for awhile to destroy.

The Scando-Gothic peoples who poured southward and westward over Europe, to shake empires and found kingdoms, to meet Greek and Roman in conflict, and levy tribute everywhere, had kept up their constantly-recruited waves of incursion, until they had raised a barrier of their own blood. It was their own kin, the sons of earlier invaders, who stayed the landward march of the Northmen in the time of Charlemagne. To the Southlands their road by land was henceforth closed. Then begins the day of the Vikings, who, for two hundred years and more, "held the world at ransom." Under many and brave leaders they first of all came round the "Western Isles" (2) toward the end of the eighth century; soon after they invaded Normandy, and harried the coasts of France; gradually they lengthened their voyages until there was no shore of the then known world upon which they were unseen or unfelt. A glance at English history will show the large part of it they fill, and how they took tribute from the Anglo-Saxons, who, by the way, were far nearer kin to them than is usually thought. In Ireland, where the old civilisation was falling to pieces, they founded kingdoms at Limerick and Dublin among other places; (3) the last named, of which the first king, Olaf the White, was traditionally descended of Sigurd the Volsung, (4) endured even to the English invasion, when it was taken by men of the same Viking blood a little altered. What effect they produced upon the natives may be seen from the description given by the unknown historian of the "Wars of the

Gaedhil with the Gaill": "In a word, although there were an hundred hard-steeled iron heads on one neck, and an hundred sharp, ready, cool, never-rusting brazen tongues in each head, and an hundred garrulous, loud, unceasing voices from each tongue, they could not recount, or narrate, or enumerate, or tell what all the Gaedhil suffered in common—both men and women, laity and clergy, old and young, noble and ignoble—of hardship, and of injury, and of oppression, in every house, from these valiant, wrathful, purely pagan people. Even though great were this cruelty, oppression, and tyranny, though numerous were the oft-victorious clans of the many-familied Erinn; though numerous their kings, and their royal chiefs, and their princes; though numerous their heroes and champions, and their brave soldiers, their chiefs of valour and renown and deeds of arms; yet not one of them was able to give relief, alleviation, or deliverance from that oppression and tyranny, from the numbers and multitudes, and the cruelty and the wrath of the brutal, ferocious, furious, untamed, implacable hordes by whom that oppression was inflicted, because of the excellence of their polished, ample, treble, heavy, trusty, glittering corslets; and their hard, strong, valiant swords; and their well-riveted long spears, and their ready, brilliant arms of valour besides; and because of the greatness of their achievements and of their deeds, their bravery, and their valour, their strength, and their venom, and their ferocity, and because of the excess of their thirst and their hunger for the brave, fruitful, nobly-inhabited, full of cataracts, rivers, bays, pure, smooth-plained, sweet grassy land of Erinn"—(pp. 52-53). Some part of this, however, must be abated, because the chronicler is exalting the terror-striking enemy that he may still further exalt his own people, the Dal Cais, who did so much under Brian Boroimhe to check the inroads of the Northmen. When a book does (5) appear, which has been announced these ten years past, we shall have more material for the reconstruction of the life of those times than is now anywhere accessible. Viking earldoms also were the Orkneys, Faroes, and Shetlands. So late as 1171, in the reign of Henry II., the year after Beckett's murder, Earl Sweyn Asleifsson of Orkney, who had long been the terror of the western seas, "fared a sea-roving" and scoured the western coast of England, Man, and the east of Ireland, but was killed in an attack on his kinsmen of Dublin. He had used to go upon a regular plan that may be taken as typical of the homely manner of most of his like in their cruising: "Sweyn had in the spring hard work, and made them lay down very much seed, and looked much after it himself. But when that toil was ended, he fared away every spring on a viking-voyage, and harried about among the southern isles and Ireland, and came home after midsummer. That he called spring-viking. Then he was at home until the corn-fields were reaped down, and the grain seen to and stored. Then he fared away on a viking-voyage, and then he did not come home till the winter was one month off, and that he called his autumn-viking." (6)

Toward the end of the ninth century Harold Fairhair, either spurred by the example of Charlemagne, or really prompted, as Snorri Sturluson tells us, resolved to bring all Norway under him. As Snorri has it in "Heimskringla": "King Harold sent his men to a girl hight Gyda.... The king wanted her for his leman; for she was wondrous beautiful but of high mood withal. Now when the messengers came there and gave their message to her, she made answer that she would not throw herself away even to take a king for her husband, who swayed no greater kingdom than a few districts; 'And methinks,' said she, 'it is a marvel that no king here in Norway will put all the land under him, after the fashion that Gorm the Old did in Denmark, or Eric at Upsala.' The messengers deemed this a dreadfully proud-spoken answer, and asked her what she thought would come of such an one, for Harold was so mighty a man that his asking was good enough for her. But although she had replied to their saying otherwise than they would, they saw no likelihood, for this while, of bearing her along with them against her will, so they made ready to fare back again. When they were ready and the folk followed them out, Gyda said to the messengers —'Now tell to King Harold these my words:—I will only agree to be his lawful wife upon the condition that he shall first, for sake of me, put under him the whole of Norway, so that he may bear sway over that kingdom as freely and fully as King Eric over the realm of Sweden, or King Gorm over Denmark; for only then, methinks, can he be called king of a people.' Now his men came back to King Harold, bringing him the words of the girl, and saying she was so bold and heedless that she well deserved the king should send a greater troop of people for her, and put her to some disgrace. Then answered the king. 'This maid has not spoken or done so much amiss that she should be punished, but the rather should she be thanked for her words. She has reminded me,' said he, 'of somewhat that it seems wonderful I did not think of before. And now,' added he, 'I make the solemn vow, and take who made me and rules over all things, to witness that never shall I clip or comb my hair until I have subdued all Norway with scatt, and duties, and lordships; or, if not, have died in the seeking.' Guttorm gave great thanks to the king for his oath, saying it was "royal work fulfilling royal rede." The new and strange government that Harold tried to enforce—nothing less than the feudal system in a rough guise —which made those who had hitherto been their own men save at special times, the king's men at all times, and laid freemen under tax, was withstood as long as might be by the sturdy Norsemen. It was only by dint of hard fighting that he slowly won his way, until at Hafrsfirth he finally crushed all effective opposition. But the discontented, "and they were a great multitude," fled oversea to the outlands, Iceland, the Faroes, the Orkneys, and Ireland. The whole coast of Europe, even to Greece and the shores of the Black Sea, the northern shores of Africa, and the western part of Asia, felt the effects also. Rolf Pad-th'-hoof, son of Harold's dear friend Rognvald, made an outlaw for a cattle-raid within the bounds of the kingdom, betook himself to France, and, with his men, founded a new people and a dynasty.

Iceland had been known for a good many years, but its only dwellers had been Irish Culdees, who sought that lonely land to pray in peace. Now, however, both from Norway and the Western Isles settlers began to come in. Aud, widow of Olaf the White, King of Dublin, came, bringing with her many of mixed blood, for the Gaedhil (pronounced "Gael", Irish) and the Gaill (pronounced "Gaul", strangers) not only fought furiously, but made friends firmly, and often intermarried. Indeed, the Westmen were among the first arrivals, and took the best parts of the island—on its western shore, appropriately enough. After a time the Vikings who had settled in the Isles so worried Harold and his kingdom, upon which they swooped every other while, that he drew together a mighty force, and fell upon them wheresoever he could find them, and followed them up with fire and sword; and this he did twice, so that in those lands none could abide but folk who were content to be his men, however lightly they might hold their allegiance. Hence it was to Iceland that all turned who held to the old ways, and for over sixty years from the first comer there was a stream of hardy men pouring in, with their families and their belongings, simple yeomen, great and warwise chieftains, rich landowners, who had left their land "for the overbearing of King Harold," as the "Landnamabok" (7) has it. "There also we shall escape the troubling of kings and scoundrels", says the "Vatsdaelasaga". So much of the best blood left Norway that the king tried to stay the leak by fines and punishments, but in vain.

As his ship neared the shore, the new-coming chief would leave it to the gods as to where he settled. The hallowed pillars of the high seat, which were carried away from his old abode, were thrown overboard, with certain rites, and were let drive with wind and wave until they came ashore. The piece of land which lay next the beach they were flung upon was then viewed from the nearest hill-summit, and place of the homestead picked out. Then the land was hallowed by being encircled with fire, parcelled among the band, and marked out with boundary-signs; the houses were built, the "town" or home-field walled in, a temple put up, and the settlement soon assumed shape. In 1100 there were 4500 franklins, making a population of about 50,000, fully three-fourths of whom had a strong infusion of Celtic blood in them. The mode of life was, and is, rather pastoral than aught else. In the 39,200 square miles of the island's area there are now about 250 acres of cultivated land, and although there has been much more in times past, the Icelanders have always been forced to reckon upon flocks and herds as their chief resources, grain of all kinds, even rye, only growing in a few favoured places, and very rarely there; the hay, self-sown, being the only certain harvest. On the coast fishing and fowling were of help, but nine-tenths of the folk lived by their sheep and cattle. Potatoes, carrots, turnips, and several kinds of cabbage have, however, been lately grown with success. They produced their own food and clothing, and could export enough wool, cloth, horn, dried fish, etc., as enabled them to obtain wood for building, iron for tools, honey, wine, grain, etc, to the extent of their simple needs. Life and work was lotted by the seasons and their changes; outdoor work—fishing, herding, hay-making, and fuel-getting—filling the long days of summer, while the long, dark winter was used in weaving and a hundred indoor crafts. The climate is not so bad as might be expected, seeing that the island touches the polar circle, the mean temperature at Reykjavik being 39 degrees.

The religion which the settlers took with them into Iceland—the ethnic religion of the Norsefolk, which fought its last great fight at Sticklestead, where Olaf Haraldsson lost his life and won the name of Saint—was, like all religions, a compound of myths, those which had survived from savage days, and those which expressed the various degrees of a growing knowledge of life and better understanding of nature. Some historians and commentators are still fond of the unscientific method of taking a later religion, in this case christianity, and writing down all apparently coincident parts of belief, as having been borrowed from the christian teachings by the Norsefolk, while all that remain they lump under some slighting head. Every folk has from the beginning of time sought to explain the wonders of nature, and has, after its own fashion, set forth the mysteries of life. The lowest savage, no less than his more advanced brother, has a philosophy of the universe by which he solves the world-problem to his own satisfaction, and seeks to reconcile his conduct with his conception of the nature of things. Now, it is not to be thought, save by "a priori" reasoners, that such a folk as the Northmen—a mighty folk, far advanced in the arts of life, imaginative, literary—should have had no further creed than the totemistic myths of their primitive state; a state they have wholly left ere they enter history. Judging from universal analogy, the religion of which record remains to us was just what might be looked for at the particular stage of advancement the Northmen had reached. Of course something may have been gained from contact with other peoples—from the Greeks during the long years in which the northern races pressed upon their frontier; from the Irish during the existence of the western viking-kingdoms; but what I particularly warn young students against is the constant effort of a certain order of minds to wrest facts into agreement with their pet theories of religion or what not. The whole tendency of the more modern investigation shows that the period of myth-transmission is long over ere history begins. The same confusion of different stages of myth-making is to be found in the Greek religion, and indeed in those of all peoples; similar conditions of mind produce similar practices, apart from all borrowing of ideas and manners; in Greece we find snake-dances, bear-dances, swimming with sacred pigs, leaping about in imitation of wolves, dog-feasts, and offering of dogs' flesh to the gods—all of them practices dating from crude savagery, mingled with ideas of exalted and noble beauty, but none now, save a bigot, would think of accusing the Greeks of having stolen all their higher beliefs. Even were some part of the matter of their myths taken from others, yet the Norsemen have given their gods a noble, upright, great spirit, and placed them upon a high level that is all their own. (8) From the prose Edda the following all too brief statement of the salient points of Norse belief is made up:—"The first and eldest of gods is hight Allfather; he lives from all ages, and rules over all his realm, and sways all things great and small; he smithied heaven and earth, and the lift, and all that belongs to them; what is most, he made man, and gave him a soul that shall live and never perish; and all men that are right-minded shall live and be with himself in Vingolf; but wicked men fare to Hell, and thence into Niithell, that is beneath in the ninth world. Before the earth "twas the morning of time, when yet naught was, nor sand nor sea was there, nor cooling streams. Earth was not found, nor Heaven above; a Yawning-gap there was, but grass nowhere.' Many ages ere the earth was shapen was Niflheim made, but first was that land in the southern sphere hight Muspell, that burns and blazes, and may not be trodden by those who are outlandish and have no heritage there. Surtr sits on the border to guard the land; at the end of the world he will fare forth, and harry and overcome all the gods and burn the world with fire. Ere the races were yet mingled, or the folk of men grew, Yawning-gap, which looked towards the north parts, was filled with thick and heavy ice and rime, and everywhere within were fog and gusts; but the south side of Yawning-gap lightened by the sparks and gledes that flew out of Muspell-heim; as cold arose out of Niflheim and all things grim, so was that part that looked towards Muspell hot and bright; but Yawning-gap was as light as windless air, and when the blast of heat met the rime, so that it melted and dropped and quickened; from those life-drops there was shaped the likeness of a man, and he was named Ymir; he was bad, and all his kind; and so it is said, when he slept he fell into a sweat; then waxed under his left hand a man and a woman, and one of his feet got a son with the other, and thence cometh the Hrimthursar. The next thing when the rime dropped was that the cow hight Audhumla was made of it; but four milk-rivers ran out of her teats, and she fed Ymir; she licked rime-stones that were salt, and the first day there came at even, out of the stones, a man's hair, the second day a man's head, the third day all the man was there. He is named Turi; he was fair of face, great and mighty; he gat a son named Bor, who took to him Besla, daughter of Bolthorn, the giant, and they had three sons, Odin, Vili, and Ve. Bor's sons slew Ymir the giant, but when he fell there ran so much blood out of his wounds that all the kin of the Hrimthursar were drowned, save Hvergelmir and his household, who got away in a boat. Then Bor's sons took Ymir and bore him into the midst of Yawning-gap, and made of him the earth; of his blood seas and waters, of his flesh earth was made; they set the earth fast, and laid the sea round about it in a ring without; of his bones were made rocks; stones and pebbles of his teeth and jaws and the bones that were broken; they took his skull and made the lift thereof, and set it up over the earth with four sides, and under each corner they set dwarfs, and they took his brain and cast it aloft, and made clouds. They took the sparks and gledes that went loose, and had been cast out of Muspellheim, and set them in the lift to give light; they gave resting-places to all fires, and set some in the lift; some fared free under it, and they gave them a place and shaped their goings. A wondrous great smithying, and deftly done. The earth is fashioned round without, and there beyond, round about it lies the deep sea; and on that sea-strand the gods gave land for an abode to the giant kind, but within on the earth made they a burg round the world against restless giants, and for this burg reared they the brows of Ymir, and called the burg Midgard. The gods went along the sea-strand and found two stocks, and shaped out of them men; the first gave soul and life, the second wit and will to move, the third face, hearing, speech, and eyesight. They gave them clothing and names; the man Ask and the woman Embla; thence was mankind begotten, to whom an abode was given under Midgard. Then next Bor's sons made them a burg in the midst of the world, that is called Asgard; there abode the gods and their kind, and wrought thence many tidings and feats, both on earth and in the Sky. Odin, who is hight Allfather, for that he is the father of all men and sat there in his high seat, seeing over the whole world and each man's doings, and knew all things that he saw. His wife was called Frigg, and their offspring is the Asa-stock, who dwell in Asgard and the realms about it, and all that stock are known to be gods. The daughter and wife of Odin was Earth, and of her he got Thor, him followed strength and sturdiness, thereby quells he all things quick; the strongest of all gods and men, he has also three things of great price, the hammer Miolnir, the best of strength belts, and when he girds that about him waxes his god strength one-half, and his iron gloves that he may not miss for holding his hammer's haft. Balidr is Odin's second son, and of him it is good to say, he is fair and: bright in face, and hair, and body, and him all praise; he is wise and fair-spoken and mild, and that nature is in him none may withstand his doom. Tyr is daring and best of mood; there is a saw that he is tyrstrong who is before other men and never yields; he is also so wise that it is said he is tyrlearned who is wise. Bragi is famous for wisdom, and best in tongue-wit, and cunning speech, and song-craft. 'And many other are there, good and great; and one, Loki, fair of face, ill in temper and fickle of mood, is called the backbiter of the Asa, and speaker of evil redes and shame of all gods and men; he has above all that craft called sleight, and cheats all in all things. Among the children of Loki are Fenris-wolf and Midgards-worm; the second lies about all the world in the deep sea, holding his tail in his teeth, though some say Thor has slain him; but Fenris-wolf is bound until the doom of the gods, when gods and men shall come to an end, and earth and heaven be burnt, when he shall slay Odin. After this the earth shoots up from the sea, and it is green and fair, and the fields bear unsown, and gods and men shall be alive again, and sit in fair halls, and talk of old tales and the tidings that happened aforetime. The head-seat, or holiest-stead, of the gods is at Yggdrasil's ash, which is of all trees best and biggest; its boughs are spread over the whole world and stand above heaven; one root of the ash is in heaven, and under the root is the right holy spring; there hold the gods doom every day; the second root is with the Hrimthursar, where before was Yawning-gap; under that root is Mimir's spring, where knowledge and wit lie hidden; thither came Allfather and begged a drink, but got it not before he left his eye in pledge; the third root is over Niflheim, and the worm Nidhogg gnaws the root beneath. A fair hall stands under the ash by the spring, and out of it come three maidens, Norns, named Has-been, Being, Will-be, who shape the lives of men; there are beside other Norns, who come to every man that is born to shape his life, and some of these are good and some evil. In the boughs of the ash sits an eagle, wise in much, and between his eyes sits the hawk Vedrfalnir; the squirrel Ratatoskr runs up and down along the ash, bearing words of hate betwixt the eagle and the worm. Those Norns who abide by the holy spring draw from it every day water, and take the clay that lies around the well, and sprinkle them up over the ash for that its boughs should not wither or rot. All those men that have fallen in the fight, and borne wounds and toil unto death, from the beginning of the world, are come to Odin in Valhall; a very great throng is there, and many more shall yet come; the flesh of the boar Soerfmnir is sodden for them every day, and he is whole again at even; and the mead they drink that flows from the teats of the she-goat Heidhrun. The meat Odin has on his board he gives to his two wolves, Geri and Freki, and he needs no meat, wine is to him both meat and drink; ravens twain sit on his shoulders, and say into his ear all tidings that they see and hear; they are called Huginn and Muninn (mind and memory); them sends he at dawn to fly over the whole world, and they come back at breakfast-tide, thereby becomes he wise in many tidings, and for this men call him Raven's-god. Every day, when they have clothed them, the heroes put on their arms and go out into the yard and fight and fell each other; that is their play, and when it looks toward mealtime, then ride they home to Valhall and sit down to drink. For murderers and men forsworn is a great hall, and a bad, and the doors look northward; it is altogether wrought of adder-backs like a wattled house, but the worms' heads turn into the house, and blow venom, so that rivers of venom run along the hall, and in those rivers must such men wade forever." There was no priest-class; every chief was priest for his own folk, offered sacrifice, performed ceremonies, and so on.

In politics the homestead, with its franklin-owner, was the unit; the "thing", or hundred-moot, the primal organisation, and the "godord", or chieftainship, its tie. The chief who had led a band of kinsmen and followers to the new country, taken possession of land, and shared it among them, became their head-ruler and priest at home, speaker and president of their Thing, and their representative in any dealings with neighbouring chiefs and their clients. He was not a feudal lord, for any franklin could change his "godord" as he liked, and the right of "judgment by peers" was in full use. At first there was no higher organisation than the local thing. A central thing, and a speaker to speak a single "law" for the whole island, was instituted in 929, and afterwards the island was divided in four quarters, each with a court, under the Al-thing. Society was divided only into two classes of men, the free and unfree, though political power was in the hands of the franklins alone; "godi" and thrall ate the same food, spoke the same tongue, wore much the same clothes, and were nearly alike in life and habits. Among the free men there was equality in all but wealth and the social standing that cannot be separated therefrom. The thrall was a serf rather than a slave, and could own a house, etc., of his own. In a generation or so the freeman or landless retainer, if he got a homestead of his own, was the peer of the highest in the land. During the tenth century Greenland was colonised from Iceland, and by end of the same century christianity was introduced into Iceland, but made at first little difference in arrangements of society. In the thirteenth century disputes over the power and jurisdiction of the clergy led, with other matters, to civil war, ending in submission to Norway, and the breaking down of all native great houses. Although life under the commonwealth had been rough and irregular, it had been free and varied, breeding heroes and men of mark; but the "law and order" now brought in left all on a dead level of peasant proprietorship, without room for hope or opening for ambition. An alien governor ruled the island, which was divided under him into local counties, administered by sheriffs appointed by the king of Norway. The Al-thing was replaced by a royal court, the local work of the local things was taken by a subordinate of the sheriff, and things, quarter-courts, trial by jury, and all the rest, were swept away to make room for these "improvements", which have lasted with few changes into this century. In 1380 the island passed under the rule of Denmark, and so continues. (9) During the fifteenth century the English trade was the only link between Iceland and the outer world; the Danish government weakened that link as much as it could, and sought to shut in and monopolise everything Icelandic; under the deadening effect of such rule it is no marvel that everything found a lower level, and many things went out of existence for lack of use. In the sixteenth century there is little to record but the Reformation, which did little good, if any, and the ravages of English, Gascon, and Algerine pirates who made havoc on the coast; (10) they appear toward the close of the century and disappear early in the seventeenth. In the eighteenth century small-pox, sheep disease, famine, and the terrible eruptions of 1765 and 1783, follow one another swiftly and with terrible effect. At the beginning of the present century Iceland, however, began to shake off the stupor her ill-hap had brought upon her, and as European attention had been drawn to her, she was listened to. Newspapers, periodicals, and a Useful Knowledge Society were started; then came free trade, and the "home-rule" struggle, which met with partial success in 1874, and is still being carried on. A colony, Gimli, in far-off Canada, has been formed of Icelandic emigrants, and large numbers have left their mother-land; but there are many co-operative societies organised now, which it is hoped will be able to so revive the old resources of the island as to make provision for the old population and ways of life. There is now again a representative central council, but very many of the old rights and powers have not been yet restored. The condition of society is peculiar absence of towns, social equality, no abject poverty or great wealth, rarity of crime, making it easy for the whole country to be administered as a co-operative commonwealth without the great and striking changes rendered necessary by more complicated systems.

Iceland has always borne a high name for learning and literature; on both sides of their descent people inherited special poetic power. Some of older Eddaic fragments attest the great reach and deep overpowering strength of imagination possessed by their Norse ancestors; and they themselves had been quickened by a new leaven. During the first generations of the "land-taking" a great school of poetry which had arisen among the Norsemen of the Western Isles was brought by them to Iceland. (11) The poems then produced are quite beyond parallel with those of any Teutonic language for centuries after their date, which lay between the beginning of the ninth and the end of the tenth centuries. Through the Greenland colony also came two, or perhaps more, great poems of this western school. This school grew out of the stress and storm of the viking life, with its wild adventure and varied commerce, and the close contact with an artistic and inventive folk, possessed of high culture and great learning. The infusion of Celtic blood, however slight it may have been, had also something to do with the swift intense feeling and rapidity of passion of the earlier Icelandic poets. They are hot-headed and hot-hearted, warm, impulsive, quick to quarrel or to love, faithful, brave; ready with sword or song to battle with all comers, or to seek adventure wheresoever it might be found. They leave Iceland young, and wander at their will to different courts of northern Europe, where they are always held in high honour. Gunnlaug Worm-tongue (12) in 1004 came to England, after being in Norway, as the saga says:—"Now sail Gunnlaug and his fellows into the English main, and come at autumntide south to London Bridge, where they hauled ashore their ship. Now, at that time King Ethelred, the son of Edgar, ruled over England, and was a good lord; the winter he sat in London. But in those days there was the same tongue in England as in Norway and Denmark; but the tongues changed when William the Bastard won England, for thenceforward French went current there, for he was of French kin. Gunnlaug went presently to the king, and greeted him well and worthily. The king asked him from what land he came, and Gunnlaug told him all as it was. 'But,' said he, 'I have come to meet thee, lord, for that I have made a song on thee, and I would that it might please thee to hearken to that song.' The king said it should be so, and Gunnlaug gave forth the song well and proudly, and this is the burden thereof—

"'As God are all folk fearing
The fire lord King of England,
Kin of all kings and all folk,
To Ethelred the head bow.'

The king thanked him for the song, and gave him as song-reward a scarlet cloak lined with the costliest of furs, and golden-broidered down to the hem; and made him his man; and Gunnlaug was with him all the winter, and was well accounted of.

The poems in this volume are part of the wonderful fragments which are all that remain of ancient Scandinavian poetry. Every piece which survives has been garnered by Vigfusson and Powell in the volumes of their "Corpus", where those who seek may find. A long and illustrious line of poets kept the old traditions, down even to within a couple centuries, but the earlier great harvest of song was never again equalled. After christianity had entered Iceland, and that, with other causes, had quieted men's lives, although the poetry which stood to the folk in lieu of music did not die away, it lost the exclusive hold it had upon men's minds. In a time not so stirring, when emotion was not so fervent or so swift, when there was less to quicken the blood, the story that had before found no fit expression but in verse, could stretch its limbs, as it were, and be told in prose. Something of Irish influence is again felt in this new departure and that marvellous new growth, the saga, that came from it, but is little more than an influence. Every people find some one means of expression which more than all else suits their mood or their powers, and this the Icelanders found in the saga. This was the life of a hero told in prose, but in set form, after a regular fashion that unconsciously complied with all epical requirements but that of verse—simple plot, events in order of time, set phrases for even the shifting emotion or changeful fortune of a fight or storm, and careful avoidance of digression, comment, or putting forward by the narrator of ought but the theme he has in hand; he himself is never seen. Something in the perfection of the saga is to be traced to the long winter's evenings, when the whole household, gathered together at their spinning, weaving, and so on, would listen to one of their number who told anew some old story of adventure or achievement. In very truth the saga is a prose epic, and marked by every quality an epic should possess. Growing up while the deeds of dead heroes were fresh in memory, most often recited before the sharers in such deeds, the saga, in its pure form, never goes from what is truth to its teller. Where the saga, as this one of the Volsungs is founded upon the debris of songs and poems, even then very old, tales of mythological heroes, of men quite removed from the personal knowledge of the narrator, yet the story is so inwound with the tradition of his race, is so much a part of his thought-life, that every actor in it has for him a real existence. At the feast or gathering, or by the fireside, as men made nets and women spun, these tales were told over; in their frequent repetition by men who believed them, though incident or sequence underwent no change, they would become closer knit, more coherent, and each an organic whole. Gradually they would take a regular and accepted form, which would ease the strain upon the reciter's memory and leave his mind free to adorn the story with fair devices, that again gave help in the making it easier to remember, and thus aided in its preservation. After a couple of generations had rounded and polished the sagas by their telling and retelling, they were written down for the most part between 1141 and 1220, and so much was their form impressed upon the mind of the folk, that when learned and literary works appeared, they were written in the same style; hence we have histories alike of kingdoms, or families, or miracles, lives of saints, kings, or bishops in saga-form, as well as subjects that seem at first sight even less hopeful. All sagas that have yet appeared in English may be found in the book-list at end of this volume, but they are not a tithe of those that remain.

Of all the stories kept in being by the saga-tellers and left for our delight, there is none that so epitomises human experience; has within the same space so much of nature and of life; so fully the temper and genius of the Northern folk, as that of the Volsungs and Niblungs, which has in varied shapes entered into the literature of many lands. In the beginning there is no doubt that the story belonged to the common ancestral folk of all the Teutonic of Scando-Gothic peoples in the earliest days of their wanderings. Whether they came from the Hindu Kush, or originated in Northern Europe, brought it with them from Asia, or evolved it among the mountains and rivers it has taken for scenery, none know nor can; but each branch of their descendants has it in one form or another, and as the Icelanders were the very crown and flower of the northern folk, so also the story which is the peculiar heritage of that folk received in their hands its highest expression and most noble form. The oldest shape in which we have it is in the Eddaic poems, some of which date from unnumbered generations before the time to which most of them are usually ascribed, the time of the viking-kingdoms in the Western Isles. In these poems the only historical name is that of Attila, the great Hun leader, who filled so large a part of the imagination of the people whose power he had broken. There is no doubt that, in the days when the kingdoms of the Scando-Goths reached from the North Cape to the Caspian, that some earlier great king performed his part; but, after the striking career of Attila, he became the recognised type of a powerful foreign potentate. All the other actors are mythic-heroic. Of the Eddaic songs only fragments now remain, but ere they perished there arose from them a saga, that now given to the readers of this. The so-called Anglo-Saxons brought part of the story to England in "Beowulf"; in which also appear some incidents that are again given in the Icelandic saga of "Grettir the Strong". Most widely known is the form taken by the story in the hands of an unknown medieval German poet, who, from the broken ballads then surviving wrote the "Nibelungenlied" or more properly "Nibelungen Not" ("The Need of the Niblungs"). In this the characters are all renamed, some being more or less historical actors in mid-European history, as Theodoric of the East-Goths, for instance. The whole of the earlier part of the story has disappeared, and though Siegfried (Sigurd) has slain a dragon, there is nothing to connect it with the fate that follows the treasure; Andvari, the Volsungs, Fafnir, and Regin are all forgotten; the mythological features have become faint, and the general air of the whole is that of medieval romance. The swoard Gram is replaced by Balmung, and the Helm of Awing by the Tarn-cap—the former with no gain, the latter with great loss. The curse of Andvari, which in the saga is grimly real, working itself out with slow, sure steps that no power of god or man can turn aside, in the medieval poem is but a mere scenic effect, a strain of mystery and magic, that runs through the changes of the story with much added picturesqueness, but that has no obvious relation to the working-out of the plot, or fulfilment of their destiny by the different characters. Brynhild loses a great deal, and is a poor creature when compared with herself in the saga; Grimhild and her fateful drink have gone; Gudrun (Chriemhild) is much more complex, but not more tragic; one new character, Rudiger, appears as the type of chivalry; but Sigurd (Siegfred) the central figure, though he has lost by the omission of so much of his life, Is, as before, the embodiment of all the virtues that were dear to northern hearts. Brave, strong, generous, dignified, and utterly truthful, he moves amid a tangle of tragic events, overmastered by a mighty fate, and in life or death is still a hero without stain or flaw. It is no wonder that he survives to this day in the national songs of the Faroe Islands and in the folk-ballads of Denmark; that his legend should have been mingled with northern history through Ragnar Lodbrog, or southern through Attila and Theodoric; that it should have inspired William Morris in producing the one great English epic of the century; (13) and Richard Wagner in the mightiest among his music-dramas. Of the story as told in the saga there is no need here to speak, for to read it, as may be done a few pages farther on, is that not better than to read about it? But it may be urged upon those that are pleased and moved by the passion and power, the strength and deep truth of it, to find out more than they now know of the folk among whom it grew, and the land in which they dwelt. In so doing they will come to see how needful are a few lessons from the healthy life and speech of those days, to be applied in the bettering of our own.

ENDNOTES:

(1) Viking (Ice. "Vikingr"; "vik", a bay or creek, "ingr", belonging to, (or men of) freebooters.

(2) "West over the Sea" is the word for the British Isles.

(3) See Todd (J. H.). "War of the Gaedhil with the Gaill".

(4) He was son of Ingiald, son of Thora, daughter of Sigurd Snake-I'-th'-eye, son of Ragnar Lodbrok by Aslaug, daughter of Sigurd by Brynhild. The genealogy is, doubtless, quite mythical.

(5) A Collection of Sagas and other Historical Documents relating to the Settlements and Descents of the Northmen on the British Isles. Ed., G. W. Dasent, D.C.L, and Gudbrand Vigfusson, M.A. "In the Press. Longmans, London. 8vo.

(6) "Orkneyinga Saga".

(7) Landtaking-book—"landnam", landtaking, from "at nema land", hence also the early settlers were called "landnamsmenn".

(8) To all interested in the subject of comparative mythology, Andrew Lang's two admirable books, "Custom and Myth" (1884, 8vo) and "Myth, Ritual, and Religion" (2 vols., crown 8vo, 1887), both published by Longmans, London, may be warmly recommended.

(9) Iceland was granted full independence from Denmark in 1944. —DBK.

(10) These pirates are always appearing about the same time in English State papers as plundering along the coasts of the British Isles, especially Ireland.

(11) For all the old Scandinavian poetry extant in Icelandic, see "Corpus Poeticum Borealis" of Vigfusson and Powell.

(12) Snake-tongue—so called from his biting satire.

(13) "Sigurd the Volsung", which seems to have become all but forgotten in this century.—DBK.

TRANSLATORS' PREFACE

In offering to the reader this translation of the most complete and dramatic form of the great Epic of the North, we lay no claim to special critical insight, nor do we care to deal at all with vexed questions, but are content to abide by existing authorities, doing our utmost to make our rendering close and accurate, and, if it might be so, at the same time, not over prosaic: it is to the lover of poetry and nature, rather than to the student, that we appeal to enjoy and wonder at this great work, now for the first time, strange to say, translated into English: this must be our excuse for speaking here, as briefly as may be, of things that will seem to the student over well known to be worth mentioning, but which may give some ease to the general reader who comes across our book.

The prose of the "Volsunga Saga" was composed probably some time in the twelfth century, from floating traditions no doubt; from songs which, now lost, were then known, at least in fragments, to the Sagaman; and finally from songs, which, written down about his time, are still existing: the greater part of these last the reader will find in this book, some inserted amongst the prose text by the original story-teller, and some by the present translators, and the remainder in the latter part of the book, put together as nearly as may be in the order of the story, and forming a metrical version of the greater portion of it.

These Songs from the Elder Edda we will now briefly compare with the prose of the Volsung Story, premising that these are the only metrical sources existing of those from which the Sagaman told his tale.

Except for the short snatch on p. 24 (1) of our translation, nothing is now left of these till we come to the episode of Helgi Hundings-bane, Sigurd's half-brother; there are two songs left relating to this, from which the prose is put together; to a certain extent they cover the same ground; but the latter half of the second is, wisely as we think, left untouched by the Sagaman, as its interest is of itself too great not to encumber the progress of the main story; for the sake of its wonderful beauty, however, we could not refrain from rendering it, and it will be found first among the metrical translations that form the second part of this book.

Of the next part of the Saga, the deaths of Sinfjotli and Sigmund, and the journey of Queen Hjordis to the court of King Alf, there is no trace left of any metrical origin; but we meet the Edda once more where Regin tells the tale of his kin to Sigurd, and where Sigurd defeats and slays the sons of Hunding: this lay is known as the "Lay of Regin".

The short chap. xvi. is abbreviated from a long poem called the "Prophecy of Gripir" (the Grifir of the Saga), where the whole story to come is told with some detail, and which certainly, if drawn out at length into the prose, would have forestalled the interest of the tale.

In the slaying of the Dragon the Saga adheres very closely to the "Lay of Fafnir"; for the insertion of the song of the birds to Sigurd the present translators are responsible.

Then comes the waking of Brynhild, and her wise redes to Sigurd, taken from the Lay of Sigrdrifa, the greater part of which, in its metrical form, is inserted by the Sagaman into his prose; but the stanza relating Brynhild's awaking we have inserted into the text; the latter part, omitted in the prose, we have translated for the second part of our book.

Of Sigurd at Hlymdale, of Gudrun's dream, the magic potion of Grimhild, the wedding of Sigurd consequent on that potion; of the wooing of Brynhild for Gunnar, her marriage to him, of the quarrel of the Queens, the brooding grief and wrath of Brynhild, and the interview of Sigurd with her—of all this, the most dramatic and best-considered parts of the tale, there is now no more left that retains its metrical form than the few snatches preserved by the Sagaman,

393

though many of the incidents are alluded to in other poems.

Chapter 30 is met by the poem called the "Short Lay of Sigurd", which, fragmentary apparently at the beginning, gives us something of Brynhild's awakening wrath and jealousy, the slaying of Sigurd, and the death of Brynhild herself; this poem we have translated entire.

The Fragments of the "Lay of Brynhild" are what is left of a poem partly covering the same ground as this last, but giving a different account of Sigurd's slaying; it is very incomplete, though the Sagaman has drawn some incidents from it; the reader will find it translated in our second part.

But before the death of the heroine we have inserted entire into the text as chapter 31 the "First Lay of Gudrun", the most lyrical, the most complete, and the most beautiful of all the Eddaic poems; a poem that any age or language might count among its most precious possessions.

From this point to the end of the Saga it keeps closely to the Songs of Edda; in chapter 32 the Sagaman has rendered into prose the "Ancient Lay of Gudrun", except for the beginning, which gives again another account of the death of Sigurd: this lay also we have translated.

The grand poem, called the "Hell-ride of Brynhild", is not represented directly by anything in the prose except that the Sagaman has supplied from it a link or two wanting in the "Lay of Sigrdrifa"; it will be found translated in our second part.

The betrayal and slaughter of the Giukings or Niblungs, and the fearful end of Atli and his sons, and court, are recounted in two lays, called the "Lays of Atli"; the longest of these, the "Greenland Lay of Atli", is followed closely by the Sagaman; the Shorter one we have translated.

The end of Gudrun, of her daughter by Sigurd and of her sons by her last husband Jonakr, treated of in the last four chapters of the Saga, are very grandly and poetically given in the songs called the "Whetting of Gudrun", and the "Lay of Hamdir", which are also among our translations.

These are all the songs of the Edda which the Sagaman has dealt with; but one other, the "Lament of Oddrun", we have translated on account of its intrinsic merit.

As to the literary quality of this work we in say much, but we think we may well trust the reader of poetic insight to break through whatever entanglement of strange manners or unused element may at first trouble him, and to meet the nature and beauty with which it is filled: we cannot doubt that such a reader will be intensely touched by finding, amidst all its wildness and remoteness, such a startling realism, such subtilty, such close sympathy with all the passions that may move himself to-day.

In conclusion, we must again say how strange it seems to us, that this Volsung Tale, which is in fact an unversified poem, should never before been translated into English. For this is the Great Story of the North, which should be to all our race what the Tale of Troy was to the Greeks—to all our race first, and afterwards, when the change of the world has made our race nothing more than a name of what has been—a story too—then should it be to those that come after us no less than the Tale of Troy has been to us.

WILLIAM MORRIS and EIRIKR MAGNUSSON.

ENDNOTES:

(1) CHAPTER viii.—DBK.

CHAPTER 1
Of Sigi, the Son of Odin

Here begins the tale, and tells of a man who was named Sigi, and called of men the son of Odin; another man withal is told of in the tale, hight Skadi, a great man and mighty of his hands; yet was Sigi the mightier and the higher of kin, according to the speech of men of that time. Now Skadi had a thrall with whom the story must deal somewhat, Bredi by name, who was called after that work which he had to do; in prowess and might of hand he was equal to men who were held more worthy, yea, and better than some thereof.

Now it is to be told that, on a time, Sigi fared to the hunting of the deer, and the thrall with him; and they hunted deer day-long till the evening; and when they gathered together their prey in the evening, lo, greater and more by far was that which Bredi had slain than Sigi's prey; and this thing he much misliked, and he said that great wonder it was that a very thrall should out-do him in the hunting of deer: so he fell on him and slew him, and buried the body of him thereafter in a snow-drift.

Then he went home at evening tide and says that Bredi had ridden away from him into the wild-wood. "Soon was he out of my sight," he says, "and naught more I wot of him."

Skadi misdoubted the tale of Sigi, and deemed that this was a guile of his, and that he would have slain Bredi. So he sent men to seek for him, and to such an end came their seeking, that they found him in a certain snow-drift; then said Skadi, that men should call that snow-drift Bredi's Drift from henceforth; and thereafter have folk followed, so that in such wise they call every drift that is right great.

Thus it is well seen that Sigi has slain the thrall and murdered him; so he is given forth to be a wolf in holy places, (1) and may no more abide in the land with his father; therewith Odin bare him fellowship from the land, so long a way, that right long it was, and made no stay till he brought him to certain war-ships. So Sigi falls to lying out a-warring with the strength that his father gave him or ever they parted; and happy was he in his warring, and ever prevailed, till he brought it about that he won by his wars land and lordship at the last; and thereupon he took to him a noble wife, and became a great and mighty king, and ruled over the land of the Huns, and was the greatest of warriors. He had a son by his wife, who was called Refir, who grew up in his father's house, and soon became great of growth, and shapely.

ENDNOTES:

(1) "Wolf in holy places," a man put out of the pale of society for crimes, an outlaw.

CHAPTER 2
Of the Birth of Volsung, the Son of Rerir,
Who Was the Son of Sigi.

Now Sigi grew old, and had many to envy him, so that at last those turned against him whom he trusted most; yea, even the brothers of his wife; for these fell on him at his unwariest, when there were few with him to withstand them, and brought so many against him, that they prevailed against him, and there fell Sigi and all his folk with him. But Rerir, his son, was not in this trouble, and he brought together so mighty a strength of his friends and the great men of the land, that he got to himself both the lands and kingdom of Sigi his father; and so now, when he deems that the feet under him stand firm in his rule, then he calls to mind that which he had against his mother's brothers, who had slain his father. So the king gathers together a mighty army, and therewith falls on his kinsmen, deeming that if he made their kinship of small account, yet none the less they had first wrought evil against him. So he wrought his will herein, in that he departed not from strife before he had slain all his father's banesmen, though dreadful the deed seemed in every wise. So now he gets land, lordship, and fee, and is become a mightier man than his father before him.

Much wealth won in war gat Rerir to himself, and wedded a wife withal, such as he deemed meet for him, and long they lived together, but had no child to take the heritage after them; and ill-content they both were with that, and prayed the Gods with heart and soul that they might get them a child. And so it is said that Odin hears their prayer, and Freyia no less hearkens wherewith they prayed unto her: so she, never lacking for all good counsel, calls to her her casket-bearing may, (1) the daughter of Hrimnir the giant, and sets an apple in her hand, and bids her bring it to the king. She took the apple, and did on her the gear of a crow, and went flying till she came whereas the king sat on a mound, and there she let the apple fall into the lap of the king; but he took the apple, and deemed he knew whereto it would avail; so he goes home from the mound to his own folk, and came to the queen, and some deal of that apple she ate.

So, as the tale tells, the queen soon knew that she big with child, but a long time wore or ever she might give birth to the child: so it befell that the king must needs go to the wars, after the custom of kings, that he may keep his own land in peace: and in this journey it came to pass that Rerir fell sick and got his death, being minded to go home to Odin, a thing much desired of many folk in those days.

Now no otherwise it goes with the queen's sickness than heretofore, nor may she be the lighter of her child, and six winters wore away with the sickness still heavy on her; so that at the last she feels that she may not live long; wherefore now she bade cut the child from out of her; and it was done even as she bade; a man-child was it, and great of growth from his birth, as might well be; and they say that the youngling kissed his mother or ever she died; but to him is a name given, and he is called Volsung; and he was king over Hunland in the room of his father. From his early years he was big and strong, and full of daring in all manly deeds and trials, and he became the greatest of warriors, and of good hap in all the battles of his warfaring.

Now when he was fully come to man's estate, Hrimnir the giant sends to him Ljod his daughter; she of whom the tale told, that she brought the apple to Rerir, Volsung's father. So Volsung weds her withal; and long they abode together with good hap and great love. They had ten sons and one daughter, and their eldest son was hight Sigmund, and their daughter Signy; and these two were twins, and in all wise the foremost and the fairest of the children of Volsung the king, and mighty, as all his seed was; even as has been long told from ancient days, and in tales of long ago, with the greatest fame of all men, how that the Volsungs have been great men and high-minded and far above the most of men both in cunning and in prowess and all things high and mighty.

So says the story that king Volsung let build a noble hall in such a wise, that a big oak-tree stood therein, and that the limbs of the tree blossomed fair out over the roof of the hall, while below stood the trunk within it, and the said trunk did men call Branstock.

ENDNOTES:

(1) May (A.S. "maeg"), a maid.

CHAPTER 3
Of the Sword that Sigmund,
Volsung's Son, Drew from the Branstock

There was a king called Siggeir, who ruled over Gothland, a mighty king and of many folk; he went to meet Volsung, the king, and prayed him for Signy his daughter to wife; and the king took his talk well, and his sons withal, but she was loth thereto, yet she bade her father rule in this as in all other things that concerned her; so the king took such rede (1) that he gave her to him, and she was betrothed to King Siggeir; and for the fulfilling of the feast and the wedding, was King Siggeir to come to the house of King Volsung. The king got ready the feast according to his best might, and when all things were ready, came the king's guests and King Siggeir withal at the day appointed, and many a man of great account had Siggeir with him.

The tale tells that great fires were made endlong the hall, and the great tree aforesaid stood midmost thereof; withal folk say that, whenas men sat by the fires in the evening, a certain man came into the hall unknown of aspect to all men; and suchlike array he had, that over him was a spotted cloak, and he was bare-foot, and had linen-breeches knit tight even unto the bone, and he had a sword in his hand as he went up to the Branstock, and a slouched hat upon his head: huge he was, and seeming-ancient, and one-eyed. (2) So he drew his sword and smote it into the tree-trunk so that it sank in up to the hilts; and all held back from greeting the man. Then he took up the word, and said—

"Whoso draweth this sword from this stock, shall have the same as a gift from me, and shall find in good sooth that never bare he better sword in hand than is this."

Therewith out went the old man from the hall, and none knew who he was or whither he went.

Now men stand up, and none would fain be the last to lay hand to the sword, for they deemed that he would have the best of it who might first touch it; so all the noblest went thereto first, and then the others, one after other; but none who came thereto might avail to pull it out, for in nowise would it come away howsoever they tugged at it; but now up comes Sigmund, King Volsung's son, and sets hand to the sword, and pulls it from the stock, even as if it lay loose before him; so good that weapon seemed to all, that none thought he had seen such a sword before, and Siggeir would fain buy it of him at thrice its weight of gold, but Sigmund said—

"Thou mightest have taken the sword no less than I from there whereas it stood, if it had been thy lot to bear it; but now, since it has first of all fallen into my hand, never shalt thou have it, though thou biddest therefor all the gold thou hast."

King Siggeir grew wroth at these words, and deemed Sigmund had answered him scornfully, but whereas was a wary man and a double-dealing, he made as if he heeded this matter in nowise, yet that same evening he thought how he might reward it, as was well seen afterwards.

ENDNOTES:

(1) Rede (A.S. raed), counsel, advice, a tale or prophecy.
(2) The man is Odin, who is always so represented, because he gave his eye as a pledge for a draught from the fountain of Mimir, the source of all wisdom.

CHAPTER 4
How King Siggeir Wedded Signy,
and Bade King Volsung and His Son to Gothland

Now it is to be told that Siggeir goes to bed by Signy that night, and the next morning the weather was fair; then says King Siggeir that he will not bide, lest the wind should wax, or the sea grow impassable; nor is it said that Volsung or his sons letted him herein, and that the less, because they saw that he was fain to get him gone from the feast. But now says Signy to her father—

"I have no will to go away with Seggeir; neither does my heart smile upon him, and I wot; by my fore-knowledge, and from the fetch (1) of our kin, that from this counsel will great evil fall on us if this wedding be not speedily undone."

"Speak in no such wise, daughter!" said he, "for great shame will it be to him, yea, and to us also, to break troth with him, he being sackless; (2) and in naught may we trust him, and no friendship shall we have of him, if these matters are broken off; but he will pay us back in as evil wise as he may; for that alone is seemly, to hold truly to troth given."

So King Siggeir got ready for home, and before he went from the feast he bade King Volsung, his father-in-law, come see him in Gothland, and all his sons with him, whenas three months should be overpast, and to bring such following with him, as he would have; and as he deemed meet for his honour; and thereby will Siggeir the king pay back for the shortcomings of the wedding-feast, in that he would abide thereat but one night only, a thing not according to the wont of men. So King Volsung gave word to come on the day named, and the kinsmen-in-law parted, and Siggeir went home with his wife.

ENDNOTES:

(1) Fetch; wraith, or familiar spirit.
(2) Sackless (A.S. "sacu", Icel. "sok".) blameless.

CHAPTER 5
Of the Slaying of King Volsung

Now tells the tale of King Volsung and his sons that they go at the time appointed to Gothland at the bidding of King Siggeir, and put off from the land in three ships, all well manned, and have a fair voyage, and made Gothland late of an evening tide.

But that same night came Signy and called her father and brothers to a privy talk, and told them what she deemed King Siggeir was minded to do, and how that he had drawn together an army no man may meet. "And," says she, "he is minded to do guilefully by you; wherefore I bid you get ye gone back again to your own land, and gather together the mightiest power ye may, and then come back hither and avenge you; neither go ye now to your undoing, for ye shall surely fail not to fall by his wiles if ye turn not on him even as I bid you."

Then spake Volsung the king, "All people and nations shall tell of the word I spake, yet being unborn, wherein I vowed a vow that I would flee in fear from neither fire nor the sword; even so have I done hitherto, and shall I depart therefrom now I am old? Yea withal never shall the maidens mock these my sons at the games, and cry out at them that they fear death; once alone must all men need die, and from that season shall none escape; so my rede is that we flee nowhither, but do the work of our hands in as manly wise as we may; a hundred fights have I fought, and whiles I had more, and whiles I had less, and yet ever had I the victory, nor shall it ever be heard tell of me that I fled away or prayed for peace."

Then Signy wept right sore, and prayed that she might not go back to King Siggeir, but King Volsung answered—

"Thou shalt surely go back to thine husband, and abide with him, howsoever it fares with us."

So Signy went home, and they abode there that night; but in the morning, as soon as it was day, Volsung bade his men arise and go aland and make them ready for battle; so they went aland, all of them all-armed, and had not long to wait before Siggeir fell on them with all his army, and the fiercest fight there was betwixt them; and Siggeir cried on his men to the onset all he might; and so the tale tells that King Volsung and his sons went eight times right through Siggeir's folk that day, smiting and hewing on either hand, but when they would do so even once again, King Volsung fell amidst his folk and all his men withal, saving his ten sons, for mightier was the power against them than they might withstand.

But now are all his sons taken, and laid in bonds and led away; and Signy was ware withal that her father was slain, and her brothers taken and doomed to death; that she called King Siggeir apart to talk with her, and said—

"This will I pray of thee, that thou let not slay my brothers hastily, but let them be set awhile in the stocks, for home to me comes the saw that says, "Sweet to eye while seen": but longer life I pray not for them, because I wot well that my prayer will not avail me."

Then answered Siggeir:

"Surely thou art mad and witless, praying thus for more bale for thy brothers than their present slaying; yet this will I grant thee, for the better it likes me the more they must bear, and the longer their pain is or ever death come to them."

Now he let it be done even as she prayed, and a mighty beam was brought and set on the feet of those ten brethren in a certain place of the wild-wood, and there they sit day-long until night; but at midnight, as they sat in the stocks, there came on them a she-wolf from out the wood; old she was, and both great and evil of aspect; and the first thing she did was to bite one of those brethren till he died, and then she ate him up withal, and went on her way.

400

But the next morning Signy sent a man to the brethren, even one whom she most trusted, to wot of the tidings; and when he came back he told her that one of them was dead, and great and grievous she deemed it, if they should all fare in like wise, and yet naught might she avail them.

Soon is the tale told thereof: nine nights together came the she-wolf at midnight, and each night slew and ate up one of the brethren, until all were dead, save Sigmund only; so now, before the tenth night came, Signy sent that trusty man to Sigmund, her brother, and gave honey into his hand, bidding him do it over Sigmund's face, and set a little deal of it in his mouth; so he went to Sigmund and did as he was bidden, and then came home again; and so the next night came the she-wolf according to her wont, and would slay him and eat him even as his brothers; but now she sniffs the breeze from him, whereas he was anointed with the honey, and licks his face all over with her tongue, and then thrusts her tongue into the mouth of him. No fear he had thereof, but caught the she-wolf's tongue betwixt his teeth, and so hard she started back thereat, and pulled herself away so mightily, setting her feet against the stocks, that all was riven asunder; but he ever held so fast that the tongue came away by the roots, and thereof she had her bane.

But some men say that this same she-wolf was the mother of King Siggeir, who had turned herself into this likeness by troll's lore and witchcraft.

CHAPTER 6
Of How Signy Sent the Children
of Her and Siggeir to Sigmund

Now whenas Sigmund is loosed and the stocks are broken, he dwells in the woods and holds himself there; but Signy sends yet again to wot of the tidings, whether Sigmund were alive or no; but when those who were sent came to him, he told them all as it had betid, and how things had gone betwixt him and the wolf; so they went home and tell Signy the tidings; but she goes and finds her brother, and they take counsel in such wise as to make a house underground in the wild-wood; and so things go on a while, Signy hiding him there, and sending him such things as he needed; but King Siggeir deemed that all the Volsungs were dead.

Now Siggeir had two sons by his wife, whereof it is told that when the eldest was ten winters old, Signy sends him to Sigmund, so that he might give him help, if he would in any wise strive to avenge his father; so the youngling goes to the wood, and comes late in evening-tide to Sigmund's earth-house; and Sigmund welcomed him in seemly fashion, and said that he should make ready their bread; "But I," said he, "will go seek firewood."

Therewith he gives the meal-bag into his hands while he himself went to fetch firing; but when he came back the youngling had done naught at the bread-making. Then asks Sigmund if the bread be ready—

Says the youngling, "I durst not set hand to the meal sack, because somewhat quick lay in the meal."

Now Sigmund deemed he wotted that the lad was of no such heart as that he would be fain to have him for his fellow; and when he met his sister, Sigmund said that he had come no nigher to the aid of a man though the youngling were with him.

Then said Signy, "Take him and kill him then; for why should such an one live longer?" and even so he did.

So this winter wears, and the next winter Signy sent her next son to Sigmund; and there is no need to make a long tale thereof, for in like wise went all things, and he slew the child by the counsel of Signy.

CHAPTER 7
Of the Birth of Sinfjotli the Son of Sigmund

So on a tide it befell as Signy sat in her bower, that there came to her a witch-wife exceeding cunning, and Signy talked with her in such wise, "Fain am I," says she, "that we should change semblances together."

She says, "Even as thou wilt then."

And so by her wiles she brought it about that they changed semblances, and now the witch-wife sits in Signy's place according to her rede, and goes to bed by the king that night, and he knows not that he has other than Signy beside him.

But the tale tells of Signy, that she fared to the earth-house of her brother, and prayed him give her harbouring for the night; "For I have gone astray abroad in the woods, and know not whither I am going."

So he said she might abide, and that he would not refuse harbour to one lone woman, deeming that she would scarce pay back his good cheer by tale-bearing: so she came into the house, and they sat down to meat, and his eyes were often on her, and a goodly and fair woman she seemed to him; but when they are full, then he says to her, that he is right fain that they should have but one bed that night; she nowise turned away therefrom, and so for three nights together he laid her in bed by him.

Thereafter she fared home, and found the witch-wife and bade her change semblances again, and she did so.

Now as time wears, Signy brings forth a man-child, who was named Sinfjotli, and when he grew up he was both big and strong, and fair of face, and much like unto the kin of the Volsungs, and he was hardly yet ten winters old when she sent him to Sigmund's earth-house; but this trial she had made of her other sons or ever she had sent them to Sigmund, that she had sewed gloves on to their hands through flesh and skin, and they had borne it ill and cried out thereat; and this she now did to Sinfjotli, and he changed countenance in nowise thereat. Then she flayed off the kirtle so that the skin came off with the sleeves, and said that this would be torment enough for him; but he said—

"Full little would Volsung have felt such a smart this."

So the lad came to Sigmund, and Sigmund bade him knead their meal up, while he goes to fetch firing; so he gave him the meal-sack, and then went after the wood, and by then he came back had Sinfjotli made an end of his baking. Then asked Sigmund if he had found nothing in the meal.

"I misdoubted me that there was something quick in the meal when I first fell to kneading of it, but I have kneaded it all up together, both the meal and that which was therein, whatsoever it was."

Then Sigmund laughed out, he said—

"Naught wilt thou eat of this bread to-night, for the most deadly of worms (1) hast thou kneaded up therewith."

Now Sigmund was so mighty a man that he might eat venom and have no hurt therefrom; but Sinfjotli might abide whatso venom came on the outside of him, but might neither eat nor drink thereof.

ENDNOTES:

(1) Serpents.

CHAPTER 8
The Death of King Siggeir and of Signy

The tale tells that Sigmund thought Sinfjotli over young to help him to his revenge, and will first of all harden him with manly deeds; so in summer-tide they fare wide through the woods and slay men for their wealth; Sigmund deems him to take much after the kin of the Volsungs, though he thinks that he is Siggeir's son, and deems him to have the evil heart of his father, with the might and daring of the Volsungs; withal he must needs think him in no wise a kinsome man, for full oft would he bring Sigmund's wrongs to his memory, and prick him on to slay King Siggeir.

Now on a time as they fare abroad in the wood for the getting of wealth, they find a certain house, and two men with great gold rings asleep therein: now these twain were spell-bound skin-changers, (1) and wolf-skins were hanging up over them in the house; and every tenth day might they come out of those skins; and they were kings' sons: so Sigmund and Sinfjofli do the wolf-skins on them, and then might they nowise come out of them, though forsooth the same nature went with them as heretofore; they howled as wolves howl, but both knew the meaning of that howling; they lay out in the wild-wood, and each went his way; and a word they made betwixt them, that they should risk the onset of seven men, but no more, and that he who was first to be set on should howl in wolfish wise: "Let us not depart from this," says Sigmund, "for thou art young and over-bold, and men will deem the quarry good, when they take thee."

Now each goes his way, and when they were parted, Sigmund meets certain men, and gives forth a wolf's howl; and when Sinfjotli heard it, he went straightway thereto, and slew them all, and once more they parted. But ere Sinfjotli has fared long through the woods, eleven men meet him, and he wrought in such wise that he slew them all, and was awearied therewith, and crawls under an oak, and there takes his rest. Then came Sigmund thither, and said—

"Why didst thou not call on me?"

Sinfjotli said, "I was loth to call for thy help for the slaying of eleven men."

Then Sigmund rushed at him so hard that he staggered and fell, and Sigmund bit him in the throat. Now that day they might not come out of their wolf-skins: but Sigmund lays the other on his back, and bears him home to the house, and cursed the wolf-gears and gave them to the trolls. Now on a day he saw where two weasels went, and how that one bit the other in the throat, and then ran straightway into the thicket, and took up a leaf and laid it on the wound, and thereon his fellow sprang up quite and clean whole; so Sigmund went out and saw a raven flying with a blade of that same herb to him; so he took it and drew it over Sinfjotli's hurt, and he straightway sprang up as whole as though he had never been hurt. Thereafter they went home to their earth-house, and abode there till the time came for them to put off the wolf-shapes; then they burnt them up with fire, and prayed that no more hurt might come to any one from them; but in that uncouth guise they wrought many famous deeds in the kingdom and lordship of King Siggeir.

Now when Sinfjotli was come to man's estate, Sigmund deemed he had tried him fully, and or ever a long time has gone by he turns his mind to the avenging of his father, if so it may be brought about; so on a certain day the twain get them gone from their earth-house, and come to the abode of King Siggeir late in the evening, and go into the porch before the hall, wherein were tuns of ale, and there they lie hid: now the queen is ware of them, where they are, and is fain to meet them; and when they met they took counsel, and were of one mind that Volsung should be revenged that same night.

Now Signy and the king had two children of tender age, who played with a golden toy on the floor, and bowled it along the pavement of the hall, running along with it; but therewith a golden ring from off it trundles away into the place where Sigmund and Sinfjotli lay, and off runs the little one to search for the same, and beholds withal where two men are sitting, big and grimly to look on, with overhanging helms and bright white byrnies; (2) so he runs up the hall to his father, and tells him of the sight he has seen, and thereat the king misdoubts of some guile abiding him; but Signy heard their speech, and arose and took both the children, and went out into the porch to them and said—

"Lo ye! These younglings have bewrayed you; come now therefore and slay them!"

Sigmund says, "Never will I slay thy children for telling of where I lay hid."

But Sinfjotli made little enow of it, but drew his sword and slew them both, and cast them into the hall at King Siggeir's feet.

Then up stood the king and cried on his men to take those who had lain privily in the porch through the night. So they ran thither and would lay hands on them, but they stood on their defence well and manly, and long he remembered it who was the nighest to them; but in the end they were borne down by many men and taken, and bonds were set upon them, and they were cast into fetters wherein they sit night long.

Then the king ponders what longest and worst of deaths he shall mete out to them; and when morning came he let make a great barrow of stones and turf; and when it was done, let set a great flat stone midmost inside thereof, so that one edge was aloft, the other alow; and so great it was that it went from wall to wall, so that none might pass it.

Now he bids folk take Sigmund and Sinfjotli and set them in the barrow, on either side of the stone, for the worse for them he deemed it, that they might hear each the other's speech, and yet that neither might pass one to the other. But now, while they were covering in the barrow with the turf-slips, thither came Signy, bearing straw with her, and cast it down to Sinfjotli, and bade the thralls hide this thing from the king; they said yea thereto, and therewithal was the barrow closed in.

But when night fell, Sinfjotli said to Sigmund, "Belike we shall scarce need meat for a while, for here has the queen cast swine's flesh into the barrow, and wrapped it round about on the outer side with straw."

Therewith he handles the flesh and finds that therein was thrust Sigmund's sword; and he knew it by the hilts, as mirk as it might be In the barrow, and tells Sigmund thereof, and of that were they both fain enow.

Now Sinfjotli drave the point of the sword up into the big stone, and drew it hard along, and the sword bit on the stone. With that Sigmund caught the sword by the point, and in this wise they sawed the stone between them, and let not or all the sawing was done that need be done, even as the song sings:

"Sinfjotli sawed
And Sigmund sawed,
Atwain with main
The stone was done."

Now are they both together loose in the barrow, and soon they cut both through stone and through iron, and bring themselves out thereof. Then they go home to the hall, whenas all men slept there, and bear wood to the hall, and lay fire therein; and withal the folk therein are waked by the smoke, and by the hall burning over their heads.

Then the king cries out, "Who kindled this fire, I burn withal?"

"Here am I," says Sigmund, "with Sinfjotli, my sister's son; and we are minded that thou shalt wot well that all the Volsungs are not yet dead."

Then he bade his sister come out, and take all good things at his hands, and great honour, and fair atonement in that wise, for all her griefs.

But she answered, "Take heed now, and consider, if I have kept King Siggeir in memory, and his slaying of Volsung the king! I let slay both my children, whom I deemed worthless for the revenging of our father, and I went into the wood to thee in a witch-wife's shape; and now behold, Sinfjotli is the son of thee and of me both! and therefore has he this so great hardihood and fierceness, in that he is the son both of Volsung's son and Volsung's daughter; and for this, and for naught else, have I so wrought, that Siggeir might get his bane at last; and all these things have I done that vengeance might fall on him, and that I too might not live long; and merrily now will I die with King Siggeir, though I was naught merry to wed him."

Therewith she kissed Sigmund her brother, and Sinfjotli, and went back again into the fire, and there she died with King Siggeir and all his good men.

But the two kinsmen gathered together folk and ships, and Sigmund went back to his father's land, and drave away thence the king, who had set himself down there in the room of king Volsung.

So Sigmund became a mighty King and far-famed, wise and high-minded: he had to wife one named Borghild, and two sons they had between them, one named Helgi and the other Hamund; and when Helgi was born, Norns came to him, (3) and spake over him, and said that he should be in time to come the most renowned of all kings. Even therewith was Sigmund come home from the wars, and so therewith he gives him the name of Helgi, and these matters as tokens thereof, Land of Rings, Sun-litten Hill, and Sharp-shearing Sword, and withal prayed that he might grow of great fame, and like unto the kin of the Volsungs.

And so it was that he grew up high-minded, and well-beloved, and above all other men in all prowess; and the story tells that he went to the wars when he was fifteen winters old. Helgi was lord and ruler over the army, but Sinfjotli was gotten to be his fellow herein; and so the twain bare sway thereover.

ENDNOTES:

(1) "Skin-changers" were universally believed in once, in Iceland no less than elsewhere, as see Ari in several places of his history, especially the episode of Dufthach and Storwolf o' Whale. Men possessing the power of becoming wolves at intervals, in the present case compelled so to

become, wer-wolves or "loupsgarou", find large place in medieval story, but were equally well-known in classic times. Belief in them still lingers in parts of Europe where wolves are to be found. Herodotus tells of the Neuri, who assumed once a year the shape of wolves; Pliny says that one of the family of Antaeus, chosen by lot annually, became a wolf, and so remained for nine years; Giraldus Cambrensis will have it that Irishmen may become wolves; and Nennius asserts point-blank that "the descendants of wolves are still in Ossory;" they retransform themselves into wolves when they bite. Apuleius, Petronius, and Lucian have similar stories. The Emperor Sigismund convoked a council of theologians in the fifteenth century who decided that wer-wolves did exist.

(2) Byrny (A.S. "byrne"), corslet, cuirass.

(3) "Norns came to him." Nornir are the fates of the northern mythology. They are three—"Urd", the past; "Verdandi", the present; and "Skuld", the future. They sit beside the fountain of Urd ("Urdarbrunur"), which is below one of the roots of "Yggdrasil", the world-tree, which tree their office it is to nourish by sprinkling it with the waters of the fountain.

CHAPTER 9
How Helgi, the Son of Sigmund, Won King Hodbrod and his Realm, and Wedded Sigrun

Now the tale tells that Helgi in his warring met a king hight Hunding, a mighty king, and lord of many men and many lands; they fell to battle together, and Helgi went forth mightily, and such was the end of that fight that Helgi had the victory, but King Hunding fell and many of his men with him; but Helgi is deemed to have grown greatly in fame because he had slain so mighty a king.

Then the sons of Hunding draw together a great army to avenge their father. Hard was the fight betwixt them; but Helgi goes through the folk of those brothers unto their banner, and there slays these sons of Hunding, Alf and Eyolf, Herward and Hagbard, and wins there a great victory.

Now as Helgi fared from the fight, he met a many women right fair and worthy to look on, who rode in exceeding noble array; but one far excelled them all; then Helgi asked them the name of that their lady and queen, and she named herself Sigrun, and said she was daughter of King Hogni.

Then said Helgi, "Fare home with us: good welcome shall ye have!"

Then said the king's daughter, "Other work lies before us than to drink with thee."

"Yea, and what work, king's daughter?" said Helgi.

She answers, "King Hogni has promised me to Hodbrod, the son of King Granmar, but I have vowed a vow that I will have him to my husband no more than if he were a crow's son and not a king's; and yet will the thing come to pass, but and if thou standest in the way thereof, and goest against him with an army, and takest me away withal; for verily with no king would I rather bide on bolster than with thee."

"Be of good cheer, king's daughter," says he, "for certes he and I shall try the matter, or ever thou be given to him; yea, we shall behold which may prevail against the other; and hereto I pledge my life."

Thereafter, Helgi sent men with money in their hands to summon his folk to him, and all his power is called together to Red-Berg: and there Helgi abode till such time as a great company came to him from Hedinsey; and therewithal came mighty power from Norvi Sound aboard great and fair ships. Then King Helgi called to him the captain of his ships, who was hight Leif, and asked him if he had told over the tale of his army.

"A thing not easy to tell, lord," says he, "on the ships that came out of Norvi Sound are twelve thousand men, and otherwhere are half as many again."

Then bade King Helgi turn into the firth, called Varin's firth, and they did so: but now there fell on them so fierce a storm and so huge a sea, that the beat of the waves on board and bow was to hearken to like as the clashing together of high hills broken.

But Helgi bade men fear naught, nor take in any sail, but rather hoist every rag higher than heretofore; but little did they miss of foundering or ever they made land; then came Sigrun, daughter of King Hogni, down on to the beach with a great army, and turned them away thence to a good haven called Gnipalund; but the landsmen see what has befallen and come down to the sea-shore. The brother of King Hodbrod, lord of a land called Swarin's Cairn, cried out to them, and asked them who was captain over that mighty army. Then up stands Sinfjotli, with a helm on his head, bright shining as glass, and a byrny as white as snow; a spear in his hand, and thereon a banner of renown, and a gold-rimmed shield hanging before him; and well he knew with what words to speak to kings—

"Go thou and say, when thou hast made an end of feeding thy swine and thy dogs, and when thou beholdest thy wife again, that here are come the Volsungs, and in this company may King Helgi be found, if Hodbrod be fain of finding him, for his game and his joy it is to fight and win fame, while thou art kissing the handmaids by the fire-side."

Then answered Granmar, "In nowise knowest thou how to speak seemly things, and to tell of matters remembered from of old, whereas thou layest lies on chiefs and lords; most like it is that thou must have long been nourished with wolf-meat abroad in the wild-woods, and has slain thy brethren; and a marvel it is to behold that thou darest to join thyself to the company of good men and true, thou, who hast sucked the blood of many a cold corpse."

Sinfjotli answered, "Dim belike is grown thy memory now, of how thou wert a witch-wife on Varinsey, and wouldst fain have a man to thee, and chose me to that same office of all the world; and how thereafter thou wert a Valkyria (1) in Asgarth, and it well-nigh came to this, that for thy sweet sake should all men fight; and nine wolf whelps I begat on thy body in Lowness, and was the father to them all."

Granmar answers, "Great skill of lying hast thou; yet belike the father of naught at all mayst thou be, since thou wert gelded by the giant's daughters of Thrasness; and lo thou art the stepson of King Siggeir, and were wont to lie abroad in wilds and woods with the kin of wolves; and unlucky was the hand wherewith thou slewest thy brethren, making for thyself an exceeding evil name."

Said Sinfjotli, "Mindest thou not then, when thou were stallion Grani's mare, and how I rode thee an amble on Bravoll, and that afterwards thou wert giant Golnir's goat-herd?"

Granmar says, "Rather would I feed fowls with the flesh of thee than wrangle any longer with thee."

Then spake King Helgi, "Better were it for ye, and a more manly deed, to fight, rather than to speak such things as it is a shame even to hearken to; Granmar's sons are no friends of me and of mine, yet are they hardy men none the less."

So Granmar rode away to meet King Hodbrod, at a stead called Sunfells, and the horses of the twain were named Sveipud and Sveggjud. The brothers met in the castle-porch, and Granmar told Hodbrod of the war-news. King Hodbrod was clad in a byrny, and had his helm on his head; he asked—

"What men are anigh, why look ye so wrathful?"

Granmar says, "Here are come the Volsungs, and twelve thousand men of them are afloat off the coast, and seven thousand are at the Island called Sok, but at the stead called Grindur is the greatest company of all, and now I deem withal that Helgi and his fellowship have good will to give battle."

Then said the king, "Let us send a message through all our realm, and go against them, neither let any who is fain of fight sit idle at home; let us send word to the sons of Ring, and to King Hogni, and to Alf the Old, for they are mighty warriors."

So the hosts met at Wolfstone, and fierce fight befell there; Helgi rushed forth through the host of his foes, and many a man fell there; at last folk saw a great company of shield-maidens, like burning flames to look on, and there was come Sigrun, the king's daughter. Then King Helgi fell on King Hodbrod, and smote him, and slew him even under his very banner; and Sigrun cried out—

"Have thou thanks for thy so manly deed! now shall we share the land between us, and a day of great good hap this is to me, and for this deed shalt thou get honour and renown, in that thou hast felled to earth so mighty a king."

So Helgi took to him that realm and dwelt there long, when he had wedded Sigrun, and became a king of great honour and renown, though he has naught more to do with this story.

ENDNOTES:

(1) Valkyrja, "Chooser of the elected." The women were so called whom Odin sent to choose those for death in battle who were to join the "Einherjar" in the hall of the elected, "Val-holl."

CHAPTER 10
The Ending of Sinfjotli, Sigmund's Son

Now the Volsungs fare back home, and have gained great renown by these deeds. But Sinfjotli betook himself to warfare anew; and therewith he had sight of an exceeding fair woman, and yearned above all things for her; but that same woman was wooed also of the brother of Borghild, the king's wife: and this matter they fought out betwixt them, and Sinfjotli slew that king; and thereafter he harried far and wide, and had many a battle and even gained the day; and he became hereby honoured and renowned above all men; but in autumn tide he came home with many ships and abundant wealth.

Then he told his tidings to the king his father, and he again to the queen, and she for her part bids him get him gone from the realm, and made as if she would in nowise see him. But Sigmund said he would not drive him away, and offered her atonement of gold and great wealth for her brother's life, albeit he said he had never erst given weregild (1) to any for the slaying of a man, but no fame it was to uphold wrong against a woman.

So seeing she might not get her own way herein, she said, "Have thy will in this matter, O my lord, for it is seemly so to be."

And now she holds the funeral feast for her brother by the aid and counsel of the king, and makes ready all things therefor or in the best of wise, and bade thither many great men.

At that feast, Borghild the queen bare the drink to folk, and she came over against Sinfjofli with a great horn, and said—

"Fall to now and drink, fair stepson!"

Then he took the horn to him, and looked therein, and said—

"Nay, for the drink is charmed drink"

Then said Sigmund, "Give it unto me then;" and therewith he took the horn and

410

drank it off.

But the queen said to Sinfjotli, "Why must other men needs drink thine ale for thee?" And she came again the second time with the horn, and said, "Come now and drink!" and goaded him with many words.

And he took the horn, and said—

"Guile is in the drink."

And thereon, Sigmund cried out—

"Give it then unto me!"

Again, the third time, she came to him, and bade him drink off his drink, if he had the heart of a Volsung; then he laid hand on the horn, but said—

"Venom is therein."

"Nay, let the lip strain it out then, O son," quoth Sigmund; and by then was he exceeding drunk with drink, and therefore spake he in that wise.

So Sinfjotli drank, and straightway fell down dead to the ground.

Sigmund rose up, and sorrowed nigh to death over him; then he took the corpse in his arms and fared away to the wood, and went till he came to a certain firth; and there he saw a man in a little boat; and that man asked if he would be wafted by him over the firth, and he said yea thereto; but so little was the boat, that they might not all go in it at once, so the corpse was first laid therein, while Sigmund went by the firth-side. But therewith the boat and the man therein vanished away from before Sigmund's eyes. (2)

So thereafter Sigmund turned back home, and drave away the queen, and a little after she died. But Sigmund the king yet ruled his realm, and is deemed ever the greatest champion and king of the old law.

ENDNOTES:

(1) Weregild, fine for man-slaying ("wer", man, and "gild", a payment).
(2) The man in the boat is Odin, doubtless.

CHAPTER 11
Of King Sigmund's Last Battle,
and of How He Must Yield up His Sword Again

There was a king called Eylimi, mighty and of great fame, and his daughter was called Hjordis, the fairest and wisest of womankind; and Sigmund hears it told of her that she was meet to be his wife, yea if none else were. So he goes to the house of King Eylimi, who would make a great feast for him, if so be he comes not thither in the guise of a foe. So messages were sent from one to the other that this present journey was a peaceful one, and not for war; so the feast was held in the best of wise and with many a man thereat; fairs were in every place established for King Sigmund, and all things else were done to the aid and comfort of his journey: so he came to the feast, and both kings hold their state in one hall; thither also was come King Lyngi, son of King Hunding, and he also is a-wooing the daughter of King Eylimi.

Now the king deemed he knew that the twain had come thither but for one errand, and thought withal that war and trouble might be looked for from the hands of him who brought not his end about; so he spake to his daughter, and said—

"Thou art a wise woman, and I have spoken it, that thou alone shalt choose a husband for thyself; choose therefore between these two kings, and my rede shall be even as thine."

"A hard and troublous matter," says she; "yet will I choose him who is of greatest fame, King Sigmund to wife, albeit he is well stricken in years."

So to him was she betrothed, and King Lyngi gat him gone. Then was Sigmund wedded to Hjordis, and now each day was the feast better and more glorious than on the day before it. But thereafter Sigmund went back home to Hunland, and King Eylimi, his father-in-law, with him, and King Sigmund betakes himself to the due ruling of his realm.

But King Lyngi and his brethren gather an army together to fall on Sigmund, for as in all matters they were wont to have the worser lot, so did this bite the sorest of all; and they would fain prevail over the might and pride of the Volsungs. So they came to Hunland, and sent King Sigmund word how that they would not steal upon him, and that they deemed he would scarce slink away from them. So Sigmund said he would come and meet them in battle, and drew his power together; but Hjordis was borne into the wood with a certain bondmaid, and mighty wealth went with them; and there she abode the while they fought.

Now the vikings rushed from their ships in numbers not to be borne up against, but Sigmund the King, and Eylimi, set up their banners, and the horns blew up to battle; but King Sigmund let blow the horn his father erst had had, and cheered on his men to the fight, but his army was far the fewest.

Now was that battle fierce and fell, and though Sigmund were old, yet most hardily he fought, and was ever the foremost of his men; no shield or byrny might hold against him, and he went ever through the ranks of his foemen on that day, and no man might see how things would fare between them; many an arrow and many a spear was aloft in air that day, and so his spae-wrights wrought for him that he got no wound, and none can tell over the tale of those who fell before him, and both his arms were red with blood, even to the shoulders.

412

But now whenas the battle had dured a while, there came a man into the fight clad in a blue cloak, and with a slouched hat on his head, one-eyed he was, (1) and bare a bill in his hand; and he came against Sigmund the King, and have up his bill against him, and as Sigmund smote fiercely with the sword it fell upon the bill and burst asunder in the midst: thenceforth the slaughter and dismay turned to his side, for the good-hap of King Sigmund had departed from him, and his men fell fast about him; naught did the king spare himself, but the rather cheered on his men; but even as the saw says, "No might 'gainst many", so was it now proven; and in this fight fell Sigmund the King, and King Eylimi, his father-in-law, in the fore-front of their battle, and therewith the more part of their folk.

ENDNOTES:

(1) Odin coming to change the ownership of the sword he had given Sigmund. See Chapter 3.

CHAPTER 12
Of the Shards of the Sword Gram,
and How Hjordis Went to King Alf

Now King Lyngi made for the king's abode, and was minded to take the king's daughter there, but failed herein, for there he found neither wife nor wealth: so he fared through all the realm, and gave his men rule thereover, and now deemed that he had slain all the kin of the Volsungs, and that he need dread them no more from henceforth.

Now Hjordis went amidst the slain that night of the battle, and came whereas lay King Sigmund, and asked if he might be healed; but he answered—

"Many a man lives after hope has grown little; but my good-hap has departed from me, nor will I suffer myself to be healed, nor wills Odin that I should ever draw sword again, since this my sword and his is broken; lo now, I have waged war while it was his will."

"Naught ill would I deem matters," said she, "if thou mightest be healed and avenge my father."

The king said, "That is fated for another man; behold now, thou art great with a man-child; nourish him well and with good heed, and the child shall be the noblest and most famed of all our kin: and keep well withal the shards of the sword: thereof shall a goodly sword be made, and it shall be called Gram, and our son shall bear it, and shall work many a great work therewith, even such as eld shall never minish; for his name shall abide and flourish as long as the world shall endure: and let this be enow for thee. But now I grow weary with my wounds, and I will go see our kin that have gone before me."

So Hjordis sat over him till he died at the day-dawning; and then she looked, and behold, there came many ships sailing to the land: then she spake to the handmaid—

"Let us now change raiment, and be thou called by my name, and say that thou art the king's daughter."

And thus they did; but now the vikings behold the great slaughter of men there, and see where two women fare away thence into the wood; and they deem that some great tidings must have befallen, and they leaped ashore from out their ships. Now the captain of these folks was Alf, son of Hjalprek, king of Denmark, who was sailing with his power along the land. So they came into the field among the slain, and saw how many men lay dead there; then the king bade go seek for the women and bring them thither, and they did so. He asked them what women they were; and, little as the thing seems like to be, the bondmaid answered for the twain, telling of the fall of King Sigmund and King Eylimi, and many another great man, and who they were withal who had wrought the deed. Then the king asks if they wotted where the wealth of the king was bestowed; and then says the bondmaid—

"It may well be deemed that we know full surely thereof."

And therewith she guides them to the place where the treasure lay: and there they found exceeding great wealth; so that men deem they have never seen so many things of price heaped up together in one place. All this they bore to the ships of King Alf, and Hjordis and the bondmaid went with them. Therewith these sail away to their own realm, and talk how that surely on that field had fallen the most renowned of kings.

So the king sits by the tiller, but the women abide in the forecastle; but talk he had with the women and held their counsels of much account.

In such wise the king came home to his realm with great wealth, and he himself was a man exceeding goodly to look on. But when he had been but a little while at home, the queen, his mother, asked him why the fairest of the two women had the fewer rings and the less worthy attire.

"I deem," she said, "that she whom ye have held of least account is the noblest of the twain."

He answered: "I too have misdoubted me, that she is little like a bondwoman, and when we first met, in seemly wise she greeted noble men. Lo now, we will make a trial of the thing."

So on a time as men sat at the drink, the king sat down to talk with the women, and said:—

"In what wise do ye note the wearing of the hours, whenas night grows old, if ye may not see the lights of heaven?"

Then says the bondwoman, "This sign have I, that whenas in my youth I was

414

wont to drink much in the dawn, so now when I no longer use that manner, I am yet wont to wake up at that very same tide, and by that token do I know thereof."

Then the king laughed and said, "Ill manners for a king's daughter!" And therewith he turned to Hjordis, and asked her even the same question; but she answered—

"My father erst gave me a little gold ring of such nature, that it groweth cold on my finger in the day-dawning; and that is the sign that I have to know thereof."

The king answered: "Enow of gold there, where a very bondmaid bore it! But come now, thou hast been long enow hid from me; yet if thou hadst told me all from the beginning, I would have done to thee as though we had both been one king's children: but better than thy deeds will I deal with thee, for thou shalt be my wife, and due jointure will I pay thee whenas thou hast borne me a child."

She spake therewith and told out the whole truth about herself: so there was she held in great honour, and deemed the worthiest of women.

CHAPTER 13
Of the Birth and Waxing of Sigurd Fafnir's-Bane

The tale tells that Hjordis brought forth a man-child, who was straightly borne before King Hjalprek, and then was the king glad thereof, when he saw the keen eyes in the head of him, and he said that few men would be equal to him or like unto him in any wise. So he was sprinkled with water, and had to name Sigurd, of whom all men speak with one speech and say that none was ever his like for growth and goodliness. He was brought up in the house of King Hjalprek in great love and honour; and so it is, that whenso all the noblest men and greatest kings are named in the olden tales, Sigurd is ever put before them all, for might and prowess, for high mind and stout heart, wherewith he was far more abundantly gifted than any man of the northern parts of the wide world.

So Sigurd waxed in King Hjalprek's house, and there was no child but loved him; through him was Hjordis betrothed to King Alf, and jointure meted to her.

Now Sigurd's foster-father was hight Regin, the son of Hreidmar; he taught him all manner of arts, the chess play, and the lore of runes, and the talking of many tongues, even as the wont was with kings' sons in those days. But on a day when they were together, Regin asked Sigurd, if he knew how much wealth his father had owned, and who had the ward thereof; Sigurd answered, and said that the kings kept the ward thereof.

Said Regin, "Dost thou trust them all utterly?"

Sigurd said, "It is seemly that they keep it till I may do somewhat therewith, for better they wot how to guard it than I do."

Another time came Regin to talk to Sigurd, and said—

"A marvellous thing truly that thou must needs be a horse-boy to the kings, and go about like a running knave."

"Nay," said Sigurd, "it is not so, for in all things I have my will, and whatso thing I desire is granted me with good will."

"Well, then," said Regin, "ask for a horse of them."

"Yea," quoth Sigurd, "and that shall I have, whenso I have need thereof."

Thereafter Sigurd went to the king, and the king said—

"What wilt thou have of us?"

Then said Sigurd, "I would even a horse of thee for my disport."

Then said the king, "Choose for thyself a horse, and whatso thing else thou desirest among my matters."

So the next day went Sigurd to the wood, and met on the way an old man, long-bearded, that he knew not, who asked him whither away.

Sigurd said, "I am minded to choose me a horse; come thou, and counsel me thereon."

"Well then," said he, "go we and drive them to the river which is called Busiltarn."

They did so, and drave the horses down into the deeps of the river, and all swam back to land but one horse; and that horse Sigurd chose for himself; grey he was of hue, and young of years, great of growth, and fair to look on, nor had any man yet crossed his back.

Then spake the grey-beard, "From Sleipnir's kin is this horse come, and he must be nourished heedfully, for it will be the best of all horses;" and therewithal he vanished away.

So Sigurd called the horse Grani, the best of all the horses of the world; nor was the man he met other than Odin himself.

Now yet again spake Regin to Sigurd, and said—

"Not enough is thy wealth, and I grieve right sore that thou must needs run here and there like a churl's son; but I can tell thee where there is much wealth for the winning, and great name and honour to be won in the getting of it."

Sigurd asked where that might be, and who had watch and ward over it.

Regin answered, "Fafnir is his name, and but a little way hence he lies, on the

416

waste of Gnita-heath; and when thou comest there thou mayst well say that thou hast never seen more gold heaped together in one place, and that none might desire more treasure, though he were the most ancient and famed of all kings."

"Young am I," says Sigurd, "yet know I the fashion of this worm, and how that none durst go against him, so huge and evil is he."

Regin said, "Nay it is not so, the fashion and the growth of him is even as of other lingworms, (1) and an over great tale men make of it; and even so would thy forefathers have deemed; but thou, though thou be of the kin of the Volsungs, shalt scarce have the heart and mind of those, who are told of as the first in all deeds of fame."

Sigurd said, "Yea, belike I have little of their hardihood and prowess, but thou hast naught to do, to lay a coward's name upon me, when I am scarce out of my childish years. Why dost thou egg me on hereto so busily?"

Regin said, "Therein lies a tale which I must needs tell thee."

"Let me hear the same," said Sigurd.

ENDNOTES:

(1) Lingworm—longworm, dragon.

CHAPTER 14
Regin's Tale of His Brothers,
and of the Gold Called Andvari's Hoard

"The tale begins," said Regin. "Hreidmar was my father's name, a mighty man and a wealthy: and his first son was named Fafnir, his second Otter, and I was the third, and the least of them all both for prowess and good conditions, but I was cunning to work in iron, and silver, and gold, whereof I could make matters that availed somewhat. Other skill my brother Otter followed, and had another nature withal, for he was a great fisher, and above other men herein; in that he had the likeness of an otter by day, and dwelt ever in the river, and bare fish to bank in his mouth, and his prey would he ever bring to our father, and that availed him much: for the most part he kept him in his otter-gear, and then he would come home, and eat alone, and slumbering, for on the dry land he might see naught. But Fafnir was by far the greatest and grimmest, and would have all things about called his.

"Now," says Regin, "there was a dwarf called Andvari, who ever abode in that force, (1) which was called Andvari's force, in the likeness of a pike, and got meat for himself, for many fish there were in the force; now Otter, my brother, was ever wont to enter into the force, and bring fish aland, and lay them one by one on the bank. And so it befell that Odin, Loki, and Hoenir, as they went their ways, came to Andvari's force, and Otter had taken a salmon, and ate it slumbering upon the river bank; then Loki took a stone and cast it at Otter, so that he gat his death thereby; the gods were well content with their prey, and fell to flaying off the otter's skin; and in the evening they came to Hreidmar's house, and showed him what they had taken: thereon he laid hands on them, and doomed them to such ransom, as that they should fill the otter skin with gold, and cover it over without with red gold; so they sent Loki to gather gold together for them; he came to Ran, (2) and got her net, and went therewith to Andvari's force, and cast the net before the pike, and the pike ran into the net and was taken. Then said Loki—

"'What fish of all fishes,
  Swims strong in the flood,
But hath learnt little wit to beware?
  Thine head must thou buy,
  From abiding in hell,
And find me the wan waters flame.'

He answered—

"'Andvari folk call me,
  Call Oinn my father,
Over many a force have I fared;
  For a Norn of ill-luck,
  This life on me lay
Through wet ways ever to wade.'

"So Loki beheld the gold of Andvari, and when he had given up the gold, he had but one ring left, and that also Loki took from him; then the dwarf went into a hollow of the rocks, and cried out, that that gold-ring, yea and all the gold withal, should be the bane of every man who should own it thereafter.

"Now the gods rode with the treasure to Hreidmar, and fulfilled the otter-skin, and set it on its feet, and they must cover it over utterly with gold: but when this was done then Hreidmar came forth, and beheld yet one of the muzzle hairs, and bade them cover that withal; then Odin drew the ring, Andvari's loom, from his hand, and covered up the hair therewith; then sang Loki—

"'Gold enow, gold enow,
  A great weregild, thou hast,
That my head in good hap I may hold;
  But thou and thy son
  Are naught fated to thrive,
The bane shall it be of you both.'

"Thereafter," says Regin, "Fafnir slew his father and murdered him, nor got I aught of the treasure, and so evil he grew, that he fell to lying abroad, and begrudged any share in the wealth to any man, and so became the worst of all worms, and ever now lies brooding upon that treasure: but for me, I went to the king and became his master-smith; and thus is the tale told of how I lost the heritage of my father, and the weregild for my brother."

418

So spake Regin; but since that time gold is called Ottergild, and for no other cause than this.

But Sigurd answered, "Much hast thou lost, and exceeding evil have thy kinsmen been! But now, make a sword by thy craft, such a sword as that none can be made like unto it; so that I may do great deeds therewith, if my heart avail thereto, and thou wouldst have me slay this mighty dragon."

Regin says, "Trust me well herein; and with that same sword shalt thou slay Fafnir."

ENDNOTES:

(1) Waterfall (Ice. "foss", "fors").
(2) Ran is the goddess of the sea, wife of Aegir. The otter was held sacred by Norsefolk and figures in the myth and legend of most races besides; to this day its killing is held a great crime by the Parsees (Haug. "Religion of the Parsees", page 212). Compare penalty above with that for killing the Welsh king's cat ("Ancient Laws and Institutes of Wales". Ed., Aneurin Owen. Longman, London, 1841, 2 vols. 8vo).

CHAPTER 15
Of the Welding Together of the
Shards of the Sword Gram

So Regin makes a sword, and gives it into Sigurd's hands. He took the sword, and said—

"Behold thy smithying, Regin!" and therewith smote it into the anvil, and the sword brake; so he cast down the brand, and bade him forge a better.

Then Regin forged another sword, and brought it to Sigurd, who looked thereon.

Then said Regin, "Belike thou art well content therewith, hard master though thou be in smithying."

So Sigurd proved the sword, and brake it even as the first; then he said to Regin—

"Ah, art thou, mayhappen, a traitor and a liar like to those former kin of thine?"

Therewith he went to his mother, and she welcomed him in seemly wise, and they talked and drank together.

Then spake Sigurd, "Have I heard aright, that King Sigmund gave thee the good sword Gram in two pieces?"

"True enough," she said.

So Sigurd said, "Deliver them into my hands, for I would have them."

She said he looked like to win great fame, and gave him the sword. Therewith went Sigurd to Regin, and bade him make a good sword thereof as he best might; Regin grew wroth thereat, but went into the smithy with the pieces of the sword, thinking well meanwhile that Sigurd pushed his head far enow into the matter of smithying. So he made a sword, and as he bore it forth from the forge, it seemed to the smiths as though fire burned along the edges thereof. Now he bade Sigurd take the sword, and said he knew not how to make a sword if this one failed. Then Sigurd smote it into the anvil, and cleft it down to the stock thereof, and neither burst the sword nor brake it. Then he praised the sword much, and thereafter went to the river with a lock of wool, and threw it up against the stream, and it fell asunder when it met the sword. Then was Sigurd glad, and went home.

But Regin said, "Now whereas I have made the sword for thee, belike thou wilt hold to thy troth given, and wilt go meet Fafnir?"

"Surely will I hold thereto," said Sigurd, "yet first must I avenge my father."

Now Sigurd the older he grew, the more he grew in the love of all men, so that every child loved him well.

CHAPTER 16
The prophecy of Grifir

There was a man hight Grifir,(1) who was Sigurd's mother's brother, and a little after the forging of the sword Sigurd went to Grifir, because he was a man who knew things to come, and what was fated to men: of him Sigurd asked diligently how his life should go; but Grifir was long or he spake, yet at the last, by reason of Sigurd's exceeding great prayers, he told him all his life and the fate thereof, even as afterwards came to pass. So when Grifir had told him all even as he would, he went back home; and a little after he and Regin met.

Then said Regin, "Go thou and slay Fafnir, even as thou hast given thy word."

Sigurd said, "That work shall be wrought; but another is first to be done, the avenging of Sigmund the king and the other of my kinsmen who fell in that their last fight."

ENDNOTES:

(1) Called "Gripir" in the Edda.

CHAPTER 17
Of Sigurd's Avenging of Sigmund His Father

Now Sigurd went to the kings, and spake thus—

"Here have I abode a space with you, and I owe you thanks and reward, for great love and many gifts and all due honour; but now will I away from the land and go meet the sons of Hunding, and do them to wit that the Volsungs are not all dead; and your might would I have to strengthen me therein."

So the kings said that they would give him all things soever that he desired, and therewith was a great army got ready, and all things wrought in the most heedful wise, ships and all war-gear, so that his journey might be of the stateliest: but Sigurd himself steered the dragon-keel which was the greatest and noblest; richly wrought were their sails, and glorious to look on.

So they sail and have wind at will; but when a few days were overpast, there arose a great storm on the sea, and the waves were to behold even as the foam of men's blood; but Sigurd bade take in no sail, howsoever they might be riven, but rather to lay on higher than heretofore. But as they sailed past the rocks of a ness, a certain man hailed the ships, and asked who was captain over that navy; then was it told him that the chief and lord was Sigurd, the son of Sigmund, the most famed of all the young men who now are.

Then said the man, "Naught but one thing, certes, do all say of him, that none among the sons of kings may be likened unto him; now fain were I that ye would shorten sail on some of the ships, and take me aboard."

Then they asked him of his name, and he sang—

> "Hnikar I hight,
> When I gladdened Huginn,
> And went to battle,
> Bright son of Volsung;
> Now may ye call
> The carl on the cliff top,
> Feng or Fjolnir:
> Fain would I with you."

They made for land therewith, and took that man aboard.

Then quoth Sigurd,(1) as the song says—

> "Tell me this, O Hnikar,
> Since full well thou knowest
> Fate of Gods, good and ill of mankind,
> What best our hap foresheweth,
> When amid the battle
> About us sweeps the sword edge."

Quoth Hnikar—

"Good are many tokens
If thereof men wotted
When the swords are sweeping:
Fair fellow deem I
The dark-winged raven,
In war, to weapon-wielder.

"The second good thing:
When abroad thou goest
For the long road well arrayed,
Good if thou seest
Two men standing,
Fain of fame within the forecourt.

"A third thing:
Good hearing,
The wolf a howling
Abroad under ash boughs;
Good hap shalt thou have
Dealing with helm-staves,
If thou seest these fare before thee.

"No man in fight
His face shall turn
Against the moon's sister
Low, late-shining,
For he winneth battle
Who best beholdeth
Through the midmost sword-play,
And the sloping ranks best shapeth.

"Great is the trouble
Of foot ill-tripping,
When arrayed for fight thou farest,
For on both sides about
Are the D?sir (2) by thee,
Guileful, wishful of thy wounding.

"Fair-combed, well washen
Let each warrior be,
Nor lack meat in the morning,
For who can rule
The eve's returning,
And base to fall before fate grovelling."

Then the storm abated, and on they fared till they came aland in the realm of
Hunding's sons, and then Fjolnir vanished away.

Then they let loose fire and sword, and slew men and burnt their abodes, and did waste all before them: a great company of folk fled before the face of them to Lyngi the King, and tell him that men of war are in the land, and are faring with such rage and fury that the like has never been heard of; and that the sons of King Hunding had no great forecast in that they said they would never fear the Volsungs more, for here was come Sigurd, the son of Sigmund, as captain over this army.

So King Lyngi let send the war-message all throughout his realm, and has no will to flee, but summons to him all such as would give him aid. So he came against Sigurd with a great army, he and his brothers with him, and an exceeding fierce fight befell; many a spear and many an arrow might men see there raised aloft, axes hard driven, shields cleft and byrnies torn, helmets were shivered, skulls split atwain, and many a man felled to the cold earth.

And now when the fight has long dured in such wise, Sigurd goes forth before the banners, and has the good sword Gram in his hand, and smites down both men and horses, and goes through the thickest of the throng with both arms red with blood to the shoulder; and folk shrank aback before him wheresoever he went, nor would either helm or byrny hold before him, and no man deemed he had ever seen his like. So a long while the battle lasted, and many a man was slain, and furious was the onset; till at last it befell, even as seldom comes to hand, when a land army falls on, that, do whatso they might, naught was brought about; but so many men fell of the sons of Hunding that the tale of them may not be told; and now whenas Sigurd was among the foremost, came the sons of Hunding against him, and Sigurd smote therewith at Lyngi the king, and clave him down, both helm and head, and mail-clad body, and thereafter he smote Hjorward his brother atwain, and then slew all the other sons of Hunding who were yet alive, and the more part of their folk withal.

Now home goes Sigurd with fair victory won, and plenteous wealth and great honour, which he had gotten to him in this journey, and feasts were made for him against he came back to the realm.

But when Sigurd had been at home but a little, came Regin to talk with him, and said—

"Belike thou wilt now have good will to bow down Fafnir's crest according to thy word plighted, since thou hast thus revenged thy father and the others of thy kin."

Sigurd answered, "That will we hold to, even as we have promised, nor did it ever fall from our memory."

ENDNOTES:

(1) This and verses following were inserted from the "Reginsmal"
by the translators.
(2) "D?sir", sing. "D?s". These are the guardian beings who
follow a man from his birth to his death. The word
originally means sister, and is used throughout the Eddaic

poems as a dignified synonym for woman, lady.

CHAPTER 18
Of the Slaying of the Worm Fafnir

Now Sigurd and Regin ride up the heath along that same way wherein Fafnir was wont to creep when he fared to the water; and folk say that thirty fathoms was the height of that cliff along which he lay when he drank of the water below. Then Sigurd spake:

"How sayedst thou, Regin, that this drake (1) was no greater than other lingworms; methinks the track of him is marvellous great?"

Then said Regin, "Make thee a hole, and sit down therein, and whenas the worm comes to the water, smite him into the heart, and so do him to death, and win thee great fame thereby."

But Sigurd said, "What will betide me if I be before the blood of the worm?"

Says Regin, "Of what avail to counsel thee if thou art still afeard of everything? Little art thou like thy kin in stoutness of heart."

Then Sigurd rides right over the heath; but Regin gets him gone, sore afeard.

But Sigurd fell to digging him a pit, and whiles he was at that work, there came to him an old man with a long beard, and asked what he wrought there, and he told him.

Then answered the old man and said, "Thou doest after sorry counsel: rather dig thee many pits, and let the blood run therein; but sit thee down in one thereof, and so thrust the worm's heart through."

And therewithal he vanished away; but Sigurd made the pits even as it was shown to him.

Now crept the worm down to his place of watering, and the earth shook all about him, and he snorted forth venom on all the way before him as he went; but Sigurd neither trembled nor was adrad at the roaring of him. So whenas the worm crept over the pits, Sigurd thrust his sword under his left shoulder, so that it sank in up to the hilts; then up leapt Sigurd from the pit and drew the sword back again unto him, and therewith was his arm all bloody, up to the very shoulder.

Now when that mighty worm was ware that he had his death-wound, then he lashed out head and tail, so that all things soever that were before him were broken to pieces.

So whenas Fafnir had his death-wound, he asked "Who art thou? And who is thy father? And what thy kin, that thou wert so hardy as to bear weapons against me?"

Sigurd answered, "Unknown to men is my kin. I am called a noble beast: (2) neither father have I nor mother, and all alone have I fared hither."

Said Fafnir, "Whereas thou hast neither father nor mother, of what wonder wert thou born then? But now, though thou tellest me not thy name on this my death-day, yet thou knowest verily that thou liest unto me."

He answered, "Sigurd am I called, and my father was Sigmund."

Says Fafnir, "Who egged thee on to this deed, and why wouldst thou be driven to it? Hadst thou never heard how that all folk were adrad of me, and of the awe of my countenance? But an eager father thou hadst, O bright eyed swain!"

Sigurd answered, "A hardy heart urged me on hereto; and a strong hand and this sharp sword, which well thou knowest now, stood me in stead in the doing of the deed; 'Seldom hath hardy eld a faint-heart youth.'"

Fafnir said, "Well, I wot that hadst thou waxed amid thy kin, thou mightest have good skill to slay folk in thine anger; but more of a marvel is it, that thou, a bondsman taken in war, shouldst have the heart to set on me, 'for few among bondsmen have heart for the fight.'"

Said Sigurd, "Wilt thou then cast it in my teeth that I am far away from my kin? Albeit I was a bondsman, yet was I never shackled. God wot thou hast found me free enow."

Fafnir answered, "In angry wise dost thou take my speech; but hearken, for that same gold which I have owned shall be thy bane too."

Quoth Sigurd, "Fain would we keep all our wealth til that day of days; yet shall each man die once for all."

Said Fafnir, "Few things wilt thou do after my counsel; but take heed that thou shalt be drowned if thou farest unwarily over the sea; so bide thou rather on the dry land, for the coming of the calm tide."

Then said Sigurd, "Speak, Fafnir, and say, if thou art so exceeding wise, who are the Norns who rule the lot of all mothers' sons."

Fafnir answers, "Many there be and wide apart; for some are of the kin of the Aesir, and some are of Elfin kin, and some there are who are daughters of Dvalin."

Said Sigurd, "How namest thou the holm whereon Surt (3) and the Aesir mix and mingle the water of the sword?"

"Unshapen is that holm hight," said Fafnir.

And yet again he said, "Regin, my brother, has brought about my end, and it gladdens my heart that thine too he bringeth about; for thus will things be according to his will."

And once again he spake, "A countenance of terror I bore up before all folk, after that I brooded over the heritage of my brother, and on every side did I spout out poison, so that none durst come anigh me, and of no weapon was I adrad, nor ever had I so many men before me, as that I deemed myself not stronger than all; for all men were sore afeard of me."

Sigurd answered and said, "Few may have victory by means of that same countenance of terror, for whoso comes amongst many shall one day find that no one man is by so far the mightiest of all."

Then says Fafnir, "Such counsel I give thee, that thou take thy horse and ride away at thy speediest, for ofttimes it falls out so, that he who gets a death-wound avenges himself none the less."

Sigurd answered, "Such as thy redes are I will nowise do after them; nay, I will ride now to thy lair and take to me that great treasure of thy kin."

"Ride there then," said Fafnir, "and thou shalt find gold enow to suffice thee for all thy life-days; yet shall that gold be thy bane, and the bane of every one soever who owns it."

Then up stood Sigurd, and said, "Home would I ride and lose all that wealth, if I deemed that by the losing thereof I should never die; but every brave and true man will fain have his hand on wealth till that last day; but thou, Fafnir, wallow in the death-pain till Death and Hell have thee."

And therewithal Fafnir died.

ENDNOTES:

(1) Lat. "draco", a dragon.
(2) "Unknown to men is my kin." Sigurd refusing to tell his
      name is to be referred to the superstition that a dying man
      could throw a curse on his enemy.
(3) Surt; a fire-giant, who will destroy the world at the
      Ragnarok, or destruction of all things. Aesir; the gods.

CHAPTER 19
Of the Slaying of Regin, Son of Hreidmar

Thereafter came Regin to Sigurd, and said, "Hail, lord and master, a noble victory hast thou won in the slaying of Fafnir, whereas none durst heretofore abide in the path of him; and now shall this deed of fame be of renown while the world stands fast."

Then stood Regin staring on the earth a long while, and presently thereafter spake from heavy mood: "Mine own brother hast thou slain, and scarce may I be called sackless of the deed."

Then Sigurd took his sword Gram and dried it on the earth, and spake to Regin —

"Afar thou faredst when I wrought this deed and tried this sharp sword with the hand and the might of me; with all the might and main of a dragon must I strive, while thou wert laid alow in the heather-bush, wotting not if it were earth or heaven."

Said Regin, "Long might this worm have lain in his lair, if the sharp sword I forged with my hand had not been good at need to thee; had that not been, neither thou nor any man would have prevailed against him as at this time."

Sigurd answers, "Whenas men meet foes in fight, better is stout heart than sharp sword."

Then said Regin, exceeding heavily, "Thou hast slain my brother, and scarce may I be sackless of the deed."

Therewith Sigurd cut out the heart of the worm with the sword called Ridil; but Regin drank of Fafnir's blood, and spake, "Grant me a boon, and do a thing little for thee to do. Bear the heart to the fire, and roast it, and give me thereof to eat."

Then Sigurd went his ways and roasted it on a rod; and when the blood bubbled out he laid his finger thereon to essay it, if it were fully done; and then he set his finger in his mouth, and lo, when the heart-blood of the worm touched his tongue, straightway he knew the voice of all fowls, and heard withal how the wood-peckers chattered in the brake beside him—

"There sittest thou, Sigurd, roasting Fafnir's heart for another, that thou shouldest eat thine ownself, and then thou shouldest become the wisest of all men."

And another spake: "There lies Regin, minded to beguile the man who trusts in him."

But yet again said the third, "Let him smite the head from off him then, and be only lord of all that gold."

And once more the fourth spake and said, "Ah, the wiser were he if he followed after that good counsel, and rode thereafter to Fafnir's lair, and took to him that mighty treasure that lieth there, and then rode over Hindfell, whereas sleeps Brynhild; for there would he get great wisdom. Ah, wise he were, if he did after your redes, and bethought him of his own weal; 'for where wolf's ears are, wolf's teeth are near.'"

Then cried the fifth: "Yea, yea, not so wise is he as I deem him, if he spareth him, whose brother he hath slain already."

427

At last spake the sixth: "Handy and good rede to slay him, and be lord of the treasure!"

Then said Sigurd, "The time is unborn wherein Regin shall be my bane; nay, rather one road shall both these brothers fare."

And therewith he drew his sword Gram and struck off Regin's head.

Then heard Sigurd the wood-peckers a-singing, even as the song says. (1)

For the first sang:

"Bind thou, Sigurd,
The bright red rings!
Not meet it is
Many things to fear.
A fair may know I,
Fair of all the fairest
Girt about with gold,
Good for thy getting."

And the second:

"Green go the ways
Toward the hall of Giuki
That the fates show forth
To those who fare thither;
There the rich king
Reareth a daughter;
Thou shalt deal, Sigurd,
With gold for thy sweetling."

And the third:

"A high hall is there
Reared upon Hindfell,
Without all around it
Sweeps the red flame aloft.
Wise men wrought
That wonder of halls
With the unhidden gleam
Of the glory of gold."

Then the fourth sang:

"Soft on the fell
A shield-may sleepeth
The lime-trees' red plague
Playing about her:
The sleep-thorn set Odin

428

Into that maiden
For her choosing in war
The one he willed not.

"Go, son, behold
That may under helm
Whom from battle
Vinskornir bore,
From her may not turn
The torment of sleep.
Dear offspring of kings
In the dread Norns' despite."

Then Sigurd ate some deal of Fafnir's heart, and the remnant he kept. Then he leapt on his horse and rode along the trail of the worm Fafnir, and so right unto his abiding-place; and he found it open, and beheld all the doors and the gear of them that they were wrought of iron: yea, and all the beams of the house; and it was dug down deep into the earth: there found Sigurd gold exceeding plenteous, and the sword Rotti; and thence he took the Helm of Awe, and the Gold Byrny, and many things fair and good. So much gold he found there, that he thought verily that scarce might two horses, or three belike, bear it thence. So he took all the gold and laid it in two great chests, and set them on the horse Grani, and took the reins of him, but nowise will he stir, neither will he abide smiting. Then Sigurd knows the mind of the horse, and leaps on the back of him, and smites and spurs into him, and off the horse goes even as if he were unladen.

ENDNOTES:

(1) The Songs of the Birds were inserted from "Reginsmal" by the translators.

CHAPTER 20
Of Sigurd's Meeting with Brynhild on the Mountain

By long roads rides Sigurd, till he comes at the last up on to Hindfell, and wends his way south to the land of the Franks; and he sees before him on the fell a great light, as of fire burning, and flaming up even unto the heavens; and when he came thereto, lo, a shield-hung castle before him, and a banner on the topmost thereof: into the castle went Sigurd, and saw one lying there asleep, and all-armed. Therewith he takes the helm from off the head of him, and sees that it is no man, but a woman; and she was clad in a byrny as closely set on her as though it had grown to her flesh; so he rent it from the collar downwards; and then the sleeves thereof, and ever the sword bit on it as if it were cloth. Then said Sigurd that over-long had she lain asleep; but she asked—

"What thing of great might is it that has prevailed to rend my byrny, and draw me from my sleep?"

Even as sings the song: (1)

> "What bit on the byrny,
> Why breaks my sleep away,
> Who has turned from me
> My wan tormenting?"

"Ah, is it so, that here is come Sigurd Sigmundson, bearing Fafnir's helm on his head and Fafnir's bane in his hand?"

Then answered Sigurd—

> "Sigmund's son
> With Sigurd's sword
> E'en now rent down
> The raven's wall."

"Of the Volsung's kin is he who has done the deed; but now I have heard that thou art daughter of a mighty king, and folk have told us that thou wert lovely and full of lore, and now I will try the same."

Then Brynhild sang—

> "Long have I slept
> And slumbered long,
> Many and long are the woes of mankind,
> By the might of Odin
> Must I bide helpless
> To shake from off me the spells of slumber.

> "Hail to the day come back!
> Hail, sons of the daylight!
> Hail to thee, dark night, and thy daughter!
> Look with kind eyes a-down,
> On us sitting here lonely,
> And give unto us the gain that we long for.

> "Hail to the Aesir,
> And the sweet Asyniur! (2)
> Hail to the fair earth fulfilled of plenty!
> Fair words, wise hearts,
> Would we win from you,
> And healing hands while life we hold."

Then Brynhild speaks again and says, "Two kings fought, one hight Helm Gunnar, an old man, and the greatest of warriors, and Odin had promised the victory unto him; but his foe was Agnar, or Audi's brother: and so I smote down Helm Gunnar in the fight; and Odin, in vengeance for that deed, stuck the sleep-thorn into me, and said that I should never again have the victory, but should be given away in marriage; but thereagainst I vowed a vow, that never would I wed one who knew the name of fear."

Then said Sigurd, "Teach us the lore of mighty matters!"

She said, "Belike thou cannest more skill in all than I; yet will I teach thee; yea, and with thanks, if there be aught of my cunning that will in anywise pleasure thee, either of runes or of other matters that are the root of things; but now let us drink together, and may the Gods give to us twain a good day, that thou mayst win good help and fame from my wisdom, and that thou mayst hereafter mind thee of that which we twain speak together."

Then Brynhild filled a beaker and bore it to Sigurd, and gave him the drink of love, and spake—

"Beer bring I to thee,
Fair fruit of the byrnies' clash,
Mixed is it mightily,
Mingled with fame,
Brimming with bright lays
And pitiful runes,
Wise words, sweet words,
Speech of great game.

"Runes of war know thou,
If great thou wilt be!
Cut them on hilt of hardened sword,
Some on the brand's back,
Some on its shining side,
Twice name Tyr therein.

"Sea-runes good at need,
Learnt for ship's saving,
For the good health of the swimming horse;
On the stern cut them,
Cut them on the rudder-blade
And set flame to shaven oar:
Howso big be the sea-hills,
Howso blue beneath,
Hail from the main then comest thou home.

"Word-runes learn well
If thou wilt that no man
Pay back grief for the grief thou gavest;
Wind thou these,
Weave thou these,
Cast thou these all about thee,
At the Thing,
Where folk throng,
Unto the full doom faring.

"Of ale-runes know the wisdom
If thou wilt that another's wife

Should not bewray thine heart that trusteth:
  Cut them on the mead-horn,
  On the back of each hand,
And nick an N upon thy nail.

"Ale have thou heed
  To sign from all harm
Leek lay thou in the liquor,
  Then I know for sure
  Never cometh to thee,
Mead with hurtful matters mingled.

"Help-runes shalt thou gather
  If skill thou wouldst gain
To loosen child from low-laid mother;
  Cut be they in hands hollow,
  Wrapped the joints round about;
Call for the Good-folks' gainsome helping.

"Learn the bough-runes wisdom
  If leech-lore thou lovest;
And wilt wot about wounds' searching
  On the bark be they scored;
  On the buds of trees
Whose boughs look eastward ever.

"Thought-runes shalt thou deal with
  If thou wilt be of all men
Fairest-souled wight, and wisest,
  These areded
  These first cut
These first took to heart high Hropt.

"On the shield were they scored
That stands before the shining God,
On Early-waking's ear,
On All-knowing's hoof,
On the wheel which runneth
Under Rognir's chariot;
On Sleipnir's jaw-teeth,
On the sleigh's traces.

"On the rough bear's paws,
And on Bragi's tongue,
On the wolf's claws,
And on eagle's bill,
On bloody wings,
And bridge's end;
On loosing palms,
And pity's path:

"On glass, and on gold,
And on goodly silver,
In wine and in wort,
And the seat of the witch-wife;
On Gungnir's point,
And Grani's bosom;
On the Norn's nail,
And the neb of the night-owl.

"All these so cut,
Were shaven and sheared,
And mingled in with holy mead,
And sent upon wide ways enow;
  Some abide with the Elves,
  Some abide with the Aesir,
Or with the wise Vanir,
Some still hold the sons of mankind.

"These be the book-runes,
And the runes of good help,
And all the ale-runes,
And the runes of much might;
  To whomso they may avail,
  Unbewildered unspoilt;
They are wholesome to have:
Thrive thou with these then.
When thou hast learnt their lore,
Till the Gods end thy life-days.

"Now shalt thou choose thee
E'en as choice is bidden,
Sharp steel's root and stem,
  Choose song or silence;
  See to each in thy heart,
All hurt has been heeded."

Then answered Sigurd—

"Ne'er shall I flee,
Though thou wottest me fey;
Never was I born for blenching,
Thy loved rede will I
  Hold aright in my heart
Even as long as I may live."

ENDNOTES:

(1) The stanzas on the two following pages were inserted here
    from "Sigrdrifasmal" by the translators.
(2) Goddesses.

CHAPTER 21
More Wise Words of Brynhild

Sigurd spake now, "Sure no wiser woman than thou art one may be found in the wide world; yea, yea, teach me more yet of thy wisdom!"

She answers, "Seemly is it that I do according to thy will, and show thee forth more redes of great avail, for thy prayer's sake and thy wisdom;" and she spake withal—

"Be kindly to friend and kin, and reward not their trespasses against thee; bear and forbear, and win for thee thereby long enduring praise of men.

"Take good heed of evil things: a may's love, and a man's wife; full oft thereof doth ill befall!

"Let not thy mind be overmuch crossed by unwise men at thronged meetings of folk; for oft these speak worse than they wot of; lest thou be called a dastard, and art minded to think that thou art even as is said; slay such an one on another day, and so reward his ugly talk.

"If thou farest by the way whereas bide evil things, be well ware of thyself; take not harbour near the highway, though thou be benighted, for oft abide there ill wights for men's bewilderment.

"Let not fair women beguile thee, such as thou mayst meet at the feast, so that the thought thereof stand thee in stead of sleep, and a quiet mind; yea, draw them not to thee with kisses or other sweet things of love.

"If thou hearest the fool's word of a drunken man, strive not with him being drunk with drink and witless; many a grief, yea, and the very death, groweth from out such things.

"Fight thy foes in the field, nor be burnt in thine house.

'Never swear thou wrongsome oath; great and grim is the reward for the breaking of plighted troth.

"Give kind heed to dead men,—sick-dead, Sea-dead; deal heedfully with their dead corpses.

"Trow never in him for whom thou hast slain father, brother, or whatso near kin, yea, though young he be; 'for oft waxes wolf in youngling'.

"Look thou with good heed to the wiles of thy friends; but little skill is given to me, that I should foresee the ways of thy life; yet good it were that hate fell not on thee from those of thy wife's house."

Sigurd spake, "None among the sons of men can be found wiser than thou; and thereby swear I, that thee will I have as my own, for near to my heart thou liest."

She answers, "Thee would I fainest choose, though I had all men's sons to choose from."

And thereto they plighted troth both of them.

CHAPTER 22
Of the Semblance and Array of Sigurd Fafnir's-Bane (1)

Now Sigurd rides away; many-folded is his shield, and blazing with red gold, and the image of a dragon is drawn thereon; and this same was dark brown above, and bright red below; and with even such-like image was adorned helm, and saddle, and coat-armour; and he was clad in the golden byrny, and all his weapons were gold wrought.

Now for this cause was the drake drawn on all his weapons, that when he was seen of men, all folk might know who went there; yea, all those who had heard of his slaying of that great dragon, that the Voerings call Fafnir; and for that cause are his weapons gold-wrought, and brown of hue, and that he was by far above other men in courtesy and goodly manners, and well-nigh in all things else; and whenas folk tell of all the mightiest champions, and the noblest chiefs, then ever is he named the foremost, and his name goes wide about on all tongues north of the sea of the Greek-lands, and even so shall it be while the world endures.

Now the hair of this Sigurd was golden-red of hue, fair of fashion, and falling down in great locks; thick and short was his beard, and of no other colour, high-nosed he was, broad and high-boned of face; so keen were his eyes, that few durst gaze up under the brows of him; his shoulders were as broad to look on as the shoulders of two; most duly was his body fashioned betwixt height and breadth, and in such wise as was seemliest; and this is the sign told of his height, that when he was girt with his sword Gram, which same was seven spans long, as he went through the full-grown rye-fields, the dew-shoe of the said sword smote the ears of the standing corn; and, for all that, greater was his strength than his growth: well could he wield sword, and cast forth spear, shoot shaft, and hold shield, bend bow, back horse, and do all the goodly deeds that he learned in his youth's days.

Wise he was to know things yet undone; and the voice of all fowls he knew, wherefore few things fell on him unawares.

Of many words he was, and so fair of speech withal, that whensoever he made it his business to speak, he never left speaking before that to all men it seemed full sure, that no otherwise must the matter be than as he said.

His sport and pleasure it was to give aid to his own folk, and to prove himself in mighty matters, to take wealth from his unfriends, and give the same to his friends.

Never did he lose heart, and of naught was he adrad.

ENDNOTES:

(1) This chapter is nearly literally the same as chapter 166 of the "Wilkinasaga"; Ed.: Perinskiold, Stockholm, 1715.

CHAPTER 23
Sigurd Comes to Hlymdale

Forth Sigurd rides till he comes to a great and goodly dwelling, the lord whereof was a mighty chief called Heimir; he had to wife a sister of Brynhild, who was hight Bekkhild, because she had bidden at home, and learned handicraft, whereas Brynhild fared with helm and byrny unto the wars, wherefore was she called Brynhild.

Heimir and Bekkhild had a son called Alswid, the most courteous of men.

Now at this stead were men disporting them abroad, but when they see the man riding thereto, they leave their play to wonder at him, for none such had they ever seen erst; so they went to meet him, and gave him good welcome; Alswid bade him abide and have such things at his hands as he would; and he takes his bidding blithesomely; due service withal was established for him; four men bore the treasure of gold from off the horse, and the fifth took it to him to guard the same; therein were many things to behold, things of great price, and seldom seen; and great game and joy men had to look on byrnies and helms, and mighty rings, and wondrous great golden stoups, and all kinds of war weapons.

So there dwelt Sigurd long in great honour holden; and tidings of that deed of fame spread wide through all lands, of how he had slain that hideous and fearful dragon. So good joyance had they there together, and each was leal to other; and their sport was in the arraying of their weapons, and the shafting of their arrows, and the flying of their falcons.

CHAPTER 24
Sigurd Sees Brynhild at Hlymdale

In those days came home to Heimir, Brynhild, his foster-daughter, and she sat in her bower with her maidens, and could more skill in handycraft than other women; she sat, overlaying cloth with gold, and sewing therein the great deeds which Sigurd had wrought, the slaying of the Worm, and the taking of the wealth of him, and the death of Regin withal.

Now tells the tale, that on a day Sigurd rode into the wood with hawk, and hound, and men thronging; and whenas he came home his hawk flew up to a high tower, and sat him down on a certain window. Then fared Sigurd after his hawk, and he saw where sat a fair woman, and knew that it was Brynhild, and he deems all things he sees there to be worthy together, both her fairness, and the fair things she wrought: and therewith he goes into the hall, but has no more joyance in the games of the men folk.

Then spake Alswid, "Why art thou so bare of bliss? this manner of thine grieveth us thy friends; why then wilt thou not hold to thy gleesome ways? Lo, thy hawks pine now, and thy horse Grani droops; and long will it be ere we are booted thereof?"

Sigurd answered, "Good friend, hearken to what lies on my mind; for my hawk flew up into a certain tower; and when I came thereto and took him, lo there I saw a fair woman, and she sat by a needlework of gold, and did thereon my deeds that are passed, and my deeds that are to come."

Then said Alswid, "Thou has seen Brynhild, Budli's daughter, the greatest of great women."

"Yea, verily," said Sigurd; "but how came she hither?"

Aswid answered, "Short space there was betwixt the coming hither of the twain of you."

Says Sigurd, "Yea, but a few days agone I knew her for the best of the world's women."

Alswid said, "Give not all thine heed to one woman, being such a man as thou art; ill life to sit lamenting for what we may not have."

"I shall go meet her," says Sigurd, "and get from her love like my love, and give her a gold ring in token thereof."

Alswid answered, "None has ever yet been known whom she would let sit beside her, or to whom she would give drink; for ever will she hold to warfare and to the winning of all kinds of fame."

Sigurd said, "We know not for sure whether she will give us answer or not, or grant us a seat beside her."

So the next day after, Sigurd went to the bower, but Alswid stood outside the bower door, fitting shafts to his arrows.

Now Sigurd spake, "Abide, fair and hale lady,—how farest thou?"

She answered, "Well it fares; my kin and my friends live yet: but who shall say what goodhap folk may bear to their life's end?"

He sat him down by her, and there came in four damsels with great golden beakers, and the best of wine therein; and these stood before the twain.

Then said Brynhild, "This seat is for few, but and if my father come."

He answered, "Yet is it granted to one that likes me well."

Now that chamber was hung with the best and fairest of hangings, and the floor thereof was all covered with cloth.

Sigurd spake, "Now has it come to pass even as thou didst promise."

"O be thou welcome here!" said she, and arose therewith, and the four damsels with her, and bore the golden beaker to him, and bade him drink; he stretched out his hand to the beaker, and took it, and her hand withal, and drew her down beside him; and cast his arms round about her neck and kissed her, and said—

"Thou art the fairest that was ever born!"

But Brynhild said, "Ah, wiser is it not to cast faith and troth into a woman's power, for ever shall they break that they have promised."

He said, "That day would dawn the best of days over our heads whereon each of each should be made happy."

Brynhild answered, "It is not fated that we should abide together; I am a shield-may, and wear helm on head even as the kings of war, and them full oft I help, neither is the battle become loathsome to me."

Sigurd answered, "What fruit shall be of our life, if we live not together: harder to bear this pain that lies hereunder, than the stroke of sharp sword."

Brynhild answers, "I shall gaze on the hosts of the war-kings, but thou shalt wed Gudrun, the daughter of Giuki."

Sigurd answered, "What king's daughter lives to beguile me? neither am I double-hearted herein; and now I swear by the Gods that thee shall I have for mine own, or no woman else."

And even suchlike wise spake she.

Sigurd thanked her for her speech, and gave her a gold ring, and now they swore oath anew, and so he went his ways to his men, and is with them awhile in great bliss.

CHAPTER 25
Of the Dream of Gudrun, Giuki's Daughter

There was a king hight Giuki, who ruled a realm south of the Rhine; three sons he had, thus named: Gunnar, Hogni, and Guttorm, and Gudrun was the name of his daughter, the fairest of maidens; and all these children were far before all other king's children in all prowess, and in goodliness and growth withal; ever were his sons at the wars and wrought many a deed of fame. But Giuki had wedded Grimhild the Wise-wife.

Now Budli was the name of a king mightier than Giuki, mighty though they both were: and Atli was the brother of Brynhild: Atli was a fierce man and a grim, great and black to look on, yet noble of mien withal, and the greatest of warriors. Grimhild was a fierce-hearted woman.

Now the days of the Giukings bloomed fair, and chiefly because of those children, so far before the sons of men.

On a day Gudrun says to her mays that she may have no joy of heart; then a certain woman asked her wherefore her joy was departed.

She answered, "Grief came to me in my dreams, therefore is there sorrow in my heart, since thou must needs ask thereof."

"Tell it me, then, thy dream," said the woman, "for dreams oft forecast but the weather."

Gudrun answers, "Nay, nay, no weather is this; I dreamed that I had a fair hawk on my wrist, feathered with feathers of gold."

Says the woman, "Many have heard tell of thy beauty, thy wisdom, and thy courtesy; some king's son abides thee, then."

Gudrun answers, "I dreamed that naught was so dear to me as this hawk, and all my wealth had I cast aside rather than him."

The woman said, "Well, then, the man thou shalt have will be of the goodliest, and well shalt thou love him."

Gudrun answered, "It grieves me that I know not who he shall be; let us go seek Brynhild, for she belike will wot thereof."

So they arrayed them in gold and many a fair thing, and she went with her damsels till they came to the hall of Brynhild, and that hall was dight with gold, and stood on a high hill; and whenas their goings were seen, it was told Brynhild, that a company of women drove toward the burg in gilded waggons.

"That shall be Gudrun, Giuki's daughter," says she: "I dreamed of her last night; let us go meet her! No fairer woman may come to our house."

So they went abroad to meet them, and gave them good greeting, and they went into the goodly hall together; fairly painted it was within, and well adorned with silver vessel; cloths were spread under the feet of them, and all folk served them, and in many wise they sported.

But Gudrun was somewhat silent.

439

Then said Brynhild, "Ill to abash folk of their mirth; prithee do not so; let us talk together for our disport of mighty kings and their great deeds."

"Good talk," says Gudrun, "let us do even so; what kings deemest thou to have been the first of all men?"

Brynhild says, "The sons of Haki, and Hagbard withal; they brought to pass many a deed of fame in the warfare."

Gudrun answers, "Great men certes, and of noble fame! Yet Sigar took their one sister, and burned the other, house and all; and they may be called slow to revenge the deed; why didst thou not name my brethren, who are held to be the first of men as at this time?"

Brynhild says, "Men of good hope are they surely, though but little proven hitherto; but one I know far before them, Sigurd, the son of Sigmund the king; a youngling was he in the days when he slew the sons of Hunding, and revenged his father, and Eylimi, his mother's father."

Said Gudrun, "By what token tellest thou that?"

Brynhild answered, "His mother went amid the dead, and found Sigmund the king sore wounded, and would bind up his hurts; but he said he grew over old for war, and bade her lay this comfort to her heart, that she should bear the most famed of sons; and wise was the wise man's word therein: for after the death of King Sigmund, she went to King Alf, and there was Sigurd nourished in great honour, and day by day he wrought some deed of fame, and is the man most renowned of all the wide world."

Gudrun says, "From love hast thou gained these tidings of him; but for this cause came I here, to tell thee dreams of mine which have brought me great grief."

Says Brynhild, "Let not such matters sadden thee; abide with thy friends who wish thee blithesome, all of them!"

"This I dreamed," said Gudrun, "that we went, a many of us in company, from the bower, and we saw an exceeding great hart, that far excelled all other deer ever seen, and the hair of him was golden; and this deer we were all fain to take, but I alone got him; and he seemed to me better than all things else; but sithence thou, Byrnhild, didst shoot and slay my deer even at my very knees, and such grief was that to me that scarce might I bear it; and then afterwards thou gavest me a wolf-cub, which besprinkled me with the blood of my brethren."

Brynhild answers, "I will arede thy dream, even as things shall come to pass hereafter; for Sigurd shall come to thee, even he whom I have chosen for my well-beloved; and Grimhild shall give him mead mingled with hurtful things, which shall cast us all into mighty strife. Him shalt thou have, and him shalt thou quickly miss; and Atli the king shalt thou wed; and thy brethren shalt thou lose, and slay Atli withal in the end."

Gudrun answers, "Grief and woe to know that such things shall be!"

And therewith she and hers get them gone home to King Giuki.

CHAPTER 26
Sigurd Comes to the Giukings
and is Wedded to Gudrun

Now Sigurd goes his ways with all that great treasure, and in friendly wise he departs from them; and on Grani he rides with all his war-gear and the burden withal; and thus he rides until he comes to the hall of King Giuki; there he rides into the burg, and that sees one of the king's men, and he spake withal—

"Sure it may be deemed that here is come one of the Gods, for his array is all done with gold, and his horse is far mightier than other horses, and the manner of his weapons is most exceeding goodly, and most of all the man himself far excels all other men ever seen."

So the king goes out with his court and greets the man, and asks—

"Who art thou who thus ridest into my burg, as none has durst hitherto without the leave of my sons?"

He answered, "I am called Sigurd, son of King Sigmund."

Then said King Giuki, "Be thou welcome here then, and take at our hands whatso thou willest."

So he went into the king's hall, and all men seemed little beside him, and all men served him, and there he abode in great joyance.

Now oft they all ride abroad together, Sigurd and Gunnar and Hogni, and ever Is Sigurd far the foremost of them, mighty men of their hands though they were.

But Grimhild finds how heartily Sigurd loved Brynhild, and how oft he talks of her; and she falls to thinking how well it were, if he might abide there and wed the daughter of King Giuki, for she saw that none might come anigh to his goodliness, and what faith and goodhelp there was in him, and how that he had more wealth withal than folk might tell of any man; and the king did to him even as unto his own sons, and they for their parts held him of more worth than themselves.

So on a night as they sat at the drink, the queen arose, and went before Sigurd, and said—

"Great joy we have in thine abiding here, and all good things will we put before thee to take of us; lo now, take this horn and drink thereof."

So he took it and drank, and therewithal she said, "Thy father shall be Giuki the king, and I shall be thy mother, and Gunnar and Hogni shall be thy brethren, and all this shall be sworn with oaths each to each; and then surely shall the like of you never be found on earth."

Sigurd took her speech well, for with the drinking of that drink all memory of Brynhild departed from him. So there he abode awhile.

And on a day went Grimhild to Giuki the king, and cast her arms about his neck, and spake—

"Behold, there has now come to us the greatest of great hearts that the world holds; and needs must he be trusty and of great avail; give him thy daughter then, with plenteous wealth, and as much of rule as he will; perchance thereby he will be well content to abide here ever."

The king answered, "Seldom does it befall that kings offer their daughters to any; yet in higher wise will it be done to offer her to this man, than to take lowly prayers for her from others."

On a night Gudrun pours out the drink, and Sigurd beholds her how fair she is and how full of all courtesy.

Five seasons Sigurd abode there, and ever they passed their days together in good honour and friendship.

And so it befell that the kings held talk together, and Giuki said —

"Great good thou givest us, Sigurd, and with exceeding strength thou strengthenest our realm."

Then Gunnar said, "All things that may be will we do for thee, so thou abidest here long; both dominion shalt thou have, and our sister freely and unprayed for, whom another man would not get for all his prayers."

Sigurd says, "Thanks have ye for this wherewith ye honour me, and gladly will I take the same."

Therewith they swore brotherhood together, and to be even as if they were children of one father and one mother; and a noble feast was holden, and endured many days, and Sigurd drank at the wedding of him and Gudrun; and there might men behold all manner of game and glee, and each day the feast better and better.

Now fare these folk wide over the world, and do many great deeds, and slay many kings' sons, and no man has ever done such works of prowess as did they; then home they come again with much wealth won in war.

Sigurd gave of the serpent's heart to Gudrun, and she ate thereof, and became greater-hearted, and wiser than ere before: and the son of these twain was called Sigmund.

Now on a time went Grimhild to Gunnar her son, and spake—

"Fair blooms the life and fortune of thee, but for one thing only, and namely whereas thou art unwedded; go woo Brynhild; good rede is this, and Sigurd will ride with thee."

Gunnar answered, "Fair is she certes, and I am fain enow to win her;" and therewith he tells his father, and his brethren, and Sigurd, and they all prick him on to that wooing.

CHAPTER 27
The Wooing of Brynhild

Now they array them joyously for their journey, and ride over hill and dale to the house of King Budli, and woo his daughter of him; in a good wise he took their speech, if so be that she herself would not deny them; but he said withal that so high-minded was she, that that man only might wed her whom she would.

Then they ride to Hlymdale, and there Heimir gave them good welcome; so Gunnar tells his errand; Heimir says, that she must needs wed but him whom she herself chose freely; and tells them how her abode was but a little way thence, and that he deemed that him only would she have who should ride through the flaming fire that was drawn round about her hall; so they depart and come to the hall and the fire, and see there a castle with a golden roof-ridge, and all round about a fire roaring up.

Now Gunnar rode on Goti, but Hogni on Holkvi, and Gunnar smote his horse to face the fire, but he shrank aback.

Then said Sigurd, "Why givest thou back, Gunnar?"

He answered, "The horse will not tread this fire; but lend me thy horse Grani."

"Yea, with all my good will," says Sigurd.

Then Gunnar rides him at the fire, and yet nowise will Gram stir, nor may Gunnar any the more ride through that fire. So now they change semblance, Gunnar and Sigurd, even as Grimhild had taught them; then Sigurd in the likeness of Gunnar mounts and rides, Gram in his hand, and golden spurs on his heels; then leapt Grani into the fire when he felt the spurs; and a mighty roar arose as the fire burned ever madder, and the earth trembled, and the flames went up even unto the heavens, nor had any dared to ride as he rode, even as it were through the deep mirk.

But now the fire sank withal, and he leapt from his horse and went into the hall, even as the song says—

"The flame flared at its maddest,

443

Earth's fields fell a-quaking
As the red flame aloft
Licked the lowest of heaven.
Few had been fain,
Of the rulers of folk,
To ride through that flame,
Or athwart it to tread.

"Then Sigurd smote
Grani with sword,
And the flame was slaked
Before the king;
Low lay the flames
Before the fain of fame;
Bright gleamed the array
That Regin erst owned.

Now when Sigurd had passed through the fire, he came into a certain fair
dwelling, and therein sat Brynhild.

She asked, "What man is it?"

Then he named himself Gunnar, son of Giuki, and said—"Thou art awarded to
me as my wife, by the good will and word of thy father and thy foster-father, and
I have ridden through the flames of thy fire, according to thy word that thou hast
set forth."

"I wot not clearly," said she, "how I shall answer thee."

Now Sigurd stood upright on the hall floor, and leaned on the hilt of his sword,
and he spake to Brynhild—

"In reward thereof, shall I pay thee a great dower in gold and goodly things?"

She answered in heavy mood from her seat, whereas she sat like unto swan on
billow, having a sword in her hand, and a helm on her head, and being clad in a
byrny, "O Gunnar," she says, "speak not to me of such things, unless thou be
the first and best of all men; for then shalt thou slay those my wooers, if thou
hast heart thereto; I have been in battles with the king of the Greeks, and our
weapons were stained with red blood, and for such things still I yearn."

He answered, "Yea, certes many great deeds hast thou done; but yet call thou
to mind thine oath, concerning the riding through of this fire, wherein thou didst
swear that thou wouldst go with the man who should do this deed."

So she found that he spoke but the sooth, and she paid heed to his words, and
arose, and greeted him meetly, and he abode there three nights, and they lay in
one bed together; but he took the sword Gram and laid it betwixt them: then she
asked him why he laid it there; and he answered, that in that wise must he
needs wed his wife or else get his bane.

Then she took from off her the ring Andvari's-loom, which he had given her aforetime, and gave it to him, but he gave her another ring out of Fafnir's hoard.

Thereafter he rode away through the same fire unto his fellows, and he and Gunnar changed semblances again, and rode unto Hlymdale, and told how it had gone with them.

That same day went Brynhild home to her foster-father, and tells him as one whom she trusted, how that there had come a king to her; "And he rode through my flaming fire, and said he was come to woo me, and named himself Gunnar; but I said that such a deed might Sigurd alone have done, with whom I plighted troth on the mountain; and he is my first troth-plight, and my well-beloved."

Heimir said that things must needs abide even as now they had now come to pass.

Brynhild said, "Aslaug the daughter of me and Sigurd shall be nourished here with thee."

Now the kings fare home, but Brynhild goes to her father; Grimhild welcomes the kings meetly, and thanks Sigurd for his fellowship; and withal is a great feast made, and many were the guests thereat; and thither came Budli the King with his daughter Brynhild, and his son Atli, and for many days did the feast endure: and at that feast was Gunnar wedded to Brynhild: but when it was brought to an end, once more has Sigurd memory of all the oaths that he sware unto Brynhild, yet withal he let all things abide in rest and peace.

Brynhild and Gunnar sat together in great game and glee, and drank goodly wine.

CHAPTER 28
How the Queens Held Angry
Converse Together at the Bathing

On a day as the Queens went to the river to bathe them, Brynhild waded the farthest out into the river; then asked Gudrun what that deed might signify.

Brynhild said, "Yea, and why then should I be equal to thee in this matter more than in others? I am minded to think that my father is mightier than thine, and my true love has wrought many wondrous works of fame, and hath ridden the flaming fire withal, while thy husband was but the thrall of King Hjalprek."

Gudrun answered full of wrath, "Thou wouldst be wise if thou shouldst hold thy peace rather than revile my husband: lo now, the talk of all men it is, that none has ever abode in this world like unto him in all matters soever; and little it beseems thee of all folk to mock him who was thy first beloved: and Fafnir he slew, yea, and he rode thy flaming fire, whereas thou didst deem that he was Gunnar the King, and by thy side he lay, and took from thine hand the ring Andvari's-loom;—here mayst thou well behold it!"

445

Then Brynhild saw the ring and knew it, and waxed as wan as a dead woman, and she went home and spake no word the evening long.

So when Sigurd came to bed to Gudrun she asked him why Brynhild's joy was so departed.

He answered, "I know not, but sore I misdoubt me that soon we shall know thereof overwell."

Gudrun said, "Why may she not love her life, having wealth and bliss, and the praise of all men, and the man withal that she would have?"

"Ah, yea!" said Sigurd, "and where in all the world was she then, when she said that she deemed she had the noblest of all men, and the dearest to her heart of all?"

Gudrun answers, "Tomorn will I ask her concerning this, who is the liefest to her of all men for a husband."

Sigurd said, "Needs must I forbid thee this, and full surely wilt thou rue the deed if thou doest it."

Now the next morning they sat in the bower, and Brynhild was silent; then spake Gudrun—

"Be merry, Brynhild! Grievest thou because of that speech of ours together, or what other thing slayeth thy bliss?"

Brynhild answers, "With naught but evil intent thou sayest this, for a cruel heart thou hast."

"Say not so," said Gudrun; "but rather tell me all the tale."

Brynhild answers, "Ask such things only as are good for thee to know—matters meet for mighty dames. Good to love good things when all goes according to thy heart's desire!"

Gudrun says, "Early days for me to glory in that; but this word of thine looketh toward some foreseeing. What ill dost thou thrust at us? I did naught to grieve thee."

Brynhild answers, "For this shalt thou pay, in that thou hast got Sigurd to thee, —nowise can I see thee living in the bliss thereof, whereas thou hast him, and the wealth and the might of him."

But Gudrun answered, "Naught knew I of your words and vows together; and well might my father look to the mating of me without dealing with thee first."

"No secret speech had we," quoth Brynhild, "though we swore oath together; and full well didst thou know that thou wentest about to beguile me; verily thou shalt have thy reward!"

Says Gudrun, "Thou art mated better than thou are worthy of; but thy pride and rage shall be hard to slake belike, and therefor shall many a man pay."

"Ah, I should be well content," said Brynhild, "if thou hadst not the nobler man!"

Gudrun answers, "So noble a husband hast thou, that who knows of a greater king or a lord of more wealth and might?"

Says Brynhild, "Sigurd slew Fafnir, and that only deed is of more worth than all the might of King Gunnar."

(Even as the song says):

> "The worm Sigurd slew,
> Nor e'er shall that deed
> Be worsened by age
> While the world is alive:
> But thy brother the King
> Never durst, never bore
> The flame to ride down
> Through the fire to fare."

Gudrun answers, "Grani would not abide the fire under Gunnar the King, but Sigurd durst the deed, and thy heart may well abide without mocking him."

Brynhild answers, "Nowise will I hide from thee that I deem no good of Grimhild."

Says Gudrun, "Nay, lay no ill words on her, for in all things she is to thee as to her own daughter."

"Ah," says Brynhild, "she is the beginning of all this hale that biteth so; an evil drink she bare to Sigurd, so that he had no more memory of my very name."

"All wrong thou talkest; a lie without measure is this," quoth Gudrun.

Brynhild answered, "Have thou joy of Sigurd according to the measure of the wiles wherewith ye have beguiled me! Unworthily have ye conspired against me; may all things go with you as my heart hopes!"

Gudrun says, "More joy shall I have of him than thy wish would give unto me: but to no man's mind it came, that he had aforetime his pleasure of me; nay not once."

"Evil speech thou speakest," says Brynhild; "when thy wrath runs off thou wilt rue it; but come now, let us no more cast angry words one at the other!"

Says Gudrun, "Thou wert the first to cast such words at me, and now thou makest as if thou wouldst amend it, but a cruel and hard heart abides behind."

"Let us lay aside vain babble," says Brynhild. "Long did I hold my peace concerning my sorrow of heart, and, lo now, thy brother alone do I love; let us fall to other talk."

Gudrun said, "Far beyond all this doth thine heart look."

And so ugly ill befell from that going to the river, and that knowing of the ring, wherefrom did all their talk arise.

CHAPTER 29
Of Brynhild's Great Grief and Mourning

After this talk Brynhild lay a-bed, and tidings were brought to King Gunnar that Brynhild was sick; he goes to see her thereon, and asks what ails her; but she answered him naught, but lay there as one dead: and when he was hard on her for an answer, she said—

"What didst thou with that ring that I gave thee, even the one which King Budli gave me at our last parting, when thou and King Giuki came to him and threatened fire and the sword, unless ye had me to wife? Yea, at that time he led me apart, and asked me which I had chosen of those who were come; but I prayed him that I might abide to ward the land and be chief over the third part of his men; then were there two choices for me to deal betwixt, either that I should be wedded to him whom he would, or lose all my weal and friendship at his hands; and he said withal that his friendship would be better to me than his wrath: then I bethought me whether I should yield to his will, or slay many a man; and therewithal I deemed that it would avail little to strive with him, and so it fell out, that I promised to wed whomsoever should ride the horse Grani with Fafnir's Hoard, and ride through my flaming fire, and slay those men whom I called on him to slay, and now so it was, that none durst ride, save Sigurd only, because he lacked no heart thereto; yea, and the Worm he slew, and Regin, and five kings beside; but thou, Gunnar, durst do naught; as pale as a dead man didst thou wax, and no king thou art, and no champion; so whereas I made a vow unto my father, that him alone would I love who was the noblest man alive, and that this is none save Sigurd, lo, now have I broken my oath and brought it to naught, since he is none of mine, and for this cause shall I compass thy death; and a great reward of evil things have I wherewith to reward Grimhild;—never, I wot, has woman lived eviler or of lesser heart than she."

Gunnar answered in such wise that few might hear him, "Many a vile word hast thou spoken, and an evil-hearted woman art thou, whereas thou revilest a woman far better than thou; never would she curse her life as thou dost; nay, nor has she tormented dead folk, or murdered any; but lives her life well praised of all."

Brynhild answered, "Never have I dwelt with evil things privily, or done loathsome deeds;—yet most fain I am to slay thee."

And therewith would she slay King Gunnar, but Hogni laid her in fetters; but then Gunnar spake withal—

"Nay, I will not that she abide in fetters."

Then said she, "Heed it not! For never again seest thou me glad in thine hall, never drinking, never at the chess-play, never speaking the words of kindness, never over-laying the fair cloths with gold, never giving thee good counsel;—ah, my sorrow of heart that I might not get Sigurd to me!"

Then she sat up and smote her needlework, and rent it asunder, and bade set open her bower doors, that far away might the wailings of her sorrow be heard; then great mourning and lamentation there was, so that folk heard it far and wide through that abode.

Now Gudrun asked her bower-maidens why they sat so joyless and downcast. "What has come to you, that ye fare ye as witless women, or what unheard-of wonders have befallen you?"

Then answered a waiting lady, hight Swaflod, "An untimely, an evil day it is, and our hall is fulfilled of lamentation."

Then spake Gudrun to one of her handmaids, "Arise, for we have slept long; go, wake Brynhild, and let us fall to our needlework and be merry."

"Nay, nay," she says, "nowise may I wake her, or talk with her; for many days has she drunk neither mead nor wine; surely the wrath of the Gods has fallen upon her."

Then spake Gudrun to Gunnar, "Go and see her," she says, "and bid her know that I am grieved with her grief."

"Nay," says Gunnar, "I am forbid to go see her or to share her weal."

Nevertheless he went unto her, and strives in many wise to have speech of her, but gets no answer whatsoever; therefore he gets him gone and finds Hogni, and bids him go see her: he said he was loth thereto, but went, and gat no more of her.

Then they go and find Sigurd, and pray him to visit her; he answered naught thereto, and so matters abode for that night.

But the next day, when he came home from hunting, Sigurd went to Gudrun, and spake—

"In such wise do matters show to me, as though great and evil things will betide from this trouble and upheaving; and that Brynhild will surely die."

Gudrun answers, "O my lord, by great wonders is she encompassed, seven days and seven nights has she slept, and none has dared wake her."

"Nay, she sleeps not," said Sigurd, "her heart is dealing rather with dreadful intent against me."

Then said Gudrun, weeping, "Woe worth the while for thy death! Go and see her; and wot if her fury may not be abated; give her gold, and smother up her grief and anger therewith!"

Then Sigurd went out, and found the door of Brynhild's chamber open; he deemed she slept, and drew the clothes from off her, and said—

"Awake, Brynhild! The sun shineth now over all the house, and thou hast slept enough; cast off grief from thee, and take up gladness!"

She said, "And how then hast thou dared to come to me? in this treason none was worse to me than thou."

Said Sigurd, "Why wilt thou not speak to folk? for what cause sorrowest thou?"

Brynhild answers, "Ah, to thee will I tell of my wrath!"

Sigurd said, "As one under a spell art thou, if thou deemest that there is aught cruel in my heart against thee; but thou hast him for husband whom thou didst choose."

"Ah, nay," she said, "never did Gunnar ride through the fire to me, nor did he give me to dower the host of the slain: I wondered at the man who came into my hall; for I deemed indeed that I knew thine eyes; but I might not see clearly, or divide the good from the evil, because of the veil that lay heavy on my fortune."

Says Sigurd, "No nobler men are there than the sons of Giuki, they slew the king of the Danes, and that great chief, the brother of King Budli."

Brynhild answered, "Surely for many an ill-deed must I reward them; mind me not of my griefs against them! But thou, Sigurd, slewest the Worm, and rodest the fire through; yea, and for my sake, and not one of the sons of King Giuki."

Sigurd answers, "I am not thy husband, and thou art not my wife; yet did a farfamed king pay dower to thee."

Says Brynhild, "Never looked I at Gunnar in such a wise that my heart smiled on him; and hard and fell am I to him, though I hide it from others."

"A marvellous thing," says Sigurd, "not to love such a king; what angers thee most? for surely his love should be better to thee than gold."

"This is the sorest sorrow to me," she said, "that the bitter sword is not reddened in thy blood."

"Have no fear thereof!" says he, "no long while to wait or the bitter sword stand deep in my heart; and no worse needest thou to pray for thyself, for thou wilt not live when I am dead; the days of our two lives shall be few enough from henceforth."

Brynhild answers, "Enough and to spare of bale is in thy speech, since thou bewrayedst me, and didst twin (1) me and all bliss;—naught do I heed my life or death."

Sigurd answers, "Ah, live, and love King Gunnar and me withal! and all my wealth will I give thee if thou die not."

Brynhild answers, "Thou knowest me not, nor the heart that is in me; for thou art the first and best of all men, and I am become the most loathsome of all women to thee."

"This is truer," says Sigurd, "that I loved thee better than myself, though I fell into the wiles from whence our lives may not escape; for whenso my own heart and mind availed me, then I sorrowed sore that thou wert not my wife; but as I might I put my trouble from me, for in a king's dwelling was I; and withal and in spite of all I was well content that we were all together. Well may it be, that that shall come to pass which is foretold; neither shall I fear the fulfilment thereof."

Brynhild answered, and said, "Too late thou tellest me that my grief grieved thee: little pity shall I find now."

Sigurd said, "This my heart would, that thou and I should go into one bed together; even so wouldst thou be my wife."

Said Brynhild, "Such words may nowise be spoken, nor will I have two kings in one hall; I will lay my life down rather than beguile Gunnar the King."

And therewith she call to mind how they met, they two, on the mountain, and swore oath each to each.

"But now is all changed, and I will not live."

"I might not call to mind thy name," said Sigurd, "or know thee again, before the time of thy wedding; the greatest of all griefs is that."

Then said Brynhild, "I swore an oath to wed the man who should ride my flaming fire, and that oath will I hold to, or die."

"Rather than thou die, I will wed thee, and put away Gudrun," said Sigurd.

But therewithal so swelled the heart betwixt the sides of him, that the rings of his byrny burst asunder.

"I will not have thee," says Brynhild, "nay, nor any other!"

Then Sigurd got him gone.

451

So saith the song of Sigurd—

"Out then went Sigurd,
The great kings' well-loved,
From the speech and the sorrow,
Sore drooping, so grieving,
That the shirt round about him
Of iron rings woven,
From the sides brake asunder
Of the brave in the battle."

So when Sigurd came into the hall, Gunnar asked if he had come to a knowledge of what great grief lay heavy on her, or if she had power of speech: and Sigurd said that she lacked it not. So now Gunnar goes to her again, and asked her, what wrought her woe, or if there were anything that might amend it.

"I will not live," says Brynhild, "for Sigurd has bewrayed me, yea, and thee no less, whereas thou didst suffer him to come into my bed: lo thou, two men in one dwelling I will not have; and this shall be Sigurd's death, or thy death, or my death;—for now has he told Gudrun all, and she is mocking me even now!"

ENDNOTES:

(1) Sunder.

CHAPTER 30
Of the Slaying of Sigurd Fafnir's-Bane

Thereafter Brynhild went out, and sat under her bower-wall, and had many words of wailing to say, and still she cried that all things were loathsome to her, both land and lordship alike, so she might not have Sigurd.

But therewith came Gunnar to her yet again, and Brynhild spake, "Thou shalt lose both realm and wealth, and thy life and me, for I shall fare home to my kin, and abide there in sorrow, unless thou slayest Sigurd and his son; never nourish thou a wolfcub."

Gunnar grew sick at heart thereat, and might nowise see what fearful thing lay beneath it all; he was bound to Sigurd by oath, and this way and that way swung the heart within him; but at the last he bethought him of the measureless shame if his wife went from him, and he said within himself, "Brynhild is better to me than all things else, and the fairest woman of all women, and I will lay down my life rather than lose the love of her." And herewith he called to him his brother and spake,—

"Trouble is heavy on me," and he tells him that he must needs slay Sigurd, for that he has failed him where in he trusted him; "so let us be lords of the gold and the realm withal."

Hogni answers, "Ill it behoves us to break our oaths with wrack and wrong, and withal great aid we have in him; no kings shall be as great as we, if so be the King of the Hun-folk may live; such another brother-in-law never may we get again; bethink thee how good it is to have such a brother-in-law, and such sons to our sister! But well I see how things stand, for this has Brynhild stirred thee up to, and surely shall her counsel drag us into huge shame and scathe."

Gunnar says, "Yet shall it be brought about: and, lo, a rede thereto;—let us egg on our brother Guttorm to the deed; he is young, and of little knowledge, and is clean out of all the oaths moreover."

"Ah, set about in ill wise," says Hogni, "and though indeed it may well be compassed, a due reward shall we gain for the bewrayal of such a man as is Sigurd."

Gunnar says, "Sigurd shall die, or I shall die."

And therewith he bids Brynhild arise and be glad at heart: so she arose, and still ever she said that Gunnar should come no more into her bed till the deed was done.

So the brothers fall to talk, and Gunnar says that it is a deed well worthy of death, that taking of Brynhild's maidenhead; "So come now, let us prick on Guttorm to do the deed."

Therewith they call him to them, and offer him gold and great dominion, as they well have might to do. Yea, and they took a certain worm and somewhat of wolf's flesh and let seethe them together, and gave him to eat of the same, even as the singer sings—

> "Fish of the wild-wood,
> Worm smooth crawling,
> With wolf-meat mingled,
> They minced for Guttorm;
> Then in the beaker,
> In the wine his mouth knew,
> They set it, still doing
> More deeds of wizards.

Wherefore with the eating of this meat he grew so wild and eager, and with all things about him, and with the heavy words of Grimhild, that he gave his word to do the deed; and mighty honour they promised him in reward thereof.

But of these evil wiles naught at all knew Sigurd, for he might not deal with his shapen fate, nor the measure of his life-days, neither deemed he that he was worthy of such things at their hands.

So Guttorm went in to Sigurd the next morning as he lay upon his bed, yet durst he not do aught against him, but shrank back out again; yea, and even so he fared a second time, for so bright and eager were the eyes of Sigurd that few durst look upon him. But the third time he went in, and there lay Sigurd asleep; then Guttorm drew his sword and thrust Sigurd through in such wise that the sword point smote into the bed beneath him; then Sigurd awoke with that wound, and Guttorm gat him unto the door; but therewith Sigurd caught up the sword Gram, and cast it after him, and it smote him on the back, and struck him asunder in the midst, so that the feet of him fell one way, and the head and hands back into the chamber.

Now Gudrun lay asleep on Sigurd's bosom, but she woke up unto woe that may not be told of, all swimming in the blood of him, and in such wise did she bewail her with weeping and words of sorrow, that Sigurd rose up on the bolster, and spake.

"Weep not," said he, "for thy brothers live for thy delight; but a young son have I, too young to be ware of his foes; and an ill turn have these played against their own fortune; for never will they get a mightier brother-in-law to ride abroad with them; nay, nor a better son to their sister, than this one, if he may grow to man's estate. Lo, now is that come to pass which was foretold me long ago, but from mine eyes has it been hidden, for none may fight against his fate and prevail. Behold this has Brynhild brought to pass, even she who loves me before all men; but this may I swear, that never have I wrought ill to Gunnar, but rather have ever held fast to my oath with him, nor was I ever too much a friend to his wife. And now if I had been forewarned, and had been afoot with my weapons, then should many a man have lost his life or ever I had fallen, and all those brethren should have been slain, and a harder work would the slaying of me have been than the slaying of the mightiest bull or the mightiest boar of the wild-wood."

And even therewithal life left the King; but Gudrun moaned and drew a weary breath, and Brynhild heard it, and laughed when she heard her moaning.

Then said Gunnar, "Thou laughest not because thy heart-roots are gladdened, or else why doth thy visage wax so wan? Sure an evil creature thou art; most like thou art nigh to thy death! Lo now, how meet would it be for thee to behold thy brother Atli slain before thine eyes, and that thou shouldst stand over him dead; whereas we must needs now stand over our brother-in-law in such a case, our brother-in-law and our brother's bane."

She answered, "None need mock at the measure of slaughter being unfulfilled; yet heedeth not Atli your wrath or your threats; yea, he shall live longer than ye, and be a mightier man."

Hogni spake and said, "Now hath come to pass the soothsaying of Brynhild; an ill work not to be atoned for."

And Gudrun said, "My kinsmen have slain my husband; but ye, when ye next ride to the war and are come into the battle, then shall ye look about and see that Sigurd is neither on the right hand nor the left, and ye shall know that he was your good-hap and your strength; and if he had lived and had sons, then should ye have been strengthened by his offspring and his kin."

454

CHAPTER 31
Of the Lamentation of Gudrun Over
Sigurd Dead, as it is Told in Ancient Songs (1)

Gudrun of old days
Drew near to dying
As she sat in sorrow
Over Sigurd;
Yet she sighed not
Nor smote hand on hand,
Nor wailed she aught
As other women.

Then went earls to her.
Full of all wisdom,
Fain help to deal
To her dreadful heart:
Hushed was Gudrun
Of wail, or greeting,
But with a heavy woe
Was her heart a-breaking.

Bright and fair
Sat the great earls' brides,
Gold arrayed
Before Gudrun;
Each told the tale
Of her great trouble,
The bitterest bale
She erst abode.

Then spake Giaflaug,
Giuki's sister:
"Lo upon earth
I live most loveless
Who of five mates
Must see the ending,
Of daughters twain
And three sisters,
Of brethren eight,
And abide behind lonely."

Naught gat Gudrun
Of wail and greeting,
So heavy was she
For her dead husband,
So dreadful-hearted
For the King laid dead there.

455

Then spake Herborg
Queen of Hunland—
"Crueller tale
Have I to tell of,
Of my seven sons
Down in the Southlands,
And the eighth man, my mate,
Felled in the death-mead.

"Father and mother,
And four brothers,
On the wide sea
The winds and death played with;
The billows beat
On the bulwark boards.

"Alone must I sing o'er them,
Alone must I array them,
Alone must my hands deal with
Their departing;
And all this was
In one season's wearing,
And none was left
For love or solace.

"Then was I bound
A prey of the battle,
When that same season
Wore to its ending;
As a tiring may
Must I bind the shoon
Of the duke's high dame,
Every day at dawning.

"From her jealous hate
Gat I heavy mocking,
Cruel lashes
She laid upon me,
Never met I
Better master
Or mistress worser
In all the wide world."

Naught gat Gudrun
Of wail or greeting,
So heavy was she
For her dead husband,
So dreadful-hearted
For the King laid dead there.

Then spake Gullrond,
Giuki's daughter—
"O foster-mother,
Wise as thou mayst be,
Naught canst thou better
The young wife's bale."
And she bade uncover
The dead King's corpse.

She swept the sheet
Away from Sigurd,
And turned his cheek
Towards his wife's knees—
"Look on thy loved one
Lay lips to his lips,
E'en as thou wert clinging
To thy king alive yet!"

Once looked Gudrun—
One look only,
And saw her lord's locks
Lying all bloody,
The great man's eyes
Glazed and deadly,
And his heart's bulwark
Broken by sword-edge.

Back then sank Gudrun,
Back on the bolster,
Loosed was her head array,
Red did her cheeks grow,
And the rain-drops ran
Down over her knees.

Then wept Gudrun,
Giuki's daughter,
So that the tears flowed
Through the pillow;
As the geese withal
That were in the homefield,
The fair fowls the may owned,
Fell a-screaming.

Then spake Gullrond,
Giuki's daughter—
"Surely knew I
No love like your love
Among all men,
On the mould abiding;
Naught wouldst thou joy in
Without or within doors,

O my sister,
Save beside Sigurd."

Then spake Gudrun,
Giuki's daughter—
"Such was my Sigurd
Among the sons of Giuki,
As is the king leek
O'er the low grass waxing,
Or a bright stone
Strung on band,
Or a pearl of price
On a prince's brow.

"Once was I counted
By the king's warriors
Higher than any
Of Herjan's mays;
Now am I as little
As the leaf may be,
Amid wind-swept wood
Now when dead he lieth.

I miss from my seat,
I miss from my bed,
My darling of sweet speech.
Wrought the sons of Giuki,
Wrought the sons of Giuki,
This sore sorrow,
Yea, for their sister,
Most sore sorrow.

"So may your lands
Lie waste on all sides,
As ye have broken
Your bounden oaths!
Ne'er shalt thou, Gunnar,
The gold have joy of;
The dear-bought rings
Shall drag thee to death,
Whereon thou swarest
Oath unto Sigurd.

Ah, in the days by-gone
Great mirth in the homefield
When my Sigurd
Set saddle on Grani,
And they went their ways
For the wooing of Brynhild!
An ill day, an ill woman,
And most ill hap!"

Then spake Brynhild,
Budli's daughter—
"May the woman lack
Both love and children,
Who gained greeting
For thee, O Gudrun!
Who gave thee this morning
Many words!"

Then spake Gullrond,
Giuki's daughter—
"Hold peace of such words
Thou hated of all folk!
The bane of brave men
Hast thou been ever,
All waves of ill
Wash over thy mind,
To seven great kings
Hast thou been a sore sorrow,
And the death of good will
To wives and women."

Then spake Brynhild,
Budli's daughter—
"None but Atli
Brought bale upon us,
My very brother
Born of Budli.

When we saw in the hall
Of the Hunnish people
The gold a-gleaming
On the kingly Giukings;
I have paid for that faring
Oft and full,
And for the sight
That then I saw."

By a pillar she stood
And strained its wood to her;
From the eyes of Brynhild,
Budli's daughter,
Flashed out fire,
And she snorted forth venom,
As the sore wounds she gazed on
Of the dead-slain Sigurd.

(1) This chapter is the Eddaic poem, called the first Lay of
Gudrun, inserted here by the translators.

CHAPTER 32
Of the Ending of Brynhild

And now none might know for what cause Brynhild must bewail with weeping
for what she had prayed for with laughter: but she spake—

"Such a dream I had, Gunnar, as that my bed was acold, and that thou didst
ride into the hands of thy foes: lo now, ill shall it go with thee and all thy kin, O
ye breakers of oaths; for on the day thou slayedst him, dimly didst thou
remember how thou didst blend thy blood with the blood of Sigurd, and with an
ill reward hast thou rewarded him for all that he did well to thee; whereas he
gave unto thee to be the mightiest of men; and well was it proven how fast he
held to his oath sworn, when he came to me and laid betwixt us the sharp-
edged sword that in venom had been made hard. All too soon did ye fall to
working wrong against him and against me, whenas I abode at home with my
father, and had all that I would, and had no will that any one of you should be
any of mine, as ye rode into our garth, ye three kings together; but then Atli led
me apart privily, and asked me if I would not have him who rode Grani; yea, a
man nowise like unto you; but in those days I plighted myself to the son of King
Sigmund and no other; and lo, now, no better shall ye fare for the death of me."

Then rose up Gunnar, and laid his arms about her neck, and besought her to
live and have wealth from him; and all others in likewise letted her from dying;
but she thrust them all from her, and said that it was not the part of any to let
her in that which was her will.

Then Gunnar called to Hogni, and prayed him for counsel, and bade him go to
her, and see if he might perchance soften her dreadful heart, saying withal, that
now they had need enough on their hands in the slaking of her grief, till time
might get over.

But Hogni answered, "Nay, let no man hinder her from dying; for no gain will
she be to us, nor has she been gainsome since she came hither!

Now she bade bring forth much gold, and bade all those come thither who
would have wealth: then she caught up a sword, and thrust it under her armpit,
and sank aside upon the pillows, and said, "Come, take gold whoso will!"

But all held their peace, and she said, "Take the gold, and be glad thereof!"

And therewith she spake unto Gunnar, "Now for a little while will I tell of that
which shall come to pass hereafter; for speedily shall ye be at one again with
Gudrun by the rede of Grimhild the Wise-wife; and the daughter of Gudrun and
Sigurd shall be called Swanhild, the fairest of all women born. Gudrun shall be

given to Atli, yet not with her good will. Thou shalt be fain to get Oddrun, but that shall Atli forbid thee; but privily shall ye meet, and much shall she love thee. Atli shall bewray thee, and cast thee into a worm-close, and thereafter shall Atli and his sons be slain, and Gudrun shall be their slayer; and afterwards shall the great waves bear her to the burg of King Jonakr, to whom she shall bear sons of great fame: Swanhild shall be sent from the land and given to King Jormunrek; and her shall bite the rede of Bikki, and therewithal is the kin of you clean gone; and more sorrows therewith for Gudrun.

"And now I pray thee, Gunnar, one last boon.—Let make a great bale on the plain meads for all of us; for me, and for Sigurd, and for those who were slain with him, and let that be covered over with cloth dyed red by the folk of the Gauls, (1) and burn me thereon on one side of the King of the Huns, and on the other those men of mine, two at the head and two at the feet, and two hawks withal; and even so is all shared equally; and lay there betwixt us a drawn sword, as in the other days when we twain stepped into one bed together; and then may we have the name of man and wife, nor shall the door swing to at the heel of him as I go behind him. Nor shall that be a niggard company if there follow him those five bond-women and eight bondmen, whom my father gave me, and those burn there withal who were slain with Sigurd.

"Now more yet would I say, but for my wounds, but my life-breath flits; the wounds open,—yet have I said sooth."

Now is the dead corpse of Sigurd arrayed in olden wise, and a mighty bale is raised, and when it was somewhat kindled, there was laid thereon the dead corpse of Sigurd Fafnir's-bane, and his son of three winters whom Brynhild had let slay, and Guttorm withal; and when the bale was all ablaze, thereunto was Brynhild borne out, when she had spoken with her bower-maidens, and bid them take the gold that she would give; and then died Brynhild, and was burned there by the side of Sigurd, and thus their life-days ended.

ENDNOTES:

(1) The original has "raudu manna blodi", red-dyed in the blood of men; the Sagaman's original error in dealing with the word "Valaript" in the corresponding passage of the short lay of Sigurd.—Tr.

CHAPTER 33
Gudrun wedded to Atli

Now so it is, that whoso heareth these tidings sayeth, that no such an one as was Sigurd was left behind him in the world, nor ever was such a man brought forth because of all the worth of him, nor may his name ever minish by eld in the Dutch Tongue nor in all the Northern Lands, while the world standeth fast.

The story tells that, on a day, as Gudrun sat in her bower, she fell to saying, "Better was life in those days when I had Sigurd; he who was far above other

461

men as gold is above iron, or the leek over other grass of the field, or the hart over other wild things; until my brethren begrudged me such a man, the first and best of all men; and so they might not sleep or they had slain him. Huge clamour made Grani when he saw his master and lord sore wounded, and then I spoke to him even as with a man, but he fell drooping down to the earth, for he knew that Sigurd was slain."

Thereafter Gudrun gat her gone into the wild woods, and heard on all ways round about her the howling of wolves, and deemed death a merrier thing than life. Then she went till she came to the hall of King Alf, and sat there in Denmark with Thora, the daughter of Hakon, for seven seasons, and abode with good welcome. And she set forth her needlework before her, and did thereinto many deeds and great, and fair plays after the fashion of those days, swords and byrnies, and all the gear of kings, and the ship of King Sigmund sailing along the land; yea, and they wrought there, how they fought, Sigar and Siggeir, south in Fion. Such was their disport; and now Gudrun was somewhat solaced of her grief.

So Grimhild comes to hear where Gudrun has take up her abode, and she calls her sons to talk with her, and asks whether they will make atonement to Gudrun for her son and her husband, and said that it was but meet and right to do so.

Then Gunnar spake, and said that he would atone for her sorrows with gold.

So they send for their friends, and array their horses, their helms, and their shields, and their byrnies, and all their war-gear; and their journey was furnished forth in the noblest wise, and no champion who was of the great men might abide at home; and their horses were clad in mail-coats, and every knight of them had his helm done over with gold or with silver.

Grimhild was of their company, for she said that their errand would never be brought fairly to pass if she sat at home.

There were well five hundred men, and noble men rode with them. There was Waldemar of Denmark, and Eymod and Jarisleif withal. So they went into the hall of King Alf, and there abode them the Longbeards and Franks, and Saxons: they fared with all their war-gear, and had over them red fur-coats. Even as the song says—

"Byrnies short cut,
Strong helms hammered,
Girt with good swords,
Red hair gleaming."

They were fain to choose good gifts for their sister, and spake softly to her, but in none of them would she trow. Then Gunnar brought unto her a drink mingled with hurtful things, and this she must needs drink, and with the drinking thereof she had no more memory of their guilt against her.

But in that drink was blended the might of the earth and the sea with the blood of her son; and in that horn were all letters cut and reddened with blood, as is

462

said hereunder—

"On the horn's face were there
All the kin of letters
Cut aright and reddened,
How should I rede them rightly?
The ling-fish long
Of the land of Hadding,
Wheat-ears unshorn,
And wild things' inwards.

In that beer were mingled
Many ills together,
Blood of all the wood
And brown-burnt acorns,
The black dew of the hearth,
The God-doomed dead beast's inwards,
And the swine's liver sodden
Because all wrongs that deadens."

And so now, when their hearts are brought anigh to each other, great cheer they made: then came Grimhild to Gudrun, and spake:

"All hail to thee, daughter! I give thee gold and all kinds of good things to take to thee after thy father, dear-bought rings and bed-gear of the maids of the Huns, the most courteous and well dight of all women; and thus is thy husband atoned for: and thereafter shalt thou be given to Atli, the mighty king, and be mistress of all his might. Cast not all thy friends aside for one man's sake, but do according to our bidding."

Gudrun answers, "Never will I wed Atli the King: unseemly it is for us to get offspring betwixt us."

Grimhild says, "Nourish not thy wrath; it shall be to thee as if Sigurd and Sigmund were alive when thou hast borne sons."

Gudrun says, "I cannot take my heart from thoughts of him, for he was the first of all men."

Grimhild says, "So it is shapen that thou must have this king and none else."

Says Gudrun, "Give not this man to me, for an evil thing shall come upon thy kin from him, and to his own sons shall he deal evil, and be rewarded with a grim revenge thereafter."

Then waxed Grimhild fell at those words, and spake, "Do even as we bid thee, and take therefore great honour, and our friendship, and the steads withal called Vinbjorg and Valbjorg."

And such might was in the words of her, that even so must it come to pass.

463

Then Gudrun spake, "Thus then must it needs befall, howsoever against the will of me, and for little joy shall it be and for great grief."

Then men leaped on their horses, and their women were set in wains. So they fared four days a-riding and other four a-shipboard, and yet four more again by land and road, till at the last they came to a certain high-built hall; then came to meet Gudrun many folk thronging; and an exceedingly goodly feast was there made, even as the word had gone between either kin, and it passed forth in most proud and stately wise. And at that feast drinks Atli his bridal with Gudrun; but never did her heart laugh on him, and little sweet and kind was their life together.

CHAPTER 34
Atli Bids the Giukings to Him

Now tells the tale that on a night King Atli woke from sleep and spake to Gudrun —

"Medreamed," said he, "that thou didst thrust me through with a sword."

Then Gudrun areded the dream, and said that it betokened fire, whenas folk dreamed of iron. "It befalls of thy pride belike, in that thou deemest thyself the first of men."

Atli said, "Moreover I dreamed that here waxed two sorb-tree (1) saplings, and fain I was that they should have no scathe of me; then these were riven up by the roots and reddened with blood, and borne to the bench, and I was bidden eat thereof.

"Yea, yet again I dreamed that two hawks flew from my hand hungry and unfed, and fared to hell, and meseemed their hearts were mingled with honey, and that I ate thereof.

"And then again I dreamed that two fair whelps lay before me yelling aloud, and that the flesh of them I ate, though my will went not with the eating."

Gudrun says, "Nowise good are these dreams, yet shall they come to pass; surely thy sons are nigh to death, and many heavy things shall fall upon us."

"Yet again I dreamed," said he, "and methought I lay in a bath, and folk took counsel to slay me."

Now these things wear away with time, but in nowise was their life together fond.

Now falls Atli to thinking of where may be gotten that plenteous gold which Sigurd had owned, but King Gunnar and his brethren were lords thereof now.

Atli was a great king and mighty, wise, and a lord of many men; and now he

464

falls to counsel with his folk as to the ways of them. He wotted well that Gunnar and his brethren had more wealth than any others might have, and so he falls to the rede of sending men to them, and bidding them to a great feast, and honouring them in diverse wise, and the chief of those messengers was hight Vingi.

Now the queen wots of their conspiring, and misdoubts her that this would mean some beguiling of her brethren: so she cut runes, and took a gold ring, and knit therein a wolf's hair, and gave it into the hands of the king's messengers.

Thereafter they go their ways according to the king's bidding; and or ever they came aland Vingi beheld the runes, and turned them about in such wise as if Gudrun prayed her brethren in her runes to go meet King Atli.

Thereafter they came to the hall of King Gunnar, and had good welcome at his hands, and great fires were made for them, and in great joyance they drank of the best of drink.

Then spake Vingi, "King Atli sends me hither, and is fain that ye go to his house and home in all glory, and take of him exceeding honours, helms and shields, swords and byrnies, gold and goodly raiment, horses, hosts of war, and great and wide lands, for, saith he, he is fainest of all things to bestow his realm and lordship upon you."

Then Gunnar turned his head aside, and spoke to Hogni—

"In what wise shall we take this bidding? might and wealth he bids us take; but no kings know I who have so much gold as we have, whereas we have all the hoard which lay once on Gnitaheath; and great are our chambers, and full of gold, and weapons for smiting, and all kinds of raiment of war, and well I wot that amidst all men my horse is the best, and my sword the sharpest, and my gold the most glorious."

Hogni answers, "A marvel is it to me of his bidding, for seldom hath he done in such a wise, and ill-counselled will it be to wend to him; lo now, when I saw those dear-bought things the king sends us I wondered to behold a wolf's hair knit to a certain gold ring; belike Gudrun deems him to be minded as a wolf towards us, and will have naught of our faring."

But withal Vingi shows him the runes which he said Gudrun had sent.

Now the most of folk go to bed, but these drank on still with certain others; and Kostbera, the wife of Hogni, the fairest of women, came to them, and looked on the runes.

But the wife of Gunnar was Glaumvor, a great-hearted wife.

So these twain poured out, and the kings drank, and were exceeding drunken, and Vingi notes it, and says—

"Naught may I hide that King Atli is heavy of foot and over-old for the warding of his realm; but his sons are young and of no account: now will he give you rule over his realms while they are yet thus young, and most fain will he be that ye have the joy thereof before all others."

Now so it befell both that Gunnar was drunk, and that great dominion was held out to him, nor might he work against the fate shapen for him; so he gave his word to go, and tells Hogni his brother thereof.

But he answered, "Thy word given must even stand now, nor will I fail to follow thee, but most loth am I to this journey."

ENDNOTES:

(1) Service-tree; "pyrus sorbus domestica", or "p. s. tormentalis.

CHAPTER 35
The Dreams of the Wives of the Giukings

So when men had drunk their fill, they fared to sleep; then falls Kostbera to beholding the runes, and spelling over the letters, and sees that beneath were other things cut, and that the runes are guileful; yet because of her wisdom she had skill to read them aright. So then she goes to bed by her husband; but when they awoke, she spake unto Hogni—

"Thou art minded to wend away from home—ill-counselled is that; abide till another time! Scarce a keen reader of runes art thou, if thou deemest thou hast beheld in them the bidding of thy sister to this journey: lo, I read the runes, and had marvel of so wise a woman as Gudrun is, that she should have miscut them; but that which lieth underneath beareth your bane with it,—yea, either she lacked a letter, or others have dealt guilefully with the runes.

"And now hearken to my dream; for therein methought there fell in upon us here a river exceeding strong, and brake up the timbers of the hall."

He answered, "Full oft are ye evil of mind, ye women, but for me, I was not made in such wise as to meet men with evil who deserve no evil; belike he will give us good welcome."

She answered, "Well, the thing must ye yourselves prove, but no friendship follows this bidding:—but yet again I dreamed that another river fell in here with a great and grimly rush, and tore up the dais of the hall, and brake the legs of both you brethren; surely that betokeneth somewhat."

He answers, "Meadows along our way, whereas thou didst dream of the river; for when we go through the meadows, plentifully doth the seeds of the hay hang about our legs."

"Again I dreamed," she says, "that thy cloak was afire, and that the flame blazed up above the hall."

Says he, "Well, I wot what that shall betoken; here lieth my fair-dyed raiment, and it shall burn and blaze, whereas thou dreamedst of the cloak."

"Methought a bear came in," she says, "and brake up the king's high-seat, and shook his paws in such a wise that we were all adrad thereat, and he gat us all together into the mouth of him, so that we might avail us naught, and thereof fell great horror on us."

He answered, "Some great storm will befall, whereas thou hadst a white bear in thy mind."

"An erne methought came in," she says, "and swept adown the hall, and drenched me and all of us with blood, and ill shall that betoken, for methought it was the double of King Atli."

He answered, "Full oft do we slaughter beasts freely, and smite down great neat for our cheer, and the dream of the erne has but to do with oxen; yea, Atli is heart-whole toward us."

And therewithal they cease this talk.

CHAPTER 36
Of the Journey of the Giukings to King Atli

Now tells the tale of Gunnar, that in the same wise it fared with him; for when they awoke, Glaumvor his wife told him many dreams which seemed to her like to betoken guile coming; but Gunnar areded them all in other wise.

"This was one of them," said she; "methought a bloody sword was borne into the hall here, wherewith thou wert thrust through, and at either end of that sword wolves howled."

The king answered, "Cur dogs shall bite me belike; blood-stained weapons oft betoken dogs' snappings."

She said, "Yet again I dreamed—that women came in, heavy and drooping, and chose thee for their mate; may-happen these would be thy fateful women."

He answered, "Hard to arede is this, and none may set aside the fated measure of his days, nor is it unlike that my time is short." (1)

So in the morning they arose, and were minded for the journey, but some letted them herein.

Then cried Gunnar to the man who is called Fjornir—

"Arise, and give us to drink goodly wine from great tuns, because mayhappen this shall be very last of all our feasts; for belike if we die the old wolf shall come by the gold, and that bear shall nowise spare the bite of his war-tusks."

Then all the folk of his household brought them on their way weeping.

The son of Hogni said—

"Fare ye well with merry tide."

The more part of their folk were left behind; Solar and Snaevar, the sons of Hogni, fared with them, and a certain great champion, named Orkning, who was the brother of Kostbera.

So folk followed them down to the ships, and all letted them of their journey, but attained to naught therein.

Then spake Glaumvor, and said—

"O Vingi, most like that great ill hap will come of thy coming, and mighty and evil things shall betide in thy travelling."

He answered, "Hearken to my answer; that I lie not aught: and may the high gallows and all things of grame have me, if I lie one word!"

Then cried Kostbera, "Fare ye well with merry days."

And Hogni answered, "Be glad of heart, howsoever it may fare with us!"

And therewith they parted, each to their own fate. Then away they rowed, so hard and fast, that well-nigh the half of the keel slipped away from the ship, and so hard they laid on to the oars that thole and gunwale brake.

But when they came aland they made their ship fast, and then they rode awhile on their noble steeds through the murk wild-wood.

And now they behold the king's army, and huge uproar, and the clatter of weapons they hear from thence; and they see there a mighty host of men, and the manifold array of them, even as they wrought there: and all the gates of the burg were full of men.

So they rode up to the burg, and the gates thereof were shut; then Hogni brake open the gates, and therewith they ride into the burg.

Then spake Vingi, "Well might ye have left this deed undone; go to now, bide ye here while I go seek your gallows-tree! Softly and sweetly I bade you hither, but an evil thing abode thereunder; short while to bide ere ye are tied up to that same tree!"

Hogni answered, "None the more shall we waver for that cause; for little methinks have we shrunk aback whenas men fell to fight; and naught shall it avail thee to make us afeard,—and for an ill fate hast thou wrought."

And therewith they cast him down to earth, and smote him with their axe-hammers till he died.

ENDNOTES:

(1) Parallel beliefs to those in the preceding chapters, and elsewhere in this book, as to spells, dreams, drinks, etc., among the English people may be found in "Leechdoms, Wortcunning, and Starcraft of the Anglo-Saxons; being a collection of Documents illustrating the History of Science in this Country before the Norman Conquest". Ed: Rev. T. O. Cockayne, M.A. (3 vols.) Longmans, London, 1864, 8vo.

CHAPTER 37
The Battle in the Burg of King Atli

Then they rode unto the king's hall, and King Atli arrayed his host for battle, and the ranks were so set forth that a certain wall there was betwixt them and the brethren.

"Welcome hither," said he. "Deliver unto me that plenteous gold which is mine of right; even the wealth which Sigurd once owned, and which is now Gudrun's of right."

Gunnar answered, "Never gettest thou that wealth; and men of might must thou meet here, or ever we lay by life if thou wilt deal with us in battle; ah, belike thou settest forth this feast like a great man, and wouldst not hold thine hand from erne and wolf!"

"Long ago I had it in my mind," said Atli, "to take the lives of you, and be lord of the gold, and reward you for that deed of shame, wherein ye beguiled the best of all your affinity; but now shall I revenge him."

Hogni answered, "Little will it avail to lie long brooding over that rede, leaving the work undone."

And therewith they fell to hard fighting, at the first brunt with shot.

But therewithal came the tidings to Gudrun, and when she heard thereof she grew exceeding wroth, and cast her mantle from her, and ran out and greeted those new-comers, and kissed her brethren, and showed them all love,—and the last of all greetings was that betwixt them.

Then said she, "I thought I had set forth counsels whereby ye should not come hither, but none may deal with his shapen fate." And withal she said, "Will it avail aught to seek for peace?"

But stoutly and grimly they said nay thereto. So she sees that the game goeth sorely against her brethren, and she gathers to her great stoutness of heart, and does on her a mail-coat and takes to her a sword, and fights by her brethren, and goes as far forward as the bravest of man-folk: and all spoke in one wise that never saw any fairer defence than in her.

Now the men fell thick, and far before all others was the fighting of those brethren, and the battle endured a long while unto midday; Gunnar and Hogni went right through the folk of Atli, and so tells the tale that all the mead ran red with blood; the sons of Hogni withal set on stoutly.

Then spake Atli the king, "A fair host and a great have we, and mighty champions withal, and yet have many of us fallen, and but evil am I apaid in that nineteen of my champions are slain, and but left six alive."

And therewithal was there a lull in the battle.

Then spake Atli the king, "Four brethren were we, and now am I left alone; great affinity I gat to me, and deemed my fortune well sped thereby; a wife I had, fair and wise, high of mind, and great of heart; but no joyance may I have of her wisdom, for little peace is betwixt us,—but ye—ye have slain many of my kin, and beguiled me of realm and riches, and for the greatest of all woes have slain my sister withal."

Quoth Hogni, "Why babblest thou thus? thou wert the first to break the peace. Thou didst take my kinswoman and pine her to death by hunger, and didst murder her, and take her wealth; an ugly deed for a king!—meet for mocking and laughter I deem it, that thou must needs make long tale of thy woes; rather will I give thanks to the Gods that thou fallest into ill."

CHAPTER 38
Of the Slaying of the Giukings

Now King Atli eggs on his folk to set on fiercely, and eagerly they fight; but the Giukings fell on so hard that King Atli gave back into the hall, and within doors was the fight, and fierce beyond all fights.

That battle was the death of many a man, but such was the ending thereof, that there fell all the folk of those brethren, and they twain alone stood up on their feet, and yet many more must fare to hell first before their weapons.

And now they fell on Gunnar the king, and because of the host of men that set on him was hand laid on him, and he was cast into fetters; afterwards fought Hogni, with the stoutest heart and the greatest manlihood; and he felled to earth twenty of the stoutest of the champions of King Atli, and many he thrust into the fire that burnt amidst the hall, and all were of one accord that such a man might scarce be seen; yet in the end was he borne down by many and taken.

Then said King Atli, "A marvellous thing how many men have gone their ways

470

before him! Cut the heart from out of him, and let that be his bane!"

Hogni said, "Do according to thy will; merrily will I abide whatso thou wrlt do against me; and thou shalt see that my heart is not adrad, for hard matters have I made trial of ere now, and all things that may try a man was I fain to bear, whiles yet I was unhurt; but now sorely am I hurt, and thou alone henceforth will bear mastery in our dealings together."

Then spake a counsellor of King Atli, "Better rede I see thereto; take we the thrall Hjalli, and give respite to Hogni; for this thrall is made to die, since the longer he lives the less worth shall he be."

The thrall hearkened, and cried out aloft, and fled away anywhither where he might hope for shelter, crying out that a hard portion was his because of their strife and wild doings, and an ill day for him whereon he must be dragged to death from his sweet life and his swine-keeping. But they caught him, and turned a knife against him, and he yelled and screamed or ever he felt the point thereof.

Then in such wise spake Hogni as a man seldom speaketh who is fallen into hard need, for he prayed for the thrall's life, and said that these shrieks he could not away with, and that it were a lesser matter to him to play out the play to the end; and therewithal the thrall gat his life as for that time: but Gunnar and Hogni are both laid in fetters.

Then spake King Atli with Gunnar the king, and bade him tell out concerning the gold, and where it was, if he would have his life.

But he answered, "Nay, first will I behold the bloody heart of Hogni, my brother."

So now they caught hold of the thrall again, and cut the heart from out of him, and bore it unto King Gunnar, but he said—

"The faint heart of Hjalli may ye here behold, little like the proud heart of Hogni, for as much as it trembleth now, more by the half it trembled whenas it lay in the breast of him."

So now they fell on Hogni even as Atli urged them, and cut the heart from out of him, but such was the might of his manhood, that he laughed while he abode that torment, and all wondered at his worth, and in perpetual memory is it held sithence. (1)

Then they showed it to Gunnar, and he said—

"The mighty heart of Hogni, little like the faint heart of Hjalli, for little as it trembleth now, less it trembled whenas in his breast it lay! But now, O Atli, even as we die so shalt thou die; and lo, I alone wot where the gold is, nor shall Hogni be to tell thereof now; to and fro played the matter in my mind whiles we both lived, but now have I myself determined for myself, and the Rhine river shall rule over the gold, rather than that the Huns shall bear it on the hands of them."

Then said King Atli, "Have away the bondsman;" and so they did.

But Gudrun called to her men, and came to Atli, and said—

"May it fare ill with thee now and from henceforth, even as thou hast ill held to thy word with me!"

So Gunnar was cast into a worm-close, and many worms abode him there, and his hands were fast bound; but Gudrun sent him a harp, and in such wise did he set forth his craft, that wisely he smote the harp, smiting it with his toes, and so excellently well he played, that few deemed they had heard such playing, even when the hand had done it. And with such might and power he played, that all worms fell asleep in the end, save one adder only, great and evil of aspect, that crept unto him and thrust its sting into him until it smote his heart; and in such wise with great hardihood he ended his life days.

ENDNOTES:

(1) Since ("sidh", after, and "dham", that.).

CHAPTER 39
The End of Atli and His Kin and Folk

Now thought Atli the King that he had gained a mighty victory, and spake to Gudrun even as mocking her greatly, or as making himself great before her. "Gudrun," saith he, "thus hast thou lost thy brethren, and thy very self hast brought it about."

She answers, "In good liking livest thou, whereas thou thrustest these slayings before me, but mayhappen thou wilt rue it, when thou hast tried what is to come hereafter; and of all I have, the longest-lived matter shall be the memory of thy cruel heart, nor shall it go well with thee whiles I live."

He answered and said, "Let there be peace betwixt us; I will atone for thy brethren with gold and dear-bought things, even as thy heart may wish."

She answers, "Hard for a long while have I been in our dealings together, and now I say, that while Hogni was yet alive thou mightest have brought it to pass; but now mayest thou never atone for my brethren in my heart; yet oft must we women be overborne by the might of you men; and now are all my kindred dead and gone, and thou alone art left to rule over me: wherefore now this is my counsel that we make a great feast, wherein I will hold the funeral of my brother and of thy kindred withal."

In such wise did she make herself soft and kind in words, though far other things forsooth lay thereunder, but he hearkened to her gladly, and trusted in her words, whereas she made herself sweet of speech.

472

So Gudrun held the funeral feast for her brethren, and King Atli for his men, and exceeding proud and great was this feast.

But Gudrun forgat not her woe, but brooded over it, how she might work some mighty shame against the king; and at nightfall she took to her the sons of King Atli and her as they played about the floor; the younglings waxed heavy of cheer, and asked what she would with them.

"Ask me not," she said; "ye shall die, the twain of you!"

Then they answered, "Thou mayest do with thy children even as thou wilt, nor shall any hinder thee, but shame there is to thee in the doing of this deed."

Yet for all that she cut the throats of them.

Then the king asked where his sons were, and Gudrun answered, "I will tell thee, and gladden thine heart by the telling; lo now, thou didst make a great woe spring up for me in the slaying of my brethren; now hearken and hear my rede and my deed; thou hast lost thy sons, and their heads are become beakers on the board here, and thou thyself hast drunken the blood of them blended with wine; and their hearts I took and roasted them on a spit, and thou hast eaten thereof."

King Atli answered, "Grim art thou in that thou hast murdered thy sons, and given me their flesh to eat, and little space passes betwixt ill deed of thine and ill deed."

Gudrun said, "My heart is set on the doing to thee of as great shame as may be; never shall the measure of ill be full to such a king as thou art."

The king said, "Worser deeds hast thou done than men have to tell of, and great unwisdom is there in such fearful redes; most meet art thou to be burned on bale when thou hast first been smitten to death with stones, for in such wise wouldst thou have what thou hast gone a weary way to seek."

She answered, "Thine own death thou foretellest, but another death is fated for me."

And many other words they spake in their wrath.

Now Hogni had a son left alive, hight Niblung, and great wrath of heart he bare against King Atli; and he did Gudrun to wit that he would avenge his father. And she took his words well, and they fell to counsel together thereover, and she said it would be great goodhap if it might be brought about.

So on a night, when the king had drunken, he gat him to bed, and when he was laid asleep, thither to him came Gudrun and the son of Hogni.

Gudrun took a sword and thrust it through the breast of King Atli, and they both of them set their hands to the deed, both she and the son of Hogni.

Then Atli the king awoke with the wound, and cried out; "no need of binding or salving here!—who art thou who hast done the deed?"

Gudrun says, "Somewhat have I, Gudrun, wrought therein, and somewhat withal the son of Hogni."

Atli said, "Ill it beseemed to thee to do this, though somewhat of wrong was between us; for thou wert wedded to me by the rede of thy kin, and dower paid I for thee; yea, thirty goodly knights, and seemly maidens, and many men besides; and yet wert thou not content, but if thou should rule over the lands King Budli owned: and thy mother-in-law full oft thou lettest sit a-weeping."

Gudrun said, "Many false words hast thou spoken, and of naught I account them; oft, indeed, was I fell of mood, but much didst thou add thereto. Full oft in this thy house did frays befall, and kin fought kin, and friend fought friend, and made themselves big one against the other; better days had I whenas I abode with Sigurd, when we slew kings, and took their wealth to us, but gave peace to whomso would, and the great men laid themselves under our hands, and might we gave to him of them who would have it; then I lost him, and a little thing was it that I should bear a widow's name, but the greatest of griefs that I should come to thee—I who had aforetime the noblest of all kings, while for thee, thou never barest out of the battle aught but the worser lot."

King Atli answered, "Naught true are thy words, nor will this our speech better the lot of either of us, for all is fallen now to naught; but now do to me in seemly wise, and array my dead corpse in noble fashion."

"Yea, that will I," she says, "and let make for thee a goodly grave, and build for thee a worthy abiding place of stone, and wrap thee in fair linen, and care for all that needful is."

So therewithal he died, and she did according to her word: and then they cast fire into the hall.

And when the folk and men of estate awoke amid that dread and trouble, naught would they abide the fire, but smote each the other down, and died in such wise; so there Atli the king, and all his folk, ended their life-days. But Gudrun had no will to live longer after this deed so wrought, but nevertheless her ending day was not yet come upon her.

Now the Volsungs and the Giukings, as folk tell in tale, have been the greatest-hearted and the mightiest of all men, as ye may well behold written in the songs of old time.

But now with the tidings just told were these troubles stayed.

CHAPTER 40
How Gudrun Cast Herself into the Sea, but was Brought Ashore Again

Gudrun had a daughter by Sigurd hight Swanhild; she was the fairest of all women, eager-eyed as her father, so that few durst look under the brows of her; and as far did she excel other woman-kind as the sun excels the other lights of heaven.

But on a day went Gudrun down to the sea, and caught up stones in her arms, and went out into the sea, for she had will to end her life. But mighty billows drave her forth along the sea, and by means of their upholding was she borne along till she came at the last to the burg of King Jonakr, a mighty king, and lord of many folk. And he took Gudrun to wife, and their children were Hamdir, and Sorli, and Erp; and there was Swanhild nourished withal.

CHAPTER 41
Of the Wedding and Slaying of Swanhild

Jormunrek was the name of a mighty king of those days, and his son was called Randver. Now this king called his son to talk with him, and said, "Thou shalt fare on an errand of mine to King Jonakr, with my counsellor Bikki, for with King Jonakr is nourished Swanhild, the daughter of Sigurd Fafnir's-bane; and I know for sure that she is the fairest may dwelling under the sun of this world; her above all others would I have to my wife, and thou shalt go woo her for me."

Randver answered, "Meet and right, fair lord, that I should go on thine errands."

So the king set forth this journey in seemly wise, and they fare till they come to King Jonakr's abode, and behold Swanhild, and have many thoughts concerning the treasure of her goodliness.

But on a day Randver called the king to talk with him, and said, "Jormunrek the King would fain be thy brother-in-law, for he has heard tell of Swanhild, and his desire it is to have her to wife, nor may it be shown that she may be given to any mightier man than he is one."

The King says, "This is an alliance of great honour, for a man of fame he is."

Gudrun says, "A wavering trust, the trust in luck that it change not!"

Yet because of the king's furthering, and all the matters that went herewith, is the wooing accomplished; and Swanhild went to the ship with a goodly company, and sat in the stern beside the king's son.

Then spake Bikki to Randver, "How good and right it were if thou thyself had to wife so lovely a woman rather than the old man there."

Good seemed that word to the heart of the king's son, and he spake to her with sweet words, and she to him in like wise.

So they came aland and go unto the king, and Bikki said unto him, "Meet and right it is, lord, that thou shouldst know what is befallen, though hard it be to tell of, for the tale must be concerning thy beguiling, whereas thy son has gotten to him the full love of Swanhild, nor is she other than his harlot; but thou, let not the deed be unavenged."

Now many an ill rede had he given the king or this, but of all his ill redes did this sting home the most; and still would the king hearken to all his evil redes; wherefore he, who might nowise still the wrath within him, cried out that Randver should be taken and tied up to the gallows-tree.

And as he was led to the gallows he took his hawk and plucked the feathers from off it, and bade show it to his father; and when the king saw it, then he said, "Now may folk behold that he deemeth my honour to be gone away from me, even as the feathers of this hawk;" and therewith he bade deliver him from the gallows.

But in that while had Bikki wrought his will, and Randver was dead-slain.

And, moreover, Bikki spake, "Against none hast thou more wrongs to avenge thee of than against Swanhild; let her die a shameful death."

"Yea," said the king, "we will do after thy counsel."

So she was bound in the gate of the burg, and horses were driven at her to tread her down; but when she opened her eyes wide, then the horses durst not trample her; so when Bikki beheld that, he bade draw a bag over the head of her; and they did so, and therewith she lost her life. (1)

ENDNOTES:

(1) In the prose Edda the slaying of Swanhild is a spontaneous and sudden act on the part of the king. As he came back from hunting one day, there sat Swanhild washing her linen, and it came into the king's mind how that she was the cause of all his woe, so he and his men rode over her and slew her.—Tr.

CHAPTER 42
Gudrun Sends Her Sons to Avenge Swanhild

Now Gudrun heard of the slaying of Swanhild, and spake to her sons, "Why sit ye here in peace amid merry words, whereas Jormunrek hath slain your sister, and trodden her under foot of horses in shameful wise? No heart ye have in you like to Gunnar or Hogni; verily they would have avenged their kinswoman!"

Hamdir answered, "Little didst thou praise Gunnar and Hogni, whereas they slew Sigurd, and thou wert reddened in the blood of him, and ill were thy brethren avenged by the slaying of thine own sons: yet not so ill a deed were it for us to slay King Jormunrek, and so hard thou pushest us on to this that we may naught abide thy hard words."

Gudrun went about laughing now, and gave them to drink from mighty beakers, and thereafter she got for them great byrnies and good, and all other weed (1) of war.

Then spake Hamdir, "Lo now, this is our last parting, for thou shalt hear tidings of us, and drink one grave-ale (2) over us and over Swanhild."

So therewith they went their ways.

But Gudrun went unto her bower, with heart swollen with sorrow, and spake—

"To three men was I wedded, and first to Sigurd Fafnir's-bane, and he was bewrayed and slain, and of all griefs was that the greatest grief. Then was I given to King Atli, and so fell was my heart toward him that I slew in the fury of my grief his children and mine. Then gave I myself to the sea, but the billows thereof cast me out aland, and to this king then was I given; then gave I Swanhild away out of the land with mighty wealth; and lo, my next greatest sorrow after Sigurd, for under horses' feet was she trodden and slain; but the grimmest and ugliest of woes was the casting of Gunnar into the Worm-close, and the hardest was the cutting of Hogni's heart from him.

"Ah, better would it be if Sigurd came to meet me, and I went my ways with him, for here bideth now behind with me neither son nor daughter to comfort me. Oh, mindest thou not, Sigurd, the words we spoke when we went into one bed together, that thou wouldst come and look on me; yea, even from thine abiding place among the dead?"

And thus had the words of her sorrow an end.

ENDNOTE:

(1) Weed (A.S. "weodo"), clothing.
(2) Grave-ale, burial-feast.

CHAPTER 43
The Latter End of All the Kin of the Giukings

Now telleth the tale concerning the sons of Gudrun, that she had arrayed their war-raiment in such wise, that no steel would bite thereon; and she bade them play not with stones or other heavy matters, for that it would be to their scathe if they did so.

And now, as they went on their way, they met Erp, their brother, and asked him

477

in what wise he would help them.

He answered, "Even as hand helps hand, or foot helps foot."

But that they deemed naught at all, and slew him there and then. Then they went their ways, nor was it long or ever Hamdir stumbled, and thrust down his hand to steady himself, and spake therewith—

"Naught but a true thing spake Erp, for now should I have fallen, had not hand been to steady me."

A little after Sorli stumbled, but turned about on his feet, and so stood, and spake—

"Yea now had I fallen, but that I steadied myself with both feet."

And they said they had done evilly with Erp their brother.

But on they fare till they come to the abode of King Jormunrek, and they went up to him and set on him forthwith, and Hamdir cut both hands from him and Sorli both feet. Then spake Hamdir—

"Off were the head if Erp were alive; our brother, whom we slew on the way, and found out our deed too late." Even as the Song says,—

> "Off were the head
> If Erp were alive yet,
> Our brother the bold,
> Whom we slew by the way,
> The well-famed in warfare."

Now in this must they turn away from the words of their mother, whereas they had to deal with stones. For now men fell on them, and they defended themselves in good and manly wise, and were the scathe of many a man, nor would iron bite on them.

But there came thereto a certain man, old of aspect and one-eyed, (1) and he spake—

"No wise men are ye, whereas ye cannot bring these men to their end."

Then the king said, "Give us rede thereto, if thou canst."

He said, "Smite them to the death with stones."

In such wise was it done, for the stones flew thick and fast from every side, and that was the end of their life-days.

And now has come to an end the whole root and stem of the Giukings. (2)

NOW MAY ALL EARLS
BE BETTERED IN MIND,
MAY THE GRIEF OF ALL MAIDENS
EVER BE MINISHED,
FOR THIS TALE OF TROUBLE
SO TOLD TO ITS ENDING.

ENDNOTES:

(1) Odin; he ends the tale as he began it.
(2) "And now," etc., inserted by translators from the Poetic
     Edda, the stanza at the end from the Whetting of Gudrun.

THE TALE OF
HOGNI AND HEDIN

CHAPTER 1
Of Freyia and the Dwarfs

East of Vanaquisl in Asia was the land called Asialand or Asiahome, but the folk
that dwelt there was called Æsir, and their chief town was Asgard. Odin was the
name of the king thereof, and therein was a right holy place of sacrifice. Niord
and Frey Odin made Temple-priests thereover; but the daughter of Niord was
Freyia, and she was fellow to Odin and his concubine.

Now there were certain men in Asia, whereof one was called Alfrigg, the second
Dwalin, the third Berling, the fourth Grerr: these had their abode but a little
space from the King's hall, and were men so wise in craftsmanship, that they
laid skilful hand on all matters; and such-like men as they were did men call
dwarfs. In a rock was their dwelling, and in that day they mingled more with
menfolk than as now they do.

Odin loved Freya full sore, and withal she was the fairest woman of that day:
she had a bower that was both fair and strong; insomuch, say men, that if the
door were shut to, none might come into the bower aforesaid without the will of
Freyia.

Now on a day went Freyia afoot by that rock of the dwarfs, and it lay open:
therein were the dwarfs a-smithying a golden collar, and the work was at point
to be done: fair seemed that collar to Freyia, and fair seemed Freyia to the
dwarfs.

Now would Freyia buy the collar of them, and bade them in return for it silver
and gold, and other good things. They said they lacked not money, yet that

479

each of them would sell his share of the collar for this thing, and nought else---
that she should lie a night by each of them: wherefore, whether she liked it
better or worse, on such wise did she strike the bargain with them; and so the
four nights being outworn, and all conditions fulfilled, they delivered the collar to
Freyia; and she went home to her bower, and held her peace hereof, as if
nought had befallen.

CHAPTER 2
Of the Stealing of Freyia's Collar,
and How She May Have it Again

There was a man called Farbauti, which carl had to wife a carline called Laufey;
she was both slim and slender, therefore was she called Needle. One child had
these, a son called Loki; nought great of growth was he, but betimes shameless
of tongue and nimble in gait; over all men had he that craft which is called
cunning; guileful was he from his youth up, therefore was he called Loki the Sly.

He betook himself to Odin at Asgard and became his man. Ever had Odin a
good word for him, whatsoever he turned to; yet withal he oft laid heavy labours
upon him, which forsooth he turned out of hand better than any man looked for:
moreover, he knew wellnigh all things that befell, and told all he knew to Odin.

So tells the tale that Loki knew how that Freyia had gotten the collar, yea and
what she had given for it; so he told Odin thereof, and when Odin heard of it he
bade Loki get the collar and bring it to him. Loki said it was not a likely
business, because no man might come into Freyia's bower without the will of
her; but Odin bade him go his ways and not come back before he had gotten
the collar. Then Loki turned away howling, and most of men were glad thereof
whenas Loki throve nought.

But Loki went to Freyia's bower, and it was locked; he strove to come in, and
might not; and cold it was without, so that he fast began to grow a-cold.

So he turned himself into a fly, and fluttered about all the locks and the joints,
and found no hole therein whereby he might come in, till up by the gable-top he
found a hole, yet no bigger than one might thrust a needle through; none the
less he wriggled in thereby. So when he was come in he peered all about to see
if any waked, but soon he got to see that all were asleep in the bower. Then in
he goeth unto Freyia's bed, and sees that she hath the collar on her with the
clasp turned downward. Thereon Loki changed himself into a flea, and sat on
Freyia's cheek, and stung her so that she woke and turned about, and then fell
asleep again. Then Loki drew from off him his flea's shape, and undid the collar,
and opened the bower, and gat him gone to Odin therewith.

Next morn awoke Freyia and saw that the doors were open, yet unbroken, and
that the goodly collar was gone. She deemed she knew what guile had wrought
it, so she goeth into the hall when she is clad, and cometh before Odin the king,
and speaketh to him of the evil he has let be wrought against her in the stealing

of that dear thing, and biddeth him give her back her jewel.

Odin says that in such wise hath she gotten it, that never again shall she have it. "Unless forsooth thou bring to pass, that two kings, each served of twenty kings, fall to strife, and fight under such weird and spell, that they no sooner fall adown than they stand up again and fight on: always unless some christened man be so bold of heart, and the fate and fortune of his lord be so great, that he shall dare go into the battle, and smite with weapons these men: and so first shall their toil come to an end, to whatsoever lord it shall befall to loose them from the pine and trouble of their fell deeds."

Hereto said Freyia yea, and gat her collar again.

CHAPTER 3
Of King Erling, and Sorli His Son

In those days, when four-and-twenty winters were worn away from the death of Peace-Frodi, a king ruled over the Uplands in Norway called Erling. He had a queen and two sons; Sorli the Strong the elder, and Erlend the younger: hopeful were they both, but Sorli was the stronger. They fell to warfare so soon as they were of age thereto; they fought with the viking Sindri, son of Sveigr, the son of Haki, the sea-king, at the Elfskerries; and there fell the viking Sindri and all his folk; and there also fell Erlend Erlingson. Thereafter Sorli sailed into the East-salt-sea, and harried there, and did so many doughty deeds that late it were ere all were written down.

CHAPTER 4
Sorli Slayeth King Halfdan

There was a king hight Halfdan, who ruled over Denmark, and abode in a stead called Roi's-well; he had to wife Hvedna the old, and their sons were Hogni and Hakon, men peerless of growth and might, and all prowess: they betook them to warfare so soon as they were come to man's estate.

Now cometh the tale on Sorli again, for on an autumn-tide he sailed to Denmark. King Halfdan was minded as at this time to go to an assembly of the kings; he was well stricken in years when these things betid. He had a dragon so good that never was such another ship in all Norway for strength's sake, and all craftsmanship. Now was this ship lying moored in the haven, but King Halfdan was a-land and had let brew his farewell drink. But when Sorli saw the dragon, so great covetise ran into his heart that he must needs have her: and forsooth, as most men say, no ship so goodly hath been in the Northlands, but it were the dragon Ellida, or Gnod, or the Long Worm.

So Sorli spake to his men, bidding them array them for battle; "for we will slay King Halfdan and have away his dragon."

Then answered his word a man called Sævar, his Forecastleman and Marshal: "Ill rede, lord," saith he; "for King Halfdan is a mighty lord of great renown, and hath two sons to avenge him, who are either of them full famous men."

"Let them be mightier than the very Gods," said Sorli, "yet shall I none the less join battle."

So they arrayed them for the fight.

Now came tidings hereof to King Halfdan, and he started up and fared down to the ships with his men, and they got them ready for battle.

Some men set before King Halfdan that it was ill rede to fight, and it were best to flee away because of the odds; but the king said that they should fall every one across the other's feet or ever he should flee. So either side arrayed them, and joined battle of the fiercest; the end whereof was such that King Halfdan fell and all his folks, and Sorli took his dragon and all that was of worth.

Thereafter heard Sorli that Hogni was come from warfare, and lay by Odins-isle; so thitherward straight stood Sorli, and when they met he told him of the fall of Halfdan his father, and offered him atonement and self-doom, and they to become foster-brethren. But Hogni gainsayed him utterly: so they fought as it sayeth in Sorli's Song. Hakon went forth full fairly, and slew Sævar, Sorli's Banner-bearer and Forecastle-man, and therewith Sorli slew Hakon, and Hogni slew Erling the king, Sorli's father.

Then they fought together, Hogni and Sorli, and Sorli fell before Hogni for wounds and weariness' sake: but Hogni let heal him, and they swore the oath of brotherhood thereafter, and held it well whiles they both lived. Sorli was the shortest-lived of them; he fell in the East-sea before the vikings, as it saith in the Sorli-Song, and here saith:---

> "Fell there the fight-greedy,
> Foremost of war-host,
> Eager in East-seas,
> All on Hells' hall-floor;
> Died there the doughty
> In dale-fishes joy-tide,
> With byrny-rod biting
> The vikings in brand-thing."

But when Hogni heard of the fall of Sorli, he went a warring in the Eastlands that same summer, and had the victory in every place, and became king thereover; and so say men that twenty kings paid tribute to King Hogni, and held their realms of him.

Hogni won so great fame from his doughty deeds and his warfare that he was as well known by name north in the Finn-steads, as right away in Paris-town; yea, and all betwixt and between.

482

CHAPTER 5
Hedinn Heareth Tell of King Hogni, and Cometh to the Northlands

Hiarandi was the name of a king who ruled over Serkland; a queen he had, and one son named Hedinn, who from his youth up was peerless of growth, and strength, and prowess: from his early days he betook him to warfare, and became a Sea-king, and harried wide about Spain and the land of the Greeks, and all realms thereabout, till twenty kings paid tribute to him, and held of him land and fief.

On a winter abode Hedinn at home in Serkland, and it is said that on a time he went into the wood with his household; and so it befell him to be alone of his men in a certain wood-lawn, and there in the wood-lawn he saw a woman sitting on a chair, great of growth and goodly of aspect: he asked her of her name, and she named herself Gondul.

Then fell they a-talking, and she asked him of his doughty deeds, and lightly he told her all, and asked her if she wotted of any king who was his peer in daring and hardihood, in fame and furtherance; and she said she wotted of one who fell nowise short of him, and who was served of twenty kings no less than he, and that his name was Hogni, and his dwelling north in Denmark.

"Then wot I," said Hedinn, "that we shall try it which of us twain is foremost."

"Now will it be time for thee to go to thy men," said Gondul; "they will be seeking thee."

So they departed and he fared to his men, but she was left sitting there.

But so soon as spring was come Hedinn arrayed his departure, and had a dragon and three hundred men thereon: he made for the Northlands, and sailed all that summer and winter, and came to Denmark in the Springtide.

CHAPTER 6
Hogni and Hedinn Meet, and Swear Brotherhood to Each Other

King Hogni sat at home this while, and when he heard tell how a noble king is come to his land he bade him home to a glorious feast, and that Hedinn took. And as they sat at the drink, Hogni asked what errand Hedinn had thither, that had driven him so far north in the world. Hedinn said that this was his errand, that they twain should try their hardihood and daring, their prowess and all their craftsmanship; and Hogni said he was all ready thereto.

So betimes on the morrow fared they to swimming and shooting at marks, and strove in tilting and fencing and all prowess; and in all skill were they so alike that none thought he could see betwixt them which was the foremost.

Thereafter they swore themselves foster-brethren, and should halve all things between them.

Hedinn was young and unwedded, but Hogni was somewhat older, and he had to wife Hervor, daughter of Hiorvard, who was the son of Heidrek, who was the son of Wolfskin.

Hogni had a daughter, Hild by name, the fairest and wisest of all women, and he loved his daughter much. No other child had he.

CHAPTER 7
The Beguiling of Hedinn, and of His Evil Deed

The tale telleth that Hogni went a-warring a little hereafter, and left Hedinn behind to ward the realm. So on a day went Hedinn into the wood for his disport, and blithe was the weather. And yet again he turned away from his men and came into a certain wood-lawn, and there in the lawn beheld the same woman sitting in a chair, whom he had seen aforetime in Serkland, and him seemed that she was now gotten fairer than aforetime.

Yet again she first cast a word at him, and became kind in speech to him; she held a horn in her hand shut in with a lid, and the king's heart yearned toward her.

She bade the king drink, and he was thirsty, for he was gotten warm; so he took the horn and drank, and when he had drunk, lo a marvellous change came over him, for he remembered nought of all that was betid to him aforetime, and he sat him down and talked with her. She asked whether he had tried, as she had bidden him, the prowess of Hogni and his hardihood.

Hedinn said that sooth it was: "For he fell short of me in nought in any mastery we tried: so now are we called equal."

"Yet are ye nought equal," said she.

"Whereby makest thou that?" said he.

"In this wise," said she; "that Hogni hath a queen of high kindred, but thou hast no wife."

He answers: "Hogni will give me Hild, his daughter, so soon as I ask her; and then am I no worse wedded than he."

"Minished were thy glory then," she said, "wert thou to crave Hogni of alliance. Better were it, if forsooth thou lack neither hardihood nor daring according to thy boast, that thou have away Hild, and slay the Queen in this wise: to wit, to lay her down before the beak of that dragon-ship, and let smite her asunder therewith in the launching of it."

Now so was Hedinn ensnared by evil heart and forgetfulness, because of the drink he had drunken, that nought seemed good to him save this; and he clean forgat that he and Hogni were foster-brethren.

So they departed, and Hedinn fared to his men; and this befell when summer was far spent.

Now Hedinn ordained his men for the arraying of the dragon, saying that he would away for Serkland. Then went he to the bower, and took Hild and the queen, one by either hand, and went forth with them; and his men took Hild's raiment and fair things. Those men only were in the realm, who durst do nought for Hedinn and his men; for full fearful of countenance was he.

But Hild asked Hedinn what he would, and he told her; and she bade him do it not: "For," quoth she, "my father will give me to thee if thou woo me of him."

"I will not do so much as to woo thee," said Hedinn.

"And though," said she, "thou wilt do no otherwise than bear me away, yet may my father be appeased thereof: but if thou do this evil deed and unmanly, doing my mother to death, then never may my father be appeased: and this wise have my dreams pointed, that ye shall fight and lay each other a-low; and then shall yet heavier things fall upon you: and great sorrow shall it be to me, if such a fate must fall upon my father that he must bear a dreadful weird and heavy spells: nor have I any joy to see thee sore-hearted under bitter toil."

Hedinn said he heeded nought what should come after, and that he would do his deed none the less.

"Yea, thou mayest none other do," said Hild, "for not of thyself dost thou it."

Then went Hedinn down to the strand, and the dragon was thrust forth, and the queen laid down before the beak thereof; and there she lost her life.

So went Hedinn aboard the dragon: but when all was dight he would fain go a-land alone of his men, and into the self-same wood wherein he had gone aforetime: and so, when he was come into the wood-lawn, there saw he Gondul sitting in a chair: they greeted each the other friendly, and then Hedinn told her of his deeds, and thereof was she well content. She had with her the horn whereof he had drunk afore, and again she bade him drink thereof; so he took it and drank, and when he had drunk sleep came upon him, and he fell tottering into her lap: but when he slept she drew away from his head and spake: "Now hallow I thee, and give thee to lie under all those spells and the weird that Odin commanded, thee and Hogni, and all the hosts of you."

Then awoke Hedinn, and saw the ghostly shadow of Gondul, and him-seemed she was waxen black and over big; and all things came to his mind again, and mighty woe he deemed it. And now was he minded to get him far away somewhither, lest he hear daily the blame and shame of his evil deed.

So he went to the ship and they unmoored speedily: the wind blew off shore, and so he sailed away with Hild.

CHAPTER 8
The Weird Falleth on These Twain, Hogni and Hedinn

Now cometh Hogni home, and comes to wot the sooth, that Hedinn hath sailed away with Hild and the dragon Halfdans-loom, and his queen is left dead there. Full wroth was Hogni thereat, and bade men turn about straightaway and sail after Hedinn. Even so did they speedily, and they had a wind of the best, and ever came at eve to the haven whence Hedinn had sailed the morning afore.

But on a day whenas Hogni made the haven, lo the sails of Hedinn in sight on the main; so Hogni, he and his, stood after them; and most sooth is it told that a head-wind fell on Hedinn, whiles the same fair wind went with Hogni.

So Hedinn brought-to at an isle called Ha, and lay in the roadstead there, and speedily came Hogni up with him; and when they met Hedinn greeted him softly: "Needs must I say, foster-brother," saith he, "how evil hath befallen me, that none may amend save thou: for I have taken from thee thy daughter and thy dragon; and thy queen I have done to death. And yet is this deed done not from my evil heart alone, but rather from wicked witchcraft and evil spells; and now will I that thou alone shear and shape betwixt us. But I will offer thee to forego both Hild and the dragon, my men and all my wealth, and to fare so far out in the world that I may never come into the Northlands again, or thine eye-sight, whiles I live."

Hogni answered: "I would have given thee Hild, hadst thou wooed her; yea, and though thou hadst borne away Hild from me, yet for all that might we have had peace: but whereas thou hast now wrought a dastard's deed in the laying down of my queen and slaying of her, there is no hope that I may ever take atonement from thee; but here, in this place, shall we try straightway which of us twain hath more skill in the smiting of strokes."

Hedinn answered: "Rede it were, since thou wilt nought else but battle, that we twain try it alone, for no man here is guilty against thee saving I alone: and nowise meet it is that guiltless men should pay for my folly and ill-doing."

But the followers of either of them answered as with one mouth, that they would all fall one upon the other rather than that they two should play alone.

So when Hedinn saw that Hogni would nought else but battle, he bade his men go up a-land: "For I will fail Hogni no longer, nor beg off the battle: so let each do according to his manhood."

So they go up a-land now and fight: full fierce is Hogni, and Hedinn apt at arms and mighty of stroke.

Soothly it is said that such mighty and evil spells went with the weird of these, that though they clave each other down to the shoulders, yet still they stood upon their feet and fought on: and ever sat Hild in a grove and looked on the play.

So this travail and torment went on ever from the time they first fell a-fighting till the time that Olaf Tryggvison was king in Norway; and men say that it was an hundred and forty and three years before the noble man, King Olaf, brought it so about that his courtman loosed them from this woeful labour and miserable grief of heart.

CHAPTER 9
Hogni and Hedinn are Loosed from Their Weird

So tells the tale, that in the first year of the reign of King Olaf he came to the Isle of Ha, and lay in the haven there on an eve. Now such was the way of things in that isle, that every night whoso watched there vanished away, so that none knew what was become of them.

On this night had Ivar Gleam-bright to hold ward: so when all on ship-board were asleep Ivar took his sword, which Iron-shield of Heathwood had owned erst, and Thorstein his son had given to Ivar, and all his war-gear he took withal, and so went up on to the isle.

But when he was gotten up there, lo a man coming to meet him, great of growth, and all bloody, and exceeding sorrowful of countenance. Ivar asked the man of his name; and he said he was called Hedinn, the son of Hiarandi, of the blood of Serkland.

"Sooth have I to tell thee," said he, "that whereas the watchmen have vanished away, ye must lay it to me and to Hogni, the son of Halfdan; for we and our men are fallen under such sore weird and labour, that we fight on both night and day; and so hath it been with us for many generations of men; and Hild, the daughter of Hogni, sitteth by and looketh on. Odin hath laid this weird upon us, nor shall aught loose us therefrom till a christened man fight with us; and then whoso he smiteth down shall rise up no more; and in such wise shall each one of us be loosed from his labour. Now will I crave of thee to go with me to the battle, for I wot that thou art well christened; and thy king also whom thou servest is of great goodhap, of whom my heart telleth me, that of him and his men shall we have somewhat good."

Ivar said yea to going with him; and glad was Hedinn thereat, and said: "Be thou ware not to meet Hogni face to face, and again that thou slay not me before him; for no mortal man may look Hogni in the face, or slay him if I be dead first: for he hath the Ægis-helm in the eyes of him, nor may any shield him thence. So there is but one thing for it, that I face him and fight him, whilst thou goest at his back and so givest him his death-blow; for it will be but easy work for thee to slay me, though I be left alive the longest of us all."

Therewith went they to the battle, and Ivar seeth that all is sooth that Hedinn hath told him: so he goeth to the back of Hogni, and smiteth him into his head, and cleaveth him down to the shoulders: and Hogni fell dead, and never rose up again.

Then slew Ivar all those men who were at the battle, and Hedinn last of all, and that was no hard work for him. But when he came to the grove wherein Hild was wont to sit, lo she was vanished away.

Then when Ivar to the ship, when it was now daybreak, and he came to the king and told him hereof: and the king made much of his deed, and said that it had gone luckily with him.

But the next day they went a-land, and thither where the battle had been, and saw nowhere any signs of what had befallen there: but blood was seen on Ivar's sword as a token thereof; and never after did the watchmen vanish away.

So after these things the king went back to his realm.

THE END OF THIS TALE

THE TALE OF ROI THE FOOL

CHAPTER 1

There was a man called Roi who was born and bred in Denmark; he was the son of a good bonder, a man of prowess, and strong enow and of good wit. Roi was ever a-going chaffering, and got money together that wise; a good smith he was to wit, and that way also he got money full oft. In those days King Swein, the son of Harald, who was called Twibeard, ruled over Denmark, and was a king well loved of his folk.

Now on a summer Roi wrecked his ship on the south parts of Denmark, and lost goods and all, though the crew were barely saved. So they went up a-land, and Roi took to smithying, and gat goods thus; he was well loved of his fellows, nor had he long followed this craft before the money grew on his hands, for a full famous smith he was; yet was the story still the same, and he fared but ill with his goods; for as soon as he had gotten together what he would he went to sea and lost it all.

Roi had a mark in the face of him whereby he was lightly known from other men, for one of his eyes was blue and the other black: but a most manly man he was, and ruled his temper well, yea even were he ill dealt with; ever he got wealth a-land, and lost it a-voyaging, and so when he had now thrice lost his

488

ship in his chaffering voyages, he thought he could see, that he was not made for that craft, and yet going from land to land with his merchandise was the thing most to his mind: so he bethought him of going to King Swein, if perchance he might have any counsel of him, for he wotted that he had been the better thereof. Wherefore he went thither, and coming before the king greeted him.

And the king asked, "Who art thou?"

"Roi am I called," said he.

Quoth the king, "Art thou Roi the Come-to-nought?"

He answered, "I am wanting somewhat else from thee than mocks such as these. I would rather of thee the help of thy money and goodhap; maybe it shall avail me, for I would fain hope that thy health and hap may perchance prevail over my ill-luck."

King Swein said: "If thou be minded to seek luck of me it were well, so please you, that we were partners together."

Then said folk to the king, that it were ill-counselled to be partner of one so unlucky as Roi, and that he would lose his money at once: but the king answered:----

"It shall be risked which may most prevail, a king's luck or his ill-luck."

Therewith he gave money to Roi that they should have together, and Roi went a chaffering on such covenant with the king, that he should pay nought if the goods were lost, and share what there was of gain, and that he should pay the king as much as he got from him to begin with. So Roi went his ways, and things went well with his voyages, and the money grew speedily, and he came back in autumn-tide to the king with much wealth; and no long time was passed before he became right wealthy, and was now called Roi the Wealthy, or the Stately, and every summer he went from land to land, chaffering, on the covenant aforesaid with the king.

CHAPTER 2

Now on a time spake Roi with the king: "Now will I that thou take thy share, lord, lest things go ill and I lose thy goods."

Said the king: "Thou art minded then that it were better for our partnership to come to an end: but I was deeming it not ill-counselled for thee to abide in the land here under my good keeping, and that thou shouldst wed and dwell quietly here, with me to further thee. Nor do I deem it hopeful, this mind of thine for trading; a slippery matter it seems to me, even as thou hast proved aforetime." Nevertheless Roi would have the money shared, and so it was done, and the king said: "This is thy rede, Roi, and not mine; and better meseems it had been since thou hast come to seek luck at my hands that it had abided by thee." Men took up the word therewith, and said how he himself had proven how the king's luck had come to him in time of need. But the king said that Roi had dealt well with him, and that it would be great scathe if he tumbled into any ill-luck: and therewithal they parted.

So Roi went on his voyage and had plenteous wealth. He sailed to Sweden this time, and made up the Low, and brought-to off certain meads: and now had Roi all the ship's lading to himself. On a day he went a-land by himself alone, and when he had gone awhile he met a man with red hair and straight, and somewhat of a brisk lad to look on. Roi asked him of his name, and he said he was called Helgi, and was a court-man of King Eric; and he asked withal who the chapman was. Roi told his name, whereon Helgi said he knew him and had seen him before; and therewith he said he would deal with him. Roi asked how much he would deal for, and Helgi answered: "I wot that ye Danes are new come a-land, and I hear say that they are all thy servants, and that all the ship's lading is thine; and I will buy the whole lading of thee if thou wilt."

Roi said he was no whit of a peddler then; and Helgi said he could deal both in small and in great. Then asked Roi: "Where are the goods that I am to take of thee?" Helgi bade him go with him, and said that he would show him that there was no fooling in that his offer. So they went till they came to a storehouse all full of merchandise, and all that was therein Helgi offered Roi for his lading: Roi deemed it good chaffer, and thought that little would be his loss therein though they made a deal of it, and that the wares were good cheap. So it came to this that they struck the bargain, and a flitting-day was appointed between them; wherewith they parted, and Roi went back to his ship.

CHAPTER 3
Earl Thorgnyr's Talk with His Daughter

The very next day came Helgi down with many men and beasts, and let flit away the lading, so that all was gone by nightfall; and soothly he had no lack either of men or of yoke beasts hereto. A few days after Roi went up a-land alone, with the mind to settle matters for the flitting of his wares: and by this time was worn by one night over and above the time that he should have let fetch them. Roi deemed it mattered nought for a night, though he had come later than was appointed; for in sooth he was busied about many things. Roi was clad full goodly, for he was a very showy man, and he had a right noble knife and belt, on either whereof had many a penny been spent: good weapons he had, and a fair scarlet kirtle, with a broidered cloak over all.

The weather was fair, and he went till he came to the bower: it stood open, but his wares were not to be seen: this seemed marvellous to him, so he went all round about the bower till he came to the place whereas Helgi slept: so Roi asked him where was his goods? but Helgi said he knew nought of any goods he had. Roi asked how was that. Quoth Helgi, that he had borne out his goods at the time agreed on. "But I saw nought of thee to fetch them away: and it was not likely that I was going to let the things stand there for any one to lay hands on; so I let flit all of it away, and I call it mine and not thine."

Roi said he dealt hastily and unjustly: "No marvel though thou get rich speedily if thou play such tricks as this often." Helgi said he had gone on in that wise for some while now, and found it availed him well enough. "But," says he, "the king hath a case against thee whereas thou heedest not thy goods: for it is the law of the land, that every man shall keep his own so that no thief may steal it, or else hath the king a case against him: now shall the king doom hereover." Roi said it looked like little making money if the king must needs charge him herewith. Therewith they parted.

Then went Roi to another court, and when he was gotten well into the garth he saw two men coming hastily after him, and one was full like to his late customer to look on. Roi had cast his belt about his neck, and thereby hung that costly knife of his. Now this first of those twain was Thorgils, brother of Helgi: he made a snatch at the belt as soon as they met, and said withal: "Every man may take his own how he may: this belt and knife thou tookest from me in Normandy, but I let smithy the things for me in England."

Said Roi: "This looks little like making money," and smiled withal. Then he went his ways and they turned back.

But he had gone no long way ere he met a man, big and ill-looking, who had but one eye: so when they met Roi asked who he was; he answered: "I ought to know thee; for I have on me a token that we have met." Roi asked what the sign might be, and the man said: "No need for thee to feign that thou knowest not: thou wert a one-eyed man; and on a time thou wentest a chaffering voyage, and layest by Samsey certain nights, whereat I chanced to be: thou hadst those men with thee, and bargained with them to bewitch me of my eye. Any man with his wits about him may see that both these eyes have been in one head: and now thou hast one, and I the other: but the king shall judge thereof tomorrow; yea, and of thy taking the knife and belt from Thorgils my brother."

"I wot not thereof," said Roi, "but belike heavy charges are flying about today;" and therewith he smiled somewhat. Therewith they parted, and Roi went to his ship: he told no man of all this, nor might any see of him but he was well content with all things.

The next morning went Roi to the town-gate, and awas all alone: and when he came thereby there was hard by a certain house wherein he heard men talking: and one took up the word, and said: "Whether will Roi the Fool come to the Thing tomorrow I wonder." Another answered: "Well, things look ugly for him, for the king ever dooms according to the urging of those brethren, whether it be right or wrong."

Roi made as if he heard not, and went his ways till he came on a young maiden going to the water, and him-seemed he had never seen a fairer woman than her: and when he came up to her she looked on him and said, "Who art thou?"

"I am called Roi," said he.

Quoth she, "Art thou Roi the Fool?"

He answered: "Well, belike it may now be a true name enough for me: yet have I borne, time was, a nobler name. What is thy name?" said he.

She said: "I am called Sigrbiorg, and I am the daughter of Thorgnyr the Lawman."

Said Roi: "Fain were I to be holpen somewhat of his wisdom: but wilt thou do anything for my helping?"

Said she: "My father hath ever little to say to men of Denmark: moreover, he is no friend to those brethren, and they have oftentimes had to bow before him."

Roi said: "But wilt thou give me some counsel herein?"

"No man hath asked my counsel heretofore," said she, "and it is not all so sure that I know aught that may avail thee, if I were to counsel thee aught: but thou art a man to be desired, so come with me, and take thy place under my loftbower, and take good heed to what thou hearest spoken; and that may avail thee, if any give counsel in thy case."

He said that so it should be; and she went her ways, but Roi abode under her loft-bower.

Now Thorgnyr knew the voice of his daughter as she came into the chamber, and asked her: "What like weather is it abroad, daughter?"

"Good is the weather," said she.

Said Thorgnyr: "Will Roi the Fool come to the Thing today?"

She said she knew not.

"Why sighest thou so heavily, daughter?" said Thorgnyr. "Hast thou met Roi the Fool? didst thou think him a goodly man, and one to be desired? wouldst thou give him help and furtherance?"

She said: "Say thou now, if thou wert so grievously bestead as he is, whither thou wouldst turn to, whenas no man would take money to further thy case?""

Thorgnyr answered: "I see nought hard to deal with herein: I would let trick meet trick: Roi will know well enow how to answer Helgi: every man may understand, that if one take another's goods by guile and treason, and do nought for him in return, the king hath a case against him, if the truth come uppermost: and he may make him a thief, and put him from all his wealth and honour; and well may Roi pay back lie for lie----forsooth he knoweth all about this already."

She answered: "He would not be Roi the Fool were he as wise as thou: but what wouldst thou do if a man claimed the eye from out thine head?" said she,

492

"or how wouldst thou answer him?"

Thorgnyr answered: "Let marvel meet marvel," and therewith he told her what he would meet either case withal; but the tale showeth hereafter what he said.

CHAPTER 4
The Strife of Roi and Helgi

After these things Sigrbiorg went away and found Roi, and asked him whether he had laid to heart that which had been counselled him; and he said he deemed he would be able to call to mind much of it. Then she said:----

"Join thyself to my father's company when he rideth to the Thing, and heed not his hard speech though he cast but cold words at thee: for he knoweth belike that I have met thee, and that my heart yearneth toward thee; wherefore I hope that he will help thee in thy need: all the more, as he wotteth that I deem the matter to touch me closely. But no counsel can I give thee if thou art not counselled herewith."

Therewithal they parted; and when Thorgnyr was ready to rides to the Thing, and Roi met him by the very towngate, and greeted him well.

Thorgnyr said: "Who art thou?" and Roi told of himself.

Thorgnyr said: "What would Roi the Fool in my company? go thou another road, I will not have thee with us."

Roi answered: "Nay, thou wilt not spare a word to bid me follow thee, and go by the road I will, whereas there nought is to hurt thee in me, and I am a stranger here, and would fain get the good of thy company: and need enough withal driveth me on this journey, and biddeth me further my case somewhat."

So men took up the word, and said that sooth it was. So they go on till they came to the Thing, and Thorgnyr had a great company, and thither were come withal many folk of the land.

So Thorgnyr spake when men were come to the Thing: "Are those brethren, Helgi and Thorgils, come hither?"

They said yea.

"Then is it due," said Thorgnyr, "to make known to the king concerning your dealings with Roi the Fool."

Then said Helgi: "I say so much, that it was agreed between us that Roi should have all the wares that were in the bower, but I should bear them out and empty the bower; and a day was appointed for his coming back again: but I was to take in return all the lading of his ship and flit it away. And now, lord," says he, "I did according to covenant; but when I had cleared the storehouse and borne out the wares Roi was not come; so I let flit it all away, for I would not that a thief should steal it: and now I claim the goods for mine own. But I say that thou, king, hast a case against him, because he took no heed of his goods, but would have other men come to ill by his wealth: so give thou judgment, lord, concerning these things."

Said the king: "A trick was this; yet it may be that thou wilt come by the money, if things went that road. Was such the covenant, Roi?"

He said that he might not gainsay it. "Yet is there a flaw herein, lord: on such terms were Helgi and I agreed, when we struck the bargain, that I was to own all that was in the storehouse: and now a part of all call I creeping things, canker-worm, and moth, and all hurtful things that were therein. All these I say he should have cleared out of his storehouse, and meseems he hath not done it: and therewithal I claim Helgi as mine own; for he was in the storehouse with me when we struck the bargain: and though he be but a sorry man, yet may I keep him for my thrall, or perchance sell him at a thrall-cheaping: so give thou judgment, lord king, concerning these things."

The king said: "With a crafty one hast thou to do now, Helgi, and no witless man."

Then said Thorgnyr: "Thou hast spoken well, Roi, and may not lightly be gainsayed: but what is to be said about thy dealings, Thorgils?"

Thorgils answered: "I say that Roi hath taken from me knife and belt, either of them dear bought things."

Thorgnyr said: "Then must Roi answer somewhat hereto, or else confess, if he knoweth it for true."

Roi said: "Well, I will answer somewhat. I was born and bred in Denmark, and had a brother called Sigurd, a likelier lad than I in all wise, but younger, as might well be seen: so on a time I fared with him chaffering in Normandy, and he was then twelve winters old. On a day the lad met a man in the wood, big and straight-haired, and they fell a-chaffering together; and a deal of money had got into the purse the lad bore, so that the other had nought to give in return: but this new-met man was keen-eyed at money, and would have the more part of what was there, wherefore he smote the lad to murder him, and when men were ware thereof they came and told me; but when I came there my brother lay dead, and the man was gone, and had left behind him this knife and belt, but all the money was gone. In such wise came I by these good things; and I say that Thorgils has stolen my money and slain my brother: doom thou, lord, concerning this."

Thorgnyr said: "Surely such men as these brethren are worthy of death."

494

CHAPTER 5
What Roi Offered unto Thorir

Now came forward Thorir, the brother of Helgi and Thorgils, and spake thus: "This that appertains unto me is a hard case;" and he told his tale, how he had lost his eye as is afore-written. "Lord," says he, "I look to thee to make my case good for me, for he may not gainsay it that even so it befell as I say: and it behoveth thee, lord, not to account outland men of more worth than we brethren, who this long while have been men useful to thee, and have not slept over any matters thou hast charged us with."

The king said: "This is a marvellous matter, and such as is seldom heard of: now, Roi, answer thou somewhat hereto."

Answereth Roi: "I know nought of it; and well might I show by ordeal that unsoothly it is said of me: yet shall there be somewhat bidden on my part for thine honour's sake, lord king."

"Let us hear it," said the king.

Said Roi: "I offer Thorir this; that the eye be pulled out of the head of each of us, and that the two of them be laid in the scales thereafter, and then if they be both come out of one head, they shall be heavy alike, and I shall atone to Thorir according to thy dooming: but if Thorir will not take this, then shall he be proven a liar in more matters than this one."

Thorir said that he would not take it.

Said Thorgnyr: "Then it comes to this, that thou liest, and ye brethren do as ever wickedly and unmanly: and belike overlong ye have woven a web of lies about you, and overlong and undeemed you have been trusted of the king, who hath deemed you better men than ye were. Now is there no need to hide the truth longer about these things: for it has now become as clear as day to all that no other doom is right, but that Roi shall do his will on the life and wealth of those brethren."

Said Roi: "Soon is my doom spoken, and I shall grow no wiser about it hereafter. The brethren Thorgils and Thorir do I doom to death, their lands to thee, king, and their chattels to me: but Helgi will I have put forth from the land so that he never show his face there again, and to be taken and slain if he ever set foot in Sweden; and all his wealth I adjudge to myself."

Then were the brethren Thorgils and Thorir taken, and a gallows was raised for them, and they were hanged thereon as thieves, according to the law of the land.

So was the Thing broken up, and each man fared thence to his own home: and now was Roi called Roi the Wise. Now he thanked Thorgnyr the Lawman for his aid, saying that he had scarce got off clear but for his counsel and wisdom. "And now," quoth he, "it may be thou wilt deem me importunate if I crave thy daughter of thee in wedlock."

Thorgnyr answered: "Well, I deem it wise to give thee a good answer herein; for betimes it was that my daughter showed me that she had set her heart upon thee to have thee."

So the wedding was done with great honour and glory, and the fairest of feasts was holden there.

Thereafter Roi arrayed him for departure, and fared to Denmark, and came to King Swein, and told him all about his voyage, and how it had gone with him: and said, that to no man was he bound to be so good as to King Swein; and therewith he gave him many good things from Sweden. King Swein said he had done well and happily, howbeit there had been close steering in the matter how it would turn out: wherewith he and the king departed, and were friends ever after while they lived. Then Roi went to Sweden, and found Thorgnyr the Lawman dead, but Thorgnyr, his son, was Lawman in his stead, and was the wisest of men: he and Roi shared the money according to the law of the land, and in all concord. Roi was accounted a right good man, and his wife had the gift of foreseeing: many noble folk in Sweden are come from them.

THE SAGA OF THORSTEIN, VIKING'S SON

CHAPTER 1
Here Begins the Saga of Thorstein, Viking's Son

The beginning of this Saga is, that a king named Loge ruled that country which is north of Norway. Loge was larger and stronger than any other man in that country. His name was lengthened from Loge to Haloge, and after him the country was called Halogeland (Hálogaland, i.e. Haloge's land). Loge was the fairest of men, and his strength and stature was like unto that of his kinsmen, the giants, from whom he descended. His wife was Glod (Glöð, glad), a daughter of Grim of Grimsgard, which is situated in Jotunheim in the north; and Jotunheim was at that time called Elivags (Elivágar in the north). Grim was a very great berserk; his wife was Alvor, a sister of Alf the Old. He ruled that kingdom which lies between two rivers, both of which were called Elfs (i.e. Elbs), taking their name from him (Alf). The river south of his kingdom, dividing it from Gautland, the country of King Gaut, was called Gaut's Elf (i.e. Gaut's River, the river Gotha in the southwestern part of th present Sweden); the one north of it was called Raum's Elf, named after King Raum, and the kingdom of the latter was called Raum's-ric. The land governed by King Alf was called Alfheim, and all his offspring are related to the Elves. They were fairer than any other people save the giants. King Alf was married to Bryngerd, a daughter of

496

king Raum of Raum's-ric; she was a large woman, but she was not beautiful, because her father, king Raum, was ugly-looking, and hence ugly looking and large men are called great "raums." King Haloge and his wife, queen Glod, had two daughters, named Eisa (glowing embers) and Eimyrja (embers). These maids were the fairest in the land, on account of their things took their names from the above-named maids. There lived with Haloge two jarls, named Vifil and Vesete, both of whom were large and strong men, and they were the warders of the king's land. One day the jarls went to the king, Vifil to woo Eimyrja and Vesete to woo Eisa; but the king refused both, on which account they grew so angry that they soon afterward carried the maids off, fleeing with them out of the land, and thus putting themselves out of his reach. But the king declared them outlaws in his kingdom, hindered them by witchcraft from every again becoming dwellers in his land, and, moreover, enchanted their kinsmen, making these also outlaws, and deprived them of hte benefit of their estates forever. Vesete settled in an island or holm, which hight Borgund's holm (Bornholm), and become the father of Bue and Sigurd, nicknamed Cape. Vifil sailed further ot the east and established himself in an island called Vifil's Isle. With his wife, Eimyrja, he got a son, Viking by name, who in his early youth became a man of great stature and extraordinary strength.

CHAPTER 2

There was a king who hight Ring, who ruled a fylke of Sweden. With his queen he had an only child, a daughter, by name Hunvor, a maiden of unrivaled beauty and education. She had a magnificent bower, and was attended by a suite of maidens. Ingeborg hight the maiden, who was next to her in position, and she was a daughter of Herfinn, jarl of Woolen Acre. Most people said that Ingeborg was not inferior to the daughter of the king in any respect, excepting in strength and wisdom, which Hunvor possessed in a higher degree than all others in the land. Many kings and princes wooed Ingeborg, but she refused them all. She was thought to be a woman of boundless pride and insolence, and it was also talked by many that her pride and insolence might some day receive a check in some way or other. Thus time passed on for a while. There was a mountain back of the king's residence so high that no human paths traversed it. One day a man—if he might be so called—came down from the mountain. He was larger and more fierce-looking than any person that had before been seen, and he looked more like a giant than like a human being. In his hand he held a bayonet-like two-pointed pike. This happened while the king was sitting at the table. This "raum" (ugly-looking fellow) came to the door of the hall and requested to be permitted to enter, but the porters refused to admit him. Then he smote the porters with his pike and pierced both of them from breast to back, on being pierced by one point of the pike and the other by the other; whereupon he lifted both of them over his head and threw their corpses down upon the ground behind him. Then, entering the door, he approached the king's throne, and thus addressed him: As I, king Ring, have honored you so much as to visit you, I think it your duty to grant my request. The king asked what the request might be, and what his name was. He answered: My name is Harek, the Ironhead, and I am a son of king Kol Kroppinbak (the humpback) of India; but my errand is that I wish you to place your daughter, your country, and

497

your subjects in my hands. And, I think, most people will say that it is better for the kingdom that I rule it instead of you, who are destitute of strength and manhood, and moreover, enfeebled by age. But, as it may seem humiliating to you to surrender your kingdom, I will agree, on my part, to marry your daughter, Hunvor. But, if this is not satisfactory to you, I will kill you, take possession of your kingdom, and make Hunvor my concubine. Now the king felt sorely perplexed, for all the people were grieved at their conversation. Then said the king: It seems to me that we ought to know what she will answer. To this Harek assented. Then Hunvor was sent for, and the matter was explained to her. She said: I like the looks of this man very well, although he seems likely to treat me with severity; but I consider him perfectly worth of me, if I marry him; nevertheless, I wish to ask whether no ransom can be paid and I be free. Yes, there can, answered Harek. If the king will try to holm-gang with me within four nights, or procure another man in his stead, then all the powers shall be surrendered to the one slaying the other in the duel. Certainly, answered Hunvor, none can be found who is able to subdue you in a duel; nevertheless, I will agree to your proposition. After this, Harek went out, but Hunvor betook herself to her bower, weeping bitterly. Then the king asked his men if there was nobody among them who regarded his daughter Hunvor a sufficient prize for which to risk his life in a holm-gang with Harek. But, although all wished to marry her, yet nobody was willing to risk the duel, looking upon it as certain death. Many also said that this fate was deserved by her, since she had refused so many, and marrying Harek would be a check to her pride. She had a man-servant, by name Eymund, a fellow faithful to her and to be rusted in all matters. This man she sent for straightway on the same day, saying to him: It will not prove advisable to keep quiet; I want to send you away take a boat and row to the island, which lies outside of Woolen Aere, and is called Vifil's Isle. On the island there is a byre (farm, farm-house); thither you must go and arrive there to-morrow at nightfall. You are to enter the western door of the byre, and when you have entered you will see a sprightly old man and an elderly woman; any other persons you will not see. They have a son by name Viking, who is now fifteen years old and a man of great ability, but he will not be present. I hope he will be able to help us out of our troubles; if not, I fear there will scarcely be any help for us. You must keep out of sight, but if you happen to see a third person, then throw this letter on his lap and hurry home. Without delay, Eymund, with a company of eleven men, went on board a ship and sailed to Vifil's Isle. He goes ashore alone and proceeds to the byre, where he finds the fire-house and places himself behind the door. The bonde (farmer) was sitting by the fire with his wife, and he seemed to Eymund a man of brave countenance. The fire was almost burnt out and the house was but faintly lighted by the embers. Said the woman: I think, my dear Vifil, that it would prove to our advantage if our son Viking should present himself, for no one seems to be offering himself for combat, and the time for the duel with Harek is close at hand. I do not think it advisable, Eimyrja, answered he, for our son is yet young and rash, ambitious and careless. It will be his sudden death if he should be induced to fight with Harek; nevertheless, it is for you to manage this matter as you think best. Presently a door oepned back of the bonde, and a man of wonderful, stature entered, taking his seat by the side of his mother. Eymund threw the letter on the lap of Viking, ran to the ship, came to Hunvor and told her how he had done his errand. Fate will now have to settle the matter, says Hunvor. Viking took the letter, in which he found a greeting from the king's daughter, and, moreover, a promise that she would be his wife if he would fight with Harek, the Ironhead. At this Viking turned pale, observing which, Vifil asked him what letter that was. Viking would showed him the letter. This I knew, said Vifil, and it would have been better, Eimyrja, if I had decided this matter myself, when we talked about it a little while ago, but what do you propose to do? Says Viking: Wopuld it not be well to save the princess? Replied Vifil: It will be sudden death to you if you fight with Harek. I will run the risk, answered Viking. Then there is no remedy, says Vifil, but I will give you an account of his family and himself.

CHAPTER 3

Tirus the Great was king of India. He was an excellent ruler in every respect, and his queen was a very superior woman, with whom he had an only daughter, who hight Trona. She was the fairest among the fair, and, unlike the majority of her sex, she excelled all other princesses in wisdom. The Saga must also mention a man by name Kol, of whom a great many good things are told: first, that he was large as a giant, ugly-looking as the devil, and so well skilled in the black art that he could pass through the earth as well as walk upon it, could glue together steeds and stars; furthermore, he was so great a ham-leaper (1) that he could burst into the shape of various kinds of animals; he would sometimes ride on the winds or pass through the sea, and he had so large a hump on his back that, although he stood upright, the hump would reach agove his head. This Kol went to India with a great army, slew Tirus, married Trona, and subjugated the land and the people. He begot many children with Trona, all of whom where more like their father than like their mother. Kol was nicknamed Kroppinbak (i.e. Humpback). He had three rare treasures. These were: a sword so mighty that none better was wielded at that time, and the name of his sword was Angervadil; another of the treasures was a gold ring, called Gleser; the third was a horn, and such was the nature of the beverage contained in the lower part of it that all who drank therefrom were attacked by an illness called leprosy, and became so forgetful that they remembered nothing of the past; but by drinking from the upper part of the horn their health and memory were restored. Their eldest child was Bjorn, the Blue-tooth. His tooth was of a blue color, and tended an ell and a half out of his mouth, with this tooth he often, in battles or when he was violently in rage, put people to death. A daughter of Kol was Dis. The third child of Kol and Trona hight Harek, whose head at the age of seven was perfectly bald, and whose skull was as hard as steel, wherefore he was called Ironhead. Their fourth child hight Ingjald, whose upper lip measured an ell from the nose whence he was called Ingjald Trana (the snout). It was the pastime of the brothers when at home that Bjorn the Blue-tooth cut his tooth into the skull of his brother Harek with all his might without hurting him. No weapon could be made to stick in the lip of Ingjald Snout. By incantations Kol the Hump-back brought about, that none of his offspring could be killed by any other weapon than by the sword Angervadil; no other iron can scathe them. But when Kol had become old enough he died a horrible death. At the time of his death Trona was pregnant, and gave birth to a son, called Kol after his father, and he was as like his father as he was asking to him. One year old, Kol as so ugly to children that he was nicknamed Kol Krappe (the crafty). Dis married Jokul Ironback, a blue berserk. She and her brothers divided their father's heritage betwixt themselves, so that Dis got the horn, but Bjorn Blue-tooth the sword, Harek the ring, Ingjald the kingdom, and Kol the personal property. Three winters after the death of king Kol, Trona married jarl Herfinn, a son of king Rodmar of Marseraland, and the first winter after they were married she bore him a son, named Framar, who was a man of great possibilities and unlike his brothers. Now it seems to me, continued Vifil, that you ought not to risk your life in a duel with this Hel-strong man, whom no iron can scathe. Not so, answered Viking; I shall urn the risk, whatsoever may be the result. And Vifil, seeing that Viking was in real earnest when he insisted on fighting with Harek, said: I can tell you still more about the sons of Kol. Vesete and I were wardens of king Haloge's country; during the summer seasons we sued to wage wars, and once we met Bjorn blue-tooth in Grening's Sound (the present Gronsun, between the Isle of Man and Falster in Denmark), and in such a manner did we fight that Veset smote Bjorn's hand with his club, so that the sword fell from his hand, and then I caught it, flung it through him, and he lost his life. From that time I have worn the sword, and now I give it to you, my son. Vifil then brought forth the sword and gave it to Viking, who liked it very much. Viking then prepared himself, went on board a boat, and came to the hall of the king on the day appointed for the duel. There everything was sad and dreary. Viking went before the king and greeted him. The king asked him his name. Viking told him the truth. Hunvor was sitting on one side of the king. Then Viking asked her whether she had requested him to come. She replied in the affirmative. Viking asked what terms he offered him for venturing a holm-gang with Harek. Replied the king: I will give you my daughter in mariage, and a suitable dowry besides. Viking gave his consent to this, and then he was betrothed to Hunvor; but it was the common opinion that it would be certain death to him if he should fight with Harek.

ENDNOTES:

1. Ham-leaper, one who is able to change his shape.

CHAPTER 4

Then Viking went to the holm, accompanied by the king and his courtiers. Thither came Harek, too, and asked who was appointed to fight with him. Viking stepped forward and said: I am the man. Whereto Harek made reply: I suppose it will be an easy matter to strike you to the ground, for I know it will be the end of you if I smite you with my fist. But I suppose, answered Viking, that you consider it no trifling matter to fight with me, since you tremble at the very sight of me. Harek replies: Not so, and I must save your life, since you go willingly into the open jaws of death; and do you smite first, according to the laws of holm-gang, for I am the challenger in this duel; but, in the meantime, I shall stand perfectly still, for I am not afraid of any danger. At this time Viking drew his sword, Angervadil, from which lightning seemed to flash. Harek seeing this, said: I would never have fought with you had I known that you were in possession of Angervadil, and most likely it will turn out as my father said, namely, that I and my brothers and my sister would all be short-lived, excepting the one bearing his own name, and it was a great misfortune that Angervadil

500

passed out of the hands of our family. At this moment Viking struck Harek's skull and split his trunk from one end to the other, so that the sword stood in the ground to the hilt. Then the men of the king burst out in loud triumphant shouting, and the king went home to his hall with great joy. Now they began to talk about preparing the wedding-feast, but Viking said he was not willing to be married yet; she shall remain betrothed, he said and not be wedded till after three years, meanwhile I am going to wage war. So was done, and Viking went abroad with two ships. He was very successful, gaining victory in every battle; and after having spent two years as a viking, he landed at an island in the autumn at a time when the weather was fair and very warm.

CHAPTER 5

The Same day as Viking landed at the island, he went ashore to amuse himself. He turned his steps to a forest and then he grew very hot. Having come to an open place in the forest, he sat down, and saw a woman of exquisite beauty walking along. She came up to him, greeted him very courteously, and he received her very kingly. They talked together a long time, and their conversation was very friendly. He asked her her name, and she said it was Solbjort (sun-bright). She then asked him if he was not thirsty, as he had walked so far, but Viking said he was not. She then took a horn, which she had kept under her cloak, offered him a drink from it, and he accepting it, and drinking therefrom, became sleepy, and bending his body into the lap of Solbjort, he fell asleep. But when he woke up again she had entirely disappeared. The drink had made him feel somewhat strange, and his whole body was shivering; the weather was gusty and cold, and he had forgotten nearly everything of the past, and least of all did he recollect Hunvor. He then went to his ship and departed from that place, and now he was confined in his bed by the disease called leprosy. He and his men frequently sailed near land, but were unwilling to go ashore and remain there. After having suffered twelve months from this sickness it grew still more severe, and his body was covered with many sores. One day sailing to land, they saw three ships passing the harbor, and at their meeting they asked for each other's names. Viking told his name, but the other chieftain said his name was Halfdan, and that he was a son of Ulf. Halfdan was a large and strong-looking man, and when he had learned the condition of Viking he went on board his ship, where he found him very weak. Halfdan asked him the cause of his illness, and Viking told him everything that happened. Halfdan answered: Here the ham-leaper, Dis, Kol's daughter, has succeeded in her tricks, and I think it will be difficult to get any assistance from her in righting this matter, for she undoubtedly thinks she has avenged her brother, Harek Ironhead. Now I will offer you foster-brotherhood, and we will try whether we cannot revenge ourselves on Dis. Answered Viking to this: Owing to my weakness, I have no hope at all of being able to kill dis and her husband, Jokul Ironback, but such is my opinion of you , that even though I were in the best circumstances, your valor makes your offer very flattering to me. And thus it was agreed that they should become foster-brothers. Halfdan had a great dragon, called Iron-ram; all of this ship that stood out of the water was iron-clad; it rose high out of the sea, and was a very costly treasure. Having spent a short time there they left the place and went home to Svafe. Then Viking's strength

501

diminished so that he became sick unto death. But when they had landed, Halfdan left the ships alone and proceeded until he came into an open space in a forest, where there stood a large rock, which he went up to and knocked at with his rod, and out of the rock there came a dwarf, who lived there and hight Lit (color), a warm friend of Halfdan, whom the dwarf greeted kindly and asked what his errand was. Replied Halfdan: It is now of great importance to me, foster-father, that you do my errand. What it is, my foster-son? Asked Lit. I want you to procure for me the good horn of Dis, Kol's daughter, said Halfdan. Risk that yourself, said Lit, for it will be my death if I attempt it; and even the sacrifice of myself would be in vain, for you know there does not exist such a troll in the whole world as Dis. Replied Halfdan; I am sure you will do as well as you can. Upon this they parted, Halfdan returning to his ships and remaining there for some time.

CHAPTER 6

Now it must be told of king Ring that he and his daughter Hunvor dwelt in his kingdom after the slaying of Harek Ironhead, which seemed to all a deed of great daring. This event was heard of in India, and Ingjald Snout was startled by the tidings of Harek's death. He began to cut the war-arrow, and dispatched it throughout the whole country, thus collecting an army containing a crowd of people, among whom there where many of the rabble, and with this army he marched toward Sweden. He came there unexpected, and offered the king battle. The challenge was accepted without delay, although the king had but a few men, and the result of his battle was soon decided. King Ring fell, together with all his courtiers; but Ingjald took Hunvor and Ingeborg and carried them away to India. Jokul Ironback went to seek after the foster-brothers, wishing to revenge the death of his brother-in-law, Harek.

Now the story goes on to tell about Viking and Halfdan staying at Svafe. Seven nights had passed away when Lit met Halfdan and brought the horn to him. This made Halfdan very glad, and he went to Viking, whom almost everybody then thought to be not far from death. Halfdan put a drop of fluid from the upper part of the horn on Viking's lips. This brought Viking to his senses; he began to grow stronger and was like unto a person awakening from a slumber; and the uncleanness fell from him as scales fall from a fish. Thus he, day by day, grew better and was restored. After this they got ready to depart from Svafe, and directed their course north of Balegard-side. There they saw eighteen ships, all of large size and covered with black tents. Said Halfdan: Here I think Jokul Ironback and his wife, the ham-leaper, are lying before us, and I do not know how Lit has parted with them, he being so exhausted that he could not speak. But now I think there is good reason for going to battle. Let everything of value be taken away from the ships, and let stones be put in instead. This was done. Then after a quick rowing to the strangers, they asked who the chieftains were. Jokul gave them his name and asked for their names in return. They said they hight Halfdan and Viking. Then we need not ask what came to pass. A very hot battle took place, and the foster-brothers lost more men than Jokul, for the latter dealt heavy blows. Then Viking, followed by Halfdan, made an attempt to board Jokul's dragon, after which a great number of the crew exchanaged blows with

each other; but although Jokul was the stronger, Halfdan succeeded in giving
him a blow across the back with his sword; yet, in spite of his being without his
coat-of-mail, the sword did not scathe him. Meanwhile Viking came to Halfdan's
assistance. He smote Jokul's shoulder and split his side, thus separating one
arm and both feet, the one above the knee, from the trunk. Then Jokul feel, but
was not yet dead, and said: I knew that when Dis had been forsaken by luck,
much of evil was in store; the first of all was that the villain Lit betrayed her, and
thus succeeded by tricks in stealing the horn from her and at the same time hurt
her, so that she is still confined to her bed from the encounter; but I should also
be inclined to think that he was not escaped without some injury himself either.
Had she been on foot, the matter would not have resulted thus. But I am glad
you have not got the princess Hunvor from my brother-in-law, Ingjald Snout.
After this he soon died, and then a cry of victory was shouted and quarter was
given to the wounded who could be cured. They got much booty there, and on
shore they found Dis almost lifeless from the encounter with Lit. Her they
seized, put a belg (whole skin) over her head, and stoned her to death.
Hereupon they went back to Svafe and cured the wounds of their men. And
having equipped twenty-four ships, all well furnished with men and weapons,
they announced that they were bound for India.

CHAPTER 7

Ingjald Snout made great preparations, fortifying the walls of his burg (town,
city) and collecting a great number of people, some of which were rabble of the
worst kind. As soon as the foster-brothers had landed they harried the country
with fire and sword; everybody was in fear of them, and before Ingjald was
aware of it they had made a great plunder. Now he goes against them; they
met, and a battle was fought. Halfdan and Viking thought they had never before
been in so great danger as in this battle. The foster-brothers showed great
bravery, and toward the end of the battle more men began to fall in Ingjald's
army. The battle lasted four days, and at last none but Ingjald remained on his
feet. He could not be wounded at all, and seemed to move through the air as
easily as on the ground. Finally, by surrounding him with shields, they
succeeded in getting him captive, put him in chains, and bound his hands with a
bow string. It was then so dark that they did not think it convenient to kill him on
the spot, Viking being unwilling to slay a man at night-time. They ran into the
burg and carried Hunvor and Ingeborg away to their ships. Here they lay during
the night; but in the morning the warders were dead, and Ingjald was not to be
found, his chains lying unbroken and the bow-string not untied. No mark of iron
could be found on the warders, and thus it was clear that Ingjald had made use
of troll-craft. Now they hoisted their sails, left this country, and directed their
course homeward to Sweden. Then Viking made preparations for the wedding,
and married Hunvor. At the same time Halfdan began his suit and asked for the
hand of Ingeborg, the daughter of the jarl. Word was sent to jarl Herfinn of
Woolen Acre. He came and gave a favorable answer, and it was agreed that
Halfdan should marry Ingeborg. Arrangements for the wedding were made, and
the marriage ceremony was performed. The foster-brothers stayed there during
the winter. The following summer they went abroad with then ships, waged wars
in the Baltic, and having got great booty they returned home in the fall. Thus

they lived as vikings three years, spending only the winters at home; and none were more famous than they. One summer they sailed to Denmark; here they harried and entered the Limfjord, where they saw nine ships and a dragon lying at anchor. They immediately directed their fleet toward these ships, and asked for the name of the commander. He said he hight Njorfe, and added: I am the ruler of the Uplands in Norway, and I have just gotten my paternal heritage; but what is the name of those who have just come? They told him this. Said Halfdan: I will offer to you, as to other vikings, two conditions: the one what you give up your fee ships and weapons, and go ashore with us. Answered Njorfe: This seems to me hard terms, and I choose rather to defend my fee, and, if need be, fall with bravery, than to flee feeless and dishonored, although you have a larger army and ships of greater size and number than mine. Said Viking: We shall not be so mean as to attack you with more ships than you have; five of our ships shall therefore lie idle during the battle. Answered Njorfe: This is bravely spoken. And so they got ready for the battle, which then began. They fought with their ships stem to stem. The attack was very violent on both sides, for Njorfe fought with great daring, and the foster-brothers also showed great bravery. Three days they fought, but sill they did not seem to know who would win. Asked then Viking: Is there much fee in your ships? Answered Njorfe: No, for from those places where we have been harrying this summer the bondes fled with their fee, and hence but little booty has been taken. Said Viking" Unwise it seems to me to fight only for the sake of outdoing each other, and thus spill the blood of many men; but are you willing to form a league with us? Answered Njorfe: It will be good for me to form a league with you , although you are not a king's son, for I know that your father was jarl, and an excellent man; and I am willing to have a foster-brotherhood formed between us on the condition that you hight jarl and I king, according to our birth-right, which must remain unchanged whether we are in my kingdom or in any other. During this talk Halfdan was silent. Viking asked why he had so little so say in the matter. Answered Halfdan: It seems to me that it may be good to make such an agreement betwixt you; but I shall not be surprised if you should get to feel that some or other of Njorfe's relatives become burdensome to you. I will however, have nothing to do with this matter—will neither dissuade nor encourage you. The result was, that Njorfe and Viking came to terms and formed a foster-brotherhood, giving oaths mutually on the terms which have before been state. They waged wars during the summer and took much booty; but in the fall they parted, Njorfe going to Norway, and Viking accompanied by Halfdan, to Sweden. But soon after Viking had come home, Hunvor was taken sick and died. They had son, who hight Ring. He was brought up in Sweden until he was full-grown, and became a king of that country. He did not live long, but had a great many descendants. The foster-brothers kept on waging wars every summer and became very famous; during their warfares they gathered so many ships that they had fifty in all.

CHAPTER 8

It must be told of Ingjald Snout, that he gathered an innumerable army and went to search for he foster-brothers, Viking and Halfdan. And one summer they met in the Baltic, Ingjald having forty ships. It came straightway to a fight, and they

504

fought in such a manner that it was not way to see which side would win. At last Viking, immediately followed by Njorfe and Halfdan, tried to board Ingjald's dragon. They made a great havoc, killing one man after the other. Then Ingjald rushed toward the stern of the dragon, with a great atgeir (a kind of javelin) ready for slaughter. Now the foster-brothers attacked Ingjald, and although they fought a large part of the day with him they did not wound him, and when the fight seemed to Ingjald to grow very hot, he sprang overboard, followed by Njorfe and Halfdan, both swimming as fast as they could. Viking did not stop fighting before he had slain every man on the dragon, after which he jumped into a boat and rowed ashore. Ingjald kept swimming till the reached the land, and then Halfdan and Njorfe were drawing near to the surf. Ingjald took a stone and threw it at Halfdan, but he dodged under the water. Meanwhile Njorfe landed, and Halfdan soon after him, in another place. They attacked Ingjald mightily, and having fought thus for a long time, they heard a great crash, and looked thither whence it they heard the crash, but on turning their faces back, Ingjald was out of sight, and instead of him there was a grim-looking boar, that left nothing undone as he attacked them, so they could do nothing but defend themselves. When this had been done some time, the boar turned upon Halfdan, bearing away the whole calf of his leg. Straightway came Viking and smote the bristles of the boar, so that his back was cut in two. Then seeing that Ingjald lay dead on the spot, they kindled a fire and burned him to ashes. Now they went back to their ships and bound up the wounds of Halfdan. After this they sailed away from this place north to an isle called Thruma, and ruled by a man who hight Refil a son of the sea-king Mefil. He had a daughter who hight Finna, a maid of surpassing fairness and accomplishments. Viking courted her, and with king Njorfe's help, and Halfdan's bravery , the marriage was agreed to. Then the foster-brothers ended their warfaring. King Njorfe established himself in his kingdom, and Viking took his abode with him and became his jarl, abut Halfdan was made a great herser and dwelt on his byre, called Vags. His land was separated by a mountain from that which was ruled by jarl Viking. They held to their friendship as long as they lived, but it was more cold between Halfdan and Njorfe.

CHAPTER 9

A King, hight Olaf, ruled Fjord-fylke (the country of the fjords). He was a son of Eystein and a brother of Onund, who was the father of Ingjald the Wicked. They were all unsafe and wicked in their dealings. King Olaf had a daughter who hight Bryngerd, whom Njorfe married, took her with him, and got with her nine sons: Olaf, Grim, Geiter, Teit, Tyrfing, Bjorn, Geir, Grane and Toke. They were all promising men, though Jokul far surpassed them all in all accomplishments. He was so haughty that he thought everything below himself . Olaf stood next to him, as a man skillful in all deeds; but he was of a noisy, troublesome and overbearing temperament, and the same might be said of all his brothers, and they boasted very much. Viking had nine sons, the eldest of whom was Thorstein, and the others hight Thorer, Finn, Ulf, Stein, Romund, Finnboge, Eystein and Thorgeir. They were hopeful men, of great skill in action , though Thorstein held the highest rank among them in everything. He was the largest and strongest of men; he was popular, steadfast in his friendship, faithful and reliable in all things. He could not easily be provoked to do harm, but when attacked he revenged himself grimly. If he was insulted, it could scarcely be seen in his daily life whether he liked it or not, but long afterward he would act as if he had just been injured. Thorer was of a most sanguine and vehement temperament; if injured or affronted he would suddenly be seized by an irresistible rage, and, no matter whom he had to do with, or what the result might be, he never hesitated to do whatsoever came into his mind. He was a most adroit man in all kinds of games, and a man of uncommon strength. He was second only to his brother Thorstein. These young men grew up together n the kingdom. In the mountain separating Viking's and Halfdan's lands there was a chasm of fearful depth and of a breadth of thirty ells at the narrowest, so that it was perfectly impassable for human beings. And hence the mountain was not crossed by any paths. It had been tried by king Njorfe and jarl Viking and Halfdan how easily they might leap over the chasm. The result was, that Viking had leaped over it in full armor, Njorfe had done it in his lightest clothes, but Halfdan had only done it by being received on the other side by Viking. Now they all kept quiet for a long time, and the friendship of jarl Viking and king Njorfe remained unimpaired.

CHAPTER 10

Njorfe and Vking became old, and their sons were reapidly advancing in growth. Jokul became in all things a violent and restless man. The sons of Njorfe were of nearly the same age as the sons of Viking, the youngest ones being at this point of our Saga about twelve years old, while Thorstein and Jokul wee at the age of twenty. The sons of Njorfe used to play with the sons of Viking, and the latter were in no way below the former. This made the sons of the king very jealous, and in their jealousy, as in all other things, Jokul surpassed all; and it was easy to see that Thorstein yielded to Jokul in all things, nor was this any reproach to him. Thorstein far surpassed all his brothers and all other men known. Jarl Viking had warned his sons not to vie with the sons of the king in any games, but rather to spare their strength and eagerness. One day the king's sons and the sons of Viking were playing ball, and the game was played very eagerly by the sons of Njorfe. Thorstein, as usual, checked his zeal. He was placed against Jokul, and Thorer was placed against Olaf, and the others were placed in the same manner, according to their age. Thus the day was spent. It happened that Thorer threw the ball on the ground so hard that it bounded over Olaf and fell down again far off. At this Olaf turned angry, thinking that Thorer was mocking him. He fetched the ball; but when he came back the game was being broken up, and the people were going home, Olaf then with the ball-club struck after Thorer, who, seeing it dodged the blow in such a manner that the club touched his head and wounded it. But Thorstein, together with many other people , hurried betwixt them and parted them. Said Jokul: I suppose you think it a thing of no great weight that Thorer got a bump on his head. Thorer blushed at Jokul's words, and thus they parted. Said Thorer then: I have left my gloves behind, and if I do not fetch them Jokul will lay it to my fear. Answered Thorstein: I do not think it advisable that you and Olaf meet. Nevertheless I will go, said Thorer, for they have gone home. So saying, he turned back at a swinging pace, and when he came to the play-ground everybody had left it. Then Thorer turned his steps toward the hall of the king. At the same moment the sons of the king also came home to the hall, and stood near the wall of the hall. Then Thorer turned toward Olaf and stabbed his waist, so that the spear passed through his body; whereupon he withdrew and escaped out of their hands. They, on the other hand, had a great ado over Olaf's corpse; but Thorer went until he found his brother. Now asked him Thorstein: Why is there blood on your spear, brother? Answered Thorer: Because I do not know whether Olaf has not perhaps been wounded by the point of it. Said Thorstein: You perhaps tell of his death. Quoth Thorer: It may be that Jokul will not be able to heal the wound of his brother Olaf, though he be a very skillful man in almost all things. Answered Thorstein: This is a sorry thing that now has happened; for I know that my father will dislike it. And when they came home jarl Viking was out-doors, and looked very stern. Said he: What I looked for from you, Thorer, has now come to pass, that you would be the most luck-forsaken of all my sons. This you have shown, as I think, by killing the son of the king himself. Answered Thorstein: Now is the time father, to help your son, although he has fallen into ill-luck; and that you know means for his purpose I think you have shown by your being aware of Olaf's death while nobody had told you of it. Answered Viking: I am unwilling to sacrifice so much to break my oaths for the life of Thorer: for both of us, king Njorfe and I, have sworn to be faithful and trusty to each other, both in private and public matters. These oaths he has kept in all matters. Now I will not, therefore, show myself worse than he has been; but this I would do if I should fight against him, for there was a time when king Njorfe was as dear to me as my own sons, and it needs not be hinted at that I should give Thorer any help; he must leave, and never more come before my eyes. Answered Thorstein: Why should not all of us brothers then leave home? For we will not part with Thorer, but will stand by one another for weal or for woe. Answered the jarl: That is a mater that rests with you, my son; but great I must call the ill-luck of Thorer, if he is the be the cause of my losing all my sons and my friendship with the king too, who is the doughtiest man in all things, and besides these, my life, which is, however, worth but little. But there is one thing that makes me glad, and that is that it will not fall to the lot of any one to put you to death, although your escape will be narrow enough, and this will all be caused by Thorer's ill-luck; nevertheless, the loss of him will be felt on account of his valor. Now, my son Thorstein, here is a sword, which I will give to you Angervadil is its name, and it has always had victory with it; my father took it from Bjorn Blue-tooth at his death. I have no other distinguished weapons except an old kesia, which I took from Harek Ironhead; but I know that nobody is able to wield it as a weapon. Now if you are going to leave home, my son Thorstein, then it is my advice that you go up to a lek named Vener; there you will find a boat belonging to me, standing in a boat-house; go in it to a holm which lies in the lake; there you will find in a shed food and clothes enough to last you twelve months; take good care of the boat, for there are no more ship in the neighborhood Hereupon the brothers parted with their father. The brother all had good clothes and armor, which had been given them by their father before this happened. Thorstein and his brothers went until they found the boat. Then they rowed to the holm, and found the shed; here enough of all things which they needed, and they took up their abode there.

CHAPTER 11

Now it is to be told that Jokul and his brothers told of the death of Olaf to their father. Said Jokul: This is the only thing to be done, that we bring together an army and march to the house of Viking and burn him and all his sons alive in their house, and even this would scarcely be vengeance enough for Olaf's death. Said Njorfe: I wholly forbid that any harm be done to Viking, for I know that my son has not been slain by his advice, and no one is guilty of this but Thorer. But Viking and I have sworn to each other an oath of brotherhood, and this oath he has kept better than anyone else, and hence I shall not wage any war against him, for I do not think Olaf will be atoned for in the least by slaying Thorer, and thus giving more grief to Viking. And so Jokul did not get any help in this matter from his father. Olaf was buried with the usual ceremonies of olden times, and from this time Jokul began to keep a suit of men. King Njorfe was already growing very old, so that Jokul for he most part had to ward the land. One day it happened that two men went before Njorfe, both dressed in blue frocks. They greeted the king. He asked them for their names. One of them said he hight Gautan, the other said he hight Ogautan, and they bade the king give them winter quarter. Answered the king: To me you look ugly, and I will not receive you. Said Jokul: have you any accomplishments: Answered Ogautan: As to that, we have not much to boast of; still we know many more things than people have spoken to us about. Said Jokul: It seems best to me then that you enter my suite and stay with me. So they did. Jokul did well by them. It had been heard at the king's hall that Viking had banished his sons. Jokul was unwilling to believe it, and went to Viking with a large suite. Viking asked what his errand was, and Jokul asked him what he knew about the miscreant Thorer. Viking told him that he had banished his sons, so that they did not live there. Jokul asked to be allowed to search the rooms of the house. Viking granted this, but said the king would not have thought that he would deceive him. They then searched the rooms, but as might be expected, found nothing; and having done this they returned home. Jokul did not like that he heard nothing of the brothers, and do he said to Ogautan and his comrade: Would not you by your cunning be able to find out where the brothers have their dwelling-place? I guess not, answered Ogautan; you are nevertheless to let me and my brother have a house to sleep in, and nobody must come there before you, nor must you visit the house until after three days. Jokul saw that this was done, and a small separate house was assigned for them to sleep in. Jokul positively forbade all people mentioned them, and he threatened the transgressor of his orders with certain death. Early on the day agreed upon Jokul dame to the house of the brothers. Said then Ogautan: You are too hasty, Jokul, for I have just awaked; still I can tell you about the sons of Viking. You know, I suppose, where there is a lake called Vener. In it is a holm, and on the holm a shed, and there are the sons of Viking. Answered Jokul: If what you say is so, then I have no hope of their being overtaken. Said Ogautan: In all things you seem to me to act like a motherless child, and I do not think you will be able to do much alone. Now I will tell you, continued Ogautan, that I have a belg (skin-bag) called the weather-belg. If I shake it, storm and wind will blow out of it, together with such biting frost and cold that within three nights the lake shall be covered with so strong an ice that you may cross it on horseback if you wish. Said Jokul: Really you are a man of great cunning; and this is the only way of reaching the holm, for there are no ships before you get to the sea, and nobody can carry them so far. Hereupon Ogautan took his belg and shook it, and out of it there came so fearful a snowstorm and such biting frost that nobody could be out of doors. This was a thing of great wonder to all; and after three nights every water and fjord was frozen. Then Jokul gathered together men to the number of thirty. King Njorfe did not like this journey, and said his mind told him it would cause him more and not less sorrow; for in this journey, he said, I will loose the most of my sons and a great many other men, It would have been better if we, according to my will in the beginning , had come to terms with Thorer, and thus kept the friendship of jarl Viking and his sons.

CHAPTER 12

Now Jokul got himself ready for the journey together with his thirty men, and besides them Gautan and Ogautan. The same morning Thorstein awoke in his shed and said: Are you awake, Thorer? Answered he: I am, but I have been sleeping until now. Said Thorstein: It is my will that we get ourselves ready for leaving the shed, for I know that Jokul will come here today together with many men. Answered Thorer: I do not think so, and I am unwilling to go at all; or have you any sign of this" I dreamt, said Thorstein, that twenty-two wolves were running hither, and besides them there were seven bears, and the eighth one, a red-cheeked bear, large and grim-looking. And besides these there were two she-foxes leading the party; the latter were very ugly-looking, and seemed to me the most disgusting of all. All the wolves attacked us, and at last they seemed to tear to pieces all my brother excepting you alone and yet you fell. Many of the bears we slew, and the wolves I killed, and the smaller one of the foxes, but then I fell. Asked Thorer" What do you think this dream means" Made answer Thorstein" I think that the large red-cheeked bear must be the fylgja (follower, guardian-spirit) of Jokul, and the other bears the fylgias of his brothers; but the wolves undoubtedly were, to my mind, as many as the men who came with them; for, certainly they are wolfishly-minded toward us. But besides them there were two she-foxes, and I do not know any men to whom such fylgias belong; I therefore suppose that some persons hated by almost everybody have lately come to Jokul, and thus these fylgias may belong to them. Now, I have told you this my thought about the matter, and we will have to act in the matter pointed out to me in my sleep, and I would that we might avoid all trouble. Says Thorer: I think your dream has been nothing but a scare-crow and idle forebodings, still it would not be uninteresting to try our mutual strength. Quoth Thorstein: I do not think so; it seems to me that an unequal meeting is intended, and I should like that we might get ready to go away from here. Thorer said he would not go away, and it had to be as he would have it. Thorstein arose and took his weapons, and all his brothers did likewise, but Thorer was very slow about it. At the very time when they had gotten themselves ready, Jokul came up with his men. The shed had two doors, one of which Thorstein guarded together with three of his brothers, the other was guarded by Thorer together with four men. A sharp attack then began; the brothers warded themselves bravely, but Jokul attacked the door warded by Thorer so strongly that three of his brothers fell, but one of them was driven out of the door to the spot where Thorstein stood. Thorer still guarded the door for a while, being by no means willing to yield. Then he turned out of the door and found his way among the enemies down upon the ice. They surrounded him, but he defended himself very bravely. Thorstein seeing this, ran out of the shed together with those of his brothers who were yet alive, went down onto the ice where Thorer was standing, and now a fierce combat took place. Thorstein and Thorer dealt many heavy blows, and at last all the brothers had fallen excepting Thorstein and Thorer; and all the sons of Njorfe had also fallen save Jokul and Grim. Then Thorstein became very weary, so that he was hardly able to stand. He saw that he would fall; and of the opposite party all had fallen but Gautan and Ogautan. Now Thorer was both weary and wounded, and the night was already growing very dark. Just then Thorstein turned against Gautan and stabbed him through his body with Angervadil, so that he fell to the ground among the other dead bodies. Then three men, Jokul, Grim, and Ogautan, arose and searched for Thorstein among the slain, and they thought they had found him, but the person they found was Jokul's brother, Finn, for they were so much like each other that it was impossible to know them apart. Grim said Thorstein was dead. Said Ogautan, That shall be put beyond a doubt, and he cut his head off, but of course it did not bleed, for he was already dead. After this they went home. King Njorfe asked them how the meeting had turned out, and learning this, he did not approve it at all, saying that now had lost much more than his son Olaf, his seven sons and many other men having died. Now Jokul kept quiet.

CHAPTER 13

In the next place it is to be told that Thorstein lay among the slain so tired out that he was wholly unable to help himself, but he was but little wounded And toward the end of the night he heard a wagon coming along the ice Then he saw a man following the wagon, and he saw that the man was his father. And when the man came to the field of battle, he cleared his way, throwing the dead out of his path, but he threw none with more force than the sons of the king. He saw that all were dead except Thorstein and Thorer. He then asked them whether they could speak at all, and Thorer said that he could. Still Viking saw that he was covered with gaping wounds. Thorstein said that he was not wounded, but very tired. Viking took Thorer in his lap, and then it seemed to Thorstein that his father, in spite of his age, showed great strength. Thorstein went to the wagon himself and laid himself in it with his weapons. Then Viking drove on with the wagon. The weather began to grow dark and cloudy, and it changed so fast that, in a very little while, the whole ice seemed to Viking to give way. Just at the time when the had landed, all the ice had melted out of the lake. Then Viking went home to his bed-chamber. Close by his bed was the entrance to an underground dwelling, and down into it he took his sons; in it was enough food and drink, and clothing, and all things that might be needed. Viking healed the wounds of his son Thorer, for he was a good leech. One end of the house stood in a forest; and here Viking very strongly warned his sons never to leave the underground dwelling, for he said it was sure that Ogautan would straightway find out that they were alive; and then, added he, we may soon look for war. As to this they made good promises. Time passed on until Thorer became altogether whole again. It was now talked abroad throughout

510

the country that all the sons of Viking were dead; but nevertheless, it was talked somewhat after Ogautan that it was not sure whether Thorer was dead or not. Then Jokul bade him seek and try to find out with certainty where Thorer had his dwelling-place. Now Ogautan fell into deep thinking, but still he did not become any surer about Thorer. One day it happened that Thorer said to Thorstein: I am getting very tired of staying in this underground dwelling, now the weather is fine, and my will is that we take a walk into the forest to amuse ourselves. Answered Thorstein: I will not, for we would then break the bidding of our father. Nevertheless, I shall go, said Thorer. Thorstein had no mind to stay behind, and so they went to the forest and spent the day there amusing themselves. But in the evening, when they were about to go home again, they saw a little she-fox scenting round about her in all directions, and snuffing under every tree. Said Thorer: What Satanic being goes there, brother? Answered Thorstein: I really do not know; it seems to me that I have once seen something like it, namely, the night before Jokul's visit to the shed, and I think that we here have the cursed Ogautan. He then took a spear, which he shot at the fox, but she crept down into the ground. After this they went home to their underground dwelling, and did not let on that anything had happened. Shortly afterward, jarl Viking came there and said: Now you have done a bad thing, having broken what I bade you, by leaving the cave, and thus Ogautan has found out that you are here. I therefore expect the brothers soon will come with war upon us.

CHAPTER 14

Shortly after this, Ogautan had a talk with Jokul and said: it is indeed true that I am your right and not your left had. What is there now about that? asked Jokul. Answered Ogautan: It is that the brothers, Thorer and Thorstein, are still alive at Viking's, and are hid by him. Answered Jokul: then I will gather together men, and not give up till we have their lives. Jokul got together eighty men, among whom there were thirty of the king's courtiers, all well busked as to clothes. In the evening they were busked for setting out, being about to leave the next morning. Two young loafers, of whom the one hight Vott and the other Thumal, had just come there, and when they had just gone to bed in the evening, Vott spoke to Thumal: Do you think it is wise brother, that we arise and go to Viking, and tell him of Jokul's plans, for I know it will be the bane of Viking if they come upon him unawares, and it is our duty to go and help him. Made answer Thumal: You are very foolish; do you not think that the watchmen will become aware of us if we travel by night, and then we shall be killed without giving any help to Viking. Said Vott: You always show that you are a coward; but although you dare not move a step, I will nevertheless go and tell Viking what is about being done, for I would gladly lose my life if I could hinder the death of Viking and his sons, for he was often been kind to me. Then Vott arose and dressed himself, and likewise did also Thumal, for the latter had no mind of staying in the bed alone. Now they went their way, and came to Viking's at midnight, and aroused him from his sleep. Vott told him that Jokul was to be looked for there with a large number of men. Said Viking: Well have you done, dear Vott, and your deed surely deserves a reward. Then Viking called together some men from the neighborhood, so that he had thirty men. Then he went down to his sons in the cave, and told them the state of things. Said Thorer: They shall be

511

withstood if they come, for we will come up out of the cave and fight together with you. Answered Viking: You shall not! Let us first see how our fight may turn out, and if it should look hopeless to me, then I will go to that place below which is your cave and make a great noise, and then you must come and help me. Thorstein said that he would do so, and so Viking went away. After daybreak Viking and all his men took their weapons. He took the kesia called Harek's loom in hand; but everybody thought he would not be able to wield it on account of its weight, he being so old. A wonderful change then seemed to take place; for as soon as Viking had put on the armor he seemed to be young a second time. A large yard was inclosed by a high wall in front of Viking's byre: it formed a very good vantage ground, and here he and his men busked themselves for the battle, and weapons were given to Vott and Thumal.

CHAPTER 15

Now it is to be told that Jokul busked himself and all his army for starting early the next morning, and he did not halt in his march before he came to the dwellings of Viking. Viking was standing outside upon the wall of the yard, and bade Jokul and all his men come in. Answered Jokul: Quite otherwise have you deserved than that we should accept your invitation; our errand here is that you give up those mishap-bringing men, Thorstein and Thorer. I will not do it, answered Viking; nevertheless I will not deny that both of them have been here, but I would sooner give up myself than them. Now you may attack us if you like, but I and my men will ward ourselves. They now made a hard attack, but Viking and his men warded themselves bravely. Thus some time passed. Then Jokul tried to scale the wall. Viking and his men slew many men; but now all his own men began to fall. Then Viking went to the place over the underground dwelling, struck his shield hard, and said to Thorstein: We ought to make haste, and for all that we may be too late, for I think our father has fallen already. Thorstein said he was quite ready, and when they came out only Vott and Thumal and three other men were standing with Viking. Nevertheless Viking was not wounded yet; he was only very tired. As soon as the brothers same out Thorstein turned to the spot where Jokul was standing, but Thorer went where Ogautan and his men stood. Twelve of king Njorfe's men attacked Viking and his men. Viking warded himself, and was not wounded by the men who were against him. Their leader hight Bjorn. In a short time Thorer slew all the followers of Ogautan, and stabbed at him with his sword, but Ogautan thrust himself down into the ground, so that only the soles of his feet could be seen. Thorstein attacked Jokul. Said Vott: It is well that you are trying each other's bravery, for Jokul never could bear to hear that Thorstein was a match for him in anything. Now there was a very hard battle between Thorstein and Jokul and it so turned out that Jokul, scarred with many wounds, bounded back, and fell down outside of the wall. But when Jokul had gone away, Viking gave quarter to the men of the king's court that still were alive, and sent them away with suitable gifts, begging them to bring his friendly greetings to king Njorfe. And when Jokul came home Ogautan was there already. Jokul blamed him bitterly for having fled before anybody else. To this made answer Ogautan: It was not possible to stay in the fight any longer, and truly it may be said that we there had to do with trolls rather than with men. But Jokul found that his words rather overdid the matter. Somewhat later king Njorfe's men, to whom quarter had been given by Viking and his men, came home, bringing Viking's greetings to kin Njorfe, and telling him of all the kind treatment they had gotten from Viking. Said the king: Truly is Viking unlike most other men, on account of his high-mindedness and all his bravery, and now, my son Jokul, I speak the truth when I solemnly forbid any war to be waged against Viking form this time forward. Answered Jokul: I cannot bear to have the slayers of my brothers in the garth next to me, and in a word, I declare that Viking and his sons shall never live in peach so far as I am concerned and I shall never cease persecuting them before they are all sent to Hel (the goddess of death). Answered the king: Then I shall try and see who of us two is the more blest of friends, for with all those who are willing to follow me I will go and help Viking; it seems to me to be of great weight that you do not become the bane of Viking, for it that should follow, I would be forced to one of two things, either to have you killed, and that would be the cause of evil talk, or to break my oaths which I have sworn, namely, that I would avenge Viking if I should outlive him. And thus he ended his speech. Viking had a talk with his sons, and said to them: Owing to Jokul's power I dare not keep you here; but there is another matter of still more weight, and that is , that I do not want any discord to arise between me and king Njorfe. Said Thorstein: What will you then advise us to do? Answered Viking: There is a man, by name Halfdan, who rules over Vags; Vags is on the other side of yonder mountain. Halfdan is my old friend and foster-brother. To him I will send you, and commend you to his good will; but there are many dangerous hindrances in the way, especially two hut-dwellers (robbers), one of whom is worse to deal with than the other the name of one of them is Sam, and the other is hight Fullafle; the latter has a dog called Gram, with which it is almost as dangerous to deal as with the robber himself. Now I am not sure that you will reach Vags, though you may escape both of these robbers, for there is a chasm along the mountain so deep and broad that I do not know any one who has passed it but my foster-brothers and myself; but I should indeed think it more likely that Thorstein night pass it, whereas I feel less hopeful about Thorer. Shortly afterward the brothers busked themselves for setting out, having all their weapons with them. Then Viking gave the kesia to Thorer; he handed a gold ring to his son Thorstein, begging him to give it to Halfdan as a token of their old friendship.

Now be patient my son Thorer, says Viking; although Halfdan may be peevish toward you, or does not look much to you or your errand. Then the sons took leave of their father, who was so deeply moved that the tears trickled down his cheeks. Viking looked after them as they were going away, and said: I shall never in my life see you again, and nevertheless you , my son Thorstein, will reach an old age, and become a very distinguished man; and now farewell, and all hail to you both. Then the old man returned home, but his sons climbed the mountain until they reached a hut in the evening. The door was half shut. Thorer stepped over to it, and by using all his strength, he pushed it open; and when they had entered the hut, they saw there a great deal of wares and supplies of all kinds. There was a large bed. And at nightfall the hut-dweller, a man of somewhat frowning look, came home. He said: Are you here, you mishap-bringing men,–you sons of Viking, Thorstein and Thorer, who have slain seven of the sons of Njorfe? And now all their ill-luck shall come to an end, for it will be an easy matter for me to strike you to the ground. Who is that, says

Thorer, who so boastingly insults us? Answered the robber: My name is Sam; I am the son of Svart; my brother's name is Fullafle; he is boss in the other hut. Said Thorstein: I see that feyness (1) calls on us two brothers, if you alone kill both of us, and therefore I do not hesitate to test our valor, but Thorer shall stand by without taking any part in our combat. At the same time Sam ran suddenly under Thorstein with so great speed, that the latter lost the hold he had gotten, but still did not fall. Then Thorer ran to Sam, stabbing him with his kesia in one side so that it came out at the other side, and thus Sam fell down dead. So they stopped there during the night and had a good rest, for there was plenty of food. They made the hut warm, but did not carry away any fee with them. In the morning they left the hut, but in the evening of the same day they came to another hut, much larger than the former one. There also the door was half shut. Thorer stepped over to the door, intending to push it open, but he could not. He used all his strength, but still the door would not open. Then Thorstein stepped over to the door, and pushed it until it gave way, and so they went into the hut. On the one side there was a stack of wares and on the other one of logs; a bed was placed in the inner part of the hut, crosswise, and it was so large that they were surprised at its size. At one end of the bed was something like a large, round bedstead, and they judged that it must be the couch of the dog Gram. They then seated themselves and built a fire before them, and long after nightfall they heard heavy footsteps outside; presently the door was opened, and a giant of stupendous stature entered, carrying bound on his back a large bear, and a string of fowl on his breast. He laid his burden down on the floor, saying: Fie! Here I have the miscreants, the sons of Viking, who, on account of their ill-fated deeds, are held in the worst repute throughout the whole land. But how did you escape the hands of my brother Sam? We escaped in such a manner, said Thorstein, that he lay dead on the spot. You have taken advantage of him in his sleep, said Fullafle. By no means, said Thorstein, for we fought with him, and my brother Thorer slew him. I shall not act as a nithing toward you tonight, says Fullafle; you shall stay till tomorrow morning, and have what good you want. Then he hut-dweller cut his game to pieces, took a table and put victuals on it, whereupon they all took to eating, and after their supper they went to bed. The two brothers slept together in some marketable cloaks. The dog growled as they passed by him. Neither party tried to deceive the other. In the morning both parties arose early. Said Fullafle: Now, Thorstein, let us try each other's strength, but let Thorer fight with my dog in another place. Answered Thorstein: That shall be according to your wish. Now they went out of the hut and over on the lawn which fronted it, and suddenly the dog, and his jaws wide open leaped upon Thorer. Both Thorer and the dog fought fiercely, for the dog warded off every blow with his tail, and when Thorer tried to pierce him with his kesia, he escaped by biting the weapon at every stab. Thus they fought for three hours and Thorer had not yet succeeded in wounding him. Once Gram suddenly darted upon Thorer and bit a slice out of his calf. At the same time Thorer stabbed the dog with the kesia, pinning him down to the ground, and soon after Gram expired. But of Fullafle it is to be told that he had a large meker (Anglo-Saxon mece, a kind of sword) in his hand, and Thorstein had his sword also. They had a long and severe struggle; for Fullafle was wont to deal heavy blows. But as Angervadil bit armor no less than flesh, he fell dead, and Thorstein was wholly without a wound.

514

ENDNOTES:

1. Feyness (Icel. Feigð) means the approach or foreboding of death.

CHAPTER 16

Now the brothers busked themselves for leaving, and continued their walk until they reached a great chasm, which it seemed to Thorstein it would be very dangerous to pass. Nevertheless, he made himself ready to leap over the abyss, and did it. He was immediately followed by Thorer, but when Thorstein had reached the other side of the chasm and looked round, Thorer had just reached the same and was falling down into the chasm. Thorstein succeeded, however, in seizing him and pulling him up again. Said Thorstein then: Brother, you always show that you are a dauntless fellow; so you did now, too, for you might know that it would be certain death to you if you should fall into the chasm. It did not happen this time, answered Thorer, for you saved me, as you have so often done before. Then they proceeded on their journey until they came to a large river, which was both deep and rapid. Thorstein said they must look for the ford, but without delay Thorer waded into the river, and not far from the bank the water was so deep that the bottom could not be reached, and therefore he had to sustain himself by swimming. Thorstein not being minded to be standing on the bank, threw himself into the river and swam after him. Thus they reached the other bank, where they wrung their wet clothes. But while they were doing this the weather grew so bitterly cold that their clothes froze hard as a stone, and so they could not put them on. At the same time a fearful snow storm arose, and it was thought that Ogautan was the cause of it. Thorstein asked Thorer what was the best thing for them to do. Answered Thorer: I think we can do nothing better than to dip our clothes in the river, for in cold water things soon thaw out. So they did, and thereby were able to put on their clothes again. Then they went on until they came tot he byre of Vags. It being night when they came there, the door of the house was locked, so they could not enter. They kept knocking at the door a long time, but nobody came to it. In the yard lay a beam twenty fathoms long. This they brought upon the roofs of the houses, and they rode upon it In such a manner that every timber began to creak, and all the inmates of the house became so frightened that they ran each into his corner. Then Halfdan went to the door and out to the front yard, and the brothers now went over to him and greeted him. Halfdan gave them a cold and reserved answer, asking them, however, for their names. They gave him their names, adding that they were the sons of jarl Viking, and that they brought greetings from the latter to him. Said Halfdan: I cannot talk about foster-brothership between us; to me it seems that many a man keeps his word of foster-brothership but middlingly well, and no more; and as for you , who have slain the most of king Njorfe's sons, it also seems to me that you have not regarded the sanctity of foster-brothership in respect to many of Njorfe's descendants. Still you may enter my house, and lodge here to-night, if you like. Then Halfdan went in at a swinging pace, followed by the brothers. They entered the stofa (sitting-room), where there but a few persons. Nobody took the clothes off the brothers, and thus they sat during the evening, till people began to go to bed; then a dish containing porridge, and a spoon in each end of it was placed on the table before them. Thorer began to eat the porridge. Said Thorstein then: You are very inconsistent in regard to your pride; and, so saying, he took the dish and threw it on the floor in the further part of the room, so that it broke to pieces. Here-upon the people went to bed. The brothers had no bed, and got but very little sleep during the night. Early in the morning they got up and busked themselves for leaving. But when they had got outside the door the old man came to them and asked them: What did you say last night, or whose sons did you say you were? Made answer Thorer: What more do you know now that when we told you we were the sons of jarl Viking: Said Thorstein: Here is a golden finger-ring, which he begged me to give to you. Said Thorer: I think he will be the worse off how shows him anything of it. Made answer Thorstein: Be not so peevish, brother! Here is the gold ring, as a token that you should receive us in such a manner that we might be comforted and protected at your house. Halfdan took the ring, became glad, and said: Why should I not receive you, and do all the good in my power for you? To do so is my duty, on account of my relations to my friend Viking. You seem to be men blest with good luck. Said Thorer: The adage is indeed a true one, that it is good to have two mouths for the two kinds of speech. Last night, soon after we had come to you, you treated us quite otherwise. I therefore am inclined to think you a coward, and you everywhere show your slyness. Said Thorstein: Let us be patient, Halfdan, with my brother, although he is cross in his words to you, for he is a reckless man in his words and doing. Answered Halfdan: I have heard that you are the most doughty of men, and that Thorer is hot-tempered and reckless; still, I think that you are in every respect a man of more spirit. Hereupon they went into the house, their clothes were taken off them, and every attention was shown them. They stayed there during the winter, and enjoyed the most hearty treatment. But in the beginning of spring Thorstein said to Halfdan: We shall now leave this place. Answered Halfdan: What is your best advice? Made answer Thorer: I wish you would give me a ship, manned with a crew, for I intend to set out and wage war and gain booty. To this Halfdan gave his consent. After busking themselves properly, they sailed to the south, along the coast of the country, until they met with two vessels, which had been sent out by their father, and were filled with men and good weapons. Now Thorstein sent back the ship which had been given to him by Halfdan, and sent the crew with it; but the brothers became skippers, one on each of the two ships. They waged wars in many places during the summer, and gained much fee and fame. In the fall they landed on an island which was ruled by the bonde, whose name was Grim. He bade them stay with him through the winter, and they accepted his offer. Grim was married and had an only daughter, by name Thora, a tall and fine-looking girl. Thorer fell in love with her, and told his brother Thorstein that he wanted to marry her. Thorstein talked about the matter to Grim, they bonde, but the latter flatly refused to give his consent. Answered Thorstein: Then I challenge you to fight with me in a holm-gang, and he who wins shall be master of your daughter. Grim said he was ready for the holm-gang. The next day they took a blanket, which they threw under their feet, and then they fought the whole day very bravely, but in the evening they parted, neither of them having received any wound. The second and the third days they fought, but the results were the same as the first day. One day Thorer asked the daughter of the bonde how it came to pass that Grim could not be vanquished. She said there was in the fore part of his helmet a stone, which made him quite invincible as long as it was not taken away from him. This Thorer told to

516

Thorstein; and on the fourth day of their fight Thorstein threw his sword, grasping the helmet of his antagonist with both his hands with so great force that the cords of the helmet were severed. Shortly after he attacked Grim, and now Thorstein's greater strength was shown. He brought Grim down, but gave him quarter. Then Grim asked who had advised him to take the helmet. Thorstein said that Thora had told it to Thorer. Then she wants to be married, answered Grim, and it shall so be. Thus it was resolved that Thorer should marry Thora. In the beginning of spring Thorstein set out to carry on wars, leaving Thorer at home. The newly married couple took to loving each other very much, and they got a son, whom they named Harald. This was their only child. He afterward took his father's kesia, after which he was nick-named and was called Harald Kesia.

CHAPTER 17

A king was named Skate, a son of Erik, who again was a son of Myndil Meitalfsson. Skate was king in Sogn, and with his queen had had two children, a son named Bele, who was a very excellent man, and a daughter who hight Ingeborg. At this time she was not in the kingdom, having been spell bound (and thus removed from the country). Skate had been a berserk and a very great viking, and he had forced his way onto the throne of Sogn. There was a man who hight Thorgrim, and who had to defend the realm against the invasion of foes. He was a great champion and a warlike man, but not over faithful. Between Thorgrim and the king's son, Bele, there was a warm friendship. Bele had great celebrity throughout all lands. It had happened, after king Skate had grown very old, both his children still being young, that two vikings, one named Gautan and the other Ogautan, had landed in his country. They had taken he king by surprise, and offered him two conditions, either to fight a battle with them, or give up his land and become a jarl under them. King Skate, though he had no troops to meet them with would rather die with honor than lie with shame; he would rather fall in his kingdom than serve his foes. He therefore went to battle, having no other troops than his courtiers. Thorgrim escaped with the king's son, Bele, but Ingeborg remained at home in her bower. In the combat with Ogautan, king Skate fell with honor, but those of his men who escaped death in the battle fled to the woods. Now Ogautan took the kingdom into his charge, and had the title of king given to himself. He asked Ingeborg to become his wife, but she flatly refused, saying she would rather kill herself than marry the bane of her father, and such a villain, too, as Ogautan; for you , she said, are more like the devil himself than like a man. At this Ogautan grew angry, and said: I shall reward you for you foul language, and I hereby enchant you, so that you shall get the same stature and look as my sister Skellinefja, and the same nature also as she, as far as you may be capable of assuming it; and spell-bound, you shall inhabit that cave which is on the deep river, and you shall never escape out of his enchanted state until some man of noble birth is willing to have you, and pledges himself to marry you; still you can never escape until I am dead. But my sister shall wear your looks. Said Ingeborg: I cause you to be so enchanted that you shall keep this kingdom only for a short time, and never have any good of your reign. The spells pronounced by Ogautan proved true, and Ingeborg disappeared. Soon afterward, the king's son, Bele, came thither again, together with Thorgrim and many other men. It was night, and they set fire to the upper story of the house in which the two brothers slept, and burnt it up, together with the people who lived in it, except the brothers who escaped through an underground passage and fled, without stopping until they came to the court of king Njorfe. Bele took possession of his country again, and Thorgrim remained in his former position as warder of the king's land.

CHAPTER 18

A king, named Vilhjalm (William), ruled over Valland. He was a wise man, and was blest with many friends. He had a daughter, who hight Olof, and was a woman of great culture. Now it is to be told that Jokul, Njorfe's son, after the departure of the sons of Viking, made Thorstein and Thorer outlaws in every place within the boundaries of his kingdom. King Njorfe did not consent to it, for he and Viking kept their friendship during their whole life. Once Ogautan had a talk with Jokul, and asked him if he would not like to get married. Jokul asked him where he saw a match for him. Answered Ogautan: Vilhjalm of Valland has a daughter named Olof, and I think a marriage with her would add to your honor. Said Jokul: why not then make up our minds as to this subject? So they busked themselves for the voyage, and together with sixty men they sailed for Valland. Here they paid a visit to king Vilhjalm, who received Jokul very heartily, for his father, Njorfe, was well known throughout all lands. Now Jokul asked for Olof in marriage, and Ogautan pleaded with the king in his behalf, but the latter appealed to his daughter. And straightway after this conversation thirty very brave-looking men entered the hall. The one who went before them was the tallest and fairest, and he went up to the king and greeted him. As soon as Ogautan saw these men his voice fell, his beard sunk, and he begged Jokul and his other men not to mention his name so long as they stayed in that land. The king asked the stately men what they hight, and the chief called himself Bele, and said he was the son of Skate, the king, who was ruler of Sogn. My errand hither, he added, is to woo your daughter. Made answer the king: Jokul, the son of Njorfe, came here before you on the same errand; now I will settle the mater in this way, that she choose herself which one of the two wooers she will have. Then the king placed Bele on one side of himself, and there was a great banquet. After three nights they took a walk to the bower of the princess, asking her which one of the two wooers, Jokul or Bele, she would marry, and it soon appeared that she would rather marry Bele; but at that moment Ogautan threw a round piece of wood into her lap, whereby her nature was suddenly changed to such an extent that she refused and married Jokul. Then Bele returned to his ships. Jokul and Bele had formerly been on good terms, so that some people say that Bele had got a reward for killing Thorstein and Thorer. Bele did not blame Jokul though the daughter of the king declined to marry him (Bele), for the matter depended upon her decision. Thereupon Bele went home to his kingdom and after the wedding Jokul also repaired homeward accompanied by Ogautan.

CHAPTER 19

Now our saga must turn to Thorstein at the time when he was returning home from his warfare, bound for Grim the bonde, for his brother Thorer resided in that island. Jokul got news of Thorstein's voyages. He spoke to Ogautan, asking him to try his tricks and by witchcraft bring about a storm against Thorstein, in order that he might be drowned, together with all his men. Ogautan said he would try, mo matter what the result might be. Then, with his incantations, he caused so tremendous a storm against Thorstein that his ships were wrecked amid the tumultuous waves, and all his crew perished. Thorstein held out well a long time, but at last he became tired of swimming, and then he had reached the surf and was beginning to sink down. At this moment he saw an old woman, of very great stature, wading from the shore out toward him. She wore a shriveled skin-cloak, which fell to her feet in front, but was very short behind, and her face was very large and like that of a monster. She stepped over to him and, seizing him up from the sea, said: Will you accept life from me, Thorstein? Answered he: Why should I not, or what is your name Said she: My name is uncommon; it is Skellenefja; but you will have to make some sacrifice in return for your life. Said he: What is it? Made answer she That you grant me the favor that I ask of you. Said thorstein: You will ask nothing from me that will not bring me good luck; but when shall the favor be granted: Answered she: Not yet. Then she bore him ashore, and now he had come to that island governed by Grim. She then wrestled with him till he grew warm, whereupon they parted, each wishing to the other success. Then she walked on, for she said she had other places to call at. But Thorstein went home to the byre, and his meeting there with his brother was the cause of great joy to both of them; and so Thorstein remained there during the winter, and very much was made of him. Now we must turn to Jokul and Ogautan as they were sailing homeward. One very fine day it happened that their ship was suddenly shrouded in darkness, accompanied by such a biting frost and cold that nobody on board dared to turn his face against the wind. They covered their faces with their clothes; but when the weather had cleared off again they saw Ogautan hanging in the hole of the mast-head, and he was dead. Jokul looked upon his death as a great loss, and returning to his kingdom he remained quite. Early the next spring Thorstein and Thorer busked themselves for a voyage, intending to visit their father, Viking; and when they came as far as to Deep River, before they knew of it, Jokul came there to them with thirty men. A combat between them straightway began. Jokul was very eager in the fight, and so was his brother Grim. Thorer and thorstein defended themselves bravely, and a long time passed before these brothers received any wounds from Jokul and his men, for not only did Thorstein deal heavy blows, but Angervadil also bit iron as well as cloth. Thorer defended himself excellently, although he did not have his kesia, which he had left at home. He and Grim met, and they fought very bravely; still the end of the fight was that Grim fell to the ground, dead. By this time Thorstein had slain eighteen men, but, as might be expected, he was both tired and wounded, and so was Thorer. Then the brothers turned their backs together and still defended themselves well. Now Jokul, with his eleven men, pursued them and made so valiant an attack that Thorer fell. Then Thorstein defended himself manfully until there remained no more than Jokul and three of his men. But then Jokul stabbed Thorstein with his sword, wounding him in the upper part of the thigh;

and Jokul being a strong man, and bearing on the sword with all his might while he stabbed him, thorstein, who was very tired, and was standing on the very edge of the riverbank, fell down from the crag, while it was all that Jokul could do to stop himself so that he did not fall also. After this Jokul went home, thinking he had slain Thorstein and Thorer; and having come home he remained quiet. But now it is to be told of Thorstein, that he, having fallen from the crag, alighted upon a grassy spot among the rocks; but, being tired and wounded, he was unable to more, and yet he was in his full senses after he had fallen. Angervadil fell out of his hand and down into the river. Thorstein was lying there betwixt life and death, and expecting soon to breathe his last. But before he had lain thus very long he saw Skellinefja coming; she was clad in her skin-gown, and looked no fairer than before. She approached the place where Thorstein was lying, and said: it seem to me, Thorstein, that your misfortunes will never come to an end, and now you seem already to be breathing your last, or will you now grant me the favor upon which we formerly agreed: Said Thorstein: I do not now find myself able to render much of any service to you. Made answer she: My request is that you promise to marry me, and then I will try to heal your wounds. Said Thorstein: I do not know as I had better make that promise, for to me you look like a monster. Said she: Still you have your choice between these two things. You must either marry me or lose your life; and in the latter case, you break, in the bargain, the oath which you swore to me when you pledged yourself to grant my favor after I had saved you at Grim's Island. Said Thorstein: There is much truth in your words, and it is better to keep one's promise; hence I vow that I will marry you, and you will prove to be my best helper in time of need; still I should like to stipulate with you that you get me my sword back, so that I may wear it in case my life is prolonged. Says she: So be it. And having taken him up in her skin-gown, she leaped, as if quite unencumbered, up over the crags and proceeded until a large cave was before them. Having entered the cave, she bandaged Thorstein's wounds and laid him on a soft bed, and within seven nights he was almost healed. One day Skellinefja had left he cave, and in he evening she came back with the sword, which was then dripping wet, and she gave it to thorstein. Said she: Now I have saved your life twice and given you your sword back, of which you are fonder than of aught else; and a fourth thing, which is of great importance to both of us, is that I hanged Ogautan. And yet you have completely rewarded me, for you have delivered me from the spell-bound condition into which Ogautan enchanted me. My name is Ingeborg; I am the daughter of king Skate and the sister of Bele, but my only means of delivery from bondage was that some man of noble birth should promise to marry me. Now you have done this, and I am freed form bondage. Now you must busk yourself for leaving he cave and follow my advices, and you will find my brother Bele and four men with him. Among the latter will be his land-warden, Thorgrim Kobbe. From Jokul they have received some money. Offered as a price for your head, and they will being a battle with you. I do not care if you do kill Thorgrim and his companions, but spare the life of my brother Bele, for I should like to have you become his foster-brother; and if you have a mind to marry me, then go with him home to Sogn and woo me. I shall be there before you, and it may be that I will look otherwise to you then that now. Then they parted, and he had not gone far before he met Bele, accompanied by four men, and, at their meeting, Thorgrim said: It is good, Thorstein, that we have found each other.

Now we shall try to win the price put upon your head by Jokul. Said Thorstein: it seems possible to me that you may lose the fee and forfeit your life too.

CHAPTER 20

Now we must tell about Thorstein that he was attacked by Bele and his men, but he defended himself well and bravely, and the result was that Thorgrim and three of his companions fell. Then Thorstein and Bele entered a new contest. Thorstein defended himself, but would not wound Bele. Bele kept attacking Thorstein, until the latter seized him and set him down at his side, saying: You are wholly in my power, but I will not only give you your life, but also offer you an opportunity to be come my foster-brother. You shall be king and I shall be herser, and in addition to this I will woo your sister Ingeborg, and get her estates in Sogn as a dowry. Said Bele: This is no very easy matter, for my sister disappeared, so that nobody knows what has become of her. Answered Thorstein: She may have come back. Said Bele: I do not see how she could get a doughtier fellow than you are, and I give my full consent to the proposition. Having settled this with their words of honor, they went home to Sogn. Bele soon became aware that his sister had come back, and that she had not lost any of that blooming beauty which she had had before in her youthful days. Thorstein began to suit, and asked that Ingeborg might become his wife. This was resolved upon. As a dowry she got from her home all the possessions lying on the other side of the fjord. The byre where Thorstein resided was called Framness, but the byre governed by Bele was called Syrstrond. The next spring Thorstein and Bele set out to wage wars, having five ships, and during the summer they harried far and wide, and got enough of booty, but in the fall they returned home again having seven ships. The next summer they went out a harrying again, but got very little booty, for all vikings shunned them; and having reached the small rocky islands called Elfarsker, they anchored in a harbor in the evening. Thorstein and Bele went ashore, and crossed that ness (peninsula) toward which their ships were lying. But having crossed the ness, they saw twelve ships covered with black tilts. On shore they saw tents, from which smoke arose, and they seemed to be sure that these tents must be occupied by cooks. Having taken on a disguise, they went thither, and having come to the door of a tent, they both placed themselves in it in such a manner that the smoke did not find any out-way. The cooks made use of abusive words, and asked what sort of beggars they were, as they were guileful enough to want them burnt alive or smothered. Bele and Thorstein made an ugly disturbance, and answered with hoarse voices that they came to get food; or, said they, who is the excellent man who commands the fleet lying here at the shore? Said they: You must be stupid old men if you have not heard of Ulfe, who is called Ufe the Unlucky, and is the son of Herbrand the Bigheaded. This Ufe is the brother of Otunfaxe, and we know there are no men under the sun more celebrated than these two brothers. Said Thorstein: You tell good tidings. Shortly after, Thorstein and Bele returned to their own men, and early the next morning, having busked themselves, they rowed around the ness and immediately shouted the cry of battle. The others the quickly busked themselves, took their weapons, and a vehement battle began. Ufe had more men, and was himself a most valiant warrior. They fought for a long time in such

521

a manner that it could not be seen which side would gain the victory. But on the third day Thorstein began to board the dragon commanded by Ufe the Unlucky, and he was followed without delay by Bele, and a great havoc they made, killing all who were between the prow and the mast of the ship. Then Ufe came from the poop and attacked Bele, and they fought for some time, until Bele began to get wounds from Ufe, who handled his weapon dexterously and dealt heavy blows. Meanwhile Thorstein came with his Angervadil, and gave Ufe a blow with it. The sword hit the helmet, split the whole body and the byrnie-clad man from head to foot, and Angervadil struck against the mast-beam so forcibly that both its edges sunk out of sight. Said Bele: This blow of yours, foster-brother, will live in the memory of men as long as the North is peopled. Hereupon they offered to the vikings two terms, either to give up and save their lives, or to have a combat. But they preferred to accept a quarter from Thorstein and Bele. The latter gave pardon to all, and they eagerly accepted it. Here much booty was taken, and having stayed three nights, during which time the wounded were healed, they repaired home in the autumn.

CHAPTER 21

At springtime the foster-brothers busked themselves for leaving home, and had fifteen ships. Bele commanded the dragon which had been owned by Ufe the Unlucky. It was a choice ship, its beak and stern being whittled and carved and extensively overlaid with gold. King Bele got the dragon, for it was the choicest part of the booty which they took when they had slain Ufe, it always being their custom to give to Bele the most costly parts of the booty. No ship was thought better than this dragon excepting Ellide, which was owned by Ufe's Brother, Otunfaxe. Ufe and Otunfaxe and inherited these ships from their father, Herbrand, and Ellide was the better one of the two in these respects, that it had fair wind wherever it sailed, and it almost understood human speech. But the reason why Otunfaxe and not Ufe had gotten Ellide was, that Ufe had fallen into so bad luck that he had killed both his father and his mother, and it seemed to Otunfaxe that if justice should be done, Ufe had forfeited his right of inheritance. Otunfaxe was the superior of the two brothers on account of his strength, stature and witchcraft. Now the foster-brothers went out a harrying, and waged wars far and wide in the waters of the Baltic, but they found but very few vikings, for everybody, upon hearing of them, fled out of their reach. At this time none were more celebrated for their harrying exploits than Thorstein and Bele. One day the foster-brothers were standing on a promontory, on the other side of which they saw twelve ships lying at anchor, and all of them were very large. They rowed rapidly toward the ships and asked who was the commander of the warriors. A man who stood leaning against the mast made answer: Angantyr is my name; I am a son of jarl Hermund of Gautland. Said Thorstein: You are a hopeful fellow; but how old are you? Made answer he: I am now nineteen years old. Asked Bele: Which do you prefer, to give up your ships and fee or to fight a battle with us? Said Angantyr: The more unequal your terms are, the more promptly I make my choice. I prefer to defend my fee, and fall, sword in hand, if such be my fate. Said Bele: busk yourself then; but we will make the attack. Then both of them busked themselves for the battle and took their weapons. Said Thorstein to Bele: There is very little of noble courage in attacking them with fifteen ships, as they have but twelve. Said Bele Why shall we not lay three of our ships aside? And so they did. A hard battle was now fought. Angantyr's warriors dealt so heavy blows, that Bele and Thorstein declared that they had never been in greater peril. They fought the whole day until evening, but in such a matter that it could not be seen which party would gain the victory. The next day they busked themselves again for the fight. Then said Angantyr: To me it seems, king Bele, that it would be wiser not to sacrifice any more of our men, but let us two fight a duel, and he who conquers the other in the holm-gang shall be the victorious party. Bele accepted this challenge; so they went ashore, and having thrown a blanket under their feet, they fought bravely until Bele became tired out and began to receive wounds. Thorstein thought it evident that Bele would not gain the victory over Angantyr, and it came to pass that Bele was not only exhausted but also nigh his last breath. Said Thorstein then: It seems best to me, Angantyr, that you cease your fighting, for I see that Bele is so exhausted that he is almost gone. On the other hand, I will not be mean enough to play the dastard toward you and assist him; but if you become the bane of Bele, then I will challenge you to fight a duel with me; and as to personal valor and strength, I think there is no less difference between me and you than there is between you and Bele. I will slay you in a holm-gang duel, and it would be a great loss if you both die. Now I offer you this condition, that if you spare Bele's life, we will enter into foster-brotherhood upon mutual oaths. Said Angantyr: To me it seems a fair offer that Bele and I enter into foster-brotherhood; but it seems to me a great favor that I may become your foster-brother. Then this was resolved upon and secured by firm pledges on both sides. They opened a vein in the hollow of their hands, crept beneath the sod, (1) and there they solemnly swore that each of them should avenge the other if any one of them should be slain by weapons. Then they reviewed their warriors, and two ships of each party had lost all their men. They healed those who were wounded, and thereupon they left the place with twenty ships, returning home in the fall. They spent the winter at home quietly, and enjoyed great honor. Now none were thought more famous on account of their weapons than these foster-brothers.

ENDNOTES:

1. There was a heathen rite of creeping under a sod partially detached from the earth, and letting the blood mix with the mould. Persons forming a foster-brotherhood would make use of this ceremony.

CHAPTER 22

When spring opened, the foster-brothers, busked themselves for departing from home, and had thirty ships. They sailed to the east and harried in Sweden and in all parts of the Baltic. As usual, they carried on their warfare in the seeming matter, slaying vikings and pirates wherever they could find them, but leaving bondes and chapmen in peace. On the other hand, it is to be told that Otunfaxe, when he heard of the death of his brother Ufe, thought it a great loss. And of him it is to be related, that for three summers together he searched for the foster-brothers. Now it is furthermore to be related, that Bele and his men one day laid their ships near some small rocky islands, called Brenner's Isles. They cast anchor and busked themselves well. Hereupon all the three foster-brothers went ashore, and proceeded until they came to a small byre. There stood a man outside the door splitting wood; he was clad in a green cloak, and was a man of astonishing corpulency. He greeted Thorstein by name. Said Thorstein: We differ widely as to our faculty of recognition; you greet me by name, but I do not remember that I have ever seen you before; what is your name? Says he: My name is an uncommon one. I hight Brenner. I am son of Vifil, and a brother of your father Viking. I was born at the time when my father was engaged in warfare, and had his home with Haloge. I was raised on this island, and have lived here since. But have you , my nephew Thorstein, heard anything about the viking Otunfaxe? Answered Thorstein: No; or what can you tell me about him? Made answer Brenner: This I can tell, that he has been searching for you during the last three years, and now he lies here on the other side of those islands with all his fleet; he wants to avenge his brother Ufe the Unlucky. He has forty ships, all of which are very large, and he himself is as big as a troll, and no weapons can bite him. Said Thorstein: What is to be done now? Made answer Brenner: I can give you no advice unless you have a chance to meet the dwarf Sindre; and moreover he will least of all be embarrassed in finding out what ought to be done. Asked Thorstein: Where can I expect to find him? Made answer Brenner: His home is in the island which lies near the shore, and is called the Smaller Brenner's Isle. He lives in a stone. I scarcely hope that you will be able to find him, but you are welcome here to-night. Said Thorstein: Something else must be done than to keep quiet. Then they went to their ships, and Thorstein launched a boat and rowed to the island. He went ashore alone, and when he came to a little stream, he saw two children, a boy and a girl, playing on its banks. Thorstein asked their names. The boy called himself Herraud, and the girl Herrid. Said she: I have lost my gold ring, and I know this will make my father, Sindre, cross, and I think I may look for punishment. Said Thorstein: Here is a gold ring, which I will give you. She accepted the gold ring and was pleased with it. Said she: I will give this to my father; but is there nothing that I might do that might be of service to you? Made answer Thorstein: Nothing; but bring your father here, that I may have a talk with him, and manage the matter in such a manner that he may advise me concerning those things which are of importance to me. Answered Herrid: I can do this only provided my brother Herraud acts according to my will, for Sindre never refused him anything. Said Herraud: You know I take your part in everything. Thorstein unbuckled a silver belt which he wore, and gave it him; to it was attached a beautifully ornamented knife. Said the boy: This is a nice present; I shall take all possible pains to promote your wish; wait here until I and my sister come back. Thorstein did so, and after a long while the dwarf Sindre came, accompanied by the boy and his sister. Sindre greeted Thorstein heartily, and said: What do you want of me, Thorstein: Made answer Thorstein: I want you to give me advice as to how I may conquer the viking Otunfaxe. Answered Sindre: It seems to me wholly impossible for any human being to vanquish Faxe, for he is worse to deal with than anybody else, and I will advise you not to fight any battle with im, for you will only lose your men, and hence the best thing for you to do is to turn your prows away from the island to-night. Made answer Thorstein: That shall never be; though I knew it before that I should lose my life, I would rather choose that then flee from danger before it has been tried. Said Sindre: I see that you are a very great champion, and I suggest to you that you unload all your ships this

524

night, bring all valuable things on shore, and that you load the ships again with wood and stones. Then busk yourself early to-morrow morning and come to them before they wake; thus you may be able to surprise them in their own tents. (1) You need all this if there shall be any show for you of gaining a victory over Faxe; for I will tell you this, that so far is common iron from biting him, that he cannot even be scathed by the sword Angervadil. Here is a belt-dirk, which my daughter Herrid will give you, and thus reward you for the gold ring, and I am of the opinion that it will bite Otunfaxe if you use it skillfully. Man son, Herraud, proposes this reward for the belt, that you shall name my name if you seem to be hard pressed. Now we must part for a while; fare you well, and good luck to you. By my power of enchanting I promise that my dises (female guardian spirits) shall always follow and assist you. Hereupon Thorstein went to his boat and rowed to his men. Straightway afterward in the night he busked himself and brought the fee out of the ships, but put stones in them instead; and when this was done the old man Brenner came down from his byre, holding in his hand a large club which was all covered with iron and large iron spikes, and so heavy that a man with common strength could scarcely lift it from the ground. Siad Brenner: This hand-weapon I will give you, my nephew Thorstein. You alone can manage it, on account of its weight; but yet, it will be rather light for the fight with Otunfaxe. Now it seems to me that it would be a wise measure if Angantyr would take the sword Angervadil, and you fight with this club, for, although it is no handy weapon, still it will prove fatal to many a man. Now my nephew, I would like to be able to help you more, but I have not the opportunity. Then Brenner went back from the shore.

ENDNOTES:

1. Come their well-arranged tent-pegs for them.

CHAPTER 23

When they had made ready they rowed quickly around the ness, and then they saw the place where Otunfaxe and all his naval force was lying. Without delay they sent forth a shower of stones so hard and vehemently that they slew more than a hundred men in their sleep, having taken them by surprise; but from the moment when the warriors awoke they made a powerful resistance. Then a bloody battle was fought. A large number of the men of the foster-brothers fell, for it could almost be said that Otunfaxe shot from every finger. So it went on until night set in; then ten of the foster-brothers ships were cleared. On the second day the battle began anew, and the slaughter was no less than on the day before. They tried several times to board Faxe's ship, and every time they made great slaughter; but never succeeded in boarding Ellide, both because Faxe defended her and because her sides were so high. But in the evening all the ships of the foster-brothers were cleared, excepting the dragon called Ufe's naut (gift). On both days they saw that two men came from the island, and that they took their positions one on one crag and the other on another, both shooting with all their might at Faxes ship. Here they saw the dwarf Sindre, every one of whose arrows brought down a man, and in this manner a great many of Faxe's men lost their lives. The one on the other crag was Brenner, who was shooting more like a bowman out against the ships. It did happen occasionally that stones came flying over the ships, and every stone thrown by Brenner was inclined to go to the bottom, and as a consequence of this, many of Faxe's ships sunk. Thus it happened that all his ships, too, had been cleared, excepting Ellide. This battle took place at that time of the year when the nights are bright, and therefore they fought the whole night. Thorstein, together with Angantyr and Bele, tried to board the dragon, but there were many men left on Ellide. Faxe ran forward against the foster-brothers, Angantyr, and Bele, and a good many blows were given and received; but no iron weapons would bite Faxe, and before they had fought very long Angantyr and Bele began to receive wounds. At this moment Thorstein approached, and with his club smote the cheek of Faxe in the way that it came handiest for him, but Faxe did not even lout the least at the blow. Thorstein smote again, just as hard as before; and now Faxe did not like the blows, but plunged himself overboard into the sea, so that only the soles of his feet could be seen. To both Bele and Angantyr it seemed disgusting to follow him; but Thorstein ran overboard, and swam after the fleeing Faxe, who looked like a whale. Thus a long time passed until Faxe, having landed, seized a stone and threw it at Thorstein just as he was swimming toward the shore. He warded off the blow by diving, and swam out of the reach of the stone, which made a great splash as it fell. Faxe took up another stone, and a third one, both of which went the same way as the first one. But meanwhile the foster-brothers, Angantyr and Bele, approached. When Thorstein sprang overboard, he threw his club backwards, but Bele had taken it up, and, having now reached the spot where Otunfaxe was standing, he smote him in the back part of the head with the club. This he did uninterrupted again, while Angantyr as the same time was pelting him with large stones. Now Faxe's skull began to ache considerably, and, not liking to receive their blows, he plunged himself form the crag down into the sea, and swam from the shore, pursued by Thorstein. Faxe, observing this, turned against Thorstein, and a wrestle between the two swimming antagonists now took place, in which there were great, fearful tussles. They were alternately drawn into the deep by each other, and yet Thorstein found out that Faxe's strength was great than his own; and it came to pass that Faxe brought Thorstein to the bottom, and thus he lost his power of swimming. Now Thorstein, being almost sure that Faxe intended to bite his throat to pieces, said: How could I ever want you more than now, dwarf Sindre? And suddenly he observed that Faxe's shoulder was seized by a grip so powerful that he soon sank to the bottom, with Thorstein upon him. Thorstein, who by this time had become very tired from the struggle, seized the belt-knife which had been given to him by Sindre, and stabbed Faxe in the breast sinking the knife into his body up to the handle, and then slashing his belly down to the lower abdomen; but still he found that Faxe was not dead yet, for now said the latter: A great deed you have done, Thorstein, in putting me to death, for I have fought ninety battles, and been victorious in all, excepting this: In duels I have been the victor eighty times, so that I certainly may say I have had a holm-gang; but now I am ninety years old. Thorstein thought it useless to let him go on prattling any longer if he could do anything to prevent it, and so he tore away everything that was loose within him. Now the saga goes to tell about Angantyr and Bele, that they took a boat and rowed in it out on the sea, searching for Faxe and Thorstein, but for along time they did not find them anywhere. At last they came to a place where the sea was mixed with blood, and quite red. They thought it must be that Faxe was at the bottom of the water, and that he had slain Thorstein, and after a while they saw some nasty thing floating upon the surface of the sea. They went nearer and saw some large, horrible looking bowels floating there. Shortly afterward Thorstein emerged from the water, but so exhausted and outdone that he could not keep himself afloat. Then they rowed over to him, and dragged him on board. At this time there was but little hope of his life, and still he was not much wounded, but the flesh of his body was almost torn from his bones into knots. They went away and procured some relief for him, after which he soon came to his senses. They went back to the islands, and made a search of the battle-field for the slain; but only thirty men were found fit to be healed. Then they went to the old man Brenner, thanking him for his assistance. Thorstein went to the lesser Brenner's Isle to call on the dwarf Sindre, to whom he made splendid presents, and thus parted in great friendship. Thorstein got the dragon Ellide as his lot of the booty, while Bele got Ufe's naut, and Angantyr as much gold and silver as he wished. Thorstein gave his uncle Brenner all those ships which they could not bring away with them. With three ships they left and went back to Sogn, where they spent the winter.

CHAPTER 24

In the spring they set out for warfare again. Angantyr asked whither they should turn their prows, saying that he thought the Baltic had already been cleared of vikings. Says king Bele: Let us then take our course into the western waters, for we have never been there a harrying before. So they did, and having reached the Orkneys, they went ashore, and waged war, destroying the inhabited parts of these islands by fire and plundering the fee; and so fearfully did they carry on their depredations that all living things fled for fear of them. Herraud hight the jarl who ruled the islands. When he heard of their depredations he gathered an army to meet hem, and marched by day and by night until he found them at an island called Pap Isle. Here it came to a battle between them, and their troops were equal. For two days they fought in such a manner that it could not be seen which party would be victorious. At last the slaughter began to lean to the disadvantage of Herraud, whose ships were cleared, so that the brothers succeeded in boarding them, and finally jarl Herraud fell, together with the most of his men. Hereupon they made expeditions through all the islands, which they subjugated, and the then busked themselves for the home journey. King Bele offered to make Thorstein jarl of all the islands, but the latter declined, saying: I would rather be a herser, and not part with you, than have the name of jarl, and live far away from you. Then he offered Angantyr the jarlship of those islands, which offer was accepted. Afterward they returned home to Sogn, where they stayed the next winter, keeping their men well, both as to weapons and clothes. And now none were thought to be superior to the foster-brothers. Children were granted to them; the sons of Bele hight Helge and Halfdan, and his daughter hight Ingeborg; she was the youngest of children. Thorstein had a son , who hight Fridthjof. Harald grew up in the island with Grim, but when he had reached the age of maturity he set out a harrying and became a most noted man, although he is not much spoken of in this saga. He kept his nick-name, being called Harald Kesia, and a large family is descended from him. Thorstein, Bele, Grim and Harald remained friends as long as they lived.

CHAPTER 25

Now we must return to Jokul, Njorfe's son, who ruled the uplands after the death of Njorfe and Viking. They had preserved their friendship well until their death. Jokul won ships and fee, and was a daring viking, treating his soldiers fairly well, but no better. A few years passed in such a manner that he was the most noted viking, harrying the most of the time in the waters of the Baltic. Thorstein and Bele had not been at home long before they busked themselves for harrying expeditions, and sailing first down along the coast of the country, then through the summer, and got a great booty, consisting of gold and silver, and many other costly things. Afterward they intended to sail home, which they did, and having reached the mouth of Lim Fjord, they were overtaken by a violent storm, which carried them out into the sea, and in a short time the ships were separated. Then the sea began to break over the ships from both sides, and all the men were engaged in baling out the water. And it came to pass that this storm drove the dragon Ellide, tossed by the waves, ashore alone at Borgund's Holm. At the same time Jokul also landed there with ten ships, all thoroughly equipped both as to weapons and crews. And now, as might be imagined, Jokul attacked Thorstein and his men. Thorstein was poorly prepared, for he and his crew were very much exhausted from hard work, and from being tossed about on the sea. A severe and bloody battle was fought, and Jokul, being very vehement, kept cheering his men on, telling them that they would never have a better chance to conquer Thorstein; and, said he, it will be an everlasting shame upon us if he escapes now. Then they attacked Thorstein and his men, not letting up until all his men had fallen, so that nobody but Thorstein alone remained standing on the dragon; but still he defended himself bravely, so that for a long time they could not give him a single wound. At last, however, it came to pass that they came so near to him that they could stab him with their spears; but the most of them he cut out of his reach, for the sword Angervadil bit as keenly as ever. Then Jokul made a desperate attack, and stabbed Thorstein with his spear through the thigh. At the same moment Thorstein dealt Jokul a blow, hitting his arm below the elbow, and cutting the hand off. Meanwhile they succeeded in surrounding Thorstein with shields and capturing him. But it was near night, so that they thought it was too late to put him to death, and so fetters were put on his feet, his hands were tied with a bow-string, and twelve men were set to watch him during the night. When all had been brought ashore excepting these twelve men, together with Thorstein, he said: Which do you prefer, that you amuse me, or that I amuse you? They said that he could not care much for amusement now, as he was to die immediately on the morrow. Now Thorstein, finding himself in close quarters, conceived a plan of escaping, and in a low, whispering voice he said: At what other time could I need you more than just now, my dear fellow Sindre, had not all our friendship already been broken off? Then darkness came upon the watch-men, and they fell asleep. Thorstein saw Sindre going along the ship, approaching him, and saying: You are in close quarters, my dear fellow Thorstein, and it certainly is high time to help you. He blew open the lock, then he cut the bow-string off from his hands; and Thorstein, who thus had become free, now seized his sword, for he knew where he had left it, and, turning against the watchmen, he killed them all. Hereupon, Sindre disappeared, but Thorstein took a boat and rowed ashore, and went home to Sogn. This meeting with Bele was a very happy one, and to the latter it seemed as if he had recovered Thorstein from the domains of Hel (death). Early the next morning (after the battle) Jokul awoke, happy in the thought that he was about to take the prisoner and kill him; but when they came to the place where they had left him, the prisoner was gone, and the watchmen dead. This was to them a very great loss. Jokul turned his prows homeward, greatly dissatisfied with his voyage, having lost Thorstein, and received scars that could never be healed. Henceforth he was called Jokul the One-handed. The foster-brothers, king Bele and Thorstein, gathered an army and went to the uplands, sending a message to Jokul, and preparing a battle-field for him. Jokul gathered men, although, on account of their friendship with Thorstein, many of his subjects sat at home, and thus, getting only a few, he durst not engage in battle, but fled out of his land, and went to Valland to his brother-in-law, Vilhjalm. The latter gave him a third part of his kingdom to rule. King Bele and Thorstein conquered the uplands, whereupon they returned home and kept quiet. Some time later there came men from Valland to meet Thorstein. They had been sent out by Jokul. Their errand was to offer Thorstein, in the name of Jokul, terms of peace. They were to have a meeting in Lim Fjord, to which both should come with three ships each, and there they should settle their dispute. Thorstein was very much pleased with this offer, confessing that it was contrary to his wish that he had had troubles with Jokul, saying that he had entered into them unwillingly on Njorfe's account, and on account of the latter's friendship with Viking. Now this was agreed upon. The ambassadors returned home, but in the summer time Thorstein busked himself for going abroad taking with him Ellide and two other ships. To Bele this voyage did not seem a hopeful one, for he looked upon Jokul as a treacherous and faithless man. He advised Thorstein to send spies ahead, and find out whether every-thing was done faithfully on Jokul's part, and having found this out, they should return and meet him in the Sound. They did so, and came back, reporting that Jokul and his part were lying at anchor in Lim Fjord, and keeping perfectly quiet. So they proceeded on their voyage till they reached the fjord. Here they held a meeting in the place agreed upon, and came to mutually satisfactory terms, on the conditions that the loss of men, the wounds and the blows, should be considered even on both sides, but Jokul should get his kingdom back, and not be tributary to anybody. Thorstein's kingdom in the uplands should fall to Jokul's lot, in compensation for the loss of his hand. On these conditions they were to be fully reconciled. Then Jokul went home to his kingdom, and kept quiet. Thorstein and Bele went home to Sogn, settled in their kingdoms, and made an end to all warfares. Ingeborg, Thorstein's wife, had already died, and Ingeborg, Bele's daughter, had her name. Fridthjof grew up with his father. Thorstein had a daughter who hight Vefreyja, who at this point of our saga had reached the age of maturity, for she was begotten in the cave of Skellinefja, and there she was born too. In wisdom she was like her mother. She got Angervadil after the death of her father, Thorstein, and many excellent men are descended from him. By all, Thorstein was considered the most distinguished and most excellent man of him time. With these contents, we now finish the saga of Thorstein, Viking's son, and it is a most amusing one.

THE SAGA OF FRIDTHJOF THE BOLD

HERE BEGINS THE SAGA OF FRIDTHJOF THE BOLD

The beginning of this saga is, that king Bele ruled over the Sogn fylke. He had three children: a son, who hight Helge, another by name of Halfdan, and a daughter called Ingeborg, a fair looking woman, of great wisdom, and the foremost of the king's children. On the coast bordering the fjord on the west side there was a large byre, called Baldershage (Balder's Meads). There was a Place of Peace and a great temple inclosed with high wooden pales. Many gods were there, yet none of them was such a favorite as Balder; and so jealous were heathen people of this place, that no harm should be done therein, either to beasts or to men; and no dealings must there take place between men or women. The place where the king dwelt hight Syrstrand, but on the other side of the fjord was a byre called Framness. There dwelt a man who hight Thorstein, the son of Viking. His byre was over against the dwelling of the king. With his wife, Thorstein had a son, by name Fridthjof, a man taller and stronger than anybody else, and even from his youth furnished with very unusual prowess. He was called Fridthjof the Bold, and so much was he beloved that all men prayed for his welfare. The children of the king were still young when their mother died. Hilding was the name of a good bonde of Sogn. He offered to foster the king's daughter, and so she was brought up in his house well and carefully. She was called Ingeborg the fair. Fridthjof was also fostered by the bonde Hilding, and thus Ingeborg was his foster-sister, and both of them were peerless among children. King Bele growing old, his personal property began to ebb away from his hands. Thorstein ruled over the third part of his kingdom, and from that man Bele got more aid than from any other source. Every third year Thorstein invited the king to a very costly banquet, while the king, on the other hand, have a feast to Thorstein the other two years. At an early age Helge, Bele's son, turned to offering to the gods, and yet neither he nor his brother was much beloved. Thorstein had a ship called Ellide, rowed on each side of fifteen oars, furnished with bow-shaped stem and stern, and strong-built like an ocean-going vessel, and its sides were clamped with iron. So strong was Fridthjof, that he, at the bow of the ship, rowed with two oars thirteen ells long, while everywhere else there were two men at each oar. Fridthjof was considered peerless among young men of that time, and the sons of the king were jealous, because he was praised more than themselves. Now king Bele was taken ill, and when he was rapidly approaching death he sent for his sons and said to them: This illness will be my bane, but this I will bid you, that you keep friendship with the friends that I have had, for it seems to me that you are inferior to Thorstein and his son Fridthjof in all things, both in good counsel and bravery. You shall raise a mound over me. Hereupon Bele died. Soon after Thorstein also was taken sick, and then he said to Fridthjof: This will I bid you, my son, that you govern your temper and yield to the sons of the king, for this is fitting on account of their dignity, and besides it seems to me that your future promises much good. I wish to be buried in a how opposite the how of king Bele, on this side of the fjord, close by the sea, so that it may be an easy thing to shout to one another about things that are about to happen. Bjorn and Asmund hight the foster brothers of Fridthjof; both of them were large and strong men. Shortly after this Thorstein died. He was buried in a how according to his request, but Fridthjof took his land and all his personal property after him.

CHAPTER 2

Fridthjof became the most famous man, and the bravest in all dangers. His foster-brother, Bjorn, he valued most, but Asmund served both of them. The best thing he got of his fathers heritage was the ship Ellide, and another costly thing was a gold ring, and a dearer one was not to be found in all Norway. So bounteous a man was Fridthjof that he was commonly said to be no less honorable than the sons of the king, excepting their royal dignity. On account of this they showed great coldness and enmity toward Fridthjof, and they could not easily bear to hear him spoken of as superior to themselves; and, furthermore, they seemed to have seen that their sister, Ingeborg, and Fridthjof had fallen into mutual love. Now the time came when the kings had to attend a banquet at Fridthjof's at Framness, and, as usual, he entertained everybody more splendidly than they were wont to be entertained. Ingeborg was also present at this feast, and Fridthjof frequently talked with her. Said the king's daughter to him: You have a good gold ring. Said Fridthjof: That is true, Hereupon, the brothers went home, and their envy of Fridthjof grew. Shortly afterward Fridthjof became very sad. Bjorn, his foster-brother, asked him what the matter was. Fridthjof answered that he had in mind to woo Ingeborg; for, said he, though my title is less than that of her brothers, still I am not inferior to them in personal worth. Says Bjorn: Let us do so. Then Fridthjof, in company with a few men, went to see the brothers. The kings were sitting on their father's how, when Fridthjof greeted them courteously. Thereupon he presented his request, saying that he prayed for their sister, Ingeborg, Bele's daughter. Said the kings: You do not show great wisdom in making this request, thinking that we will give her in marriage to a man who is without dignity. We therefore most positively refuse to give our consent. Said Fridthjof: Then my errand Is quickly done; but this shall be given in return, that hereafter I shall never give you my help though you may want it. They said they did not care about it at all. Then Fridthjof returned home, and got back his cheerful mind.

CHAPTER 3

There was a king, by name Ring, who ruled over Ring-ric, which also is a part of Norway. He was a mighty fylke-king, of great ability, but as this time somewhat advanced in age. Spoke he to his men: I have heard that the sons of Bele have broken off their friendship with Fridthjof, a man of quite uncommon excellence. Now I will send some men to the kings, and offer them this choice,—either they must become subject and tributary to me, or I will equip an army against them; and I think it will be easy to capture their kingdom, for they are not my peers either in forces or in wisdom, and yet it would be a great honor to me in my old age to put them to death. Hereupon king Ring's messengers left, and, meeting the brothers, Helge and Halfdan, in Sogn, they spoke to them as follows: This message does king ring send you, that you must either pay a tribute to him, or he will come and harry your kingdom. They made answer that they were unwilling to learn in their youth that which they had no mind to know in their old age, namely, to serve him with shame; and now, said they, we shall gather all the army that we may be able to get together. And so they did; but, as it seemed to them that their army would be small, they sent Hilding's foster-father to Fridthjof, asking him to come and help the kings. Fridthjof was sitting at the knave-play (1) when Hilding came. Said Hilding: Our kings send you their greetings, and request your help for the battle with king Ring, who is going to invade their kingdom with arrogance and wrong. Fridthjof answered nothing, but said to Bjorn with him he was playing: There is an open place there, foster-brother, and you will not be able to mend it; bit I will attack the red piece, and see whether it can be saved. Said Hilding then again: King Helge bade me say this to you, Fridthjof, that you should go into this warfare together with them, or you might look for a severe treatment from them when they come back. Said Bjorn: There is a choice between two, foster-brother, and there are two moves by which you may escape. Says Fridthjof: Then I think it advisable to attack the knave first, and yet the double game is sure to be doubtful. No other answer to his errand did Hilding get, and so, without delay, he went back and told the kings what Fridthjof had said. They asked Hilding what meaning he could make out of those words. Answered he: When he spoke of the open place, he thought, in my opinion, of leaving his place in your expedition open; but when he pretended to attack the red piece, I think he by this meant your sister, Ingeborg; watch her, therefore, as well as you can. But when I threatened him with severe treatment from you, Bjorn considered it a choice between two, but Fridthjof said the knave must be attacked first, and by this he meant king Ring. Then the kings busked themselves for departure, but before they went they brought Ingeborg to Baldershage, and eight maidens with her. Said they that Fridthjof would not be so daring that he would go thither to meet her, for nobody is so rash as to injure anybody there. But the brothers went south to Jadar, and met king Ring in Sokn-Sound. What most of all made king Ring angry was that they brothers had said that they though it a shame to fight with a man so old that he was unable to mount his horse without help.

ENDNOTES:

1. Knave-play, chess.

CHAPTER 4

When the kings had gone away Fridthjof took his robes of state, and put his good gold ring on his hand; then the foster-brothers went down to the sea and launched Ellide. Said Bjorn: Whither shall we now turn the prow, foster-brother: Answered Fridthjof: To Baldershage. And amuse ourselves with Ingeborg. Said Bjorn: It is not a proper thing to do, to provoke the gods. Said Fridthjof: Yet that risk shall now be run; besides, I rate the favor of Ingeborg or more account than that of Balder. Hereupon they rowed over the fjord, walked up to Baldershage and entered Ingeborg's bower, where she sat, together with eight maidens, and they, too, were eight. But when they came there all the place was covered with cloth of pall and other fine woven stuff. Then Ingeborg arose and said: Why are you so overbold, Fridthjof, that you have come here without the consent of my brothers, and thus provoke the wrath of the gods: Made answer Fridthjof: However this may be, I consider your love of more account than the wrath of the gods. Answered Ingeborg: You shall be welcome here, and all your men. Then she made room for him to sit at her side, and drank his toast of the best wine, and they sat and were merry together. Then Ingeborg, seeing the gold ring on his hand, asked whether he was the owner of that precious thing. Fridthjof said it was his. She praised the ring very much. Said Fridthjof: I will give you the ring if you promise not to part with it, and will send it to me when you no longer care to keep it, and with it we pledge our troth and love to each other. With this pledging of troth they exchanged rings. Fridthjof spent many nights at Baldershage, and every day he went over there now and then to be merry with Ingeborg.

CHAPTER 5

Now it is to be told of the brothers, that they met king Ring, who had more forces than they; then some people went between them, trying to bring about an agreement, so that there should be no battle. King Ring said he was willing to settle with them, on the condition that they brothers submit to him and give him their sister, Ingeborg the Fair, in marriage, together with the third part of all their possessions. The kings consented to this, for they saw that they had to do with a force far superior to their own. This peace was firmly established by oaths, and the wedding was to be in Sogn, when king Ring came to meet his betrothed. The brothers fared home again with their troops, right ill content with the result. When Fridthjof thought the time had come when the brothers might be expected home, he said to the daughter of the king: Well and handsomely you have treated us, nor has the bonde Balder been angry with us. But as soon as you know that your kings have come home, then spread your bed-sheets on the hall of the goddesses, for that is the highest of all the houses in this place, and we can easily see it from our byre. Said the king's daughter: You have not followed the example of other men in this matter, but we certainly must welcome our friends when you come to us. Then Fridthjof went home and early the next morning he went out-doors, and when he came in again he sang:

Tell I must,
Our good people,
That our pleasure trips
Wholly are ended;
Men shall no more
Go aboard the ships,
For now are the sheets
Spread out to bleach.

So they went out, and saw that all the hall of the goddesses was thatched with bleached linen. Said Bjorn then: Now the kings must have come home, and for us I think there will be but a short peace; to me it seems advisable that we gather folks together This was done, and many men flocked together there. Soon the brothers heard of the ways of Fridthjof, and of his men and forces. Said king Helge then: It seems a wonder to me that Balder must endure every disgrace from Fridthjof. Now I will send messengers to him, and know what kind of atonement he is willing to offer us, or else he is to be driven from the land, for I do not see that we have men enough at our command now to fight with him. Fridthjof's friends and his foster-father, Hilding, brought the message to him. Said they: The kings ask as an atonement from you, Fridthjof, that you go and collect the tribute from the Orkneys, which has never been paid since the death of Bele, for they are in want of the money just now, as they are about to give their sister Ingeborg in marriage, and a large amount of wealth with her. Makes answer Fridthjof: The only thing urging peace between us is regard for our deceased relatives, but the brothers will show us no trustiness. But this I will reserve, that all our possessions shall be left in peace during our absense. This was promised and bound with an oath. Now Fridthjof made preparations for his voyage, choosing his men in reference to their bravery and ability to render service. The company consisted of eighteen men. Fridthjof's men asked him if he would not before setting out go to king Helge and make peace with him, and pray Balder to take his wrath away from him. Says Fridthjof: I make s solemn vow that I shall never ask for peace from king Helge. Hereupon he went aboard Ellide, and so they sailed out of the Sogn-Fjord. But when Fridthjof had departed from home and king Halfdan to his brother Helge as follows: Our rule would be better and greater if Fridthjof was paid for his misdoings. Let us burn up his byre, and bring such a storm upon him and his men that they perish. Helge said this was a thing to be done. Thereupon they burnt up the whole byre at Framness, and robbed it of all its fee. Then they sent for two witch-wives, Heid and Hamglom, and gave them fee to send upon Fridthjof and his men so mighty a tempest that they should all be wrecked. So the witches sang their songs of witchcraft, and ascended the witch-scaffold with sorcery and incantations.

CHAPTER 6

But when Fridthjof and his men had gotten out of the Sogn-Fjord there fell upon them a violent storm and a great tempest, and the sea rolled heavily. The ship sped on swiftly, for it glided smoothly over the waters, and had an excellent form for breasting the sea. Sang Fridthjof then:

> My tarred horse of the sea
> I let swim out of Sogn,
> While the maids were drinking mead
> In the midst of Baldershage.
> The tempest now increases,
> Farewell, my brides, I bid you,
> Who have a mind to love us,
> Though Ellide should be filled.

534

Said Bjorn: It would be well if you could find something else to do than to sing about the maids of Baldershage. Made answer Fridthjof: My songs will not give out so soon, though. Then they were driven northward to the sounds near the islands called the Solunds. And now the storm had reached its highest pitch. Sang then Fridthjof:

> High now the sea is swelling;
> The waves and clouds unite,
> Old spells are the causes
> That call forth the breakers;
> With Æger shall I not
> Content in the tempest.
> Let the ice-clad Solunds
> Shelter our people!

Then they stood toward the islands that are called the Solunds, and intended to stop there; and now the storm suddenly abated. Then they took another course, and turned their prow away from the islands, having fair prospects for the voyage, for they had favorable wind for awhile; but the fair wind soon freshened into a gale. Sand Fridthjof then:

> In former days
> At Framness
> I rowed to meet
> My Ingeborg.
> Now I shall sail
> In the tempest cold,
> Making the horse of the wave
> Smoothly speed on.

And Then they had sped before the wind far into the sea the waters began to be violently agitated again, and a gale blew up, accompanied by so great a snow-storm that the stem could not be seen from the stern, but the seas rushed over the ship so that the water had to be baled out constantly. Said Fridthjof then:

> The waves are hid from sight,
> For witch-wrought is the weather.
> Heroes we of a well-famed band
> Far out on the sea have come.
> Stand we now all—
> Disappeared have the Solunds—
> Eighteen men a-bailing
> And Ellide sustaining.

Said Bjorn: Varied will be his fortunes who fares far. That is certainly so, says Fridthjof, and sings:

> Helge it is who causes
> The rime-maned waves to swell,
> This is not like kissing

535

The bride so fair in Baldershage;
Otherwise quite does love me
Ingeborg than the king.
I know no greater happiness
Than her wishes to fulfill.

Said Bjorn: Maybe she is looking to something higher for you than your present position, and this is not unpleasant to know. Says Fridthjof: Now is the time to test good companions, though it would be more agreeable to be in Baldershage. They busked themselves bravely for valiant men had gathered there, and the ship was the best that ever had bee in the Northlands. Said Fridthjof then this stave:

The waves are hid from sight,
Far west in the sea we are come.
Seems to ocean to me
Like embers all blazing;
Hows are tossed up
By the swan-feathered billows.
On the rising ridges
Now Ellide rides.

Now huge seas were shipped, so that all had to be baling out water. Said Fridthjof:

Much must there now be drunk
To me by the maid's fair lips
East, where the sheets lay bleaching,
If it shall make me sink
'Neath the swan-feathered waves.

Said Bjorn: Do you think the maids of Sogn will shed many tears for you when you are dead? Made answer Fridthjof: That certainly comes into my mind. Then a huge sea broke over the bow of the ship. So that streams of water rushed in; but this saved them, that the ship was so excellent and the crew so hardy. Sang Bjorn then a stave:

It seems not that a widow
To you does drink,
Nor that the ring-keeper fair
Bids you draw near to her.
Salt are our eyes,
Soaked in the brine;
Our strong arms are failing,
Our eyelids are sore.

Answered Asmund: it does not matter though you do try your arms somewhat, for you did not pity us when we rubbed our eyes every morning when you rose so early to go to Baldershage. Said Fridthjof: Well, why do you not make a stave, Asmund? That shall not be said Asmund, but still he sang this stave:

> Tight was the tug round the mast,
> When the seas broke over the ship:
> I alone 'gainst eight men
> Within board had to work.
> Better to the maiden's bower
> Than to be baling out Ellide
> Mid the roaring waves.

Said Fridthjof, laughing: You do not speak of your help in lower terms than it deserves, nevertheless you now showed something of the thrall-blood in you, when you were willing to be a table-waiter. The storm still kept increasing, so that the breakers that roared round the ship seemed to the men who were on board more like huge peaks and mountains than like waves. Said Fridthjof then:

> On cushioned seat I sat
> In Baldershage,
> Singing the songs I knew
> For the king's fair daughter.
> Now am I really
> To Ran's bed going.
> And another shall own
> My Ingeborg.

Said Bjorn: Great fear is now before us, foster-brother, and your words betoken anxiety, and that is too bad for such a brave fellow as you are. Says Fridthjof: There is neither fear nor anxiety, though ditties are made of our pleasure voyages, but it may be that they are spoken of oftener than need be, but most men would think themselves nearer to death than life if they were in our place; and still I will answer you with a stave:

> That did I get to my gain;
> With the maidens eight
> Of Ingeborg did I, not you,
> Succeed in negotiations.
> At Baldershage we laid
> Bright rings together;
> Nor far away was then
> The warder (1) of Halfdan's land.

Said Bjorn: Such things as are already done, foster-brother, we must be content with. Now the seas dashed over the ship so violently that the bulwarks and both the sheets were broken, and four men were washed overboard and all were lost. Sand Fridthjof then:

> Broken are both the sheets
> Mid the ocean's great waves;
> four swains did sink
> In the sea so deep.

Said Fridthjof: Reasonable it now seems to me that some of our men will go to Ran; but in my opinion we will not be considered fit to be sent thither unless we may come there busked like men, and it therefore seems good to me that every one of us have some gold on him. The he cut the ring, Ingeborg's gift, asunder, distributed the pieces among his men, and sang this stave:

> Before we are lost by Æger,
> Asunder shall be hewed the ring,
> By the wealthy father of Halfdan owned.
> Red as it is,
> Gold shall glitter on the guests,
> If of guesting we have need,
> That will be fitting
> For men of might
> In the midst of Ran's halls.

Said Bjorn then: Now it is not to be looked for with any certainty that we come there, although it is not unlikely. At this moment Fridthjof and his men observed that the ship was gliding over the waves very rapidly, but before them was a wholly unknown sea, and it was growing dark on all sides, so that no one could see the stem or stern form the middle of the ship, and the darkness was accompanied by sea-spray, storm, frost, snow and piercing cold. Then Fridthjof climbed the mast, and when he came down again said he to his companions: A wondrous sight I have seen: a large whale was swimming round the ship, and I have no doubt we must have come near to some land, and that this whale intends to keep us from reaching it. King Helge, I think, does not deal kindly with us, and he has undoubtedly sent us anything but a friendly messenger. I saw two women on the back of the whale, and they methinks, cause this fearful tempest by witchcraft and sorcery of the worst sort. Now lest us try whether our good luck of their witchcraft is more powerful, and you shall steer ashore as straightly as possible, but I shall smite these monsters with beams. Sang he then this stave:

> Witches two
> On the wave I see.
> Has them hither
> Helge sent.
> Their backs shall Ellide
> Cut in twain
> E'er she her voyage
> Completed has.

It is said that the ship Ellide had by enchantment gotten the power of understanding human speech. Said Bjorn then: Now men can see the disposition of the brothers toward us. Then Bjorn took the command of the ship; but Fridthjof seized a forked beam, ran to the prow and sang this stave:

> Hail, Ellide!
> Leap on the wave!
> Break of the witches
> The teeth and brow!
> The cheeks and jaw-bones
> Of the cursed woman,

One foot or both
Of this horrible witch!

Then he shot a fork at one of the ham-leapers (skin-changers), but the beak of
Ellide struck the back of the other, and the backs of both were broken; but the
whale dove down and swam away, and they saw him no more. Now the
weather grew calmer, but the ship was water logged, and then Fridthjof called to
his men requesting them to bale the ship dry. Bjorn said that this work was not
needed. Whereto made answer Fridthjof: Have a care, foster-brother, and do
not fall into despair; it has, you know, heretofore been the custom of brave men
to give aid as long as possible, no matter what the result may be. Fridthjof sang
this stave:

> My brave men! You need not
> Have fear of death.
> Exult with joy,
> My thanes!
> For this my dreams
> Full well do know,
> That I shall own
> My Ingeborg.

Having then baled the ship dry, and being near land, a rainy wind still blew
against them. Then Fridthjof took two oars, seated himself in the foremost part
of the prow and rowed rather vigorously. Thereupon the weather cleared off,
and now they saw the had gotten out of the sound of Effia, and there they
landed. The crew were very much exhausted, but so stout was Fridthjof that he
bore eight men over the fore-shore; Bjorn bore two, but Asmund one. Sang
Fridthjof then:

> Up to the hearth
> Myself did bear
> My brave men, exhausted
> By the raging snow-storm.
> Now on the sand
> The sail I have brought;
> With the might of the sea
> It's not easy to deal.

ENDNOTES:

1.   Balder; i.e they were betrothed in the presence of Balder.

CHAPTER 7

Angantyr was in Effia when Fridthjof landed there with his men. It was his
custom when he drank that some man should sit at the watch-window of his
drinking-hall, and look toward the wind and keep watch there. This man was to
drink form a horn, and whenever one horn was emptied by him another was

filled. He who was keeping watch at the time when Fridthjof landed hight Hallvard. Hallvard saw the coming of Fridthjof and his men, and sang this stave:

> In the violent storm
> I see on board Ellide
> Six men a-bailing
> And seven a-rowing.
> The man in the prow,
> Is like Fridthjof the Bold,
> The valiant in battle.

And when he had drunk from the horn he threw it in through the window, and said to the woman who gave him drink:

> Thou fair-walking woman!
> Take from the floor
> The horn turned over,
> Which I have emptied!
> Men I see on the sea,
> Exhausted by storm and rain,
> Who our help may need
> Ere the harbor they reach.

The jarl heard what Hallvard said, and asked for tidings. Says Hallvard: Some men have landed here; they are quite exhausted, but I think they are good fellows, and one of them is so doughty that he is carrying the other men ashore. Said the jarl then: Go to meet them, and receive them in a seemly manner, if it should happen to be Fridthjof, son of my friend, the herser Thorstein; he is a most excellent man in respect to every accomplishment. Then took up the word the man who hight Atle, a great viking, and said he: Now it shall be found out whether Fridthjof, as it is said, has made a solemn vow never to be the first in praying for peace from anybody. Together with Atle there were ten bad and ambitious men, who often went into berserks-gang. When they met Fridthjof they took their weapons. Said Atle then: Now it seems good. Fridthjof, that you turn this way, for as eagles fight face to face with their claws, so must we also, Fridthjof: and moreover, now is the time for you to keep your word, and not be the first to ask for peace. Fridthjof turned to meet them, and sang this stave:

> Succeed shall you never
> In cowing us down,
> You fainting cowards,
> Dwellers of these isles!
> Rather would I go
> Alone to fight
> With you men ten
> Than sue for peace.

Then Hallvard came to them and said: the jarl desires me to bid you all welcome, and no one shall insult you. Fridthjof said that he heartily accepted this greeting of welcome, and yet he was prepared to take either peace or war. Thereupon they went to call on the jarl, who received Fridthjof and all his men

540

kindly. They spent the winter with the jarl, and were held in great honor by him; the latter frequently made questions about their voyages. This stave sang Bjorn:

> During ten whole days,
> And eight days more,
> We, fellows so merry,
> Continued a-baling,
> While billows dashed o'er us
> From both sides.

Made answer the jarl: Greatly has king Helge vexed you, and evil are such kings as do nothing but put people to death by witchcraft: but I know, Fridthjof, says Angantyr, what your errand hither is; you are sent hither to gather tribute, and thereto I can speedily give the answer, that king Helge shall have no tribute from me, but you may have as much fee from me as you please, and you may call it tribute or anything else you have a mind to. Fridthjof said he would accept the fee.

CHAPTER 8

Now it shall be told what came to pass in Norway after Fridthjof had gone abroad. The brothers burn up all the byre at Framness. But while the weird sisters were performing their spells they fell down from the witch-scaffold on which they were seated, and both of them broke their backs. This autumn king Ring came north to Sogn to have his wedding, and a great feast was prepared for his nuptials with Ingeborg. Says king Ring to Ingeborg: Whence has come that excellent ring that you wear on your hand? She said her father had been its owner. Answered he: It is a gift of Fridthjof; take it off your hand straightway, for you shall not be in want of gold when you come to Alfheim. Then she handed the ring to Helge's wife, and bade her give it to Fridthjof when he came back. King Ring then went home with his wife, and his love of her was exceedingly great.

CHAPTER 9

The next spring Fridthjof departed from the Orkneys, and parted with Angantyr on the most friendly terms. Hallvard went with Fridthjof. But when they came to Norway they learned that his byre had been burnt up, and when Fridthjof came to Framness he said:

> Stout fellows, we
> Formerly did drink
> At Framness
> With my father.
> Now burnt I see
> That same byre;
> Repay must I
> The king's ill deeds.

Then he consulted his men as to what was not to be done, but they bade him look to that himself; whereunto he made answer that he would first hand over tribute. Afterward they rowed the boat over and came to Syrstrand. There they learn that the kings were at Baldershage, sacrificing to the dises (goddesses). Bjorn and Fridthjof then went up thither; and the latter bade Hallvard, Asmund and the other men break in pieces all the ships, large and small, that were to be found thereabout. So they did. Fridthjof wanted to enter. Bjorn bade him go warily, as he wanted to go in alone. Fridthjof bade Bjorn remain outside and keep watch while he entered. Sang he then this stave:

> Alone will I go
> And enter the byre;
> Little help do I need
> The kings to find.
> You shall throw fire
> On the byre of the kings,
> If I do not come
> Back to-night.

Says Bjorn: That stave was well sung. Then Fridthjof went in and saw that there were but a few people in the hall of the dises: the kings were there at the time sacrificing, and sat drinking. Fire was burning on the floor, and the wives of the kings sat at the fires and warmed the gods, whereas other women were anointing the gods and wiping them with napkins. Fridthjof went before king Helge and said: Here you have tribute. Herewith he swung the purse wherein was the silver, and threw it at this nose so violently that two teeth were broken out of his mouth, and he fell into a swoon in his high seat; but Halfdan caught him, so that he did not fall into the fire. Sang Fridthjof then this stave:

> Take here your tribute,
> King of men!
> Take it with your fore-teeth
> Lest more you demand.
> At the bottom of this belg
> You find silver abounding,
> O'er which have ruled together
> Bjorn and I.

There were but few men in the room, for in another place there was drinking going on. But as Fridthjof walked over the floor toward the door, he saw that goodly ring on the hand of Helge's wife while she was warming Balder by the fire. Fridthjof took after the ring, but it stuck fast to her hand, and so he dragged her along the floor toward the door, and then Balder fell into the fire. But when Halfdan's wife caught after her quickly, the god that she had been warming also fell into the fire. The flame now blazed up around both the gods, as they had previously been anointed, and thence it ran up into the roof, so that the whole house was wrapped in flames. Fridthjof got hold of the ring before he went out. Asked Bjorn then what had taken place during his visit in the house. But Fridthjof held the ring up and sang this stave:

542

A blow received Helge;
Smote the purse the villain's nose;
Down fell the brother of Halfdan
In the midst of the high seat.
Balder had to burn,
But first got I the ring.
Then from the fire-place I
Fearlessly wended by way.

People say that Fridthjof flung a flaming fire-brand at the roof, so that all the house was wrapped in flames, and that he then sang this stave:

Wend we our way to the strand!
Then let our aims be high!
For the blue flame is bickering
In the midst of Baldershage.

Hereupon they went down to the sea.

CHAPTER 10

When king Helge had come to his senses he gave orders to follow quickly after Fridthjof and kill him and all his companions. That man, said he, has forfeited his life, as he has spared no Place of Peace. Now the trumpet was blown, and all the king's men came together; and when they came out to the hall, they saw that it stood in flames. King Halfdan and some of his men went to the fire, but king Helge followed after Fridthjof and his men. The latter had already got on board their ships and were lying on their oars. Helge and his men found that all their ships had been damaged, so they were forced to row ashore again, and lost some men. (1) then king Helge grew angry that the became stark mad. Thereupon, with an arrow on the string, he stretched his bow with so much force that both ends of it suddenly snapped off. When Fridthjof saw this, he seized two of Ellide's oars and plied them so mightily that both of them broke. Said he then this stave:

Kissed I the young Ingeborg,
Bele's daughter,
In Baldershage.
This shall the oars
Of Ellide
Both be broken
Like Helge's bows.

After this the wind began to blow out of the inner part of the fjord, so they hoisted the sails and sailed on. Fridthjof said to his men that they might busk themselves not to stay there very long. Afterward they sailed out of Sogn. Sang Fridthjof then this stave:

Sailed we out of Sogn,

Here sailed we a short time ago;
When flames consumed the byre
My father left to me.
But now in the midst of Baldershage
The flames have begun to blaze.
I now am an outlaw for sooth
I know that it has been sworn.

Said Bjorn to Fridthjof: What shall we do now? Foster-brother, said Fridthjof, I shall not remain here in Norway; I will try the life of warriors, and go on viking expeditions. Then they explored islands and skerries during the summer, and thus gained for themselves free and fame; but in the fall they repaired to the Orkneys, where they were heartily welcomed by Angantyr, and they spent the winter there. But when Fridthjof had left Norway the kings held a thing, and declared Fridthjof an outlaw in all their realms, and made all his possessions their own. King Halfdan settled at Framness, and rebuilt the byre which had been burnt down; and likewise they restored the whole Baldershage, but it took a long time before the fire was put out. That which most touched the heart of Helge was that the gods had been burnt up, and it cost much to build Baldershage up again as it had been before. Sat king Helge now at Syrstrand.

ENDNOTES:

1. Hallvard, Asmund and the other men had scuttle all the ships of king Helge while Fridthjof went to Baldershage. See Chapter 9.

CHAPTER 11

Fridthjof was successful in gaining fee and fame wheresoever he came; villains and savage vikings he slew; the bondes and chapmen (merchants) he left in peace; and he was now a second time called Fridthjof the Bold. He had gotten by this time a large and well arrayed army, and had become exceedingly rich in chattels. But when Fridthjof had spent three winters in viking expeditions, he sailed west and steered up the Vik. (1) Fridthjof said he had a mind to go ashore; but you, said he, will have to go a harrying this winter; for I am growing tired of warfare, and I am going to the uplands to find king Ring, and have a talk with him; but you shall come back next summer and get me, and I will be here on the first day of summer. Says Bjorn: This is no wise plan; however, your will must prevail; my wish it would be to go north to Sogn, and kill both the kings Halfdan and Helge. Makes answer Fridthjof: That is of no use; I prefer to go and find king Ring and Ingeborg. Says Bjorn: I am unwilling to run the risk of sending you alone into his hands, for although he is somewhat advanced in age, Ring is a wise man and of noble birth. Fridthjof said he must have his own way; and you, Bjorn, said he, will have to be the commander of our company in the meantime. They did as he would have it. So Fridthjof went to the uplands in the fall, for he was curious to see the love betwixt king Ring and Ingeborg. Before he came thither he put on a large cowled cloak over the other clothes, all shaggy. He had two staves in his hands, a mask over his face, and made himself look as old as possible. Afterward he met some herd-swains, and going

544

heavily he asked them: Whence are you? Made answer they: We have our homes in Streitaland (Struggle-land), at the king's dwelling. Asks the old man: Is Ring a mighty king: Made answer they: To us you seem to be so old a man that you ought to know what manner of man king Ring is in all respects. The old man said he had been thinking more about salt-boiling than about the manner of kings. After this he went up the king's hall. Toward the close of the day he went in, assumed a very feeble look, and stopping near the door he pulled the cowl over his head and his face. Said then king Ring to Ingeborg: There went a man into the hall much larger than other men. Answered the queen: Such are insignificant tidings here. The king then spoke to the man-servant who stood before the table: Go ask the cowl-man who he is, whence he comes, and where his kinsmen dwell. The swain then ran over the floor to the stranger and said: What is your name, my man? Or where were you last night? Or where are your kinsmen? Says the cowl-man: You ask your questions rapidly, my fellow' but will you be able to understand if I tell you about these things: Certainly I can, said the swain. Says the cowl-man: Thjof (thief) is my name, at Ulf's (wolf's) I spent last night, and in Anger (2) (grief) I am brought up. The swain hastened before the king, and told him the answers of the stranger. Says the king: You understood admirably, swain. I know the land called Anger; besides, it may be that this man's mind is not at ease. I think he is a wise man, and a man of great worth. Says the queen: This is a remarkable manner of yours to be so eager to talk with every carle that comes here, whosoever he may be; but so far as this man is concerned, I should like to know of what account he is. Says the king: You do not know any better than I do. I see he is a man that thinks more than he talks, and makes good use of his eyes. Thereupon the king sent a man for him, and the cowled man went to the inner part of the hall before the king; he bent forward somewhat, and greeted the king in a low voice. Said the king: What hight you, my large man? Made answer the cowled man by singing this stave:

> FRIDTHJOF (peace-thief) I hight
> When I fared with the vikings;
> HERTHJOF (war-thief) when
> The widows I grieved;
> GEIRTHJOF (spear-thief) when I
> The barbed shafts threw;
> GUNNTHJOF (battle-theif) when I
> 'Gainst the kings went;
> EYTHJOF (isle-theif) when I
> The skerries did plunder;
> HELTHJOF (death-theif) when I
> The babies did toss up;
> VALTHJOF (slain-theif) when I
> Higher than men was;
> But now since then
> With salt-boilers about
> Have I been wandering;
> With needy salt-carles,
> Until hither I came.

Said then the king: From many things you have taken the theif's (Thjof's) name; but where were you last night? And where is your home? Made answer the cowled man: in Anger (grief) I am born, my mind urged me hitherward, but my home is nowhere. Says the king: It may be that you have been brought up in sorrow for awhile, but I may also be that you were born in peace. You must, I think, have spent last night in the forest, for there is no bonde near this place who hight Ulf (wolf); but when you say you have no home, you undoubtedly mean that you think your home of little consequence, since your heart drove you hitherward. Said Ingeborg now: Go theif (Thjof)! Get yourself other night-quarters, or betake yourself to the guest-chamber! Said the king: I am now old enough to arrange seats for my guests; come, stranger, put off your cloak and take a seat at my other hand. Said the queen: Yea, in your dotage you are, when you ask beggars to sit down by your side.

Said Thjof: It is not becoming sir; better is that which the queen says; I am more accustomed to be among salt-boilers than to sit by the side of rulers. Said the king Do as I will it; for I think my will must prevail this time. Thjof doffed his cloak, under which he was clad in a dark blue kirtle, and had a goodly ring on his hand; a large silver belt was about his waist; down from the belt hung a large purse full of bright silver coins, and a sword was girt at his side; but on his head he wore a large skin cap; his eyes looked dim and his face was all shaggy. Says the king: Now I dare say that things look as we would wish to have them; give him, my queen, a good mantle, and such a one as may be becoming to him. Answered the queen: Your will shall prevail, my lord, but I do not like this Thjof (thief) much. Then a good mantle was given to him, which he donned and sat down in the high seat beside the king. The queen's face blushed red as blood when she saw the goodly ring, but still she was unwilling to converse with him, while the king was exceedingly cheerful and said: A goodly ring you have on your hand, and you must have been boiling salt a long time before your earned it. Made answer Thjof: this is my whole paternal heritage. Says the king: May be you have more than that, but few salt-boilers are your equal; so I think, lest it should be that old age is fast creeping into my eyes. So Thjof spent the winter here, heartily treated and highly esteemed by all. He was liberal with his fee and cheerful to everybody. The queen seldom talked to him, but the king and he were always happy when they were together.

ENDNOTES:

1. The main part of the present Christiania fjord.

2. Angr also means a narrow firth, and in this sense it is still found in some noted fjord-names on the coast of Norway, as Stavanger (Icel. Stafangr), and Hardanger.

CHAPTER 12

The saga tells that king Ring and his queen and a large company once were to go to a feast. Said king Ring then to Thjof: Will you go along, or will you stay at home? He said he would rather go along. Said the king: That suits me better.

So they started, and had to cross a frozen lake. Said Thjof to the king: Untrustworthy seems to me the ice, and we seem to be going unwarily. Said the king: It is often to be observed that you have much forethought concerning us. A little while afterward all the ice broke down; then Thjof leaped to the place that was broken, and pulled up the sled and all that were in it. Both the king and the queen were sitting in the sled. All these, together with the horses hitched to the sled, Thjof suddenly pulled up onto the ice, and then said the king: That was a right good lift, Thjof; and Fridthjof the Bold, had he been here, would not have been able to do it with stronger hands; the doughtiest companions are such men as you. Now they came to the feast, from which we have no tidings, and the king fared home loaded with seemly gifts. Midwinter had passed, and when spring began the weather grew milder, the forests took to blooming, the grass to growing, and the ships were able to glide betwixt the lands.

CHAPTER 13

It was one day that the king said to his courtier: I want you to go with me to the woods to-day, that we may amuse ourselves and see how fair is the country; and so they did, a large number of men rambled out into the woods with the king. It happened that the king and Fridthjof were both together in the woods, far from the other men. Said the king that he was heavy, and would fain sleep. Answers Thjof: Go home, my lord, for that is more becoming to a man of noble estate than to lie out-of-doors. Said the king: I cannot do that. Then he laid himself down, fell asleep and snored loudly. Thjof sat near him, drew his sword from the sheath and threw it far away from him. A little while afterward the king sat up and said: Is it not true, Fridthjof, that many things entered your mind? But you dealt wisely with those thoughts, and henceforth you shall be held in great honor with us. But I knew immediately the first evening when you came into our hall, and you shall not speedily leave us; and I think a great future lies before you. Said Fridthjof: My lord, you have treated me well and friendly, but now I must soon be off, for my troops are soon coming to meet me, according to a previous arrangement that I have with them. Therewith they rode home from the woods, and now the king's folk crowded around them. All went home to the hall and drank freely. At the drinking it was made known to all that Fridthjof the Bold had spent the winter there.

CHAPTER 14

One morning early there was a knock at that door of the hall where the king, the queen and many others were sleeping. Asked the king who was calling at the door. Said he who was outside: Fridthjof is here. I am now busk and bowne for my departure. Then the door was opened. In stepped Fridthjof and sang this stave:

> Now must I thank you,
> Bountifully you have feasted
> The feeder of the eagle.
> Bowne am I for departure.

> Ingeborg can I ne'er forget
> While to both of us life is granted.
> Fare she well! And take she
> This costly gift for many kisses.

Therewith he threw the goodly ring to Ingeborg and bade her accept it. The king smiled at this stave and said: So, after all, it came to pass that she got more thanks for your winter quarters than I, and yet she has not been more kind to you than I. The king then sent his servants for drink and food, saying that they should eat and drink before Fridthjof went away. Sit up, queen, he added, and be of good cheer. She said she had not mind to eat so early. Says king Ring: Let us now all eat together, and so they did. But when they had been drinking a while said king Ring: I wish you might stay here, Fridthjof, for my sons are as yet nothing but children, but I am old and unfit to ward my land, if anybody should seek it for the purpose of harrying. Soon must I be off, my lord; and he sang this stave:

> Live, king Ring,
> Hale and long!
> The highest of kings
> 'Neath the northern skies!
> Guard well, my king,
> Your queen and land.
> Nevermore shall meet again
> Ingeborg and I.

Sang king Ring then:

> Fare not thus from hence,
> My Fridthjof! dearest
> Son of kings,
>   So sad in mind!
> Your costly gifts
> I shall reward
> Better far
> Than you are aware.

Sang he this too:

> Give I the famous
> Fridthjof my wife,
> And therewith all
> That belongs to me.

Interrupted him straightaway Fridthjof, and sang:

> I will not accept
> Those gifts from you,
> Lest fatal illness
> Threatens my king.

Says the king: I should not have given these things to you had I not thought that this was the case; for I am sick, and I wish you to enjoy this in preference to all others, for you are above all men in Norway. I give you a king's name, too; for her brothers, I think, will be less willing than I am to grant honor to you and give you the wife. Said Fridthjof: Accept many thanks form me, my lord, for your kindness, which is more than I could ask or even think; but as to my rank, I will take nothing more than a jarl's name. Herewith king Ring, taking Fridthjof's hand, gave him the government of the kingdom, which he had rued over, and jarl's name therewith. Fridthjof was to rule until the sons of king Ring kept his sick-bed but a short time, and when he died there was great sorrow in his kingdom. A howe was raised over him, and, according to his wish, much fee was buried with him. Then Fridthjof made a great feast, which his folk came to. At this feast king Ring's funeral and Ingeborg's and Fridthjof's wedding were celebrated together. Hereafter Fridthjof began to rule this kingdom, and was thought a most excellent man. He and Ingeborg had many children.

CHAPTER 15

The kings in Sogn, the brothers of Ingeborg, heard these tidings, that Fridthjof had become the ruler of Ring-ric, and that he had married Ingeborg, their sister. Said Helge to Halfdan, his brother, that it was a great shame and an overbold act, that the son of a herser should marry her. So they gathered together much folk and went with them to Ring-ric with a view to slaying Fridthjof and conquering all the kingdom for themselves. When Fridthjof became aware of this he also gathered together folk and said to the queen: A new war has come upon our realm, but, whatever the end of it may be, we do not like to see you in low spirits. Said she: It has now come to this, what we must look to you above all others. Bjorn had them come from the east to aid Fridthjof. They preceded to battle, and, as he formerly had been wont, Fridthjof was foremost where the danger was the greatest. He and Helge came to a hand-to-hand struggle, and Fridthjof slew king Helge. Then Fridthjof held up the shield (1) of peace, and thus the battle ceased. Said Fridthjof then to king Halfdan: Two important choices are now in your hands, the one that you surrender everything to me, the other that you get your bane like your brother. It is clear that I am stronger then both of you. Then Halfdan chose to surrender himself and his kingdom to Fridthjof. Now Fridthjof took the rule of Sogn-fylke, but Halfdan should be herser in Sogn, and pay tribute to Fridthjof as long as he ruled over Ring-ric. The title of king of Sogn was given to Fridthjof from the time when he gave up Ring-ric to the sons of king Ring, and thereupon he added Hordaland by conquest. Fridthjof and Ingeborg had two sons, Gunnthjof and Hunthjof. Both o f these became men of might. And now here ends the saga of Fridthjof the Bold.

ENDNOTES:

1. A white shield lifted up in the battle was a sign of peace. During the battle the red shields or war waved over the contending armies.

THE STORY OF THE GREENLANDERS

CHAPTER 1
Discovery and Colonization of Greenland

A man was named Þorvaldr, son of Ásvaldr, son of Úlfr, son of Oxen-Þórir [Öxna-Þórir]. Þorvaldr and his son Eiríkr the Red [Eiríkr rauði] removed from Jæderen to Iceland, in consequence of murder. At that time Iceland was settled wide around. They lived at Drangar on Hornstandir; there died Þorvaldr. Eiríkr then married Þjóðhildr, the daughter of Jörundr son of Úlfr and Þorbjörg Knarrarbringa, who was then married to Þorbjörn of Haukadalur. Then went Eiríkr northwards and lived at Eiríksstaðir near Vatnshorn. The son of Eiríkr and Þjóðhildr was named Leifr.

But after the killing of Eyjólfr Saurr [mud/dirt/excrement] and Duel-Hrafn [Hólmgöngu-Hrafn], Eiríkr was banished from Haukadalur, and he removed westwards to Breiðafjörður, and lived at Öxney at Eiríksstaðir. He lent Þorgestr at Breiðabólstaður his seat-posts, and could not get them back again when he demanded them. Upon this arose disputes and frays between him and Þorgestr, as is told in Eiríks saga. Styrr, son of Þorgrímr, assisted Eiríkr and so did Eyjólfr of Svíney, and the sons of Brandr of Álftafjörður, and Þorbjörn son of Vífill. But supporting Þorgestr's people were the sons of Þórðr Gellir and also Þorgeirr of Hítardalur.

Eiríkr was declared outlawed by the Þórsnes assembly, and he then made ready his ship in Eiríksvágr [Eiríkr's creek], and when he was ready, Styrr and the others followed him out past the islands. Eiríkr told them that he intended to go in search of the land, which Gunnbjörn, son of Úlfr kráka [crow] saw, when he was driven out to the westward in the sea, the time when he found Gunnbjarnarsker [Gunnbjörn's rock]. He said he would come back to his friends if he found the land.

Eiríkr sailed out from Snæfellsjökull; he found the land, and came in from the sea to the place which he called Miðjökull [middle glacier]; it is now called Bláserkr. He then went southwards to see whether it was there habitable land. The first winter he was at Eiríksey [Eiríkr's isle], nearly in the middle of the eastern settlement; the spring after repaired he to Eiríksfjörðr [Eiríkr's fjord], and took up there his abode. He removed in summer to the western settlement, and gave names to many places.

He was the second winter at Hólmar in Hvarfsgnípa, but the third summer went he to Iceland, and came with his ship into Breiðafjörður. He called the land which he had found Greenland [Grænland], because he said it people would be attracted there if the land had a good name.

550

Eiríkr was in Iceland for the winter, but the summer after, went he to colonize the land; he dwelt at Brattahlíð in Eiríksfjörðr. Informed people say that the same summer Eiríkr the Red went to colonize Greenland, thirty-five ships sailed from Breiðafjörður and Borgarfjörður, but only fourteen arrived; some were driven back, and others were lost. This was fifteen winters before Christianity was established by law in Iceland. The following men who went out with Eiríkr took land in Greenland: Herjólfr took Herjólfsfjörður [Herjólfr's fjord] (he lived at Herjólfsnes), Ketil Ketilsfjörðr, Hrafn Hrafnsfjörðr, Sölvi Sölvadalr [Sölvi's valley], Helgi, son of Þorbrandr, Álftafjörðr, Hafgrímr Hafgrímsfjörðr and Vatnahverfi, Arnlaugr Arnlaugsfjörðr, but some went to the western settlement.

CHAPTER 2
Bjarni Herjólfsson Seeks Greenland

Herjólfr was the son of Bárðr son of Herjólfr; he was kinsman to Ingólfr the settler. To Herjólfr and his people gave Ingólfr land between Vogur and Reykjanes. Herjólfr lived first at Drepstock; Thorgerd hight his wife, and Bjarne was their son, a very hopeful man. He conceived, when yet young, a desire to travel abroad, and soon earned for himself both riches and respect, and he was every second winter abroad, every other at home with his father. Soon possessed Bjarne his own ship, and the last winter be was in Norway, Herjulf prepared for a voyage to Greenland with Erik. In the ship with Herjulf was a Christian from the Hebrides, who made a hymn respecting the whirlpool, in which was the following verse:--

O thou who triest holy men!
Now guide me on my way,
Lord of the earth's wide vault, extend
Thy gracious hand to me!

Herjulf lived at Herjulfsness; he was a very respectable man. Erik the Red lived at Brattahlid; he was the most looked up to, and every one regulated themselves by him. These were Erik's children: Leif, Thorvald and Thorstein, but Freydis hight his daughter; she was married to a man who Thorvard hight; they lived in Garde, where is now the Bishop's seat; she was very haughty, but Thorvard was narrow-minded; she was married to him chiefly on account of his money. Heathen were the people in Greenland at this time. Bjarne carne to Eyrar with his ship the summer of the same year in which his father had sailed away in spring. These tidings appeared serious to Bjarne, and he was unwilling to unload his ship. Then his seamen asked him what he would do; he answered that he intended to continue his custom, and pass the winter with his father; "and I will," said he, "bear for Greenland if ye will give me your company." All said that they would follow his counsel. Then said Bjarne: "Imprudent will appear our voyage since none of us has been in the Greenland ocean."

However, they put to sea so soon as they were ready and sailed for three days, until the land was out of sight under the water; but then the fair wind fell, and there arose north winds and fogs, and they knew not where they were, and thus it continued for many days. After that saw they the sun again, and could discover the sky; they now made sail, and sailed for that day, before they saw land, and counselled with each other about what land that could be, and Bjarne said that he thought it could not be Greenland. They asked whether he wished to sail to this land or not. "My advice is," said he, "to sail close to the land;" and so they did, and soon saw that the land was without mountains, and covered with wood, and had small heights. Then left they the land or their larboard side, and let the stern turn from the land. Afterwards they sailed two days before they saw another land. They asked if Bjarne thought that this was Greenland, but he said that he as little believed this to be Greenland as the other; "because in Greenland are said to be very high ice hills." They soon approached the land, and saw that it was a flat land covered with wood. Then the fair wind fell, and the sailors said that it seemed to them most advisable to land there; but Bjarne was unwilling to do so. They pretended that they were in want of both wood and water. "Ye have no want of either of the two," said Bjarne; for this, however, he met with some reproaches from the sailors. He bade them make sail, and so was done; they turned the prow from the land, and, sailing out into the open sea for three days, with a southwest wind, saw then the third land; and this land was high, and covered with mountains and ice-hills. Then asked they whether Bjarne would land there, but he said that he would not: "for to me this land appears little inviting." Therefore did they not lower the sails, but held on along this land, and saw that it was an island; again turned they the stern from the land, and sailed out into the sea with the same fair wind; but the breeze freshened, and Bjarne then told them to shorten sail, and not sail faster than their ship and ship's gear could hold out. They sailed now four days, when they saw the fourth land. Then asked they Bjarne whether he though that this was Greenland or not. Bjarne answered: "This is the most like Greenland, according to what I have been told about it, and here will we steer for land." So did they, and landed in the evening under a ness; and there was a boat by the ness, and just here lived Bjarne's father, and from him has the ness taken its name, and is since called Herjulfsness. Bjarne now repaired to his father's, and gave up seafaring, and was with his father so long as Herjulf lived, and afterwards he dwelt there after his father.

CHAPTER 3
Voyage of Leif Erikson (A. D. 1008)

THE next thing now to be related is that Bjarne Herjulfson went out from Greenland and visited Erik Jarl, and the Jarl received him well. Bjarne told about his voyages, that he had seen unknown lands, and people thought he had shown no curiosity, when he had nothing to relate about these countries, and this became somewhat a matter of reproach to him. Bjarne became one of the Jarl's courtiers, and came back to Greenland the summer after. There was now much talk about voyages of discovery. Leif, the son of Erik the Red, of Brattahlid, went to Bjarne Herjulfson, and bought the ship of him, and engaged men for it, so that there were thirty-five men in all. Leif asked his father Erik to be the leader on the voyage, but Erik excused himself, saying that he was now pretty well stricken in years, and could not now, as formerly, hold out all the hardships of the sea. Leif said that still he was the one of the family whom good fortune would soonest attend; and Erik gave in to Leif's request, and rode from home so soon as they were ready; and it was but a short way to the ship. The horse stumbled that Erik rode, and he fell off, and bruised his foot. Then said Erik, "It is not ordained that I should discover more countries than that which we now inhabit, and we should make no further attempt in company." Erik went home to Brattahlid, but Leif repaired to the ship, and his comrades with him, thirty-five men. There was a southern 1 on the voyage, who Tyrker hight (named). Now prepared they their ship, and sailed out into the sea when they were ready, and then found that land first which Bjarne had found last. There sailed they to the land, and cast anchor, and put off boats, and went ashore, and saw there no grass. Great icebergs were over all up the country, but like a plain of flat stones was all from the sea to the mountains, and it appeared to them that this land had no good qualities. Then said Leif, "We have not done like Bjarne about this land, that we have not been upon it; now will I give the land a name, and call it Helluland." Then went they on board, and after that sailed out to sea, and found another land; they sailed again to the land, and cast anchor, then put off boats and went on shore. This land was flat, and covered with wood, and white sands were far around where they went, and the shore was low. Then said Leif, "This land shall be named after its qualities, and called Markland 2 (woodland.)" They then immediately returned to the ship.

Now sailed they thence into the open sea, with a northeast wind, and were two days at sea before they saw land, and they sailed thither and came to an island (Nantucket?) which lay to the eastward of the land, 1 and went up there, and looked round them in good weather, and observed that there was dew upon the grass; and it so happened that they touched the dew with their hands, and raised the fingers to the mouth, and they thought that they had never before tasted anything so sweet.

After that they went to the ship, and sailed into a sound, which lay between the island and a ness (promontory), which ran out to the eastward of the land; and then steered westwards past the ness. It was very shallow at ebb tide, and their ship stood up, so that it was far to see from the ship to the water.
But so much did they desire to land, that they did not give themselves time to wait until the water again rose under their ship, but ran at once on shore, at a place where a river flows out of a lake; but so, soon as the waters rose up under the ship, then took they boats, and rowed to the ship, and floated it up to the river, and thence into the lake, and there cast anchor, and brought up from the ship their skin cots, 2 and made their booths.

After this took they counsel, and formed the resolution of remaining there for the winter, and built there large houses. There was no want of salmon either in the river or in the lake, and larger salmon than they had before seen. The nature of the country was, as they thought, so good that cattle would not require house feeding in winter, for there came no frost in winter, and little did the grass wither there. Day and night were more equal than in Greenland or Iceland, for on the shortest day was the sun above the horizon from half-past seven in the forenoon till half-past four in the afternoon.

But when they had done with the house building, Leif said to his comrades:--"Now will I divide our men into two parts, and have the land explored, and the half of the men shall remain at home at the house, while the other half explore the land; but however, not go further than that they can come home in the evening, and they should not separate." Now they did so for a time, and Leif changed about, so that the one day he went with them, and the other remained at home in the house. Leif was a great and strong man, grave and well favoured, therewith sensible and moderate in all things.

CHAPTER 4
Leif Finds Shipwrecked Men

It happened one evening that a man of the party was missing, and this was Tyrker the German. This took Leif much to heart, for Tyrker had been long with his father and him, and loved Leif much in his childhood. Leif now took his people severely to task, and prepared to seek for Tyrker, and took twelve men with him. But when they had gotten a short way from the house, then came Tyrker towards them, and was joyfully received. Leif soon saw that his foster-father was not in his right senses. Tyrker had a high forehead, and unsteady eyes, was freckled in the face, small and mean in stature, but excellent in all kinds of artifice. Then said Leif to him: "Why wert thou so late my fosterer, and separated from the party?" He now spoke first, for a long time, in German, and rolled his eyes about to different sides, and twisted his mouth, but they did not understand what he said. After a time he spoke Norse. "I have not been much further off, but still have I something new to tell of; I found vines and grapes." "But is that true, my fosterer?" quoth Leif. "Surely is it true," replied he, "for I was bred up in a land where there is no want of either vines or grapes." They slept now for the night, but in the morning, Leif said to his sailors: "We will now set about two things, in that the one day we gather grapes, and the other day cut vines and fell trees, so from thence will be a loading for my ship," and that was the counsel taken, and it is said their long boat was filled with grapes. Now was a cargo cut down for the ship, and when the spring came they got ready and sailed away, and Leif gave the land a name after its qualities, and called it Vinland, or Wineland.

They sailed now into the open sea, and had a fair wind until they saw Greenland, and the mountains below the joklers. Then a man put in his word and said to Leif: "Why do you steer so close to the wind?" Leif answered: "I attend to my steering, and something more, and can ye not see anything?" They answered that they could not observe anything extraordinary. "I know not," said Leif, "whether I see a ship or a rock." Now looked they, and said it was a rock. But he saw so much sharper than they that he perceived there were men upon the rock. "Now let us," said Leif, "hold our wind so that we come up to them, if they should want our assistance, and the necessity demands that we should help them; and if they should not be kindly disposed, the power is in our hands, and not in theirs." Now sailed they under the rock, and lowered their sails, and cast anchor, and put out another little boat, which they had with them. Then asked Tyrker who their leader was? He called himself Thorer, and said he was a Northman; "but what is thy name?" said he. Leif told his name. "Art thou a son of Erik the Red, of Brattahlid?" quoth he. Leif answered that so it was. "Now will I," said Leif, "take ye all on board my ship, and as much of the goods

554

as the ship can hold." They accepted this offer, and sailed thereupon to Eriksfjord with the cargo, and thence to Brattahlid, where they unloaded the ship. After that, Leif invited Thorer and his wife Gudrid, and three other men to stop with him, and got berths for the other seamen, as well Thorer's as his own, elsewhere. Leif took fifteen men from the rock; he was, after that, called Leif the Lucky. Leif had now earned both riches and respect. The same winter came a heavy sickness among Thorer's people, and carried off as well Thorer himself as many of his men. This winter died also Erik the Red. Now was there much talk about Leif's voyage to Vinland, and Thorvald, his brother, thought that the land had been much too little explored. Then said Leif to Thorvald: "Thou can'st go with my ship, brother! if thou wilt, to Vinland, but I wish first that the ship should go and fetch the timber, which Thorer had upon the rock;" and so was done.

CHAPTER 5
Thorvald Repairs to Vinland (A. D. 1002)

Now Thorvald made ready for this voyage with 30 men, and took counsel thereon with Leif his brother. Then made the their ship ready, and put to sea, and nothing is told of their voyage until they came to Leif's booths in Vinland. There they laid up their ship, and spent a pleasant winter, and caught fish for their support. But in the spring, said Thorvald, that they should make ready the ship, and that some of the men should take the ship's long boat round the western part of the land, and explore there during the summer. To them appeared the land fair and woody, and but a short distance between the wood and the sea, and white sands; there were many islands, and much shallow water. They found neither dwellings of men nor beasts, except upon an island, to the westward, where they found a corn-shed of wood, but many works of men they found not; and they then went back and came to Leif's booths in the autumn. But the next summer, went Thorvald eastward with the ship, and round the land to the northward. Here came a heavy storm upon them when off a ness, so that they were driven on shore, and the keel broke off from the ship, and they remained here a long time, and repaired their ship. Then said Thorvald to his companions: "Now will I that we fix up the keel here upon the ness, and call it Keelness (Kjalarness), and so did they. After that they sailed away round the eastern shores of the land, and into the mouths of the firths, which lay nearest thereto, and to a point of land which stretched out, and was covered all over with wood. There they came to, with the ship, and shoved out a plank to the land, and Thorvald went up the country with all his companions. He then said: "Here it is beautiful, and here would I like to raise my dwelling." Then went they to the ship, and saw upon the sands within the promontory three elevations, and went thither, and saw there three skin boats (canoes), and three men under each. Then divided they their people, and caught them all, except one, who got away with his boat. They killed the other eight, and then went back to the cape, and looked round them, and saw some heights inside of the frith, and supposed that these were dwellings. After that, so great a drousiness came upon them that they could not keep awake, and they all fell asleep. Then came a shout over them, so that they all awoke. Thus said the shout: "Wake thou! Thorvald! and all thy companions, if thou wilt preserve life, and return thou to thy ship, with all thy men, and leave the land without delay." Then rushed out from the interior of the frith an innumerable crowd of skin boats, and made towards them. Thorvald said then: "We will put out the battle-skreen, and defend ourselves as well as we can, but fight little against them." So did they, and the Skrælings shot at them for a time, but afterwards ran away, each as fast as he could. Then asked Thorvald his men if they had. gotten any wounds; they answered that no one was wounded. "I have gotten a wound under the arm," said he, "for an arrow fled between the edge of the ship and the shield, in under my arm, and here is the arrow, and it will prove a mortal wound to me. Now counsel I ye, that ye get ready instantly to depart, but ye shall bear me to that cape, where I thought it best to dwell; it may be that a true word fell from my mouth, that I should dwell there for a time; there shall ye bury me, and set up crosses at my head and feet, and call the place Krossaness for ever in all time to come." Greenland was then Christianized, but Erik the Red died before Christianity was introduced. Now Thorvald died, but they did all things according to his directions, and then went away, and returned to their companions, and told to each other the tidings which they knew, and dwelt there for the winter, and gathered grapes and vines to load the ship. But in the spring they made ready to sail to Greenland, and came with their ship in Eriksfjord, and could now tell great tidings to Leif.

CHAPTER 6
Unsuccessful Voyage of Thorstein Erikson (A. D. 1005)

MEANTIME it had happened in Greenland that Thorstein in Eriksfjord married Gudrid, Thorbjorn's daughter, who had been formerly married to Thorer the Eastman, as is before related. Now Thorstein Erikson conceived a desire to go to Vinland after the body of Thorvald his brother, and he made ready the same ship, and chose great and strong men for the crew, and had with him 25 men, and Gudrid his wife. They sailed away so soon as they were ready, and came out of sight of the land. They drove about in the sea the whole summer, and knew not where they were; and when the first week of winter was past, then landed they in Lysefjord in Greenland, in the western settlement. Thorstein sought shelter for them and procured lodging for all his crew; but he himself and his wife were without lodging, and they, therefore, remained some two nights in the ship. Then was Christianity yet new in Greenland. Now it came to pass one day that some people repaired, early in the morning, to their tent, and the leader of the party asked who was in the tent. Thorstein answered: "Here are two persons, but who asks the question?" "Thorstein is my name," said the other, "and I am called Thorstein the Black, but my business here is to bid ye both, thou and thy wife, to come and stop at my house." Thorstein said that he would talk the matter over with his wife, but she told him to decide, and he accepted the bidding. "Then will I come after ye in the morning with horses, for I want nothing to entertain ye both; but it is very wearisome at my house, for we are there but two, I and my wife, and I am very morose; I have also a different religion from yours, and yet hold I that for the better which ye have." Now came he after them in the morning with horses, and they went to lodge with Thorstein the Black, who shewed them every hospitality. Gudrid was a grave and dignified woman, and therewith sensible, and knew well how to carry herself among strangers. Early that winter came sickness amongst Thorstein Erikson's men, and there died many of his people. Thorstein had coffins made for the bodies of those who died, and caused them to be taken out to the ship, and there laid; "for I will," said he, "have all the bodies taken to Eriksfjord in the summer." Now it was not long before the sickness came also into Thorstein's house, and his wife, who hight Grimhild took the sickness first; she was very large, and strong as a man, but still did the sickness master her. And soon after that, the disease attacked Thorstein Erikson, and they both lay ill at the same time, and Grimhild, the wife of Thorstein the Black, died. But when she was dead, then went Thorstein out of the room, after a plank to lay the body upon. Then said Gudrid: "Stay not long away, my Thorstein!" he answered that so it should be. Then said Thorstein Erikson: "Strangely now is our house-mother 1 going on, for she pushes herself up on her elbows, and stretches her feet out of bed, and feels for her shoes." At that moment came in the husband Thorstein, and Grimhild then lay down, and every beam in the room creaked. Now Thorstein made a coffin for Grimhild's body, and took it out, and buried it; but although he was a large and powerful man, it took all his strength to bring it out of the place. Now the sickness attacked Thorstein Erikson and be died, which his wife Gudrid took much to heart. They were then all in the room; Gudrid had taken her seat upon a chair beyond the bench upon which Thorstein her husband, had lain; then Thorstein the host took Gudrid from the chair upon his knees, and sat down with her upon another bench, just opposite Thorstein's body. He comforted her in many ways, and cheered her up, and promised to go with her to Eriksfjord, with her husband's body, and those of his companions; "and I will also," added he, "bring many servants to comfort and amuse thee." She thanked him. Then Thorstein Erikson sat himself up on the bench, and said: "Where is Gudrid?" Three times said he that, but she answered not. Then said she to Thorstein the host: "Shall I answer his questions or not?" He counselled her not to answer. After this, went Thorstein the host across the floor, and sat himself on a chair, but Gudrid sat upon his knees, and he said: "What wilt thou, Namesake?" After a little he answered: "I wish much to tell Gudrid her fortune, in order that she may be the better reconciled to my death, for I have now come to a good resting place; but this can I tell thee, Gudrid! that thou wilt be married to an Icelander, and ye shall live long together, and have a numerous posterity, powerful, distinguished, and excellent, sweet and well favoured; ye shall remove from Greenland to Norway, and from thence to Iceland; there shall ye live long, and thou shalt outlive him. Then wilt thou go abroad, and travel to Rome, and come back again to Iceland, to thy house; and then will a church be built, and thou wilt reside there, and become a nun, and there wilt thou die." And when he had said these words, Thorstein fell back, and his corpse was set in order, and taken to the ship. Now Thorstein the host kept well all the promises which he had made to Gudrid; in the spring (1006) he sold his farm, and his cattle, and betook himself to the ship, with Gudrid, and all that he possessed; he made ready the ship, and procured men therefor, and then sailed to Eriksfjord. The bodies were now buried by the Church. Gudrid repaired to Leif in Brattahlid, but Thorstein the Black made himself a dwelling at Eriksfjord, and dwelt there so long as he lived, and was looked upon as a very able man.

CHAPTER 7

That same summer a ship came from Norway to Greenland. The man was called Thorfinn Karlsefne, who steered the ship. he was a son of Thord the Horsehead, son of Snorre, son of Thor from (-- -- --). Thorfinn Karlsefne was very rich in goods, and stayed during the winter at Brattalid with Leif Ericsson. Soon he fell in love with Gudrid and wooed her, but she made Leif answer for her. Afterwards she was betrothed to him, and their bridal was made that winter. At the same time mention was made of a Wineland voyage as before. And called people much upon Karlsefne to make this voyage, both Gudrid and others. Now was settled his voyage and hired he ship soldiers, LX men, and V women. Then the agreement was made by Karlsefne and his crew, that even shares should they have in all, that they got of good things. They had with them all sorts of cattle, because they intended to settle in the country, if they were mighty to do that. Karlsefne asked Leif for his houses in Wineland, but he replied that he might lend him the houses, but give them not. Afterwards they put to sea with the ship and came to Leif's booths whole and sound, and bore there up their leather bags. They got soon in hand a large and good catch, for a whale was driven up there, both large and good; they went hither and cut the whale. Were then not short of food. The cattle went up on the land there, but it soon happened, that the males became unruly and caused much trouble. They had had with them one bull. Karlsefne let trees fell and hew for his ship, and laid the wood on a rock for drying. They profited by all the products of the land, that there were, both of grapes and deer and fish and all good things. After this first winter came summer, they became aware of Skralings, and came there out from the wood a great troop of men. There was near cattle of theirs, and the bull took to bellow and roar extremely, but this frightened the Skralings, and they ran away with their burdens, but those were greyfur and sable and all sorts of skin-wares; and they turned towards Karlsefne's abode and would there enter the houses; but Karlsefne made defend the doors. Neither understood the other's language. Then the Skralings took down their packs and loosened them, and offered them and desired weapons especially for them, but Karlsefne forbade them to sell weapons, and now he takes the counsel, that he bade the women carry out milk to them, and as soon as they saw the milk, then would they buy that and nothing else. Now was this the purchasing of the Skralings, that they carried their bargain away in their stomachs. But Karlsefne and his followers kept their packs and skinwares. Went they thus away. Now is this to be told, that Karlsefne let make a strong fence of pales round his abode and made all ready there. At this time Gudrid, Karlsefne's wife, brought forth a male child, and the boy was called Snorre. At the beginning of the next winter the Skralings came to meet with them,and were many more than before, and had the same wares as before. Then said Karlsefne to the women: now you shall carry out such meat, as was before most asked for, and nothing else. And when they saw it, they cast their packs in over the fence. But Gudrid sat within the door with the cradle of her son Snorre. Then fell a shadow through the door, and entered there a woman in a black narrow kirtle, rather low-built, and she had a ribbon round her head, and light brown hair, pale and large-eyed, so that nobody had seen so large eyes in any human skull. She went up there, where Gudrid sat and asked: what is thy name, says she. My name is Gudrid, but what is thy name. My name is Gudrid, says she.

Then Gudrid the housewife stretched out her hand to her, that she should sit by her, but it happened in the same moment, that Gudrid heard a great crack, and was then the woman lost to sight, and at the same time one Skraling was killed by a house carle of Karlsefne's, because he would have taken their weapons. And went they now away as usual, and their clothes lay there behind, and their wares; no man had seen this woman, but Gudrid alone. Now we may be in need of counsel taking, says Karlsefne, for I think, that they may call at ours the third time with un-peace and with many men. Now we shall take that counsel, that X men go forth on this ness, and show themselves there, but another part of ours shall go into the woods and hew there a road for our cattle, when the troop comes out from the wood; we shall also take our bull and let him go ahead of us. But there were such conditions, where their meeting was planned, that water was on one side but a wood on the other side. Now was this counsel taken, which Karlsefne proposed. Now the Skralings came to the place, which Karlsefne had fixed for the battle. Now was there battle, and were slain many of the Skralings host. One man was tall and fair inthe Skralings host, and Karlsefne thought, he might be headman of them. Now one of them, the Skralings, had taken up an axe, and looked at for a while, and lifted it against his comrade and struck at him. He fell at once dead; then that tall man took the axe and looked at for a while, and hurled it after that into the sea as far as he could. But then they fled into the wood, every one as best he could, and ends now their encounter. Stayed Karlsefne and his men there all the winter, but in the spring Karlsefne announces, that he will there no longer remain, and will go to Greenland. now they make ready for the voyage, and had with them many goods in wine-wood and berries and skin-wares. Now they sail out on the sea and came to Ericsfirth, the ship whole, and stayed there in the winter.

CHAPTER 8
Voyage of Freydis, Helgi and Finnbogi (A. D. 1011)

Now began people again to talk about expeditions to Vinland, for voyages thereto appeared both profitable and honourable. The same summer that Karlsefni came from Vinland, came also a ship from Norway to Greenland; this ship steered two brothers, Helgi and Finnbogi, and they remained for the winter in Greenland. These brothers were Icelanders by descent, and from Austfjord. It is now to be told that Freydis, Erik's daughter, went from her home at Garde to the brothers Helgi and Finnbogi, and bade them that they should sail to Vinland with their vessels, and go halves with her in all the profits which might be there made. To this [232] they agreed. Then went she to Leif her brother, and begged him to give her the houses, which he had caused to be built in Vinland; but he answered the same as before, that he would lend the houses, but not give them. So was it settled between the brothers and Freydis, that each should have thirty fighting men in the ship, besides women. But Freydis broke this agreement, and had five men more, and hid them; so that the brothers knew not of it before they came to Vinland. Now sailed they into the sea, and had before arranged that they should keep together, if it could so be, and there was little difference, but still came the brothers somewhat before, and had taken up their effects to Leif's houses. But when Freydis came to land, then cleared they out their ships, and bore up their goods to the house. Then said Freydis: "Why bring ye in your things here?" "Because we believed," said they, "that the whole agreement should stand good between us." "To me lent Leif the houses," quoth she, "and not to you." Then said Helgi: "In malice are we brothers easily excelled by thee." Now took they out their goods, and made a separate building, and set that building further from the strand, on the edge of a lake, and put all around in good order; but Freydis had trees cut down for her ship's loading. Now began winter, and the brothers proposed to set up sports, and have some amusement. So was done for a time, until evil reports and discord sprung up amongst them, and there was an end of the sports, and nobody came from the one house to the other, and so it went on for a long time during the winter. It happened one morning early that Freydis [233] got up from her bed, and dressed herself, but took no shoes or stockings, and the weather was such that much dew had fallen. She took her husband's cloak, and put it on, and then went to the brothers' house, and to the door; but a man had gone out a little before, and left the door half open. She opened the door, and stood a little time in the opening, and was silent; but Finnbogi lay inside the house, and was awake, and said: "What wilt thou here, Freydis?" She said: "I wish that thou wouldest get up, and go out with me, for I will speak with thee." He did so; they went to a tree that lay near the dwellings, and sat down there. "How art thou satisfied here?" said she; he answered: "Well think I of the land's fruitfulness, but ill do I think of the discord that has sprung up betwixt us, for it appears to me that no cause has been given." "Thou sayest as it is," said she, "and so think I; but my business here with thee, is that I wish to change ships with thy brother, ye have a larger ship than I, and it is my wish to go from hence." "That must I agree to," said he, "if such is thy wish." Now with that they separated; she went home, and Finnbogi to his bed. She got into the bed with cold feet, and thereby woke Thorvard, and he asked why she was so cold and wet. She answered, with much vehemence: "I was gone," said she, "to the brothers, to make a bargain with them about their ship, for I wished to buy the large ship; but they took it so ill that they beat me, and used me shamefully; but thou! miserable man! wilt surely, neither avenge my disgrace nor thine own, and it is easy to see that I am no longer in Greenland, and [234] I will separate from thee if thou avengest not this." And now could he no longer withstand her reproaches, and bade his men to get up, with all speed, and take their arms; and so did they, and went straightway to the brothers' house, and went in, and fell upon them sleeping, and then took and bound them, and thus led out one after the other; but Freydis had each of them killed as he came out. Now were all the men there killed, and only women remained, and them would no one kill. Then said Freydis: "Give me an axe!" So was done; upon which she killed the five women that were there, and did not stop until they were all dead. Now they went back to their house after this evil work, and Freydis did not appear otherwise than as if she had done well, and spoke thus to her people: "If it be permitted us to come again to Greenland," said she, "I will take the life of that man who tells of this business; now should we say this, that they remained behind when we went away." Now early in the spring made they ready the ship that had belonged to the brothers, and loaded it with all the best things they could get, and the ship could carry. After that they put to sea, and had a quick voyage, and came to Eriksfjord with the ship early in the summer. Now Karlsefni was there, and had his ship quite ready for sea, and waited for a fair wind; and

560

it is generally said, that no richer ship has ever gone from Greenland than that which he steered.

CHAPTER 9
Thorfinn Goes to Iceland

Freydis repaired now to her dwelling, which, in the meantime, had stood uninjured; she gave great gifts to all her companions, that they should conceal her misdeeds and sat down now in her house. All were not, however, so mindful of their promises to conceal their crimes and wickedness but that it came out at last. Now finally it reached the ears of Leif, her brother, and he thought very ill of the business. Then took Leif three men of Freydis's band. and tortured them to confess the whole occurrence, and all their statements agreed. "I like not," said Leif, "to do that to Freydis, my sister, which she has deserved, but this I will predict, that thy posterity will never thrive." Now the consequence was, that no one, from that time thought otherwise than ill of them.

Now must we begin from the time when Karlsefni got ready his ship, and put to sea; he had a prosperous voyage, and came safe and sound to Norway, and remained there for the winter and sold his goods, and both he and his wife were held in great honor by the most respectable men in Norway. But the spring after, fitted he out his ship for Iceland; and when he was all ready, and his ship lay at the bridge waiting for a fair wind, then came there a southern to him, who was from Bremen in Saxony, and wanted to buy from Karlsefni his house broom. "I will not sell it," said he. "I will give thee a half mark gold for it," said the German. Karlsefni thought this was a good offer, and they closed the bargain. The southern went off with the house [236] broom, but Karlsefni knew not what wood it was; but that was mausur, brought from Vinland. Now Karlsefni put to sea, and came with his ship to Skagafjord, on the northern coast, and there was the ship laid up for the winter. But in spring bought he Glaumbæland, and fixed his dwelling there, and lived there, and was a highly respected man, and from him and Gudrid his wife has sprung a numerous and distinguished race. And when Karlsefni was dead, took Gudrid the management of the house with her son Snorri, who was born in Vinland. But when Snorri was married, then went Gudrid abroad, and travelled southwards, and came back again to the house of Snorri her son, and then had he caused a church to be built at Glaumbæ. After this, became Gudrid a nun and recluse, and remained so whilst she lived. Snorri had a son who Thorgeir hight; he was father to Ingveld, mother of Bishop Brand. The daughter of Snorri Karlsefnesson hight Hallfrid; she was mother to Runolf, father to Bishop Thorlak. Bjorn hight a son of Karlsefni and Gudrid; he was father to Thorunn, mother of Bishop Bjarn. A numerous race are descended from Karlsefni, and distinguished men; and Karlsefni has accurately related to all men the occurrences on all these voyages, of which somewhat is now recited here.

THE TALE OF THORSTEIN STAFF-SMITTEN

There was a man called Thorarin, who dwelt in Sunnudale, an old man and feeble of sight: he had been a red-hand viking in his younger days, nor was he a man good to deal with though he were old. One son he had, hight Thorstein, a big man, sturdy, but well ruled, who worked in such wise about his father's house that three men else would not have turned out more work. Thorstein was not a wealthy man, but good weapons he had: stud-horses also that father and son owned, that brought them in the most of their money, whereas they would sell away the horse-colts, who were such that they never failed either in bottom or courage.

There was one Thord, a house-carle of Biarni of Hof: he took heed of Biarni's riding-horses, for a horse-learned man he was accounted. Thord was a very unjust man, and would let many a man feel that he was house-carle of a mighty man: yet was he not of better worth therefor, nor better befriended.

Two others also abode with Biarni, one named Thorhall, the other Thorvald: great tale-bearers about all that they heard in the countryside.

Now Thorstein and Thord set afoot a horse fight for the young horses, and when they drave them together Thord's horse was put to the worse: so Thord smote Thorstein's horse on the nose with a great stroke when he saw he was getting the worst of it; which thing Thorstein saw, and smote Thord's horse in return a stroke bigger yet, so that Thord's horse ran away, and men fell a-whooping hugely.

Then Thord smote Thorstein with his horse-staff, and the stroke came on the brow so that the skin fell over the eyes. So Thorstein tore a clout from his shirt and bound up his brow, and made as if nought had happened, and bade men hide this from his father; and so the matter dropped. But Thorhall and Thorvald made a mock of this, and called him Thorstein Staff-smitten.

A little before Yule that winter the women rose up early to their work at Sunnudale, and then stood up Thorstein and bare in hay, and afterward lay down on a bench. Now cometh in old Thorarin, his father, and asked who lay there, and Thorstein told of himself.

"Why art thou so early afoot, son?" said old Thorarin.

Thorstein answered: "There are few to mate with me in the work I win here."

"Art thou not ailing in the head-bone, son?" said Thorarin.

"I know nought thereof," said Thorstein.

"What canst thou tell me, son, of the Horse-meet last summer? Wert thou not beaten into swooning like a hound, kinsman?"

"I think it not worth while," said Thorstein, "to account it a stroke; it was a chance hap rather."

Thorarin said: "I should not have thought it, that I could have a faint-heart for a son."

"Father," said Thorstein, "speak thou nought but what thou wilt not think overmuch said in time to come."

"I will not say so much as my heart would," said Thorarin.

Now rose up Thorstein and taketh his weapons, and went his ways from home till he came to the horse-house where Thord was a-heeding the horses of Biarni, and there he found Thord.

So Thorstein came up to him and said to him: "I would wot, friend Thord, whether that was a chance blow that I gat from thee last summer at the Horse-meet, or if it were done wilfully of thee?"

Thord answereth: "If thou hast two mouths, thrust thou thy tongue now in one, now in the other and call the one a chance stroke and the other a wilful: lo, there all the boot thou gettest of me."

"See to it," said Thorstein, "that I most like shall not claim boot of thee again." And he fell on him therewith and smote him his death-blow. Then he went to the house at Hof, and met a woman without and said to her: "Tell thou to Biarni that a beast hath gored Thord, his horse-boy, and that he will abide him there by the horse-house till he cometh."

"Go thy ways home, man," said she, "and I will tell it when it seemeth good to me."

So Thorstein went home and the woman went to her work.

Biarni rose up that morning, and when he was gotten to table he asked where Thord was, and men answered that he must have gone to work the horses.

"I should have thought he would have been home by now if he were well," said Biarni.

Then the woman whom Thorstein had met took up the word: "True it is what is oft said of us womanfolk, that there is little of wits at work where we women are. Here came this morning Thorstein Staff-smitten, and said that a beast had gored Thord so that he might not help himself: but I was loth to wake thee, and so it slipped out of my head."

Then Biarni went from the table and out to the horse-house, and found Thord slain; and he was buried thereafter.

Biarni set a-foot a bloodsuit, and had Thorstein made guilty of the slaying: but Thorstein abode at home in Sunnudale and worked for his father, and Biarni let things be.

In the autumn sat men by the singeing-fires at Hof, but Biarni was lying outside the wall of the fire-hall, and hearkened thence the talk of men.

Now those brethren Thorhall and Thorvald take up the word: "We thought not when we first took up abode with Slaying Biarni that we should have been singeing lambs' heads here, while Thorstein, Biarni's outlaw, was singeing wethers' heads at Sunnudale: better had it been to have spared his kin something more in Bodvarsdale rather than to have let his outlaw hold his head so high in Sunnudale; but 'most men are foredone when wounds befall them:' nor wot we when he will wipe this stain from his honour."

A certain man answered: "It is worse to say such words than to hold peace over them: like it is that the trolls have set the tongues wagging in the heads of you. For we deem that Biarni is loth to take the help and sustenance from the sightless father and other helpless creatures at Sunnudale. Marvellous I shall deem it if ye are oft a-singeing lambs' heads here, or laughing over what betid in Bodvarsdale."

Now go men to table and so to sleep, and nought was it seen of Biarni that he had taken to heart what had been talked.

But the next morning Biarni waked Thorhall and Thorvald, and bade them ride to Sunnudale, and bring him at breakfast-tide the head of Thorstein sheered from his body: "For meseemeth ye are the most like to wipe the stain from my honour if I have not heart to do it myself."

Now deem they that they have assuredly spoken overmuch, but they go their ways nevertheless till they come to Sunnudale.

Thorstein stood in the door there whetting a sax, and when they came thereto he asked them what they would, and they said they must needs seek their horses: so Thorstein said they had but a little way to seek, "For here they are by the garth."

"It is not sure," say they, "that we shall find the horses, unless thou show us of them clearly."

So Thorstein went out; and when they were come down into the garth Thorvald hove up his axe and ran at him: Thorstein smote him with his hand so that he fell forward, and then put the sax through him. Then would Thorhall be on him, and fared in likewise with Thorvald. Then Thorstein bindeth them both a-horseback, and layeth the reins on the horses' necks, and bringeth them all on to the road, and home now go the horses to Hof.

The house-carles were without at Hof, and they go in and tell Biarni that Thorvald and his fellow were come home, and they said that they had not gone for nought. So Biarni goeth out and seeth how their dealings have gone; and he made no words about the matter, but had them laid in earth, and all is now quiet till Yule over.

Then Rannveig took up the word one night, when they came into bed together, Biarni and she----

"What thinkest thou is most talked of in the countryside?" saith she.

"I wot not," saith Biarni: "many men are unnoteworthy of their words," saith he.

"Well," says she, "this is oftenest in men's mouths, 'What will Thorstein Staff-smitten do that thou wilt think thou must needs avenge?' He hath now slain three of thy house-carles: and thy Thingmen think that there is no upholding in thee if this be unavenged; and the hands laid on knee are ill-laid for thee."

Biarni answereth: "Now it comes to that which is said: 'None will be warned by another's woe;' yet will I hearken to what thou sayest. Few men though hath Thorstein slain sackless."

Therewith they drop this talk and sleep away the night.

On the morrow wakeneth Rannveig as Biarni took down his shield, and asked him what he would?

He answereth: "We shall shift and share honour between us in Sunnudale today, Thorstein and I."

"How many in company?" saith she

"I will not drag a host against Thorstein," saith he. "I shall fare alone."

"Do it not," saith she, "to risk thyself alone under the weapons of that man of Hell!"

Said Biarni: "Yea, dost thou not after the fashion of women, bewailing now what ye egged on to then? A long while oft I bare the taunts both of thee and of others, but it will not avail to stay me when I will be afoot."

So fareth now Biarni to Sunnudale, where stood Thorstein in the door, and certain words went between them. Said Biarni: "Today shalt go with me, Thorstein, to the single-fight on yonder knoll amidst the home-mead."

"All is lacking to me," said Thorstein, "that I might fight with thee: but I will get me abroad so soon as a ship saileth: for I know of thy manliness, that thou wilt get work done for my father if I fare from him."

"It availeth not to cry off," said Biarni.

"Give me leave then to see my father first," said Thorstein.

"Yea, sure," saith Biarni.

So Thorstein went in and told his father that Biarni was come thither, who bade him to single-fight. Old Thorarin answered---

"A man must look for it if he have to do with one mightier than he, and abide in the same countryside with him, and hath done him some dishonour, that he will not live to wear out many shirts. Nor may I mourn for thee, for meseemeth thou hast earned it: so take thy weapons and do thy manliest. Time has been when I would not have budged before such as Biarni: yet is he the greatest of champions. Now would I rather lose thee than have a coward son."

So Thorstein went out, and then they went to the Knoll, and fell a-fighting eagerly, smiting the armour sorely from each other. And when they had fought a long while, Biarni said to Thorstein: "I am athirst, for I am more unwont to the work than thou."

"Go thou to the brook and drink, then," said Thorstein.

That did Biarni, and laid his sword down beside him. Thorstein took up the sword and looked on it, and said: "This sword thou wilt not have had in Bodvarsdale."

Biarni answered not, and they went up again on to the Knoll, and fought for an hour's space; and Biarni deemed the man skilled of fight, and faster on foot than he had looked for.

"Many haps hinder me today," said Biarni: "now is my shoe-tie loose."

"Bind it up, then," said Thorstein.

So Biarni stoops down; but Thorstein went in and brought out two shields and a sword, and went to the Knoll to Biarni, and said to him----

"Here is a shield and a sword which my father sendeth thee, and the blade will not dull more in smiting than that which thou hast had heretofore. And for me, I am loth to stand shieldless any longer before thy strokes; nay, I were fain to leave this play, for I fear me that thy luck will go further than my lucklessness: and every lad listeth to live if he may rule the rede."

"It availeth not to beg off," said Biarni; "we shall fight on yet."

"I will not smite first," said Thorstein.

Then Biarni smote away all the shield from Thorstein, and after Thorstein smote the shield from Biarni.

"A great stroke," said Biarni.

Thorstein answered: "Thine was no less."

Biarni said: "Better biteth now that same weapon of thine which thou hast borne all day afore."

Thorstein said: "I would spare myself an illhap if I might; and with thee I fight afeard: I will let all the matter lie under thy dooming."

And now it was Biarni's turn to smite, and they were both shieldless. So Biarni said: "It will be an ill bargain to take a crime to one instead of a good-hap: I shall deem me well paid for my three house-carles by thee alone if thou wilt be true to me."

Thorstein answereth: "Time and place served me today that I might have bewrayed thee, if so be my haplessness had been mightier than thy good hap: I will not bewray thee."

"I see of thee," said Biarni, "that thou art peerless among men. Give me leave to go in to thy father, and tell him such things as I will."

"Go thou in as for me," said Thorstein, "but fare thou warily."

So Biarni went in, and to the shut-bed wherein lay the carle Thorarin. Thorarin asked who went there; and Biarni named himself.

"What tidings tellest thou me, my Biarni?" said Thorarin.

"The slaying of Thorstein thy son," said Biarni.

"Made he any defence?" said Thorarin.

"I think no man hath been better man at arms than was Thorstein thy son."

"Nought woundrous," said the old man; "though thou wert hard to deal with in Bodvarsdale if thou hast overcome my son."

Then said Biarni: "I bid thee to Hof, and thou shalt sit in the second high-seat whiles thou livest, and I will be to thee in a son's stead."

"So it fareth with me," said the old man, "as with them who have no might, that: 'Oft is the fool fain of promise.' But such are the promises of you great men, when ye will appease a man after such haps as this, that it is a month's rest to us, and thereafter are we held even as worthy as other poor wretches, and no sooner for all that do our sorrows wear out. Nevertheless, he who taketh handsel of such a man as thee may be well content with his lot, when matters are to be doomed on; and this handsel will I take of thee. So come thou on to my shut-bed floor, and draw very nigh, for the old carle tottereth on his feet now with eld and feebleness; nor deem it so but my dead son yet runneth in my head."

567

So Biarni went up on to the shut-bed floor, and took old Thorarin by the hand, and found him fumbling with a sax which he had a mind to thrust into Biarni. So he drew aback his hand and said: "Wretchedest of old carles! now shall it go as meet is betwixt us! Thorstein thy son lives, and shall home with me to Hof: but I will get thee thralls to work for thee, nor shalt thou want for aught while thou livest."

So Thorstein fared home to Hof with Biarni, and served him till his death-day, and was deemed peerless of any man for manhood and courage.

Biarni kept his honour still, and waxed ever in friendship and good conditions the older he grew; and was the best proven of all men, and was a man of great faith in his latter days. He fared abroad and went south, and in that journey died, and resteth in the burg called Valeri, a little way hitherward from Rome-town. Biarni was a man happy of kin: his son was Skeggbroddi, much told of in tale, a man peerless in his days.

So here an end of telling of Thorstein Staff-smitten.

INTRODUCTION TO THE ORKNEYINGERS' SAGA

SHETLAND, THE ORKNEYS, AND CAITHNESS

The two groups of islands, in which the events narrated in the Orkneyingers' Saga for the most part happened, are widely different in their geographical confirmation. While the Orkneys lie like Cyclades round Hrossey or the Mainland, and are tolerably equal in size and shape, Shetland may be said to be altogether overpowered by its Mainland, which is larger than all the other islands put together, only two or three of which are of any importance. Added to this the Orkneys are, with the exception of a part of Hoy, "the tall island," generally flat; and the hills even in Hrossey rarely rise to any great elevation. When we have named Wideford Hill, the Keely Long Hills, the Ward Hill of Orfir, and the uplands of Rowsay, we have almost exhausted the hills of Orkney. In Shetland, on the other hand, the Mainland is full of high hills and headlands culminating in North Mavin at the extreme north-west of the island in Rona's Hill. Between the two groups politically united in the days described in the Orkneyingers' Saga, but thus physically distinct, lies the waste of waters called Sumburgh Roost in modern times, and "Dynraust," or Dynröst, that is the "thundering, roaring roost" by the Northmen who saw in its wild waves and rushing tides an apt occasion for the name. In the midst of this Race lies the Fair Isle, the Friðarey of the Saga, an isle shunned by travellers and steamers at the present time, and memorable in the story of the Armada for Spanish shipwrecks, but not so inhospitable in older days when its bays and creeks afforded frequent shelter to the small craft in which the Northmen ran from one group of islands to the other. There is probably no part of the British Isles which now plays a less part and is more rarely heard of than the Fair Isle or Fair Hill as it is sometimes incorrectly called, but there was certainly none which in the time of earl Rognvald-Kali was more conspicuous in Orkney story. Then Friðarey formed the point on which the earl's operations against the Orkneys turned, and it was on Friðarey that the beacons were to have been lighted which were to warn earl Paul and his adherents that mischief was threatening them from Shetland. The Fair Isle, therefore, forms in the Saga a geographical link between the two groups of Orkney and Shetland, and we can hardly understand the story unless we keep the position of Friðarey on the map steadily in view.

Having thus roughly sketched in outline the two groups and their connecting link, let us enter more fully into the geographical description of the two groups themselves, and let us begin with Shetland, as the group which the Northmen first made as they ran over from Norway, and which we may be sure was known to their vikings and sea-rovers before the more westerly group.

Whatever may be the case with the name of Orkney, it is certain that the name which Shetland bore before the Northmen called it Hjaltland or Hjaltaland is lost. Some, indeed, have thought with Munch that these islands never had any fixed population before the Northmen, except those Papæ or Irish Anchorites and Hermits, whose cells are found on all the islands of the west as far as Iceland. But it is clear that this view is unfounded. Not to mention the existence in Shetland of those burghs or castles, of which that on the isle of Moussa alone remains in something like its full proportions, the underground dwellings and "weems" in which the Shetland as well as the Orkney Isles abound afford evidence to prove that both groups of islands were inhabited in early times by one, and probably two distinct races, to one of which the subterranean earth dwellings and underground weems are to be assigned, while to the other and more advanced race the burghs and castles, which tower above the soil like Moussa, are due. What these races were, whether the first which dwelt underground, in what the Icelandic Sagas call "jarðhúsa," were Esquimaux of Turanian race, while the burghs, or castles, or Picts' houses, are the handiwork of that mysterious race of Picts so long the terror of British antiquaries, may be matter of doubt. But certain it is, from the evidence of our eyes, that both the dwellers in the earthhouses and weems and the builders of the burghs existed long before the arrival of the Northmen. How those races perished and passed away is also a matter of which we are in complete ignorance. It would seem from the silence of the Sagas, and still more perhaps from the fact that the anchorites referred to only chose the waste places of the earth for their ascetic abodes, that the Northmen really found those islands empty and desolate, and that it was not before their swords that the ancient races vanished away. If so this only throws these questions further up the stream of time. Who were the races who built these subterranean dwellings and these towering burghs? By what name did they call the country? And how did they vanish, leaving no trace of their nationality behind?

As soon as the Northmen came they gave the new found land a name, and they called it "Hjaltaland," or "Hjaltland," from "Hjalt," the knob or guard of the hilt of a sword. It is idle to ask why the name was given, for the Northmen, as Munch well says, gave names to places from the most trivial accidents; as when Auda, the Deeply-wealthy, who passed from Scotland to Iceland by way of Shetland, called a headland or "ness" "Kambnes," or Combness, because she had lost her comb there. In the same way Shetland may have been called "Hjaltland," or "Hjaltaland" because some sea-rover lost the pommel of his sword there. It is easier to show how the modern Shetland ---not Zetland, which is a barbarous distortion--- arose out of the ancient Hjaltland. First of all the pronunciation of the word went over in Norway itself to Hjeltland and Hjetland; the inhabitants of Shetland were called by their Norwegian cousins, "Hjelter" instead of Hjalter; and even at this day we have the authority of Munch for saying that boats built in Norway for sale in Shetland are called "Hjeltebaade," while the northern entrance to Bergen Sound, the point for which ships from Shetland usually steered, is still called "Hjeltefjord." At the same time, as the pronunciation of "Hj" in many Norwegian dialects is very nearly "Sh" or "Sch," the name of the group must have sounded to Scotch and English ears as "Shatland" or "Shetland," and thus "Hjaltaland" or "Hjeltland," written phonetically, would have become Shatland or Shetland, and so passed into legal deeds and documents. Just in the same way the supposed name of the Orkney Island, "Hjálpandisey," was turned into "Shapandsey," "Shapensey," and "Shapinsay." It can also be shown that this change of name occurred early, for in a deed of the year 1289, given in Rymer's Fœdera, I. 2, p. 706, we find the name of Thorvaldus de Shetland, and in a letter of the year 1319, in the Acts of the Parliament of Scotland, vol. I., and also printed in the Diplomatarium Norwegicum, II. No. 114, the form "Syettelandia" occurs. In the same way the ponies which come from Shetland are called "Shelties," which is only another form of the word "Hjelte" or "Hjalte," and means "Shetlander," just in the same way, as Munch well observes, Norwegian horses are called "Norbagger," that is, "Norwegians," and horses from Arabia "Arabs." In another point of view the form "Sheltie" is curious as retaining the "l" of the original name, which is thus preserved in common speech, though it has dropped out of the name of the country itself.

Passing from the common appellation of the whole group of islands to each in particular, we find the principal islands mentioned in our Saga, or in old deeds and documents to be the following: --- Meginland, Mainland, Jalda, or Ála, the modern Yell; Örnist or Örmstr, the modern Unst; Fetilar or Fætilör, the modern Fetlar; Hvalsey, the modern Whalesay; Nös, the modern Noss; Brúsey, the modern Bressay; Mosey or Morsey, the modern Moussa; two called Papey, the big and the little; Glumsey; Fugley, the modern Foula; and Friðarey, the modern Fair Isle or Fair Hill.

Of these after the Mainland, the ancient Meginland, Jala is often named as well as Jalasund or Álasund, the modern Yell Sound, which arose out of the ancient name by a very natural corruption. Munch has pointed out that as the form "Jala" occurs in a list of islands and firths given in Skálda, and printed in the Ann. for North. Archæol. 1846, p. 86, it is probably the true form, and not, Ála, in both of which the final –a is another of those old indeclinable endings in –a which also occur in "Gula" and "Aga," and must not be confounded with the feminine ending –a which forms u in the genitive. The Saga, p. 107, speaks of Álasund, and not Jalasund, on the authority of a good MS., 325. As to the original meaning of the word we have no information, but any one who has lain in Yell Sound and seen the rush of its tideway and heard the roaring which it makes both in flood and ebb, will acknowledge that the modern "yell" is very suggestive of the character of its waters. It was in Álasund that earl Paul seized the ships of his rival earl Rognvald, Tr. p. 114.

We next come to Örnist, or "Onyst," or "Örmstr," as our text of the Saga gives it, p. 93. This island is the modern Unst. In the list given in Skálda the form "Ormstr" occurs. While Munch decides for the form Örnist, which he thinks may be derived from the Eagles Örn, which may build in the high cliffs of Unst, the Saga, as well as Skálda, speak for Örmstr. Unst is mentioned in the Saga, and it is remarkable that several of the cures at the shrine of St. Magnus were worked on afflicted persons who came from this island. In this island lies Haroldswick, the ancient Haraldsvík, said to have been called after Harold Fairhair, who lay there on his expedition to the Hebrides. If he lay there at all, it is more likly that he lay in Baltasound, which forms a splendid harbour. Ballastead, Ballastaðir, is mentioned in the Saga, p. 93, in the accounts of the miracles of earl Magnus; but as the modern name of the "sound" is Baltasound it is not unlikely that the true reading should be Baltastaðir.

Fætilör, the modern Fetlar, occurs in the list from the Skálda, but the short Saga of St. Magnus reads "Fetilar," as we have corrected the false reading "Færeyjum," of the Cod. Flat. Saga, p. 91. Munch thinks the name is derived from fót, leg or foot, and that the "lör" of the ending should be "laer," a thigh, in which case the name might come from a fanciful resemblance in the shape of the island to a human thigh.

Passing over the minor islands, we come to Brúsey or Brúsi's island, the modern representative of which is the modern Bressay, which helps to make the magnificent harbour of Lerwick off the Mainland. It perhaps takes its name from Brúsl, one of the earlier Orkney earls, and earl Rognvald's father.

The two islands called Papa Stour and Papa Little recall the anchorites, recall the anchorites, who have left evidence of thier ancient occupation of them in those names. Papa Stour means the big Papa, as Papa Little means the small Papa. In the Icelandic they would be Papey Stora and Papey Littla.

The Mainland of Shetland though preponderating in size over all the other islands, plays no such part in the Orkneyingers' Saga as that assumed by Hrossey of the Mainland of Orkney. That was the abode of mighty earls who had their seats at various times in different parts of the island. But the Mainland of Shetland, so far as the Orkney Saga is concerned, seems rather to have been used by those great chiefs as a house of call or a harbour of refuge. So it was that Harold Fairhair and a long line of kings of his race who followed him steered for Shetland on their voyages west, and after laying in Bressay Sound off the modern Lerwick, or in some other convenient haven for a while, passed on to conquest or piracy further west. The case was nearly the same with the Orkney earls and with the chiefs and bishops who passed west from Norway. When earl Rognvald-Kali, the kinsman of Saint Magnus set out on his expeditions against earl Paul Hacon's son, he twice made Shetland his halting place, once to return inglorious to his politic father's house, and once again to pass on victorious to the Orkneys. So again when earl Paul had been seized and carried off, and when earl Rognvald at the height of his power resolved on a pilgrimage to the Holy Land, he sailed for Shetland from Norway in his two ships Help and Arrow and lost them both in the breakers of Gullberwick near the modern Lerwick. (Tr. p. 154, 155.) The loss of his ships delayed him long in Shetland. The Saga expressly says that "the earl stayed very long in Shetland" that autumn, and it was then that the romantic episode occurred which is described in the Story of Earl Rognvald.

On other occasions when we hear of any of the earls going to Shetland it is only to stay there for a comparatively short time, and never with a view to a fixed above. It follows from this that but very few Shetland names are mentioned in the Saga even on the Mainland, and though we can in most cases restore the old Norse names from their modern equivalents, we can but rarely point to the old names themselves in the pages of the Saga. One of these cases in which we can fix the locality of the ancient name with certainty is Borgarfjörðr now Burrafirth on the Mainland, of which we read at p. 75 of our Saga, Tr. p. 76, that while earl Hacon and earl Magnus held the joint wardship of the land, they made an expedition to Shetland and put to death Thorbjorn, a nobleman in "Burrafirth." On a holm near the "voe" stands the ruins of the "Borg" or "Burgh" which gave a name to the Firth, which seems to have been a castle of the same kind as that on the isle of Moussa, and if so erected long before the arrival of the Northmen in Shetland. (1) Munch supposes that it was in this castle that the noble Thorbjorn lived when he was cut off about the year 1100 by the cousins, and that from its strength he must have made a long resistance. But the Saga simply says that the two earls went against him together and put him to death.

Another place to which we can assign its ancient name is Gulberwick, not far from Lerwick, which is a town of comparatively modern origin. This, beyond doubt, is the Gullberuvík of the Saga mentioned in p. 151 as the place where, at the house of a man named Einar, earl Rognvald-Kali and twelve of his men were hospitably received after his shipwreck.

But perhaps the most interesting place in all Shetland is the burgh of Moussa which lies near Sandwick (Sandvík) in the southern part of the Shetland Main. Here, on a little island, stands the "Burgh" of which we have already spoken, and the only one of those ancient castles which exists in tolerable preservation. It was famous for its strength before the period of which the Saga treats, for in the Egils Saga, ch. 32 and 33, we read that about the year 900 Björn the freeman from Aurland in Sogn, in Norway, who had run away with Thora Hladhand, the sister of Thorir, a hersir or baron from the district called the Firths, and was on his voyage with her to Iceland, suffered shipwreck in Shetland, and took refuge in this castle while his ship was being repaired. In that Saga it is called Morseyjarborg or Moseyjarborg, a name which we find in our Saga, p. 189, where oddly enough, we find another pair of fugitive lovers taking shelter in its strong walls. In the year 1153 Erlend the young, a noble chief, but not, as some have supposed, the young earl of that name, carried off, or rather run off with earl Harold Maddadson's mother Margaret, who is described as rather a forward woman. The pair fled from the wrath of the earl and shut themselves up in the burgh on Moussa, where they were besieged for some time by earl Harold, until peace was made between him and them, and Erlend was allowed to marry the widow of Maddad who had been earl of Athole.

These are almost the only places which can be identified in Shetland, and which are mentioned in the Saga. All the names in these islands are

572

corruptions of old Norse names as Scalloway and Thingwell, which are clearly the old "Skálavágr" and "Þingvöll." The latter was the place where the solemn assemblies of the freeman were held, as was invariably the case in early Northern times, under the free and open air of heaven; while the former was the bay or "voe" on which the booths and huts were erected for the convenience and shelter of those who attended the assemblies, and which temporary shelter gradually grew into a village, and a town. In later times when the fashion of open-air Parliaments went out, Scalloway became the place of meeting, and there in a building the later assemblies were held. These and many other old names have been identified by Munch in his exhaustive essays on this subject in the Annals for Northern Archæology; but our purpose here is with the names and places actually mentioned in the Saga. Before we pass on from Shetland to the Fair Isle, across Sumburgh Roost, which takes its name from Sumburgh, the southernmost point of the island, let us pause to remark that as the troubled sea between Shetland and Orkney was called "Dynröst" (Saga, p. 192), and as the modern name for the southernmost parish of the Shetland mainland, is Dunrossness, it is plain that this modern application is only a distortion of "Dynrastarnes," the first part of which is the genitive of "Dynröst." Dynrastarnes does not occur in the text of the Saga, but in the new matter printed in this edition we find both Dynrastar höfcti and Dynrastarvágr, Dynröst-head and Dynrost-voe, as the old names for the headland now called Sumburgh Head and the voe beneath it, out of which earl Rognvald rowed in disguise with the poor fisherman to fish at the very edge of the dangerous race (pp. 155-7). The word "Sumburgh," is to be found in the old Norse "Svínborg" and in earlier deeds is called not "Sumburgh" but "Swynburgh." The "Fitful Head," separated from its sister headland by Quendal Bay, which all readers of the "Pirate" know, has unfortunately nothing to do with the capricious nature of the winds, but is derived, as Munch has shown, from the old "Fitfuglahöfði," that is, the head covered with sea-foul, or "web-footed birds," "fitfuglar," which may still be seen sitting in myriads on the ledges of the noble promontory which rises more than 900 feet into the air.

From all that we have said of Shetland, it will be seen that to the Orkneyingers it was always more or less a foreign land. The one group seems to have clung more closely to Norway, and to have been far more dependent on that country than the other. We hear little there of risings against the power of the kings of Norway, and Norwegians seem always to have been welcome in Shetland, as may be seen by the way in which Rognvald-Kali, a pure Norwegian on his father's side, was welcomed on his expeditions against Orkney, and from the dread which earl Paul had of landing and fighting out his quarrel with his rival, even after he had seized his ships in Yell Sound. The Saga, p. 114, expressly says that the reason why earl Paul would not land was that he put no trust in the Shetlanders, and the best proof that his power over these islands was merely nominal is to be found in the fact that earl Rognvald stayed there the whole summer after the loss of his ships in the autumn, only to return to Shetland the summer after on a more successful expedition. It is evident, therefore, that geographically as well as politically the Shetlanders were more dependent on Norway. Lying north-east and not far from the Faroes, both their politics and position were Norwegian, while the Orkneys, lying more to the west and farther from the mother country of the first settlers, were more independent, and besides politically attracted towards Scotland and the British Isles. Much, no doubt, was due to the seat of rule being in the Orkneys, from which the earls ruled Shetland as a dependency, but still more was owing to the geographical position of the group of isles, and to the temper of the people, which in Shetland remained more purely Norse than the inhabitants of the sister group. At last, in the days of king Sverrir, at the end of the 12th century, in the year 1194, just at the period when the Orkneyingers' Saga ends, Shetland was separated by that king altogether from Orkney, and associated, for the purpose of government, with the Faroe islands, and thus the earls of Orkney lost for some years the rights of lordship and the power of taxation which they had so long held over Shetland as vassals of the Kings of Norway. pp. 231, 235-6.

We now leave Shetland, and pass on our way to the Orkneys, stopping for a while at the Fair Isle or Fairhill, the Friðarey of the Saga, in which, at one period, the little island became suddenly famous. The position of the Fair Isle midway between Orkney and Shetland made it a very important place when the power of earl Paul Hacon's son was threatened by the expeditions of Rognvald-Kali, who claimed to be one of the rightful earls of the Orkneys, not only because of the grant which King Harold Gilli had made to him, but because he was the son of the sister of the saint, earl Magnus, and thus came into the land strong both from a political and a religious point of view. In those days the proverb was as true as it has ever been before and since, "forewarned is forearmed." It was everything to earl Paul to know when earl Rognvald, whom he knew had arrived among the untrusty Shetlanders, would start on his expedition against the Orkneys. For this purpose, as our Saga informs us, p. 115, a system of beacons was established, the first of which was to be on the Fair Isle, a second on Rínansey, or North Ronaldsay, a third on Sanday, a fourth on Westray, and a fifth on Rowsay. But all the others rested on the first, so that the beacon on the Fair Isle was the most important of all. These several beacons were entrusted to the care of earl Paul's most faithful adherents, and not the least interesting portion of the Saga is that which describes how this system of beacons was turned to the gain, instead of the harm of earl Rognvald, by the good counsel of his father, the politic Kol. At that time the chief householder on the Fair Isle was Dagfinn Hlodver's son, described at p. 122 of the Saga as "a brisk stirring man." So long as he had charge of the beacon it was sure to be lighted at the first approach of an enemy. But at p. 124 foll. we are informed how even the wary Dagfinn was deceived by the guile of Kol into lighting the beacon on a false alarm; how the warning lights spread from isle to isle, and earl Paul's host flocked together, only to find themselves gathered for no purpose; and at last how quarrels and recriminations arose, in the course of which Dagfinn was slain. After that false alarm a man named Eric succeeded to the care of the beacon on the Fair Isle, who, not so wary as Dagfinn, was beguiled into handing over the beacon to the care of Uni, a confederate of Kol, who took care to drench it so thoroughly with water that it would not catch fire when earl Rognvald really started with his expedition (p. 127). The result was that no beacons were lighted on the other islands, and earl Rognvald established himself in Westray, whither his friends and kinsmen soon flocked to him in sufficient numbers to enable him to hold his own against earl Paul. After this sudden blaze, like that of its own beacon, the Fair Isle, or Friðarey, passed out of the story, and is scarcely mentioned again, except at p. 195, when Sweyn Asleif's son bore up for it when he and earl Erlend the young

574

were caught and parted in Sumburgh Roost in such a violent storm that each gave the other up as lost.

From the Fair Isle we pass on to Rínansey or North Ronaldsay, the first of the Orkney islands. But before we proceed farther, let us, as we have given the etymology of the name Shetland, spend a little time in the consideration of the name Orkney. If we can believe that Shetland was a nameless land till the Northmen came and called it after the pommel of a sword, the same cannot be said of the Orkneys, which were already called Orcades by Pliny the elder in his Natural History, I. 4. ch. 10., and Juvenal in his second Satire, II. 161, (2) quotations which show that the name did not arise with the Northmen who came more than 700 years after Pliny, but that it is only their adaptation of the old Celtic name which the islands received from their earliest inhabitants. The Irish and Gaelic tribes called the group "Innsi'h Orce," or Innish Orc, that is the Ork isles; the Northmen Orkn-eyjar, that is the Orkn-isles, where Orkn- seems to be a contraction of Orkan, for the Anglo-Saxons called the group Orcan-ig, where "an" is only a derivative ending, and has nothing to do with the root. That root is "Ork" or "Orc," and, as we must look to the Celtic tribes for the first application of the term to the Orkneys, we must see what "Orc" means in those dialects. Now "Orc" in Gaelic means a smaller sort of whale, a grampus or bottle-nose whale, the Delphinus orca of Linnæus, which is still found in large shoals, in the seas round Orkney, Shetland, and Faroe. Pliny himself calls this kind of whale "orca," and when Ptolemy calls a promontory, supposed to be Dunnet Head in Caithness opposite the Orkneys, "Tarvedum or Orcas," we recognise with Munch in the first word the Gaelic "Tarbat," (3) and in the second the singular of Orcades. So, too, this primæval or aboriginal "Ork" may be seen in the "Orkahaugr" or Orkahow of the Saga, p. 187; Tr. 190. It was the name which the Northmen gave to the huge barrow, now called the Maes Howe, which stands near "the Stones of Stennes," and they gave it a name from the largest animal which they knew on land or in the sea; much in the same way as the Americans speak in modern times of "Mammoth" caves and trees to express natural objects of huge size.

There can be no room for doubt then that in the words "Orkneyjar" and "Orkney" we have a Celtic derivative, and that the islands were so called from the shoals of a particular kind of whale which in earlier times were much more numerous than they are at present. The Northmen, as was their common practice, took the ancient name of the islands as they found it adopted by the Anglo-Saxons. They turned the "Orc" of the Celts into Orkn and added "ey," their word for an island, to the Celtic appellation.

As they had adopted the Celtic term for the whole group they proceeded in the same way with each island. When it had what they called Örnefni, that is, an old ariginal received name of its own, they adopted it, merely putting "ey" after it to mark its insular character. In cases where an island had no old name of its own, or when its ancient appellation was unknown, they gave it a new one of their own sometimes descriptive of its natural features, and sometimes taken from the name of a person. In process of time the termination "ey" in the names of each of the islands has been transformed into ay or a; thus "Shapinsay" or "Shapinsa," while certain combinations of letters are slurred over in utterance; "alp" or "olp" or "alb" in particular have lost their "l," so that the old Skálpeið, the neck or isthmus between Kirkwall and Scapa Bay, is now pronounced Scapa, and Kolbeinsey has become Copinsay and Cobesa. At the same time the same change has taken place with regard to names beginning with Hj, as we have already remarked as being the origin of the name "Shetland." Thus "Hjálpandisey," which it is conjectured is the old form of one of the Orkney isles, has become Shapinsay, and the rule holds good in other cases. But as this perversion of the ending of the names of each isle has given rise to two forms in ay and a, both plainly derived from the old Norse "ey," it was proposed by Munch in his essay on this subject in the Annals for Northern Archæology for 1852, to revert to the old form "ey;" and in fact this change had already been made, even before that learned historian suggested it, on the excellent charts of the Orkneys, published by the late Captain Thomas, R.N., under the direction of the Admiralty. We cannot learn, however, that this suggestion has been accepted by the inhabitants of the islands themselves, and we have therefore in general adhered to the more usually received form.

After these introductory remarks let us give a list of the Orkney isles as we find them mentioned in the Saga with their ancient names, and then direct our attention to each island in its turn, beginning from the North.

The names are North Ronaldsay, Rínansey; Sanay, Sandey; Papa Westray, Papey Meiri; Westray, Vestrey; Stronsay, Strjónsey; Papa Stronsay, Papey Minni; Egilsay or Egelsha, Egilsey; Rowsay, Hrólfsey; Mainland, Hrossey; Eynhallow, Eyinhelga; Weir, Vigr; Gairsay, Gareksey; Damsay, Daminsey; Eller or Hellier Holm, Hellisey; Burray, Borgarey; Græmsay, Grímsey; How with Walls, Háey with Vágar or Vágaland; South Ronaldsay, Rögnvaldsey; Svonay, Svíney; Stromay or Stroma, Straumey, and the Pentland Skerries, Pettland-sker. Two of the larger islands, Eday, Eiðey, and Shapinsay, Hjálpandisey, together with many smaller ones, are not mentioned in the Saga.

In this list there are some which, at the very first sight, betray a Celtic and a Christian origin. Just as in the "Orkn" or "Ork" of the Orkneys we perceive a Celtic root, so is a Celtic and a religious appellations as plainly discernible in Papey, the name given to two islands. We have seen that the Irish anchorites of St. Columba's rule had left traces of their cells and ascetic life in Shetland and Iceland. These anchorites the Northmen believed to have been "Westmen" or Irishmen. (4) Thus there were Papar or anchorites in Orkney and Shetland, where islands were named after them, and even farms such as Papuli or Papýli, now Paplay. When the heathen Northmen came to disturb them in their hermitages these anchorites vanished before them, leaving behind them their cells and churches, as the Dwarfie Stone on Hoy, and the old church on Egilsay. In Iceland we are told they left behind them books and staves and rings, and Ari Fróði in his Islendíngabók expressly says of Iceland, when it was discovered by his countrymen, "Then there were here Christian men, those whom the Northmen call Papa; but afterwards they went away for that they would not be here with heathen men, and they left behind them Irish books" (that is manuscripts), and staves and rings, from that it might be known that they were Irishmen." Besides this we know from Dicuil's Treatise De Mensurâ Orbis, that about the year 795 several priests had resided in Iceland from the 1st of February to the 1st of August. What happened in Iceland, Faroe, and Shetland had more frequently happened in the Orkneys, and we may be sure, as indeed the names Papey and Papýli sufficiently prove, that this group of isles, so long as they were waste, in what may be supposed to be the interval between the coming of the Northmen and the disappearance of the earlier races, was a favourite resort for Irish anchorites of St. Columba's rule.

And here let us remark that the same problem remains to be solved in Orkney that was left unsolved in Shetland. The testimony of the soil shows that this group of islands was inhabited in early times by races which burrowed in the earth in weems and Picts' houses and erected stately burghs like that at Moussa. But whoever they were and in whatever way they disappeared, it is certain that at one time these isles were inhabited by races which possessed considerable skill in construction, and in the case of the burgh-dwellers had made great advances to civilisation.

Returning to the traces of Celtic influence in the names of the Orkneys, we find it in Rínansey, Rinarsey, or Ronansey, all ancient names for North Ronaldsay. This is one of the first islands mentioned in the Saga, in the time of Turf-Einar the fourth Orkney earl, and there can be little doubt that it took its name from St. Ninian whom the Scots also called Ringan and Ronan. In later times Rínansey or Ronansey was perverted into Ronaldsay, and as there was another Ronaldsay in the south of the group, it became necessary to distinguish one as North, and the other as South Ronaldsay; but originally the name of the northern island was Rínansey after the saint, and that of the southern Ronaldsey after one of the earl Rognvalds. (5)

In Daminsey we find another name derived from St. Damian; and in the case of Egilsey, though it seems thoroughly Norse at first sight, and to have come from the well-known Norse name Egill, and to be the island of Egill, Munch has endeavoured to show that the name is derived from the ancient church which still stands with its round tower on the little island. This church has indeed been a puzzle to ecclesiastical antiquaries. While some have thought it so like the Irish churches of the same supposed age and character that it seems to them to have been transported from Ireland; others like Sir Henry Dryden have refused to see in it a building earlier than the 12th century. According to the first view, Egilsey would be called not from Egill but from the Irish ecclais or the Welsh eglaus, a church, and was so named by the Northmen because they found the venerable church standing on the island when they first arrived in the Orkney waters. In after times, the origin of the name was forgotten, though the church still stood, memorable for the martyrdom of St. Magnus which happened hard by, and Egilsey came to be looked on as the island of Egill. But in the midst of this controversy one fact remains that there was a church on Egilsey when St. Magnus was slain in the year 1116, and from this church whether it were that now existing or not the name of the island may have been derived. If this be so in the collective name of Orkney itself, as well as in the particular names, Papey, Papýli, Rínansey, Daminsey, and Egilsey, we have unmistakeable evidence of Celtic origin. (6)

After these general remarks we return to our list of islands beginning from the north. And first of North Ronaldsay, Rínansey, a low flat island, the northernmost of the group and lying well to the east. This is one of the earliest of all the islands to be mentioned in the Saga, and in the old edition which is very imperfect in the beginning, it is the first of all mentioned. As it is, the Mainland, Hrossey, is the first named at p. 6 of this edition of the Saga, where it is said that earl Hallad, the do-nothing son of earl Rognvald of Mœren, sate down in Hrossey while the Vikings harried his realm. But after earl Hallad came Turf-Einar, who thus mentions Rínansey after his battle with Halfdan Longlegs: "I know not what I see in Rínansey, sometimes it lifts itself up, but sometimes it lays itself down; that is either a bird or a man, and we will go to it." --- P. 8. The battle itself, which ended in Halfdan's disastrous defeat and death, probably took place in the firth between Sanday and North Ronaldsay, and from Toftsness on the former island it would be possible for a sharp-sighted man, as we are told earl Einar was, to see across to the opposite island. But we are not reduced to this supposition, as he might well have been on board his ship the morning after the battle when the search for his routed enemies began. At the present time, North Ronaldsay with its beautiful lighthouse and dangerous reefs is shunned by voyagers, but in the days of the Saga it was easy of approach to the light craft of the islanders, and was a place of importance. There it was, in the days of earl Paul, that the second beacon was to be lighted on the approach of earl Rognvald-Kali, and Thorstein Ragna's son was to have charge of it (p. 115). His mother was the outspoken Ragna, who at page 121 foll., entertained earl Paul at a banquet in her house on the island, and gave him such offence by her bold advice. After earl Paul was carried off by Sweyn Asleif's son, the very man whom the wise widow advised the earl to make his friend, Ragna and her son became firm friends of earl Rognvald-Kali. At p. 144, we are told, how when Hall, the son of Thorarin Broadpaunch came from Iceland to spend the winter with Ragna and her son, and was ill at ease, and wished to be passed on to the earl's court, Ragna and her son did their best to further his wishes at first without success. The earl had warriors enough and said, "No, to neighbour of the brawn." But Ragna was not a woman to be put off, for the Saga goes on to tell us that she provoked the earl's satire by paying him a visit in a new fashioned head dress. After that they began to talk, and the end was that Ragna got her way, and Hall was long afterwards with earl Rognvald, with whom, as they were both excellent skalds, he made what the Icelanders called the Old Key to Metres.

We next come to Vestrey, Westray, the Western isle, about the Norse derivation of which there can be no doubt. It and the West Firth, Vestfjörðr, that is, the troubled strait between it and Rowsay, are often mentioned in the Saga. There, at Rapness, Hreppisnes, p. 89, lived Kugi, a powerful man, and an adherent of earl Paul, while at Höfn lived Helgi, who was inclined to earl Rognvald; for the earl came to his house when he got a fair wind from Shetland, while Kugi was thrown into fetters and badly beaten by the earl's men (p. 127 fol.) Rapness is also mentioned at p. 209 as the place where earl Rognvald met John Wing when he had carried off Sweyn Aslief's son Olaf. It is called also the "Bull" of Rapness, that is, the "ból" or farm of Rapness, and lies on the south-east side of the island, while Höfn, that is, the "Haven," was on the north-east side, where the modern Pier o' Wall lies. Close by are the "Links," the Norse "lykkjur," where a number of old interments, described in Wilson's Archæology, pp. 552-555, were discovered in 1849. Not far from Pier o' Wall, or the ancient Höfn, called also the thorpe or village, lies Trenaby, from which Mr. Balfour of Balfour takes one of his territorial titles. On the west of the island, not far from the Noup Head, the Icelandic Gnúpr, stands Noltland Castle, also owned by Mr. Balfour. This, in John Ben's description of Orkney in 1529, is described as "excellentissia arx sive castellum sed nondum tamen adhuc completa." In this unfinished state it has remained ever since, with its walls of immense thickness, its two round towers, and its arched portal. The name of the place, "Noltland" or "Nowtland," seems plainly derived from the Norse Nautaland, that is, "neat" or "cattle land." It was on the West Firth, between Westray and Rowsay, that Waltheof Olaf's son was lost in a ten-oared boat in the year 1135, when on his way to a yule feast given by earl Paul at Orfir. He was brother of the powerful and unruly Sweyn Asleif's son, with whose adventures the last part of our Saga is full. At p. 116 will be found an account of Waltheof's loss. There is a farm called Rackwick on the north-east of Westray, which has been supposed by some to be the Rekavík of the Saga, where Thorliot, the father of Oliver the unruly, lived; but it is certain that the Rekavík where that powerful family lived was the other Rackwick in Hoy, for all the relations of Thorliot and Oliver lay in the south, and not in the north isles. At p. 87 of our Saga will be found an account of Thorliot and his kindred, who were in reality rather Scotch than Orkneyingers.

To the north-east of Westray and just opposite to the little harbour of Pier o' Wall or Höfn, the thorpe where Helgi lived, and where earl Rognvald-Kali first landed in Orkney, lies Papey Meiri, the bigger Papey, now called Papa Westray to distinguish it from Papey Minni, the lesser Papey, now called Papa Stronsay. Both these isles, as we have seen, take their names from the cells of Irish anchorites, and not from any Norse derivatives. As soon as the Orkneys became Christian, shortly after the days of Olaf Tryggvi's son, that is, about the year 1000, Papey Meiri became a holy place, and until the great cathedral in Kirkwall was built it is probable taht St. Tredwall's chapel (7) on Papey Meiri was considered the holiest spot in all the isles. In the days described by our Saga, St. Tredwall's chapel has an interest as being the burial place of the gallant earl Rognvald Brúsi's son, whose body, after he had been slain on Papey Minni or the lesser Papey off Stronsay, was brought to St. Tredwall's chapel to be interred. Our Saga, p. 53, foll., tells the story of his death, which for interest and truth may vie with any scene in any Saga.

We now pass by Eday, the ancient name of which is to be restored as Eiðey, that is, the island of the eið or aith, or isthmus, from the neck or waist of land which joins the two ends of the island together, and along with it its satellites Kalfr the Calf, Færey the Sheep isle, Hólmr the Holm of Farey, and Grænuholmr the Greenholms; for all these are never mentioned in the Saga, though it is easy to restore, as Munch has done, their ancient form from their modern names.

Next in order and position is Sandey, Sanday, which is often mentioned in the Saga, and lies east of Westray and north-east of Eday. Here it was, off the northern end of the island, which looks on Rínansey or North Ronaldsay, that Turf-Einar lay with his ships when he had that engagement with Halfdan Longlegs, the son of the mighty Harold Fairhair, which ended in his defeat and death by immolation to Odin, the God of battles. With regard to the possibility of that sharp-sighted though one-eyed earl being able to see from Sanday as far as Rínansey, Munch tells us that it is no more than 6,000 paces from Toftsness in Sanday to Stromness in Rínansey, a distance to which earl Einar's sharp eyes might perhaps have reached; but we have already remarked that, in all probability, the earl was on board his ships when he uttered the words given in the Saga, which besides would seem to have been caused by something seen on land from the water. After the bloody rite of cutting a spread-eagle on the back of the victim with a sword by severing the ribs from the backbone on each side and drawing the lungs out, earl Einar made his men cast a "howe" or cairn over his enemy, and burst out into a song of triumph on having revenged his father, earl Rognvald of Mæren, on the son of the great king Harold. It is probable that, as the battle was fought in Sanday, that the sacrifice to Odin took place on that island, and not on Rínansey; and that the cairn of Halfdan Longlegs must be sought for among the many barrows which still exist on Sanday.

In later times Sanday was the abode of a great chief, Thorstein Havard's son, one of earl Paul's most active followers, and when the care of the beacon on Rínansey was entrusted to his namesake the son of Ragna, (8) his brother Magnus was to attend to that on Sanday; later on in the Saga earl Rognvald sent for him and his namesake from Sanday, p. 129, that they try to arrange matters between himself and earl Paul. Still farther on in the Saga we read of Sanday and a farm on it called Völuness or Valeness, in the account of Swein Asleif's son's flight from earl Harold, when the earl seized his house on Gairsay, p. 206. It was on Sanday that, as the Saga tells us, p. 195, Sweyn Asleif's son and earl Erlend met after they had parted in Dynröst or sumburgh Roost in so violent a storm that each gave up the other as lost. It was in Sanday too that Sweyn Asleif's son forced his kinsman John Wing the younger to fly from Völuness in the bitter winter night, because he abused earl Erlend, p. 206.

Next in order is Strjónsey, Stronsay, which is frequently mentioned in the Saga. The chief house on it in old times, seems to have been "the Brink," Brekkar or í Brekkum, where Richard lived, one of Sweyn Asleif's son's kinsmen, of whom we read, p. 130, that he and John Wing of the Uplands in Hoy fell on Thorkell flat or the flayer, to whom earl Paul had given the land in Stronsay which Waltheof Sweyn's brother had owned, and burnt him in it with nine men. Before that Thorkell had lived in Westray with his sons, not much beloved by his neighbours, p. 89. Munch has recognised the old Hofsness in the modern Hvipsness on Stronsay where earl Erelend met Sweyn Asleif's son on his return from Norway at the house of Sweyn's brother-in-law, Thorfinn Brúsi's son, who had married his sister Ingigerd, whom Thorbjörn the clerk had repudiated (Saga, p. 187). There the old feud between the young earl and the old Viking, which arose out of the burning of Frakok, was finally arranged, and Sweyn became Erelend's chief adviser. In Rousholmhead or the Red Head of Stronsay, may also be recognised the old name Rauðholmshöfði. Off Stronsay, too, lay Papey Minni, now Papa Stronsay, where earl Rognvald Brúsi's son was slain.

Shapinsay, which may be restored to Hjálpandisey, is, as we have said, not mentioned in the Saga by name, but the modern name of the island is well known to all visitors to Orkney as the principal seat of Mr. Balfour of Trenaby, the owner of this island as well as of so many others in the Orkneys. But close to Ellwick, the ancient Ellidavík, on the south side of the island, lies Ellerholm, or Hellierholm, the ancient Hellisey, where, according to Captain Thomas, quoted by Munch, the cave may still be seen in which the shifty Sweyn Asleif's son hid his boat when escaping from the pursuit of earl Harold Maddad's son (Saga, p. 205). At that time there must have been a monastery on one or other of the islands, for as Sweyn's boat was high and dry in the cave, Sweyn sailed away to Sanday in an old ship of burden belonging to the monks.

We next come to Egilsey, of which we have already shown that it possibly derives its name, not from any "Egill" but from the Irish "ecclais" or the Welsh "eglws," meaning a church, and was called Church island by the Northmen because, when they first came into the islands, they saw a church standing on it; just as they called Stennis "Steinsnes" because of the large circle of stones which they beheld standing on that promontory between the two lakes on the Mainland. Here, at any rate, until the cathedral in Kirkwall was built, the bishops of Orkney seem to have had their residence. That old church was what may be called their peculiar as opposed to the earl's churches at Birsay and Orfir, and St. Olaf's church in Kirkwall, which was the church of the burghers. On various occasions in the Saga when bishop William was wanted, and especially twice at Christmans (Saga, p. 119, 137), when the proper place for a bishop would be at his own church, we find him at Egilsay. On the last of these occasions bishop John of Athole visited bishop William at Egilsay before his interview with earl Rögnvald as the bearer of Margaret's proposals as to the claim of her son Harold to half the Orkneys. This church, therefore, remained the bishop's church, though his cathedral was the Earl's church at Birsay, till the relics of St. Magnus were translated from that church, where he was first buried, to St. Olaf's church in Kirkwall, to be again translated to the stately minster which the piety of earl Rognvald-Kali reared in obedience to his vow to the honour of his holy kinsman. And there on the island which was called after it still stands the venerable church, a silent witness of so much that has happened in the isles besides the martyrdom of St. Magnus which threw over it an additional sanctity throughout Catholic times. At p. 78 foll. of the Saga will be found an account of the treacherous attack of earl Hacon Paul's son on his cousin Magnus, which ended in the death of the pious earl, who so soon afterwards was revered as the patron saint of the isles.

Next we come to Gairsay, the ancient Gareksey, famous in the Saga as the chief abode of the adventurous Sweyn Asleif's son, though he had other farms in Stronsay and Caithness, where on the Scotch mainland he held Duncansby, and the strong castle of Lambaborg close to Þrasvík, the modern Freswick. It was on gairsay that he built himself a house, the drinking hall of which was so long that it could contain eighty retainers. Here it was that, when he was at feud with earl Harold, when the earl had seized his house and wasted his corn and goods, Sweyn fell on him unawares, and sought to burn the house over his head, even though his own wife and children were in it, and it was fortunate for the earl that he was just then away hare hunting (Saga, p. 204). Here too, when the long feud between Harold and himself had burnt itself out and they were reconciled, Sweyn entertained the earl at a great banquet about the year 1171, when the earl advised him to leave off sea roving, and in the words of the proverb, "to drive home with a whole wain." The Saga tells, p. 222, how Sweyn neglected the earl's advice, said he would leave off after one more voyage, set off on a cruise to Dublin and there perished by treachery. After his death his sons parted their father's goods and his hall between them, and built up a wall which cuts the large room in two. (9) All certain traces of this large drinking hall, which surpassed in size all others in the Orkneys, have now perished, but the name lingers, perhaps, in the farm Langskeal on the south-west side of the island, which may be restored to Lángskáli, that is the Long Hall.

On Vígr, now Wyre or Weir, lived another great chief, Kolbeinn the Burly, a Norwegian, who, as the Saga tells us, p. 151, built a strong stone castle on it which was known as hard to take. As for Kolbeinn himself he seems to have been a prudent man and to have kept himself, as much as he could, out of strife. He was the friend of Sweyn Asleif's son, his neighbour in Gairsay, and fostered his son Olaf (Saga. p. 209). After Sweyn's death his son Andrew married Kolbein's daughter Frida. At the end of his life he sided with earl Harold Maddad's son, and together with his son Bjarni, called in the Saga both Bjarni Skáld and Bjarni Bishop, was a firm adherent of that earl. By their mother Herbjorg Kolbein's children were descended from earl Paul Thorfinn's son. Some remains of his castle are still to be seen on Weir, where they are pointed out as "Cobbe Row's castle," that is, Kolbein Hruga's Castle. In popular tradition he has become a giant, and his burliness is shown in throwing rocks at churches, after the fashion of the trolls in the popular tales of Norway.

West of Egilsay lies Rowsay, the ancient Hrólfsey, often confounded by careless scribes in the MSS. of the Saga with Hrossey or the Mainland. After Hoy it is the hilliest of all the islands, and its dark upland moors are seen over the green fields of Gairsay and Weir, as the voyager enters Kirkwall Bay. Here at Westness, Vestnes, then, as now, the chief house on the island, lived in the time described in the latter part of the Saga, Sigurd of Westness, the husband of Ingibjörg the honourable, earl Paul's warmest adherent in his feud with earl Rognvald. Here it was while that ill-fated earl was on a visit to his friend that he was seized and carried off to perish miserably in Scotland by the daring Sweyn Asleif's son; a feat which is described in the Saga, p. 131 foll., with a force and liveliness nowhere surpassed in northern story. At Swendro near the "Urð," the "Ord" or heap of stones where the earl was seized after a fierce struggle when out otter-hunting, remains have been found in recent times which may well have been the bones of those nineteen men of the earl's followers whom Sigurd knew when he went to look at the slain and those six "whom he did not know" who had fallen on Sweyn's side (Saga, p. 133). Between Rowsay and the Mainland is Evie Sound, the ancient Efjusund so called from efja, the backwater which is to be found at both ebb and flow in sounds where the stream runs out and in so violently as it does in Evie Sound. There may be seen and heard that terrific bore or wall of water caused by the waves of the deep Atlantic when borne by the tide over shallower ground. It may, perhaps be seen best in Yell Sound in Shetland; but it is seen more or less in all the Orkney and Shetland firths and sounds, and certainly in a most remarkable degree in Evie Sound.

In Evie Sound, between Rowsay and the mainland, lies the little island of Eyn-hallow, that is, Eyin Helga, the Holy Isle, the ground of which was said to be so holy that neither rats nor mice could live on it, and where the straw dripped blood when corn was cut after sunset. All which are doubtless traditions from the days of the anchorites, who may have had their abode on it. In the Saga Eyn-hallow is mentioned, p. 209, as the place where John Wing the younger, Sweyn Asleif's son's kinsman, seized Olaf Sweyn's son, and carried him off as a hostage to Rapness in Westray, where he met earl Rognvald. The boy had been fostered by Kolbein the Burly at Weir close by, and as soon as the earl heard of the seizure he made John Wing carry him back with the warning that, unless he did so, John would have no peace either at Sweyn's or Kolbein's hands.

We now come to the Mainland called by the Northmen Hrossey (10) or the Horse Island. What induced them to call it by this name is as doubtful as the occassion which gave rise to the name Hjaltland for Shetland. Perhaps it was because they found ponies running wild there; perhaps because they turned horses loose themselves as they did in Iceland. "Mainland," the modern name of the central island, is the old Norse "Meginland" which they gave in the case of both Orkney and Shetland to the largest island in each group.

Having thus considered the origin of the ancient and modern names of the Main island we step into it from Rowsay across Evie Sound and find ourselves in Evie parish, which stretches from Costa Head all along the troubled sound to Woodwick opposite to Gairsay. At that point the parish of Rendale (11) meets us; the ancient Rennadalr, somewhere in which lay Flugunes or Flyðrunes, where Thorstein lived with his cross-grained sons, Asbjörn and Berlian or Blánn, the latter of whom seems to have been warder of the strong castle in Damsay, Rennadalr is again mentioned in our Saga (p. 201), on the occasion of earl Erlend's violent death at Damsay. Southward Rendale extends as far as Isbister, the ancient Ossabólstaðr, where the inland parish of Harray(12) begins, from which the lake of that name is called; while beyond Costa Head, the most northerly point of the island, the parish of Birsay begins and stretches along the coast as far as the high ground of Westrafold in the south-west. The name Birsay comes from Birgisey, that is, the isle off the ancient district Birgishera ð, still called the Barony or Lordship of Birsay; off the coast, and joined to it at low tide lies the isle itself, the Brock or Burgh of Birsay. The district is famous in the Saga as the residence of the mighty earl Thorfinn and his descendants, the chief seat of their power and the burial place of their race till the translation of the relics of St. Magnus to Kirkwall deprived the earl's church at Birsay of most of its peculiar sanctity. Before that translation that church, built by earl Thorfinn, p. 59, and called "Christ's Church," was reckoned as the cathedral of the bishop (Saga, p. 89). On the Brock are still to be seen not only some remains of earl Thorfinn's castle, but also the ruins of another church said to have been dedicated to St. Peter, and all who have visited this remarkable spot, looking out on the West Atlantic, under the guidance of the late Mr. George Getrie, will know how much of interest still lingers round that little islet. The existing Christ Church is a comparatively recent erection, but close by are the foundations of the older church, of which close by are the foundations of the older church, of which a portion of the walls and traces of the apse were detected by the sharp eyes of Mr. Petrie.

After Birsay comes Sandwick parish, the ancient Sandvík, remarkable in modern times as the site of the discovery of those massive silver rings and brooches, the hoard of some Viking, which were found some years ago, and may be seen in the Museum at Edinburgh. This Sandwick must not be confounded with another place of the same name near Deerness in the south-east of the island, where Amundi, the father of Thorkel Fosterer lived, and where Earl Einar was slain by Thorkell at the feast which was to have reconciled them (Saga, p. 22). On the east the parish of Sandwick is bounded by the Lakes of Harray and Stennis, between which it ends near Brogar Bridge, west of which on a ness stand or lie the famous circles of stones which gave its name to the lake and the parish. The larger circle, also called the "Ring of Brogar," where Brogar is no doubt a corruption of Brúargarðr "the farm by the bridge," has been described by Captain Thomas in the Archæologia, vol. xxxiv., to which the curious reader is referred for more precise details. Let it suffice here to say, that it consisted originally of 60 stones, erected about 18 feet apart, and forming a circle 366 feet in diameter. Of these rough unhewn stones, which are about 13 feet in height, 36 remain in a more or less perfect state of preservation. The area, comprising 2 1/2 acres, within the circle has been artificially raised and levelled, and is surrounded outside the stones by a ditch 6 feet deep and 29 feet wide. The smaller circle, called the Ring of Stennis, originally consisted of 12 stones enclosing an area of about 100 feet in diameter; only two of these stones remain standing, and a third has been thrown down. This circle too was surrounded by a broad and deep ditch now nearly obliterated. In character these circles of stones are identical with those of Callernish in the Lewes, and may be ascribed to the same race, though what that race may have been is hard to say. Round these circles standing-stones and barrows are irregularly scattered on both the nesses or peninsulas between the lakes of Harray and Stennis. About a mile and a half from the Stones of Stennis, on the south east shore of the lake of that name, towers the "Maes Howe," the great mound with a sepulchral chamber, excavated in 1861 by Mr. Farrer by the permission of Mr. Balfour, the owner of the property, and with the assistance of Mr. George Petrie and other distinguished antiquaries. Both those circles of stones and those huge barrows were found by the Northmen when they came into the Orkneys, and they at once called the ness or headland on which the principal circle stands Steinsnes or Stoneness, of which the modern Stennis is a corruption. After that it became the place of meeting for the inhabitants, whether in council or for single combat. And here it was in the days of one of the most ancient earls, that Havard the "harvest happy," the son of earl Thorfinn Skull-splitter, was attacked and slain by his sister's son, Einar Hardchaft, on a spot called Hávarðsteigar in the Saga, p. 12, which we are assured by Mr. George Petrie, as quoted by Munch, is still called "Havardsteg," after the ill fated earl.

For readers of the Saga, the most interesting fact connected with these Celtic monuments is the strange discovery when the "Maes Howe" was excavated, that the stones of its central sepulchral chamber were scored with runes which have been variously read. One fact, however, remains clear, that the Howe was broken open by the followers of earl Rognvald-Kali to the Holy Land. This appears plain from one of the very few readings on which the antiquaries seem all agreed. In inscription 20 occurs the line "Iorsalafarar bruto "Orkhaug," "The Jewryfarers broke into Orkhow;" but the wise men are wrong in seeking Orkhaug or "Orkhaugr" anywhere else than in the Maes Howe itself. (13) In spite of the opinions expressed by authorities on runic inscriptions who venture to ascribe various dates to the inscriptions in question, it is probable that they were all done at the same time, and before the expedition to the Holy Land started. That was part of the sport of that idle winter which earl Rognvald and his unruly Norwegian comrades spent in the Orkneys, when, as we are told, that bold band was full of outrage and frolic. There has always been a tendency to make more of runic inscriptions that they deserve. They were as often as not the production of whim or caprice, and no more meant to be serious than the scrawlings of modern tourists after their own names on national monuments. Thus when we read in one of these inscriptions "Ingigerð is the loveliest woman," this may mean earl Rognvald's only child Ingigerð; but then Ingigerd is not at all an uncommon name, and just as when we read "Mary is a pretty girl" on the Pyramids we do not think it means a Princess Mary, but some Mary whom the tourist knows, it is probable that this Ingigerd was another maiden than the earl's daughter.

So also when another of the inscriptions says, "This was cut with the axe which Gauk Trandil's son from the south country owned," that is an allusion indeed to a weapon owned by one of the chiefs named in the Njal's Saga as alive two hundred years before; but it was probably only scored as a joke or hoax on generations to come. It seems pretty plain that if, as these inscriptions expressly assert, the voyagers to the Holy Land broke into the Howe, that the inscriptions would be all after their time, the middle of the twelfth century. With regard to the Maes Howe itself, the evidence of the Saga, as well as of the inscriptions, seems to show that it was called "Orkahaugr" or Orkahow in the time of the Saga. At p. 190, it is mentioned that when earl Harold Maddad's son set off on one of his expeditions against earl Erlend who then lay at Damsay, two of his men went mad, and delayed them much, owing to the inclemency of the wintry weather while they were in "Orkahow," where they had taken shelter. This is the Howe now known as the Maes Howe, and it was open, because a year or two before at most it had been broken into by the followers of earl Rognvald. On the occasion in question as earl Harold was on an adventure the success of which depended on secrecy, nothing could be more appropriate than that he should use the deserted chamber of the Howe as a place of shelter after landing from his ship on the shore of the lake of Stennis on his straight road to Aurriðafirth or Wideford Bay, in which the isle of Damsay lies. On the other hand, had he been staying at a farm, his sick men would not have delayed him; he would have left them there, and passed on. The Howe was called Orkahaugr because it was the largest of the great barrows which surround the Stones of Stennis.

The south west point of the peninsula beyond Sandwick forms Stromness parish, a name no doubt derived from the stream or tide which rushes in between the isles of Hoy and Græmsay and the Mainland. In ancient times a farm called Kjarrekstaðir stood near the site of the modern Stromness, which has been identified with the modern Cairston or Carstone. (14)

The southern extremity of this part of the island forms the parish of Orphlr or Orfir, the ancient Orfjara or Örfjara, the meaning of which is a flat or foreshore left bare at the ebb tide, a character which the coast still remains. Here it was that earl Paul Hacon's son kept his court, and here was a stately hall and a round church close by it, which also has been identified by the skill of Mr. George Petrie; for their position see the Saga p. 117, foll., where the earl's court and the events which led Sweyn Asleif's son to slay his namesake Sweyn Breastrope are graphically described. The hall lay near the modern Swanbister under what is now called the Ward Hill of Orfir, that is to say, the beacon hill of Orfir, and the highest in the island, which rises behind it to a height of 700 feet. But Munch has well pointed out that the Saga is wrong when it says that the Bay of Firth or Aurriðafjörðr, in which Damsay lies, can be seen from that hill, for the prospect in that direction is intercepted by the Keely Long Hills, the Norse Kilir, and Wideford Hill. At the extreme southern point of Orfir parish lies a little island, between which and the mainland is formed what is called in modern times Midland Harbour, in which we at once recognise the Meðallandshöfn of the Sagas. (15)

Munch thinks that the "voe" or "vágr" which runs up into the mainland protected by this island was called Hafnarvágr, that is the "voe of the harbour or haven" the modern Hamnavoe, and he quotes the Saga, p. 190, where it is said, that when earl Harold Maddad's son attempted to surprise earl Erlend, he sailed first to Græmsay, where he lay two nights. After that they landed at Hafnarvágr in Hrossey, and crossed to Firth, that is, Wideford Firth. Then it was that they were caught in that storm which drove them to take shelter in "Orkahaugi," which Munch calls a farm, and identifies as the modern "Orkhill," but we have already seen that the Orkahaugr here mentioned is probably no other than the How now called Maes Howe, and that it was within its sepulchral chambers, then recently broken into by earl Rognvald's companions, that the earl took refuge. He was on a secret expedition, bent on seizing his unwary enemy by a sudden dash, and the site of the modern Orkhill is too near Orfir to have rendered it a suitable stopping place. It is probable, therefore, that the site of Hafnarvágr is to be sought further up in the bight of the bay, where the stream from the Lake of Stennis meets the sea. There Harold Maddad's son landed, and thence he started to traverse the district between the Stones of Stennis and the bay of Firth. Overtaken by a storm, he sought shelter in Orkahow, and there it was that two of his men went mad.

East of Orfir parish lies that of St. Olaf, which comprises the waist of the Orkney Mainland, and in which lies Kirkwall, the heart of the islands, as fortunate in its position between two seas as the ancient Corinth. The parish was called after the royal Norwegian saint from the church which was erected to his honour on the shores of the "voe" which runs into the mainland on the north side of the isthmus. From the church the town which sprang up round it took its name Kirkjuvágr "the voe of the church," which modern pronunciation has turned into Kirkwall. From the "voe of the church" across the isthmus to the southern bay it is hardly so much as an English mile. That isthmus or "eið" is the Skálpeið so often mentioned in the Saga, and the bay itself is called Skálpaflói or "Skálpeiðsflói," which have both degenerated in modern speech into "Scapa," and "Scapa bay." On this isthmus, at or close to the town , but near enough to the bay to see ships sailing up, Things and gatherings of the freemen were frequently held. No doubt as Kirkwall rose into importance after the translation thither of the relics of St. Magnus and the building of the cathedral, (16) the ancient place of assembly at the Stones of Stennis was deserted for the more frequented locality near the capital, and as Scapa Bay became the great landing place of travellers from the south to Kirkwall, the place of meeting was transferred to the spot where men most congregated. So it was that after earl Paul was spirited away in that mysterious manner by Sweyn Asleif's son we find earl Rognvald, p. 134, assembling a Thing to discuss matters near Kirkwall, where the text shows that the place of meeting was close enough to the shore to see and even to recognize travellers as they landed. Not far from the landing place on the western side of Scapa Bay lay the ancient "Knarrarstaðir," Knarstead, that is, the "stead of ships" and especially merchant ships, from the ancient "Knörr." This was a farm which belonged to the earls, or at least to earl Rognvald-Kali, p. 137, and where there was according to the Saga, p. 188, some sort of fortification or castle. The Saga, p. 198 foll., shows how narrowly the earls, on more than one occasion, escaped the attacks of their enemies at this very farm. On the east side of the bay, where the land is higher, lies the modern Gatnip, where the Saga, p. 134, tells us that Borgar, the son of earl Erlend's base-born daughter, Jadvör, lived. The ancient name was Geitaberg or "Goathill" or Jadvarastaðr, Jadvorstead, and from that elevation Borgar saw Sweyn Asleif's son as he sailed from Caithness through the South Isles on his adventurous voyage to seize earl Paul. The same sharp eyes saw the bold Viking return with his prey after he had accomplished his daring feat.

Now let us return to Kirkwall. The position of the town is peculiar. To the north and west it is bounded by water. To the north by the open sea of the voe, and on the west by a backwater called the "Oyce" or "Peerie Sea," that is, the Little Sea. This backwater is cut off from the open sea by a bank of sand and shingle called the "air," derived from the ancient Norse "eyrr," the old English form of which is "ere" or "or." (17)

Along the east side of this "Oyce" or Peerie Sea straggles the town of Kirkwall abutting on the open sea of the voe at its northern extremity. Of public buildings, the remains of the old St. Olaf's Church lie nearest the sea at the northern end of the town, and no doubt in early times the dwellings of the inhabitants were clustered round that ancient church. In later days when earl Rognvald's magnificent cathedral rose in all its beauty further south, other public buildings sprang up about it. So arose what used to be called till it was pulled down a few years since, the King's Castle, but which was in reality the ancient palace of the earls, though it was probably not the work of any of the earls mentioned in the Saga, but erected by one of the St. Clairs in the fourteenth century. Later still as the town stretched itself still further south another earl's palace was built by the tyrannical Patrick Stewart at the beginning of the seventeenth century; it stands a little beyond the bishop's palace, which lay between it and the older earl's palace.

We now come to the cathedral, which is the glory of the Orkneys and indeed of all the north. It stands nobly on an open space to the east of the long straggling high street, pretty nearly at the end of the town, and south east of the king's castle or ancient earl's palace. The Saga relates how this splendid church arose in obedience to a vow suggested by the politic Kol, the father of earl Rognvald-Kali. It also tells us that Kol was the master mason, in which case he was as skilled in architecture as in policy, and how, when money fell short, the work was carried on by allowing the freemen to redeem their allodial holdings for a fixed sum (Saga, p. 137). But in spite of all efforts the work after the first start proceeded slowly, as was often the case with mediæval buildings; and there was a great gap in the west end of the church which was not filled up till the time of bishop Thomas Tulloch, about the year 1450. In it, till the Reformation, was that magnificent shrine of St. Magnus of which we read so much in the Saga. In that religious revolution it perished with all its treasures. The bones of the saint and his skull, bearing marks of the fracture made by Lifolf's axe (Saga, p. 81), were then immured in one of the massive pillars of the choir, whence they were broken out a few years ago by an English nobleman, and having been inspected, and as far as possible identified, they were returned to the resting place in which they had so long remained. In this respect the relics were more fortunate than those of any saint, either in North or South Britain, except perhaps those of Cuthbert at Durham, and of Edward the

Confessor, which last are supposed still to rest at Westminster in the wooden shrine to which they were restored by Abbot Feckenham in the time of Queen Mary. For those of St. Cuthbert inquire of the Benedictines. In the cathedral too rested the bones of bishop William, whom the Saga calls the first bishop of the Orkneys. After having held the see for the long space of 60 years, he was buried there in the year 1168. In 1848, when the church was repaired, his bones were found enclosed in a stone cist along with a leaden plate, on which was inscribed "Hic requiescit Willielmus senex, felicis memoria, primus Episcopus." The bones and the cist were carted away as rubbish, but the plate and the bone head of the bishop's pastoral staff are preserved in the Museum of the Society of Antiquaries of Scotland.

On the south side of the cathedral and just opposite to it, nearer to the sea shore, stand the venerable remains of Saint Olaf's church and the cathedral, the oldest building in the town. For Norwegian history it has great interest, as being the abode and death place of king Hacon Hacon's son, in the year 1263. His remains found a resting place in St. Magnus Church till they were removed to Norway.

With regard to the earls and their residence in Kirkwall, it is probable that, in the times of which the Saga treats, they seldom took up their abode in the town. The earliest mention of Kirkwall in our Saga is at p. 53, where it is said that earl Rognvald established himself there, and how earl Thorfinn, after slaying earl Rognvald Brúsi's son and his followers on the Greater Papey, sailed for Kirkwall, where, by a stratagem, he induced the remaining adherents of his rival on land to meet him at the landing place unarmed, when he seized them and put them all to death but one. At the end of the Saga and especially in the quarrels between the earls Rognvald and Harold and Sweyn Asleif's son, we hear much of Kirkwall in connexion with the cathedral, which was used both as a sanctuary for fugitives and a storehouse for sails and the tackling of ships which the earls had seized.

Leaving Kirkwall and Thievisholm, which no doubt may be restored to þiofahólmr from the thieves who met their deaths on the gallows there, but which is not mentioned in the Saga, we come to Quanterness on the west side of the voe, with its Picts' house, first described by Barry and since scientifically examined along with so many others in the Orkneys by the late lamented Mr. George Petrie. Looking west from Quanterness and Kirkwall the horizon is intercepted by Wideford Hill, in which "Wideford" is a corruption of "Aurriðafjörðr," that is Troutfirth, otherwise called simply Fjörðr or Firth in the Saga. From this hill, which almost rivals the Ward Hill of Orfir in height, an extended prospect is afforded over the whole archipelago and especially north and west towards Westray and Stronsay. Its sides are hollow with those weems and Picts' houses already described, which seem more common in this neighbourhood than anywhere else in the Orkneys. Close under the feet of the beholder as he stands on the top of Wideford Hill lies Aurriðafjörðr, the bay or firth already mentioned. It is often mentioned in the Saga and was the scene of the death of the ill fated earl Erlend, who lay in his ship off Damsay, the ancient Daminsey. Of the strong castle on that island a few remains are visible. On the north side of the Bay of Firth we return to Rendale parish, the ancient Rennadalr, from which we started, and we have now completed our perambulation of Hrossey or the Mainland west of the isthmus at Scapa Bay. The districts east of that isthmus remain to be described.

Off Inganess lies Shapinsay, which is not mentioned in the Saga, but which, as has been already said, may be with certainty restored to the ancient Hjálpandisey. On its southern side which protects the entrance to Kirkwall Harbour lies Ellwick, the ancient Elliðavík which is mentioned in Hacon Hacon's son's Saga.

Returning to the Mainland east of Scapa Bay we come after Inganess Bay to Tankarness, a peninsula which juts out into the sea, the north point of which was called Tannskaranes, off which earl Paul Hacon's son (Saga, p. 112 foll.), met the ships of Oliver the Unruly and Frakok and signally defeated them, having first descried them rounding the Mull Head off Deerness on their way to join his rival earl Rognvald. Here, on a farm of the same name, lived a freeman named Erling, who, with his stalwart sons, helped the earl by bringing stones, the rude artillery of those times, to hurl at his foes, down to his ship. Passing on from Tankarness we come to the easternmost peninsula of the Mainland, Deerness, the ancient Dýrnes, which is almost an island, being only joined to the Mainland by a narrow neck, probably called in ancient times Sandeið from the nature of the soil, and now called "Sandaysand." Off the Mull Head (Múli) of Deerness, the bloody sea fight took place between earl Thorfinn and the Scot-king, Karl Hound's son, and in the verses of Arnor Earlskald, the name of the promontory is given (Saga, p. 33). This Dýrnes is not to be mistaken for another Dýrnes or Djurnes near Cape Wrath, which is also mentioned in the Sagas.

On Deerness lies a spot memorable in the early days of the Orkney earls. Here at Sandvík now Sandwick, that is Sandy Bay, on the east side of the peninsula, lived Ámundi or Amund in the days of earl Einar Brúsi's son. The words of the Saga are (p. 17) that he lived in Hrossey at Sandwick, on Laupandanes or Lopness. It seems probable that the last name is that of the district, and Sandvik that of the abode of Ámundi, but whichever it be, there with his father lived Thorkel the fosterer of earl Thorfinn, and there at Sandwick Thorkel slew earl Einar Wrymouth at a feast. Thither, too, a little afterwards earl Thorfinn fled when surprised by king Karl, and there he was met by Thorkel "under Deerness" with reinforcements.

Off Deerness lies Copinsay, the first islet which the traveller passes when steering for Kirkwall. It is not mentioned in the Saga, but there is no doubt that its ancient name was Kolbeinsey, as Munch has restored it, and not "Kaupmannaey island" or "Merchant's island" as some have supposed.

Last of all we come to the south easternmost part of Mainland, the parish of Holm or Paplay. Munch supposes that Holm is a mispronunciation of "Heimr," but it might have arisen from the Holms which lie off the coast. The "Papýli" or "Papuli" mentioned in our Saga was probably this Paplay in Hrossey, and not another farm of the same name in the neighbouring island of South Ronaldsay. See Saga, page 198. Whichever it was, it was part of the landed property which belonged to the family of earl Erlend, the father of Saint Magnus, for Paplay is mentioned by the Saga, p. 74, as part of the dower which Gunhilda, the sister of the saint, brought to her husband Kol, the son of Kali; and here, too lived the saint's mother, and after her her son Hacon churl.

We now leave the Mainland, and passing rapidly over Lambholm, Glimsholm, and Burray, on the last of which there are the remains of a fine burgh, like that at Moussa, from which no doubt the island took its ancient name of Borgarey, "the island of the burgh or castle," we come to South Ronaldsay, which is often mentioned in the Saga. We have already seen that, in modern times, South Ronaldsay took its prefix "South" to distinguish it from North Ronaldsay; but in ancient times there was no such ambiguity. The northern island was called Rínansey and the southern Rögnvaldsey, though, as the MSS. sometimes write both names R-ey, some confusion has arisen from the carelessness of transcribers, both ancient and modern. After Hrossey no island is named so often in our Saga as South Ronaldsay, a fact easily accounted for by its nearness to the Scottish main, whence so many expeditions against the Isles were planned and executed. On this island was Barðsvik, now Barswick, where Sweyn Asleif's son (p. 207) saw a ship of war sailing from Hrossey to South Ronaldsay, and from the same place, (p. 208) earl Rognvald and Sweyn saw earl Harold Maddad's son sailing over from Caithness to Vágaland, or Walls or Waas, that is to the low lying portion of Hoy. On the northwest side of the island lies Ronaldsvoe, the ancient Rognvaldsvágr, which, according to Munch, is the inner bight of the great bay now called "Widewall Bay," and in ancient times Víðivágr. Ronaldsvoe is interesting as being the harbour in which king Hacon Hacon's son lay from the 1st to the 10th of August in 1263, when he witnessed the annular eclipse of the sun which happened on the 5th of August in that year. (18)

Hoxa, the ancient Haugseið (the Cod. Flat. reads "Haugaheiði," Howheath), is an outlying peninsula on the north west of South Ronaldsay, which forms one arm of Widewall harbour. It was in all probability so called from the Haugr or Howe of earl Thorfinn Skullsplitter (Saga, p. 11), whose resting place may, perhaps, be identified with the great barrow called the "Howe of Hoxa;" though it is probable, as Munch suggests, that the Howe existed before the Northmen came to Orkney, and was utilized by the followers of the Orkney earl as his burial place.

Here, too, on the east side of the island, is another Papýli or Paplay, which, with the other Paplay already mentioned in Hrossey, claims to be the farm described in the Saga, p. 74, as part of the possessions of the descendents of earl Magnus the Saint. In any case the name is another proof of the abode of Irish anchorites in the Orkneys. Off South Ronaldsay lies Swanay, the ancient Swíney, mentioned in the Saga, p. 89, as the abode of Grim, a man of small means, whose sturdy sons Asbjorn and Margad were the constant followers of Sweyn Asleif's son.

After South Ronaldsay we have only one considerable island of the group left to describe. This is Hoy, the ancient Háey, or "high island," which answers to its name as being, in part at least, the only really mountainous island of the group. The southeastern extremity of the island is, however, flat; cut off from the hilly part by a narrow neck of land, just where the "voe," which forms part of the splendid harbour of Longhope, indents the shore, it is almost considered a distinct island, and is called "Walls," from the ancient vágar, from vágr, a "voe." In the Saga it is called repeatedly Vágaland. Here is the voe or haven called Osmondswall in modern and Ásmundarvágr in ancient times; where the Saga tells us that earl Sigurd was caught weatherbound by king Olaf Tryggvi's son, in the year 995, and forced to become an unwilling convert to Christianity (Saga, p. 15). here too earl Einar Wrymouth caught and slew Eyvind Urarhorn, king Olaf's dear friend (Saga, p. 20). By some it has been supposed that Osmondswall is to be sought on South Ronaldsay opposite, but Munch has shown that it is more properly placed on Walls. The remainder of Hoy is so hilly as to be scarcely habitable, though there on the "Upland," no doubt a hill farm, lived John WIng, the friend and kinsman of Sweyn Asleif's son (Saga, p. 89). His brother was Richard of the Brink on Stronsay, and the Saga tells us (p. 130) how the two fell on Thorkel the flayer, and burnt him and nine men in the house which their kinsman Waltheof had owned. At Rackwick, the ancient Rekavík, on the northwest side lived Thorljót, the father of Oliver the Unruly, and the son in law of Frakok, whose fate is described, Saga, p. 140. In a valley on the side of the highest hill on Hoy is the famous Dwarfie Stone which contains three chambers hewn by human hands, and in which we, no doubt, see one of those cells to which the Papæ or anchorites retired to spend their ascetic lives. Here in Hoy the legends of the North laid the scene of that endless mythical combat mentioned in the Skálda as Hjaðnínga-víg, where day by day the followers of Högni and Heðinn fought and fell, only to rise up at dawn next day to renew the struggle, which was to last till the day of doom. This is not the only tale which shows that to the Northmen those islands of the West were holy ground, but it is remarkable that the last remains of Norse poetry in these islands, rescued by Low in 1774, should have turned on one of the episodes in this Hjaðnínga-víg.

We now leave the Orkneys and pass on across the Pentland Firth, but let us pause to point out that the true name of that stormy strait is not Pentland, but Petland or Pettland, that is "the Firth of the land of 'the Picts.'" Whatever may be said to the contrary, the name thus given by the Northmen to the strait which separated them from a foreign and hostile race is a proof that the Picts or Pihte or Peohte or Peti, as the Latinized form ran, were in existence as a people or race when the first sea rovers and settlers reached those waters from Norway. In those days the term Scotland had not extended to the northernmost part of the country. The Picts in fact had not yet disappeared before the advance of the Scots from Ireland and the West. For a long period these two races, the Picts in the north and east and the Scots --- the Dalriad Scots as they were called --- in the west, co-existed in Scotland, and during the events narrated in the earlier portion of our Saga a continuous struggle for supremacy went on between the older Pictish royal race in Moray and the younger line of the Scots in the south, which at last terminated in the victory of the latter. Then, and not till then, the Picts disappeared, that is to say, they were amalgamated with the victorious race. But for centuries the dwellers beyond Caithness, and Sutherland, in Ross, and Moray, were known to the Northmen as Picts, and not as Scots, and so the stormy water which parted them from the Scottish mainland was called the Pettland, or Pictland Firth. In it, between South Ronaldsay and Caithness, lies the Pettlands Sker, now called "the Pentland Skerries," and nearer to the Scottish shore lies Stromay or Stroma, the ancient Straumey, "the island in the stream" or tideway, mentioned in the Njáls Saga, as well as in the Saga, p. 208, as the abode of Ámundi the son of Hnefi, who reconciled earl Harold and Sweyn Asleif's son.

Finally, before we land on Caithness, we must mention "Svelgr" a dangerous whirlpool or "maelstrom," which may, perhaps, be identified with the eddy off

Swelchie or Swilchie Point in the island of Stroma. It was in this famous whirlpool that Grotti the mill of the mythic king Fróði, which could grind all things, was sunk by the sea rover who carried it off; a story which still lingers in the Norse popular tale, "Why the Sea is Salt," and there at the bottom of the "Swelchie," Fróði's mill is supposed still to lie and to grind all the salt in the sea.

Landing in Caithness we shall not be suprised to find the Northmen simultaneously with their colonization of the Orkneys established on various parts of the north of Scotland. On jutting headlands and in deep bays and along the winding dales and straths of the rivers, Northern names still linger to witness their ancient occupation by this stirring race. Of Caithness, the ancient Katanes or more shortly Nes, the Naze or promontory par excellence, it may be said that it was in those times purely Norse. It seems always to have been held by the Orkney earls, and notably by earl Harold Maddad's son, as a fief from the Scottish king, who, even when most exasperated against his vassal, gave vent to his wrath rather on the population and freemen than on the earl (Saga, p. 230). When there were joint earls in the Orkneys and they were good friends, they went annually over to Caithness to hunt deer, as when earls Rognvald and Harold set out on that hunting party which ended in Rognvald's death (Saga p. 214-5). Sutherland, too, the ancient Suðrlönd took its name from the Northmen. It was south to them though north to almost all the rest of Scotland. Over both these counties, which, by the conformation of the coasts east and west, form as it were a promontory by themselves, for a long period the Northmen held more sway than any other rulers in Scotland. In the time of the earls their power naturally varied on the Mainland as they were strong and aggressive, or weak and peaceful at home. The power wielded by a Sigurd or a Thorfinn differed much from that claimed by a Brúsi or a Paul. Speaking generally, we may say that the rule of the Northmen in early times extended as far as the Dornoch Firth and the Oikel; and on the banks of the latter river it is expressly said of Sigurd, one of the earliest earls, that he was buried under a "howe" (19) there (Saga, p. 6). The Torfnes, where earl Einar first cut turf as we are told, and whence he took his nickname, is supposed to be the same as Tarbetness which divides the Dornoch from the Moray Firth. Arnor Earlskald sings of it as south of Oikel, p. 35. That this influence of the Northmen existed in later times, is shown by the account of the route pursued by Sweyn Asleif's son when he went out to take vengeance on the carline Frakok. He sailed from the Orkneys east of the Swelchie in the Pentland Firth to the Moray Firth, the ancient Breiðafjörðr, and on to Elgin and the valley of the Oikel, (20) and so up the country to Athole, where he got guides, and then fell on his enemy by a back blow in Sutherland, where he wreaked his vengeance to the full.

In both Caithness and Sutherland a glance at the map will show from the names the prevalence of Northern settlers in the country. Along the coast, Cape Wrath is a distortion of cape Hvarf, that is Turnagain Point, because after it the coast trends away south. Close to it was a Djurnes or Dýrnes, not to be confounded with the headland of the same name in Hrossey. Then there is Force or Fors, the "waterfall" at the mouth of the river which runs down from Loch Caldell, the ancient Kalfadals-vatn, through the side dale of the same name, in which Earl Rognvald-Kali met his death by the hands of the unruly Thorbjorn Clerk (Saga, p. 215). Next comes Thurso, the ancient þórsá, mentioned in the Saga, p. 130, as the abode of earl Ottar Frakok's brother and afterwards of his kinsman, earl Harold Maddad's son. Not far off is Staur, supposed to be Broom Ness. At Scrabster, Skarabólstaðr, they had a castle. Not far from Scrabster lies Murkle, the ancient Myrkholl, where Ragnhilda, Eric Bloodaxe's bloodthirsty daughter, caused her husband earl Arnfinn to be murdered (Saga, p. 11). Dunnet Head is probably the Rauðabjörg or Red Head of the Sagas. Between it and Duncansby Head is the Dungalsbœr of the Saga, in which it is mentioned often as one of the possessions of Sweyn Asleif's son, and on the east coast was Lambaborg, Lamburg, the strong castle whence he and Margad escaped when besieged by earl Rognvald. It is clear from the Saga, pp. 186, 191, that this castle was close to Freswick, the ancient þrasvík. Further down the coast is Víkr the modern Wick. It is uncertain where Skidmire, the ancient Skiðamýri, lay, where the rival earls of Northern and Scottish or Pictish race met to settle their quarrels in staked lists. It was probably in the interior of Caithness, in the district called the Dales. (21) There in the Dales at one time dwelt the treacherous and intriguing Frakok till her designs against earl Paul made both Caithness and Sutherland too hot to hold her, and she retired to Athole, where her niece Margaret had married earl Maddad. Afterwards she returned to Helmsdale, Hjalmundalr, in Sutherland, and there it was that her implacable foe, Sweyn Asleif's son, fell on her after a circuitous expedition, and burnt her and all who were in the house (Saga, p. 139, 140). Besides these and many others in Caithness and Sutherland, which last was the border country between the Northmen and the Scottish races, numberless names of places along the coasts east and west attest the extent to which their expeditions reached when they were bent on conquest or sea roving. Not to speak of the invasions both of Scotland, England, and Ireland by earl Thorfinn, the life of Sweyn Asleif's son, so graphically told in the Saga, proves how wide a flight the old Viking took in his private wars. Sometimes he is harrying and burning either alone or in partnership, in the Southern Isles and Scotland's Firths, that is the Firths on the west coast, where dwelt the great race of which Somerled was the chief, whom Sweyn was said to have slain. Sometimes he is on an expedition into the heart of Scotland as far as Athole, bent on vengeance in a blood feud. Now he is plundering monks or merchants in the Firth or Forth, and seizing, in company with Anakol, on the goods of Canute, a merchant of North Berwick; for it is plain from the context that it is North Berwick, and not Berwick-on-Tweed, which is meant when the Saga in several places talk of Beruvík. At another time he is in the Scilly Isles at Port St. Mary's, or off Ireland robbing English traders of their broadcloth. Going regularly out to rob and plunder twice in each year, in spring after he had sown his crops, and in autumn after he had reaped them, he dies at last in Dublin, the victim of treachery; and so ended the career of one who may be called the last of the Vikings. Wherever the Northman went he left his mark, and one of his marks was giving names to places which to his day all over Scotland and the West bear witness to his enterprize and power.

But this geographical account would be incomplete were we to pass over in silence those expeditions by the Northmen which went beyond the Narrow Seas away from Norway and the islands of the West, and entered what to them was the ocean of the Mediterranean. Such were the fleets fitted out by king Sigurd for a pilgrimage to the Holy Land, whence he got his nickname "Jewryfarer," and by earl Rognvald-Kali expressly in imitation of that monarch. Those pilgrimages followed the Crusades and the establishment of the Latin kingdom of Jerusalem, and as in the days of the earlier earls, such as Thorfinn and Hacon, a pilgrimage to Rome followed by absolution from the Holy Father for direful sins was looked on as the fitting end of an earthly career too often debased by ambition; so in the days of their successors it was thought that to visit Jerusalem and to see the Holy Places in that city and in Palestine was a voyage which might atone for many crimes. In those days the northern pilgrims, like the modern Syrians and Copts, swam across the muddy Jordan in token that their sins were washed out by the waves of that holy stream, and not one of the least curious facts recorded in the pilgrimage of earl Rognvald is his swimming across that river with Sweyn Asleif's son's stepson, the dashing Sigmund angle, and twisting the knot of shame in the hoary willows on the opposite bank as a brand of disgrace for the false Eindrid who had deserted them on the way. These expeditions in another way were connected with the Crusades. As the Crusaders had often lingered at Constantinople sometimes aiding, sometimes expelling, the emperors of the East, so king Sigurd and earl Rognvald after him thought it right to show themselves and their trim ships and bold crews at the Byzantine court, and as they neared the imperial city, which to their eyes was greater and richer far than any capital in the world, they strained every nerve and put on all their bravery of apparel to present themselves as great kings and mighty earls before the eyes of the Greeks and their master. Nor, assuredly, was it without a flush of pride as they sailed through the Dardanelles and across the sea of Marmora that those hardy children of the North remembered that the mainstay of all the pomp and pride of the empire of the East was that chosen band of Varangians, on whom, of all their legions, the emperors most relied, and to whom the most exclusive rights and the most sweeping privileges were granted as the reward of their unflinching allegiance. With regard to these expeditions the Orkneyingers' Saga affords the most curious information. In it we can follow such a design through every stage from its very conception to its perfect accomplishment. Here we see how Eindrid the young, who had served long among the Varangians, first incited earl Rognvald to gain glory by deeds in the East; then how earl Rognvald's friends and relations rallied round him as soon as he had made up his mind to make the pilgrimage; next how the ships were built and how long they took to build, how jealously earl Rognvald's rights as leader of the expedition were guarded in the stipulation that no one but he was to have a gaily painted and decorated ship, no one but he one of more than sixty oars; (22) both of which conditions were broken by the ambition of Eindrid, whose ship alone of all the squadron rivalled in burden and beauty the longship of the earl.

At last after the ships had been built and his plans matured, earl Rognvald started, late in the summer of 1151 --- for they had to wait for the traitor Eindrid's new ship --- for his voyage to the east. Besides bishop William, who, as a clerk of Paris, was supposed to know all things, and whom they took with them as an interpreter, the earl was followed by his Orkney chiefs and his Norse kinsmen and friends. In all they had a fleet of fifteen ships, as well built and fitted out as ships in that age could be. Our purpose here is only with the geography of their voyage, --- the places they passed rather than the feats they performed are what we wish to describe. As they passed the Vesla-sands off the Northumbrian coast, that is, the northeast coast of England, as far as the Humber, one of the skalds who accompanied the earl burst out into song, the words of his verse fix the spot as off Humber-mouth, and perhaps one of the many shoals which fringe the mouth of that estuary and the Wash may be the sand meant. (23) After this we hear of them sailing south along the coast of England till they come to Valland, that is, France, or some country peopled by a Romance race; and next we find them at Nerbon, according to all the best MSS. That this Nerbon is the same as Narbonne in the Gulf of Lyons, in the south of France, seems impossible, for that city is just the last spot on the shores of the Mediterranean in which we should expect to find these adventurers, as it lay entirely out of their course. That, however, it was some place in the wine-growing country is clear from the fact that Ermingard pours out wine to the earl and his captains rather than mead or ale; and, on the whole, it seems not unlikely that "Nerbon" is the river Nerbion or Nervion, and that the sea burg is the modern Bilbao in the north of Spain; but wherever it was, that lovely lady received the Northmen most hospitably, and whatever might be the case with her, it is plain from earl Rognvald's verses, long after their parting and when much of that salt water which proverbially washes out love was between them, that she made a great impression on him. But their aim was the Holy Land, not to make love in Nerbon, and so earl Rognvald tore himself away and we next hear of him as sailing west off Thrasness, which may mean Capes La Hogue, Ortegal, or Finisterre in Spain, according to the position of the doubtful "Nerbon" on the map of Europe. Next they came, still sailing west, to Galicia in Spain, and there they wintered, spending part of it, till the weather allowed them to sail in the spring of 1152, in ridding the inhabitants of the district of a tyrant named Godfrey who oppressed them terribly. Having taken his castle, they sailed thence west along the shore of heathen Spain, that is, along the districts possessed by the Moors, landing and harrying the country, and encountering a violent storm before they could beat through the Gut at Gibraltar. As soon as they had passed it the treacherous nature of Eindrid was revealed. He sailed away with six ships for Marseilles, while earl Rognvald and the rest lay to in the Straits. After that the earl sailed along the Barbary coast till he came off the island of Sardinia, where he fell in with a huge Dromond, or ship of burden, which had been driven to sea from Tripoli, Tunis, or Algiers, having on board of her a Moorish chief and untold wealth in wares and gold and silver. The Northmen took her after a sharp struggle, and then, after a custom not uncommon in those times, put into a port in Barbary to dispose of the prisoners they had spared, and some of the goods which they had taken out of their prize. Thence they sailed south to Crete, again encountering heavy weather, and there they lay under the lee of the island till they got a fair wind for Acre in Palestine, where they arrived early on a Friday morning. (24)

There they landed after their long voyage, but sickness as was not unlikely, broke out among them, and many died. From Acre earl Rognvald and his men visited all the "halidoms" or holy places in Jewry, and as we have already seen bathed in Jordan, and swam across it, as it seems on St. Laurence's Day, August 10th, 1152. Soon after that they left the Holy Land and completed their adventures by a visit to the city of cities, Constantinople. On their way thither they came in the autumn to a place which is in its way as puzzling as Nerbon. This was "Imbolum," which some have thought to be the island of Imbros, while the late Gudbrand Vigfusson thought it to be only a distortion of "ej tan polin." In the account of their stay at this place, another puzzling word occurs in "miðhœfi," which the inhabitants called out to one another when they met in a narrow place. This, too, Mr. Vigfusson explains in the Icelandic Dictionary by the Greek metabhqi, "get down," or "get out of the way," and whatever it was, ignorance of it caused Erling, the second in command of the expedition, a fall and roll in the mud. A more tragical event happened there in the murder of John Peter's son, the earl's brother in law, who seems to have been slain by some of the inhabitants after he had missed his way when drunk at night.

Leaving "Imbolum" they passed "Engilsness," or Cape St. Angelo, though another reading is Ægisness, said to be the point at the end of the Thracian Chersonese, at the mouth of the Dardanelles, where they lay some nights waiting for a fair south wind to carry them across the sea of Marmora to the great city. As soon as it came, they sailed up with great pomp, just after the pattern of king Sigurd, and when they came to Constantinople they were made much of by the emperor Manuel and the Varangians, though the traitor Eindrid, whom they found there in great favour, did everything in his power to set men against them. About winter the earl began his voyage home, sailing first to Bulgaria and Durazzo, and thence across the Adriatic to Apulia. There he left his ships, and with the noblest of his company ended his journey home by land, clearly leaving the rest of his force to bring the ships home by sea. From Apulia he took horse and rode to Rome, where, though it is not mentioned, he no doubt got absolution for his sins. From Rome he went "Rome way," that is, by the usual route of pilgrims to that city, and so passing through Germany he came to Denmark and to Norway. No wonder after such a voyage and such exploits men were glad to see them safe back, and thought that their voyage had been most glorious, and they were much greater men then than they had been before. This must have been early in 1153. Many things kept earl Rognvald most of that year in Norway. When the winter was far spent he reached his realm in a merchant ship with a great train. Ships of war were being built for him in Norway, and his old ships seem never to have returned from the Mediterranean; at least they are never heard of. During his absence there had been many changes in the Orkneys, and he found a new pretender to the earldom in Erlend, the son of earl Harold smooth-tongue. Whatever they might have thought of him in Norway, earl Rognvald must have felt that to come home in a merchant ship, after having sailed from the Isles with such a goodly fleet, and to return to find strife where he had left peace, was a downfall in his position and power which it would require all his skill and tact to retrieve. How he did this and kept his predominance in the Orkneys till his death will be seen in that Story of Earl Rognvald which forms the third portion of the Orkney Sagas.

The late Mr. Vigfusson having elaborately described in the preface to the Norse text, of which the translation is contained in this volume, the process whereby he was enabled to build up from various sources the structure of the Orkneyingers' Saga, and having also most carefully examined and estimated the value which, in point of historical credibility, attaches to each fragment, it is unnecessary for the translator to add anything to the information which has already been laid before the student of this period of English History. It may, however, be pointed out that this volume and the translation of the Hacon Saga and its Appendices should, with the Norse text and Mr. Vigfusson's laborious introductions, be treated as a whole, as between them they contain nearly all that is known from northern sources as to the dominion claimed and exercised by the Northmen over portions of Great Britain from the reign of Harold Fairhair, in the latter half of the ninth century, until the collapse of King Hacon's great expedition to Scotland in 1263.

ENDNOTES:

1. It is described in Hibbert's book on Shetland, p. 544, as built of stones, without cement. In the walls, which are thirteen feet thick, are eleven small round rooms, each five feet in diameter, with a separate entrance from the inner court, which is 31 feet in diameter. This "burgh" seems to have differed from that at Moussa in having single, and not double walls.

2. The lines in Juvenal, II. 159-161 --- "Arma quidem ultra...... Littora Juvernæ promovimus, et modo captas Orcadas, ac minimâ contentos nocte Britannos." were written after A.D. 84, when Agricola sailed round Britain and discovered the Orkneys. They are also important as marking the quantity Orcades with a short pen- ultimate like Strophades, Pleiades, and Symplegandes.

3. The meaning of this word is a portage, or place where boats and ships are dragged across a narrow isthmus from sea to sea. Any one acquainted with Scotland, will recall several Tarbats, or Tarbets, as for instance, that across the neck of the Mull of Cantire, that at the head of Loch Lomond, where a narrow neck of land separates It from Loch Long, and another on the east coast in the Dornoch Firth.

4. See Munch's essay in the Annals: and Introduction to Burnt Njal, Edinburgh, 1861.

5. Great confusion has arisen between these two islands from the custom In MSS. of using the abreviation R-ey for both of them. This abreviation when expanded under the pen of a careless scribe often turned Rinansey into Rögnvaldsey, and vice versa.

6. It is remarkable that the Horæ for the Feast of St. Magnus (p. 311) as found in the Aberdeen Breviary contain the form Eglissei and not Egilssei, as though the name of the isle on which the Saint was martyred were derived from a church and not from Egil.

7. So holy was this church considered, that the first reformed minister could scarcely prevent his parishioners from saying their prayers in the ruins before they came to the parish church. St. Tredwall is the Scottish form of St. Triduana, a saint once much revered across the border. She was said to have come from Achaia with Saint Regulus, to Scotland; in the course of her journey her beauty so inflamed a Gaulish chief, that to escape his advances, she cut out her own eyes. After this mutilation, she came to Scotland and died, and was buried at Restalrig near Edinburgh. Many miracles were wrought at her grave, and she was especially sought for diseases and injuries of the eyes. At p. 229 of our Saga will be found a proof of this in the case of Bishop John of Caithness, whom earl Harold Maddad's son, mutilated both in eyes and tongue, who when brought to the shrine of St. Tredwall, it is uncertain whether at her chapel in Papey Meiri, or her shrine at Restalrig, recovered both sight and speech. In Norse utterance, St. Triduana or St. Tredwall became Trollhæna, pronounced Trodlhæna. Barry says, p. 63, that St. Tredwall's chapel in Papey

Meiri was built over an old Pict's house; and in all probability, the chapel was in existence as a place of worship, like the church at Egilsay, long before the arrival of the Northmen in the Orkneys.

8. The text of the Saga, p. 111, says that Thorstein Havard's son Gunnis son was to have charge of the beacon on Rínansey, but this probably arises out of a confusion between the two Thorstein's, for at p. 121 it is said that Thorstein Ragna's son fired the beacon on Rínansey.

9. This seems to be the meaning of the words (p. 221), "Þeir (his sons Olaf and Andres) gjörðu hit næsta sumar eptir er Sveinn var látinn gaflhlöd í drikkjuskála þann hinn mikla er hann hafði áttan i Gareksey." Munch says that the meaning of the words is that Andrew and Olaf built an upper story to the house when their father died, but the sense of the context plainly is that the hall which Sweyn built was too long for them, they therefore cut it in half and divided it between them.

10. Munch has shown that the strange name, Pomona, identical with that of the Roman goddess of Fruit and Plenty, which Buchanan gave to the mainland of Orkney when he says, "Orcadum maxima multis veterum Pomona vocatur," arose out of a mistake in some MS. of Solinus, who, in speaking of the Orcades and Thyle, says, "Secundum a continenti stationem Orcades præbent .... vacant homine, non habent silvas, tantum junceis herbis inhorrescunt. Cætera eorum nudæ arenæ. Ab Orcadibus Thylen usque 5 dierum ac noctium navigatio est; sed Thyle larga et diutinâ copiosa est." In this passage both diutina and pomona have been taken as local names at various times, as when Torfæus tells us that Hrossey or the Mainland was called Diutina by Solinus, and when the MS. which Fordun and Buchanan preferred read Pomona. In the one case, the passage in Solinus would have run, "Sed Thyle larga, et Diutina pomonâ copiosa est," and in the other "Sed Thyle larga et diutina Pomona copiosa est." Solinus was as Munch well says, a geographical oracle all through the middle ages, but it is clear that in the passage in question he says nothing whatever about the Orkneys, but only that "Thyle, which was distant from that group by a voyage of five days and nights, was fruitful and abundant in the lasting yield of its crops." It follows, therefore, that "Pomona," of which Barry says "This appellation has been traced, ridiculously enough to a word in the Roman (i.e., Latin) language, that implies the core or heart of an apple, an allusion to the situation of this with regard to the rest of the islands," should be banished from the geography of the Orkneys, as well as the Celtic derivation from "po," little, and "mon," country. It is remarkable that Solinus describes the Orkneys as uninhabited in his day, but when he flourished is very doubtful; about the middle of the third century of the Christian era seems the most probable date.

11. In this parish the old Norse dialect seems to have maintained itself a long time. John Ben, as quoted by Munch and Anderson, found it in full force there in 1529. "Utuntur idiomate proprio," he says, "veluti quum dicimus 'guid 'day, guidman,'" illi dicunt 'goand da, boundæ.'" That is, "godan dag, bóndi."

12. The name of this parish is probably derived from the word herad, which forms the last part of the compound Birgis-herad, now Birsay. In old times both the parishes of Harray and Birsay were united in the district called Birgis-herad. Munch thinks that Birsay does not come from Birgis-ey, the isle or brock of Birsay, but Birgis-á, the stream which falls into the sea at that spot.

13. See Farrer's beautiful book, Maes Howe, 1862. Compare also this translation of the Saga, p. 190.

14. The conjecture of Munch is no doubt right that for "Kjarrekstöðum," p. 185 of the text of the Saga, we should read "Hnarrarstum" Knarstead. Arni could never have run so far with his shield on his back without being aware of it.

15. Hacon Hacon's son's Saga, p. 352, new ed.

16. The Saga, p. 92, expressly says of Kirkwall, before the translation of the relics of St. Magnus, from Christ Church in Birsay, that it "had few houses."

17. This "or" or "ere" forms the ending of many names of places in the British Isles, as Upn-or, Bogn-or, Walm-er, in each of which there is a natural bank of sand or shingle protecting a low tract of land, sometimes, as in the case of Walmer, below high-water mark; compare also Ravensere, the old Hrafuseyrr, Saga, p. 63, near the Spurn Head at the north of the Humber.

18. Hacon Hacon's son's Saga, p. 333-4, 352, new ed.

19. Mr. Anderson in Hjaltalins translation of the Saga, p. 107,has identified Sigurd's Howe through Siward hoch, and Siddera with the modern Cyder hall "near the ferry on the north bank of the Dornoch Firth into which the Oykel runs." Mr. Skene, however, does not agree with this view.

20. This route by the Oikel is a stumbling block to Mr. Anderson, who proposes to read "Atjöklabakki" for Ekkjals-bakki; but there seems no good reason for the alteration.

21. Mr. Anderson places it at Skitten.

22. The longships, that is, the warships of the Northmen, were vessels with one mast and one sail of a lug shape; they must also have carred a jib or foresail. Aft there seems to have been a half deck, on which was a poop, lypting, where the cabin of the captain was. In the waist, they were undecked, and here on benches, sessur, sat the rowers two on a bench. Hence, when a ship is said to be a twitugsessa, or twenty benches, that means she had forty oars, halfþritugt, like earl Rognvald's ship fifty oars, and so on, some ships being said to have had 100 oars on each side, though that, no doubt, is a fabulous number. The way in which the rowers sat is not clear, though it is not quite such a puzzle as the position of the oarsmen in the ancient trireme. It is not improbable, if the oars were long and the longship high out of the water, that the rower who pulled the oar on the starboard side sat over to larboard and his mate on the bench who pulled on the larboard in his turn over to starboard, so that each might have more purchase and control over his oar. Across the undecked part of the ships were thwarts or planks, þoptur; whether these were the benches on which the rowers sat is uncertain. Passing on to the forepart of the ship, that, too, was decked, and under the deck, in what would now be called the forecastle, some of the crew were lodged at night. The rest found shelter under the awnings, tjöld, with which the ships of the Northmen seem always to have been covered at night when strife was not looked for. See Saga, p. 192, and Sweyn Asleif's son's advice to his companions. The word "forecastle" exactly implied what the bow or forepart of the Northmen's ships were. It was raised like the poop, and on it stood in action the picked men of the crew who were

called stafnbúar that is, stem-men or bowmen. On either side of the prow or true bow, where the bowsprit projected, were two cat heads, brandar, which were often, together with the figure-head of the ship, much carved and decorated, and hence often taken as trophies and erected at the doors of the conquerors' houses as signs of victory; just as was the case with the prows of galleys in ancient times, and even among the Anglo-Saxons, as when earl Harold Godwin's son sent similar trophies to Edward the Confessor after he had slain Griffith and taken his ship. As the waists of the ships were low compared with the stem and stern means were taken to raise the sides before action by temporary bulwarks, this "clearing the decks for action" was called víggyrðla skipit. At other times this waist of the ship was decorated with the shields of the crew which were hung along them on a rail which is even found in trading ships or býrðinger, see the account in the Saga, page 54, of the surprise of earl Rognvald's men in Kirkwall by earl Thorfinn. In shape and look these longships or warships were long and narrow, and so less seaworthy than the byrðings, in which the ordinary traffic of the time was carried on. t is also a question whether the true byrðingr or trading ship, also called Knörr, was ever rowed unless in very exceptional cases. Sometimes a warship was called Snekkja, a snake, or Dreki, a drake or dragon; a ship of this name probably differed in nothing from the mould of other warships, except that it had, as in Eindrid's ship, which is expressly called a Drake, a figurehead carved like a dragon, and that at the taffrail at the sterm, it was carved into coils resembling the folds and tail of a serpent. Besides the thirty, forty, fifty, or more rowers that each longship carried, her crew consisted of a greater number, some to fight while the oarsmen rowed the ship into action, some to relieve the rowers when they had rowed a certain time, Thus, to take one instance out of many, earl Harold's ship, mentloned in the Saga, page 184, was one of forty oars, and yet her crew was made up of eighty men; and again, page 48, seventy dead are mentioned as having been taken out of earl Thorfinn's ship, though it had been said before that his ships were not large. One hundred and twenty men was no unusual number for a longship to carry. It seems to have been an invariable practice when Northmen fought against Northmen that the attacking side rowed up to their adversaries, who awaited them, having first lashed their ships together in line. As soon as the attacking ships came close enough to begin the action, they too were lashed together, and after a struggle which lasted some time with missiles, in which stones were largely and constantly employed, the two lines closed together by the action of wind or tide, and then when the decks of either side had been sufficiently cleared to allow them to board, those who had the best of it boarded, gengu upp, much in our old English way, and then cleared the enemy's deck by a struggle hand to hand. All round the ship on both sides a gangway seems to have run, and when these and the poop and forecastle were cleared the ship was said to be "hroðit," and the conquerors passed on from her to the next ship in the enemy's line to which she was as has been said, lashed. In this way action went on, till one side had so much the best of it and had cleared or captured so many of the enemy that the day was won. The sign of this stage was the contest was the signal given on the beaten side to cut away the lashings, höggva tengslin, and to fly. Then as the line was broken every ship of the worsted party rowed or sailed off and shifted for itself. This was followed by a similar sundering of the lashings in the conqueror's line, which then ship by ship chased the flying foe. Very graphic accounts of such actions will be found in the Saga, page 33, fol., where the sea fight near

Dyrness between earl Thorfinn and king Karl of Scotland is described, and also at page 47, fol., where the action between earls Thorfinn and Rognvald off Dunnet Head in the Pentland Firth is minutely detailed. Compare also the account of the battle at Hjoring voe, in the Iomsvíkinga Saga. These were the fights of Northmen against Northmen, but an action very nearly resembling a boarding expedition in large boats against a galleon of great size will be found at page 173, fol., where earl Rognvald with his seven ships attacked the Moorish Dromond, which was so huge that she loomed through the fog like an island, while her sides were so tall and round that they could not board her when they closed with her broadside to broadside, and at last had to hew their way into her through her ironbound sides. This combat with the Dromond reminds one much of Drake or Hawkins or Cavendish capturing the huge galleons or carracks of the Spaniards off the Spanish Main.

23. The Flatey Book reads for Humrumynni Hverumynni, that is, "Wearmouth." If so, the sand in question must be sought for off the mouth of the Wear in Durham; and as even the Flatey Book may have sometimes a good reading, this may be one of the exceptional merits of that text.

24. The text says only Föstumorgin snemma, "Friday morning early," but it was probably Good Friday morning, as that was the day by which all pilgrims desired to be in the Holy Land.

THE ORKNEYINGERS' SAGA

CHAPTER 1

There was a king named Fornjot, he ruled over those lands which are called Finland and Kvenland; that is to the east of that bight of the sea which goes northward to meet Gandvik; that we call the Helsingbight. Fornjot had three sons; one was named Hler, whom we call Ægir, the second Logi, the third Kari; he was the father of Frost, the father of Snow the old, his son's name was Thorri; he (Thorri) had two sons, one was named Norr and the other Gorr; his daughter's name was Goi. Thorri was a great sacrificer, he had a sacrifice every year at midwinter; that they called Thorri's sacrifice; from that the month took its name. One winter there were these tidings at Thorri's sacrifice, that Goi was lost and gone, and they set out to search for her, but she was not found. And when that month passed away Thorri made them take to sacrifice, and sacrifice for this, that they might know surely where Goi was hidden away. That they called Goi's sacrifice, but for all that they could hear nothing of her. Four winters after those brothers vowed a vow that they would search for her; and so share the search between them, that Norr should search on land, but Gorr should search the outscars and islands, and he went on board ship. Each of those brothers had many men with him. Gorr held on with his ships out along the sea-bight, and so into Alland's (1) sea; after that he views the Swedish scars far and wide, and all the isles that lie in the East salt sea; after that to the Gothland scars, and thence to Denmark, and views there all the isles; he found there his kinsmen, they who were come from Hler the old out of Hler's isle, (2) and he held on then still with his voyage and hears nothing of his sister. But Norr his brother bided till snow lay on the heaths, and it was good going on snow-shoon. After that he fared forth from Kvenland and inside the sea-bight, and they came thither where those men were who are called Lapps, that is at the back of Finmark. But the Lapps wished to forbid them a passage, and there arose a battle; and that might and magic followed Norr and his men; that their foes became as swine (3) as soon as they heard the war-cry and saw weapons drawn, and the Lapps betook themselves to flight. But Norr fared thence west on the Keel, (4) and was long out, so that they knew nothing of men, and shot beasts and birds for meat for themselves; they fared on till they came where the waters turned to the westward from the fells. Then they fared along with the waters, and came to a sea; there before them was a firth as big as it were a sea-bight; there was a mickle tilths, and great dales came down to the firth. There was a gathering of folk against them, and they straightway made ready to battle with Norr, and their quarrel fared as was to be looked for. All that folk either fell or fled, but Norr and his men overcame them as weeds over cornfields. Norr fared round all the firth and laid it under him, and made himself king over those districts that lay there inside the firth. Norr tarried there the summer over till it snowed upon the hearths; then he shaped his course up along the dale which goes south from the firth; that firth is now called Drontheim. Some of his men he lets fare the coast way round Mæren; he laid under him all withersoever he came. And when he comes south over the fell that lay to the south of the dalebight, he went on still south along the dales, until he came to a great water which they called Mjösen. Then he turns west again on to the fell, because it had been told him that his men had come off worsted before that king whose name was Sokni. Then they came into that district which they called Valders. Thence they fared to the sea, and came into a long firth and a narrow, which is now called Sogn; there was their meeting with Sokni, and they had there a mickle battle, because their witchcraft had no hold on Sokni. Norr went hard forward, and he and Sokni came to handstrokes. There fell Sokni and many of his folk.

CHAPTER 2

After that Norr fared on into the firth that goes north from Sogn. There Sokni had ruled before in what is now called Sokni's dale. There Norr tarried a long time, and that is now called Norafirth. There came to meet him Gorr his brother, and neither of them had then heard anything of Goi. Gorr too had laid under him all the outer land as he had fared from the south, and then those brothers shared the lands between them. Norr had all the mainland, but Gorr shall have all those isles between which and the mainland he passes in a ship with a fixed rudder. And after that Norr fares to the Uplands, and came to what is now called Heidmörk (5); there that king ruled whose name was Hrolf of the Hill; he was the son of Svadi the giant from north of the Dovrefell. Hrolf had taken away from Kvenland Goi, Thorri's daughter; he went at once to meet Norr, and

602

offered him single combat; they fought long together and neither was wounded. After that they made their quarrel up, and Norr got Hrolf's sister, but Hrolf got Goi to wife. Thence Norr turned back to the realm which he had laid under him, that he called Norway; he ruled that realm while he lived, and his sons after him, and they shared the land amongst them, and so the realms began to get smaller and smaller as the kings got more and more numerous, and so they were divided into provinces.

CHAPTER 3

Gorr had the isles, and for that he was called a sea-king; his sons were they Heiti and Beiti, they were sea-kings and mighty overbearing men. They made many inroads on the realm of Norr's sons, and they had many battles, and now one, now the other won the day. Beiti ran into Drontheim and warred there; he lay where it is now called Beitsea and Beitstede; thence he made them drag his ship from the innermost bight of Beitstede, and so north over Elduneck, that is where the Naumdales come down from the north. He sat himself on the poop and held the tiller in his hand, and claimed for his own all that land that then lay on the larboard, and that is many tilths and much land. Heiti, Gorr's son, was father of Sveiði the sea-king, the father of Halfdan the old, the father of Ivar the Uplanders' earl, the father of Eystein the noisy, the father of earl Rognvald the mighty and the wise in council. (6)

CHAPTER 4

Earl Rognvald joined Harold fair-hair when he seized the land, but he (Harold) gave him lordship over both the Mæren and Romsdale; (7) he had to wife Ragnhilda the daughter of Hrolf nosy; their son was Hrolf who won Normandy, he was so tall that horses could not carry him; for that he was called Ganging-Hrolf; from him are come the Rouen Jarls and the English Kings; their son was also Ivar, and Thorir the silent. Rognvald had also base-born sons, their names were Hallad and Hrollaug and Einar, he was the youngest. Harold fair-hair fared one summer west across the sea to chastise the Vikings, when he was weary at the peacelessness of those who harried in Norway in summer, but were in the winter in Shetland or the Orkneys. He laid under him Shetland and the Orkneys and the Southern Isles; he fared west too as far as Man, and laid waste the tilths of Man. He had there many battles, and took as his own lands so far west that no king of Norway has ever owned land further west since. And in one battle, Ivar, son of earl Rögnvald, fell. But when king Harold sailed from the west, then he gave to earl Rognvald, as an atonement for his son, Shetland and the Orkneys; but earl Rognvald gave both lands to Sigurd his brother: he was one of king Harold's forecastle men. The king gave Sigurd the title of earl when he went from the west, and Sigurd stayed behind there in the west.

CHAPTER 5

Earl Sigurd made himself a mighty chief; he joined his fellowship with Thorstein the red, son of Olaf the white and Aud the deep-minded, (8) and they won all Caithness and much else of Scotland, Moray and Ross; there he caused to be built a burg southward of Moray. These two agreed between themselves to meet, Sigurd and Melbricta toothy the Scot-earl, that they should meet and settle their quarrel at a given place, each with forty men. And when the day named came, Sigurd thought to himself that the Scots were faithless. He made them mount eighty men on forty horses; and when Melbricta got to see them, he said to his men: "Now are we cheated by Sigurd, for I see two feet of a man on each horse's side, and the men must be twice as many again as the steeds that bear them. Let us now harden our hearts, and let us see that each has a man for himself ere we die;" and they got ready after that. And when Sigurd saw their plan, he said to his men: "Now half of our force shall get off horseback and come on them in flank when the battle is joined; but we will ride at them as hard as we can, and break in sunder their array." And so they met and there was a hard battle, and not long ere Melbricta fell and his followers, and Sigurd caused the heads to be fastened to his horses' cruppers as a glory for himself. And then they rode home, and boasted of their victory. And when they were come on the way, then Sigurd wished to spur the horse with his foot, and he struck his calf against the tooth which stuck out of Melbricta's head and grazed it; and in that wound sprung up pain and swelling, and that led him to his death. And Sigurd the mighty is buried under a "how" at Ekkjalsbakka. (9) Guttorm was the name of Sigurd's son; he ruled the lands one winter and died childless. And when earl Rognvald of Mæren learnt the death of that father and son, he sent his son Hallad west, and king Harold gave him the title of earl. And when Hallad came west, he sate down in Hrossey, but Vikings went about the isles and over in Caithness; they slew and robbed men. But when the yeomen brought their scathe before earl Hallad, then he thought it hard to right their lot, and he grew weary of the dignity; he turned himself out of the earldom, and took up his freehold right, and went back to Norway; and his journey was thought the greatest mark for mockery.

CHAPTER 6

Two Dansk Vikings set themselves down in the lands; the name of the one was Thorir tree-beard, but the other's Kalf Skurvy; and when earl Rognvald learnt this, he took it very ill to heart, and fetched before him his sons Thorir and Hrollaug. Hrolf was then out warring. Rögnvald asked which of them would go west into the isles. Thorir bade him see about his passage. "So says my mind about this," says the earl, "that thy thriving will be most here, and thy ways lie not hence." Then Hrollaug asked, "Wilt thou that I go?" The earl says, "Not for thee will the earldom be destined, and the spirits that follow thee lie towards Iceland; there wilt thou increase thy race and be a famous man in that land.'" Then Einar went forward, the youngest of his sons, and said, "Wilt thou that I go to the isles? I will promise that I will never come back into thy eyesight; besides I have here little good to part from, and it is not to be looked for that my thriving will be less anywhere else than here." The earl says, "Unlikely art thou for a chief for thy mother's sake, for she is thrall born on all sides, but true it is that I should think it all the better that thou goest soon away and comest late back." Rögnvaldr gave Einar a ship of twenty benches fully maned, but king Harold gave him the title of earl.

CHAPTER 7

Einar sailed west to Shetland, and there folk gathered to him; after that he went south into the Orkneys, and held on at once to meet Kalf and his companion. There a battle arose, and both those Vikings fell. Then this stave was sung: "He gave Treebeard to Trolls. Turf-Einar slew Skurvy." After that he laid the lands under him, and made himself the greatest chief. He first of men found out how to cut turf out of the earth for firewood on Turfness in Scotland, for they were ill off for wood in the isles. Einar was a tall man and ugly, one-eyed, and yet the sharpest-sighted of men.

CHAPTER 8

When the sons of Harold fair-hair had grown to man's estate, they became most overbearing men and unruly within the land; they fell on the king's earls, some they slew, but some they drove from their owndoms. Snowfrid's sons, Halfdan long-leg, and Gudred the bright, fell on earl Rognvald of Mœren, and slew him, and took to themselves his realm. But when king Harold heard that, he grew very wrath, and went out against his sons. Halfdan rushed on shipboard and sailed west across the sea, but Gudred gave himself up to his father's power. King Harold gave Thorir as an atonement for his father, Alofa harvest-heal his daughter, and the title of earl, and all that his father left behind him. Halfdan long-leg came into the Orkneys, and as soon as it was known that a son of king Harold was come thither, then men became full of fear. Some became Halfdan's liegemen, but earl Einar fled away out of the isles and up into Scotland. Halfdan laid the isles under him, and made himself king over them. Einar came back that same year, and he and Halfdan met; there arose then a great battle, and Einar gained the victory, but Halfdan leapt overboard in the dusk at eventide. Then Einar sang a stave:

"I see not from Hrolf's hand,

Nor Hrollaug's eke, fly

Dart on the foeman flock,

Father-vengeance befits us;

But while we the battle

This even urged on,

Earl Thorir in Mæren

O'er mead-cup sits mute."

Next morning when it was light they went to look for runagate men among the isles if any had got away; and each was slain on the spot as he stood. Then earl Einar took to saying these words: "I know not what I see in Rinansey, sometimes it lifts itself up, but sometimes it lays itself down, that is either a bird or a man, and we will go to it." There they found Halfdan long-leg, and Einar made them carve an eagle on his back with a sword, and cut the ribs all from the backbone, and draw the lungs there out, and gave him to Odin for the victory he had won (10) then Einar sung this:

> "Man broad-bearded oft is outlawed,
>
> Many a one, for stealing sheep;
>
> But in isles here I for felling
>
> Mighty Harold's youthful son:
>
> Risk hangs o'er me, say the freemen,
>
> From the king so courage-full,
>
> Harold's shield I've hewn a hole in,
>
> None can call that dint in doubt."

And again this:

> "Ever am I glad since spears,
>
> ----Good 'tis daring deeds to do,---
>
> Spears of warriors fond of fight,
>
> Bit the boy-son of the king;
>
> Him I hide not they mislike,
>
> There flew gray across the isles
>
> Bird that feasts on body-wounds,
>
> Wounds of Halfdan, joy of hawks."

After that he made them cast Halfdan's "how," and sang:

> "Wreakt I reckon Rognvald's death,
>
> Right in this the Norns have shapen.
>
> Now the people's prop hath fallen
>
> To my fourth share of revenge;
>
> Scatter stones ye lissom lads,
>
> For a victory we have won,
>
> Scatt to Long-legs here I scatter,
>
> Scatt of stones of grit so hard."

And when this news was heard in Norway, then his brothers took it very ill, and vowed a vow to fare to the Orkneys and avenge him, but king Harold made them put off their voyage. Einar sung when he heard of their vow:

"For my life forsooth are many

Eager, as I hear them say,

Mighty men of no mean race,

From divers mansions of the earth;

But for that they do not know,

These, until they lay me low,

Which of us the eagle's claws

Shall bow beneath ere all be o'er."

But sometime after king Harold fared west across the sea and came to the isles. Einar fled away out of the isles and over to Caithness; after that men came between them and they made up their quarrel. King Harold laid a fine upon the isles, and bade them pay sixty marks of gold. Earl Einar offered to bring out the fine alone, and then to own all the allodial holdings, and the freeholders were willing to do that; for the wealthy thought they would be able to buy back their holdings, but the poor had no money to pay the fine with. Einar paid up the fine, and so it was long after that the earls had all the allodial lands, till earl Sigurd gave back to the Orkneyingers their allodial lands. King Harold fared back to Norway, but earl Einar ruled over the Orkneys a long time, and died of sickness. He had three sons. One's name was Arnkell, another Erlend, a third Thorfinn skull-splitter. When Harold the fair-haired breathed his last, Eric blood-axe was king two winters.

Then came Hacon Athelstane's foster-child from England, but Eric fared out of the land. He sailed west over the sea, and harried in Scotland and England. But when king Athelstane heard that he sent men to Eric, and offered to give him some land; he said he had been a great friend of king Harold, and said that he would show that by honouring his son. He said also that he would set him at one with king Hacon his foster son. King Eric accepted this choice, and he gave him Northumberland to rule over; that is a fifth of England. But for that, Eric had little land and many men, he grew short of money. For that he harried during the summers, but in the winters he sat at home on his lands; he kept on doing that while king Athelstane lived. After him his brother Edmund took the realm; he was not such a friend of the Northmen as king Athelstane, he thought it ill that Eric should have Northumberland. And one spring king Eric fared north along Scotland, and thence to the Orkneys, and took with him the earls of the Orkneys, the sons of Turf-Einar, Arnkell and Erlend. Thence he fared to the Southern Isles, and there too he got a great force. Thence he fared to Ireland and harried, and he did the like in Bretland (Wales). Thence he fared to England, and there he harried as he had done elsewhere. Olaf was the name of the king whom Edmund had set there to ward the land. But for that Eric had a great force, he landed and went up away from his ships. Olaf also gathered an overwhelming force and fared against king Eric, and there was a mighty battle. At the beginning of the day the Englishmen fell fast, but where one fell

607

three came in his stead. But towards the close of the day the loss of men turned on the side of the Northmen, and the end of it was that king Eric fell and five kings with him. One of them was called Guthrum; there fell also the earls Arnkell and Erlend, the sons of Turf-Einar. But when queen Gunnhilda and her sons were ware that Eric had fallen and that he had before harried the land of the king of England, they thought they knew that there was no hope of peace for them in England; so they busked them in haste for the Orkneys. Thorfinn Skullsplitter was then earl there. Then the sons of Gunnhilda took the isles under them, and were there in the winters but fared a-warring in the summers. But while Gunnhilda and her sons were in the Orkneys, they heard that there was strife between the king of the Danes and king Hacon Athelstane's foster-child. Then they thought there was some hope that they might get help from Harold Gorm's son. Then they began their voyage to the Dane king. But before they fared out of the Orkneys they gave away Ragnhilda, the daughter of king Eric and Gunnhilda, to Arnfinn the son of earl Thorfinn, and then Thorfinn took up his seat (established his rule) in the isles. (11)

CHAPTER 9

Thorfinn had five sons. The name of the first was Havard the harvest happy, the second was Hlodver, the third Ljot, the fourth Skuli, the fifth Arnfinn, Ragnhilda Eric's daughter wrought her husband Arnfinn's death at Murkle in Caithness; but she gave herself away to Havard the harvest-happy, his brother. Harvard took the earldom, and was a good chief; and in his days were good harvests. Einar oily-tongue was the name of a man, Harvard's sister's son. He was a great chief, and had a great following, and went a-warring in the summers. He was guest at a feast at Havard's, and at that feast they, Ragnhilda and Einar, talked much together. She said such a man was well worthy to be a chief, and better fitted for the earldom than Havard, his kinsman; she called, too, that woman well wedded who had such a husband. Einar bade her not to take to such words; said he (Harvard) was the noblest man in the isles, and she full well wedded. Ragnhild answers: "Short henceforth shall be my and Harvard's wedded life; true it is that there must be men in the isles who will not let everything grow in their eyes, even if thou puttest aside the honour from thee." With such upbraidings Einar's mind turned to greed and guile against the earl his kinsman, and they settled it between them that he should slay the earl, but that she should be wedded to him. And sometime after Einar busked himself to that journey, and then a spaeman spoke, who was with him: "Don't do this work today, but rather tomorrow, else kin-killing will last long in your family." Einar made as though he heard it not. Havard was then at Stoneness (12) in Hrossey; there they met one another, and there was a hard battle, and not long ere the earl fell. That place is now called Havard's crofts. And when these tidings were heard, Einar was thought to have been a mickle dastard for this deed; then Ragnhilda would have no fellowship with him, and said it was all a lie that she had ever given him word. Then she sent for Einar hardchaft; he was son of another sister of Harvard's; and when they met, she said 'twas shame on such kinsmen of his who would not avenge him, and she said she would do anything that the earl might be avenged. "Besides, too," she said, "it is well known that he must be most honoured by all good men who avenges the earl, and that man, too, will have won his way to his realm." Einar answers: "About this it is said," he says, "that ye sometimes say other things than what you have in your heart, but whoso does this work must have for it that thou holdest in hand for him the realm and those other things too, which will not be thought less worth having." So they break off their speech. After this Einar hardchaft fell on Einar oily-tongue, and slew him; but Ragnhilda sent for Ljot their (Havard's and Arnkell's) brother, and wedded him. Ljot took the earldom, and became a mighty chief. Einar hardchaft had now slain his kinsman, but was no nearer the earldom than before. Now he is very ill pleased with his lot, and would gather men to him, and seek to have the isles by main force; but he was ill off for men, for the Orkneyingers would only serve the sons of Thorfinn skull-splitter; and sometime after the earl let Einar hardchaft be slain.

CHAPTER 10

Skuli, Ljot's brother, fared away up into Scotland, and there the title of earl was given him by the Scot-king. After that he came down on Caithness, and gathered folk to him there; and thence he fared into the isles, and there strove against his brother Ljot for the realm. Ljot gathers folk, and fared to meet Skuli, and had more men on his side; but when they met, Skuli would hear of nothing but fighting, so there was a hard battle, and Ljot won the victory; but Skuli fled over to the Ness and up into Scotland, and thither Ljot fares after him, and stayed there a while, and had more men on his side. And then Skuli rides down from Scotland with a mighty host, which the Scot-king and earl Macbeth had given him, and he and Ljot met in the Dales in Caithness, and there arose a mickle battle. And the Scots were most hot at the beginning of the fight. Earl Ljot bade his men to keep under their shields, but still to stand as fast as they could. But when the Scots could do nothing, Ljot egged on his men, and was himself the hottest. And when things had stood so for a while, then the array of those Scots was broken, and after that they fly; but Skuli kept up the battle, though he fell at last. Ljot took Caithness under him, and then there was strife between the King of Scots and earl Ljot, for the Scots were ill pleased at their bad luck. When earl Ljot was in Caithness with few men, then earl Macbeth came down from Scotland with a mighty host, and he and Ljot met on Skidmoor in Caithness; and earl Ljot had no great force against them, but still Ljot went so fast forward, that the Scots they yielded before him, and there was a short battle ere they fled, who chose life, but many were wounded. Ljot turned back with victory, but his men were much wounded. Earl Ljot also had gotten that wound which led him to his death, and his death was much mourned.

ENDNOTES FOR CHAPTERS 1-10:

1. The sea in which are the Åland Isles in the Gulf of Bothnia.

2. Now Læssö in the Cattegat.

3. That is, were panic stricken and rushed wildly about.

4. Keel: The ridge of mountains which forms the watershed, backbone, or keel, between Sweden and Norway.

5. Now Hedemark.

6. "He was called Rognvald the mighty and wise in council, and men say both were true names." R. L.

7. "Both the Mæren" are North and South Mæren, which are divided the one from the other by the Romsdale firth. They stretch north-eastward along the coast from Stadt to Naumdale."

8. Fl. reads "very wealthy," as Aud was more commonly called.

9. The banks of the Oikel in Sutherland.

10. The Run. Lex. quotes this passage thus: "Then earl Einar went to Halfdan and carved a blood-eagle on his back in this wise, that he thrust a sword into his trunk by the backbone and cut all the ribs away, from the backbone down to the loins, and drew the lungs out there;" omitting the interesting words as to the sacrifice to Odin.

11. The text of this account of Eric blood-axe has been turned into Icelandic from the Danish Translation, aided by the Heimskringla. In Fl. it is abridged thus: "Then came Hacon Athelstane's foster-child into the land, but Eric fled away as is before said. Earls Arnkell and Erlend, sons of Turf-Einar, fell in England with King Eric blood-axe, as is written before. Gunnhilda and her sons fared afterwards to the Orkneys, and took them under her, and dwelt there awhile. Then they fared to Denmark, but before they went gave away Ragnhilda, daughter of Eric and Gunnhilda, to Arnfinn, son of earl Thorfinn, and earl Thorfinn established himself in the isles."

12. Now Stennis.

CHAPTER 11

Hlodver Thorfinn's son took the earldom after Ljot, and was a great chief; he had to wife Edna, daughter of Kjarval, the Irish king; their son was Sigurd the stout. Hlodver died of sickness, and is buried under a "how" at Hofn in Caithness. Sigurd, his son, took the earldom after him; he was a great chief and wide of lands. He held by main force Caithness against the Scots, and had a host out every summer. He harried in the Southern Isles, in Scotland and Ireland. It chanced one summer that Finnleik, the Scot-earl, staked in a battle-field for Sigurd on Skidmoor by a day named, but Sigurd went to ask his mother's counsel, for she knew many things. (1) The earl told her that there would not be less odds against him than seven men for one. She answers: "I had reared thee up long in my wool-bag had I known thou wouldest like to live for ever; and fate rules life, but not where a man is come; better it is to die with honour than to live with shame. Take thou here hold of this banner which I have made for thee with all my cunning and I ween it will bring victory to those before whom it is borne, but speedy death to him who bears it." The banner was made with mickle needlecraft and famous skill. It was made in raven's shape; and when the wind blew out the banner, then it was as though the raven spread his wings for flight. Earl Sigurd was very wrath at the words of his mother, and gave the Orkneyingers their allodial holdings for their help, and so he fared to meet earl Finnleik on Skidmoor, and each drew up his host in battle array. And when the battle was joined, the banner bearer of earl Sigurd was shot to death. The earl bade another man go and bear the banner, and after they had fought a while that man fell. So three banner bearers of the earl fell, but he had the victory, and then the Orkneyingers got back their allodial rights.

CHAPTER 12

Olaf Tryggvi's son was four years in warfare in the western lands since he had come from Vindland--- the land of the Wends--- ere he let himself be baptized in the Scilly isles. Thence he fared to England --- read Ireland--- and got there to wife Gyda, the daughter of Kvaran the Irish king. After that he stayed a while in Dublin until earl Hacon sent Thorir the whiner to lure him thence. Olaf sailed from the west with four ships and came first to the Orkneys. There he met earl Sigurd in Osmund's voe in South Rognvaldsey with three ships, and he was boun for warfare. King Olaf let the earl be called on board his ship and said he wished to talk with him; and when they met king Olaf spoke to him, "It is my will that thou lettest thyself be baptized and all the folk that serve thee, else thou shalt die here at once, but I will fare with fire and flame over all the isles." But when the earl saw into what a strait he had come he gave up all his suit into the king's power. The king then let him be baptized, and took as a hostage his son whose name was Hound or Whelp, but the king let him be baptized in the name of Hlodvir. Then all the Orkneys became Christian. But king Olaf then sailed east to Norway, and Hlodvir fared with him, but he lived a short while. But after that earl Sigurd yielded no obedience to king Olaf. He went into a marriage with a daughter of Malcolm the king of the Scots, and their son was earl Thorfinn.
  Earl Sigurd had before had three sons who were then alive, the name of one of them was Summerled, of the second Brusi, the third Einar. (2)

CHAPTER 13

A little while after the agreement between king Olaf and earl Sigurd Hlodverson, the earl took to wife the daughter of Malcolm, the Scot-king, and their son was earl Thorfinn. Earl Sigurd had three other sons, one was called Brusi, the second Summerled, the third Einar wry-mouth. Five winters (3) after the battle at Svolder, earl Sigurd fared to Ireland, to help king Sigtrygg silk-beard, but he set up his elder sons over the lands, but his son Thorfin, he gave over into the hands of the Scot-king, his mother's father, to foster. But when earl Sigurd came to Ireland, he and king Sigtrygg marched with that host to meet Brian, the Irish king, and their meeting was on Good Friday. Then it fell out that there was no one left to bear the raven banner, and the earl bore it himself, and fell there, but king Sigtrygg fled. King Brian fell with victory and glory.

CHAPTER 14

After the fall of earl Sigurd, his sons took the realm and shared it into trithings among Summerled, Brusi, and Einar. Thorfinn was with the Scot-king five winters old when his father Sigurd fell. Then the Scot-king gave Thorfinn, his daughter's son, Caithness and Sutherland and the title of earl, and set up men to rule the land with him. Earl Thorfinn was early in coming to his full growth, the tallest and strongest of men; his hair was black, his features sharp, and his brows scowling, and as soon as he grew up it was easy to see that he was forward and grasping. Those brothers, Brusi and Einar, were unlike in temper. Einar was a man stern and grasping, unfriendly, and a mighty man for war. Brusi was a meek man, he kept his feelings well in hand and was humble, and ready-tongued. Summerled was like to Brusi in temper; he was the eldest of those brothers, and lived shortest, and died of sickness. After his death earl Thorfinn claimed a share of the realm in the Orkneys. Einar said that Thorfinn had Caithness and Sutherland, that realm which their father had owned, and called it more than a trithing of the isles, and would not grant Thorfinn a share after Summerled; but Brusi was willing to grant it, and gave over the share for his part. "I will not," he said, "covet more of the realm than that trithing which I own by right." Then Einar took two lots of the isles under him; then he made himself mighty, and had many followers, was oft a-warring in the summers, and had a great levy of men out of the land, but it was quite another story with the spoil. Then the freemen began to be weary of that toil; but the earl held boldly on with his burdens, and suffered no man to speak a word against him. Einar was the most overbearing of men. A great dearth arose in his realm from the toil and outgoings which the freemen had; but in that lot of the land that Brusi had was great peace and plenty, and the freemen had an easy life; for that he had many friends.

CHAPTER 15

There was a powerful and wealthy man named Amund, he dwelt at Hrossey, at Sandwick on Lopness. His son's name was Thorkell, the properest man of all men who were then growing up in the Orkneys. Asmund was a wise man, and one of the men most esteemed in the islands. It fell out one spring that the earl had a mighty levy, as was his wont, but the freemen grumbled and took it ill, and brought the matter before Amund, and bade him speak to the earl for a little forbearance. Amund said the earl would turn a deaf ear, "and little will come of it; as it is the earl and I are good friends, but methinks there is a great risk if we two should come to a quarrel with our tempers. No," says he, "I will have nothing to do with it." Then they told their story to Thorkell; he was loath to do anything, but still promised them his good offices, after being egged on by the men. Amund thought he had been too hasty in promising. But when the earl held a Thing, then Thorkell spoke on behalf of the freemen, told the need of the men, and bade the earl spare his people. Einarr answers well, and says he will give heed to his words: "I had meant now to have six ships out of the land, but now no more than three shall go; but as for thee, Thorkell, don't now ask this any more." The freemen thanked Thorkell well for his help. The earl fared away on a Viking voyage, and came back at autumn. But after that, in the spring, the earl had again a levy and held a Thing with the freemen. Then Thorkell spoke again, and bade the earl spare the freemen. The earl answers wrathfully, and said that the lot of the freemen should much worsen for his speech. He made himself so wood and wrath, that he said they should not be both there another spring safe and sound at the Thing. And so the Thing broke up. But when Amund became ware of what had passed between the earl and Thorkell, he begged Thorkell to go away. So he fared over to Caithness to earl Thorfinn, and was there long afterwards, and fostered him, when the earl was young, and was afterwards called Thorkell fosterer; and he was a man of mark. Many were the men of might who fled away out of the Orkneys for the overbearing of earl Einarr. Most fled to earl Thorfinn, some to Norway and to divers lands.

CHAPTER 16

As soon as earl Thorfinn was grown up, then he sent a message to Einar his brother, and asked of him that share of the realm which he thought belonged to him in the Orkneys, but that was a trithing. Einar was in no hurry to lessen himself so. But when earl Thorfinn hears that, then he calls out force from Caithness. But when earl Einar was ware of that, then he gathers force, and goes against Thorfinn, and means to fight with him. Earl Brusi also gathers force, goes to meet them, and brings about an agreement that Thorfinn should have a trithing of the realm in the Orkneys which he owned by right, but earl Brusi and earl Einarr laid their lots together. Einar was to have the leadership over them, and the wardship of the land. But if either of them died before the other, then that one of them who lived longer should take the lands after the other. But that settlement was thought to be unfair, for Brusi had a son, whose name was Rognvald, but Einar was sonless. Earl Thorfinn sets men to keep watch and ward over that realm which he owned in the Orkneys; but he was most often in Caithness.

CHAPTER 17

Earl Einar (4) was most often in the summers in warfare round Ireland and Scotland and Wales. It happened one summer when he was warring on Ireland that he fought in Ulfreksfirth (5) with Konufogur the Irish king. Earl Einar there got a mighty defeat and loss of men. The next summer after Eyvind Urarhorn fared from the west from Ireland, and meant to steer for Norway. The weather was sharp, and there was a great storm. Then Eyvind put in to Osmund's voe, (6) and lay there weather bound a while. But when earl Einar learns that, then he went thither with a great force, and he took there Eyvind, and made them slay him, but gave peace to most of his men. They fared home to Norway about autumn, and went to find king Olaf, and told him how Eyvind had been taken off. The king answers little about it, and yet it could be found out that he thought this a mickle manscathe, and wrought more against himself than any one else. The king was short of words whenever he thought anything much against his mind. Earl Thorfinn sent Thorkell, his fosterer, out into the isles to get together his scatts and tolls. Earl Einar laid at Thorkell's door much of that rising against him which had happened when earl Thorfinn laid his claim out in the isles. Thorkell fared hastily out of the isles over to the Ness, and told earl Thorfinn that he had become sure of this, that earl Einar meant death for him, if his friends or kinsmen had not given him warning. "Now I must choose one of these two things, either to let the earl's and my meeting be so that we may settle our business once for all; or that other to fare further away, and thither where the earl shall never have power over me." Earl Thorfinn was very eager that he should fare east to Norway to meet King Olaf. "Thou wilt," says the earl, "be made much of wherever thou art with honourable men; but I know both your tempers, the earl's and thine, that ye two would be but a scant time before ye came to blows." Then Thorkell busked him to go to king Olaf, and fared about autumn to Norway, and was with king Olaf that winter in great love; the king took Thorkell much into his counsel. He thought, as was true, that Thorkell was a wise and very able man. The king found out from his talk that he was very uneven in his stories about the earls, and that he was a great friend of Thorfinn, but slow to praise earl Einar. And early next spring the king sent a ship west over the sea to find earl Thorfinn, and this bidding, by word of mouth, that the earl should come to see him. He did not lay the journey under his pillow, for words of friendship came along with the message.

CHAPTER 18

Earl Thorfinn fared east to Norway and came to see king Olaf. He got there a good welcome, and stayed there long on in the summer. But when he made ready to go west, then king Olaf gave him a great and good longship, with all her tackling. Thorkell fosterer made up his mind to go with earl Thorfinn, and the earl gave him that ship which he had brought from the west that summer. The king and the earl parted the best of friends with great love. Earl Thorfinn came back about autumn to the Orkneys. But when earl Einar heard this, he got many men together and lay aboard ship. Earl Brusi went to meet those brothers, and tried to bring about a settlement between them, and so it came about that they were set at one again, and bound that with oaths. Thorkell fosterer was then to be taken into that settlement, and into friendship with earl Einar, and that was also said that each of them should make the other a feast, and the earl was to come first to pay Thorkell a visit at Sandwick. But when the earl was there at the feast, he was treated in the bravest way. The earl was not cheerful. There was a mickle hall there, and doors at both ends. That day on which the earl was to go away, and was busking himself, Thorkell was to go along with him to the feast, Thorkell sent men forward to spy out on the road along which they were to fare that day; but when they came back they told

Thorkell that they found there three ambushes and men with weapons; "and we think, to say thee sooth, that treachery must lie under this." But when Thorkell learned that he put off his busking and got his men together. The earl bade him busk himself and said 'twas high time to ride. Thorkell said he had much to look after. He went sometimes out and sometimes in. Fires were on the floor. Then Thorkell went in at one of the doors and with him a man who is named Hallvard. He was a man from Iceland, an Eastfirther by kin. He shut the door after them. Thorkell went inside along the hall between the fire and where the earl sate. The earl asked, "Art thou boun now?" Thorkell answers, "I am boun now." Then Thorkell hewed at the earl on his head. The earl fell forward stooping on the floor. Hallvard said, "Here I see the worst of all wrestling tricks, that ye do not draw the earl from the fire." Then he thrust an Irish axe (7) under the nape of the earl's neck, and jerked him up on the bench. Then both those comrades Thorkell and Hallvard, went out hastily, by the other doorway facing that by which they went in, and there outside stood Thorkell's men armed to the teeth. The earl's men looked to him, but he was then dead, and the hands of all failed them to avenge him; besides, it was all done in a hurry, for no man looked for such a deed from Thorkell; for they all thought that it would be, as was already agreed, that there should be friendship between the earl and Thorkell. Most of the men too were weaponless who were inside the hall, and many of them good friends of Thorkell of yore. It happened too by that fate by which longer life was allotted to Thorkell. When Thorkell came out he had no less force than the earl's men. Then Thorkell fared to his ship, but the earl's men went away. Thorkell sailed away that day east into the sea, and that was after the winter had begun. Then they came safe and sound to Norway. Thorkell went at once to find king Olaf, and he got there a good welcome: The king showed himself well pleased at this deed. Thorkell was with him that winter.

CHAPTER 19

After the falling away of earl Einar, earl Brusi took that lot of the lands which earl Einar had before had, for it was with many men's witness on what terms Brusi and Einar had gone into partnership. It seemed most right to earl Thorfinn that each of them should have half the isles; but still Brusi had that winter both lots of the isles. But the spring after Thorfinn laid claim to the land against Brusi, saying that he will have half the lands, but Brusi would not say yes to that; so they summoned meetings about those matters. Then their friends went about to settle the business, and so it came out not only that Thorfinn would let nothing else please him than to have half the isles; but he says at the same time that Brusi, with the temper he had, had no need of more than a trithing. "I grudged not," says he (Brusi), "to have a trithing of the land which I took after my father as my heritage; and no one challenged my right to that; but now I have taken another trithing after my brother by lawful agreement. But though I am unable to strive in rivalry with you, kinsman, yet I will look to some one else rather than consent to give away my realm in such a way." When things had gone so far at that parley they parted. But when Brusi saw that he could not stand on even feet against Thorfinn, for that he had a much greater realm, besides the trust that he had in the Scot-king, his mother's father, then he, Brusi, made up his mind to fare away out of the land east to find king Olaf, and he had with him his son Rognvald, who was then ten winters old. But when the earl met the king, he gave him a good welcome. But when the earl unfolded his errand, and tells the king the whole story of what had happened between his brother and himself, and begged the king to lend him strength to hold his realm, he offered him at the same time in return his entire friendship. The king answers, and began first to say how Harold fair-hair had owned all the allodial land in the Orkneys, "but the earls have held it since in fief, but never as their owndom; and that is a token," says he, "that when Eric blood-axe and his sons were in the Orkneys, then the earls were bound to do them service. But when Olaf, Tryggvi's son, my kinsman, came there, then earl Sigurd, your father, made himself his man. Now I have taken all the heritage after him. Now I will make thee that choice that thou becomest my man; then will I give over to thee the isles in fief; then we two will try, if I lend thee my strength, whether it shall stand thee in better stead, or whether his trust in the Scot-king, to thy brother Thorfinn. But if thou wilt not take this choice, then must I look after those rights and owndoms which our kinsmen have held there away west.'" The earl bore these sayings in his mind, and laid them before his friends, and asked counsel of them to what he should consent, and whether he should strike a bargain with king Olaf on those terms and become his man. "But it is not at all plain to me what my lot will be when we part, if I say nay; for the king has made bare to me his claim, that he thinks he owns the isles. But with his boldness of purpose, and bearing in mind this too that we have come here, it will be a little thing for him to do just as he pleases with our affair." But though the earl found manifest fault with both courses, whichever way he went, still he took that choice, to lay all in the king's power, both himself and his realm. Then king Olaf took from the earl power and lordship over all his lands of heritage, and then the earl was made the king's man, and bound that with oaths.

CHAPTER 20

Earl Thorfinn learnt that Brusi his brother had fared east to find king Olaf, to seek trust from him; but because Thorfinn had before fared to find king Olaf and got himself into friendship there, then he thought he had made it all right there beforehand, and knew that many there would back his cause; so earl Thorfinn takes this counsel: he makes ready his voyage as speedily as he can and fared to Norway, and thought that he should make the passage almost as soon as Brusi, and that his errand would not be brought to an end. But when Thorfinn met the king, it was another way than he had thought; for when he came to see king Olaf, all that bargain between the king and Brusi was made and struck. Besides, earl Thorfinn did not know that Brusi had given up his realm before ever earl Thorfinn had come to see king Olaf. But as soon as they met, the earl and king Olaf, then the king raised the same claim to the realm in the Orkneys which he had already made to Brusi, and bade Thorfinn do the same thing, that he should yield over to the king those lots of the lands which he already owned. The earl answers well to the king's words, and spoke so as to show that he set great store on his friendship. "And if ye, lord," said the earl, "think that ye need my help against other chiefs, then ye have won it fully; but it is not in my power to yield you homage, for I am already the Scot-king's earl, and bound to do him service." But when the king found that there was drawing back in the earl's answers as to this question which he had raised, then the king spoke: "If thou, earl, wilt not become my man, there is yet another choice, that I set that man up over the Orkneys whom I will, and my will then is that thou take oath to lay no claim to their lands, and to let them be in peace for thee whom I set up. But if thou wilt have none of these choices, then it must so seem to those whom I set up, as though strife were to be looked for them from thee; then mayest thou not think it wonderful though the dale comes to meet the hill." (8) The earl answers, and bade the king give him time to think over that matter. The king did so, and gave the earl time and leave to take counsel with his friends as to this. Then the earl begged the king to grant him time till the next summer, and that he might fare home first of all. "All my councillors are at home," (9) he says, "and I am but a child for my years' sake." But the king bade him choose one of the two courses there and then. Thorkell fosterer was then with the king; he sent men stealthily to the earl, and besought him not to think, whatever might be on his mind, of parting so with king Olaf that they were not good friends, just when he had put himself in the king's hands. He (Thorkell) thought he could see that the only choice left him was to let the king have his will in everything. It seemed to them (Thorkell and his friends) though not at all a good choice to have no hope one's self of one's heritage, and to take an oath to the effect that they might have that realm in peace who were not born to it. But because that he thought it uncertain about his going away, then he made that choice to give himself over into the king's hand, and become his man as his brother Brusi had done. The king found out that Thorfinn was of a much higher spirit than Brusi, and for that sake he trusted Thorfinn less; the king saw too that he would think he might look for strength from the Scot-king, even though he broke this agreement; the king understood that out of his wisdom. Brusi went unwillingly into all the agreement, but spoke nothing but what he meant to hold; but where Thorfinn was he went gladly at everything; as soon as ever he had made up his mind what part he should take, (then he went gladly into every condition) (10) and did not stickle in the least at what the king asked the first evening; but the king doubted that he must mean to go back on some of his undertakings.

ENDNOTES FOR CHAPTERS 11-20

1. That is "by witchcraft."

2. The true text here is preserved only in the Danish Translation, in its place Fl. has a long chapter out of the Saga of king Olaf, Tvyggvi's son, as contained in Fms. That chapter will be found in the Appendix.

3. Thus, according to the chronology of the Icelandic writers, it was in reality fourteen years afterwards.

4. The Fl. begins here a new section of the Saga thus: "The chapter of those Orkneyingers. A mighty man of war in the Orkneys was earl Einar, earl Sigurd's son. He was thought no fair man. He warred in Ireland, etc."

5. Lough Larne in Ireland.

6. Now Osmondswall in the Orkneys.

7. In the original Sparða, some sort of bill or pole-axe. The word occurs as "spart" or "spert" in mediæval lists of arms in England. See Hist. Com. Report for 1877. I. p. 491.

8. A proverb meaning that Thorfinn must not be surprised if the natural result followed.

9. In the Runic Lex. the whole passage runs thus: "earl Thorfinn said, as was true, that most of his councillors were at home."

10. The sentence in brackets is a repetition.

CHAPTER 21

When king Olaf had thought over with himself the whole matter, he let them blow the trumpets for a great gathering of men, and made them call both the earls thither. Then he spoke thus: "I will now declare before the whole people the settlement between the Orkney earls and myself. They have now agreed to my absolute right over the Orkneys and Shetland, and made themselves my men, and bound that with oaths, and I will now give them in fief, to Brusi one trithing and to Thorfinn another as they have had before; but that trithing which earl Einar owned, that I make fall to me, for that sake that he slew Eyvind Urarhorn, my henchman and dear brother in arms. For that lot of the lands, I will take care as I think good. That, too, I lay on both ye brethren, my earls, that ye take an atonement from Thorkell, Amund's son, for the slaying of your brother Einar; and I wish to lay down the terms of the atonement if ye will say yes to that." But it was now as it was in other things; they said yes to everything the king said. Then Thorkell went forward and bound himself by the king's award, and so that Thing broke up. King Olaf awarded an atonement for earl Einar as though for three kings' thanes, but for cause given a trithing of the fine was to fall to the ground. Earl Thorfinn begged leave of the king to go away, but as soon as he got that he busked him speedily. But when he was all-boun, it fell upon a day when the earl was a-drinking on his ship, that there came to him stealthily Thorkell Amund's son, and laid his head upon his knees, and bade him do with it as he would. The earl asked why he did so, "now that we are already set at one by the king's doom. Stand up, pray." He did so, and said, "That atonement which the king made between us I may trust between Brusi and me; but so far as you have any share in it, you alone shall have your way. Though the king has awarded me my estates and right to stay in the Orkneys, still I know your frame of mind so well that I can never go into the isles unless I fare thither on your good faith. I will bind myself to you," he says,

"never to come to the Orkneys, whatever the king may have said about that."
The earl held his peace, and was slow to speak, and then he spoke thus: "Wilt
thou, Thorkell, that I speak my doom about our matter, and not rest on the
king's doom. Then must I have this beginning of our atonement, that thou shallt
fare with me to the Orkneys, and be with me, and never part from me, unless
thou hast my leave; that thou shalt be bound to guard my land, and do all
things that I will have done so long as we two both live." Thorkell answers:
"That shall be in your power, lord, as well as everything else in which I may
have any voice." Then Thorkell went up (to earl Thorfinn), and bound himself to
the earl in everything that the earl laid down. The earl says that he will utter his
doom as to the payment of the fine (for Einar) afterwards, but he took there and
then oaths from Thorkell, and he turned him then at once to fare away with the
earl. Then the earl fared away at once, as soon as ever he was boun, and he
and king Olaf never saw each other more. Earl Brusi stayed then after him and
took more time to busk himself; but ere he fared away, king Olaf had a meeting
with him, and said, "It looks to me, earl, that I am like to have thee for a faithful
liegeman there away over the western sea, and so I purpose that thou shalt
have two lots of the lands to rule over, those two I mean which thou hadst of
yore; and my will is that thou shouldest not be a less man, nor a less powerful,
now that thou hast given thyself into my hand, than thou wast before; but I will
clench thy faithfulness with this, that I will that thy son Rognvald be here
behind. I see then, if thou hast any trust and two lots of the lands, that thou
mayest well hold thy own by right against earl Thorfinn." Brusi took that with
thanks to have two lots of the lands. Brusi stayed there a little while longer ere
he fared away, and came about autumn west to the Orkneys. Rognvald, Brusi's
son, stayed behind with king Olaf. He was of all men fairest; his hair was full
and yellow, like silk. He was soon tall and strong; the most perfect man was he
both for wit's sake and courtesy. He was long with king Olaf. Ottar the black
makes mention of these things in that ode which he made on king Olaf:

"Among thy thanes are reckoned

Bold lads of Hialti's land,

Thou gotten hast a handy realm

Of princes of the people;

There was no king on earth,

Ere thou cam'st, warlike lord,

Who underneath his yoke could bow

Those islands of the west."

When those brothers came west to the Orkneys, Thorfinn and Brusi, then Brusi
took two lots of the lands under his lordship, but Thorfinn a trithing. He was
ever in Caithness and Scotland, but set up his men over the isles. At that time
Brusi alone kept watch and ward over the isles. But in that time they were
much warred on, for Northmen and Danes harried much in the west, sea-roving,
and came often to the isles when they fared west, or from the west, and seized
this or that ness. Brusi complained that Thorfinn had no force out to guard the
Orkneys or Shetland, but kept the scatts and dues all to his share. Then

Thorfinn made him that offer, that Brusi should have a trithing of the lands, but Thorfinn two lots, and alone keep watch and ward over the land. But though this arrangement was not made all at once, yet at last this settlement came about, that Brusi had a trithing and Thorfinn two lots. This was when Canute had rule in Norway, but Olaf had been forced to fly out of the land.

CHAPTER 22

Earl Thorfinn (1) made himself a great chief; he was the tallest and strongest of men, ugly, black-haired, sharp-featured, and big-nosed, and with somewhat scowling brows. He was a mighty man of strife, and greedy both of money and honour; he was lucky in battle, and skilful in war, and good in onslaught; he was then five winters old when Malcolm the Scot-king, his mother's father, gave him the title of earl and Caithness as his lordship, as was written above; but he was fourteen winters when he had war levies out of his land, and harried on the realms of other chiefs. So says Arnor Earlskald:

> "The king amid the crash of helms
>
> Died red his broadsword's edge,
>
> Ere fifteen winters he had filled,
>
> Reddener of raven's feet;
>
> Brave chief, of Einar's brothers last,
>
> Lands good to win and guard
>
> He proved himself, a properer man
>
> Is no man 'neath the sky."

Earl Thorfinn had much strength from his kinsman the Scot-king; it was a great help to his power in the Orkneys that that strength was so near. The Scot-king breathed his last just when those brothers, Brusi and Thorfinn, were set at one again. Then Karl Houndson took the rule over Scotland; he thought he ought to own Caithness too, like the former Scot-kings; and he would have scatt from that part of the realm as from other places, but earl Thorfinn thought he had not too great a heritage after his mother's father, though he had Caithness. He said that realm had been given to him, and he would pay no scatt for it; now out of this arose a mighty feud, and each harried the other's realm. King Karl would set up in Caithness that chief whose name was Mumtan or Muddan; he was his sister's son, and he gave him the title of earl. Then Muddan rode down on Caithness, and gathered force together in Sutherland; then news came to earl Thorfinn; and then he drew together a host all over Caithness; there came too out from the Orkneys Thorkell fosterer, with much force to meet the earl; then Thorfinn fared to meet Muddan, and had then the greater host. And as soon as the Scots knew that they had fewer men, they would not fight, (2) and rode up back to Scotland. Then earl Thorfinn fared after them and laid under him Sutherland and Ross, and harried far and wide over Scotland; thence he turned back to Caithness, but Thorkell went out to the isles. The levies of the people also went home. The earl sate in Caithness at Duncansby, and had there five long-ships, and just so much force as was enough to man them well. Muddan came to see king Karl in Berwick, and tells him how his paths had not been smooth. King Karl then got very wrath when he learned that his land was harried; he went then at once on ship-board, and had eleven long-ships and much people; then he held on north along Scotland. Muddan he sent back to Caithness with a great force, and he rode the upper way through Scotland; it was so settled that he should come down thence, and then Thorfinn would be in a cleft stick. Now it must be told of Karl that he never slackened sail before he came to Caithness; and then there was scant space between him and Thorfinn. Then Thorfinn took that counsel to go on ship-board and hold out into the Pentland firth, and he meant to go to the Orkneys; by that time there was so scant space between them, that Karl and his men saw Thorfinn's sails as he sailed east across the firth, and they sailed after them at once. Thorfinn and his men had not seen their sails, and so east he steered along the isles, and meant to go to Sandwick. He ran in from the east under Deerness, and sent word at once to Thorkell that he should gather force together. Brusi had the northermost lot of the isles, and was then there. Thorfinn lay under Deerness, as was written before, and had come thither late. But next morning when it was light, the first thing they found out was that Karl and his men were rowing up to them with eleven ships. There were then two choices on hand: the one was to jump ashore and leave the ships and all his goods to his foes; the other is to put out to meet them and then let destiny have her sway. Thorfinn called then on his men, and bade them get out their weapons; he said he would not run away, and bade them row against them manfully. And after that each side lashed their ships together. Earl Thorfinn egged on his men much, and bade them be hot, and make the first bout hard. As for the Scots, he said few of them would stand. This fight was both hard and long, and it was long before it could be seen which way the day would turn. Of this battle Arnor makes mention in Thorfinn's ode:

"At last I trow our lord hath taught

To mail-linked Karl a lesson,

Away east off Deerness,

The prince's rule prospered:

With war-snakes five the wrathful chief

Rushed 'gainst eleven of the king,

And hating flight himself held on

His course with constant heart.

The seamen laid their ships aboard,

Along the thwarts the foemen fell,

Sharp-edged steel in blood was bathed,

Black blood of Scottish men.

The hero's heartstrings did not quake,

> Bowstrings sung and blades were biting,
>
> Shafts were shot and sweat was streaming,
>
> Spear-heads quivered, bright and gleaming."

Now earl Thorfinn egged on his men hotly; then he ran his ship aboard of Karl's ship, and there was a very hard fight. Then the Scots held together, just before the mast on the king's ship, and then earl Thorfinn leaps out of the poop and forward on the ship, and fought most bravely. And when he saw that men grew thin on board Karl's ships, he egged on his men to board; and when king Karl saw that, he bade them cut the lashings and hold away. (3) Then Thorfinn and his men cast grappling hooks on board the king's ship. Then Thorfinn bade them bear up his banner, and he followed it thither himself, and a great company of men with him. Then Karl leapt from his ship with those men that were left upstanding; but the most part had fallen on board that ship. Karl leapt on board another ship, and bade them take to their oars, and then the Scots laid themselves out to fly, but Thorfinn chased them. So says Arnor:

> So much shorter was the onslaught,
>
> For my lord to honour dear,
>
> Speedy drove at point of spear,
>
> With less force the foe to flight:
>
> O'er that army sorely smitten
>
> Screamed the seamew bird of battle
>
> Ere their red brands sheathed the king's men;
>
> From Sandwick south he fought and won."

Karl held on away south to Broadfirth, (4) and went on shore there and gathered force anew. Thorfinn turned back after the battle. Then came Thorkell fosterer to meet him, and then they had much people; then they sailed south to Broadfirth after Karl and his men, and as soon as ever they came off Scotland they began to harry. Then they were told how Muddan was north in Caithness at Thurso, and had there a great host; he had also sent to Ireland after men, for he had there many friends and kinsmen, and there he waited for this force. Then Thorfinn and Thorkell took this counsel, that Thorkell fosterer should go north along Caithness with some of the host, while Thorfinn lay behind off Scotland and harried there. Thorkell went stealthily; besides all the land-folk was true and trusty to him in Caithness; no news of him went before him until he came into Thurso at dead of night, and took the house over the heads of Muddan and his men and set fire to it. Muddan slept up in a loft, and just as he leapt out and down out of the loft gallery, Thorkell hewed at him, and the blow came on his neck and took off his head. After that the men gave themselves up, but some got away by running. There many men were slain, but there were a very great many to whom peace was given. Thorkell stayed there a short while ere he fared back to Broadfirth; he had then a whole host with him which he had got in Caithness and out of Sutherland and Ross; then he met earl Thorfinn south of Moray, and tells him what had been done in his travels. The earl thanked him well for his toil; then they both lay there a while and harried the land.

Now it must be told about king Karl, that he fared up into Scotland after the battle which he had with earl Thorfinn, and there gathered forces anew. He drew together a host all from the south of Scotland, both east and west, and from the south all the way to Cantire. Then also came to meet him that host from Ireland which Muddan had sent after; he sends too far and wide to chiefs for force, and summoned all that host to meet him against earl Thorfinn; and the place where he and Thorfinn met was at Turfness, south of Broadfirth. There arose a mighty battle, and the Scots had a far greater host. Earl Thorfinn was at the head of his battle array; he had a gilded helmet on his head, and was girt with a sword; a great spear in his hand, and he fought with it, striking right and left. So it is said that he was the foremost of all his men. He went thither at first where the battle of those Irish was; so hot was he with his train, that they gave way at once before him, and never afterwards got into good order again. Then Karl let them bring forward his banner to meet Thorfinn; there was a hard fight, and the end of it was, that Karl laid himself out to fly, but some men say that he has fallen. But Arnor says thus:

"Gleaming edge of swords grew gory,

Turfness hight the battle-field,

Young in years the chieftain wrought it,

'Twas on Monday that it fell;

Then to battle there were singing

Blades so thin near Oikel south,

When the sea-king sharp and shifty

Fared to fight with Scotland's lord.

High aloft bore Shetland's lord

Helm amid the crash of spears,

First in fight in Irish blood

The warrior bathed his ruddy brand.

My bounteous lord put forth his might

Under his British shield,

And Hlodver's kinsman caught the host

And set their farms on fire."

Earl Thorfinn drove the flight before him a long way up into Scotland, and after that he fared about far and wide over the land and laid it under him. He fared then so far south as Fife, and laid the land under him; men went under him wherever he fared. And then while he was staying in Fife he sent away from him Thorkell fosterer with some of his force. And when the Scots knew that, how the earl had sent away from him some of his host, those very same came

623

against him who had already given themselves up to him; and as soon as ever the earl was ware of their guile, he fetched together his force and fared to meet them; then the Scots were slower in their onslaught when they knew the earl was ready for them. Earl Thorfinn made ready to fight as soon as ever he met the Scots; but then they did not dare to defend themselves, but broke off at once into flight, and fled wide away to woods and wastes. And when Thorfinn had chased the fleers, he got together his men, and says that then he will let them burn all that district in which they were then were, and so pay the Scots for their enmity and treachery. Then the earl's men fared among thorpes and farms, and so burned everything, that not a cot stood after them; they slew too all the fighting-men they found, but women and old men dragged themselves off to woods and wastes with weeping and wailing. Much folk too they made captives of war and put them into bonds, and so drove them before them. So says Arnor:

"Homesteads then in blaze were blasted,

Danger that day did not fail them,

Ruddy flame o'er reeking roofs

Leapt throughout the Scottish land;

Manslayers paid their footing painful

To men, and in one summer's space

Thrice they got the lesser lot

Before our chief, the caitiff Scots."

After that earl Thorfinn fared north along Scotland to his ships, and laid under him the land wherever he went. He fared then north to Caithness, and sate there that winter; but every summer thenceforth he had his levies out, and harried about the West lands, but sat most often still in the winters.

CHAPTER 23

Earl Thorfinn did that noble deed in the Orkneys, that he furnished all his body-guard and many other powerful men all the winter through, both with meat and drink, so that no man needed to go into inn or boarding-house; just as it is the custom with kings or earls in other lands to furnish their body-guard and guests with meat and drink at Yule. So says Arnor:

"All throughout the scourge of serpents, (5)

Rognvald's royal progeny

Drank the lake of barleycorn,

Then the chieftain gleamed in glory."

At this time earl Brusi breathed his last, and then Thorfinn took under him all the Orkneys. But it must be told of Rognvald Brusi's son, that he was in the battle at Sticklestead when the saint king Olaf fell; Rognvald got away with the rest of the men who fled. He brought out of the battle Harold Sigurd's son, king Olaf's brother; Harold was very much wounded. Rognvald left him to be healed at a small freeman's house, but Rognvald then fared east across the Keel to Jemtland, and thence to Sweden, to find King Œnund. Harold was with the freeman till he was healed; the freeman then gave his son for a guide to Harold, and they fared east to Jemtland, and thence to Sweden, and fared much with hooded head. (6) Harold sung this stave as they ride over some thickets. (7)

> Now pass I wood on wood,
>
> Wandering little worth;
>
> Who knows whether I may be
>
> Widely known hereafter."

Harold went in Sweden to meet Rognvald Brusi's son. Thence they both fared east to Russia, and much folk beside who had been with king Olaf. They did not stop till they came east into Holmgard (8) to meet king Jarizleif; he made them welcome for the sake of the saint king Olaf. Then they were made land-warders over Russia, all of them, and earl Eilif, the son of earl Rognvald Wolf's son.

CHAPTER 24

Rognvald Brusi's son stayed behind in Russia when Harold Sigurd's son fared out to Micklegarth (Constantinople); Rognvald had then the wardenship of the land in the summers, but was in Holmgard in the winters. King Jarizleif esteemed him much, and all the people too. Rognvald was, as was written before, taller and stronger than any man; he was the fairest too of men in his face, and a most gifted man both in mind and body, so that his match was not to be found. So says Arnor earlskald, that Rognvald had in Russia ten pitched battles.

> "He flourished as a fruitful tree,
>
> And fierce in fight as battle's God,
>
> Ten storms of swords that file the shield
>
> In Russia's regions won."

When they, Einar Thambaskelfir (9); and Kalf Arni's son, sought out Magnus Olaf's son, east in Russia, Rognvald met them at Aldeigjuborg; (10) then he was just about falling on Kalf until Einar made him aware in what way it stood with their journey. Einar let Rognvald be told that Kalf repented him of that wickedness that he had killed the saint king Olaf from off the face of the land, and now he will atone for that in his son; says that Kalf then wishes to raise Magnus to rule in Norway and strengthen him against the Knutlings. And after that Rognvald softened down; then Einar begs him to make up his mind to a journey with them up to Holmgard, and to back their suit with king Jarizleif, and

Rognvald says yea to that. After that they hire themselves carriage in Aldeigjuborg and drive up to Holmgard, and find there king Jarizleif, then they bring forward their errand, and say that the rule of the Knutlings and of Alfifa most of all had got so wearisome to them, that they cannot at all bear to serve them any longer. Then they beg that king Jarizleif would give over to them Magnus Olaf's son as a chief. Then Rognvald backs their suit with them, and so does Ingigerd the queen, and many other chiefs. The king was slow to give over Magnus into the hands of the Northmen, after what they had done towards the saint king Olaf his father: but still it came about in this way, that twelve of the most noble men swore to king Jarizleif this oath, that all was true and trustworthy, but king Jarizleif forbore to take the oath of Rognvald for his faithfulness' sake. Kalf swore that oath to Magnus, that he would follow him without the land and within the land, and do all those things that Magnus thought more or safer for his power. After that the Northmen took Magnus for their king, and became hand-bound to him. Kalf and his friends stayed at Holmgard until Yule went by; then they fared down to Aldeigjuborg and got ship there; they fared at once from the east as soon as the ice loosened in the spring; then Rognvald Brusi's son, made up his mind to journey with the king. They fared first to Sweden, as is said in king Magnus' saga, and thence to Jemtland, and so from the east across the Keel to Verdale. And as soon as Magnus came into Drontheim, all the people came under his power. Then he fared to Nidaros, and was there taken to be king over all the land at the Eyra Thing. After that came about the dealings which he had with king Sweyn, as is said in the Lives of the kings of Norway.

CHAPTER 25

When Rognvald Brusi's son came into Norway, he heard of the death of earl Brusi his father; he heard also this, that earl Thorfinn had taken under him all the Orkneys. Then Rognvald was eager to go to his own land, and begged that King Magnus would give him leave to do that. King Magnus saw that this was needful to Rognvald, and stood well with him in this matter. Then king Magnus gave Rognvald the title of earl, and three longships, and all well manned; he gave him also in fief that trithing which king Olaf had owned in the Orkneys, and which he had given to Brusi, Rognvald's father. Then king Magnus promised to Rognvald his foster-brother his entire friendship, and said he might reckon his strength his own whenever he needed it. Thus they parted with such like love-tokens as now were written.

CHAPTER 26

Rognvald Brusi's son sailed west to the Orkneys, and fared first to those homesteads which his father had owned; then he sent a message to earl Thorfinn his kinsman, and begged to have that trithing of the isles which his father had owned. He made them also tell Thorfinn that king Magnus gave him in fief that trithing of the lands which king Olaf had owned. He begged to have those two lots of the lands at his will of his kinsman Thorfinn. But at that time earl Thorfinn had great quarrels with the Southislanders and the Irish; he thought he had much need of help in men, and he made these answers to Rognvald's messengers, that he shall take of a surety that trithing of the isles which he owned by right, "but that trithing which Magnus claims as his, then we yielded in that to king Olaf, more for that we were come within his grasp, than because we thought it right; and so we and our kinsman Rognvald will agree all the more if we two talk little to each other about that trithing of the lands; it has long been a cause of quarrel. But if Rognvald will be a trusty kinsman and strengthener to me, then methinks my realm will be well bestowed if he has that trithing as a pastime for himself and a strength for both of us. In short, his help is worth more to me than the scatts which I get from it." After that the messengers fared back, and said to Rognvald that Thorfinn had yielded to him two lots of the lands, if he will be his strengthener, as ought to be for kinship's sake. Rognvald says that he had only laid claim to what he thought he owned. But for that Thorfinn gave the lands up so readily, he said he would of a surety be willing to lend him help and to be his entire friend, just as their kinship bound them. Now Rognvald took under him two lots of the lands, and so things stood that winter. But very early in the spring earl Thorfinn sent word to his kinsman Rognvald, and begs him to fare a-roving with him, and to bring as many men as he could get with him. And when these words came to Rognvald, he got ready at once and drew a host together, and gathered to himself all the ships he could get; and when that host was boun, he fared to meet earl Thorfinn; then Thorfinn had also got his host boun; and he gave his kinsman Rognvald a good welcome, and then they went into fellowship together.

CHAPTER 27

Those kinsmen Thorfinn and Rognvald harried that summer over the Southern isles and Ireland, and far and wide about Scotland's firths. Thorfinn laid the land under him wherever they fared. In the summer they had a great fight in the place called Waterfirth; (11) there was a great loss of men. They took to battle speedily, and those kinsmen won a bright victory. Of this battle Arnor earlskald makes mention in Thorfinn's ode: He was there in the battle.

> "There was I where Waterfirth
>
> The place is hight in mickle risk,
>
> With my Lord the friend of man,
>
> Of his works I know the tokens;
>
> From the ships the warriors speedy
>
> Bore the shieldburg, Friday morning
>
> There I saw the gray wolf gaping
>
> O'er wounded corse of many a man."

627

After this battle they turned back to the Orkneys, and sate still through that winter. And so eight winters went by that Rognvald had two lots of the isles, so that earl Thorfinn made no complaint about it. But every summer they were a-roving, sometimes both together, but sometimes each of them by himself, as Arnor says:

> "He who loved was often working,
>
> Ireland's offspring fell before him,
>
> When he fell on British races,
>
> Fire flew o'er Scotland's realm."

CHAPTER 28

With those kinsmen everything went always well when they met; but if bad (worse) men went between them (tale-bearing) the disputes were always talked out. Earl Thorfinn sate long in Caithness, and Rognvald in the isles. It fell out one summer that earl Thorfinn harried in the Southern isles and about the West Coast of Scotland. He lay at the place called Galloway, there Scotland and England meet. He had sent away from him a force south to England to land and seize and slaughter cattle, for there where he lay with his force all the folk had fled away, and all the cattle were driven away from him. But when the Englishmen were ware of the Vikings, they gathered themselves together and fell upon them, and took from them all the cattle, but slew of them all the men who were fit for anything, but sent back some runagates, and bade them tell earl Thorfinn how they made Vikings sick of wrong and robbery; and they had besides about it many scornful words. So they fared to find earl Thorfinn, and told him how ill they had fared. He took it ill that his men were lost, but said he could not help it; but this he said he was well able to do, and that was to pay off the Englishmen for all the gibes and jeers which they made out of the matter; and he said he must first of all part from them for a while, but if he were safe and sound next summer he said he and they should meet.

CHAPTER 29

At that time Hardicanute was (king) over England and Denmark. After that earl Thorfinn fared to the Orkneys and sate there that winter. Early in the spring he called out his levies over all his realm; then he sent a message to his kinsman Rognvald, and Rognvald agrees to it. Rognvald had a levy over all his realm. Earl Thorfinn drew together a host from the Orkneys and Caithness; he had also a mighty host from Scotland and Ireland, and from all the Southern isles people flocked to him. He held on with all that host to England just as he had promised them the autumn before. Hardicanute was in Denmark when these tidings happened. But as soon as ever the earls came to England they began to harry and waste; but those chiefs who were set there to watch the land fared against them with force, and there was a great and hard battle, and the earls got the victory. After that they fared far and wide over England, and harried, slew men, and burned the farms wherever they went. This Arnor mentions in Thorfinn's ode:

"One there was that Angles mind

Storm of spears, nor evermore

Shall the lord of rings come thither

WIth a greater force to battle.

Thin-ground swords bit sturdy people,

But the child of ancient Rognvald

Rushed beneath his buckler thither,

South from Man across the main.

On English native land his banner

Bore the earl, and often reddened

Tongue of eagles, troops to carry

Ensigns onward still he ordered,

Fire waxed and homes were blazing,

As the army chased the fleers,

Flames spread fast, and near to heaven

Smote the glare of forest's foeman. (12)

Many blasts of horns were blowing,

Through the burgs when bold to battle

Rushed the ruler, while his banner

Fluttered bravely in the breeze.

'Twas on a rainy Friday morning,

When the day scarce beamed for battle,

That the foeman fierce he scattered;

Weapons flew and wolves were fattened."

Earl Thorfinn had two pitched battles in England, but on the other hand he gave them many defeats and man-slayings. He lay there almost all the summer through, but at autumn he fared hom to the Orkneys, and was there that winter.

629

CHAPTER 30

At this time Kalf Arni's son fled out of the land before king Magnus. He fared west across the sea to his nephew-in-law earl Thorfinn. Thorfinn had then to wife Ingibiorg earlsmother, the daughter of earl Finn Arni's son. Then Kalf was in great love with earl Thorfinn. He held about him a great following of men; that was very costly to the earl. There were many, too, then who said out before him that he should not let Rognvald have two lots of the isles, when he had to spend so much money himself. And after that earl Thorfinn sent men out into the isles, and asked for that trithing from earl Rognvald, which earl Einar wrymouth had owned. But when that message came, the earl brought it before his friends and counsellors. After that he calls thither earl Thorfinn's messengers. Rognvald says, that as for that lot of the isles which they claim, he had taken it in fief from king Magnus, and that the king called it his father's heritage. Now he said king Magnus had power to say which of them should own that lot; but he said he would not let it go if it were the king's will that he should have it. On this the messengers fared away, and tell earl Thorfinn those words. They said, too, it was surely to be looked for that this would not be got without a struggle. But when earl Thorfinn heard that, he grew very wrath, and said it was a likely story that king Magnus was to have his brother's heritage. He said, too, that had been agreed to more because he and earl Brusi were then come into king Olaf's grasp than because it was a fair and rightful sharing of the inheritance. "Now methinks Rognvald doth not repay me well when I have now let him have that realm in freedom for a while, if I shall not now come near the heritage my brother has left me unless I fight for it." Earl Thorfinn was so wrath at this, that no long time after he sends men into the Southern isles, and up into Scotland, and drew a force together. He gave it out too, that he meant to come to blows with earl Rognvald, and then take that without forbearance which he could not get when he sought for it in peace. And now, when this is told to earl Rognvald, that earl Thorfinn was gathering a force against him, he summoned his friends about him, and moots this with them, that earl Thorfinn his kinsman means to come to blows with him with a host and strife. He asked then what force they will furnish him with, and says he is not willing to lose his own without one trial of strength. But when he begged for their judgment on this matter then men gave it in very different ways. Some spoke after earl Rognvald, and said it was to be forgiven him that he did not wish to share his realm; but there were some who said it was to be forgiven to Thorfinn that he wished to have the realm for a while, when Rognvald had already had that lot which earl Einar had owned. They said, too, it was bad counsel that Rognvald should lay himself out to fight against Thorfinn with that force which he could get from two lots of the isles, when Thorfinn had a trithing and Caithness, and a great share of Scotland and all the Southern isles. There were men, too, who spoke and said that a peaceful settlement must be sought, who beg that Rognvald would offer earl Thorfinn a half of the isles, and so in that way their kinship might still be saved. But when Rognval found that each had a way of his own, but all were against his resisting, then he laid bare his will, and said that he will not cut his realm asunder by any settlement; that he would far rather give up the realm at once, and go to seek king Magnus his fosterbrother, and look after what strength the king will give him to hold his realm. After that he makes ready for his voyage, and fares east to Norway, nor does he slacken his course before he comes into the presence of king Magnus. And when he is come thither, he tells the king the whole story. The king made earl Rognvald good cheer, and bade him be with him so long as he liked, and to take a fief of him so large that he could well maintain himself and his people; but earl Rognvald told the king that he wished he would give him strength enough to seek back his realm. King Magnus said of a surety he would aid him with strength to get what he asked. Rognvald stayed a short time in Norway ere he began his voyage west to the Orkneys. He had then many picked men whom king Magnus had granted him. And this went with him too; he (the king) sent word to Kalf Arni's son, that he should have his lands and leave to live in Norway, if he would stand by earl Rognvald in this quarrel between him and earl Thorfinn.

ENDNOTES FOR CHAPTERS 21-30

1. The Fl. heads this chapter with the following passage: "King Olaf, Harold's son, got no service from earl Thorfinn, since they parted after earl Brusi and they came to a settlement all together.

2. Fl. "They were slower about an onslaught."

3. Fl. "and get all his fleet of ships under way as fast as they could, take to their oars and row away."

4. The Moray firth.

5. The scourge of serpents "the winter."

6. with hooded head, very secretly.

7. "when they parted in a thicket."

8. Holmgard, probably Novgorod.

9. Thambaskelfir, "paunch-shaker," from his fatness, or "good archer," "string twanger," for his skill with the bow.

10. Aldeigjuborg, the burg on the Aldeiga, or Ladoga lake.

11. A firth in the Isle of Skye.

12. forest's foeman; fire.

CHAPTER 31

Earl Rognvald sailed from Norway west towards the Orkneys, and made Shetland from the sea, and drew force to himself, and thence fared south into the Orkneys. There he summoned his friends to meet him, and gathered force thence. Earl Thorfinn was over in Caithness, and news came to him at once of Rognvald's doings, and he drew force to himself from Scotland and the

Southern isles. Earl Rognvald sent at once the message of king Magnus to Kalf Arni's son, and Kalf took in a kind way all that the king had spoken. Earl Rognvald drew his host together in the Orkneys, and meant to cross over into the Ness. But when he came into the Pentland firth, then he had thirty war-ships, all big and in good trim. There came against him earl Thorfinn, and had sixty ships, and most of them small. Their meeting was off the Red Head, and they ran into battle at once. There, too, was come Kalf Arni's son, and had six ships, and all great, and did not run into the fight. And now arises the hardest battle; either earl egged on his people. But when things had gone on so for a while, the loss of men turns on earl Thorfinn's side, and that was most because the difference in the height of the ship's sides was great. Thorfinn had a great ship, and in good trim, and in that he ran forward most bravely. But when the decks of the smaller ships were cleared, then the earl's ship was run aboard of on both sides; and then they stood in very great need. Then numbers of men fell on board the earl's ship, but some were very badly wounded. Earl Rognvald then egged on his men to board; but when earl Thorfinn saw into what a bad plight they were come, he made them cut his ship away from her lashings and rowed to land. He made them bear out of his ship seventy corpses. There, too, went out all those who were unfightworthy for their wounds' sake. Then earl Thorfinn begged Arnor earlskald to go out of the ship; he was in the earl's train, and held in great love. He went on shore and chaunted a song:

"This man is loath to go against

Brusi's son, one's lord to follow

Is good, that lesson to the people

Ne'er shall I be found gainsaying;

Hard the choice we have before us

If these earls so full of fury

Fall to blows, a time of trial

For friendship we shall surely see."

Earl Thorfinn mans his ship with the best men he had left. After that he fares to find Kalf, and asked him for help. He said thus, that Kalf could not get bought back the friendship of king Magnus when he had already been forced to flee out of the land. "When thou foundest it no good that thou hadst already been taken into very great love. So mayest thou make up thy mind if Rognvald is victorious over us, and if the power of king Magnus and of him spreads here over the western sea, that then thou wilt not be welcome here. But if we win the day, then nothing shall fall short to you that I have power to give. We two shall be at no man's mercy here across the western sea, if we two are both of one mind. And thou wilt not surely like to have that on your mind that thou liest here like a cat in a cave, while I fight for the freedom of us both. Besides, there are those ties between us two, that it beseems each of us better to lend the other help, since men who are bound to you by no ties are against us." But when Kalf heard the egging on of Thorfinn, he called on his men, and bade them put out to battle together with earl Thorfinn. As Bjarni Gullbrar-Skald says:

"We have heard, O Kalf, to hurly

How Finn's son-in-law thou followedst,

And thy war-snakes o'er the waters

Swiftly swept against the earl;

Gold-begetter, vengeance-mindful,

All unwilling to attack

Brusi's son so bold in battle;

Thorfinn had thy help at last."

Now they made an onslaught by rowing, both of them together, earl thorfinn and Kalf. And when they came to the fight, Thorfinn's host was ready to flee, but very many of them were fallen. The earl ran his ship against the ship of earl Rognvald, and there arose the hardest fight. So says Arnor:

"I saw both my goldbestowers,

Each the other's henchmen hewing,

On the fitful firth of Pentland;

Thence my grief grew more and more;

Sea was blood-stained, black kept dripping

Gore between the gaping seams,

Sweat was shed on rim of shield,

All the sides with blood were dabbled."

Kalf ran up against the smaller ships of Rognvald and cleared their decks quickly, for there was a great difference in the height of their sides. But when the levies who had come from Norway saw ships cleared hard by them, they then loosed their ships from their lashings and laid themselves out to fly, so that scarce a ship was left behind with the earl's ship. Then the fight began to turn. So says Arnor earlskald:

"The lord, so brave in burst of battle,

Then had surely laid beneath him

All that ancient land of Orkney,

--- He had far less loss of men, ---

If the sea-king son of Endil

Could have brought that host to help him,

Island-born, but Shetland's lord,

By his army was betrayed."

And now that the main host had fled, then they, Kalf and Thorfinn, both ran aboard of earl Rognvald's ship, and then many men of earl Rognvald's fell. And when earl Rognvald saw in what a straight he was come, and that he could not conquer Thorfinn and Kalf both, then he made them hew the lashings asunder, and laid himself out to fly. Then the day was far spent, and it began to grow dark. Earl Rognvald sailed at once that night into the main, and so east to Norway; he did not slacken his course till he came into king Magnus' presence; he made him welcome now as before, and bade him be with him; and there earl Rognvald stayed a while.

CHAPTER 32

Now it is to be said of earl Thorfinn, that on the morning after the fight he made them row about all the isles to search for the men who had fled. Many were slain, but some came to terms of peace; then earl Thorfinn laid under him all the isles, and made every man come into his hand, (1) and those as well who had been before bound by an oath to Rognvald. He sat himself up then in the Orkneys with a very great band of men, and drew his supplies from Caithness on the other side. But Kalf Arni's son, he sends into the Southland isles, and let him sit there as a means of strength for himself. But when earl Rognvald had stayed in Norway awhile with king Magnus, he said to the king that he would try back to the Orkneys. But when the king heard that, he called it unwise to fare before the winter abated and ice loosened and the sea began to thaw; said he then would give him ships and crews as many as he needed. Rognvald speaks thus, and said now he was not willing to lose king Magnus' men; said, too, that it could not be carried out unless with great loss of men, if he gathered a host to come to blows with Thorfinn and Karl, such a large realm as they have there west: "I mean now," he said, "to hold on west with one ship, and to man it as well as I can; then I ween that no news of us will be borne before us. Then it will either be, that we shall come upon them unawares, and then we may speedily win that victory which we should win hardly or not at all with a great force. But if they become aware of our voyage, then we will let the sea still take care of us." King Magnus bade him fare as he liked, but to come back to him again as soon as he chose. And after that earl Rognvald makes ready his voyage and takes pains in choosing men to go with him; and some of the king's bodyguard made up their minds to go with him; then he had a picked force. And when they were boun they sailed away to sea. That was about the beginning of winter. (2)

CHAPTER 33

Earl Rognvald made Shetland from the sea; then he learnt that earl Thorfinn was in the Orkneys and had no very great force with him; he had then no fear of war in high-winter. Now Rognvald held on straightway south to the Orkneys. Earl Thorfinn was then in Hrossey, and had no fear for himself. But as soon as Rognvald came into the Orkneys he held on thither where he heard Thorfinn was, and came upon him so unawares, that nothing was heard of them before they had seized all the doors of the house which Thorfinn and his men were in. It was night then, and most men were asleep, but the earl sat then still a-

634

drinking. Rognvald and his men bore fire to the homestead; but when earl Thorfinn was ware of the strife, he sent men to the doors and let them ask, who had sway over the strife. Then it was said that Earl Rognvald was come thither. Then men sprung to their arms. Then nothing could be done in the way of defence, because outlet was shut to all. The house began soon to blaze. Thorfinn gave counsel that men should beg for leave to go of the earl, and he allowed it to all women and unfree men, but said most of earl Thorfinn's bodyguard would be no better to him alive than dead. So those men were drawn out to whom peace was given and then the whole house was soon burning. Earl Thorfinn broke away a wainscot panel at the back of the house, and sprung out there; he had Ingibjorg his wife in his arms. The night was pitch dark and moonless, and he got away under the smoke, so that the earl's men were not ware of him. He rowed at once that night alone in a boat over to the Ness. Earl Rognvald burned down the whole homestead, and all those men who were inside it, to whom leave was not given to go out. Now no man thought anything else than that earl Thorfinn had lost his life there. After this earl Rognvald fared about over all the isles and laid them under him. He sent also those words over to Caithness and to the Southern isles, that he meant to claim all that realm that earl Thorfinn had owned. No man gainsaid him in this. Earl Thorfinn was in divers places in hiding in Caithness with his friends, and no news went abroad that he had got away from the burning.

CHAPTER 34

Earl Rognvald sat in Kirkwall, and drew thither the stores which he needed to have for his winter quarters. He had a great band of men, and much good cheer. But a little before Yule earl Rognvald fared with a great following into the Little Papey to fetch malt, to be brewed for Yule. And at even, as they were on the isle, they sate long over a roasting fire, and he who made up the fire spoke and said that the firewood began to fall short. Then the earl made a slip of the tongue, and these were the words he spoke: "Then are we full old when these fires are burnt out." But he meant so to have spoken, that they would then be full warmed. And as soon as ever he found it out, he said "I have not made a slip of the tongue before this so that I call it to mind; it comes into my mind what king Olaf my foster-father said at Sticklestead when I took him up for a slip of the tongue: If it ever happens that I made a slip of the tongue I might make up my mind that I should then have but a short time unlived. May be that my kinsman Thorfinn is yet alive." And just then they heard how that the homestead was girt round by men. There was come earl Thorfinn. They bore fire at once to the house, and laid up a pile of fuel before the doors. They allowed all to go out save the earl's men. And when most of the men were drawn out, a man went out into the doorway in linen underclothes, and begged earl Thorfinn to stretch out his hand toward the deacon. But that man rested his hands on the balk of wood across the doorway, and vaulted out over the balk and the ring of men, so that he came down ever so far off all of them, and was lost in the darkness of night. Thorfinn bade them hold on after him, and says there went earl Rognvald, "this is his nimbleness, and no one's else." Then they fared to hunt for him, and parted themselves into companies, and Thorkell fosterer went along the sea-shore to search. They heard how a dog barked among the rocks on the seashore. Earl Rognvald had his lapdog with him, and he betrayed the earl. (3) They put him to death at once among the rocks, and it is the story of some men that Thorkell fosterer slew him, because there were no other men who would do it. But he had sworn to do all those deeds which seemed to Thorfinn more for his realm's safety than otherwise. Thorfinn and his men stayed that night on the isle, and there all the train that had followed Rognvald thither were slain. But the morning after they took a ship of burden and laded her with malt. After that they went on board, and left the shields at stem and prow which Rognvald and his men had owned. They let, too, no more men be seen in the ship than had followed the earl. Then they rowed to Kirkwall. And when the followers of Rognvald who were in the town saw that, they thought that there earl Rognvald must be coming and his men; then they went to meet him, and most of them unarmed. Earl Thorfinn let them there take about thirty men and slay them. They were most of them of king Magnus' bodyguard and his friends. The earl gave peace to one of king Magnus' bodyguard, and bade that man fare east to Norway and tell these tidings to king Magnus.

CHAPTER 35

The body of earl Rognvald was carried to the Greater Papey, and there buried; and it was the saying of men that he has been by far the best bred man and with most friends of all the Orkney earls, and his death was a great grief to many a man. After that earl Thorfinn laid all the isles under him, and now no man gainsaid him in that. Early in the spring came these tidings east to Norway, and king Magnus thought the loss of Rognvald, his foster-brother, the greatest scathe, and said he would avenge him as soon as ever he had time. But he had at that time great strife with king Sweyn Ulfson, who had then let himself be chosen to be king over Denmark.

CHAPTER 36

At that time came into Norway Harold Sigurd's son, the kinsman of king Magnus, and king Magnus gave him half Norway. They were both kings in Norway one winter. Then they called out a levy over all Norway and meant to go south to Denmark. But when they lay in the Selisles two long-ships ran into the haven, and up to king Magnus' ship. A man went from the long ship in a white cowl, and aft along the ship and up into the poop. The king sate over meat. This man hailed the king, and bowed before him, took up a loaf of bread and broke a bit off and ate. The king took his greeting, and reached out to him the bowl when he saw that he ate the bread. This man took the bowl, and said: "We want peace, messmate." The king looked at him, and said, "Who art thou?" "I am Thorfinn, Sigurd's son." "Art thou earl Thorfinn," says the king. "So I am called west yonder," says he, "but I am come hither with two ships of twenty benches each, and rather well manned, so far as we are able. Now I will

636

row on this levy with you, if ye will take help of me. But all my matter and I myself shall be at God's command and yours, lord, for the sake of those great misdeeds which I have broken against your will." Then men went up and heard their talk. The king was slow in answering, and spoke thus: "True it is, earl Thorfinn, that I had not meant, if the meeting of us two ever took place as it has now done, that thou shouldst be able to tell of our parting. But now things have happened so, that it beseems not my honour that I should take and kill thee, now thou shalt fare with me, but the terms of our atonement I will utter at my leisure."" Earl Thorfinn bade the king good-bye, and went to his ships. The king lay a very long time in the Selisles. Then a host gathered thither to him out of the Bay. He meant to sail thence south under Jutland as soon as he got a fair wind. Earl Thorfinn was then often long a-talking with the king. The king treated him well, and took him much into his counsels. It fell out one day that the earl went on board the king's ship, and aft into the poop. The king bade him sit by him. The earl sat him down, and they both drank together and were merry. A tall brisk man in a red kirtle came into the poop, that man hailed the king. The king took his greeting blithely; that was one of the king's bodyguard. This man began to speak, and said, "Thee am I come to find, earl Thorfinn." "What wilt thou of me," says the earl. "I want to know with what thou wilt atone to me for my brother, whom thou letst to be slain west in Kirkwall, along with other thanes of king Magnus." "Hast thou not heard that," says the earl, "that I am not wont to atone for those men with money whom I cause to be slain. And this is how it is, that methinks I have always had good cause when I have let men be slain." "It is no business of mine how thou hast done by other men, if thou atonest for this one, on whose behalf I make this claim. Besides, I left behind me there some goods of my own, and for myself I was shamefully treated. I have the best right, therefore, to make this claim in my brother's name and my own, and I will have amends for it. But the king may as well forgive everything that is done against him, if he thinks it nothing worth when his thanes are led out and hewn down like sheep." The earl answers: "I see plainly that it is all the better for me here that thou hast not had power over me. Art thou not that man to whom I gave peace yonder." "Sure enough I am," says he; "it was in thy choice to slay me there and then like other men." Then the earl answers: "Sooth it is, as the saying goes, that 'many things happen that one least looks for.' I thought then that I could never be so placed that I should have to pay for being too peaceable to my foes; but now I am to smart for having given thee mercy. Thou wouldest not be able to cry out against me today before princes if I had let thee be slain like the rest of thy companions." The king looked at the earl and said: "There it comes out though, earl Thorfinn, that thou thinkest thou hast slain too few of my thanes without atonement." The king was then as red as blood. The earl sprang up then, and went down out of the poop and on board his ship. Then all was quiet that evening. But next morning, when men were woke, a fair breeze was come. Then men rowed straightway out of the haven. The king sailed then south into Jutland's sea with all the fleet. The earl's ship sailed a good deal westward to the open sea at the beginning of the day; but when the day began to wear away, the earl steered west into the main. There is nothing to be said about him before he came to the Orkneys and sate down there in his realm. King Magnus and Harold sailed to Denmark, and stayed there that summer. King Sweyn would not come out to meet them; he was in Scanör with his host. In that summer king Magnus took that sickness which led him to his death. He gave it out then before all the people that he gave all the realm of Norway to his father's brother Harold. (4)

CHAPTER 37

Earl Thorfinn now ruled over the Orkneys and all the rest of his realms. Kalf, Arni's son, was also mostly with him. Sometimes he went west sea-roving, and harried the coasts of Scotland and Ireland; he was also in England, and was for a while over the Thingmen's band. When earl Thorfinn heard of the death of king Magnus, he sent then men east to Norway to find king Harold and greet him with friendly words; he says, thus, that he wishes to become his friend. But when that message came to the king, he took it well, and the king promised him his friendship. And when this message came back to the earl, he made ready his voyage, and had with him from the west two ships of twenty benches each, and more than a hundred men, all fine picked fellows. Then he fared east to Norway, and found the king in Hördaland. He gave him a very hearty welcome; and at their parting the king gave him good gifts. Thence the earl sailed south along the land and so to Denmark. There he fared round the land, and found king Sweyn in Aalborg; he asked the earl to his house, and made him a grand feast. Then the earl laid bare his purpose how he meant to go south to Rome. But when he came to Saxony, he met there the kaiser Henry, and he gave the earl a very hearty welcome, and gave him many great gifts. He got him, too, many horses, and then he made ready his journey south. Then he fared to Rome and saw the pope there, and there he took absolution from him for all his misdeeds. The earl turned thence to his journey home, and came back safe and sound into his realm; and that journey was most famous. Then the earl sat down quietly and kept peace over all his realm. Then he left off warfare; then he turned his mind to ruling the people and land, and to law-giving. He sate almost always in Birsay, and let them build there Christchurch, a splendid minster. There first was set up a bishop's seat in the Orkneys. Earl Thorfinn had to wife Ingibjorg earlsmother; they had two sons, who grew up out of childhood; the name of one was Paul and the other's Erlend; they were tall men and fair, and took more after their mother's side. They were men wise and meek. The earl loved them much, and so too did all the people.

CHAPTER 38

Earl Thorfinn held all his realms till his death day; it is soothly said that he has been the most powerful of all the Orkney earls. He owned nine earldoms in Scotland, and all the Southern isles, and he had a great realm in Ireland. So says Arnor earlskald:

> "All the way from Tuskar-skerry
>
> Down to Dublin hosts obeyed him,
>
> Royal Thorfinn, raven-feeder;

True I tell how liegemen loved him."

Earl Thorfinn was then five winters old when Malcolm the Scot-king, his mother's father, gave him the title of earl; but afterwards he was sixty (5) winters earl. He breathed his last about the end of king Harold Sigurd's son's days. He is buried at Christchurch in Birsay, which he let be built. The earl's death was a great grief in the Orkneys and in his lands of heritage. But in those lands which he had laid under him with war, then many thought it great thraldom to abide under his power. Then many realms fell away which the earl had laid under him, and men looked for trust under those chiefs who were there homeborn to rule in those realms. So losses were very soon plainly seen when earl Thorfinn fell away.

These songs were sung about the battle between earl Rognvald Brusi's son, and earl Thorfinn:

> "Loath am I to tell the story,
>
> How I witness was when men
>
> Broke the truce between the earls,
>
> Equal corpses got the corbies:
>
> Off the isles the mighty monarch
>
> Tore the sea's blue tent in twain,
>
> Storm-cold waters then were stiffened,
>
> Striking ships with buffets sore.
>
> Hard mishap uprose triumphant
>
> As the earls in onslaught strove,
>
> Many a man then learnt the lesson
>
> How to fall in bloody fight;
>
> Hard beneath the headland ruddy
>
> Hearty friends of ours fought,
>
> Storm of spear-points followed after,
>
> Many mild folk there met grief.
>
> Gloom o'er gleaming sun shall gather,
>
> Earth 'neath billow black be merged,
>
> Austri's burden (6) break to pieces,
>
> Main-sea mount above the mountains;
>
> Ere among those isles a fairer
>
> Chieftain shall again be born,
>
> Thorfinn trusty lord of thanes

THE STORY OF EARL MAGNUS
CHAPTER 39

Now (7) the sons of earl Thorfinn took the realm after him. Paul was the elder of them, and he took the lead over them. They did not share the lands between them, and yet were a very long time well agreed in their dealings. Ingibjorg earlsmother gave herself away, after the death of earl Thorfinn, to Malcolm the Scot-king, who was called long-neck; their son was Duncan the Scot-king, father of William the nobleman. His son's name again was William the prince, whom all the Scots wished to take for the king. Earl Paul, Thorfinn's son, got to wife the daughter of earl Hacon Ivar's son, and they had many children. Their son's name was Hacon. They had a daughter whose name was Thora; she was given away in Norway to Haldor, the son of Brynjulf (the old) camel. Their son's name was Brynjulf; his son's name was Haldor, who had to wife Gyrid Dag's daughter. Another daughter of Paul's was named Ingirid, whom Einar Vorsacrow had to wife. Herbjorg was the name of Paul's third daughter; she was the mother of Ingibjorg the honourable, whom Sigurd of Westness had to wife, and their sons were Hacon pick and Brynjulf. Sigrid was another daughter of Herbjorg, the mother of Hacon bairn and Herborg, whom Kolbeinn the burly had to wife. Ragnhilda was the name of a fourth daughter of earl Paul, she was the mother of Benedict, the father of Ingibjorg, the mother of Erling the archdeacon. Bergliot was the name of another ? daughter of Ragnhilda, whom Havard Gunni's son had to wife; their sons were Magnus and Hacon claw, and Dufnjal and Thorstein. These are all earls' kin, and noblemen in the Orkneys, and all these men come into the story afterwards. Earl Erlend Thorfinn's son had to wife that woman whose name was Thora and was the daughter of Summerled the son of Ospak. The mother of Ospak was Thordis, daughter of Hall o' the Side. Erling and Magnus were their (Erlend's and Thora's) sons, but their daughters were Gunnhilda and Cecilia, whom Isaac had to wife, and their sons (Cecilia's and Isaac's), were Endridi and Kol. Jatvor was the name of a base-born daughter of Erlend, her son's name was Borgar.

CHAPTER 40

When those brothers Paul and Erlend had taken the rule in the Orkneys, Harold Sigurd's son came from the east out of Norway with a great host. He came first to Shetland. Thence he fared to the Orkneys. There he left behind him Elspeth his queen and their daughters Maria and Ingigerd. Out of the Orkneys he had much force. Both the earls made ready to go with the king. The king fared thence south to England, and landed in the place called Cleveland, and won Scarborough. After that he ran in at Hallorness, and had there a battle and won the victory. On the mid-week day (Wednesday) next before Matthiasmass he had a battle in York against earls Waltheof and Morcar. There Morcar fell. The Sunday after that burg was given into the power of king Harold which stood by

Stamford-bridge. The Monday after he went on land to settle things in the town. At the ships he left behind him his son Olaf, and earls Paul and Erlend, and Eystein gorcock his brother-in-law, and Thorberg Arni's son. In that land journey came Harold, Godwin's son, against king Harold with an overwhelming host. A great battle arose at once, and in that battle fell Harold Sigurd's son. After the king's fall came Eystein gorcock from the ships, and the earls, and made a very hard onslaught. That battle was called the gorcock's storm or the gorcock's bout. There fell Eystein gorcock and well nigh the whole host of the Northmen. After those fights king Harold gave Olaf Harold's son, and the earls leave to go away out of England, and also to all that host that had not already fled. Olaf sailed out about autumn from Ravensere, and so to the Orkneys. And there they heard these tidings, that on that day and at that hour when Harold fell, his daughter Maria died a sudden death, and it is the talk of men that they have had but one man's life between them. Olaf was that winter in the Orkneys, and he was the greatest friend of the earls his kinsmen. They were brother's daughters, Thora king Olaf's mother and Ingibjorg the earls' mother. Olaf fared when the spring came east to Norway, and was there taken to be king with Magnus his brother.

But when those brothers ruled the Orkneys, then was their agreement great and good a long while. But when their sons began to grow up, then they became very overbearing men, Hacon and Erling. Magnus was the quietest tempered of them. They were all of them tall and strong, and proper men in all things. Hacon, Paul's son, would be the leader over those brothers (his cousins); he thought he was more by birth than the sons of Erlend, because he was the daughter's son of earl Hacon Ivar's son and Ragnhilda daughter of king Magnus the good. Hacon would have it that his friends should have a larger lot when there was anything to share than they allowed to the sons of Erlend; but Erlend would not that his sons should have the worst of it there in the isles. Then it so came about that those kinsmen could not be together in peace, and there was danger with them. Then their fathers took a share in the matter; they were to try and make matters up; then a meeting was fixed, and it was soon found out that each of them leant towards his own sons, and they could make no settlement. Now disagreement arose between those brothers, and they parted bad friends, and that many thought great scathe.

ENDNOTES FOR CHAPTERS 31-40

1. come into his hand, become his liegeman.

2. Fl. adds, "and got a fair wind."

3. Fl. adds, "Thorkell made him captive, and bade men put an end to the earl, and offered them money to do it; but no one would do it any more for money. Then Thorkell did the deed himself, for that he knew that one or other of them must bow before the other. Then earl Thorfinn came up, and did not blame the deed."

4. The Fl. has here left out a long passage which runs thus in the Danish translation: "But to kjing Sweyn he gave Denmark. He also sent his brother

Thorir and many other of his friends whom he wished to be well treated to king Sweyn. But after king Magnus was dead, king Harold gave out that he would make for Veborg Thing, and let himself be chosen there king over all Denmark; and said that then the Norwegians would be for ever over the Danes, and made a long speech about it. But Einar Paunchshaker answered him, and said, 'It is more to my mind, and I am more bound, to bear the body of king Magnus north to Norway to the saint king Olaf, his father, than to fight along with king Harold for other kings' realms.' And at the same time he ended his speech by saying he thought it better to follow king Magnus dead than any other king alive; and there and then Einar went to his ship, and as he went all the chiefs whose homes lay north of Stad in Norway, went with him. Then king Harold saw no other way than to sail first to Norway, and first take the kingdom under him. King Sweyn was in Skanör at the time that he heard that king Magnus was dead. He had it then in his mind to ride east into Sweden, and to give up the name of king which he had taken; and just as he was ready to start there came a man to him who told him that king Magnus was dead, and all the Norwegian host had gone out of Denmark. Then king Sweyn swore by God that he would never give up Denmark for any man so long as he was alive. Then he crossed over to Zealand, and laid the realm under him wherever he came. There he met Thorir and many other of king Magnus' men whom he had sent together. He took very kindly to them, and Thorir was with him a long time afterwards."

5. Fifty would seem to be the true reading, for Thorfinn seems to have reigned from AD 1014 till 1064, in which latter year the earl apears to have died.

6. burden; Heaven, "the burden of Austri," one of the four Dwarves who bore up the heavens.

7. Here begins the second part of the Orkneyingers' Saga, containing an abridgement of the Life of St. Magnus.

CHAPTER 41

After that kindly men came between them, and seek to settle things; so there was a peace-meeting fixed for them in Hrossey. At that meeting a settlement was made in this way, that then the isles were shared into halves as they had been between Thorfinn and Brusi. So things stood awhile. Hacon was then almost always away war-roving since he had grown up. He became then a very overbearing man, and they (Hacon and his men) were hard on those men who served under those kinmen, Erlend and his sons. So it came about again that the settlement was broken, and they fared against each other a great force. Havard Gunni's son and all the other noblemen of the earls came one day between them and again brought them together and tried to bring about a settlement. Then Erlend and his sons would not make matters up, so that Hacon was to be there in the isles. But because it seemed to their friends that there was great risk in their quarrels, then they prayed Hacon not to let this stand in the way of peace; but that he would rather fare away out of the isles. They said it would be good counsel if he fared east across the sea to visit his kinsmen, both in Norway and Sweden. And at the beseeching of his men, and also that Hacon was envious of his kinsmen there in the isles, and thought it good to learn the ways of other chiefs, then he granted them their prayer that he would fare away at once out of the isles. Then the settlement was again made by the counsel of good men. After that Hacon fared away out of the isles, first east to Norway, and he found there king Olaf the quiet. This was about the end of his days. There Hacon stayed some time. After that he fared east to Sweden to see king Ingi, Steinkel's son, and he made him welcome. He found there his friends and kinsmen. He reaped there the greatest honour from the friendships of Hacon, his mother's father. He had held rule there from Steinkel, the Swede king, after he had to fly the land before king Harold Sigurd's son. He had grown there to be the greatest friend, both of the king and the men of the land. Another daughter's son of earl Hacon Ivar's son, was Hacon, who called the Northman; he was father of Eric the wise, who was king in Denmark after king Eric the ever-memorable. Hacon stayed in Sweden a while, and king Ingi was good to him. But when things had gone on so a while then home-sickness came over him to seek west to the isles. Christianity was then young in Sweden; there were then many men who went about with witchcraft, and thought by that to become wise and knowing of many things which had not yet come to pass. King Ingi was a thorough Christian man, and all wizards were loathsome to him. He took great pains to root out those evil ways which had long gone hand in hand with heathendom, but the rulers of the land and the great freeholders took it ill that their bad customs were found fault with. So it came about that the freemen chose them another king, Sweyn, the queen's brother, who still held to his sacrifices to idols, and was called Sacrifice-Sweyn. Before him king Ingi was forced to fly the land into West-Gothland; but the end of their dealings was, that king Ingi took the house over Sweyn's head and burnt him inside it. After that he took all the land under him. Then he still went on rooting out many bad ways.

CHAPTER 42

When Hacon Paul's son was in Sweden, he had heard say that there in the land was a man who went about with wisdom and spaedom, whether he got it by witchcraft or other things. He had a great longing to find out this man, and to know whether he could be made wise as to his future fate. And after that he fared to that man, and found him at last dwelling in the woods. There he used to go about to feasts, and told the freemen about their crops and other things. But when he found that man, then he asked him he might come to power or other good luck. The wizard asked him what manner of man he was. He told him his name and kin, that he was the daughter's son of Hacon Ivar's son. Then said the wizard: "Why wilt thou take of me wisdom or sayings; thou knowest that those kinsmen of thine of old have had little mind for such like men as I am, and it may serve thy need that thou shouldest seek to know thy fate from Olaf the stout, they kinsman, the king of Norway, whom ye set all faith in. But I rather doubt that he would not have humble-mindness enough to tell thee what thou art eager to know, or perhaps be not so mighty either as ye say he is." Then Hacon answers: "I will not speak ill of him. I think it more likely that I may not have worthiness enough to take wisdom from him, than that he may not be so powerful, that for that reason I should not take wisdom from him. But this is why I have come to see thee, because it hath come into my mind that here neither of us will need to envy the other for the sake of matters of virtue or belief." That man answers: "It likes me well that I find that thou thinkest that thou hast all trust where I am, and before that faith which ye have followed, you and your other kinsmen. So it is, too, that with you those who lay themselves out for such things go wondrously to work. They go about with fasts and wakes, and deem that therefore those things must be granted to them which they are eager to know. But though they take such pains, yet are they all the less wise of what they desire to know, the more they mix themselves up with them; but we lay ourselves under no penance, and yet we are always wise as to those things of which our friends think it worth while that they should not go on in ignorance. Now things will so go with us two that thou shalt get this gain from me, as I see clearly that thou thinkest thyself better able to get the truth from me than from king Ingi's priestly teachers, whom he thinks he may put all trust in. Thou shalt come in three nights' space, and then we two will try if I can tell thee anything which thou art eager to know."

After that they part, and Hacon stays there in those parts, and when three nights were gone by he fared to meet the wizard. He was then in a certain house all alone, and drew his breath heavily when he (Hacon) went in, stroked his brow with his hand, and said it cost him much ere he became wise of those things which he was to know beforehand. Hacon says he was willing to hear his future fate. The spaeman began to say: "If thou wilt know thy fate, then is it long to tell about, for that it is great and because from thy life and labour very great tidings will come to pass; and it is my belief that thou wilt come to be sole chief over the Orkneys at last, but it may be that thou wilt think it long to wait. I trow, also, that thy offspring will rule there. But from thy western voyage, which thou farest next of all to the Orkneys, very great tidings will come about when those things are fulfilled which will spring from it. Thou wilt also in thy days let that wickedness be done which thou must either make atonement for or not to that God in whom thou believest. But thy footsteps lie further out into the world than I can get to see, but still I think that thou wilt bring back thy bones here to the northern half of the world. Now have I told thee those things that I can at this time, and now say how thou wilt like thy day's work." Hacon answers: "A great story is this thou tellest, if it be sooth, but I think it will go better with my lot than thou sayest. May be, too, that thou has not seen all this of a truth." The spaeman bade him believe it or not as he chose, but said that it would come to pass.

CHAPTER 43

After that Hacon went away to see king Ingi, and stayed with him a short time ere he set his heart on faring to the western lands. Then he took leave of the king to go away. Hacon fared first to Norway to see his kinsman king Magnus, and he made him welcome. Then he learnt those tidings from the Orkneys, that earl Erlend and his sons had it almost all their own way there, and had won very many friends, but Paul his father had little or nothing to do with ruling the land. He thought, too, he made out from those men who came from the west, and in whose words he could put most faith, that the Orkneyingers would long very

644

little for his coming thither west; for they had already good peace and quietness, but feared if Hacon came west that strife and uproar would arise from him. But when Hacon thought of this to himself, then he thought it not unlikely that those kinsmen would hold the realm from him, but let it not be without risk to him if he came thither west without a great force. So he took that counsel to seek to king Magnus that he would bring him to power in the Orkneys.

This was after that king Magnus had made them put to death Steigar-Thorir and Egil, and freed the land from all strife. Hacon was a wise man, and he thought he could see by king Magnus' talk when they spoke together, that the king would be high-minded and eager to attack the realms of other chiefs. Hacon fell to saying this before the king, that it would be a brave deed for a prince to have out the levy and harry west across the sea, and lay the isles under him, as Harold fair-hair did. Says, too, if he could get rule in the Southern isles, it would be handy to harry thence in Ireland and Scotland; and if he put the western lands under him, that thence it would be good to strive with the strength of the Northmen against the Englishmen, "and so avenge Harold Sigurd's son, thy father's father." But when they spoke of this, it was found that this jumped well with the king's temper; he said it was well and bravely spoken, and near his mind. "But that thou shalt keep in mind Hacon," says the king, "if I were to do this after thy words and egging on, to fare with a host west over the sea, that it must not come on thee unawares, though I bore on with a bold claim to those realms which lie away there west, and make in that no distinction of men." But when Hacon heard this utterance, he grew cold and said very little more about it, and doubted for what these words could be spoken. He left off after that egging on the king to any voyage; but then little was needed, for after this speech the king sent messengers over all his realm that the levy should be out. He laid it bare before all the people that he meant to hold on with that host west over the sea, whatever tidings might happen afterwards in his voyages. So men made ready for this voyage all over the land. King Magnus had with him his son on this voyage, eight winters old, whose name was Sigurd; he was much of a man for his years.

CHAPTER 44

When those brothers Paul and Erlend ruled over the Orkneys, king Magnus, the son of Olaf the quiet, came from the east out of Norway. He had a mighty host, and many liegemen followed him. Vidkun Johnson, Sigurd Hranis' son, Sark out of Sogn, Dag Eilif's son, Skopti of Gizki, Œgmund, Finn, and Thord; Eyvind elbow the king's marshal. There was also Kali of Agdir Seabear's son, the son of Thorleif the wise, whom Hallfred maimed, and Kol his son. Kali was a very wise man, and dear to the king, and a good rhymer. Now when king Magnus came to the Orkneys, then he seized the earls Paul and Erlend, and sent them east to Norway, but set up his son Sigurd over the isles, and gave him councillors. King Magnus fared to the Southern isles and the earls' sons, Magnus and Erling, sons of earl Erlend, and Hacon, Paul's son, went along with him. But when king Magnus came into the isles, he fell to harrying first in the Lewes, and won them; and in that voyage he won all the Southern isles, and took captive Lögman, the son of Gudred, the king of the Southern isles. Thence he fared south under Bretland (Wales), and had a great battle in Anglesey-sound with two British earls, Hugh the stout and Hugh the proud. They were brothers of Costnami, who was then king in Ireland in Ulster. And when men were getting out their weapons and busking themselves for the fight, Magnus, Erlend's son, sate him down aft in the forecastle, and did not arm himself. The king asked why he sate. He said he had no quarrel with any man there; "that's why I will not fight." The king said: "Get thee away down under the thwarts, and don't lie here before men's feet, if thou darest not to fight, for I do not think that faith drives thee to this." Magnus took a psalter, and sung while the battle lasted, but did not shield himself. This battle was both hard and long, and both spears were thrown and blows struck; it was long so that it could not be seen between them which way the fight would turn. King Magnus shot with a crossbow, and another man from Helgeland by his side. Hugh the proud fought most sturdily; he was so clad and byrnied that there was no bare spot on him save the eyes. King Magnus bade the man from Helgeland that they should both shoot at him at once, and so they did, and one arrow struck him on his nose-guard, but the other went in at the eye, and flew afterwards through the head. That shot was reckoned to the king.

CHAPTER 45

There fell Hugh the proud. After that the British fled and had lost many men; but king Magnus had won a great victory, but had yet lost many good men, and very many were wounded. So this was made about it:

> "Bolts on byrnies then came rattling,
>
> Might and main the monarch fought,
>
> Agdir's ruler bent his crossbow,
>
> Blood on helmets there was sprinkled:
>
> Bowstrings' hail on mail came flying,
>
> Men fell fast, and Hordas' king,
>
> Seeking land with onslaught hard,
>
> Dealt his deathblow to the earl."

Then king Magnus made Anglesea his own as far south as ever the kings of Norway of old had ever owned it. Anglesea is a trithing of Bretland (Wales). Kali Seabear's son had got many wounds in Anglesea sound, though none of them at once mortal. Afterwards king Magnus turned back by the south course along Scotland.

King Magnus had made Magnus Erlend's son his page, and he served always at the king's board. But after the battle in Anglesey-sound king Magnus took a great dislike to him. He said he had behaved like a coward. It fell on a night when king Magnus lay off Scotland that Magnus Erlend's son ran away from king Magnus' ship when he thought he had the best chance of flying from the king. He jumped overboard and swam to land, and made up his berth so that it seemed as if a man lay there. But when he came to land he ran into the woods, and was in his under-clothing. He struck his foot, and hurt himself much, as he was bare-foot, and so he could walk no longer at that time. He came to a great tree, and climbed up there into the branches, and there bound up his foot, and hid himself there in the branches for some time. But in the morning when men went to meat on board the king's ship, the king asked where Magnus Erlend's son was. He was told that he was asleep in his berth. The king bade them wake him, and said something else than sleep must have come over him when he lay longer than other men. But when they came to his place, then he was missing. Then the king bade them search for him and let loose the slot hounds. But when the hounds were loose, they came at once on his track, and ran off to the wood, and came to that tree in which Magnus was up. Then one hound ran round and round the oak and bayed. Magnus had a stick in his hand, and threw it at the hound, and hit him on the side. The hound laid his tail between his legs and ran down to the ships, and the others after it. The king's men could not find Magnus. He lay hid for a while in the wood, and was next heard of in the court of Malcolm the king of Scots, and stayed there a while, but sometimes he was in Bretland with a certain bishop. He was sometimes in England, or in other places with his friends, but he did not come back to the Orkneys while king Magnus lived.

King Magnus held on his course from the south along Scotland, and then came to meet him messengers from Malcolm the king of Scots, and offered him peace. They said thus that the king of Scots would give up to him all those isles that lie to the west of Scotland, between which and the mainland he could sail in a ship with a fixed rudder. But when king Magnus ran in from the south to Cantire, he let them drag a cutter over the neck of Cantire, he held the tiller, and so took as his own all Cantire. That is better than the best isle in the Southern isles save Man. It goes from the west of Scotland, and has a narrow neck of land at the top of it, so that there ships are very often drawn over. King Magnus held on thence into the Southern isles, but sent his men into Scotland's firths; they were to row in hugging the land on one side, and out hugging it on the other, and so King Magnus claimed as his own all the isles to the west of Scotland. Then the king gave it out that he would sit that winter in the Southern isles, but gave leave to those men who he thought had most need of it to fare home. But when the levies knew that, they became home-sick, and grumbled badly about their being so long away. The king then had a talk with his men and councillors. he went and looked at the wounds of his men. Then the king went to see Kali Seabear's son and asked after his wounds. Kali said they healed very little, and let him know that he could not tell how they would turn out. The king asked counsel of him. Kali asked: "Is it not so king that now your friends steal away from you." The king made as though he thought that were not so. Kali bade him call them under arms, and so muster his men. The king did so, and then missed many men. And when the king told this to Kali, then Kali chaunted this:

"How thy wary chiefs reward thee

For those precious gifts of thine?

West the vessel's sides are shaking,

Try our trustiness, O king!"

Then the king answers:

"Ill have I my boons bestowed,

Boons that brighten face of man,

Buoyant keel to climb the billow,

Now must I command in vain."

After this the king kept watch and ward if men ran from him, and let none ....
(1) When king Magnus was in the Southern isles, then he got as a bride for his son Sigurd, Bjadmunja, daughter of Moorkiartan, Thialbi's son, the Irish king of Connaught. Sigurd was then nine winters old and the maiden five. This winter Kali Seabear's son breathed his last of his wounds. In Anglesey-sound had fallen Sigurd skewer, Kali's kinsman. He was liegeman in Agdir.

Next spring early king Magnus fared away from the Southern isles. He fared first to the Orkneys. There he heard from the east across the sea of the death of the earls, and how Erlend had died in Nidaros, and was buried there, and Paul in Bergen. In the spring in the Orkneys king Magnus gave away Gunnhilda, the daughter of earl Erlend, to Kol Kali's son, as an atonement for the loss of his father, and some estates in the Orkneys went with her as her dowry, and a homestead in Paplay. Of Erling, the son of earl Erlend, some men say that he had fallen in Anglesey sound, but Snorri Sturla's son says he has fallen in Ulster with king Magnus. Kol Kali's son became king Magnus' liegeman, and fared east into Norway with the king, and home to Agdir with his wife, and settled down on his farms. They, Kol and Gunnhilda, had two children; their son's name was Kali, but their daughter's name was Ingirid. they were both of the greatest promise, and reared up with much love.

CHAPTER 46

When king Magnus had ruled the land nine winters, he fared away out of the land west across the sea and harried in Ireland, and was the winter in Connaught. But the summer after he fell in Ulster on Bartholomew's day. But when king Sigurd in the Orkneys heard of his father's fall, he fared at once to Norway, and was there taken to be king with his brothers Eystein and Olaf. Sigurd left behind him over the western sea the daughter of the Irish king. One winter or two after the fall of king Magnus, Hacon Paul's son came from the west across the sea, and the kings gave him the title of earl and such power, as was due to his birth. Then he fared west across the sea and took the realm under him in the Orkneys; he had always followed king Magnus while he lived. He was with him in his warfare east in Gothland, as is said in that lay which was made on Hacon Paul's son.

CHAPTER 47

When earl Hacon had taken the rule in the Orkneys, Magnus earl Erlend's son came down from Scotland and asked to take his father's heritage. That pleased the freemen well, for he had very many friends. He had there many kinsmen and connexions who were glad to raise him to power. A worthy man named Sigurd then had his mother to wife; their son was Hacon churl; they kept house in Paplay. When earl Hacon heard that earl Magnus was come into the isles, he drew force to himself, and would not give up the Orkneys or share that realm which he had there. After that friends came between them and tried to settle matters. So it came about that they were made friends on those terms, that Hacon gave up half the realm if that were the award of the kings of Norway, and with that this strife was stayed. Magnus fared straightway in the spring to Norway to find king Eystein, for Sigurd had then fared out abroad to Jerusalem. King Eystein made him a hearty welcome, and gave him up his father's inheritance, half the Orkneys and the title of earl. Earl Magnus fared west over the sea to take up his power, and his kinsmen and friends and all the people were glad at that; then the kinship of Hacon and Magnus throve well when friends took part in it. There was then peace and plenty in the Orkneys so long as their friendship lasted.

CHAPTER 48

Saint Magnus the isle earl was the most peerless of men, tall of growth, manly, and lively of look, virtuous in his ways, fortunate in fight, a sage in wit, ready-tongued and lordly-minded, lavish of money and high-spirited, quick of counsel and more beloved of his friends than any man; blithe and of kind speech to wise and good men, but hard and unsparing against robbers and sea-rovers; he let many men be slain who harried the freemen and landfolk; he made murderers and thieves be taken, and visited as well on the powerful as on the weak robberies and thieveries and all ill deeds. He was no favourer of his friends in his judgments, for he valued more godly justice than the distinctions of rank. He was open-handed to chiefs and powerful men, but still he showed most care for poor men. In all things he kept straitly God's commandments, and kept down his body in many things which in his praiseworthy life where bright before God, but hidden before men. He then showed his purpose when he asked the hand of a maiden of the most noble race of Scotland, and drank the bridal feast with her; he lived ten years with her so that he fulfilled neither of their lusts, but was pure and spotless of all carnal sins. And when he felt temptation coming over him, then he went into cold water, and asked support of God for himself. Many were those other things and noble virtues which he showed to God himself, but hid from men.

CHAPTER 49

Those kinsmen Magnus and Hacon held the wardship of the land for some while, so that they were well agreed. So it is said in that song which is made of them, that they fought against that chief whose name was Duffnjal, and who was one step further off than the earl's brother's son, (2) and he fell before them. Thorbjorn was the name of a noble man whom they put to death in Burra-firth in Shetland; it is the story of many men that they took the house over his head and burnt him inside it. There are more tidings on which songs have been made which show that they must have been both together, though here it is not fully told about them. But when those kinsmen had ruled the land some time, then again happened, what often and always can happen, that many ill-willing men set about spoiling their kinship. Then unlucky men gathered more about Hacon, for that he was very envious of the friendships and lordliness of his kinsman Magnus.

CHAPTER 50

Two men are they who are named, who were with earl Hacon, and who were the worst of all the tale-bearers between those kinsmen, Sigurd and Sighvat sock. This slander came so far with the gossip of wicked men, that those kinsmen again gathered forces together, and each earl fared against the other with a great company. Then both of them held on to Hrossey, where the place of meeting of those Orkneyingers was. But when they came there, then each drew up his men in array, and they made them ready to battle. There were then the earls and all the great men, and there too were many friends of both who did all they could to set them at one again. Many then came between them with manliness and goodwill. This meeting was in Lent, a little before Palm Sunday. But because many men of their well-wishers took a share in clearing up these difficulties between them, but would stand by neither to do harm to the other, then they bound their agreement with oaths and handsels. (3) And when some time had gone by after that, then earl Hacon, with falsehood and fair words, settled with the blessed earl Magnus to meet him on a certain day; so that their kinship and steadfast new-made peace should not be turned aside or set at naught. This meeting for a steadfast peace and thorough atonement between them was to be in Easter week that spring on Egil's isle. This pleased earl Magnus well, being, as he was, a thoroughly whole-hearted man, far from all doubt, guile, or greed; and each of them was to have two ships, and each just as many men; this both swore, to hold and keep those terms of peace which the wisest men made up their minds to declare between them. But when Eastertide was gone by, each made him ready for this meeting. Earl Magnus summoned to him all those men whom he knew to be kindest-hearted and likeliest to do a good turn to both those kinsmen. He had two longships and just as many men as was said. And when he was ready he held on his course to Egil's isle. And as they were rowing in calm over the smooth sea, there rose a billow against the ship which the earl steered and fell on the ship just where the earl sate. The earl's men wondered much at this token, that the billow fell on them in a calm where no man had ever known it to fall before, and where the water under was deep. Then the earl said: "It is not strange that ye wonder at this, but my thought is, that this is a foreboding of my life's end; may be that may happen which was before spaed about earl Hacon. We should so make up our minds about our undertaking, that I guess my kinsman Hacon must not mean to deal fairly by us at this meeting." The earl's men were afraid at these words, when he said he had so short hope as to his life's end, and bade him take heed for his life, and not fare farther trusting in earl Hacon. Earl Magnus answers: "We shall fare on still, and may all God's will be done as to our voyage."

ENDNOTES FOR CHAPTERS 41-50

1. The end of this sentence is illegible in the MS.

2. That is, he was their second cousin.

3. The Danish Translation adds "and the wisest men were to decide between them."

CHAPTER 51

Now it must be told about earl Hacon, that he summoned to him a great company, and has many warships, and all manned and trimmed as though they were to run out to battle. And when the force came together, the earl makes it clear to the men that he meant at that meeting so to settle matters between himself and earl Magnus, that they should not both of them be over the Orkneys. Many of his men showed themselves well pleased at this purpose, and added many fearful words; and they, Sigurd and Sighvat sock, were among the worst in their utterance. Then men began to row hard, and they fared furiously. Havard Gunni's son was on board the earl's ship, a friend and counsellor of the earls', and a fast friend to both alike. Hacon had hidden from him this bad counsel, which Havard would surely not join in. And when he knew the earl was so steadfast in this bad counsel, then he jumped from the earl's ship and took to swimming, and swam to an isle where no man dwelt. Earl Magnus came first to Egil's isle with his company, and when they saw Hacon coming, they knew that treachery must be meant. Earl Magnus then betook himself up on the isle with his men, and went to the church to pray, and was there that night, but his men offered to defend him. The earl answers: "I will not lay your life in risk for me, and if peace is not to be made between us two kinsmen, then be it as God wills." Then his men thought that what he had said when the billow fell on them was coming true. Now for that he felt sure as to the hours of his life beforehand, whether it was rather from his shrewdness or of godly foreshadowing, then he would not fly nor fare far from the meeting of his foes. (1) He prayed earnestly, and let a mass be sung to him.

CHAPTER 52

Hacon and his men jumped up in the morning and ran first to the church, and ransacked it, and did not find the earl. He had gone another way on the isle with two men into a certain hiding place. And when the saint earl Magnus saw that they sought for him, then he calls out to them, and says where he was; he bade them look nowhere else for him. And when Hacon saw him, then they ran thither with shouts and crash of arms. Earl Magnus was then at his prayers when they came to him, and when he had ended his prayers, then he signed himself (with the cross), and said to earl Hacon, with steadfast heart: "Thou didst not well, kinsman, when thou wentest back on thy oaths, and it is much to be hoped that thou doest this more from others badness than thine own. Now will I offer thee three choices, that thou doest some one of these rather than break thy oaths and let me be slain guiltless." Hacon's men asked what offer he made. "That is the first, that I will go south to Rome, or out far as Jerusalem, and visit holy places, and have two ships with me out of the land with what we need to have, and so make atonement for both of our souls. This I will swear, never to come back to the Orkneys." To this they said "Nay" at once. Then earl Magnus spoke: "Now seeing that my life is in your power, and that I have in many things made myself an outlaw before Almighty God, then send thou me up into Scotland to some of both our friends, and let me be there kept in ward, and two men with me as a pastime. Take thou care then that I may never be able to get out of that wardship." To this they said "Nay" at once. Magnus spoke: "One choice is still behind, which I will offer thee, and God knows that I look more to your soul than to my life; but still it better beseems thee than to take away my life. Let me be maimed in my limbs as thou pleasest, or pluck out my eyes, and set me in a dark dungeon." Then earl Hacon spoke: "This settlement I am ready to take, nor do I ask anything farther." Then the chiefs sprang up and said to earl Hacon: "We will slay now either of you twain, and ye two shall not both from this day forth rule the lands." Then answers earl Hacon: "Slay ye him rather, for I will rather rule the realm and lands than die so suddenly." So says Holdbodi, a truthful freeman from the Southern isles, of the parley they had. he was then with Magnus, and another man with him, when they took him captive.

CHAPTER 53

So glad was the worthy earl Magnus as though he were bidden to a feast; he neither spoke with hate nor words of wrath. And after this talk he fell to prayer, and hid his face in the palms of his hands, and shed out many tears before God's eyesight. When earl Magnus the saint was done to death, Hacon bade Ofeig his banner-bearer to slay the earl, but he said "Nay" with the greatest wrath. Then he forced Lifolf his cook to kill Magnus, but he began to weep aloud. "Thou shalt not weep for this," said the earl, "for that there is fame in doing such deeds; be steadfast in thy heart, for thou shalt have my clothes, as is the wont and law of men of old (2) and thy will, and he who forces thee misdoes more than thou." But when the earl had said this, he threw off his kirtle and gave it to Lifolf. After that he begged leave to say his prayers, and that was granted him. He fell to earth, and gave himself over to God, and brought himself as an offering to him. He not only prayed for himself or his friends, but rather there and then for his foes and banemen, and forgave them with all his heart what they had misdone towards him, and confessed his own misdeeds to God, and prayed that they might be washed off him by the outshedding of his blood, and commended his soul into God's hand, and prayed that God's angels would come to meet his soul, and bear it into the rest of Paradise. Some men say that he took the Lord's Body when the mass was sung to him. When the friend of God was led out to slaughter, he spoke to Lifolf: "Stand thou before me, and hew me on my head a great wound, for it beseems not to chop off chiefs' heads like thieves'; strengthen thyself, wretched man, for I have prayed for thee to God that he may have mercy on thee." After that he signed himself (with the cross), and bowed himself to the stroke. And his spirit passed to heaven.

CHAPTER 54

That spot was before mossy and stony. But in a little after the worthiness of earl Magnus before God was so bright that there sprung up a green sward where he was slain, and God showed that, that he was slain for righteousness' sake, and inherited the fairness and greenness of Paradise, which is called the earth of living men. Earl Hacon did not allow the earl to be borne to the church. The death-day of earl Magnus is two nights after Tiburce mass. He had then been earl over the Orkneys seven winters, he and Hacon both together. There had then passed since the fall of king Olaf seventy four winters. Sigurd and Eystein and Olaf were the kings over Norway. There had been passed since the birth of Christ one thousand and ninety and one winters. (3)

CHAPTER 55

After the meeting, Thora, the mother of earl Magnus, had bidden both earls to a feast, (4) and now came earl Hacon to the feast after the slaying of earl Magnus the saint. Thora went about waiting on the guests herself, and bore drink to the earl and his men, those who had been at the slaying of her son. And when the drink took hold of the earl, then Thora went before him and said: "Now art thou come hither alone, lord, but I looked for you both; wilt thou now gladden me before the witness of God and men; be now to me in a son's stead, and I will be to thee in a mother's stead; I much need now thy pity, and that thou givest me leave that my son may be borne to church; be now so with me in my prayers as thou wouldest wish God to be with thee at doomsday." The earl holds his peace and thinks over the matter, and was sorry for those ill deeds when she begged so meekly with tears that she might have her way about bearing her son to church. He looked at her, and dropped tears, and said to her: "Bury thy son where it pleases thee." After that earl Magnus was borne to Hrossey, and buried at that Christchurch (in Birsay) which earl Thorfinn made them make. Straightway after that a heavenly light was often seen shining over his grave. Afterwards men began to call upon him often, if they were placed in danger, and their matter was granted at once as they prayed. In the same way a heavenly fragrance was often perceived at his grave, and sick men got back their health thence. Then next men made journeys thither both from the Orkneys and Shetland, who were in weak health, and watched at the tomb of earl Magnus the saint, and got healing for their ailments. But yet men did not dare to spread this abroad while earl Hacon lived. It is also so said, that those men who were most in the treachery against earl Magnus the saint, most of them died ill and harrowing deaths. At that time William was bishop in the Orkneys; he was the first bishop there. The bishop's seat was then at Christchurch in Birsay. William was bishop sixty-six years. He doubted long the holiness of earl Magnus. (5) After the slaying of earl Magnus, Hacon took all the realm under him in the Orkneys; he then made all men take an oath to him who had before served earl Magnus; then he became a great chief, and laid heavy burdens on the friends of earl Magnus, whom he thought had been most against him in their quarrels. But some winters after, Hacon began his voyage out of the land, and fared south to Rome; in that journey he fared out to Jerusalem, thence he sought the halidoms, and bathed in the river Jordan, as is palmers' wont. After that he turned back to his own land, and took under him the realm in the Orkneys. He then became a good ruler, and kept his realm well at peace. Then he set up in the Orkneys new laws, which pleased the freemen much better than those that had been before. With such things his friendships began to grow; and so it came about that the Orkneyingers cared for nothing else than to have Hacon for their chief, and his offspring after him.

CHAPTER 56

At that time, when earl Hacon had rule in the Orkneys, that man dwelt at the Dale in Caithness whose name was Moddan, a man of rank and very wealthy; his daughters were these, Helga and Frakok and Thorleif. Helga, Moddan's daughter, was the concubine of earl Hacon, and their son was Harold, who was called the smooth-tongued, but their daughter was Ingibjorg, whom Olaf bitling (6) the Southern isle king had to wife, and Margaret was also their daughter. Frakok, Moddan's daughter, was given away to that man in Sutherland whose name was Ljot the dastard, and their daughter was Steinvor the stout, whom Thorljot in Rackwick had to wife. Their sons were Oliver the unruly and Magnus, and Orm, and Moddan and Eindrid; and Audhild (was their daughter). Another daughter of Frakok was Gudrun, whom Thorstein the freeman, dribblemouth, had to wife; their son was Thorbjorn the clerk. Thorleif, Moddans' daughter, had also a daughter whose name was Gunnhilda. (Audhild?) Earl Hacon had also another son, whose name was Paul, and was called hold-tongue; he was gloomy, but had many friends. Between those brothers there was never much love lost when they grew up. Earl Hacon Paul's son was smitten to death by sickness there in the isles, and men thought that great scathe, for at the end of his days there was good peace, but the freemen misdoubted much whether those brothers, Paul and Harold, would be of one mind.

654

CHAPTER 57

After the death of earl Hacon, his sons took the rule, and they were soon of two minds, and shared the realm into halves. There soon arose great divisions among the great men, and the chieftains threw themselves very much into two sides. Earl Harold held Caithness from the Scot-king, and he was almost always there, but sometimes he was up in Scotland, for he had there many kinsmen and friends. When earl Harold was seated in Sutherland, there came to him that man whose name was Sigurd, who was said to be the son of Ethelbert the priest; he was called snap-deacon; he came down then from Scotland, and had been with David the Scot-king, and he had laid upon him great honours. Earl Harold gave him a very hearty welcome. Sigurd fared out to the Orkneys with earl Harold, and so did Frakok, Moddan's daughter, for that Ljot the dastard, her husband was then dead. She and her sister Helga had then a great share in ruling the land with earl Harold. Sigurd snap was in great love with all of them. Then Audhild the daughter of Thorleif, Moddan's daughter, followed him as his leman, and their daughter was Ingigerd, whom Hacon claw afterwards had to wife. Eric the straight had before had Audhild to wife; their son was Eric stay-brails. When they, Sigurd and Frakok, came into the isles, a great sundering of followers arose, and each of the earls gather as many of his friends about him as he could. These were dearest to earl Paul, Sigurd of Westness, who had to wife Ingibjorg the honourable, the earl's kinswoman, and Thorkel Summerled's son, who was always with earl Paul, and was called fosterer. He was near of kin to Magnus the saint, and was more beloved of his friends than any man. Now the friends of earl Harold deemed that Thorkell would be the last man to spare those brothers strife for the sake of those griefs which he had suffered from earl Hacon their father. So it came about at last that earl Harold and Sigurd snap fell on Thorkell fosterer and slew him. But when earl Paul heard that, he took the tidings very ill, and gathered force together to him. But then the news came at once to earl Harold, and he, too, drew force to him. But when the friends of both of them were aware of this, they came up and tried to settle matters, and then all men had a share in setting them at one again. Earl Paul was so wrath that he would hear of no terms, unless all those men were sent away who had been at the slaying. But inasmuch as it seemed to the freemen that great harm would come of their strife, then all men threw in their word that they should make friends. So it came about that Sigurd was sent away out of the isles, and those other men whom earl Paul thought were most guilty of the deed. Earl Harold paid up the fines that followed on Thorkell's slaying. It was also said at this peace-making that the kinship of those brothers, Paul and Harold, should be bettered, and they were both to be together at Yule and all the other greatest high-days. Sigurd snap fared away out of the Orkneys, and up into Scotland, and dwelt there awhile with Malcolm the Scot-king in good cheer, and he was there thought to be the doughtiest man in all manly feats. He stayed for a time in Scotland ere he fared out to Jewry.

CHAPTER 58

It fell out once in the days of those brothers, earl Harold and earl Paul, that they were to keep the Yule feast at Orfir, in the house of earl Harold, and he was to find the fare for both of them. He was busy there working hard in getting ready for the feast. Those sisters were there, Frakok and Helga, the earl's mother, and they were sitting in the little room at their sewing. Then earl Harold went into the room, but those sisters sat on the cross-bench, and a new-sewn linen shirt lay between them, white as driven snow. The earl took up the shirt and saw that it was thickly stitched with gold. He asked: "Who owns this precious thing?" Frakok says: "'Tis meant for thy brother Paul." The earl says: "Why work ye so hard at clothes for him? Ye do not take as much pains in making me clothes." The earl was just risen up from his bed, and was only in a shirt and linen breeks, and had cast a cloak over his shoulders. He threw off the cloak and unfolded the linen shirt. His mother caught at it, and bade him not be envious though his brother had good clothes. The earl jerked it out of her hand, and got ready to put it on. Then they threw off their wimples and tore their hair, (7) and said, his life lay on it if he put on the shirt. They both then wept sore. The earl put it on nevertheless, and let it fall down over him. But as soon as ever the cloth clung about his body, a shiver came over his skin, and straightway after that followed great pain. And from that the earl took to his bed, and lay but a short while ere he breathed his last. That his friends thought great scathe. But at once after the death of earl Harold, earl Paul his brother took all the realm under him with the consent of all the freemen in the Orkneys. Earl Paul reckoned as if Frakok and her sister had meant that precious thing for him which earl Harold had put on, and for that sake he would not have them live there in the isles. Then they fared away with all their kith and kin, first to Caithness, and thence up into Sutherland, to those homesteads which Frakok owned there. There was reared up with her Erlend son of Harold the smoothed-tongued, while he was a youngster. There, too, was reared up Oliver the unruly, the son of Thorljot of Rackwick, and of Steinvor Frakok's daughter. Oliver was the tallest of men, and of very great strength, and wantonly quarrelsome, and a great manslayer; there too was reared up Thorbjorn the clerk, son of Thorstein the freeman and Gudrun Frakok's daughter. There, too was reared up Margaret, daughter of earl Hacon and Helga Moddan's daughter, and Eric staybrails, Frakok's kinsman. These men were all of great family and great for their own sakes, and they all thought they had a great claim in the Orkneys to those realms which their kinsman earl Harold had owned. The brothers of Frakok were Angus of the open-hand, and earl Otter in Thurso; he was a man of birth and rank.

CHAPTER 59

Then Earl Paul ruled the Orkneys, and had very many friends. He was a man of few words, and no speaker at the Things. He let many other men rule the land with him. The earl was courteous and kind to all the land-folk, liberal of money, and spared nothing to his friends. He was not fond of war, and sate much in quiet. There were then in the Orkneys many men of rank who were

656

come from the stock of the earls. There then dwelt at Westness, in Rowsay, a man of rank, whose name was Sigurd; he had to wife Ingibjorg the honourable, but her mother's name was Herbjorg, daughter of earl Paul Thorfinn's son. Their sons were these, Brynjulf and Hacon pike. They were all chieftains of earl Paul. The sons of Havard Gunni's son, were also friends of earl Paul, Magnus, and Hacon claw, and Thorstein and Dufnjal. Their mother was Bergljot, but her mother was Ragnhilda, daughter of earl Paul. (8) Erling was the name of a man; he dwelt at Tankarnes, in Hrossey; he had four sons, all of them proper men. Olaf was the name of a man, and he was Hrolf's son, who dwelt in Gairsay; he had another house at Duncansby in Caithness. Olaf was a man of the greatest strength and power, and had great honours given him by earl Paul. Asleif was the name of his wife. She was wise, and of great family, and was much thought of for her own sake. Waltheof was the name of one of their sons, Sweyn was another, a third Gunni; all these were tall and proper men. Their sister's name was ingigerd. Sigurd earl's-father-in-law had to wife Thora, the mother of Magnus the saint; their son was Hacon churl; that father and son were mighty chiefs. In Rinansey (9) dwelt that woman whose name was Ragna, a worthy housewife. Her son's name was Thorstein, a fine man of good parts. Kugi was the name of a householder in Westray, a wise man and wealthy, at Rapness. Helgi was the name of a householder, a man of worth and power, who lived there in Westray, in a thorpe that was then there. Thorkel flat was the name of a householder in Westray, cross-grained and high and mighty; Thorstein and Haflidi were his sons; they had not many friends. In Swanay in the Pentland firth, dwelt Grim, a man of small means; his sons were these, Asbjorn and Margad, the briskest of men. In the Fair Isle dwelt that man whose name was Dagfinn. Thorstein was the name of a man who dwelt at Flydruness in Hrossey; his sons were Asbjorn crook-eye and Blian; they were all unfriendly cross-grained men. Jaddvor, she was the bastard daughter of earl Erlend, born of a thrall, dwelt at Knarstead, and her son Borgar with her; they were not much beloved. John wing dwelt in Hoy at the Upland. Richard his brother dwelt at the Brink in Stronsay; they were grand men, and kinsmen of Olaf Hrolf's son. Grimkel was the name of a man who dwelt at Gletness. These were all friends of earl Paul, and all the people along with them. These men all come into the story afterwards. --- William was then bishop of the Orkneys, (10) and the bishop's seat was at Christchurch in Birsay. There then were wrought ever and anon great tokens from the holiness of earl Magnus when men watched over his tomb, but little stir was made about it because of the rule of earl Paul. Bishop William too took the edge off of what men said about the tokens of earl Magnus, and said it was great misbelief to go about with such things. Now we will first of all let the story stop awhile and rather say something of those glorious tokens which God hath granted for the worth's sake of earl Magnus the saint.

CHAPTER 60

Bergfinn Skati's son was the name of a householder in Shetland, and he was blind; he brought two cripples south into the Orkneys; the name of the one was Sigurd and the other's Thorbjorn; they all watched over the tomb of earl

Magnus. To all of them earl Magnus the saint appeared, and gave them their health with God; and Bergfinn became so clear-sighted that he saw and knew his right hand from his left, but both the others stood straight up. But some time after, on the eve of the death day of earl Magnus, four and twenty men in weak health watched over the tomb, and all got cured. Then many men craved that of the bishop, that he would let earl Paul be spoken to, that he would give leave that the tomb should be searched and the halidom (the relics) of earl Magnus taken up. The bishop took that heavily when it was said. It happened one summer that bishop William fared east to Norway, and when he fared back he was late boun, and came to Shetland in autumn, a little before winter set in. Then foul weather arose and mighty storms, but the bishop could not bear to spend his time there, and was eager to get home. After that gales burst upon them, and the winter was come. Then the captain spoke to the bishop, and asked if he would vow for a fair wind not to say anything against taking up the halidom of earl Magnus; the bishop said yea to that, if the weather bettered so that he might sing mass at home on the second Sunday at his bishop's seat.

And as soon as ever that vow was fast made, the weather began to change, and came round to their mind, and they had a fair wing to the Orkneys, and such a quick one that the bishop sung mass at home the next Sunday. But even when such things were granted to him, still he would not for all that believe in the holiness of earl Magnus. Earl Paul too laid his displeasure on all those men who spread such stories about. This event happened in Christchurch at Birsay one day that the bishop went into the church, and was at his prayers; he was all alone in the church, but when he stood up and meant to go away, then he became blind, and could not find his way to the doors; he went about a long time seeking if he might get away. Then great fear fell upon him, and with that he fared to the tomb of earl Magnus, and there prayed with tears, and vowed that he would take up the halidom of earl Magnus, whether earl Paul liked it well or ill. And after that he got back his sight there over the tomb. After that the bishop sent to fetch to him all the most noble men in the Orkneys, and made it plain to them that he was ready then to search the tomb of earl Magnus. And when it was dug into, the coffin was taken out of the ground; the bishop then let the bones be washed, and they were of a right fair hue. He let them take a knuckle-bone and proves it thrice in hallowed fire, and it burnt not, but rather became of a hue as though it were gold. It is the story of some men that it had then run into the shape of a cross. Then many tokens were there wrought at the halidom of earl Magnus. Then the body was laid in a shrine and set over the altar. That was on St. Lucia's day. (11) He had then lain in the mould twenty-one winters. Then it was taken as law that each day should be kept holy, --- the day that he was taken up and the day of his death. The halidom of earl Magnus was kept there for some time. --- It happened once that a man dreamed a dream in Westray, whose name was Gunni, a good yeoman, that Magnus the saint came to him and said to him: "This shalt thou say to bishop William, that my will is to fare away from Birsay and east to Kirkwall, and I trow that Almighty God will grant me of his mercy that those men shall be healed of their ailments who seek thither past hope of cure with right faith. This dream shalt thou boldly tell." But when Gunni awoke it came all at once into his mind that he must not tell the dream, for that he was afraid that earl Paul would lay his displeasure on him. But the next night after earl Magnus showed himself to him when he slumbered; he was then very wrath (and said): "Thou shalt fare

658

to Birsay and tell thy dream when most men are by; but if thou farest not, thou shalt have punishment for it in this world and more in the other world."" Then Gunni woke and was full of fear, and fared at once until he came to Birsay to tell his dream before all the people at mass; and earl Paul was there and many other mighty men. Then many begged that the bishop would set about it and bear the halidom east to Kirkwall as the earl had revealed. Earl Paul held his peace as though he had water in his mouth, and turned as red as blood. After that bishop William fared east to Kirkwall with a gallant company, and flitted thither the halidom of earl Magnus, and they set the shrine over the high altar in the church. At that time the market town at Kirkwall had few houses. Then many signs and tokens were straightway wrought there. --- A little after Bergfinn Skati's son fared from the north from Shetland the second time to watch over the halidom of earl Magnus, and had with him his leprous son, whose name was Halfdan. Earl Magnus appeared to both of them, and passed his hands over them, and then Halfdan was made thoroughly whole; but Bergfinn got back his sight, so that he became a sharp-sighted man. --- Amundi was the name of a man from the north of Shetland; he had leprosy over all his body; he fared to Kirkwall, and watched at the shrine of earl Magnus the saint, and prayed for help and health for himself; but the holy servant of God, earl Magnus, showed himself to him as he slumbered, and passed his hands over all his body, and when he awoke he was whole and well, and knew no ailment anywhere, and all praised God and earl Magnus the saint. --- Thorkel was a man's name who kept house in the Orkneys; he fell down from off his barley-stack right down to the ground, and was all crushed on one side; he was brought to the shrine of the blesséd earl Magnus, and there he got back his health. --- Sigurd was the name of a man from the north out of Fetlar. His hand was cramped, so that all his fingers lay in the palm; he fared to Kirkwall, and was there made whole. --- Thorbjorn was the name of a man, but Gurth was the name of his father; he was from Shetland, and was mad, and was brought to earl Magnus, and became straightway whole. --- Thord was the name of a man whose nickname was dragon-shot; he was Bergfinn's hireling of Shetland; he thrashed corn from the halm in the barley barn the next day before St. Lucia's and St. Magnus' day. But when the daylight began to change, then Bergfinn the master went out thither into the barn and bade him strike off work. Thord says: "It doesn't often happen that thou thinkest I work over long." Bergfinn said: "Tomorrow is St. Magnus' day, which we ought to hold with all such honour as we best can." Then Bergfinn went away, but Thord worked still as hard as he could. But when a short time had gone by then Bergfinn went a second time and spoke to Thord in mickle wrath, and said he thought there was spite in that, "that thou workest now at holy tides, and now leave off at once."

Then Bergfinn went away in a rage. But Thord worked on as before. But when men had sat down to the board, and had eaten and were full, Thord came in in his workaday clothes, just when men took to drinking, and began to drink at once. But when he had drained one full cup, then he lost his wits at once and got wild, so that men had to hold him and to put him into bonds, and so it went on for three days and nights. Then Bergfinn vowed for him to give half a mark of silver to the shrine of earl Magnus, and to let Thord watch for three nights if he might become whole. But Thord became whole on that night, on the evening of which the vow had just been made. Two men took gold from the shrine of earl Magnus, one an Orkney and the other a Caithness man; the

Caithness man was lost in the Pentland firth; his name was Gilli. The Orkney man went mad, and said in his fits what they had done, and then a vow was made for him to go on a pilgrimage south (to Rome), if he might be made whole at the shrine of earl Magnus. Now he was brought thither and became whole at once. — Ogmund was the name of a Shetlander on whose head a crossbeam fell and crushed his skull much, but Bergfinn vowed for him, and cast lots whether the vow should be to go south on a pilgrimage, or to set a slave free, or to give money to earl Magnus' shrine if he were made whole. But the lot turned up to give money for earl Magnus' shrine. But the lot turned up to give money for earl Magnus' shrine, and there he became whole. But Bergfinn, his mother's brother, gave half a mark as he had vowed. Sigrid Sigurd's daughter was the name of a woman from the north out of Shetland, who was blind from childhood and until she was twenty; then her father went with her to earl Magnus, and let her watch there, and gave much goods to the shrine of Magnus, and there she got her sight. --- Sigrid was again the name of a woman from Shetland whose leg broke in two bits; she was taken to Magnus and she got back there her health. --- Sigrid was the name of a third woman from the north out of Shetland in the island of Unst; she was with Thorlak, who kept house at Baltastead; (12) she sewed when other men left off work on the eve of earl Magnus' mass; but Thorlak asked why she worked so long; she said she would leave off there and then. He went away, but she sewed on as before. Then Thorlak went a second time, and asked why she did so ill; "and away with thee," he says, "and don't work in my house." She said she had only a little bit unsewn, and worked on as before until it got dark, and she sate in her place. But when fires were made, and men busked them to eating and drink, then she fell mad and was thrown into bonds, and she was mad until Thorlak vowed a vow for her. He cast lots whether the vow should be a pilgrimage south, or setting a slave free, or giving money to the shrine of earl Magnus the saint, but the lot came up to give money to earl Magnus' shrine. Thorlak brought her thither, and there she became whole, and went south afterwards. --- In England were two men who staked much money on casting of dice, and one of them had already lost a large sum. Then he staked a ship of burden and all that he had against all that he had already lost. But the other man threw first two sixes. Then that man thought things looked badly for him, and called on earl Magnus the saint that he might not lose all that he had, and then threw his throw. But one of the dice burst asunder, and there turned up two sixes and and ace, and he gained all that lay upon the throw, and after that he gave earl Magnus much goods. --- Groa was a woman's name in Hrossey; she became raving mad, and was brought to earl Magnus the saint, and got there her health, and was there all her life after and praised God. --- Sigurd was the name of a man; he was Tand's son, he kept house north in Shetland, he became devil-mad; and was sewn up in a hide, and was brought afterwards from the north to Kirkwall to earl Magnus the saint, and there he got back his health, and all praised God who were by and his holy bosom-friend earl Magnus.

Now is done telling here of those glorious tokens which God grants for the sake of saint Magnus the isle-earl. Now also we must make an end of these stories with this prayer, that he who wrote this Saga, and he who dictated it, and everyone who listened to it, may have intercession and help in their prayers from the holy knight of God earl Magnus, to the absolution of their sins and to everlasting joy; but of our almighty Lord Jesus Christ may they have help and mercy, peace and joy, both now and for ever, from him who is and was and shall be, one true and everlasting God, granting and willing and mighty to give all good things for ever and ever. Amen.

ENDNOTES FOR CHAPTERS 51-60

1. The Danish Translation here adds "He did not go into the church for any other reason than that he wished to preserve his life. (sic) There he made his prayers heartily to God, and commended himself into his hands. Early the morning after he went out of the church, and two others with him by another way down to the shore into a secret place, and then said his prayers again to God."

2. The Danish Translation adds, "that he shall have one's weapons and clothes who puts him to death."

3. This date is wrong, to agree with the others it should be 1116.

4. Instead of this sentence the Translation runs thus: --- "Wise men say that in the spring after they should have been set at one, Thora, the mother of Magnus, had bidden them both to be her guests, and they were to come straightway to her when they were reconciled, and came back from Egil's isle."

5. Fl. adds, "until his worthiness was so plainly revealed that God let his holiness wax higher in the same proportion as it was more tried, as is said in his Book of Tokens and Wonders."

6. bitling; i.e., "the little bit" or "the tiny."

7. Fl. reads, "Then Frakok threw off her wimple and tore her hair."

8. earl Paul; that is, of earl Paul the 1st, grandfather of earl Paul Hacon's son.

9. Rinansy; North Ronaldsay.

10. Comp. above ch. 55, and Isl. Ann. under the year 1168.

11. St. Lucia's day; Comp. Magn. S. Eyjajarls, ch. 31. and ch. 54 above.

12. Baltastead for Ballaslead in the MS., which would answer to the neighbourhood of the present Baltasound in Unst.

THE STORY OF EARL ROGNVALD
CHAPTER 61

Cecilia (1) was the name of a sister of earl Magnus, born in wedlock. She was given away east in Norway, and that man whose name was Isaac had her to wife. Their son's name was Kol. Kol (Kali's son) sate on his farms in Agdir, as was written before, and was the wisest of all men. He did not fare into the Orkneys. Kol was a very shrewd man. Kali his son grew up there, and was the most hopeful (2) man, a middleman in growth, well set up, one of the best limbed of men, with light brown hair. He had more friends than most men, and was a more proper man, both in body and mind, than most of the other men of his time. He made this song:

> "Draughts I play with open hand,
>
> Games and feats so skilful nine;
>
> Writing runes to me comes ready;
>
> Books I read and smith's work furnish;
>
> I can glide on snow-shoon swift;
>
> Doughtily I shoot and row;
>
> Either stands at my behest,
>
> Sweep of harp or burst of song."

Kali was almost always with Solmund his kinsman, the son of Sigurd supple. He was (the king's) steward at Tunsberg, and had a house of his own at East Agdir. He was a chief, and had a great following. They were much of an age, those kinsmen.

CHAPTER 62

Kali was fifteen winters old when he fared with chapmen west to England, and had good wares for traffic. They held on their course to that town which is called Grimsby. Thither came a very great crowd of men both from Norway, the Orkneys, and from Scotland, and so also from the Southern isles. There Kali met that man who went by the name of Gillikrist. (3) He asked then much about Norway, and talked most with Kali; there was a great fellowship sprung up (between them). He told Kali as a secret that his name was Harold, and that king Magnus barelegs was his father, but that his mother's stock was in the Southern isles, and some of them in Ireland. He asked Kali how he thought he would be welcomed if he came to Norway. Kali says he thought king Sigurd likely to give him a good welcome if other men did not spoil matters between them. They, Gillikrist and Kali, exchanged gifts at their parting; each promised the other his thorough friendship wherever their next meeting might be. But Gillikrist does not tell his secret to more men in that place.

CHAPTER 63

After that Kali fared from the west on board the same ship, and they came from abroad at Agdir, and held on thence north to Bergen. Then Kali sang this song:

> Weeks of grimmest walking five
>
> We have waded through the mud;
>
> In mid Grimsby where we were,
>
> Was no want of mud and mire.
>
> Now it is with merry minds,
>
> O'er the sea-moors (4) that we let,
>
> Beaked elk (5) across the billow,
>
> Blithely bound to Bergen home."

But when they came to the town, they found there a great crowd of men out the land, both from the north and from the south, and many, too, from other lands, who had flitted thither much goods. Then those shipmates went into the taverns to make merry. Kali was then a great man for dress, and had many braveries with him as he was newly come from England. Then he thought much of himself, and many others thought so too, for he came of a good stock, and was a well-bred man in himself. But in that tavern where he drank he found a young man of rank whose name was John; he was the son of Peter Sark's son of Sogn. He was then one of the king's liegemen. His mother's name was Helga, a daughter of Harek of Sæter. John was a very showy man in his dress. Unna was the name of a worthy housewife who owned the house in which they drank. Then there arose a great fellowship between those two, John and Kali, and they parted with love; John fared then south (6) to Sogn, to his abode, but Kali east to Agdir, to his father. Kali was also often with Solmund his kinsman. So it went on for some half years, that Kali was in the summers on trading voyages, but at home in the winters or with his kinsman Solmund.

CHAPTER 64

So it fell out one summer, when Kali had fared north to Drontheim, that he lay weather-bound under that island which is called Doll. (7) In the isle was a great cave, which is called Doll's cave. In the cave was great hope of treasure. The chapmen made ready, and went into the cave, and had the hardest work to make their way there. They came where water stood across the cave, and none dared to fare across the water save Kali and another man, whose name was Havard, Solmund's house-carle. They swam across the water, and had a rope between them. Kali swam first, and had in his hand a blazing torch and a tinder-box between his shoulders. (8) So they swam over the water and came to land. That place was rough and rugged, and there was a great stench, and they could scarce get the light struck. Then Kali gave out that they would go no farther, and said they should make a beacon there as a memorial. Then Kali sang a song:

"Here have I built in darksome cave

Of Doll a beacon high

To goblin grim of sternest mood,

So golden store I sought,

None knows what man of those who work

The water-skates (9) will wend his way,

His long and weary path, once more

Across this water wide."

After that they turned back and came safe and sound to their men, then they fared out of the cave; it is not told about their journey that any tidings happened that summer. They came back to Bergen, and Kali turned into the same tavern to Unna the housewife. There too he found again John Peter's son and his serving-man, whose name was Brynjulf. There were there besides many others of his men, though they are not named. It happened one evening that they John Peter's son and Kali, were gone to sleep, but many sat behind and drank. Then there was much talk, when men were well drunk; and it came about that they spoke of matching one man with another, and of who were thought to be noblest of the king's liegemen in Norway. Brynjulf stood up that John Peter's son was the best bred and best born of the younger men south of Stad; (10) but Havard Kali's companion spoke up for Solmund, and said he was no worse bred than John, and declared that the dwellers in the Bay would set much greater store by him than by John Peter's son. Out of this a great strife arose, and when the ale spoke in them, then no better heed was taken than this, that up jumped Havard and got him a cudgel and gave Brynjulf there and then such a blow on the head that he fell down at once senseless, and men ran to help him up; but Havard was packed off to see Kali, and Kali sent him south into Alvidra to a priest whose name was Richard, "and bring him," he says, "my message that I beg him to take thee in till I go home east." Kali got him a man to bear him company, and a boat, and they row away south till they come to Græning Sound. Then Havard said to his fellow-traveller: "Now we two are come beyond the bark of hounds, and we will rest ourselves here," and with that they lie down to sleep. Now we must take up our story and say that Brynjulf came to his wits, and he was carried to see John, and he tells him all that had happened, and how the man had been packed off there and then. John guessed the truth as to his doings, and made them take a rowing-cutter, and ten men got into her; Brynjulf was there to lead the men. After that they row south, and come south into Græning Sound, (11) when it was getting daylight. Then they saw that a boat lay before them on the beach, "and may be," says Brynjulf, "that these men will be able to tell us something of Havard." So they went up on land and found them; Havard and his mate were then just awake. Brynjulf fell on Havard at once with the sword, and both those companions were slain at that meeting. And now Brynjulf and his men fared back to Bergen after these tidings, and tell them to John; and after that all the townsfolk knew them. Kali took the tidings of these slayings very ill; and when men came between him and John, John says that his wish is that Kali shall alone make his award as to the wrong which he thinks he has suffered, but that should be saving the king's right and that of the next of kin to take the feud up. And Kali agreed to those terms, but still there was no love between him and John. Then Kali fared home east very soon after that; and when he and his father met, and Kali had told about those tidings and the close of his quarrel, then Kol says: "Methought thou wert showing thyself in a strange light when thou tookest any atonement before thy kinsman Solmund were by; now methinks thou has come into a strait, and canst take little part in the matter, except to ask for atonement; and so would not Solmund do if thy house-carle were slain and his shipmate." Kali says: "Thou speakest the truth, no doubt, father, when thou sayest that I have been too hasty in looking at the matter; but thou wert too far off to teach me what to do. It will often be shown too that I am not so deep-witted as thou, but still I thought this, that Solmund would be never the nearer his due though I forsook that which was offered to me; and I do not call it a disgrace either to Solmund or to thee to accept the right to fix your own terms from John for your share in the suit, if he offers it you, though I very much doubt whether there is any need for you to take up the matter. But as for myself, I call myself quite free as to Brynjulf, so long as I have come to no final utterance in the matter, and taken no money in atonement." So that father and son talked much together, and each of them drew his own way about it; (12) then they sent men to tell Solmund those tidings. After that Kol and Kali and Solmund met; Kol wished that men should be sent to John to seek for an atonement; but Solmund and Hallvard, Havard's brother, would hear of nothing but revenge, man for man; and said it was unseemly to ask a Sogn man for atonement. But for all that the plan was taken which Kol wished, with this understanding, that Kol gave his word not to withdraw from this suit before Solmund got what was due to his honour. Kol too was to have the whole management of the matter in his hands. But when the messengers came back, they say that their business was taken up slowly and unwillingly; and John refused right out to atone for that man with money who had before made himself an outlaw by his deeds. Solmund said that had gone just after his guess, that it would bring them little honour to ask John for an atonement; and now he begged Kol to give them some advice that was worth having. Kol says: "Will Hallvard run any risk to get revenge for "his brother, and may be that after all there may be little brought about." Hallvard said he would not spare himself to get revenge for his brother, even though there were risk of life in it. Kol says: "Then shalt thou fare north stealthily to Sogn to that man whose name is Uni; he dwells hard by John: he is a wise man and rather short of money, for John has long elbowed him out of his means. He is a great friend (of mine), and now rather stricken in years. To him thou shalt bring six marks weighed, which I send him that he may lay some plan how thou mayest wreak thy revenge on Brynjulf, or some other man of John's household, whom he will think not less loss (than Brynjulf.) But if this deed be fulfilled, then Uni shall send thee on to Studla (13) to Kyrping-Worm my kinsman, and his sons Ogmund and Erling, and then methinks thou art as good as come home. Bid Uni after that to sell his land, and change his abode hither to me." Now Hallvard busked him to this journey, and nothing is told of how he fared, or where his night-quarters were, before he came one day at evening to Uni's house, and did not call himself by his own name. Uni and his household asked him about the news of the day, and at night when men sat by the fires, then the guest asked much about high-born men there in Sogn and Hördaland. Uni said that none of the king's liegemen there was thought more powerful than John, both for his birth's sake, but still more for his unfairness, and asked whether they had not some keepsakes of that down south in the land. The guest he said little when he (Uni) spoke thus; and after that men dropped off from the fires one by one, so that at last they two were left behind. Then Uni began to speak, and said thus: "Is thy name Hallvard, pray?" says he. "Nay," says the guest, and again gave the name he had given in the evening. Then Uni said: "Off then is my difficulty," says he, "and yet I would have thought that if my name were Brynjulf, thine would be Hallvard; but still we two will now go to sleep." Then the guest took hold of him, and said: "No, we two will not go yet," and with that he handed him over the bag of money, and says that Kol sent him that silver, with his greeting, "and why he sends it is that thou mayest lay a plan with me that I may fulfil my revenge for my brother," and then he tells him all Kol's counsel. Uni said: "Kol were worthy of good from me, but I cannot tell how it is fated as to revenge on Brynjulf; but he is looked for hither tomorrow to fetch clothes from his sweetheart." And now Uni led him out to the horse-stable which stood before the door outside, and stowed him away there in the manger. That was before men rose, but he had lain indoors during the night. Now, when Hallvard had been a little while in the horse stable, he saw how a huge man had come up to the homestead, and calls out that the woman must be quick; she took her clothes, and carries them out. Then Hallvard thinks he knows who it must be. So he goes out. Brynjulf had laid aside his arms while he tied up the clothes which the woman brought, and as soon as ever they meet, Hallvard smites Brynjulf his death-blow, and then went back again into the horse stable, and hid himself there. While the slaying was going on the woman had gone into the house to kiss and take leave of her friends in the household; and when she came out she saw the tokens of the deed, and ran in with a great shriek, and was in such a fright that she was just about to faint away, but still she told them what had happened. Goodman Uni ran out, and said that the guest must have been a hired murderer, and sent a man at once to John to tell these tidings, and egged on men as much as he could to search for the man, and for that no man suspected him of having anything to do with the deed. Hallvard was in the horse stable till the hottest of the chase had passed off, but after that he fared by Uni's help and counsel till he came to Studla to Worm and his sons, and they got him company home east. Kol and Solmund made him welcome, and were well pleased with their share in the matter; and now these tidings are noised abroad, and men became aware of the truth. Now John is heavily displeased at this, and so that winter and the summer after pass away; and thenext winter when Yule was drawing on, John busked him from home with thirty men, and gave it out that he meant to go on a journey to see his kinsfolk up at Sæter to the house of Harek, his mother's father, and so he did, and gets there a hearty welcome. And when those kinsmen were talking together, John says that he means to go thence to East Agdir to look up Solmund. Harek tried to turn him from this, and said he had not got the worst of it, though they (John and Solmund) parted as they were. John said he would not be content that Brynjulf should be unavenged. Harek said he thought his lot would not be bettered, though they (John and Solmund) had any further dealings in the matter; but still he had with him away thence thirty men, and so they fared east with half a hundred men (14) by the upper road, and thought to

666

come unawares upon Solmund and Kol. But when John was newly gone from home, Uni bestirred himself and fared south to Studla to see Worm, and that father and son got him company south to Kol, and he came there at Yule, and told them he thought that John was on his way to attack them. Kol sends out spies at once on all the ways about him, by which he looked that John might come, and he fared to find Solmund; and those kinsmen sat with a great company. News came to them about John's journey, and they fared against him; their meeting was in a wood; they fell at once to battle; Kol and his men were far more in number, and had the victory. But John lost many men and fled himself into the woods. He got a wound in his leg, and that healed so ill that he was halt ever after, and was called limp-leg John. He came home north in Lent, and his journey was thought most shameful. So now this winter wore away. But the summer after John made them slay two of Kol's kinsmen, Gunnar and Aslak. A little after king Sigurd came to the town, (15) and this difficulty was brought before him. After that the king sent word to both sides, and summoned them to him. Then they came to the king, with their kinsfolk and friends; then an atonement was sought, and the end of it was that the king's doom should pass upon all their quarrels, and either side plighted their troth to the other. King Sigurd made a settlement between them with the advice of the best men. It was so fixed in that settlement that John Peter's son should take Ingirid Kol's daughter to wife, and then friendship would spring up with those ties, while the manslaughters (of Havard and Brynjulf) were to be set off one against the other. The attack on Kol and John's wound were set off against the loss of men away there east, but the wounds on either side were matched together and set off, and those that were odd were atoned for in money. Each side too was to yield help to the other both at home and abroad. It followed also on this settlement that king Sigurd gave Kali Kol's son half the Orkneys with earl Paul Hacon's son, and the title of earl too. He also gave him the name of earl Rognvald Brusi's son, because his mother Gunnhilda said that he had been the most proper man of all the Orkney earls, and thought the name would bring good luck. This share of the Orkneys Saint Magnus had owned, Rognvald-Kali's mother's brother. After this atonement they parted with great love-tokens; they who had erewhile been foes.

CHAPTER 65

That winter after king Sigurd sat in Oslo, (16) but about the spring in Lent he took a sickness, and breathed his last one night after Lady-day. His son Magnus was then in the town there, and held a Thing at once, and was taken to be king over all the land according to the oath which men had sworn to king Sigurd. Then he took the king's treasures into his power. Harold Gilli was then at Tunsberg, (17) when he heard of king Sigurd's death, then he held meetings with his friends. Then he sent for Rognvald and his kindred, for he had always been his friend (18) since they met in England. That father and son too had most hand in Harold's clearing himself by ordeal before king Sigurd, with the help of other liegemen, Ingimar Sweyn's son and Thiostolf Ali's son. The counsel of Harold and his friends was to hold the Hauga-Thing there in Tunsberg. There Harold was taken to be king over half the land. Then those were called force-oaths (19) by which he had sworn away his fathers inheritance out of his hands before they would let him take the ordeal. Then men flocked to him and became hand-bound to him, and he gathered a very great company. Then words passed between those kinsmen. And it was so that seven nights passed ere a settlement was brought about on these terms, that each of them should have half the land against the other; but king Magnus had (beside) king Sigurd's longship and his table furniture and all his treasures, and yet he still was not content with his share. He fastened feuds on all Harold's friends. King Magnus too would not let that gift hold good by which king Sigurd gave the Orkneys and the earldom to Rognvald, because he clung very fast to Harold's cause in all their quarrels, and would never leave his cause till all their quarrels were brought to an end. They, Magnus and Harold, were three winters kings over Norway, so that their settlement might be said to hold good, but the fourth summer they fought at Fyrileif; (20) then king Magnus had near sixty hundred men, but Harold had fifteen hundred. These chiefs were with Harold: Kristred his brother, earl Rognvald, Ingimar of Ask, Thiostolf Ali's son, and Solmund. King Magnus got the victory, but king Harold fled. There fell Kristred and Ingimar. He (Ingimar) chanted this song: ---

> "Friends befooled me
>
> To Fyrileif field,
>
> Aye was I unwilling
>
> For onslaught of war;
>
> Me bit bolts bitter
>
> From crossbow sped,
>
> Ne'er again shall I
>
> To Ask (21) go back."

King Harold fled east to the Bay to his ships, and fared south to Denmark to find king Eric the ever-memorable. He gave him Halland as a lordship and eight longships without tackle. Thiostolf Ali's son sold his lands for ships and arms, and went to seek king Harold south in Denmark that autumn. King Harold came towards Yule to Bergen, and lay over Yule-tide in Floru-voe. (22) But after Yule they run up to the town, and there was but a little struggle; king Magnus was taken captive on board his ship and maimed, but king Harold took all the land under his sway. But the next spring after king Harold renewed the gift to Rognvald about the isles, and the title of earl as well.

CHAPTER 66

Kol gave this advice to send men to the Orkneys at once after this, and (Rognvald) begged earl Paul that he would give up half the isles as king Harold had given them to him; then friendship and thorough kinship should spring up between them. But if earl Paul refused these things, then these very same men should fare to find Frakok and Oliver the unruly, and offer them half the lands with earl Rognvald, if they would seek to get it from earl Paul with a host. But when these men came to the Orkneys and saw earl Paul, and brought forward their errand there, then earl Paul answers: "I understand this claim, how it is made with mickle cunning and forethought; they have betaken themselves to the kings of Norway to get the realm away from under me. Now I will not reward that faithlessness by giving up my realm to those who come no nearer to me than Rognvald, and by refusing it to my brother's son and my sister's son. There is no need here of long words, for I will guard the Orkneys by the strength of my friends and kinsfolk while God grants me life to do so." Then the messengers saw how their errand was likely to turn out there. So they fared away, and went south over the Pentland firth to Caithness, and so into Sutherland to find Frakok, and tell their errand there, how earl Rognvald and Kol offer Oliver and Frakok half the Orkneys if they will win them back from earl Paul. Frakok speaks thus: "True it is that Kol is a very wise man, and wisely has it been seen to in this plan to look hither for strength, because we kinsfolk have great strength, and many men bound to us by ties. I have now given away Margaret Hacon's daughter to earl Moddan of Athole, who is noblest of all the Scottish-chiefs by birth. Melmari his father was brother of Malcolm the Scot-king, father of David, who is now the Scot-king. We have also," she said, "many true claims to the Orkneys, but we are ourselves something of schemers, and we are said to be rather deep-witted, so that this strife does not come upon us unawares; but still it seems good to me to join fellowship with that father and son for many things' sake. Ye shall say these words to Kol and Rognvald that we two, Oliver and I, will come to the Orkneys next summer at midsummer with a host to fall on earl Paul; let Rognvald and his men come thither then to meet us, and let us then fight it out with earl Paul; but this winter I will draw strength to me out of Scotland and the Southern isles from my kinsfolk and friends and connexions." Now the messengers fare back east to Norway, and tell that father and son how they had sped.

CHAPTER 67

That winter after this earl Rognvald busked him to fare west, and these chiefs with him, Solmund and John; they fared in the course of the summer after, and had picked men, though not many; (and) five or six ships. They come off Shetland at midsummer and heard nothing of Frakok. Then high and foul winds arose, and they laid their ships up in Alasound, (23) but fared about to feasts and free-quarters over the land and the freemen made them good cheer. But of Frakok it must be told that she fares in the spring out to the Southern isles, and she and Oliver gather force thence to themselves in men and ships; they got twelve ships, and all of them small and rather thinly manned. And near midsummer they held on for the Orkneys, and mean to meet earl Rognvald, as was said; they were slow in getting a wind. There Oliver the unruly was leader of that host, and the earldom in the Orkneys was meant for him if they could get it. Frakok was there in the fleet too, and many of her kith and kin.

CHAPTER 68

Earl Paul was then at Westness in Rowsay at a feast with Sigurd, when he heard that earl Rognvald was come to Shetland; then too was heard how a host was gathering together in the Southern isles to attack them. Then the earl sent word to Kugi in Westray, and to Thorkell flayer, they were wise men; and many other chieftains he summoned to him. At this meeting the earl asked counsel of his friends, but they did not all look on the matter in one way; some wished to share the realm with one or other (of the foe), and not to have both against them, but some advised that the earl should fare over to the Ness to his friends, and see what force he could get there. Earl Paul answers: "I will not now offer my realm to those to whom I refused it then right out when they sought it by fair means; methinks too it is unchieftainlike to fly my land without one trial of strength; I will take that counsel to send men tonight round all the isles to gather force, and let us fare against Rognvald and his men as soon as we can, and let our quarrel come to the sword" point ere the South-islanders come."" This plan was taken which the earl spoke of. That man was then with earl Paul, whose name was Sweyn breastrope; he was one of the earl's bodyguard, and well honoured of him; he was ever on viking voyages in the summer, but the winters he spent with earl Paul. Sweyn was a tall, strong man, swarthy and rather unlucky-looking; he was very fond of the old faith, and had all his life lain out at night (to follow his black arts). He was one of the earl's forecastle men. These chiefs came at once that night to earl Paul; Eyvind Melbrigdi's son; he had a longship fully manned. Olaf Hrolf's son of Gairsay had another, Thorkell flayer a third, Sigurd the master of the house there a fourth, the fifth the earl had himself. With these five ships they hold on to Hrossey, and come there on the evening of the fifth day of the week (Thursday evening) at sundown; then force flocked to them during the night, but they got no more ships. They meant the day after to sail to Shetland against Rognvald and his men. But next morning, when it had got light, and the sun was just up, those men came to the earl, who said they had seen longships fairing from the south on the Pentland firth; they said they could not tell whether there were ten or twelve of them. The earl and his men made up their minds that there must be coming Frakok's host. Then the earl bade them to get ready to row against them as hard and as fast as they could. Then they, Olaf and Sigurd begged him to take time about it, and said men would come into them every hour. And lo! as they rowed east from Tankarness, longships come sailing against them from the east round the Mull, and they were twelve in all. Then the earl and his men lashed their ships together. Then came to him Erling, the master of Tankarness, and his sons, and offered him his help. By that time they were so thronged on board their ships that they thought they could find room for no more men. Then the earl bade Erling to bring down stones for them while they were in no risk of attack. And when they had made all clear for fight, Oliver and his side came up, and gave them an onslaught by rowing at once, and they had far more men, but smaller ships. Oliver had a great ship, and he laid that against the earl's ship. There was then the hardest fight. Olaf Hrolf's son, laid his ship against the smaller ships of Oliver, and there was a great difference in the height of the sides, and in a short while he cleared the decks of three ships. Oliver made such a hard onslaught on the earl's ship, that all the forecastle men gave way and fled aft of the mast. Then Oliver egged on his men to board, and goes himself the first man up. Sweyn breastrope was the foremost of all the earl's men, and fought most stoutly. Earl Paul sees now that Oliver was come up on board his ship, and eggs on his men fast; he leaps down himself from the poop, and springs forward in the ship, and when Oliver saw that, he snatched up a boat-hook, and hurled it at the earl, and it fell upon his shield, and down he fell at once on the planks. Then there was a great shout. And at that moment Sweyn breastrope snatched up a great stone and hurled it at Oliver, and hit him full in the breast; the blow was so great that he tumbled at once overboard, and sank in the sea. His men got hold of him, and then he was drawn up into his ship, and he lay there senseless, and men knew not whether he were dead or alive. Then some ran and hewed the lashings asunder, and were for flying, and then all Oliver's men were driven down from the earl's ship. Then they took to flying. Just then Oliver came to himself, and bade them not to fly; but then no one made as though he knew what he said: The earl chased the flying ships east of Hrossey, and so farther east of Hrossey and Rognvaldsey, and so into the Pentland firth; then they drew away from one another. Then the earl turns back, and where they had fought five ships of Oliver's fleet lay empty and unmanned. The earl took them for his own, and manned them with his followers. The fight took place on the Fastday (Friday), but that night the earl made them put their ships into trim. Then many men gathered to him, and two longships. Next morning he had twelve ships, and all in good trim and well manned. Saturday he sailed to Shetland, and came by night into Alasound unawares to those who watched earl Rognvald's ships; then earl Paul made them slay the men, but took the ships and the goods to himself. But next morning news came to Rognvald and his men; they rushed together and had a great gathering of the freemen; after that they fared down to the strand, and then egg on Paul and his men to come on shore and fight with them. But earl Paul put no trust in the Shetlanders, and therefore would not go on land, but offered that they should get them ships and fight it out on shipboard. But Rognvald and his men saw that they could get no ships in which they could fight on fair terms. And so they parted as things stood. Earl Paul and his men fared back to the Orkneys, but earl Rognvald and his men were in Shetland all that summer, but at autumn they got carried in ships to Norway by divers chapmen, and their voyage was thought rather shameful. But when earl Rognvald came home, and he and his father met, Kol asks whether Rognvald was ill content with his lot. He says he thinks very little had come of his errand, and that little rather unworthily. Kol says: "I do not think so though; methinks the errand has been good, and that much has been done if the Shetlanders are your friends, and that it is better to have gone than not to have gone." Rognvald says: "If thou praisest this voyage, then it must either be that thou must care less about our lot than I thought, or thou must see something in our voyage which we have not yet thought of seeing. I should be very glad now that thou shouldest lay down a plan for us and be thyself on the voyage with us." Kol says: "Both of these things now shall not be done; say all your work is easy, but come one self's never near the spot. I shall be very glad to use my counsel so as not to swerve from your honour." Rognvald answers: "We will willingly follow the advice thou givest." Kol says: "My first advice is that thou sendest word to king Harold and other of thy friends that they get thee force and ships for a western voyage early in the spring, but we will draw to us all the strength we can get this winter, and let us so lay our plans this second time that one of two things may be, either that we get the Orkneys, or else lay our bones there." Rognvald answers: "The thought dwells in my mind not to fare on many more such voyages as this which we have now fared; and such, I ween, is the thought of most of those who lately fared with us."

CHAPTER 69

Earl Paul fared to the Orkneys after that he had taken the ships of earl Rognvald and his men; he had then to boast over a great victory. Then he had a great feast and bade to him his chieftains. There then was taken that counsel to pile up (24) a beacon in the Fair Isle; fire was to be put to it if a host were seen sailing from Shetland. Then there was another on Rinansey (North Ronaldsay), and so on in more of the isles, so that it might be seen all over the isles if war were coming on them. Then too men were set to call out men round all the islands; Thorstein Havard's son, Gunni's son, was to have Rinansey, but his brother Magnus was to have Sanday, Kugi (was to be on the watch) round Westray, Sigurd of Westness on Rowsay, Olaf Hrolf's son fared to Duncansby in Caithness, and had the wardship there. His son Waltheof dwelt then in Stronsay. Then earl Paul granted gifts to his friends, and all promised him their thorough friendship. He kept many men about him that autumn, until he learned that Rognvald and his men were away from Shetland. Then no tidings happened in the islands, and so it went on up to Yule. Earl Paul had a great Yule-feast, and made ready for it at that homestead of his which is called Orfir; he bade thither many noble men. Thither was bidden Waltheof Olaf's son out of Stronsay. (25) They set off ten of them in a ten-oared boat, and they were all lost in the West-firth the day before Yule, and that was thought great tidings, for Waltheof one of the best-bred of men. His father Olaf had a great train of followers in Caithness; there were his sons Sweyn and Gunni, and the sons of Grim of Swanay, Asbjorn and Margad, but Asleif the mistress of the house and her son Gunni had gone to a feast at a friend's house no long way off. These tidings happened at Duncansby three nights before Yule that Sweyn Olaf's son had rowed out to fish, and those brothers Asbjorn and Margad with him. They always went about with him, and were the briskest and bravest of men. But in the night after they had gone away came Oliver the unruly to Duncansby with that train which had followed him on his viking voyage that summer, and seized the house over Olaf's head and set fire to it at once, and burned him inside it and six men with him, but allowed the others in the house to go out. They took there all the chattels and goods, and went away after they had done that deed. Sweyn, who was afterwards called Asleif's son, came home before the first day of Yule, and fared at once north on the Pentland firth; he came about midnight to Swanay to the house of Grim, the father of Asbjorn and his brother. Grim got into a ship with them, and they put Sweyn across to Knarstead on Scapa-neck. Arnkell was the name of the man who kept house there, and his sons' names were Hanef and Sigurd. Grim and his sons turned back thence, and Sweyn gave Grim a gold finger-ring. Hanef and his brother Sigurd brought Sweyn to Orfir; there he had a hearty welcome; men guided him to Eyvind Melbrigdi's son, Sweyn's kinsman. Eyvind led Sweyn before earl Paul, and the earl greeted Sweyn well and asked him what news, but Sweyn tells the death of his father, with all that had happened. The earl was ill pleased at that, and said that

672

he had suffered a great loss; he asked Sweyn to be with him, and said that he would do him great honour. Sweyn thanks the earl kindly for his bidding, and said he would willingly accept it.

CHAPTER 70

After that men went to even-song. There was a great homestead there, and it stood on the side of a slope, and there was a steep hill at the back of the house, and when one came on to the brow of the hill, Orrida-firth lay down below. In it lies Damsay. There was a castle in the island, and that man guarded it whose name was Blann, a son of Thorstein of Flidruness. There in Orfir was a great drinking hall, and there was a door at the east gable from the south in the side wall, and a noble church stood before the hall door, and one went down steps from the hall into the church. But as one went into the hall, there was on the left hand a great flat stone, and further on inside ale-casks, both many and great, but when one passed through the doorway there was a small room facing one. (26) When men were come from even-song, they were ranged in seats. The earl made Sweyn Asleif's son sit next to him on the inside, but on the outside of the earl Sweyn breastrope sat next him, and then John the kinsman of Sweyn breastrope. When the board was cleared those men came who told of the drowning of Waltheof Olaf's son; and the earl thought that great news. Then the earl bade that no one should tease Sweyn Asleif's son while Yule lasted, and said that even then he would have enough to think on. And at even, when men had drunk, the earl and most men with him went to sleep. But Sweyn breastrope went out, and sat out all night, in heathen rites, as was his wont. And during the night men rose and went to church and heard prayers, and after high mass men sat down at the board. Eyvind Melbrigdi's son had most of the management of the feast with the earl, and did not sit down himself. The waiting-men and torch-bearers stood before the earl's table, but Eyvind poured out the drink into the cup of each of those namesakes. Then Sweyn breastrope thought that Eyvind filled his cup higher, and would not touch it before Sweyn Asleif's son had drunk off his cup, and said Sweyn (Asleif's son) drank unfairly. There had long been no love lost between Sweyn breastrope and Olaf Hrolf's son, and so too between those namesakes since Swein Asleif's son grew up to be a man. And when drinking had gone on a while, then they went to Nones. But when men came in again, then healths and memories were solemnly spoken of, and horns were drained. Then Sweyn breastrope would change horns with his namesake, and said he thought it was a little one. Then Eyvind thrust a great horn into Sweyn Asleif's son's hand, and he offered that to his namesake. Then Sweyn breastrope got wrath, and said to himself between his lips, so that some men, and the earl among the rest, heard him: "Sweyn will be Sweyn's death, and Sweyn shall be Sweyn's death." This was hushed up at once, and now the drinking went on up to even-song. And when the earl went out, then Sweyn Asleif's son went before him, but Sweyn breastrope sat behind and drank. But when they came out into the ale-room, Eyvind came after them, and led Sweyn aside to talk. "Heardest thou," he asked, "what thy namesake said when thou hadst offered him the horn?" "No," he said. Then Eyvind repeated the words, and said that the fiend must have put those words into his mouth during the night. "He must mean thee death, but thou shalt be beforehand with him in the deed, and slay him."" Eyvind put an axe into his hand, and bade him stand by the flat stone in the shade, and told him to give Sweyn the blow in front if John went before him, but if John went behind, then he bade Sweyn to deal his namesake the blow behind. The earl went to church, and no one gave heed to Eyvind and Sweyn. But Sweyn breastrope and John went out a little later than the earl. Sweyn breastrope had a sword in his hand, for he always bore his sword, though others were weaponless, and John went first. It was light up to the doorway, but the weather was thick. And when Sweyn breastrope came to the doorway, Sweyn Asleif's son smote him in front on the forehead, and he stumbled forward at the blow, but did not fall. And when he stood straight again, then he saw a man standing at the door, and thought it must be he that had wounded him. Then he drew his sword, and dealt him a blow with it on the head, and clave him down to the shoulders; but it was his kinsman John on whom the blow fell, and there they both fell down. Then Eyvind came up and led Sweyn Asleif's son into that room which was over against the doorway, and he was there drawn out at a window-slit. (27) There Magnus Eyvind's son has a horse ready saddled, and guided him away at the back of the homestead, and so to Orrida-firth. Then they took ship, and Magnus carried Sweyn to Damsay, and brought him to the castle; but Blann carried him next morning north to Egil's isle to meet bishop William. The bishop was then at prayers when they came thither. And after mass Sweyn was brought by stealth to the bishop, and Sweyn tells him the tidings, the death of his father Olaf and of Waltheof, and the slaying of Sweyn and John, and called on the bishop to shelter him. The bishop thanked him for the slaying of Sweyn breastrope, and said that had been a cleansing of the land. The bishop let Sweyn stay there till Yule was over; but after that he sent him into the Southern isles to Tyree, to that man whose name was Holdbodi, and who was Hundi's son; he was a great chief there, and gave Sweyn a very hearty welcome. He stayed there that winter, and was thought of much worth by all the people.

ENDNOTES FOR CHAPTERS 61-70

1. This passage from "Cecilia" to "Kol" is an addition of the Danish Translation, M.O. reads, "Kali was the name of a man, Kol's son, Kali's son, Seabear's son. Kali was a son of Gunnhilda, daughter of earl Erlend, the son of Thorfinn, the Orkney earl, who (Kali) after a time was called Rognvald."

2. hopeful; that is, "of the greatest promise," as in the English expression "young hopeful."

3. Gillikristi; i.e., "the servant of Christ," one of a series of Celtic names which came in with the conversion of the heathen, and which still remains in the surname Gilchrist, Gillespie, "the bishop's servant," is another; Gillicallum, "St. Columba's servant," another; Gilpatrick, "St. Patrick's servant," another. Of the same character are Melbride (Melbrigði), Malise, Malcolm, and Melmari, which mean respectively St. Bride's, Jesus', St. Columba's and the Virgin Mary's servant; Mail or Maoile, like Gilli or Giolla, being Celtic for servant. Comp. an

excellent essay by Munch, on the Runic Inscriptions in the Isle of Man, in the Mémoires de la Soc. Roy. des Antiquaires du Nord. Copenh. 1845-49.

4. sea-moors; the waste surface of the sea.

5. beaked elk; the ship.

6. So the MS., it should be "north."

7. This island was also called Sandey, Fornm. S. xii. 344. It belongs to the province of South Mæren, near Drontheim. The cave is still to be seen on its western shore. Comp. Munch. N.H. iii. 688.

8. shoulders; That is, the materials for striking a light were fastened at the nape of his neck and remained dry.

9. water-skates; ships, i.e., what sailor will ever again, &c.

10. Stad; Stað or Staðir, the westernmost headland in Norway, away from which the coast trends north and south. The expression answers to our "south of the Tweed," or "in the south country."

11. The sound near the island of Græning, now Gröningen, north of Mostr, in South Hördaland.

12. Fl. "each thought his own way about it."

13. Now Stöle in South Hördaland.

14. That is with sixty, half the long hundred of 120. Thirty of his own people and thirty of Harek's.

15. That is to the town of Bergen.

16. Oslo; Now Christiania, a town of much importance in ancient times.

17. Tunsberg; Now Tönsberg, a great mart in ancient times on the western shore of "the Bay." By "the Bay" was meant the great Gulf in the south of Norway, the entrance to which is the Skaw, and at the bottom of which lies the Christiania firth. The district round the Gulf was also called "the Bay," and the inhabitants were called "Bay-dwellers."

18. The Danish Translation reads he sent messengers after Kali, who at that time was called Rognvald, and his father Kol, for Rognvald had always been his friend.

19. As we should say oaths taken under duress, and therefore not binding.

20. Fyrileif; A place on the east side of "the Bay," in the Norwegian province, called of old Ránríki, but to which the Swedish Båhuslen now answers.

21. Now Asköe, an island off the town of Bergen.

22. A creek, or "voe," near Bergen.

23. Alasound; Yell Sound.

24. The Danish Translation paraphrases the passage: "Then that counsel was taken that they should bring together heath, wood, and tar on the highest hills in

the Fair Isle, and make out of them a pile or heap of wood; that they called a beacon."

25. So the Danish Translation. Fl. reads "Stroma" (badly).

26. The Danish Translation reads, "A great slab or flat stone; between it and the hall (stoffven) were many and great ale-casks; but just opposite the door as one went in was another little room."

27. Literally "bladder-window," a narrow window covered with bladder to supply the place of glass. Comp. Sturl. S. i. 168. The Run. Lex s.v. ljóri reads, "he was drawn up through the louvre."

CHAPTER 71

A little while after those manslayings had taken place in Orfir men ran up from the church, and Sweyn was borne inside the house, for he had not yet drawn his last breath, though he had lost his senses. He died in the course of the night. Then the earl made every man take his seat, and wanted to be sure who it was that had caused the slayings; and then Sweyn Asleif's son was missing. Then men thought it clear that Sweyn had slain them. Then Eyvind came up and said: "Any man can see that Sweyn breastrope must have given John his death." The earl said that no man should blow a hair off Sweyn's (1) head, and says he would not have done this without a cause. "But if he takes himself off from meeting me," says he, "then he will be doing himself an ill turn by that." (2) Men thought it most likely that Sweyn would have gone to Paplay to Hacon churl, brother of earl Magnus the saint; he was a great chief, mild and gentle. The earl heard no news of Sweyn that winter, and made them make him an outlaw. When the spring began the earl fared far and near about the north isles to get in his rents. He made great friends with the great men, and gave away almost with both hands. The earl came into Stronsay, and gave Thorkell flayer that farm which Waltheof Olaf's son had owned, for the sake of knowing where Sweyn had settled down. Thorkell spoke and said: "It does not turn out now as the saying goes, 'Many are a king's ears.' But though thou beest earl, still it seems to me wonderful that though hast heard no tidings of Sweyn, for I knew at once that bishop William sent him to the Southern isles to Holdbodi Hundi's son, and there he has been this winter." The earl said: "What shall I do to the bishop who has dared to do this?" Thorkell answers: "No blame must be given to the bishop for this in the face of what now lies at the door; thou wilt need all thy friends if Rognvald and his men come from the east." The earl says, "that what he says is true." Earl Paul fared thence to Rinansey (North Ronaldsay), and accepted feast at mistress Ragna's house and Thorstein's her son. Ragna was a wise woman. They had another farm in Papay. (3) The earl sat there three nights, for he could not get a wind to Kugi's house in Westray. They, Ragna and the earl, talked much, and she says to the earl that he had little loss in Sweyn breastrope, even though he was a great warrior. "Thou gottest from him many feuds; it were my counsel, in the face of that trouble which stares you in the face, that ye make you as many friends as you can, and not be fault-finding. I would too that ye laid no blame on bishop William or the other kinsmen of Sweyn Asleif's son; but I would rather that thou wouldest forgive the bishop thy wrath, and this besides, that thou wouldest let word be sent to the Southern isles for Sweyn, and forgive him thy wrath too, and give him back his estates on condition that he will be to thee such a man as his father was. It has always been the custom of the noblest men to do much for the sake of their friends, and so to gather to themselves force and friendship." The earl answers: "Thou art a wise wife, Ragna, but still thou has not yet gotten the title of earl in the Orkneys; thou shalt not rule the land here. A pretty thing indeed that I should give Sweyn goods for an atonement, and think that I should win victory for my side in that way!" He gets wrath about this, and said: "God settle matters between my kinsman earl Rognvald and me, and let things so go as each has deserved by his deeds. If I have misdone towards him, then it is time that I should atone for it; but if so be his aim is to get my realm, then methinks that man my best friend who aids me, that I may be able to hold my realm. Rognvald I have never yet seen; and this is why, so far as my knowledge goes, I have all the less done him any wrong, because whatever our kinsfolk may have caused to be done, men know well enough that I had no share in those things." Many answered that it was quite unpardonabl for any one to try and strive with him for the realm, but no one spoke against him. When the spring began to wear away, earl Paul made them pile up the beacons in the Fair Isle and Rinansey, and in almost all the isles, so that each might be seen from the other. There was a man named Dagfinn Hlodver's son, who kept house on the Fair Isle, a brisk stirring man; he was to watch that beacon and set fire to it if a host were seen faring from Shetland.

Earl Rognvald sat that winter at home in Agdir on the farms of that father and son, and sent word to his friends and kinsfolk; but some he went to see, and begged that they would aid him in his voyage west both in men and ships, and most of them turned a willing ear to his wants. But about February Kol sent two ships of burden out of the land, one west to England to buy stores and weapons, but in the other Solmund sailed south to Denmark to buy there what Kol bade him, for he has now all the business of fitting them out in his hands. It was so meant that these ships of burden should come back to Norway at Easter, but they mean to set sail on the voyage after Easter week. So it was done, and they held on from the east after Easter week. Each of that pair, father and son, had his own long-ship, but Solmund had the third. Kol and his son had besides a ship of burden laden with stores. But when they came to Bergen, they found king Harold there; he gave Rognvald a long-ship fully trimmed and manned. John limp-leg had also a long-ship. The sixth Aslak, son of Erlend of Hern had; he was a daughter's son of Steigar-Thorir. He too had a ship of burden laden with stores. They had six large ships, five cutters, and three ships of burden. When they lay waiting for a wind at Hern, a ship ran in from the west, and they heard news from the Orkneys and Shetland, and what preparations earl Paul was taking, if earl Rognvald came thither west with a host that summer.

677

CHAPTER 72

Earl Rognvald let them blow the trumpets to call together a house-Thing (4) while they lay in Hern, (5) and spoke then of earl Paul's preparations, and how great feud the Orkneyingers showed towards him when they meant to keep him from the inheritance of his kinsfolk, after the kings of Norway had given it to him as the rightful heir. And so he makes them a long and clever speech, --- I meant, he said, "so to go to the Orkneys as either to get them or else die." Men gave him great praise for his speech, and promised him trustier following. Then Kol stood up and said: "We have heard from the Orkneys how all men there will rise up against you, and keep you from your realm, siding with earl Paul; and be sure, kinsman, that they will be slow to lay down that feud which they have taken up against you. Now, it is my counsel to look for trust thither where there is enough of it and to spare, that he may give you your realm who owns it by right; but that is the saint earl Magnus, your mother's brother. My wish is that though vowest to him, if he will grant thee the inheritance of thy kindred and make thee his heir, that thou wilt let a stone minster be built in the Orkneys at Kirkwall if thou canst get that realm, so that there shall not be another as splendid in that land, and let it be hallowed in the name of Saint Magnus the earl thy kinsman, and that thou wilt lay out money, so that the church may grow and thrive, and that thither may come his halidom, together with the bishop's seat." This all thought good advice. And that vow was fast made. After that they put to sea, and they got a fair wind, and made Shetland, and each were glad at meeting the others. The Shetlanders were able to tell them many tidings from the Orkneys, and so they stayed there some time.

CHAPTER 73

It chanced once that Kol asks Uni, for he was then there, and had changed his abode to that of Kol and his son, after he had taken part in the plot against Brynjulf. Then Kol asks: "Whether of the twain wilt thou, Uni, give counsel how the beacon in the Fair Isle may be set on fire for naught, or undertake that work that another beacon may not be lighted. I speak to thee about this because I know that thou art wiser than most of the others who are now here, though we have here many men of worth." Uni answers: "I am no man for advice, but still less would I make a rush to war by my plans. I will therefore rather choose what shall be done last, because I mean to take the doing of it all on myself." (6) And a little after, one day when the weather was fair, Kol made them fit out many small ships, and turned his course towards the Orkneys. There were no chiefs on board the ships but Kol. And when they come so far that they think their fleet might be seen from the Fair Isle, then Kol made them hoist the sails on all the ships, and set men to back water with the oars, so that the ships might move as slowly as possible, though the wind was right aft; and he made them set the sails no higher than half-mast, and so hoist them higher and higher up as they had gone further on. Kol says that then their fleet would be seen from the Fair Isle, "[and it would seem] as though the ships were coming near to the isle. (7) May be then that they will set fire to the beacon, and there will be a rush to arms all over the islands." Then Dagfinn of the Fair Isle saw the ships sailing and he set fire to the beacon at once, but fared himself to the earl and told him the news. And as soon as ever the beacon was seen on the Fair Isle, then Thorstein Ragna's son made them kindle the beacon on Rinansey. And after that all the others were lit one after the other over all the isles. But all the freemen fared to meet the earl, and that was the greatest war-gathering. But when Kol saw that the beacon was a-blaze, he bade his men fare back; and said it might so happen that this would be a cause of quarrel to some of them; Kol fares back to Shetland after he had done thus much, and says that now Uni shall betake himself to his plans. Uni calls three Shetlanders to go along with him; they take a six-oared boat and a few stores beside and fishing-tackle. They fared to the Fair Isle, and Uni said he was a Norseman, but gives out that he had wedded in Shetland and had sons there; he says too he had been robbed by earl Rognvald's men, and speaks the hardest things of them. He takes up his abode in a house there, and his sons row out to fish; but he stays at home to watch their stores and catch. He gets to speaking with and to knowing those men who take the lead there, and they are well pleased with him.

CHAPTER 74

After that Dagfinn had set fire to the beacon, he set off to find earl Paul, as was before said, and thither came all the earl's chieftains. Then they took to asking every one about the doings of earl Rognvald and his men; and men thought it wonderful when they showed themselves nowhere. But still they kept the force together three days. Then the freemen began to take it ill, and say that it was great folly to burn the beacons, though fishermen were seen sailing in their boats. Then blame was laid on Thorstein Ragna's son that he had done a bad thing when he kindled the beacon on Rinansey. Thorstein answers, and says he could do nothing else than fire the beacon, when he saw the blaze on the Fair Isle, and said this had been all Dagfinn's doing. Dagfinn answers: "Men far more often get ill from thee than though art able to say the same of me." Thorstein bade him hold his tongue, and sprang up to him with an axe, and smote him there and then his death-blow. Then men sprang to arms and a battle arose. This was in Hrossey, a little way from Kirkwall. Sigurd of Westness and his sons Hacon pike and Brynjulf aided Hlodver Dagfinn'' father, but his own kin helped Thorstein. Then this was told the earl, and he came up, but it was long ere he could get them parted. Then Kugi of Westray speaks a long speech, and says thus: "Do not do the earl this shame, that ye fall to blows among yourselves, for ye will need all your men within a little time. Let us take heed then that we be not unhandy or quarrelsome. But as for this, it must have come about by the will and plan of our foes, and it must have been a trick of theirs to waste the beacons thus. But now they may be looked for to come every day, and so let us take counsel and make our plans. No ill-will could have driven Dagfinn to do as he did, but he was a little more hasty than he ought to have been." This guess of Kugi was the very truth, and so he went on with many wise words. So it came about that each side was willing that the earl should settle the matter; but still it was thought best to break up the gathering, and men went home. But that man was set to watch the beacon in the Fair Isle whose name was Eric. And when Uni had been a little while in the Fair Isle, he came to Eric and said: "Wilt thou that I watch the beacon? since I do naught else, and I may well sit and spend all my time on it." Eric accepted that. But as soon as ever no men were near to the spot, Uni threw water on the beacon, and made it so wet that fire had no hold of it anywhere.

CHAPTER 75

Earl Rognvald and his men agreed that they would wait until the spring tides and east wind set in together, for then it is scarcely possible to pass between Westray and Hrossey, but with an east wind one may sail from Shetland to Westray. And so earl Rognvald and his men profited by this, and came on Friday evening to Westray into Hofn, to the house of Helgi, who lived there. No signs were then given by the beacons, for when the sails were seen from the Fair Isle, Eric busked him to go to earl, and sent men to Uni to bid him fire the beacon, but when that man came thither, Uni was off and away. And when that man wanted to fire the beacon, then it was so wet that the fire would not catch it. And when Eric hears this, he thinks he sees how things have gone. After that he fares to find earl Paul, and tells him. But when earl Rognvald was come into Westray, all the island blades gathered together, and they, Kugi and Helgi, take counsel for them. The first thing was to seek for peace from the earl. And the end of this business was that the Westrayingers come under earl Rognvald's power, and swear oaths to him.

CHAPTER 76

On the Sunday after earl Rognvald heard mass there in the thorpe, and they were standing outside by the church. Then they saw how sixteen men walked without weapons and bald. Them they thought wonderously boun. The earl's men talked together, and asked who these men might be. Then the earl sang a song:

> "Sixteen have I seen at once---
>
> Topknots fell about their brows,
>
> Shield or weapon bore they none, ---
>
> Women all together walk;
>
> We bore witness now to this,
>
> That here west are far the most
>
> Shaveling maidens in this isle,
>
> In the main it lies in tempests."

When the Sunday was over earl Rognvald's men fared there about the country round, and all men came under the earl's power. It fell out one night in Westray that the earl's men had news that the islanders were to have a secret meeting to plot against earl Rognvald. But when the earl got news of that, then he arose and went to the meeting. But it happened that the earl's men had beaten many of the island blades, and taken master Kugi and put him in fetters, and said he was at the bottom of this plot. But when earl Rognvald came to the meeting Kugi fell at his feet and laid all his cause in God's hand and the earl's; he said he had been brought to the meeting against his will, for all the freemen wished him to be foreman in the plot. Kugi pleaded his own cause well and glibly, and many others pleaded with him, and tried to prove what he said to be true. Then the earl chanted this:

"Crooked fetters I see lying

On the legs of greybeard Kugi,

Kugi, worst of midnight plotters,

Fetters now forbid thy straying!

Kugi! never hold again

Midnight tryst nor bargain break,

Thou shalt be shut out from guile,

Take an oath and keep it too."

The earl gave all the men there peace. Then they bound their fellowship anew [with oaths].

CHAPTER 77

When earl Rognvald had come into the Orkneys and many men had come under his power, Paul was in Hrossey, and he and his friends held a Thing and took counsel with their men. The earl asked for advice as to how he should behave in this strait. But men handled it in various ways, and it was counsel of some that the lands should be shared with earl Rognvald; but most of the mighty men, and the freemen too, wished to buy earl Rognvald off with money, and offered there and then help to do it. Some were eager to have a fight for it, and said that had turned out well before. Earl Rognvald had had spies at the meeting, and when they come to him, the earl asked the news. A skald who had been at the Thing answered the earl: (8)

"Mighty chief! I hear that our

Foemen hide a hostile mind,

From the freemen at the meeting

This report I also heard,

That the feeders of the wolf,

Many masters too of ships,

681

Wished thy ships to keep the sea,

But for Paul to hold the land."

After that earl Rognvald sent men to find the bishop and begged him to become a daysman (9) between them, and (he) sent for Thorstein Ragna's son, and Thorstein Havard's son out of Sanday, and bade them to go with him and try to make a settlement and to stand by neither side in making any strife; and when they came to the bishop they fared altogether to find earl Paul, and he (the bishop) tried to make a settlement between those kinsmen. The bishop brought this about, that peace was fixed for half a month, that they might try to make a more lasting settlement. Then the isles were shared into lots, where either earl should have his living during that time. Then earl Rognvald fared to Hrossey, but earl Paul fared to Rowsay. And in that time these tidings happened in the isles, that those kinsmen of Swein Asleif's son, John wing of the Upland in Hoy, and Richard of the Brink in Stronsay, fared against Thorkell flayer to that farm which Waltheof had owned, and burned him inside it, and nine men with him. They fared after that to find earl Rognvald, and gave him that choice, that they would join earl Paul with all their kin if earl Rognvald would not take to them. The earl did not turn them away from him. And when Haflidi Thorkell's son heard that, he fared at once to find earl Paul, as soon as he heard of his father's burning, and earl Paul took to him. After that John and his kinsfolk bound themselves as earl Rognvald's liegemen. He soon had a great following there in the isles, and was much beloved. Earl Rognvald gave John and Solmund and Aslak and many other of his helpers leave to go home; but they wished to stay and see how things would turn out. Then earl Rognvald said: "My thought is, if God wills that I should get rule in the Orkneys, that he will give me strength, and so will the saint earl Magnus, my kinsman, to hold it, even though ye fare home to your estates." After that they fared home to Norway, each of them to his own abode.

CHAPTER 78

That spring early Sweyn Asleif's son had fared away from the Southern isles up into Scotland to see his friends. He stayed a long time in Athole with earl Moddad and Margaret Hacon's daughter, and they talked about many things in secret. There Sweyn heard of strife from the Orkneys, and he grew eager to fare thither and find his kinsfolk. He fared first to Caithness to Thurso, and a noble man with him whose name was Ljotolf; with him Sweyn had been long that spring. They came to earl Ottar's house in Thurso, Frakok's brother, and Ljotolf tried to bring about a settlement between Ottar and Sweyn for what Frakok had caused to be done, and earl Ottar paid down the fines for the atonement on his own behalf. The earl also gave his word that he would be friends with Sweyn, but Sweyn promised earl Ottar to strengthen Erlend the son of Harold smooth-tongue, so that he might get back his father's inheritance in the Orkneys when he laid claim to it. Sweyn there changed ships, and had a ship of burden thence, and thirty men on board her. Thence he took a northwest wind across the Pentland firth, and so west of Hrossey, and so to Evie sound, and so up the sound to Rowsay. At the isle's end was a high headland, and a great heap of stones under it beneath; and there otters often lay among the rocks. And as Sweyn and his men were rowing along the sound, he began to speak, and said: "There are men yonder on the headland, and we will run in thither and learn the news of them. My will now is that men should change their trim a little; we will take to our hammocks; and there twenty men shall lie down, but ten shall row; (10) we will go softly and slowly." But when they neared the isle, men call out from the head that they must row to Westness, and bring to earl Paul what they had on board ship. They thought they were speaking to chapmen. But earl Paul had been that night at Westness to a feast in Sigurd's house. The earl had risen up betimes, and he and nineteen men had gone south on the isle to hunt otters which lay among the rocks under the head. They meant to be back home in time for their morning draught. The men on board the ship of burden rowed to land, and they asked one another of this thing and that, and what the men were called whom they had met. The men in the ship of burden told whence they had come; they ask also where the earl might be. They tell them that he was there on the rocks. Sweyn and his men heard that as they lay in their hammocks; and Sweyn then told them to run the ship in so that she might not be seen from the head. Then Sweyn said that they must arm themselves, and fall at once on the earl's men when they met. And so they do. There they slew nineteen men, but six of Sweyn's men fell. They took earl Paul by force, and led him on board their ship, and turned their stem to the sea, and fared back the same way west of Hrossey, and ran in between Hoy and Grimsey, and so east of Swelg, (11) thence south to Broad firth, and up it to Ekkjalsbakka. (12) There he left his ship and twenty men, but he and the rest fared till he came to Athole and met earl Maddad and Margaret earl Paul's sister. There they had a hearty welcome, and earl Maddad set earl Paul in his own high-seat. And when they had sat down, in came Margaret walking with a great train of women, and threw her arms round her brother. After that men were brought in to amuse them. Earl Paul was rather short of words, as was not wonderful that he should have great misgivings. Nothing has been handed down of earl Paul's words, or of Sweyn's as they were faring both together. Earl Maddad and Margaret and Sweyn Asleif's son went into a room and talked together. But at even after drink Sweyn and his captive were shown the way to a sleeping-house all alone, and they were locked in there, and so it went on every evening while they were there.

CHAPTER 79

It happened one day that Margaret gave out that Sweyn Asleif's son was going to the Orkneys to see earl Rognvald, and give him his choice whether he would rather have earl Paul to rule with him in the Orkneys, or Harold, son of Maddad and herself, who was three winters old. And when earl Paul heard of that, he answers: "As to my mind, it is to be said that I fared away so from my realm that men will never have heard of such doings before: nor will I ever go back to the Orkneys. I see that this vengeance must be given of God for the robbery of me and my kinsmen; but if it seems to God that the realm is mine, then will I give it to Harold, if he may live to enjoy it; but as for me, I wish that money may be given me to settle me in some cloister, and then keep ye watch and ward, so that I do not get away thence. But my wish is, Sweyn, that thou farest to the Orkneys, and sayest that I am blinded, or even more maimed, for my friends will seek me out if I am sound and hale in all my limbs. It may then be that I may not be able to forego faring back to my realm with them, for I guess they will think there is more harm in our parting than will really befall them." No more words of the earl are handed down than these. After that Sweyn Asleif's son fared to the Orkneys, but earl Paul stayed behind in Scotland. And this is the story that Sweyn told of what had happened. But some men tell a story which is less seemly, that Margaret had led Sweyn Asleif's son by her counsel to blind earl Paul her brother, and put him into a dark dungeon; but after that she got another man to take his life there. But we do not know which of the two stories is more true; but all men know that he never afterwards came back to the Orkneys, nor held he any rule in Scotland.

CHAPTER 80

These tidings happened at Westness, when the earl's home-coming grew late, then Sigurd, the master of the house, made them send men to look for them; but when they got to where the pile of rocks was, they saw the bodies of the slain. Then they thought the earl must have fallen there; fared home and told these tidings. Sigurd fared at once to the spot to see and reckon the dead, and they found there nineteen of the earl's men, but there were six men besides there whom they knew not. After that Sigurd sent men to Egil's isle to find the bishop and to tell him these tidings. And the bishop fared at once to see Sigurd, and they fell to talk of these tidings, and Sigurd guessed that this must have been by the plotting of earl Rognvald. But the bishop answers that some other proof must be brought forward before he would believe that earl Rognvald had betrayed earl Paul his kinsman. "I guess," says the bishop, "that some others must have wrought this ill deed." Borgar the son of Jatvor Erlend's daughter, who dwelt at Goathill, (13) he had seen the ship of burden when it fared from the south, and fared back south. But when that was heard, then men thought that this must have been by the plotting of Frakok and Oliver the unruly. But when these tidings were noised about the isles, that earl Paul was away and gone, and no man knew what was become of him, then they sought counsel among themselves, and there were very many who then fared to find earl Rognvald, and swore fealty to him. But Sigurd of Westness, and his sons Brynjulf and Hakon pike, said they would swear oaths to no man, while they were without news of earl Paul, whether he were to be looked for back or not. There were more men too who refused to take oaths to earl Rognvald, but there were some who laid down a time or a day when they would come over into his hand if nothing was then heard of earl Paul. But when earl Rognvald saw that he had to do with many mighty men, then he took crossly nothing that the freemen asked. And so time went on, that every now and then he held Things with the freemen, and from time to time some of them came over to his hand at each Thing.

Now it happened one day at Kirkwall, that earl Rognvald had a Thing with the freemen, and when men were at the Thing, it was seen how nine armed men came from Scapa-neck to the Thing. And when they came to the Thing, there they knew Sweyn Asleif's son, and men were eager to know what tidings he had to tell. Sweyn had sailed in his ship from the south to Scapa-neck, and there left his ship, but he and his men walked to Kirkwall afterwards. And so when they came on the place of meeting, then his friends and kinsfolk flocked round him, and asked him what news, but he answered little, and bade them call the bishop to him. But the bishop greeted Sweyn well, for they had long been friends. They two went aside to talk, and Sweyn tells the bishop all the truth about his doings, and bade him now take counsel with him about these knotty points. The bishop said: "These are mickle tidings that thou tellest Sweyn, and it is more than likely that we two shall not be able to settle this matter by ourselves; and now my will is that thou bidest for me here, but I will go and back thy suit before all the people and earl Rognvald." Then the bishop goes to the meeting, and craves for a hearing, and when he got it, then the bishop pleads Sweyn's cause, and said for what cause he had fared away from the Orkneys, and what penalties earl Paul had laid on him for the slaying of Sweyn breastrope, that worst of men. Then the bishop begged of earl Rognvald for peace on Sweyn" part, and he begs it too of all the people. Then earl Rognvald answers: "I give my word that Sweyn shall have peace from me for three nights, but methinks, bishop, thou bearest that look beneath thy brow, as though ye two, Sweyn and thou, will be able to tell us of some great tidings which have not yet come out. My will is that thou takest Sweyn into thy keeping and be answerable for him, but I will have a talk with him on the morrow."" "Yes, yes," said the bishop, "willingly will he talk with you, and that as soon as may be, and he will become thy man if ye will take to him." The earl answers: "Methinks there are not over many friends of mine in this land, but still we must talk more together ere I agree to that." After that those four went aside to talk, earl Rognvald, Kol his father, the bishop, and Sweyn Asleif's son; then Sweyn tells them the lieve and the loath (14) of all that had passed between him and earl Paul; but they took that counsel to let most of the crowd of men fare away from the Thing. The earl stands up the morning after, and gave the men then leave to go home. But when the crowd of men broke up from the Thing, then he fetched this man and that man by himself to come and talk with them, and made all men first promise Sweyn peace who were by before he told the tidings. But the morning after Hacon churl, brother of earl Magnus the saint, was got to go and tell Sigurd of Westness and his sons of what had befallen the earl, and this too that he was not to be looked for to take up his rule, and that he was maimed. Sigurd says: "This methinks is great tidings about the earl's going away, but that methinks is heaviest of all that he is maimed, for there is no place whither he could have gone that I would not fare to find him out if he were hale." And so he had said to his friends afterwards, that Hacon should not have gone away unmaimed if he had had force enough when he [Hacon] told him this story, he took it so much to heart.

But after these tidings, all men in the Orkneys went over into earl Rognvald's hands, and now he became sole chief over that realm which earl Paul had owned. And not long after the ground plan was marked out for Magnus' church, and builders were gathered for it; and the work went on so fast in three years, that less was done in four or five thenceforth. Kol was the man who looked most after the workmanship of the building, and had most of the guidance as to the plan. But as the building went on, it grew costly to the earl, and his money was far spent. Then the earl sought for counsel to his father. But Kol gave him that advice that the earl should bring in a law to the effect that the earls had taken all freehold lands in inheritance after men, but that the heirs had to redeem them for their own, and that was thought rather hard. Then earl Rognvald made them call together a Thing, and offered the freemen the choice of buying their freeholds out and out, so that there was no need to redeem them. And that they agreed on among themselves, so that all were well pleased. But a mark was to be paid to the earl for every plough-land over all the isles. But thenceforth money was not lacking for the church building, and that building is wrought with much toil and pains.

ENDNOTES FOR CHAPTERS 71-80

1. Sweyn's; i.e. Sweyn Asleif's son's.

2. The Danish Translation reads: "Then he must have something on his conscience, and knows that he is guilty; else I will not believe that he has done this without cause."

3. Papay; Probably in Papay Westray.

4. The original of our "husting" or "hustings."

5. A group of islands near Bergen off the coast of Hördeland.

6. The Translation runs thus: "still less would I go thither with warriors, and therefore I will come afterwards with my plan, if I can think anything out by myself."

7. In the Translation the stratagem of Kol is thus described. "As if the ships were coming ever nearer and nearer as they hoisted the sails, though they scarcely moved on at all."

8. Fl. reads, "the earl asked the news of a skald who had been there."

9. daysman] "Neither is there any daysman betwixt us." --- Job ix. 33.

10. The Danish Translation adds, "and we will take in our sail."

11. Swelg] The "Swelchie," a wellknown eddy or whirlpool off the Caithness coast.

12. Ekkjalsbakka] No doubt Strath Oikel.

13. In chapter 59 they are said to have lived at Knarstead.

14. the lieve and the loath] that is he made a clean breast of it; he told them everything, whether it were pleasing or displeasing to them.

CHAPTER 81

When earl Rognvald had ruled two winters over the Orkneys, then he kept the Yule feast at one of his farms which is called Knarstead. It was the sixth Yule day, that a ship was seen faring from the south from the Pentland firth. The weather was good, and the earl stood out of doors, and many men by him, and looked and thought what that ship might be. That man was there whose name was Hrolf, and he was the earl's body-priest. And when these men came to land, then they went up from their ship, and the earl's men kept count of them and reckoned that they might be fifteen or sixteen men. But at the head of the band walked a man in a blue cape, and he had tucked his hair under the hood; he had shaven the beard from his chin in front, but his jaws and cheeks were unshaven, and there (the hair) hung down full and long. This man seemed rather strange to them (the earl's men), but Hrolf the Priest knew that man, and says that that was bishop John who had come down from Scotland out of Athole. Then the earl went to meet them, and gives the bishop a hearty welcome. The earl seated the bishop on his own high-seat, but waits himself at the board before him like a page. Next morning the bishop held mass early, and then he fared north to Egil's isle to see bishop William, and was there till the tenth Yule day. Then both the bishops fared to see earl Rognvald with a worthy following, and brought out their errand. They tell him of that agreement between Sweyn's Asleif's son and earl Maddad, that their son Harold should fare out into the Orkneys to be fostered by earl Rognvald, with this understanding that Harold should bear the title of earl, and have half the Orkneys with earl Rognvald, but they should both have one court, and that earl Rognvald should rule for both of them, and do so though Harold grew to be a man; and if each had a will of his own, then earl Rognvald was to have his way. Sweyn was there too, and brought this matter forward along with the bishop. So earl Rognvald and his friends took this counsel, that a meeting was fixed for the spring at Lent in Caithness, and then an agreement was made on those terms, and was bound by the oaths of the best men of the Orkneys and of Scotland. Then Harold Maddad's son fared out into the Orkneys with earl Rognvald, and there and then the title of earl was given him. Then Thorbjorn clerk fared unto the isles with earl Harold; he was a son of Thorstein the freeman and Gudrun Frakok's daughter; he was a wise man and of great weight; he then fostered earl Harold, and had great power over him. Thorbjorn took to himself a wife in the Orkneys, and got Ingirid (1) Olaf's daughter, Sweyn Asleif son's sister. Thorbjorn was then by turns either out there in the Orkneys or up in Scotland, and he was the boldest of men, and the most unfair overbearing man in most things. Sweyn Asleif's son took under him all those estates which his father Olaf and his brother Waltheof had owned; he then became a mighty chief, and always had a great company of men with him. He was a wise man and foresighted (2) about many things; an unfair overbearing man, and reckless towards others. There were not at that time those two men west across the sea, who were not of greater birth, who were thought of more power and weight than those brothers-in-law Sweyn and Thorbjorn. There was then between them great love.

687

CHAPTER 82

It fell out once that Sweyn Asleif's son came to talk with earl Rognvald, and asked that he would give him strength of men and ships to avenge on Oliver and Frakok the burning of his father Olaf. The earl spoke and said: "Do not think, Sweyn, that either of us need now look for harm at the hands of either Oliver or Frakok, a carline, who is fit for nothing." Sweyn answers: "There will always be harm at their hands so long as they live; and I must say I then looked for other things when I did my utmost for thy sake, than that thou shouldest not grant me such things [as I now ask]." The earl answers: "What help then shall I give thee which will please thee?" Sweyn answers: "Two ships well fitted and manned." The earl said it should be as he asked. And after that Sweyn busked him for that voyage, and when he was "boun" he sailed south to Broadfirth, and took the north-west wind to Dufeyra. (3) That is a market town in Scotland. But thence he sailed into the land along the shore of Murray and to Ekkjalsbakka. Thence he fared next of all to Athole to earl Maddad and lay at the place called Elgin. Then he [the earl] gave Sweyn guides, who knew the paths over fells and wastes, whither he wished to go. Thence he fared the upper way over fells and wood, above all places where men dwelt, and came out in Helmsdale, near the middle of Sutherland. But Oliver and his men had spies out everywhere where they thought that strife was to be looked for from the Orkneys, but on this way they did not at all look for warriors. So they were not ware of the host before Sweyn and his men had come to a slope at the back of Frakok's homestead. There came against them Oliver the unruly with sixty men; then they fell to battle at once, and there was a short struggle. Oliver and his men gave way towards the homestead, for they could not get to the wood. Then there was a great slaughter of men, but Oliver he fled away up to Helmsdale water, and swam across the river and so up on to the fell, and thence he fared to Scotland's firth, and so out to the Southern isles. And he is out of the story. But when Oliver drew off, Sweyn and his men fared straight up to the house and plundered it of everything, but after that they burnt the homestead, and all those men and women who were inside it. And there Frakok lost her life. Sweyn and his men did there the greatest harm in Sutherland ere they fared to their ships. After that they lay out that summer, and harried round Scotland. Sweyn came home at autumn to the Orkneys to see earl Rognvald; and he gave Sweyn a hearty welcome; then Sweyn fared across to the Ness to Duncansby, and sat there that winter. At that time came a message by word of mouth to Sweyn from Holdbodi out of the Southern isles, that Sweyn should come to help him, for thither to Tyree had come a Freeman from Wales, and had chased Holdbodi out of house and home, and had robbed him of much goods. That man was called Robert who was sent, English by kin. Sweyn bestirred himself at once when the message was sent to him, and came out into the Orkneys to meet earl Rognvald, and begged earl Rognvald that he would give him force and ships. The earl asked what Sweyn wanted to take in hand. He said that man had sent him word, to whom of all others he ought to be the last to say "nay," and who had stood him then in best stead, when he had most need when almost every one turned against him. The earl answers: "It were well then if ye two parted friends, but most South-islanders are untrue; but thou wilt be able to show thy manliness, and I will give thee two ships thoroughly manned." This pleases Sweyn well, and they fared then to the

Southern isles, and he did not find Holdbodi before he got as far west as Man, for he [Holdbodi] had fled away thither. But when Sweyn came to Man, then Holdbodi was fain to see him. And there in Man that Freeman from Wales had done great harm in plunderings and manslayings, and so wide about in the Southern-isles. Before him had fallen a man of birth and worth, whose name was Andrew; he left behind him a wife whose name was Ingirid, and a son whose name was Sigmund angle. Ingirid the housewife had much goods and a great homestead. Holdbodi gave Sweyn that advice to ask for her hand, but when that question was put to her, then she said that Sweyn must do that deed for his match, to avenge her husband Andrew. Sweyn answers that he might do the Welshmen some harm, "but I cannot tell how it will be fated as to loss of life." And after that those two, Sweyn and Holdbodi, went on warfare and had five ships. They harried round Wales, and went up on land at the place called Earlsness, and did there great mischief. It was one morning that they went up into a certain thorpe, and there was but a little struggle. The householders fled out of the thorpe, but Sweyn and his men plundered it of everything, and burnt six homesteads before their breakfast. There was then with Sweyn a man from Iceland, whose name was Eric, and he sang this stave: "Farms are in flames, But farmers are robbed; So hath Sweyn willed it, Six in one morning: Wild work enough too He wrought there to one man, Letting the leaseholder Livecoal on lease." After that they fared to their ship, and lay out that summer and got much war-spoil, but the Freeman ran away to that isle which is called Lund. (4) There was a good stronghold; Sweyn and Holdbodi sat before it for some time, and could do nothing. And they fared home in the autumn to Man.

CHAPTER 83

That winter Sweyn made his wedding-feast with Ingirid, and then sat there in great honour. Next spring he gathered men to him, and fared to see Holdbodi, and asked him for force of men, but he begged off, and said the men were many of them at work, but some were on trading voyages, and Sweyn got nothing of what he asked. But there was proof plain that the Freeman and Holdbodi had come to terms by stealth, and bound their bargain by gifts. But Sweyn fared away nevertheless, and had then three ships, and they got little spoil in goods at the beginning of the summer. But as time went on they fared south under Ireland, and took there a bark which the monks of the Scilly Isles owned and plundered it. He harried also far and wide on Ireland, and took there much goods, and they fared home at autumn to Man, and had a great force. Sweyn Asleif's son had sat there at home but a scant time, when he heard this rumour that Holdbodi would not be true to him but Sweyn would not hear of such a thing. And one night about winter those tidings happened, that Sweyn's watchmen came and said that strife was coming upon them. Sweyn and his men ran to their weapons and out of doors. They saw where men were coming with fire to the homestead, and they had a great band. Then Sweyn and his men sprung up on a hillock and defended themselves thence; they had horns and blew them. But that place is thickly peopled, and men flocked to help Sweyn and his band, so that the end of it was, that those who had come against them fell off. Sweyn and his men followed them up and chased them. There many men fell in the flight, but a crowd were wounded on either side ere they parted. But Holdbodi was the leader of this band, and he had taken himself off in the flight. He fared away till he came to Lundy; the Freeman gave him a hearty welcome, and they held together. Sweyn fared home, and had many men with him and kept good watch and ward, for he put little faith in the South-islanders. When the stores of Sweyn and his men began to fail, the folk quarrelled with him; and he sold his lands when the winter went on for money and goods, and fared early in the spring from the South to the Lewes, and stayed there a long time. He had done much mischief in this voyage.

CHAPTER 84

When Sweyn was in the Southern isles, earl Rognvald had fared to Caithness, and went to a feast at Wick with that man whose name was Hroald, his wife's name was Arnljot. Sweyn was the name of their son, and he was the briskest of men. But when the earl was at the feast, Thorbjorn clerk and his men came down from Scotland, and told these tidings that Thorstein the freeman his father was slain, and that a Scottish earl had slain him, but that earl's name was Waltheof. But men made that a matter of talk what a deal earl Rognvald and Thorbjorn had to say to one another, for the earl could scarce finish the business he had in hand for their talk. Thorbjorn fared thence out into the isles with the earl, but Sweyn Hroald's son then became the earl's waiting-man. Thorbjorn had then been for a while in Scotland; he had let two men be slain who had been at the burning of Frakok with Sweyn Asleif's son. But when Sweyn came out of the Southern isles, then he fared home to Gairsay to his house, but he did not go to see earl Rognvald as he was wont when he came off warfare. But when the earl heard that he was come home, he asked Thorbjorn if he thought he knew why it was that Sweyn would not come to see him. Thorbjorn answers: "This I guess, that Sweyn mislikes me, for that I let those men be slain who were with him at the burning of Frakok." The earl said: "I will not that ye two be at strife." And after that earl Rognvald fared to Gairsay, and tried to bring about an atonement between them, and that was easy, for they both were willing that the earl should settle the matter. After that he made them good friends for that time, and that settlement was kept a long time after.

CHAPTER 85

In that time a vessel from Iceland came to the Orkneys, and that man was on board whose name was Hall, son of Thorarin broad-paunch; he fared to live and lodge in Rinansey with Ragna and her son Thorstein. He was ill at ease there, and begged Thorstein that he would take him to earl Rognvald. They fared to find him, but the earl would not take him into his service; but when they came home, then Ragna asks how they had fared. Then Hall sang a song: "I sent thy son on an errand, Ragna, Man to man speaks words of truth; This his weighty calling was Place at court for me to ask; But the prince, of rings the waster, He who rules with glory highest, Says he has warriors enough; Said

'No' to neighbour of the brawn." A little after Ragna fared to see earl Rognvald on some errand of her own. She was so "boun" that she had a red cap on her head made of horsehair. And when the earl saw that, he sang: "Never have I heard that ladies, All of them if highly born, Wimples wore upon their heads; Soft-tongued grows not rings' assassin; (5) But now Ragna, gold-lands' fury, (6) Binds a mare's tail round her brow; She a bride in gay attire Goes to meet the wound-goose feeder." (7) Ragna said: "Now it comes to that which is often said that no man is so wise as to see everything as it is, for this is of a horse and not of a mare." She took then a silken cloth, and threw it over her head as a wimple, and still went on talking of her affairs. The earl was rather slow in listening to her at first, but afterwards softened down his speech as she went on, and she got her business settled as she wished, and leave for Hall to live at the earl's court. And he was there long afterwards with earl Rognvald. They made both of them together the old Key to Verse-making, and let there be five strophes in each metre, but then the song seemed too long, and now two strophes are sung in each metre.

CHAPTER 86

It is said that Sweyn Asleif's son heard how Holdbodi was come into the Southern isles, then he begged Earl Rognvald to give him strength to avenge himself. The earl gave him five ships, and Thorbjorn clerk steered one of them, but Haflidi son of Thorkell flayer the second, Duffnjal son of Havard Gunni's son the third, Richard Thorleif's son the fourth, Sweyn Asleif's son the fifth. But as soon as ever Holdbodi heard of Sweyn, then he fled back south to Lundy; and his fellows took him to them. Sweyn and his companions slew many men in the Southern isles, but plundered and burnt far and wide. They got much goods, but they could not get at Holdbodi, and he never came back to the Southern isles afterwards. Sweyn wanted to be in the Southern isles that winter, but Thorbjorn and the rest wished to go home, and so late in the autumn they fared from the south to Caithness, and came to Duncansby. And when they were to share their war-spoil, then Sweyn said that all should have an even share, save himself, who was to have a chief's share, for he said he alone had led them, and said the earl had given them to him as help. He said too he was the only one who had any quarrel with the South-islanders, but they had none. But Thorbjorn thought he had not done a bit less work, and been not a whit less a leader than Sweyn. They wished also that all the ship-captains should have an even share. But the end of it was that Sweyn had his way, for he had many more men to back him there on the Ness. But Thorbjorn fared out to the Orkneys to find earl Rognvald, and told him how things had gone between them and Sweyn, and how ill pleased they were that he had robbed them of their shares. The earl said it would not be the only time that Sweyn would be found to be no fair man in his dealings, "but still the day will come when he will take his pay for his wrong-doings. But ye shall not strive with him about this. I will give you as much out of my goods as ye lose by him; my will also is that ye make no claim against him for this, and it will be well if greater difficulties do not flow from him; though I fear that we shall not have long to wait for this." Thorbjorn answers: "God thank you, lord, for this honour which ye do to us, and we will not strive with Sweyn about this, but never hereafter will I be his friend, and I will do him some dishonour instead of this." And after that Thorbjorn declares himself parted from Ingirid Sweyn's sister, and sent her over to the Ness to Sweyn. He gave her a hearty welcome, but thought great shame had been done to him. Then there was feud between them, and it came to what the saw says, "Set a thief to catch a thief." But still neither now plotted openly against the other.

When Sweyn was in the Souther-isles, he had set Margad Grim's son in Duncansby to govern it, and given into his hand that charge (8) which he held of earl Rognvald. But Margad was quibbling and quarrelsome, and he became hated for his unfairness. But those who were most sufferers by his unfairness ran off to find master Hroald and kept themselves there with him. From that a feud arose between Hroald and Margad. A little after Sweyn had come home Margad fared south to Wick with nineteen men on some business of his own. And ere he came from the south he made an onslaught on master Hroald's house and slew him and some men more. After that they fared to Duncansby to find Sweyn. Then Sweyn gathers men and fares to Lambburg, and got the place ready. There was a good stronghold, and there he sat with sixty men, and flitted thither for himself food and other stores, which they needed to have. The burg stood on some sea-crags, but at the top on the land side there was a stone wall well built. The rocks went far along the sea the other way. They did there much mischief in Caithness in robberies, and flitted thither their spoil into the burg, and they became much hated.

CHAPTER 87

These tidings came to the ears of earl Rognvald and Sweyn Hroald's son; Sweyn begged the earl for help that he might set this matter straight; many men backed this prayer with Sweyn. So it came about that earl Rognvald bestirred himself and fared over to the Ness, and these chiefs with him; Thorbjorn, Haflidi Thorkel's son, Duffnjal Havard's son, and Richard, and they were the worst in their counsel against Sweyn. They fared to Duncansby, and Sweyn was then away. It was said that he had fared south to Wick, and they fared thither. But when they came there they heard that Sweyn was in Lambburg. Then the earl and his men fared thither. And when they came to the burg, then Sweyn asks who ruled over the band. He was told that Earl Rognvald ruled over it. Sweyn greeted him well and asked the earl after his errand. The earl answers that he wills that he should hand over Margad into their power. Sweyn asks whether he shall have peace. The earl said he would not promise that. Then Sweyn said: "I cannot find it in my heart to give Margad up to the power of Sweyn Hroald's son and his band, or any other of my foes, those I mean who are with you, but willingly would I be atoned with you, lord." Then Thorbjorn clerk answers: "Hear now what the lord's traitor says, that he will willingly be atoned; but he has already robbed his land, and lain out like a thief. Ill repayest thou the earl the many honours which he has done to thee, as thou wilt [repay] all those over whom thou mayest be able to come." Sweyn answers: "Thou hast no need Thorbjorn, to throw in so much talk here, for it will not be done after thy words. But that is my foreboding that thou wilt repay him in the worst way the honour that he has done thee ere ye two part, for that none will ever reap luck from thee who have aught to do with thee." Then earl Rognvald bade that men should not rail at one another. After that they sat themselves down round the burg, and forbade all ingoings of food, and so it went on for a long time that they could do nothing in the way of attack. And when their food was wellnigh spent, then Sweyn called his men together and sought counsel of them, but all men spoke with one mouth that they would have his guidance and foresight while they had the choice of it. Then Sweyn took to words, and said: "It seems to me most unworthy to starve here, but after all to fall into the power of one's foes. And this too has gone, as was likely, [and proves] that we lack both wit and luck when matched with earl Rognvald. And here now it was tried to bring about peace and atonement, but neither could be got for Margad my companion; but though I know that all other men here will have a choice of peace, yet I cannot find it in my heart to hand him over [to fall] under the axe. Now it is not right that so many should pay for his perplexity, though I dare not part from him even yet." And after this Sweyn took that counsel to knit together those ropes that they had. But at night then they let Sweyn and Margad slip down out of the burg into the sea. And after that they took to swimming, and struck out along the rocks till the cliffs broke off. After that they stepped on land, and fared up into Sutherland, and so to Murray, and thence to Dufeyri. There they found some Orkneymen in a ship of burden; the man's name was Hallvard who was their chief, but the second's name was Thorkell; they were ten in all. Sweyn and Margad went on board ship with them, and they twelve together fared in the ship of burden south off Scotland till they came to the isle of May. There was then a monastery. Baldwin was the abbot's name who ruled over it. There Sweyn and his men were seven nights weather-bound, and said that they were sent to find the Scot-king from earl Rognvald. The monks doubted their story, and thought they were robbers, and sent to the land for men. But when Sweyn and his men were ware of that, then they sprang on shipboard and plundered the place of much goods. They fared away and in up Murkfirth. (9) They found in Edinburgh David the Scot-king; he gave Sweyn a hearty welcome, and bade them stay with him. Sweyn told the king the whole story of his coming thither, and how things had gone between him and earl Rognvald ere they parted, and so also that they had robbed in the isle of May. Sweyn and his men were there for a while with the Scot-king in good cheer. King David sent men to those men who had lost goods at Sweyn's hands in his voyage, and let them put their own worth on their scathe, but made good with his own money to each his loss. King David offered Sweyn to send and fetch his wife from the Orkneys, but to give him such honour in Scotland as he might well be pleased with. Sweyn laid bare his will before the king, and spoke thus that his wish was that Margad should be there behind with the king, but that he should send word to earl Rognvald that he should take an atonement at his hand, but Sweyn says that he was ready to lay all his suit in earl Rognvald's power; he said he would ever be well-pleased if they were good friends, but ill-pleased if they were foes. King David answers: "It is now clear both that this earl must be worthy, and besides that ye think that only worth having which looks towards him; for now thou riskest all on his good faith, but givest up that which we offer thee." Sweyn says he will never give up his friendship, but still says that he must beg the king to grant him this. The king said so it should be. King David sent men north into the Orkneys with gifts, and this message, that the earl should take atonement from Sweyn. Then

Sweyn too fared north into the isles, but Margad stayed behind with the king. King David's messengers fared to find earl Rognvald. He gave them a hearty welcome, took the gifts too which the king sent him, and gave his word as to the atonement. He took Sweyn after that into his peace and full friendship, and then he [Sweyn] fared back to his house.

CHAPTER 88

When Sweyn and Margad were away out of Lambburg, those who were in the burg took that counsel to give up the place into earl Rognvald's power. He asked what was the last they knew of Sweyn and Margad; but they told him all about it. And when the earl heard that, he said: "Sooth it is to say that no man is Sweyn's match of all those men of whom we have a choice here with us; such deeds are both manly and hardy. But I will not be a dastard towards you, though ye have been woven up in this difficulty with Sweyn; each of you shall fare away in peace from before me." The earl fared home thence to the Orkneys, but sent Thorbjorn clerk with forty men on board a ship south to Broadfirth to look after Sweyn and Margad, and naught could be heard of him. Then Thorbjorn speaks out and tells them that they are going on wondrously: "Here we are driving along ever so far at Sweyn's heels, but we have heard that earl Waltheof my father's bane-man is but a short way hence with a small following of men. And now if ye will fare with me against him, then will I give you my word that I shall not behave as Sweyn, that I should make you robbed of your share if war-spoil falls into our hands; for those goods which we shall get ye shall have, but allot me that only which ye please, for methinks fame is better than fee." After that they fared to where earl Waltheof was at a feast, and took the house over their heads, and set fire to it at once. Waltheof and his men ran to the doors, and asked who was master of that fire. Thorbjorn said who he was. Waltheof offered atonement for the slaying of Thorstein, but Thorbjorn said there was no need to seek for a settlement. Waltheof and his men defended themselves well for a while. But when the fire pressed them hard, they sprang out, and then their defence lasted but a short while, for they were much worn out by the fire. There fell earl Waltheof and thirty men with him. There Thorbjorn and his men got much goods, and he kept all his promise manfully by his men; they fared after that out to the Orkneys to find earl Rognvald, and he showed that he was well pleased at their errand. Then it was quiet in the isles, and there was good peace.

In that time dwelt at Wyre, in the Orkneys, Kolbein the burly, a man from Norway, and he was a very mighty man; he built him a good stone-castle there; that was a safe stronghold. Kolbein had to wife Herbjorg, a sister of Hacon bairn, but their mother was Sigrid a daughter of Herborg, Paul's daughter. These were their children: Kolbein carle, Bjarni skald, Summerled, Aslak, Frida. They were all of might and mark.

CHAPTER 89

In that time the sons of Harold Gilli ruled over Norway. Ingi and Sigurd were children in years. Then liegemen were chosen as councillors to those brothers. Eystein was the eldest of them. But Ingi was lawfully begotten, and the liegemen paid most honour to him; he let them have their own way in everything as they chose. In that time these liegemen had most to do with his counsel, Ogmund and Erling, the sons of Kyrping-Worm. They took that counsel with king Ingi, that he should send word to earl Rognvald, and give him a seemly bidding to come and see him. They said, as was true, that the earl had been a great friend of his father, and they bade him to behave as lovingly as he could to the earl, so that he might be more his friend than his brothers', whatever might arise between them. The earl was a kinsman of those brothers, (10) and one of their greatest friends. But when these words came to earl Rognvald, he listened to them quickly, and busks him for his voyage, for he was eager to fare to Norway to see his kinsfolk and friends. On this voyage earl Harold begged to go for the sake of curiosity and pastime; he was then fourteen or fifteen years old. And when the earls were "boun," they fared from the west with chapmen, and had a proper following, and came in the spring early to Norway. They found king Ingi in Bergen, and king Ingi gave them a very hearty welcome; there earl Rognvald found many of his kinsfolk and friends; he stayed there very long that summer. That summer came from abroad, from Micklegarth, (11) Eindrid the young; he had been there long in [the Emperor's] service; he was able to tell them many tidings thence, and men thought it a pastime to ask him about things that had happened abroad out in the world. The earl often talked with him. And once on a time when they were talking, then Eindrid said: "Methinks it is wonderful, earl, that thou wilt not fare out to Jewry, and not have stories alone as to the tidings which are to be told thence. That is the fittest place for such men as thou for the sake of your skill; thou wilt be best honoured there when thou fallest in with men of rank." And when Eindrid had said that, many others backed it with him, and egged the earl on that he should become the leader of this voyage. Erling threw in many words in favour of it, and said that he would make up his mind to join the voyage, if the earl would become their leader. And so, when so many men of rank and birth were eager, then the earl gave his word to go on the voyage. And when the earl and Erling made up their minds to this, then many great men chose to go on this voyage. These liegemen: Eindrid the young shall tell them the way, John Peter's son, Aslak Erlend's son, and Gudorm Mjola-pate of Helgeland. It was agreed that none of them should have a larger ship than one but the earl should have a carved or painted or gilded ship. That should be done so that no man might envy another for that one had fitted out his ship or his crew better than another; John limp-leg shall get a ship made for the earl to sail abroad in, and take the greatest pains with it.

Earl Rognvald fared home west in the autumn, and meant to sit two winters in his realm. King Ingi gave the earl two long-ships, rather small but very handsome, and made most for rowing, and they were the fastest of all ships. Earl Rognvald gave one ship to earl Harold; that was named "Arrow," but the other was named "Help." In these ships the earls held on west across the sea. Earl Rognvald had also taken great gifts from his friends. It was on Tuesday evening that the earl's put to sea, and they sailed with a very good wind that night; and the wind began to get high. Midweek-day (Wednesday) there was a mighty storm, but on Thursday night they were ware of land. It was then very dark. They saw the surf of breakers on every side about them. They had sailed in company up to this. Then there was no other choice than to sail on and dash both ships to pieces, and so they did. There were rocks a-head, and a little strip of foreshore, but all the rest above cliffs. There all the men were saved, but they lost much goods; some of it was thrown ashore in the night. Earl Rognvald behaved himself then still best of all men, as he ever did. He was so merry, that he played with his fingers and made verses nearly at every word. He drew his finger-ring off his finger with his lips and sang a song:

> "Here I hang with hammer bent
>
> The hanger of the falcon's seat, (12)
>
> On the gallows of the hawk's bridge (13)
>
> Golden ring to Odin's draught; (14)
>
> Cave-dwellers of giant voice
>
> Me so glad your pine hath made,
>
> That I play now with my fingers,
>
> Perch of hawk that harries geese."

And when they had got together their baggage, they fared up into the country to look for dwellings, for they thought they knew that they must have come to Shetland. They found homesteads speedily, and then the men were shared out amongst the houses of the district. Men were fain to see the earl where he came, and the mistress asked about his voyage. The earl sang a song:

> "There was a crash when ocean billow
>
> Crushed to pieces, Help and Arrow;
>
> To those wives the storm brought sorrow,
>
> Wild waves threatened men with scathe;
>
> I see this voyage of ready-witted
>
> Earls, will long be had in mind;
>
> Hard work surely had the seamen
>
> To withstand the watery shock."

The housewife bore a cloak of skin to the earl instead of a cloak; he took it laughingly, and reached out his hands towards her and sang:

> "Here I shake a wrinkled skin-cloak,
>
> Strangely scanty is my dress;
>
> That ship-plain that stands o'er our
>
> Plaids and mantles rises high;

Still perhaps attired more bravely

From the eel-mead's briny horse (15)

We may go; against the rocks

Dashed the surf the yardarm's steed."

Then great fires were made for them, and they roasted themselves at the fires. Asa was the name of the waiting-maid. She went out for water, and another woman with her. But when they came to the water Asa stumbled into the well in the fog; but she ran home much chilled and spoke between her shiverings, and men could not make out what she said. The earl says he knows her tongue, and sang:

"Be quiet, now, alas! but Asa

Atatata! in water lieth;

Hutututu! where by the fire

Shall I sit? I'm very cold."

The earl sends twelve of his men to Einar in Gullberwick, but he said he would not take them in unless the earl came himself. And when earl Rognvald hears that, then he sang:

"Einar says that he will nourish

None of Rognvald's trusty men

Save the earl himself; now Odin's

Ocean(16) rises in my throat;

Well I know the stout of heart

Ne'er yet broke his word to men;

Late at even in I went

Where the fires brightly blazed."

This even happened one day south in Dynröstvoe in Shetland, that an old and poor householder waited long for his mate, but all the boats rowed out, each as it was manned. Then came a man to the old householder in a white cowl; and asked why he did not row out a-fishing like other men. The householder says that his mate was not come. "Master," says the cowl-man wilt "thou that I row with thee?" "That I will" says the householder, "but still I must have the lot which falls to my boat; for I have many bairns at home, and I work for them as well as I can." After that they rowed out off Dynrösthead and inside the Hundholms. There was a strong current there where they lay and great eddies; they had to lie in the eddy and fish in the race. The cowl-man sat in the bow and paddled against the tide; but the householder was to fish. The householder bade him mind that they were not borne into the race; for then he said they would run great risks. The cowl-man did not behave as he bade him, and cared not though the householder came into a little danger. A little after they were borne into the race, and the householder was very scared and said "Wretch that I was

697

for my ill-luck when I took you today to row; for here I must die; but my folk at home have no one to help them, and will all come to beggary if I am lost." And the householder was so afraid that he wept, and he dreaded that his death was nigh. The cowl-man answers, "Be cheerful master, and do not weep; for he will pull us two out of the race who let us fall into it." After that the cowl-man rowed out of the race, and the householder was very glad at that. Then they rowed to land, and put up the boat. And the householder bade the cowl-man to go with him and share the fish. But the cowl-man told the householder to share them as he liked; he says he will not have more than his third. There was much folk come down to the strand, both men and women, and many needy folk. The cowl-man gave the poor all the fish which had fallen to his lot that day; and then he made ready to go away. There was a steep slope to walk up, and many woman sat on the slope. But as he went up the slope his foot slipped, for it was slippery after rain, and he fell down from the slope. A woman was the first to see that and laughed loud at him, and after her other folk. But when the cowl-man heard that he sang:

> "The nymph of silk with eyes of fire,
>
> Louder laughs the lovely may,
>
> Than she aught at my array:
>
> Few can tell an earl indeed,
>
> Thus disguised in fisher's weed,
>
> Yet through billows danger scorning,
>
> I drew the boat this early morning."

After that the cowl-man went away; and men became aware later that this cowl-man had been earl Rognvald. It became also known afterwards to many men that there had been many such feats of his which were both helpful in the sight of God, and pleasant in the eyes of men. Men reckoned (to him) also as a proverb what stood in the verse that "Few can tell an earl in fisher's weeds."

The earl stayed very long in Shetland, and fared in the autumn south to the Orkneys, and sat in his realm. That autumn two Iceland men came to him, the one's name was Armod, and he was a skald; the other's Oddi the little Glum's son, a man from Broadfirth, and he too made good verses. The earl took to them both and gave them board and lodging in his train. The earl had a great Yule feast, and bade men to it and gave gifts. He reached out a spear inlaid with gold to Armod skald, and shook it as he did that, and bade him make a song in return. [Armod sang]:

> "The best of chiefs, of Odin's storm
>
> The rouser, does not trust his gifts
>
> To other men to bring to me,
>
> The poet who will sound his praise;
>
> The noble warder of the land,
>
> The first of kings, to Armod bore

This best blood-taper (17) bright with gold,

And placed the weapon in his hand."

It fell out one day about Yule that men were looking at the hangings; then the earl said to Oddi the little: "Make thou a song about the behaviour of that man who is there on the hanging, and have thou thy song sung when I have ended my song; and mind and have none of those words in thy song that I have in my song." The earl sang:

"The ring lord of the falcon's seat

Who, old in years, stands on the hanging

Down from his shoulder by his side;

Bandy-legs will not move forward,

Through the grove of Ocean's brightness

Waxes wrath with him who loves

The icicle of battle-hour."

Oddi sang:

"Sword-god here with stooping shoulders

Stands, and thinks to hew with sword

His rival in a woman's love

At the door of yonder tent;

He will do the men a mischief

With his sword; and now 'tis time

For the loaders of the sea-skates

To make friends ere wounds are given."

It happened one day that a mad man got loose from his bonds, and rushed at earl Rognvald; and clutched him so fast that the earl all but tottered to his fall. Then the earl sang a song:

"At the mantle of the monarch

The sturdy beggar caught and clutched,

The carle was on the eve of hurling

Hard to earth the liberal lord;

Still the tree of steel stood upright,

Though men said they saw him stagger;

Might enow the sword-edge scatterer

Careful keeps to hold his own."

The earl had also bishop William at his feast that Yule, and many of his chieftains. Then he laid bare his plans how he meant to go away from the land and out to Jewry; he begged the bishop to go with him on his voyage. The bishop was a Paris clerk, and the earl wished above all things that he should be their spokesman. The bishop promised to go with him.

CHAPTER 90

These men made ready to go with earl Rognvald: Magnus, son of Havard Gunni's son, and Sweyn Hroald's son. They were captains of ships both of them. These fared of the lesser men, so far as they are named: Thorgeir Scotpoll, Oddi the little, Thorbjorn the swarthy, and Armod. These were the earl's skalds. Then there were also these men: Thorkell crook-eye, and Grimkel of Glettness, and Blian, son of Thorstein of Flydruness. --- And when those two winters were spent which they were to have to get ready, earl Rognvald fared out of the Orkneys east to Norway early in the spring, and wished to know how those liegemen got on with their outfit. And when the earl came to Bergen, he found there Erling wryneck and John limp-leg the earl's brother-in-law. There too had come Aslak, but Gudorm came a little after. There too was that ship off the wharf which John had got made for the earl; it had five-and-thirty seats for rowers, and was a very careful piece of work, and the figure-head and taffrail and weather-vanes were all overlaid with gold, and she was carved and painted in many other places; the ship was the greatest treasure of her kind. Eindrid came also from time to time to the town that summer, and always says that he would be boun the week after; but men were ill-pleased when they had to wait so long. Some wished that he should not be waited for, and said that men had sailed on such voyages before though Eindrid were not with them. And a little while after Eindrid came to the town and gave out that he was then boun, and then the earl bade him set sail as soon as ever he thought he was like to get a fair wind. And when that day came that they thought they had a good chance, they pulled out of the town and took to their sails. The wind was rather light, and the earl's ship made little way, for she needed a good breeze. The other chiefs slackened sail, and would not sail away from the earl. But as they drew away from among the isles, the wind began to get sharp, and then it grew so high that they had to reef sail on board the smaller ships, but the earl's ship began to walk fast. Then they saw two big ships sailing after them and at once by and beyond them. One of those ships was a work of much pains, it was a drake; both the head forward and the coils aft were much gilded. It was gay and gaudy, and painted all above the water-line wherever it seemed to look well. The earl's men said that there must Eindrid be sailing, "and he has kept little to that which was laid down, that no one should have a carved or gilded ship but thou, lord." The earl says: "Great is Eindrid's pride. But now there is this excuse for his refusing to be equal with us that we have been so far wrong in our opinion as to him; but it is hard to see whether luck goes before him or after him; we will not shape our course after his haste." Then Eindrid bore speedily away from them in that big ship, but the earl kept in company with his ships, and they had a good passage. They came about autumn to the Orkneys safe and sound. Then it was thought best that they should sit there that winter; some sat at their own cost, but some were with the householders, and many with the earl. --- In the isles there was great stir that winter, and the Easterlings and the Orkneyingers fell asunder about bargains and love-matters, and many quarrels sprang up. The earl took great pains to keep watch on those on both sides who thought they wre bound to repay him for all the good he had done them, and that they were worthy of all good from him. --- Of Eindrid and his messmates that is to be told that they came to Shetland; and he dashed there that good ship to splinters and lost much goods, but the lesser ship was saved. Eindrid was that winter in Shetland, and sent men east to Norway to let them build him a ship for his voyage abroad.

There was a man named Arni spindleshanks, a messmate of Eindrid's; he fared south into the Orkneys that winter and nine of his companions with him. Arni was a very unfair man and bold and strong. He and his companions sat at his own cost in one of the isles that winter. Arni buys malt and cattle for slaughter from a tenant of Sweyn Asleif's son; but when he asked for the price, Arni put him off. And a second time, when he asked for it, he was paid with threats, and ere they parted Arni gave him a blow with the back of his axe and said this: "Go now and tell that champion Sweyn with whom thou art ever threatening us, and let him set thy lot straight; thou wilt not need more than this." The husbandman went and told Sweyn and bade him set his lot straight. Sweyn answers shortly about it, and said he could make no promise about it. It was one day about spring that Sweyn fared to get in his rents; they were four of them in an eight-oared boat. Their course lay by that isle in which Arni and his men sat. Sweyn told his men to pull in towards the land, but there was a strong ebb tide on. Sweyn went on shore alone, and had his hand-axe in his hand and no other weapons. He bade them watch the boat so that the ebb did not leave it high and dry. Arni and his men sat in an outhouse a short way from the sea. Sweyn went up to the outhouse and into it. Arni and five of his men were inside and hailed Sweyn; he took their greeting, and spoke to Arni, and told him that he must pay up his debt to the husbandman. Arni said there was good time still for that. Sweyn bade him do as he asked him, and pay up the debt. Arni said he would not do so for all that. Sweyn said he would only ask him for a little more, and with that he struck his axe against Arni's head, so that it went up to the back of the blade, and he lost his hold of the axe. Sweyn sprang out, but Arni's messmates looked to him, but some ran after Sweyn down into the mud. So they ran along the shore and one was fleetest; Sweyn and his pursuer were then at very close quarters. Great sea-weed tangles lay on the shore in the mud. Sweyn caught up one of the tangles and dashed it into the face of him who was nearest to him, sand and all. This man took to rubbing his eyes with both hands, and wiped the sand out of them. But Sweyn got clear off to his boat, and fared home to Gairsay to his house. A little while after Sweyn fared over to the Ness on an errand of his own; he sent word to earl Rognvald that he should take an atonement for the slaying of Arni spindleshanks. And as soon as these words came to him, he [the earl] summoned to him all those who had the blood feud for the slaying of Arni, and made matters up with them, so that they were pleased, and he paid up the fine himself. Much other mischief the earl made good with his own money that was wrought that winter both by the Easterlings and Orkneyingers, for they had pulled very ill together. In the spring very early the earl summoned a crowded Thing in Hrossey; thither came all the chiefs who were in his realm. Then he made it bare to them that he meant to go out of the land to Jewry, and says that he would give over his realm into the hands of Harold Maddod's son, his kinsman. He begged this that all would follow him like true men in whatever he might need while he was away. Earl Harold was then nearly a man of twenty. (18) He was a tall man of growth, and stout and strong, an ugly man and wise enough, and men thought him a likely man for a chief. Thorbjorn clerk had then most share in ruling the land with him when earl Rognvald first fared out of the Orkneys.

ENDNOTES FOR CHAPTERS 81-90

1. Thus in the text and in the Danish Translation. In chap. 59. she is called Ingigerd, cf. ch. 86, below.

2. foresighted] This word implies that he had a supernatural foreknowledge of many things which were about to happen. We have the remnant of this old belief in the Scottish "second sight."

3. Deveron. (?)

4. Lund] Lundy island in the Bristol Channel.

5. A "kenning" or periphrasis for king or earl.

6. A periphrasis for lady.

7. A periphrasis for hawk, and "the wound-goose feeder," a periphrasis for chief or earl.

8. charge] Swayn was earl Rognvald's sýslumaðr, i.e. his "steward" or "bailiff," in Caithness, whose office it was to collect the earl's income from taxes, fines, and dues. When Sweyn went to the Southern isles he handed over these duties to Margad as his deputy.

9. Murk-firth] The Firth of Forth.

10. i.e. of Ogmund and Erling.

11. Constantinople.

12. A periphrasis for ring which hangs on the hand, the falcon's seat.

13. Another periphrasis for the hand.

14. A periphrasis for "poetry."

15. This and "the yard-arm's steed" are periphrasis for "a ship."

16. A periphrasis for "song."

17. A periphrasis for a sword.

18. man of twenty] He was then between eighteen and nineteen.

CHAPTER 91

Earl Rognvald busked him that summer to leave the Orkneys, and he was rather late boun, for they had a long while to wait for Eindrid, as his ship did not come from Norway which he had let be made there the winter before. But when they were boun, they held on their course away from the Orkneys in fifteen big ships. These were then the ship-captains; earl Rognvald, bishop William, Erling wry-neck, Aslak Erlend's son, Gudorm, Mjola-pate of Helgeland, Magnus Havard's son, Sweyn Hroald's son, Eindrid the young, John Peter's son limpleg, and those five whose names are not told. They were Eindrid's men. They sailed away from the Orkneys, and south to Scotland, and so on to England, and as they sailed by Northumberland, off Humbermouth, Armod sang a song:

> "The sea was high off Humbermouth
>
> When our ships were beating out,
>
> Bends the mast and sinks the land
>
> 'Neath our lee off Vesla-sand;
>
> Wave with veil of foam that rises
>
> Drives not in the eyes of him
>
> Who now sits at home; the stripling
>
> From the meeting rideth dry."

They sailed thence south round England and to France. (1) Nothing is said of their voyage before that they came to that seaburg which is named Nerbon. (2) There these tidings had happened, that the earl who before had ruled the town was dead; his name was Germanus; he left behind him a daughter young and fair, whose name was Ermingerd. She kept watch and ward over her father's inheritance with the counsel of the most noble men of her kinsfolk. They gave that counsel to the queen that she should bid the earl to a worthy feast, and said that by that she would be famous if she welcomed heartily such men of rank who had come so far to see her, and who would bear her fame still further. The queen bade them see to that. And when this counsel had been agreed on by them, men were sent to the earl and he was told that the queen bade him to a feast with as many of his men as he chose to bring with him. The earl of his men bidding with thanks; he chose out all his best men for this journey with him. And when they came to the feast, there was the best cheer, and nothing was spared which could do the earl more honour than he had ever met before. One day it happened as the earl sat at the feast that the queen came into the hall and many women with her, she held a beaker of gold in her hand. She was dressed in the best clothes, had her hair loose as maidens wont to have, and had put a golden band round her brow. She poured the wine into the earl's cup, but her maidens danced before them. The earl took her hand and the beaker too and set her on his knee, and they talked much that day. Then the earl sang a song:

703

"Sure it is, O lady lovely,

That thy stature far outvies

Form of women whose attire

Gleams well fringed with Frodi's meal; (3)

Locks as soft as yellow silk,

Lets the maiden downward fall

On her shoulders; I have reddened

Eager eagles' crooked claws."

The earl stayed there very long in the best of cheer. The townsmen pressed the earl to settle down there, and spoke out loudly about how they would give him the lady to wife. The earl said he would fare on that voyage which he had purposed, but said he would come thither as he fared back, and then they could carry out their plan [or not] as they pleased. After that the earl busked him away thence with his fellow voyagers. And as they sailed west of Thrasness they have a good wind; then they sat and drank and were very merry. Then the earl sang a song:

"Noble youth will long remember

Words which Ermingerda spoke;

Brave bride wills that we should ride

O'er Ran's home to Jordan's stream;

But when back the water-horse's

Woods (4) fare north across the wave,

He will cut the whale-land then

Home to Nerbon at the fall."

This Armod sang:

"Unless changes my fate hard,

I shall fair Ermingerd

Ne'er meet again;

Many nurseth for that noble maiden his pain;

Were I not blessed in slumbering ---

'Twere luck past all numbering ---

One night by her side;

The fairest of faces hath surely that bride."

Oddi the little sang a song:

"We are scarcely, as I ween,

Worthy of fair Ermingerd;

Well I know that noble crown-land

May be called the king of queens;

For it well befits that goddess

Of the ringfield's fire to find

A better husband altogether;

May she live blest 'neath seat of sun."

CHAPTER 92

They fared till they came west to Galicialand in the winter before Yule, and meant to sit there Yule over. They dealt with the landsmen and begged them to set them a market to buy food; for the land was barren and bad for food; for the land was barren and bad for food, and the landsmen thought it hard to feed that host of men. Now these tidings had happened there, that in that land sat a chief, who was a stranger, in a castle, and he had laid on the landsmen very heavy burdens. He harried them on the spot if they did not agree at once to all that he asked, and he offered them the greatest tyranny and oppression. And when the earl spoke to the landsmen about bringing him food to buy, they made him that offer, that they would set them up a market thenceforth on till Lent, but they must rid them in some way or other of the men in the castle; but earl Rognvald was to bear the brunt in return for the right of having all the goods that were gotten from them. The earl laid this bare before his men, and sought counsel from them as to which choice he should take, but most of them were eager to fall on the castlemen, and thought it bid fair for spoil. And so earl Rognvald and his host went into that agreement with the landsmen. But when it drew near to Yule, earl Rognvald called his men to a talk and said: "Now have we sat here awhile, and yet we have had nothing to do with the castlemen, but the landsmen are getting rather slack in their dealings with us; methinks they think that what we promised them will have no fulfilment; but still that is not manly not to turn our hands to what we have promised. Now, kinsman Erling will I take counsel from you in what way we shall win the castle, for I know that ye are here some of you the greatest men for good counsel; but still I will beg all those men who are here that each will throw in what [he thinks] is likeliest to be worth trying." Erling answered the earl's speech: "I will not be silent at your bidding, but I am not a man for counsel; and it would be better rather to call on those men for that who have seen more, and are more wont to such exploits, as is Eindrid the young. But here it will be as the saying goes, 'You must shoot at a bird before you get him.' And so we will try to give some counsel whatever comes of it. We shall today, if it seems to you not bad counsel or to the other shipmasters, go all of us to the wood, and bear each of us three shoulder-bundles of faggots on our backs under the castle; for it seems to me as though the lime will not be trusty if a great fire is brought to it. We shall let this go on for the three next days and see what turn things take." They did as Erling bade.

And when that toil was over, it was come right on to Yule. The bishop would not let them make their onslaught while the Yule high feast stood over them.

That chief's name was Godfrey who dwelt in the castle; he was a wise man and somewhat stricken in years. He was a good clerk, and had fared far and wide, and knew many tongues. He was a grasping man and a very unfair man. He calls together his men when he saw their [Rognvald's] undertakings, and said to them: "This scheme seems to me clever and harmful to us which the Northmen have taken in hand; it will befall us thus if fire is borne against us, that the stone wall round the castle will be untrusty, but the Northmen are strong and brave; we shall have to look for a sharp fight from them if they get a chance. I will now take counsel with you what shall be done in this strait which has befallen us." But his men all bade him see to that for them. Then he began to speak, and said: "My first counsel is that ye shall bind a cord round me and let me slide down the castle wall tonight. I shall have on bad clothes and fare into the camp of the Northmen, and know what I can find out." This counsel was taken as he had laid it down. And when Godfrey came to earl Rognvald, and said he was an old beggar carle, and spoke in Spanish; they understood that tongue best. He fared about among all the booths and begged for food. He found out that there was great envy and splitting into parties amongst the Northmen. Eindrid was the head of one side, but the earl of the other. Godfrey came to Eindrid and got to talk with him, and brought that before him that the chief who held the castle had sent him thither. "He will have fellowship with thee, and he hopes that thou wilt give him peace if the caste be won; he would rather that thou shouldst have his treasures, if thou wilt do so much in return for them, than those who would rather see him a dead man." Of such things they talked and much besides. But the earl was kept in the dark; all this went on by stealth at first. And when Godfrey had stayed a while with the earl's men, then he turned back to his men. But this was why they did not flit what they owned out of the castle, because they did not know whether the storm would take place at all; besides they could not trust the landfolk.

CHAPTER 93

It was the tenth day of Yule that earl Rognvald rose up. The weather was good. Then he bade his men put on their arms, and let the host be called up to the castle with the trumpet. Then they drew the wood towards it, and piled a bale (5) round about the wall; the earl drew up his men for the onslaught where each of them should go. The earl goes against it from the south with the Orkneyingers; Erling and Aslak from the west; John and Gudorm from the east; Eindrid the young from the north, with his followers. And when they were boun for the storm they cast fire into the bale. Then the earl sang:

> "Ermingerd's white handmaid bore
>
> Wine to men, the goddess bright
>
> Of driven snow, so fair she seemed
>
> To my vision when we met;

Now the warrior band resolves

To rush onward and attack

Castle-garrison with fire;

Sharp-swords spring from out the sheaths."

Now they begin to press on fast both with fire and weapons. Then they shot hard into the work, for they could not reach them by any other attack. The castlemen stood loosely here and there on the wall, for they had to guard themselves against the shots. They poured out too burning pitch and brimstone, and the earl's men took little harm by that. Now it turned out, as Erling had guessed, that the castle wall crumbled before the fire when the lime would not stand it, and there were great breaches in it. Sigmund angle was the name of a man in the earl's body-guard; he was Sweyn Asleif's son's stepson; he pressed on faster than any man to the castle, and ever went on before the earl; he was then scarcely grown up. And when the storm had lasted awhile, then all men fled from the castle wall. The wind was on from the south, and the reek of the smoke lay towards Eindrid and his men. And when the fire began to spread very fast, then the earl made them bring water, and cool the rubble that was burned. And then there was a lull in the assault. (6) Then earl Rognvald sang a song:

"Aye shall I that Yule remember,

Warrior! which we spent at Agdir,

East among the fells with Solmund,

Steward strong of Norway's king;

Now again at that same season

Of another year as then

Stunning din of swords I make

On the castle's southern verge."

And again he sang:

"Well pleased was I when the wine-tree (7)

Listened to my winning words;

Past all hope then was I given

At harvest to the foreign maid;

Now again I sate the eagles,

Since full well we love the girl

Nobly born; and now the freestone

Set in mortar must give way."

Then Sigmund angle sang this:

"Bear these words back when the spring comes

To the goddess needle-plying,

Wearing gems from fell-side won,

Bear them o'er the sea to Orkney;

That no warrior, though he were

Wight of elder years, went farther

Forward 'neath the castle walls,

When strokes sung high at early morn."

After that the earl made ready to storm, and Sigmund angle with him. There was then but a little struggle, and they got into the castle. There many men were slain, but those who would take life gave themselves up to the earl's power. There they took much goods, but they did not find the chief, and scarcely any precious things. Then there was forthwith much talk how Godfrey could have got away; and then at once they had the greatest doubt of Eindrid the young, that he must have passed him away somehow, and that he [Godfrey] must have gone away under the smoke to the wood.

After that earl Rognvald and his host stayed there a short time in Galicialand, and held on west off Spain. They harried wide in that part of Spain which belonged to the heathen, and got there much goods. They ran up into a thorpe there, as the earl told them. But those who dwelt in the thorpe ran together and made ready to battle; then there was a hard struggle, and the landfolk fled at last, but many were slain. Then the earl sang a song:

"Lady-meeting now I long for;

Out away in Spain was driven

Foe in speedy flight, and many

Ring-trees (8) panting rushed before me;

We were worthy Ermingerda,

For that then sweet songs were chaunted

In our praises to the people;

Corses covered all the field."

After that they sailed west off Spain, and got there a great storm, and lay three days at anchor, so that they shipped very much water, and it lay near that they had lost their ships. Then the earl sang:

"Cool fields goddess! (9) never shall I

Free afraid in wintry storm

If along the good ship's sides

Hemp and cable do not snap;

To the white-hued clad in linen,

To lady proud my word when sailing

South I gave; and now the wind

To the Sound soon bears my ship."

After that they hoisted their sails, and beat out to Njorfa Sound (10) with a very cross wind. (11) Then Oddi the little sang:

"Hearty friend of men, who drinketh

Mead in-doors, hath often spent

Seven much more cheerful days

With the captain of the sound-tree; (12)

But today the high-souled Rognvald,

With his band of shielded men,

On his bright-hued wooden horse

Ran for Njorvi's narrow Sound."

And as they were just beating into the Sound, the earl sang:

"Eastern wind hath borne along

Our ships at winter-tide

Far from the French lady's hands;

Come, run out our boom to tack;

We shall have to gird our sea-stag

Half-mast high off Spain today;

Soon to Svidrir's stormy Sound,

Speeds the gale our ships along."

They sailed through Njorfa Sound, and then the weather began to get better. And then as they bore out of the Sound, Eindrid the younger parted company from the earl with six ships. He sailed over the sea to Marseilles, but Rognvald and his ships lay behind at the Sound, and men talked much about it, how Eindrid helped Godfrey away. Then the earl made them hoist their sails; they sailed on the main, and steered a south course along Sarkland. (13) Then Rognvald sang a song:

"North away the land still trends,

Brave ship spares not now the wave,

Nor shall now this man be slow

To break out in burst of song;

This soft belt of earth (14) I cut

709

Off the Spanish shore today;

With thin keel, this hateful bight

To a lazy longshoreman."

Nothing is told of the voyage of the earl and his men before they came south off Sarkland, and lay in the neighbourhood of Sardinia, and knew not what land they were near. The weather had turned out in this wise, that a great calm set in and mists and smooth seas --- though the nights were light --- and they saw scarcely at all from their ships, and so they made little way. One morning it happened that the mist lifted. Men stood up and looked about them. Then the earl asked if men saw anything new. They said they saw naught but two islets, little and steep; and when they looked for the islets the second time, then one of the islets was gone. They told this to the earl; he began to say: "That can have been no islets, that must be ships which men have out here in this part of the world, which they call Dromonds; (15) those are ships big as holms to look on. But there where the other Dromond lay a breeze must have come down on the sea, and they must have sailed away, but these must be wayfaring men, either chapmen or faring in some other way on their business." After that the earl lets them call to him the bishop and all the shipmasters; then he began to say: "I call you together for this, lord bishop and Erling my kinsman; see ye any scheme or chance of ours that we may win victory in some way over those who are on the Dromond." The bishop answers: "Hard, I guess, will it be for you to run your longships under the Dromond, for ye will have no better way of boarding than by grappling the bulwarks with a broad axe, but they will have brimstone and boiling pitch to throw under your feet and over your heads. Ye may see, earl, so wise as ye are, that it is the greatest rashness to lay one's self and one's men in such risk." Then Erling began to speak: "Lord bishop," he says, "likely it is that ye are best able to see this that there will be little hope of victory in rowing against them. But somehow it seems to me that though we try to run under the Dromond, so methinks it will be that the greatest weight of weapons will fall beyond our ships, if we hug her close, broadside to broadside. But if it be not so, then we can put off from them quickly, for they will not chase us in the Dromond." The earl began to say: "That is spoken like a man and quite to my mind. I will now make that clear to the shipmasters and all the crews, that each man shall busk him in his room, and arm himself as he best can. After that we will row up to them. But if they are Christian chapmen, then it will be in our power to make peace with them; but if they are heathen, as I feel sure they are, then Almighty God will yield us that mercy that we shall win the victory over him. But of the war-spoil which we get there, we shall give the fiftieth penny to poor men." After that men got out their arms and heightened the bulwarks of their ships, and made themselves ready according to the means which they had at hand. The earl settles where each of his ships should run in. Then they made an onslaught on her by rowing, and pulled up to her as briskly as they could.

CHAPTER 94

But when those who were on board the Dromond saw that ships were rowing up to them, and that men meant to make an onslaught on them, they took silken stuffs and costly goods and hung them out on the bulwarks, and then made great shoutings and hailings; and it seemed to the earl's men as though they dared the Northmen to come on against them. Earl Rognvald laid his ship aft alongside the Dromond on the starboard, but Erling aft too on the larboard. John and Aslak, they laid their ships foreward each on his own board, but the others amidships on both boards, and all the ships hugged her close, broadside to broadside. And when they came under the Dromond, her sides were so high out of the water that they could not reach up with their weapons. But they [the foe] poured down blazing brimstone and flaming pitch over them. And it was as Erling guessed it would be, that the greatest weight of weapons fell out beyond the ships, and they had no need to shield themselves on that side which was next to the Dromond, but those who were on the other side held their shields over their heads and sheltered themselves in that way. And when they made no way with their onslaught, the bishop shoved his ship off and two othes, and they picked out and sent thither their bowmen, and they law within shot, and shot thence at the Dromond, and then that onslaught was the hardest that was made. Then those [on board the Dromond] got under cover, but thought little about what those were doing who had laid their ships under the Dromond. Earl Rognvald called out then to his men that they should take their axes and hew asunder the broadside of the Dromond in the parts where she was least iron-bound. But when the men in the other ships saw what the earls men were about, they also took the like counsel. Now where Erling and his men had laid their ship a great anchor hung on the Dromond, and the fluke was hung by the crook over the bulwark, but the stock pointed down to Erling's ship. Audun the red was the name of Erling's bowman; he was lifted up on the anchor-stock. But after that he hauled up to him more men, so that they stood as thick as every they could on the stock, and thence hewed at the sides as they best could, and that hewing was by far the highest up. And when they had hewn such large doors that they could go into the Dromond, they made ready to board, and the earl and his men got into the lower hold, but Erling and his men into the upper. And when both their bands had come up on the ship, there was a fight both great and hard. On board the Dromond were Saracens, what we call Mahomet's unbelievers. There were many blackamoors, and they made the hardest struggle. Erling got there a great wound on his neck near his shoulders as he sprang up into the Dromond. That healed so ill, that he bore his head on one side ever after. That was why he was called wryneck. And when they met, earl Rognvald and Erling, the Saracens gave way before them to the forepart of the ship, but the earl's men then boarded her one after another. Then they were more numerous, and they pressed the enemy hard. They saw that on board the Dromond was that one man who was both taller and fairer than the others; the Northmen held it to be the truth that that man must be their chief. Earl Rognvald said that they should not turn their weapons against him, if they could take him in any other way. Then they hemmed him in and bore him down with their shields, and so he was taken, and afterwards carried to the bishop's ship, and few men with him. They slew there much folk, (16) and got much goods and many costly things. When they had ended the greatest part of their toil, they sat down and rested themselves. Then the earl sang this:

> "Famous in victorious glory,
>
> Erling, brave in battle, went
>
> 'Gainst the galleon, tree of spears, (17)
>
> When our banners dripped with blood;
>
> Low we laid the swarthy champions,
>
> Blood of foemen then was shed
>
> Far and wide, and soldiers brave
>
> Died their keen-edged faulchions red."

And again he sang:

> "We make up our minds to win
>
> The galleon, slaughter this I call;
>
> At early dawn the warrior crew
>
> Reddened all their blades with gore;
>
> North and from the north the lady
>
> Of this shower of spears will hear
>
> Up to Nerbon; from our people
>
> Foemen loathsome life-loss bore."

Men spoke of these tidings which had happened there. Then each spoke of what he thought he had seen; and men talked about who had been the first to board the Dromond, and could not agree about it. Then some said that it was foolish that they should not all have one story about these great tidings; and the end of it was that they agreed that earl Rognvald should settle the dispute; and afterwards they should all back what he said. Then the earl sang:

> "First upon the gloomy galleon
>
> Ruddy Audun went with eager
>
> Daring, and the warrior dauntless
>
> Swift dashed on to seize the spoil;
>
> There at last we reached to redden
>
> Weapons in our foeman's blood;
>
> Mankind's God hath ruled it so;
>
> On the planks fell corses black."

When they had stripped the Dromond, they put tire into her and burnt her. And when that tall man whom they had made captive saw that, he was much stirred and changed colour, and could not hold himself still. But though they tried to make him speak, he said never a word, and made no manner of sign, nor did he pay any heed to them whether they promised him good or ill. But when the Dromond began to blaze, they saw as though blazing molten ore ran down into the sea. That moved the captive man much. They were quite sure then that they had looked for goods carelessly, and now the metal had melted in the heat of the fire, whether it had been gold or silver. Earl Rognvald and his men sailed thence south under Sarkland, and lay under a sea-burg, and made a seven nights' truce with the townsmen, and had dealings with them, and sold them the men whom they had taken. No man would buy the tall man. And after that the earl gave him leave to go away, and four men with him. He came down the next morning with a train of men, and told them that he was a prince of Sarkland, and had sailed thence with the Dromond and all the goods that were aboard her. He said too he thought that worst of all that they burnt the Dromond, and made such waste of that great wealth, that it was of no use to any one. "But now I have great power over your affairs. Now ye shall have the greatest good from me for having spared my life, and treated me with such honour as ye could; but I would be very willing that we saw each other never again. And so now live safe and sound and well." After that he rode up the country, but earl Rognvald sailed thence south to Crete, and they lay there in very foul weather. Then Armod sang a song when he kept watch at night on board the earl's ship.

> "On the keel-horse we keep watch,
>
> Where below the stiff ribs dashes
>
> Wave on wave; this weary work
>
> Have we here to win till morning;
>
> O'er my shoulder now I look
>
> Back on Crete, while milksop soft
>
> Sleeps to night with sleek-skinned maiden,
>
> Kind in her close-fitting smock."

CHAPTER 95

The earl and his men lay under Crete till they got a fair wind for Jewry-land, and came to Acreburg early on a Friday morning, and landed then with such great pomp and state as was seldom seen there. Thorbjorn the swarthy then made a song:

> "In the Orkneys for a winter
>
> Was I serving with the chief;
>
> Feeder of the bird of battle
>
> First arose to strive in fight;

Now the shield on Friday morning

Here we bear with eager haste,

With the earl in battle proven,

In watery port of Acre town."

The earl and his men stayed in Acreburg a while. There sickness came into their ranks, and many famous men breathed their last. There Thorbjorn the swarthy a liegeman breathed his last. Oddi the little sang:

"Barks of chieftains

Thorbjorn bore,

Swarthy of hue,

By Thrasness swift;

Under the best of skalds

Woodbear (18) trode

Ati's acres

To Acreburg.

Then saw I him,

The hero's friend,

Sprinkled with mould

In mother church;

Now the soil stony,

By sunbeam blest,

Lies heavy o'er him

In southern land."

Earl Rognvald and his men then fared from Acreburg, and sought all the holiest places in the land of Jewry. They all fared to Jordan and bathed there. Earl Rognvald and Sigmund angle swam across the river, and went up on the bank there, and thither where was a thicket of brushwood, and there they twisted great knots. Then the earl sang:

"For the men a coil I twisted

Of the way-thong on the heath,

Out on Jordan's further bank;

Clever woman this will learn;

But I trow that it will seem

Long to go so far as this

714

To all lazy stay-at-homes;

On wide field the blood falls warm."

Then Sigmund sang:

"I will wreathe another knot

For the sloth who sits at home;

Sooth to say that we have set

For his child a snare today."

The earl sang:

"To the coward here we twine

In the thicket close a knot,

On this feast of holy Laurence;

Tired to quarters good I came."

After that they fared back to Jerusalem. And when they came close to the city, then earl Rognvald sang:

"At this bard's breast hangs a cross,

Twixt his shoulder-blades a palm;

Pride of heart shall be laid low;

Soldiers scale the cliffs in order."

CHAPTER 96

Earl Rognvald and his men fared that summer from the land of Jewry, and meant to go north to Micklegarth, and came about autumn to that town which is called Imbolar. (19) They stayed there a very long time in the town. They had that watchword in the town if men met one another walking where it was throng and narrow, and the one thought it needful that the other who met him should yield him the path, then he says thus: "Out of the way," "Out of the way." One evening as the earl and his men were coming out of the town, and Erling wryneck went out along the whart to his ship, some of the townsmen met him and called out, "Out of the way," "Out of the way." Erling was very drunk, and made as though he heard them not, and when they ran against one another, Erling fell off the wharf, and down into the mud which was below, and his men ran down to pick him up, and had to strip off every stitch of his clothes, and wash him. Next morning when he and the earl met, and he was told what had happened, he smiled at it and sang:

" 'Mid-street' my friend would not call

So he had in filth to fall

Head and heels, and thus in that

Great misfortune nearly followed;

Then I trow the king's own cousin

Little comely looked when rolling

midst the mud in Imbolar;

To his breeks the blue clay clung."

These tidings happened a little while after there in the town, when they came out of the town very drunk that John limpleg's men missed him, but no man else. They sent at once to look for him on board the other ships that night, and he could not be found, but they could not look for him upon the land in the night. But next morning they rose up as soon as ever it was light, and found him a little way from the burg-wall, and he had breathed his last, and they found wounds on him. But it was never known who had given him his hurt. Then they bestowed burial on his body, and found him a grave at the church. After that they fared away thence. And nothing is told of their voyage before they come north to Engilsness [Cape St. Angelo]. There they lay some nights and waited for a wind which would seem fair to them to sail north along the sea to Micklegarth. They took great pains then with their sailing, and so sailed with great pomp just as they had heard that Sigurd Jewryfarer had done. And as they sailed north along the sea, earl Rognvald sang a song:

"Let us ride on Refil's steed (20)

Out to Micklegarth with speed;

From the field draw not the plough,

Ear the main with dripping prow;

Take we bounty of the king,

Push we on while weapons ring,

Redden maw of wolf with gore,

Mighty monarch bow before."

CHAPTER 97

When earl Rognvald and his men came to Micklegarth, they had a hearty welcome from the emperor and the Varangians. Menelaus was then emperor over Micklegarth, whom we call Manuel; he gave the earl much goods, and offered them bounty-money if they would stay there. They stayed there awhile that winter in very good cheer. There was Eindrid the young, and he had very great honour from the emperor. He had little to do with earl Rognvald and his men, and rather tried to set other men against them. Earl Rognvald set out on his voyage home that winter from Micklegarth, and fared first west to Bulgaria-land to Dyrrachburg. (21) Thence he sailed west across the sea to Poule. (22)

There earl Rognvald and bishop William and Erling and all the nobler men of their band landed from their ships, and got them horses, and rode thence first to Rome, and so homewards on the way from Rome until they come to Denmark, and thence they fared north to Norway. There men were glad to see them, and this voyage was most famous, and they who had gone on it were thought to be men of much more worth after than before. While they had been on their travels Ogmund the gallant, Erling wryneck's brother had died; he was thought of most worth of those brothers while they were both alive. Erling threw in his lot at once with king Ingi, because he leant most to him of those brothers in all friendship, and they never parted so long as they both lived.

But after king Ingi's fall Magnus was chosen to be king over that band, the son of Erling and Kristina, daughter of king Sigurd Jewryfarer; but Erling alone had then the whole rule over the land in Norway. Waldemar the Dane-king gave Erling the title of earl; he became the greatest man after that, and a mighty chief, as is written in his saga. Eindrid the young came from abroad some winters later than earl Rognvald and his men, and he threw in his lot then with king Eystein, for he would have nothing to do with Erling. But after the fall of king Eystein, these, Eindrid the young and Sigurd son of Havard the freeman of Reyrir, got together a band, and chose as king Hacon broadshoulders, son of king Sigurd Harold's son. They slew Gregory Dag's son and king Ingi. Those two, Eindrid and Hacon, fought with Erling wryneck under Sekk; there Hacon fell but Eindrid fled. Earl Erling let Eindrid the young be slain sometime after away east in the Bay.

CHAPTER 98

Earl Rognvald stayed a very long time in Hordaland that summer when he came into the land, and heard then many tidings out of the Orkneys. It was told him that there was great strife, and the chieftains had gone into two bands, but there were few who sat by so that they had no share in the strife. Earl Harold was on one side, but on the other earl Erlend and Sweyn Asleif's son. And when the earl heard that said, he sang this song:

> "Now the princes of the people
>
> Have gone back on many an oath;
>
> That is blasphemy 'gainst God;
>
> Men's ill redes now come to light;
>
> But this evil will not lessen
>
> In those who guile devise at home;
>
> So let us on lissom leg
>
> Step light so long as beard will wag."

The earl had no ships at his command. Then he looked to his kinsfolk and friends that they should get him some longships made that winter. They took that well upon them, and granted him in that matter just what he asked. The earl busked him that summer to fare west into the Orkneys to his realm, and he was very late boun, for he lingered much. He fared west on board that trading-ship which Thorhall Asgrim's son owned; he was an Icelander, and of great kindred, and had a house south at Bishopstongues. The earl had for all that a great train on board the ship and a noble band of companions. They made Scotland when the winter was far spent, and long lay off Scotland under Turfness. The earl came a little before Yule into the Orkney to his realm.

CHAPTER 99

Now shall be told what tidings happened in the Orkneys while earl Rognvald was abroad on his travels.

That same summer that the earl had fared away from the land, came east from Norway king Eystein son of Harold Gilli; he had a great host. And when he came into the Orkneys he steered with his host for South Ronaldshay. Then he heard that earl Harold Maddad's son had fared over to Caithness with a twenty-benched ship, and had eighty men with him; he lay in Thurso. But when king Eystein heard of him, he manned three cutters and fared west over the Pentland-firth, and so to Thurso. He came there so that the earl and his men were not ware of it before the king's men boarded their ship and made the earl captive. He was led before the king, and their dealings turned out so, that the earl ransomed himself with three marks of gold, but his realm he gave over into king Eystein's hands, so that he was to hold it of him ever after. Then the earl became king Eystein's man, and bound that with oaths. And after that king Eystein fared to Scotland, and harried there that summer. He harried far and wide too round England on that voyage, and he was thought to aveng king Harold Sigurd's son. After that king Eystein fared east into his realm to Norway, and very various stories were told of his doings. Earl Harold stayed behind in the Orkneys in his realm, and he was in good favour with most men. Earl Maddad his father was then dead, but his mother Margaret had come out into the Orkneys. She was a fair woman and very proud and haughty. At that time David the Scot-king died, and Malcolm his grandson (23) was taken to be king; he was a child in years when he took the realm.

CHAPTER 100

Erlend, son of Harold smooth-tongue, was most of his time in Thurso, but sometimes he was in the Southern isles, or a-roving after earl Ottar was dead. He was the most promising man, and thoroughly trained and skilled in most things, bountiful of money, blithe and ready to listen to good advice, and of all men most beloved by his followers. He had a great train. Anakol was the name of a man, he was Erlend's fosterer, and had most weight in his counsels. Anakol was a viking and a man of good birth and great hardihood, a Southislander by kin; he was Erlend's counsellor.

When Erlend heard that earl Rognvald was gone away from his realm abroad to Jerusalem, he went to him to give him the title of earl and Caithness as a lordship, as his father Harold had held it from king David, king Malcolm's grandfather. King Malcolm was then a child in years, but for that Erlend had there many noble kinsfolk who backed his cause, it came about that the Scot-king gave Erlend the title of earl, and granted him half Caithness with his kinsman Harold. Then Erlend fared to Caithness and met his friends there. After that he gathered force to himself and fared out into the Orkneys. There he bade them do homage to him, but earl Harold Maddad's son got a force together at once, when he heard of Erlend, and had many men on his side. Then men went between those kinsman, and tried to set them at one. Erlend asked for half the isles with Harold, but he will not give them up, and the end of it was that peace was fixed for that year. But the plan was that Erlend shall fare east into Norway to find king Eystein and ask for that half which earl Rognvald owned, and then Harold said he would give it up. Then Erlend fared east into Norway, but Anakol and some of his train were behind in the Orkneys. Gunni Olaf's son, Sweyn Asleif's son's brother, had got a child by Margaret earl Harold's mother, but the earl made him an outlaw. From that unfriendliness sprung up between Sweyn and earl Harold, and Sweyn sent Gunni south into the Lewes to his friend Ljotolf, with whom Sweyn had been before. Fogl was the name of Ljotolf's son; he was with earl Harold, and he and Sweyn had little to say to one another. When earl Erlend fared east to Norway, earl Harold fared over to Caithness, and sat that winter in Wick. Sweyn Asleif's son was then in Thraswick in Caithness, and had under his charge the farms of his stepsons. He had first to wife Ragnhild Ogmund's daughter; they were but a short while together. Olaf was their son. After that he had to wife Ingirid Thorkel's daughter. Andrew was their son. It was on Wednesday in Passion week that Sweyn had gone up into Lambaburg with some men. They saw where a ship of burden fared from the east off the Pentland firth, and Sweyn thought he knew that there must be earl Harold's men, whom he had sent after his scatts to Shetland. Sweyn bade his men go on board ship, and pull out to the ship of burden, and so they did. They took the ship of burden and all that was worth anything, but shoved earl Harold's men ashore, and they went east to Wick and told him. Earl Harold said little in answer, and says that he and Sweyn would take it by turns to have each other's goods, and he quartered his men about at different houses during Easter. Then the Caithness men said that the earl was on his visitations. But as soon as ever Easter was over, Sweyn fared away with the ship of burden and a rowing cutter to the Orkneys. And when they came to Scapa-neck, they took there a ship from Fogl Ljotolf's son; he was then come from the south out of the Lewes from his father, and meant to go to earl Harold. And in that trip they took about twelve ounces of gold from Sigurd cloven-foot, earl Harold's house-carle; that money had been brought into his house, but they were in Kirkwall who owned it. After that Sweyn fared over to the Ness and up into Scotland, and found Malcolm the Scot-king at Aberdeen. He was then nine winters old. (24) There Sweyn was a month in very good cheer, and the Scot-king bade him take all those rights and easements in Caithness which he had owned ere he fell out with earl Harold. Sweyn thanked the king. After that Sweyn busked him to go away, and he and the Scot-king parted with great love. Then Sweyn fared to his ships, and sailed from the south to the Orkneys. Anakol was then in Deerness when Sweyn and his men sailed from the south, and they saw his sails off the east side of the Mull. They sent to Sweyn and his

719

men Gauti the Master of Skeggbjornsstead, and Anakol begged that Sweyn would come to terms with Fogl about taking the ship, for there was kinship between them, and Fogl was then with Anakol. But when Gauti found Sweyn and his men, and told him Anakol's words, then Sweyn bade them sail to Sanday and meet him there, for he said he must sail thither at once. There was a very numerous meeting there to make matters up, and the atonement was only brought about slowly. But the end of it was that Sweyn alone was to make what award he chose. After that Anakol threw in his force with Sweyn, and they bound themselves to try to bring about an atonement between him and earl Erlend when he came from the east, for there was feud between them for the burning of Frakok. Sweyn and Anakol fared to Stronsay, and lay by Hofsness some nights. Thorfinn Brusi's son then dwelt in Stronsay; he had then to wife Ingigerd Sweyn's sister, whom Thorbjorn clerk had left to herself. When Sweyn and Anakol lay by Hofsness, earl Erlend sailed up from off the main, and Anakol and Thorfinn Brusi's son fared out at once to meet him, and tried to bring about an atonement between him and Sweyn, and the earl took the offer of atonement heavily, and said Sweyn had always gone against the stream towards his kinsfolk and himself, but not kept to what he [Sweyn] and earl Ottar had settled as to lending him [Erlend] strength to get the realm for himself. (25) Then Sweyn offered to the earl his following and counsel, and they were trying to bring the atonement about all day, but it was not brought about before they both of them, Anakol and Thorfinn, gave out that they would follow Sweyn out of the islands if the earl would not be atoned with him. Earl Erlend brings back from the east that message from king Eystein, that he should have that lot of the Orkneys which earl Harold had owned before. Sweyn gave that counsel, when he and the earl were set at one, that they should fare at once to find earl Harold ere he heard that of others, and bid him give up the realm to him. It was done as Sweyn said. They met earl Harold off Kjarrekstead, (26) and he lay on shipboard. It was on Michaelmas morning that earl Harold and his men saw that longships were faring up to them, and they doubted that there would be strife. They ran from their ships and into the castle that was then there. Arni Hrafn's son was the name of a man who ran from earl Harold's ship and to Kirkwall; he was so scared that he did not know that he had his shield at his back before he stuck fast in the church-door. Thorgeirr was the name of a man who was there inside and saw him Arni's messmates thought that he was lost, and looked for him two days. Earl Erlend and Sweyn ran from their ships to the castle after earl Harold and his men, and attacked them all that day both with fire and weapons. They made a very stout defence, and the darkness of night parted them. There many men were wounded on either side, but earl Harold and his men had surely been worn out and forced to give themselves up to them if the onslaught had lasted longer. But next morning freemen came up, friends of both sides, and tried to bring about an atonement between them, and Sweyn and earl Erlend were loath to make matters up. But still it came about that they were set at one on these terms, that earl Harold swore oaths that Erlend should have his (Harold's), share of the isles, and that he would never make any claim against him for that realm. These oaths were taken before many of the best men then in the isles as witnesses, and after that earl Harold fared over to the Ness, and so on up to Scotland to his kinfolk, then few Orkneyingers fared with him. Earl Erlend and Sweyn and his companions summoned a Thing of the freemen in Kirkwall, and the freemen came to it from all the isles. Earl Erlend pleaded his cause, and so too did many others of his friends and kinsfolk. Then the earl said that king Eystein had given him that realm in the Orkneys which earl Harold had before had in his keeping; then he begged the freemen to do him homage. He had there with him Eystein's letters, which proved that he spoke sooth. So it came about that the freemen yielded obedience to earl Erlend, and then he took under him all the Orkneys, and made himself chief over them. But it was so settled between earl Erlend and the freemen, that he should not withhold from earl Rognvald that half of the realm which he owned, if it were fated that he should come back. But if earl Rognvald claimed more than half, then the freemen should hold that against him along with earl Erlend. Sweyn Asleif's son was ever with earl Erlend, and bade him be wary, and not trust too well earl Harold or the Scots. They lay most part of the winter on shipboard, and kept spies out away from them. But when Yule drew on, and the weather began to grow hard, then Sweyn fared home to Gairsay to his house, but bade the earl be not the less wary though they were parted, and so the earl did, for he lay long on shipboard, and gathered stores together in no one place for his Yule feast.

ENDNOTES FOR CHAPTERS 91-100

1. France] Valland in its widest sense means all the Romano-Celtic nations in the west of Europe, and is used just as the Germans speak of Welschland. In a more restricted sense it is used of the north-west of France, or of Brittany and Normandy. Fm. S. iv. 59. Here it seems to include both France and Spain.

2. This is probably the best reading: The "seaburg" might be Bilbao on the "Nerbion" or "Nervion."

3. A periphrasis for "gold."

4. A periphrasis for "ships."

5. bale] The old meaning of the word was a heap of fuel for a fire, a pyre, whence all the other meanings of the word and its compounds, as "baleful" and "balefire" are derived.

6. M.O. reads thus: "and cool the grit that had run (been fused by the heat) before they made ready to the storm. But while the lull lasted the earl sang this song."

7. A periphrasis for "woman."

8. Ring-trees, a periphrasis for men.

9. Cool fields goddess, a periphrasis for lady, i.e. Ermengarda.

10. The Gut of Gibraltar.

11. The Danish Translation reads, "for the wind was very much on one side." Fl. reads "a very fair wind."

12. A periphrasis for "a ship."

13. Barbary.

14. A periphrasis for "sea."

15. Also called "Dromons" from the Greek "dromwn," used at first for a swift ship of war, and afterwards for any large vessel. See Du Cange, s.v. "Dromones."

16. Fl. reads, "but every other man's child they slew," which is wrong. Compare the sale of the prisoners further on.

17. Periphrasis for man, i.e. Erling.

18. A periphrasis for "ship."

19. Imbolar] It is very hard to identify this place. If Ægissness be the true reading at the end of this chapter, Imbolar may very well be the island of Imbros at the mouth of the Dardanelles, for Ægisness is said to be the extreme point of the Thracian Chersonese. On the other hand, if Engilsness be the true reading in the passage referred to, Imbolar must be sought for in the south-western part of Asia Minor, or even in Crete, for Engilsness, or Egilsness, is identified with Cape Malea or St. Angelo in the Peloponese. Munch inclines to the latter view, N. H. iii, 840, note. G. V. supposes, in the Icel. Dict., that Imbolum is a mistake of the Northmen for "empolij" as "miðhæfi" a little further on is a distortion of "metabhqi" "get down" or "out of the way."

20. A periphrasis for "ship."

21. Durazzo.

22. Apulia.

23. Grandson] The Cd. reads "son," the Tr. "grandson" correctly.

24. nine winters old] King Malcolm was born in 1140, and was therefore about twelve years old at this time. The Chron. de Melrose says that he was twelve years old at his accession. Comp. Munch, N. H. iii, 848, note, who places these events in the year 1154.

25. himself] Comp. ch. 78.

26. Kjarrekstead] Munch N. H. iii., 849, note, has well pointed out that Knarrarstöðum, the present Knarstane, is probably the right reading here. Kjarrekstödum, answering to the present Cairston or Stromness, would be too far off the Arni's flight, while Knarstane is within easy reach of Kirkwall.

CHAPTER 101

It happened on the tenth day of Yule that Sweyn sat in Gairsay and drank with his house-carles; he began to speak and rubbed his nose: "It is my meaning that now earl Harold is on his voyage to the isles." His house-carles say that that were unlikely for the storms' sake that then lay over them. He said he knew that they would think so. "And now," says he, "I will not send the earl news of this for my foreboding all alone, but I doubt though that there is worse counsel in that." So that talk fell to the ground, and they drank on as before. Earl Harold began his voyage out to the Orkneys at Yule. He had four ships and one hundred men; he lay two nights off Grimsay. They landed at Hamnavoe in Hrossey; thence they went the thirteenth day of Yule to Firth. They were in Orkahow while a snow-storm drove over them, and there two men of their band lost their wits and that was a great hindrance to their journey. It was in the night that they came to Firth; it happened then that earl Erlend had gone on board his ship, but he had drunk that day up at the house. Earl Harold and his men slew two men there, and the name of one of them was Kettle; (1) but they took prisoners four men: Arnfinn Anakol's brother, Ljot was the name of the second, and two others. Earl Harold fared back to Thurso, and Thorbjorn clerk and his men. But those brothers Benedict and Eric fared to Lambaburg, and had Arnfinn along with them. At once that very night, as soon as earl Erlend was ware of the strife, then he sent men to Gairsay to tell Sweyn, and he [Sweyn] made them run down to his ships to the sea the day after, and fared to find earl Erlend, as he had sent word, and they were then on shipboard most of the winter. Benedict and his brother sent that message, that Arnfinn would only be set loose on those terms, if earl Erlend and his men would let them have that ship which they had taken off Kjarrekstead. The earl was rather eager that the ship should be given up; but Anakol set his face against it, and said that Arnfinn should get away not a whit the less that winter, though that were not granted. It was on the midweekday (Wednesday) next before the Fast that they Anakol and Thorstein Ragna's son, fared over to the Ness with twenty men in a cutter, and came off the coast in the night. They drew the cutter into a hidden cove under a certain burg. (2) They go up on shore, and hide themselves in thickets a short way from the house in Thraswick, but they dressed up the ship so, that it looked just as if men lay in every seat. Men had come to the ship in the morning, and had no doubt as to what she was. Anakol and his men saw men row in a ship away from the burg and land at the oyce. (3) Then they saw a man too ride out from the burg, and another walking, and knew it was Eric. Then Anakol and his men parted their force, and ten of them went to the sea, down the river, and watched that no one should come to the ship, but the other ten went to the house. Eric came to the homestead a little before them, and went up to the hall, there he heard the sound of armed men, and then ran into the hall, and out at the other door, and wanted to go to the ship, but there the men were in his way, and he got taken captive there, and was carried out into the isles to earl Erlend. Then men were sent to earl Harold, and it was told him that Eric would not be set free till Arnfinn and his companions came safe and sound to earl Erlend, and that was done as he was told. Next spring earl Harold busked him from Caithness, and fared north to Shetland; he meant to take the life of Erlend the young, for he had asked the hand of Margaret the earl's mother, but she had refused. After that he got himself a train of followers, and took her away from the Orkneys, and bore her north to Shetland, and sat himself down in Moussaburg; there he had laid in great stores. But when earl Harold came to Shetland, he sat down round the burg and forbade all supplies, but it is an unhandy place to get at by storm. Then men came up and tried to bring about an atonement between them. Erlend asked that the earl should give him the woman in marriage, but offered himself to strengthen the earl's hands, and said that it was worth more to him to get back his realm, but said too that the likeliest way to do that was to make himself as many friends as he could. That prayer many backed with Erlend, and this was the end of the matter, that they were set at one, and Erlend got Margaret, and after that made ready to follow the earl, and they fared that summer east to Norway. And when that was heard in the Orkneys, then earl Erlend and his men laid their plans, and Sweyn was eager that they should fare a sea-roving, and so get money. And so they did, and fared south to Broadfirth, and harried off the east of Scotland. They fared south to Berwick. (4)

Canute the wealthy was the name of a man, he was a chapman, and sat very often in Berwick. Sweyn and his companions took a ship large and good, which Canute owned, and much goods aboard her; there too his wife was on board. After that they fared south under Blyholm. Canute was then in Berwick when he heard of the robbery; he made a bargain with the men of Berwick for a hundred marks of silver, that they go out to get back the goods. They were most of them chapmen who went out to look for the goods. They fared in fourteen ships to look for them. Now when Erlend and Sweyn lay under Blyholm, Sweyn spoke to them, and told them that men should lie with no awning over their ships; said he had got it into his head that the men of Berwick would come in a great company to look them up at night. But there was a sharp wind on, and men gave no heed to what he said, and all men lay under their awnings, save that on Sweyn's ship there was no awning aft of the mast. Sweyn sat up on the poop in a hairy cloak on a chest and said he was so boun to spend the night. Einar skew was the name of a man on board Sweyn's ship; he spoke and said that far too many stories had been told of Sweyn's bravery; "he is called a better man than other men, but now he dares not throw an awning over his ship." Sweyn made as though he heard not. There were watchmen upon the holm; Sweyn heard how they could not agree as to what they saw. He went up to them and asked about what they strove. They said they could not tell what they saw. Sweyn was the sharpest-sighted of all men, and when he looked steadfastly at the spot, he saw that there were fourteen ships coming on them from the north all together. He went on board his ship and bade the watchmen go on board the ships and tell what had happened. Sweyn bade his men wake up and throw off their awnings. After that a great cry arose, and most men shouted out to Sweyn, and asked what counsel should be taken; he bade men be still, but said his counsel was to lay their ships between the holm and the land, "and try if they will so sail round away from us; but if that may not be, then let us row against them as hard as we can." But other counsellors spoke against that, and said the only plan was to sail away, and so it was done. Then Sweyn spoke: "If ye will sail away, then beat out to sea." Sweyn was last boun. Anakol waited for him. But when Sweyn's ship went faster, then he made them slacken sail, and waited for Anakol, and would not that he should be left behind with a single ship. Then Einar skew said, as Sweyn and his men sailed with all sail: "Sweyn," says he, "is it not so that our ship stands still?" Sweyn says: "I do not think that," says he, "but I counsel thee that thou speakest no more against my bravery, if thou canst not tell for fear's sake whether the ship walks under thee or not, for this is the fastest of all ships under sail." The men of Berwick sailed south away from them, but Sweyn and his fleet then turned in under the mainland. And when they came under the Isle of May, then Sweyn sent men to Edinburgh to tell the Scot-king of the spoil they had taken, but ere they came to the burg, twelve men rode to meet them, and they had bags full of silver at their cruppers. And when they met, the Scottish men asked after Sweyn Asleif's son; they said where he was, and asked what they wanted of him. The Scots said that they had been told that Sweyn was taken prisoner, and the Scot-king had sent them to set him free with that money which they carried with them. Sweyn's men told them the news in return, and fared to find the Scot-king, and told him their errand. The king spoke lightly of the loss of Canute's money, and sent Sweyn a costly shield and other good gifts more. Earl Erlend and Sweyn fared that autumn to the Orkneys and came back rather late.

That summer earl Harold fared to Norway, as was before told. Then too earl Rognvald came back from abroad from Micklegarth into Norway, and Erling wryneck with him, as was before written. And earl Rognvald came into the Orkneys a little before Yule.

CHAPTER 102

Then men at once came between earl Rognvald and earl Erlend, and tried to set them at one. Then men brought forward that understanding which had passed between freemen and earl Erlend, that he should not withhold his share of the Isles from earl Rognvald. Then things came to a fixed meeting between those earls in Kirkwall, and at that meeting they made matters up and bound that by oaths. That was two nights before Yule, and the terms of the settlement were that each of them should have half of the isles, and both should guard them against earl Harold or any others if they laid claim to them. Earl Rognvald had then no force of ships before the summer after, when his ships came from the east out of Norway. That winter all stood quiet, but in the spring after the earls laid their plans against earl Harold if he should come from the east, and earl Erlend and Sweyn Asleif's son fared to Shetland, and were to lie in wait for him there if he showed himself. Earl Rognvald fared over to Thurso, for they thought that Harold might make thither when he came from the east, for he had many kinsfolk and friends there. Earl Erlend and Sweyn were in Shetland that summer, and stopped all ships so that no one might go to Norway. Earl Harold fared that summer from the east out of Norway, and had seven ships; he made the Orkneys, but three of his ships were driven into Shetland by stress of weather, and Erlend and Sweyn took them. When earl Harold came into the Orkneys, there he heard those tidings, that earl Rognvald and earl Erlend were atoned, and that each of them was to have half the isles. Then earl Harold thought he saw that as for his choice, nothing was meant for him. Then he took that counsel to fare over to the Ness at once to find earl Rognvald ere earl Erlend and Sweyn came back from Shetland. Earl Erlend and Sweyn were then in Shetland, when they heard that earl Harold was come into the Orkneys with five ships; they held on south at once into the isles with five ships, and got caught in Dynrace, (5) in dangerous tides and a storm of wind, and there they parted company. Then Sweyn bore up for the Fair isle in two ships, and they thought the earl lost. Thence they held on their course south under Sanday, and there earl Erlend lay before them with three ships, and that was a very joyful meeting. Thence they fared to Hrossey, and heard there that earl Harold had fared over to the Ness. But that is to be said of earl Harold's doings, that he came to Thurso and had six ships. Earl Rognvald was then up the country in Sutherland, and sat there at a wedding, at which he gave away his daughter Ingirid to Eric staybrails. News came to him at once that earl Harold was come into Thurso. Earl Rognvald rode down with a great company from the bridal to

Thurso. Eric staybrails was Harold's kinsman, and he did all he could to set them at one again, and many others backed that with him, and said that it was as clear as day to them that they ought not to let themselves be parted for the sake of that kinship and those foster-ties and that fellowship which had been between them. So it came about that a meeting was brought to pass between them and peace given, and they were to meet in a castle at Thurso, and they two talk alone, but each of them was to have as many men as the other hard by the castle. They talked long, and things went well with them. They had not met before since earl Rognvald came into the land. And when the day was far spent, earl Rognvald was told that earl Harold's people were flocking thither with arms. Earl Harold said that no harm would come of that. Next after that they heard great blows struck outside, and then they ran out. There was come Thorbjorn clerk with a great train of men, and he began straightway to wound and maimearl Rognvald's men when they met. The earls called out that they should not fight. Then men ran up out of the town and parted them. There fell thirteen of earl Rognvald's house-carles, but he himself was wounded in the face. After that their friends did their best to set them at one again, and so it came about that they were atoned and bound anew their friendship with oaths. This was four nights before Michaelmas. Then too that counsel was taken that they should fare at once that night out into the Orkneys against earl Erlend and Sweyn. They held on with thirteen ships west on the Pentland firth, and ran across to Rognvaldsey, (6) and made the land in Vidvoe, and there went on shore. Earl Erlend and his men lay on shipboard in Bardswick, and thence they saw a great company in Rognvaldsey, and sent out spies thither, and then they had sure news that the earls had been set at one. It was also told them that they would not let them have the power either of strand-slaughter or any other stores of food, and must so mean then and there to cut off their food in the isles. Then earl Erlend and his men went to talk, and he sought counsel of his men. But they all agreed with one voice that Sweyn should see to it what counsel should be taken. But Sweyn gave utterance to this decision, that they should at once that very night sail over to the Ness, and said that they had no strength to strive with both of them there in the isles. He made that show before the people at large, that they would fare to the Southern isles, and be there that winter. That was Michaelmas eve when they sailed on the firth, but as soon as ever they came to Caithness, they hastened up into the country, and drove down to the shore great droves of cattle to slaughter and slaughtered them, and put them on board their ships. Great storms were on and foul weather, and the firth was always impassable. But as soon as ever there was a fair wind, Sweyn sent men in a boat to the other side from the Ness to say that earl Erland had slaughtered cattle on the shore in Caithness, and that they lay boun to sail to the Southern isles as soon as ever they got a breeze. And when these tidings came to earl Rognvald's ears, he brought them before a meeting of householders, and spoke to his people. He bade his men be wary and keep good watch, and lie every night on board their ships, "for there is not an hour of the day or night that I do not look for Sweyn here in the Orkneys, and so much the rather that he made so many words about how he would fare out of the land."

At the beginning of winter Sweyn and his companions fared out of Thurso, and turned west round the coast of Scotland. They had seven ships, and all well manned and trimmed and big. They began their passage by the help of oars alone. But when they were come on their course away from the Ness, earl Rognvald's spies fared out into the isles, and told him these tidings. The earls then rowed their ships to Scapaneck, and earl Rognvald would that they should lie on board their ships a while. Now when Sweyn and his companions had got about as far west as Staur, Sweyn spoke and said that they would not plague themselves any longer by rowing, and bade them put their ships about and hoist their sails. This plan the men thought rather foolish, but still it was done as Sweyn would. But when they had sailed about, the war-snakes ran swiftly before the wind. (7) And nothing is told of their voyage before they come to Vogland (8) in the Orkneys. There they heard that the earls lay at Scapa-neck with fourteen ships off Knarstead. There was then Erlend the young and Eric staybrails, and many other noble men.

CHAPTER 103

Thorbjorn clerk had gone east to Paplay at Firth to the house of Hacon churl, his father-in-law. Thorbjorn then had his daughter Ingigerd to wife. It was four nights before Simon's mass that Sweyn uttered that decision, that he would row up and make an onslaught on the earls at night. But that seemed rather foolhardy considering the difference of force which there was. Still Sweyn would have his way, and so it was, for the earl too was rather eager for it.

At even a storm of soft melting sleet set in; then earl Rognvald went away from his ship and meant to go to Ofir to his house; he knew no cause for fear; he was with six men. They came to Knarstead in the sleet storm. There dwelt Botolf bungle, a man from Iceland and a good skald. He asked earl Rognvald to be there with him the night over, and tried to talk him over with many words. They went in, and their clothes were pulled off them; they lay down to sleep, but Botolf was to keep watch. That self same night earl Erlend and his men pulled up against earl Harold and his men, and came upon them unawares, so that they knew nothing of their coming before they heard the warcry. Then they ran to their arms, and defended themselves like men. There was great slaughter, and the onslaught ended so that earl Harold fled away up on shore, when only five men were left upstanding on board the ship. There fell Bjarni Erlend the young's brother, a man of rank and worth, and a hundred men with him, but a whole crowd were wounded. All men ran from their ships and fled up on the land. Few fell of earl Erlend's men, but the earl took there fourteen ships that the earls owned, and all the goods that were on board them. When the most of the work was done, they heard that earl Rognvald had gone away from his ship that evening, and first up to Knarstead, and thither they fared. Botolf the master was outside before the door when they came there, and he gave them a hearty greeting. They asked whether earl Rognvald were there by chance. Botolf said he had been there that night. But they behaved wildly, and asked where he then was, and said he must know. Botolf stretched out his hand up and round about the yard, and sang a song:

"After fowls the chieftain fares;

Soldiers shoot their weapons well;

Yonder heath-hen 'neath the hill

May have hope of blow on neck;

There the cross-bow crushes heath-poults

Wondrously when warriors meet,

Warrior stems that wound the snake; (9)

The king defends his land with sword."

The earl's men ran headlong out of the "town," (10) and he thought he had the best of it who ran fastest and first got power over the earl. But Botolf went indoors and woke up the earl, and tells him those tidings that had happened in the night, and also what the earl's men were after. Then they jumped up and clothed themselves, and fared away at once, and to Orfir to the earl's house, and when they came there, earl Harold was there before them in hiding. Then they fared at once over to the Ness each in his boat, the one with three men and the other with four men. All their men fared over to the Ness as they got passages. Earl Erlend and Sweyn took all the earl's ships and very much goods. Sweyn Asleif's son made them hand over to him as his share all earl Rognvald's treasures that were taken on board his ship, and he sent them to earl Rognvald over to the Ness. Sweyn was very eager that earl Erlend and his men should station their ships out in Vogaland, and that they should lie in that part of the Firth (11) where they could see any sailing of ships as soon as ever they put out from the Ness. He thought it good thence to lie in wait for attacks, if there were any chance of a passage. But earl Erlend made up his mind, for the sake of the egging on of his levies, that they should fare north to Damsay, and there they drank by day in a great hall, but lashed their ships together every evening, and slept in them by night. And so it went up to the Yule fast. It was five nights before Yule, that Sweyn Asleif son fared east to Sandwick to Sigrid his kinswoman; he was to make up a quarrel between her and her neighbour, whose name was Bjorn. But ere he fared away, he spoke to earl Erlend that he should sleep on shipboard by night, and be then not less wary though he [Sweyn] were not with him. Sweyn was one night at the house of his kinswoman Sigrid.

CHAPTER 104

Gisl was the name of a man; he was Sweyn's tenant and dear friend. He made a prayer to Sweyn that he should come as a guest to his house, and see how matters stood with him. He had made them brew liquor, and wated to tap it for Sweyn and his men. When they came at even to Gil's (12) house, it was told them that earl Erlend had not gone to the ships the evening before. As soon as ever Sweyn heard this, he sent Margad Grim's son and two other men to the earl, and bade him take heed to his counsel, though he had not done so the night before; "but," says he, "methinks it is to be dreaded that I shall need to take counsel for this earl but a short while longer." Margad and his companions fared to find earl Erlend, and told him Sweyn's words. The earl's men said he [Sweyn] had wondrous ways; they said that one while he thought nothing too dangerous, but sometimes he was so afraid that he scarce knew how to keep himself or others safe. They said that they would sleep in peace on land, and not fare to the ships. The earl said it should be so as Sweyn had laid it down; and the end of it was, that the earl went on board his own ship with four-and-twenty men, but all the others lay up at the house. Margad and those who were on board Sweyn's ship lay in another bay a short way off thence.

This very same night earl Rognvald and earl Harold came unawares upon earl Erlend, so that those watchmen who watched on the isle and on the ship were none of them aware of it before they boarded the ship. Orm was the name of a man, and Ufi was another; they were in the forehold on board earl Erlend's ship. Ufi jumped up, and would wake the earl, and could not get him awakened, so dead drunk was he. Ufi caught up the earl in his arms, and leapt overboard with him, and into the after boat which floated by the ship's side; but Orm leapt over on the other side, and he got safe to land. But the earl lost his life, and most of the other men who were in the ships. (13) The men on board Sweyn's ship wakened at the war cry, and cut the cable asunder, and pulled out off the ness, but the full moon gave a strong light, and then they saw that the earls were pulling away. Then they thought they could tell that they must have settled their business with earl Erlend. Sweyn's house carles then rowed away, and fared first to Rendale, but sent a man to Sweyn to tell him such things as they had then seen and heard. Earl Harold was for giving peace to earl Erlend's men, but earl Rognvald would wait first to see whether his body were found, or whether he had got away. Earl Erlend's body was found two nights before Yule; the shaft of a spear was seen standing up out of the seaweed, and when they got to it, that spear stood right through him. His body was borne to the church, but then peace was given to the earl's men, and so too to four of Sweyn's house carles who were taken. John was the name of a man who was called wing; he was a sister's son of John wing, of whom it was spoken before, he had been with Hacon churl, and had got his sister with child, and then ran away a sea roving with Anakol, but now he was with earl Erlend, and yet he had not been at the battle. Earl Erlend's men made their way to Kirkwall, and took shelter in Magnus' church. The earls also fared thither, and then a meeting for a settlement was fixed in the church. Then John could not get an atonement with the earls before he had given his word to keep his wedding with the woman. There all men took oaths to the earls, and they settled that matter rather easily. John wing bound himself over into earl Harold's hand, and became his steward.

CHAPTER 105

When Sweyn Asleif's son heard of the fall of earl Erlend, he fared to Rendale, and met his house carles there. (14) They were able to tell him plainly of the tidings that had happened in Damsay. After that Sweyn and his men fared to Rowsay, and came there at the flood-tide; they took all the tackling out of the ship, and laid her up; they shared the men about among the houses, and kept spies out between them and the earls and others of the great men to know what each were doing. Sweyn Asleif's son went there up on the fell, and five men with him, and so down the other side to the sea shore, and stole right up to a homestead thereabouts in the darkness. They heard a great chattering inside. There were that father and son, Thorfinn and Ogmund, and Erlend their brother in law. Erlend, he was boasting about that to that father and son, that he had given earl Erlend his death blow, but they all thought they had fought very well. And when Sweyn heard that, he springs inside into the house at them, and his companions after him. Sweyn was quickest, and he smote Erlend at once his death blow; but they took Thorfinn prisoner, and had him off along with them, but Ogmund was slightly wounded. Sweyn and his men fared to Thingwall; there dwelt then Helgi Sweyn's father's brother, and they were there at the beginning of Yule in hiding. Earl Rognvald fared to Damsay at Yule, but earl Harold stayed behind at Kirkwall. Earl Rognvald sent men to Thingwall to Helgi, and bade him tell his kinsman Sweyn if he knew anything as to where he was, that the earl wanted to bid him to stay with him at Yule, and said he was willing to have a hand in setting him and earl Harold at one again. And when these words came to Sweyn, he fared to meet earl Rognvald with five men, and was with him the latter part of Yule. (15) But after Yule a meeting to make friends was fixed between Sweyn and the earls; there all those quarrels were to be put an end to which had not been already made up. And when they met, earl Rognvald did his best to make Sweyn and earl Harold friends, but most men there were very hard in their counsel against him, who were not already either kinsfolk or friends of Sweyn; but those men said that trouble would always arise from Sweyn if he were not made away with out of the isles. But that settlement was made, that Sweyn should pay a mark of gold to each of the earls, and lose half his lands and his good longship. Sweyn answers when he hears the award: "This atonement will be best kept if I am not treated with dishonour." Earl Rognvald would not take the fine from Sweyn. He says he will in no wise disgrace him, he says, too, he thinks there is much more gain to be got from his friendship than from his goods. Earl Harold fared after the atonement to Gairsay to Sweyn's house, and dealt there rather wastefully with his corn and other gear that he had. But when Sweyn heard that he brought it before earl Rognvald, and called it a breach of the atonement, and said he would fare home and see after his stores. Earl Rognvald said; "Be with me, Sweyn and I will send word to the earl, and again bring him to speak about your affairs; but I will not that thou shouldst think to strive against earl Harold, for he will be too much of a man for thee in strife, though thou art a mighty man in thyself, and a bold brisk man." But Sweyn would not let himself be hindered, and fared with nine men in a cutter to Gairsay, and came there late at even. They saw fire in the bake house; (16) Sweyn fared thither to it. He wished that they should take the fire and lay it to the hall, and burn the homestead and the earl inside it. Sweyn Blakari's son was the name of a man; he was the man of most weight of all those that were there with Sweyn; he set his face most against this, and said might be the earl were not in the house. But even though he were there, he says that they would not let his wife or his daughters come out; but says that it would never do to burn them inside the house. Then Sweyn and his men went to the doorway, and so in towards the hall door; then those men sprang up who were in the hall, and shut to the door. Then Sweyn and his men became aware that the earl was not in the homestead. But those who were inside gave up their defence, and handed over their weapons to Sweyn and his men, and came out all unarmed, and Sweyn gave peace to all the earl's house carles. Sweyn broached all his drink, and had away with him his wife and daughters. He asked Ingirid his wife where Harold was, but she

730

would not tell him: "Hold thy peace then and point it out to us." She would not do that either. She was the earl's kinswoman. Sweyn gave up some of their arms when they came on shipboard. There was an end of the atonement between Sweyn and the earl when this news was heard. Earl Harold had gone to a little isle to hunt hares. Sweyn held on his course to Hellis isle, (17) that is a craggy isle towards the sea, and there is a great cave in the rock, and the sea came right up into the mouth of the cave at flood-tide. When earl Harold's house carles got their weapons from Sweyn and his men, they fared straightway to find earl Harold, and told him of their dealings with Sweyn. The earl made them launch his ship at once, and egged on his men to row after them, "and let us now bring matters to the sword's point." Then they fell to rowing after them, and each saw the other and knew one another. And when Sweyn sees that the earl and his men were drawing up to them, Sweyn spoke and said: "We must try and seek some plan, for I have no mind to meet him when matters are so hot between us, with the difference in force which there will be; we will take that counsel," says he, "to fare to the cave, and see what turn our matters then take." So Sweyn and his men did. They came to the cave at the flood, laid the ship up there, for the cave sloped up into the rock; then the sea rose and flowed into the mouth of the cave. Earl Harold and his men fared all day about the isle looking for them and found them not; they saw too no sailing of ships from the isle. They wondered much at that; they thought it unlikely that Sweyn should have foundered and sunk. They rowed round and round the isle to look for Sweyn and could not find him, as was likly. Then the most they could make of it was that Sweyn and his men must have borne up for other islands; then they rowed thither to seek them where they thought likeliest. Almost as soon as ever the earl and his men rowed away, the sea fell from the cave's mouth. Sweyn and his men had heard the talk of the earl and his men. Sweyn left his ship behind in the cave, (18) but they took an old ship of burden on the isle, which the monks owned, and held on in her to Sanday. There they went on land, but shoved off the ship of burden and she drove about from strand to strand until she broke up. But Sweyn and his men went up into the isle, and came to that homestead which is called Valaness, there that man dwelt whose name was Bard, Sweyn's kinsman. They called him out by stealth, and Sweyn said that he wished to stay there. Bard said he should do so if he pleased "but I dare not that ye be here save in hiding." They went in and were alone in [a room in] the house, so that only a wall of wattle was between them and other men. There was a secret doorway in the house in which Sweyn was, and stones were loosely piled up in it. That afternoon came John wing earl Harold's steward and seven of them together. Bard gave them a hearty welcome, and fires were made for them, and they roasted themselves at them. John was very wild in his words, and talked about the tidings that had happened in those dealings which the earls had had with Sweyn; he blamed Sweyn much, and said he was a dastardly trucebreaker and true to no man; he had but just now made peace with earl Harold, and yet he would fare forthwith and burn the house over his head: he said too there would never be peace in the land before Sweyn were driven out of the land. The master Bard and John's companions rather spoke up for Sweyn. After that John took to speaking ill of earl Erlend, and said that was no scathe though he had lost his life; he called him such an overbearing man, that no one dared to call his head his own for him. And when Sweyn heard that, then he could not stand it, and snatched up his weapons and ran at the secret doorway, and hurled down the stones out of it. Then there was a great clatter. Sweyn meant to run round to the hall door. John sat in his shirt and linen breeks. And when he heard the noise that Sweyn made he lost no time in lacing up his shoon, but jumped up from the fire, and set off at once away from the house. But it was moonless and pitch dark, and a sharp frost. He came that night to another homestead, and was much frostbitten on his feet, so that some of his toes dropped off. Sweyn gave peace to John's companions for master Bard's words' sake. Sweyn was there that night, but afterwards next morning they fared away thence with a cutter which Bard owned and gave to Sweyn. Then they fared south to Bardswick, and were there at a cave. Sweyn was sometimes during the day at the house and drank there, but slept by his ship at night, and so guarded himself against his foes.

CHAPTER 106

It happened one morning early that Sweyn and his men saw a great longship fare from Hrossey to Rognvaldsey, and Sweyn knew at once that it was earl Rognvald's ship, that he was wont to steer himself, and they ran into Rognvaldsey, and thither where Sweyn's cutter lay, and five men went on shore from the earl's ship, but Sweyn and his men were on a height, and pelted the earl's men with stones thence. And when they saw that from the ship, men got out their arms. But when Sweyn and his men saw that they ran down from the height and to the beach, and shoved off the cutter and jumped into her. The longship had run up on shore, so that she was fast. Sweyn stood up in his cutter as they rowed out by the longship, and had a spear in his hand. But when earl Rognvald saw that, then he took a shield and held it before him, but Sweyn did not throw the spear. But when the earl saw that they were about to part, he made them hold up a truce shield, (19) and begged that Sweyn and his men would come to land. But when Sweyn saw that, he bade his men pull to land, and says he would still be best pleased if he could be made friends with earl Rognvald.

CHAPTER 107

After that earl Rognvald and Sweyn went on shore, and they two talked long together, and things went smoothly with them. And as they sat a talking then they saw earl Harold's sailing, as he fared from Caithness and to Vogaland. (20) And when the ship bore away under the island, then Sweyn asked the earl what counsel should be taken now. The earl says that Sweyn should fare over to the Ness then and there. This was in Lent. They fared both at the same time out of Rognvaldsey, the earl he fared to Hrossey, but Sweyn fared west to Stroms, and earl Harold and his men saw the ship, and thought they knew that Sweyn owned her. They put out at once into the firth after them. And when Sweyn and his men saw that the earl and his men held on after them; then they left their ship and hid themselves away. But when earl Harold came to Stroms, they saw Sweyn's ship, and doubted then that the abodes of men must be too near, and for that they would not land from their ship. Amundi was a man's name the son of Hnefi; he was a friend of earl Harold, but a father's brother of Sweyn Asleif's son's step-children; he came between them then, and got it brought about that the same atonement should be held which had been made the winter before. Then a storm of wind sprung up; and each side had to stay there that night; and Amundi stowed away earl Harold and Sweyn both in one bed. In that house many men of each of them took their rest. After this atonement Sweyn fared over to the Ness, but earl Harold over to the Orkneys. Sweyn heard that the earl had said that he called their peace making rather loosely made. Little heed paid Sweyn to that. He fared south into the Dales, and was that Easter with Summerled his friend; but earl Harold fared north to Shetland, and was there very long that spring. Sweyn fared from the south after Easter, and met on the way John wing's two brothers, the name of the one was Peter down-at-heel, (21) but the other's Blane. Sweyn and his men took them captive and stripped them of all their goods, but brought them to land; then a gallows tree was hewn for them. And when all was ready, Sweyn said that they should run away up the country; he said it would be more shame to their brother John that they should live. They were long out in the cold and much frozen when they got to a homestead. Sweyn fared thence to the Southern isles to the Lewes, and stayed there a while. But when John wing heard that Sweyn had taken his brothers captive, but knew not what he had done with them, then he fared to Enhallow, (22) and there seized Olaf Sweyn's son, Kolbein the burly's fosterchild, and fared with him to Westray. Then earl Rognvald and he met at Rapness, and when the earl saw Olaf there, he said: "Why art thou here, Olaf?" He answers: "It is John wing's doing." The earl looked to John, and said: "Why broughtest thou Olaf hither?" He answered: "Sweyn seized my brothers, and I know not that he has not slain them." The earl said: "Carry thou him back as fast as thou canst, and do not dare to do him any harm, whatever has become of thy bretheren; for thou wilt have no peace in the isles, either at Sweyn's or Kolbein's hands, if thou doest aught to him."

CHAPTER 108

After Easter in the spring Sweyn began his voyage from the Southern isles, and had sixty men. He held on his course to the Orkneys, and first to Rowsay. There he seized that man whose name was Hacon churl; he had been with earl Harold when earl Erlend fell. Hacon bought himself off with three marks of gold, and so freed himself from Sweyn. There in Rowsay Sweyn and his men found that ship which the earls had awarded that Sweyn should give up, and the bulwarks on both sides had been hewn out of her. That earl Rognvald had made them do, for no one had been willing either to buy or beg the ship from the earls. Sweyn held on then to Hrossey, and found earl Rognvald in Birsay. The earl gave him a hearty welcome, and Sweyn was with him that spring. Earl Rognvald says that was why he had hewn the bulwarks out of the ship, because he did not wish him to do any hasty deed there in the isles when he came back from the Southern isles. Sweyn was there with earl Rognvald and fourteen men besides himself. Earl Harold came from Shetland that spring at Whitsuntide, and as soon as ever he came into the Orkneys, earl Rognvald sent men to him to say that his will was that he and Sweyn should make friends anew. And then the meeting for an atonement was fixed for the Friday in the Holy Week in Magnus' church, and earl Rognvald went with a broad axe to the meeting and Sweyn with him. Then the self same atonement was agreed upon which had been brought about the winter before.

CHAPTER 109

Then earl Rognvald gave to earl Harold that ship which Sweyn had owned, but he gave to Sweyn all else that had been awarded from him and came to his share. Earl Rognvald and Sweyn stood by the church door while the sail was being borne out; for it had been laid up in Magnus' church; and Sweyn looked rather cross when they bore out the sail. The Saturday after, when nones were over, earl Harold's men came to see Sweyn Asleif's son, and said that he would that Sweyn should come and talk with him. Sweyn brought that message before earl Rognvald, and he was not very eager that Sweyn should go on this quest; he says he does not know whether he might trust them. But Sweyn went nevertheless, and six of them together. The earl sat in a little room on a cross bench, and Thorbjorn clerk by him. There were few other men with the earl. They greeted the earl worthily; and he took their greeting well. They made room for Sweyn to sit; so they sat a while and drank. After that Thorbjorn went away, and Sweyn and his men said that they then doubted much as to what the earl was about to take in hand. Thorbjorn came back a little after and gave Sweyn a scarlet kirtle and cloak and sword; he said he did not know whether he would call them a gift, for those precious things had been taken from Sweyn the winter before. Sweyn accepted these gifts. Earl Harold gave Sweyn the longship which he had owned, and half his lands and estates. He asked Sweyn to come and be with him, and said their friendship should never fail. Sweyn took this well, and went at once that night, and told earl Rognvald how things had gone with earl Harold and himself. Earl Rognvald showed that he was glad at that, and bade Sweyn take heed that they did not fall out again.

CHAPTER 110

Sometime after these three chiefs made up their minds to go a sea roving, Sweyn, Thorbjorn, and Eric. They fared first to the Southern isles. They fared as far west as the Scilly isles, and won there a great victory in Mary Haven (23) on Columba's mass, and got very much war spoil. After that they fared to the Orkneys, and were well agreed.

After the atonement of earl Rognvald and earl Harold and Sweyn Asleif's son, the earls were always both together, and earl Rognvald had the leadership, but they were very good friends. When they came home from Scilly, Thorbjorn clerk fared to earl Harold, and became his chief councillor. Sweyn fared home to Gairsay, and sat there with a great band of men in the winters, and had his war spoil to keep up his household expenses, along with his other stores, which he had there in the isles. He had most leaning to earl Rognvald. Every summer he was out roving. It was said that Thorbjorn clerk made things no better between earl Rognvald and earl Harold. Thorarin cod-nose was the name of one of earl Rognvald's body guard and his friend too; he was always with the earl. Thorkell was the name of one of Thorbjorn clerk's followers and friends. Those Thorarin and Thorkell, quarrelled over their drink in Kirkwall, and Thorkell gave Thorarin a wound, and got away afterwards to Thorbjorn. Thorarin's messmates followed Thorkell up, but he and Thorbjorn defended themselves out of a loft. Then that was told to the earls, and they came to the spot to part them. Thorbjorn would not let earl Rognvald utter an award in this quarrel, and found fault with the hue and cry that had been made to his house. But when Thorarin was whole of his wounds, then he slew Thorkell as he went to church. Thorarin ran into the church, but Thorbjorn and his men ran after him and his followers. Then that was told to earl Rognvald, and he went thither with a great company, and asked whether Thorbjorn meant to break open the church. Thorbjorn said that the church had no right to hold those who were inside it. Earl Rognvald said once for all the church must not be broken into, and Thorbjorn was hustled away from the church by the throng of men. No atonement was made for this. Thorbjorn fared over to the Ness, and was there a while. Then there was much heard of their doings, for Thorbjorn did much mischief both in the ravishing of women and in slaughter of men. Thorbjorn fared by stealth into the Orkneys, in a cutter, with thirty men with him. He rushed in by himself alone in the evening into the tavern where Thorarin was a drinking. Thorbjorn smote him at once his death blow; after that he ran off in the dark far away. For this sake earl Rognvald made Thorbjorn clerk an outlaw over all his realm. Thorbjorn fared over to the Ness, and was with his brother in law Hosvir in hiding; he was called "the strong"; he had to wife Ragnhilda, Thorbjorn's sister; their son was Stephen councillor, Thorbjorn's follower. A little while after Thorbjorn fared to see Malcolm the Scot-king, and was with him in good cheer. With the Scot-king was the man whose name was Gilli-Odran; he was of great kindred and a very unfair man; he fell under the wrath of the Scot-king for the mischief and manslaying which he wrought in his realm. Gilli-Odran ran away into the Orkneys, and the earls took him into their service. Gilli-Odran was in Caithness, and had the earl's stewardship there. Helgi was the name of a man of rank and a householder in Caithness, he was earl Rognvald's friend. He and Gilli-Odran quarrelled about the stewardship, and1 Gilli-Odran fell upon him and slew him. But after the manslaughter he fared away west to Scotland's firths, and that chief took him in whose name was Summerled the freeman, he had rule in the Dales, in Scotland's firths. Summerled had to wife Ragnhilda daughter of Olaf bitling, (24) the Southern isle king. The mother of Ragnhilda was Ingibjorg, the daughter of earl Hacon Paul's son. These were the children of Summerled and Ragnhilda: Dougal the king, Rognvald, and Angus, that is called the Dale-dwellers' kin. Earl Rognvald summoned to him Sweyn Asleif's son ere he went on his roving cruise. And when they met, earl Rognvald begged him to keep a look out for Gilli-Odran if he had a chance. Sweyn said he could not tell what might be fated to come of it.

ENDNOTES FOR CHAPTERS 101-110

1. Fl. adds, "but the other is not named."

2. Fl. reads, "some rocks."

3. i.e., River's mouth. Oyce is the modern Orkney word for this.

4. This Berwick appears from the context not to be Berwick-upon-Tweed, but North Berwick, at the mouth of the Firth of Forth.

5. Dynrace] Sumburg Roost.

6. South Ronaldshay.

7. Fl. reads, "the war-snakes began to walk swiftly for there was a good breeze."

8. Vogland] Walls in Hoy in the Orkneys.

9. A periphrase for "men."

10. i.e. "homefield."

11. i.e. the Pentland Firth.

12. Thus, by transposition, for "Gisl's."

13. Fl. "ship."

14. Fl. reads, "After the fall of earl Erlend, Sweyn Asleif's son fared to Rendale and found there Margad, and his house-carles."

15. Fl. adds, "in good cheer."

16. Fl. reads, "they fared to the back of the house, Sweyn wished that they should light a fire."

17. Hellis isle] Ellarholm, near Shapinsay.

18. Because they could not launch her as she was high and dry.

19. i.e. a white shield as opposed to the red war shield.

20. Vogaland] Walls in Hoy.

21. The Translation reads "whining-Peter."

22. Eyin Helga, i.e., the Holy Island, now Enhallow, between Rowsay and the Mainland.

23. Port St. Mary.

24. i.e., the tiny, an allusion probably to his stature.

CHAPTER 111

After that Sweyn fared off on his viking cruise, and had five longships. And when he came west off Scotland's firths, Sweyn heard that Summerled the freeman was gone on board ship, and meant to go a roving; he had seven ships. There Gilli-Odran steered one ship, and he was gone higher up the firths after that force which had not yet come. As soon as ever Sweyn heard of Summerled, he ran in to battle against him, and there was a hard battle. And in that fight fell Summerled the freeman, and much folk with him. There Sweyn became sure that Gilli-Odran had not been there. Then Sweyn fared to look him up, and found him in Murkfirth, and there he slew Gilli-Odran and fifty men with him. After that Sweyn fared a sea roving, and back at autumn, as he was wont. And when he came home he was not long in meeting earl Rognvald, and he showed himself well pleased at those deeds.

CHAPTER 112

It was the earl's custom nearly every summer to fare over to Caithness, and there to go up into the woods and wastes to hunt red deer or reindeer. (1) Thorbjorn clerk was with Malcolm the Scot-king, but sometimes he fared down to the Ness, and was with his friends by stealth. He had three friends in Caithness, in whom he placed most trust. One was Hosvir his brother in law; the second Lifolf, who dwelt in Thorsdale; the third was Halvard Dufa's son, who dwelt at Force in Calfdale which goes off from Thorsdale. These were his bosom friends.

CHAPTER 113

When earl Rognvald had been earl two and twenty winters since earl Paul was made captive, then the earls fared over to Caithness, when the summer was far spent, after their wont. And when they came to Thurso, then they heard some rumour that Thorbjorn clerk must be up Thorsdale in hiding, and not at all short-handed, and how he must mean an onslaught thence if he got a chance. Then the earls got men together to them, and fared with a band of one hundred, and twenty of them ride, but the others were on foot. They fared in the evening up the dale and turned in as guests somewhere where there was (what the Celts call) "erg," but we call "setr" (a shieling on the hill). That evening, as men sat by the fires, earl Rognvald sneezed very often. Earl Harold spoke and said: "Shrill sneezing kinsman." They fared on up the dale the next morning, and earl Rognvald rode always on in front that day, and that man with him whose name was Asolf; another man who was with him was Jomar his kinsman. Five of them together so ride a head up along Calfdale. (2) And as they fared to the homestead which is called Force, master Halvard was up on a corn-rick, and piled it up, but his house carles bore the sheaves up to him. Earl Harold and his men rode somewhat behind. But when Halvardk knew earl Rognvald, he hailed him by name, and bawled out very loud, and asked him after news, and his voice might have been heard just as well though he were farther off. This was a little way from the sitting room, and the house stood on a high brink; but there was a narrow fenced path to ride along up to the house, and it was very steep. In this homestead was Thorbjorn clerk inside, and sat at drink. The fenced path led up to the house end at the gable, and there was a doorway in the house and another doorway in the gable, and stones heaped up loosely in it. When Thorbjorn and his men heard the words that passed, and how Halvard hailed earl Rognvald and his men, they ran at once to their arms, and broke down the stones out of the secret door, and sprang out at it. Thorbjorn runs round the gable, and to the fence of the path. Just then the earl and his men had come to the door. Then Thorbjorn smote at once at the earl, but Asolf threw his arms in the way, and the stroke toomk off his hand. Afterwards the sword came on the earl's chin, and that was a great wound. Asolf said, when he got the stroke: "Let those follow the earl better who have more gifts to pay him for." He was then eighteen winters old, and was newcome to the earl. Earl Rognvald wanted to jump off his horse's back when he saw Thorbjorn, but his foot got fast in the stirrup. At that moment up came Stephen and thrust at the earl with a spear. Then Thorbjorn gave the earl another wound. But Jomar just then thrust a spear into Thorbjorn's thigh, and the blow passed on into his small entrails. Then Thorbjorn and his men turned to the back of the house, and there they had to run down a great steep brink, and on to a soft moor. Just then up came earl Harold and his men, and their course was so shaped that they came right in the way of Thorbjorn and his men, and then each knew the others. Then the earl's men said, those who knew what was in the wind, that they should turn after Thorbjorn and his men; but earl Harold set his face against it, and says he will wait and hear what earl Rognvald says about this matter: "For Thorbjorn is a very great friend of mine as ye know, for kinship's sake, and many other ties which are between us." But those men who were with earl Rognvald thronged about him dead, (3) and rather a long time passed ere earl Harold and his men heard the tidings. Then they [Thorbjorn and his men] were come on to the moor, and across the quagmire which ran along through the moor. But for the egging on of the earls' companions, earl Harold and his men ran down on the moor, and the two bands met at the quagmire, so that each band was on its own side, and Thorbjorn and his men held the bank of the dike against them. Then those men flocked to him from the homestead who had followed him thither, and all together they made up fifty men. Then they defended themselves manfully, and had a good stronghold to fight from, for the quagmire was both broad and deep, and the moor was soft up to it in front, and the only way they could make an onslaught on them was, that they shot at them with spears. Thorbjorn told his men that they should not shoot any of them back. And when the shots died away, then they began to speak to one another, and Thorbjorn called out to earl Harold and spoke thus: "This I will pray of you, kinsman, that ye give me peace; but I will offer to give over this matter into your power, that ye alone may doom it; and I will then shrink from no one thing that is in my power, that your honour may be then more than it was before. I hope also, kinsman, that thou wilt bear in mind that those strifes have been, in which thou wouldst not have made such a difference between us two, earl Rognvald and me, that thou wouldst have slain me though I had done this deed, I mean when he kept thee most under his elbow, and let thee have no voice in anything any more than his knave; but I gave thee the best gifts, and looked to do thee honour in all that I could. But this deed that I have done in

738

great wickedness, and that lies on me, but the whole realm is fallen into your power. You may also know this, that earl Rognvald meant the same lot for me which I have now given to him; and it is my foreboding, kinsman, though things had turned out so that I were dead, but earl Rognvald were alive, that you would treat him as a man who had done a deed which you must put up with, but me ye now wish to make a dead man." Thorbjorn went on so that many and fair spoken words, and many men backed that with him, and begged for peace for him. So it came that the earl began to listen to what he said when many backed it. Then Magnus the son of Havard Gunni's son, a chieftain of the earls' and their kinsman. He was the man of most birth and worth in the band with earl Harold. He spoke thus: "It is no business of ours to teach you what to do, earl, after these great deeds which we see before us. But I must say how the common fame will run about them, if peace be given to Thorbjorn after this work; and this besides I will say, that when he dares to say to your face nearly at every word that he hath done this his ill deed for thee, or wrought it for thy honour, it will be an everlasting shame and dishonour to thee, and to all the earl's kinsfolk, if he be not avenged. I think that earl Rognvald's friends will hold it for sooth that thou must for a long while have been plotting the earl's death; but now hast brought it about. Or thinkest thou that he will clear thy conscience when he has to throw off the blame from himself, but when no one makes an answer for you, when he now tells you to your face that he has wrought this misdeed for your sake; or how couldest thou better prove the truth of that but by now giving him peace. As for me, my mind is made up, that he shall never have peace from me, if any good men and true will follow me, whether it believe or loath to you." Just in the same way spoke his brothers, Thorstein and Hacon, and Sweyn Hroald's son. Then they turned away from the earl, and went up along the bank of the dike, and tried where they might get across. And when Thorbjorn and his men saw that Magnus and his followers turn away along the dike, then Thorbjorn began to speak and said: "Now they must have split about the counsel to take, the earl will wish to give me peace, but Magnus will speak against it." But while they were speaking about that, Thorbjorn and his men fell away from the dike. Earl Harold and his men stood on the dike bank. And when he saw that nothing would come of the peace giving, he leapt over the quagmire with all his weapons, and it was nine ells across the dike. His companions leapt after him, and no one got to leap clear over, but most of them got hold of the bank and so floundered to land. Thorbjorn's men egged him on that they should turn either against the earl and his men or against Magnus and his men, and let their quarrel be settled, there and then. Then Thorbjorn said: "Methinks the best plan is that each man should choose what he thinks likeliest to stand him in stead, but as for me, I will still look to meeting with earl Harold." Most men set their faces against this, and begged him rather to take to the woods and save himself. Thorbjorn would not take that counsel. So those men his companions dropped off from him, and looked for help for themselves in divers ways. But Thorbjorn and eight men together with him were left behind. And when he sees that earl Harold is come over the dike, he goes to meet him, and fell on his knees before him, and says he brings him his head. Many of the earl's men still begged for peace for Thorbjorn. Then the earl began to speak, and said: "Away and save thyself, Thorbjorn, I have no heart to slay thee, but I will not see thee henceforth." Then they were faring down along Calfdale's river, when these words passed between them. Magnus and his men pressed on hard after them, and when the earl saw that, he spoke: "Save thyself, Thorbjorn; I cannot fight for thee against my men." Then Thorbjorn and his men parted from the earl's company, and went to some empty shielings, which are called Asgrim's "erg"; Magnus and his men followed Thorbjorn and his men up, and forthwith set fire to the house. Thorbjorn and his men defended themselves manfully. And when the house began to fall down over their heads from the fire, Thorbjorn and his men came out, and every weapon was at once brought to bear upon them that could reach them; they were already much worn out by the force of the flames. There all those nine brothers in arms lost their lives. And when they came to look what wounds Thorbjorn had, his entrails had slipt out into that wound which Jomar had given him. Earl Harold went his way down along the dale, but Magnus and his men turned back to Force, and laid out earl Rognvald's body and brought it down to Thurso.

Earl (4) Harold and his men fared with the body away thence out into the Orkneys with a goodly company, and bestowed burial on it in St. Magnus' church in the choir; and there he rested until Bishop Bjarni caused his halidom (relics) to be taken up by the Pope's leave. (5) There on the stone on which earl Rognvald's blood had come when he died, it may still be seen at this very day as fair as though it were new shed blood. Earl Rognvald's death was a great grief, for he was very much beloved there in the isles, and far and wide elsewhere. He had been a very great helper to many men, bountiful of money, gentle, and a steadfast friend; a great man for feats of strength and a good skald. He had a daughter his only child alive, Ingigerd, whom Eric staybrails had to wife. Their children were these: Harald the young, and Magnus mannikin, Rognvald, and Ingibjorg, Elin, and Ragnhilda.

CHAPTER 114

After the fall of earl Rognvald, earl Harold took all the isles under his rule, and became the sole chief over them. Earl Harold was a mighty chief, one of the tallest and strongest of men, "dour" and hard-hearted; he had to wife Afreka; (6) their children were these: Henry and Hacon, Helena and Margaret. When Hacon was but a few winters old, Sweyn Asleif's son offered to take him as his foster child, and he was bred up there, and as soon as ever he was so far fit, that he could go about with other men, then Sweyn had him away with him a sea roving every summer, and led him on to the worthiness in everything. It was Sweyn's wont at that time, that he sat through the winter at home in Gairsay, and there he kept always about him eighty men at his beck. He had so great a drinking hall, that there was not another as great in all the Orkneys. Sweyn had in the spring hard work, and made them lay down very much seed, and looked much after it himself. But when that toil was ended, he fared away every spring on a viking voyage, and harried about among the Southern isles and Ireland, and came home after midsummer. That he called spring-viking. Then he was at home until the corn fields were reaped down, and the grain seen to and stored. Then he fared away on a viking voyage, and then he did not come home till the winter was one month spent and that he called his autumn viking.

CHAPTER 115

These tidings happened once on a time, that Sweyn Asleif's son fared away on his spring cruise, then Hacon earl Harold's son fared with him; and they had five ships with oars, and all of them large. They harried about among the Southern isles. Then the folk was so scared at him in the Southern isles, that men hid all their goods and chattels in the earth or in piles of rocks. Sweyn sailed as far south as Man, and got ill off for spoil. Thence they sailed out under Ireland and harried there.But when they came about south under Dublin, then two keels sailed there from off the main, which had come from England, and meant to steer for Dublin; they were laden with English cloths, and great store of goods was aboard them. Sweyn and his men pulled up to the keels, and offered them battle. Little came of the defence of the Englishmen before Sweyn gave the word to board. Then the Englishmen were made prisoners. And there they robbed them of every penny which was aboard the keels, save that the Englishmen kept the clothes they stood in and some food, and went on their way afterwards with the keels, but Sweyn and his men fared to the Southern isles, and shared their war spoil. They sailed from the west with great pomp. They did this as a glory for themselves when they lay in harbours, that they threw awnings of English cloth over their ships. But when they sailed into the Orkneys, they sewed the cloth on the fore part of the sails, so that it looked in that wise as though the sails were made altogether of broadcloth. This they called the broadcloth cruise. Sweyn fared home to his house in Gairsay. He had taken from the keels much wine and English mead. Now when Sweyn had been at home a short while, he bade to him earl Harold, and made a worthy feast against his coming. When earl Harold was at the feast, there was much talk amongst them of Sweyn's good cheer. The earl spoke and said: "This I would now, Sweyn, that thou wouldest lay aside thy sea rovings; 'tis good now to drive home with a whole wain. But thou knowest this, that thou hast long maintained thyself and thy men by sea roving, but so it fares with most men who live by unfair means, that they lose their lives in strife, if they do not break themselves from it." Then Sweyn answered, and looked to the earl, and spoke with a smile, and said thus: "Well spoken is this, lord, and friendly spoken, and it will be good to take a bit of good counsel from you; but some men lay that to your door, that ye too are men of little fairness." The earl answered: "I shall have to answer for my share, but a gossiping tongue drives me to say what I do." Sweyn said: "Good, no doubt, drives you to it, lord. And so it shall be, that I will leave off sea roving, for I find that I am growing old, and strength lessens much in hardships and warfare. Now I will go out on my autumn cruise, and I would that it might be with no less glory than the spring cruise was; but after that my warfaring shall be over." The earl answers: "'Tis hard to see, messmate, whether death or lasting luck will come first." After that they dropped talking about it. Earl Harold fared away from the feast, and was led out with fitting gifts. So he and Sweyn parted with great love-tokens.

CHAPTER 116

A little after Sweyn busks him for his roving cruise; he had seven longships and all great. Hacon earl Harold's son went along with Sweyn on his voyage. They held on their course first to the Southern isles, and got there little war spoil; thence they fared out under Ireland, and harried there far and wide. They fared so far south as Dublin, and came upon them there very suddenly, so that the townsmen were not ware of them before they had got into the town. They took there much goods. They made prisoners there those men who were rulers in the town. The upshot of their business was that they gave the town up into Sweyn's power, and agreed to pay as great a ransom as he chose to lay upon them. Sweyn was also to hold the town with his men and to have rule over it. The Dublin men swear an oath to do this. They fared to their ships at even, but next morning Sweyn was to come into the town, and take the ransom, place his men about the town, and take hostages from the townsmen. Now it must be told of what happened in the town during the night. The men of good counsel who were in the town held a meeting among themselves, and talked over the straits which had befallen them; it seemed to them hard to let their town come into the power of the Orkneyingers, and worst of all of that man whom they knew to be the most unjust man in the Western lands. So they agreed amongst themselves that they would cheat Sweyn if they might. They took that counsel, that they dug great trenches before the burg gate on the inside, and in many other places between the houses where it was meant that Sweyn and his men should pass; but men lay in wait there in the houses hard by with weapons. They laid planks over the trenches, so that they should fall down as soon as ever a man's weight comes on them. After that they strewed straw on the planks so that the trenches might not be seen, and so bided the morrow.

CHAPTER 117

On the morning after Sweyn and his men arose and put on their arms; after that they went to the town. And when they came inside beyond the burg gate the Dublin men made a lane from the burg gate right to the trenches. Sweyn and his men saw not what they were doing, and ran into the trenches. The townsmen they ran straightway to hold the burg gate, but some to the trenches, and brought their arms to bear on Sweyn and his men. It was unhandy for them to make any defence, and Sweyn lost his life there in the trenches, and all those who had gone into the town. So it was said that Sweyn was the last to die of all his messmates, and spoke these words ere he died: "Know this all men, whether I lose my life today or not, that I am one of the saint earl Rognvald's bodyguard, and I now mean to put my trust in being there where he is with God." (7) Sweyn's men fared at once to their ships and pulled away, and nothing is told about their voyage before they come into the Orkneys. There now is an end of telling about Sweyn; and it is the talk of men that he hath been most of a man for his own sake in the Western lands, both of yore and now a days, of those men who had no higher titles of honour than he. (8)

After the fall of Sweyn, his sons Olaf and Andrew shared his inheritance between them. They made the next summer after Sweyn lost his life a party-wall in that great drinking hall which he had owned in Gairsay. Andrew Sweyn's son had to wife Frida Kolbein the burly's daughter, sister of Bjarni, bishop of the Orkneyingers.

Earl Harold now ruled over the Orkneys, and was the greatest chief; he had to wife afterwards Hvarflada (9) earl Malcolm's daughter of Moray. Their children were these: Thorfinn, David, and John, Gunhilda, Herborga, and Longlife.

ENDNOTES FOR CHAPTERS 111-117

1. See Dr. Smith in the 8th vol. of the Proceedings of the Society of Antiquaries of Scotland.

2. Calfdale] Calder, in Caithness.

3. The Danish Translation reads, "while he was a dying."

4. Fl., quoting some collection of annals, reads thus, "The death-day of earl Rognvald---Kali is five nights after Mary's mass the former , in summer."

5. Fl. reads, "until God revealed his worthiness by many and great miracles."

6. Afreka] She was sister of Duncan, earl of Fife. When earl Harold quarrelled with the Scottish Court, during earl Rognvald's absence in the Holy Land, he repudiated her, and married Hvarflada, daughter of Malcolm McHeth, earl of Moray. See below, ch. 119 comp. also Munch, N. H. iii. 847 note.

7. G. V. thinks that this passage from "So it was said" to "with God," is a later interpolation.

8. Here the Danish Translation ends, adding "Finis. A final historical conclusion to this chronicle." The following sentences are from the Fl.

9. Hvarflada] Comp. ch. 115 above, and note.

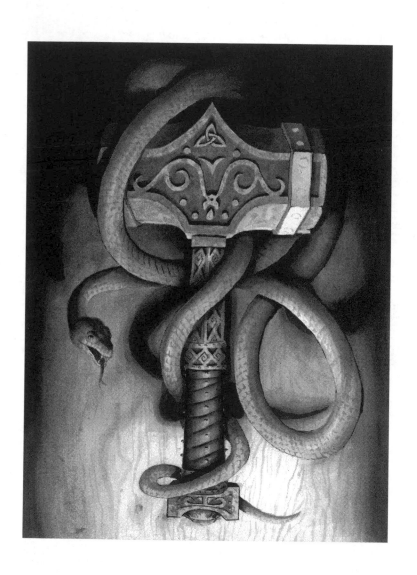

33731125R00417

Made in the USA
San Bernardino, CA
09 May 2016